GESENIUS'
HEBREW GRAMMAR

AS EDITED AND ENLARGED BY THE LATE

E. KAUTZSCH

PROFESSOR OF THEOLOGY IN THE UNIVERSITY OF HALLE

SECOND ENGLISH EDITION

REVISED IN ACCORDANCE WITH THE TWENTY-EIGHTH GERMAN
EDITION (1909) BY

A. E. COWLEY

WITH A FACSIMILE OF THE SILOAM INSCRIPTION BY J. EUTING, AND
A TABLE OF ALPHABETS BY M. LIDZBARSKI

OXFORD
AT THE CLARENDON PRESS

Oxford University Press, Ely House, London W. 1

GLASGOW NEW YORK TORONTO MELBOURNE WELLINGTON
CAPE TOWN SALISBURY IBADAN NAIROBI LUSAKA ADDIS ABABA
BOMBAY CALCUTTA MADRAS KARACHI LAHORE DACCA
KUALA LUMPUR HONG KONG

SECOND ENGLISH EDITION 1910

REPRINTED LITHOGRAPHICALLY IN GREAT BRITAIN
AT THE UNIVERSITY PRESS, OXFORD
FROM CORRECTED SHEETS OF THE SECOND EDITION
1946, 1949, 1952, 1956, 1960, 1966

TRANSLATOR'S PREFACE

THE translation of the twenty-sixth German edition of this grammar, originally prepared by the Rev. G. W. Collins and revised by me, was published in 1898. Since that date a twenty-seventh German edition has appeared; and Prof. Kautzsch was already engaged on a twenty-eighth in 1908 when the English translation was becoming exhausted. He sent me the sheets as they were printed off, and I began revising the former translation in order to produce it as soon as possible after the completion of the German. The whole of the English has been carefully compared with the new edition, and, it is hoped, improved in many points, while Prof. Kautzsch's own corrections and additions have of course been incorporated. As before, the plan and arrangement of the original have been strictly followed, so that the references for sections and paragraphs correspond exactly in German and English. Dr. Driver has again most generously given up time, in the midst of other engagements, to reading the sheets, and has made numerous suggestions. To him also are chiefly due the enlargement of the index of subjects, some expansions in the new index of Hebrew words, and some additions to the index of passages, whereby we hope to have made the book more serviceable to students. I have also to thank my young friend, Mr. Godfrey R. Driver, of Winchester College, for some welcome help in correcting proofs of the Hebrew index and the index of passages. בֶּן חָכָם יְשַׂמַּח אָב. Many corrections have been sent to me by scholars who have used the former English edition, especially the Rev. W. E. Blomfield, the Rev. S. Holmes, Mr. P. Wilson, Prof. Witton Davies, Mr. G. H. Skipwith, and an unknown correspondent at West Croydon. These, as well as suggestions in reviews, have all been considered, and where possible, utilized. I am also much indebted to the Press-readers for the great care which they have bestowed on the work.

Finally, I must pay an affectionate tribute to the memory of Prof. Kautzsch, who died in the spring of this year, shortly after finishing the last sheets of the twenty-eighth edition. For more than thirty years he was indefatigable in improving the successive editions of the Grammar. The German translation of the Old Testament first published by him in 1894, with the co-operation of other scholars, under the title *Die Heilige Schrift des A Ts*, and now (1910) in the third and much enlarged edition, is a valuable work which has been widely appreciated: the *Apocryphen und Pseudepigraphen des A Ts*, edited by him in 1900, is another important work: besides which he published his *Grammatik des Biblisch-Aramäischen* in 1884, two useful brochures *Bibelwissenschaft und Religionsunterricht* in 1900, and *Die bleibende Bedeutung des A Ts* in 1903, six popular lectures on *Die Poesie und die poetischen Bücher des A Ts* in 1902, his article 'Religion of Israel' in Hastings' *Dictionary of the Bible*, v. (1904), pp. 612–734, not to mention minor publications. His death is a serious loss to Biblical scholarship, while to me and to many others it is the loss of a most kindly friend, remarkable alike for his simple piety and his enthusiasm for learning.

A. C.

MAGDALEN COLLEGE, OXFORD,
Sept. 1910.

FROM THE GERMAN PREFACE

THE present (twenty-eighth) edition of this Grammar,[1] like the former ones, takes account as far as possible of all important new publications on the subject, especially J. Barth's *Sprachwissenschaftliche Untersuchungen zum Semitischen*, pt. i, Lpz. 1907 ; the important works of C. Brockelmann (for the titles see the heading of § 1 ; vol. i of the *Grundriss* was finished in 1908) ; P. Kahle's *Der masoretische Text des A Tᵉ nach der Überlieferung der babylonischen Juden*, Lpz. 1902 (giving on p. 51 ff. an outline of Hebrew accidence from a Babylonian MS. at Berlin) ; R. Kittel's *Biblia Hebraica*, Lpz. 1905 f., 2 vols. (discriminating between certain, probable, and proposed emendations ; see § 3 g, end) ; Th. Nöldeke's *Beiträge zur semit. Sprachwissenschaft*, Strassburg, 1904 ; Ed. Sievers' *Metrische Studien* (for the titles of these striking works see § 2 r). The important work of J. W. Rothstein, *Grundzüge des hebr. Rhythmus*, &c. (see also § 2 r), unfortunately appeared too late to be used. The two large commentaries edited by Nowack and Marti have been recently completed; and in P. Haupt's Polychrome Bible (*SBOT.*), part ix (Kings) by Stade and Schwally was published in 1904.

For full reviews of the twenty-seventh edition, which of course have been considered as carefully as possible, I have to thank Max Margolis (in *Hebraica*, 1902, p. 159 ff.), Mayer

---

[1] The first edition appeared at Halle in 1813 (202 pp. small 8vo) ; twelve more editions were published by W. Gesenius himself, the fourteenth to the twenty first (1845–1872) by E. Rödiger, the twenty-second to the twenty-eighth (1878–1910) by E. Kautzsch. The first abridged edition appeared in 1896, the second at the same time as the present (twenty-eighth) large edition. The first edition of the 'Übungsbuch' (Exercises) to Gesenius-Kautzsch's Hebrew Grammar appeared in 1881, the sixth in 1908.

Lambert (*REJ.* 1902, p. 307 ff.), and H. Oort (*Theol. Tijd-schrift,* 1902, p. 373 ff.). For particular remarks and corrections I must thank Prof. J. Barth (Berlin), Dr. Gasser, pastor in Buchberg, Schaffhausen, B. Kirschner, of Charlottenburg, (contributions to the index of passages), Pastor Köhler, of Augst, Dr. Liebmann, of Kuczkow, Posen, Prof. Th. Nöldeke, of Strassburg, Pastor S. Preiswerk junior, of Bâle, Dr. Schwarz, of Leipzig, and Prof. B. Stade, of Giessen (died in 1906). Special mention must be made of the abundant help received from three old friends of this book, Prof. P. Haupt, of Baltimore, Prof. Knudtzon, of Kristiania, and Prof. H. Strack, of Berlin, and also, in connexion with the present edition, Prof. H. Hyvernat, of the University of Washington, who has rendered great service especially in the correction and enlargement of the indexes. I take this opportunity of thanking them all again sincerely. And I am no less grateful also to my dear colleague Prof. C. Steuernagel for the unwearying care with which he has helped me from beginning to end in correcting the proof-sheets.

Among material changes introduced into this edition may be mentioned the abolition of the term *Š^ewâ medium* (§ 10 *d*). In this I have adopted, not without hesitation, the views of Sievers. I find it, however, quite impossible to follow him in rejecting all distinctions of quantity in the vowels. It is no doubt possible that such matters may in the *spoken* language have worn a very different appearance, and especially that in the period of nearly a thousand years, over which the Old Testament writings extend, very great variations may have taken place. Our duty, however, is to represent the language in the form in which it has been handed down to us by the Masoretes; and that this form involves a distinction between unchangeable, tone-long, and short vowels, admits in my opinion of no doubt. The discussion of any earlier stage of development belongs not to Hebrew grammar but to comparative Semitic philology.

The same answer may be made to Beer's desire (*ThLZ.* 1904,

col. 314 f.) for an 'historical Hebrew grammar describing the actual growth of the language on a basis of comparative philology, as it may still be traced within the narrow limits of the Old Testament'. Such material as is available for the purpose ought indeed to be honestly set forth in the new editions of Gesenius; but Beer seems to me to appraise such material much too highly when he refers to it as necessitating an 'historical grammar'. In my opinion these historical differences have for the most part been obliterated by the harmonizing activity of the Masoretes.

.   .   .   .

E. KAUTZSCH.

HALLE,
July, 1909.

ADDITIONS AND CORRECTIONS

Page 42, line 13 from below, *for* note 1 *read* note 3.

Page 63, § 15 *p*. [See also Wickes, *Prose Accentuation*, 130 f., 87 *n*. (who, however, regards the superlinear, Babylonian system as the earlier); and Ginsburg, *Introduction to the Hebrew Bible*, 76, 78. In Ginsburg's *Hebrew Bible*, ed. 2 (1908), pp. 108 f., 267 f., the two systems of division are printed *in extenso*, in parallel columns—the 10 verses of the superlinear (Babylonian) system consisting (in Exodus) of v. [2.3-6.7.8-11.12.13.14.15.16.17] (as numbered in ordinary texts), and the 12 verses of the sublinear (Palestinian) system, consisting of v. [2-3.4.5.6.7.8.9.10.11.12.13-16.17].—S. R. D.]

Page 65, note 1, *for* אֲנָּ֗א *read* אֲנָּ֗א (as § 105 *a*).

[Editions often vary in individual passages, as regards the accentuation of the first syllable: but in the 7 occurrences of אנא, and the 6 of אנה, Baer, Ginsburg, and Kittel agree in having an accent on both syllables (as אֲנָּא) in Gn 50¹⁷, Ex 32³¹, ψ 116¹⁶, and Metheg on the first syllable and an accent on the second syllable (as אָנָּה) in 2 K 20³=Is 38³, Jon 1¹⁴, 4², ψ 116⁴, 118²⁵·²⁵, Dn 9⁴, Ne 1⁵·¹¹, except that in ψ 116⁴ Ginsburg has אָנָּה.—S. R. D.]

Page 79, § 22 *s*, *before* הִרְדִּיפֻהוּ *insert* exceptions to *b* are. *After* Jer 39¹² *add* ψ 52⁶; *and for* Ez 9⁶ *read* Ezr 9⁶.

[So Baer (cf. his note on Jud 20⁴³; also on Jer 39¹², and several of the other passages in question): but Ginsburg only in 10 of the exceptions to *b*, and Jacob ben Ḥayyim and Kittel only in 5, viz. Jer 39¹², Pr 11²¹, 15¹, ψ 52⁵, Ezr 9⁶.—S. R. D.]

Page 111, line 12, *for* הַהוּה *read* הַהוּא.

Page 123, § 45 *e*, *add*: cf. also מַהְפֵּכָה followed by אֵת, Is 13¹⁹, Am 4¹¹ (§ 115 *d*).

Page 175, § 67. *See* B. Halper, 'The Participial formations of the Geminate Verbs' in *ZAW*. 1910, pp. 42 ff., 99 ff., 201 ff. (also dealing with the regular verb).

Page 177, at the end of § 67 *g* the following paragraph has been accidentally omitted:

Rem. According to the prevailing view, this strengthening of the first radical is merely intended to give the bi-literal stem at least a tri-literal appearance. (Possibly aided by the analogy of verbs פ"ן, as P. Haupt has suggested to me in conversation.) But cf. Kautzsch, ' Die sog. aramaisierenden Formen der Verba ע"ע im Hebr.' in *Oriental. Studien zum 70. Geburtstag Th. Nöldekes*, 1906, p. 771 ff. It is there shown (1) that the sharpening of the 1st radical often serves to emphasize a particular meaning (cf. יִפֻּר, but יָחֵל, יַגְלֵהוּ and יַחֵל, יִסֹּב and יְסֹב, יִשֹּׁם and תֵּשַׁם), and elsewhere no doubt to dissimilate the vowels (as יִדַּל יִפֻּר, never יִדַּל יְגֵּר, &c.): (2) that the sharpening of the 1st radical often appears to be occasioned by the nature of the first letter of the stem, especially when it is a sibilant. Whether the masoretic pronunciation is based on an early tradition, or the Masora has arbitrarily adopted aramaizing forms to attain the above objects, must be left undecided.

Page 193, the second and third paragraphs should have the marginal letters *d* and *e* respectively.

Page 200, § 72 *z*, line 2, *after* Est 2[18] *add* 4[14].

Page 232, § 84[a] *s*, *add* שְׁמֵמָה 2 S 13[20].

Page 236, § 85 *c*, *add* הֻנְּקָה Ezr 4[22].

Page 273, § 93 *qq* end, *add* מוֹסֵרוֹת Jer 5[5], שָׁלֵשִׁים, רְבֵעִים Ez 20[5], שְׁמֵמוֹת Is 49[8], שָׁמֵמִים La 1[16] (cf. König, ii. 109).

LIST OF ABBREVIATIONS

The following abbreviations have occasionally been used for works and periodicals frequently quoted :—

AJSL. = American Journal of Semitic Languages.

CIS. = Corpus Inscriptionum Semiticarum.

Ed.Mant. = Biblia Hebraica ex recensione Sal. Norzi edidit Raphael Hayyim Basila, Mantuae 1742–4.

Jabl. = Biblia Hebraica ex recensione D. E. Jablonski, Berolini, 1699.

JQR. = Jewish Quarterly Review.

*KAT.*³ = Die Keilinschriften und das Alte Testament, 3rd ed. by H. Zimmern and H. Winckler, 2 vols., Berlin, 1902 f.

Lexicon = A Hebrew and English Lexicon of the Old Testament, based on the Thesaurus and Lexicon of Gesenius, by F. Brown, S. R. Driver, and C. A. Briggs, Oxford, 1906.

NB. = J. Barth, Die Nominalbildung in den semitischen Sprachen. Lpz. 1889–94.

NGGW. = Nachrichten der Göttinger Gesellschaft der Wissenschaften.

OLZ. = Orientalistische Literaturzeitung. Vienna, 1898 ff.

PRE. = Realencyclopädie für protestantische Theologie und Kirche, 3rd ed. by A. Hauck. Lpz. 1896 ff.

PSBA = Proceedings of the Society of Biblical Archæology. London, 1879 ff.

REJ. = Revue des Études Juives. Paris, 1880 ff.

Sam. = The (Hebrew) Pentateuch of the Samaritans.

SBOT. = Sacred Books of the Old Testament, ed. by P. Haupt. Lpz. and Baltimore, 1893 ff.

ThLZ. = Theologische Literaturzeitung, ed. by E. Schürer. Lpz. 1876 ff.

VB. = Vorderasiatische Bibliothek, ed. by A. Jeremias and H. Winckler. Lpz. 1907 ff.

ZA. = Zeitschrift für Assyriologie und verwandte Gebiete, ed. by C. Bezold. Lpz. 1886 ff.

ZAW. = Zeitschrift für die alttestamentliche Wissenschaft, ed. by B. Stade, Giessen, 1881 ff., and since 1907 by K. Marti.

ZDMG. = Zeitschrift der deutschen morgenländischen Gesellschaft, Lpz. 1846 ff., since 1903 ed. by A. Fischer.

ZDPV. = Zeitschrift des deutschen Palästinavereins, Lpz. 1878 ff., since 1903 ed. by C. Steuernagel.

CONTENTS

FIRST PART

ELEMENTARY PRINCIPLES, OR THE SOUNDS AND CHARACTERS

CHAPTER I. THE INDIVIDUAL SOUNDS AND CHARACTERS

CHAPTER II. PECULIARITIES AND CHANGES OF LETTERS: THE SYLLABLE AND THE TONE

SECOND PART

ETYMOLOGY, OR THE PARTS OF SPEECH

CHAPTER I. THE PRONOUN

CHAPTER II. THE VERB

I. The Strong Verb.

A. *The Pure Stem, or Qal.*

Contents

Contents

CHAPTER IV. THE PARTICLES

THIRD PART

SYNTAX

CHAPTER I. THE PARTS OF SPEECH

I. Syntax of the Verb.

A. *Use of the Tenses and Moods.*

Contents

B. *The Infinitive and Participle.*

C. *The Government of the Verb.*

II. Syntax of the Noun.

III. Syntax of the Pronoun.

Contents

Chapter II. The Sentence

I. The Sentence in General.

II. Special Kinds of Sentences.

. . . . . תעשׂו . העבדה . דבר . היה . היה . החבה . [. חם]

ק . אשׁ . לק . [הק]רדה . אמר . בשׁא . וישׁבע . לקחה . [. חם]

ה . הים . . . . ישׂב . . . הרד . . . בל . הרד . ונזל . [רזל]

אש . אשׁ . לג . לג . ד . ג . ב . וזנב . לגל . ונזל . ונזל .

חמצב . הכה . הכה . אשׁ . המצבר . לב . הים . . . . . .

חבה . לאשׁ . הככהה . ככהבה . אל . המצבה . וכב . . . . .

ה . אמר . חבב . הבב . על . הרד . הדל . הרב . בגב . לבב .

[חמצב]ה . לאשׁ . על . הרד . . . . .

Rem.—Line 1 probably began with חם, cf. § 145 o, since there is hardly room for שׁכם.

Line 2. The reading לקחה is supported by the fact that a trace of the top of the ק is visible; cf. Lidzbarski, *Ephemeris*, i. 53. The next word was probably, as P. Haupt suggests, וישׁבע, the imperf. consec. Qal or Niph'al.

Line 3. רדה, not found in the Old Testament, most probably means a *cleft, crack*, but the etymology and consequently the pronunciation of it [רדֶה?] are still doubtful.

THE SILOAM INSCRIPTION. From Müller-Benzinger, *Landschaftsbilderbibel* (H. Grund : Berlin).

HEBREW GRAMMAR

INTRODUCTION

§ 1. *The Semitic Languages in General.*

B. Stade, *Lehrb. der hebr. Gramm.*, Lpz. 1879, § 2 ff. ; E. König, *Hist.-krit. Lehrgeb. der hebr. Spr.*, i. Lpz. 1881, § 3 ; H. Strack, *Einl. in das A. T.*, 6th ed., Munich, 1906, p. 231 ff. (a good bibliography of all the Semitic dialects) ; Th. Nöldeke, article 'Semitic Languages', in the 9th ed. of the *Encycl. Brit.* (*Die semit. Sprachen*, 2nd ed., Lpz. 1899), and *Beitr. zur sem. Sprachwiss.*, Strassb., 1904 ; W. Wright, *Lectures on the Comparative Grammar of the Semitic Languages*, Cambr. 1890 ; H. Reckendorf, 'Zur Karakteristik der sem. Sprachen,' in the *Actes du Xme Congrès internat. des Orientalistes* (at Geneva in 1894), iii. 1 ff., Leiden, 1896 ; O. E. Lindberg, *Vergl. Gramm. der sem. Sprachen*, i A : *Konsonantismus*, Gothenburg, 1897 ; H. Zimmern, *Vergl. Gramm. der sem. Sprachen*, Berlin, 1898 ; E. König, *Hebräisch und Semitisch: Prolegomena und Grundlinien einer Gesch. der sem. Sprachen*, &c., Berlin, 1901 ; C. Brockelmann, *Semitische Sprachwissenschaft*, Lpz. 1906, *Grundriss der vergl. Gramm. der sem. Sprachen*, vol. i (Laut- und Formenlehre), parts 1–5, Berlin, 1907 f. and his *Kurzgef. vergleichende Gramm.* (Porta Ling. Or.) Berlin, 1908.—The material contained in inscriptions has been in process of collection since 1881 in the Paris *Corpus Inscriptionum Semiticarum.* To this the best introductions are M. Lidzbarski's *Handbuch der Nordsem. Epigraphik*, Weimar, 1898, in 2 parts (text and plates), and his *Ephemeris zur sem. Epigraphik* (5 parts published), Giessen, 1900 f. [G. A. Cooke, *Handbook of North-Semitic Inscriptions*, Oxford, 1903].

1. The Hebrew language is one branch of a great family of lan- *a* guages in Western Asia which was indigenous in Palestine, Phoenicia, Syria, Mesopotamia, Babylonia, Assyria, and Arabia, that is to say, in the countries extending from the Mediterranean to the other side of the Euphrates and Tigris, and from the mountains of Armenia to the southern coast of Arabia. In early times, however, it spread from Arabia over Abyssinia, and by means of Phoenician colonies over many islands and sea-boards of the Mediterranean, as for instance to the Carthaginian coast. No comprehensive designation is found in early times for the languages and nations of this family; the name *Semites* or *Semitic* [1] *languages* (based upon the fact that according to Gn 10[21 ff.] almost all nations speaking these languages are descended from Shem) is, however, now generally accepted, and has accordingly been retained here.[2]

---

[1] First used by Schlözer in Eichhorn's *Repertorium für bibl. u. morgenl. Literatur*, 1781, p. 161.

[2] From Shem are derived (Gn 10[21 ff.]) the Aramaean and Arab families as well as the Hebrews, but not the Canaanites (Phoenicians), who are traced back to Ham (vv. [6. 15 ff.]), although their language belongs decidedly to what is now called Semitic. The language of the Babylonians and Assyrians also was long ago shown to be Semitic, just as Aššur (Gn 10[22]) is included among the sons of Shem.

b　　**2.** The better known Semitic languages may be subdivided[1] as follows :—

I. **The South Semitic or Arabic branch.** To this belong, besides the classical literary language of the Arabs and the modern vulgar Arabic, the older southern Arabic preserved in the Sabaean inscriptions (less correctly called Himyaritic), and its offshoot, the Ge'ez or Ethiopic, in Abyssinia.

II. **The Middle Semitic or Canaanitish branch.** To this belongs the Hebrew of the Old Testament with its descendants, the New Hebrew, as found especially in the Mishna (see below, § 3 *a*), and Rabbinic ; also Phoenician, with Punic (in Carthage and its colonies), and the various remains of Canaanitish dialects preserved in names of places and persons, and in the inscription of Měša', king of Moab.

c　　III. **The North Semitic or Aramaic branch.** The subdivisions of this are—(1) The Eastern Aramaic or Syriac, the literary language of the Christian Syrians. The religious books of the Mandaeans (Nasoraeans, Sabians, also called the disciples of St. John) represent a very debased offshoot of this. A Jewish modification of Syriac is to be seen in the language of the Babylonian Talmud. (2) The Western or Palestinian Aramaic, incorrectly called also 'Chaldee'.[2] This latter dialect is represented in the Old Testament by two words in Gn 31[47], by the verse Jer 10[11], and the sections Dn 2[4] to 7[28] ; Ezr 4[8] to 6[18], and 7[12-26], as well as by a number of non-Jewish inscriptions and Jewish papyri (see below, under *m*), but especially by a considerable section of Jewish literature (Targums, Palestinian Gemara, &c.). To the same branch belongs also the Samaritan, with its admixture of Hebrew forms, and, except for the rather Arabic colouring of the proper names, the idiom of the Nabataean inscriptions in the Sinaitic peninsula, in the East of Palestine, &c.

For further particulars about the remains of Western Aramaic (including those in the New Test., in the Palmyrene and Egyptian Aramaic inscriptions) see Kautzsch, *Gramm. des Biblisch-Aramäischen*, Lpz. 1884, p. 6 ff.

d　　IV. **The East Semitic branch,** the language of the Assyrio-Babylonian cuneiform inscriptions, the third line of the Achaemenian inscriptions.

On the importance of Assyrian for Hebrew philology especially from a lexicographical point of view cf. Friedr. Delitzsch, *Prolegomena eines neuen*

---

[1] For conjectures as to the gradual divergence of the dialects (first the Babylonian, then Canaanite, including Hebrew, lastly Aramaic and Arabic) from primitive Semitic, see Zimmern, *KAT.*[3], ii. p. 644 ff.

[2] In a wider sense *all* Jewish Aramaic is sometimes called 'Chaldee'.

hebr.-aram. Wörterbuchs zum A. T., Lpz. 1886 ; P. Haupt, 'Assyrian Phonology, &c.,' in *Hebraica,* Chicago, Jan. 1885, vol. i. 3 ; Delitzsch, *Assyrische Grammatik,* 2nd ed., Berlin, 1906.

If the above division into four branches be reduced to two principal groups, No. I, as South Semitic, will be contrasted with the three North Semitic branches.[1]

All these languages stand to one another in much the same relation as those *e* of the Germanic family (Gothic, Old Norse, Danish, Swedish ; High and Low German in their earlier and later dialects), or as the Slavonic languages (Lithuanian, Lettish ; Old Slavonic, Serbian, Russian ; Polish, Bohemian). They are now either wholly extinct, as the Phoenician and Assyrian, or preserved only in a debased form, as Neo-Syriac among Syrian Christians and Jews in Mesopotamia and Kurdistan, Ethiopic (Ge'ez) in the later Abyssinian dialects (Tigrê, Tigriña, Amharic), and Hebrew among some modern Jews, except in so far as they attempt a purely literary reproduction of the language of the Old Testament. Arabic alone has not only occupied to this day its original abode in Arabia proper, but has also forced its way in all directions into the domain of other languages.

The Semitic family of languages is bounded on the East and North by another of still wider extent, which reaches from India to the western limits of Europe, and is called Indo-Germanic[2] since it comprises, in the most varied ramifications, the Indian (Sanskrit), Old and New Persian, Greek, Latin, Slavonic, as well as Gothic and the other Germanic languages. With the Old Egyptian language, of which Coptic is a descendant, as well as with the languages of north-western Africa, the Semitic had from the earliest times much in common, especially in grammatical structure ; but on the other hand there are fundamental differences between them, especially from a lexicographical point of view ; see Erman, ' Das Verhältnis des Aegyptischen zu den semitischen Sprachen,' in the *ZDMG.* xlvi, 1892, p. 93 ff., and Brockelmann, *Grundriss,* i. 3.

3. The *grammatical structure* of the Semitic family of languages, *f* as compared with that of other languages, especially the Indo-Germanic, exhibits numerous peculiarities which collectively constitute its distinctive character, although many of them are found singly in other languages. These are—(*a*) among the consonants, which in fact form the substance of these languages, occur peculiar gutturals of different grades; the vowels are subject, within the same consonantal framework, to great changes in order to express various modifications of the same stem-meaning ; (*b*) the word-stems are almost invariably triliteral, i.e. composed of three consonants; (*c*) the verb is restricted to two tense-forms, with a peculiarly regulated use; (*d*) the noun has only two genders (masc. and fem.) ; and peculiar expedients are adopted for the purpose of indicating the case-relations; (*e*) the

---

[1] Hommel, *Grundriss der Geogr. und Gesch. des alten Orients,* Munich, 1904, p. 75 ff., prefers to distinguish them as Eastern and Western Semitic branches. Their geographical position, however, is of less importance than the genealogical relation of the various groups of dialects, as rightly pointed out by A. Jeremias in *Th.LZ.* 1906, col. 291.

[2] First by Klaproth in *Asia Polyglotta,* Paris, 1823 ; cf. Leo Meyer in *Nachrichten d. Gött. Gesellschaft,* 1901, p. 454.

oblique cases of the personal pronoun, as well as all the possessive pronouns and the pronominal object of the verb, are denoted by forms appended directly to the governing word (suffixes); (*f*) the almost complete absence of compounds both in the noun (with the exception of many proper n⸺s) and in the verb; (*g*) great simplicity in the expression of sy�ºal relations, e. g. the small number of particles, and the prevalen⸍ simple co-ordination of clauses without periodic structure.   Clas⸍ Arabic and Syriac, however, form a not un-important except⸍ regards the last-mentioned point.

g   4. From a lexi⸍ ⸍hical point of view also the vocabulary of the Semites differs es⸍ 'ly from that of the Indo-Germanic languages, although there is a⸍ ⸍tly more agreement here than in the grammar. A considerable nu⸍ of Semitic roots and stems agree in sound with synonyms in ⸍ndo-Germanic family.   But apart from ex-pressions actually ⸍ ved (see below, under *i*), the real similarity may be reduced to ⸍ative words (onomatopoetica), and to those in which one and tl⸍ ⸍ne idea is represented by similar sounds in consequence of a f⸍ ⸍ve instinct common to the most varied families of language.⸍ ⸍ither of these proves any *historic* or *generic* relation, for which an⸍ ⸍ement in grammatical structure would also be necessary.

Comp. Friedr. Delitzsc⸍ *lien über indogermanisch-semitische Wurzelverwandt-schaft*, Lpz. 1873; Nöld⸍ *Semit. Glossen zu Fick und Curtius*, Magdeb. 1876 f.; McCurdy, *Aryo-⸍ Speech*, Andover, U. S. A., 1881. The phonetic relations have been tho⸍ y investigated by H. Möller in *Semitisch und Indogermanisch*, Teil i, Kö⸍ *en*, Copenhagen and Lpz. 1907, a work which has evoked considerable ⸍ m.

h   As onomatopoetic word⸍ ⸍ stem-sounds of a similar character, we may compare, e. g. לָקַק, לָחַךְ א⸍ 'lingo, Skt. *lih*, Eng. *to lick*, Fr. *lécher*, Germ. lecken; גָּלַל (cf. עָגַל, אָגַל)⸍ , *volvo*, Germ. *quellen*, *wallen*, Eng. *to well*; חָרַט, חָרַת, גָּרַד, χαράττω, 1⸍ ⸍*háridan*, Ital. *grattare*, Fr. *gratter*, Eng. *to grate*, *to scratch*, Germ. kratz⸍ ₚ *frango*, Germ. *brechen*, &c.; Reuss, *Gesch.* der hl. Schriften A. T.'s, Bra⸍ w. 1881, p. 38, draws attention moreover to the Semitic equivalents 1⸍ ⸍h, *six*, *seven*, *horn*, *to sound*, *to measure*, *to mix*, *to smell*, *to place*, *clear*, *to kneel*,⸍ *goat*, *ox*, &c. An example of a somewhat different kind is am, ham (sa⸍ ⸍m, *kam*, in the sense of the German *samt*, zusammen, *together*; in Hebrew⸍ (whence אֻמָּה *people*, properly *assembly*), עַם (*with*) samt, גַּם *also*, *moreover*,⸍ גָּמַע *to collect*; Pers. *ham*, *hamah* (*at the same time*); Skt. samâ (*with*),⸍ ⸍ıa (ἄμφω), ὁμός, ὁμοῦ (ὅμιλος, ὅμαδος), and harder samós, Lat. *cum*, *cumulu*⸍ *tus*; with the corresponding sibilant Skt. sam, Gk. σύν, ξύν, ξυνός = κοινός,⸍ *sama*, Germ. *samt*, *sammeln*; but many of these instances are doubtful.

i   Essentially different fro⸍ ⸍s internal connexion is the occur-rence of the same words in⸍ ⸍ent languages, where one language has borrowed directly from tl⸍ ⸍er.   Such *loan-words* are—

(a) In Hebrew: some names of objects which were originally indigenous in Babylonia and Assyria (see a comprehensive list of Assyrio-Babylonian loan-words in the Hebrew and Aramaic of the Old Testament in Zimmern and Winckler, *KAT.*[3], ii. p. 648 ff.), in Egypt, Persia, or India, e. g. יְאֹר (also in the plural) *river*, from Egyptian *yoor*, generally as the name of the Nile (late Egypt. *yaro*, Assyr. *yaru'u*), although it is possible that a pure Semitic יְאֹר has been confounded with the Egyptian name of the Nile (so Zimmern); אָחוּ (Egyptian) Nile-reed (see Lieblein, ' Mots égyptiens dans la Bible,' in *PSBA.* 1898, p. 202 f.); פַּרְדֵּם (in Zend *pairidaêza*, circumvallation = παράδεισος) *pleasure-garden, park*; אֲדַרְכּוֹן *daric*, Persian gold coin; תֻּכִּיִּים *peacocks*, perhaps from the Malabar *tôgai* or *tôghai*. Some of these words are also found in Greek, as כַּרְפַּס (Pers. *karbás*, Skt. *karpâsa*) cotton, κάρπασος, *carbasus*. On the other hand it is doubtful if קוֹף corresponds to the Greek κῆπος, κῆβος, Skt. *kapi*, ape.

(b) In Greek, &c. : some originally Semitic names of Asiatic products and articles of commerce, e. g. בּוּץ βύσσος, *byssus* ; לְבֹנָה λίβανος, λιβανωτός, *incense* ; קָנֶה κάνη, κάννα, *canna*, cane ; כַּמֹּן κύμινον, *cuminum*, cumin ; קְצִיעָה κασσία, *cassia*; גָּמָל κάμηλος, *camelus*; עֵרָבוֹן ἀρραβών, *arrhabo, arrha*, pledge. Such transitions have perhaps been brought about chiefly by Phoenician trade. Cf. A. Müller, 'Semitische Lehnworte im älteren Griechisch,' in Bezzenberger's *Beiträge zur Kunde der Indo-germ. Sprachen*, Göttingen, 1877, vol. i. p. 273 ff. ; E. Ries, *Quae res et vocabula a gentibus semiticis in Graeciam pervenerint*, Breslau, 1890; Muss-Arnolt, 'Semitic words in Greek and Latin,' in the *Transactions of the American Philological Association*, xxiii. p. 35 ff. ; H. Lewy, *Die semitischen Fremdwörter im Griech.*, Berlin, 1895 ; J. H. Bondi, *Dem hebr.-phöniz. Sprachzweige angehör. Lehnwörter in hieroglyph. u. hieratischen Texten*, Lpz. 1886.

5. No system of writing is ever so perfect as to be able to reproduce *k* the sounds of a language in all their various shades, and the *writing of the Semites* has one striking fundamental defect, viz. that only the consonants (which indeed form the substance of the language) are written as real letters,[1] whilst of the vowels only the longer are indicated by certain representative consonants (see below, § 7). It was only later that special small marks (points or strokes below or above the consonants) were invented to represent to the eye all the vowel-sounds (see § 8). These are, however, superfluous for the practised reader, and are therefore often wholly omitted in Semitic manuscripts and printed texts. Semitic writing, moreover, almost invariably proceeds from right to left.[2]

---

[1] So also originally the Ethiopic writing, which afterwards represented the vowels by small appendages to the consonants, or by some other change in their form. On the Assyrio-Babylonian cuneiform writing, which likewise indicates the vowels, see the next note, ad fin.

[2] The Sabaean (Himyaritic) writing runs occasionally from left to right, and even alternately in both directions (*boustrophedon*), but as a rule from right to left. In Ethiopic writing the direction from left to right has become the rule ; some few old inscriptions exhibit, however, the opposite direction. The cuneiform writing also runs from left to right, but this is undoubtedly borrowed from a non-Semitic people. Cf. § 5 d, note 3.

With the exception of the Assyrio-Babylonian (cuneiform), all varieties of Semitic writing, although differing widely in some respects, are derived from one and the same original alphabet, represented on extant monuments most faithfully by the characters used on the stele of Mêša', king of Moab (see below, § 2 *d*), and in the *old* Phoenician inscriptions, of which the bronze bowls from a temple of Baal (*CIS*. i. 22 ff. and Plate IV) are somewhat earlier than Mêša'. The old Hebrew writing, as it appears on the oldest monument, the Siloam inscription (see below, § 2 *d*), exhibits essentially the same character. The old Greek, and indirectly all European alphabets, are descended from the old Phoenician writing (see § 5 *i*).

l See the Table of Alphabets at the beginning of the Grammar, which shows the relations of the older varieties of Semitic writing to one another and especially the origin of the present Hebrew characters from their primitive forms. For a more complete view, see Gesenius' *Scripturae linguaeque Phoeniciae monumenta*, Lips. 1837, 4to, pt. i. p. 15 ff., and pt. iii. tab. 1-5. From numerous monuments since discovered, our knowledge of the Semitic characters, especially the Phoenician, has become considerably enlarged and more accurate. Cf. the all but exhaustive bibliography (from 1616 to 1896) in Lidzbarski's *Handbuch der Nordsemitischen Epigraphik*, i. p. 4 ff, and on the origin of the Semitic alphabet, ibid., p. 173 ff., and *Ephemeris* (see the heading of § 1 *a* above), i. pp. 109 ff., 142, 261 ff., and his 'Altsemitische Texte', pt. i, *Kanaanäische Inschriften* (Moabite, Old-Hebrew, Phoenician, Punic), Giessen, 1907.—On the origin and development of the *Hebrew* characters and the best tables of alphabets, see § 5 *a*, last note, and especially § 5 *e*.

m **6.** As regards the relative *age* of the Semitic languages, the oldest literary remains of them are to be found in the Assyrio-Babylonian (cuneiform) inscriptions,[1] with which are to be classed the earliest Hebrew fragments occurring in the old Testament (see § 2).

The earliest non-Jewish *Aramaic* inscriptions known to us are that of זכר king of Hamath (early eighth cent. B.C.), on which see Nöldeke, *ZA*. 1908, p. 376, and that found at Teima, in N. Arabia, in 1880, probably of the fifth cent. B.C., cf. E. Littmann in the *Monist*, xiv. 4 [and Cooke, *op. cit.*, p. 195]. The monuments of Kalammus of Sam'al, in the reign of Shalmanezer II, 859–829 B.C. (cf. A. Šanda, *Die Aramäer*, Lpz. 1902, p. 26), and those found in 1888–1891 at Zenjîrlî in N. Syria, including the Hadad inscription of thirty-four lines (early eighth cent. B.C.) and the Panammu inscription (740 B.C.), are not in pure Aramaic. The Jewish-Aramaic writings begin about the time of Cyrus (cf. Ezr 6³ ff.), specially important being the papyri from Assuan ed. by Sayce and Cowley, London, 1906 (and in a cheaper form by Staerk, Bonn, 1907), which are precisely dated from 471 to 411 B.C., and three others of 407 B.C. ed. by Sachau, Berlin, 1907.

---

[1] According to Hilprecht, *The Babylonian Expedition of the University of Pennsylvania*, i. p. 11 ff., the inscriptions found at Nippur embrace the period from about 4000 to 450 B.C.

Monuments of the *Arabic* branch first appear in the earliest centuries A. D. (Sabaean inscriptions, Ethiopic translation of the Bible in the fourth or fifth century, North-Arabic literature from the sixth century A. D.).

It is, however, another question which of these languages has adhered longest and most faithfully to the original character of the Semitic, and which consequently represents to us the earliest phase of its development. For the more or less rapid transformation of the sounds and forms of a language, as spoken by nations and races, is dependent on causes quite distinct from the growth of a literature, and the organic structure of a language is often considerably impaired even before it has developed a literature, especially by early contact with people of a different language. Thus in the Semitic group, the Aramaic dialects exhibit the earliest and greatest decay, next to them the Hebrew-Canaanitish, and in its own way the Assyrian. Arabic, owing to the seclusion of the desert tribes, was the longest to retain the original fullness and purity of the sounds and forms of words.[1] Even here, however, there appeared, through the revolutionary influence of Islam, an ever-increasing decay, until Arabic at length reached the stage at which we find Hebrew in the Old Testament.

Hence the phenomenon, that in its grammatical structure the ancient *n* Hebrew agrees more with the modern than with the ancient Arabic, and that the latter, although it only appears as a written language at a later period, has yet in many respects preserved a more complete structure and a more original vowel system than the other Semitic languages, cf. Nöldeke, 'Das klassische Arabisch und die arabischen Dialekte,' in *Beiträge zur semitischen Sprachwissenschaft*, p. 1 ff. It thus occupies amongst them a position similar to that which Sanskrit holds among the Indo-Germanic languages, or Gothic in the narrower circle of the Germanic. But even the toughest organism of a language often deteriorates, at least in single forms and derivatives, while on the contrary, in the midst of what is otherwise universal decay, there still remains here and there something original and archaic ; and this is the case with the Semitic languages.

Fuller proof of the above statements belongs to the comparative Grammar of the Semitic languages. It follows, however, from what has been said : (1) that the Hebrew language, as found in the sacred literature of the Jews, has, in respect

---

[1] Even now the language of some of the Bèdawi is much purer and more archaic than that of the town Arabs. It must, however, be admitted that the former exalted estimate of the primitiveness of Arabic has been moderated in many respects by the most recent school of Semitic philology. Much apparently original is to be regarded with Nöldeke (*Die semit. Spr.*, p. 5 [= *Encycl. Brit.*, ed. 9, art. SEMITIC LANGUAGES, p. 642]) only as a modification of the original. The assertion that the Arabs exhibit Semitic characteristics in their purest form, should, according to Nöldeke, be rather that 'the inhabitants of the desert lands of Arabia, under the influence of the extraordinarily monotonous scenery and of a life continually the same amid continual change, have developed most exclusively some of the principal traits of the Semitic race '.

to its organic structure, already suffered more considerable losses than the Arabic, which appears much later on the historical horizon ; (2) that, notwithstanding this fact, we cannot at once and in all points concede priority to the latter ; (3) that it is a mistake to consider with some that the Aramaic, on account of its simplicity (which is only due to the decay of its organic structure), is the oldest form of Semitic speech.

§ 2. *Sketch of the History of the Hebrew Language.*

See Gesenius, *Gesch. der hebr. Sprache u. Schrift*, Lpz. 1815, §§ 5–18 ; Th. Nöldeke's art., 'Sprache, hebräische,' in Schenkel's *Bibel-Lexikon*, Bd. v, Lpz. 1875 ; F. Buhl, 'Hebräische Sprache,' in Hauck's *Realencycl. für prot. Theol. und Kirche*, vii (1899), p. 506 ff.; A. Cowley, 'Hebrew Language and Literature,' in the forthcoming ed. of the *Encycl. Brit.* ; W. R. Smith in the *Encycl. Bibl.*, ii. London, 1901, p. 1984 ff. ; A. Lukyn Williams, 'Hebrew,' in Hastings' *Dict. of the Bible*, ii. p. 325 ff., Edinb. 1899.

a 1. The name *Hebrew Language* usually denotes the language of the sacred writings of the Israelites which form the canon of the *Old Testament*. It is also called *Ancient Hebrew* in contradistinction to the New Hebrew of Jewish writings of the post-biblical period (§ 3 *a*). The name Hebrew language (לְשׁוֹן עִבְרִית‎ *γλῶσσα τῶν Ἑβραίων, ἑβραϊστί*) does not occur in the Old Testament itself. Instead of it we find in Is 19¹⁸ the term *language of Canaan*,¹ and יְהוּדִית‎ *in the Jews' language* 2 K 18²⁶·²⁸ (cf. Is 36¹¹·¹³) Neh 13²⁴. In the last-cited passage it already agrees with the later (post-exilic) usage, which gradually extended the name *Jews, Jewish* to the whole nation, as in Haggai, Nehemiah. and the book of Esther.

b The distinction between the names *Hebrew* (עִבְרִים‎ *Ἑβραῖοι*) and *Israelites* (בְּנֵי יִשְׂרָאֵל‎) is that the latter was rather a national name of honour, with also a religious significance, employed by the people themselves, while the former appears as the less significant name by which the nation was known amongst foreigners. Hence in the Old Testament *Hebrews* are only spoken of either when the name is employed by themselves as contrasted with foreigners (Gn 40¹⁵, Ex 2⁶ f. 3¹⁸ &c., Jon 1⁹) or when it is put in the mouth of those who are not Israelites (Gn 39¹⁴·¹⁷ 41¹² &c.) or, finally, when it is used in opposition to other nations (Gn 14¹³ 43³², Ex 2¹¹·¹³ 21²). In 1 S 13³·⁷ and 14²¹ the text is clearly corrupt. In the Greek and Latin authors, as well as in Josephus, the name *Ἑβραῖοι*, Hebraei,² &c., alone occurs. Of the many explanations of the gentilic עִבְרִי‎, the derivation from עֵבֶר‎ *a country on the other side* with the derivative suffix יִ‍‍ָ‍ (§ 86 *h*) appears to be the only one philologically possible. The name accordingly denoted the Israelites as being those who inhabited the *'eber*, i. e. the district on the other side of the Jordan (or according to others the Euphrates), and would therefore originally be only appropriate when used by the nations on this side of the Jordan or Euphrates. We must, then, suppose that after the crossing of the river in question it had been retained by the Abrahamidae as an old-established name, and within certain limits

---

¹ That Hebrew in its present form was actually developed in Canaan appears from such facts as the use of *yām* (sea) for the west, *nègeb* (properly *dryness*, afterwards as a proper name for the south of Palestine) for the south.

² The Graeco-Roman form of the name is not directly derived from the Hebrew עִבְרִי‎, but from the Palestinian Aramaic *'ebrāyā*, 'the Hebrew.'

(see above) had become naturalized among them. In referring this name to the patronymic Eber, the Hebrew genealogists have assigned to it a much more comprehensive signification. For since in Gn 10²¹ (Nu 24²⁴ does not apply) Shem is called the *father of all the children of Eber*, and to the latter there also belonged according to Gn 11¹⁴ ᶠ. and 10²⁵ ᶠ. Aramean and Arab races, the name, afterwards restricted in the form of the gentilic *'ibrî* exclusively to the Israelites, must have originally included a considerably larger group of countries and nations. The etymological significance of the name must in that case not be insisted upon.[1]

The term ἑβραϊστί is first used, to denote the old Hebrew, in the prologue **C** to Jesus the son of Sirach (about 130 B.C.), and in the New Testament, Rv 9¹¹. On the other hand it serves in Jn 5², 19¹³·¹⁷ perhaps also in 19²⁰ and Rv 16¹⁶ to denote what was then the (Aramaic) vernacular of Palestine as opposed to the Greek. The meaning of the expression ἑβραΐς διάλεκτος in Acts 21⁴⁰, 22², and 26¹⁴ is doubtful (cf. Kautzsch, *Gramm. des Bibl.-Aram.*, p. 19 f.). Josephus also uses the term *Hebrew* both of the old Hebrew and of the Aramaic vernacular of his time.

The Hebrew language is first called the *sacred language* in the Jewish-Aramaic versions of the Old Testament, as being the language of the sacred books in opposition to the *lingua profana*, i. e. the Aramaic vulgar tongue.

2. With the exception of the Old Testament (and apart from the **d** Phoenician inscriptions; see below, *f–h*), only very few remains of old Hebrew or old Canaanitish literature have been preserved. Of the latter—(1) an inscription, unfortunately much injured, of thirty-four lines, which was found in the ancient territory of the tribe of Reuben, about twelve miles to the east of the Dead Sea, among the ruins of the city of Dîbôn (now Dîbân), inhabited in earlier times by the Gadites, afterwards by the Moabites. In it the Moabite king Mêša' (about 850 B.C.) recounts his battles with Israel (cf. 2 K 3⁴ ᶠ.), his buildings, and other matters.[2] Of old Hebrew: (2) an inscription

---

[1] We may also leave out of account the linguistically possible identification of the 'Ibriyyim with the Ḫabiri who appear in the Tell-el-Amarna letters (about 1400 B.C.) as freebooters and mercenaries in Palestine and its neighbourhood.

[2] This monument, unique of its kind, was first seen in August, 1868, on the spot, by the German missionary F. A. Klein. It was afterwards broken into pieces by the Arabs, so that only an incomplete copy of the inscription could be made. Most of the fragments are now in the Louvre in Paris. For the history of the discovery and for the earlier literature relating to the stone, see Lidzbarski, *Nordsemitische Epigraphik*, i. pp. 103 f., 415 f., and in the bibliography (under Me), p. 39 ff. The useful reproduction and translation of the inscription by Smend and Socin (Freiburg in Baden, 1886) was afterwards revised and improved by Nordlander, *Die Inschrift des Königs Mesa von Moab*, Lpz. 1896; by Socin and Holzinger, 'Zur Mesainschrift' (*Berichte der K. Sächsischen Gesell. d. Wiss.*, Dec. 1897); and by Lidzbarski, 'Eine Nachprüfung der Mesainschrift' (*Ephemeris*, i. 1, p. 1 ff.; text in his *Altsemitische Texte*, pt. 1, Giessen, 1907); J. Halévy, *Revue Sémitique*, 1900, pp. 236 ff., 289 f., 1901, p. 297 ff.; M. J. Lagrange, *Revue biblique internationale*, 1901, p. 522 ff.; F. Prätorius in *ZDMG.* 1905, p. 33 ff., 1906, p. 402. Its genuineness was attacked by A. Löwy, *Die Echtheit der Moabit. Inschr. im Louvre* (Wien, 1903), and G. Jahn in *Das Buch Daniel*, Lpz. 1904, p. 122 ff. (also in *ZDMG.* 1905, p. 723 ff.), but without justification, as shown by E. König in *ZDMG.* 1905, pp. 233 ff. and 743 ff. [Cf. also Driver, *Notes on the Hebrew Text of the Books of Samuel*, Oxford, 1890, p. lxxxv ff.; Cooke, *op. cit.*, p. 1 ff.]

of six lines (probably of the eighth century B.C.[1]) discovered in June, 1880, in the tunnel between the Virgin's Spring and the Pool of Siloam at Jerusalem; (3) about forty engraved seal-stones, some of them pre-exilic but bearing little except proper names[2]; (4) coins of the Maccabaean prince Simon (from 'the 2nd year of deliverance', 140 and 139 B.C.) and his successors,[3] and the coinage of the revolts in the times of Vespasian and Hadrian.

e 3. In the whole series of the ancient Hebrew writings, as found in the Old Testament and also in non-biblical monuments (see above, *d*), the language (to judge from its consonantal formation) remains, as regards its general character, and apart from slight changes in form and differences of style (see *k* to *w*), at about the same stage of development. In this form, it may at an early time have been fixed as a literary language, and the fact that the books contained in the Old Testament were handed down as *sacred* writings, must have contributed to this constant uniformity.

f To this old Hebrew, the language of the Canaanitish or Phoenician[4] stocks came the nearest of all the Semitic languages, as is evident partly from the many Canaanitish names of persons and places with a Hebrew form and meaning which occur in the Old Testament (e.g. קִרְיַת סֵפֶר, מַלְכִּי־צֶדֶק, &c. ;

---

[1] Of this inscription—unfortunately not dated, but linguistically and palaeographically very important—referring to the boring of the tunnel, a facsimile is given at the beginning of this grammar. See also Lidzbarski, *Nordsemitische Epigraphik*, i. 105, 163, 439 (bibliography, p. 56 ff. ; facsimile, vol. ii, plate xxi, 1) ; on the new drawing of it by Socin (*ZDPV.* xxii. p. 61 ff. and separately published at Freiburg i. B. 1899), see Lidzbarski, *Ephemeris*, i. 53 ff. and 310 f. (text in *Altsemit. Texte*, p. 9 f.). Against the view of A. Fischer (*ZDMG.* 1902, p. 800 f.) that the six lines are the continuation of an inscription which was never executed, see Lidzbarski, *Ephemeris*, ii. 71. The inscription was removed in 1890, and broken into six or seven pieces in the process. It has since been well restored, and is now in the Imperial Museum at Constantinople. If, as can hardly be doubted, the name שִׁלֹחַ (i. e. *emissio*) Is 8⁶ refers to the discharge of water from the Virgin's Spring, through the tunnel (so Stade, *Gesch. Isr.* i. 594), then the latter, and consequently the inscription, was already in existence about 736 B.C. [Cf. Cooke, *op. cit.*, p. 15 ff.]

[2] M. A. Levy, *Siegel u. Gemmen, &c.*, Bresl. 1869, p. 33 ff. ; Stade, *ZAW.* 1897, p. 501 ff. (four old-Semitic seals published in 1896) ; Lidzbarski, *Handbuch*, i. 169 f. ; *Ephemeris*, i. 10 ff. ; W. Nowack, *Lehrb. d. hebr. Archäol.* (Freib. 1894), i. 262 f. ; I. Benzinger, *Hebr. Archäol.*[2] (Tübingen, 1907), pp. 80, 225 ff., which includes the beautiful seal inscribed לשמע עבד ירבעם from the castle-hill of Megiddo, found in 1904 ; [Cooke, p. 362].

[3] De Saulcy, *Numismatique de la Terre Sainte*, Par. 1874 ; M. A. Levy, *Gesch. der jüd. Münzen*, Breslau, 1862 ; Madden, *The Coins of the Jews*, Lond. 1881 ; Reinach, *Les monnaies juives*, Paris, 1888.—Cf. the literature in Schürer's *Gesch. des jüd. Volkes im Zeitalter J. C.*[3], Lpz. 1901, i. p. 20 ff. ; [Cooke, p. 352 ff.].

[4] כְּנַעֲנִי, כְּנַעַן is the native name, common both to the Canaanitish tribes in Palestine and to those which dwelt at the foot of the Lebanon and on the Syrian coast, whom we call Phoenicians, while they called themselves כנען on their coins. The people of Carthage also called themselves so.

on 'Canaanite glosses'[1] to Assyrian words in the cuneiform tablets of Tell-el-Amarna [about 1400 B.C.] cf. H. Winckler, 'Die Thontafeln von Tell-el-Amarna,' in *Keilinschr. Bibliothek*, vol. v, Berlin, 1896 f. [transcription and translation]; J. A. Knudtzon, *Die El-Amarna-Tafeln*, Lpz. 1907 f. ; H. Zimmern, *ZA.* 1891, p. 154 ff. and *KAT.*[3], p. 651 ff.), and partly from the numerous remains of the Phoenician and Punic languages.

The latter we find in their peculiar writing (§ 1 *k, l*) in a great number of inscriptions and on coins, copies of which have been collected by Gesenius, Judas, Bourgade, Davis, de Vogüé, Levy, P. Schröder, v. Maltzan, Euting, but especially in Part I of the *Corpus Inscriptionum Semiticarum*, Paris, 1881 ff. Among the inscriptions but few public documents are found, e. g. two lists of fees for sacrifices ; by far the most are epitaphs or votive tablets. Of special importance is the inscription on the sarcophagus of King Ešmûnazar of Sidon, found in 1855, now in the Louvre ; see the bibliography in Lidzbarski, *Nordsem. Epigr.*, i. 23 ff. ; on the inscription, i. 97 ff., 141 f., 417, ii. plate iv, 2 ; [Cooke, p. 30 ff.]. To these may be added isolated words in Greek and Latin authors, and the Punic texts in Plautus, *Poenulus* 5, 1–3 (best treated by Gildemeister in Ritschl's edition of Plautus, Lips. 1884, tom. ii, fasc. 5). From the monuments we learn the native orthography, from the Greek and Latin transcriptions the pronunciation and vocalization ; the two together give a tolerably distinct idea of the language and its relation to Hebrew.

Phoenician (Punic) words occurring in inscriptions are, e. g. אל *God, g* אדם *man,* בן *son,* בת *daughter,* מלך *king,* עבד *servant,* כהן *priest,* זבח *sacrifice,* בעל *lord,* שמש *sun,* ארץ *land,* ים *sea,* אבן *stone,* כסף *silver,* ברזל *iron,* שמן *oil,* עת *time,* קבר *grave,* מצבת *monument,* מקם *place,* משכב *bed,* כל *all,* אחד *one,* שנים *two,* שלש *three,* ארבע *four,* חמש *five,* שש *six,* שבע *seven,* עשר *ten,* כן (= Hebr. היה) *to be,* שמע *to hear,* פתח *to open,* נדר *to vow,* ברך *to bless,* בקש *to seek,* &c. Proper names : צדן *Sidon,* צר *Tyre,* חנא *Hanno,* חנבעל *Hannibal,* &c. See the complete vocabulary in Lidzbarski, *Nordsem. Epigr.*, i. 204 ff.

Variations from Hebrew in Phoenician orthography and inflection are, *h* e. g. the almost invariable omission of the vowel letters (§ 7 *b*), as בת for בית *house,* קל for קול *voice,* צדן for צידון, כהנם for כֹּהֲנִים *priests,* אלנם (in Plaut. *alonim*) *gods* ; the fem., even in the absolute state, ending in ת (*ath*) (§ 80 *b*) as well as א (*ô*), the relative אש (Hebr. אֲשֶׁר), &c. The differences in pronunciation are more remarkable, especially in Punic, where the וֹ was regularly pronounced as *û*, e. g. שֹׁפֵט *sûfeṭ* (judge), שָׁלֹשׁ *sâlûs* (three), רש *rûs* = רֹאשׁ *head* ; *i* and *e* often as the obscure dull sound of *y*, e. g. הִנְנּוּ *ynnynnu* (ecce eum), אֵת (אית) *yth* ; the ע as *o*, e. g. מעקר *Mocar* (cf. מַעֲכָה LXX, Gn 22²⁴ Μωχά). See the collection of the grammatical peculiarities in Gesenius, *Monumenta Phoenicia*, p. 430 ff. ; Paul Schröder, *Die phöniz. Sprache*, Halle, 1869 ; B. Stade, 'Erneute Prüfung des zwischen dem Phönic. und Hebr. bestehenden Verwandtschaftsgrades,' in the *Morgenländ. Forschungen*, Lpz. 1875, p. 169 ff.

4. As the Hebrew writing on monuments and coins mentioned *i* in *d* consists only of consonants, so also the writers of the Old

---

[1] Cf. inter alia : *aparu,* also *ḥaparu* (Assyr. *epru, ipru*) = עָפָר ; *ḥullu* = עֹל (with hard ע ; cf. § 6 *c*, and Assyr. *ḥumri* = עָמְרִי, *ḥazzatu* = עַזָּה) ; *iazkur* = יִזְכֹּר, *zuruḥu* = זְרֹעַ, *abadat* = אֲבְדָה, *šaḥri* = שַׁעַר, *gate* ; *baṭnu* = בֶּטֶן, *belly* ; *kilûbi* = כְּלוּב, *net* ; *ṣaduk* = צָדֹק (צַדִּיק), &c. [Cf. Böhl, *Die Sprache d. Amarnabriefe*, Lpz. 1909.]

Testament books used merely the consonant-signs (§ 1 *k*), and even now the written scrolls of the Law used in the synagogues must not, according to ancient custom, contain anything more. The present pronunciation of this consonantal text, its vocalization and accentuation, rest on the tradition of the Jewish schools, as it was finally fixed by the system of punctuation (§ 7 *h*) introduced by Jewish scholars about the seventh century A.D.; cf. § 3 *b*.

k An earlier stage in the development of the Canaanitish-Hebrew language, i.e. a form of it anterior to the written documents now extant, when it must have stood nearer to the common language of the united Semitic family, can still be discerned in its principal features :—(1) from many archaisms preserved in the traditional texts, especially in the names of persons and places dating from earlier times, as well as in isolated forms chiefly occurring in poetic style; (2) in general by an *a posteriori* conclusion from traditional forms, so far as according to the laws and analogies of phonetic change they clearly point to an older phase of the language; and (3) by comparison with the kindred languages, especially Arabic, in which this earlier stage of the language has been frequently preserved even down to later times (§ 1 *m*, *n*). In numerous instances in examining linguistic phenomena, the same—and consequently so much the more certain—result is attained by each of these three methods.

Although the systematic investigation of the linguistic development indicated above belongs to comparative Semitic philology, it is nevertheless indispensable for the scientific treatment of Hebrew to refer to the ground-forms [1] so far as they can be ascertained and to compare the corresponding forms in Arabic. Even elementary grammar which treats of the forms of the language occurring in the Old Testament frequently requires, for their explanation, a reference to these ground-forms.

l 5. Even in the language of the Old Testament, notwithstanding its general uniformity, there is noticeable a certain progress from an earlier to a later stage. Two periods, though with some reservations, may be distinguished: the *first*, down to the end of the Babylonian exile; and the *second*, after the exile.

m To the former belongs, apart from isolated traces of a later revision, the larger half of the Old Testament books, viz. (*a*) of the prose and historical writings, a large part of the Pentateuch and of Joshua, Judges, Samuel, and Kings; (*b*) of the poetical, perhaps

---

[1] Whether these can be described simply as 'primitive Semitic' is a question which may be left undecided here.

a part of the Psalms and Proverbs; (*c*) the writings of the earlier prophets (apart from various later additions) in the following chronological order: Amos, Hosea, Isaiah I, Micah, Nahum, Zephaniah, Habakkuk, Obadiah (?), Jeremiah, Ezekiel, Isaiah II (ch. 40–55).

n The beginning of this period, and consequently of Hebrew literature generally, is undoubtedly to be placed as early as the time of Moses, although the Pentateuch in its present form, in which very different strata may be still clearly recognized, is to be regarded as a gradual production of the centuries after Moses. Certain linguistic peculiarities of the Pentateuch, which it was once customary to regard as archaisms, such as the epicene use of נַעַר *boy, youth*, for נַעֲרָה *girl*, and הוּא for הִיא, are merely to be attributed to a later redactor; cf. § 17 *c*.

o The linguistic character of the various strata of the Pentateuch has been examined by Ryssel, *De Elohistae Pentateuchici sermone*, Lpz. 1878; König, *De criticae sacrae argumento e linguae legibus repetito*, Lpz. 1879 (analysis of Gn 1–11); F. Giesebrecht, 'Der Sprachgebr. des hexateuchischen Elohisten,' in *ZAW.* 1881, p. 177 ff., partly modified by Driver in the *Journal of Philology*, vol. xi. p. 201 ff. ; Kräutlein, *Die sprachl. Verschiedenheiten in den Hexateuchquellen*, Lpz. 1908.—Abundant matter is afforded also by Holzinger, *Einleitung in den Hexateuch*, Freib. 1893 ; Driver, *Introduction to the Literature of the Old Testament* [8], Edinburgh, 1908; Strack, *Einleitung ins A. T.* [6], Munich, 1906 ; König, *Einleitung in das A. T.*, Bonn, 1893.

p 6. Even in the writings of this first period, which embraces about 600 years, we meet, as might be expected, with considerable differences in linguistic form and style, which are due partly to differences in the time and place of composition, and partly to the individuality and talent of the authors. Thus Isaiah, for example, writes quite differently from the later Jeremiah, but also differently from his contemporary Micah. Amongst the historical books of this period, the texts borrowed from earlier sources have a linguistic colouring perceptibly different from those derived from later sources, or passages which belong to the latest redactor himself. Yet the structure of the language, and, apart from isolated cases, even the vocabulary and phraseology, are on the whole the same, especially in the prose books.

q But the *poetic language* is in many ways distinguished from prose, not only by a *rhythm* due to more strictly balanced (parallel) members and definite metres (see *r*), but also by peculiar *words* and *meanings, inflexions* and *syntactical constructions* which it uses in addition to those usual in prose. This distinction, however, does not go far as, for example, in Greek. Many of these poetic peculiarities occur in the kindred languages, especially in Aramaic, as the ordinary modes of expression, and probably are to be regarded largely as archaisms which poetry retained. Some perhaps, also, are embellishments which the Hebrew poets who knew Aramaic adopted into their language.[1]

The prophets, at least the earlier, in language and rhythm are to be regarded almost entirely as poets, except that with them the sentences are often more extended, and the parallelism is less regular and balanced than is the case with the poets properly so called. The language of the later prophets, on the contrary, approaches nearer to prose.

r   On the *rhythm* of Hebrew poetry, see besides the Commentaries on the poetical books and Introductions to the O.T., J. Ley, *Grundzüge des Rhythmus, &c.*, Halle, 1875; *Leitfaden der Metrik der hebr. Poesie*, Halle, 1887; 'Die metr. Beschaffenheit des B. Hiob,' in *Theol. Stud. u. Krit.*, 1895, iv, 1897, i; Grimme, 'Abriss der bibl.-hebr. Metrik,' *ZDMG.* 1896, p. 529 ff., 1897, p. 683 ff.; *Psalmenprobleme, &c.*, Freiburg (Switzerland), 1902 (on which see Beer in *ThLZ.* 1903, no. 11); 'Gedanken über hebr. Metrik,' in Altschüler's *Vierteljahrschrift*, i (1903), 1 ff.; Döller, *Rhythmus, Metrik u. Strophik in d. bibl.-hebr. Poesie*, Paderborn, 1899; Schloegl, *De re metrica veterum Hebraeorum disputatio*, Vindobonae, 1899 (on the same lines as Grimme); but especially Ed. Sievers, *Metrische Studien* : i *Studien zur hebr. Metrik*, pt. 1 *Untersuchungen*, pt. 2 *Textproben*, Lpz. 1901 : ii *Die hebr. Genesis*, 1 *Texte*, 2 *Zur Quellenscheidung u. Textkritik*, Lpz. 1904 f. : iii *Samuel*, Lpz. 1907 ; *Amos metrisch bearbeitet* (with H. Guthe), Lpz. 1907 ; and his *Alttest. Miszellen* (1 Is 24-27, 2 Jona, 3 Deutero-Zechariah, 4 Malachi, 5 Hosea, 6 Joel, 7 Obadiah, 8 Zephaniah, 9 Haggai, 10 Micah), Lpz. 1904-7.—As a guide to Sievers' system (with some criticism of his principles) see Baumann, ' Die Metrik u. das A.T.,' in the *Theol. Rundschau*, viii (1905), 41 ff. ; W. H. Cobb, *A criticism of systems of Hebrew Metre*, Oxford, 1905 ; Cornill, *Einleitung ins A.T.*[5], Tübingen, 1905, p. 11 ff. ; Rothstein, *Zeitschr. für d. ev. Rel.-Unterricht*, 1907, p. 188 ff. and his *Grundzüge des hebr. Rhythmus*, Lpz. 1909 (also separately *Psalmentexte u. der Text des Hohen Liedes*, Lpz. 1909) ; W. R. Arnold, 'The rhythms of the ancient Heb.,' in *O. T. and Semitic Studies in memory of W. R. Harper*, i. 165 ff., Chicago, 1907, according to whom the number of syllables between the beats is only limited by the physiological possibilities of phonetics ; C. v. Orelli, ' Zur Metrik der alttest. Prophetenschriften,' in his *Kommentar zu den kl. Propheten*[3], p. 236 ff., Munich, 1908.— In full agreement with Sievers is Baethgen, *Psalmen*[3], p. xxvi ff., Göttingen, 1904. [Cf. Budde in *DB.* iv. 3 ff. ; Duhm in *EB.* iii. 3793 ff.]

Of all views of this matter, the only one generally accepted as sound was at first Ley's and Budde's discovery of the Qina- or Lamentation-Verse (*ZAW.* 1882, 5 ff. ; 1891, 234 ff. ; 1892, 31 ff.). On their predecessors, Lowth; de Wette, Ewald, see Löhr, *Klagelied*[2], p. 9. This verse, called by Duhm 'long verse', by Sievers simply ' five-syllabled ' (Fünfer), consists of two members, the second at least one beat shorter than the other. That a regular repetition of an equal number of syllables in *arsis* and *thesis* was observed by other poets, had been established by Ley, Duhm, Gunkel, Grimme, and others, especially Zimmern, who cites a Babylonian hymn in which the members are actually marked (*ZA.* x. 1 ff., xii. 382 ff. ; cf. also Delitzsch, *Das babyl. Weltschöpfungsepos*, Lpz. 1896, pp. 60 ff.). Recently, however, E. Sievers, the recognized authority on metre in other branches of literature, has indicated, in the works mentioned above, a number of fresh facts and views, which have frequently been confirmed by the conclusions of Ley and others. The most important are as follows :—

Hebrew poetry, as distinguished from the quantitative Classical and Arabic

---

[1] That already in Isaiah's time (second half of the eighth century B. C.) educated Hebrews, or at least officers of state, understood Aramaic, while the common people in Jerusalem did not, is evident from 2 K 18²⁶ (Is 36¹¹).

and the syllabic Syriac verse, is *accentual.* The number of unstressed syllables between the beats (*ictus*) is, however, not arbitrary, but the scheme of the verse is based on an irregular anapaest which may undergo rhythmical modifications (e. g. resolving the ictus into two syllables, or lengthening the arsis so as to give a double accent) and contraction, e. g. of the first two syllables. The foot always concludes with the ictus, so that toneless endings, due to change of pronunciation or corruption of the text, are to be disregarded, although as a rule the ictus coincides with the Hebrew wordaccent. The metrical scheme consists of combinations of feet in *series* (of 2, 3 or 4), and of these again in *periods*—double threes, very frequently, double fours in narrative, fives in Lamentations (see above) and very often elsewhere, and sevens. Sievers regards the last two metres as catalectic double threes and fours. Connected sections do not always maintain the same metre throughout, but often exhibit a mixture of metres.

It can no longer be doubted that in the analysis of purely poetical passages, this system often finds ready confirmation and leads to textual and literary results, such as the elimination of glosses. There are, however, various difficulties in carrying out the scheme consistently and extending it to the prophetical writings and still more to narrative : (1) not infrequently the required number of feet is only obtained by sacrificing the clearly marked parallelism, or the grammatical connexion (e. g. of the construct state with its genitive), and sometimes even by means of doubtful emendations ; (2) the whole system assumes a correct transmission of the text and its pronunciation, for neither of which is there the least guarantee. To sum up, our conclusion at present is that for poetry proper some assured and final results have been already obtained, and others may be expected, from the principles laid down by Sievers, although, considering the way in which the text has been transmitted, a *faultless* arrangement of metres cannot be expected. Convincing proof of the *consistent* use of the same metrical schemes in the prophets, and *a fortiori* in narrative, can hardly be brought forward.

The great work of D. H. Müller, *Die Propheten in ihrer ursprüngl. Form* (2 vols., Vienna, 1896 ; cf. his *Strophenbau u. Responsion*, ibid. 1898, and *Komposition u. Strophenbau*, ibid. 1907), is a study of the most important monuments of early Semitic poetry from the point of view of strophic structure and the use of the refrain, i. e. the repetition of the same or similar phrases or words in corresponding positions in different strophes.

The arrangement of certain poetical passages in verse-form required by early scribal rules (Ex 15¹⁻¹⁹ ; Dt 32¹⁻⁴³ ; Ju 5 ; 1 S 2¹⁻¹⁰ ; 2 S 22, 23¹⁻⁷ ; ψ 18, 136 ; Pr. 31¹⁰⁻³¹ ; 1 Ch 16⁸⁻³⁶ : cf. also Jo 12⁹⁻²⁴ ; Ec 3²⁻⁸ ; Est 9⁷⁻¹⁰) has nothing to do with the question of metre in the above sense.

Words are used in poetry, for which others are customary in prose, e. g. ‫שׁ‬ ‫אֱנוֹשׁ‬ *man* = ‫אָדָם‬ ; ‫אֹרַח‬ *path* = ‫דֶּרֶךְ‬ ; ‫מִלָּה‬ *word* = ‫דָּבָר‬ ; ‫חָזָה‬ *to see* = ‫רָאָה‬ ; ‫אָתָה‬ *to come* = ‫בּוֹא.‬

To the poetic *meanings of words* belongs the use of certain poetic *epithets* as substantives ; thus, for example, ‫אָבִיר‬ (only in constr. st. ‫אֲבִיר)‬ *the strong one* for *God* ; ‫אַבִּיר‬ *the strong one* for *bull, horse* ; ‫לְבָנָה‬ *alba* for *luna* ; ‫צָר‬ *enemy* for ‫אֹיֵב.‬

Of word-forms, we may note, e. g. the longer forms of prepositions of place (§ 103 *n*) ‫עֲלֵי‬ = ‫עַל‬, ‫אֱלֵי‬ = ‫אֶל‬, ‫עֲדֵי‬ = ‫עַד‬ ; the endings ‫יָ‬___, ‫וֹ‬ in the noun (§ 90) ; the pronominal suffixes ‫מוֹ‬, ‫מוֹ‬___, ‫מוֹ‬___, ‫מוֹ‬___ for ‫ם‬, ‫ם‬___, ‫ם‬___ (§ 58) ; the plural ending ‫ין‬___ for ‫ים‬___ (§ 87 *e*). To the *syntax* belongs the far more sparing use of the article, of the relative pronoun, of the accusative particle ‫אֵת‬ ; the construct state even before prepositions ; the shortened imperfect with the same meaning as the ordinary form (§ 109 *i*) ; the wider governing power of prepositions ; and in general a forcible brevity of expression.

t **7.** The *second* period of the Hebrew language and literature, after the return from the exile until the Maccabees (about 160 B.C.), is chiefly distinguished by a constantly closer approximation of the language to the kindred western Aramaic dialect. This is due to the influence of the Aramaeans, who lived in close contact with the recent and thinly-populated colony in Jerusalem, and whose dialect was already of importance as being the official language of the western half of the Persian empire. Nevertheless the supplanting of Hebrew by Aramaic proceeded only very gradually. Writings intended for popular use, such as the Hebrew original of Jesus the son of Sirach and the book of Daniel, not only show that Hebrew about 170 B.C. was still in use as a literary language, but also that it was still at least understood by the people.[1] When it had finally ceased to exist as a living language, it was still preserved as the *language of the Schools*—not to mention the numerous Hebraisms introduced into the Aramaic spoken by the Jews.

> For particulars, see Kautzsch, *Gramm. des Bibl.-Aram.*, pp. 1–6. We may conveniently regard the relation of the languages which co-existed in this later period as similar to that of the High and Low German in North Germany, or to that of the High German and the common dialects in the south and in Switzerland. Even amongst the more educated, the common dialect prevails orally, whilst the High German serves essentially as the literary and cultured language, and is at least understood by all classes of the people. Wholly untenable is the notion, based on an erroneous interpretation of Neh 8⁸, that the Jews immediately after the exile had completely forgotten the Hebrew language, and therefore needed a translation of the Holy Scriptures.

u The Old Testament writings belonging to this second period, in all of which the Aramaic colouring appears in various degrees, are : certain parts of the Pentateuch and of Joshua, Ruth, the books of Ezra, Nehemiah, Chronicles, Esther ; the prophetical books of Haggai, Zechariah, Isaiah III (56–66), Malachi, Joel, Jonah, Daniel; of the poetical books, a large part of Proverbs, Job, Song of Songs, Ecclesiastes, and most of the Psalms. As literary compositions, these books are sometimes far inferior to those of the first period, although work was still produced which in purity of language and aesthetic value falls little short of the writings of the golden age.

v *Later words* (Aramaisms) are, e.g. אֶחְוָה *declaration*, אָנַס *compel*, בַּר *son*, גִּיר *chalk*, עֵת = זְמָן *time*, זְקַף *raise up*, חסד Pi. *reproach*, טלל Pi. *roof over*,

---

[1] The extensive use of Hebrew in the popular religious literature which is partly preserved to us in the Midrašim, the Mišna, and the Liturgy, indicates, moreover, that Hebrew was widely understood much later than this. Cf. M. H. Segal, 'Mišnaic Hebrew and its relations to Biblical Hebrew and Aramaic,' in *J. Q. R.*, 1908, p. 647 ff. (also separately).

טָעָה *stray*, בֵּף *rock*, מָלֵךְ *advise*, סוֹף=קֵץ *end*, קָבַל=לָקַח *take*, רָעַע=רָצַץ *break*,
שָׂנֵא *be many*, שָׁלַט=מָלַךְ *rule*, תָּקַף=אָמֵץ *be strong*.—Later *meanings* are, e. g.
אָמַר (to say) *to command*; עָנָה (to answer) *to begin speaking*.—*Orthographical*
and *grammatical* peculiarities are, the frequent *scriptio plena* of וֹ and יֵ—,
e. g. דָּוִיד [1] (elsewhere דָּוִד), even קוֹדֶשׁ for קֹדֶשׁ, רוֹב for רֹב ; the interchange
of הָ— and אָ— *final*; the more frequent use of substantives in וֹן, וֹן—, וּת,
&c. Cf. Dav. Strauss, *Sprachl. Studien zu d. hebr. Sirachfragmenten*, Zürich, 1900,
p. 19 ff.; for the Psalms Cheyne, *Origin of the Psalter*, p. 461 ff., and especially
Giesebrecht in *ZAW.* 1881, p. 276 ff. ; in general, Kautzsch, *Die Aramaismen
im A. T.* (i, Lexikal. Teil), Halle, 1902.

But all the peculiarities of these later writers are not Aramaisms. Several
do not occur in Aramaic and must have belonged at an earlier period to
the Hebrew vernacular, especially it would seem in northern Palestine.
There certain parts of Judges, amongst others, may have originated, as is
indicated, e. g. by שֶׁ, a common form in Phoenician (as well as אֵשׁ), for
אֲשֶׁר (§ 36), which afterwards recurs in Jonah, Lamentations, the Song of
Songs, the later Psalms, and Ecclesiastes.

Rem. 1. Of dialectical varieties in the old Hebrew language, only one *w*
express mention occurs in the O. T. (Ju 12[6]), according to which the
Ephraimites in certain cases pronounced the שׁ as ס. (Cf. Marquart in
ZAW. 1888, p. 151 ff.) Whether in Neh 13[24] by the *speech of Ashdod* a Hebrew,
or a (wholly different) Philistine dialect is intended, cannot be determined.
On the other hand, many peculiarities in the North Palestinian books
(Judges and Hosea) are probably to be regarded as differences in dialect,
and so also some anomalies in the Moabite inscription of Mêša' (see above, *d*).
On later developments see L. Metman, *Die hebr. Sprache, ihre Geschichte u.
lexikal. Entwickelung seit Abschluss des Kanons u. ihr Bau in d. Gegenwart,*
Jerusalem, 1906.

2. It is evident that, in the extant remains of old Hebrew literature,[2] the
entire store of the ancient language is not preserved. The canonical books
of the Old Testament formed certainly only a fraction of the whole Hebrew
national literature.

§ 3. *Grammatical Treatment of the Hebrew Language.*

Gesenius, *Gesch. der hebr. Sprache*, §§ 19–39 ; Oehler's article, 'Hebr. Sprache,'
in Schmid's *Encykl. des ges. Erziehungs- u. Unterrichtswesens*, vol. iii. p. 346 ff.
(in the 2nd ed. revised by Nestle, p. 314 ff.). Cf. also the literature cited
above in the headings of §§ 1 and 2 ; also Böttcher, *Lehrb. der hebr. Spr.*, i. Lpz.
1866, p. 30 ff. ; L. Geiger, *Das Studium der Hebr. Spr. in Deutschl. vom Ende des
XV. bis zur Mitte des XVI. Jahrh.*, Breslau, 1870 ; B. Pick, 'The Study of the
Hebrew Language among Jews and Christians,' in *Bibliotheca Sacra*, 1884,
p. 450 ff., and 1885, p. 470 ff. ; W. Bacher, article 'Grammar' in the *Jew.
Encyclopaedia*, vol. vi, Now York and London, 1904. Cf. also the note on *d*.

1. At the time when the old Hebrew language was gradually *a*
becoming extinct, and the formation of the O. T. canon was

---

[1] דָּוִיד in the Minor Prophets throughout (Ho 3[5], &c.) is due merely to
a caprice of the Masoretes.

[2] According to the calculation of the Dutch scholar Leusden, the O. T.
contains 5,642 different Hebrew and Aramaic words ; according to rabbinical
calculations, 79,856 altogether in the Pentateuch. Cf. also E. Nestle, *ZAW.*
1906, p. 283 ; H. Strack, *ZAW.* 1907, p. 69 ff.; Blau, 'Neue masoret. Studien,'
in *JQR.* xvi. 357 ff., treats of the number of letters and words, and the verse-
division in the O. T.

approaching completion, the Jews began to explain and critically
revise their sacred text, and sometimes to translate it into the
vernacular languages which in various countries had become current
among them. The oldest *translation* is the Greek of the *Seventy*
(more correctly *Seventy-two*) Interpreters (LXX), which was begun
with the Pentateuch at Alexandria under Ptolemy Philadelphus, but
only completed later. It was the work of various authors, some of
whom had a living knowledge of the original, and was intended for
the use of Greek-speaking Jews, especially in Alexandria. Somewhat
later the Aramaic translations, or Targums (תַּרְגּוּמִים i. e. *interpreta-
tions*), were formed by successive recensions made in Palestine and
Babylonia. The *explanations*, derived in part from alleged tradition,
refer almost exclusively to civil and ritual law and dogmatic theology,
and are no more scientific in character than much of the textual
tradition of that period. Both kinds of tradition are preserved
in the *Talmud*, the first part of which, the *Mišna*, was finally brought
to its present form towards the end of the second century ; of the
remainder, the *Gemāra*, one recension (the *Jerusalem* or *Palestinian
Gem.*) about the middle of the fourth century, the other (the *Babylonian Gem.*) about the middle of the sixth century A.D. The Mišna
forms the beginning of the New-Hebrew literature; the language of
the Gemaras is for the most part Aramaic.

b   2. To the interval between the completion of the Talmud and
the earliest grammatical writers, belong mainly the vocalization and
accentuation of the hitherto unpointed text of the O. T., according to
the pronunciation traditional in the Synagogues and Schools (§ 7 *h, i*),
as well as the greater part of the collection of critical notes which
bears the name of Masōra (מְסוֹרָה *traditio* ?).[1] From this the text
which has since been transmitted with rigid uniformity by the MSS.,

---

[1] On the name Masora (or Massora, as e. g. E. König, *Einleitung in das A. T.*,
p. 38 ff. ; *Lehrgeb. d. hebr. Sprache*, ii. 358 ff.), and the great difficulty of satis-
factorily explaining it, cf. De Lagarde, *Mitteilungen*, i. 91 ff. W. Bacher's
derivation of the expression (in *JQR*. 1891, p. 785 ff. ; so also C. Levias in
the *Hebrew Union College Annual*, Cincinnati, 1904, p. 147 ff.) from Ez 20³⁷
(מָסֹרֶת הַבְּרִית ; מסרה, i. e. מוֹסֵרָה, being an equally legitimate form) is
rightly rejected by König, l. c. The correctness of the form מָסֹרָה (by the
side of the equally well-attested form מַסֹּרֶת) does not seem to us to be
invalidated by his arguments, nor by Blau's proposal to read מְסוֹרֶת (*JQR*. xii.
241). The remark of Levias (l.c.) deserves notice, that with the earlier Masoretes
מסורת is equivalent to orthography, i. e. *plene-* and *defective* writing, and only
later came to mean *traditio*.—G. Wildboer, in *ZAW*. 1909, p. 74, contends
that as מסר *to hand on* is not found in the O.T., it must be a late denominative in this sense.

and is still the received text of the O. T., has obtained the name of the Masoretic Text.

E. F. K. Rosenmüller already (*Handbuch für d. Liter. der bibl. Kritik u. C Exegese*, 1797, i. 247; *Vorrede zur Stereotyp-Ausg. des A. T.*, Lpz. 1834) maintained that our O. T. text was derived from Codices belonging to a single recension. J. G. Sommer (cf. Cornill, *ZAW*. 1892, p. 309), Olshausen (since 1853), and especially De Lagarde (*Proverbien*, 1863, p. 1 ff.), have even made it probable that the original Masoretic text was derived from a single standard manuscript. Cf., however, E. König in *Ztschr. f. kirchl. Wiss.*, 1887, p. 279 f., and especially his *Einleitung ins A. T.*, p. 88 ff. Moreover a great many facts, which will be noticed in their proper places, indicate that the Masora itself is by no means uniform but shows clear traces of different schools and opinions; cf. H. Strack in *Semitic Studies in memory of . . . Kohut*, Berlin, 1897, p. 563 ff. An excellent foundation for the history of the Masora and the settlement of the masoretic tradition was laid by Joh. Buxtorf in his *Tiberias seu Commentarius Masorethicus*, first published at Basel in 1620 as an appendix to the Rabbinical Bible of 1618 f. For more recent work see Geiger, *Jüdische Ztschr.*, iii. 78 ff., followed by Harris in *JQR*. i. 128 ff, 243 ff.; S. Frensdorff, *Ochla W'ochla*, Hanover, 1864; and his *Massor. Wörterb.*, part i, Hanover and Lpz. 1876; and Ch. D. Ginsburg, *The Massora compiled from Manuscripts, &c.*, 3 vols., Lond. 1880 ff., and *Introduction to the Massoretico-critical edition of the Hebr. Bible*, Lond. 1897 (his text, reprinted from that of Jacob b. Ḥayyîm [Venice, 1524–5] with variants from MSS. and the earliest editions, was published in 2 vols. at London in 1894, 2nd ed. 1906; a revised edition is in progress); H. Hyvernat, 'La langue et le langage de la Massore' (as a mixture of New-Hebrew and Aramaic), in the *Revue biblique*, Oct. 1903, p. 529 ff. and B: 'Lexique massorétique,' *ibid.*, Oct. 1904, p. 521 ff., 1905, p. 481 ff., and p. 515 ff. In the use of the Massora for the critical construction of the Text, useful work has been done especially by S. Baer, in the editions of the several books (only Exod.-Deut. have still to appear), edited from 1869 conjointly with Fr. Delitzsch, and since 1891 by Baer alone. Cf. also § 7 *h*.

The various readings of the Q°rê (see § 17) form one of the oldest and most important parts of the Masora. The punctuation of the Text, however, is not to be confounded with the compilation of the Masora. The former was settled at an earlier period, and is the result of a much more exhaustive labour than the Masora, which was not completed till a considerably later time.

3. It was not until about the beginning of the tenth century that *d* the Jews, following the example of the Arabs, began their grammatical compilations. Of the numerous grammatical and lexicographical works of R. Saʿadya,[1] beyond fragments in the commentary on the Sepher Yeṣira (ed. Mayer-Lambert, pp. 42, 47, 75, &c.), only the explanation in Arabic of the seventy (more correctly ninety) *hapax legomena* in the O. T. has been preserved. Written likewise in Arabic, but frequently translated into Hebrew, were the still extant works of the grammarians R. Yehuda Ḥayyûg (also called Abu Zakarya Yaḥya, about the year 1000) and R. Yona (Abu 'l-Walîd Merwân ibn Ǵanâḥ, about 1030). By the aid of these earlier labours, Abraham ben Ezra (commonly called Aben Ezra, ob. 1167) and R. David Qimḥi (ob. c. 1235) especially gained a classical reputation by their Hebrew grammatical writings.

---

[1] On his independent attitude towards the Masoretic punctuation, see Delitzsch, *Comm. zu den Psalmen*[4], p. 39.

From these earliest grammarians are derived many principles of arrangement and technical terms, some of which are still retained, e. g. the naming of the conjugations and weak verbs according to the paradigm of פָּעַל, certain *voces memoriales*, as בְּנַדְכְּפַת and the like.[1]

e 4. The father of Hebrew philology among Christians was John Reuchlin (ob. 1522),[2] to whom Greek literature also is so much indebted. Like the grammarians who succeeded him, till the time of John Buxtorf the elder (ob. 1629), he still adhered almost entirely to Jewish tradition. From the middle of the seventeenth century the field of investigation gradually widened, and the study of the kindred languages, chiefly through the leaders of the Dutch school, Albert Schultens (ob. 1750) and N. W. Schröder (ob. 1798), became of fruitful service to Hebrew grammar.

f 5. In the nineteenth century[3] the advances in Hebrew philology are especially connected with the names of W. Gesenius (born at Nordhausen, Feb. 3, 1786; from the year 1810 Professor at Halle, where he died Oct. 23, 1842), who above all things aimed at the comprehensive observation and lucid presentation of the actually occurring linguistic phenomena; H. Ewald (ob. 1875, at Göttingen; *Krit. Gramm. der Hebr. Spr.*, Lpz. 1827; *Ausführl. Lehrb. d. hebr. Spr.*, 8th ed., Gött. 1870), who chiefly aimed at referring linguistic forms to general laws and rationally explaining the latter; J. Olshausen (ob. 1882, at Berlin; *Lehrb. der hebr. Sprache*, Brunswick, 1861) who attempted a consistent explanation of the existing condition of the language, from the presupposed primitive Semitic forms, preserved according to him notably in old Arabic. F. Böttcher (*Ausführl. Lehrb. d. hebr. Spr.* ed. by F. Mühlau, 2 vols., Lpz. 1866–8) endeavoured to present an exhaustive synopsis of the linguistic phenomena, as well as to give an explanation of them from the sphere of Hebrew

---

[1] On the oldest Hebrew grammarians, see Strack and Siegfried, *Lehrb. d. neuhebr. Spr. u. Liter.*, Carlsr. 1884, p. 107 ff., and the prefaces to the Hebrew Lexicons of Gesenius and Fürst; Berliner, *Beiträge zur hebr. Gramm. im Talmud u. Midrasch*, Berlin, 1879; Baer and Strack, *Die Dikduke ha-ṭeamim des Ahron ben Moscheh ben Ascher u. andere alte grammatisch-massorethische Lehrstücke*, Lpz. 1879, and P. Kahle's criticisms in *ZDMG.* lv. 170, n. 2; Ewald and Dukes, *Beiträge z. Gesch. der ältesten Auslegung u. Spracherklärung des A. T.*, Stuttg. 1844, 3 vols.; Hupfeld, *De rei grammaticae apud Judaeos initiis antiquissimisque scriptoribus*, Hal. 1846; W. Bacher, 'Die Anfänge der hebr. Gr.,' in *ZDMG.* 1895, 1 ff. and 335 ff.; and *Die hebr. Sprachwissenschaft vom 10. bis zum 16. Jahrh.*, Trier, 1892.

[2] A strong impulse was naturally given to these studies by the introduction of printing—the Psalter in 1477, the Bologna Pentateuch in 1482, the Soncino O. T. complete in 1488: see the description of the twenty-four earliest editions (down to 1528) in Ginsburg's *Introduction*, p. 779 ff.

[3] Of the literature of the subject down to the year 1850, see a tolerably full account in Steinschneider's *Bibliogr. Handb. f. hebr. Sprachkunde*, Lpz. 1859.

alone. B. Stade, on the other hand (*Lehrb. der hebr. Gr.*, pt. i. Lpz.
1879), adopted a strictly scientific method in endeavouring to reduce
the systems of Ewald and Olshausen to a more fundamental unity.
E. König[1] in his very thorough researches into the phonology and
accidence starts generally from the position reached by the early
Jewish grammarians (in his second part ' with comparative reference
to the Semitic languages in general ') and instead of adopting the usual
dogmatic method, takes pains to re-open the discussion of disputed
grammatical questions. The syntax König has ' endeavoured to treat
in several respects in such a way as to show its affinity to the common
Semitic syntax '.—Among the works of Jewish scholars, special attention may be called to the grammar by S. D. Luzzatto written in
Italian (Padua, 1853–69).

The chief requirements for one who is treating the grammar of
an ancient language are—(1) that he should *observe* as fully and
accurately as possible the existing linguistic phenomena and *describe*
them, after showing their organic connexion (the empirical and
historico-critical element); (2) that he should try to *explain* these
facts, partly by comparing them with one another and by the analogy
of the sister languages, partly from the general laws of philology
(the logical element).

Such observation has more and more led to the belief that the *g*
original text of the O. T. has suffered to a much greater extent than
former scholars were inclined to admit, in spite of the number of
variants in parallel passages : Is $2^{2\,\text{ff.}}$=Mi $4^{1\,\text{ff.}}$, Is 36–39=2 K 18^{13}–
20^{19}, Jer 52 = 2 K 24^{18}–25^{30}, 2 S 22=ψ 18, ψ 14=ψ 53, ψ $40^{14\,\text{ff.}}$=
ψ 70, ψ 108=ψ $57^{8\,\text{ff.}}$ and $60^{7\,\text{ff.}}$. Cf. also the parallels between the
Chronicles and the older historical books, and F. Vodel, *Die konsonant.
Varianten in den doppelt überlief. poet. Stücken d. masoret. Textes*,
Lpz. 1905. As to the extent and causes of the corruption of the
Masoretic text, the newly discovered fragments of the Hebrew
Ecclesiasticus are very instructive; cf. Smend, *Gött. gel. Anz.*, 1906,
p. 763.

The causes of *unintentional* corruption in the great majority of
cases are :—Interchange of similar letters, which has sometimes taken
place in the early ' Phoenician ' writing; transposition or omission of

---

[1] *Historisch-krit. Lehrgeb. der hebr. Sprache mit steter Beziehung auf Qimchi und
die anderen Autoritäten*: I, 'Lehre von der Schrift, der Aussprache, dem Pron.
u. dem Verbum,' Lpz. 1881 ; II. 1, 'Abschluss der speziellen Formenlehre u.
generelle Formenl.,' 1895 ; ii. 2, 'Historisch-kompar. Syntax d. hebr. Spr.,'
1897.

single letters, words, or even whole sentences, which are then often
added in the margin and thence brought back into the text in the
wrong place; such omission is generally due to homoioteleuton (cf.
Ginsburg, *Introd.*, p. 171 ff.), i. e. the scribe's eye wanders from the
place to a subsequent word of the same or similar form. Other
causes are dittography, i. e. erroneous repetition of letters, words,
and even sentences; its opposite, haplography; and lastly wrong
division of words (cf. Ginsburg, *Introd.*, p. 158 ff.), since at a certain
period in the transmission of the text the words were not separated.[1]—
Intentional changes are due to corrections for the sake of decency or
of dogma, and to the insertion of glosses, some of them very early.

Advance in grammar is therefore closely dependent on progress
in *textual criticism*. The systematic pursuit of the latter has only
begun in recent years: cf. especially Doorninck on Ju 1–16, Leid.
1879; Wellhausen, *Text der Bb. Sam.*, Gött. 1871; Cornill, *Ezechiel*,
Lpz. 1886; Klostermann, *Bb. Sam. u. d. Kön.*, Nördl. 1887; Driver,
Notes on the Hebr. text of the Books of Sam., Oxf. 1890; Klostermann, *Deuterojesaja*, Munich, 1893; Oort, *Textus hebr. emendationes*,
Lugd. 1900; Burney on *Kings*, Oxf. 1903; the commentaries of Marti
and Nowack; the *Internat. Crit. Comm.*; Kautzsch, *Die heil.
Schriften des A.T.*[2], 1909–10. A critical edition of the O.T. with full
textual notes, and indicating the different documents by colours, is
being published in a handsome form by P. Haupt in *The Sacred Books
of the Old Test.*, Lpz. and Baltimore, 1893 ff. (sixteen parts have
appeared: Exod., Deut., Minor Prophets, and Megilloth are still to
come); Kittel, *Biblia hebraica*[2], 1909, Masoretic text from Jacob b.
Ḥayyim (see *c*), with a valuable selection of variants from the
versions, and emendations.

§ 4. *Division and Arrangement of the Grammar.*

The division and arrangement of Hebrew grammar follow the
three constituent parts of every language, viz. (1) articulate *sounds*
represented by *letters*, and united to form *syllables*, (2) *words*, and
(3) *sentences*.

The first part (the elements) comprises accordingly the treatment
of *sounds* and their representation in writing. It describes the nature
and relations of the sounds of the language, teaches the pronunciation

---

[1] This *scriptio continua* is also found in Phoenician inscriptions. The
inscription of Mêʻaʼ always divides the words by a point (and so the Siloam
inscription; see the facsimile at the beginning of this grammar), and frequently marks the close of a sentence by a stroke.

of the written signs (orthoepy), and the established mode of writing (orthography). It then treats of the sounds as combined in syllables and words, and specifies the laws and conditions under which this combination takes place.

The second part (etymology) treats of words in their character as parts of speech, and comprises: (1) the principles of the *formation of words,* or of the derivation of the different parts of speech from the roots or from one another; (2) the principles of *inflexion,* i. e. of the various forms which the words assume according to their relation to other words and to the sentence.

The third part (syntax, or the arrangement of words): (1) shows how the word-formations and inflexions occurring in the language are used to express different shades of ideas, and how other ideas, for which the language has not coined any forms, are expressed by periphrasis; (2) states the laws according to which the parts of speech are combined in sentences (the principles of the sentence, or syntax in the stricter sense of the term).

FIRST PART

ELEMENTARY PRINCIPLES OR THE SOUNDS AND CHARACTERS

CHAPTER I

THE INDIVIDUAL SOUNDS AND CHARACTERS

§ 5. *The Consonants: their Forms and Names.*

(Cf. the Table of Alphabets.)

Among the abundant literature on the subject, special attention is directed to : A. Berliner, *Beiträge zur hebr. Gramm.*, Berlin, 1879, p. 15 ff., on the names, forms, and pronunciation of the consonants in Talmud and Midrash; H. Strack, *Schreibkunst u. Schrift bei d. Hebräern*, *PRE.³*, Lpz. 1906, p. 766 ff. ; Benzinger, *Hebr. Archäologie²*, Tübingen, 1907, p. 172 ff. ; Nowack, *Lehrbuch d. hebr. Archäol.*, Freiburg, 1894, i. 279 ff.; Lidzbarski, *Handbuch d. nordsem. Epigraphik*, Weimar, 1898, i. 173 ff. ; also his art. 'Hebrew Alphabet,' in the *Jewish Encyclopaedia*, i, 1901, p. 439 ff. (cf. his *Ephemeris*, i. 316 ff.) ; and 'Die Namen der Alphabet-buchstaben', in *Ephemeris*, ii. 125 ff.; Kenyon, art. 'Writing,' in the *Dictionary of the Bible*, iv. Edinb. 1902, p. 944 ff. ; Nöldeke, 'Die semit. Buchstabennamen,' in *Beitr. zur semit. Sprachwiss.*, Strassb. 1904, p. 124 ff. ; F. Praetorius, *Ueber den Ursprung des kanaan. Alphabets*, Berlin, 1906 ; H. Grimme, 'Zur Genesis des semit. Alphabets,' in *ZA.* xx. 1907, p. 49 ff. ; R. Stübe, *Grundlinien zu einer Entwickelungsgesch. d. Schrift*, Munich, 1907 ; Jermain, *In the path of the Alphabet*, Fort Wayne, 1907.—L. Blau, *Studien zum althebr. Buchwesen, &c.*, Strassb. 1902 ; and his 'Ueber d. Einfluss d. althebr. Buchwesens auf d. Originale', &c., in *Festschr. zu Ehren A. Berliners*, Frkf. 1903.

The best tables of alphabets are those of J. Euting in G. Bickell's *Outlines of Heb. Gram.* transl. by S. I. Curtiss, Lpz. 1877 ; in Pt. vii of the *Oriental Series* of the Palaeographical Soc., London, 1882 ; and, the fullest of all, in Chwolson's *Corpus inscr. Hebr.*, Petersburg, 1882; also Lidzbarski's in the *Jewish Encycl.*, see above.

a   1. The Hebrew letters now in use, in which both the manuscripts of the O. T. are written and our editions of the Bible are printed, commonly called the *square character* (כְּתָב מְרֻבָּע), also the *Assyrian character* (כְּ׳ אַשּׁוּרִי),[1] are not those originally employed.

Old Hebrew (or *Old Canaanitish*[2]) writing, as it was used on

---

[1] The name אַשּׁוּר (Assyria) is here used in the widest sense, to include the countries on the Mediterranean inhabited by Aramaeans; cf. Stade in *ZAW.* 1882, p. 292 f. On some other names for Old Hebrew writing. cf. G. Hoffmann, ibid. 1881, p. 334 ff. ; Buhl, *Canon and Text of the O. T.* (transl. by J. Macpherson), Edinb. 1892, p. 200.

[2] It is tacitly assumed here that this was the mother of *all* Semitic alphabets. In *ZDMG.* 1909, p. 189 ff., however, Prätorius has shown good

public monuments in the beginning of the ninth and in the second half of the eighth century B.C., is to be seen in the inscription of Mêša', as well as in that of Siloam. The characters on the Maccabaean coins of the second century B.C., and also on ancient gems, still bear much resemblance to this (cf. § 2 *d*). With the Old Hebrew writing the Phoenician is nearly identical (see § 1 *k*, § 2 *f*, and the Table of Alphabets). From the analogy of the history of other kinds of writing, it may be assumed that out of and along with this monumental character, a less antique and in some ways more convenient, rounded style was early developed, for use on softer materials, skins, bark, papyrus, and the like. This the Samaritans retained after their separation from the Jews, while the Jews gradually [1] (between the sixth and the fourth century) exchanged it for an Aramaic character. From this gradually arose (from about the fourth to the middle of the third century) what is called the *square character*, which consequently bears great resemblance to the extant forms of Aramaic writing, such as the Egyptian-Aramaic, the Nabatean and especially the Palmyrene. Of Hebrew inscriptions in the older square character, that of 'Arâq al-Emîr (15½ miles north-east of the mouth of the Jordan) probably belongs to 183 B.C.[2]

The Jewish sarcophagus-inscriptions of the time of Christ, found in Jerusalem in 1905, almost without exception exhibit a pure square character. This altered little in the course of centuries, so that the age of a Hebrew MS. cannot easily be determined from the style of the writing. The oldest known biblical fragment is the Nash papyrus (found in 1902), containing the ten commandments and the beginning of Dt 6⁴ᶠ·, of the end of the first or beginning of the second century A.D. ; cf. N. Peters, *Die älteste Abschr. der 10 Gebote*, Freibg. i. B. 1905. Of actual MSS. of the Bible the oldest is probably one of 820–850 A.D. described by Ginsburg, *Introd.*, p. 469 ff., at the head of his sixty principal MSS. ; next in age is the codex of Moses ben Asher at Cairo (897 A.D., cf. the art. 'Scribes' in the *Jew. Encycl.* xi and Gottheil in *JQR.* 1905, p. 32). The date (916 A.D.) of the Codex prophetarum Babylon. Petropol. (see § 8 *g*, note) is quite certain.—In the synagogue-rolls a distinction is drawn between the Tam-character (said to be so called from Rabbi Tam, grandson of R. Yiṣḥáqî, in the twelfth century) with its straight strokes, square corners and 'tittles' (tāgîn), in German and Polish MSS., and the *foreign* character with rounded letters and tittles in Spanish MSS. See further E. König, *Einl. in das A. T.*, Bonn, 1893, p. 16 ff.

---

grounds for believing that the South Semitic alphabet is derived not from the Mêša' character, or from some kindred and hardly older script, but from some unknown and *much* earlier form of writing.

[1] On the effect of the transitional mixture of earlier and later forms on the constitution of the text, see R. Kittel, *Ueber d. Notwendigk. d. Herausg. einer neuen hebr. Bibel*, Lpz. 1901, p. 20 ff.—L. Blau, ' Wie lange stand die althebr. Schrift bei den Juden im Gebrauch ? ' in *Kaufmanngedenkbuch*, Breslau, 1900, p. 44 ff.

[2] Not 176, as formerly held. Driver and Lidzbarski now read ערביה, correctly, not טוביה.

b　**2.** The Alphabet consists, like all Semitic alphabets, solely of consonants, twenty-two in number, some of which, however, have also a kind of vocalic power (§ 7 *b*). The following Table shows their form, names, pronunciation, and numerical value (see *k*):—

FORM.	NAME.	PRONUNCIATION.	NUMERICAL VALUE.
א	'Ālĕph	' *spiritus lenis*	I
ב	Bêth	*b* (*bh*, but see § 6 *n*)	2
ג	Gimĕl (*Giml*)	*g* (*gh*, ,, ,, ,,)	3
ד	Dālĕth	*d* (*dh*, ,, ,, ,,)	4
ה	Hē	*h*	5
ו	Wāw (*Wāu*)	*w* (*u*) [1]	6
ז	Záyĭn	*z*, as in English (soft *s*)	7
ח	Ḥêth	*ḥ*, a strong guttural	8
ט	Ṭêth	*ṭ*, emphatic *t*	9
י	Yôd	*y* (*i*) [1]	I O
כ, final ך	Kaph	*k* (*kh*, but see § 6 *n*)	20
ל	Lāmĕd	*l*	30
מ, final ם	Mêm	*m*	40
נ, final ן	Nûn	*n*	50
ס	Sāmĕkh	*s*	60
ע	'Áyĭn	' a peculiar guttural (see below)	70
פ, final ף	Pê	*p* (*f*, see § 6 *n*)	80
צ, final ץ	Ṣādê	*ṣ*, emphatic *s*	90
ק	Qôf	*q*, a strong *k* [2] formed at the back of the palate	100
ר	Rêš	*r*	200
שׂ	Śin	*ś*	300
שׁ	Šĭn [3]	*š*, pronounced *sh*	
ת	Tāw (*Tāu*)	*t* (*th*, but see § 6 *n*)	400

---

[1] Philippi, 'Die Aussprache der semit. Consonanten ו und י,' in *ZDMG*. 1886, p. 639 ff., 1897, p. 66 ff., adduces reasons in detail for the opinion that 'the Semitic ו and י are certainly by usage consonants, although by nature they are vowels, viz. *u* and *i*, and consequently are consonantal vowels'; cf. § 8 *m*.

[2] As a representation of this sound the Latin *q* is very suitable, since it occupies in the alphabet the place of the Semitic ק (Greek κόππα).

[3] Nestle (*Actes du onzième Congrès . . . des Orientalistes*, 1897, iv. 113 ff.) has shown that the original order was שׂ, שׁ.

3. As the Table shows, five letters have a special form at the end *c*
of the word.　They are called final letters, and were combined by the
Jewish grammarians in the mnemonic word בְּמַנְפֵּץ *Kamnèphäṣ,* or
better, with A. Müller and Stade, בַּמַנְפֵּץ i. e. *as the breaker in pieces.*[1]
Of these, ך, ן, ף, ץ are distinguished from the common form by the
shaft being drawn straight down, while in the usual form it is bent
round towards the left.[2]　In the case of ם the letter is completely
closed.

4. Hebrew is read and written from right to left.[3]　Words must *d*
not be divided at the end of the lines ;[4] but, in order that no empty
space may be left, in MSS. and printed texts, certain letters suitable
for the purpose are dilated at the end or in the middle of the line.
In our printed texts these *literae dilatabiles* are the five following :
ם ת ל ה א (mnemonic word אֲהַלְתֶּם *'aháltèm*).　In some MSS. other
letters suitable for the purpose are also employed in this way, as
ר, כ, ד ; cf. Strack in the *Theol. Lehrb.,* 1882, No. 22; Nestle, *ZAW.*
1906, p. 170 f.

Rem. 1.　The forms of the letters originally represent the rude outlines of *e*
perceptible objects, the names of which, respectively, begin with the consonant
represented (akrophony).　Thus *Yôd,* in the earlier alphabets the rude picture
of a hand, properly denotes *hand* (Heb. יָד), but as a letter simply the sound
י (y), with which this word begins; *'Ayin,* originally a circle, properly an
eye (עַיִן), stands for the consonant ע.　In the Phoenician alphabet, especially,
the resemblance of the forms to the objects denoted by the name is still for
the most part recognizable (see the Table).　In some letters (ג, ו, ז, ט, ש) the
similarity is still preserved in the square character.

It is another question whether the present names are all original.　They
may be merely due to a later, and not always accurate, interpretation of the
forms.　Moreover, it is possible that in the period from about 1500 to 1000 B. C.
the original forms underwent considerable change.

The usual explanation of the present names of the letters[5] is : אָלֶף *ox,*　*f*

---

[1] In the Talmud, disregarding the alphabetical order, מִן־צֹפֶךְ *of thy watcher,*
i. e. *prophet.*　See the discussions of this mnemonic word by Nestle, *ZAW.*
1907, p. 119 ff., König, Bacher (who would read מִן־צֹפַיִךְ = proceeding *from thy
prophets,* Is 52⁸), Krauss, Marmorstein, ibid. p. 278 ff.　All the twenty-two
letters, together with the five final forms, occur in Zp 3⁸.

[2] Chwolson, *Corpus Inscr. Hebr.,* col. 68, rightly observes that the more
original forms of these letters are preserved in the *literae finales.*　Instances of
them go back to the time of Christ.

[3] The same was originally the practice in Greek, which only adopted the
opposite direction exclusively about 400 B.C.　On the *boustrophēdon* writing
(alternately in each direction) in early Greek, early Sabaean, and in the
Safa-inscriptions of the first three centuries A. D., cf. Lidzbarski, *Ephemeris,* i.
116 f.

[4] This does not apply to early inscriptions or seals.　Cf. Mêša‘, ll. 1–5,
7, 8, &c., Siloam 2, 3, 5, where the division of words appears to be customary.

[5] We possess Greek transcriptions of the Hebrew names, dating from the
fifth century B. C.　The LXX give them (in almost the same form as Eusebius,
Praep. Evang. 10. 5) in La 1–4, as do also many Codices of the Vulgate (e. g. the

בֵּית *house,* גָּמֶל *camel* (according to Lidzbarski, see below, perhaps originally גָּרְזֶן *axe or pick-axe*), דֶּלֶת *door* (properly *folding door* ; according to Lidzbarski, perhaps דַּד *the female breast*), הֵא *air-hole* (?), *lattice-window* (?), וָו *hook, nail,* זַיִן *weapon* (according to Nestle, comparing the Greek ζῆτα, rather זַיִת *olive-tree*), חֵית *fence, barrier* (but perhaps only differentiated from ה by the left-hand stroke), טֵית *a winding* (?), according to others a *leather bottle* or a *snake* (but perhaps only differentiated from ת by a circle round it), יוֹד *hand,* כַּף *bent hand,* לָמֶד *ox-goad,* מַיִם *water,* נוּן *fish* (Lidzbarski, 'perhaps originally נָחָשׁ *snake,*' as in Ethiopic), סָמֶך *prop* (perhaps a modification of ז), עַיִן *eye,* פֶּא (also פֵּי) *mouth,* צָדִי *fish-hook* (?), קוֹף *eye of a needle,* according to others *back of the head* (Lidzb., 'perhaps קֶשֶׁת *bow* '), רֵישׁ *head,* שִׁין *tooth,* תָּו *sign, cross.*

g   With regard to the origin of this alphabet, it may be taken as proved that it is not earlier (or very little earlier) than the fifteenth century B. C., since otherwise the el-Amarna tablets (§ 2 *f*) would not have been written exclusively in cuneiform.[1] It seems equally certain on various grounds, that it originated on Canaanitish soil. It is, however, still an open question whether the inventors of it borrowed

(*a*) From the Egyptian system—not, as was formerly supposed, by direct adoption of hieroglyphic signs (an explanation of twelve or thirteen characters was revived by J. Halévy in *Rev. Sémit.* 1901, p. 356 ff., 1902, p. 331 ff., and in the *Verhandlungen des xiii. . . . Orient.-Kongr. zu Hamb.*, Leiden, 1904, p. 199 ff.; but cf. Lidzbarski, *Ephemeris*, i. 261 ff.), or of hieratic characters derived from them (so E. de Rougé), but by the adoption of the *acrophonic* principle (see *e*) by which e. g. the hand, in Egyptian *tot*, represents the letter *t*, the lion = *laboi*, the letter *l*. This view still seems the most probable. It is now accepted by Lidzbarski ('Der Ursprung d. nord- u. südsemit. Schrift' in *Ephemeris*, i (1900), 109 ff., cf. pp. 134 and 261 ff.), though in his *Nordsem. Epigr.* (1898) p. 173 ff. he was still undecided.

(*b*) From the Babylonian (cuneiform) system. Wuttke's and W. Deecke's derivation of the old-Semitic alphabet from new-Assyrian cuneiform is impossible for chronological reasons. More recently Peters and Hommel have sought to derive it from the old-Babylonian, and Ball from the archaic Assyrian cuneiform. A vigorous discussion has been aroused by the theory of Frdr. Delitzsch (in *Die Entstehung des ält. Schriftsystems od. der Urspr. der Keilschriftzeichen dargel.*, Lpz. 1897; and with the same title 'Ein Nachwort ', Lpz. 1898, preceded by a very clear outline of the theory) that the old-Semitic alphabet arose in Canaan under the influence both of the Egyptian system (whence the acrophonic principle) and of the old-Babylonian, whence the principle of the graphic representation of objects and ideas by means of simple, and mostly rectilinear, signs. He holds that the choice of the objects was probably (in about fifteen cases) influenced by the Babylonian system. The correspondence of names had all the more effect since, according to Zimmern (*ZDMG.* 1896, p. 667 ff.), out of twelve names which are certainly identical, eight appear in the same order in the Babylonian arrangement of signs. But it must first be shown that the present names of the

---

Cod. Amiatinus) in ψψ 111, 112, 119, but with many variations from the customary forms, which rest on the traditional Jewish pronunciation. The forms *Deleth* (and *delth*), *Zai*, *Sen* (LXX also χσεν, cf. Hebr. שֵׁן *tooth*) are to be noticed, amongst others, for *Daleth*, *Zain*, *Šin*. Cf. the tables in Nöldeke, *Beiträge zur sem. Sprachwiss.*, p. 126 f. In his opinion (and so Lidzbarski, *Ephemeris*, i. 134) the form and meaning of the names point to Phoenicia as the original home of the alphabet, since *alf, bêt, dalt, wāw, tāw, pei = pê, pi*, mouth, and the vowel of *ρ̂ω̂ = rōš*, head, are all Hebraeo-Phoenician.

[1] In the excavations at Jericho in April, 1907, E. Sellin found a jar-handle with the Canaanite characters יה, which he dates (probably too early) about 1500 B C.

'Phoenician' letters really denote the original picture. The identity of the objects may perhaps be due simply to the choice of the commonest things (animals, implements, limbs) in both systems.

The derivation of the Semitic alphabet from the signs of the Zodiac and their names, first attempted by Seyffarth in 1834, has been revived by Winckler, who refers twelve fundamental sounds to the Babylonian Zodiac. Hommel connects the original alphabet with the moon and its phases, and certain constellations; cf. Lidzbarski, *Ephemeris*, i. 269 ff., and in complete agreement with him, Benzinger, *Hebr. Archäologie*[2], p. 173 ff. This theory is by no means convincing.

(*c*) From the hieroglyphic system of writing discovered in 1894 by A. J. Evans in inscriptions in Crete (esp. at Cnossus) and elsewhere. According to Kluge (1897) and others, this represents the 'Mycenaean script' used about 3000–1000 B. c., and according to Fries ('Die neuesten Forschungen über d. Urspr. des phöniz. Alph.' in *ZDPV*. xxii. 118 ff.) really supplies the original forms of the Phoenician alphabet as brought to Palestine by the Philistines about 1100 B. c., but 'the Phoenician-Canaanite-Hebrews gave to the Mycenaean signs names derived from the earlier cuneiform signs'. The hypothesis of Fries is thus connected with that of Delitzsch. But although the derivation of the Phoenician forms from 'Mycenaean' types appears in some cases very plausible, in others there are grave difficulties, and moreover the date, 1100 B.C., assigned for the introduction of the alphabet is clearly too late. [See Evans, *Scripta Minoa*, Oxf. 1909, p. 80 ff.]

(*d*) From a system, derived from Asia Minor, closely related to the Cypriote syllabary (Praetorius, *Der Urspr. des kanaan. Alphabets*, Berlin, 1906). On this theory the Canaanites transformed the syllabic into an apparently alphabetic writing. In reality, however, they merely retained a single sign for the various syllables, so that e. g. ק is not really *q*, but *qa*, *qe*, *qi*, &c. Of the five Cypriote vowels also they retained only the star (in Cypriote = *a*) simplified into an *'ālef* (see alphabetical table) to express the vowels at the beginning of syllables, and *i* and *u* as Yod and Waw. Praetorius claims to explain about half the twenty-two Canaanite letters in this way, but there are various objections to his ingenious hypothesis.

2. As to the *order* of the letters, we possess early evidence in the alphabetic[1] *h* poems: ψ 9 (א–כ, cf. ψ 10[1] ל, and vv[12–17] ק–ת; cf. Gray in the *Expositor*, 1906, p. 233 ff., and Rosenthal, *ZAW*. 1896, p. 40, who shows that ψ 9[3.15.17] ב, ל, נ exactly fit in between ח, ט, י, and that ψ 10[1.3.5] therefore has the reverse order ל, כ, י); also ψψ 25 and 34 (both without a separate ו-verse and with פ repeated at the end[2]); 37, 111, 112, 119 (in which every eight verses begin with the same letter, each strophe, as discovered by D. H. Müller of Vienna, containing the eight leading words of ψ 19[8 ff.], *tōrā*, *'ēdûth*, &c.); La 1–4 (in 2–4 פ before ע[3], in chap. 3 every three verses with the same initial, see Löhr, *ZAW*. 1904, p. 1 ff., in chap. 5 at any rate as many verses as letters in the alphabet); Pr 24[1.3.5], 31[10–31] (in the LXX with פ before ע[3]); also in Na 1[2–10] Pastor Frohnmeyer of Württemberg (ob. 1880) detected traces of an alphabetic arrangement, but the attempt of Gunkel, Bickell, Arnold (*ZAW*. 1901,

---

[1] On the supposed connexion of this artificial arrangement with magical formulae ('the order of the letters was believed to have a sort of magic power') cf. Löhr, *ZAW*. 1905, p. 173 ff., and *Klagelieder*[2], Gött. 1907, p. vii ff.

[2] On this superfluous פ cf. Grimme, *Euphemistic liturgical appendices*, Lpz. 1901, p. 8 ff., and Nestle, *ZAW*. 1903, p. 340 f., who considers it an appendage to the Greek alphabet.

[3] [Perhaps also originally in ψ 34.] פ before ע is probably due to a magic alphabet, see above, n. 1. According to Böhmer, *ZAW*. 1908, p. 53 ff., the combinations אב, גד, הו, &c., were used in magical texts; עם was excluded, but by a rearrangement we get סף and עץ.

p. 225 ff.), Happel (*Der Ps. Nah*, Würzb. 1900) to discover further traces, has not been successful. [Cf. Gray in *Expositor*, 1898, p. 207 ff.; Driver, in the Century Bible, *Nahum*, p. 26.]—Bickell, *Ztschr f. Kath. Theol.*, 1882, p. 319 ff., had already deduced from the versions the alphabetical character of Ecclus 51¹³⁻³⁰, with the omission of the ו-verse and with פ¹ at the end. His conjectures have been brilliantly confirmed by the discovery of the Hebrew original, although the order from נ to ל is partly disturbed or obscured. If ו before צ is deleted, ten letters are in their right positions, and seven can be restored to their places with certainty. Cf. N. Schlögl, *ZDMG.* 53, 669 ff.; C. Taylor in the appendix to Schechter and Taylor, *The Wisdom of Ben Sira*, Cambr. 1899, p. lxxvi ff., and in the *Journ. of Philol.*, xxx (1906), p. 95 ff.; *JQR.* 1905, p. 238 ff.; Löhr, *ZAW.* 1905, p. 183 ff.; I. Lévy, *REJ.* 1907, p. 62 ff.

The sequence of the three softest labial, palatal, and dental sounds ב, ג, ד, and of the three liquids ל, מ, נ, indicates an attempt at classification. At the same time other considerations also appear to have had influence. Thus it is certainly not accidental, that two letters, representing a hand (*Yôd, Kaph*), as also two (if *Qôph* = back of the head) which represent the head, and in general several forms denoting objects naturally connected (*Mêm* and *Nûn, 'Ayin* and *Pê*), stand next to one another.

i   The order, names, and numerical values of the letters have passed over from the Phoenicians to the Greeks, in whose alphabet the letters A to Υ are borrowed from the Old Semitic. So also the Old Italic alphabets as well as the Roman, and consequently all alphabets derived either from this or from the Greek, are directly or indirectly dependent on the Phoenician.

k   3. *a.* In default of special arithmetical figures, the consonants were used also as numerical signs; cf. G. Gundermann, *Die Zahlzeichen*, Giessen, 1899, p. 6 f., and Lidzbarski, *Ephemeris*, i. 106 ff. The earliest traces of this usage are, however, first found on the Maccabean coins (see above, § 2 *d*, end). These numerical letters were afterwards commonly employed, e.g. for marking the numbers of chapters and verses in the editions of the Bible. The units are denoted by ט–א, the tens by צ–י, 100-400 by ת–ק, the numbers from 500-900 by ן (= 400), with the addition of the remaining hundreds, e. g. תק 500. In compound numbers the greater precedes (on the right), thus יא 11, קכא 121. But 15 is expressed by טו 9 + 6, not יה (which is a form of the divine name, being the first two consonants of יהוה).² For a similar reason טז is also mostly written for 16, instead of יו, which in compound proper names, like יואל, also represents the name of God, יהוה.

The thousands are sometimes denoted by the units with two dots placed above, e. g. א 1000.

l   *b.* The reckoning of the years in Jewish writings (generally ליצירה *after the creation*) follows either the *full chronology* (לפרט גדול or לפ׳ ג׳), with the addition of the thousands, or the *abridged chronology* (לפ׳ קטון), in which they are omitted. In the dates of the first thousand years after Christ, the Christian era is obtained by the addition of 240, in the second thousand years by the addition of 1240 (i. e. if the date falls between Jan. 1 and the Jewish new year; otherwise add 1239), the thousands of the Creation era being omitted.

m   4. Abbreviations of words are not found in the text of the O. T., but they occur on coins, and their use is extremely frequent amongst the later Jews.³

---

¹ See note 3 on p. 29.

² On the rise of this custom (יה having been originally used and afterwards הי), cf. Nestle in *ZAW.* 1884, p. 250, where a trace of this method of writing occurring as early as Origen is noted.

³ Cf. Jo. Buxtorf, *De abbreviaturis Hebr.*, Basel, 1613, &c.; Pietro Perreau.

A point, or later an oblique stroke, serves as the sig.ı of abridgement in old MSS. and editions, e. g. יִשְׂרָאֵל for יְשִׂ', פְּלֹנִי for פ', דָּבָר for דְּ aliquis, דָּבָר for ד aliquid, וְגוֹמֵר for וְגוֹ et complens, i.e. *and so on.* Also in the middle of what is apparently a word, such strokes indicate that it is an abbreviation or a *vox memorialis* (cf. e. g. § 15 *d* תא״ם). Two such strokes are employed, from § 41 *d* onward, to mark the different classes of weak verbs.—Note also וַ or וָ (also ה') for יְהוָֹה.

5. Peculiarities in the tradition of the O. T. text, which are already *n* mentioned in the Talmud, are—(1) The 15 *puncta extraordinaria,* about which the tradition (from Siphri on Nu 9[10] onwards) differs considerably, even as to their number; on particular consonants, Gn 16[5], 18[9], 19[33·35], Nu 9[10]; or on whole words, Gn 33[4], 37[12], Nu 3[39], 21[30], 29[15], Dt 29[28], 2 S 19[20], Is 44[9], Ez 41[20], 46[22], ψ 27[13],—all no doubt critical marks; cf. Strack, *Prolegomena Critica,* p. 88 ff.; L. Blau, *Masoretische Untersuchungen,* Strassburg, 1891, p. 6 ff., and *Einleitung in die hl. Schrift,* Budapest, 1894; Königsberger, *Jüd. Lit.-Blatt,* 1891, nos. 29–31, and *Aus Masorah u. Talmudkritik,* Berlin, 1892, p. 6 ff.; Mayer-Lambert, *REJ.* 30 (1895), no. 59; and especially Ginsburg, *Introd.,* p. 318 ff.; also on the ten points found in the Pentateuch, see Butin (Baltimore, 1906), who considers that they are as old as the Christian era and probably mark a letter, &c., to be deleted. (2) The *literae majusculae* (e. g. ב Gn 1[1], ו Lv 11[42] as the middle consonant of the Pentateuch, י Nu 14[17]), and *minusculae* (e. g. ה Gn 2[4]). (3) The *literae suspensae* (Ginsburg, *Introd.,* p. 334 ff.) נ Ju 18[30] (which points to the reading מֹשֶׁה for מְנַשֶּׁה), ע ψ 80[14] (the middle of the Psalms [1]) and Jb 38[13·15]. (4) The 'mutilated' *Wāw* in שׁלום Nu 25[12], and ק Ex 32[25] (בקמיהם), and Nu 7[2] (הפקודים). (5) *Mêm clausum* in למרבה Is 9[6], and *Mêm apertum* in הם פרוצים Neh 2[13]. (6) *Nûn inversum* before Nu 1c[35], and after ver. 36, as also before ψ 107[23–28] and ⁴⁰; according to Ginsburg, *Introd.,* p. 341 ff., a sort of bracket to indicate that the verses are out of place; cf. Krauss, *ZAW.* 1902, p. 57 ff., who regards the inverted *Nûns* as an imitation of the Greek obelus.

§ 6. *Pronunciation and Division of Consonants.*

P. Haupt, 'Die Semit. Sprachlaute u. ihre Umschrift,' in *Beiträge zur Assyrio-logie u. vergleich. semit. Sprachwissenschaft,* by Delitzsch and Haupt, i, Lpz. 1889, 249 ff.; E. Sievers, *Metrische Studien,* i, Lpz. 1901, p. 14 ff.

1. An accurate knowledge of the original phonetic value of each *a* consonant is of the greatest importance, since very many grammatical peculiarities and changes (§ 18 ff.) only become intelligible from the nature and pronunciation of the sounds. This knowledge is obtained partly from the pronunciation of the kindred dialects, especially the still living Arabic, partly by observing the affinity and interchange

---

Oceano delle abbreviature e sigle[2], Parma, 1883 (appendix, 1884); Ph. Lederer, *Hebr. u. Chald. Abbreviaturen,* Frankf. 1893; Händler, *Lexicon d. Abbreviaturen* (annexed to G. Dalman's *Aram.-neuhebr. WB.,* Frankf. 1897); Levias, art. 'Abbreviations,' in the *Jew. Encycl.,* i. 39 ff.; F. Perles, 'Zur Gesch. der Abbrev. im Hebr.' (*Archiv f. Stenogr.,* 1902, p. 41 ff.). On abbreviations in biblical MSS. see Ginsburg, *Introd.,* 165 ff.

[1] According to Blau, *Studien zum althebr. Buchwesen,* Strassburg, 1902, p. 167, properly a large ע, called *t'lūyā* because *suspended* between the two halves of the Psalter, and then incorrectly taken for a *littera suspensa.*

of sounds on Hebrew itself (§ 19), and partly from the tradition of the Jews.[1]

The pronunciation of Hebrew by the modern German Jews, which partly resembles the Syriac and is generally called 'Polish', differs considerably from that of the Spanish and Portuguese Jews, which approaches nearer to the Arabic. The pronunciation of Hebrew by Christians follows the latter (after the example of Reuchlin), in almost all cases.

b   The oldest tradition is presented in the transcription of Hebrew names in Assyrian cuneiform ; a later, but yet in its way very important system is seen in the manner in which the LXX transcribe Hebrew names with Greek letters.[2] As, however, corresponding signs for several sounds (ט, ע, צ, ק, שׁ) are wanting in the Greek alphabet, only an approximate representation was possible in these cases. The same applies to the Latin transcription of Hebrew words by Jerome, according to the Jewish pronunciation of his time.[3]

On the pronunciation of the modern Jews in North Africa, see Bargès in the *Journ. Asiat.*, Nov. 1848 ; on that of the South Arabian Jews, J. Dérenbourg, *Manuel du lecteur*, &c. (from a Yemen MS. of the year 1390), Paris, 1871 (extrait 6 du *Journ. Asiat.* 1870).

c   2. With regard to the pronunciation of the several gutturals and sibilants, and of ט and ק, it may be remarked :—

1. Among the gutturals, the glottal stop א is the lightest, corresponding to the *spiritus lenis* of the Greeks. It may stand either at the beginning or end of a syllable, e. g. אָמַר *'ámár*, יֵאָשֵׁם *yā'šám*. Even *before* a vowel א is almost lost to our ear, like the *h* in *hour* and in the French *habit*, *homme*. *After* a vowel א generally (and at the end of a word, always) coalesces with it, e. g. קָרָא *qārā* for an original *qārā'*, Arab. *qārā'ă* ; see further, § 23 *a*, 27 *g*.

d   ה before a vowel corresponds exactly to our *h* (spiritus asper) ; after a vowel it is *either* a guttural (so always at the end of a syllable which is not final, e. g. נֶהְפַּךְ *náhpakh* ; at the-end of a word the consonantal ה has a point —Mappîq—in it, see § 14), *or* it stands inaudible at the end of a word, generally as a mere orthographic indication of a preceding vowel, e. g. גָּלָה *gālā* ; cf. §§ 7 *b* and 75 *a*.

e   ע is related to א, but is a much stronger guttural. Its strongest sound is a rattled, guttural *g*, cf. e. g. עַזָּה, LXX Γάζα, עֲמֹרָה Γόμορρα ; elsewhere, a weaker sound of the same kind, which the LXX reproduce by a *spiritus (lenis* or *asper*), e. g. עֵלִי 'Ηλί, עֲמָלֵק 'Αμαλέκ.[4] In the mouth of the Arabs one hears in the former case a sort of guttural *r*, in the latter a sound peculiar to themselves formed in the back of the throat.—It is as incorrect to omit the ע

---

[1] Cf. C. Meinhof, 'Die Aussprache des Hebr.,' in *Neue Jahrb. f. Philol. u. Pädag.*, 1885, Bd. 132, p. 146 ff. ; M. Schreiner, 'Zur Gesch. der Ausspr. des Hebr.,' in *ZAW.* 1886, p. 213 ff.

[2] Cf. Frankel, *Vorstudien zu der Septuag.*, Lpz. 1841, p. 90 ff. ; C. Könneke, 'Gymn.-Progr.,' Stargard, 1885. On the transcription of eleven Psalms in a palimpsest fragment of the Hexapla at Milan, see Mercati, *Atti della R. Accad.*, xxxi, Turin, 1896. [Cf. Burkitt, *Fragments of . . . Aquila*, Cambr. 1897, p. 13.]

[3] Numerous examples occur in *Hieronymi quaestiones hebraicae in libro geneseos*, edited by P. de Lagarde, Lpz. 1868 ; cf. the exhaustive and systematic discussion by Siegfried, 'Die Aussprache des Hebr. bei Hieronymus,' in *ZAW.* 1884, pp. 34–83.

[4] It is, however, doubtful if the LXX always consciously aimed at reproducing the actual differences of sound.

entirely, in reading and transcribing words (עֵלִי *Eli*, עֲמָלֵק *Amalek*), as to pronounce it exactly like *g* or like a nasal *ng*. The stronger sound might be approximately transcribed by *gh* or *ʾg*; but since in Hebrew the softer sound was the more common, it is sufficient to represent it by the sign ʾ, as אַרְבַּע *ʾarbaʿ*, עַד *ʿad*.

f ח is the strongest guttural sound, a deep guttural *ch*, as heard generally in Swiss German, somewhat as in the German *Achat, Macht, Sache, Docht, Zucht* (not as in *Licht, Knecht*), and similar to the Spanish *j*. Like ע it was, however, pronounced in many words feebly, in others strongly.

g As regards ר, its pronunciation as a palatal (with a vibrating uvula) seems to have been the prevailing one. Hence in some respects it is also classed with the gutturals (§ 22 *q, r*). On the *lingual* ר, cf. *o*.

h 2. The Hebrew language is unusually rich in sibilants. These have, at any rate in some cases, arisen from dentals which are retained as such in Aramaic and Arabic (see in the *Lexicon* the letters ז, צ and שׁ).

i שׁ and שׂ were originally represented (as is still the case in the unpointed texts) by only *one* form שׁ; but that the use of this one form to express two different sounds (at least in Hebrew) was due only to the poverty of the alphabet, is clear from the fact that they are differentiated in Arabic and Ethiopic (cf. Nöldeke in *Ztschr. f. wissensch. Theol.*, 1873, p. 121; Brockelmann, *Grundriss*, i. 133). In the Masoretic punctuation they were distinguished by means of the diacritical point as שׁ (*sh*) and שׂ (*ś*).[1]

k The original difference between the sounds שׂ and ס [2] sometimes marks a distinction in meaning, e. g. סָכַר *to close*, שָׂכַר *to hire*, סָכַל *to be foolish*, שָׂכַל *to be prudent, to be wise*. Syriac always represents both sounds by ס, and in Hebrew also they are sometimes interchanged; as סָכַר for שָׂכַר *to hire*, Ezr 4⁵; שִׂכְלוּת for סִכְלוּת *folly*, Ec 1¹⁷.

l ז (transcribed ζ by the LXX) is a soft whizzing *s*, the French and English *z*, altogether different from the German *z* (*ts*).

m 3. ט, ק, and probably צ are pronounced with a strong articulation and with a compression of the larynx. The first two are thus essentially different from ת and כ, which correspond to our *t* and *k* and also are often aspirated (see below, *n*). צ is distinguished from every other *s* by its peculiar articulation, and in no way corresponds to the German *z* or *ts*; we transcribe it by *ṣ*; cf. G. Hüsing, 'Zum Lautwerte des צ,' in *OLZ*. x. 467 ff.

n **3.** Six consonants, the weak and middle hard Palatals, Dentals, and Labials

(בְּגַדְכְּפַת) ב ג ד כ פ ת

have a twofold pronunciation, (1) a harder sound, as mutes, like

---

[1] The modern Samaritans, however, in reading their Hebrew Pentateuch pronounce שׂ invariably as שׁ.

[2] The original value of ס, and its relation to the original value of שׂ and שׁ, is still undetermined, despite the valuable investigations of P. Haupt, *ZDMG*. 1880, p. 762 f.; D. H. Müller, 'Zur Geschichte der semit. Zischlaute,' in the *Verhandlungen des Wiener Orient. Congresses*, Vienna, 1888, Semitic section, p. 229 ff.; De Lagarde, 'Samech,' in the *NGGW*. 1891, no. 5, esp. p. 173; Aug. Müller, *ZAW*. 1891, p. 267 ff.; Nöldeke, *ZDMG*. 1893, p. 100 f.; E. Glaser, *Zwei Wiener Publicationen über Habaschitisch-punische Dialekte in Südarabien*, Munich, 1902, pp. 19 ff.—On the phonetic value of צ see G. Hüsing, *OLZ*. 1907, p. 467 ff.

k, p, t, or initial *b, g* (hard), *d;* and (2) a softer sound as *spirantes.*[1] The harder sound is the original. It is retained at the beginning of syllables, when there is no vowel immediately preceding to influence the pronunciation, and is denoted by a point, *Dageš lene* (§ 13), placed in the consonants, viz. בּ *b,* גּ *g,* דּ *d,* כּ *k,* פּ *p,* תּ *t.* The weaker pronunciation appears as soon as a vowel sound immediately precedes. It is occasionally denoted, esp. in MSS., by *Rāphè* (§ 14 *e*), but in printed texts usually by the mere absence of the *Dageš.* In the case of בּ, כּ, פּ, תּ, the two sounds are clearly distinguishable even to our ear as *b* and *v, k* and German (weak) *ch, p* and *ph, t* and *th* (in *thin*). The Greeks too express this twofold pronunciation by special characters : כּ *κ,* כ *χ;* פּ *π,* פ *φ;* תּ *τ,* ת *θ.* In the same way ג should be pronounced like the North German *g* in *Tage, Wagen,* and ד like *th* in *the,* as distinguished from גּ and דּ.

For more precise information on the cases in which the one or the other pronunciation takes place, see § 21. The modern Jews pronounce the aspirated בּ as *v,* the aspirated תּ as *s,* e.g. רַב *rav* (or even *raf*), בַּיִת *bais.* The customary transcription (used also in this Grammar) of the spirants בּ, כּ, תּ by *bh, kh, th* is only an unsatisfactory makeshift, since it may lead (esp. in the case of *bh* and *kh*) to an erroneous conception of the sounds as real aspirates, *b-h, k-h.*

o   **4.** According to their special character the consonants are divided into—

(*a*) Gutturals	א ע ה ח ;
(*b*) Palatals	ג כ ק ;
(*c*) Dentals	ד ט ת ;
(*d*) Labials	ב פ ;
(*e*) Sibilants	ז שׁ שׂ ס צ ;
(*f*) Sonants	נ מ, רל, יו.

In the case of ד its hardest pronunciation as a *palatal* (see above, *g,* end) is to be distinguished from its more unusual sound as a lingual, pronounced in the front of the mouth.

On the twofold pronunciation of *r* in Tiberias, cf. Delitzsch, *Physiol. und Musik,* Lpz. 1868, p. 10 ff.; Baer and Strack, *Dikduke ha-ṭᵉamim,* Lpz. 1879, p. 5, note *a,* and § 7 of the Hebrew text, as well as p. 82.

p   In accordance with E. Sievers, *Metrische Studien,* i. 14, the following scheme of the Hebrew phonetic system is substituted for the table formerly given in this grammar :—

i. Throat sounds (Gutturals) : א ה ע ח.

---

[1] So at any rate at the time when the present punctuation arose.

ii. Mouth-sounds:		w.	m.	e.	w.	m.
1. Mutes and Spirants:	Palatal	גּ	כּ	ק	ג	כ
	Dental	דּ	תּ	ט	ד	ת
	Labial	בּ	פּ	—	ב	פ
2. Sibilants:		...	ז	שׁ שׂ ס	צ	
3. Sonants:		...	וּ י	ר ל	נ מ	

Rem. 1. The meaning of the letters at the top is, w. = weak, m. = middle hard, e. = emphatic. Consonants which are produced by the same organ of speech are called *homorganic* (e.g. ג and כ as palatals), consonants whose sound is of the same nature *homogeneous* (e.g. ו and י as semi-vowels). On their homorganic character and homogeneity depends the possibility of interchange, whether within Hebrew itself or with the kindred dialects. In such cases the soft sound generally interchanges with the soft, the hard with the hard, &c. (e.g. ד = ז, ת = שׂ, ט = צ). Further transitions are not, however, excluded, as e.g. the interchange of ת and ק (ת = כ = ק). Here it is of importance to observe whether the change takes place in an initial, medial, or final letter; since e.g. the change in a letter when medial does not always prove the possibility of the change when initial. That in certain cases the character of the consonantal sound also influences the preceding or following vowel will be noticed in the accidence as the instances occur.

Rem. 2. Very probably in course of time certain nicer distinctions of pronunciation became more and more neglected and finally were lost. Thus e.g. the stronger ע *ʿg*, which was known to the LXX (see above, *e*), became in many cases altogether lost to the later Jews; by the Samaritans and Galileans ע and ח were pronounced merely as א, and so in Ethiopic, ע like א, ח like *h*, שׁ like *s*.

Rem. 3. The consonants which it is usual to describe especially as *weak*, are those which readily coalesce with a preceding vowel to form a long vowel, viz. א, ו, י (as to ה, cf. § 23 *k*), or those which are most frequently affected by the changes described in § 19 *b–l*, as again א, ו, י, and נ, and in certain cases ה and ל; finally the gutturals and ר for the reason given in § 22 *b* and *q*.

§ 7. *The Vowels in General, Vowel Letters and Vowel Signs.*

1. The original vowels in Hebrew, as in the other Semitic tongues, are *a*, *i*, *u*. *E* and *o* always arise from an obscuring or contraction of these three pure sounds, viz. *ĕ* by modification from *ĭ* or *ă*; short *ŏ* from *ŭ*; *ê* by contraction from *ai* (properly *ay*); and *ô* sometimes by modification (obscuring) from *â*, sometimes by contraction from *au* (properly *aw*).[1]

In Arabic writing there are vowel signs only for *a*, *i*, *u*; the combined sounds *ay* and *aw* are therefore retained uncontracted and pronounced as diphthongs (*ai* and *au*), e.g. שׁוֹט Arab. *sauṭ*, and עֵינַיִם Arab. *ʿainain*. It was

---

[1] In proper names the LXX often use the diphthongs *ai* and *aυ* where the Hebrew form has *ê* or *ô*. It is, however, very doubtful whether the *ai* and *aυ* of the LXX really represent the true pronunciation of Hebrew of that time; see the instructive statistics given by Kittel in Haupt's *SBOT.*, on 1 Ch 1²·²⁰.

only in later Arabic that they became in pronunciation *ê* and *ô*, at least after weaker or softer consonants; cf. בֵּין Arab. *bain, bên,* יוֹם Arab. *yaum, yôm.* The same contraction appears also in other languages, e. g. in Greek and Latin (θαῦμα, Ionic θῶμα ; *plaustrum = plostrum*), in the French pronunciation of *ai* and *au*, and likewise in the German popular dialects (*Oge* for *Auge*, &c.). Similarly, the obscuring of the vowels plays a part in various languages (cf. e. g. the *a* in modern Persian, Swedish, English, &c.).[1]

b **2.** The partial expression of the vowels by certain consonants (ה, ו, י; א), which sufficed during the lifetime of the language, and for a still longer period afterwards (cf. § 1 *k*), must in the main have passed through the following stages [2] :—

(*a*) The need of a written indication of the vowel first made itself felt in cases where, after the rejection of a consonant, or of an entire syllable, a long vowel formed the final sound of the word. The first step in such a case was to retain the original final consonant, at least as a vowel letter, i. e. merely as an indication of a final vowel. In point of fact we find even in the Old Testament, as already in the Mêša' inscription, a ה employed in this way (see below) as an indication of a final *o*. From this it was only a step to the employment of the same consonant to indicate also other vowels when final (thus, e. g. in the inflection of the verbs ל"ה, the vowels *ā̆*,[3] *ē*, *è*). After the employment of ו as a vowel letter for *ô* and *û*, and of י for *ê* and *î*, had been established (see below, *e*) these consonants were also employed—although not consistently—for the same vowels at the end of a word.

c According to § 91 *b* and *d*, the suffix of the 3rd sing. masc. in the noun (as in the verb) was originally pronounced הֻ. But in the places where this הֻ with a preceding *a* is contracted into *ô* (after the rejection of the ה), we find the ה still frequently retained as a vowel letter, e. g. עִירֹה סֻתֹה Gn 49[11], cf. § 91 *e*; so throughout the Mêša' inscription אַרְצֹה, בֵּיתֹה (also בֵּתֹה), הִלְתֲחֲמֹה לֹה, בֹּה, בְּנֹה ; on the other hand already in the Siloam inscription רֵעֹו.[4] יְמֹה Mêša', l. 8 = יְמָיו *his days* is unusual, as also רֹשׁה l. 20 if it is for רָאשׁיו *his chiefs.* The verbal forms with ה suffixed are to be read וַיַּחְלְפֶהָ (l. 6), וְאֶסְחָבֶהָ (l. 12 f.) and וַיִּגְרְשֶׁהָ (l. 19).

d As an example of the original consonant being retained, we might also include the י of the constr. state plur. masc. if its *ê* (according to § 89 *d*) is

---

[1] In Sanskrit, in the Old Persian cuneiform, and in Ethiopic, short *a* alone of all the vowels is not represented, but the consonant by itself is pronounced with short *a*.

[2] Cf. especially Stade, *Lehrb. der hebr. Gr.*, p. 34 ff.

[3] According to Stade, the employment of ה for *ā̆* probably took place first in the case of the locative accusatives which originally ended in ה- , as קָדֹימָה, אַרְצָה.

[4] The form רֵעֹו contradicts the view of Oort, *Theol. Tijds.*, 1902, p. 374, that the above instances from the Mêša'-inscription are to be read *benhu, bahu, lahu,* which were afterwards vocalized as *beno, bo, lo.*

contracted from an original *ay*. Against this, however, it may be urged that the Phoenician inscriptions do not usually express this *ê*, nor any other final vowel.[1]

(*b*) The employment of ו to denote *ô*, *û*, and of י to denote *ê*, *î*, may *e* have resulted from those cases in which a ו with a preceding *a* was contracted into *au* and further to *ô*, or with a preceding *u* coalesced into *û*, and where י with *a* has been contracted into *ai* and further to *ê*, or with a preceding *i* into *î* (cf. § 24). In this case the previously existing consonants were retained as vowel letters and were further applied at the end of the word to denote the respective long vowels. Finally א also will in the first instance have established itself as a vowel letter only where a consonantal א with a preceding *a* had coalesced into *â* or *ā*.

The orthography of the Siloam inscription corresponds almost exactly with *f* the above assumptions. Here (as in the Mêša‘ inscr.) we find all the long vowels, which have not arisen from original diphthongs, *without* vowel letters, thus אִשׁ, חֹצְבָם, מִימָן (or מִיֽמָן); אַמֹּת, קֹל, שְׁלֹשׁ, צֻר. On the other hand מוֹצָא (from *mauṣa’*), עוֹד (from *‘aud*) ; מימן also, if it is to be read מִימָן, is an instance of the retention of a י which has coalesced with *i* into *î*. Instances of the retention of an originally consonantal א as a vowel letter are מָאֿתַֿיִם, מוֹצָא, and קְרָא, as also רֹאשׁ. Otherwise final *ā* is always represented by ה : נִקְבָה, זִדֶה, הָיָה, אַמָּה. To this סֿ‘ alone would form an exception (cf. however the note on יֹם, § 96), instead of יֹם (Arab. *yaum*) *day*, which one would expect. If the reading be correct, this is to be regarded as an argument that a consciousness of the origin of many long vowels was lost at an early period, so that (at least in the middle of the word) the vowel letters were omitted in places where they should stand, according to what has been stated above, and added where there was no case of contraction. This view is in a great measure confirmed by the orthography of the Mêša‘ inscription. There we find, as might be expected, דיבן (= *Daibōn*, as the Δαιβών of the LXX proves), חוֹרֹנָן (*ô* from *au*), and בֵּיתֹה (*ê* from *ai*), but also even הִשְׁעַנִי[2] instead of הוֹשַׁעַנִי (from *hauš-*), בֵּת = וָאֹשֵׁיב = וָאֵשֵׁב four times, בֵּתֹה once, for בֵּית and בֵּיתֹה (from *bait*); לַיְלָה = לְלָה = אִן = אֵין or אֵין.

---

[1] Thus there occurs, e.g. in Melit. I, l. 3 שׁנבן = שְׁנֵי בְנֵי *the two sons*; elsewhere כ for כִּי (but כי in the Mêša‘ and Siloam inscrr.), ז for זֶה (the latter in the Siloam inscr.), בנת = בְּנָתִי (so Mêša‘) or בְּנִיתִי, &c. Cf. on the other hand in Mêša‘, אנכי = אנכ (unless it was actually pronounced *‘anôkh* by the Moabites!). As final *ā* is represented by ה and א and final *i* by י, so final *û* is almost everywhere expressed by ו in Mêša‘, and always in the Siloam inscription. It is indeed not impossible that Hebrew orthography also once passed through a period in which the final vowels were left always or sometimes undenoted, and that not a few strange forms in the present text of the Bible are to be explained from the fact that subsequently the vowel letters (especially ו and י) were not added in all cases. So Chwolson, ‘Die Quiescentia הוי in der althebr.Orthogr.,’ in *Travaux du Congrès . . . des Orientalistes*, Petersb. 1876 ; cf. numerous instances in Ginsburg, *Introd.*, p. 146 ff.

[2] השׁעני is the more strange since the name of king הוֹשֵׁעַ is represented as *A·u si’* in cuneiform as late as 728 B.C.

g   (c) In the present state of Old Testament vocalization as it appears in the Masoretic text, the striving after a certain uniformity cannot be mistaken, in spite of the inconsistencies which have crept in. Thus the final long vowel is, with very few exceptions (cf. § 9 *d*, and the very doubtful cases in § 8 *k*), indicated by a vowel letter—and almost always by the same letter in certain nominal and verbal endings. In many cases the use of ו to mark an *ô* or *û*, arising from contraction, and of י for *ê* or *î*, is by far the more common, while we seldom find an originally consonantal א rejected, and the simple phonetic principle taking the place of the historical orthography. On the other hand the number of exceptions is very great. In many cases (as e.g. in the plural endings ◌ִים and וֹת) the vowel letters are habitually employed to express long vowels which do not arise through contraction, and we even find short vowels indicated. The conclusion is, that if there ever was a period of Hebrew writing when the application of fixed laws to all cases was intended, either these laws were not consistently carried out in the further transmission of the text, or errors and confusion afterwards crept into it. Moreover much remained uncertain even in texts which were plentifully provided with vowel letters. For, although in most cases the context was a guide to the correct reading, yet there were also cases where, of the many possible ways of pronouncing a word, more than one appeared admissible.[1]

h   3. When the language had died out, the ambiguity of such a writing must have been found continually more troublesome ; and as there was thus a danger that the correct pronunciation might be finally lost, the vowel signs or vowel points were invented in order to fix it. By means of these points everything hitherto left uncertain was most accurately settled. It is true that there is no historical account of the date of this vocalization of the O. T. text, yet we may at least infer, from a comparison of other historical facts, that it was gradually developed by Jewish grammarians in the sixth and seventh centuries A.D. under the influence of different Schools, traces of which have been preserved to the present time in various differences of tradition.[2] They mainly followed, though with independent regard to

---

[1] Thus e. g. קטל can be read *qāṭal, qāṭāl, qāṭōl, qᵉṭōl, qōṭēl, qiṭṭēl, qaṭṭēl, quṭṭal, qᵉṭel,* and several of these forms have also different senses.

[2] The most important of these differences are, (*a*) those between the Orientals, i. e. the scholars of the Babylonian Schools, and the Occidentals, i. e. the scholars of Palestine (Tiberias, &c.) ; cf. Ginsburg, *Introd.*, p. 197 ff. ; (*b*) amongst the Occidentals, between Ben-Naphtali and Ben-Asher, who flourished in the first half of the tenth century at Tiberias ; cf. Ginsburg, *Introd.,* p. 241 ff. Both sets of variants are given by Baer in the appendices

the peculiar nature of the Hebrew, the example and pattern of the older Syrian punctuation.[1]

See Gesenius, *Gesch. d. hebr. Spr.*, p. 182 ff. ; Hupfeld, in *Theol. Studien u. Kritiken*, 1830, pt. iii, who shows that neither Jerome nor the Talmud mentions vowel signs ; Berliner, *Beiträge zur hebr. Gramm. im Talm. u. Midrasch*, p. 26 ff. ; and B. Pick, in *Hebraica*, i. 3, p. 153 ff. ; Abr. Geiger, 'Zur Nakdanim-[Punctuators-]Literatur,' in *Jüd. Ztschr. für Wissensch. u. Leben*, x. Breslau, 1872, p. 10 ff. ; H. Strack, *Prolegomena critica in Vet. Test. Hebr.*, Lips. 1873 ; 'Beitrag zur Gesch. des hebr. Bibeltextes,' in *Theol. Stud. u. Krit.*, 1875, p. 736 ff., as also in the *Ztschr. f. die ges. luth. Theol. u. K.*, 1875, p. 619 ff. ; 'Massorah,' in the *Protest. Real.-Enc.*[3], xii. 393 ff. (a good outline) ; A. Merx, in the *Verhandlungen des Orientalistenkongresses zu Berlin*, i. Berlin, 1881, p. 164 ff. and p. 188 ff. ; H. Graetz, 'Die Anfänge der Vokalzeichen im Hebr.,' in *Monatsschr. f. Gesch. u. Wissensch. d. Judenth.*, 1881, pp. 348 ff. and 395 ff. ; Hersmann, *Zur Gesch. des Streites über die Entstehung der hebr. Punktation*, Ruhrort, 1885 ; Harris, 'The Rise... of the Massorah,' *JQR*. i. 1889, p. 128 ff. and p. 223 ff. ; Mayer-Lambert, *REJ*. xxvi. 1893, p. 274 ff. ; J. Bachrach, *Das Alter d. bibl. Vocalisation u. Accentuation*, 2 pts. Warsaw, 1897, and esp. Ginsburg, *Introd.* (see § 3 c), p. 287 ff. ; Budde, 'Zur Gesch. d. Tiberiens. Vokalisation,' in *Orient. Studien zu Ehren Th. Nöldekes*, i. 1906, 651 ff. ; Bacher, 'Diakrit. Zeichen in vormasoret. Zeit,' in *ZAW*. 1907, p. 285 ; C. Levias, art. 'Vocalization,' in the *Jewish Encycl.*—On the hypothesis of the origin of punctuation in the Jewish schools for children, cf. J. Dérenbourg in the *Rev. Crit.*, xiii. 1879, no. 25.

4. To complete the historical vocalization of the consonantal text *i* a phonetic system was devised, so exact as to show all vowel-changes occasioned by lengthening of words, by the tone, by gutturals, &c., which in other languages are seldom indicated in writing. The pronunciation followed is in the main that of the Palestinian Jews of about the sixth century A.D., as observed in the solemn reading of the sacred writings in synagogue and school, but based on a much older tradition. That the real pronunciation of early Hebrew is consistently preserved by this tradition, has recently been seriously questioned on good grounds, especially in view of the transcription of proper names in the LXX. Nevertheless in many cases, internal reasons, as well as the analogy of the kindred languages, testify in a high degree to the faithfulness of the tradition. At the same recension of the text, or soon after, the various other signs for reading (§§ 11–14, 16) were added, and the accents (§ 15).

§ 8. *The Vowel Signs in particular.*

P. Haupt, 'The names of the Hebrew vowels,' *JAOS*. xxii, and in the *Johns Hopkins Semitic Papers*, Newhaven, 1901, p. 7 ff. ; C. Levias in the *Hebr. Union Coll. Annual*, Cincinnati, 1904, p. 138 ff.

---

to his critical editions. Our printed editions present uniformly the text of Ben-Asher, with the exception of a few isolated readings of Ben-Naphtali, and of numerous later corruptions.

[1] See Geiger, 'Massorah bei d. Syrern,' in *ZDMG*. 1873, p. 148 ff. ; J. P. Martin, *Hist. de la ponctuation ou de la Massore chez les Syriens*, Par. 1875 ; E. Nestle, in *ZDMG*. 1876, p. 525 ff. ; Weingarten, *Die syr. Massora nach Bar Hebraeus*, Halle, 1887.

Preliminary Remark.

The next two sections (§§ 8 and 9) have been severely criticized (Philippi, *ThLZ*. 1897, no. 2) for assigning a definite quantity to each of the several vowels, whereas in reality ⵗ, ⵗ, ⵗ are merely signs for *ă, e, o*: 'whether these are long or short is not shown by the signs themselves but must be inferred from the rules for the pause which marks the breaks in continuous narrative, or from other circumstances.' But in the twenty-fourth and subsequent German editions of this Grammar, in the last note on § 8 *a* [English ed. p. 38, note 4], it was stated : 'it must be mentioned that the Masoretes are not concerned with any distinction between long and short vowels, or in general with any question of quantity. Their efforts are directed to fixing the received pronunciation as faithfully as possible, by means of writing.

For a long time only שִׁבְעָה מְלָכִים *seven kings* were reckoned (*vox memor.* in Elias Levita וַיֹּאמֶר אֵלָיְהוּ), Šureq and Qibbuṣ being counted as one vowel. The division of the vowels in respect of quantity is a later attempt at a scientific conception of the phonetic system, which was not invented but only represented by the Masoretes (Qimchi, *Mikhlol*, ed. Rittenb. 136 *a*, distinguishes the five long as *mothers* from their five daughters).'

I have therefore long shared the opinion that 'the vowel-system represented by the ordinary punctuation (of Tiberias) was primarily intended to mark only differences of quality' (Sievers, *Metrische Studien*, i. 17). There is, however, of course a further question how far these 'later' grammarians were mistaken in assigning a particular quantity to the vowels represented by particular signs. In Philippi's opinion they were mistaken (excluding of course *i, ê, ô* when written *plene*) in a very great number of cases, since not only does ⵗ stand, according to circumstances, for *ā̆* or *ă*, and ⵗ for *ā̆* or *ă*, but also ⵗ for *ē* or *ĕ*, and ⵗ for *ō̆* or *ŏ*, e. g. כָּבֵד and קָטֹל, out of pause *kåbéd*, *qā̆ṭón* (form קְטֹל), but in pause *kåbéd*, *qā̆ṭón*.

I readily admit, with regard to Qameṣ and Seˢgol, that the account formerly given in § 8 f. was open to misconstruction. With regard to Ṣere and Ḥolem, however, I can only follow Philippi so long as his view does not conflict with the (to me inviolable) law of a long vowel in an open syllable before the tone and (except Pathaḥ) in a final syllable with the tone. To me כָּבֵד = *kåbéd*, &c., is as impossible as e. g. עֲנָב = '*ĕnab* or בָּרֶךְ = *bŏrakh*, in spite of the analogy cited by Sievers (p. 18, note 1) that 'in old German e. g. original *ĭ* and *ŭ* often pass into *ĕ* and *ŏ* dialectically, while remaining in a closed syllable.

a   1. The full vowels (in contrast to the half-vowels or vowel trills, § 10 *a–f*), classified according to the three principal vowel sounds (§ 7 *a*), are as follows :—

First Class. *A-sound.*

A {
1. ⵗ [1] Qāmĕṣ denotes either *ā, â*, more strictly *ā̆* (the obscure Swedish *å*) and *å̂*,[2] as יָד *yā̆d* (hand), רָאשִׁים *rā̆'šîm* (heads), or *ă* (in future transcribed as *ŏ*), called Qāmĕṣ *ḥāṭûph*, i. e. hurried Qameṣ. The latter occurs almost exclusively as a modification of *ŭ*; cf. *c* and § 9 *u*.

2. ⵗ *Páthaḥ, ă*, בַּת *băth* (daughter).
}

---

[1] In early MSS. the sign for Qames is a stroke with a point underneath, i. e. according to Nestle's discovery (*ZDMG*. 1892, p. 411 f.), Pathaḥ with *Ḥolem*, the latter suggesting the obscure pronunciation of Qameṣ as *å*. Cf. also Ginsburg, *Introd.*, p. 609.

[2] Instead of the no doubt more accurate transcription *ā̆, å̂* we have

Also 3. ֶ *Sĕgôl*, an open *e, ê* (*ā̆* or *ā̆*), as a modification of *ă*,[1] either
in an untoned closed syllable, as in the first syllable of יֶדְכֶם *yădkhèm*
(your hand) from *yădkhèm*—or in a tone-syllable as in פֶּסַח *pĕsaḥ*;
cf. πάσχα, and on the really monosyllabic character of such formations, see § 28 *e*. But *Sĕgôl* in an open tone-syllable with a following
י, as in גָּלִינָה *gĕlènā* (cf. § 75 *f*), יָדְיִךְ *yādèkhā* (cf. § 91 *i*), is due
to contraction from *ay*.

Second Class. I- and E-sounds.

I {

1. ִי־ *Ḥîrĕq* with *yod*, almost always *î*, as צַדִּיק *ṣaddîq* (righteous). *b*

2. ִ either *î* (see below, *i*), as צַדִּיקִים *ṣaddîqîm*, only orthographically different from צדיקים (צַדִיקֶם),—or *ĭ*, as צִדְקוֹ
ṣidqô (his righteousness).

E {

3. ֵי־ *Ṣerî* or *Ṣerê* with *yod*=*ê*, e. g. בֵּיתוֹ *bêthô* (his house).

ֵ either *ê*, but rarely (see below, *i*), or *ē* as שֵׁם *šēm* (name).
Ṣere can only be *ĕ*, in my opinion, in few cases, such as
those mentioned in § 29 *f*.

4. ֶ *Sĕgôl, ě*, a modification of *ĭ*, e.g. חֶפְצִי *ḥäfṣî* (ground-form
ḥifṣ); שֶׁן *šän* (ground-form *šin*).

Third Class. U- and O-sounds.

U {

1. וּ *Šûrĕq*, usually *û*, מוּת *mûth* (to die), rarely *ŭ*.   *c*

2. ֻ *Qibbûṣ*, either *ŭ*, e.g. סֻלָּם *sŭllām* (ladder), or *û*, e.g. קֻמוּ
qûmû (rise up), instead of the usual קוּמוּ.

O {

3. וֹ and ֹ *Ḥōlĕm, ô* and *ō*, קוֹל *qôl* (voice), רֹב *rōbh* (multitude).
Often also a defective ֹ for *ô*; rarely וֹ for *ō*.
On the question whether ֹ under some circumstances
represents *ŏ*, see § 93 *r*.

4. ָ On *Qāmĕṣ ḥāṭûph*=*ŏ*, generally modified from *ŭ*, as חָק
ḥŏq (statute), see above, *a*.

---

retained *ā, á* in this grammar, as being typographically simpler and not
liable to any misunderstanding. For *Qameṣ ḥaṭuph*, in the previous German
edition expressed by *ā̆*, we have, after careful consideration, returned to *ŏ*
The use of the same sign ָ for *ā̆* (*ā̆*) and *ā̆*, shows that the Massoretes did
not intend to draw a sharp distinction between them. We must not, however, regard the Jewish grammarians as making a merely idle distinction
between *Qāmeṣ rāḥāb*, or broad Qameṣ, and *Qāmeṣ ḥaṭuph*, or light Qameṣ. It
is quite impossible that in the living language an *ā* lengthened from *ă*, as in
dābār, should have been indistinguishable from e.g. the last vowel in וַיֵּשֶׁב
or the first in קָרָשִׁים.—The notation *â, ê, ô* expresses here the vowels essentially long, either naturally or by contraction; the notation *ā, ē, ō* those
lengthened only by the tone, and therefore changeable; *ă, ĕ, ŏ* the short
vowels. As regards the others, the distinction into *i* and *î*, *û* and *ŭ* is
sufficient; see § 9.—The mark ˊ stands in the following pages over the tone-
syllable, whenever this is not the last, as is usual, but the penultimate
syllable of the word, e. g. יֵ֫שֶׁב.

[1] These *Sĕgôls*, modified from *ă*, are very frequent in the language. The

d The names of the vowels are mostly taken from the form and action of the mouth in producing the various sounds, as פָּתַח *opening* ; צֵרִי *a wide parting* (of the mouth), also שֶׁבֶר (= *ĭ*) *breaking, parting* (cf. the Arab. *kasr*) ; חִירֶק (also חֶרֶק) *narrow opening* ; חֹולֶם *closing*, according to others *fullness*, i. e. of the mouth (also מְלֹא פוּם [1] *fullness of the mouth*). קָמֵץ [2] also denotes a slighter, as שׁוּרֶק and קִבּוּץ (also קְבוּץ פוּם) a firmer, compression or contraction of the mouth. *S⁰gôl* (סֶגֹּול *bunch of grapes*) takes its name from its form. So שָׁלֹשׁ נְקֻדֹּות (*three points*) is another name for *Qibbúṣ*.

e Moreover the names were mostly so formed (but only later), that the sound of each vowel is heard in the first syllable (קָמֵץ for קְמֵץ, פַּתַח for פְּתַח, צֵרִי for צְרִי) ; in order to carry this out consistently some even write *Ṣägôl, Qomeṣ-ḥaṭúf, Qŭbbús.*

f **2.** As the above examples show, the vowel sign stands regularly *under* the consonant, *after* which it is to be pronounced, רָ *rā*, רַ *rŭ*, רֵ *rē*, רֻ *rŭ*, &c. The *Pathaḥ* called *furtivum* (§ 22 *f*) alone forms an exception to this rule, being pronounced *before* the consonant, רוּחַ *rûᵃ̯ḥ* (wind, spirit). The *Ḥōlĕm* (without *wāw*) stands on the left above the consonant; רֹ *rō* (but לֹ = *lō*). If א, as a vowel letter, follows a consonant which is to be pronounced with *ō*, the point is placed over its right arm, thus רֹאשׁ, בֹּא ; but e.g. בָּאָם, since א here begins a syllable.

g No dot is used for the Ḥolem when *ō* (of course without *wāw*) is pronounced after *sin* or before *šin*. Hence שֹׂנֵא *śōnē* (hating), נְשֹׂא *n⁰śō* (to bear), מֹשֶׁה *môśè* (not מֹשֶׁה) ; but שֹׁמֵר *śōmēr* (a watchman). When *ō* precedes the *sin*, the dot is placed over its right arm, e.g. יִרְפֹּשׂ *yirpōś* (he treads with the feet), הַנֹּשְׂאִים *hannōś⁰ʾîm* (those who carry).

In the sign וֹ, the ו may also be a consonant. The וֹ is then either to be read *ōw* (necessarily so when a consonant otherwise without a vowel precedes, e.g. לֹוֶה *lōwè*, lending) or *wō*, when a vowel already precedes the ו, e.g. עָוֹן *ʿāwôn* (iniquity) for עָוֹן. In more exact printing, a distinction is at least made between וֹ (*wo*) and וֹ (i. e. either *ō* or, when another vowel follows the *wāw, ōw* [3]).

Babylonian punctuation (see § 8 *g*, note 1) has only one sign for it and tone-bearing Pathaḥ ; see also Gaster, 'Die Unterschiedslosigkeit zwischen Pathach u. Segol,' in *ZAW.* 1894, p. 60 ff.

[1] On the erroneous use of the term *melo pum*, only in Germany, for *šúreq* (hence also pronounced *melu pum* to indicate *ú*), see E. Nestle, *ZDMG.* 1904, p. 597 ff. ; Bacher, ibid., p. 799 ff., Melopum ; Simonsen, ibid., p. 807 ff.

[2] The usual spelling קָמֵץ and פַּתַח takes the words certainly rightly as Hebrew substantives ; according to De Lagarde (*Gött. gel. Anz.* 1886, p. 873, and so previously Luzzatto), קָמֵץ and פַּתַח are rather Aram. participles, like *Dageš*, &c., and consequently to be transliterated *Qàmēṣ* and *Páthah.*

[3] Since 1846 we have become acquainted with a system of vocalization different in many respects from the common method. The vowel signs, all except וֹ, are there placed *above* the consonants, and differ almost throughout in form,

3. The vowels of the first class are, with the exception of $'_{\overline{\tau}}$ in *h* the middle and $\Pi_{\overline{\tau}}$, $\aleph_{\overline{\tau}}$, $\Pi_{\overline{\tau}}$ at the end of the word (§ 9 *a–d, f*), represented *only* by vowel signs, but the long vowels of the I- and U-class largely by vowel letters. The vowel sound to which the letter

---

and some even as regards the sound which they denote: $\overset{\angle}{} = \acute{a}, \bar{a},$ $\overset{\mathscr{L}}{} = $ tone-bearing $\breve{a}$ and $\grave{e}$, $\overset{..}{\overline{}} = \hat{e}, \bar{e}, \overset{.}{\overline{}} = \hat{i}, \mathring{}$, $\overset{.}{\underline{}} = \hat{o}, \bar{o}, \overset{.}{\underline{}}$ or $\daleth = \hat{u}$. In an unsharpened syllable $\overset{\angle}{} = $ toneless $\breve{a}$ and $\grave{e}$, and also Ḥaṭeph Pathaḥ; $\overset{..}{\underline{}} = $ toneless $\breve{e}$ and Ḥaṭeph Seghôl; $\overset{.}{} = \hat{i}, \overset{.}{\underline{}} = \hat{u}, \overset{\mathit{3}}{} = \breve{o}$, and Ḥaṭeph Qameṣ. Lastly in toneless syllables before Dageš, $\overset{\mathscr{L}}{} = \breve{a}, \overset{..}{\overline{}} = \breve{e}, \overset{.}{\overline{}} = i, \overset{.}{\underline{}} = \breve{u}, \overset{\mathit{3}}{} = \breve{a}$. Šewâ is $\overset{.}{=}$ The accents differ less and stand in some cases under the line of the consonants. Besides this complicated system of the Codex Babylonicus (see below) and other MSS., there is a simpler one, used in Targums. It is still uncertain whether the latter is the foundation of the former (as Merx, *Chrest. Targ.* xi, and Bacher, *ZDMG.* 1895, p. 15 ff.), or is a later development of it among the Jews of South Arabia (as Praetorius, *ZDMG.* 1899, p. 181 ff.). For the older literature on this *Babylonian punctuation* (נִקּוּד בַּבְלִי), as it is called, see A. Harkavy and H. L. Strack, *Katalog der hebr. Bibelhandschr. der Kaiserl. öffentl. Bibliothek zu St. Petersb.*, St. Petersb. and Lpz., 1875, parts i and ii, p. 223 ff. A more thorough study of the system was made possible by H. Strack's facsimile edition of the *Prophetarum posteriorum codex Babylonicus Petropolitanus* (St. Petersb., 1876, la. fol.) of the year 916, which Firkowitsch discovered in 1839, in the synagogue at Tschufutkale in the Crimea. The MS. has been shown by Ginsburg (*Recueil des travaux rédigés en mémoire . . . de Chwolson*, Berlin, 1899, p. 149, and *Introd.*, pp. 216 ff., 475 f.) to contain a recension of the Biblical text partly Babylonian and partly Palestinian; cf. also Barnstein, *The Targum of Onkelos to Genesis*, London, 1896, p. 6 f. Stràck edited a fragment of it in *Hosea et Joel prophetae ad fidem cod. Babylon. Petrop.*, St. Petersb. 1875. Cf. also the publication by A. Merx, quoted above, § 7 *h*, and his *Chrestomathia Targumica*, Berlin, 1888; G. Margoliouth, in the *PSBA.* xv. 4, and M. Gaster, ibid.; P. Kahle, *Der masoret. Text des A. T. nach d. Überlief. der babyl. Juden*, Lpz. 1902, with the valuable review by Rahlfs in *GGA.* 1903, no. 5; Nestle, *ZDMG.* 1905, p. 719 (Babylonian $\overset{\mathscr{L}}{} = $ 𝔶. According to the opinion formerly prevailing, this Babylonian punctuation exhibits the system which was developed in the Eastern schools, corresponding to and contemporaneous with the Western or Tiberian system, although a higher degree of originality, or approximation to the original of both systems of punctuation, was generally conceded to the latter. Recently, however, Wickes, *Accents of the Twenty-one Books*, Oxford, 1887, p. 142 ff, has endeavoured to show, from the accents, that the 'Babylonian' punctuation may certainly be *an* Oriental, but is by no means *the* Oriental system. It is rather to be regarded, according to him, as a later and not altogether successful attempt to modify, and thus to simplify, the system common to all the Schools in the East and West. Strack, *Wiss. Jahresb. der ZDMG.* 1879, p. 124, established the probability that the vowels of the superlinear punctuation arose under *Arab* influence from the vowel letters אוי (so previously Pinsker and Graetz), while the Tiberian system shows *Syrian* influence.

A third, widely different system (Palestinian), probably the basis of the other two, is described by A. Neubauer, *JQR.* vii. 1895, p. 361 ff., and Friedländer, ibid., p. 564 ff., and *PSBA.* 1896, p. 86 ff.; C. Levias, *Journ. of Sem. Lang. and Lit.*, xv. p. 157 ff.; and esp. P. Kahle, *Beitr. zu der Gesch. der hebr. Punktation*, in *ZAW.* 1901, p. 273 ff. and in *Der masoret. Text des A. T.* (see above), chiefly dealing with the Berlin MS. Or. qu. 680, which contains a number of variants on the biblical text, and frequently agrees with the transcriptions of the LXX and Jerome.

points is determined more precisely by the vowel sign standing before, above, or within it. Thus—

י may be combined with *Ḥireq*, *Ṣerê*, *Seĝôl* ('ִ‎, 'ֵ‎, 'ֶ‎).

ו with *Šûreq* and *Ḥōlĕm* (וּ and וֹ).[1]

> In Arabic the long *a* also is regularly expressed by a vowel letter, viz. '*Aleph* (اَ‎), so that in that language three vowel letters correspond to the three vowel classes. In Hebrew א is rarely used as a vowel letter; see § 9 *b* and § 23 *g*.

i 4. The omission of the vowel letters when writing *î, û, ê, ô* is called *scriptio defectiva* in contrast to *scriptio plena.* קוֹל, קוּם are written *plene*, קֹל, קֻם *defective*.

> Cf. Bardowitz, *Studien zur Gesch. der Orthogr. im Althebr.*, 1894 ; Lidzbarski, *Ephem.*, i. 182, 275 ; Marmorstein, ' Midrasch der vollen u. defekt. Schreibung,' in *ZAW.* 1907, p. 33 ff.

k So far as the choice of the full or defective mode of writing is concerned, there are certainly some cases in which only the one or the other is admissible. Thus the full form is necessary at the end of the word, for *û, ô, ō, î, ê, ē,* as well as for *e* in חֹזֶה &c. (§ 9 *f*), also generally with *â, ā* (cf. however § 9 *d*), e.g. קָטְלוּ, קָטַלְתִּי, יָדִי, מַלְכֵי. (But the Masora requires in Jer 26⁶, 44⁸; Ezr 6²¹; 2 Ch 32¹³ גוֹי instead of גּוֹיִי ; Zp 2⁹ גּוֹי [perhaps an error due to the following י‎] for גּוֹיִי; Is 40³¹ וְקוֹי [followed by י‎] for וְקוֹיִי; Jer 38¹¹ בְּלוֹי for בְּלוֹיִי.) On the other hand the defective writing is common when the letter, which would have to be employed as a vowel letter, immediately precedes as a strong consonant, e.g. גּוֹיִם (*nations*) for גּוֹיִים, מִצְוֹת (*commandments*) for מִצְווֹת.

l That much is here arbitrary (see § 7 *g*), follows from the fact that sometimes the same word is written very differently, e.g. הַקִּימוֹתִי Ez 16⁶⁰ : הֲקִמֹתִי and also הֲקִמוֹתִי Jer 23⁴ ; cf. § 25 *b*. Only it may be observed,

(*a*) That the scriptio plena in two successive syllables was generally avoided ; cf. e.g. נָבִיא but נְבִאִים; צַדִּיק, but צַדְּקִים; קוֹל, קֹלוֹת; יְהוֹשֻׁעַ; מְצָאֻהוּ.

(*b*) That in the later Books of the O. T. (and regularly in post-biblical Hebrew) the full form, in the earlier the defective, is more usual.

m 5. In the cognate dialects, when a vowel precedes a vowel-letter which is not kindred (heterogeneous), e.g. וְ‎ֱ‎, וֹ‎ֲ‎, יְ‎ִ‎, יֵ‎ֱ‎, יַ‎ֲ‎, a diphthong (*au, ai*)[2] is formed if the heterogeneous vowel be *a*. This is also to be regarded as the Old Hebrew pronunciation, since it

---

[1] After the example of the Jewish grammarians the expression, 'the vowel letter rests (*quiesces*) in the vowel-sign,' has become customary. On the other hand, the vowel letters are also called by the grammarians, *matres lectionis* or *supports* (*fulcra*).

[2] Cf. T. C. Foote, *The diphthong ai in Hebrew* (Johns Hopkins Univ. Circulars, June, 1903, p. 70 ff.).

agrees with the vocalic character of ן and י (§ 5 b, note 2). Thus such words as וָו, חַי, גּוֹי, עָשׂוּי, גֵּו, בַּיִת are not to be pronounced according to the usual Jewish custom [1] as *vāv, ḥay, gôy, ʿāsûy, gēv, bayith* (or even as *vaf, &c.* ; cf. modern Greek *av af, ev ef* for αὐ, εὐ), but with the Italian Jews more like *wāu, ḥai, &c.* The sound of יְ⫶ is the same as יִ⫶, i.e. almost like *āu*, so that יִ⫶ is often written defectively for יְ⫶.

§ 9. *Character of the several Vowels.*

Numerous as are the vowel signs in Hebrew writing, they are yet *a* not fully adequate to express all the various modifications of the vowel sounds, especially with respect to length and shortness. To understand this better a short explanation of the character and value of the several vowels is required, especially in regard to their length and shortness as well as to their changeableness (§§ 25, 27).

I. *First Class. A-sound.*

1. *Qameṣ* (⫶), when it represents a long *a*, is, by nature and origin, of two kinds :—

(1) The essentially long *â* (in Arabic regularly written אָ⫶), which is not readily shortened and never wholly dropped (§ 25 c), e.g. כְּתָב *kᵉthâbh* (writing); very seldom with a following א, as רָאשׁ 2 S 12^{1.4} (see the examples in § 72 p).[2]

The writing of קָאם Ho 10¹⁴ for קָם would only be justifiable, if the *â* *b* of this form were to be explained as a contraction of *ăă*; cf. however § 72 a; דָּאג Neh 13¹⁶ for דָּג (*dāg*) is certainly incorrect.—The rarity of the *â* in Hebrew arises from the fact that it has for the most part become an obtuse *ô*; see below, *q*.

(2) *ā*, lengthened only by position (i.e. tone-long or at all events *c* lengthened under the influence of the tone, according to the laws for the formation of syllables, § 27 *e–h*), either in the tone-syllable itself (or in the secondary tone-syllable indicated by *Mèthĕg*, see below), or just before or after it. This sound is invariably lengthened from an original *ă*,[3] and is found in open syllables, i.e. syllables ending in a vowel (§ 26 b), e.g. לְךָ, קָטַל, יָקוּם, אָסִיר (Arab. *lăkă, qătălă, yăqûmŭ, ʾăsîrŭ*), as well as in closed syllables, i.e. those ending in

---

[1] In MSS. ן and י, in such combinations as גֵּו, חַי, are even marked with Mappîq (§ 14 a).

[2] Of a different kind are the cases in which א has lost its consonantal sound by coalescing with a preceding *a*, § 23 a–d.

[3] In Arabic this *ă* is always retained in an open syllable.

a consonant, as יָד, בּוֹכָב (vulgar Arab. *yăd, kaukăb*). In a closed syllable, however, it can only stand when this has the tone, דָּבָר, עוֹלָם; whereas in an open syllable it is especially frequent *before* the tone, e.g. דָּבָר, לָבֶם, זְקַן. Where the tone is moved forward or weakened (as happens most commonly in what is called the construct state of nouns, cf. § 89 *a*) the original short *ă* (*Pathaḥ*) is retained in a closed syllable, while in an open syllable it becomes *S̆ewâ* (§ 27 *i*): חָכָם, constr. state חֲכַם (*ḥᵃkhăm*); דְּבַר, דְּבָר (*dᵉbhăr*); קָטַל, קְטָלָם. For examples of the retention, in the secondary tone-syllable, of *ā* lengthened from *ă*, see § 93 *xx*.

d   In some terminations of the verb (תָ in the 2nd sing. masc. perf., נָ in the 2nd pl. fem. of the imperat., as well as in the 3rd and 2nd pl. fem. of the imperf.), in אַתָּ *thou* (masc.) and in the suffixes ךָ and ךָ, the final *ā* can stand even without a vowel letter. A ה is, however, in these cases (except with ךָ) frequently added as a vowel letter.

On ◌ָ for *ŏ* see below, *f*.

e   2. *Pathaḥ*, or short *ă*, stands in Hebrew almost exclusively in a closed syllable with or without the tone (קָטַל, קְטַלְתֶּם). In places where it now appears to stand in an open syllable the syllable was originally closed, and a helping vowel (*ă*, *ĭ*) has been inserted after the second radical merely to make the pronunciation easier, e.g. נַחַל (ground-form *naḥl*), בַּיִת (Arab. *bait*), see § 28 *d*, and with regard to two cases of a different kind, § 26 *g*, *h*. Otherwise *ă* in an open syllable has almost without exception passed into *ā* (◌ָ), see above, *c*.

On the very frequent attenuation of *ă* to *ĭ*, cf. below, *h*. On the rare, and only apparent union of Pathaḥ with א (אֲ‌◌), see § 23 *d*, end. On *ă* as a helping-vowel, § 22 *f* (*Pathaḥ furtivum*), and § 28 *e*.

f   3. Segôl (*ĕ, è* [*ä̆*]) by origin belongs sometimes to the second, but most frequently to the first vowel class (§ 27 *o, p, u*). It belongs to the first class when it is a modification of *a* (as the Germ. *Bad*, pl. *Bäder*; Eng. *man*, pl. *men*), either in a toneless syllable, e.g. יֶדְכֶם (for *yadkhèm*), or with the tone, e.g. אֶרֶץ from *'arṣ*, קֶרֶן Arab. *qărn*, קֶמַח Arab. *qămḥ*. This *Segôl* is often retained even in the strongest tone-syllable, at the end of a sentence or of an important clause (in *pause*), as צֶדֶק מֶלֶךְ (*mălăkh, sădăq*). As a rule, however, in such cases the *Pathaḥ* which underlies the *Segôl* is lengthened into *Qameṣ*, e.g. קָמַח, קָרֶן. A *Segôl* apparently lengthened from *S̆ewâ*, but in reality traceable to an original *ă*, stands in pausal forms, as פֶּרִי (ground-form *păry*), יֶהִי (*yăhy*), &c. On the cases where a י (originally consonantal) follows this Segôl, see § 75 *f*, and § 91 *k*.

II.　*Second Class. I- and E-sounds.*

4. The long *î* is frequently even in the consonantal writing indicated *g*
by י (a *fully* written *Ḥireq* י֖—) ; but a naturally long *î* can be also
written *defectively* (§ 8 *i*), e. g. צַדִּיק (*righteous*), plur. צַדִּקִים *ṣaddîqîm* ;
יִרָא (*he fears*), plur. יִרְאוּ. Whether a *defectively* written *Ḥireq* is long
may be best known from the origin of the form ; often also from the
nature of the syllable (§ 26), or as in יִרְאוּ from the *Metheg* attached to
it (§ 16 *f*).

5. The *short Ḥireq* (always[1] written *defectively*) is especially frequent *h*
in sharpened syllables (אִמִּי, קִטֵּל) and in toneless closed syllables (מִזְמוֹר
psalm); cf. however וַיִּשְׁבְּ in a closed tone-syllable, and even וַיִּפֶן, with
a helping Segôl, for *wayyiphn*. It has arisen very frequently by
attenuation from *ă*, as in דִּבְרֵי from original *dăbărê*, צִדְקִי (ground-form
ṣădq),[2] or else it is the original *ĭ*, which in the tone-syllable had
become *ē*, as in אֹיִבְךָ (*thy enemy*) from אֹיֵב (ground-form *'ăyĭb*).[3] It
is sometimes a simple helping vowel, as in בַּיִת, § 28 *e*.

The earlier grammarians call every *Ḥireq* written *fully*, *Ḥireq magnum* ; every
one written *defectively*, *Ḥireq parvum*,—a misleading distinction, so far as
quantity is concerned.

6. The longest *ê* י֗— (more rarely defective —֗, e. g. עֵנִי for עֵינִי *i*
Is 3[8]; at the end of a word also ה—) is as a rule contracted from י— *ay*
(*ai*), § 7 *a*, e. g. הֵיכָל (*palace*), Arab. and Syriac *haikal*.

7. The *Ṣere* without Yôdh mostly represents the tone-long *ē*, which, *k*
like the tone-long *ā* (see *c*), is very rarely retained except *in* and *before*
the tone-syllable, and is always lengthened from an original *ĭ*. It
stands in an open syllable with or before the tone, e. g. סֵפֶר (ground-
form *sĭphr*) *book*, שֵׁנָה (Arab. *sĭnăt*) *sleep*, or with Metheg (see § 16 *d, f*)
in the secondary tone-syllable, e. g. שְׁאֵלָתִי *my request*, נֵלְכָה *let us go*.
On the other hand in a closed syllable it is almost always with the
tone, as בֵּן *son*, אֵלֶם *dumb*.

Exceptions : (*a*) *ē* is sometimes retained in a toneless closed syllable, in *l*
monosyllabic words before Maqqeph, e. g. עֵץ־ Nu 35[18], as well as in the
examples of *nāsôg 'āḥôr* mentioned in § 29 *f* (on the quantity cf. § 8 *b* 3 end) ;
(*b*) in a toneless open final syllable, Ṣere likewise occurs in examples of the
nāsôg 'āḥôr, as יֵצֵא Ex 16[29] ; cf. Ju 9[39].

8. The Segôl of the I(E)-class is most frequently an *ĕ* modified from *m*
original *ĭ*, either replacing a tone-long *ē* which has lost the tone, e. g.

---

[1] At least according to the Masoretic orthography ; cf. Wellhausen, *Text
der Bb. Sam.*, p. 18, Rem.

[2] Jerome (cf. Siegfried, *ZAW.* 1884, p. 77) in these cases often gives *ă* for *ĭ*.

[3] Cf. the remarks of I. Guidi, ' La pronuncia del ṣērē,' in the *Verhandl. des
Hamburger Orient.-Kongr.* of 1902, Leiden, 1904, p. 208 ff., on Italian *e* for
Latin *i*, as in *fede = fidem*, *pece = pĭcem*.

תֵּן from תֵּת (*give*), יֹצְרֶךָ (*thy creator*) from יָצַר, or in the case discussed in § 93 *o*, עֶזְרִי, חֶלְקִי from the ground-forms *ḥilq*, '*izr* ; cf. also § 64 *f*. *Seġôl* appears as a simple helping-vowel in cases such as סֵפֶר for *siphr*, יָגֶל for *yigl* (§ 28 *e*).

III.   Third Class.   U- and O-sounds.

n   **9.** For the U-sound there is—

(1) the *long û*, either (*a*) written fully, וּ *Šureq*, e.g. גְּבוּל (*boundary*), or (*b*) defectively written —ֻ *Qibbûṣ* גְּבֻלוֹ, יְמֻתוּן ;

(2) the short *ŭ*, mostly represented by *Qibbûṣ*, in a toneless closed syllable and especially common in a sharpened syllable, in e.g. שֻׁלְחָן (*table*), סֻכָּה (*booth*).

O   Sometimes also *ŭ* in a sharpened syllable is written וּ, e.g. הֻפְּכָה ψ 102⁵, יֻלַּד Jb 5⁷, כֻּלָּם Jer. 31³⁴, מָשׁוּבָתוֹ Is 5⁵, עֲרוּמִּים Gn 2²⁵ for הֻכָּה, &c.

For this *u* the LXX write *o*, e.g. עֲרֻלָּם 'Οδολλάμ, from which, however, it only follows, that this *ŭ* was pronounced somewhat indistinctly. The LXX also express the sharp *Ḥireq* by ε, e.g. אָמֵר ='Εμμήρ. The pronunciation of the *Qibbûṣ* like the German *ü*, which was formerly common, is incorrect, although the occasional pronunciation of the U-sounds as *ü* in the time of the punctators is attested, at least as regards Palestine[1] ; cf. the Turkish *bülbül* for the Persian *bulbul*, and the pronunciation of the Arabic *dunyā* in Syria as *dünyā*.

p   **10.** The O-sound bears the same relation to U as the E does to I in the second class. It has four varieties :—

(1) The *ô* which is contracted from *aw* (=*au*), § 7 *a*, and accordingly is mostly written fully ; וֹ (*Ḥolem plenum*), e.g. שׁוֹט (*a whip*), Arab. *saut̤*, עַוְלָה (*iniquity*) from עַוְלָה. More rarely *defectively*, as שֹׁרְךָ (*thine ox*) from שׁוֹר Arab. *t̤aur*.

q   (2) The long *ô* which arose in Hebrew at an early period, by a general process of obscuring, out of an original *â*,[2] while the latter has been retained in Arabic and Aramaic. It is usually written *fully* in the tone-syllable, *defectively* in the toneless, e.g. קֹטֵל Arab. *qâtil*. Aram. *qâṭēl*, אֱלוֹהַּ Arab. '*ilâh*, Aram. '*elâh*, plur. אֱלֹהִים; שׁוֹק (*leg*), Arab. *sâq* ; גִּבּוֹר (*hero*), Arab. *gâbbâr* ; חוֹתָם (*seal*), Arab. *ḥâtäm* ; רִמּוֹן (*pomegranate*), Arab. *rŭmmân* ; שִׁלְטוֹן (*dominion*), Aram. שָׁלְטָן and שָׁלְטָן Arab. *sŭltân* ; שָׁלוֹם (*peace*), Aram. שְׁלָם, Arab. *sălâm*. Sometimes the form in *â* also occurs side by side with that in *ô* as שִׁרְיָן and שִׁרְיוֹן (*coat of mail* ; see however § 29 *u*). Cf. also § 68 *b*.

r   (3) The tone-long *ō* which is lengthened from an original *ŭ*, or from an *ŏ* arising from *ŭ*, by the tone, or in general according to the

---

[1] Cf. Delitzsch, *Physiologie u. Musik*, Lpz. 1868, p. 15 f.
[2] Cf. above, *b*, end. On Jerome's transliteration of *o* for *â*, see *ZAW*. 1884, p. 75.

laws for the formation of syllables. It occurs not only in the tone-
syllable, but also in an open syllable before the tone, e. g. קֹ֫דֶשׁ (ground-
form *qŭdš*) *sanctuary*; בָּרֵ֑ךְ for *burrakh*, יִלְקְטוּן ψ 104²⁸, as well as
(with *Metheg*) in the secondary tone-syllable ; אָהֳלִים, בְּעֶלוֹ. But the
original ŏ (ŭ) is retained in a toneless closed syllable, whereas in
a toneless open syllable it is weakened to *Šᵉwâ*. Cf. כֹּל *all*, but
כָּל־ (*kŏl*), כֻּלָּם (*kŭllām*); יִקְטֹל, יְקַטְּלָה and יִקְטְלוּ, where original ŭ is
weakened to *Šᵉwâ*: *yiqᵉtᵉlû*, Arab. *yaqtŭlû*. This tone-long ō is only
as an exception written fully.

(4) ◌ָ *Qameṣ-ḥaṭuph* represents ŏ (properly ă, cf. § 8 a, note 2) modified *s*
from ŭ and is therefore classed here. It stands in the same relation to
Ḥolem as the *Sᵉgôl* of the second class to *Sere*, כָּל־ *kŏl*, וַיָּ֫קָם *wayyāqŏm*.
On the distinction between this and *Qameṣ*, see below, *u*.

11. The following table gives a summary of the gradation of the *t*
three vowel-classes according to the quantity of the vowels :—

First Class : A.	*Second Class* : I and E.	*Third Class* : U and O.
◌ָ original *á* (Arabic אָ).	◌ֵי *ê*, from original *ay* (*ai*). ◌ִי or ◌ִ long *i*.	וֹ *ô*, from original *aw* (*au*). וֹ or ◌ֹ *ô* obscured from *â*. וּ or ◌ֻ *û*.
◌ָ tone-long *ā* (from original ă) chiefly in the tone-syllable but also just before it.	◌ֵ tone-long *ē* (from *i*) generally in the tone-syllable but also just before it.	◌ֹ tone-long *ō* (from original ŭ) in the tone-syllable, otherwise in an open syllable.
◌ֶ (as a modification of ă) sometimes a tone-long *è*, sometimes *ĕ*. ◌ַ short *ă*. [◌ִ *i* attenuated from ă ; see *h*.] Utmost weakening to ◌ֲ *a*, ◌ֱ *ĕ*, ◌ְ *e*.	◌ֶ *ĕ*. ◌ִ short *i*. Utmost weakening to ◌ֲ *a*, ◌ֱ *ĕ*, or ◌ְ *e*.	◌ָ *ŏ*, modified from ŭ. ◌ֻ short *ŭ*, especially in a sharpened syllable. Utmost weakening to ◌ֲ *a*, ◌ֱ *ĕ*, ◌ֳ *o*, or ◌ְ *e*.

Rem. *On the distinction between Qameṣ and Qameṣ-ḥaṭuph.*[1]   *u*
According to § 8 a, long *ā* or *ā̊* (*Qameṣ*) and short ŏ or ă̊ (*Qameṣ-ḥaṭuph*) are in
manuscripts and printed texts generally expressed by the same sign (◌ָ), e. g.
קָם *qām*, כָּל־ *kŏl*. The beginner who does not yet know the grammatical

---

[1] These statements, in order to be fully understood, must be studied in
connexion with the theory of syllables (§ 26) and *Metheg* (§ 16 c–i).

origin of the words in question (which is of course the surest guide), may depend meanwhile on the following principal rules : —

1. *The sign* —ָ [1] *is* ŏ *in a toneless closed syllable*, since such a syllable can have only a short vowel (§ 26 *o*). The above case occurs—

(*a*) When *S̆ewâ* follows as a syllable-divider, as in חָכְמָה *ḥŏkh-má* (wisdom), אָכְלָה *'ŏkh-lá* (food). With *Metheg* —ָ is *ā* (*ā̆*) and according to the usual view stands in an open. syllable with a following *S̆ewâ mobile*, e.g. אָכְלָה *'ā-kh^elá* (she ate) ; but cf. § 16 *i*.

(*b*) When a closed syllable is formed by *Dageš forte*, e. g. חָנֵּנִי *ḥŏnnēnî* (have mercy upon me); but בָּתִּים (with *Metheg*, § 16 *f* ζ) *bâttîm*.

(*c*) When the syllable in question loses the tone on account of a following *Maqqēph* (§ 16 *a*), e. g. כָּל־הָאָדָם *kŏl-hā-'ādám* (all men).

In ψ 35¹⁰ and Pr 19⁷ *Maqqēph* with כָּל is replaced by a conjunctive accent (*Mer^ekha*) ; so by *Darga*, Ju 19⁵ with סָעַד, and Ez 37⁸ with וַיִּקְרַם (so Baer after Qimḥi ; ed. Mant., Ginsburg, Kittel וַיְקְרַם).

(*d*) In a closed final syllable without the tone, e.g. וַיָּקָם *wayyắqŏm* (and he stood up).—In the cases where *ắ* or *ā̆* in the final syllable has become toneless through *Maqqēph* (§ 16 *a*) and yet remains, e.g. כְּדָּת־הַדָּת Est 4⁸, שְׁתִי־לִי Gn 4²⁵, it has a *Metheg* in correct manuscripts and printed texts.

In cases like הֲלָאָה, לָמָּה *lámmā*, the tone shows that —ָ is to be read as *ā*.

v 2. The cases in which —ָ appears to stand in an open syllable and yet is to be read as ŏ require special consideration. This is the case, (*a*) when *Ḥaṭeph-Qameṣ* follows, e. g. פָּעֳלוֹ *his work*, or simple vocal *S̆ewâ*, e.g. דָּרְבָן *ox goad* ; בְּעָבְרוֹ Jo 4⁷ ; שָׁמְרָה (so ed. Mant., Ginsb.) *preserve* ψ 86², cf. 16¹ and the cases mentioned in § 48 *i*, n., and § 61 *f*, n. ; other examples are Ob 11, Ju 14¹⁸); *Ḥaṭeph-Pathaḥ* follows in לְמִשְׁחָה (so Ginsburg ; Baer לְמָשְׁחֳךָ) 1 S 15¹, לַהֲרָגְךָ 24¹¹, and יִפְנָשֶׁךָ (so Baer, Gn 32¹⁸, others יִפְגָּשֶׁךָ) ; (*b*) before another *Qameṣ-ḥaṭuph*, e. g. פָּעָלְךָ *thy work* ; on אָרְחֶ־לִי and קָבֳהֶ־לִי Nu 23⁷, see § 67 *o* ; (*c*) in the two plural forms קָדָשִׁים *sanctuaries* and שָׁרָשִׁים *roots* (also written קָדֳ and שָׁרֳ). In all these cases the Jewish grammarians regard the *Metheg* accompanying the —ָ as indicating a Qāmeṣ raḥabh (broad Qāmeṣ) and therefore read the —ָ as *ā* ; thus *pā-ʾlŏ, dā-r^ebān, pā-ŏl^ekhā, qā-dāšim*. But neither the origin of these forms, nor the analogous formations in Hebrew and in the cognate languages, nor the transcription of proper names in the

---

[1] In the Babylonian punctuation (§ 8 *g*, note) *ā* and ŏ are carefully distinguished. So also in many MSS. with the ordinary punctuation and in Baer's editions of the text since 1880, in which —ֳ is used for ŏ as well as for ŏ. Cf. Baer-Delitzsch, *Liber Jobi*, p. 43. But the identity of the two signs is certainly original, and the use of —ֳ for ŏ is misleading.

LXX, allows us to regard this view as correct. It is just possible that Qameṣ
is here used loosely for *ā̆*, as the equivalent of *ō̆*, on the analogy of בָּעֳלוֹ &c.,
§ 93 *q*. As a matter of fact, however, we ought no doubt to divide and read
pŏ̆'ŏ-lô (for *pŏ̆'-lô*), *pŏ̆'ŏ-lᵉkhā*, *qŏdā-šîm*.—Quite as inconceivable is it for *Metheg* to
be a sign of the lengthening into *ā* in בְּחָרִי־אָף (Ex 11⁸), although it is so in בָּאֳנִי
bā-'ŏnî (in the navy), since here the *ā* of the article appears under the ב.

§ 10. *The Half Vowels and the Syllable Divider* (Šᵉwâ).

1. Besides the full vowels, Hebrew has also a series of vowel *a*
sounds which may be called *half vowels* (Sievers, *Murmelvokale*).
The punctuation makes use of these to represent extremely slight
sounds which are to be regarded as remains of fuller and more distinct
vowels from an earlier period of the language. They generally take
the place of vowels *originally short* standing in *open syllables*. Such
short vowels, though preserved in the kindred languages, are not
tolerated by the present system of pointing in Hebrew, but either
undergo a lengthening or are weakened to Šᵉwâ. Under some
circumstances, however, the original short vowel may reappear.

To these belongs first of all the sign ָ, which indicates an ex- *b*
tremely short, slight, and (as regards pronunciation) indeterminate
vowel sound, something like an obscure half *ĕ* (ְ). It is called *Šᵉwâ*,[1]
which may be either *simple Šᵉwâ* (*Šᵉwâ simplex*) as distinguished
from the compound (see *f*), or *vocal Šᵉwâ* (*Šᵉwâ mobile*) as distinguished from *Šᵉwâ quiescens*, which is silent and stands as a mere
syllable divider (see *i*) under the consonant which closes the syllable.

The vocal *Šᵉwâ* stands under a consonant which is closely united, as *c*
a kind of grace-note, with the following syllable, either (*a*) at the
beginning of the word, as קְטֹל *qᵉtōl* (to kill), מְמַלֵּא *mᵉmallē* (filling),
or (*b*) in the middle of the word, as קוֹטְלָה *qô-tᵉlā*, יִקְטְלוּ *yiq-tᵉlû*.

In former editions of this Grammar *Šᵉwâ* was distinguished as *medium* *d*
when it followed a short vowel and therefore stood in a supposed 'loosely
closed' or 'wavering' syllable, as in בְּנָפֵּל, מַלְכֵי. According to Sievers,
Metrische Studien, i. 22, this distinction must now be abandoned. These
syllables are really closed, and the original vowel is not merely shortened,
but entirely elided. The fact that a following Bᵉgadkᵉphath letter (§ 6 *n*)
remains spirant instead of taking *Dageš lene*, is explained by Sievers on the
'supposition that the change from hard to spirant is older than the elision

---

[1] On שְׁוָא, the older and certainly the only correct form (as in Ben Asher),
see Bacher, *ZDMG*. 1895, p. 18, note 3, who compares Šewayya, the name of
the Syriac accentual sign of similar form ֗ (= Hebr. Zaqeph). The form
שְׁבָא, customary in Spain since the time of Menaḥem b. Sarûq, is due
to a supposed connexion with Aram. שְׁבָת *rest*, and hence would originally
have denoted only *Šᵉwâ quiescens*, like the Arabic *sukûn* (rest). The derivation
from שֵׁבָה, שִׁיבָה (stem יָשַׁב, Levias, *American Journ. of Philol.*, xvi. 28 ff.) seems
impossible.

of the vowel, and that the prehistoric *malakai* became *malakhai* before being shortened to *malkhē'*.   In cases like בְּמָאוֹ (from בְּמָא), יִקְחוּ (from יִקַּח) the dropping of the *Dageš forte* shows that the original vowel is completely lost.

e   The sound *ĕ* has been adopted as the normal transcription of simple *Šᵉwâ mobile*, although it is certain that it often became assimilated in sound to other vowels. The LXX express it by *ε*, or even by *η*, כְּרוּבִים Χερουβίμ, הַלְלוּיָהּ ἀλληλούια, more frequently by *a*, שְׁמוּאֵל Σαμουήλ, but very frequently by assimilating its indeterminate sound to the following principal vowel, e.g. סְדֹם Σόδομα, שְׁלֹמֹה Σολομών (as well as Σαλωμών), צְבָאוֹת Σαβαώθ, נְתַנְאֵל Ναθαναήλ.[1] A similar account of the pronunciation of *Šᵉwâ* is given by Jewish grammarians of the middle ages.[2]

How the *Šᵉwâ* sound has arisen through the vanishing of a full vowel is seen, e.g. in בְּרָכָה from *bărăkă*, as the word is still pronounced in Arabic. In that language the full short vowel regularly corresponds to the Hebrew *Šᵉwâ mobile*.

f   **2.** Connected with the *simple Šᵉwâ mobile* is the compound *Šᵉwâ* or *Ḥâṭēph (correptum)*, i.e. a *Šᵉwâ* the pronunciation of which is more accurately fixed by the addition of a short vowel. There are three *Šᵉwâ*-sounds determined in this way, corresponding to the three vowel classes (§ 7 a):—

(⸗) *Ḥâṭēph-Pắthăḥ*, e.g. חֲמוֹר *ḥᵃmôr*, ass.

(⸗) *Ḥâṭēph-Sᵉgôl*, e.g. אֱמֹר *'ᵉmōr*, to say.

(⸗) *Ḥâṭēph-Qāmĕṣ*, e.g. חֳלִי *ḥᵒlî*, sickness.

These *Ḥâṭēphs*, or at least the first two, stand especially under the four guttural letters (§ 22 l), instead of a *simple Šᵉwâ mobile*, since these letters by their nature require a more definite vowel than the indeterminate *simple Šᵉwâ mobile*. Accordingly a guttural at the beginning of a syllable, where the *Šᵉwâ* is necessarily vocal, can never have a mere *Šᵉwâ simplex*.

On ⸗ the shorter Ḥatef as compared with ⸗ cf. § 27 v.

g   **Rem. A.** Only ⸗ and ⸗ occur under letters which are not gutturals. *Ḥaṭeph-Pathaḥ* is found instead of *simple Šᵉwâ* (especially *Šᵉwâ mobile*), chiefly (a) under strengthened consonants, since this strengthening (commonly called doubling) causes a more distinct pronunciation of the *Šᵉwâ mobile*, שַׁבְּלֵי *branches*, Zc 4¹². According to the rule given by Ben-Asher (which, however, appears to be unknown to good early MSS. and is therefore rejected by Ginsburg, *Introd.*, p. 466; cf. Foote, *Johns Hopkins Univ. Circulars*, June 1903,

---

[1] The same occurs frequently also in the Greek and Latin transcriptions of Phoenician words, e.g. מַלְכָא Malaga, גֻּבֻלִים gubulim (Schröder, *Die phöniz. Spr.*, p. 139 ff.). Cf. the Latin augment in *momordi, pupugi*, with the Greek in τέτυφα, τετυμμένος, and the old form *memordi*.

[2] See especially *Yehuda Ḥayyûǵ*, pp. 4 f. and 130 f. in Nutt's edition (Lond. 1870), corresponding to p. 200 of the edition by Dukes (Stuttg. 1844); Ibn Ezra's *Ṣaḥoth*, p. 3; Gesenius, *Lehrgebäude der hebr. Sprache*, p. 68. The *Manuel du lecteur*, mentioned above, § 6 b, also contains express rules for the various ways of pronouncing *Šᵉwâ mobile*: so too in the *Dikduke ha-ṭᵉamim*, ed. by Baer and Strack, Lpz. 1879, p. 12 ff. Cf. also Schreiner, *ZAW.* vi. 236 ff.

p. 71 f.), the *Ḥaṭeph* is necessary[1] when, in a strengthened *medial* consonant with Š^ewâ (consequently not in cases like וַיְהִי, &c.), preceded by a Pathaḥ, the sign of the strengthening (*Dageš forte*) has fallen away, e. g. הַלְלוּ (but ed. Mant. and Ginsb.) הַלְלוּ) *praise ye!* וַתְּאָלְצֵהוּ Ju 16¹⁶; no less universally, where after a consonant with Š^ewâ the same consonant follows (to separate them more sharply, and hence with a *Metheg* always preceding), e. g. סוֹרְרִים ψ 68⁷; קִלְלָתְךָ (ed. Mant. and Ginsb. קִלְלְ) Gn 27¹³ (but not without exceptions, e. g. חָקְקִי Ju 5¹⁵, Is 10¹; צָלְלִי Jer 6⁴, and so always הִנְנִי *behold me*, הִנְנוּ *behold us*; on כְ before the suffix ךָ, see § 20 *b*); also in certain forms under Kaph and Reš after a long vowel and before the tone, e. g. תֹּאכַלְנֶּה Gn 3¹⁷; בָּרֲכִי ψ 103¹; וַתִּשְׁרָתֵהוּ 1 K 1⁴ (but וְיִתְבָּרְכוּ ψ 72¹⁷, cf. Jer 4², 1 Ch 29²⁰, because the tone is thrown back on to the *ā*. After *ē* Š^ewâ remains even before the tone, as בָּרְכוּ, &c.; but before Maqqef אֶלְכָה־נָּא Baer Ex 4¹⁸, 2 S 15⁷, Jer 40¹⁵, but ed. Mant., Jabl., Ginsb. 'אֶל)² ; (*b*) under initial sibilants after ו copulative, e. g. וְזָהָב Gn 2¹²; cf. Jer 48²⁰; וּסְחַר Is 45¹⁴; וּשְׂדֵה Lv 25³⁴; Gn 27²⁶; וּשְׁמַע Nu 23¹⁸, Is 37¹⁷, Dn 9¹⁸, cf. Ju 5¹², 1 K 14²¹, 2 K 9¹⁷, Jb 14¹, Ec 9⁷—to emphasize the vocal character of the Š^ewâ. For the same reason under the emphatic ט in הֻטְּלוּ Jer 22²⁸; cf. Jb 33²⁵; after *Qôph* in וְקִדַּרְתִּי (so Baer, but ed. Mant., Jabl., Ginsb. 'וְק) Ez 23⁴¹; וְקָרַב־ ψ 55²²; cf. Jer. 32⁹; under Reš in אֶרְדָה (ed. Mant. 'אֶר) Gn 18²¹; וְגָרַע ψ 28⁹; even under ח Ezr 26¹; under ב Est 2⁸; וּבֵרַכְךָ so Jabl., Ginsb., but ed. Mant. (וּבֵר') Dt 24¹³; (*c*) under sonants, sibilants or *Qôph* after *i*, e. g. יִצְחָק Gn 21⁶, cf. 30³⁸ and Ez 21²⁸ (under ק); אִמְּרוּת ψ 12⁷; הִתְמַלֵּךְ Jer 22¹⁵; בְּנֵרוֹת Jos 11²; בְּכֶסֶף־ ψ 74⁶,—for the same reason as the cases under *b*³; according to Baer also in שְׁמַוֹת 1 S 30²⁸; יִפְנֶךָ Gn 32¹⁸ after *ŏ* (cf. § 9 *v*), as well as after *a* in הַקְּשִׁיבָה Dn 9¹⁹; הַבְרָכָה Gn 27³⁸; הַמְצֹרָעִים 2 K 7⁸.

B. The *Ḥaṭeph-Qameṣ* is less restricted to the gutturals than the first two, *h* and stands more frequently for a simple Š^ewâ *mobile* when an original O-sound requires to be partly preserved, e. g. at the beginning, in רְאִי (ground-form *rŏ'y*) *vision* (cf. § 93 *z*); בְּנָיְהוּ 2 Ch 31¹², &c., *Q^erê* (*K^eth.* כון'); עֳמָנִיּוֹת *Ammonitish women*, 1 K 11¹ (sing. עֲמוֹנִית); יִרְדְּפֶךָ for the usual יִרְדְּפֶךָ Ez 35⁶, from יִרְדֹּף; תִּקְבְּנוּ Nu 23²⁵, Jer 31³³, and elsewhere before suffixes, cf. § 60 *a*; קָדְקֳדוֹ *his pate* (from קָדְקֹד) ψ 7¹⁷, &c.; אֶשְׁקֳטָה Is 18⁴ *Q^erê*. Further, like ◌ָ, it stands under consonants, which ought to have *Dageš forte*, as in לְקָחָה (for לְקָּחָה) Gn 2²³. In this example, as in וְסָעֳדָה 1 K 13⁷; וּסְאָה 2 K 7¹⁸; and וְצָעֳקִי Jer 22²⁰, the *Ḥaṭeph-Qameṣ* is no doubt due to the influence of the

---

[1] See Delitzsch, 'Bemerkungen über masoretisch treue Darstellung des alttestam. Textes,' in the *Ztschr. f. luth. Theol. u. Kirche*, vol. xxiv. 1863, p. 409 ff.

[2] On the uncertainty of the MSS. in some cases which come under *a*, see *Minḥat shay* (the Masoretic comm. in ed. Mant.) on Gn 12³ and Ju 7⁶.

[3] Ben-Asher requires ◌ָ for ◌ֳ (even for Š^ewâ *quiescens*) generally before a guttural or ר; hence Baer reads in 2 S 15⁵ בְּקָרֳב־, ψ 18⁷ אֶקְרָא; 49¹⁵ לִשְׁאוֹל; 65⁵ תְּבָחַר; 68²⁴ תִּמְחַץ; Pr 30¹⁷ תִּלְעַג; Jb 29²⁵ אֶבְחַר; cf. Delitzsch, *Psalms*, 12⁷, note.

following guttural as well as of the preceding U-sound. (Elsewhere indeed after וּ in similar cases *Ḥaṭeph-Pathaḥ* is preferred, see above, *b*; but with לְקָחָה cf. also סַבְלוֹ Is 9³, 10²⁷, 14²⁵, where the U-sound must necessarily be admitted to have an influence on the *Šᵉwâ* immediately following.) In וּטְהָר־ (*û-ṭᵉhŏr*) Jb 17⁹ it is also influenced by the following O-sound. In קָסְמִי 1 S 28⁸ *Qᵉrê*, the original form is קְסָם, where again the *ŏ* represents an *ŏ*. It is only through the influence of a following guttural that we can explain the forms נִקְרָאָה Est 2¹⁴; נִבְהַל Pr 28²²; נִסְרְחָה Jer 49⁷; אֶפְשְׁעָה Is 27⁴; וָאֶשְׁמְעָה Dn 8¹³; שְׁמְעָה ψ 39¹³; בְּסָעְרָה 2 K 2¹ (Baer's ed. also in ver. 11); הַקְהָתִים 2 Ch 34¹² (ed. Mant., Opitius, &c. 'הַקְ). Finally in most of the examples which have been adduced, the influence of an emphatic sound (ק, ט, cf. also אֶלְקֻטָה Ru 2²·⁷), or of a sibilant is also to be taken into account.

i   3. The sign of the *simple Šᵉwâ* — serves also as a mere syllable divider. In this case it is disregarded in pronunciation and is called *Šᵉwâ quiescens*. In the middle of a word it stands under every consonant which closes a syllable; at the end of words on the other hand it is omitted except in *final* ך (to distinguish it better from final ן), e.g. מֶלֶךְ *king*, and in the less frequent case, where a word ends with a mute after another vowelless consonant as in נֵרְדְּ *nard*, אַתְּ *thou* fem. (for *'ant*), קָטַלְתְּ *thou* fem. *hast killed*, וַיַּשְׁקְ *and he watered*, וַיִּשְׁבְּ *and he took captive*, אַל־תֵּשְׁתְּ *drink thou not*; but וַיֵּרְא, חֵטְא.¹

k   However, in the examples where a mute closes the syllable, the final *Šᵉwâ* comes somewhat nearer to a vocal *Šᵉwâ*, especially as in almost all the cases a weakening of a final vowel has taken place, viz. אַתְּ *'attᵉ* from אַתִּי *'atti* (*'anti*), קָטַלְתְּ from קָטַלְתִּי (cf. in this form, the 2nd sing. fem. perf. Qal, even בָּאת, after a vowel, Gn 16⁸, Mi 4¹⁰, &c., according to the readings of Baer), יֵשְׁבְּ *yišᵉ* from יֵשְׁבָה, &c. The Arabic actually has a short vowel in analogous forms. In נֵרְדְּ borrowed from the Indian, as also in קֹשְׁטְ (*qŏšṭ*) Pr 22²¹; and in אַל־תּוֹסְףְ *ne addas* (for which we should expect תּוֹסֵף) Pr 30⁶ the final mute of itself attracts a slight vowel sound.

l   Rem. The proper distinction between *simple Šᵉwâ mobile* and *quiescens* depends on a correct understanding of the formation of syllables (§ 26). The beginner may observe for the present, that (1) *Šᵉwâ* is always *mobile* (*a*) at the beginning of a word (except in שְׁתֵּי, שְׁתַּיִם § 97 *b*, note); (*b*) under a consonant with *Dageš forte*, e.g. גִּדְּפוּ *gid-dᵉphû*; (*c*) after another *Šᵉwâ*, e.g. יִקְטְלוּ *yiqtᵉlû* (except at the end of the word, see above, *i*). (2) *Šᵉwâ* is *quiescens* (*a*) at the end of a word, also in the ך; (*b*) before another *Šᵉwâ*.

§ 11. *Other Signs which affect the Reading.*

Very closely connected with the vowel points are the *reading-signs*, which were probably introduced at the same time. Besides the diacritical point over שׁ and שׂ, a point is placed *within* a consonant

---

¹ On יתְ— as an ending of the 2nd sing. fem. perf. Qal of verbs ל″ה, see § 75 *m*.

to show that it has a stronger sound. On the other hand a horizontal stroke (*Rāphè*) *over* a consonant is a sign that it has *not* the stronger sound. According to the different purposes for which it is used the point is either (1) *Dageš forte*, a sign of strengthening (§ 12); or (2) *Dageš lene*, a sign of the harder pronunciation of certain consonants (§ 13); or (3) *Mappîq*, a sign to bring out the full consonantal value of letters which otherwise serve as vowel letters (§ 7 *b*), especially in the case of ה at the end of the word (§ 14 *a*). The *Rāphè*, which excludes the insertion of any of these points, has almost entirely gone out of use in our printed texts (§ 14 *e*).

§ 12. *Dageš in general,[1] and Dageš forte in particular.*

Cf. Graetz, 'Die mannigfache Anwendung u. Bedeut. des Dagesch,' in *Monatsschr. für Gesch. u. Wiss. d. Judent.*, 1887, pp. 425 ff. and 473 ff.

1. *Dageš*, a point standing in the middle of a consonant,[2] denotes, *a* according to § 11, (*a*) the *strengthening*[3] of a consonant (*Dageš forte*), e. g. קִטֵּל *qiṭṭēl* (§ 20); or (*b*) the *harder* pronunciation of the letters בְּגַדְכְּפַת (*Dageš lene*). For a variety of the latter, now rarely used in our printed texts, see § 13 *c*.

The root דגשׁ in Syriac means *to pierce through, to bore through* (with sharp *b* iron); hence the name *Dageš* is commonly explained, solely with reference to its form, by *puncture, point.* But the names of all similar signs are derived rather from their grammatical significance. Accordingly דגשׁ may in the Masora have the sense : *acuere (literam)*, i. e. to *sharpen* a letter, as well as to *harden* it, i. e. to pronounce it as hard and without aspiration. דָּגֵשׁ *acuens (literam)* would then be a sign of sharpening and hardening (like *Mappîq* מַפִּיק *proferens*, as *signum prolationis*), for which purposes a *prick* of the pen, or *puncture*, was selected. The opposite of *Dageš* is רָפֶה *soft*, § 14 *e*, and § 22 *n*.

2. In grammar *Dageš forte*, the *sign of strengthening*, is the more *c* important. It may be compared to the *sicilicus* of the Latins (*Luculus* for *Lucullus*) or to the stroke over *m̄* and *n̄*. In the unpointed text it is omitted, like the vowels and other reading signs.

For the different kinds of *Dageš forte*, see § 20.

---

[1] Oort, *Theol. Tijdschr.* 1902, p. 376, maintains that 'the Masoretes recognized no distinction between *Dageš lene* and *forte*. They used a *Dageš* where they considered that a letter had the sharp, not the soft or aspirated sound.' This may be true; but the old-established distinction between the two kinds of *Dageš* is essential for the right understanding of the grammatical forms.

[2] *Wāw* with *Dageš* (וּ) cannot in our printed texts be distinguished from a *wāw* pointed as *Šûrĕq* (וּ); in the latter case the point should stand higher up. The ו *û* is, however, easily to be recognized since it cannot take a vowel before or under it.

[3] Stade, *Lehrb. der hebr. Gr.*, Lpz. 1879, pp. 44, 103, rightly insists on the expression *strengthened pronunciation* instead of the older term *doubling*, since the consonant in question is only written once. The common expression arises from the fact that in transcription a *strengthened* consonant can only be indicated by writing it as double.

§ 13. *Dageš lene.*

Ginsburg, *Introd.*, p. 114 ff. : Dagesh and Raphe.

a 1. *Dageš lene*, the sign of *hardening*, is in ordinary printed texts placed only within the בְּגַדְכְּפַת letters (§ 6 *n*) as a sign that they should be pronounced with their original hard sound (without aspiration), e.g. מֶלֶךְ *mĕlĕkh*, but מַלְכּוֹ *ma'-kô*; תָּפַר *tāphár*, but יִתְפֹּר *yith-pōr*; שָׁתָה *šāthā*, but יִשְׁתֶּה *yiš-tè*.

b 2. The cases in which a *Dageš lene* is to be inserted are stated in § 21. It occurs almost exclusively at the beginning of words and syllables. In the middle of the word it can easily be distinguished from *Dageš forte*, since the latter always has a vowel before it, whereas *Dageš lene* never has; accordingly the *Dageš* in אַפִּי *'appî*, רַבִּים *rabbîm* must be *forte*, but in יִגְדַּל *yigdal* it is *lene*.

c A variety of the *Dageš lene* is used in many manuscripts, as well as in Baer's editions, though others (including Ginsburg in the first two cases, *Introd.*, pp. 121, 130, 603, 662) reject it together with the Ḥaṭefs discussed in § 10 *g*. It is inserted in consonants other than the *Begadkephath* to call attention expressly to the beginning of a new syllable : (*a*) when the same consonant precedes in close connexion, e. g. בְּכָל־לִבִּי *ψ* 9², where, owing to the *Dageš*, the coalescing of the two *Lameds* is avoided ; (*b*) in cases like מַחְסִי *ψ* 62⁸ = *maḥ-si* (not *mäḥᵃ-si*) ; (*c*) according to some (including Baer ; not in ed. Mant.) in לֹא in the combination לֹא לוֹ Dt 32⁵, or לוֹ לֹא Hb 1⁶, 2⁶ &c. (so always also in Ginsburg's text, except in Gn 38⁹) ; see also § 20 *e* and *g*.—Delitzsch appropriately gives the name of *Dageš orthophonicum* to this variety of *Dageš* (*Bibl. Kommentar*, 1874, on *ψ* 94¹²) ; cf. moreover Delitzsch, *Luth. Ztschr.*, 1863, p. 413 ; also his *Complutensische Varianten zu dem Alttest. Texte*, Lpz. 1878, p. 12.

d 3. When *Dageš forte* is placed in a *Begadkephath*, the strengthening necessarily excludes its aspiration, e. g. אַפִּי, from אַנְפִּי.

§ 14. *Mappîq and Rāphè.*

a 1. *Mappîq*, like *Dageš*, also a point *within* the consonant, serves in the letters א ה ו י as a sign that they are to be regarded as full consonants and not as vowel letters. In most editions of the text it is only used in the consonantal ה at the end of words (since ה can never be a vowel letter in the middle of a word), e.g. גָּבַהּ *gābháh* (to be high), אַרְצָהּ *'arṣāh* (her land) which has a consonantal ending (shortened from -*hā*), different from אַרְצָה *'árṣā* (to the earth) which has a vowel ending.

b Rem. 1. Without doubt such a *Hē* was distinctly aspirated like the Arabic *Hā* at the end of a syllable. There are, however, cases in which this ה has lost its consonantal character (the Mappîq of course disappearing too), so that it remains only as a vowel letter ; cf. § 91 *e* on the 3rd fem. sing.

c The name מַפִּיק means *proferens*, i. e. a sign which brings out the sound of the letter distinctly, as a consonant. The same sign was selected for this and for *Dageš*, since both are intended to indicate a hard, i. e. a strong, sound. Hence *Râphè* (see *e*) is the opposite of both.

2. In MSS. Mappîq is also found with א, ו, י, to mark them expressly as *d* consonants, e. g. גּוֹי (*gôy*), קָו (*qāw, qāu*), for which ו is also used, as עָשׂוּ, &c. For the various statements of the Masora (where these points are treated as *Dageš*), see Ginsburg, *The Massorah, letter* א, § 5 (also *Introd.*, pp. 557, 609, 637, 770), and ' The Dageshed Alephs in the Karlsruhe MS.' (where these points are extremely frequent), in the *Verhandlungen des Berliner Orientalisten-Kongresses*, Berlin, i. 1881, p. 136 ff. The great differences in the statements found in the Masora point to different schools, one of which appears to have intended that every audible א should be pointed. In the printed editions the point occurs only four times with א (אַ or אָ), Gn 43²⁶, Lv 23¹⁷, Ezr 8¹⁸ and Jb 33²¹ (רָאוּ; where the point can be taken only as an orthophonetic sign, not with König as *Dageš forte*). Cf. Delitzsch, *Hiob*, 2nd ed., p. 439 ff.

2. *Râphè* (רָפֶה i. e. weak, soft), a horizontal stroke over the letter, *e* is the opposite of both kinds of *Dageš* and *Mappîq*, but especially of *Dageš lene*. In exact manuscripts every בגדכפת letter has either *Dageš lene* or *Râphè*, e. g. מֶלֶךְ *mĕlĕkh*, תָּפַר, שָׁתָה. In modern editions (except Ginsburg's 1st ed.) *Râphè* is used only when the absence of a *Dageš* or *Mappîq* requires to be expressly pointed out.

§ 15. *The Accents.*

On the ordinary accents (see below, *e*), cf. W. Heidenheim, מִשְׁפְּטֵי הַטְּעָמִים *a* [*The Laws of the Accents*], Rödelheim, 1808 (a compilation from older Jewish writers on the accents, with a commentary); W. Wickes (see also below), טעמי כ״א ספרים [*The Accents of the Twenty-one Books*], Oxford, 1887, an exhaustive investigation in English ; J. M. Japhet, *Die Accente der hl. Schrift* (exclusive of the books אמ״ת), ed. by Heinemann, Frankf. a. M. 1896; Prätorius, *Die Herkunft der hebr. Accente*, Berlin, 1901, and (in answer to Gregory's criticism in the *TLZ*. 1901, no. 22) *Die Uebernahme der früh-mittelgriech. Neumen durch die Juden*, Berlin, 1902 ; P. Kahle, ' Zur Gesch. der hebr. Accente,' *ZDMG*. 55 (1901), 167 ff. (1, on the earliest Jewish lists of accents; 2, on the mutual relation of the various systems of accentuation ; on p. 179 ff. he deals with the accents of the 3rd system, see above, § 8 *g*, note) ; Margolis, art. ' Accents,' in the *Jewish Encycl.* i (1901), 149 ff. ; J. Adams, *Sermons in Accents*, London, 1906.—On the accents of the Books תא״ם (see below, *h*), S. Baer, תורת אמת [*Accentual Laws of the Books* אמ״ת], Rödelheim, 1852, and his appendix to Delitzsch's *Psalmencommentar*, vol. ii, Lpz. 1860, and in the 5th ed., 1894 (an epitome is given in Baer-Delitzsch's *Liber Psalmorum hebr.*, Lpz. 1861, 1874, 1880); cf. also Delitzsch's most instructive ' Accentuologischer Commentar' on Psalms 1–3, in his *Psalmencommentar* of 1874, as well as the numerous contributions to the accentual criticism of the text, &c., in the editions of Baer and Delitzsch, and in the commentaries of the latter ; W. Wickes, טעמי אמ״ת [*Accents of the Poet. Books*], Oxford, 1881 ; Mitchell, in the *Journal of Bibl. Lit.*, 1891, p. 144 ff. ; Baer and Strack, *Dikduke ha-ṭeamim*, p. 17 ff.

1. As Prätorius (see above) has convincingly shown, the majority of *b* the Hebrew accents, especially, according to Kahle (see above), the ' Conjunctivi', were adopted by the Jews from the neums and punctuation-marks found in Greek gospel-books, and, like these, their primary purpose was to regulate minutely the public reading of the sacred

text. The complete transformation and amplification of the system (in three different forms, see § 8 *g*, note), which soon caused the Jews to forget its real origin, is clearly connected with the gradual change from the speaking voice in public reading to chanting or singing. The accents then served as a kind of musical notes.[1] Their value as such has, however, with the exception of a few traces, become lost in transmission. On the other hand, according to their original design they have also a twofold use which is still of the greatest importance for grammar (and syntax), viz. their value (*a*) as *marking the tone*, (*b*) as *marks of punctuation* to indicate the logical (syntactical) relation of single words to their immediate surroundings, and thus to the whole sentence.[2]

c   2. As a mark of the tone the accent stands almost invariably (but see below, *e*) with the syllable which has the principal tone in the word. This is usually the ultima, less frequently the penultima. Amongst the Jewish grammarians a word which has the tone on the ultima is called *Milra'* (Aram. מִלְרַע i.e. accented below[3]), e.g. קָטַל *qāṭál*; a word which has the tone on the penultima is *Mil'êl* (Aram. מִלְעֵיל, accented above), e.g. מֶ֫לֶךְ *mèlĕkh*. Besides this, in many cases a *secondary tone* is indicated in the word by *Mèthĕg* (cf. § 16). Examples such as נֶעֶמְדָה יַ֫חַד Is 50[8] (cf. 40[18], Ex 15[8], Jb 12[15], La 2[16]) are regarded by the Jewish grammarians as even *proparoxytone*.[4]

d   3. As marks of interpunctuation the accents are subdivided into those which *separate* (*Distinctivi* or *Domini*) and those which *connect* (*Conjunctivi* or *Servi*). Further a twofold system of accentuation is to be noted : (*a*) the common system found in twenty-one of the Books (the כ״א i.e. twenty-one), and (*b*) that used in the first three Books of the *Hagiographa*, viz. Psalms, Proverbs, and Job, for which the *vox memor.* is אֱמֶת, from the initial consonants of the names, תְּהִלִּים Psalms, מִשְׁלֵי Proverbs, אִיּוֹב Job, or more correctly, according to their original sequence, תְּאָם (תְּאָם *twin*), so that טַעֲמֵי תא״ם means the accents (sing. טַעַם) of these three Books. The latter system is not only richer and more complicated in itself, but also musically more significant than the ordinary accentuation.

---

[1] On the attempts of Christian scholars of the sixteenth century to express the Hebrew accents by musical notes, cf. Ortenberg, *ZDMG.* 1889, p. 534.

[2] At the same time it must not be forgotten that the value of the accent as a mark of punctuation is always relative; thus, e. g. '*Athnâḥ* as regards the logical structure of the sentence may at one time indicate a very important break (as in Gn 1[4]); at another, one which is almost imperceptible (as in Gn 1[1]).

[3] 'Above' in this sense means what comes before, 'below' is what comes after; cf. Bacher, *ZAW.* 1907, p. 285 f.

[4] Cf. Delitzsch on Is 40[18].

I. *The Common Accents.*

Preliminary remark. The accents which are marked as *prepositive* stand to *e* the right over or under the initial consonant of the word ; those marked as *postpositive*, to the left over or under the last consonant. Consequently in both cases the tone-syllable must be ascertained independently of the accent (but cf. below, *l*).

A. DISJUNCTIVE ACCENTS (*Distinctivi* or *Domini*).[1]

1. (⊥) סִלּוּק Sillûq (*end*) always with the tone-syllable of the last word before Sôph pāsûq (:), the verse-divider, e.g. : הָאָֽרֶץ.

2. (⊥) אַתְנָח 'Athnâḥ or אַתְנַחְתָּא 'Athnaḥtā (*rest*), the principal divider within the verse.

3 *a.* (⸴) סְגוֹלְתָּא Segôltā, *postpositive*, marks the fourth or fifth sub-ordinate division, counting backwards from 'Athnâḥ (e.g. Gn 1[7.28]).

3 *b.* (| ⊥) שַׁלְשֶׁלֶת Šalšèleth (i.e. *chain*), as disjunctive, or Great Šalšèleth, distinguished by the following stroke[2] from the conjunctive in the poetic accentuation, is used for

---

[1] All the disjunctives occur in Is 39[2].—The earlier Jewish accentuologists already distinguish between מְלָכִים *Reges* and מְשָׁרְתִים *Servi*. The division of the disjunctive accents into Imperatores, Reges, Duces, Comites, which became common amongst Christian grammarians, originated in the *Scrutinium S. S. ex accentibus* of Sam. Bohlius, Rostock, 1636, and, as the source of manifold confusion, had better be given up. The order of the accents in respect to their disjunctive power is shown in general by the above classification, following Wickes. In respect to the height of tone (in chanting) 1, 2, 5, 4, 8, which were *low* and long sustained notes, are to be distinguished from the *high* notes (7, 3[a], 6, 13, 9), and the highest (3[b], 11, 12, 10); cf. Wickes, כ״א ט׳ p. 12 ff.—The name טְעָמִים (later = *accents* in general) was originally restricted to the disjunctives, see Kahle, l. c., p. 169.

[2] This stroke is commonly confused with *Paseq*, which has the same form. But Pàsēq (= *restraining, dividing*, also incorrectly called Pᵉsîq) is neither an independent accent, nor a constituent part of other accents, but is used as a mark for various purposes; see the Masoretic lists at the end of Baer's editions, and Wickes, *Accents of the Twenty-one Books*, p. 120 ff., where Pàsēq is divided into *distinctivum, emphaticum, homonymicum*, and *euphonicum*. The conjecture of Olshausen (*Lehrb.*, p. 86 f.), that Pàsēq served also to point out marginal glosses subsequently interpolated into the text, has been further developed by E. von Ortenberg, 'Die Bedeutung des Paseq für Quellenscheidung in den BB. d. A. T.,' in *Progr. des Domgymn. zu Verden*, 1887, and in the article, 'Paseq u. Legarmeh,' in *ZAW.* 1887, p. 301 ff. (but see Wickes, ibid. 1888, p. 149 ff.; also E. König, in the *Ztschr. f. kirchl. Wiss. u. kirchl. Leben*, 1889, parts 5 and 6; Maas, in *Hebraica*, v. 121 ff., viii. 89 ff.). Prätorius, *ZDMG.* 1899, p 683 ff., pointed out that *Paseq* (which is pre-masoretic and quite distinct from Lᵉ*garmēh*) besides being a divider (used especially for the sake of greater clearness) also served as a sign of abbreviation. For further treatment of *Paseq* see H. Grimme, 'Pasekstudien,' in the *Bibl. Ztschr.*, i. 337 ff., ii. 28 ff., and *Psalmenprobleme*, &c., Freiburg (Switzerland), 1902, p. 173, where it is argued that *Paseq* indicates variants in a difficult sentence ; J. Kennedy, *The Note-line in the Heb. Scriptures*, Edinb. 1903, with an index of all the occurrences of *Paseq*, p. 117 ff. According to Kennedy the 'note-line', of which he distinguishes sixteen different kinds, is intended to draw attention to some peculiarity in the text ; it existed long before the Masoretes, and was no longer understood by them. See, however, the reviews of E. König, *Theol.*

Segôltā (seven times altogether) when this would stand
at the head of the sentence ; cf. Gn 19¹⁶, &c.

4 *a.* (—ֺ) זָקֵף גָּדוֹל Zâqēph gādôl, and

4 *b.* (—ֺ) זָקֵף קָטוֹן Zâqēph qāṭôn. The names refer to their musical
character. As a disjunctive, Little Zâqēph is by nature
stronger than Great Zâqēph; but if they stand together,
the one which comes first is always the stronger.

5. (—֖) טִפְחָא Ṭiphhā or טַרְחָא Ṭarhā, a subordinate disjunctive
before Sillûq and 'Athnâḥ, but very often the principal
disjunctive of the whole verse instead of 'Athnâḥ ; always
so when the verse consists of only two or three words
(e. g. Is 2¹⁸), but also in longer verses (Gn 3²¹).

6. (—֗) רְבִיעַ Rᵉbhîaʻ.

7. (—֮) זַרְקָא Zarqā, *postpositive.*

8 *a.* (—֙) פַּשְׁטָא Paštā, *postpositive,*[1] and

8 *b.* (—֚) יְתִיב Yᵉthibh, *prepositive,* and thus different from Mᵉhuppākh. Yᵉthibh is used in place of Paštā when the latter
would stand on a monosyllable or on a foretoned word,
not preceded by a conjunctive accent.

9. (—֛) תְּבִיר Tᵉbhîr.

10 *a.* (—֜) גֶּרֶשׁ Gèreš or טֶרֶם Ṭères, and

10 *b.* (—֞) גֵּרְשַׁיִם Gᵉrāšáyim[2] or Double Gèreš, used for Gèreš, when
the tone rests on the ultima, and 'Azlā does not precede.

11 *a.* (—֡) פָּזֵר Pâzēr, and

11 *b.* (—֟) פָּזֵר גָּדוֹל Pâzēr gādôl (Great Pâzēr) or קַרְנֵי פָרָה Qarnê phārā
(*cow-horns*), only used 16 times, for special emphasis.

12. (—֠) תְּלִישָׁא גְדוֹלָה Tᵉlišā gᵉdôlā or Great Tᵉlišā, *prepositive.*

13. (|—֧) לְגַרְמֵהּ Lᵉgarmēh, i.e. Mûnaḥ (see below) with a following
stroke.

Stud. u. Krit., 1904, p. 448 ff., G. Beer, *TLZ.* 1905, no. 3, and esp. A. Klostermann, *Theol. Lit.-blatt,* 1904, no. 13, with whom Ginsburg agrees (*Verhandlungen des Hamb. Or.-kongresses von 1902,* Leiden, 1904, p. 210 ff.) in showing
that the tradition with regard to the 479 or 480 uses of *Paseq* is by no means
uniform. The purpose of *Paseq* is clearly recognizable in the five old rules :
as a divider between identical letters at the end and beginning of two words ;
between identical or very similar words ; between words which are absolutely
contradictory (as *God* and *evil-doer*) ; between words which are liable to be
wrongly connected ; and lastly, between heterogeneous terms, as ' Eleazar the
High Priest, and Joshua '. But the assumption of a far-reaching critical
importance in *Paseq* is at least doubtful.—Cf. also the important article by
H. Fuchs, ' Pesiq ein Glossenzeichen,' in the *Vierteljahrsschrift f. Bibelkunde,*
Aug. 1908, p. 1 ff. and p. 97 ff.

[1] If the word in question has the tone on the penultima, Paštā is placed
over it also, e. g תֹהוּ Gn 1² ; cf. below, *l.*

[2] Wickes requires Geršáyim (גְּרְשַׁיִם).

B. Conjunctive Accents (*Conjunctivi* or *Servi*).

g

14. (⸜) מוּנַח Mûnaḥ.

15. (⸝) מְהֻפָּךְ Mᵉhuppākh or מַהְפָּךְ Mahpākh.

16 *a.* (⸝) מֵירְכָא or מֵארְכָא Mêrᵉkhā, and

16 *b.* (⸟) מ׳ כְפוּלָה Mêrᵉkhā khᵉphûlā or Double Mêrᵉkhā.

17. (⸜) דַּרְגָּא Dargā.

18. (⸍) אַזְלָא 'Azlā, when associated with Gèreš (see above) also called Qadmā.

19. (⸍) תְּלִישָׁא קְטַנָּה Tᵉlišā qᵉtannā or Little Tᵉlišā, *postpositive.*

20. (⸹) גַּלְגַּל Galgal or יֶרַח Yèraḥ.

[21. (⸏) מְאַיְלָא Mᵉ'ayᵉlā or מָאיְלָא Mâyᵉlā, a variety of Ṭiphḥa, serves to mark the secondary tone in words which have Sillûq or 'Athnâḥ, or which are united by Maqqēph with a word so accentuated, e.g. וַיֵּצֵא־נֹחַ Gn 8¹⁸.]

II. *The Accents of the Books* תא״ם.

A. Distinctivi.

h

1. (⸜) Sillûq (see above, I, 1).

2. (⸍) עוֹלֶה וְיוֹרֵד 'Ôlè wᵉyôrēd,[1] a stronger divider than

3. (⸝) 'Athnâḥ (see above, I, 2). In shorter verses 'Athnâḥ suffices as principal distinctive; in longer verses 'Ôlè wᵉyôrēd serves as such, and is then mostly followed by 'Athnâḥ as the principal disjunctive of the second half of the verse.

4. (⸎) Rᵉbhîaꜥ gādôl (Great Rᵉbhîaꜥ).

5. (⸎) Rᵉbhîaꜥ mugrāš, i.e. Rᵉbhîaꜥ with Gèreš on the same word.

6. (⸣) Great Šalšèleth (see above, I. 3 *b*).

7. (⸞) צִנּוֹר Ṣinnôr (Zarqā), as *postpositive,* is easily distinguished from צִנּוֹרִית Ṣinnôrîth similarly placed, which is not an independent accent, but stands only over an open syllable before a consonant which has Mêrᵉkhā or Mahpākh.

8. (⸎) Rᵉbhîaꜥ qāṭôn (Little Rᵉbhîaꜥ) immediately before 'Ôlè wᵉyôrēd.

9. (⸏) דְּחִי Dᵉḥî or Ṭiphḥa, *prepositive,* to the right underneath the initial consonant, e.g. הַגּוֹי (consequently it does not mark the tone-syllable).

---

[1] Wrongly called also Mêrᵉkhā mᵉhuppākh (*Mêrᵉkha mahpakhatum*), although the accent underneath is in no way connected with Mêrᵉkhā; cf. Wickes, l. c., p. 14.

10. (᷷) Pâzēr (see above, I, 11 *a*).

11 *a*. (|᷈) Mᵉhuppākh lᵉgarmēh, i.e. Mahpākh with a following stroke.

11 *b*. (|᷈) 'Azlā lᵉgarmēh, i.e. 'Azlā with a following stroke.

i
B. CONJUNCTIVI.

12. (᷍.) Mêrᵉkhā (see above, I. 16 *a*).

13. (᷎) Mûnaḥ (see above, I. 14).

14. (᷍) עִלּוּי 'Illûy or Mûnaḥ superior.

15. (᷍) טַרְחָא Ṭarḥā (under the tone-syllable, and thus easily distinguished from No. 9).

16. (᷷) Galgal or Yèraḥ (see above, I. 20).

17. (᷈) Mᵉhuppākh or Mahpākh (see above, I. 15).

18. (᷈) 'Azlā (see above, I. 18).

19. (᷈) Šalšèleth qᵉṭannā (Little Šalšèleth).

The last three are distinguished from the disjunctives of the same name by the absence of the stroke.

[20. (᷍) Ṣinnôrîth, see above under No. 7.]

REMARKS ON THE ACCENTS.

I. *As Signs of the Tone.*

k 1. As in Greek and English (cf. εἰμί and εἶμι, cómpact and compáct) so also in Hebrew, words which are written with the same consonants are occasionally distinguished by the position of the tone, e.g. בָּנוּ banú (they built), בָּנוּ bánu (in us) ; קָמָה qáma (she stood up), קָמָה qamá (standing up, *fem.*).

l 2. As a rule the accent stands on the tone-syllable, and properly on its initial consonant. In the case of prepositives and postpositives alone (see above, *e*) the tone-syllable must be ascertained independently of the accent. In many MSS. as well as in Baer's editions of the text, the postpositive sign in foretoned words stands also over the tone-syllable after the analogy of Paštā (see above, I. 8 *a*, note) ; e.g. טֶרֶם יִשְׁכָּבוּ Gn 19⁴ ; so the prepositive sign in cases like וַיְהִי Gn 8¹³.

II. *As Signs of Punctuation.*

m 3. In respect to this use of the accents, every verse is regarded as a period which closes with Sillûq, or in the figurative language of the grammarians, as a province (*ditio*) which is governed by the great distinctive at the end. According as the verse is long or short, i.e. the province great or small, there are several subordinate *Domini* of different grades, as governors of greater and smaller divisions. When possible, the subdivisions themselves are also split up into parts according to the law of dichotomy (see Wickes, *The Accents of the Twenty-one Books*, p. 29 ff).—When two or more *equivalent* accents (Zâqēph, Rᵉbhia') occur consecutively, the accent which precedes marks a greater division than the one which follows ; cf. e.g. the Zàqēph, Gn 1²⁰ ᵃ.

n 4. In general a conjunctive (*Servus*) unites only such words as are closely connected in sense, e.g. a noun with a following genitive or a noun with an adjective. For the closest connexion between two or more words *Maqqēph* is added (§ 16 *a*).

5. The consecution of the several accents (especially the correspondence of *O* disjunctives with their proper conjunctives) conforms in the most minute details to strict rules, for a further investigation of which we must refer to the above-mentioned works. Here, to avoid misunderstanding, we shall only mention further the rule that in the accentuation of the books אמ״ת, the *Rᵉbhiaᵃ' mugrāš* before *Silluq*, and the *Dᵉḥi* before *'Athnāḥ*, must be changed into conjunctives, unless at least two toneless syllables precede the principal disjunctive. For this purpose Šᵉwâ *mobile* after Qames, Sere, or Ḥolem (with Metheg) is to be regarded as forming a syllable. After 'Ôlè wᵉyōrēd the 'Athnāḥ does not necessarily act as pausal (cf. Delitzsch on ψ 45⁶). The condition of our ordinary texts is corrupt, and the system of accents can only be studied in correct editions [see Wickes' two treatises].

6. A double accentuation occurs in Gn 35²², from וישכב onward (where *p* the later accentuation, intended for public reading, aims at uniting vv. 22 and 23 into *one*, so as to pass rapidly over the unpleasant statement in v. 22); and in the Decalogue, Ex 20² ᶠᶠ·; Dt 5⁶ ᶠᶠ· Here also the later (mainly superlinear) accentuation which closes the first verse with עֲבָדִים (instead of פְּנֵי) is adopted simply for the purposes of public reading, in order to reduce the original twelve verses (with sublinear accentuation) to ten, the number of the Commandments. Thus עֲבָדִים at the end of v. 2 has Silluq (to close the verse) in the lower accentuation, but in the upper, which unites vv. 2-6 (the actual words of God) into a single period, only Rᵉbhiaᵃ'. Again פְּנֵי, regarded as closing v. 3, is pointed פָּנַי (pausal Qames with Silluq), but in the upper accentuation it is פָּנַי with Pathaḥ because not in pause. (Originally there may have been a third accentuation requiring עֲבָדִים and פָּנַי, and thus representing vv. 2 and 3 as the first commandment.) Further the upper accentuation unites vv. 8-11 into one period, while in vv. 12-15 the lower accentuation combines commandments 5-8 into one verse. Cf. Geiger, *Urschrift u. Übersetzungen der Bibel*, p. 373; Japhet, *op. cit.*, p. 158, and esp. K. J. Grimm, *Johns Hopkins Univ. Circ.* xix (May, 1900), no. 145.

§ 16. *Of Maqqēph and Mèthĕg.*

These are both closely connected with the accents.   *a*

1. Maqqēph (מַקֵּף i.e. *binder*) is a small horizontal stroke between the upper part of two words which so connects them that in respect of tone and pointing they are regarded as one, and therefore have only one accent. Two, three, or even four words may be connected in this way, e.g. כָּל־אָדָם *every man*, אֶת־כָּל־עֵשֶׂב *every herb*, Gn 1²⁹, אֶת־כָּל־אֲשֶׁר־לוֹ *all that he had*, Gn 25⁵.

Certain monosyllabic prepositions and conjunctions, such as אֶל־ *to*, עַד־ *b until*, עַל־ *upon*, עִם־ *with*, אַל־ *ne*, אִם־ *if, whether*, מִן־ *from*, פֶּן־ *lest*, are almost always found with a following Maqqēph, provided they have not become independent forms by being combined with prefixes, e.g. מֵעַל, מֵעִם, in which case Maqqēph as a rule does not follow. Occasionally Maqqēph is replaced by a conjunctive accent (see above, § 9 *u*, 1 *c*), as, according to the Masora, in Dt 27⁹, 2 S 20²³, Jer 25³⁰, 29²⁵, Ec 9⁴ in the case of אֶל־כָּל־; ψ 47⁵, 60², Pr 3¹² in the case of אֶת־, the objective particle. Longer words are, however, connected by Maqqēph with a following monosyllable, e.g. הִתְהַלֶּךְ־נֹחַ Gn 6⁹, וַיְהִי־בֶן Gn 1⁷.; or two words of more than one syllable, e.g. שִׁבְעָה־עָשָׂר *seventeen*, Gn 7¹¹. Cf. the Greek proclitics ἐν, ἐκ, εἰς, εἰ, ὡς, οὐ, which are *atonic*, and lean on the following word.

c   **2.** Mètheg (מֶתֶג i.e. *a bridle*), a small perpendicular stroke under the consonant to the left of the vowel, indicates most frequently the secondary stress or counter-tone, as opposed to the principal tone marked by the accents. It serves, however, in other cases to point out that the vowel should not be hastily passed over in pronunciation, but should be allowed its full sound. Hence other names of *Mèthĕg* are *Ma'ᵃrîkh*, i.e. *lengthener*, and *Ga'yā*, i.e. *raising* of the voice, which is *Great Ga'yā* with long vowels, otherwise *Little Ga'yā*.¹

d   It is divided into: 1. The *light Mèthĕg*. This is subdivided again into (*a*) the ordinary Mèthĕg of the counter-tone, as a rule in the second (open) syllable before the tone, e.g. הָאָדָם (cf. also such cases as מֶלֶךְ־צֹר); but also in the third when the second is closed, e.g. הָאַרְבָּעִים (also in such cases as עֶבֶד־הַמֶּלֶךְ), and when the third is not suitable for it, even in the fourth (open) syllable before the tone. This Mèthĕg may be repeated in the fourth syllable before the tone, when it already stands in the second, e.g. שָׁבַעֲתִיכֶם. Finally it is always added to the vowel of an open ultima, which is joined by Maqqēph to a word beginning with a toneless syllable and so without Mèthĕg (e.g. בְּנֵי־יִשְׂרָאֵל, on the other hand רִשְׁפֵי־קֶשֶׁת, לֹא־אֶהְיֶה), or to a word beginning with *Šᵉwâ* before the tone-syllable, e.g. מִי־לְךָ, שְׁלֹמֹה־בְּנִי, &c. ; the object being to prevent the *Šᵉwâ* from becoming *quiescent*.

e   The ordinary *light Mèthĕg* is omitted with a movable וּ *copulative*, consequently we do not find וּבְנִים, &c. (nor even וּבְנֵי, &c., contrary to b, a; but וְזָהָב, &c., according to b, δ, cf. § 10 g. b).

f   (*b*) The *firm* or *indispensable Mèthĕg*. (*a*) With all long vowels (except in certain cases, וּ *copulative*, see above), which are followed by a *Šᵉwâ mobile* preceding the tone-syllable; e.g. יְרָאוּ, יֵשְׁנוּ, &c. (β) To emphasize a long vowel in a closed syllable immediately before Maqqēph, e.g. שְׁתֵל־לִי Gn 4²⁵ (not *ŏth-li*); hence also with כָּל־ ψ 138², and אֶת־ Jb 41²⁶ (for כָּל־ and אֶת־; cf. also מֵאֵת־ Jo 15¹⁸, &c.). (γ) With Ṣere, which has become toneless through retraction of the tone, in order to prevent its being pronounced as *Sᵉghôl*, e.g. אֹהֵב דַּעַת Pr 12¹ (not *'ôhĕbh*). (δ) With all vowels before composite *Šᵉwâ*, e.g. יַעֲמֹד, צְעָקִים, &c. (except when the following consonant is strengthened, e.g. יְקֻבְּנּוּ Is 62², because the strengthening by Dageš excludes the retarding of the vowel by Mèthĕg); so in the cases discussed in § 28 c, where a short vowel has taken the place of a Ḥateph, as עָמְדוּ, &c. (ε) In the preformative syllable of all forms of הָיָה *to be*, and חָיָה *to live*, when *Šᵉwâ quiescens* stands under the ה or ח, e.g. יִהְיֶה, תִּחְיֶה (*yih-yè, tiḥ-yè*), &c., cf.

---

¹ Cf. as the source of this account of *Mèthĕg*, the exhaustive treatment by S. Baer, 'Mèthĕg-Setzung nach ihren überlieferten Gesetzen,' in A. Merx's *Archiv für die wissenschaftl. Erforschung des A. Test.*, Heft i, Halle, 1867, p. 56 ff., and Heft ii. 1868, p. 194 ff. ; Baer and Strack, *Dikduke ha-ṭᵉamim*, p. 30 ff.

§ 63 q. (ζ) With the Qameṣ of the plural forms of בַּיִת *house* (thus בָּתִּים *báttim*, cf. § 96 under בַּיִת), and with אָנָּה [1] *prithee!* to guard against the pronunciation *bŏttim, ŏnnā*.—Every kind of light Mètheg may in certain circumstances be changed into a conjunctive accent, e. g. בָּתִּים 2 Ch 34[11], &c.

2. The grave *Mètheg* (*Ga'yā* in the more limited sense) is especially employed *g* in the following cases in order more distinctly to emphasize a short vowel or an initial Šᵉwâ : (*a*) with the Pathaḥ of the article or of the prefixes בְּ, כְּ, לְ, when followed by Šᵉwâ under a consonant without Dageš, e. g. הַמְסַפֵּה, לַמְסַפֵּה, &c., but not before יְ (before which וְ also remains without Mèthĕg, with the exception of וַיְהִי and וַיְחִי, when they are followed by Maqqēph, or accented with Paštā), nor before the tone-syllable of a word, and neither *before* nor *after* the common *Mèthĕg*; likewise not in words which are connected by a conjunctive accent with the following word ; (*b*) with the interrogative הֲ with Pathaḥ (except when it precedes יְ, Dageš forte or the tone-syllable of the word), e. g. הַאֵלֶךְ. When a Šᵉwâ follows the הֲ and after the Šᵉwâ there is an untoned syllable, Baer places the Mèthĕg to the right of the Pathaḥ, e. g. הֲבָרְכָה Gn 27[38] (but ed. Mant. and Ginsb. הֲבְרַ); (*c*) with the Pathaḥ or Sᵉgol of the article before a guttural (which cannot take Dageš), e. g. הֶהָרִים, הַחַיִּים.—The *Šᵉwâ-Ga'yā* (ֽ) is especially important in the accentuation of the תא"ם, for purposes of musical recitation ; it stands chiefly in words whose principal tone is marked by a disjunctive without a preceding conjunctive, e. g. וְהָיָה ψ 1[3].

3. The *euphonic Ga'yā*, to ensure the distinct pronunciation of those con- *h* sonants which in consequence of the loss of the tone, or because they close a syllable, might easily be neglected, e. g. וַיִּשְׁבַע לוֹ Gn 24[9]; פֶּדֶּנָה אֲרָם (here to avoid a hiatus) 28[2], or in such cases as רוּחַ־אֵל Jb 33[4], &c. ; תַּדְשֵׁא Gn 1[11].

Mètheg (especially in the cases mentioned in 1, *b*, *a*) is a guide to correct *i* pronunciation, since it distinguishes *ā* from *ŏ* (except in the case noted in § 9 *v*, *b*) and *î* from *ĭ* ; e. g. אָכְלָה *'ā-khᵉlā* (she has eaten), but אָכְלָה *'ŏkhlā* (food), since the ָ stands here in a toneless closed syllable, and must therefore be a short vowel ; thus also יִרְאוּ *yĭ-rᵉ'û* (they fear), but יִרְאוּ *yir'û* (they see), יִשְׁנוּ (they sleep), but יִשְׁנוּ (they repeat). The Jewish grammarians, however, do not consider the syllables lengthened by Mèthĕg as open. They regard the Šᵉwâ as *quiescent* in cases like אָכְלָה, and belonging to the preceding vowel ; cf. Baer, *Thorat 'Emeth*, p. 9, and in Merx's *Archiv*, i. p. 60, Rem. 1, and especially *Dikduke ha-ṭᵉamim*, p. 13.

§ 17. *Of the Qᵉrê and Kᵉthîbh. Masora marginalis and finalis.*

On Qᵉrê and Kᵉthîbh see Ginsburg, *Intr.*, p. 183 ff.]

1. The margin of Biblical MSS. and editions exhibits variants *a* of an early date (§ 3 *c*), called קְרִי [2] *to be read*, since, according to

---

[1] The common form is אָנָּא, with an accent on both syllables, in which case, according to Qimḥi, the tone is always to be placed on the former. For the above mode of writing and position of the tone cf. Is 38[3], Jon 1[14], 4[2], ψ 116[4].

[2] On the necessity of the punctuation קְרִי as passive participle (= *legendum*)

the opinion of the Jewish critics, they are to be preferred to the כְּתִיב, i.e. what is *written* in the text, and are actually to be read instead of it.

On this account the vowels of the marginal reading (the *Qᵉrê*) are placed under the consonants of the text, and in order to understand both readings properly, the vowels in the text must be applied to the marginal reading, while for the reading of the text (the *Kᵉthîbh*) its own vowels are to be used. Thus in Jer 42⁶ אֲנוּ occurs in the text, in the margin אנחנו קרי. Read אֲנוּ *we* (or according to Jewish tradition אָנוּ) in the text, in the margin אֲנַחְנוּ. A small circle or asterisk in the text always refers to the marginal reading.

b 2. Words or consonants which are to be passed over in reading, and are therefore left unpointed, are called כְּתִיב וְלֹא קְרֵי (*scriptum et non legendum*), e.g. את Jer 38¹⁶, אם 39¹², ידרך 51³. Conversely, words not contained in the text, but required by the Masora (as indicated by the insertion of their vowels), are called קְרֵי וְלֹא כְתִיב, e.g. 2 S 8³, Jer 31³⁸. See further Strack, *Prolegomena Critica*, p. 85 ; *Dikduke ha-ṭᵉamim*, §§ 62, 64 ; Blau, *Masoretische Untersuchungen*, p. 49 ff.

c 3. In the case of some very common words, which are *always* to be read otherwise than according to the *Kᵉthîbh*, it has not been considered necessary to place the *Qᵉrê* in the margin, but its vowels are simply attached to the word in the text. This *Qᵉrê perpetuum* occurs in the Pentateuch in הוּא (Qᵉrê הִיא) wherever הוא stands for the feminine (§ 32 *l*), and in נַעַר (Kᵉthîbh נער, Qᵉrê נַעֲרָה) always, except in Dt 22¹⁹ (but the Sam. text always has נערה, הִיא). The ordinary explanation of this supposed archaism, on the analogy of Greek ὁ παῖς and ἡ παῖς, our *child*, is inadequate, since there is no trace elsewhere of this epicene use ; נער for נערה is rather a survival of a system of orthography in which a final vowel was written defectively, as in קָטַלְתְּ ; cf. § 2 *n*.— Other instances are : יִשָּׂשׂכָר (Q. יִשָּׂכָר) Gn 30¹⁸ &c., see the *Lexicon*, and Baer and Delitzsch, *Genesis*, p. 84, and below, note to § 47 *b*; יְרוּשָׁלֵַם (Q. יְרוּשָׁלַיִם), properly יְרוּשָׁלֵם ; יְהֹוָה (Q. אֲדֹנָי *the Lord*), or (after אֲדֹנָי) יֱהֹוִה (Q. אֱלֹהִים) properly יַהְוֶה *Yahwè* (cf. § 102 *m*, and § 135 *q*, note) ; on שְׁנַיִם שְׁתַּיִם for שְׁנֵי, שְׁתֵּי, see § 97 *d*, end.

d 4. The masoretic apparatus accompanying the biblical text is divided into (*a*) *Masora marginalis*, consisting of (α) *Masora (marginalis) magna* on the upper and lower margins of MSS. ; (β) *Masora (marginalis) parva* between and on the right and left of the columns ;

---

instead of קְרִי *Qᵉri*, which was formerly common but is properly a past tense (= *lectum est*), see Kautzsch, *Gramm. des Bibl.-Aram.*, p. 81, note.

(b) *Masora finalis* at the end of the several books, counting Samuel, Kings, Minor Prophets, Ezra-Nehemiah, Chronicles, each as one book. On all three varieties see especially Ginsburg, *Introd.*, p. 423 ff., and the appendices containing (p. 983 ff.) the masoretic treatise from the St. Petersburg MS. of A.D. 1009, and (p. 1000 ff.) specimens of the *Masora parva* and *magna* on two chapters.

In nearly all printed editions only the *Masora finalis* is found, indicating *e* the number of verses, the middle point of the book, &c., and a scanty selection from the *Masora parva*. The following alphabetical list of technical expressions (some of them Aramaic) and abbreviations, may suffice with the help of the lexicon to elucidate the subject. Further details will be found in the appendix to Teile's edition of the Hebrew O. T., p. 1222 ff.

אוֹת *letter.* אֶלָּא *nisi, except.* אֶמְצַע *middle.* אס״ף=פָּסוּק סוֹף אַתְנָח in the formula בְּלָא אס״ף *without* 'Athnaḥ *or* Soph-pasuq i.e. *although no* 'Athnaḥ *or* Soph-pasuq *is written.*

בְּ *with,* before names of vowels or accents, as קָמֵץ בְּזָקֵף *Qames with Zaqeph* used instead of Pathaḥ (§ 29 *i*).—בְּ as a numeral=*two,* as in ב׳ טְעָמִים *two accents.* במקצת, see מִקְצָת. בנ״א=בְּנֻסְחָא אַחֲרִינָא (Aramaic) *in another copy;* pl. בְּנֻסְחָן אַחֲרִינָן.—בס״א=בִּסְפָרִים אַחֵרִים *in other books.* בָּתַר (Aram.) *after.* דְּגֻשָׁה fem. דְּגֻשָׁה *marked with Dageš (or Mappiq).* דַּף *leaf, page.*

זְעִיר fem. זְעִירָא (Aram.) *small.*

חֹל *profane, not sacred,* e.g. אֲדֹנָי Gn 19² because not referring to God. חוּץ *except.* חָסֵר *written defectively,* also *wanting* as ח׳ א׳ *'aleph is omitted.*

טַעַם *accent* (see ב); טָעַם in Hiphil *to chant an accent.*

יַתִּיר *superfluous.*

כַּאן *here.* כְּלָל (Aram.) *total,* as adv. *in general.*

לֵית=לָא אִית (Aram., from לָא אִית *non est*)=the form *is not found elsewhere.*

מְדֻיָּק *accurately corrected.* מָלֵא *full* i.e. written *plene.* מִלְּמַטָּה *below*=מִלְּרַע (§ 15 c). מִלְעֵיל=מִלְמַעְלָה (§ 15 c). מְנֻזָּרוֹת *separated,* the name of the strangely formed Nûns before ψ 107²³ ff. (§ 5 n). מִקְרָא *that which is read,* the name for all the O. T. scriptures. מִקְצָת *part.*

נָח fem. נָחָה *quiescent,* i.e. not sounded. נֶעְלָם *concealed,* i.e. only retained orthographically. נָקוּד *a point.* נָקֻד *pointed.*

ס״א see בְּ. סִימָן σημεῖον, *sign,* esp. *a mnemonic word* or, frequently, *sentence.* סך=סְכוּם *total.* ס״ף=סוֹף פָּסוּק (§ 15 f).

עַמּוּד *column of a page.*

פָּסוּק *a masoretic verse.* פִּסְקָא *a space,* esp. in the phrase פ׳ בְּאֶמְצַע פָּסוּק *a space within a verse,* e.g. Gn 35²²; cf. H. Grätz, *Monatschrift für Gesch. u. Wiss. des Judentums,* 1878, p. 481 ff., and H. Strack, ibid. 1879, p. 26 ff.

ק=קְרִי, see above, *c.* קוֹדֵם properly קָדָם *before.* קָמוּץ fem. קְמוּצָה *poin'ed with Qames.* קוֹרֵא *reader of the sacred text.*

רַבָּתִי, רַבְּתָה, רַבְּתָא (Aram., all fem. sing.) *large.*

תֵּיבָה *word* (consisting of more than one letter). תְּלוּיָה *suspensa* (§ 5 n, 3). תְּרֵי (Aram.) *two.*

CHAPTER II

PECULIARITIES AND CHANGES OF LETTERS: THE SYLLABLE AND THE TONE

§ 18.

THE changes which take place in the forms of the various parts of speech, depend partly on the peculiar nature of certain classes of letters and the manner in which they affect the formation of syllables, partly on certain laws of the language in regard to syllables and the tone.

§ 19. *Changes of Consonants.*

a   The changes which take place among consonants, owing to the formation of words, inflexion, euphony, or to influences connected with the progress of the language, are *commutation, assimilation, rejection, addition, transposition, softening.*

1. *Commutation*[1] may take place between consonants which are either *homorganic* or *homogeneous* (cf. § 6 *q*), e.g. עָלֵץ, עָלַס, עָלַז to *exult,* לָאָה, לָהָה, Aram. לְעָא to be *weary,* לָחַץ and נָחַץ to *press,* סָגַר and סָכַר to *close,* מָלַט and פָּלַט to *escape.* In process of time, and partly under the influence of Aramaic, the harder and rougher sounds especially were changed into the softer, e.g. צָחַק into שָׂחַק to *laugh,* גָּעַל into גָּאַל to *reject,* and the sibilants into the corresponding mutes: ז into ד, שׁ into ת, צ into ט. In many cases these mutes may be regarded as a return to an earlier stage of the pronunciation.

The interchange of consonants, however, belongs rather to the lexicographical treatment of stems[2] than to grammatical inflexion. To the latter belong the interchange (*a*) of ת and ט in *Hithpaʿēl* (§ 54 *b*); (*b*) of ו and י in verbs *primae Yôd* (§ 69), יָלַד for וָלַד, &c.

b   2. *Assimilation* usually takes place when one consonant which closes a syllable passes over into another beginning the next syllable, and forms with it a strengthened letter, as *illustris* for *inlustris, affero* for *adfero,* συλλαμβάνω for συνλαμβάνω. In Hebrew this occurs,

---

[1] Cf. Barth, *Etymologische Forschungen,* Lpz. 1893, p. 15 ff. ('Lautverschiebungen').

[2] See in the *Lexicon,* the preliminary remarks on the several consonants.

(a) most frequently with נ, e.g. מִשָּׁם (for min-šām) *from there*, מִזֶּה c
(for min-zè) *from this*, יִתֵּן (for yintēn) *he gives.* נ is *not* assimilated
after the prefix לְ, e.g. לִנְפֹּל, nor as a rule before gutturals (except
sometimes before ה), nor when it is the third consonant of the stem,
e.g. שָׁכַנְתְּ (cf. however נָתַתְּ for nāthántā) except when another *Nun*
follows, cf. § 44 o; nor in some isolated cases, as Dt 33⁹, Is 29¹, 58³,
all in the principal pause; on הִנְדֹּף and תִּנְדֹּף ψ 68³, see § 51 k, and
§ 66 f.

(b) Less frequently and only in special cases with ל, ת, ד, e.g. יִקַּח d
(for yilqaḥ) *he takes;* מְדַבֵּר for mithdabbēr; יִטַּמָּא ʿfor yithṭammā; תִּכּוֹנֵן
for tithkônēn; תִּכַּשֵּׂא for תִּתְכַּשֵּׂא; אַחַת for 'aḥadt; but in 1 S 4¹⁹ for לָלַת
read probably לָלֶדֶת.

(c) In isolated cases with ה, ו, י, e.g. אָנָּא *prithee!* if from אָה נָא; c
ו and י mostly before sibilants in the verbal forms enumerated in § 71.

In all these cases, instead of the assimilated letter, a *Dageš forte* f
appears in the following consonant. *Dageš,* however, is omitted when
the strengthened consonant would stand at the end of a word, since
the strengthening would then be less audible (§ 20 l), e.g. אַף *nose*
(from 'anp), תֵּת *to give* (from tint).

The cases are less frequent where a weak letter is lost in pronunciation,[1]
and in place of it the preceding stronger sound is sharpened, i. e. takes *Dageš,*
e.g. קְטַלְתִּנוּ from קְטַלְתָּהוּ (§ 59 g). אֶסָּק for אֶסְלַק (§ 66 e) is an Aramaism.

3. Complete *rejection* takes place only in the case of weaker con- g
sonants, especially the sonants נ and ל, the gutturals א and ה, and the
two half vowels ו and י. Such rejection takes place,

(a) at the beginning of a word (*aphaeresis*), when these weak con- h
sonants (א, י, ל, נ) are not supported by a full vowel, but have only
Šewâ, e.g. נַחְנוּ *we,* also אֲנַחְנוּ; דַּע for וְדַע; קַח for לְקַח; גַּשׁ for נְגַשׁ,
הִי for נְהִי Ez 2¹⁰.

Aphaeresis of a weak consonant with a full vowel is supposed to occur in רַד i
Ju 19¹¹ for יָרַד; in תָּתֵּה 2 S 22⁴¹ for נָתַתָּה; in שׁוֹב for יָשׁוֹב Je 42¹⁰; on קַח
Ez 17⁵ for לְקַח, and on קָחָם Ho 11³ for לְקָחָם, see § 66 g, end. In reality,
however, all these forms are to be regarded merely as old textual errors.

(b) In the middle of a word (*syncope*), when Šewâ precedes the k
weak consonant[2]; thus in the case of א (see further § 23 b-f, and

---

[1] Such a suppression of a letter is sometimes inaccurately called ʿbackward
assimilation'.

[2] Syncope of a strong consonant (ע) occurs in בִּי *prithee!* if this stands for
בְּעִי (see *Lexicon*), also in וַנִּשְׁקָה Am 8⁸, Kᵉthibh for וְנָשְׁקָה (cf. וְשָׁקְעָה 9⁵), and

§ 68 *b–k*), e.g. in מוּם for מְאוּם. As a rule in such cases, however, the א is orthographically retained, e.g. לִקְרַאת for לִקְרַאת. Syncope occurs frequently in the case of ה, e.g. לַמֶּלֶךְ for לְהַמֶּלֶךְ (§ 23 *k* and § 35 *n*), יַקְטִיל for יְהַקְטִיל (§ 53 *a*).

Syncope of א with Šᵉwâ occurs in such cases as בַּאדֹנָי for בַּאֲדֹנָי (cf. § 102 *m*); וַיֵּעֶשׂ Zc 11⁵.[1] On the cases in which א is wholly omitted after the article, see § 35 *d*.

Finally, the elision of ו and י in verbs ל״ה (§ 75 *h*) is an instance of syncope.—On the syncope of ה between two vowels, see § 23 *k*.

l   (c) At the end of a word (*apocope*), e.g. גִּלֹה pr. name of a city (cf. גִּילֹנִי Gilonite); וַיַּרְא, where א though really rejected is orthographically retained, &c. On the apocope of ו and י in verbs ל״ה, see § 24 *g*, and § 75 *a*.

> Bolder changes (especially by violent apocope), took place in earlier periods of the language, notably the weakening of the feminine ending ת__ *ith* to ה__ *â*, see § 44 *a*, and § 80 *f*.

m   **4.** To avoid harshness in pronunciation a helping sound, Aleph prosthetic[2] with its vowel, is prefixed to some words, e. g. אֶזְרוֹעַ and זְרוֹעַ *arm* (cf. χθές, ἐχθές; *spiritus*, French *esprit*).—A prosthetic ע occurs probably in עַקְרָב *scorpion*; cf. Arab. *'uṣfûr* bird (stem *ṣafara*).

n   **5.** *Transposition*[3] occurs only seldom in the grammar, e. g. הִשְׁתַּמֵּר for הִתְשַׁמֵּר (§ 54 *b*) for the sake of euphony; it is more frequent in the lexicon (כֶּבֶשׂ and כֶּשֶׂב *lamb*, שִׂמְלָה and שַׂלְמָה *garment*), but is mostly confined to sibilants and sonants.

o   **6.** *Softening* occurs e.g. in כּוֹכָב *star*, from *kaukabh=kawkabh* for *kabhkabh* (cf. Syriac *raurab = rabrab*); טוֹטָפוֹת *phylacteries* for *ṭaph-ṭâphôth*; according to the common opinion, also in אִישׁ *man* from *'inš*, cf. however § 96.

§ 20. *The Strengthening (Sharpening) of Consonants.*

a   **1.** The strengthening of a consonant, indicated by *Dageš forte*, is necessary and essential (*Dageš necessarium*)

(a) when the same consonant would be written twice in succession

---

in בָּלָה Jos 19³ for בַּעֲלָה (as in 15²⁹). Probably, however, ונשקה and בלה are only clerical errors, as is undoubtedly כָּאֹר Am 8⁸ for כַּיְאֹר (9⁵).

[1] Frensdorff, *Ochla W'ochla*, p. 97 f., gives a list of forty-eight words with quiescent א.

[2] This awkward term is at any rate as suitable as the name *Alef protheticum* proposed by Nestle, *Marginalien u. Materialien*, Tübingen, 1893, p. 67 ff.

[3] Cf. Barth, *Etymologische Studien*, Lpz. 1893, p. 1 ff.; Königsberger, in *Zeitschrift f. wissenschaftliche Theologie*, 1894, p. 451 ff.

without an intermediate vowel or *S͏̌ᵉwâ mobile*; thus we have נָתַנּוּ for

נָתַנְנוּ *nāthăn-nû* and שַׁתִּי for שָׁתְתִּי.

(*b*) in cases of assimilation (§ 19 *b–f*), e.g. יִתֵּן for *yintēn*.

In both these cases the *Dageš* is called *compensativum*.

(*c*) When it is characteristic of a grammatical form, e.g. לָמַד *he has learned*, לִמַּד *he has taught* (*Dageš characteristicum*). In a wider sense this includes the cases in which a consonant is sharpened by Dageš forte, to preserve a preceding short vowel (which in an open syllable would have to be lengthened by § 26 *e*), e.g. גְּמַלִּים *camels* for *gᵉmālīm*; cf. § 93 *ee* and *kk*, § 93 *pp*.

This coalescing of two consonants as indicated above does not take place *b* when the first has a vowel or *S͏̌ᵉwâ mobile*. In the latter case, according to the correct Masora, a *compound S͏̌ᵉwâ* should be used, preceded by Methĕg, e.g. קִלֲלַת, הַגֲּלִים, &c. (cf. §§ 10*g*, 16*f*). This pointing is not used before the suffix ךָ, e.g. תְּבָרֶכְךָ Gn 27⁴, but the first כ has a vocal *S͏̌ᵉwâ*, otherwise the second כ would have *Dageš lene*. Also when the former of the two consonants has been already strengthened by *Dageš forte*, it can only have a vocal *S͏̌ᵉwâ*, and any further contraction is therefore impossible. This applies also to cases where *Dageš forte* has been omitted (see below, *m*), e.g. הַלֲלוּ properly = *hal-lᵉlû*. The form חָנֲנֵנִי ψ 9¹⁴ (not חָנְנֵנִי) might be explained as imperat. Pi‘ēl = חַנֲּנֵנִי; if it were imperat. Qal the non-contraction of the monosyllabic root would be as strange as it is in שְׁדָדוּ Jer 49²⁸, and in the imperf. יְשָׁדְּרֵם Jer 5⁶.

2. A consonant is sometimes strengthened merely for the sake of *c* euphony (*Dageš euphonicum*), and the strengthening is then not so essential. This occurs [1]—

(*a*) when two words are closely united in pronunciation by *Dageš forte conjunctivum*: (1) in the first letter of a monosyllable or of a word having the tone (or occasionally the counter-tone) on the first syllable,[2] when closely connected with the preceding word, if that word ends in a tone-bearing *Qameṣ* (הָ‍ָ) with *S͏̌ᵉwâ mobile* preceding, or a tone-bearing הָ‍ֶ,—called דְּחִיק (i. e. *compressed*) by the Jewish grammarians.

The term monosyllable here and in *f* (by § 28 *e*) includes Segholates like בֶּסֶף, שַׁחַד, &c., as well as forms like פְּרִי, שְׁאָל, שְׁמוֹ, and even כְּנָעַן.

---

[1] Cf. Baer, 'De primarum vocabulorum literarum dagessatione,' in his *Liber Proverbiorum*, Lpz. 1880, pp. vii–xv; F. Prätorius, 'Über den Ursprung des Dag. f. conjunctivum,' in *ZAW*. 1883, p. 17 ff. (ascribed to an original assimilation of ת or נ).

[2] לֵאמֹר alone, although having the tone on the ultima, invariably takes the *Dageš forte conj.* when מֹשֶׁה with a conjunctive accent precedes, Ex 6¹⁰·²⁹, 15²⁴, &c.

Some limit the use of the *Dᵉḥiq* to the closest connexion of a monosyllable with a following *Bᵉgadkᵉphath*. However, it also applies to cases like לְכָה־נָּא Nu 22⁶; לְקָחַת־זֹּאת Gn 2²³; יָצְאָה־לָּךְ ψ 91¹¹; and even with *Rêš*, מַעֲנֵה־רַּךְ Pr 15¹; וּמִשְׁנֶה־כֶּסֶף Gn 43¹⁵. In all these examples the tone, were it not for the Maqqēph, would be on the ultima of the first word.

d   Rem. 1. When זֶה *this* has Maqqēph after it, a *Dageš forte conj.* always follows, even if the next word is neither a monosyllable nor has the tone on the initial syllable; thus not only in זֶה־שְּׁמוֹ but also in זֶה־פִּרְיָה Nu 13²⁷, זֶה־פִּרְיָה Jer 23⁶, but also in זֶה־פִּרְיָה Nu 13²⁷, 1 Ch 22¹. In הִנֵּה־נָּא Gn 19² (where Maqqēph is represented by a conjunctive accent, § 9 *u*, 1 *c*, and § 16 *b*), the Sᵉghôl coincides with the secondary tone-syllable. On the origin of *Dag. f. conj.* after מַה־ (for מָה) *what?*, see § 37 *b*, *c*.

e   2. Such cases as נָאָה גָּאֹה Ex 15¹·²¹, the 2nd בְּמֹכָה in ver. 11, גָּאַלְתָּ ver. 13, כָּאֶבֶן ver. 16, do not belong here. In these the *Dageš* can only be intended for *Dag. lene*, see § 21 *d*.

f   (2) In the first letter of a monosyllable, or of a word with the tone on the first syllable after a closely connected *milʿêl* ending in הָ—, or הֶ—. Such a milʿêl is called by the Jewish grammarians אָתֵי מֵרָחִיק (Aram. = Heb. אָתֶה מֵרָחוֹק) *veniens e longinquo* (in respect of the tone). The attraction of the following tone-syllable by *Dageš forte conj.* is here also due to the exigencies of rhythm, e.g. שָׁבִיתָ שֶּׁבִי ψ 68¹⁹; הוֹשִׁיעָה נָּא ψ 118²⁵ (so ed. Mant., but Ginsburg and Kittel (וְ)הוֹשִׁיעָה נָּא); הִרְחִיבָה שְּׁאוֹל Is 5¹⁴; אַרְצָה כְּנַעַן Gn 11³¹. The Milʿêl may, however, also be due to a subsequent retraction of the tone (*nāsôg ʾaḥôr*, § 29 *e*), as in עֹשֶׂה פֶּרִי Gn 1¹¹.—The prefixes בְ, כְ, לְ, and וְ alone do not take a Dageš in this case, except in לְךָ, always, and לְלַיְלָה ψ 19³. Such forms as הִשָּׁבְעָה לִּי Gn 21²³, מָלְאָה שָּׁחַד ψ 26¹⁰, רָחֲקָה מֶּנִּי Jb 21¹⁶, and even נֶעֶמְדָה יָּחַד Is 50⁸ (i.e. the cases where the tone is thrown back from the ultima on to the syllable which otherwise would have *Metheg*), are likewise regarded as *milʿêl*. On the other hand, e.g. חָרָה לָךְ Gn 4⁶, not לָּךְ since the first *ā* of חָרָה could not have *Metheg*. When words are closely united by Maqqēph the same rules apply as above, except that in the first word *Metheg*, in the secondary tone, takes the place of the accent, cf. עֹשֶׂה־פְּרִי Gn 1¹²; הַגִּידָה־נָּא Gn 32³⁰, &c. Finally, the *Dageš* is used when the attracted word does not begin with the principal tone, but with a syllable having *Metheg*, הַמָּה יִירְשׁוּ ψ 37⁹; אֵלֶּה יַעֲקֹב Is 44²¹; עָשִׂיתָ קַעֲרֹתָיו Ex 25²⁹, provided that the second word does not begin with a *Bᵉgadkᵉphath* letter (hence e.g. אֵלֶּה תוֹלְדוֹת Gn 2⁴).

g   Rem. Such cases as קֻבֵּנֶךְ Dt 32⁶, and כָּשִׁיתָ 32¹⁵, and נָעוֹת (so Baer, but not ed. Mant., &c.) 1 S 1¹³ are therefore anomalous; also, because beginning with

a B⁼gadk⁼phath, בְּאֵלִם Ex 15¹¹ (cf. however above, *e*); תֵּל־ Jos 8²⁸; בְּזָרוֹעַ
ψ 77¹⁶; בֶּן־הִיא Jb 5²⁷.—It is doubtful whether we should include here those
cases in which *Dageš forte* occurs after a word ending in a toneless *û*, such as
קוּמוּ צְאוּ Gn 19¹⁴, Ex 12³¹; Ex 12¹⁵ (שְׂאֹר), Dt 2²⁴; also לֹּא Gn 19², 1 S 8¹⁹;
לֹּו Ju 18¹⁹, Est 6¹³ (where P. Haupt regards the *Dageš* as due to the enclitic
character of the לֹו); מֵעַט Ho 8¹⁰; גֹּרוּ Jer 49⁸⁰; רְדוּ 1 S 15⁶. When we
explained the *Dageš* in these examples not as conjunctive, but orthophonic
(see above, § 13 c, and Delitzsch, *Psalmen*, 4th ed. on ψ 94¹² ᵃ), we especially
had in view those cases in which the consonant with *Dageš* has a *Š⁼wâ*. The
extension of the use of *Dageš* to consonants with a strong vowel, seems,
however, to indicate that these are cases of the אָתֵי מֵרַחִיק, which was
required by some Masoretes but not consistently inserted. On the other
hand, the *Dageš forte* in י after a preceding *î* (ψ 118⁵·¹⁸), and even after *û*
(ψ 94¹²), is due to an attempt to preserve its consonantal power; see König,
Lehrgeb., p. 54 *b*.

(*b*) When a consonant with *Š⁼wâ* is strengthened by *Dageš forte h
dirimens* to make the *Š⁼wâ* more audible. In almost all cases the
strengthening or sharpening can be easily explained from the character
of the particular consonant, which is almost always a sonant, sibilant,
or the emphatic *Qôph*; cf. עִנְבֵי Lv 25⁵, Dt 32³² (for עֲנָבֵי); כִּנְּתָךְ Is 33¹
(where, however, כְּכַלּוֹתְךָ is to be read); cf. Na 3¹⁷, Jb 9¹⁸, 17², Jo 1¹⁷
(with מ); Is 57⁶ (with ל); Ju 20⁴³,¹ 1 S 1⁶ (with ר); Gn 49¹⁰·¹⁷ (and
so always in עָקְבֵי Ju 5²², Ct 1⁸ and עַקְּבוֹת ψ 77²⁰, 89⁵²); Ex 15¹⁷, Dt 23¹¹,
Ju 20³², 1 S 28¹⁰ (ק)²; Ex 2³, Is 58³, Am 5²¹, ψ 141³, Pr 4¹³ (צ); Pr 27²⁵
(שׂ); Is 5²⁸, ψ 37¹⁵, Jer 51⁵⁶, Neh 4⁷ (שׁ). Also, with כ Ho 3²; with ב
Is 9³, Jer 4⁷; with ת 1 S 10¹¹. In many instances of this kind the
influence of the following consonant is also observable.

(*c*) When a vowel is to be made specially emphatic, generally in *î*
the principal *pause*, by a *Dageš forte affectuosum* in the following
consonant. Thus in a following sonant, Ju 5⁷ (חָדְלּוּ), Jb 29²¹ (וַיִּחֵלּוּ),
22¹² (רָמּוּ); Ez 27¹⁹ (in נ); in ת Is 33¹², 41¹⁷, Jer 51⁵⁸, perhaps also
Jb 21¹³ (יֵחַתּוּ).

(*d*) When the sonants ל, מ, נ are strengthened by *Dageš forte firma- k
tivum* in the pronouns הֵמָּה, הֵנָּה, אֵלֶּה, and in לָמָּה *why ?* cf. also בַּמֶּה,
בַּמָּה *whereby ?* בַּמָּה *how much ?* (§ 102 k, l), to give greater firmness
to the preceding tone-vowel.

3. Omission of the strengthening, or at least the loss of the *Dageš l
forte* occurs,

(*a*) *almost always* at the end of a word, since here a strengthened

---

¹ The ordinary reading הִרְדִיפֻהוּ, where ר is without *Dageš*, is only intelligible if the ר has *Dageš*.

² Also in ψ 45¹⁰ read בִּיקְרוֹתֶיךָ with Baer and Ginsburg, following Ben
Asher, and in Pr 30¹⁷ לִיקֲהַת (Ben Naphthali בִּיקֲ׳ and לִיקֳ׳).

consonant cannot easily be sounded.[1]　In such cases the preceding vowel is frequently lengthened (§ 27 *d*), e. g. רֹב *multitude*, from רבב; עָם *people*, with a distinctive accent or after the article, עָם, from עמם; but e. g. גַּן *garden*, בַּת *daughter*, with the final consonant virtually sharpened. On the exceptions אַתְּ *thou* (fem.) and נָתַתְּ *thou* (fem.) *hast given* Ez 16³³, see § 10 *k*.

m　(*b*) Very frequently in certain consonants with *Šᵉwâ mobile*, since the absence of a strong vowel causes the strengthening to be less noticeable. This occurs principally in the case of ו and י (on יְ and יִ after the article, see § 35 *b*; on יְ after מַה־, § 37 *b*); and in the sonants מ,[2] נ and ל; also in the sibilants, especially when a guttural follows (but note Is 62⁹, מְאַסְפָיו, as ed. Mant. and Ginsb. correctly read, while Baer has מְאָסְ׳ with compensatory lengthening, and others even מְאָסָ׳; מְשַׁמְּמֵי Gn 27²⁸·³⁹; מְשַׁלֵּשׁ 38²⁴ for מְשַׁ׳, הַשְׁלַבִּים 1 K 7²⁸; אֶשְּׁקָה־ 1 K 19²⁰ from נָשַׁק, הַשְּׁפַתַּיִם Ez 40⁴³ and לַשְׁפַּנִּים ψ 104¹⁸; מִשְׁתִּים Jon 4¹¹, הַצְּפַרְדְּעִים Ex 8¹ &c.) ;—and finally in the emphatic ק.[3]

Of the *Bᵉgadkᵉphath* letters, ב occurs without *Dageš* in מִבְצִיר Ju 8²; נ in מִנְגִּוּרָתָם Ez 32³⁰; ד in נִדְחֵי Is 11¹² 56⁸, ψ 147² (*not* in Jer 49⁵⁶), supposing that it is the Participle Niphʿal of נָדַח; lastly, ת in תִּתְצוּ Is 22¹⁰. Examples, עוֹרִים, וַיְהִי (so always the preformative יְ in the *imperf.* of verbs), יְקְחוּ, יִשְׂאוּ, בְּסַאי, מְלְאוּ, הֲלֹלוּ, הִנְנִי, לַמְנַצֵּחַ, מִלְמַעְלָה, מִקְצָה, מַקְלֹות, &c. In correct MSS. the omission of the *Dageš* is indicated by the *Rāphè* stroke (§ 14) over the consonant. However, in these cases, we must assume at least a *virtual* strengthening of the consonant (*Dageš forte implicitum*, see § 22 *c*, end).

(*c*) In the Gutturals, see § 22 *b*.

n　Rem. 1. Contrary to rule the strengthening is omitted (especially in the later Books), owing to the lengthening of the preceding short vowel, generally *ḥireq* (cf. *mîle* for *mille*), e. g. יְחִתָּן *he makes them afraid*, for יְחִתֵּן Hb 2¹⁷ (where, however, it is perhaps more correct to suppose, with König, a formation on the analogy of verbs ע׳׳וּ, and moreover to read יְחִיתֶךָ with the LXX), וִיקֹות Is 50¹¹ for וְקֹות.

o　2. Very doubtful are the instances in which compensation for the strengthening is supposed to be made by the insertion of a following נ. Thus for

---

[1] So in Latin *fel* (for *fell*), gen. *fellis*; *mel, mellis*; *os, ossis*. In Middle High German the doubling of consonants never takes place at the end of a word, but only in the middle (as in Old High German), e g. *val* (*Fall*), gen. *valles*; *swam* (*Schwamm*, &c., Grimm, *Deutsche Gramm.*, 2nd ed., i. 383.

[2] *Dageš forte* is almost always omitted in מְ when it is the prefix of the participle Piʿel or Puʿal, hence ψ 104³ הַמְקָרֶה *who layeth the beams*, but הַמְּקָרֶה *the roof* Ec 10¹⁸ (cf. הַמְּלָאכָה *the work*, &c.).

[3] According to some also in ט in תִּטְּעֵי Is 17¹⁰; but see Baer on the passage.

מְעֹנֶיהָ Is 23¹¹, read מָעֻזֶּיהָ (or מְעֹזֶנֶיהָ); and for תָּמְנוּ La 3²², read תַּמּוּ. In Nu 23¹³ קָבְנוֹ is not an instance of compensation (see § 67 *o*, end).

§ 21. *The Aspiration of the Tenues.*[1]

The *harder* sound of the six *B*ᵉ*gadk*ᵉ*phath* letters, indicated by *a* Dageš lene, is to be regarded, according to the general analogy of languages, as their older and original pronunciation, from which the softer sound was weakened (§ 6 *n* and § 13). The original hard sound is maintained when the letter is initial, and after a consonant, but when it immediately follows a vowel or *Š*ᵉ*wā mobile* it is softened and aspirated by their influence, e. g. פָּרַץ *pāraṣ*, יִפְרֹץ *yiphrōṣ*, כֹּל *kōl*, לְכֹל *l*ᵉ*khōl*. Hence the *B*ᵉ*gadk*ᵉ*phath* take Dageš lene

(1) at the beginning of words : (*a*) without exception when the *b* preceding word ends with a vowelless consonant, e. g. עַל־כֵּן *ʿal-kēn* (*therefore*), עֵץ פְּרִי *ʿēṣ p*ᵉ*rî* (*fruit-tree*); (*b*) at the beginning of a section, e. g. בְּרֵאשִׁית Gn 1¹, or at the beginning of a sentence, or even of a minor division of a sentence after a distinctive accent (§ 15 *d*), although the preceding word may end with a vowel. The distinctive accent in such a case prevents the vowel from influencing the following tenuis, e. g. וַיְהִי כַּאֲשֶׁר *and it was so, that when*, Ju 11⁵ (but וַיְהִי כֵן Gn 1⁷).

Rem. 1. The vowel letters ה, י, ו, א, as such, naturally do not close a *C* syllable. In close connexion they are therefore followed by the aspirated *B*ᵉ*gadk*ᵉ*phath*, e. g. וּמָצָא בָהּ, &c. On the other hand, syllables are closed by the consonantal ו and י (except קָרָתֹהוּ Is 34¹¹ ; שָׁלֵו בָהּ Ez 23⁴² ; ψ 68¹⁸), and by ה with *Mappiq* ; hence e. g. there is Dageš lene in פִּיהֶם עָלַי and always after יְהֹוָה, since the *Q*ᵉ*rê perpetuum* of this word (§ 17) assumes the reading אֲדֹנָי.

2. In a number of cases Dageš lene is inserted, although a vowel precedes in *d* close connexion. This almost always occurs with the prefixes בְּ and כְּ in the combinations בְּב, כְּכ, פְּפ (i. e. when a *B*ᵉ*gadk*ᵉ*phath* with Š*ᵉ*wâ precedes the same or a kindred aspirate) and בְּמ (see Baer, *L. Psalmorum*, 1880, p. 92,[2] on ψ 23³) ; cf. e. g. 1 S 25¹, Is 10⁹, ψ 34², Jb 19² ; כְּנ is uncertain ; כְּד, בְּד, and בְּכ according to David Qimḥi do not take Dageš, nor כְּנ, כְּב, and כְּפ according to the *Dikduke ha-ṭ*ᵉ*amim*, p. 30. Sometimes the *B*ᵉ*gadk*ᵉ*phath* letters, even with a full vowel, take Dageš before a spirant (and even before ח in בַּחֲמִשָּׁה 1 K 12³²) ; cf. the instances mentioned above, § 20 *e* (mostly *tenues* before א). In all these cases the object is to prevent too great an accumulation of aspirates. The LXX, on the other hand, almost always represent the כ and

---

[1] Cf. Delitzsch, *Ztschr. f. luth. Theol. u. Kirche*, 1878, p. 585 ff.
[2] Also *L. Proverbiorum*, 1880, Praef. p. ix ; and *Dikduke ha-ṭ*ᵉ*amim*, p. 30 (in German in König's *Lehrgeb.*, i. p. 62).

ב, even at the beginning of a syllable, by χ and φ; Χερούβ, Χαλδαῖοι, Φαρφάρ, &c.—The forms בְּדֹלַח (after וְשַׂמְתִּי) Is 54¹¹, and בִּלְבַל (after וְנִלְאֵיתִי) Jer 20⁹ are doubly anomalous.

e   (2) In the middle of words after *Šᵉwâ quiescens*, i.e. at the beginning of a syllable immediately after a vowelless consonant,[1] e.g. יִרְפָּא *yirpā* (*he heals*), קְטַלְתֶּם *ye have killed*; but after *Šᵉwâ mobile*, e.g. רְפָא *rᵉphā* (*heal thou*), כָּבְדָה *she was heavy*.

f   On וַיִּשֶׁב, קְטַלְתְּ and similar forms, see § 10 *i*.

Whether *Šᵉwâ* be vocal and consequently causes the aspiration of a following *tenuis*, depends upon the origin of the particular form. It is almost always vocal

   (*a*) When it has arisen from the weakening of a strong vowel, e.g. רְדְפוּ *pursue ye* (not רָדְפוּ) from רְדֹף; מַלְכֵי (not מַלְכֵּי), because originally *mălăkhê*, but מַלְכִּי from the ground-form *malk*.

   (*b*) With the כ of the pronominal suffixes of the 2nd pers. ךָ—, כֶם—, כֶן—, since Šᵉwâ mobile is characteristic of these forms (see § 58 *f*; § 91 *b*).

Rem. Forms like שָׁלַחַתְּ *thou* (fem.) *hast sent*, in which we should expect an aspirated ת after the vowel, cf. וְלַחַתְּ Ex 18⁹, have arisen from שָׁלַחְתְּ, יִחַדְ, &c.; Pathaḥ being here simply a helping vowel has no influence on the tenuis; cf. § 28 *e*.

§ 22. *Peculiarities of the Gutturals.*

a   The four gutturals ח, ה, ע, א, in consequence of their peculiar pronunciation, have special characteristics, but א, as the weakest of these sounds, and sometimes also ע (which elsewhere as one of the harder gutturals is the opposite of א), differ in several respects from the stronger ה and ח.

b   1. They do not admit of *Dageš forte*, since, in consequence of a gradual weakening of the pronunciation (see below, note 2), the strengthening of the gutturals was hardly audible to the Masoretes. But a distinction must be drawn between (*a*) the complete omission of the strengthening, and (*b*) the mere *echo* of it, commonly called *half* doubling, but better, *virtual* strengthening.

c   In the former case, the short vowel before the guttural would stand in an open syllable, and must accordingly be lengthened or modified.[2]

---

[1] The exceptions יְקַתְאֵל Jos 15³⁸ (see *Minḥat shay*, on this passage), 2 K 14⁷, and יָקְדְעָם Jos 15⁵⁶ may perhaps be due to the character of the ק.

[2] Cf. *terra* and the French *terre*, the German *Rolle* and the French *rôle*; German *drollig* and French *drôle*. The omission of the strengthening shows a deterioration of the language. Arabic still admits of the strengthening of gutturals in all cases.

For a distinction must again be drawn between the full lengthening of
Pathaḥ into *Qameṣ*—mostly before א (*always* under the ה of the
article, see § 35), as a rule also before ע, less frequently before ה, and
least often before ח—and the modification of *Pathaḥ* to *Sᵉghôl*,
mostly before a guttural with *Qameṣ*. In the other case (*virtual
strengthening*) the *Dageš* is still omitted, but the strengthening is
nevertheless regarded as having taken place, and the preceding vowel
therefore remains short. This *virtual* strengthening occurs most
frequently with ח, usually with ה, less frequently with ע, and very
seldom with א. Examples of (*a*) מֵאֵן, הָאָדָם, הָעָם, הָהָר, יֶחֱבָא (for
yiḥḥābhē'); also אֶחָד, הֶחָג, הֶהָרִים, הֶעָנִי (see more fully on the pointing
of the article before ע in § 35).—Of (*b*) מָחוּט, הַחֹדֶשׁ (from *minḥûṭ*),
הַהוּא, בְּעֵר, נְאֵץ, &c.—In all these cases of virtual strengthening the
Dageš forte is to be regarded at least as implied (hence called *Dageš
forte implicitum, occultum,* or *delitescens*).

2. They prefer before them, and sometimes after them (cf. *h*), *d*
a short A-sound, because this vowel is organically the nearest akin
to the gutturals. Hence

(*a*) before a guttural, *Pathaḥ* readily (and always before ה, ח, ע
closing a syllable) takes the place of another short vowel or of
a rhythmically long *ē* or *ō*, e.g. זֶבַח *sacrifice*, not *zĕbĕḥ*; שֵׁמַע *report*,
not *šēmĕ'*. This is more especially so when *a* was the original vowel
of the form, or is otherwise admissible. Thus in the Imperat. and
Imperf. Qal of guttural verbs, שְׁלַח *send thou*, יִשְׁלַח *he will send* (not
yišlŏḥ); Perf. Pi'el שִׁלַּח (but in Pausa שִׁלֵּחַ); יַחְמֹד *he will desire* (not
yiḥmōd); וַיָּנַח *and he rested* (not *wayyānŏḥ*); נַעַר *a youth*. In שְׁלַח
and יַחְמֹד *ă* is the original vowel.

Rem. In such cases as דְּשֵׁא, טֶנֶא, פֶּלֶא, פֶּרֶא, the א has no consonantal *e*
value, and is only retained orthographically (see § 23 *a*).

(*b*) After a heterogeneous long vowel, i. e. after all except *Qameṣ*, *f*
the hard gutturals[1] (consequently not א), when standing at the end
of the word, require the insertion of a rapidly uttered *ă* (*Pathaḥ
furtivum*) between themselves and the vowel. This *Pathaḥ* is placed
under the guttural, but sounded *before* it. It is thus merely an
orthographic indication not to neglect the guttural sound in pronunciation, e.g. רוּחַ *rûᵃḥ*, נוֹעַ, רֵעַ, הִשְׁלִיחַ, נָבוֹהַּ (when consonantal ה is

---

[1] Prätorius, *Ueber den rückweich. Accent im Hebr.*, Halle, 1897, p. 17, &c.,
remarks that Pathaḥ furtivum has not arisen merely under the influence of
the guttural, but is due to a duplication of the accented syllable, so that e.g.
יָצוּר, יָשִׁיב would also be pronounced *yaṣiⁱbh*, *yaṣûᵘdh* although the short
intermediate vowel was not so noticeable as before a guttural.

final it necessarily takes Mappíq), but e. g. רוּחִי, &c., since here the rapidly uttered *ă* is no longer heard.

g *I^a ch* for *ich*, &c., in some Swiss dialects of German, is analogous ; a *furtive Pathaḥ* is here involuntarily intruded before the deep guttural sound. In Arabic the same may be heard in such words as *mesiaḥ*, although it is not expressed in writing. The LXX (and Jerome, cf. *ZAW.* iv. 79) write ε, sometimes α, instead of *furtive Pathaḥ*, e. g. נֹחַ Νῶε, יָדוּעַ Ἰεδδουά (also Ἰαδδού).

h Rem. 1. The guttural may also have an influence upon the *following* vowel, especially in Segholate forms, e. g. נַעַר (not na'ĕr) a *youth*, בַּעַל (not pō'ĕl) *deed*. The only exceptions are רֶחֶם, לֶחֶם, בֹּהֶן, אֹהֶל.

i 2. Where in the present form of the language an *ĭ*, whether original or attenuated from *Pathaḥ*, would stand before or after a guttural in the first syllable of a word, a *Sᵉghôl* as being between *ă* and *ĭ* is frequently used instead, e. g. יֶחְבַּשׁ (also יַחְבֹּשׁ), יֶהְגּוּ, חֶבְלֵי, נֶאְדָּר, עֶזְרִי, &c.

k On the other hand, the slighter and sharper *Ḥireq* is retained even under gutturals when the following consonant is sharpened by *Dageš forte*, e. g. הָלֵּל, הִנֵּה, חִטָּה ; but when this sharpening is removed, Sᵉghôl is again apt to appear, e.g. הַפִּיוֹן constr. הֶנְיוֹן, חִזָּיוֹן constr. חֶזְיוֹן.

l 3. Instead of *simple Šᵉwâ mobile*, the gutturals take without exception à *compound Šᵉwâ*, e. g. אֲנִי, אֱמֹר, אֲקַטֵּל, שְׁחַטוּ, &c.

m 4. When a guttural with *quiescent Šᵉwâ* happens to close a syllable in the middle of a word, the strongly closed syllable (with *quiescent Šᵉwâ*) may remain ; necessarily so with ח, ע, and ה at the end of the tone-syllable, e. g. יָדַעְתָּ, שָׁלַחְתִּי, but also *before* the tone (see examples under *i*), even with א.

But in the syllable before the tone and further back, the closed syllable is generally opened artificially by a *Ḥaṭeph* (as being suited to the guttural) taking the place of the *quiescent Šᵉwâ*, and in particular that *Ḥaṭeph* which repeats the sound of the preceding vowel, e. g. יַחֲשֹׁב (also יַחְשֹׁב) ; יֶחֱזַק (also יֶחְזַק) ; פָּעֳלוֹ *pŏ'ŏlô* (for *pŏ'lô*). But when, owing to a flexional change, the strong vowel following the *Ḥaṭeph* is weakened into *Šᵉwâ mobile*, then instead of the *Ḥaṭeph* its full vowel is written, e. g. יַעַמְדוּ (from יַעֲמֹד), נֶעֶרְמוּ, פְּעֻלָּה (from פֹּעַל). The original forms, according to § 28 *c*, were *ya'mᵉdhû, ne'rᵉmû, pŏ'lᵉkhā*. Hence יַעַמְדוּ, &c., are really only different orthographic forms of יַעֲמְדוּ, &c., and would be better transcribed by *ya'ᵃmᵉdhû*, &c.

n Rem. 1. On the use of simple or compound Šᵉwâ in guttural verbs, see further §§ 62–65.

o 2. Respecting the choice between the three *Ḥaṭephs*, it may be remarked :
(a) ח, ה, ע at the beginning of a syllable prefer ⁔, but א prefers ⁔, e. g. חֲמוֹר *ass*, הֲרֹג *to kill*, אֱמֹר *to say* ; when farther from the tone syllable, however, the ⁔ even under א changes into the lighter ⁔, e. g. אֱלִי (poetic for אֶל־) *to*, but אֲלֵיכֶם *to you*, אֱכֹל *to eat*, but אֲכָל־ ('ᵃkhŏl, toneless on account

of Maqqēph). Cf. § 27 *w*. The 1st pers. sing. imperf. Pi‘ēl regularly has ⸺.
Likewise ⸺ is naturally found under א in cases where the *Ḥaṭeph* arises
from a weakening of an original *ă* (e. g. אֲרִי *lion*, ground-form *'ary*), and ⸺
if there be a weakening of an original *u* (e. g. אֳנִי *a fleet*, עֳנִי *affliction*, cf.
§ 93 *q, z*).

(*b*) In the middle of a word after a long vowel, a *Ḥaṭeph-Pathaḥ* takes the *p*
place of a *simple Šᵉwâ mobile*, e. g. הֶעֱלָה מֵאֲנָה (see § 63 *p*); but if a short
vowel precedes, the choice of the *Ḥaṭeph* is generally regulated by it, e.g.
Perf. Hiph. הֶעֱמִיד (see above, *i*), Infin. הַעֲמִיד (regular form הַקְטִיל); Perf.
Hoph. הָעֳמַד (regular form הָקְטַל); but cf. שְׁחֲדוּ Jb 6²² (§ 64 *a*).

5. The ר, which in sound approximates to the gutturals (§ 6 *g*), *q*
shares with the gutturals proper their first, and to a certain extent
their second, peculiarity, viz.

(*a*) The exclusion of the strengthening, instead of which the preceding vowel is almost always lengthened, e. g. בֵּרַךְ *he has blessed* for
birrakh, בָּרֵךְ *to bless* for *barrēkh*.

(*b*) The preference for *ă* as a preceding vowel, e. g. וַיַּרְא *and he saw r*
(from יִרְאֶה); וַיָּסַר both for וַיָּ֫סָר *and he turned back*, and for וַיָּ֫סֶר *and
he caused to turn back*.

The exceptions to *a* are מָרַּת *mŏrrăth*, Pr 14¹⁰; כָּרַּת *khŏrrăth* and שָׁרֵךְ *šŏrrēkh*, S
Ez 16⁴ (cf. Pr 3⁸); שֵׁרָאשִׁי Ct 5²; הָרֵעֲמָהּ 1 S 1⁶; הִרְאִיתֶם 1 S 10²⁴, 17²⁵,
2 K 6³²; הִרְדִּיפֻהוּ Ju 20⁴³ (cf. § 20 *h*); מִרְדֹּף 1 S 23²⁸, 2 S 18¹⁶; also on account
of דָּחִיק (§ 20 *c*), Pr 15¹, 20²², 2 Ch 26¹⁰; and on account of אַתֵּי מְרַחִיק
(§ 20 *f*) 1 S 15⁶, Jer 39¹², Hb 3¹³, Pr 11²¹, Jb 39⁹, Ez 9⁶. A kind of virtual
strengthening (after מַ for מִן) is found in מִרְנְוָךְ Is 14³. In Samaritan and
Arabic this strengthening has been retained throughout, and the LXX write
e. g. Σάῤῥα for שָׂרָה.

§ 23. *The Feebleness of the Gutturals* א *and* ה.

1. The א, a light and scarcely audible guttural breathing, as a rule *a*
entirely loses its slight consonantal power whenever it stands without
a vowel at the end of a syllable. It then remains (like the German
h in *roh, geh, nahte*) merely as a sign of the preceding long vowel, e.g.
מָצָא, מָלֵא, הוֹצִיא (but when a syllable is added with an introductory
vowel, according to *b* below, we have, e.g. הוֹצִיאַנִי, מְצָאַנִי, since the א
then stands at the beginning of the syllable, not הוֹצִיאנִי, מְצָאנִי), מָצָא,
כָּלוּא (cf., however, § 74 *a*) מָצָאתָ (for *māṣa'tā*), תִּמָּצֶאנָה. Similarly
in cases like חֵטְא, וַיִּרָא, שָׁוְא, &c. (§ 19 *l*), and even in פֶּלֶא, דְּשֶׁא (see
above, § 22 *e*), the א only retains an orthographic significance.

2. On the other hand, א is in general retained as a strong con- *b*
sonant whenever it begins a syllable, e. g. אָמַר, מָאֲסוּ, or when it is
protected by a *Ḥaṭeph* after a short syllable, e. g. לֶאֱכֹל, and finally,

when it stands in a closed syllable with quiescent *Šᵉwâ* after a preceding *Sᵉghôl* or *Pathaḥ*, e.g. וַיֶּאְסֹר, נֶאְדָּר *näʾdār*, יַאְדִּ֫ימוּ *yaʾdîmû.* Even in such cases the consonantal power of א may be entirely lost, viz.

c　(*a*) when it would stand with a long vowel in the middle of a word after *Šᵉwâ mobile.* The long vowel is then occasionally thrown back into the place of the *Šᵉwâ*, and the א is only retained orthographically, as an indication of the etymology, e.g. רָאשִׁים *heads* (for *rᵉʾâšîm*), מָאתַ֫יִם *two hundred* (for *mᵉʾātháyim*), שָׁ֫אטְךָ Ez 25⁶ for שְׁאָטְךָ; בּוֹדְאָם Neh 6⁸ for בְּדְאָם; מַאֻם Jb 31⁷, Dn 1⁴ for מְאוּם; פֵּארָה for פְּאֵרָה Is 10³³; חֹטָאים *ḥôṭîm*, 1 S 14³³ for חֹטְאִים (cf. § 74 *h*, and § 75 *oo*); הָרֵאוּבֵנִי Nu 34¹⁴, from רְאוּבֵן; so always חַטּאת or חַטָּאות 1 K 14¹⁶, Mi 1⁵, &c., for חַטָּאות. Sometimes a still more violent suppression of the א occurs at the beginning of a syllable, which then causes a further change in the preceding syllable, e.g. מְלָאכָה *work* for מַלְאָכָה (as in the Babylonian punctuation), יִשְׁמָעֵאל for יִשְׁמְעֵאל; שְׂמֹאל or שְׂמֹאול *the left hand*, ground form *simʾâl.*

d　(*b*) When it originally closed a syllable. In these cases א is generally (by § 22 *m*) pronounced with a *Ḥaṭeph*, ◌ֲ or ◌ֱ. The preceding short vowel is, however, sometimes lengthened and retains the following א only orthographically, e.g. וַיָּ֫אצֶל Nu 11²⁵ for וַיֶּאֱצֶל (cf. Ju 9⁴¹), and פָּארוּר Jo 2⁶ for בַּאֲרוּר; לֵאמֹר for לֶאֱמֹר; לֵאלֹהִים for לֶאֱלֹהִים; but the contraction does not take place in לֶאֱלִֽילֶיהָ Is 10¹¹. The short vowel is retained, although the consonantal power of א is entirely lost, in וָארֵד, &c. (see § 102 *m*), וַיַּאת Is 41²⁵, וְאֶבְּדֶךָ Ez 28¹⁶ for וָאַאַבֶּדְךָ; cf. Dt 24¹⁰, 1 K 11³⁹, Is 10¹³.

e　Instead of this א which has lost its consonantal value, one of the vowel letters ו and י is often written according to the nature of the sound, the former with *ô* and the latter with *ê* and *î*, e.g. רֵים *buffalo* for רְאֵם. At the end of the word ה also is written for א, יִמְלֶה *he fills* for יִמְלָא Jb 8²¹ (see below, *l*).

f　3. When א is only preserved orthographically or as an indication of the etymology (quiescent), it is sometimes entirely dropped (cf. § 19 *k*), e.g. יָצָ֫תִי Jb 1²¹ for יָצָ֫אתִי; מָלֵ֫תִי Jb 32¹⁸ for מָלֵ֫אתִי; מָצָ֫תִי Nu 11¹¹; וַתֵּחֶז 2 S 20⁹; וַיַּרְפֻּ Jer 8¹¹ for וַיְרַפְּאוּ; וַתֻּזְרֵ֫נִי 2 S 22⁴⁰, but וַתְּאַזְּרֵ֫נִי ψ 18⁴⁰; תּוֹמִם Gn 25²⁴ for תְּאוֹמָם; אַחֲטֶ֫נָּה 31³⁹ for אַחַטְּאֶ֫נָּה; שְׁלֹתֶךָ 1 S 1¹⁷ for שָׁאֵל״; רֵמִים ψ 22²² for רְאֵמִים; גֵּוָה Jb 22²⁹ for גֵּאֲוָה; הֻבְּרֵ֫תִי 1 Ch 11³⁹ for הַבְּאֵר״, and so 2 S 23³⁷; שֵׁרִית 1 Ch 12³⁸ for שְׁאֵרִית; לַהְשׁוֹת 2 K 19²⁵ *Kᵉthîbh* for לְהַשְׁאוֹת (cf. Is 37²⁶); חֶמְאָה¹ Jb 29⁶ for חֵמָה. In מַבֹּלֶת

---

¹ In Jer 22²³, נֵחַנְתְּ is unquestionably a corruption of נחנת for נֶאֱנַחַתְּ.

1 K 5²⁵ (for "מְאָכ) the strengthening of the following consonant by Dageš compensates for the loss of the א; in מְסֹרֶת Ez 20³⁷, if for "מְאָס (but read מוּסָר, with Cornill), the preceding vowel is lengthened; cf. above, *c*. On אֹמַר for אָאמַר, see § 68 *g*.

Rem. 1. In Aramaic the א is much weaker and more liable to change than in Hebrew. In literary Arabic, on the other hand, it is almost always a firm consonant. According to Arabic orthography, א serves also to indicate a long *a*, whereas in Hebrew it very rarely occurs as a mere vowel letter after Qames; as in קָאם Ho10¹⁴ for קָם *he rose up*; רֹאשׁ Pr10⁴, 13²³ for רֹשׁ *poor*; but in 2 S 11¹ the *Kᵉthibh* הַמַּלְאָכִים *the messengers*, is the true reading; cf. § 7 *b*.

2. In some cases at the beginning of a word, the א, instead of a compound *Šᵉwâ*, takes the corresponding full vowel, e. g. אֱזוֹר *girdle* for אֲזוֹר; cf. § 84 *a*, *q*, and the analogous cases in § 52 *n*, § 63 *p*, § 76 *d*, § 93 *r* (אֹהָלִים).

3. An א is sometimes added at the end of the word to a final *û*, *î*, or *ô*, e. g. הָלְכוּא for הָלְכוּ Jos 10²⁴(before א !), אָבוּא Is 28¹². These examples, however, are not so much instances of 'Arabic orthography', as early scribal errors, as in יִשָּׁוְא Je 10⁵ for יִנָּשֵׂאוּ; and in נָשֹׂוא ψ 139²⁰ for נָשְׂאוּ. Cf. also יֵהוּא Ec 11³ (§ 75 *s*); נָקִיא for נָקִי *pure*; לוּא for לוּ *if*; אֵפוֹא for אֵפוֹ *then (enclitic)*; רִבּוֹא for רִבּוֹ *myriad*, Neh 7⁶⁶·⁷¹. On הוּא and הִיא see § 32 *k*.

4. The ה is stronger and firmer than the א, and never loses its consonantal sound (i. e. *quiesces*) in the middle of a word [1] except in the cases noted below, in which it is completely elided by syncope. On the other hand, at the end of a word it is always a mere vowel letter, unless expressly marked by *Mappîq* as a strong consonant (§ 14 *a*). Yet at times the consonantal sound of ה at the end of a word is lost, and its place is taken by a simple ה or more correctly הֿ, with *Rāphè* as an indication of its non-consonantal character, e. g. לָהֿ *to her* for לָהּ, Zc 5¹¹, &c. (cf. § 103 *g*, and §§ 58 *g*, 91 *e*); cf. also יָהֿ for יָהּ (from יְהוּ) in proper names like יִרְמְיָהֿ, &c.—Finally, in very many cases a complete elision of the consonantal ה takes place by *syncope*: (*a*) when its vowel is thrown back to the place of a preceding *Šᵉwâ mobile* (see above, *c*, with א), e. g. לַבֹּקֶר for לְהַבֹּקֶר (the ה of the article being syncopated as it almost always is); כַּיּוֹם for כְּהַיּוֹם [but see § 35 *n*], בַּשָּׁמַיִם for בְּהַשָּׁמַיִם; יוֹנָתָן for יְהוֹנָתָן; perhaps also בְּנֵיהֶם for בְּנֵיהֶם Ez 27³². (*b*) By contraction of the vowels preceding and following the ה, e. g. סוּסוֹ (also written סוּסֹה) from *sûsahu* (*a + u = ô*).—A violent suppression of ה together with its vowel occurs in בָּם (from בְּהֶם), &c.

---

[1] Only apparent exceptions are such *proper names* as עֲשָׂהאֵל, פְּדָהצוּר, which are compounded of two words and hence are sometimes even divided. Cf. forms like חֲזָאֵל for חֲזָהאֵל. Another exception is יְפֶהפִיָּה, the reading of many MSS. for the artificially divided form יְפֶה־פִיָּה in the printed texts, Je 46²⁰.

l   Rem. In connexion with ō and ē, a ה which only marks the vowel ending is occasionally changed into ו or י (רָאוֹ = רָאֹה, חַפֵּי = חַפֵּה Ho 6⁹), and with any vowel into א in the later or Aramaic orthography, but especially with ā, e. g. שֵׁנָא *sleep*, ψ 127² for שֵׁנָה; נָשֹׂא Jer 23³⁹ for נָשֹׂא, &c. Thus it is evident that final ה as a vowel letter has only an orthographical importance.

§ 24. *Changes of the Weak Letters* ו *and* י.

Philippi, *Die Aussprache der semit. Konsonanten* ו *und* י (mentioned above, § 5 *b*, note 1), a thorough investigation of their phonetic value as consonantal, i. e. non-syllabic, vowel-sounds, not palatal or labial fricatives ; cf. also E. Sievers, *Metrische Studien*, i. 15.

a   ו and י are, as consonants, so weak, and approach so nearly to the corresponding vowels *u* and *i*, that under certain conditions they very readily merge into them. This fact is especially important in the formation of those weak stems, in which a ו or י occurs as one of the three radical consonants (§ 69 ff., § 85, § 93).

1. The cases in which ו and י lose their consonantal power, i. e. merge into a vowel, belong almost exclusively to the middle and end of words ; at the beginning they remain as consonants.[1]

The instances may be classified under two heads :

b   (*a*) When either ו or י with *quiescent Šᵉwâ* stands at the end of a syllable immediately after a *homogeneous* vowel (*u* or *i*). It then merges in the homogeneous vowel, or more accurately it assumes its vowel-character (ו as *u*, י as *i*), and is then contracted with the preceding vowel into *one* vowel, necessarily long, but is mostly retained orthographically as a (quiescent) vowel letter. Thus הוּשַׁב for *huwšab*; יִיקַץ for *yiyqaṣ*; so also at the end of the word, e. g. עִבְרִי *a Hebrew*, properly *'ibrîy*, fem. עִבְרִיָּה, pl. עִבְרִים (and עִבְרִים); עָשׂוּ Jb 41²⁵ for עָשׂוּ (cf. עָשׂוּוֹת 1 S 25¹³ *Kᵉthîbh*). On the other hand, if the preceding vowel be heterogeneous, ו and י are retained as full consonants (on the pronunciation see § 8 *m*), e. g. שָׁלֵו *quiet*, זִו *the month of May*, גּוֹי *nation*, גְּלוּי *revealed*. But with a preceding ă the ו and י are mostly contracted into ô and ê (see below, *f*), and at the end of a word they are sometimes rejected (see below, *g*).

Complete syncope of ו before î occurs in אִי *island* for אֱוִי; עִי *ruins* for עֱוִי; רִי *watering* Jb 37¹¹ for רְוִי; [כִּי *burning* Is 3²⁴ for כְּוִי, cf. §§ 84ᵃ *c, e*, 93 *y*].

---

[1] Or as consonantal vowels (see above), and are then transcribed by P. Haupt, Philippi, and others, as ṷ, i̯, following the practice of Indogermanic philologists. ו for וּ *and*, alone is a standing exception, see § 26. 1 and § 104 *e*. On י = *i* at the beginning of a word, cf. § 47 *b*, note. According to § 19 *a*, end, *initial* ו in Hebrew almost always becomes י ; always in verbs originally פ״ו, § 69 *a*. Apart from a few proper names, initial ו occurs only in וָו *hook*, וָלָד *child* Gn 11³⁰, 2 S 6²³ *Kᵉthîbh* [elsewhere יֶלֶד], and the doubtful וָזָר Pr 21⁸.

Thus an initial יְ after the prefixes בְּ, וְ, כְּ, לְ, which would then be *c*
pronounced with ĭ (see § 28 *a*), and also almost always after מִ (see
§ 102 *b*), coalesces with the ĭ to î, e. g. בִּיהוּדָה *in Judah* (for בְּיְ),
וִיהוּדָה *and Judah*, בִּיאֹר *as the Nile*, לִיהוּדָה *for Judah*, מִידֵי *from the
hands of.*

(*b*) When ו and י without a vowel would stand at the end of the *d*
word after *quiescent Šᵉwâ*, they are either wholly rejected and only
orthographically replaced by ה (e.g. בְּכֵה from *bikhy*, as well as the
regularly formed בְּכִי *weeping*; cf. § 93 *x*) or become again vowel
letters. In the latter case י becomes a homogeneous *Ḥireq*, and also
attracts to itself the tone, whilst the preceding vowel becomes *Šᵉwâ*
(e.g. פְּרִי from *piry*, properly *pary*); ו is changed sometimes into
a toneless *u* (e.g. תֹּהוּ from *tuhw*).

Rem. In Syriac, where the weak letters more readily become vowel sounds, *c*
a simple *i* may stand even at the beginning of words instead of י or יְ. The
LXX also, in accordance with this, write Ἰουδά for יְהוּדָה, Ἰσαάκ for יִצְחָק.
Hence may be explained the *Syriac usage* in Hebrew of drawing back the
vowel *i* to the preceding consonant, which properly had a simple *vocal Šᵉwâ*,
e. g. (according to the reading of Ben-Naphtali[1]) וִילֶּלַת Jer 25³⁶ for וְיִלֶּלַת (so
Baer), בִּיתְרוֹן Ec 2¹³ for בְּיִתְרוֹן, cf. also the examples in § 20 *h*, note 2 ; even
וִיחַלּוּ Jb 29²¹ (in some editions) for וְיִחַלּוּ. According to Qimḥi (see § 47 *b*)
יִקְטֹל was pronounced as *iqṭōl*, and therefore the 1st pers. was pointed אֶקְטֹל
to avoid confusion. In fact the Babylonian punctuation always has ĭ for ă
in the 1st pers.

2. With regard to the *choice* of the long vowel, in which ו and י *f*
quiesce after such vocalization and contraction, the following rules
may be laid down :

(*a*) With a short *homogeneous* vowel ו and י are contracted into the
corresponding long vowel (û or î), see above, *b*.

(*b*) With short ă they form the diphthongs ô and ê according to
§ 7 *a*, e.g. מֵיטִיב from מַיְטִיב ; יוֹשִׁיב from יַוְשִׁיב, &c.[2]

Rem. The rejection of the half vowels ו and י (see above, *b*) occurs especially *g*
at the end of words after a heterogeneous vowel (ă), if according to the
nature of the form the contraction appears impossible. So especially in

---

[1] According to Abulwalid, Ben-Naphtali regarded the *Yodh* in *all* such cases
as a vowel letter.

[2] Instances in which no contraction takes place after ă are, מַיְמִינִים 1 Ch 12² ;
אַיְסִירֵם Ho 7¹² (but cf. § 70 *b*) ; הַיְשֵׁר ψ 5⁹ Qᵉrê ; the locatives בַּיְתָה, מִצְרַיְמָה,
&c.—On the suffix יְכִ֑י for יֶךְ֑ see § 91 *l*.—Sometimes both forms are
found, as עַוְלָה and עוֹלָה ; cf. חַי *living*, constr. state חֵי. Analogous is the
contraction of מָוֶת (ground-form *mawt*) *death*, constr. מוֹת ; עַיִן (ground-form
'*ayn* ['*ain*]) *eye*, constr. עֵין.

verbs ה״ל, e. g. originally גְּלֶה = (גְּלַי) = גְּלָי, since ă after the rejection of the י stands in an open syllable, and consequently must be lengthened to ā. The ה is simply an orthographic sign of the long vowel. So also שָׁלָה for *šālaw*.[1] On the origin of יִגְלֶה, see § 75 *e*; on קָם as perf. and part. of קוּם, see § 72 *b* and *g*; on יֵלֵד, &c., from וָלַד, see § 69 *b*.—On the weakening of ו and י to א, see § 93 *x*.

§ 25. *Unchangeable Vowels.*

a   What vowels in Hebrew are unchangeable, i.e. are not liable to attenuation (to Šᵉwâ), modification, lengthening, or shortening, can be known with certainty only from the nature of the grammatical forms, and in some cases by comparison with Arabic (cf. § 1 *m*). This holds good especially of the *essentially* long vowels, i. e. those long by *nature* or *contraction*, as distinguished from those which are only lengthened *rhythmically*, i. e. on account of the special laws which in Hebrew regulate the tone and the formation of syllables. The latter, when a change takes place in the position of the tone or in the division of syllables, readily become short again, or are reduced to a mere *vocal* Šᵉwâ.

b   1. The essentially long and consequently, as a rule (but cf. § 26 *p*, § 27 *n, o*), unchangeable vowels of the *second* and *third* class, *î, ê, û, ô*, can often be recognized by means of the vowel letters which accompany them (יִ_, ֵי, וּ, וֹ); e.g. יֵיטִיב *he does well*, הֵיכָל *palace*, גְּבוּל *boundary*, קוֹל *voice*. The *defective* writing (§ 8 *i*) is indeed common enough, e.g. יֵטִב and יֵטִיב for יֵיטִיב; גְּבֻל for גְּבוּל; קֹל for קוֹל, but this is merely an orthographic licence and has no influence on the quantity of the vowel; the *û* in גְּבֻל is just as necessarily long, as in גְּבוּל.

As an exception, a merely tone-long vowel of both these classes is sometimes written *fully*, e. g. יְקֹטוֹל for יְקֹטֹל.

c   2. The essentially or naturally long *â* (*Qameṣ impure*),[2] unless it has become *ô* (cf. § 9 *q*), has as a rule in Hebrew no representative among the consonants, while in Arabic it is regularly indicated by א; on the few instances of this kind in Hebrew, cf. § 9 *b*, § 23 *g*. The naturally long *â* and the merely tone-long *ā* therefore can only be distinguished by an accurate knowledge of the forms.

---

[1] The Arabic, in such cases, often writes etymologically גָּלְי, but pronounces *galā*. So the LXX סִינַי Σινᾶ, Vulg. *Sina*; cf. Nestle, *ZAW.* 1905, p. 362 f. But even in Arabic שְׁלָא is written for שָׁלַי and pronounced *salā*.

[2] By *vocales impurae* the older grammarians meant vowels properly followed by a vowel letter. Thus כְּתָב *kᵉthâbh* was regarded as merely by a licence for כְּתָאב, &c.

3. Short vowels in closed syllables (§ 26 *b*), which are not final, are *d* as a rule unchangeable, e. g. מַלְבּוּשׁ *garment,* מִדְבָּר *wilderness,* מַמְלָכָה *kingdom*; similarly, short vowels in sharpened syllables, i. e. before *Dageš forte,* e. g. גַּנָּב *thief.*

4. Finally, those long vowels are unchangeable which, owing to *e* the omission of the strengthening in a guttural or ר, have arisen by lengthening from the corresponding short vowels, and now stand in an open syllable, e. g. מֵאֵן for *mi̓"ēn*; בֹּרַךְ for *burrakh.*

§ 26. *Syllable-formation*[1] *and its Influence on the Quantity of Vowels.*

Apart from the unchangeable vowels (§ 25), the use of short or long *a* vowels, i.e. their lengthening, shortening, or change into vocal *Šᵉwâ,* depends on the *theory of syllable-formation.* The initial and final syllables especially require consideration.

1. The *initial* syllable. A syllable regularly begins with a consonant, or, in the case of initial ו and י (cf. note on § 5 *b*), a consonantal vowel.[2] The copula is a standing exception to this rule. According to the Tiberian pronunciation וְ *and* is resolved into the corresponding vowel וּ before *Šᵉwâ,* and the labials, e.g. וּמֶלֶךְ, וּדְבַר; the Babylonian punctuation in the latter cases writes וֹ, i.e. ו before a full vowel.

2. The *final* syllable. A syllable may end— *b*

(*a*) With a vowel, and is then called an *open* or *simple* syllable, e. g. in קָטְלָה where the first and last are open. See below, *e.*

(*b*) With *one* consonant, and is then called a *simple closed* or *com-* *c* *pound* syllable, as the second in לֵבָב, קָטַל. See below, *o, p.* Such are also the syllables ending in a strengthened consonant, as the first in קַטֵּל *qaṭ-ṭēl.* See below, *q.*

(*c*) With *two* consonants, a *doubly closed* syllable, as קֹשְׁטְ *qōšt,* קָטַלְתְּ. *d* Cf. below, *r,* and § 10 *i–l.*

3. *Open* or *simple* syllables have a long vowel, whether they have *e* the tone as in בְּךָ *in thee,* יֵלֵךְ *he goes,* or are toneless as in קָטַל, עֵנָב *a bunch of grapes.*[3] A long vowel (Qameṣ, less frequently Ṣere) is

---

[1] Cf. C. H. Toy, 'The Syllable in Hebrew,' *Amer. Journal of Philol.,* 1884, p. 494 ff. ; H. Strack, 'The Syllables in the Hebrew Language,' *Hebraica,* Oct. 1884, p. 73 ff.

[2] We are not taking account here of the few cases in which initial *Yodh* is represented as simple *i,* by being written אִי or אִ, see § 24 *e,* and especially § 47 *b,* note ; nor of certain other cases in which א with an initial vowel has only a graphic purpose, though it is indispensable in an unpointed text.

[3] In opposition to this fundamental law in Hebrew (a *long* vowel in an *open* syllable), the original short vowel is found always in Arabic, and sometimes

especially common in an open syllable before the tone (pretonic vowel),
e. g. רְכַב¹, קְטַל, יְקוּם, לְהֶם.

f *Short* vowels in *open* syllables occur :

(*a*) In apparently dissyllabic words formed by means of a helping vowel
from monosyllables, as נַחַל *brook*, בַּיִת *house*, יֶרֶב *let him increase*, from *naḥl,
bayt, yirb* ; cf. also ־ַיִם the ending of the dual (§ 88). But see § 28 *e*.

g (*b*) In the verbal suffix of the 1st pers. sing. (־ַנִי *me*), e. g. קְטָלַנִי (Arab.
qătălăni). The uncommon form ־ַנְ־, however (Gn 30⁶, cf. § 59*f*), proves that
the tone-bearing *Pathaḥ* produces a sharpening of the following sonant, and
thus virtually stands in a closed syllable, even when the *Nun* is not expressly
written with *Dageš*. In cases like וַאדֹנָי (§ 102 *m*) *Pathaḥ* is retained in the
counter-tone after the א has become quiescent.

h (*c*) Sometimes before the toneless ה‍ָ *local* (§ 90 *c*), e. g. מִדְבָּרָה *towards the
wilderness* ; only, however, in the constr. state (1 K 19¹⁵), since the toneless
suffix ה‍ָ does not affect the character of the form (especially when rapidly
pronounced in close connexion) ; otherwise it is מִדְבָּרָה.

In all these cases the short vowel is also supported by the tone, either the
principal tone of the word, or (as in *h*) by the secondary tone in the constr.
st., or by the counter-tone with *Metheg*, as in וַאדֹנָי above, *g* ; cf. the effect of
the *arsis* on the short vowel in classical prosody.

i (*d*) In the combinations ־ֲ־ַ, ־ֳ־ָ, ־ֱ־ֶ, e. g. נַעֲרוֹ *his boy*, יֶאְסֹר
he will bind, פָּעֳלוֹ *his deed*. In all these cases the syllable was at first really
closed, and it was only when the guttural took a *Ḥateph* that it became in
consequence open (but cf. e. g. יֶאְסֹר and יֶאֱסֹר). The same vowel sequence
arises wherever a preposition בְּ, כְּ, לְ, or וְ copulative is prefixed to an
initial syllable which has a *Ḥateph*, since the former then takes the vowel

---

in the other Semitic languages, except of course in the case of *naturally* long
vowels. The above examples are pronounced in Arabic *bĭkă, qătălă, 'ĭnăb*.
Although it is certain therefore that in Hebrew also,·at an earlier period,
short vowels were pronounced in open syllables, it may still be doubted
whether the present pronunciation is due *merely* to an artificial practice
followed in the solemn recitation of the O. T. text. On this hypothesis we
should have still to explain, e. g. the undoubtedly very old lengthening of *ĭ*
and *ŭ* in an open syllable into *ē* and *ō*.

¹ That these pretonic vowels are really *long* is shown by Brockelmann, *Z A.*
xiv. 343 f., from the transcription of Hebrew proper names in the Nestorian
(Syriac) punctuation, and e. g. from the Arabic 'Ibrâhim = אַבְרָהָם. He
regards their lengthening in the syllable before the tone as a means adopted
by the Masoretes to preserve the pronunciation of the traditional vowels.
This explanation of the pretonic vowels as due to a precaution against their
disappearing, is certainly right ; as to whether the precaution can be ascribed
to the Masoretes, see the previous note. For the pretonic vowel the Arabic
regularly has a short vowel (*lăhŭm, yăqûm*, &c.), the Aramaic simply a vocal
Šewâ (לְהוֹן, יְקוּם, קְטַל, רְכַב); and even in Hebrew, when the tone is thrown
forward the pretonic vowel almost always becomes *Šewâ*, see § 27. It would,
however, be incorrect to assume from this that the pretonic vowel has taken
the place of *Šewâ* only on account of the following tone-syllable. It always
arises from an original short vowel, since such a vowel is mostly lengthened
in an open syllable before the tone, but when the tone is moved forward it
becomes *Šewâ*.

contained in the *Ḥaṭeph* (see § 102 *d* and § 104 *d*). To the same category belong also the cases where these prepositions with Hireq stand before a consonant with simple Šᵉwâ mobile, e. g. בִּדְבַר, כִּדְבַר, &c.

(e) In forms like יֶחֶזְקוּ *yăḥă-zᵉ-qû* (they are strong), פָּעָלְךָ *põ'ŏ lᵉkhă* (thy *k* deed). These again are cases of the subsequent opening of closed syllables (hence, e. g. יֶחֶזְקוּ also occurs) ; פָּעָלְךָ is properly *põ'lᵉkhă* ; cf. generally § 22 *m*, end, and § 28 *c*.

Such cases as אָחִים הֶחָדָשׁ (§ 96), הַחְתֹּת (§ 67 *w*) do not come under this *l* head, since they all have *ă* in a virtually sharpened syllable ; nor does the tone-bearing *Sᵉghôl* in suffixes (e.g. דְּבָרֶךָ), nor *Sᵉghôl* for *ă* before a guttural with *Qameṣ* (§ 22 *c*). On קֳדָשִׁים and שֳרָשִׁים, see § 9 *v*.

4. The independent syllables with a firm vowel which have been *m* described above, are frequently preceded by a single consonant with vocal Šᵉwâ, simple or compound. Such a consonant with vocal Šᵉwâ never has the value of an independent syllable, but rather attaches itself so closely to the following syllable that it forms practically one syllable with it, e. g. לְחִי (cheek) *lᵉḥî* ; חֳלִי (sickness) *ḥŏlî* ; יִלְמְדוּ *yil-mᵉdhû*. This concerns especially the prefixes וְ, בְּ, כְּ, לְ. See § 102.

The *Šᵉwâ mobile* is no doubt in all such cases weakened from an original *n* full vowel (e. g. יִקְטְלוּ Arab. *yaqtŭ'û*, בֵּךְ Arab. *bĭkă*, &c.) ; from this, however, it cannot be inferred that the Masoretes regarded it as forming a kind of *open* syllable, for this would be even more directly opposed to their fundamental law (viz. that a long vowel should stand in an open syllable), than are the exceptions cited above, *f–k*. Even the use of Metheg with Šᵉwâ in special cases (see § 16 *f*) is no proof of such a view on the part of the Masoretes.

5. *Closed* syllables ending with one consonant, when without the *o* tone, necessarily have *short* vowels, whether at the beginning or at the end of words,[1] e. g. מַלְכָּה *queen*, חֶשְׁבּוֹן *understanding*, חָכְמָה *wisdom*, וַיָּסָר *and he turned back*, וַיָּקֶם, וַיָּקָם (*wayyāqŏm*).

A *tone-bearing* closed syllable may have either a long or short vowel, *p* but if the latter, it must as a rule be either Pathaḥ or Sᵉghôl.[2] The tone-bearing closed penultima admits, of the *long* vowels, only the tone-long *ā, ē, ō*, not the longest *î, ê, ô, û*; of the *short* vowels, only *ă, ĕ*, not *ĭ, ŭ, ŏ* (but on *ĭ* and *ŭ*, see § 29 *g*). Thus יַקְטִילוּ (3rd pl. masc. Imperf. Hiph.) but תִּקְטֹלְנָה 3rd pl. fem., and קֹלוּ (2nd pl. masc. Imperat. Qal) but קֹמְנָה fem.

---

[1] In exceptions such as שְׁת־לִי Gn 4²⁵ (where *šăt* is required by the character of the form, although the closed syllable has lost the tone owing to the following Maqqeph), Metheg is used to guard against a wrong pronunciation ; similarly *ē* is sometimes retained before Maqqeph, e.g. שֵׁם־ Gn 2¹³ ; עֵץ־ Gn 2¹⁶.

[2] See § 9 *e, f*. *ĭ* occurs thus only in the particles אִם, עִם, מִן ; but these usually (מִן always) are rendered toneless by a following Maqqeph. Cf. also such forms as וַיֵּשֶׁב § 26 *r* and § 75 *q*.

q **6.** A special kind of closed syllables are the *sharpened*, i. e. those which end in the same (strengthened) consonant with which the following syllable begins, e. g. אִמִּי *'im-mî*, כֻּלּוֹ *kŭl-lô*. If without the tone, they have, like the rest, short vowels; but, if bearing the tone, either short vowels as כֻּלּוֹ, הִנֵּנוּ, or long, as הֵמָּה שָׁמָּה, הֵמָּה.

On the omission of the strengthening of a consonant at the end of a word, see § 20 *l*.

r **7.** Syllables ending with *two* consonants occur only at the end of words, and have most naturally short vowels, קָטַלְתְּ, וַיֵּשְׁבְּ; but sometimes *Ṣere*, as נֵרְדְּ, וַיֵּבְךְּ, or *Ḥolem*, תּוֹסְףְּ קֹשְׁטְ. Cf., however, § 10 *i*. Usually the harshness of pronunciation is avoided by the use of a helping vowel (§ 28 *e*).

§ 27. *The Change of the Vowels, especially as regards Quantity.*

a The changes in sound through which the Hebrew language passed, before it assumed the form in which we know it from the Masoretic text of the O.T. (see § 2 *k*), have especially affected its vowel system. A precise knowledge of these vowel changes, which is indispensable for the understanding of most of the present forms of the language, is derived partly from the phenomena which the language itself presents in the laws of derivation and inflexion, partly from the comparison of the kindred dialects, principally the Arabic. By these two methods, we arrive at the following facts as regards Hebrew:

b 1. That in an open syllable the language has frequently retained only a half-vowel (*Šewâ mobile*), where there originally stood a full short vowel, e. g. עֲגָלָה (ground-form *'ăgălăt*) *a waggon*, צְדָקָה (ground-form *ṣădăqăt*) *righteousness*, קְטָלוֹ (Arab. *qătălû*), יְקַטְּלוּ (Arab. *jŭqattĭlû*).

c 2. That vowels originally short have in the tone-syllable, as also in the open syllable preceding it, been generally changed into the corresponding tone-long vowels, *ă* into *ā*, *ĭ* into *ē*, *ŭ* into *ō* (see § 9, *a–e, k, r*). If, however, the tone be shifted or weakened, these tone-long vowels mostly revert to their original shortness, or, occasionally, are still further shortened, or reduced to mere *Šewâ mobile*, or, finally, are entirely lost through a change in the division of syllables; e. g. מָטָר (Arab. *măṭăr*) *rain*, when in close dependence on a following genitive in the *construct state*), becomes מְטַר; עָקֵב (Arab. *'ăqĭb*) *heel*, dual עֲקֵבַיִם, dual *construct* (with attenuation of the original *ă* of the first syllable to *ĭ*) עִקְּבֵי [on the פ, see § 20 *h*]; יָקְטֹל (Arab. *yăqtŭl*), plur. יִקְטְלוּ (Arab. *yăqtŭlû*). For instances of complete loss, as in כַּסְפִּי, cf. § 93 *m*.

According to § 26, the following details of vowel-change must be observed :

1. The original, or a kindred short vowel reappears— *d*

(*a*) When a closed syllable loses the tone (§ 26 *o*). Thus, יָד *hand*, but יַד־יְהוָֹה *the hand of Yahwe*; בֵּן *son*, but בֶּן־הַמֶּלֶךְ *the son of the king*; כֹּל *the whole*, but כָּל־הָעָם *the whole of the people* ; so also when a tone-bearing closed syllable loses the tone on taking a suffix, e. g. אֹיֵב *enemy*, but אֹיִבְךָ *thy enemy*; finally, when the tone recedes, יָקָם, but וַיָּ֫קָם (*wayyāqŏm*); יֵלֵךְ, but וַיֵּ֫לֶךְ.

(*b*) To the same category belong cases like סֵפֶר *book*, but סִפְרִי *my book*; קֹדֶשׁ *holiness*, but קָדְשִׁי *my holiness*. In spite of the helping vowel, סֵפֶר and קֹדֶשׁ are really closed syllables with a tone-long vowel; when the syllable loses the tone, the original *ĭ* or *ŏ* (properly *ŭ*) reappears.

The same is true of syllables with a virtually sharpened final consonant: the lengthening of original *ĭ* to *ē* and *ŭ* to *ō* takes place only in a tone-bearing syllable; in a toneless syllable the *ĭ* or *ŏ* (or *ŭ*) remains, e. g. אֵם *mother*, but אִמִּי *my mother*; חֹק *law*, plur. חֻקִּים; but עֹז *strength*, עֻזִּי (and עָזִּי) *my strength*.

2. The lengthening of the short vowel to the corresponding long, *e* takes place—

(*a*) When a closed syllable becomes open by its final consonant being transferred to a suffix beginning with a vowel, or in general to the following syllable, e. g. קְטָלוֹ, קָטַל *he has killed him* ; סוּקָתִי primarily from סֻקַּת. Similarly *ă* mostly becomes *ā* even before a suffix beginning with *Š^ewâ mobile*; e. g. קְטָלְךָ from קָטַל, סוּקָתְךָ from סֻקַּת.

(*b*) When a syllable has become open by complete loss of the *f* strengthening of its final consonant (a guttural or *Rêš*), e. g. בֵּרַךְ for *bĭrrakh*, see § 22 *c*. Cf. also § 20 *n*.

(*c*) When a weak consonant (א, ו, י) following the short vowel *g* quiesces in this vowel, according to § 23 *a, c, d*, § 24 *f*, e. g. מָצָא for מַצְא, where the א, losing its consonantal value, loses also the power of closing the syllable, and the open syllable requires a long vowel.

(*d*) Very frequently through the influence of the *pause*, i. e. the *h* principal tone in the last word of a sentence or clause (§ 29 *k*). Sometimes also through the influence of the article (§ 35 *o*).

3. When a word increases at the end and the tone is consequently *i* moved forward, or when, in the *construct state* (see § 89), or otherwise in close connexion with the following word, its tone is weakened, in such cases a full vowel (short or tone-long) may, by a change in the

division of syllables, be weakened to *Šᵉwâ mobile*, or even be entirely lost, so that its place is taken by the mere syllable-divider (*Šᵉwâ quiescens*). Examples of the first case are, שֵׁם *name*, pl. שֵׁמוֹת, but שְׁמִי *my name*, שְׁמוֹתָם *their names*, דָּבָר *word*, constr. st. דְּבַר; צְדָקָה *righteousness*, constr. st. צִדְקַת; an example of the second case is, בְּרָכָה *blessing*, constr. st. בִּרְכַּת. Whether the vowel is retained or becomes *Šᵉwâ* (דָּם, דָּמִי, but שֵׁם, שְׁמִי), and which of the two disappears in two consecutive syllables, depends upon the character of the form in question. In general the rule is that only those vowels which stand in an open syllable can become *Šᵉwâ*.

Thus the change into *Šᵉwâ* takes place in—

k ⁀ (*a*) The *ā* and *ē* of the first syllable, especially in the inflexion of nouns, e. g. דָּבָר *word*, plur. דְּבָרִים; גָּדוֹל *great*, fem. גְּדוֹלָה; לֵבָב *heart*, לְבָבִי *my heart*; but also in the verb, תָּשׁוּב *she will return*, plur. תְּשׁוּבֶינָה, and so always, when the originally short vowel of the prefixes of the Imperfect comes to stand in an open syllable which is not pretonic. On the other hand, an *ā* lengthened from *ă* before the tone is retained in the *Perfect consecutive* of Qal even in the secondary tone, e. g. וְקָטַלְתָּ; cf. § 49 *i*.

l (*b*) The short, or merely tone-long, vowels *a*, *e*, *o* of the ultima, especially in verbal forms, e. g. קָטַל, fem. קָטְלָה *qāṭᵉlā*; יִקְטֹל, יִקְטְלוּ *yiqṭᵉlû*; but note also יִלְקְטוּן, תִּרְדְּפִין, &c., according to § 47 *m* and *o*. The helping vowels are either entirely omitted, e. g. מֶלֶךְ *king* (ground-form *malk*), מַלְכִּי *my king*; or, under the influence of a guttural, are weakened to Ḥaṭeph, e. g. נַעַר *boy*, נַעֲרוֹ *his boy*. If the tone remains unmoved, the vowel also is retained, notwithstanding the lengthening of the word, e. g. יְקֹטְלוּ pausal-form for יִקְטְלוּ.

m Where the tone moves forward two places, the former of the two vowels of a dissyllabic word may be shortened, and the second changed into *Šᵉwâ*. Cf. דָּבָר *word*; in the plur. דְּבָרִים; with heavy suffix דִּבְרֵיהֶם (cf. § 28 *a*) *their words*. On the attenuation of the *ă* to *ĭ*, see further, *s*, *t*.

n Rem. I. An *ô* arising from *aw = au*, or by an obscuring of *â* (see § 9 *b*), sometimes becomes *û*, when the tone is moved forward, e. g. נְקוּמוֹת, נָקוּם (see Paradigm *Perf. Niph.* of קוּם); מָנוֹס *flight*, fem. מְנוּסָה, with suffix, מְנוּסִי. The not uncommon use of ו in a sharpened syllable, as בְּחֻקֵּי Ez 20¹⁸ (for בְּחֻקֵּי, cf. also the examples in § 9 *o*), is to be regarded as an orthographic licence, although sometimes in such cases *û* may really have been intended by the *Kᵉthibh*.

o Of the vowels of the *U*-class, *û* and tone-long *ō* stand in a tone-bearing closed final syllable, and *ŏ* in a toneless syllable, e.g. יָקוּם *he will arise*, יָקֹם jussive, *let him arise*, וַיָּקָם *and he arose*. The only instance of *ŭ* in an ultima which has lost the tone is וַיֻּרְם Ex 16²⁰ (see § 67 *n*). Similarly, of vowels of the *I*-class, *ê*, *i*, and *ē* stand in a tone-bearing closed final syllable, and *ĕ* in a toneless syllable, e.g. יָקִים *he will raise*, יָקֵם *let him raise*, וַיָּקֶם *and he raised*. The only instance of *ĭ* in an ultima which has lost the tone is וַתָּרֶץ Ju 9⁵³ (see § 67 *p*).

2. In the place of a *Pathaḥ* we not infrequently find (according to § 9 *f*) *p* a *Seghôl* (*ĕ*, *è*) as a modification of *ă* :

(*a*) In a closed antepenultima, e.g. in the proper names אֲבִיתָר and אֶבְיָסָף, where LXX 'Αβι-='אֲבִי, which is certainly the better reading, cf. Ulmer, *Die semit. Eigennamen*, 1901, p. 12 ; or in a closed penultima, e.g. יֶהְדֹּף, but also יֶדְכֶם *your hand*, for *yadᵉkhèm*. In all these cases the character of the surrounding consonants (see § 6 *q*) has no doubt had an influence.

(*b*) Regularly before a guttural with *Qameṣ* or *Ḥaṭeph Qameṣ*, *q* where the strengthening has been dropped, provided that a lengthening of the *Pathaḥ* into *Qameṣ* be not necessary, e.g. אֶחָיו *his brothers*, for *'aḥâw* ; כָּחָשׁ *false*, for *kaḥâš* ; פֶּחָה *governor*, constr. st. פַּחַת ; פֶּחָם *coal* ; הֶחָי *the living* (with the article, הֶ for הַ) ; יִתְנֶחָם Nu 23¹⁹, &c., and so always before חָ and חֳ, as הֶחֳדָשִׁים *the months*, see § 35 *k*. Before הָ and עָ *Seghôl* generally stands only in the second syllable before the tone, e.g. הֶהָרִים *the mountains*; הֶעָוֹן *the guilt*; immediately before the tone *Pathaḥ* is lengthened into a (pretonic) *Qameṣ*, e.g. הָהָר, הָעָם ; but cf. also הִטַּהֲרוּ Nu 8⁷. Before the weak consonants א and ר (cf. § 22 *c*, *q*), the lengthening of the *Pathaḥ* into *Qameṣ* almost always takes place, e.g. הָאָב *the father*, pl. הָאָבוֹת ; הָרֹאשׁ *the head*, pl. הָרָאשִׁים. Exceptions, הָרָה *towards the mountain*, Gn 14¹⁰, in the tone-syllable, for *hárrā* ; יְבָרֲכֵהוּ (pr. name) for יְבָרֲכְיָהוּ. On הֶ as a form of the interrogative הֲ (הַ), see § 100 *n* ; on מֶה for מָה (מַה), § 37 *e*, *f*. Finally, אֲכָלְךָ Ex 33³ also comes partly under this head, in consequence of the loss of the strengthening, for אַכֶּלְךָ, and יְחֶזְקֵאל *Ezekiel* for יְחַזְקֵאל=יֶחֱזַק־אֵל *God strengthens*.

(*c*) As a modification of the original *Pathaḥ* in the first class of the segholate *r* forms (§ 93 *g*), when a helping vowel (§ 28 *e*) is inserted after the second consonant. Thus the ground-form *kalb* (*dog*), after receiving a helping *Seghôl*, is modified into כֶּלֶב (also in modern Arabic pronounced *kelb*),¹ *yarḥ* (*month*), with a helping *Pathaḥ*, יֶרַח. The same phenomenon appears also in the formation of verbs, in cases like יֶגֶל (jussive of the Hiph'il of גָּלָה), with a helping *Seghôl*, for *yagl*.

3. The attenuation of *ă* to *ĭ* is very common in a toneless closed syllable. *s*
(*a*) In a firmly closed syllable, מִדּוֹ *his measure*, for מַדּוֹ (in a sharpened syllable) ; יְלִדְתִּיךָ *I have begotten thee*, from יָלַדְתִּי with the suffix ךָ ; cf. Lv 11⁴⁴, Ez 38²³, and § 44 *d*. Especially is this the case in a large number of *segholates*

---

¹ So the LXX write Μελχισεδέκ for מַלְכִּי־צֶדֶק.

from the ground-form *qaṭl*, when combined with singular suffixes, e.g. צִדְקִי *my righteousness*, for *ṣadqi*.

t (*b*) In a loosely-closed syllable, i.e. one followed by an aspirated *Begadkᵉphath*, as דִּמְכֶם *your blood*, for דַּמְכֶם, and so commonly in the *st. constr. plur.* of segholates from the ground-form *qaṭl*, e.g. בִּגְדִי from בֶּגֶד (ground-form *bagd*) *a garment*. In most cases of this kind the attenuation is easily intelligible from the nature of the surrounding consonants. It is evident from a comparison of the dialects, that the attenuation was consistently carried out in a very large number of noun and verb-forms in Hebrew, as will be shown in the proper places.[1]

u 4. *Sᵉghôl* arises, in addition to the cases mentioned in *o* and *p*, also from the weakening of *ā* of the final syllable in the isolated cases (הֶ–ָ– for הָ–ָ–) in 1 S 28¹⁵ (? see § 48 *d*), ψ 20⁴ (?), Is 59⁵, Pr 24¹⁴ (see § 48 *l*); for examples of Locative forms in הָ–ָ– see § 90 *i* end.

v 5. Among the *Ḥaṭeph*-sounds –ֲ– is shorter and lighter than –ֱ–, and consequently the vowel group –ֲ– –ַ– is shorter than –ֱ– –ֶ–; e.g. אֱדוֹם *Edom*, but אֲדֹמִי (*Edomite*), shortened at the beginning because the tone is thrown forward; אֱמֶת (*ᵉmèth*) *truth*, אֲמִתּוֹ *his truth*; נֶעְלָם *hidden*, pl. נֶעְלָמִים; הֶעֱבַרְתִּי but וְהַעֲבַרְתִּי; but also conversely נַעֲשָׂה *fem.* נֶעֶשְׂתָה, cf. § 63 *f*, 3.

w 6. To the chapter on vowel changes belongs lastly the *dissimilation* of vowels, i.e. the change of one vowel into another entirely heterogeneous, in order to prevent two similar, or closely related vowels, from following one another in the same word.[2] Hence לוּלֵא for *lū lō* (*unless*). Cf. also חִיצוֹן from חוּץ; רִאשׁוֹן from רֹאשׁ; תִּיכוֹן from תּוֹךְ; נְכָחוֹ from נֹכַח; עֵילָם from stem עוּר; most probably also יִלּוֹד *offspring*, קִפּוֹד *porcupine*, for יָלְ', קָפְ', see § 68 *c*, note.— On the proper names יְהוֹא and יֵשׁוּעַ, which were formerly explained in the same way, see now Prätorius, *ZDMG.* 1905, p. 341 f.

§ 28. *The Rise of New Vowels and Syllables.*

a 1. According to § 26 *m a* half-syllable, i.e. a consonant with Šᵉwâ mobile (always weakened from a short vowel), can only occur in close dependence on a full syllable. If another half-syllable with simple Šᵉwâ follows, the first takes a full short vowel again.[3] This vowel is almost always *Ḥireq*. In most cases it is probably an attenuation of an original *ă*, and never a mere helping vowel. In some instances analogy may have led to the choice of the *ĭ*. Thus, according to § 102 *d*, the prefixes בְּ, כְּ, לְ before a consonant with Šᵉwâ mobile become בִּ, כִּ, לִ, e.g. לִפְרִי, בִּפְרִי, כִּפְרִי; before יְ they are pointed as in בִּיהוּדָה (from *bi-yᵉhûdā*, according to § 24 *c*); so too with *Wāw* copulative, e.g. וִיהוּדָה for וִיְ' attenuated from וַיְ'. The first half-

---

[1] Analogous to this attenuation of *ă* to *ĭ* is the Lat. *tango, attingo; laxus, prolixus*; to the transition of *ă* to *ĕ* (see above, *a*), the Lat. *carpo, decerpo; spargo, conspergo*.

[2] Cf. Barth, *Die Nominalbildung in den semit. Spr.*, p. xxix; A. Müller, *Theol. Stud. u. Krit.*, 1892, p. 177 f., and Nestle, ibid., p. 573 f.

[3] Except וְ *and*, which generally becomes וּ before a simple Šᵉwâ, cf. § 104 *e*.

syllable, after the restoration of the short vowel, sometimes combines with the second to form a firmly closed syllable, e. g. לִנְפֹּל Nu 14³ for *lin*ᵉ*phōl*, and so almost always in the infin. constr. after לְ (§ 45 *g*); in isolated cases also with כְּ, as כְּפֻּר Jer 17².

2. If a guttural with *Ḥaṭeph* follows, the original *ă* of the prefixes *b* is retained before Ḥaṭeph Pathaḥ, but before Ḥaṭeph Seghol or Ḥaṭeph Qameṣ it is modified to the short vowel contained in the *Ḥaṭeph*. Thus arise the vowel groups ⹂⹂, ⹂⹂, ⹂⹂, e. g. וַאֲנִי and I, כַּאֲשֶׁר as, לַעֲבֹד to serve, לֶאֱכֹל to eat, לֳחֳלִי in sickness. On the Metheg with every such short vowel, see § 16 *f*, δ. Sometimes here also a fully closed syllable is formed. In such a case, the prefix takes the short vowel, which would have belonged to the suppressed *Ḥaṭeph*, e. g. לַחְטֹב for לַחֲטֹב; לַחְמָם Is 47¹⁴ for לַחֲמָם (see § 67 *cc*); לֶאְסֹר but also לֶאֱסֹר; and even וַעְצֹר Jb 4², cf. Gn 32¹⁶. So always in the Infin. and Imperat. Qal of the verbs הָיָה to be and חָיָה to live, e. g. לִהְיוֹת to be, וִהְיִי and be ye; even with מִן, as מִהְיוֹת, on which cf. § 102 *b*; but וֶהְיֵה and be, וֶחְיֵה and live, have *ĕ* instead of *ĭ* under the prefix. For the Metheg, cf. § 16 *f*, ε.

3. When a *Ḥaṭeph* in the middle of a word, owing to flexional *c* changes, would stand before a vocal *Šᵉwâ*, it is changed into the short vowel, with which it is compounded. This applies especially to cases in which the *Ḥaṭeph* stands under a guttural instead of quiescent *Šᵉwâ*, as an echo of the preceding short vowel, e. g. יַעֲמֹד *he will stand* (for יַעְמֹד), but plur. יַעַמְדוּ for *yaʿᵃmᵉdhû*, and הָפְכוּ for *nĕhᵃphᵉkhû* (*they have turned themselves*), פָּעָלְךָ *thy work*, cf. § 26 *k*. The syllables are to be divided *yăʿă-mᵉdhû*, and the second *ă* is to be regarded exactly as the helping *Pathaḥ* in נַעַר, &c.¹

4. At the end of words, syllables occur which close with two con- *d* sonants (§ 10 *i*, § 26 *r*), but only when the latter of the two is an emphatic consonant (ט, ק) or a tenuis (viz. בּ, דּ, ךּ, תּ²), e. g. יֵשְׁטְ *let him turn aside*, וַיַּשְׁקְ and *he caused to drink*, אָמַרְתְּ *thou* (fem.) *hast said*, וַיֵּבְךְּ *and he wept*, וְיֵרְדְּ *and let him have dominion*, וַיִּשְׁבְּ *and he took captive*.

This harsh ending is elsewhere avoided by the Masora,³ which *c* inserts between the two final consonants a helping vowel, usually

---

¹ In Ju 16¹³ read הָאֶרֶג not (with Opitius, Hahn and others) תָּאַרְגִי.

² With a final ךּ, the only example is תֹּסְףּ Pr 30⁶, where several MSS. and printed editions incorrectly have ךְ without Dageš. Instead of this masoretic caprice we should no doubt read תֹּסַף.

³ An analogy to this practice of the Masora is found among the modern Beduin, who pronounce such a helping vowel before *h, ḥ, ḫ, ġ*; cf. Spitta, *Gramm. des arab. Vulgärdialektes von Aegypten*, Lpz. 1880, § 43 *d*.

S^eghôl, but with medial or final gutturals a *Pathaḥ*,¹ and after י a *Ḥireq*, e. g. וַיְגֶל and *he revealed*, for *wayyiḡl*; יֶרֶב *let it multiply*, for *yirb*; קֹדֶשׁ *holiness*, ground-form *quds̆*; נַחַל *brook*, ground-form *naḥl*; שָׁלַחַתְּ ² for שָׁלַחְתְּ *thou hast sent*; בַּיִת *house*, ground-form *bayt*. These helping vowels are, however, to be regarded as exactly like *furtive Pathaḥ* (§ 22 *f, g*); they do not alter the monosyllabic character of the forms, and they disappear before formative suffixes, e. g. קָדְשִׁי *my holiness*, בַּיְתָה *home-ward*.

f   5. On the rise of a full vowel in place of a simple *S^ewâ*, under the influence of the *pause*, see § 29 *m*; on initial אֲ for אֳ, see § 23 *h*.

§ 29. *The Tone, its Changes and the Pause.*

a   1. The principal tone rests, according to the Masoretic accentuation (cf. § 15 *c*), as a rule on the final syllable, e. g. קָטַל, דָּבָר, דְּבָרוֹ, דְּבָרִים, קְדֹרָן, קְטָלוּ, קְטַלְתֶּם—in the last five examples on the formative additions to the stem. Less frequently it rests on the penultima, as in לַיְלָה *night*, קָטַלְתְּ, כֶּלֶּה, כְּמוֹ; but a closed penultima can only have the tone if the ultima is open (e. g. קָטַלְתָּ, קָטְלָה, לָכֶנָה, קֹמְנָה), whilst a closed ultima can as a rule only be without the tone if the penultima is open, e. g. וַיָּקָם, וַיִּקֶם; see also below, *e*.

b   A kind of counter-tone or secondary stress, as opposed to the principal tone, is marked by *Metheg* (§ 16 *c*). Words which are closely united by *Maqqeph* with the following word (§ 16 *a*) can at the most have only a secondary tone.

c   2. The original tone of a word, however, frequently shifts its place in consequence either of changes in the word itself, or of its close connexion with other words. If the word is increased at the end, the tone is moved forward (*descendit*) one or two places according to the length of the addition, e. g. דָּבָר *word*, plur. דְּבָרִים; דִּבְרֵיכֶם *your words*; קֹדֶשׁ *holy thing*, plur. קְדָשִׁים; קָטַלְתָּ with suffix קְטַלְתֵּהוּ, with *Wāw* consecutive וְקָטַלְתָּ. On the consequent vowel-changes, see § 27 *d, i–m*.

d   3. On the other hand, the original tone is shifted from the ultima to the penultima (*ascendit*):

---

¹ On the apparent exceptions שֶׁדְּךָ, &c., cf. § 22 *e*; other instances in which א has entirely lost its consonantal value, and is only retained orthographically, are חֵטְא *sin*, גֵּיא *valley* (also גֵּ), שָׁוְא *vanity* (Jb 15³¹ *K^ethibh* שֵׁו).

² In this form (§ 65 *g*) the *Dageš lene* remains in the final *Tāw*, although a vowel precedes, in order to point out that the helping *Pathaḥ* is not to be regarded as a really full vowel, but merely as an orthographic indication of a very slight sound, to ensure the correct pronunciation. An analogous case is יֵחַד *yiḥad* from חָדָה (§ 75 *r*).

(a) In many forms of the Imperfect, under the influence of a prefixed *Wāw consecutive* (וְ see § 49 c–e), e. g. יֹאמַר *he will say*, וַיֹּאמֶר *and he said*; יֵלֵךְ *he will go*, וַיֵּלֶךְ *and he went*.   Cf. also § 51 n on the impf. Niphʻal, and § 65 g, end, on the impf. Piʻel; on these forms in Pause, when the וּ *consec.* does not take effect, see below, *p*.

(b) For rhythmical reasons (as often in other languages), when *e* a monosyllable, or a word with the tone on the first syllable, follows a word with the tone on the ultima, in order to avoid the concurrence of two tone-syllables.[1] This rhythmical retraction of the tone, however (נָסוֹג אָחוֹר *receding*, as it is called by the Jewish grammarians), is only admissible according to *a*, above, provided that the penultima, which now receives the tone, is an open syllable (with a long vowel; but see *g*), whilst the ultima, which loses the tone, must be either an open syllable with a long vowel, e. g. קָרָא לַיְלָה, Gn 1⁵, 4¹⁷, 27²⁵, Ex 16²⁹, ψ 5¹¹, 104¹⁴, Dn 11¹³, or a closed syllable with a short vowel, e. g. תֹּאכַל לֶחֶם Gn 3¹⁹, Jb 3³, 22²⁸. [2] The *grave* suffixes ־כֶם, ־כֶן, ־הֶם, ־הֶן are exceptions, as they never lose the tone. Moreover a fair number of instances occur in which the above conditions are fulfilled, but the tone is not retracted, e. g. esp. with הָיָה, and before א; cf. Qimḥi, *Mikhlol*, ed. Rittenberg (Lyck, 1862), p. 4ᵇ, line 13 ff.

Although *Ṣere* can remain in a closed ultima which has lost the tone, it *f* is perhaps not to be regarded in this case (see § 8 b) as a long vowel. At any rate it then always has, in correct editions, a retarding *Metheg*, no doubt in order to prevent its being pronounced as *Sᵉghôl*, e. g. לְבָעֵר קַיִן Nu 24²²; cf. Nu 17²³, Ju 20², Is 66³, Jer 23²⁹, Ez 22²⁵, ψ 37⁷, and even with a following *furtive Pathaḥ* Pr 1¹⁹, 11²⁶, &c., although there is no question here of two successive tone-syllables.   In other cases the shortening into *Sᵉghôl* does take place, e. g. הוֹלֶם פָּעַם *who smiteth the anvil*, Is 41⁷, for הוֹלֶם פַּעַם; מֵאֵת שֶׁמֶר 1 K 16²⁴.—The retraction of the tone even occurs when a half-syllable with a Šᵉwâ mobile precedes the original tone-syllable, e. g. וַיֹּאמְרוּ לוֹ Gn 19⁵, and frequently; ψ 28¹; יֹרְדֵי בוֹר שָׁמְנוּ לִי

---

[1] Even Hebrew *prose* proceeds, according to the accentuation, in a kind of iambic rhythm. That this was intended by the marking of the tone, can be seen from the use of Metheg.—Jos. Wijnkoop in *Darche hannesigah sive leges de accentus Hebraicae linguae ascensione*, Ludg. Bat. 1881, endeavours to explain, on euphonic and syntactical grounds, the numerous cases in which the usual retraction of the tone does not occur, e. g. וּבוֹרֵא חֹשֶׁךְ Is 45⁷, where the object probably is to avoid a kind of hiatus; but cf. also Am 4¹³. Prätorius, *Ueber den rückweich. Accent im Hebr.*, Halle, 1897, has fully discussed the *nasog 'aḥor*.

[2] The reading עֲדָיִם (so even Opitius and Hahn) Ez 16⁷ for עֲדִים is rightly described by Baer as 'error turpis'.—That an unchangeable vowel in a closed final syllable cannot lose the tone is shown by Prätorius from the duplication of the accent (see above, § 22 f).

מְטֹעֲנֵי חָרֶב ‎ 31⁵ψ; Is 14¹⁹; as also when the tone-syllable of the second word is preceded by a half-syllable, e. g. עֹשֵׂה פְּרִי Gn 1¹¹ (on the *Dag. f.*, cf. § 20 *f*) ; לָקַחַת לְךָ Gn 15⁷ (cf. § 20 *c*).

g According to the above, it must be regarded as anomalous when the Masora throws back the tone of a closed ultima upon a *virtually* sharpened syllable with a short vowel, e.g. אַחַר כֵּן 1 S 10⁵, § 101 *a* ; וּבְחֻשׁ בּוֹ Jb 8¹⁸, cf. Lv 5²², Ho 9² ; לְצָחָק בָּנוּ Gn 39¹⁴·¹⁷ ; whereas it elsewhere allows a closed penultima to bear the tone only when the ultima is open. Still more anomalous is the placing of the tone on a *really* sharpened syllable, when the ultima is closed, as in הֵקִם עַל 2 S 23¹ ; נִכַּר שׁוֹעַ Jb 34¹⁹ ; cf. also יִקַּם־קָיִן Gn 4²⁴, with Metheg of the secondary tone. We should read either הֻקַם, or, with Frensdorff, *Massora Magna*, p. 167, Ginsb., Kittel, after Bomb., הֻקָם. Other abnormal forms are וַיְחַזֶּק בּוֹ Ex 4⁴ (for similar instances see § 15 *c*, end) and וַיְהִי שָׁם Dt 10⁵.

h (*c*) In *pause*, see *i–v*.

The meeting of two tone-syllables (see *e*, *f*) is avoided also by connecting the words with Maqqeph, in which case the first word entirely loses the tone, e. g. וַיִּכְתָּב־שָׁם *and he wrote there*, Jos 8³².

i 4. Very important changes of the tone and of the vowels are effected by the *pause*. By this term is meant the strong stress laid on the tone-syllable in the last word of a sentence (verse) or clause. It is marked by a great *distinctive accent*, Sillûq, 'Athnâḥ, and in the accentuation of the books תא״ם, '*Ôlè wᵉyôrēd* (§ 15 *h*). Apart from these principal pauses (*the great pause*), there are often pausal changes (*the lesser pause*) with the lesser distinctives, especially *Sᵉgolta*, *Zaqeph qaṭon*, *Rᵉbhîaʿ*, and even with *Pašṭa*, *Tiphḥa*, *Gereš*, and (Pr 30⁴) *Pazer*.[1] The changes are as follows :

k (*a*) When the tone-syllable naturally has a short vowel, it as a rule becomes tone-long in *pause*, e. g. קָטַל, קָטָל ; כַּיָּם, מַיִם ; קָטַלְתְּ, קָטָלְתָּ. An *ă* which has been modified to *Sᵉghôl* usually becomes *ā* in *pause*, e. g. קֶשֶׁר (ground-form *qašr*) in *pause* קָשֶׁר 2 K 11¹⁴ ; אֶרֶץ אָרֶץ Jer 22²⁹ ;

----

[1] In most cases, probably on account of a following guttural or (at the end of a sentence) ו (cf. e.g. Ex 21³¹, Jer 3⁹ [but Ginsb. וַתְּחַנֵּף], Ru 4⁴, Ec 11⁶ [but Ginsb. יֹבְשָׁר] ; before ו Jer 17¹¹) [see also § 29 *w*]. שָׁפַט אֶת־ 1 S 7¹⁷, וָאֶרֶץ Is 65¹⁷, Pr 25³, where *ā* has *munaḥ*, are very irregular, but the lengthening here is probably only to avoid the cacophony *šāphăṭ 'ĭt*. In the same way הִיצַּלֵח Ez 17¹⁵ (with Maḥpakh before הַ) and וַיִּקְרַם Ez 37⁸ (with Darga before ע) are to be explained. The four instances of אֲנִי for אֲנִי apparently require a different explanation ; see § 32 *c*.—The theory of Olshausen and others that the phenomena of the *pause* are due *entirely* to liturgical considerations, i. e. that it is 'a convenient way of developing the musical value of the final accents by means of fuller forms' in liturgical reading (Sievers, *Metr. Studien*, i. 236, also explains pausal forms like יִקְטֹלוּ, קָטָלָה, as 'late formations of the grammarians'), is contradicted by the fact that similar phenomena are still to be observed in modern vulgar Arabic, where they can only be attributed to rhythmical reasons of a general character.

also in 2 K 4³¹ read קֶשֶׁב with ed. Mant., &c. (Baer קָשֶׁב).—דְּבַּר becomes in *pause* דִּבֵּר.

Sometimes, however, the distinct and sharper *ă* is intentionally retained *l* in *pause*, especially if the following consonant is strengthened, e. g. יִבַּתּוּ Jb 4²⁰, or ought to be strengthened, e. g. כְּבַת 2 S 12³, בֶּן Is 8¹, &c.; but also in other cases as זָקַנְתִּי Gn 27², because from זָקֵן, cf. below, *q*; עַד Gn 49²⁷; וְתִקְנֻשְׁנוּ 2 Ch 29¹⁹ (so Baer, but Ginsb. הקְדָ׳, ed. Mant. הקְדָ׳); and regularly in the numeral אַרְבַּע *four*, Lv 11²⁰, &c. In the accentuation of the three poetical books (§ 15 *d*) the use of *Pathaḥ* with *'Athnaḥ* is due to the inferior pausal force of *'Athnaḥ*, especially after *'Ôlè weyôred* (§ 15 *o*); cf. ψ 100⁸, Pr 30⁹, and Qimḥi, *Mikhlol*, ed. Rittenberg, p. 5ᵇ, line 4 from below. Compare the list of instances of pausal *ă* and *ĕ* in the appendices to Baer's editions.

(*b*) When a full vowel in a tone-bearing final syllable has lost the *m* tone before an afformative, and has become vocal *Šewâ*, it is restored in *pause* as tone-vowel, and, if short, is lengthened, e. g. קָטֹל, *fem.* קְטֻלָה (*qāṭelā*), in *pause* קָטֵלָה; שָׁמְעוּ (*šimeʿû*), in *pause* שָׁמֵעוּ (from sing. שְׁמַע); יִקְטֹלוּ, יִקְטְלוּ ¹, מָלָאָה, מָלֵאָה (sing. יִקְטֹל). The fuller endings of the Imperfect וּן and וּ— (§ 47 *m* and *o*) alone retain the tone even when the original vowel is restored. In segholate forms, like פְּרִי, לְחִי (ground-form *laḥy*, *pary*), the original *ă* returns, though under the form of a tone-bearing *Seghôl*, thus פֶּרִי, לֶחִי; original *i* becomes *ē*, e.g. חֲצִי, in *pause* חֵצִי; original *ŏ* (*ŭ*) becomes *ō*, חֳלִי (ground-form *ḥuly*), in *pause* חֹלִי (§ 93 *x*, *y*, *z*).

On the analogy of such forms as לֶחִי, &c., the shortened Imperfects *n* יְהִי and יְחִי become in *pause* יֶהִי, יֶחִי, because in the full forms יִהְיֶה *he will be*, and יִחְיֶה *he will live*, the *i* is attenuated from an original *ă*· Similarly שְׁכֶם *shoulder*, in *pause* שֶׁכֶם (ground-form *šakhm*), and the pron. אֲנִי *I*, in *pause* אָנִי; cf. also the restoration of the original *ă* as *ĕ* before the suffix ךָ— *thy*, *thee*, e. g. דְּבָרְךָ *thy word*, in *pause* דְּבָרֶךָ; יִשְׁמָרְךָ *he guards thee*, in *pause* יִשְׁמָרֶךָ; but after the prepositions בְּ, לְ, (אֶת) אֵת the suffix ךָ— in *pause* becomes ךָ—, e. g. אִתְּךָ, לָךְ, בָּךְ.

(*c*) This tendency to draw back the tone in *pause* to the *penultima O* appears also in such cases as אָנֹכִי *I*, in *pause* אָנֹכִי; אַתָּה *thou*, in *pause* אָתָּה (but in the three poetically accented books also אַתָּה, since in those books *'Athnaḥ*, especially after *'Ôlè weyôred*, has only the force of a *Zaqeph*; hence also יְמַלְאוּ Pr 24⁴ instead of יְמַלְּאוּ)²; עַתָּה *now*, עָתָּה; and in other sporadic instances, like כָּלוּ ψ 37²⁰ for כָּלוּ; but in 1 S 12²⁵

---

¹ Such a pausal syllable is sometimes further emphasized by strengthening the following consonant, see § 20 *i*.

² יִפְלוּ ψ 45⁶, cf. also יִבָּלְמוּ ψ 40¹⁵, is to be explained in the same way, but not הַמְלָטִי Zc 2¹¹, where, on the analogy of הַשָּׁמְרוּ Je 9³, we should expect הַפָּלְטִי.

תִּסְפְּפוּ with Baer and Ginsb., is to be preferred to the reading of ed. Mant., &c.

p (*d*) Conversely all forms of imperfects consecutive, whose final syllable, when not in *pause*, loses the tone and is pronounced with a short vowel, take, when in *pause*, the tone on the ultima with a tone-long vowel, e. g. וַיָּמָת and *he died*, in *pause* וַיָּמֹת.

q Of other effects of the *pause* we have still to mention, (1) the transition of an *ĕ* (lengthened from *i*) to the more distinct *ă* (see above, *l*), e. g. תַּחַת for תַּחַת Is 18⁵ (cf. § 67 *v*; § 72 *dd*); קָמָל Is 33⁹; אָצַל 1 Ch 8³⁸ (beside אָצֵל [, see *v*. 37. Cf. : טָבְאָל Is 7⁶ טָבְאַל Ezr 4⁷); : שָׁשָׁר Jer 22¹⁴; סָפָרַד Ob 20; : וַיִּנָּפַשׁ Ex 31¹⁷; : וַיֵּאָנַשׁ 2 S 12¹⁵ (below, § 51 *m*)—S. R. D.]); הֵפַר Gn 17¹⁴; הַפָּצַר 1 S 15²³; תֵּאָחַר ψ 40¹⁸; הַרְחַק Jb 13²¹, mostly before liquids or sibilants (but also הֹשֵׁב Is 42²², and without the *pause* תֵּרַד La 3⁴⁸). So also וַיֵּלֶךְ (shortened from יֵלֵךְ) becomes in *pause* וַיֵּלַךְ; cf. וַיֵּלַךְ La 3²; תֵּלַךְ for תֵּלֵךְ Ju 19²⁰. On *Sĕghôl* in *pause* instead of Ṣere, cf. § 52 *n*, 60 *d*, and especially § 75 *n*, on וְחָיָה Pr 4⁴ and 7².

r (2) The transition from *ă* to *ĕ* in the ultima; so always in the formula לְעוֹלָם וָעֶד (for עַד) *for ever and ever*.

s (3) The *pausal Qameṣ* (according to § 54 *k*, lengthened from original *ă*) in *Hithpa'ēl* (but not in *Pi'ēl*) for Ṣere, e. g. יִתְהַלָּךְ Jb 18⁸ for יִתְהַלֵּךְ. But pausal forms like סָתֶר, שָׁבֶט (in the *absol. st.* סֵתֶר, שֵׁבֶט) go back to a secondary form of the *abs. st.* סֵתֶר, שֵׁבֶט.

t (4) The restoration of a final *Yodh* which has been dropped from the stem, together with the preceding vowel, e. g. בְּעָיוּ, אֱתָיוּ Is 21¹², for בְּעוּ, אֱתוּ, the latter also without the *pause* Is 56⁹·¹²; cf. Jb 12⁶, and the same occurrence even in the word *before* the *pause* Dt 32³⁷, Is 21¹².

u (5) The transition from *ô* or *ō* to *â* in *pause*: as שְׁאָלָה Is 7¹¹, if it be a locative of שְׁאוֹל, and not rather imperat. Qal of שָׁאַל; שְׁכָלְתִּי Gn 43¹⁴ for עָז; שָׁכֹלְתִּי Gn 49³; יִטְרָף Gn 49²⁷; perhaps also שֹׁרָץ 1 K 22³⁴, Is 59¹⁷, and מִשְׁקֹלֶת Is 28¹⁷, cf. 2 K 21¹³. On the other hand the regular pausal form יַחְפָּץ (ordinary imperfect יַחְפֹּץ) corresponds to a perfect חָפֵץ (see § 47 *h*).

v (6) When a *Pathaḥ* both precedes and follows a virtually strengthened guttural, the second becomes *â* in *pause*, and the first *Sĕghôl*, according to § 22 *c* and § 27 *q*, e. g. אַחַי *my brothers*, in *pause* אֶחָי. Similarly in cases where an original *Pathaḥ* after a guttural has been attenuated to *i* out of *pause*, and then lengthened to *ē* with the tone (cf. § 54 *k*), e. g. יִתְנַחֵם, but in *pause* יִתְנֶחָם Dt 32³⁶; cf. Nu 8⁷, 23¹⁹, Ez 5¹³, ψ 135¹⁴.—On pausal Ṣere, for *Sĕghôl*, in infin., imperat., and imperf. of verbs לֹ״ה, see § 75 *hh*.

w [Other instances of the full vowel in lesser pause, where the voice would naturally rest on the word, are Gn 15¹⁴ יַעֲבֹדוּ, Is 8¹⁵, 40²⁴, Ho 4¹², 8⁷, Dn 9¹⁵, and very often in such cases.]

SECOND PART

ETYMOLOGY, OR THE PARTS OF SPEECH

§ 30. *Stems and Roots*[1]: *Biliteral, Triliteral, and Quadriliteral.*

1. Stems in Ḥebrew, as in the other Semitic languages, have this *a* peculiarity, that by far the majority of them consist of three consonants. On these the meaning essentially depends, while the various modifications of the idea are expressed rather by changes in the vowels, e. g. עָמֵק (עָמֵק or עָמֹק; the 3rd pers. sing. perf. does not occur) *it was deep,* עָמֹק *deep,* עֹמֶק *depth,* עֵמֶק, *a valley, plain.* Such a stem may be either a verb or a noun, and the language commonly exhibits both together, e. g. זָרַע *he has sown,* זֶרַע *seed* ; חָכַם *he was wise,* חָכָם *a wise man.* For practical purposes, however, it has long been the custom to regard as the stem the 3*rd pers. sing. Perf. Qal* (see § 43), since it is one of the simplest forms of the verb, without any formative additions. Not only are the other forms of the verb referred to this stem, but also the noun-forms, and the large number of particles derived from nouns ; e. g. קָדֵשׁ *he was holy,* קֹדֶשׁ *holiness,* קָדוֹשׁ *holy.*

Sometimes the language, as we have it, exhibits only the verbal *b* stem without any corresponding noun-form, e. g. סָקַל *to stone,* נָהַק *to bray* ; and on the other hand, the noun sometimes exists without the corresponding verb, e. g. אֶבֶן *stone,* נֶגֶב *south.* Since, however, the nominal or verbal stems, which are not now found in Hebrew, generally occur in one or more of the other Semitic dialects, it may be assumed, as a rule, that Hebrew, when a living language, also possessed them. Thus, in Arabic, the verbal stem *'ăbĭnă* (*to become compact, hard*) corresponds to אֶבֶן, and the Aramaic verb *nᵉgab* (*to be dry*) to נֶגֶב.

Rem. 1. The Jewish grammarians call the stem (i.e. the 3rd pers. sing. *c* Perf. Qal) שֶׁרֶשׁ *root.* Hence it became customary among Christian grammarians to call the stem *radix,* and its three consonants *litterae radicales,* in contradistinction to the *litterae serviles* or *formative letters.* On the correct use of the term *root,* see *g.*

---

[1] On the questions discussed here compare the bibliography at the head of § 79.

H 2

d   2. Others regard the three stem-consonants as a *root*, in the sense that, considered as *vowelless* and unpronounceable, it represents the common foundation of the verbal and nominal stems developed from it, just as in the vegetable world, from which the figure is borrowed, stems grow from the hidden root, e. g.

Root : מֶלֶךְ, the indeterminate idea of *ruling*.

Verb-stem, מָלַךְ *he has reigned.*   Noun-stem, מֶלֶךְ *king.*

For the historical investigation of the language, however, this hypothesis of unpronounceable roots, with indeterminate meaning, is fruitless. Moreover, the term *root*, as it is generally understood by philologists, cannot be applied to the Semitic triliteral stem (see *f*).[1]

e   3. The 3rd sing. Perf. Qal, which, according to the above, is usually regarded, both lexicographically and grammatically, as the ground-form, is generally in Hebrew a dissyllable, e.g. קָטַל. The monosyllabic forms have only arisen by contraction (according to the traditional explanation) from stems which had a weak letter (ו or י) for their middle consonant, e.g. קָם from *qāwăm* ; or from stems whose second and third consonants are identical, e.g. צַר and צָרַר (but see below, §§ 67, 72). The dissyllabic forms have themselves no doubt arisen, through a loss of the final vowel, from trisyllables, e. g. קָטַל from *qătălă*, as it is in literary Arabic.

f   2. The law of the triliteral stem is so strictly observed in the formation of verbs and nouns in Hebrew (and in the Semitic languages generally), that the language has sometimes adopted artificial methods to preserve at least an appearance of triliteralism in monosyllabic stems, e.g. שֶׁבֶת for the inf. constr. of verbs פ״י; cf. § 69 *b*. Conversely such nouns, as אָב *father*, אֵם *mother*, אָח *brother*, which were formerly all regarded as original monosyllabic forms (*nomina primitiva*), may, in some cases at least, have arisen from mutilation of a triliteral stem.

g   On the other hand, a large number of triliteral stems really point to a biliteral base, which may be properly called a *root* (*radix primaria, bilitteralis*), since it forms the starting-point for several triliteral modifications of the same fundamental idea. Though in themselves unpronounceable, these roots are usually pronounced with *ă* between the two consonants, and are represented in writing by the sign √, e. g. √כר as the root of אָכַר, כּוּר, כָּרָה, כָּרָה, בָּרַר. The reduction of a stem to the underlying root may generally be accomplished with certainty when the stem exhibits one weak consonant with two strong ones, or when the second and third consonants are identical. Thus e. g. the stems דָּכָה, דָּכָא, דּוּךְ, דָּכַךְ may all be traced to the idea of *striking, breaking,* and the root common to them all is evidently the two strong consonants דך (*dakh*). Very frequently, however, the development of the root into a stem is effected by the addition of

---

[1] Cf. Philippi, 'Der Grundstamm des starken Verbums,' in *Morgenländische Forschungen,* Leipz. 1875, pp. 69-106.

a strong consonant, especially, it seems, a sibilant, liquid or guttural.[1]
Finally, further modifications of the same root are produced when
either a consonant of the root, or the letter which has been added,
changes by phonetic laws into a kindred letter (see the examples
below). Usually such a change of sound is accompanied by a modification of meaning.

Examples: from the root קִיק (no doubt *onomatopoetic*, i.e. imitating the *h*
sound), which represents the fundamental idea of *carving off, cutting in pieces*,
are derived directly: קָצַץ and קָצָה *to cut, to cut off*; the latter also metaph. *to*
decide, to judge (whence קָצִין, Arab. *qâḍi, a judge*); also קָצַב *to cut off, to shear*,
קָצַף *to tear, to break*, קָצַע *to cut into*, קָצַר *to cut off, to reap*. With a dental instead
of the sibilant, קַד, קַט, whence קָטַב *to cut in pieces, to destroy*, קָטַל *to cut down,*
to kill, קָטַף *to tear off, to pluck off*. With the initial letter softened,
the root becomes כס, whence בָּסַח *to cut off*, and בָּסַם *to shave*; cf. also נכס
Syr. *to slay* (*sacrifice*), *to kill*. With the greatest softening to גו and גד: גָּזַז *to*
cut off, to shear; גָּזָה *to hew stone*; גּוּז, גָּזַם, גָּזַע, גָּזַל, גָּזַר *to cut off, to tear off, eat up*;
similarly גָּדַר *to cut into*, גָּדַע *to cut off*; cf. also גָּדָה, גָּדַף, גָּדַד. Allied to this
root also is the series of stems which instead of a palatal begin with a
guttural (ח), e.g. חָדַד *to split, cut*; cf. also חדל, חדר, חדק, חרד, חדש, and further
חצר, חצץ, חצה, חצב, חסף, חסם, חסל, חסף, חטף, חטם, חטב, חזה, חזז, חץ, חוץ, חום
in the Lexicon.

The root הם expresses the sound of *humming*, which is made with the
mouth closed (μύω); hence הָמַם, הוּם, הָמָה, נָהַם (נָאַם), Arab. *hámhama, to buzz,*
to hum, to snarl, &c.

As developments from the root רע cf. the stems רָעַד, רָעַל, רָעַם, רָעַע, רָעַע,
רָעַשׁ. Not less numerous are the developments of the root (פר, פל) בר and
many others.[2]

Closer investigation of the subject suggests the following observations:

(*a*) These roots are mere *abstractions* from stems in actual use, and are *i*
themselves not used. They represent rather the hidden germs (*semina*) of the
stems which appear in the language. Yet these stems are sometimes so
short as to consist simply of the elements of the root itself, e.g. תַּם *to be*
finished, קַל *light*. The ascertaining of the root and its meaning, although in
many ways very difficult and hazardous, is of great lexicographical importance.
It is a wholly different and much contested question whether there ever was
a period in the development of the Semitic languages when purely *biliteral*
roots, either isolated and invariable or combined with inflexions, served for
the communication of thought. In such a case it would have to be admitted,
that the language at first expressed extremely few elementary ideas, which
were only gradually extended by additions to denote more delicate shades of
meaning. At all events this process of transformation would belong to
a period of the language which is entirely outside our range. At the most
only the gradual multiplication of *stems* by means of phonetic change (see
below) can be historically proved.

(*b*) Many of these monosyllabic words are clearly imitations of sounds, and *k*

---

[1] That *all* triliteral stems are derived from biliterals (as König, *Lehrg.* ii. 1,
370; M. Lambert in *Studies in honour of A. Kohut*, Berl. 1897, p. 354 ff.) cannot
be definitely proved.

[2] Cf. the interesting examination of the Semitic roots QR, KR, XR, by
P. Haupt in the *Amer. Journ. of Sem. Lang.*, xxiii (1907), p. 241 ff.

sometimes coincide with roots of a similar meaning in the Indo-Germanic family of languages (§ 1 *h*). Of other roots there is definite evidence that Semitic linguistic consciousness regarded them as onomatopoetic, whilst the Indo-Germanic instinct fails to recognize in them any imitation of sound.

l   (*c*) Stems with the harder, stronger consonants are in general (§ 6 *r*) to be regarded as the older, from which a number of later stems probably arose through softening of the consonants; cf. פּוּר and בּוּר, צָחַק and שָׂחַק, צָעַק and זָעַק, עָלַץ and עָלַז, עָלַס; רָקַק and רָכַךְ, and the almost consistent change of initial ו to י. In other instances, however, the harder stems have only been adopted at a later period from Aramaic, e. g. טָעָה, Hebr. תָּעָה. Finally in many cases the harder and softer stems may have been in use together from the first, thus often distinguishing, by a kind of sound-painting, the intensive action from the less intensive; see above קָצַץ *to cut*, גָּזַז *to shear*, &c.

m   (*d*) When two consonants are united to form a root they are usually either both emphatic or both middle-hard or both soft, e. g. קִק, קֵט, כֵּס, גֵּו, גֵּר never בֵּין, גֵּין, גֵּט, גֵּם, קֵן. Within (triliteral) stems the first and second consonants are never identical. The apparent exceptions are either due to reduplication of the root, e. g. דָּדָה (ψ 42⁵, Is 38¹⁵), Arabic רָאֵד, or result from other causes, cf. e. g. בָּבָה in the Lexicon. The first and third consonants are very seldom identical except in what are called concave stems (with middle ו or י), e. g. נוּן, צוּץ; note, however, גָּגַן נָתַן, שָׁמַשׁ, שָׁרַשׁ, and on עָלַע Jb 39³⁰ see § 55 *f*. The second and third consonants on the other hand are very frequently identical, see § 67.¹

n   (*e*) The softening mentioned under *l* is sometimes so great that strong consonants, especially in the middle of the stem, actually pass into vowels: cf. § 19 *o*, and עֲזָאזֵל Lv 16⁸ ᶠᶠ. if it is for עֲזַלְזֵל.

o   (*f*) Some of the cases in which triliteral stems cannot with certainty be traced back to a biliteral root, may be due to a combination of two roots—a simple method of forming expressions to correspond to more complex ideas.

p   3. Stems of *four*, or even (in the case of nouns) of *five* consonants ² are secondary formations. They arise from an extension of the triliteral stem: (*a*) by addition of a fourth stem-consonant; (*b*) in some cases perhaps by composition and contraction of two triliteral stems, by which means even *quinquiliterals* are produced. Stems which have arisen from reduplication of the biliteral root, or from the mere repetition of one or two of the three original stem-consonants, e. g. כִּלְכֵּל from כּוּל or כִּיל, סְחַרְחַר from סָחַר, are usually not regarded as *quadri-literals* or *quinqueliterals*, but as *conjugational* forms (§ 55); so also the few words which are formed with the prefix שׁ, as שַׁלְהֶבֶת *flame* from לָהַב, correspond to the Aramaic conjugation *Šaphʿēl*, שַׁלְהֵב.

q   Rem. on (*a*). The letters *r* and *l*, especially, are inserted between the first and second radicals, e. g. כָּסַם, כִּרְסֵם *to eat up*; שַׁרְבִּיט = שֵׁבֶט *sceptre* (this insertion of an *r* is especially frequent in Aramaic); זַלְעָפָה *hot wind* from זָעַף

---

¹ Consonants which are not found together in roots and stems are called *incompatible*. They are chiefly consonants belonging to the same class, e. g. גב, גק, כב, דט, מף, בף, זד, זס, צם, צע, אע, חע, and ה, &c., or in the reverse order.

² In Hebrew they are comparatively rare, but more numerous in the other Semitic languages, especially in Ethiopic.

to be hot. Cf. Aram. עַרְגֵּל *to roll*, expanded from עַגֵּל (conjugation *Paʽēl*,
corresponding to the Hebrew *Piʽēl*). In Latin there is a similar expansion
of *fid, scid, tud, jug* into *findo, scindo, tundo, jungo*. At the end of words the
commonest expansion is by means of ל and ן, e. g. גַּרְזֶן *axe*, כַּרְמֶל *garden-land*
(from כֶּרֶם), גִּבְעֹל *corolla* (גָּבִיעַ *cup*); cf. § 85, xi.

Rem. on (*b*). Forms such as צְפַרְדֵּעַ *frog*, חֲבַצֶּלֶת *meadow-saffron*, צַלְמָוֶת *shadow* *r*
of death,[1] were long regarded as compounds, though the explanation of them
all was uncertain. Many words of this class, which earlier scholars attempted
to explain from Hebrew sources, have since proved to be *loan-words* (§ 1 *i*),
and consequently need no longer be taken into account.

4. A special class of formations, distinct from the fully developed *s*
stems of three or four consonants, are (*a*) the *Interjections* (§ 105),
which, as being direct imitations of natural sounds, are independent
of the ordinary formative laws; (*b*) the *Pronouns*. Whether these
are to be regarded as the mutilated remains of early developed stems,
or as relics of a period of language when the formation of stems followed
different laws, must remain undecided. At all events, the many
peculiarities of their formation[2] require special treatment (§ 32 ff.).
On the other hand, most of the particles (adverbs, prepositions, conjunctions) seem to have arisen in Hebrew from fully developed stems,
although in many instances, in consequence of extreme shortening,
the underlying stem is no longer recognizable (see § 99 ff.).

§ 31. *Grammatical Structure.*

P. Dörwald, 'Die Formenbildungsgesetze des Hebr.' (*Hilfsbuch für Lehrer
des Hebr.*), Berlin, 1897, is recommended for occasional reference.

1. The formation of the parts of speech from the stems (derivation), *a*
and their inflexion, are effected in two ways : (*a*) internally by changes
in the stem itself, particularly in its vowels: (*b*) externally by the
addition of formative syllables before or after it. The expression of
grammatical relations (e. g. the comparative degree and some case-
relations in Hebrew) periphrastically by means of separate words
belongs, not to etymology, but to syntax.

The external method (*b*) of formation, by affixing formative syllables, *b*
which occurs e. g. in Egyptian, appears on the whole to be the more ancient.
Yet other families of language, and particularly the Semitic, at a very early
period had recourse also to the internal method, and during their youthful
vigour widely developed their power of forming derivatives. But the continuous decay of this power in the later periods of language made syntactical
circumlocution more and more necessary. The same process may be seen
also e. g. in Greek (including modern Greek), and in Latin with its Romance
offshoots.

---

[1] So expressly Nöldeke in *ZAW.* 1897, p. 183 ff. ; but most probably it is to
be read צַלְמֻת *darkness* from the stem צלם [Arab. *zalima*, to be dark].

[2] Cf. Hupfeld, 'System der semitischen Demonstrativbildung,' in the
Ztschr. f. d. Kunde des Morgenl., vol. ii. pp. 124 ff., 427 ff.

c **2.** Both methods of formation exist together in Hebrew. The internal mode of formation by means of vowel changes is tolerably extensive (קָטַל, קֵטֵל, קֹטֶל; קִטֵּל, קֻטַּל, קַטֵּל, &c.). This is accompanied in numerous cases by external formation also (נִקְטַל, הִקְטִיל, הִתְקַטֵּל, &c.), and even these formative additions again are subject to internal change, e.g. הָקְטַל, הָתְקַטַּל. The addition of formative syllables occurs, as in almost all languages, chiefly in the formation of the persons of the verb, where the meaning of the affixed syllables is for the most part still perfectly clear (see §§ 44, 47). It is also employed to distinguish gender and number in the verb and noun. Of case-endings, on the contrary, only scanty traces remain in Hebrew (see § 90).

CHAPTER I

THE PRONOUN

Brockelmann, *Semit. Sprachwiss.*, p. 98 ff. ; *Grundriss*, i. 296 ff. L. Reinisch,
'Das persönl. Fürwort u. die Verbalflexion in den chamito-semit. Sprachen'
(*Wiener Akad. der Wiss.*, 1909).

§ 32. *The Personal Pronoun. The Separate Pronoun.*

1. The personal pronoun (as well as the pronoun generally) belongs *a*
to the oldest and simplest elements of the language (§ 30 *s*). It must
be discussed *before* the verb, since it plays an important part in verbal
inflexion (§§ 44, 47).

2. The independent principal forms of the personal pronoun serve *b*
(like the Gk. ἐγώ, σύ, Lat. *ego, tu*, and their plurals) almost exclusively
to emphasize the nominative-subject (see, however, § 135 *d*). They
are as follows:

Singular.	Plural.
1. *Com.* אָנֹכִי, in *pause* אָנֹכִי ; $\left.\right\} I.$ אֲנִי, in *pause* אָנִי	1. *Com.* אֲנַחְנוּ, in *pause* אֲנָחְנוּ $\left.\right\}$ we. (אנו), נַחְנוּ, in *pause* נָחְנוּ
2. $\left\{\begin{array}{l} m. \text{ אַתָּה (אַתְּ), in } pause \\ \text{ אָתָּה or אַתָּה} \\ f. \text{ אַתִּי(אַתְּ) properly (אַתְּי),} \\ \text{ in pause אָתְּ} \end{array}\right\}$ thou.	2. $\left\{\begin{array}{l} m. \text{ אַתֶּם} \\ f. \text{ אַתֵּנָה (אַתֵּנָּה) ; (אַתֵּן) אַתֵּן (אַתֶּן)} \end{array}\right\}$ ye.
3. $\left\{\begin{array}{l} m. \text{ הוּא } he \ (it). \\ f. \text{ הִיא } she \ (it). \end{array}\right.$	3. $\left\{\begin{array}{l} m. \text{ הֵמָּה (הֵם־), הֵם} \\ f. \text{ הֵנָּה after } prefixes \text{ הֵן, הֶן,} \end{array}\right\}$ they.

The forms enclosed in parentheses are the less common. A table of these
pronouns with their shortened forms (*pronominal suffixes*) is given in Paradigm
A at the end of this Grammar.

REMARKS.

I. *First Person.*

1. The form אָנֹכִי is less frequent than אֲנִי.[1] The former occurs in *c*

---

[1] On the prevalence of אָנֹכִי in the earlier Books compare the statistics
collected by Giesebrecht in *ZAW.* 1881, p. 251 ff., partly contested by Driver
in the *Journal of Philology*, 1882, vol. xi. p. 222 ff. (but cf. his *Introduction*, ed.
6, p. 135, line 1 f.), but thoroughly established by König in *Theol. Stud. u. Krit.*,
1893, pp. 464 ff. and 478, and in his *Einleitung in das A. T.*, p. 168, &c. In some
of the latest books אנכי is not found at all, and hardly at all in the Talmud.
[For details see the Lexicon, s. v. אֲנִי and אָנֹכִי.]

Phoenician, Moabite, and Assyrian, but in no other of the kindred dialects;[1] from the latter the suffixes are derived (§ 33). The *ô* most probably results from an obscuring of an original *á* (cf. Aram. אֲנָא, Arab. *'ána*). The pausal form אֲנִי occurs not only with small disjunctive accents, but even with conjunctives; so always in אָנֹכִי חַי *as I live!* also Is 49[18] with Munaḥ, ψ 119[125] with Merkha (which, however, has been altered from D[e]ḥî), and twice in Mal 1[6]. In all these cases there is manifestly a disagreement between the vocalization already established and the special laws regulating the system of accentuation.

d 2. The formation of the plural, in this and the other persons, exhibits a certain analogy with that of the noun, while at the same time (like the pronouns of other languages) it is characterized by many differences and peculiarities. The short form אֲנוּ (אֲנוּ) from which the suffix is derived occurs only in Jer 42[6] K[e]thibh. The form נַחְנוּ (cf. § 19 *h*) only in Ex 16[7.8], Nu 32[32], La 3[42]; נַחְנוּ in *pause*, Gn 42[11]; in Arabic *náḥnu* is the regular form. In the Mišna אֲנוּ (אֲנוּ) has altogether supplanted the longer forms.

e 3. The pronoun of the 1st person only is, as a rule in languages, of the *common gender*, because the person who is present and speaking needs no further indication of gender, as does the 2nd person, who is addressed (in Greek, Latin, English, &c., this distinction is also lacking), and still more the 3rd person who is absent.

II. *Second Person.*

f 4. The forms of the 2nd person אַתָּה, אַתְּ, אַתֶּם, אַתֵּנָה, &c., are contracted from *'antā*, &c. The kindred languages have retained the *n* before the ן, e. g. Arab. *'ántā*, fem. *'ánti*, thou; pl. *'ántum*, fem. *'antúnna*, ye. In Syriac אַנְתְּ, fem. אַנְתִּי are written, but both are pronounced *'at*. In Western Aramaic אַנְתְּ is usual for both genders.

g אַתְּ (without ה) occurs five times, e. g. ψ 6[4], always as K[e]thibh, with אַתָּה as Q[e]rê. In three places אַתְּ appears as a masculine, Nu 11[15], Dt 5[24], Ez 28[14].

h The feminine form was originally אַתִּי as in Syriac, Arabic, and Ethiopic. This form is found seven times as K[e]thibh (Ju 17[2], 1 K 14[2], 2 K 4[16.23], 8[1], Jer 4[30], Ez 36[13]) and appears also in the corresponding personal ending of verbs (see § 44 *f*), especially, and necessarily, before suffixes, as קְטַלְתִּינִי, § 59 *a* [*c*]; cf. also *î* as the ending of the 2nd fem. sing. of the imperative and imperfect. The final *î* was, however, gradually dropped in pronunciation, just as in Syriac (see above, *f*) it was eventually only written, not pronounced. The י therefore finally disappeared (cf. § 10 *k*), and hence the Masoretes, even in these seven passages, have pointed the word in the text as אַתִּי to indicate the Q[e]rê אַתְּ (see § 17). The same final ִי appears in the rare (Aramaic) forms of the suffix כִי, יְכִי ִ (§§ 58, 91).

i 5. The plurals אַתֶּם (with the second vowel assimilated to the fem. form) and אַתֵּן (אַתֶּן), with the tone on the ultima, only partially correspond to the assumed ground-forms *'antumú*, fem. *'antinná*, Arab. *'ántüm* (Aram. אַתּוּן, אַנְתּוּן) and *'antúnna* (Aram. אַתֵּין, אַנְתֵּין). The form אַתֵּן is found only in Ez 34[31] (so Qimḥi expressly, others אַתֶּן); אַתֵּנָה (for which some MSS. have

---

[1] In Phoenician and Moabite (inscription of Mêša', line 1) it is written אנך, without the final ִי. In Punic it was pronounced *anec* (Plaut. *Poen.* 5, 1, 8) or *anech* (5, 2, 35). Cf. Schröder, *Phöniz. Sprache*, p. 143. In Assyrian the corresponding form is *anaku*, in old Egyptian *anek*, Coptic *anok*, *nok*.

אַתֵּ֫נָה) only four times, viz. Gn 31⁶, Ez 13¹¹·²⁰, 34¹⁷; in 13²⁰ אַתֵּם (before a מ) is even used as feminine.

III. *Third Person.*

6. (*a*) In הוּא and הִיא (*hû* and *hî*) the א (corresponding to the *'Elif of pro-* *k* *longation* in Arabic, cf. § 23 *i*) might be regarded only as an orthographic addition closing the final long vowel, as in לוּא, נָקִיא, &c. The א is, however, always written in the case of the separate pronouns,[1] and only as a toneless suffix (§ 33 *a*) does הוּא appear as הו, while הִיא becomes הָ. In Arabic (as in Syriac) they are written הו and הי but pronounced *huwă* and *hiyă*, and in Vulgar Arabic even *huwwa* and *hiyya*. This Arabic pronunciation alone would not indeed be decisive, since the vowel complement might have arisen from the more consonantal pronunciation of the ו and י; but the Ethiopic *weʾetû* (= *huʾa-tû*) for הוּא, *yeʾetî* (= *hiʾa-tî*) for הִיא (cf. also the Assyrian *ya-u-a* for יְהוּא) show that the א was original and indicated an original vocalic termination of the two words. According to Philippi (*ZDMG.* xxviii. 172 and xxix. 371 ff.) הוּא arose from a primitive Semitic *ha-ra*, הִיא from *ha-ya*.

(*b*) The form הוּא also stands in the consonantal text (*Kᵉthibh*) of the *l* Pentateuch[2] (with the exception of eleven places) for the *fem.* הִיא. In all such cases the Masora, by the punctuation הִוא, has indicated the Qᵉrê הִיא (*Qᵉrê perpetuum*, see § 17). The old explanation regarded this phenomenon as an archaism which was incorrectly removed by the Masoretes. This assumption is, however, clearly untenable, if we consider (1) that no other Semitic language is without the quite indispensable distinction of gender in the separate pronoun of the 3rd pers.; (2) that this distinction does occur eleven times in the Pentateuch, and that in Gn 20⁵, 38²⁵, Nu 5¹³·¹⁴ הוּא and הִיא are found close to one another; (3) that outside the Pentateuch the distinction is found in the oldest documents, so that the הִיא cannot be regarded as having been subsequently adopted from the Aramaic; (4) that those parts of the book of Joshua which certainly formed a constituent part of the original sources of the Pentateuch, know nothing of this epicene use of הוּא. Consequently there only remains the hypothesis, that the writing of הוא for הִיא rests on an orthographical peculiarity which in some recension of the Pentateuch-text was almost consistently followed, but was afterwards very properly rejected by the Masoretes. The orthography was, however, peculiar to the Pentateuch-text alone, since it is unnecessary to follow the Masora in writing הִיא for הוּא in 1 K 17¹⁵, Is 30³³, Jb 31¹¹, or הוּא for הִיא in ψ 73¹⁶, Ec 5⁸, 1 Ch 29¹⁶. The Samaritan recension of the Pentateuch has the correct form in the *Kᵉthibh* throughout. Levy's explanation of this strange practice of the Masoretes is evidently right, viz. that originally הא was written for both forms (see *k*, note), and was almost everywhere, irrespective of gender, expanded into הוא. On the whole question see Driver, *Leviticus* (in Haupt's Bible), p. 25 f. In the text Driver always reads הא.

7. The plural forms הֵם (הֵ֫מָּה) and הֵ֫נָּה (after *prefixes* הֵן, הֶן) are of doubt- *m* ful origin, but הֵ֫מָּה, הֵם have probably been assimilated to הֵ֫נָּה which goes back to a form *hinnâ*. In Western Aram. הִמּוֹן, הִמּוֹ (הִנּוּן, (אִנּוּן), Syr. *henûn*

---

[1] In the inscription of King Mêšaʿ (see § 2 *d*), lines 6 and 27, we find הא for הוא, and in the inscription of 'Ešmunʿazar, line 22, for הִיא, but in the Zenjirli inscriptions (see § 1 *m*) both הא and הו occur (Hadad i, l. 29).

[2] Also in twelve places in the Babylonian Codex (Prophets) of 916 A. D.; cf. Baer, *Ezechiel*, p. 108 f.; Buhl, *Canon and Text of the O. T.* (Edinb. 1892), p. 240.

('enûn), Arab. *humû* (archaic form of *hum*), and Ethiop. *hômû*, an *ô* or *ú* is appended, which in Hebrew seems to reappear in the poetical suffixes וֹמ‍ָ, ‍ָ‍מוֹ, ‍ֵ‍מוֹ (§ 91 *l*, 3).

n In some passages הֵמָּה stands for the feminine (Zc 5¹⁰, Ct 6⁸, Ru 1²²; cf. the use of the suffix of the 3rd masc. for the 3rd fem., § 135 *o* and § 145 *t*). For the quite anomalous עָדֶ־הֶם 2 K 9¹⁸ read עָדֵיהֶם (Jb 32¹²).

O 8. The pronouns of the 3rd person may refer to *things* as well as persons. On their meaning as *demonstratives* see § 136.

§ 33. *Pronominal Suffixes.*

Brockelmann, *Semit. Sprachwiss.*, p. 100 f.; *Grundriss*, i. 306 ff. J. Barth, 'Beiträge zur Suffixlehre des Nordsemit.,' in the *Amer. Journ. of Sem. Lang.*, 1901, p. 193 ff.

a 1. The independent principal forms of the personal pronoun (the *separate pronoun*), given in the preceding section, express only the nominative.[1] The accusative and genitive are expressed by forms, usually shorter, joined to the end of verbs, nouns, and particles (*pronominal suffixes* or simply *suffixes*); e. g. הוּ (toneless) and וֹ (from *āhû*) *eum* and *eius*, קְטַלְתִּיהוּ *I have killed him* (also קְטַלְתִּיו), קְטַלְתָּהוּ or (with *āhû* contracted into *ô*) קְטַלְתּוֹ *thou hast killed him*; אוֹרוֹ (also אוֹרֵהוּ) *lux eius*.

The same method is employed in all the other Semitic languages, as well as in the Egyptian, Persian, Finnish, Tartar, and others; in Greek, Latin, and German we find only slight traces of the kind, e. g. German, *er gab's* for *er gab es*; Greek, πατήρ μου for πατὴρ ἐμοῦ; Latin, *eccum, eccos*, &c., in Plautus and Terence for *ecce eum, ecce eos*.

b 2. The *case* which these suffixes represent is—

(*a*) When joined to verbs, the accusative (cf., however, § 117 *x*), e. g. קְטַלְתִּיהוּ *I have killed him.*

c (*b*) When affixed to substantives, the genitive (like πατήρ μου, *pater eius*). They then serve as *possessive pronouns*, e. g. אָבִי ('ābh-î) *my father*, סוּסוֹ *his horse*, which may be either *equus eius* or *equus suus*.

d (*c*) When joined to particles, either the genitive or accusative, according as the particles originally expressed the idea of a noun or a verb, e. g. בֵּינִי, literally *interstitium mei*, *between me* (cf. *mea causa*); but הִנְנִי *behold me, ecce me*.

e (*d*) Where, according to the Indo-Germanic case-system, the dative or ablative of the pronoun is required, the suffixes in Hebrew are joined to prepositions expressing those cases (לְ sign of the dative, בְּ *in*, מִן *from*, § 102), e. g. לוֹ *to him* (*ei*) and *to himself* (*sibi*), בּוֹ *in him*, מִנִּי (usually מִמֶּנִּי) *from me.*

---

[1] On apparent exceptions see § 135 *d*.

3. The suffixes of the 2nd person (ךָ‑ָ, &c.) are all formed with *f* a *k*-sound, not, like the *separate* pronouns of the 2nd person, with a *t*-sound.

So in all the Semitic languages, in Ethiopic even in the verbal form (*qatalka, thou hast killed* = Hebr. קְטַלְתָּ).

4. The *suffix of the verb* (the accusative) and the *suffix of the noun* (the *g* genitive) coincide in most forms, but some differ, e. g. נִי— *me*, ־ִי *my*.

Paradigm A at the end of the Grammar gives a table of all the forms of the *separate pronoun* and the *suffixes*; a fuller treatment of the *verbal suffix* and the mode of attaching it to the verb will be found in § 58 ff., of the *noun-suffix* in § 91, of the prepositions with suffixes in § 103, of adverbs with suffixes § 100 *o*.

§ 34. *The Demonstrative Pronoun.*

1. Sing. $\begin{cases} m.\ \text{זֶה}^1 \\ f.\ \text{זֹאת} \ (\text{זֹה, זוֹ})^2 \end{cases}$ *this*.   Plur. com. אֵלֶּה (rarely אֵל) *these*. *a*

Rem. 1. The feminine form זֹאת has undoubtedly arisen from זָאת, by *b* obscuring of an original *â* to *ô* (for זֶה = זָא cf. the Arab. *hâ-ḏâ, this*, masc. ; for ת as the feminine ending, § 80), and the forms זֹה, זוֹ, both of which are rare,[3] are shortened from זֹאת. In ψ 132[12] זוֹ is used as a *relative*, cf. זוּ below. In Jer 26[6], K*ethibh*, הַזֹּאתָה (with the article and the demonstrative termination ה‑ָ) is found for זֹאת. The forms אֵלֶּה and אֵל are the plurals of זֶה and זֹאת by usage, though not etymologically. The form אֵל occurs only in the Pentateuch (but not in the Samaritan text), Gn 19[8.25], 26[3.4], &c. (8 times), always with the article, הָאֵל [as well as הָאֵלֶּה, אֵלֶּה frequently], and in 1 Ch 20[8] without the article [cf. Driver on Dt 4[42]].[4] Both the singular and the plural may refer to things as well as persons.

2. In combination with prepositions to denote the oblique case we find לָזֶה *c* *to this* (cf. for לְ, § 102 *g*), לָזֹאת, לְזֹאת *to this* (fem.), לָאֵלֶּה, לְאֵלֶּה *to these* ; אֶת־זֶה *hunc*, אֶת־זֹאת *hanc*, אֶת־אֵלֶּה *hos*, also without אֶת־, even *before* the verb ψ 75[8], &c. Note also מְחִיר זֶה *pretium huius* (1 K 21[2]), &c.

---

[1] In many languages the demonstratives begin with a *d*-sound (hence called the *demonstrative sound*) which, however, sometimes interchanges with a sibilant. Cf. Aram. דֵּן, דֶּן *masc.*, דָּא, דָּךְ, *fem.* (this); Sansk. *sa, sâ, tat*; Gothic *sa, sô, thata* ; Germ. *da, der, die, das* ; and Eng. *the, this, that,* &c. Cf. J. Barth, 'Zum semit. Demonstr. *ḏ*,' in *ZDMG.* 59, 159 ff., and 633 ff.; *Sprachwiss. Untersuchungen zum Semit.*, Lpz. 1907, p. 30 ff. [See the Lexicon, s. v. זֶה, and Aram. דִּי, דָא.]

[2] That זֶה may stand for the feminine, cannot be proved either from Ju 16[28] or from the certainly corrupt passage in Jos 2[17].

[3] זֹה 2 K 6[19], and in seven other places ; זוֹ only in Hos 7[16], ψ 132[12].

[4] According to Kuenen (cf. above, § 2 *n*) and Driver, on Lev 18[27] in Haupt's Bible, this אֵל is due to an error of the punctuators. It goes back to a time when the vowel of the second syllable was not yet indicated by a vowel letter, and later copyists wrongly omitted the addition of the ה. In Phoenician also it was written אל, but pronounced *ily* according to Plautus, *Poen*, v, 1, 9.

d   **2.** The secondary form זוּ occurs only in poetic style, and mostly for the relative, like our *that* for *who* [see Lexicon, s. v.]. Like אֲשֶׁר (§ 36), it serves for all numbers and genders.

e   Rem. 1. This pronoun takes the article (הָאֵל, הָאֵלֶּה, הַזֹּאת, הַזֶּה) according to the same rule as adjectives, see § 126 *u*; e. g. הָאִישׁ הַזֶּה *this man*, but זֶה הָאִישׁ *this is the man*.

f   2. Rarer secondary forms, with strengthened demonstrative force, are הַלָּזֶה Gn 24⁶⁵, 37¹⁹; הַלָּזוּ *fem.* Ez 36³⁵; and shortened הַלָּז, sometimes *masc.*, as in Ju 6²⁰, 1 S 17⁷⁶, 2 K 23¹⁷, Zc 2⁸, Dn 8¹⁶, sometimes *fem.*, 2 K 4²⁵ : cf. 1 S 14¹ [and 20¹⁹ LXX; see Commentaries and Kittel].

g   3. The personal pronouns of the 3rd person also often have a demonstrative sense, see § 136.

§ 35. *The Article.*

J. Barth, ' Der heb. u. der aram. Artikel,' in *Sprachwiss. Untersuch. zum Semit.*, Lpz. 1907, p. 47 ff.

a   **1.** The article, which is by nature a kind of demonstrative pronoun, never appears in Hebrew as an independent word, but always in closest connexion with the word which is defined by it. It usually takes the form הַ־, with *ă* and a strengthening of the next consonant, e. g. הַשֶּׁמֶשׁ *the sun*, הַיְאֹר *the river*, הַלְוִים *the Levites* (according to § 20 *m* for הַלְוִים, הַיְאֹר).

b   Rem. With regard to the *Dageš* in י after the article, the rule is, that it is inserted when a ה or ע follows the י, e. g. הַיְּהוּדִים *the Jews*, הַיְּעֵפִים *the weary* (בַּיְעֵנִים La 4³ *Qᵉrê* is an exception), but הַיְאוֹר, הַיְלָדִים, הַיְסוֹד, &c. *Dageš forte* also stands after the article in the prefix מְ in certain nouns and in the participles *Piʿēl* and *Puʿal* (see § 52 *c*) before ה, ע and ר, except when the guttural (or ר) has under it a short vowel in a sharpened syllable; thus הַמְהֻגְמָה Ez 22⁵, הַמְּעָרָה *the cave*, בַּמְּרֵעִים ψ 37¹ (cf. Jb 38⁴⁰, 1 Ch 4⁴¹); but הַמְהַלֵּךְ ψ 104³ (Ec 4¹⁵, 2 Ch 23¹²; before ע ψ 103⁴); הַמְעַשָּׂקָה Is 23¹²; חַמְרֻגְּלִים Jos 6²². Before letters other than gutturals this מְ remains without *Dageš*, according to § 20 *m*.

c   **2.** When the article stands before a guttural, which (according to § 22 *b*) cannot properly be strengthened, the following cases arise, according to the character of the guttural (cf. § 27 *q*).

(1) In the case of the weakest guttural, א, and also with ר (§ 22 *c* and *q*), the strengthening is altogether omitted. Consequently, the *Pathaḥ* of the article (since it stands in an open syllable) is always lengthened to *Qameṣ*; e. g. הָאָב *the father*, הָאַחֵר *the other*, הָאֵם *the mother*, הָאִישׁ *the man*, הָאוֹר *the light*, הָאֱלֹהִים ὁ θεός, הָרֶגֶל *the foot*, הָרֹאשׁ *the head*, הָרָשָׁע *the wicked*.

d   So also הָאֲשָׁפוֹת Neh 3¹³, because syncopated from הָאַשְׁפוֹת (cf. verse 14 and Baer on the passage); הָאֻזְקִים (as in Nu 11⁴, Ju 9⁴¹, 2 S 23³³, with the א

orthographically retained), for הָאָז֗ Jer 40⁴ (cf. בָּאז֗ verse 1) ; הַסוּרִים Ec 4¹⁴
for הָאַס֗ ; הָרֵמִים 2 Ch 22⁵ for הָאָר֗ (cf. 2 K 8²⁸).

(2) In the case of the other gutturals either the virtual strengthen- *e*
ing takes place (§ 22 c)—especially with the stronger sounds ח and
ה, less often with ע—or the strengthening is wholly omitted. In
the former case, the *Pathaḥ* of the article remains, because the syllable
is still regarded as closed; in the second case, the *Pathaḥ* is either
modified to *Sᵉghôl* or fully lengthened to *Qameṣ*. That is to say :—

A. When the guttural has any other vowel than *ā* (—) or *ŏ* (—), *f*
then

(1) before the stronger sounds ח and ה the article regularly remains
הַ ; e.g. הַהוּא *that,* הַחֹדֶשׁ *the month,* הַחַיִל *the force,* הַחָכְמָה *the wisdom.*
Before ח, *ā* occurs only in הָחַי Gn 6¹⁹ [not elsewhere], הֶחָרִיטִים Is 3²²,
הֶחָמָנִים Is 17⁸ [not elsewhere] ; before ה, always in הָהֵם, הָהֵמָּה.

(2) before ע the *Pathaḥ* is generally ¹lengthened to *Qameṣ*, e.g. הָעַיִן *g*
the eye, הָעִיר *the city,* הָעֶבֶד *the servant,* plur. הָעֲבָדִים ; לְעֲלִים 1 K 12³² ;
also in Gn 10¹⁷ הָעַרְקִי is the better reading. Exceptions are בְּעוֹפֶרֶת
Ex 15¹⁰, הַעִוְרִים 2 S 5⁶˙⁸, Is 42¹⁸, בַּעֶבֶד Is 24², הַעֹרְכִים Is 65¹¹, בַּעֶשֶׁק
Ez 22⁷, הַעֹזְבִים Pr 2¹³ and הַעֹזֶבֶת Pr 2¹⁷, לָעֵינַיִם 1 S 16⁷, Ec 11⁷ ; but
לָעֵינ֗ Gn 3⁶, Pr 10²⁶. Cf. Baer on Is 42¹⁸.

B. When the guttural has *ā* (—) then *h*

(1) immediately before a tone-bearing הָ or עָ the article is always
הָ, otherwise it is הֶ ; e.g. הָעָם *the people,* הָהָר *the mountain,* הָעָיִן (in
pause) *the eye,* הָהָרָה *towards the mountain* ; but (according to § 22 c)
הֶהָרִים *the mountains,* הֶעָוֹן *the iniquity.*

(2) before חָ the article is invariably הֶ without regard to the tone ; *i*
e.g. הֶחָכָם *the wise man,* הֶחָג *the festival.*

C. When the guttural has — the article is הֶ before חֳ ; e.g. *k*
הֶחֳדָשִׁים *the months* ; בֶּחֳרָבוֹת *in the waste places* (without the article בָּחֳ֗
bŏḥŏrābhôth) Ez 33²⁷, הֶחֳרָבוֹת Ez 36³⁵˙³⁸, cf. 2 Ch 27⁴ ; but הָ before עֳ, as
הָעֳמָרִים *the sheaves* Ru 2¹⁵.

The gender and number of the noun have no influence on the form
of the article.

Rem. 1. The original form of the Hebrew (and the Phoenician) article הַ· *l*
is generally considered to have been הַל, the ל of which (owing to the proclitic
nature of the article) has been invariably assimilated to the following consonant, as in יַקַּח from *yilqaḥ,* § 19 d. This view was supported by the form
of the Arabic article אַל (pronounced *hal* by some modern Beduin), the ל of
which is also assimilated at least before all letters like *s* and *t* and before *l, n,*
and *r,* e.g. *'al-Qur'ân* but *'as-sắnă* (Beduin *has-sana*) = Hebr. הַשָּׁנָה *the year.*

But Barth (*Amer. Journ. of Sem. Lang.*, 1896, p. 7 ff.), following Hupfeld and Stade, has shown that the Hebrew article is to be connected rather with the original Semitic demonstrative *hā*,[1] cf. Arab. *hāḏa*, Aram. *hāḏēn*, &c. The sharpening of the following consonant is to be explained exactly like the sharpening after וְ consecutive (§ 49 *f*; cf. also cases like כַּמָּה, בַּמֶּה, &c., § 102 *k*), from the close connexion of the *ha* with the following word, and the sharpening necessarily involved the shortening of the vowel.[2]

m　The Arabic article is supposed to occur in the Old Testament in אַלְמֻגִּים 1 K 10[11.12] (also אַלְגּוּמִּים 2 Ch 2[7], 9[10.11]), *sandal-wood* (?), and in אֶלְגָּבִישׁ *hail, ice* = גָּבִישׁ (Arab. *ǧibs*) Ez 13[11.13], 38[22], but this explanation can hardly be correct. On the other hand, in the proper name אֱלְמוֹדָד Gn 10[26] the first syllable is probably אֵל *God*, as suggested by D. H. Müller (see Lexicon, s. v.) and Nöldeke, *Sitzungsber. der Berl. Akad.*, 1882, p. 1186. אַלְקוּם Pr 30[31], commonly explained as = Arab. *al-qaum*, the militia, is also quite uncertain.

n　2. When the prefixes בְּ, לְ, כְּ (§ 102) come before the article, the ה is elided, and its vowel is thrown back to the prefix, in the place of the Šⁿwâ (§ 19 *k*, and § 23 *k*), e. g. בַּשָּׁמַיִם *in the heaven* for בְּהַשָּׁמַיִם (so ψ 36[6]) ; לָעָם for לְהָעָם *to the people*, בֶּהָרִים *on the mountains*, בֶּחֳדָשִׁים *in the months* ; also in Is 41[2], read כֶּעָפָר instead of the impossible כֶּהֱעָפָר. Exceptions to this rule occur almost exclusively in the later Books : Ez 40[25], 47[22], Ec 8[1], Dn 8[16], Neh 9[19], 12[3⁴], 2 Ch 10[7], 25[10], 29[27]; cf., however, 1 S 13[21], 2 S 21[20]. Elsewhere, e. g. 2 K 7[12], the Masora requires the elision in the *Qⁿrê*. A distinction in meaning is observed between כְּהַיּוֹם *about this time* (Gn 39[11], 1 S 9[13], &c.) and כַּיּוֹם *first of all* (Gn 25[31], &c.). After the copula וְ (*and*) elision of the ה does not take place, e. g. וְהָעָם.

o　3. The words אֶרֶץ *earth*, הַר *mountain*, חַג *feast*, עַם *people*, פַּר *bull*, always appear after the article with a long vowel (as in *pause*) ; הָעָם, הֶחָג, הָהָר, הָאָרֶץ, הַפָּר ; cf. also אֲרוֹן *ark* (so in the absol. st. in 2 K 12[10], 2 Ch 24[8], but to be read אָרוֹן), with the article always הָאָרוֹן.

§ 36. *The Relative Pronoun.*

The relative pronoun (cf. § 138) is usually the indeclinable אֲשֶׁר (*who, which,* &c.), originally a demonstrative pronoun ; see further §§ 138 and 155. In the later books, especially Eccles. and the late Psalms, also Lam. (4 times), Jon. (1[7]), Chron. (twice), Ezra (once),—and always in the Canticle (cf. also Ju 7[12], 8[26], 2 K 6[11]), שֶׁ is used instead ; more rarely שַׁ Ju 5[7], Ct 1[7] (Jb 19[29]?) ; once שָׁ before א Ju 6[17] (elsewhere שֶׁ before a guttural), before ה even שׁ Ec 3[18], and according to some (e. g. Qimḥi) also in Ec 2[22].[3] [See Lexicon, s. v.]

---

[1] An original form *han*, proposed by Ungnad, 'Der hebr. Art.,' in *OLZ.* x (1907), col. 210 f., and *ZDMG.* 1908, p. 80 ff., is open to grave objections.

[2] In the Liḥyanitic inscriptions collected by Euting (ed. by D. H. Müller in *Epigraphische Denkmäler aus Arabien*, Wien, 1889) the article is ה, and also in a North Arabian dialect, according to E. Littmann, *Safa-inschriften*, p. 2, Rem., and p. 34.

[3] The full form אשר does not occur in Phoenician, but only אש (= אֲשֶׁי ?), pronounced *asse, esse* (also *as, es, is, ys, us*), or—especially in the later Punic

§ 37. *The Interrogative and Indefinite Pronouns.*

1. The interrogative pronoun is מִי *who?* (of persons, even before *a*
plurals, Gn 33[5], Is 60[8], 2 K 18[35], and sometimes also of things Gn 33[8],
Ju 13[17], Mi 1[5]; cf. also בַּת־מִי *whose daughter ?* Gn 24[23]; לְמִי *to whom ?*
אֶת־מִי *whom?*)—מָה, מַה (see *b*) *what?* (of things).—אֵי־זֶה *which? what?*

The form ·מָה, מַ, &c. (followed by *Dageš forte conjunct.*: even in יְ, Hb 2[1], &c., *b*
against § 20 *m*) may be explained (like the art. הַ· § 35 *l*, and ·וַ in the *imperf.*
consec.) from the rapid utterance of the interrogative in connexion with the
following word. Most probably, however, the *Dageš forte* is rather due to
the assimilation of an originally audible ה (מַה, as Olshausen), which goes
back through the intermediate forms *math, mat* to an original *mant*: so
W. Wright, *Comparative Grammar*, Cambridge, 1890, p. 124, partly following
Böttcher, *Hebräische Grammatik*, § 261. A ground-form *mant* would most easily
explain מָן (*what?*), used in Ex 16[15] in explanation of מָן *manna*, while מַן is
the regular Aramaic for *who*. Socin calls attention to the Arabic *mah* (in
pause with an audible *h*: *Mufaṣṣal*, 193, 8). Observe further that—

(*a*) In the closest connexion, by means of *Maqqeph*, מַה־ takes a following *c*
Dageš (§ 20 *d*), e.g. מַה־לָּךְ *what is it to thee?* and even in *one* word, as מַלָּכֶם
what is it to you? Is 3[15]; cf. Ex 4[2], Mal 1[13], and even before a guttural, מֵהֶם
Ez 8[6] *K*ᵉ*thîbh*.

(*b*) Before gutturals in close connexion, by means of *Maqqeph* or (e.g. Ju 14[18], *d*
1 S 20[1]) a conjunctive accent, either מַה is used with a virtual strengthening
of the guttural (§ 22 *c*), so especially before ה, and, in Gn 31[36], Jb 21[21], before ח
—or the doubling is wholly omitted. In the latter case either (cf. § 35 *e–k*)
ă is fully lengthened to *Qames* (so always before the ה of the article, except in
Ec 2[12]; also before הָמָה, הֵנָּה, and so ה (Hb 2[18]), א (2 S 18[22], 2 K 8[14]),
ע (Gn 31[22], 2 K 8[13]), or modified to *Sᵉghôl*, especially before ע, ח, and generally
before ה. The omission of the strengthening also takes place as a rule with
ה, ח, ע, when they have not *Qames*, and then the form is either מָה or מֶה,
the latter especially before ה or ע, if *Maqqeph* follows.

The longer forms מָה and מֶה are also used (מֶה even before letters which *e*
are not gutturals) when not connected by *Maqqeph* but only by a *conjunctive*
accent. As a rule מָה is then used, but sometimes מֶה when at a greater distance from the principal tone of the sentence, Is 1[5], ψ 4[3]. (On מֶה in the
combinations בַּמֶּה, כַּמֶּה, and even לְמֶה, 1 S 1[8], cf. § 102 *k* and *l*.)

(*c*) In the principal pause מָה is used without exception; also as a rule *f*
with the smaller *disjunctives*, and almost always before gutturals (מֶה only in
very few cases). On the other hand, מֶה more often stands before letters
which are not gutturals, when at a greater distance from the principal tone
of the sentence, e.g. 1 S 4[6], 15[14], 2 K 1[7], Hag 1[9] (see Köhler on the passage),
ψ 10[13], Jb 7[21]; cf., however, Pr 31[2], and Delitzsch on the passage.

2. On מִי and מָה as indefinite pronouns in the sense of *quicunque, g*
quodcunque, and as relatives, *is qui, id quod*, &c., see § 137 *c*.

---

and in the *Poenulus* of Plautus—שׂ (*sa, si, sy, su*). Also in New Hebrew ·שֶׁ
has become the common form. Cf. Schröder, *Phön. Sprache*, p. 162 ff. and
below, § 155; also Bergsträsser, ' Das hebr. Präfix שׁ,' in *ZAW*. 1909, p. 40 ff.

CHAPTER II

THE VERB

§ 38. *General View.*

a　Verbal stems are either original or derived. They are usually divided into—

(a) Verbal stems proper (*primitive verbs*), which exhibit the stem without any addition, e, g. מָלַךְ *he has reigned.*

b　(b) *Verbal derivatives*, i. e. *secondary* verbal stems, derived from the pure stem (letter *a*), e. g. קִדֵּשׁ *to sanctify,* הִתְקַדֵּשׁ *to sanctify oneself,* from קָדַשׁ *to be holy.* These are usually called *conjugations* (§ 39).

c　(c) *Denominatives,*[1] i. e. verbs derived from nouns (like the Latin *causari, praedari,* and Eng. *to skin, to stone*), or even from particles (see *d*, end) either in a primitive or derivative form, e. g. אָהַל, *Qal* and *Pi'ēl, to pitch a tent,* from אֹהֶל *tent*; הִשְׁרִישׁ and שֵׁרֵשׁ *to take root,* and שֵׁרֵשׁ *to root out,* from שֹׁרֶשׁ *root* (§ 52 *h*).

d　This does not exclude the possibility that, for nouns, from which denominative verbs are derived, the corresponding (original) verbal stem may still be found either in Hebrew or in the dialects. The meaning, however, is sufficient to show that the denominatives have come from the noun, not from the verbal stem, e. g. לְבֵנָה *a brick* (verbal stem לבן *to be white*), denomin. לְבַּן *to make bricks*; דָּג *a fish* (verbal stem דָּנָה *to be prolific*), denomin. דּוּג *to fish*; חָרַף *to winter* (from חֹרֶף *autumn, winter,* stem חָרַף *to pluck*); קוּץ *to pass the summer* (from קַיִץ *summer,* stem קִיץ *to be hot*).

On 'Semitic verbs derived from particles' see P. Haupt in the *Amer. Journ. of Sem. Lang.,* xxii (1906), 257 ff.

§ 39. *Ground-form and Derived Stems.*

Brockelmann, *Sem. Sprachwiss.,* p. 119 ff.; *Grundriss,* p. 504 ff.

a　1. The 3rd sing. masc. of the *Perfect* in the form of the pure stem (i. e. in *Qal,* see *e*) is generally regarded, lexicographically and grammatically, as the ground-form of the verb (§ 30 *a*), e. g. קָטַל *he has killed,* כָּבֵד *he was heavy,* קָטֹן *he was little.*[2] From this form the other

---

[1] Cf. W. J. Gerber, *Die hebr. Verba denom., insbes. im theol. Sprachgebr. des A. T.,* Lpz. 1896.

[2] For the sake of brevity, however, the meaning in Hebrew-English Lexicons is usually given in the Infinitive, e. g. לָמַד *to learn,* properly *he has learnt.*

persons of the *Perfect* are derived, and the *Participle* also is connected
with it. קְטֹל or קְטַל, like the Imperative and Infinitive construct in
sound, may also be regarded as an alternative ground-form, with
which the Imperfect (see § 47) is connected.

In verbs ע״וּ (i.e. with וּ for their second radical) the stem-form, given both *b*
in Lexicon and Grammar, is not the 3rd sing. masc. Perfect (consisting of two
consonants), but the form with medial וּ, which appears in the Imperative
and Infinitive; e.g. שׁוּב *to return* (3rd pers. perf. שָׁב): the same is the case
in most stems with medial יּ, e.g. דִּין *to judge*.

2. From the pure stem, or *Qal*, the derivative stems are formed *c*
according to an unvarying analogy, in which the idea of the stem
assumes the most varied shades of meaning, according to the changes
in its form (intensive, frequentative, privative, causative, reflexive,
reciprocal; some of them with corresponding passive forms), e.g.
לָמַד *to learn,* לִמַּד *to teach*; שָׁכַב *to lie,* הִשְׁכִּיב *to lay*; שָׁפַט *to judge,*
נִשְׁפַּט *to contend.* In other languages such formations are regarded
as new or *derivative* verbs, e.g. Germ. *fallen* (to fall), *fällen* (to fell);
trinken (to drink), *tränken* (to drench); Lat. *lactere* (to suck, Germ.
saugen), *lactare* (to suckle, Germ. *säugen*); *iacĕre* (to throw), *iacēre*
(to lie down); γίνομαι, γεννάω. In Hebrew, however, these formations
are incomparably more regular and systematic than (e.g.) in Greek,
Latin, or English; and, since the time of Reuchlin, they have usually
been called *conjugations* of the primitive form (among the Jewish
grammarians בִּנְיָנִים, i.e. *formations*, or more correctly *species*), and are
always treated together in the grammar and lexicon.[1]

3. The changes in the primitive form consist either in internal *d*
modification by means of vowel-change and strengthening of the middle
consonant (קִטֵּל, קָטַל; קוֹטֵל, קוֹטַל; cf. *to lie, to lay; to fall, to fell*), or
in the repetition of one or two of the stem-consonants (קְטַלְטַל, קְטַלֵל),
or finally in the introduction of formative additions (נִקְטַל), which may
also be accompanied by internal change (הִתְקַטֵּל, הִקְטִיל). Cf. § 31 *b*.

In Aramaic the formation of the conjugations is effected more by formative
additions than by vowel-change. The vocalic distinctions have mostly become
obsolete, so that, e.g. the reflexives with the prefix הִת, אִת, אֶת have entirely
usurped the place of the passives. On the other hand, Arabic has preserved
great wealth in both methods of formation, while Hebrew in this, as in other
respects, holds the middle place (§ 1 *m*).

4. Grammarians differ as to the *number* and *arrangement* of these *e*
conjugations. The common practice, however, of calling them by the

---

[1] The term *Conjugation* thus has an entirely different meaning in Hebrew
and Greek or Latin grammar.

old grammatical terms, prevents any misunderstanding. The simple form is called *Qal* (קַל *light*, because it has no formative additions) ; the others (כְּבֵדִים *heavy*, being weighted, as it were, with the strengthening of consonants or with formative additions) take their names from the paradigm of פָּעַל *he has done*,[1] which was used in the earliest Jewish grammatical works. Several of these have passives which are distinguished from their actives by more obscure vowels. The common conjugations (including *Qal* and the passives) are the seven following, but very few verbs exhibit them all :

		Active.			Passive.
f	1. Qal	קָטַל *to kill*.			(Cf. § 52 *e*.)
	2. Niph'al	נִקְטַל *to kill oneself* (rarely passive).			
	3. Pi'ēl	קִטֵּל *to kill many, to massacre*.	4. Pu'al	קֻטַּל.
	5. Hiph'îl	הִקְטִיל *to cause to kill*.	6. Hoph'al	הָקְטַל.
	7. Hithpa'ēl	הִתְקַטֵּל *to kill oneself*.	[Very rare, Hothpa'al	הָתְקַטַּל.]

g There are besides several less frequent conjugations, some of which, however, are more common in the kindred languages, and even in Hebrew (in the weak verb) regularly take the place of the usual conjugations (§ 55).

In Arabic there is a greater variety of conjugations, and their arrangement is more appropriate. According to the Arabic method, the Hebrew conjugations would stand thus: 1. *Qal*; 2. *Pi'ēl* and *Pu'al*; 3. *Pô'ēl* and *Pô'al* (see § 55 *b*); 4. *Hiph'îl* and *Hoph'al*; 5. *Hithpa'ēl* and *Hothpa'al*; 6. *Hithpô'ēl* (see § 55 *b*); 7. *Niph'al*; 8. *Hithpa'ēl* (see § 54 *l*); 9. *Pi'lēl* (see § 55 *d*). A more satisfactory division would be into three classes: (1) The intensive *Pi'ēl* with the derived and analogous forms *Pu'al* and *Hithpa'ēl*. (2) The causative *Hiph'îl* with its passive *Hoph'al*, and the analogous forms (*Šaph'ēl* and *Tiph'ēl*). (3) The reflexive or passive *Niph'al*.

---

[1] This paradigm was borrowed from the Arabic grammarians, and, according to Bacher, probably first adopted throughout by Abulwalîd. It was, however, unsuitable on account of the guttural, and was, therefore, usually exchanged in later times for פָּקַד, after the example of Moses Qimḥi. This verb has the advantage, that all its conjugations are actually found in the Old Testament. On the other hand, it has the disadvantage of indistinctness in the pronunciation of some of its forms, e. g. פָּקַדְתְּ, פְּקַדְתֶּם. The paradigm of קָטַל, commonly used since the time of Danz, avoids this defect, and is especially adapted for the comparative treatment of the Semitic dialects, inasmuch as it is found with slight change (Arab. and Ethiop. קתל) in all of them. It is true that in Hebrew it occurs only three times in *Qal*, and even then only in poetic style (ψ 139[19], Jb 13[15], 24[14]); yet it is worth retaining as a model which has been sanctioned by usage. More serious is the defect, that a number of forms of the paradigm of קְטַל leave the beginner in doubt as to whether or not there should be a *Dageš* in the B*e*gadk*e*phath letters, and consequently as to the correct division of the syllables.

§ 40. *Tenses. Moods. Flexion.*

A. Ungnad, ' Die gegenseitigen Beziehungen der Verbalformen im Grund-stamm des semit. Verbs,' in *ZDMG.* 59 (1905), 766 ff., and his ' Zum hebr. Verbalsystem ', in *Beiträge zur Assyriologie* ed. by Fr. Delitzsch and P. Haupt, 1907, p. 55 ff.

1. While the Hebrew verb, owing to these derivative forms or *a* conjugations, possesses a certain richness and copiousness, it is, on the other hand, poor in the matter of *tenses* and *moods.* The verb has only two *tense*-forms (*Perfect* and *Imperfect,* see the note on § 47 *a*), besides an *Imperative* (but only in the active), two *Infinitives* and a *Participle.* All relations of time, absolute and relative, are expressed either by these forms (hence a certain diversity in their meaning, § 106 ff.) or by syntactical combinations. Of moods properly so called (besides the *Imperfect Indicative* and *Imperative*), only the *Jussive* and *Optative* are sometimes indicated by express modifications of the Imperfect-form (§ 48).

2. The *inflexion* of the *Perfect, Imperfect,* and *Imperative* as to *b* persons, differs from that of the Western languages in having, to a great extent, distinct forms for the two genders, which correspond to the different forms of the *personal pronoun. It is from the union of the pronoun with the verbal stem that the personal inflexions of these tenses arise.*

The following table will serve for the beginner as a provisional *c* scheme of the formative syllables (*afformatives* and *preformatives*) of the two *tenses.* The three stem-consonants of the strong verb are denoted by dots. Cf. § 44 ff. and the Paradigms.

PERFECT.

	Singular.					Plural.			
3. *m.*		•	•	•	3. *c.*	וּ	•	•	•
3. *f.*	הָ	•	•	•					
2. *m.*	תָּ	•	•	•	2. *m.*	תֶּם	•	•	•
2. *f.*	תְּ	•	•	•	2. *f.*	תֶּן	•	•	•
1. *c.*	תִּי	•	•	•	1. *c.*	נוּ	•	•	•

IMPERFECT.

	Singular.					Plural.				
3. *m.*	•	•	•	י	3. *m.*	י	•	•	•	י
3. *f.*	•	•	•	ת	3. *f.*	נָ	•	•	•	ת
2. *m.*	•	•	•	ת	2. *m.*	י	•	•	•	ת
2. *f.*	יְ	•	•	•	ת	2. *f.*	נָ	•	•	•	ת
1. *c.*	•	•	•	א	1. *c.*	•	•	•	נ	

§ 41. *Variations from the Ordinary Form of the Strong Verb.*

a   The same laws which are normally exhibited in stems with strong (unchangeable) consonants, hold good for all other verbs. Deviations from the model of the strong verb are only modifications due to the special character or weakness of certain consonants, viz. : —

(*a*) When one of the stem-consonants (or *radicals*) is a guttural. In this case, however, the variations only occur in the vocalization (according to § 22), not in the consonants. The *guttural verbs* (§§ 62–65) are, therefore, only a variety of the *strong verb*.

b   (*b*) When a stem-consonant (*radical*) disappears by assimilation (§ 19 *b–f*), or when the stem originally consisted of only two consonants (*verbs* פ״נ, ע״ע, and ע״י, as נַגֵּשׁ, קַל, קוּם, §§ 66, 67, 72).

c   (*c*) When one of the stem-consonants (*radicals*) is a weak letter. In this case, through aphaeresis, elision, &c., of the weak consonant, various important deviations from the regular form occur. Cf. § 68 ff. for these verbs, such as יָשַׁב, מָצָא, גָּלָה.

d   Taking the old paradigm פָּעַל as a model, it is usual, following the example of the Jewish grammarians, to call the first radical of any stem פ, the second ע, and the third ל. Hence the expressions, *verb* פ״א for a verb whose first radical is א (*primae radicalis* [*sc. literae*] א); ע״ו for *mediae radicalis* ו; ע״ע for a verb whose second radical is repeated to form a third.

I.   The Strong Verb.

§ 42.

As the formation of the strong verb is the model also for the weak verb, a statement of the general formative laws should precede the treatment of special cases.

Paradigm B, together with the Table of the personal preformatives and afformatives given in § 40 *c*, offers a complete survey of the normal forms. A full explanation of them is given in the following sections (§§ 43–55), where each point is elucidated on its first occurrence ; thus e. g. the inflexion of the Perfect, the Imperfect and its modifications, will be found under Qal, &c.

A.   The Pure Stem, or Qal.

§ 43. *Its Form and Meaning.*

a   The common form of the 3rd sing. masc. of the *Perfect Qal* is קָטַל, with *ă* (*Pathaḥ*) in the second syllable, especially in *transitive* verbs (but see § 44 *c*). There is also a form with *ē* (*Ṣere*, originally *ĭ*), and another with *ō* (*Ḥolem*, originally *ŭ*) in the second syllable, both of which, however, have almost always an *intransitive*[1] meaning,

---

[1] But cf. such instances as Jer 48⁵. In Arabic also, transitive verbs are found with middle *ĭ*, corresponding to Hebrew verbs with *ē* in the second

and serve to express states and qualities, e.g. כָּבֵד *to be heavy,* קָטֹן *to be small.*

In Paradigm B a verb *middle a,* a verb *middle ē,* and a verb *middle ō* are accordingly given side by side. The second example כָּבֵד is chosen as showing, at the same time, when the *Dageš lene* is to be inserted or omitted.

Rem. 1. The vowel of the second syllable is the principal vowel, and hence *b* on it depends the distinction between the transitive and intransitive meaning. The *Qameṣ* of the first syllable is lengthened from an original ă (cf. Arabic *qătălă*), but it can be retained in Hebrew only immediately before the tone, or at the most (with an open ultima) in the counter-tone with *Metheg*; otherwise, like all the pretonic vowels (ā, ē), it becomes *Šᵉwâ,* e. g. קְטַלְתֶּם 2nd *plur. masc.* In the Aramaic dialects the vowel of the first syllable is always reduced to Šᵉwâ, as קְטַל = Hebr. קָטַל. The intransitive forms in Arabic are *qătĭlă, qătŭlă*; in Hebrew (after the rejection of the final vowel) ĭ being in the tone-syllable has been regularly lengthened to ē, and ŭ to ō.

2. Examples of *denominatives* in Qal are: חָמַר *to cover with pitch,* from חֵמָר *c pitch*; מָלַח *to salt,* from מֶלַח *salt*; שָׁבַר (usually *Hiph.*) *to buy or sell corn,* from שֶׁבֶר *corn*; see above, § 38 *c.*

§ 44. *Flexion of the Perfect of Qal.*[1]

1. The formation of the persons of the Perfect is effected by the *a* addition of certain forms of the personal pronoun, and marks of the 3rd fem. sing. and 3rd pl. (as *afformatives*) to the *end* of the verbal-stem, which contains the idea of a predicate, and may be regarded, in meaning if not in form, as a *Participle* or *verbal adjective.* For the 3rd *pers. sing. masc. Perfect,* the pronominal or subject idea inherent in the finite verb is sufficient: thus, קָטַל *he has killed,* קָטַלְתָּ *thou hast killed* (as it were, *killing thou,* or *a killer thou*), *a killer wast thou* = קטל אַתָּה; יָרֵא *he was fearing,* יְרֵאתֶם *ye were fearing* = ירא אַתֶּם. The ending of the 1st pers. plur. (נוּ—) is also certainly connected with the termination of אֲנַחְנוּ, אנו *we* (§ 32 *b, d*). The afformative of the 1st pers. sing. (תִּי) is to be referred, by an interchange of כ and ת (cf. § 33 *f*), to that form of the pronoun which also underlies אָנֹכִי, I.[2] In the *third* person ה— (originally ת—, cf. below, *f*) is the mark of the feminine, as in a great number of nouns (§ 80 *c*), and ו is the termination of the plural; cf., for the latter, the termination of the 3rd and 2nd pers. plur. Imperf. *ûna* in Arabic and *û* (often also וּן)

syllable. Hence P. Haupt (*Proc. Amer. Or. Soc.,* 1894, p. ci f.) prefers to distinguish them as *verba voluntaria* (actions which depend on the will of the subject) and *involuntaria* (actions or states independent of the will of the subject).

[1] Cf. Nöldeke, 'Die Endungen des Perfects' (*Untersuchungen zur semit.* Gramm. ii.), in *ZDMG.* vol. 38, p. 407 ff., and more fully in *Beiträge zur sem. Sprachwiss.,* Strassb. 1904, p. 15 ff.

[2] According to Nöldeke, *l.c.,* p. 419, the original Semitic termination of the 1st sing. Perf. was most probably *kû*; cf. the Ethiopic *qatalku,* Arabic *qataltu.*

in Hebrew, also *ûna* (in the construct state *û*) as the plural termination of masc. nouns in literary Arabic.

b 2. The characteristic *Pathaḥ* of the second syllable becomes *Šᵉwâ* before an afformative beginning with a vowel, where it would otherwise stand in an open syllable (as קָטְלָה, קָטְלוּ; but in *pause* קָטָלָה, קָטָלוּ). Before an afformative beginning with a consonant the *Pathaḥ* remains, whether in the tone-syllable (קָטַלְתְּ, קָטַלְתְּ, קָטַלְתִּי, קָטַלְנוּ; in *pause* קָטָלְתְּ &c.) or *before* it. In the latter case, however, the *Qameṣ* of the first syllable, being no longer a pretonic vowel, becomes vocal *Šᵉwâ*; as קְטַלְתֶּם, קְטַלְתֶּן; cf. § 27 *i* and § 43 *b*. On the retention of *ā* with *Metheg* of the counter-tone in the *Perf. consecutive*, cf. § 49 *i*.

c Rem. 1. Verbs *middle ē* in Hebrew (as in Ethiopic, but not in Arabic or Aramaic) generally change the *E*-sound in their inflexion into *Pathaḥ* (frequently so even in the 3rd sing. masc. Perf.). This tendency to assimilate to the more common verbs *middle a* may also be explained from the laws of vocalization of the tone-bearing closed penultima, which does not readily admit of *Ṣere*, and never of *Ḥireq*, of which the *Ṣere* is a lengthening (cf. § 26 *p*). On the other hand, *Ṣere* is retained in an open syllable; regularly so in the weak stems ל״א (§ 74 *g*), before suffixes (§ 59 *i*), and in the pausal forms of the strong stem in an open tone-syllable, e. g. דָּבֵקָה *it cleaveth*, Jb 29¹⁰ (not דָּבְקָה), cf. 2 S 1²³, Jb 41¹⁵; even (contrary to § 29 *q*) in a *closed* pausal syllable, e. g. שָׁבֵן, Dt 33¹² (out of pause שָׁכַב, Is 32¹⁶); but קָרֵאל Is 33⁹, &c., according to § 29 *q*.

d 2. In some weak stems *middle a*, the *Pathaḥ* under the second radical sometimes, in a closed toneless syllable, becomes ⸺, and, in one example, ⸺. Thus from יָרֵשׁ: וִירִשְׁתָּהּ *and thou shalt possess it*, Dt 17¹⁴; וִירִשְׁתָּם Dt 19¹; וִירִשְׁתֶּם Dt 4¹, and frequently; from יָלַד *to bring forth, to beget*; יְלִדְתִּיךָ ψ 2⁷ (cf. Nu 11¹², Jer 2²⁷, 15¹⁰); from פּוּשׁ; וּפִשְׁתֶּם Mal 3²⁰; from שָׁאַל; שְׁאִלְתִּיו *I have asked him*, 1 S 1²⁰ (Ju 13⁶), and three times שְׁאֶלְתֶּם 1 S 12¹³, 25⁵, Jb 21²⁹. Qimḥi already suggests the explanation, that the *i* (*ĕ*) of these forms of שָׁאַל and יָרֵשׁ is the original vowel, since along with שָׁאַל and יָרֵשׁ are also found שָׁאֵל and יָרֵשׁ (see the Lexicon). The possibility of this explanation cannot be denied (especially in the case of יָרֵשׁ, see § 69 *s*); the *i* in these forms might, however, equally well have arisen from an attenuation of *ă* (§ 27 *s*), such as must in any case be assumed in the other instances. Moreover, it is worthy of notice that in all the above cases the *i* is favoured by the character of the following consonant (a sibilant or dental), and in most of them also by the tendency towards assimilation of the vowels (cf. § 54 *k* and § 64 *f*).

e 3. In verbs *middle ō*, the *Ḥolem* is retained in the tone-syllable, e. g. יָנֹרְתָּ *thou didst tremble*; יָכֹלוּ in *pause* for יָכְלוּ *they were able*; but in a toneless closed syllable the original short vowel appears in the form of a *Qameṣ ḥaṭuph*; יָכָלְתִּיו *I have prevailed against him*, ψ 13⁵; וְיָכָלְתָּ (see § 49 *h*) *then shalt thou be able*, Ex 18²³; in a toneless open syllable it becomes vocal *Šᵉwâ*, e. g. יְכְלָה, יְכְלוּ.

f 4. Rarer forms¹ are: Sing. 3rd *fem.* in ת⸺ (as in Arabic, Ethiopic, and

¹ Many of these forms, which are uncommon in Hebrew, are usual in the

Aramaic), e. g. אָזְלַת *it is gone*, Dt 32³⁶; וְנִשְׁבַּחַת Is 23¹⁵ (in the Aramaic form, for וְנִשְׁכָּחָה); from a verb ע״וׁ, וְשָׁבַת, cf. § 72 *o*. This original feminine ending -*ath* is regularly retained before suffixes, see § 59 *a*; and similarly in stems ל״ה, either in the form *āth* (which is frequent also in stems ל״א § 74 *g*), or with the *Pathaḥ* weakened to *vocal Šᵉwâ* before the pleonastic ending ה‿, e. g. גָּלְתָה § 75 *i*. In Ez 31⁵ the Aramaic form גָּבְהָא occurs instead of גָּבְהָה.

2nd *masc.* תָּה for תָּ (differing only orthographically), e. g. בָּגַדְתָּה *thou hast* **g** *dealt treacherously*, Mal 2¹⁴; cf. 1 S 15³, Gn 3¹² (נָתַתָּה which is twice as common as נָתַתָּ, cf. § 66 *h*); Gn 21²³, 2 S 2²⁶, 2 K 9³, Is 2⁶, ψ 56⁹ (so also in *Hiph'il*; 2 K 9⁷, Is 37²³, ψ 60⁴).

2nd *fem.* has sometimes a Yodh at the end, as in הָלַכְתִּי *thou wentest*, Jer 31²¹; **h** cf. 2³³, 3⁴·⁵, 4¹⁹ (but read the ptcp. שֹׁמַעַת, with the LXX, instead of the 2nd fem.), 46¹¹, and so commonly in Jeremiah, and Ez (16¹⁸, &c.); see also Mi 4¹³, Ru 3³·⁴. הָלַכְתִּי, &c., is really intended, for the vowel signs in the text belong to the marginal reading הָלַכְתְּ (without י)[1] as in the corresponding pronoun אַתִּי (אַתְּ) § 32 *h*. The ordinary form has rejected the final *i*, but it regularly reappears when pronominal suffixes are added (§ 59 *a*, *c*).

1st *pers. comm.* sometimes without Yodh, as יָדַעְתְּ ψ 140¹³, Jb 42², 1 K 8⁴⁸, **i** Ez 16⁵⁹ (all in Kᵉthîbh), ψ 16², without a Qᵉrê; in 2 K 18²⁰ also אָמַרְתְּ is really intended, as appears from Is 36⁵. The Qᵉrê requires the ordinary form, to which the vowels of the text properly belong, whilst the Kᵉthîbh is probably to be regarded as the remains of an earlier orthography, which omitted vowel-letters even at the end of the word.

תֶן as the termination of the 2nd *plur. m.* for תֶּם Ez 33²⁶, might just possibly **k** be due to the following ה (cf., for an analogous case, Mi 3¹², § 87 *e*), but is probably a copyist's error. Plur. 2nd *fem.* in תֶּנָה- (according to others תֶּנָּה-) Am 4³, but the reading is very doubtful; since ה follows, it is perhaps merely due to dittography; cf., however, אַתֵּנָה § 32 *i*.

3rd *plur. comm.* has three times the very strange termination וּן[2]; יְדָעוּן Dt **l** 8³·¹⁶ (both before א, and hence, no doubt, if the text is correct, to avoid a hiatus), and in the still more doubtful form עָקוּן Is 26¹⁶; on וּן in the Imperf. see § 47 *m*; on the affixed א in Jos 10²⁴, Is 28¹², see § 23 *i*.

It is very doubtful whether, as in most Semitic languages (see § 47 *c*, note), **m** the 3rd-*fem. plur.* in Hebrew was originally distinguished from the 3rd *masc.*

---

other Semitic dialects, and may, therefore, be called Aramaisms (Syriasms) or Arabisms. They must not, however, be regarded as cases of borrowing, but as a return to original forms.

[1] Where the Masora apparently regards the תִּי as the termination of the 2nd *sing. fem.*, e. g. in Jer 2²⁰ (twice), Mi 4¹³, it has rather taken the form as 1st *pers. sing.* (cf. Stade, *Gramm.*, p. 253); so in Ju 5⁷, where קַמְתִּי, on account of verse 12, must either have originally been intended as 2nd *sing. fem.*, or is due to an erroneous pronunciation of the form קמת as קַמְתְּ instead of 3rd *sing. fem.* קָמַת (as LXX).

[2] That these examples can hardly be referred to a primitive Semitic ending *ûn* in the 3rd plur. Perf., has been shown by Nöldeke in *ZDMG.* vol. 38, p. 409 ff.; cf. also *ZDMG.* vol. 32, p. 757 f., where G. Hoffmann proves that the terminations in *Nûn* of the 3rd plur. in Aramaic, formerly adduced by us, are secondary forms. [See also Driver, *Heb. Tenses*³, p. 6 *note*.]

plur. by the termination הָ‎‗, as in Biblical Aramaic. Nöldeke (*ZDMG.* 38
[1884], p. 411) referred doubtfully to the textual readings in Dt 21⁷, Jos 15⁴,
18¹².¹⁴.¹⁹, Jer 2¹⁵, 22⁶, where the Masora uniformly inserts the termination *û*,
and to Gn 48¹⁰ in the Samaritan Pentateuch, Gn 49²², 1 S 4¹⁵, ψ 18³⁵, Neh 13¹⁰.
In his *Beiträge zur sem. Sprachwiss.*, p. 19, however, he observes that the construction of a fem. plural with the 3rd sing. fem. is not unexampled, and also
that ה‎ is often found as a mistake for וֹ. On the other hand Mayer Lambert
(*Une série de Qeré ketib*, Paris, 1891, p. 6 ff.) explains all these Kᵉthîbh, as well
as ψ 73², Jer 50⁶ (?), and (against Nöldeke) 1 K 22⁴⁹ (where ה‎ is undoubtedly
the article belonging to the next word), Jb 16¹⁶ (where the *masc.* פָּנָי requires the
marginal reading), also Jer 48⁴¹, 51⁵⁶, Ez 26², ψ 68¹⁴, as remains of the 3rd *fem.*
plur. in הָ‎‗. The form was abandoned as being indistinguishable from the
(later) form of the 3rd *fem. sing.*, but tended to be retained in the perfect of
verbs ה″ל, as הָיָה‎ Kᵉthîbh six times in the above examples.

n 5. The afformatives תָּ, (תְּ), תִּי, נוּ are generally toneless, and the forms
with these inflexions are consequently *Milʿēl* (קָטַלְתְּ, &c.) ; with all the other
afformatives they are *Milraʿ* (§ 15 *c*). The place of the tone may, however, be
shifted : (*a*) by the *pause* (§ 29 *i–v*), whenever a vowel which has become
vocal Šᵉwâ under the second stem-consonant is restored by the *pause* ; as
קָטָלָה for קָטְלָה, דָּבֵקָה for (דְּבֵקָה), and קָטָלוּ for קָטְלוּ, מָלֵאוּ for (מִלְאוּ) ; (*b*) in
certain cases after *wāw consecutive* of the Perfect (see § 49 *h*).

o 6. Contraction of a final ת with the ת of the afformative occurs e. g. in
כָּרַתִּי Hag 2⁵, &c. ; cf. Is 14²⁰, &c., in the *Perf. Poʿel* ; Dt 4²⁵ in the *Hiphʿîl* of
שָׁחַת ; Is 21², &c., in the *Hiphʿîl* of שָׁבַת. Contraction of a final נ with the
afformative נוּ occurs in נָתַנּוּ Gn 34¹⁶ ; in Niph. Ezr 9⁷, cf. 2 Ch 14¹⁰ ; in Hiph.
2 Ch 29¹⁹ ; with the afformative נָה in the *Imperfect Qal* Ez 17²³ ; *Piʿēl* ψ 71²³,
where with Baer and Ginsburg תְּרַנֶּנָּה is to be read, according to others
תְּרַנֶּנָה (cf. in *Polel* תְּקוֹנֶנָּה Ez 32¹⁶), but certainly not תְּרַנֶּנָה with the Mantua
ed., Opitius and Hahn ; with נָה in the *Imperat. Hiph.* Gn 4²³, Is 32⁹.

§ 45. *The Infinitive.*

F. Prätorius, 'Ueber den sog. Inf. absol. des Hebr.,' in *ZDMG.* 1902, p. 546 ff.

a 1. The Infinitive is represented in Hebrew by two forms, a shorter
and a longer ; both are, however, strictly speaking, independent *nouns*
(*verbal substantives*). The shorter form, *the Infinitive construct* (in Qal
קְטֹל,¹ sometimes incorrectly קְטוֹל), is used in very various ways, sometimes in connexion with pronominal suffixes, or governing a substantive
in the genitive, or with an accusative of the object (§ 115), sometimes
in connexion with prepositions (לִקְטֹל *to kill*, § 114 *f*), and sometimes
in dependence upon substantives as genitive, or upon verbs as accusative of the object. On the other hand, the use of the longer form,
the *Infinitive absolute* (in Qal קָטוֹל, sometimes also קָטֹל, obscured from
original *qâtâl*), is restricted to those cases in which it emphasizes

---

¹ Cf. the analogous forms of the noun, § 93 *t*.

the abstract verbal idea, without regard to the subject or object of the action. It stands most frequently as an adverbial accusative with a finite verb of the same stem (§ 113 *h–s*).[1]

The flexibility and versatility of the Infin. constr. and the rigidity *b* and inflexibility of the Infin. absol. are reflected in their vocalization. The latter has unchangeable vowels, while the ō of the Infin. constr. may be lost. For קְטֹל, according to § 84*a*, *e*, goes back to the ground-form *qŭṭŭl*.

Other forms of the Infin. constr. Qal of the strong verb are—   *c*

(*a*) קְטַל, e. g. שְׁכַב *to lie*, Gn 34⁷; שְׁפַל *to sink*, Ec 12⁴; especially with verbs which have ă in the second syllable of the Imperf.: hence sometimes also with those, whose second or third radical is a guttural (frequently besides the ordinary form). All the examples (except שְׁכַב, see above) occur in the closest connexion with the following word, or with suffixes (see § 61 *c*). In Ez 21³³ the Masora seems to treat לְטֶבַח (verse 20, in *pause* לְטָבַח) as an Infinitive = לִטְבֹּחַ; probably לְטֶבַח should be read.

(*b*) קַטְלָה and, attenuated from it, קִטְלָה; קָטְלָה and קְטֻלָה (which are *d* feminine forms[2] of קְטַל and קְטֹל, mostly from intransitive verbs, and sometimes found along with forms having no feminine ending in use), e. g. לְאַשְׁמָה *to be guilty*, Lv 5²⁶, אַהֲבָה *to love*, שִׂנְאָה *to hate*; לְיִרְאָה, often in Dt., *to fear*; זִקְנָה *to be old*; קִרְאָה *to meet* (in לִקְרַאת § 19 *k*); לְרִבְעָה *to lie down*, Lv 20¹⁶; לְמָשְׁחָה *to anoint*, Ex 29²⁹; לְרָחְצָה *to wash*, Ex 30¹⁸, &c.; לְטֻמְאָה (also a subst. = *uncleanness*, like טֻמְאָה) *to be unclean*, Lv 15³²; לְקָרְבָה *to approach*, Ex 36², &c.; cf. Lv 12⁴·⁵, Dt 11²², Is 30¹⁹, Ez 21¹⁶, Hag 1⁶; also רָחֳקָה *to be far off*, Ez 8⁶; חֶמְלָה *to pity*, Ez 16⁵; cf. Ho 7⁴. On the other hand in חָמְלָה Gn 19¹⁶, the original ă has been modified to ŏ; cf. חָזְקָה Is 8¹¹, &c.

(*c*) In the Aramaic manner (מִקְטַל but cf. also Arab. *maqtal*) there occur as *e* *Infin. Qal*: מִשְׁלוֹחַ *to send*, Est 9¹⁹; מִקְרָא *to call* and מַסַּע *to depart*, Nu 10² (Dt 10¹¹); מִקַּח *to take*, 2 Ch 19⁷, &c.; מַשָּׂא *to carry*, Nu 4²⁴, &c. (cf. even לְמַשָּׂאוֹת Ez 17⁹); also with a feminine ending מַעֲלָה *to go up*, Ezr 7⁹, &c.; cf. for these forms (almost all very late) Ryssel, *De Elohistae Pentateuchici sermone*, p. 50, and Strack on Nu 4²⁴.

(*d*) קְטֹלֶת in יָבֹשֶׁת Gn 8⁷; יְבֹלֶת Nu 14¹⁶; probably also חֲרֹשֶׁת Ex 31⁵, 35³³.

2. A kind of *Gerund* is formed by the *Infin. constr.* with the prepo- *f* sition לְ; as לִקְטֹל *ad interficiendum*, לִנְפֹּל *ad cadendum* (see § 28 *a*).

---

[1] The terms *absolute* and *construct* are of course not to be understood as implying that the Infin. constr. קְטֹל forms the *construct state* (see § 89) of the Infin. absol. (קָטוֹל ground-form *qăṭâl*). In the Paradigms the *Inf. constr.*, as the principal form, is placed before the other, under the name of Infinitive simply.

[2] According to the remark of Elias Levita on Qimḥi's *Mikhlol*, ed. Rittenb., 14 *a*, these feminine forms occur almost exclusively in connexion with the preposition לְ.

g The blending of the לְ with the *Infin. constr.* into a single grammatical form seems to be indicated by the firmly closed syllable, cf. לִשְׁכַּב Gn 34⁷; לִנְפֹּל ψ 118¹³, with *Dageš lene* in the פ = *lin-pōl*; hence, also *liq-ṭōl*, &c.; but בִּנְפֹל *binᵉphōl*, Jb 4¹³; בִּנְפֹּל 2 S 3³⁴. Exceptions לִצְבָא Nu 4²³, 8²⁴; לִנְתוֹשׁ וְלִנְתוֹץ Jer 1¹⁰, 18⁷, 31²⁸; לִשְׁדוֹד Jer 47⁴; לִטְבוֹחַ Jer 11¹⁹, &c., ψ 37¹⁴; לִבְדֹּק 2 Ch 34¹⁰; according to some also לִסְבֹב Nu 21⁴ and לִכְבֹּשׁ 2 Ch 28¹⁰ (Baer לִכְבּֽשׁ); on the other hand בִּשְׁכֹּן Gn 35²²; כִּזְבֹּר Jer 17². For the meaningless לִדְרִיוֹשׁ Ezr 10¹⁶ read לִדְרֹשׁ.

§ 46. *The Imperative.*

a 1. The ground-forms of the Imperative, קְטֹל (properly *qᵉṭŭl*, which is for an original *quṭŭl*), and קְטַל (see below, *c*), the same in pronunciation as the forms of the Infin. constr. (§ 45), are also the basis for the formation of the Imperfect (§ 47).[1] They represent the *second* person, and have both fem. and plur. forms. The third person is supplied by the Imperfect in the Jussive (§ 109 *b*); and even the second person must always be expressed by the Jussive, if it be used with a negative, e. g. אַל־תִּקְטֹל *ne occidas* (not אַל־קְטֹל). The passives have no Imperative, but it occurs in the reflexives, as Niphʻal and Hithpaʻēl.[2]

b 2. The Afformatives of the *2nd sing. fem.* and the *2nd plur. masc.* and *fem.* are identical in every case with those of the Imperfect (§ 47 *c*). In the same way, the Imperative of the *2nd sing. masc.*, in common with the Imperfect, admits of the lengthening by the ה‗ *paragogicum* (§ 48 *i*), as, on the other hand, there are certain shortened forms of this person analogous to the Jussive (§ 48. 5).

c Rem. 1. Instead of the form קְטֹל (sometimes also *plene*, e. g. שְׁמוֹר Ec 12¹³; before *Maqqeph* קְטָל־ with *Qameṣ ḥaṭuph*), those verbs which have an *a* in the final syllable of the *Imperf.* (i. e. especially verbs middle *ē*) make their Imperative of the form קְטַל, e. g. לְבַשׁ *dress!* (Perf. לָבַשׁ and (לְבֵשׁ); שְׁכַב *lie down!* in *pause* שְׁכָ֑ב 1 S 3⁵·⁶·⁹.

d 2. The first syllable of the sing. fem. and plur. masc. are usually to be pronounced with *Šᵉwâ mobile* (*qiṭᵉlî, qiṭᵉlû*, and so שִׁכְבִי, &c., without *Dageš lene*, and even מְשְׁכוּ with *Metheg*, Ex 12²¹; but cf. אִסְפִּי Jer 10¹⁷, and with the same phonetic combination חִשְׂפִּי Is 47²; see analogous cases in § 93 *m*); less frequently we find an *ŏ* instead of the *ĭ*, e. g. מָלְכִי *rule*, Ju 9¹⁰; מָשְׁכוּ *draw*, Ez 32²⁰; חָרְבוּ Jer 2¹² (cf. חָרְבִי Is 44²⁷); on קָסְמִי 1 S 28⁸ *Qᵉrê*, צָעֳקִי Jer. 22²⁰ (cf. 1 K 13⁷), see § 10 *h*. This *ŏ* arises (see above, *a*) from a singular ground-form *quṭŭl*, not from a retraction of the original *ŭ* of the second syllable. We must abandon the view that the forms with *ĭ* in the first syllable (cf. also

---

[1] The *Infin. absol.*, like the Greek Infin., is also sometimes used for the Imperative (§ 113 *bb*). Cf. in general, Koch, *Der semitische Inf.* (Schaffhausen, 1874).

[2] In *Hophʻal* an Imperative is found only twice (Ez 32¹⁹, Jer. 49⁸), and closely approximating in meaning to the reflexive.

עִבְרִי, מִכְרִי, חִגְרִי, אִמְרִי) arise from a weakening of the characteristic vowel ŏ. They, or at least some of them, must rather be regarded with Barth (*ZDMG.* 1889, p. 182) as analogous to the original *ĭ*-imperfects. See further analógies in §§ 47 *i* and 48 *i*; 61 *b*, 63 *n*.

The *pausal* form of the 2nd plur. masc. is גְּזֹרוּ 1 K 3²⁶; from שְׁמַע שְׁמָעוּ, *e* &c.; similarly the 2nd sing. fem. in *pause* is עֲבֹרִי Is 23¹²; even without the *pause* מְלֹוכִי Ju 9¹⁰·¹², *Keth.*; קְסֹומִי 1 S 28⁸, *Keth.* (cf. with this also מְלֹוכָה, &c., § 48 *i*); from שְׂמַח שְׂמָחִי Jo 2²¹.

3. In the 2nd plur. fem. שְׁמַעַן occurs once, in Gn 4²³ (for שְׁמַעְנָה) with loss *f* of the ה and insertion of a helping vowel, unless it is simply to be pointed שְׁמַעַן. Also instead of the abnormal קְרֶאָן Ex 2²⁰ (for קְרֶאנָה) we should perhaps read as in Ru 1²⁰ קְרֶאָן (cf. מְצֶאָן 1⁹ and לֵכְן, 1¹²).

On the examples of a 2nd plur. fem. in ‑ָ, Is 32¹¹, see § 48 *i*.

§ 47. *The Imperfect and its Inflexion.*

1. The persons of the Imperfect,[1] in contradistinction to those of *a* the Perfect, are formed by placing abbreviated forms of the personal pronoun (preformatives) *before* the stem, or rather before the abstract form of the stem (קְטֹל). As, however, the tone is retained on the characteristic vowel of the Stem-form, or even (as in the *2nd sing. fem.* and the *3rd* and *2nd plur. masc.*) passes over to the afformatives, the preformatives of the Imperfect appear in a much more abbreviated form than the afformatives of the Perfect, only *one* consonant (י, ת, א, נ) remaining in each form. But as this preformative combined with the

---

[1] On the use of the Semitic Perfect and Imperfect cf. § 106 ff. and the literature cited in § 106. For our present purpose the following account will suffice :—The name *Imperfect* is here used in direct contrast to the Perfect, and is to be taken in a wider sense than in Latin and Greek grammar. The Hebrew (Semitic) *Perf.* denotes in general that which is *concluded, completed*, and *past*, that which has happened and has come into effect ; but at the same time, also that which is *represented* as accomplished, even though it be continued into present time or even be actually still future. The *Imperf.* denotes, on the other hand, the *beginning*, the *unfinished*, and the *continuing*, that which is just happening, which is conceived as in process of coming to pass, and hence, also, that which is yet future ; likewise also that which occurs repeatedly or in a continuous sequence in the past (Latin Imperf.). It follows from the above that the once common designation of the Imperf. as a *Future* emphasizes only *one* side of its meaning. In fact, the use of Indo-Germanic tense-names for the Semitic tenses, which was adopted by the Syrians under the influence of the Greek grammarians, and after their example by the Arabs, and finally by Jewish scholars, has involved many misconceptions. The Indo-Germanic scheme of three periods of time (past, present, and future) is entirely foreign to the Semitic tense-idea, which regards an occurrence only from the point of view of completed or incomplete action.—In the formation of the two tenses the chief distinction is that in the Perfect the verbal stem precedes and the indication of the person is added afterwards for precision, while in the Imperf. the subject, from which the action proceeds or about which a condition is predicated, is expressed by a prefixed pronoun.

stem-form was not always sufficient to express at the same time differences both of gender and number, the distinction had to be further indicated, in several cases, by special *afformatives*. Cf. the table, § 40 *c*.

b 2. The derivation and meaning, both of the preformatives and the afformatives, can still, in most cases, be recognized.

In the *first* pers. אֶקְטֹל, plur. נִקְטֹל, א is probably connected with אֲנִי, and נ with נַחְנוּ; here no indication of gender or number by a special ending was necessary. As regards the vocalization, the Arabic points to the ground-forms *'ăqṭŭl* and *năqṭŭl*: the *ĭ* of the 1st plur. is, therefore, as in the other preformatives, attenuated from *a*. The *Sᵉghôl* of the 1st sing. is probably to be explained by the preference of the א for this sound (cf. § 22 *o*, but also § 51 *p*); according to Qimḥi, it arises from an endeavour to avoid the similarity of sound between אֶקְטֹל (which is the Babylonian punctuation) and יִקְטֹל, which, according to this view, was likewise pronounced *iqṭōl*.[1]

c The preformative ת of the *second* persons (תִּקְטֹל, ground-form *tăqṭŭl*, &c.) is, without doubt, connected with the ת of אַתָּה, אַתֶּם. &c., and the *afformative* ־ִי of the 2nd fem. sing. תִּקְטְלִי with the *i* of the original feminine form אַתִּי (see § 32 *h*). The *afformative* ו of the 2nd masc. plur. תִּקְטְלוּ (in its more complete form, ן, see *m*) is the sign of the plural, as in the 3rd pers., and also in the Perfect (§ 44 *a*). In the Imperfect, however, it is restricted in both persons to the masculine,[2] while the afformative נָה (also ־ֶן) of the 3rd and 2nd plur. fem. is probably connected with הֵנָּה *eae* and אַתֵּנָה *vos* (fem.).

d The preformatives of the *third* persons (י in the masc. יִקְטֹל, ground-form *yăqṭŭl*, plur. יִקְטְלוּ, ground-form *yăqṭŭlû*; ת in the fem. תִּקְטֹל, plur. תִּקְטֹלְנָה) have not yet met with any satisfactory explanation. With ת might most obviously be compared the original feminine

---

[1] Cf. § 24 *e*. In favour of the above view of Qimḥi may be urged the phonetic orthography אֵשׁ (in Pr 18²⁴ אִישׁ), 2 S 14¹⁹ (unless, with Perles, אֵשֶׁב is to be read), Mi 6¹⁰, for יֵשׁ, and יְשִׁי 1 Ch 2¹³ for יִשַׁי (as verse 12). Also הָאָזְכָּה Mi 6¹¹ is probably for הַיִן/ = הֲיֵין, הַיִן; אֶפְקֹד Is 10¹² for יִפְקֹד; אֶנְחֲמֵךְ Is 51¹⁹ for יְנַחֲמֵךְ; and conversely יִשָּׂשְׂכָר is for אִשְׁשָׂכָר = אִישׁ שָׂכָר. Similarly, יְשׁוּי 1 S 14⁴⁹ is probably for אֲשִׁיו or אֲשִׁיָה; in 2 S 23⁸ ישׁב בשׁבת is, according to the LXX, an error for יֹשְׁבֶת = אֶשְׁבָּעַת. In Assyrian also the simple *i* corresponds to the Hebrew י as the preformative of the Impf. Qal.

[2] This is also the proper gender of the plural syllable *û*, *ûn*. In Hebrew, indeed, it is used in the 3rd plur. *Perfect* for both genders, but in the kindred languages even there only for the masculine, e.g. in Syriac *qᵉṭălû*, *qᵉṭălûn*, with the feminine form *qᵉṭălên*, in Western Aram. *qᵉṭălû*, fem. *qᵉṭălā*; in Arab. *qătălû*, fem. *qătălnă*. Eth. *qătălû*, *qătălā*.

ending ◌ָה of nouns, and of the 3rd fem. sing. perfect. For the afformatives וֹ (וֹ) and נָה, see *c*.

3. The characteristic vowel of the second syllable becomes *Šewâ e* before tone-bearing afformatives which begin with a vowel, but is retained (as being in the tone-syllable) before the toneless afformative נָה.　Thus : תִּקְטְלִי, תִּקְטְלוּ, יִקְטְלוּ (but in *pause* תִּקְטֹלִי, &c.), תִּקְטֹלְנָה.

Rem. 1. The *ō* of the second syllable (as in the inf. constr. and imperat.), *f* being lengthened from an original *ŭ* in the tone-syllable, is only tone-long (§ 9 *r*). Hence it follows that : (*a*) it is incorrectly, although somewhat frequently, written *plene*; (*b*) before *Maqqeph* the short vowel appears as *Qameṣ ḥaṭuph*, e.g. וַיִּכְתָּב־שָׁם *and he wrote there*, Jos 8³² (but cf. also Ex 21³⁷, Jos 18²⁰); (*c*) it becomes *Šewâ* before the tone-bearing afformatives ◌ִי and וֹ (see above, *e*; but Jerome still heard e.g. *iezbuleni* for יִזְבְּלֵנִי; cf. *ZAW.* iv. 83).

Quite anomalous are the three examples which, instead of a shortening to *g Šewâ*, exhibit a long *û* : יִשְׁפּוֹטוּ הֵם Ex 18²⁶, immediately before the principal pause, but according to Qimḥi (ed. *Rittenb.* p.18ᵇ), ed. Mant., Ginsb., Kittel against the other editions, with the tone on the ultima; likewise לֹא־תַעֲבוּרִי מִזֶּה Ru 2⁸; תִּשְׁמוּרֻם (in principal pause) Pr 14³. In the first two cases perhaps יִשְׁפּוֹטוּ and תַּעֲבוּרִי (for יִשְׁפְּטוּ, &c.) are intended, in virtue of a retrogressive effect of the pause; in Pr 14³ תִּשְׁמְרֻם is to be read, with August Müller.

2. The *ō* of the second syllable is to be found almost exclusively with transi- *h* tive verbs middle *a*, like קָטַל. Intransitives *middle a* and *ē* almost always take *ă* (*Pathaḥ*)[1] in the impf., e.g. רָבַץ, יִרְבַּץ *to couch*, שָׁכַב, יִשְׁכַּב *to lie down*, לָמַד, יִלְמַד *to learn* is also originally intransitive = *to accustom oneself*); גָּדַל, יִגְדַּל *to become great* (but cf. שָׁכֵן and שָׁכֵן imperf. יִשְׁכֹּן *to dwell* and *to inhabit*, נָבֵל imperf. יִבֹּל *to wither*); also from verbs *middle ō*, as קָטֹן *to be small*, the imperf. has the form יִקְטַן.

Sometimes both forms occur together; those with *ō* having a transitive, *i* and those with *ă* an intransitive meaning, e.g. יִקְצֹר *he cuts off*, יִקָּצֵר *he is cut off*, i.e. *is short*; חָלַשׁ impf. *ō*, to overcome, Ex 17¹³; impf. *ă*, to be overcome, Jb 14¹⁰. More rarely both forms are used without any distinction, e.g. יֹשֵׁךְ and יִשֹּׁךְ *he bites*, יַחְפֹּץ and יֶחְפַּץ *he is inclined* (but only the latter with a transitive meaning = *he bends*, in Jb 40¹⁷). On the *a* of the impf. of verbs middle and third guttural, cf. § 64 *b*; § 65 *b*. In some verbs first guttural (§ 63 *n*), ע״ע (§ 67 *p*), פ״י (§ 69 *b*), and פ״א (§ 68 *c*), and in יִתֵּן for *yintēn* from נָתַן *to give*, instead of *ă* or *ō* a movable *Ṣere* (originally *ĭ*) is found in the second syllable. A trace of these *i*-imperfects[2] in the ordinary strong verb is probably to be found in וַיִּטְמְנוּ 2 K 7⁸, since טמן otherwise only occurs in Qal. We call these three forms of the imperfect after their characteristic vowel impf. *o*, impf. *a*, impf. *e*.

3. For the *3rd sing. fem.* תִּקְטֹל (= *tiq-ṭōl*), Baer requires in 1 S 25²⁰ תִּפְנֹשׁ *k* (but read with ed. Mant.,&c. תִּפְגֹּשׁ). For the *2nd sing. fem.* (תִּקְטְלִי) the form

---

[1] This *ă* is, however, by no means restricted to intransitive *strong* verbs; apart from verbs third guttural (§ 65 *b*), it is to be found in פ״ן and ע״ע, and in many verbs פ״א and פ״י (§§ 69-71).

[2] Cf. Barth, 'Das *ĭ*-Imperfekt im Nordsemitischen,' *ZDMG.* 1889, p. 177 ff.

תִּקְטֹל is found in Is 57⁸, Jer 3⁵, Ez 22⁴, 23³² , in every case after the regular form; but cf. also Ez 26¹⁴. In Is 17¹⁰, where the 2nd fem. precedes and follows, probably וּב׳ תִּזְרָעִין is to be read with Marti for תִּזְרָעֶנּוּ.—For the 3rd plur. *fem.* תִּקְטֹלְנָה we find in Jer 49¹¹, in pause תִּבְטָחוּ (for תִּבְטַחְנָה), and thrice (as if to distinguish it from the 2nd pers.) the form יִקְטֹלְנָה with the preformative י (as always in Western Aram., Arab., Eth., and Assyr.), in Gn 30³⁸, 1 S 6¹², Dn 8²². On the other hand, תִּקְטֹלְנָה appears in some cases to be incorrectly used even for the fem. of the 3rd pers. or for the masc. of the 2nd pers. *sing.* as תִּשְׁלַחְנָה Ju 5²⁶ (where, however, perhaps תִּשְׁלָחֶנָּה is to be read), and Ob¹³, for 2nd sing. masc., according to Olshausen a corruption of תִּשְׁלַח יָד; in Pr 1²⁰, 8³ for תָּרֹנָּה read תִּרְנֶה as in Jb 39²³; in Ex 1¹⁰ read תִּקְרֶאנָּ with the Samaritan.—In Is 27¹¹, 28³, as also in Jb 17¹⁶ (if we read טוֹבָתִי with LXX for the 2nd תִּקְוֹת), it is equally possible to explain the form as a plural. This small number of examples hardly justifies our finding in the above-mentioned passages the remains of an emphatic form of the Impf., analogous to the Arab. *Modus energicus I*, with the termination *ännä*.

l For נָה we frequently find, especially in the Pentateuch and mostly after *wāw consecutive*, simply וַ, e.g. Gn 19³³·³⁶, 37⁷, Ex 1¹⁸·¹⁹, 15²⁰, Nu 2⁵², Ez 3²⁰, 16⁵⁵; in Arab. always *nă*. According to Elias Levita תִּלְבַּשְׁן (2 S 13¹⁸) is the only example of this kind in the strong verb. The form וַתִּגְבְּהֶינָה (so also Qimḥi and ed. Mant.; but Baer, Ginsb. וַתִּגְבֹּהֶנָה) for *they were high*, Ez 16⁵⁰, is irregular, with יֶ inserted after the manner of verbs ע״ע and ע״וּ, § 67 *d*; § 72 *i*; according to Olshausen it is an error caused by the following form.

m 4. Instead of the plural forms in וּ there are, especially in the older books, over 300 forms[1] with the fuller ending וּן (with *Nûn paragogicum*), always bearing the tone; cf. § 29 *m* and § 44 *l*; on its retention before suffixes, see § 60 *e*; also defectively יְרִבֻן Ex 21¹⁸, 22⁸, &c. This usually expresses marked emphasis, and consequently occurs most commonly at the end of sentences (in the principal pause), in which case also the (pausal) vowel of the second syllable is generally retained. Thus there arise full-sounding forms such as יִלְקֹטוּן *they collect*, ψ 104²⁸; יִרְגָּזוּן *they tremble*, Ex 15¹⁴; תִּשְׁמָעוּן *ye shall hear*, Dt 1¹⁷; cf. Ex 34¹³, with Zaqeph qaṭon, Athnaḥ, and Silluq; Jos 24¹⁵, with Segolta; Is 13⁸ and 17¹³ with Zaqeph qaṭon, 17¹² with Athnaḥ and Silluq, 41⁵ after *wāw consec.* Without the pause, e.g. ψ 11² קֶשֶׁת יִדְרְכוּן, cf. 4³, Gn 18²⁸·²⁹·³⁰ ff·, 44¹, Nu 32²³, Jos 4⁶ (יִשְׁאָלוּן); Is 8¹², 1 S 9¹³, Ru 2⁹ (יִקְצֹרוּן and יִשְׁאָבוּן); Ju 11¹⁸ after *wāw consec.*

Some of these examples may be partly due to euphonic reasons, e.g. certainly Ex 17², Nu 16²⁹, 32²⁰, 1 S 9¹³, 1 K 9⁶, and often, to avoid a hiatus before א or ע. It was, however, the pause especially which exerted an influence on the restoration of this older and fuller termination (cf. § 159 *c*, note), as is manifest from Is 26¹¹ : בַּל־יֶחֱזָיוּן יֶחֱזוּ וְיֵבֹשׁוּ *they see not; may they see and become*

---

[1] [See details in F. Böttcher, *Lehrb.*, § 930; and cf. Driver on 1 S 2¹⁵.]

ashamed. All this applies also to the corresponding forms in the Imperfect of the derived conjugations.[1] In Aramaic and Arabic this earlier ‏ן‎ (old Arabic *ŭnă*) is the regular termination; but in some dialects of vulgar Arabic it has also become *ú*.

With an affixed ‏א‎ we find (in the imperf. Niph‘al) ‏יִנָּשֹׂא‎ Jer 10[5], evidently *n* an error for ‏יִנָּשֵׂא‎, caused by the preceding ‏נָשׂוֹא‎.—In ‏יְשִׁישׂוּם‎ Is 35[1], since ‏מ‎ follows, the ‏ם‎ is no doubt only due to dittography.

5. Corresponding to the use of ‏ן‎ for ‏ו‎ there occurs in the 2nd sing. fem., *o* although much less frequently, the fuller ending ‏ין__‎ (as in Aram. and Arab.; old Arab. *ină*), also always with the tone, for ‏י__‎, generally again in the principal pause, and almost in all cases with retention of the vowel of the penultima; thus ‏תִּדְבָּקִין‎ Ru 2[8.21], cf. 3[4.18], 1 S 1[14] (‏תִּשְׁתַּבָּרִין‎), Jer 31[22], Is 45[10].

6. On the reappearance in pause of the *ō* which had become *Sewâ* in the *p* forms ‏תִּקְטְלִי‎, &c., see above, *e*; similarly, the imperfects with *ă* restore this vowel in pause and at the same time lengthen it (as a tone-vowel) to *ā*, hence, e.g. ‏יִגְדְּלִי‎, ‏תֶּחֶזְלוּ‎. This influence of the pause extends even to the forms without afformatives, e.g. ‏יִגְדַּל‎, in pause ‏וַיִּגְדָּל‎. But the fuller forms in *ún* and *ín* have the tone always on the ultima, since the vowels *ú* and *í* in a closed final syllable never allow of the retraction of the tone.

7. On the numerous instances of passive forms in the imperfect, mostly *q* treated as Hoph‘al, see § 53 *u*.

§ 48. *Shortening and Lengthening of the Imperfect and Imperative. The Jussive and Cohortative.*

1. Certain modifications which take place in the form of the *a* imperfect, and express invariably, or nearly so, a distinct shade of meaning, serve to some extent as a compensation for the want of special forms for the *Tempora relativa* and for certain *moods* of the verb.

2. Along with the usual form of the imperfect, there exists also *b* a lengthened form of it (the *cohortative*), and a shortened form (the *jussive*).[2] The former occurs (with few exceptions) only in the 1st person, while the latter is mostly found in the 2nd and 3rd persons, and less frequently in the 1st person. The laws of the tone, however, and of the formation of syllables in Hebrew, not infrequently precluded the indication of the jussive by an actual shortening of the form; consequently it often—and, in the imperfect forms with afformatives, always—coincides with the ordinary imperfect (*indicative*) form.

In classical Arabic the difference is almost always evident. That language distinguishes, besides the indicative *yăqtŭlŭ*, (*a*) a subjunctive, *yăqtŭlă*; (*b*) a

---

[1] It is to be observed that the Chronicles often omit the *Nûn*, where it is found in the parallel passage in the Books of Kings; cf. 1 K 8[38.43] with 2 Ch 6[29.33]; 1 K 12[24], 2 K 11[5] with 2 Ch 11[4], 23[4].

[2] The perfect has only *one* form, since it cannot be used, like the imperfect, to express mood-relations (see § 106 *p*).

jussive, *yăqtŭl*; (*c*) a double 'energetic' mood of the impf., *yăqtŭlănnă* and *yăqtŭlăn*, in pause *yăqtŭlā*, the last form thus corresponding to the Hebrew cohortative.

c 3. The characteristic of the cohortative form is an *ā* (ה‍ָ‍ֿ) affixed to the 1st pers. sing. or plur., e. g. אֶקְטְלָה from אֶקְטֹל.[1] It occurs in almost all conjugations and classes of the strong and weak verb (except of course in the passives), and this final ה‍ָ‍ֿ has the tone wherever the afformatives וֹ and י‍ָ‍ֿ would have it. As before these endings, so also before the ה‍ָ‍ֿ cohortative, the movable vowel of the last syllable of the verbal form becomes *Šewâ*, e. g. in Qal אֶשְׁמְרָה *I will observe*, in Pi'el נִתְּקָה *let us break asunder*, ψ 2³; on אֶשְׁקְטָה Is 18⁴ *Qerê* (cf. also 27⁴, Ezr 8²⁵, &c.), see § 10 *h*; with the *Kethîbh* of these passages, compare the analogous cases יִשְׁפּוֹטוּ, &c., § 47 *g*.—On the other hand, an unchangeable vowel in the final syllable is retained as tone-vowel before the ה‍ָ‍ֿ, as (e. g.) in Hiph. אַזְכִּירָה *I will praise*. In pause (as before *û* and *î*), the vowel which became *Šewâ* is restored as tone-vowel; thus for the cohortative אֶשְׁמְרָה the pausal form is אֶשְׁמֹרָה ψ 59¹⁰; cf. Gn 18²¹, Is 41²⁶.

d The change of ה‍ָ‍ֿ into the obtuse ה‍ֶ‍ֿ seems to occur in 1 S 28¹⁵, unless, with Nestle, we are to assume a conflate reading, וָאֶקְרָא and וָאֶקְרֶה; and with the 3rd pers. ψ 20⁴, in a syllable sharpened by a following *Dageš forte conjunct.*; cf. similar cases of the change of ה‍ָ‍ֿ into the obtuse ה‍ֶ‍ֿ in *l* and in §§ 73 *d*, 80 *i*, 90 *i*. In ψ 20⁴, however, יְרַשְּׁנֶה—with suffix—is probably intended. An ה‍ֶ‍ֿ cohort. is also found with the 3rd pers. in Is 5¹⁹ (twice); Ez 23²⁰, and again in verse 16 according to the *Qerê*, but in both these cases without any effect on the meaning. Probably another instance occurs in Jb 11¹⁷, although there תָּעֻפָה might also, with Qimḥi, be regarded as 2nd masc. For the doubly irregular form תְּבוֹאָתָה Dt 33¹⁶ (explained by Olshausen and König as a scribal error, due to a confusion with תבואת in verse 14), read תָּבֹאֶנָה. For תְבוּאָתְךָ Jb 22²¹ the noun תְּבוּאָתְךָ *thine increase*, might be meant, but the Masora has evidently intended an imperfect with the ending *ath*, instead of ה‍ָ‍ֿ, before the suffix, on the analogy of the 3rd sing. fem. perfect, see § 59 *a*; on ותבאתי 1 S 25³⁴, see § 76 *h*.

e The *cohortative* expresses the direction of the will to an action and thus denotes especially self-encouragement (in the 1st plur. an exhortation to others at the same time), a resolution or a wish, as an *optative*, &c., see § 108.

f 4. The general characteristic of the *jussive* form of the imperfect is rapidity of pronunciation, combined with a tendency to retract

---

[1] Probably this *ā* goes back to the syllable *an*, which in Arabic (see above, Rem. to *b*) is used for the formation of the 'energetic' mood, and in Hebrew (see the footnote to § 58 *i*) often stands before suffixes.

the tone from the final syllable, in order by that means to express the urgency of the command in the very first syllable. This tendency has, in certain forms, even caused a material shortening of the termination of the word, so that the expression of the command appears to be concentrated on a single syllable. In other cases, however, the jussive is simply marked by a shortening of the vowel of the second syllable, without its losing the tone, and very frequently (see above, *b*) the nature of the form does not admit of any alteration. It is not impossible, however, that even in such cases the jussive in the living language was distinguished from the indicative by a change in the place of the tone.

In the strong verb the jussive differs in *form* from the indicative *g* only in *Hiph'il* (juss. יַקְטֵל, ind. יַקְטִיל), and similarly in the weak verb, wherever the imperfect indicative has *î* in the second syllable, e. g. from יָשַׁב impf. *Hiph.* יוֹשִׁיב, juss. יוֹשֵׁב; from מוּת יָמִית and יָמֵת; also in *Qal* of the verbs ע״י and ע״ו, as יָמֻת, ind. יָמוּת; יָגֵל, ind. יָגִיל; in all conjugations of verbs ל״ה, so that the rejection (*apocope*) of the ending הָ‍ in *Qal* and *Hiph.* gives rise to monosyllabic forms, with or without a helping vowel under the second radical, e. g. *Qal* ind. יִגְלֶה, juss. יִגֶל; *Hiph.* ind. יַגְלֶה, juss. יֶגֶל; and in the *Pi'ēl* יְצַו from the indic. יְצַוֶּה (called apocopated imperfects). But almost all [1] the plural forms of the jussive coincide with those of the indicative, except that the jussive excludes the fuller ending וּן. Neither do the forms of the 2nd sing. fem., as תִּגְלִי, תָּמֹתִי, תַּקְטִילִי, &c., admit of any change in the jussive, nor any forms, whether singular or plural, to which suffixes are attached, e. g. תְּמִיתֵנִי as ind. Jer 38¹⁵, as jussive Jer 41⁸.

The meaning of the jussive is similar to that of the cohortative, *h* except that in the jussive the command or wish is limited almost exclusively to the 2nd or 3rd pers. On special uses of the jussive, e. g. in hypothetical sentences (even in the 1st pers.), see § 109 *h*.

5. The imperative, in accordance with its other points of connexion *i* with the imperfect in form and meaning, admits of a similar lengthening (by הָ‍, Arab. *imper. energicus*, with the ending -*ănnă* or -*ăn*, in pause -*ā*) and shortening. Thus in *Qal* of the strong verb, the lengthened form of שְׁמֹר *guard* is שָׁמְרָה [2] (*šŏmᵉrâ*, cf. קְטָלִי *qiṭᵉlî*, § 46 *d*); עֲזָב, עֲזֹב Jer 49¹¹; שִׁכְבָה, שְׁכַב *lie down*; שְׁמַע, שָׁמְעָה *hear*, in lesser pause שָׁמְעָה

---

[1] Only in 1st plur. do we find a few shortened forms, as נִשְׁאָר 1 S 14³⁶, parallel with cohortatives; and נֵרָא Is 41²³ *Kᵉth*.

[2] On the reading שָׁמְרָה (i. e. *šāmᵉra*, according to the Jewish grammarians), required by the Masora in ψ 86², 119¹⁶⁷ (cf. also Is 38¹⁴, and שָׁמְרֵנִי ψ 16¹), see § 9 *v*; on מַלוּכָה, Ju 9⁸ *Kᵉth.*, see § 46 *e*.

Dn 9¹⁹; in Niph'al הִשָּׁבְעָה Gn 21²³. Cf., however, also מִכְרָה *sell*,
Gn 25³¹, notwithstanding the impf. יִמְבֹּר; עֶרְכָה Jb 33⁵ (cf. עֶרְכוּ Jer 46³),
but impf. יַעֲרֹךְ; אֶסְפָה *collect*, Nu 11¹⁶ (for אֱסֹ׳ cf. § 63 *l* and the plural
אִסְפוּ), but 2nd masc. אֱסֹף; נִצְרָה ψ 141³. Barth (see above, § 47 *i*
note) finds in these forms a trace of old imperfects in *i*, cf. § 63 *n*.
On the other hand, קָרְבָה ψ 69¹⁹ (also Imperat. קְרַב Lv 9⁷, &c.), but
impf. יִקְרַב. Without ה, we have the form לֵךְ *go*, Nu 23¹³, Ju 19¹³,
2 Ch 25¹⁷. The form קְטֹל in pause becomes קְטֹלָה, the form קְטַל
becomes קְטָלָה, e. g. יְרָשָׁה Dt 33²³. But also without the pause we find
מְלוֹכָה Ju 9⁸ *Keth*. and צְרוּפָה ψ 26²ᵛ *Keth*., on which see § 46 *e*. On
the other hand חֲנוֹרָה, עֹרָה, פְּשֹׁטָה, רְגָזָה Is 32¹¹ are to be explained as
aramaizing forms of the 2nd plur. fem.; also for חִרְדוּ v. 11 read חֲרָדָה,
and for סְפֹדִים v. 12 read סְפֹדָה.

k   The shortened imperative is found only in verbs ל״ה, e. g. in *Pi'ēl*
גַּל from גַּלֵּה. The shade of meaning conveyed by the imperatives
with ָה_ is not always so perceptible as in the cohortative forms of the
imperfect, but the longer form is frequently emphatic, e. g. קוּם *rise up*,
קוּמָה *up!* תֵּן *give*, תְּנָה *give up!*

l   Rem. The form דְּעֶה for דְּעָה, best attested in Pr 24¹⁴ (where it is taken
by the Masora as imperat., not as infin., דֵּעָה) is evidently due to the influence
of the ה which follows it in close connexion (so Strack, on the analogy of
Jb 31²); for other examples of this change of *a* to S°ghol, see above, under *d*,
§ 73 *d*, and § 80 *i*. On the other hand, it is doubtful whether רַבֶּה Ju 9²⁹ (from
רָבָה) is intended for רַבָּה, and not rather for the common form of the
imperative *Pi'ēl* רַבֵּה. In favour of the former explanation it may be urged
that the imperative צֵאָה (from יָצָא) follows immediately after; in favour of
the latter, that the ending ָה_, with imperatives of verbs ל״ה, is not found
elsewhere, and also that here no guttural follows (as in Pr 24¹⁴).

§ 49. *The Perfect and Imperfect with Wāw Consecutive.*

a   1. The use of the two tense-forms, as is shown more fully in the
Syntax (§§ 106, 107, cf. above, § 47, note on *a*), is by no means
restricted to the expression of the past or future. One of the most
striking peculiarities in the Hebrew *consecution* of tenses¹ is the
phenomenon that, in representing a series of past events, only the first

---

¹ The other Semitic languages do not exhibit this peculiarity, excepting
the Phoenician, the most closely related to Hebrew, and of course the
Moabitish dialect of the *Mēša'* inscription, which is practically identical with
Old Hebrew. It also appears in the inscription of זכר of Hamâth (cf.
Nöldeke, *ZA*. 1908, p. 379) where we find ואשׂא ידי *and I lifted up my hand*,
ויענני *and he answered me*, after a perfect of narration.

verb stands in the perfect, and the narration is continued in the imperfect. Conversely, the representation of a series of future events begins with the imperfect, and is continued in the perfect. Thus in 2 K 20[1], *In those days was Hezekiah sick unto death* (perf.), *and Isaiah . . . came* (imperf.) *to him, and said* (imperf.) *to him,* &c. On the other hand, Is 7[17], *the Lord shall bring* (imperf.) *upon thee . . . days,* &c., 7[18], *and it shall come to pass* (perf. וְהָיָה) *in that day . . .*

This progress in the sequence of time, is regularly indicated by *b* a pregnant *and* (called *wāw consecutive*[1]), which in itself is really only a variety of the ordinary *wāw copulative,* but which sometimes (in the imperf.) appears with a different vocalization. Further, the tenses connected by *wāw consecutive* sometimes undergo a change in the tone and consequently are liable also to other variations.

2. The *wāw consecutive* of the *imperfect* is (*a*) pronounced with *c* Pathaḥ and a *Dageš forte* in the next letter, as וַיִּקְטֹל *and he killed;* before א of the 1st pers. sing. (according to § 22 *c*) with Qameṣ, as וָאֶקְטֹל *and I killed.* Exceptions are, וָאֲכַפֵּךְ Ez 16[10] according to the *Dikduke ha-ṭeamim,* § 71 ; also וַאֲמֹתְתֵהוּ 2 S 1[10] according to Qimḥi ; but in Ju 6[9] וָאֲגָרֵשׁ should be read according to Baer, and 'וָאֲ in both places in Ju 20[6]. *Dageš forte* is always omitted in the preformative ׳, in accordance with § 20 *m.*

(*b*) When a shortening of the imperfect form is possible (cf. § 48 *g*), *d* it takes effect, as a rule (but cf. § 51 *n*), after *wāw consec.,* e.g. in Hiphil וַיַּקְטֵל (§ 53 *n*). The tendency to retract the tone from the final syllable is even stronger after *wāw consec.* than in the jussive. The throwing back of the tone on to the penultima (conditional upon its being an open syllable with a long vowel, § 29 *a*), further involves the greatest possible shortening of the vowel of the ultima, since the vowel then comes to stand in a toneless closed syllable, e.g. יָקֻם, juss.

---

[1] This name best expresses the prevailing syntactical relation, for by *wāw consecutive* an action is always represented as the direct, or at least temporal *consequence* of a preceding action. Moreover, it is clear from the above examples, that the *wāw consecutive* can only be thus used in immediate conjunction with the verb. As soon as *wāw,* owing to an insertion (e. g. a negative), is separated from the verb, the imperfect follows instead of the perfect *consecutive,* the perfect instead of the imperfect *consecutive.* The fact that whole Books (Lev., Num., Josh., Jud., Sam., 2 Kings, Ezek., Ruth, Esth., Neh., 2 Chron.) begin with the imperfect *consecutive,* and others (Exod., 1 Kings, Ezra) with *wāw copulative,* is taken as a sign of their close connexion with the historical Books now or originally preceding them. Cf., on the other hand, the independent beginning of Job and Daniel. It is a merely superficial description to call the wāw consecutive by the old-fashioned name *wāw conversive,* on the ground that it always converts the meaning of the respective tenses into its opposite, i.e. according to the old view, the future into the preterite, and vice versa.

יָקֹם, with *wāw consec.* וַיָּ֫קָם *and he arose* (§ 67 n and x, § 68 d, § 69 p, § 71, § 72 t and aa, § 73 e).[1]

e In the *first* pers. sing. alone the retraction of the tone and even the reducing of the long vowel in the final syllable (*û* to *ō*, *î* to *ē*, and then to *ŏ* and *ĕ*) are not usual,[2] at least according to the Masoretic punctuation, and the apocope in verbs ל״ה occurs more rarely ; e.g. always וָאָק֫וּם (or וָאָקֻ֫ם, a merely orthographic difference) *and I arose*; *Hiph.* וָאָקִ֫ים (but generally written וָאָקֶם, implying the pronunciation *wā'āqem*, as וָאָקֶם implies *wā'āqŏm*); וָאֶרְאֶה *and I saw*, more frequently than וָאֵ֫רֶא, § 75 t. On the other hand, the form with final ◌ָה is often used in the 1st pers. both sing. and plur., especially in the later books, e. g. וָאֶשְׁלְחָה *and I sent*, Gn 32⁶, 41¹¹, 43²¹, Nu 8¹⁹ (וָאֶתְּנָה), as in Ju 6⁹, 1 S 2²⁸, and often, probably a sort of compensation for the lost נ); Ju 6¹⁰, 12³, 2 S 22²⁴, ψ 3⁶, 7⁵, 90¹⁰, 119⁵⁵, Jb 1¹⁵ ff·, 19²⁰, Ez 7²⁸, 8²⁵, 9³, Neh 2¹³, 5⁷·⁸·¹³, 6¹¹, 13⁷⁻¹¹·²¹ f·, &c.—Sometimes, as in ψ 3⁶, with a certain emphasis of expression, and probably often, as in Ju 10¹², וָאוֹשִׁ֫יעָה before א, for euphonic reasons. In Is 8² וָאָעִ֫ידָה may have been originally intended ; in ψ 73¹⁶ וָאֵ֫ח׳ and in Jb 30²⁶ וָאֲיַ׳. In Ez 3³ read וָאֹכְלָה or וָאֹֽכְלָה.

f This ־ו is in meaning a strengthened *wāw copulative*, and resembles in pronunciation the form which is retained in Arabic as the ordinary copula (*wă*).[3] The close connexion of this *wă* with the following consonant, caused the latter in Hebrew to take Dageš, especially as *ă* could not have been retained in an open syllable. Cf. בָּמָּה, בַּמֶּה, לָמָּה (for לַמֶּה), where the prepositions בְּ and לְ, and the particle בְּ, are closely connected with מָה in the same way (§ 102 k).

g The retraction of the tone also occurs in such combinations, as in לָמָּה (for לַמֶּה § 102 l).—The identity of many *consecutive* forms with jussives of the same conjugation must not mislead us into supposing an intimate relation between the moods. In the consecutive forms the shortening of the vowel (and the retraction of the tone) seems rather to be occasioned solely by the strengthening of the preformative syllable, while in the jussives the shortening (and retraction) belongs to the character of the form.

h 3. The counterpart of *wāw consecutive* of the *imperfect* is *wāw consecutive* of the *perfect*, by means of which perfects are placed as

---

[1] The plural forms in ן also occur less frequently after *wāw consecutive* ; cf., however, וַיָּרִ֫יבוּן Ju 8¹, 11¹⁸, Am 6³, Ez 44⁸, Dt 4¹¹, 5²⁰. The 2nd fem. sing. in ◌ִין never occurs after *wāw consecutive*.

[2] In the 1st plur. וַנַּעֲמִיד Neh 4³ is the only instance in which the vowel remains unreduced (cf. וְנָשׁוּב, i. e. וְנַשּׁוּב, 4⁹ K⁶th. ; Q⁶rê וַנָּ֫שָׁב). On the treatment of the tone in the imperfect, imperative, and infinitive *Niph'al*, see § 51 n.

[3] In usage the Hebrew *wāw* does duty for the Arabic *fă* (*wāw apodosis*, see § 143 d) as well as *wă*.

the sequels in the future to preceding actions or events regarded as incomplete at the time of speaking, and therefore in the imperfect, imperative, or even participle. This *wāw* is in form an ordinary *wāw copulative*, and therefore shares its various vocalization (וַ, וָ, וְ, as 2 K 7⁴, and וּ); e.g. וְהָיָה, after an imperfect, &c., *and so it happens = and it will happen*. It has, however, the effect, in certain verbal forms, of shifting the tone from the penultima, generally on to the ultima, e.g. הָלַכְתִּי *I went*, consecutive form וְהָלַכְתִּי *and I will go*, Ju 1³, where it is co-ordinated with another *perfect consecutive*, which again is the consecutive to an *imperative*. See further on this usage in § 112.

As innumerable examples show, the *Qameṣ* of the first syllable is retained *i* in the strong perf. consec. Qal, as formerly before the tone, so now in the secondary tone, and therefore necessarily takes *Metheg*. On the other hand, the ō of the second syllable in verbs *middle* ō upon losing the tone necessarily becomes ŏ, e.g. וִיכָלְתָּ Ex 18²³.

The shifting forward of the tone after the *wāw consecutive* of the *perfect* is, *k* however, not consistently carried out. It is omitted—(*a*) always in the 1st pers. pl., e.g. וְיָשַׁבְנוּ Gn 34¹⁶; (*b*) regularly in Hiph'il before the afformatives הָ_ and וּ, see § 53 *r*; and (*c*) in many cases in verbs ל״א and ל״ה, almost always in the 1st sing. of ל״א (Jer 29¹⁴), and in ל״ה if the vowel of the 2nd syllable is *i*, Ex 17⁶, 26⁴·⁶·⁷·¹⁰ ff., Ju 6²⁶, &c., except in Qal (only Lv 24⁵, before א) and the 2nd sing. masc. of Hiph'il-forms before א, Nu 20⁸, Dt 20¹³, 1 S 15³, 2 K 13¹⁷; similarly in Pi'ēl before א, Ex 25²⁴, Jer 27⁴. On the other hand the tone is generally moved forward if the second syllable has *ê* (in ל״א Gn 27¹⁰ &c., in ל״ה Ex 40⁴, Jer 33⁶, Ez 32⁷); but cf. also וְיָרֵאתָ Lv 19¹⁴·³² and frequently, always before the counter-tone, Jo 4²¹, ψ 19¹⁴.[1] With *ā* in the penultima the form is וְנָשָׂאתָ Is 14⁴, and probably also וְקָרָאתָ Jer 2², 3¹², 1 S 10² with little *T°lîšā*, a postpositive accent.

But before a following א the ultima mostly bears the tone on phonetic *l* grounds, e.g. וּבָאתָ־אֶל Gn 6¹³, Ex 3¹⁸, Zc 6¹⁰ (by the side of וּבָאתָ), &c. (cf., however, וְקָרָאתָ, before א, Gn 17¹⁹, Jer 7²⁷, Ez 36²⁹); וְהִפִּיתָ אֶת־ Ju 6¹⁶, cf. Ex 25¹¹, Lv 24⁵ (but also וְצִוִּיתִי אֶת־ Lv 25²¹). Likewise, before ה, Am 8⁹, and ע, e.g. Gn 26¹⁰, 27¹², Lv 26²⁵ (cf., however, וְקָרָאתִי עָלָיו, Ez 38²¹); on verbs ע״ע, see § 67 *k* and *ee*.

(*d*) The tone always keeps its place when such a perfect stands in *pause*, *m* e.g. וְשָׂבַעְתָּ Dt 6¹¹, 11¹⁵; וְאָמַרְתָּ Is 14⁴, Ju 4⁸; sometimes even in the lesser pause, as Dt 2²⁸, Ez 3²⁶, 1 S 29⁸ (where see Driver), with *Zaqeph qaṭon*; and frequently also immediately *before* a tone-syllable (according to § 29 *e*), as in וְיָשַׁבְתָּה בָּהּ Dt 17¹⁴, Ez 14¹³, 17²², Am 1⁴·⁷·¹⁰·¹²—but also וְחָשַׁקְתָּ בָּהּ Dt 21¹¹, 23¹⁴, 24¹⁹, 1 K 8⁴⁶.

---

[1] The irregularity in the tone of these perfects manifestly results from following conflicting theories, not that of Ben Asher alone.

§ 50. *The Participle.*

a 1. Qal has both an active participle, called *Pô'ēl* from its form (פֹּעֵל), and a passive, *Pā'ûl* (פָּעוּל).[1]

Pā'ûl is generally regarded as a survival of a passive of Qal, which still exists throughout in Arabic, but has been lost in Hebrew (see, however, § 52 *e*), just as in Aramaic the passives of *Pi'ēl* and *Hiph'il* are lost, except in the participles. But instances of the form *quṭṭāl* are better regarded as remnants of the passive participle Qal (see § 52 *s*), so that פָּעוּל must be considered as an original verbal noun ; cf. Barth, *Nominalbildung*, p. 173 ff.

b 2. In the intransitive verbs *mid. e* and *mid. o*, the form of the participle active of Qal coincides in form with the 3rd sing. of the perfect, e. g. יָשֵׁן *sleeping*, from יָשֵׁן ; יָגוֹר (only orthographically different from the perf. יָגֹר) *fearing*; cf. the formation of the participle in *Niph'al*, § 51 *a*. On the other hand, the participle of verbs *mid. a* takes the form קָטֵל (so even from the *transitive* שָׂנֵא *to hate*, part. שֹׂנֵא). The *ô* of these forms has arisen through an obscuring of the *â*, and is therefore unchangeable, cf. § 9 *q*. The form קָטָל (with a changeable *Qameṣ* in both syllables), which would correspond to the forms יָשֵׁן and יָגֹר, is only in use as a noun, cf. § 84ᵃ *f*. The formation of the participle in *Pi'ēl*, *Hiph'il*, and *Hithpa'ēl* follows a different method.

c 3. Participles form their feminine (קֹטְלָה or קֹטֶלֶת) and their plural like other nouns (§ 80 *e*, § 84ᵃ *r*, *s*, § 94).

d Rem. 1. From the above it follows, that the *ā* of the form יָשֵׁן is lengthened from *ă*, and consequently changeable (e.g. *fem.* יְשֵׁנָה) ; and that the *ô* of קָטֵל on the other hand is obscured from an unchangeable *â*.[1] In Arabic the verbal adjective of the form *qătĭl* corresponds to the form *qāṭēl*, and the part. *qātĭl* to *qôṭēl*. In both cases, therefore, the *ē* of the second syllable is lengthened from *ĭ*, and is consequently changeable (e. g. קְטֵל, plur. קְטֵלִים ; כָּבֵד, constr. pl. כִּבְדֵי).

e תּוֹמִיךְ ψ 16⁵, instead of the form *qôṭēl*, is an anomaly ; it is possible, however, that תּוֹמֵיךְ (incorrectly written fully) is intended (cf. סָבִיב 2 K 8²¹), or even the *imperfect Hiph'il* of יָמַךְ. The form יֹסֵף in Is 29¹⁴, 38⁵ appears to stand for יֹסֵף, but most probably the Masora here (as certainly in יוֹסִיף Ec 1¹⁸) intends the 3rd sing. imperf. Hiph., for which the better form would be יוֹסֵף ; אֹבִיל 1 Ch 27³⁰, being a proper name and a foreign word, need not be considered.—אֹבֵד (constr. state of אֹבֵד), with *ă* in the second syllable, occurs in Dt 32²⁸ (cf. moreover, § 65 *d*). On הֹלֵם Is 41⁷ (for הֹלְם), see § 29 *f*.

f 2. A form like the pass. ptcp. *Pā'ûl*, but not to be confused with it, is sometimes found from *intransitive verbs*, to denote an inherent quality, e. g. אָמוּן *faithful* ; אָנוּשׁ *desperate*, Jer 15¹⁸, &c. ; בָּטוּחַ *trustful*, Is 26³, ψ 112⁷ ; עָצוּם *strong* ; שָׁכוּר *drunken*, Is 51²¹ ; and even from transitive verbs, אָחוּז *handling*, Ct 3⁸ ; זָכוּר *mindful*, ψ 103¹⁴ ; יָדוּעַ *knowing*, Is 53³ ; cf. § 84ᵃ *m*.

---

[1] The constr. st. נְאֻם in the formula נְאֻם יְהוָֹה, *the word* (properly the *whispering*) *of the Lord*, &c., is always written defectively.

[2] Cf. Vollers, ' Das Qâtil-partizipium,' in *ZA.* 1903, p. 312 ff.

B. Verba Derivativa, or Derived Conjugations.

§ 51. *Niph'al.*[1]

1. The essential characteristic of this conjugation consists in a *a* prefix[2] to the stem. This exists in two forms : (*a*) the (probably original) prepositive *nă*, as in the Hebrew perfect and participle, although in the strong verb the *ă* is always attenuated to *ĭ* : נִקְטַל for original *nă-qăṭăl*, participle נִקְטָל, infinitive absolute sometimes נִקְטֹל; (*b*) the (later) proclitic *in* (as in all the forms of the corresponding Arabic conjugation VII. '*inqătălă*), found in the imperfect יִקָּטֵל for *yinqāṭēl*, in the imperative and infinitive construct, with a secondary ה added, הִקָּטֵל (for *hinqāṭēl*), and in the infinitive absolute הִקָּטֹל   The inflexion of *Niph'al* is perfectly analógous to that of Qal.

The features of *Niph'al* are accordingly in the perfect and participle the *b* prefixed *Nûn*, in the imperative, infinitive, and imperfect, the *Dageš* in the first radical. These characteristics hold good also for the weak verb. In the case of an initial guttural, which, according to § 22 *b*, cannot take *Dageš forte*, the omission of the strengthening invariably causes the lengthening of the preceding vowel (see § 63 *h*).

2. As regards its meaning, *Niph'al* bears some resemblance to the *c* Greek *middle voice*, in being—(*a*) primarily *reflexive* of Qal, e.g. נִלְחַם *to thrust oneself* (*against*), נִשְׁמַר *to take heed to oneself*, φυλάσσεσθαι, נִסְתַּר *to hide oneself*, נִגְאַל *to redeem oneself*; cf. also נַעֲנֶה *to answer for oneself.* Equally characteristic of *Niph'al* is its frequent use to express emotions which react upon the mind ; נִחַם *to trouble oneself*, נֶאֱנַח *to sigh* (*to bemoan oneself*, cf. ὀδύρεσθαι, *lamentari, contristari*); as well as to express actions which the subject allows to happen to himself, or to have an effect upon himself (*Niph'al tolerativum*), e. g. דָּרַשׁ *to search, to inquire*, Niph. *to allow oneself to be inquired of*, Is 65[1], Ez 14[3], &c.; so the Niph. of מָצָא *to find*, יָסַר *to warn, to correct*, Jer 6[8], 31[18], &c.

(*b*) It expresses *reciprocal* or mutual action. e.g. דִּבֶּר *to speak*, Niph. *d to speak to one another*; שָׁפַט *to judge*, Niph. *to go to law with one another*; יָעַץ *to counsel*, Niph. *to take counsel*, cf. the *middle* and *deponent* verbs βουλεύεσθαι (נוֹעַץ), μάχεσθαι (נִלְחַם), *altercari, luctari* (נָצָה *to strive with one another*) *proeliari.*

(*c*) It has also, like *Hithpa'ēl* (§ 54 *f*) and the Greek *middle*, the *c* meaning of the active, with the addition of *to oneself* (*sibi*), *for one-*

---

[1] Cf. A. Rieder, *De linguae Hebr. verbis, quae vocantur derivata nifal et hitpael,* Gumbinnen (Progr. des Gymn.), 1884, a list of all the strong Niph'al forms (81) and Hithpa'ēl forms (36) in the Old Testament; and especially M. Lambert, 'L'emploi du Nifal en Hébreu,' *REJ.* 41, 196 ff.

[2] See Philippi in *ZDMG.* 1886, p. 650, and Barth, ibid. 1894, p. 8 f.

self, e. g. נִשְׁאַל to ask (something) *for oneself* (1 S 20⁶·²⁸, Neh 13⁶), cf. αἰτοῦμαί σε τοῦτο, ἐνδύσασθαι χιτῶνα, *to put on* (oneself) *a tunic.*

f   (d) In consequence of a looseness of thought at an early period of the language, *Niphʻal* comes finally in many cases to represent the *passive* [1] of *Qal*, e. g. יָלַד *to bear*, Niph. *to be born*; קָבַר *to bury*, Niph. *to be buried.* In cases where *Qal* is intransitive in meaning, or is not used, *Niphʻal* appears also as the passive of *Piʻēl* and *Hiphʻîl*, e. g. כָּבֵד *to be in honour*, Piʻēl *to honour*, Niph. *to be honoured* (as well as Puʻal כֻּבַּד); כָּחַד Piʻēl *to conceal*, Hiph. *to destroy*, Niph. passive of either. In such cases *Niphʻal* may again coincide in meaning with Qal (חָלָה Qal and Niph. *to be ill*) and even take an accusative.

g   Examples of denominatives are, נִזְכַּר *to be born a male*, Ex 34¹⁹ (from זָכָר; but probably הַזָּכָר should here be read); נִלְבַּב *cordatum fieri*, Jb 11¹² (from לֵבָב *cor*); doubtless also נִבְנָה *to obtain children*, Gn 16², 30³.

h   The older grammarians were decidedly wrong in representing *Niphʻal* simply as the *passive* of Qal; for *Niphʻal* has (as the frequent use of its imperat. shows), in no respect the character of the other passives, and in Arabic a special conjugation ('*inqátálá*) corresponds to it with a passive of its own. Moreover, the forms mentioned in § 52 *e* point to a differently formed passive of *Qal*.— The form נְגְאֲלוּ Is 59³, La 4¹⁴, is not to be regarded as a passive of Niphʻal, but with König and Cheyne as a *forma mixta*, in the sense that the punctuators intended to combine two optional readings, נִגְאֲלוּ, perf. Niph., and גֹּאֲלוּ, perf. Puʻal [cf. also Wright, *Compar. Gramm.*, p. 224]. Although the passive use of Niphʻal was introduced at an early period, and became tolerably common, it is nevertheless quite secondary to the reflexive use.

i   Rem. 1. The *infin. absol.* נִקְטוֹל is connected in form with the perfect, to which it bears the same relation as קָטוֹל to קָטַל in Qal, the ô in the second syllable being obscured from an original *á*. Examples are, נִכְסֹף Gn 31³⁰; נִלְחֹם Ju 11²⁵; נִשְׁאֹל 1 S 20⁶·²³, all in connexion with the perfect.

k   Examples of the form הִקָּטֵל (in connexion with imperfects) are, הִנָּתֹן Jer 32⁴; הֵאָכֵל Lv 7¹⁸; once אִדָּרֹשׁ Ez 14³, where, perhaps, the subsequent אִדָּרֶשׁ has led to the substitution of א for ה.—Moreover, the form הִקָּטֵל is not infrequently used also for the infin. absol.,[2] e. g. Ex 22³, Nu 15³¹, Dt 4²⁶, 1 K 20³⁹. On the other hand, כְּהִנָּדֵף should simply be read for the wholly abnormal כְּהִנְדֹּף *ψ* 68³ (commonly explained as being intended to correspond in sound with the subsequent תִּנְדֹּף, but probably a 'forma mixta', combining the readings כְּהִנָּדֵף and כְּנְדֹּף).

---

[1] Cf. Halfmann, *Beiträge zur Syntax der hebräischen Sprache*, I. Stück, Wittenb., 1888, 2. St. 1892 (Gymn.-Programm), statistics of the Niphʻal (Puʻal, Hophʻal, and qātûl) forms at different periods of the language, for the purpose of ascertaining the meaning of Niph. and its relation to the passive; the selection of periods is, however, very questionable from the standpoint of literary criticism.

[2] But, like הִקָּטֵל, *only* in connexion with imperfects, except Jer 7⁹. Barth is therefore right in describing (*Nominalbildung*, p. 74) both forms as later analogous formations (in addition to the original Semitic נַקְטוֹל), intended to assimilate the infinitive to the imperfect which it strengthens.

Elision of the ה after prepositions is required by the Masora in בְּכִשְׁלוֹ Pr *l*
24¹⁷ (for בְּהִכָּ'), בֵּהָרֵג Ez 26¹⁵ and בֵּעָטֵף La 2¹¹; also in verbs ל״ה Ex 10³
(לְעֵנוֹת); 34²⁴, Dt 31¹¹, Is 1¹² (לֵרָאוֹת); in verbs ע״י Jb 33³⁰ (לֵאוֹר). It is, however, extremely doubtful whether the *infin. Qal* of the *K^ethîbh* is not rather
intended in all these examples; it certainly is so in La 2¹¹, cf. ψ 61³.

2. Instead of the *Ṣere* in the ultima of the imperfect, *Pathaḥ* often occurs *m*
in pause, e.g. וַיִּגְמָל Gn 21⁸; cf. Ex 31¹⁷, 2 S 12¹⁵ (with final שׁ); 17²³ (with
ק); Jon 1⁶ (with מ); see § 29 *q*. In the 2nd and 3rd plur. fem. *Pathaḥ* predominates, e.g. תִּוָּבַרְנָה Is 65¹⁷; *Ṣere* occurs only in תֵּעָגֵנָה Ru 1¹³, from עגן,
and hence, with loss of the doubling, for תֵּעָגֵנָה; cf. even תֵּאָמַנָה Is 60⁴.—
With *Nûn paragogicum* (see § 47 *m*) in the 2nd and 3rd plur. masc. are found,
תִּלָּחֲמוּן, יִלָּכְדוּן, &c., in *pause* יִבָּהֵלוּן, תִּשָּׁמֵדוּן, &c.; but Jb 19²¹ (cf. 24²⁴)
יַחְצְבוּן.

3. When the imperfect, the infinitive (in *ē*), or the imperative is followed *n*
in close connexion by a monosyllable, or by a word with the tone on the first
syllable, the tone is, as a rule (but cf. וַיֵּאָבֵק אִישׁ Gn 32²⁵), shifted back from
the ultima to the penultima, while the ultima, which thus loses the tone,
takes *S^eghôl* instead of *Ṣere*; e.g. יִבָּשֶׁל בָּהּ Ez 33¹²; וַיֵּעָתֶר לוֹ Gn 25²¹; in the
imperative, 13⁹.—So always הִשָּׁמֶר לְךָ (since לְךָ counts as *one* syllable) Gn
24⁶, &c., cf. 1 S 19²; and even with *Pathaḥ* in the ultima, תֵּעָב אֶרֶץ Jb 18⁴
(but cf. וַיֵּעָתֶר אֱלֹהִים 2 S 21¹⁴). Although in isolated cases (e.g. Gn 32²⁵, Ezr
8²³) the tone is not thrown back, in spite of a tone-syllable following, the
retraction has become usual in certain forms, even when the next word
begins with a toneless syllable; especially after ו *consec.*, e.g. וַיִּשָּׁאֶר Gn 7²³;
וַיִּלָּחֶם Nu 21¹ and frequently, וַיִּצָּמֶד 25⁹; and always so in the imperative
הִשָּׁמֶר Ex 23²¹, Jb 36²¹, and (before Metheg of the counter-tone) Dt 24⁸, 2 K 6⁹.
On the avoidance of pausal-forms in the imperative (Am 2¹² with *Silluq*, Zc
2¹¹ with *Athnaḥ*), and imperfect (Pr 24⁴, &c.), see § 29 *o*, and note; on the
other hand, always הִפָּלֵט, יִפָּלֵט, &c.

In the *imperative*, נְקַבְּצוּ, for הִקָּבְצוּ, with the rejection of the initial ה, *o*
occurs in Is 43⁹, and in Joel 4¹¹ in *pause* נִקְבָּצוּ (cf. נִלְווּ Jer 50⁵); but in these
examples either the reading or the explanation is doubtful. The 2nd sing.
imperat. of נִשְׁבַּע is always (with ה־ *paragogicum*) הִשָּׁבְעָה לִּי *swear to me*,
Gn 21²³, &c. (also הִשָּׁבְעָה לִּי Gn 47³¹, 1 S 30¹⁵).

4. For the 1st sing. of the *imperfect*, the form אֶקָּטֵל is as frequent as אֶקָּטֵל, *p*
e.g. אִדָּרֵשׁ *I shall be inquired of*, Ez 14³; אִשָּׁבֵעַ *I will swear*, Gn 21²⁴; cf. 16²,
Nu 23¹⁵, Ez 20³⁶, and so always in the cohortative, e.g. אִנָּקְמָה *I will avenge
me*, Is 1²⁴; cf. 1 S 12⁷, Ez 26², and in the impf. Niph. of פ״י (§ 69 *t*). The
Babylonian punctuation admits only *ĭ* under the preformative of the 1st
person.

§ 52. *Pi'ēl and Pu'al.*

1. The *characteristic* of this conjugation consists in the strengthening *a*
of the middle radical. From the simple stem *qaṭal* (cf. § 43 *b*) the
form קַטֵּל (cf. the Arabic conj. II. *qattălă*) would naturally follow as

the *perfect* of the active (*Pi'ēl*). The *Pathaḥ* of the first syllable is, however, with one exception (see *m*), always attenuated to *ĭ* in the *perfect*. In the second syllable, *ă* has been retained in the majority of cases, so that the conjugation should more correctly be called *Pi'al*; but very frequently [1] this *ă* also is attenuated to *ĭ*, which is then regularly lengthened to *ē*, under the influence of the tone. Cf. in Aram. קַטֵּל; but in Biblical Aramaic almost always קַטֵּל. On the three cases in which *ă* before a final ר or ם has passed into *S⁰ghôl*, see below, *l.*— Hence, for the *3rd sing. masc. perfect*, there arise forms like אִבֵּד, כִּבֵּד, גִּדֵּף, קִדֵּשׁ; לִמַּד, &c.—Before afformatives beginning with a consonant, however, *ă* is always retained, thus קִטַּלְתָּ, קִטַּלְתֶּם, קִטַּלְנוּ, &c. In the *infinitives* (*absol.* קַטֹּל, obscured from *qaṭṭâl*; *constr.* קַטֵּל), *imperfect* (יְקַטֵּל), *imperative* (קַטֵּל), and *participle* (מְקַטֵּל) the original *ă* of the first syllable reappears throughout. The vocal *S⁰wâ* of the preformatives is weakened from a short vowel; cf. the Arabic imperfect *yŭqăttĭl*, participle *mŭqăttĭl*.

b   The *passive* (*Pu'al*) is distinguished by the obscure vowel *ŭ*, or very rarely *ŏ*, in the first syllable, and *ă* (in pause *ā*) always in the second. In Arabic, also, the passives are formed throughout with *ŭ* in the first syllable. The inflexion of both these conjugations is analogous to that of *Qal*.

c   Rem. 1. The preformative מ, which in the remaining conjugations also is the prefix of the participle, is probably connected with the interrogative or indefinite (cf. § 37) pronoun מִי *quis? quicunque* (fem. i. e. neuter, מָה); cf. § 85 *e*.

d   2. The Dageš *forte*, which according to the above is characteristic of the whole of *Pi'ēl* and *Pu'al*, is often omitted (independently of verbs *middle guttural*, § 64 *d*) when the middle radical has *S⁰wâ* under it (cf. § 20 *m*), e. g. שָׁלְחָה for שִׁלְּחָה Ez 17¹⁷; בִּקְשֻׁהוּ 2 Ch 15¹⁵ (but in the *imperative* always בַּקְּשׁוּ 1 S 28⁷, &c.), and so always in הַלְלוּ *praise*. The vocal character of the *S⁰wâ* under the *litera dagessanda* is sometimes in such cases (according to § 10 *h*) expressly emphasized by its taking the form of a *Ḥaṭeph*, as in לְקְחָה Gn 2²³, with ‗ owing to the influence of the preceding *u*, cf. פֻּעֲלוֹ for פֻּעֲלוֹ, &c.; Gn 9¹⁴, Ju 16¹⁶. In the *imperfect* and *participle* the *S⁰wâ* under the preformatives (*Ḥaṭeph-Pathaḥ* under א in the *1st sing. imperfect*) serves at the same time as a characteristic of both conjugations (Gn 26¹⁴ f·).

e   3. According to the convincing suggestion of Böttcher[2] (*Ausführliches Lehrbuch*, § 904 ff. and § 1022), many supposed perfects of *Pu'al* are in reality

---

[1] So in all verbs which end in *Nûn*, and in almost all which end in *Lamed* (Olsh. p. 538). Barth is probably right in supposing (*ZDMG.* 1894, p. 1 ff.) that the vowels of the strengthened perfects have been influenced by the *imperfect*.

[2] As Mayer Lambert observes, the same view was already expressed by Ibn Ġanâḥ (see above, § 3 *d*) in the *Kitāb el-luma'*, p. 161. Cf. especially Barth, 'Das passive Qal und seine Participien,' in the *Festschrift zum Jubiläum Hildesheimer* (Berlin, 1890), p. 145 ff.

passives of Qal. He reckons as such all those *perfects*, of which the *Pi'ēl* (which ought to express the corresponding active) is either not found at all, or only (as in the case of יֻלַּד) with a different meaning, and which form their *imperfect* from another conjugation, generally Niph'al. Such *perfects* are the *quṭṭal* form of the stems אֻבַּל (*imperfect* תְּאָכְּלוּ Is 1²⁰), חֻפַּשׂ, טֹרַף, יֻלַּד, יֻצַּר, שֻׁפַּךְ, שֻׁטַּף, שֻׁנַּל, עֻבַּד, לֻקַּח. Barth (see below) adds to the list the apparent *Pu'al-perfects* of אֻסַּר, בֻּוַּז, זֻנָּה, חֻצַּב, כֻּרַת, נֻפַּח, עֻזַּב, עֻשָּׂה, רֹאָה, and of verbs with middle ו (hence with *ŭ* of the first syllable lengthened to *ō*), הֻרַג, הֻרָה Jb 3³ [זֹרָה, see § 67 *m*], זֹרַע, זֹרַק, טֹרַף, מֹרַט, קֹרָא, שֹׁרַף; also the infinitives absolute הֹרוֹ וְהֹגוֹ Is 59¹³. In these cases there is no need to assume any error on the part of the punctuators; the sharpening of the second radical may have taken place in order to retain the characteristic *ŭ* of the first syllable (cf. Arab. *qŭtĭlă* as passive of *qătălă*), and the *a* of the second syllable is in accordance with the vocalization of all the other passives (see § 39 *f*). Cf. § 52 *s* and § 53 *u*.

2. The fundamental idea of *Pi'ēl*, to which all the various shades *f* of meaning in this conjugation may be referred, is *to busy oneself eagerly* with the action indicated by the stem. This intensifying of the idea of the stem, which is outwardly expressed by the strengthening of the second radical, appears in individual cases as—(*a*) a *strengthening* and *repetition* of the action (cf. the *intensive* and *iterative* nouns with the middle radical strengthened, § 84*b*),¹ e. g. צָחַק *to laugh*, Pi'ēl *to jest*, *to make sport* (to laugh repeatedly); שָׁאַל *to ask*, Pi'ēl *to beg*; hence when an action has reference to *many*, e. g. קָבַר *to bury* (a person) Gn 23⁴, Pi'ēl *to bury* (many) 1 K 11¹⁵, and often so in Syr. and Arab. Other varieties of the *intensive* and *iterative* meaning are, e. g. פָּתַח *to open*, Pi'ēl *to loose*; סָפַר *to count*, Pi'ēl *to recount*: [cf. כָּתַב, חִשֵּׁב, הָלַךְ, מִרַצֵּחַ, מְאַהֵב, תִּפֵּשׂ, חִפֵּשׂ, רִפֵּא].

The eager pursuit of an action may also consist in *urging* and *g* *causing* others to do the same. Hence *Pi'ēl* has also—(*b*) a *causative* sense (like *Hiph'îl*), e. g. לָמַד *to learn*, Pi'ēl *to teach*. It may often be turned by such phrases as *to permit to, to declare* or *hold as* (*the declarative Pi'ēl*), *to help to*, e. g. חִיָּה *to cause to live*, צָדֵּק *to declare innocent*, יִלֵּד *to help in child-bearing*.

(*c*) *Denominatives* (see § 38 *b*) are frequently formed in this conjugation, and generally express a being occupied with the object expressed by the noun, either to form or to make use of it, e. g. קִנֵּן *to make a nest, to nest* (from קֵן), עִפַּר *to throw dust, to dust* (from עָפָר),

---

¹ Analogous examples, in which the strengthening of a letter has likewise an *intensive* force, are such German words as *reichen*, *recken* (Eng. *to reach, to rack*); *streichen* (*stringo*), *strecken*: cf. *Strich* (a *stroke*), *Strecke* (a *stretch*), *wacker* from *wachen*; others, in which it has the *causative* sense, are *stechen*, *stecken* (*wachen* (*watch*), *wecken* (*wake*); τέλλω *to bring to an end* (cf. the stem τέλω *to end*, in τέλος, τελέω); γεννάω *to beget*, from the stem γένω *to come into being* (cf. γένος).

עָנַן to gather the clouds together (from עָנָן), שִׁלֵּשׁ to divide in three parts, or to do a thing for the third time (from שָׁלֹשׁ); probably also דִּבֶּר to speak, from דָּבָר a word. Or again, the denominative may express taking away, injuring, &c., the object denoted by the noun (*privative Pi'ēl*, cf. our to skin, to behead, to bone), e. g. שֵׁרֵשׁ, from שֹׁרֶשׁ to root out, to extirpate, זִנֵּב prop. to injure the tail (זָנָב), hence to rout the rear of an army, to attack it; לִבֵּב to ravish the heart; דִּשֵּׁן to remove the ashes (דֶּשֶׁן), חִטֵּא to free from sin (חֵטְא), עִצֵּם to break any one's bones (עֶצֶם; cf., in the same sense, גֵּרֵם from גֶּרֶם); סָעֵף to lop the boughs, Is 10³³ (from סָעִיף a bough). Some words are clearly denominatives, although the noun from which they are derived is no longer found, e. g. סִקֵּל to stone, to pelt with stones (also used in this sense in *Qal*), and to remove stones (from a field), to clear away stones; cf. our to stone, used also in the sense of taking out the stones from fruit.

The meaning of the passive (*Pu'al*) follows naturally from the above, e. g. בִּקֵּשׁ Pi'ēl to seek, Pu'al to be sought.

i In *Pi'ēl* the literal, concrete meaning of the verb has sometimes been retained, when *Qal* has acquired a figurative sense, e. g. גִּלָּה, Pi'ēl to uncover, Qal to reveal, also to emigrate, i. e. to make the land bare.

k Also with an intransitive sense *Pi'ēl* occurs as an intensive form, but only in poetic language, e. g. חִתַּת in Pi'ēl to be broken in pieces, Jer 51⁵⁶; פָּחַד to tremble, Is 51¹³, Pr 28¹⁴; רִוָּה to be drunken, Is 34⁵·⁷; [מִעֵט to be few, Ec 12³]; but in Is 48⁸, 60¹¹ instead of the Pi'ēl of פתח the Niph'al is certainly to be read, with Cheyne.

l Rem. 1. The (more frequent) form of the perfect with *Pathaḥ* in the second syllable appears especially before *Maqqeph* (Ec 9¹⁵, 12⁹) and in the middle of sentences in continuous discourse, but at the end of the sentence (in pause) the form with *Ṣere* is more common. Cf. גִּדַּל Is 49²¹ with גִּדֵּל Jos 4¹⁴, Est 3¹; מִלַּט Ez 33⁵ with מִלֵּט Ec 9¹⁵; קִצַּץ 2 K 8¹⁶ with קִצֵּץ ψ 129⁴; but Qameṣ never appears in this pausal form. The 3rd sing. fem. in pause is always of the form קִטְּלָה, except קָבְצָה Mi 1⁷; the 3rd plur. always as קִטְּלוּ; the 2nd and 1st sing. and 1st plur. of course as קִטַּלְתְּ, קִטְּלָה, קִטַּלְתִּי (but always דִּבַּרְתִּי and לִמַּדְתִּי), קִטַּלְנוּ. In the 3rd sing. perf. דִּבֵּר to speak, כִּפֵּר to pardon, and כִּבֵּם to wash clothes (also כִּבֵּם Gn 49¹¹) take *Sᵉghôl*, but become in pause דִּבֵּר, כִּבֵּם (2 S 19²⁵); the pausal form of כִּפֵּר does not occur.

m Pathaḥ in the first syllable (as in Aramaic and Arabic) occurs only once, Gn 41⁵¹, נַשַּׁנִי he made me forget, to emphasize more clearly the play on the name מְנַשֶּׁה.

n 2. In the imperfect (and jussive Ju 16²⁵), infinitive, and imperative Pi'ēl (as also in Hithpa'ēl) the Ṣere in the final syllable, when followed by *Maqqeph*, is usually shortened into Sᵉghôl, e. g. יְבַקֶּשׁ־לֹו he seeks for himself, Is 40²⁰; קַדֶּשׁ־לִי sanctify unto me, Ex 13². Pausal-forms with Sᵉghôl instead of Ṣere, as יְרַחֵף Dt 32¹¹, אֲרַחֵם Ho 2⁶ (cf. Ex 32⁶ in the infinitive, and Gn 21⁹ in the participle), owe their origin to some particular school of Masoretes, and are wrongly accepted by Baer; cf. the analogous cases in § 75 *n* and *hh*. If the final syllable of the imperfect Pi'ēl has Pathaḥ (before a guttural or ר), it remains even in *pause*; cf. § 29 s and 65 e. In the 1st sing. imperfect the *e*-sound occurs in two words for *Ḥateph-Pathaḥ*, under the preformative א; אֲזָרֵה Lv 26³³, Ez 5¹², 12¹⁴ and וָאֲסָעֵרֵם Zc 7¹⁴ (in accordance with § 23 h).—Before the full plural ending וּן (see § 47 m) the *Ṣere* is retained in *pause*, e. g. תֻּרַבְּרוּן ψ 58² (but Gn 32²⁰ תְּדַבְּרוּן), cf. 2 K 6¹⁹, Dt 12³; so before *Silluq* ψ 58³, Jb 21¹¹ and even before *Zaqeph qaṭon* Dt 7⁵. Instead of תֻּקְפַלְנָה, forms like תִּקְפַּלְנָה are also found, e. g. Is 3¹⁶, 13¹⁸, in both cases before a sibilant and in pause. Also פַּלֵּג ψ 55¹⁰ occurs as the 2nd sing. imperative (probably an intentional imitation of the sound of the preceding בַּלַּע) and קָרַב (for *qarrabh*) Ez 37¹⁷.

3. The *infinite absolute* of *Pi'ēl* has sometimes the special form קַטֹּל given in the paradigm, e. g. יַסֹּר *castigando*, ψ 118¹⁸; cf. Ex 21¹⁹, 1 K 19¹⁰ (from a verb ל״א); ψ 40² (from a verb ל״ה); but much more frequently the form of the *infinitive construct* (קַטֵּל) is used instead. The latter has also, in exceptional cases, the form קִטֵּל (with *ă* attenuated to *ĭ* as in the *perfect*), e. g. in 1 Ch 8⁸ שִׁלְחוֹ; perhaps also (if not a substantive) קִטֵּר Jer 44²¹; and for the sake of assonance even for *infinitive absolute* in 2 S 12¹⁴ (נִאֵץ נִאַצְתָּ). On the other hand, שַׁלֵּם Dt 32³⁵ and דַּבֵּר Jer 5¹³ are better regarded as substantives, while דִּבֶּר Ex 6²⁸, Nu 3¹, Dt 4¹⁵ (in each case after בְּיוֹם), Ho 1² (after תְּחִלַּת), in all of which places it is considered by König (after Qimḥi) to be *infinitive construct*, is really perfect of *Pi'ēl*.

The infinitive construct *Pi'ēl*, with the *fem.* ending (cf. § 45 d), occurs in יַסְּרָה Lv 26¹⁸; זַמְּרָה ψ 147¹; with ת of the *fem.* before a suffix צַדְּקָתֵךְ Ez 16⁵². On the verbal nouns after the form of the Aram. inf. *Pa'il* (קַטָּלָה), see § 84ᵇ e.

Instead of the abnormal מְאַסְפָּיו (so Baer, Is 62⁹) as ptcp. Pi'el, read מְאַסְּ׳ with ed. Mant. and Ginsburg.

4. In Pu'al *ŏ* is sometimes found instead of *ŭ* in the initial syllable, e. g. מָאֳדָם *dyed red*, Ex 25⁵, &c., Na 2⁴, cf. 3⁷ שֹׁדֳרָה; Ez 16⁴, ψ 72²⁰, 80¹¹. According to Baer's reading also in תֻּרְצָחוּ ψ 62⁴, and so also Ben Ašer, but Ben Naphtali תְּרָצָחוּ. It is merely an orthographic licence when *ŭ* is written fully, e. g. יוּלַּד Ju 18²⁹.

5. As *infinitive absolute* of Pu'al we find גֻּנֹּב Gn 40¹⁵.—No instance of the *inf. constr.* occurs in the strong verb in Pu'al; from ל״ה with suffix עֻנּוֹתוֹ ψ 132¹.

6. A few examples occur of the *participle Pu'al* without the preformative (מ), e. g. אֻכָּל Ex 3²; יֻלַּד (for מְיֻלָּד) Ju 13⁸; לֻקַּח 2 K 2¹⁰; סֹעֲרָה Is 54¹¹. These *participles* are distinguished from the *perfect* (as in Niph'al) by the *ā* of the final syllable. For other examples, see Is 30²⁴, Ec 9¹² (where יֻקָּשִׁים, according to § 20 n, stands for יֻקְּ׳ = מְיֻקָּ׳); but, according to the Masora, *not* Ez 26¹⁷, since הָהֻלָּלָה as *Mil'ēl* can only be the *perfect*. The rejection of the מ may be favoured by an initial מ, as in Is 18²·⁷ (but also מְמֻשָּׁךְ); Pr 25¹⁹ (where, however, read מוֹעֶדֶת); so also in the participle *Pi'ēl* מְאָן Ex 7²⁷, 9² (always after אִם, but cf. also הַמְּאָנִים Jer 13¹⁰, where, however, הַמְמָאֲנִים = הַמְמָאֲנִים is to be read, with Brockelmann, *Grundriss*, p. 264 f.) and מַהֵר Zp 1¹⁴ (and Is 81·³ ?). Notice, however, Barth's suggestion (*Nominalbildung*, p. 273) that, as the active of forms like אֻכָּל only occurs in Qal, they are perfect participles of former passives of Qal (see e), and in Jer 13¹⁰, 23³², perfect participles of Pi'ēl.—On מְרֻבָּע Ez 45², see § 65 d.

§ 53. *Hiph'il and Hoph'al.*

a 1. The characteristic of the active (*Hiph'îl*) is a prefixed הַ (on its origin see § 55 *i*) in the perfect הִ (with the *ă* attenuated to *ĭ*, as in *Pi'ēl*), which forms a closed syllable with the first consonant of the stem. The second syllable of the perfect had also originally an *ă*; cf. the Arabic conj. IV. *'aqtălă*, and in Hebrew the return of the *Pathaḥ* in the 2nd and 1st pers. הִקְטַ֫לְתָּ, &c. After the attenuation of this *ă* to *ĭ*, it ought by rule to have been lengthened to *ē* in the tone-syllable, as in Aramaic אַקְטֵל, beside הַקְטֵל in Biblical Aramaic. Instead of this, however, it is always replaced in the strong verb by *ĭ*,[1] ־ִי, but sometimes written defectively ־ִ; cf. § 9 *g*. Similarly in the infinitive construct הַקְטִיל, and in the imperfect and participle יַקְטִיל and מַקְטִיל, which are syncopated from יְהַקְטִיל and מְהַקְטִיל; § 23 *k*. The corresponding Arabic forms (*juqtĭl* and *muqtĭl*) point to an original *ĭ* in the second syllable of these forms. In Hebrew the regular lengthening of this *ĭ* to *ē* appears in the strong verb at least in the *jussive* and in the *imperfect consecutive* (see *n*), as also in the *imperative* of the 2nd sing. masc. (see *m*); on הַקְטֵלְנָה, תַּקְטֵלְנָה cf. § 26 *p*. On the return of the original *ă* in the second syllable of the *Imperat., Jussive,* &c , under the influence of a guttural, cf. § 65 *f*.

b In the *passive* (*Hoph'al*) the preformative is pronounced with an obscure vowel, whilst the second syllable has *ă* (in pause *ā*), as its characteristic, thus :—*Perf.* הָקְטַל or הֻקְטַל, *Imperf.* יָקְטַל (syncopated from יְהָקְטַל) or יֻקְטַל, *Part.* מָקְטָל or מֻקְטָל (from מְהָקְטָל); but the *infinitive absolute* has the form הָקְטֵל.

Thus the characteristics of both conjugations are the ה preformative in the *perfect, imperative,* and *infinitive*; in the *imperfect* and *participle Hiph'il,* Pathaḥ under the preformatives, in the *Hoph'al ŏ* or *ŭ*.

c 2. The *meaning* of *Hiph'il* is primarily, and even more frequently than in *Pi'ēl* (§ 52 *g*), causative of *Qal*, e. g. יָצָא *to go forth,* Hiph. *to bring forth, to lead forth, to draw forth* ; קָדֵשׁ *to be holy,* Hiph. *to sanctify.* Under the *causative* is also included (as in *Pi'ēl*) the *declarative* sense; e. g. הִצְדִּיק *to pronounce just* ; הִרְשִׁיעַ *to make one an evil doer (to pronounce guilty)* ; cf. עֲשׁק, in *Hiph'îl,* Jb 9²⁰, *to represent as perverse.* If Qal has already a transitive meaning, *Hiph'îl* then takes two accusatives (see § 117 *cc*). In some verbs, *Pi'ēl* and *Hiph'îl* occur side by side in the same sense, e. g. אָבַד *periit,* Pi'ēl and Hiph'il, *perdidit* ; as a rule,

---

[1] This *ĭ* may have been transferred originally from the imperfects of verbs ע״וּ, as a convenient means of distinction between the indicative and jussive, to the *imperfect* of the strong verb and afterwards to the whole of *Hiph'îl*; so Stade, Philippi, Praetorius, *ZAW.* 1883, p. 52 f.

however, only one of these two conjugations is in use, or else they differ from one another in meaning, e. g. כָּבֵד *gravem esse*, Pi'ēl *to honour*, Hiph'il *to bring to honour*, also *to make heavy*. Verbs which are intransitive in *Qal* simply become transitive in *Hiph'il*, e. g. נָטָה *to bow oneself*, Hiph. *to bow, to bend*.

d   Among the ideas expressed by the *causative* and *transitive* are included, moreover, according to the *Hebrew* point of view (and that of the Semitic languages in general, especially Arabic), a series of actions and ideas, which we have to express by periphrasis, in order to understand their being represented by the Hiph'il-form. To these *inwardly transitive* or *intensive* Hiph'ils belong: (*a*) Hiph'il stems which express the obtaining or receiving of a concrete or abstract quality. (In the following examples the *Qal* stems are given, for the sake of brevity, with the addition of the meaning which—often together with other meanings—belongs to the *Hiph'il*.) Thus יפע, זהר, אהל, צוץ *to be bright, to shine* (to give forth brightness); opposed to חשׁך *to become dark*; חזק, גבר, אמץ *to be strong* (to develop strength), עטף *to be weak*; ארך *to be long* (to acquire length); גבה *to be high*; הום *to be in tumult*, זעק *to cry out*, רוע, רנן *to make a noise, to exult*; חלף *to sprout* (to put forth shoots), cf. פרח *to bloom*, עדף, שׁוק *to overflow*; חרשׁ, חשׁה, סכת, צמת *to be silent* (silentium facere, Pliny); מתק *to be sweet*; צלח *to have success*; שׁפל *to be low*; אדם *to become red*, לבן *to become white*.

e   (*b*) Stems which express in *Hiph'il* the entering into a certain condition and, further, the being in the same: אמן *to become firm, to trust in*; באשׁ *to become stinking*; זוד *to become boiling, to boil over*; חלה *to become ill*; הסר *to come to want*; חרה *to become hot*; יבשׁ *to become dry, to become ashamed*; יתר *to attain superiority*; סכן *to become familiar*; עור, קוץ *to become awake*; קשׁה *to become hard*; רגע, שׁקט *to become quiet* (to keep quiet); שׁמם *to be astonished*. The Hiph'il forms of some verbs of motion constitute a variety of this class: נגשׁ *to draw near*; קרב *to come near*; רחק *to withdraw far off* (all these three are besides used as causatives); קדם *to come before*.

f   (*c*) Stems which express action in some particular direction: חטא *to err*; חלק *to flatter* (to act smoothly); יטב *to act well, to do good*; סכל *to act foolishly*, שׂכל *to act wisely*; ערם *to act craftily*; צנע *to act submissively*; רשׁע, רעע *to act wickedly, godlessly*; תעב, שׁחת *to act corruptly, abominably*; שׁלם *to act peacefully, to be at peace, to be submissive*.

g   Further, there are in *Hiph'il* a considerable number of *denominatives* which express the *bringing out*, the *producing* of a thing, and so are properly regarded as causatives,[1] e. g. אצר *to set over the treasury*, Neh 13[13] (unless וַאֲצַוֶּה is to be read, as in Neh 7[2]); בכר *to bring forth a firstborn*; גשׁם *to cause to rain*; זרע *to produce seed*; ימן (Hiph'il הֵימִין) *to go to the right*, cf. הִשְׂמְאִיל *to go to the left*; פרס *to get or to have hoofs*; קרן *to get or to have horns*; שׁכל *to produce abortion*; שׁלג *to become snow-white*; שׁמן *to grow fat*; שׁרשׁ *to put forth roots*, &c.; so also according to the ordinary acceptation הֶאֱזְנִיחוּ Is 19[6], *they have become stinking*, from אֲזֵנָה *stinking* or *stench*, with retention of the א prosthetic, § 19 *m* (but see below, *p*).

---

[1] The same ideas are also paraphrased by the verb עָשָׂה (*to make*), e. g. *to make fat, for, to produce fat upon his body*, Jb 15[27]; *to make fruit, to make branches, for, to put forth, to yield*, Jb 14[9], Ho 8[7], cf. the Lat. *corpus, robur, sobolem, divitias facere*, and the Ital. *far corpo, far forze, far frutto*.

Of a different kind are the *denominatives* from: אָזַן (scarcely *to prick up the ears*, but) *to act with the ears, to hear*; cf. לָשַׁן *to move the tongue, to slander*, and the German *äugeln* (to make eyes), *füsseln, näseln, schwänzeln*; שָׁבַר *to sell corn*; שָׁכַם *to set out early* (to load the back [of the camel, &c.]?); opposed to הֶעֱרִיב.

h 3. The meaning of *Hophʿal* is (*a*) primarily that of a *passive* of *Hiphʿil*, e.g. הִשְׁלִיךְ *proiecit*, הָשְׁלַךְ or הֻשְׁלַךְ *proiectus est*; (*b*) sometimes equivalent to a passive of *Qal*, as נָקַם *to avenge*, Hoph. *to be avenged* (but see below, *u*).

i Rem. 1. The *i* of the 3rd sing. masc. perf. Hiphʿil remains, without exception, in the 3rd fem. (in the tone-syllable). That it was, however, only lengthened from a short vowel, and consequently is changeable, is proved by the forms of the *imperative* and *imperfect* where *ē* (or, under the influence of gutturals, *ă*) takes its place. In an open syllable the *i* is retained almost throughout; only in very isolated instances has it been weakened to *Šᵉwâ* (see *n* and *o*).

k 2. The *infinitive absolute* commonly has Ṣere without *Yodh*, e.g. הַקְדֵּשׁ Ju 17³; less frequently it takes יִ‸, e.g. הַשְׁמֵיד Am 9⁸; cf. Dt 15¹⁴, Is 59⁴, Jer 3¹⁵, 23³², 44²⁵, Jb 34³⁵, Ec 10¹⁰. With א instead of ה (probably a mere scribal error, not an Aramaism) we find אַשְׁפֵּים Jer 25³. Rare exceptions, where the form with Ṣere stands for the *infinitive construct*, are, e.g. Dt 32⁸ (Sam. בְּהַנְחִיל; read perhaps בְּהַנְחֵל), Jer 44¹⁹·²⁵, Pr 25², Jb 13³ (?); on the other hand, for לַעְשֵׂר Dt 26¹² (which looks like an infinitive Hiphʿil with elision of the ה, for לְהַעְשִׂיר) the right reading is simply לְעַשֵּׂר, since elsewhere the Piʿēl alone occurs with the meaning *to tithe*; for בַּעְשֵׂר Neh 10³⁹ perhaps the inf. Qal (בַּעְשֹׂר) was intended, as in 1 S 8¹⁵·¹⁷ (= *to take the tithe*). At the same time it is doubtful whether the present punctuation does not arise from a conflation of two different readings, the Qal and the Piʿēl.

l Instead of the ordinary form of the *infinitive construct* הַקְטִיל the form הַקְטֵיל sometimes occurs, e.g. הַשְׁמֵיד *to destroy*, Dt 7²⁴, 28⁴⁸; cf. Lv 14⁴⁶, Jos 11¹⁴, Jer 50³⁴, 51³³ and הַקְצֹות for הַקְצֵות Lv 14⁴³ from קָצָה; scarcely, however, Lv 7³⁵ (see § 155 *l*), 2 S 22¹ (ψ 18¹), 1 K 11¹⁶ (after עַד), and in the passages so explained by König (i. 276) where הִשְׁאֵיר appears after prepositions[1]; [cf. Driver on Dt 3³, 4¹⁵, 7²⁴, 28⁵⁵].

With *ă* in the second syllable there occurs הַוְבֵּרְכֶם Ez 21²⁹ (cf. the substantival infin. הַפְצַר 1 S 15²³).—In the Aram. manner לְהַשְׁמָעוּת is found in Ez 24²⁶ (as a construct form) for the *infinitive Hiphʿil* (cf. the *infinitive Hithpaʿel*, Dn 11²³). On the elision of the ה after prefixes, see *q*.

m 3. In the *imperative* the *i* is retained throughout in the open syllable, according to *i*, and consequently also before suffixes (see § 61 *g*) and ה‸ paragogic, e.g. הַקְשִׁיבָה *attend to*, הוֹשִׁיעָה נָּא ψ 118²⁵, as in ed. Mant., Jabl., Baer, not הוֹשִׁיעָה נָּא as Ginsb. and Kittel; with the tone at the end only הַצְלִיחָה ibid. v. 25ᵇ. On the other hand, in the 2nd sing. masc. the original *i* (cf. Arabic *ʾáqtil*) is lengthened to *ē*, e.g. הַשְׁמֵן *make fat*, and becomes Sᵉghôl before *Maqqeph*, e.g. הַסְכֶּן־נָא Jb 22²¹.—The form הַקְטֵיל for הַקְטֵל appears anomalously a few times: ψ 94¹, Is 43⁸, Jer 17¹⁸ (cf. § 69 *v* and § 72 *y*); elsewhere the Masora has preferred the punctuation הַקְטִיל, e.g. 2 K 8⁶; cf. ψ 142⁵.—In La 5¹ הַבִּיטָה is required by the Qᵉrê for הבים.

---

[1] As to the doubtfulness, on general grounds, of this form of the Inf. Hiph., see Robertson Smith in the *Journ. of Philol.*, xvi. p. 72 f.

4. In the *imperfect Hiph'îl* the *shorter* form with Ṣere prevails for the jussive *n* in the 3rd masc. and *fem.* and 2nd masc. sing., e. g. אַל־תַּגְדֵּל *make not great,* Ob ¹²; יַכְרֵת *let Him cut off!* ψ 12⁴; even incorrectly תַּגֵּיד Ex 19³ and יַגִּיד Ec 1c²⁰; cf. also יַבְעֶר־ Ex 22⁴, where the jussive form is to be explained according to § 109 *h*, and יַאֲבֵר Jb 39²⁶ before the principal pause. Similarly, after ו consec., e. g. וַיַּבְדֵּל *and He divided,* Gn 1⁴. On the other hand, *i* is almost always retained in the 1st sing., e. g. וָאַשְׁמִיד Am 2⁹ (but generally without י, as וָאַסְתֵּר Ez 39²³ ʳ., &c.); cf. § 49 *e* and § 74 *l*, but also § 72 *aa*; in 1st plur. only in Neh 4³; in the 3rd sing. ψ 105²⁸. With *ă* in the principal pause וַתּוֹתַר Ru 2¹⁴, and in the lesser pause, Gn 49⁴; before a sibilant (see § 29 *q*) וַיַּגֵּשׁ Ju 6¹⁹; in the lesser pause וַיַּקֵּף La 3⁵. Before *Maqqeph* the Ṣere becomes *Sᵉghôl,* e. g. וַיְחַזֶּק־בּוֹ Ju 19⁴. In the plural again, and before suffixes, *i* remains in the forms תַּקְטִילוּ יַקְטִילוּ, even in the jussive and after ו consecutive, e. g. וַיַּדְבִּיקוּ Ju 18²². The only exceptions, where the *i* is weakened to *Sᵉwâ,* are וַיַּדְרִכוּ Jer 9²; וַיַּדְבִּקוּ 1 S 14²², 31², 1 Ch 10²; יַעֲבְרוּ Jer 11¹⁵; וָאוֹצְרָה Neh 13¹³, if it is *Hiph'îl* of אצר, but probably וָאֲצַוֶּה is to be read, as in 7²; perhaps also תַּהְפְּכוּ Jb 19³ (according to others, *imperfect Qal*). The same weakening occurs also in the imperfect in 3rd and 2nd masc. sing. before suffixes, 1 S 17²⁵, 1 K 20³³, ψ 65¹⁰, and in Jb 9²⁰, unless the form be *Pi'ēl*וַיַּעַקְשֵׁנִי, since the *Hiph'îl* is not found elsewhere. It is hardly likely that in these isolated examples we have a trace of the ground-form, *yaqtil,* or an Aramaism. More probably they are due partly to a misunderstanding of the defective writing, which is found, by a purely orthographic licence, in numerous other cases (even in 3rd sing. יֵשָׁלֵם Is 44²⁸), and partly are intended, as *formae mixtae,* to combine the forms of *Qal* and *Hiph'îl.* Instead of the firmly closed syllable, the Masora requires in Gn 1¹¹ תַּדְשֵׁא, with euphonic Ga'ya (see § 16 *h*).

5. In the *participle,* מוֹצִא ψ 135⁷ appears to be traceable to the ground-form, *O maqtîl*; yet the Ṣere may also possibly be explained by the retraction of the tone. The Masora appears to require the weakening of the vowel to *Sᵉwâ* (see above, *n*) in מֵהֲלָכִים Zc 3⁷ (probably, however, מַהְלְכִים should be read), also in מַחֲלָמִים Jer 29⁸, מַעֲוָרִים 2 Ch 28²³ (but as מ precedes, and accordingly dittography may well have taken place, the participle Qal is probably to be read in both places; the reading of the text is perhaps again intended to combine Qal and Hiph'îl, see above, *n*), and in the *Qᵉrê* מַחֲצְרִים 1 Ch 15²⁴ &c. (where the *Kᵉthîbh* מְחַצְּרִים is better).—The fem. is ordinarily pointed as מַזְכֶּרֶת Nu 5¹⁵, מַשְׁנֶת Lv 14²¹; in pause מַשְׁכֶּלֶת Pr 19¹⁴.

6. In the *perfect* there occur occasionally such forms as הִכְלִמְנוּ 1 S 25⁷; *p* cf. Gn 41²⁸, 2 K 17¹¹, Jer 29¹, Mi 6³, Jb 16⁷; with the original *ă* in the first syllable וְהִרְאִיתִי Na 3⁵.—In אֶנְאַלְתִּי ¹ *I have stained,* Is 63³, א stands at the beginning instead of ה, cf. above, *k,* on אַשְׁפַּיִם. On the other hand, וְהַאֲוֹנִיחַ

---

¹ Most probably, however, גֵּאַלְתִּי (*perfect Pi'ēl*) is to be read, and the א is only an indication of the change of the *perfect* into the *imperfect,* as also previously, by a change of punctuation, וְאֶרְדְּכֵם and וְיִן (instead of וְאֶרְ and וַיִן) are made future instead of past. Jewish exegesis applied these Edom-oracles to the Roman (i. e. Christian) empire. So G. Moore in *Theol. Literaturzeitung,* 1887, col. 292.

Is 19⁶ (see above, *g*) is a mere error of the scribe, who had the Aramaic form in mind and corrected it by prefixing ה.

q 7. In the *imperfect* and *participle* the characteristic ה is regularly elided after the preformatives, thus יַקְטִיל, מַקְטִיל; but it is retained in the *infinitive* after prepositions, e.g. לְהַקְטִיל. The exceptions are in the imperfect, יְהוֹשִׁיעַ *He will save* for יוֹשִׁיעַ 1 S 17⁴⁷, ψ 116⁶ (in pause); יוֹדֶה *He will praise* for יוֹדֶה Neh 11¹⁷, ψ 28⁷, 45¹⁸ (cf. the proper name יְהוֹנָכָל Jer 37³, for which 38¹ יוּכַל [and יְהוֹסֵף ψ 81⁶]); יְהֵילִלוּ (§ 70 *d*) Is 52⁵, יֶהֱתַלּוּ Jer 9⁴, תְּהָחֵל Jb 13⁹] and מֵהִקְצָעוֹת Ez 46²²; in the *infinitive* (where, however, as in *Niph'al*, § 51 *l*, the infinitive *Qal* is generally to be read) לַסְתֻּר Is 29¹⁵ for לְהַסְתִּיר; לַנְפֹּל and לַצְבּוֹת Nu 5²²; לַעֲבִיר 2 S 19¹⁹; לְהַלְק Jer 37¹²; לַחֲטִיא Ec 5⁵; לַבֵּן (doubly anomalous for לְהַלְבִּין) Dn 11³⁵; לַשְׁמֵעַ ψ 26⁷; לְאַדְרִיב 1 S 2³³; לַשָׁמֵד Is 23¹¹; וְלַשְׁבִּית Am 8⁴ (certainly corrupt); בָּעִיר for בְּהָעִיר ψ 73²⁰ (but *in the city* is probably meant); לָבִיא Jer 39⁷ (2 Ch 31¹⁰); לְמֵרוֹת Is 3⁸, ψ 78¹⁷; לַנְחֹתָם Ex 13²¹; כַּגְּלוֹת (see, however, § 20 *h*) Is 33¹; לְרֹאתְכֶם Dt 1³³: cf. further, from verbs ל״ה, Nu 5²², Jer 27²⁰; on Dt 26¹² and Neh 10³⁹, see above, *k*; for לְמֹחוֹת Pr 31³ read לְמֹחוֹת or לְמִמְחוֹת.

r 8. With regard to the tone it is to be observed that the afformatives וּ and ‍ָה‍ in Hiph'îl have *not* the tone, even in the *perfect* with *waw consecutive* (except in Ex 26³³ before ה, Lv 15²⁹ before א, to avoid a hiatus); but the plural ending וּן (see § 47 *m*) always has the tone, e.g. תַּקְרִבוּן Dt 1¹⁷.

s 9. The passive (Hoph'al) has *ŭ* instead of Qameṣ-ḥaṭuph in the first syllable (הֻקְטַל), in the strong verb less frequently in the perfect and infinitive, but generally in the participle, through the influence of the initial מ (but cf. מָשְׁחַת Pr 25²⁶); e.g. הֻשְׁבַּב Ez 32³² (beside הֻשְׁכְּבָה 32¹⁹); הֻשְׁלַךְ *impf.* יֻשְׁלַךְ, part. מֻשְׁלָךְ 2 S 20²¹ (beside הָשְׁלַכְתְּ Is 14¹⁹) הֻמְלַחַתְּ Ez 16⁴; in the partic. Hoph. without elision of the ה: מֵהִקְצָעוֹת Ez 46²²; on the other hand, verbs פ״ן always have *ŭ* (in a sharpened syllable): הֻגַּד, יֻגַּד (cf. § 9 *n*).

t 10. The *infinitive absolute* has in Hoph'al (as in Hiph'îl) Ṣere in the last syllable, e.g. הָחְתֵּל and הָמְלֵחַ Ez 16⁴; הֻגֵּד Jos 9²⁴. An *infinitive construct* does not occur in the strong verb.

  11. With regard to the *imperative* Hoph'al, see above, § 46 *a*, note.

u 12. According to Böttcher (*Ausführliches Lehrbuch*, § 906) and Barth (see above, § 52 *e*) a number of supposed imperfects Hoph'al are, in fact, imperfects of the passive of *Qal*. As in the case of the perfects passive of Qal (see above, § 52 *e*) the question is again of verbs of which neither the corresponding causative (i.e. here the Hiph'îl), nor the other tense of the same conjugation (i.e. here the perfect Hoph'al) is found; so with יֻקַּם (for יֻנְקַם, cf. *yuqtălŭ* as imperfect Qal in Arabic) and יֻתַּן, from נָתַן and נָחַן, נָתַן; יֻקַּח from לָקַח (cf. § 66 *g*); יוּאָר Nu 22⁶ from אָרַר; יֻחַן from חָנַן; יוּשַּׁד Ho 10¹⁴ (cf. Is 33¹) from שָׁדַד; Barth adds the verbs פ״ן: תֻּתַּשׁ Ez 19¹² from נתשׁ; יֻתַּץ Lev 11³⁵ from נתץ; the verbs ע״ע: יֻחַקוּ Jb 19²³ from חקק; יֻכַּת &c. from כתת; the verb יוּרַשׁ ע״ו: from דּוּשׁ; the verbs ע״ו: יֻשַּׁר, יֻוחַל from יֻשַּׁת, חִיל, יָשִׁיר and שִׁית. On וַיִּישֶׂם &c., § 73 *f*. In point of fact it would be very strange, especially in the case of יֻתַּן and יֻקַּח, that of these frequently used verbs, amongst all the forms of Hiph'îl and Hoph'al, only the *imperfect* Hoph'al should have been preserved. A passive of Qal is also indicated in the Tell-el-Amarna letters, according to Knudtzon, by a number of imperfect forms, which are undoubtedly due to Canaanite influence, cf. *Beitr. zur Assyriologie,* iv. 410.

§ 54. *Hithpaʿēl.*

1. The *Hithpaʿēl* [1] is connected with *Piʿēl*, being formed by prefixing *a* to the *Piʿēl*-stem (*qattēl, qattal*) the syllable הִת (Western Aramaic אֶת, but in Biblical Aramaic הִת; Syr. *'et* [2]). Like the preformative נ (הִנ) of *Niph'al*, הִת has also a reflexive force.

2. The ת of the prefix in this conjugation, as also in *Hothpa'al b* (see *h*), *Hithpōʿēl, Hithpaʿlēl* and *Hithpalpel* (§ 55), under certain circumstances, suffers the following changes:

(*a*) When the stem begins with one of the harder sibilants ס, צ, or שׂ, the ת and the sibilant change places (cf. on this *metathesis,* § 19 *n*), and at the same time the ת after a צ becomes the corresponding emphatic ט: thus הִשְׁתַּמֵּר *to take heed to oneself,* for הִתְשַׁמֵּר; הִסְתַּבֵּל *to become burdensome,* for הִתְסַבֵּל; הִצְטַדֵּק *to justify oneself,* from צָדַק. The only exception is in Jer 49³, וְהִתְשׁוֹטַטְנָה, to avoid the cacophony of three successive *t*-sounds.

(*b*) When the stem begins with a *d*- or *t*-sound (ד, ט, ת), the ת of *c* the preformative is assimilated to it (§ 19 *d*), e. g. מְדַבֵּר *speaking, conversing;* הִדַּכָּא *to be crushed,* הִטַּהֵר *to purify oneself,* הִטַּמֵּא *to defile oneself,* הִתַּמֵּם *to act uprightly.* (An exception occurs in Ju 19²².) The assimilation of the ת occurs also with נ and כ, e. g. הִנַּבֵּא *to prophesy,* as well as הִתְנַבֵּא (cf. Nu 24⁷, Ez 5¹³, Dn 11¹⁴); תִּכַּוֵּן Nu 21²⁷ (cf. Is 54¹⁴, ψ 59⁵); תִּכַּפֶּה Pr 26²⁶; with שׁ Ec 7¹⁶; with ר Is 33¹⁰.

Rem. Metathesis would likewise be expected, as in the cases under *b,* *d* when ת and ז come together, as well as a change of ת to ד. Instead of this, in the only instance of the kind (הֻזַּכּוּ Is 1¹⁶) the ת is assimilated to the ז, —unless indeed הֻזַּכּוּ, *imperative Niph'al* of זכך, is intended.

3. As in form, so also in meaning, *Hithpaʿēl* is primarily (*a*) *reflexive* of *Piʿēl*, e. g. הִתְאַזֵּר *to gird oneself,* הִתְקַדֵּשׁ *to sanctify oneself.* Although in these examples the intensive meaning is not distinctly marked, it is so in other cases, c. g. הִתְנַקֵּם *to show oneself revengeful (Niph.* simply *to take revenge*), and in the numerous instances where the *Hithpaʿēl* expresses *to make oneself* that which is predicated by the stem, *to conduct oneself* as such, *to show oneself, to imagine oneself, to*

---

[1] A. Stein, *Der Stamm des Hithpael im Hebr.* pt. 1, Schwerin, 1893, gives alphabetical statistics of the 1151 forms.

[2] So also in Hebrew אֶתְחַבַּר 2 Ch 20³⁵; cf. ψ 76⁶ (אֶשְׁתּוֹלְלוּ).

affect to be of a certain character. E. g. הִתְגַּדֵּל *to make oneself great, to act proudly*; הִתְחַכֵּם *to show oneself wise, crafty*; הִתְחַלָּה *to pretend to be ill*; הִתְעַשֵּׁר *to make, i. e. to feign oneself rich*; הִשְׁתָּרֵר Nu 16¹³, *to make oneself a prince*; הִתְנַבֵּא 1 S 18¹⁰, *to act in an excited manner like a prophet, to rave*. The meaning of *Hithpaʻēl* sometimes coincides with that of *Qal*, both forms being in use together, e. g. אָבַל *to mourn*, in Qal only in poetic style, in *Hithpaʻēl* in prose. On the accusative after Hithpaʻēl (regarded as a transitive verb), see § 117 *w*.

f　　(*b*) It expresses *reciprocal* action, like *Niphʻal*, § 51 *d*, e. g. הִתְרָאָה *to look upon one another*, Gn 42¹; cf. ψ 41⁸;—but

(*c*) It more often indicates an action less directly affecting the subject, and describes it as performed *with regard to* or *for* oneself, in one's own special interest (cf. *Niphʻal*, § 51 *e*). Hithpaʻēl in such cases readily takes an accusative, e. g. הִתְפָּרֵק Ex 32³ and הִתְנַצֵּל Ex 33⁶ *to tear off from oneself*; הִתְפַּשֵׁט *exuit sibi* (*vestem*), הִתְפַּתַּח *solvit sibi* (*vincula*); הִצְטַיֵּד Jos 9¹², *to take* (*something*) *as one's provision*; without an accusative, הִתְהַלֵּךְ *to walk about for oneself* (*ambulare*); הִתְפַּלֵּל *sibi intercedere* (see Delitzsch on Is 1¹⁵); הִתְחַקָּה *to draw a line for oneself,* Job 13²⁷; on Is 14², see § 57, note.

g　　(*d*) Only seldom is it *passive*, e. g. הִיא תִתְהַלָּל Pr 31³⁰ *she shall be praised*; הִשְׁתַּבַּח *to be forgotten,* Ec 8¹⁰, where the reflexive sense (*to bring oneself into oblivion*) has altogether disappeared. Cf. Niphʻal, § 51 *f*.

h　　The passive form *Hothpaʻal* is found only in the few following examples : הֻטַּמָּא *to be defiled*, Dt 24⁴; *infinitive* הֻכַּבֵּס *to be washed*, Lv 13⁵⁵.⁵⁶; הֻדַּשְׁנָה (for הִתְדַּשְּׁנָה, the נָה being treated as if it were the afformative of the *fem. plur.*) *it is made fat*, Is 34⁶. On הָתְפָּקְדוּ, see *l*.

i　　Denominatives with a reflexive meaning are הִתְיַהֵד *to embrace Judaism,* from יְהוּד (יְהוּדָה) *Judah*; הִצְטַיֵּד *to provision oneself for a journey*, from צֵידָה *provision for a journey* (see § 72 *m*).

k　　Rem. 1. As in *Piʻēl*, so in *Hithpaʻēl*, the perfect very frequently (in stems ending in ג, ק, מ, פ) has retained the original *Pathaḥ* in the final syllable (while in the ordinary form it is attenuated, as in *Piʻēl*, to *ĭ* and then lengthened to *ē*), e. g. הִתְאַנַּף Dt 4²¹, &c. ; cf. 2 Ch 13⁷, 15⁸; with ו *consecutive* Is 8²¹; so also in the imperfect and imperative, e. g. תִּתְחַכָּם Ec 7¹⁶; cf. Dt 9⁸·¹⁸, 1 S 3¹⁰, 2 S 10¹², 1 K 11⁹, Is 55², 58¹⁴, 64¹¹, ψ 55²; הִתְחַזָּק 1 K 20²², ψ 37⁴, Est 5¹⁰; וָאֶתְאַפַּק 1 S 13¹².—In Lv 11⁴⁴, 20⁷ and Ez 38²³, *ĭ* takes the place of *ă* in the final syllable of the stem before שׁ (cf. § 44 *d*), and in the last passage before לְ. In the *perfect, imperfect* (with the exception of Ec 7¹⁶), and *imperative* of Hithpaʻēl (as well as of Hithpōʻēl, Hithpaʻlēl, Hithpalpēl, § 55) the original *ă* always returns in *pause* as *Qames*, e. g. הִתְאָנֶּף ψ 93¹; יִתְאַבָּל Ez 7²⁷; יִתְהַלָּךְ Jb 18⁸; הִתְקַדָּשׁוּ Jos 3⁵; cf. Jb 33⁵ and § 74 *b*.—The *ā* also appears before the fuller ending ן־ in the plural of the imperfect (cf. § 47 *m*) in ψ 12⁹, Jb

9⁶, 16¹⁰.—Like the *Piʿēl* תְּקַטֵּלְנָה (§ 52 *n*), forms occur in *Hithpaʿēl* like תִּתְהַלַּכְנָה Zc 6⁷; cf. Am 8¹³, and so in *Hithpoʿēl*, Jer 49³, Am 9¹³; with *ē* only in La 4¹.— In the Aramaic manner an *infinitive Hithpaʿēl* הִתְחַבְּרוּת occurs in Dn 11²³ (cf. the *Hiphʿil* inf. הַשְׁמָעוּת in Ez 24²⁶).

2. As instances of the *reflexive* הִתְקַטֵּל (connected with *Piʿēl*) a few reflexive *l* forms of the verb פָּקַד (*to examine*) are also probably to be reckoned. Instead of a *Pathaḥ* in a sharpened syllable after the first radical, these take *Qameṣ* in an open syllable, e. g. הִתְפָּקְדוּ Ju 20¹⁵.¹⁷, *imperfect* יִתְפָּקֵד 20¹⁵, 21⁹. The corresponding passive form הָתְפָּקְדוּ also occurs four times, Nu 1⁴⁷, 2³³, 26⁶², 1 K 20²⁷. According to others, these forms are rather reflexives of *Qal*, in the sense of *to present oneself for review, to be reviewed*, like the Aramaic *'Ithpeʿēl* (Western Aramaic אִתְקְטֵל, Syr. אֶתְקְטֶל) and the Ethiopic *taqatᵉla*, Arab. *'iqtatala*, the last with the *t* always placed after the first radical (cf. above, *b*); but they are more correctly explained, with König, as *Hithpaʿēl* forms, the doubling of the ק being abnormally omitted.—Such a reflexive of *Qal*, with the ת transposed, occurs in הלתחם (on the analogy of O. T. Hebrew to be pronounced הִלָּתְחֶם) in the inscription of the Moabite king *Mêšaʿ*, with the meaning of the O. T. *Niphʿal* נִלְחַם *to fight, to wage war*: see the inscription, lines 11, 15, 19, and 32; in the first two places in the *imperfect* with *wāw consecutive* וָאֶלָּתְחֶם; in line 19 in the *infinitive* with suffix, בְּהִלָּתְחֹמֹה בִי *in his fighting against me*.

§ 55. *Less Common Conjugations.*

Of the less common conjugations (§ 39 *g*) some may be classed with *a Piʿēl*, others with *Hiphʿil*. To the former belong those which arise from the lengthening of the vowel or the repetition of one or even two radicals, in fact, from an internal modification or development of the stem; to the latter belong those which are formed by prefixing a consonant, like the ה of Hiphʿil. Amongst the conjugations analogous to *Piʿēl* are included the *passive* forms distinguished by their vowels, as well as the reflexives with the prefix הִת, on the analogy of *Hithpaʿēl*.

The following conjugations are related to *Piʿēl*, as regards their *b* inflexion and partly in their meaning:

1. *Pôʿēl* קוֹטֵל, passive *Pôʿal* קוֹטַל, reflexive *Hithpôʿēl* הִתְקוֹטֵל, corresponding to the Arabic conj. III. *qâtălă*, pass. *qûtĭlă*, and conj. VI. reflexive *tăqâtălă*; *imperfect* יְקוֹטֵל, *participle* מְקוֹטֵל, *imperfect passive* יְקוֹטַל &c. Hence it appears that in Hebrew the *ô* of the first syllable is in all the forms obscured from *â*, while the passive form is distinguished simply by the *a*-sound in the second syllable. In the strong verb these conjugations are rather rare. Examples: *participle* מְשֹׁפְטִי *mine adversary, who would contend with me*, Jb 9¹⁵; מְלוֹשְׁנִי (denominative from לָשׁוֹן *the tongue*) *slandering* (as if *intent on injuring with the tongue*) ψ 101⁵ *Kᵉth.* (The *Qᵉré* requires מְלָשְׁנִי *mᵉlošni* as Na 1³ גִּנְדּוּל); זֹרְמוּ *they have poured out*, ψ 77¹⁸ (if not rather *Puʿal*); יוֹדַעְתִּי *I have appointed*, 1 S 21³ (unless הוֹדַעְתִּי should be read); יְסֹעֵר Ho 13³; שֹׁרֵשׁ *to take root*, passive

שׁוֹרֵשׁ, *denominative* from שֶׁרֶשׁ *root* (but שָׁרֵשׁ *to root out*); in Hithpōʿēl הִתְגֹּעֲשׁוּ *they shall be moved*, Jer 25¹⁶; imperf. 46⁸; from a verb ל״ה, שׁוֹשֵׂתִי Is 10¹³. The *participle* מְנָאֵץ Is 52⁵ is probably a *forma mixta* combining the readings מְנָאֵץ and מִתְנָאֵץ.

c Poʿel proper (as distinguished from the corresponding conjugations of verbs ע״וּ § 67 *l* and ע״י § 72 *m*, which take the place of the ordinary causative *Piʿēl*) expresses an aim or endeavour to perform the action, especially with hostile intent, and is hence called, by Ewald, the stem expressing *aim* (Ziel-stamm), *endeavour* (Suche-stamm) or *attack* (Angriffs-stamm); cf. the examples given above from Jb 9¹⁵, ψ 101⁵, and עוֹיְן 1 S 18⁹ Qᵉrê (probably for מְעוֹיֵן, cf. § 52 *s*; § 55 *f*: *seeking to cast an evil eye*).

With קוֹטֵל is connected the formation of quadriliterals by the insertion of a consonant between the first and second radicals (§ 30 *p*, § 56).

d 2. *Paʿlēl*, generally with the ă attenuated to ĭ = *Piʿlēl* [1] (*Piʿlal*), קְטַלֵל and קְטְלֵל; the ē in the final syllable also arises from ĭ, and this again from ă; passive *Puʿlal* קְטְלֵל, reflexive *Hithpaʿlēl* הִתְקַטְלֵל, like the Arabic conjugations IX. ʾiqtállă and XI. ʾiqtāllă, the former used of permanent, the latter of accidental or changing conditions, e. g. of colours; cf. שָׁאַנֵן *to be at rest*, רַעֲנַן *to be green*, passive אֻמְלַל *to be withered*, all of them found only in the *perfect* and with no corresponding *Qal* form. (For the barbarous form צְמָתְּתֻנִי ψ 88¹⁷ read צְמַתְּתֻנִי; for נִפְלַל Ez 28²³, which has manifestly arisen only from confusion with the following חלל, read נָפַל). These forms are more common in verbs ע״וּ, where they take the place of *Piʿēl* and *Hithpaʿēl* (§ 72 *m*). Cf. also § 75 *kk.*

e 3. *Pᵉʿalʿal*: קְטַלְטַל with repetition of the last two radicals, used of movements repeated in quick succession; e. g. סְחַרְחַר *to go about quickly, to palpitate* (of the heart) ψ 38¹¹, from סָחַר *to go about*; passive חֲמַרְמַר *to be in a ferment, to be heated, to be red*, Jb 16¹⁶, La 1²⁰, 2¹¹. Probably this is also the explanation of חֲצֹצֵר (denom. from חֲצֹצְרָה *a trumpet*, but only in the *participle*, 1 Ch 15²⁴ &c. Kᵉth.) for חֲצַרְצֵר, by absorption of the first ר, lengthening of ă in the open syllable, and subsequent obscuring of ā to ô. On the other hand, for the meaningless אֲהַבוּ הֵבוּ Ho 4¹⁸ (which could only be referred to this conjugation if it stood for אֲהַבְהֵבוּ) read אֲהֵבוּ, and for the equally meaningless יְפֵיפִיתָ ψ 45³ read יָפִיתָ. In both these cases a scribal error (*dittography*) has been perpetuated by the punctuation, which did not venture to alter the Kᵉthîbh. On the employment of *Pᵉʿalʿal* in the formation of nouns, cf. § 84ᵇ *n*. Closely related to this form is—

f 4. *Pilpēl* (pass. *Pōlpal*), with a strengthening of the two essential radicals in stems ע״וּ, ע״י, and ע״ע, e. g. גִּלְגֵּל *to roll*, from גַּל = גָּלַל; *reflexive* הִתְגַּלְגֵּל *to roll oneself down*; כִּלְכֵּל from כּוּל, *passive* כָּלְכַּל; cf. also טִאטֵא (so Baer and Ginsb. after Qimḥi; others טָאטֵא) Is 14²³, and with ă in both syllables owing to the influence of ר, קַרְקַר from קוּר Nu 24¹⁷ (cf. however, in the parallel passage, Jer 48⁴⁵ קָדְקֹד) and Is 22⁵, in the *participle*; שׁוֹרֵשׁ Is 17¹¹ *to hedge in*, acc. to others *make to grow*. Probably to this form also belongs יְלַעְלְעוּ, the emended reading of Jb 39³⁰ instead of the impossible יְעַלְעוּ; also

---

[1] Cf. Wolfensohn, 'The Piʿlel in Hebrew,' *Amer. Journ. of Or. Studies*, xxvii (1907), p. 303 ff.

סָאפְאָה Is 27[8], if that form is to be referred to an *infinitive* סָאסָא ; perhaps also שִׁשָּׁא Ez 39[2] for שָׁאשָׁא. This form also commonly expresses rapidly repeated movement, which all languages incline to indicate by a repetition of the sound,[1] e.g. צִפְצֵף *to chirp*; cf. in the Lexicon the nouns derived from עוּף, גָּרַר, and צָלַל.

g As *Hithpalpel* we find יִשְׁתַּקְשְׁקוּן Na 2[5]; וַתְּתְחַלְחַל Est 4[4]; וַיִּתְמַרְמַר Dn 8[7], 11[11]. Of the same form is אֶדַּדֶּה Is 38[15], if contracted from אֶתְדַּוְדֶּה or אתדידה from the root דו or (דיַ), and also הִתְמַהְמְהוּ *tarry ye*, Is 29[9] (but read probably הִתְפַּהוּ), וַיִּתְמַהְמָהּ (in *pause*) Gn 19[16], &c., if it is to be derived from מָהַהּ, and not Hithpaʿel from מָהַהּ.

Only examples more or less doubtful can be adduced of— *h*

5. *Tiphʿēl* (properly *Taphʿēl* [2]): תִּקְטֵל, with ת prefixed, cf. תִּרְגַּלְתִּי *to teach to walk, to lead* (denominative from רֶגֶל *a foot?*) Ho 11[3]; from a stem לֵ"ה, the *imperfect* יִרְחָרֶה *to contend with*, Jer 12[5]; *participle*, 22[15] (from חָרָה *to be hot, eager*). Similarly in Aramaic, תַּרְגֵּם *to interpret*, whence also in Hebrew the *passive participle* מְתֻרְגָּם Ezr 4[7].

6. *Šaphʿēl* : שִׁקְטֵל, frequent in Syriac, e.g. שַׁלְהֵב from לְהב *to flame*; whence *i* in Hebrew שַׁלְהֶבֶת *flame*. Perhaps of the same form is שַׁבְלוּל *a snail* (unless it be from the stem שׁבל), and שַׁעֲרוּרֹת *hollow strakes*, cf. § 85, No. 50. This conjugation is perhaps the original of *Hiphʿîl*, in which case the ה, by a phonetic change which may be exemplified elsewhere, is weakened from a sibilant.

* * *

Forms of which only isolated examples occur are:— *k*

7. קֻטְלַט, *passive* : קָטְלַט ; as מְחֻסְפָּס *peeled off, like scales*, Ex 16[14], from חָסַף, חָשַׂף *to peel, to scale*.

8. קַטְקֵל, in זַרְזִיף *a rain-storm*, from זָרַף.

9. נִתְקַטֵּל (regularly in Mishnic Hebrew [3]) a form compounded of *Niphʿal* and *Hithpaʿēl*; as וְנִתְוַסְּרוּ for וְנִוָּסְרוּ *that they may be taught*, Ez 23[48]; נִכַּפֵּר probably an error for הִתְכַּפֵּר *to be forgiven*, Dt 21[8]. On נִשְׁתַּוָּה Pr 27[15], see § 75 *x*.

§ 56. *Quadriliterals.*

On the origin of these altogether secondary formations cf. § 30 *p*. While quadriliteral *nouns* are tolerably numerous, only the following examples of the verb occur:

---

[1] Cf. Lat. *tinnio, tintinno*, our *tick-tack, ding-dong*, and the German *wirrwarr, klingklang*. The repetition of the radical in verbs ע"ע also produces this effect; as in לָקַק *to lick*, דָּקַק *to pound*, טָפַף *to trip along*. The same thing is expressed also by *diminutive* forms, as in Latin by the termination -*illo*, e.g. *cantillo*, in German by -*eln*, -*ern*, e.g. *flimmern, trillern, tröpfeln, to trickle*.

[2] The existence of a *Taphʿēl* is contested on good grounds by Barth, *Nominalbildung*, p. 279.

[3] [See Segal, *Mišnaic Hebrew*, Oxf. 1909, p. 30 ff.]

(a) On the analogy of *Pi'ēl* : פִּרְסֵם, *imperfect* יְכַרְסְמֶ֫נָּה *he doth ravage it*, ψ 80¹⁴ from כָּסַם, cf. גֹּם. *Passive* רֻטֲפַשׁ *to grow fresh again*, Jb 33²⁵. *Participle* מְכֻרְבָּל *girt, clothed* (cf. Aramaic כְּבַל *to bind*), 1 Ch 15²⁷. It is usual also to include among the quadriliterals פַּרְשֵׁז Jb 26⁹, as a *perfect* of Aramaic form with *Pathaḥ* not attenuated. It is more correctly, however, regarded, with Delitzsch, as the *infinitive absolute* of a *Pi'lel* formation, from פָּרַשׁ *to spread out*, with euphonic change of the first שׁ to שׂ, and the second to ז. Moreover, the reading פַּרְשֵׂז also is very well attested, and is adopted by Baer in the text of Job ; cf. the Rem. on p. 48 of his edition.

(b) On the analogy of *Hiph'il* : הִשְׂמִאיל, by syncope הִשְׂמִאיל and הִשְׂמִיל *to turn to the left* (denom. from שְׂמֹאל) Gn 13⁹, Is 30²¹, &c. On הֶאֱזִינוּ cf. § 53 *p*.

C. Strong Verb with Pronominal Suffixes.[1]

§ 57.

The accusative of the personal pronoun, depending on an active verb,[2] may be expressed (1) by a separate word, אֵת the accusative sign (before a suffix אֹת, אָת) with the pronominal suffix, e. g. קָטַל אֹתוֹ *he has killed him*; or (2) by a mere suffix, קְטָלָ֫הוּ or קְטָלוֹ *he has killed him*. The latter is the usual method (§ 33), and we are here concerned with it alone.[3] Neither of these methods, however, is employed when the accusative of the pronoun is *reflexive*. In that case a reflexive verb is used, viz. Niph'al or Hithpa'ēl (§§ 51 and 54), e. g. הִתְקַדֵּשׁ *he sanctified himself*, not קִדְּשׁוֹ, which could only mean *he sanctified him*.[4]

Two points must be specially considered here : the form of the suffix itself (§ 58), and the form which the verb takes when suffixes are added to it (§§ 59–61).

---

[1] This subject of the verbal suffixes is treated here in connexion with the strong verb, in order that both the forms of the suffixes and the general laws which regulate their union with verbal forms may be clearly seen. The rules which relate to the union of the suffixes with weak verbs will be given under the several classes of those verbs.

[2] An accusative suffix occurs with *Niph'al* in ψ 109³ (since נִלְחַם is used in the sense of *to attack*), and according to some, in Is 44²¹; with *Hithpa'ēl* Is 14² (הִתְנַחֵל to appropriate somebody *to oneself as a possession*); cf. above, § 54 *f*, and § 117 *w*.

[3] On the cases where אֵת is necessary, see § 117 *e*.

[4] The exceptions in Jer 7¹⁹, Ez 34².⁸.¹⁰ are only apparent. In all these instances the sharp antithesis between אֹתָם (*themselves*) and another object could only be expressed by retaining the same verb ; also in Ex 5¹⁹ אֹתָם after an active verb serves to emphasize the idea of *themselves*.

§ 58.   *The Pronominal Suffixes of the Verb.*

Cf. the statistics collected by H. Petri, *Das Verbum mit Suffixen im Hebr.*, part ii, in the נביאים ראשונים, Leipzig, 1890.   W. Diehl, *Das Pronomen pers. suff. . . . des Hebr.*, Giessen, 1895.   J. Barth, 'Beiträge zur Suffixlehre des Nordsem.,' *AJSL.* xvii (1901), p. 205 f.   Brockelmann, *Semit. Sprachwiss.*, i. 159 f.; *Grundriss*, p. 638 ff.

1. The *pronominal suffixes* appended to the verb express the *a* accusative of the *personal pronoun*.   They are the following :—

A.	B.	C.	
To a form ending in a Vowel.	*To a form in the Perf. ending in a Consonant.*	*To a form in the Imperf. ending in a Consonant.*	
Sing. 1. com. נִי	נִי (in *pause* נִי)	נִי	*me.*
2. m. ךָ	ךָ (in *pause* ךָ, also ךָ)	ךָ	*thee.*
f. ךְ	ךְ, ךָ, rarely ךְ	ךְ	
3. m. הוּ, ו	הוּ, ו (הֹ)	הוּ	*him.*
f. הָ	הָ	הָ	*her.*
Plur. 1. com. נוּ	נוּ	נוּ	*us.*
2. m. כֶם		כֶם	*you* (*vos*).
f. . . . . .[1]			
3. m. הֶם, ם	ם (from הֶם), ם	ם (from הֶם)	*eos.*
poet. מוֹ	מוֹ	מוֹ	
f. ן	ן, ן	. . . . .[1]	*eas.*

2. That these suffixes are connected with the corresponding *forms b* *of the personal pronoun* (§ 32) is for the most part self-evident, and only a few of them require elucidation.

The suffixes נִי, נוּ, הוּ, הָ (and ךָ, when a long vowel in an open *c* syllable precedes) never have the tone, which always rests on the preceding syllable; on the other hand, כֶם and הֶם always take the tone.

In the 3rd pers. masc. הוּ, by contraction of *a* and *u* after the *d* rejection of the weak ה, frequently gives rise to *ô* (§ 23 *k*), ordinarily written ו, much less frequently הֹ (see § 7 *c*).   In the *feminine*, the suffix הָ should be pronounced with a preceding *a* (cf. below, *f*, note), as הָ or הָ, on the analogy of *āhû*; instead of הָ, however, it was simply pronounced הָ, with the rejection of the final vowel,

---

[1] According to Diehl (see above), p. 61, כֶם occurs only once with the perfect (see § 59 *e*), 7 times with the imperfect, but never in pre-exilic passages, whereas the accus. אֶתְכֶם occurs 40 times in Jer. and 36 times in Ezek.—הֶם occurs only once as a *verbal* suffix (Dt 32²⁶, unless, with Kahan, *Infinitive u. Participien*, p. 13, אַפְאֵיהֶם from פָּאָה is to be read), while the forms כֶן (2nd *f. pl.*) and ן and הֶן (3rd *f. pl.*), added by Qimḥi, never occur.

and with *Mappiq*, since the ה is consonantal; but the weakening to
ה‗ is also found, see below, *g*.

e 3. The *variety* of the suffix-forms is occasioned chiefly by the fact
that they are modified differently according to the form and tense of the
verb to which they are attached. For almost every suffix three forms
may be distinguished:

(*a*) One beginning with a consonant, as נִי‗, הוּ‗, וֹ (only after *î*),
נוּ‗, (הֶם) ם, &c. These are attached to verbal forms which end with
a vowel, e.g. יִקְטְלוּנִי; קְטַלְתִּיהוּ, for which by absorption of the ה we
also get קְטַלְתִּיו, pronounced *qᵉṭaltîu*; cf. § 8 *m*.

f (*b*) A second and third with what are called *connecting vowels* [1]
(נִי‗, נִי‗), used with verbal forms ending with a consonant (for
exceptions, see § 59 *g* and § 60 *e*). This *connecting vowel* is *a* with
the forms of the perfect, e.g. קְטָלַנִי, קְטָלָנוּ, קְטָלָם (on קְטָלַתְהֻ, the ordinary
form of the 3rd masc. perf. with the 2nd fem. suffix, cf. below, *g*); and
e (less frequently *a*) with the forms of the imperfect and imperative, e.g.
יִקְטְלֵהוּ, קָטְלֵם; also with the infinitive and participles, when these do
not take noun-suffixes (cf. § 61 *a* and *h*). The form י also belongs to
the suffixes of the perfect, since it has arisen from הוּ‗ (cf., however,
§ 60 *d*). With ך, כֶם, the connecting sound is only a vocal *Šᵉwâ*,
which has arisen from an original short vowel, thus ך‗, כֶם‗, e.g.
קְטָלְךָ (*qᵉṭālᵉkhā*), or when the final consonant of the verb is a guttural,
ך‗, e.g. שְׁלָחֲךָ. In *pause*, the original short vowel (*ă*) reappears as
Sᵉghôl with the tone ך‗ (also ך‗, see *g*). On the appending of
suffixes to the final ן of the imperfect (§ 47 *m*), see § 60 *e*.

g Rem. 1. As *rare* forms may be mentioned *sing.* 2nd pers. *masc.* כָה‗ Gn 27[7],
1 K 18[44], &c., in *pause* also כָּה‗ (see below, *i*); *fem.* כִי, כִי‗ ψ 103[4], 137[6].
Instead of the form ך‗, which is usual even in the perfect (e.g. Ju 4[20],
Ez 27[26]), ך‗ occurs as *fem.* Is 60[9] (as *masc.* Dt 6[17], 28[45], Is 30[19], 55[5] always in
pause); with *Munaḥ* Is 54[6], Jer 23[37].—In the 3rd *masc.* ה Ex 32[25], Nu 23[8];
in the 3rd *fem.* ה‗ without *Mappiq* (cf. § 91 *e*) Ex 2[3], Jer 44[19]; Am 1[11], with

---

[1] We have kept the term *connecting* vowel, although it is rather a superficial
description, and moreover these vowels are of various origin. The connective
a is most probably the remains of the old verbal termination, like the *i* in
the 2nd pers. *fem.* sing. קְטַלְתִּיהוּ. Observe e.g. the Hebrew form *qᵉṭāl-ani* in
connexion with the Arabic *qatala-ni*, contrasted with Hebrew *qᵉṭālat-ni* and
Arabic *qatalat-ni*. König accordingly prefers the expression 'vocalic ending
of the stem', instead of 'connecting syllable'. The connective ē, ā, as
Prätorius (*ZDMG*. 55, 267 ff.) and Barth (ibid. p. 205 f.) show by reference to
the Syriac connective *ai* in the imperf. of the strong verb, is originally due
to the analogy of verbs ל״ה (מְחִינִי=מְחַנִי from *mᵉḥaini*), in which the final *ê*
was used as a connecting vowel first of the imperat., then of the impf.
(besides many forms with *a*, § 60 *d*), and of the infin. and participle.

retraction of the tone before a following tone-syllable, but read certainly
שָׁמַר לְנֶצַח.—The forms מוֹ-ֵ֫-, מוֹ-ֵ֫-, מוֹ-ֵ֫- occur 23 times, all in poetry [1]
(except Ex 23³¹) [viz. with the perfect Ex 15¹⁰, 23³¹, ψ 73⁶; with the imperfect
Ex 15⁵ (מוֹ for מוֹ), 15⁷·⁹·⁹·¹²·¹⁵·¹⁷·¹⁷, ψ 2⁵, 21¹⁰·¹³, 22⁵, 45¹⁷, 80⁶, 14c¹⁰; with the
imperative ψ 5¹¹, 59¹²·¹², 83¹²]. On the age of these forms, see § 91 *l* 3; on
ן_ and ן_ as suffixes of the 3rd fem. plur. of the imperfect, § 60 *d*.—
In Gn 48⁹ קָחֶם־נָא (cf. שָׁם וַיֻּכַּם־ 1 Ch 14¹¹ according to Baer), ם__ has lost
the tone before *Maqqeph* and so is shortened to ם_‍:.—In Ez 44⁸ וַתְּשִׂימוּן is
probably only an error for וַתְּשִׂימוּם.

2. From a comparison of these verbal suffixes with the noun-suffixes (§ 91) *h*
we find that (*a*) there is a greater variety of forms amongst the verbal than
amongst the noun-suffixes, the forms and relations of the verb itself being
more various ;—(*b*) the verbal suffix, where it differs from that of the noun,
is longer; cf. e.g. נִי-ֵ֫-, נִי-ֵ֫-, נִי-ֵ֫- (*me*) with י__ (*my*). The reason is that
the pronominal object is less closely connected with the verb than the
possessive pronoun (the genitive) is with the noun; consequently the former
can also be expressed by a separate word (אֵת in אֹתִי, &c.).

4. A verbal form with a suffix gains additional strength, and some- *i*
times intentional emphasis, when, instead of the mere connecting vowel,
a special connecting-syllable [2] (*ăn*) [3] is inserted between the suffix and
the verbal stem. Since, however, this syllable always has the tone,
the *ă* is invariably (except in the 1st pers. sing.) modified to tone-
bearing *Seghôl*. This is called the *Nûn energicum* [4] (less suitably
demonstrativum or *epentheticum*), and occurs principally (see, however,
Dt 32¹⁰ *bis*) in pausal forms of the imperfect, e. g. יְבָרֲכֶנְהוּ *he will bless
him* (ψ 72¹⁵, cf. Jer 5²²), אֶתְקׇנֶנְךָ Jer 22²⁴; יְכַבְּדֶנְנִי *he will honour me*
(ψ 50²³) is unusual; rarely in the perfect, Dt 24¹³ בֵּרֲכֶךָ. On examples
like דָּנַּנִּי Gn 30⁶, cf. § 26 *g*, § 59 *f*. In far the greatest number of
cases, however, this *Nûn* is assimilated to the following consonant
(נ, כ), or the latter is lost in pronunciation (so ה), and the *Nûn*
consequently sharpened. Hence we get the following series of suffix-
forms :—

---

[1] Thus in ψ 2 מוֹ__ occurs five times [four times attached to a noun or
preposition, §§ 91 *f*, 103 *c*], and ם__ only twice.

[2] It is, however, a question whether, instead of a connecting syllable, we
should not assume a special verbal form, analogous to the Arabic *energetic mood*
(see *l*, at the end) and probably also appearing in the Hebrew cohortative (see the footnote on § 48 *c*).—As M. Lambert has shown in *REJ.* 1903,
p. 178 ff. (' De l'emploi des suffixes pronominaux . . .'), the suffixes of the 3rd
pers. with the impf. without *waw* in prose are נּוּ-ֵ֫- and נָּה-ֵ֫-, but with
waw consec. הוּ-ֵ֫- and הָ-ֵ֫- or הָ__ ; with the jussive in the 2nd and 3rd pers.
always הוּ-ֵ֫-, הָ-ֵ֫-, in the 1st pers. more often נּוּ-ֵ֫- than הוּ-ֵ֫-, and always
נָּה-ֵ֫-.

[3] According to Barth ' n-haltige Suffixe' in *Sprachwiss. Untersuchungen*, Lpz.
1907, p. 1 ff., the connecting element, as in Aramaic, was originally *in*, which
in Hebrew became *en* in a closed tone-syllable.

[4] So König, *Lehrgeb.*, i. p. 226.

1st pers. נִּ֫־ (even in pause, Jb 7¹⁴, &c.), נִּ֫־ (for נְנִי֫־, נְנִי֫־).

2nd pers. ךָּ֫־ (Jer 22²⁴ in pause ךָּ֫־) and, only orthographically different,

כָּ֫ה־ (Is 10²⁴, Pr 2¹¹ in *pause*).

3rd pers. נּוּ֫־ (for נְהוּ֫־),[1] *fem.* פֶּ֫ה־ for נְהָ֫־.

[*1st pers. plur.* נּוּ֫־ (for נְנוּ֫־), see the Rem.]

In the other persons Nûn energetic does not occur.

k　Rem. The uncontracted forms with *Nûn* are rare, and occur only in poetic or elevated style (Ex 15², Dt 32¹⁰ [*bis*], Jer 5²², 22²⁴); they are never found in the *3rd fem. sing.* and *1st plur.* On the other hand, the contracted forms are tolerably frequent, even in prose. An example of נּוּ֫־ as *1st plur.* occurs perhaps in Jb 31¹⁵ [but read נּוּ֫־ and cf. § 72 *cc*], hardly in Ho 12⁵; cf. הִנֶּ֫נּוּ *behold us*, Gn 44¹⁶, 50¹⁸, Nu 14⁴⁰ for הִנְנוּ (instead of הִנֵּ֫נוּ; see § 20 *m*).— In Ez 4¹² the Masora requires תְּעֻגֶ֫נָה, without Dageš in the Nûn.

l　That the forms with *Nûn energicum* are intended to give greater emphasis to the verbal form is seen from their special frequency in *pause*. Apart from the verb, however, *Nûn energicum* occurs also in the union of suffixes with certain particles (§ 100 *o*).

This Nûn is frequent in Western Aramaic. In Arabic the corresponding forms are the two *energetic moods* (see § 48 *b*) ending in *an* and *anna*, which are used in connexion with suffixes (e. g. *yaqtulan-ka* or *yaqtulanna-ka*) as well as without them.

§ 59. *The Perfect with Pronominal Suffixes.*

a　1. The endings (*afformatives*) of the perfect occasionally vary somewhat from the ordinary form, when connected with pronominal suffixes; viz. :—

(*a*) In the 3rd *sing. fem.* the original feminine ending הֹ־ or הַ־ is used for הָ־.

(*b*) In the 2nd *sing. masc.* besides תָ we find תְ, to which the connecting vowel is directly attached, but the only clear instances of this are with נִי֫־.[2]

(*c*) In the 2nd *sing. fem.* תִי, the original form of תְ, appears; cf. אַתִּי, קָטַלְתִּי, § 32 *f*; § 44 *g*. This form can be distinguished from the 1st pers. only by the context.

(*d*) 2nd *plur. masc.* תוּ for תֶּם. The only examples are Nu 20⁵, 21⁵, Zc 7⁵. The *fem.* קְטַלְתֶּן never occurs with suffixes; probably it had the same form as the masculine.

b　We exhibit first the forms of the perfect *Hiph'îl*, as used in connexion with suffixes, since here no further changes take place in the stem itself, except as regards the tone (see *c*).

---

[1] On נוּ = נּוּ֫־ Nu 23¹³, see § 67 *o*.

[2] On the *ă* as an original element of the verbal form, see § 58 *f*, note.

	Singular.		Plural.
3. *m.*	הִקְטִיל	3. *c.*	הִקְטִילוּ
3. *f.*	הִקְטִילַת		
2. *m.*	הִקְטַלְתְּ, הִקְטַלְתָּ	2. *m.*	הִקְטַלְתּוּ
2. *f.*	הִקְטַלְתְּ, הִקְטַלְתִּי		
1. *c.*	הִקְטַלְתִּי	1. *c.*	הִקְטַלְנוּ

The beginner should first practise connecting the suffixes with these *Hiph'il* forms and then go on to unite them to the *Perfect Qal* (see *d*).

2. The addition of the suffix generally causes the tone to be thrown *c* forward towards the end of the word, since it would otherwise fall, in some cases, on the ante-penultima; with the *heavy* suffixes (see *e*) the tone is even transferred to the suffix itself. Considerations of tone, especially in the Perfect *Qal*, occasion certain vowel changes: (*a*) the *Qameṣ* of the first syllable, no longer standing *before* the tone, always becomes vocal *Š^ewâ*; (*b*) the original *Pathaḥ* of the second syllable, which in the 3rd *sing. fem.* and 3rd *plur.* had become *Šewâ*, reappears before the suffix, and, in an open syllable before the tone, is lengthened to *Qameṣ*; similarly original *ĭ* (as in the 3rd *sing. masc. without* a suffix) is lengthened to *ē*, e. g. אֲהֵבוּךְ 1 S 18²², Pr 19⁷.

The forms of the perfect of Qal consequently appear as follows:— *d*

	Singular.		Plural.
3. *m.*	קָטַל	3. *c.*	קָטְלוּ
3. *f.*	קָטְלָה (קָטְלַת, see *g*)		
2. *m.*	קָטַלְתָּ (קָטַלְתְּ, see *h*)	2. *m.*	קְטַלְתּוּ
2. *f.*	קָטַלְתְּ (קָטַלְתִּי, see *h*)		
1. *c.*	קָטַלְתִּי	1. *c.*	קָטַלְנוּ

The connexion of these forms with all the suffixes is shown in *Paradigm C*. It will be seen there also, how the *Ṣere* in the Perfect *Pi'ēl* changes sometimes into *S^eghôl*, and sometimes into vocal *Šewâ*.

Rem. 1. The suffixes of the 2nd and 3rd pers. plur. כֶם and הֶם, since they *e* end in a consonant and also always have the tone, are distinguished as *heavy* suffixes (*suffixa gravia*) from the rest, which are called *light* suffixes. Compare the connexion of these (and of the corresponding feminine forms כֶן and הֶן) with the *noun*, § 91. With a perfect כֶם alone occurs, ψ 118²⁶. The form קְטָל which is usually given as the connective form of the 3rd sing. masc. before כֶם and כֶן is only formed by analogy, and is without example in the O. T.

2. In the 3rd *sing. masc.* קְטָלְהוּ (especially in verbs ל״ה; in the strong verb *f* only in Jer 20¹⁵ in *Pi'ēl*) is mostly contracted to קְטָלוֹ, according to § 23 *k*; likewise in the 2nd sing. masc. קְטַלְתָּהוּ to קְטַלְתּוֹ.—As a suffix of the 1st sing. נִי_ֵ_ occurs several times with the 3rd sing. masc. perf. Qal of verbs ל״ה, not only in *pause* (as עָנָנִי ψ 118⁵; קָנָנִי Pr 8²² with *D^eḥi*), but even with a con-

junctive accent, as הֹרֵנִי עָנְנִי Jb 30¹⁹; עָנֵנִי 1 S 28¹⁵ (where, however, the reading עֲנֵנִי is also found). With a sharpened נ: דָּנַּנִּי Gn 30⁶, יְסֹבְבֻ֫נִי ψ 118¹⁸.

g   3. The 3*rd sing. fem.* קְטָלַת (= קְטָלָה) has the twofold peculiarity that (*a*) the ending *ath* always takes the tone,[1] and consequently is joined to those suffixes which form a syllable of themselves (נוּ, הָ, הוּ, ֵנִי), without a connecting vowel, contrary to the general rule, § 58 *f*; (*b*) before the other suffixes the connecting vowel is indeed employed, but the tone is drawn back to the *penultima*, so that they are pronounced with shortened vowels, viz. ךָ_ _ _⌣,
ם_ _ _⌣, e. g. אֲהֵבַ֫תְךָ *she loves thee,* Ru 4¹⁵, cf. Is 47¹⁰; גְּנָבָ֫תַם *she has stolen them,*
Gn 31³²; שְׂרָפַ֫תַם *it burns them,* Is 47¹⁴, Jos 2⁶, Ho 2¹⁴, ψ 48⁷. For ⌣_ _ךָ, ⌣_ _ךְ
&c., in *pause* חִנַ֫ _ _ is found, Jer 8²¹, ψ 69¹⁰, and תְךָ_ _ Ct 8⁵; and also without the *pause* for the sake of the assonance חִבְּלַ֫תְךָ, *she was in travail with thee,* ibid.
The form קְטָלַ֫תּוּ (e. g. Ru 4¹⁵) has arisen, through the loss of the ה and the consequent sharpening of the ת (as in נוּ⌣_ _ and נָה⌣_ _ for נְהוּ and נָ֫הֶ_ ⌣_,
cf. § 58 *i*), from the form קְטָלַתְהוּ, which is also found even in *pause* (אֲהֵבַ֫תְהוּ
1 S 18²⁸; elsewhere it takes in *pause* the form סְמָכַ֫תְהוּ Is 59¹⁶); so קְטָלָ֫תָה from קְטָלַ֫תְהָ; cf. 1 S 1⁶, Is 34¹⁷, Jer 49²⁴, Ru 3⁶; in *pause* Ez 14¹⁵, always, on the authority of Qimḥi, without *Mappiq* in the ה, which is consequently always a mere vowel-letter.

h   4. In the 2*nd sing. masc.* the form קְטַלְתָּ֫ is mostly used, and the suffixes have, therefore, no connecting vowel, e. g. וְהִנַּחְתָּ֫נוּ פְּרַצְתָּ֫נוּ *thou hast cast us off, thou hast broken us down,* ψ 60³; but with the suff. of the 1st sing. the form קְטַלְתַּ֫נִי is used, e. g. חֲקַרְתַּ֫נִי ψ 139¹; in *pause,* however, with *Qameṣ,* e. g. עֲזַבְתָּ֫נִי ψ 22²; Ju 1¹⁵ (with *Zaqeph qaṭon*); but cf. also צְרַפְתָּ֫נִי ψ 17³ with *Mer̥kha.*—In the 2*nd sing. fem.* תְּ_ _ is also written defectively, רְמִיתִ֫נִי 1 S 19¹⁷, Ju 11³⁵, Jer 15¹⁰, Ct 4⁹. Occasionally the suffix is appended to the ordinary form תְּ_ _, viz. הִשְׁבַּעְתָּ֫נוּ *thou (fem.) dost adjure us,* Ct 5⁹, Jos 2¹⁷·²⁰; cf. Jer 2²⁷, and, quite abnormally, with *Ṣere* הֹורַדְתֵּ֫נוּ *thou (fem.) didst let us down,* Jos 2¹⁸, where הֹורַדְתֵּ֫נוּ would be expected. In Is 8¹¹ וְיִסְּרֵ֫נִי is probably intended as an *imperfect.*

i   5. In verbs *middle ē,* the *ē* remains even before suffixes (see above, *c*), e. g. אֲהֵבְךָ Dt 15¹⁶, אֲהֵבַתְהוּ 1 S 18²⁸, cf. 18²²; יִרְאֻ֫הוּ Jb 37²⁴. From a verb *middle ō* there occurs יָכֹ֫לְתִּיו *I have prevailed against him,* ψ 13⁵, from יָכֹל with *ŏ* instead of *ō* in a syllable which has lost the tone (§ 44 *e*).

§ 60. *Imperfect with Pronominal Suffixes.*

a   In those forms of the *imperfect* Qal, which have no afformatives, the vowel *ō* of the second syllable mostly becomes _⌐_ (simple *S̆ewâ mobile*), sometimes _⌐_; thus in the principal *pause,* Nu 35²⁰, Is 27³, 62², Jer 31³³, Ez 35⁶, Ho 10¹⁰; before the principal *pause,* ψ 119³³; before a secondary *pause,* Ez 17²³; even before a conjunctive accent, Jos 23⁵. Before ךָ_⌐_,

---

[1] חִבְּלָ֫תְךָ Ct 8⁵ is an exception. כֶם would probably even here have the tone (see *e*); but no example of the kind occurs in the O.T. In Is 51² the *imperfect* is used instead of the *perfect* with a suffix.

כֶם‎_, however, it is shortened to Qameṣ ḥaṭuph, e. g. יִשְׁמָרְךָ‎ (but in pause יִשְׁמְרֶ֑ךָ‎ or יִשְׁמָרֶ֑ךָ‎; with *Nûn energicum*, see § 58 *i*), יִשְׁמָרְכֶם‎, &c. Instead of תִּקְטֹלְנָה‎, the form תִּקְטְלִי‎[1] is used for the 2nd and 3rd *fem. plur.* before suffixes in three places : Jer 2¹⁹, Jb 19¹⁵, Ct 1⁶.

Rem. I. יְחָבְּרֶךָ‎ ψ 94²⁰ is an anomalous form for יְחָבְּרֶךָ‎ (cf. the analogous *b* יָחָנֶ֑ךָ‎ § 67 *n*) and יִפְנֶ֫שֶׁךָ‎ (so Baer ; others יִפְנְשֶׁ֑ךָ‎) Gn 32¹⁸ for יִפְנָ֑שֶׁךָ‎. To the same category as יְחָבְּרֶךָ‎ belong also, according to the usual explanation, תֶּעֶבְדֵם‎ (from תַּעֲבֹד‎), Ex 20⁵, 23²⁴, Dt 5⁹, and נֶעֱב/‎ Dt 13³. As a matter of fact, the explanation of these forms as imperfects of *Qal* appears to be required by the last of these passages ; yet why has the retraction of the ŏ taken place only in these examples (beside numerous forms like יַֽעַבְדֵ֫נִי‎)? Could the Masora in the two Decalogues and in Ex 23²⁴ (on the analogy of which Dt 13³ was then wrongly pointed) have intended an imperfect *Hophʿal* with the suffix, meaning *thou shalt not allow thyself to be brought to worship them* ?

Verbs which have *a* in the second syllable of the *imperfect*, and imperative, *c Qal* (to which class especially *verba tertiae* and *mediae gutturalis* belong, § 64 and § 65) do *not*, as a rule, change the *Pathaḥ* of the *imperfect* (nor of the imperative, see § 61 *g*) into *Šewâ* before suffixes ; but the Pathaḥ, coming to stand in an open syllable before the tone, is lengthened to Qameṣ, e. g. וַיְלַבִּשֵׁ֫נִי‎ Jb 29¹⁴ ; יִנְאָלֹֽהוּ‎ 3⁵ ; וַיִּשְׁלָחֵם‎ Jos 8³ ; יִקְרָאֵ֫הוּ‎ ψ 145¹⁸ ; but יִקְרָא֫וּ‎ Jer 23⁶, is probably a *forma mixta* combining the readings יִקְרָא֫וּ‎ and יִקְרָ֫אוּ‎, cf. § 74 *e*.

2. Not infrequently suffixes with the connecting vowel *a* are also found *d* with the imperfect, e. g. תְּדַבְּקַ֫נִי‎ Gn 19¹⁹, cf. 29³², Ex 33²⁰, Nu 22³³, 1 K 2²⁴ *Qᵉrê*, Is 56³, Jb 9¹⁸ ; also ‑ַ֫נִי‎, Gn 27¹⁹·³¹, Jb 7¹⁴, 9³⁴, 13²¹ (in principal *pause*) ; וַיִּפְדָ֫רָה‎ Gn 37³³, cf. 16⁷, 2 S 11²⁷, Is 26⁵, Jb 28²⁷, 1 Ch 20² ; יַכִּירֶ֫נּוּ‎ Is 63¹⁶ (manifestly owing to the influence of the preceding וְיָֽדַעְתָּ‎) ; וְלָֽבַשְׁתָּם‎ Ex 29⁵·⁰, cf. 2¹⁷, Nu 21³⁰, Dt 7¹⁵, ψ 74⁸ ; even אֲמִילַם‎ 118¹⁰⁻¹² ; וַיּֽוֹשִׁיעֵן‎ Ex 2¹⁷, and יֲחִיתַן‎ Hb 2¹⁷ (where, however, the ancient versions read יְחִתֶּ֫ךָ‎ ; even יִרְדְּפוֹ‎ (ô from *âhu*) Ho 8³ ; cf. Ex 22²⁹, Jos 2⁴ (but read וּתִצְפְּנֵם‎) ; 1 S 18¹ *Kᵉth.*, 21¹⁴ (where, however, the text is corrupt ; 2 S 14⁶ (where read with the old versions וַיַּךְ‎) ; Jer 23⁶ (see § 74 *e*), ψ 35⁸, Ec 4¹².—On pausal *Sᵉghôl* for *Ṣere* in וַֽאֲבָרֲכֶם‎ Gn 48⁹ and וּתִֽאַלְצֵהוּ‎ (so Baer, but ed. Mant., Ginsb. וַתְּאַלְצֵ֫הוּ‎) Ju 16¹⁶, see § 29 *q*.

3. Suffixes are also appended in twelve passages to the plural forms in וּן‎, *e* viz. תְּרַכְּאוּנֲנִי‎ *will ye break me in pieces?* Jb 19² ; יְשָׁרְתוּנֶ֑ךָ‎ (here necessarily with a connecting vowel) Is 60⁷·¹⁰ ; Pr 5²² (וּ‎ but probably corrupt) ; elsewhere always without a connecting vowel ; יִקְרָאֻ֫נְנִי‎ with two other examples Pr 1²⁸, 8¹⁷, Ho 5¹⁵ ; cf. ‑וּ֫נְךָ‎ ψ 63⁴, 91¹² ; ‑ֻ֫הוּ‎ Jer 5²² ; ‑וּ֫נָה‎ Jer 2²⁴, all in principal pause. [See Böttcher, *Lehrb.*, § 1047 f.]

4. In *Piʿēl*, *Pôʿēl*, and *Poʿlēl*, the *Ṣere* of the final syllable, like the ŏ in Qal, *f* becomes vocal *Šewâ* ; but before the suffixes ךָ‑‎ and כֶם‑‎ it is shortened to *Sᵉghôl*, e. g. יְקַבְּצֶ֑ךָ‎ Dt 30⁴, ψ 34¹², Is 51². With a final guttural, however, אֲשַׁלֵּֽחֲךָ‎ Gn 32²⁷ ; also in Pr 4⁸, where with Qimḥi תְּכַבֶּ֫דְךָ‎ is to be read. *ē* is

---

[1] This form is also found as feminine without a suffix, in Jer 49¹¹, Ez 37⁷. In the latter passage וַתִּקְרְבוּ‎ is probably to be regarded, with König, as a clumsy correction of the original וַיִּק‎, intended to suggest the reading וַתִּקְרַ֫בְנָה‎, to agree with the usual gender of עֲצָמוֹת‎.

retained in the tone-syllable; an analogous case in *Hiph'îl* is וַיֻּגַּד־לְךָ Dt 32[7].
Less frequently *Ṣere* is sharpened to *Ḥireq*, e. g. אֲאַמִּצְכֶם Jb 16[5], cf. Ex 31[18],
Is 1[15], 52[12]; so in *Po'lēl*, Is 25[1], ψ 30[2], 37[34], 145[1], and probably also in *Qal* אֹסְפֵּךְ
1 S 15[6]; cf. § 68 *h*.

g   5. In *Hiph'îl* the *i* remains, e. g. תַּלְבִּישֵׁנִי Jb 10[11] (after *wāw consecutive* it is
often written defectively, e.g. וַיַּלְבִּשֵׁם Gn 3[21] and often); but cf. above, *f*,
Dt 32[7]. Forms like תַּעְשְׁרֶנָּה *thou enrichest it*, ψ 65[10], 1 S 17[25], are rare.
Cf. § 53 *n*.

h   6. Instead of the suffix of the 3rd plur. fem. (ן), the suffix of the 3rd plur.
masc. (ם) is affixed to the afformative וּ, to avoid a confusion with the personal
ending וּן; cf. וַיְמַלְאוּם Gn 26[15] (previously also with a perf. סְתָמוּם) ; Gn 26[18],
33[13], Ex 2[17] (where וַיּוֹשִׁעָן occurs immediately after); 39[18.20], 1 S 6[10] (where
also בְּנֵיהֶם is for בְּנֵיהֶן, a neglect of gender which can only be explained by
§ 135 *o*).—For יַהְרְגֻן Zc 11[5] read perhaps יַהַרְגֵן with M. Lambert.

§ 61. *Infinitive, Imperative and Participle with Pronominal Suffixes.*

a   1. The *infinitive construct* of an *active verb* may be construed with
an accusative, and therefore can also take a *verbal suffix*, i. e. the
accusative of the personal pronoun. The only undoubted instances of
the kind, however, in the O. T. are infinitives with the verbal suffix
of the 1st pers. sing., e. g. לְדָרְשֵׁנִי *to inquire of me*, Jer 37[7]. As a rule
the infinitive (as a *noun*) takes *noun*-suffixes (in the *genitive*, which
may be either subjective or objective, cf. § 115 *c*), e. g. עָבְרִי *my passing
by*; מָלְכוֹ *his reigning*, see § 115 *a* and *e*. The infinitive *Qal*, then,
usually has the form *qŏṭl*, retaining the original short vowel under the
first radical (on the probable ground-form *qŭṭŭl*, see § 46 *a*). The
resulting syllable as a rule allows a following Begadkephath to be
spirant, e. g. בְּכָתְבוֹ *in his writing*, Jer 45[1]; cf., however, הָפְכִּי Gn 19[21];
נָפְפוֹ (so ed. Mant.; others נָפְפוֹ) Ex 12[27]; עָצְבִּי 1 Ch 4[10]; before ךָ — and
כֶם — also the syllable is completely closed, e. g. בְּאָסְפְּךָ Ex 23[16], Lv 23[39]
(but in pause לְהָרְגֶךָ Gn 27[42]), unless the vowel be retained in the
second syllable; see *d*. With the form קְטֹל generally, compare the
closely allied nouns of the form קֹטֶל (before a suffix קָטְל or קֻטְל),
§ 84[a] *a*; § 93 *q*.

b   Rem. 1. The infin. of verbs which have *ō* in the last syllable of the *imperfect*
of *Qal*, sometimes takes the form *qiṭl* before suffixes, e. g. מָכְרָם Ex 21[8]; בְּבִגְדוֹ
Am 2[6] (but מָכְרָהּ Ex 21[8]), נִפְלוֹ 2 S 1[10] (but נָפְלוֹ 1 S 29[3]), לְשָׁטְנוֹ Zc 3[1], שָׁבְרִי
Lv 26[26], Ez 30[18] &c. According to Barth (see above, § 47 *i* with the note)
these forms with *i* in the first syllable point to former *i*-imperfects.

c   Infinitives of the form קְטַל (§ 45 *c*) in verbs middle or third guttural (but
cf. also שָׁכְבָהּ Gn 19[33.35]—elsewhere שָׁכְבְּךָ and שָׁכְבוֹ) before suffixes sometimes
take the form *qaṭl*, as וַעֲפוֹ Jon 1[15] (and, with the syllable loosely closed.

פַּעֲמוֹ Ju 13²⁵), מַחְאֲךָ and רַקְעֲךָ Ez 25⁶; sometimes *qiṭl*, with the *a* attenuated to *i*, especially in verbs third guttural; as פִּתְחִי, פִּגְעוֹ, בִּקְעָם, בִּלְעִי, בְּטַחֲךָ, רִבְעָה.—Contrary to § 58 *f* ־ֵנִי (1 Ch 12¹⁷) and ־ֵנוּ (Ex 14¹¹) are sometimes found with the *infinitive* instead of ־ֵנִי and ־ֵנוּ. On רְדוּפִי *my following* ψ 38²¹ (but *Q°rê* רָדְפִי), cf. the analogous examples in § 46 *e*.

2. With the suffixes ךָ and כֶם, contrary to the analogy of the corre- *d* sponding nouns, forms occur like אֲכָלְךָ *thy eating*, Gn 2¹⁷; אֲכָלְכֶם Gn 3⁵; עֲמָדְךָ (others עָמְדְךָ) Ob ¹¹, i.e. with *ŏ* shortened in the same way as in the *imperfect*, see § 60. But the analogy of the nouns is followed in such forms as קֻצְרְכֶם *your harvesting*, Lv 19⁹, 23²² (with retention of the original *ŭ*), and מָאָסְכֶם (read *mŏ'ŏs°khèm*) *your despising*, Is 30¹²; cf. Dt 20²; on בְּמֹצַאֲכֶם Gn 32²⁰ (for /בְּמֹצְ), see § 74 *h*.—Very unusual are the infinitive suffixes of the 2nd sing. masc. with נ *energicum* (on the analogy of suffixes with the imperfect, § 58 *i*), as יָפָרְךָ Dt 4³⁶, cf. 23⁵, Jb 33³², all in principal pause.

Examples of the *infinitive Niph'al* with suffixes are, הִכָּבְדִי Ex 14¹⁸; הִשָּׁמֶרְךָ *e* Dt 28²⁰ (in pause, הִשָּׁמֶרְךָ verse 24); הִשָּׁפְטוֹ ψ 37³³; הִכָּרֶכֶם Ez 21²⁹; הִשָּׁמְדָם Dt 7²³. In the *infinitive* of *Pi'ēl* (as also in the *imperfect*, see § 60 *f*) the *ē* before the suff. ךָ, כֶם becomes *S°ghôl*, e.g. דַּבֶּרְךָ Ex 4¹⁰, and with a sharpening to *i* פֶּרְשְׁכֶם Is 1¹⁵ (see § 60 *f*). In the *infinitive Pô'ēl*, בּוֹשַׁסְכֶם occurs (with *a* for *ĕ* or *i*) Am 5¹¹, but probably בּוּסְכֶם, with Wellhausen, is the right reading; the correction ם has crept into the text alongside of the *corrigendum* שׁ.

2. The leading form of the *imperative Qal* before *suffixes* (קְטָל) is *f* due probably (see § 46 *d*) to the retention of the original short vowel of the first syllable (ground-form *qŭṭŭl*). In the *imperative* also *ŏ* is not followed by *Dageš lene*, e.g. כָּתְבֶם *kŏthbhēm* (not *kŏthbēm*), &c.[1] As in the *imperfect* (§ 60 *d*) and *infinitive* (see above, *c*), so also in the *imperative*, suffixes are found united to the stem by an *a*-sound; e.g. כָּתְבָה Is 30⁸; cf. 2 S 12²⁸.—The forms קְטָלִי, קְטָלוֹ, which are not exhibited in Paradigm C, undergo no change. Instead of קְטֹלְנָה, the masc. form (קְטְלוּ) is used, as in the *imperfect*.

In verbs which form the *imperative* with *a*, like שְׁלַח (to which class *g* belong especially verbs *middle* and *third guttural*, §§ 64 and 65), this *a* retains its place when pronominal suffixes are added, but, since it then stands in an open syllable, is, as a matter of course, lengthened to *Qameṣ* (just as in *imperfects Qal* in *a*, § 60 *c*), e.g. שְׁלָחֵנִי *send me*, Is 6⁸, בְּחָנֵנִי ψ 26², קְרָאֵנִי ψ 50¹⁵, שְׁמָעֵנִי Gn 23⁸. In Am 9¹ בְּצָעָם (so ed. Mant., Baer, Ginsb., instead of the ordinary reading בְּצַעַם) is to be explained, with Margolis, *AJSL.* xix, p. 45 ff., from an original בִּצָעֵמוֹ, as וְהִרַגְתֶּם Am 9⁴ from original וַהֲרַגְתֵּמוֹ.—In the imperative *Hiph'îl*, the form used in conjunction with suffixes is not the 2nd *sing. masc.*

---

[1] שָׁמְרֵנִי *šām°rēni* required by the Masora in ψ 16¹ (also שָׁמְרָה ψ 86², 119¹⁶⁷; cf. Is 38¹⁴ and עָמְדְךָ Ob ¹¹), belongs to the disputed cases discussed in § 9 *c* and § 48 *i* note.

הַקְטֵל, but הַקְטִיל (with *î* on account of the open syllable, cf. § 60 *g*),
e. g. הַקְרִיבֵהוּ *present it*, Mal 1⁸.

h 3. Like the infinitives, the participles can also be united with either
verbal or noun-suffixes; see § 116 *f*. In both cases the vowel of the
participles is shortened or becomes *Šᵉwâ* before the suffix, as in the
corresponding noun-forms, e. g. from the form קֹטֵל: רֹדְפִי, רֹדְפוֹ, &c.;
but before *Šᵉwâ mobile* יֹצְרֶךָ, &c., or with the original *î*, אֹיִבְךָ Ex 23⁴,
&c., אֹסְפְךָ 2 K 22²⁰ (coinciding in form with the 1st *sing. imperfect Qal*,
1 S 15⁶; cf. § 68 *h*); with a middle guttural (גֹּאַלְיֹ), גֹּאַלְךָ; with a third
guttural, בֹּרַאֲךָ Is 43¹, but שֹׁלְחֵךְ, מְשַׁלְחֵךְ Jer 28¹⁶, cf. § 65 *d*. The form
מְקַטֵּל, with suffix מְקַטְּלִי; before *Šᵉwâ* sometimes like מְלַמֶּדְךָ Is 48¹⁷,
מְנַחֶמְכֶם 51¹², sometimes like מְאַסְּפְכֶם 52¹². In Is 47¹⁰ רֹאָנִי is irregular
for רֹאֵנִי; instead of the meaningless מְקַלְלְוֹנִי Jer 15¹⁰ read כְּלָהֶם קִלְלוּנִי.

Also unusual (see above, *d*) with participles are the suffixes of the 2nd sing.
masc. with נ *energicum*, as עוֹנֶךָ Jb 5¹; cf. Dt 8⁵, 12¹⁴·²⁸.

§ 62. *Verbs with Gutturals.*

Brockelmann, *Grundriss*, p. 584 ff.

Verbs which have a guttural for one of the three radicals differ
in their inflexion from the ordinary strong verb, according to the
general rules in § 22. These differences do not affect the consonantal
part of the stem,‒ and it is, therefore, more correct to regard the
guttural verbs as a subdivision of the strong verb. At the most, only
the entire omission of the strengthening in some of the verbs *middle
guttural* (as well as in the *imperfect Niph'al* of verbs *first guttural*)
can be regarded as a real weakness (§§ 63 *h*, 64 *e*). On the other
hand, some original elements have been preserved in guttural stems,
which have degenerated in the ordinary strong verb; e. g. the *ă* of the
initial syllable in the *imperfect Qal*, as in יַחְמֹד, which elsewhere is
attenuated to *ĭ*, יִקְטֹל.—In guttural verbs א and ה are only taken
into consideration when they are actual consonants, and not vowel-
letters like the א in some verbs פ״א (§ 68), in a few ע״א (§ 73 *g*),
and in most ל״א (§ 74). In all these cases, however, the א was at
least originally a full consonant, while the ה in verbs ל״ה was never
anything but a vowel letter, cf. § 75. The really consonantal ה at
the end of the word is marked by *Mappîq*.—Verbs containing a ר
also, according to § 22 *q*, *r*, share some of the peculiarities of the
guttural verbs. For more convenient treatment, the cases will be
distinguished, according as the guttural is the first, second, or third
radical. (Cf. the Paradigms D, E, F, in which only those conjugations
are omitted which are wholly regular.)

§ 63. *Verbs First Guttural*, e.g. עָמַד *to stand*.

In this class the deviations from the ordinary strong verb may be *a* referred to the following cases:—

1. Instead of a *simple Šewâ mobile*, the initial guttural takes a *compound Šewâ* (*Ḥaṭeph*, § 10 *f*, § 22 *l*). Thus the *infinitives* עֲמֹד, אֱכֹל *to eat*, and the *perfects*, 2nd *plur. masc.* חֲפַצְתֶּם, עֲמַדְתֶּם from חָפֵץ *to be inclined*, correspond to the forms קְטֹל and קְטַלְתֶּם; also אֲכָלוֹ to קְטָלוֹ, and so always with initial ◌ֲ before a suffix for an original *ă*, according to § 22 *o*.

2. When a preformative is placed before an initial guttural, either *b* the two may form a closed syllable, or the vowel of the preformative is repeated as a *Ḥaṭeph* under the guttural. If the vowel of the preformative was originally *a*, two methods of formation may again be distinguished, according as this *a* remains or passes into Seghôl.

Examples: (*a*) of firmly closed syllables after the original vowel *c* of the preformative (always with *ō* in the second syllable, except וַתַּעֲגַּב Ez 23⁵, תַּעֲדֶה &c. from עָדָה *to adorn oneself*, and יַעֲטֶה; but cf. *e*): יַעֲקֹב, יַחֲשֹׁב, יַחֲשֹׁךְ, יַחֲמֹל, יַחֲמֹד Jer 9⁸ (probably to distinguish it from the name יַעֲקֹב, just as in Jer 10¹⁹, &c., the participle fem. Niph'al of חָלָה is נַחֲלָה to distinguish it from נֶחֱלָה), &c., and so generally in the *imperfect Qal* of stems beginning with ח, although sometimes parallel forms exist, which repeat the *ă* as a *Ḥaṭeph*, e.g. יַחֲשֹׁב, &c. The same form appears also in the *imperfect Hiph'îl* יַחֲסִיר, &c. Very rarely the original *ă* is retained in a closed syllable under the preformative נ of the *perfect Niph'al*: נַחְבֵּאתָ Gn 31²⁷; cf. 1 S 19², Jos 2¹⁶; also the *infinitive absolute* נַחְתּוֹם Est 8⁸, נַעְתּוֹר 1 Ch 5²⁰, and the *participle fem.* נַחְלָה (see above), *plur.* נַעְתָּרוֹת Pr 27⁶. In these forms the original *ă* is commonly kept under the preformative and is followed by *Ḥaṭeph-Paṭhaḥ*; thus in the *perfect* of some verbs ל״ה, e.g. נַעֲשָׂה, &c.; in the *infinitive absolute*, נַהֲפוֹךְ Est 9¹; in the *participle* נַעֲרָץ, ψ 89⁸, &c.

(*b*) Of the corresponding *Ḥaṭeph* after the original vowel: יַחֲבֹשׁ *d* (but יֶחְבַּשׁ Jb 5¹⁸ in pause), יַחֲלֹם, יַעֲמֹד, יַהֲרֹם, and so almost always with ע and often with ה in the *imperfects* of *Qal* and *Hiph'îl*; in *Hoph'al*, הָעֳמַד, יָעֳמַר; but cf. also הֶחְבָּאוּ Is 42²², הָחְתֵּל Ez 16⁴.

The *ă* of the preformative before a guttural almost always (§ 22 *i*, *c* cf. § 27 *p*) becomes Seghôl (cf., however, *q*). This Seghôl again appears sometimes

(*c*) in a closed syllable, e.g. יֶאְשַׁם, יֶעְתַּר, יֶחְסַר, יֶחְבַּשׁ, always with *ă* in the second syllable, corresponding to the imperfects of verbs ע״ע,

with original *ĭ* in the first and *ă* in the second syllable, § 67 *n*, and also to the imperfects of verbs ע״וּ, § 72 *h*; but cf. also יֶאֱסֹר, and יֶהְדֹּף; in *Niph.*, e.g. נֶהְפַּךְ; נֶחֱלוּ Am 6⁶, &c.; in *Hiph.* הֶחֱסִיר, הֶעֱלִים 2 K 4ᵛ⁷, &c.: sometimes

(*d*) followed by *Ḥaṭeph-Sᵉghôl*, e.g. יַחֲזֵק, יֶאֱסֹף, יַחֲשֹׁף, יַעֲרֹב in *imperfect Qal*; הֶעֱמִיד *Hiph'îl*; נֶעֱנַשׁ *Niph'al*.

f　Rem. With regard to the above examples the following points may also be noted : (1) The forms with a firmly closed syllable (called the hard combination) frequently occur in the same verb with forms containing a loosely closed syllable (the soft combination). (2) In the 1st *sing. imperfect Qal* the preformative א invariably takes *Sᵉghôl*, whether in a firmly or loosely closed syllable, e. g. אֶחֱבשׁ (with the cohortative אֶחְבְּשָׁה), אֶחְסָר (in *pause*), &c. In Jb 32¹⁷ אֶעֱנֶה must unquestionably be *Hiph'îl*, since elsewhere the pointing is always אַעַ׳. Cohortatives like אַהֲרְגֶנָה Gn 27⁴¹ and אֶחְדְּלָה Jb 16⁶, are explained by the next remark. (3) The shifting of the tone towards the end frequently causes the *Pathaḥ* of the preformative to change into *Sᵉghôl*, and vice versa, e. g. נַעֲשָׂה, but נֶעֶשְׂתָה 3rd *sing. fem.*; יֶאֱסֹף, but תַּאַסְפִי; הֶעֱמִיד, but with *wāw consecutive* וְהֶעֱמַדְתָּ, &c. ; so וַיַּחְסְרוּ Gn 8³ the plur. of וַיֶּחְסַר, cf. Gn 11⁸ ; and thus generally a change of the stronger *Ḥaṭeph-Sᵉghôl* group (⹁⹁⹁⹁) into the lighter *Ḥaṭeph-Pathaḥ* group takes place whenever the tone is moved one place toward the end (cf. § 27 *v*).

g　3. When in forms like יַעֲמֹד, נֶעֱמַד, the vowel of the final syllable becomes a *vocal Šᵉwâ* in consequence of the addition of an afformative (וּ, ◌ִ⹁, ה◌ָ⹁) or suffix, the *compound Šᵉwâ* of the guttural is changed into the corresponding short vowel, e. g. יַעֲמֹד, *plur.* יַעַמְדוּ (*ya-'a-mᵉ-dhû* as an equivalent for *ya'-mᵉ-dhû*) ; נֶעֶזְבָה *she is forsaken*. But even in these forms the hard combination frequently occurs, e. g. יַחְבְּלוּ *they take as a pledge* (cf. in the *sing.* תַּחְבֹּל, also יַחְבֹּל); יֶחְזְקוּ (also יֶחֱזְקוּ) *they are strong.* Cf. *m* and, in general, § 22 *m*, § 28 *c*.

h　4. In the *infinitive, imperative,* and *imperfect Niph'al*, where the first radical should by rule be strengthened (יִקָּטֵל, הִקָּטֵל), the strengthening is always omitted, and the vowel of the preformative lengthened to *Ṣere*; יֵעָמֵד for *yi''āmēd*,[1] &c. Cf. § 22 *c*.—For תֵּיעָשֶׂה Ex 25³¹ (according to Dillmann, to prevent the pronunciation תֵּעָשֶׂה, which the LXX and Samaritan follow) read תֵּעָשֶׂה.

REMARKS.

I. On Qal.

i　1. In verbs פ״א the *infinitive construct* and *imperative* take *Ḥaṭeph-Sᵉghôl* in the first syllable (according to § 22 *o*), e. g. אֱזֹר *gird thou*, Jb 38³, אֱהַב *love thou*,

---

[1] אֶעֱנֶה Jb 19⁷ (so even the Mantua ed.) is altogether abnormal : read אֵעָנֶה, with Baer, Ginsb.

Ho 3¹, אֱחֹז *seize thou*, Ex 4⁴ (on אֵפוּ *bake ye*, Ex 16²³, see § 76 *d*); אֱכֹל *to eat*; infinitive with a prefix בֶּאֱכֹל, לֶאֱכֹל, לֶאֱחֹז Is 5²⁴; לֶאֱהֹב Ec 3⁸. Sometimes, however, Ḥaṭeph-Pathaḥ is found as well, e. g. *infinitive* אֱחֹז 1 K 6⁶; בֶּאֱכֹל הָאִישׁ Nu 26¹⁰ (before a suffix אֲמָרְךָ, אֲבֶלְכֶם, אֲמָרְכֶם, אֲבֶלְךָ § 61 *d*); cf. Dt 7²⁰, 12²³, Ez 25⁸, ψ 102⁵, Pr 25⁷ (אֲמָר־לָךְ), Jb 34¹⁸, always in close connexion with the following word. With a firmly closed syllable after לְ cf. לַחְסוֹת Is 30²; לַחְפֹּר Jos 2²ᶠ. (on Is 2²⁰, cf. § 84ᵇ *n*); לַחְתּוֹת Is 30¹⁴, Hag 2¹⁶; קַחְשַׁב Ex 31⁴, &c.; לַעְזוֹר 2 S 18³ *Qᵉrê*, but also בַּעְזֹר 1 Ch 15²⁶.

הֶחֳדַלְתִּי Ju 9⁹·¹¹·¹³ is altogether anomalous, and only a few authorities give *k* הֶחֳדַלְתִּי (Hiphʿil), adopted by Moore in Haupt's Bible. According to Qimḥi, Olshausen, and others, the Masora intended a *perfect Hophʿal* with syncope of the preformative after the ה interrogative = הֶהָחֳדַלְתִּי, or (according to Olshausen) with the omission of the ה interrogative. But since the *Hiphʿil* and *Hophʿal* of חָדַל nowhere occur, it is difficult to believe that such was the intention of the Masora. We should expect the *perfect Qal*, הֶחָדַלְתִּי. But the Qameṣ under the ה, falling between the tone and counter-tone, was naturally less emphasized than in חָדַלְתִּי, without the ה interrogative. Consequently it was weakened, not to simple Šᵉwâ, but to ⟨ḥ⟩, in order to represent the sound of the Qameṣ (likewise pronounced as *â*) at least in a shortened form. The Sᵉghôl of the ה interrogative is explained, in any case, from § 100 *n* (cf. the similar pointing of the article, e. g. in הֶחֳדָשִׁים, § 35 *k*). For the accusative after חָדַל, instead of the usual מִן, Jb 3¹⁷ affords sufficient evidence.

Also in the other forms of the *imperative* the guttural not infrequently *l* influences the vowel, causing a change of *ĭ* (on this *ĭ* cf. § 48 *i*) into Sᵉghôl, e. g. אֶסְפָה *gather thou*, Nu 11¹⁶; עֶרְכָה *set in order*, Jb 33⁵; חֶשְׂפִּי *strip off*, Is 47² (on this irregular Dageš cf. § 46 *d*), especially when the second radical is also a guttural, e. g. אֶהֱבוּ Am 5¹⁵, ψ 31²⁴; cf. Zc 8¹⁹; אֶחֱזוּ Ct 2¹⁵; cf. also in verbs ל"ה, עֶנוּ *sing ye*, Nu 21¹⁷, ψ 147⁷ (compared with עֲנוּ *answer ye*, 1 S 12³) and אֶלָי Jo 1⁸.—*Pathaḥ* occurs in חַבְלֵהוּ *hold him in pledge*, Pr 20¹⁶, and probably also in ψ 9¹⁴ (חַנְנֵנִי).—As a pausal form for חָרְבִי (cf. the *plur.* Jer 2¹²) we find in Is 44²⁷ חֳרָבִי (cf. the *imperf.* יֶחֱרָב) with the *ŏ* repeated in the form of a Ḥaṭeph-Qameṣ. For other examples of this kind, see § 10 *h* and § 46 *e*.

2. The pronunciation (mentioned above, No. 2) of the imperfects in *ă* with *m* Sᵉghôl under the preformative in a firmly closed syllable (e. g. יַחְדַּל, יֶחְכַּם) regularly gives way to the soft combination in verbs which are at the same time ל"ה, e. g. יֶחֱזֶה יֶחֱצֶה &c. (but cf. יֶהְגֶּה &c., אֶעֱשֶׂה Pr 6²⁷, יַחְתֶּה Pr 6²⁷, ed. Mant., Ex 3²⁰). Even in the strong verb וַיֶּחֱזַק is found along with יַחֲזָק. Cf. also וַתֶּעֱצַב Ez 23⁵; וַיַּעְקְבֵנִי Gn 27³⁶ (so Ben-Asher; but Ben-Naphtali וַיַּעְקֹב); וַתַּחְלְקֵם Neh 9²², and so always in the *imperfect Qal* of עוּר with suffixes, Gn 49²⁵, &c.—תֶּאֱהֲבוּ Pr 1²² is to be explained from the endeavour to avoid too great an accumulation of short sounds by the insertion of a long vowel, but it is a question whether we should not simply read תֶּאֱהֲבוּ with Haupt in his Bible, *Proverbs*, p. 34, l. 44 ff.; cf. the analogous instances under *p*, and

such nouns as בְּאֵר, זְאֵב, § 93 *t.*—On יְחָבְּרֶךָ ψ 94²⁰ for יַחְבָּרְךָ (according to Qimḥi, and others, rather *Puʿal*) cf. § 60 *b*.

n יַאְשֵׁם ψ 58⁵ and יַעְרֵם *to deal subtilly*, 1 S 23²², Pr 15⁵, 19²⁵, may be explained with Barth (*ZDMG.* 1889, p. 179) as *i*-imperfects (see above, § 47 *i*),—the latter for the purpose of distinction from the causative עֲרִים ψ 83⁴.—Instead of the unintelligible form וַיְחֶלְקֵם (so ed. Mant.; Baer and Ginsb. as in 24³) 1 Ch 23⁶ and וַיַּחֵץ׳ 24³ (partly analogous to תֶּעְבְּרֵם § 60 *b*) the Qal וַיְחַלְּקֵם is to be read. The form יְרֹדֵף ψ 7⁶ which is, according to Qimḥi (in *Mikhlol*; but in his Lexicon he explains it as *Hithpaʿēl*), a composite form of Qal (יִרְדֹּף) and Piʿēl (יְרַדֵּף), can only be understood as a development of יִרְדֹּף (cf. § 64 *h* on יִצְחָק, and § 69 *x* on תְּהֵלַךְ Ex 9²³, ψ 73⁹). Pathaḥ has taken the place of *Ḥaṭeph-Pathaḥ*, but as a mere helping-vowel (as in שָׁמַעְתָּ § 28 *e*, note 2) and without preventing the closing of the syllable. It is much simpler, however, to take it as a *forma mixta*, combining the readings יִרְדֹּף (impf. Qal) and יְרַדֵּף (impf. Piʿēl).

II. *On Hiph'îl and Hoph'al.*

o 3. The above-mentioned (*f*, 3) change of ____ to ____ occurs in the *perfect Hiph'îl*, especially when *wāw consecutive* precedes, and the tone is in consequence thrown forward upon the afformative, e. g. הֶעֱמַדְתָּ, but וְהֶעֱמַדְתָּ Nu 3⁶, 8¹³, 27¹⁹; הֶעֱבַרְתִּי, but וְהַעֲבַרְתִּי Jer 15¹⁴, Ez 20³⁷; even in the 3rd *sing.* וְהָאֲזִין ψ 77².—On the contrary ____ occurs instead of ____ in the *imperative Hiph'îl*, Jer 49⁸·³⁰; and in the *infinitive* Jer 31³². The preformative of עתר in *Hiph'îl* always takes *a* in a closed syllable: Ex 8⁴ הַעְתִּירוּ; verse 5 אַעְתִּיר; also verse 25 and Jb 22²⁷.

p 4. In the *perfect Hiph'îl* ____ is sometimes changed into ____, and in *Hoph'al* ____ into ____ (cf. § 23 *h*); הֶעֱבַרְתְּ Jos 7⁷, הֶעֱלָה Hb 1¹⁵, הֶעֱלָה Ju 6²⁸, 2 Ch 20³⁴, Na 2⁸, always before ע, and hence evidently with the intention of strengthening the countertone-syllable (הֶ or הָ) before the guttural. On a further case of this kind (זְעָמָה) see § 64 *c*. Something similar occurs in the formation of segholate nouns of the form *qŏṭl*; cf. § 93 *q*, and (on אֱמוּן &c. for אֱמוּן) § 84ᵃ *q*.—In the imperfect consecutive וַיֶּחֱזַק בּוֹ the tone is thrown back on to the first syllable. On the *Hoph'al* תֶּעְבְּרֵם Ex 20⁵, &c., see § 60 *b*.

III. הָיָה *and* חָיָה.

q 5. In the verbs הָיָה *to be*, and חָיָה *to live*, the guttural hardly ever affects the addition of preformatives; thus *imperfect Qal* יִהְיֶה and יִחְיֶה, *Niph'al* נִהְיָה; but in the *perfect Hiph'il* הֶחֱיָה (2nd *plur.* וְהַחֲיִתֶם Jos 2¹³, and even without *wāw consecutive*, Ju 8¹⁹). Initial ה always has *Ḥaṭeph-Seghôl* instead of *vocal Šewâ*; הֱיֵה, הֱיוֹת, הֱיִיתֶם 1 S 25⁷, הֱיִיתֶם (except הֱיִי *be thou! fem.* Gn 24⁶⁰). The 2nd *sing. fem. imperative* of חָיָה is חֲיִי *live thou*, Ez 16⁶; the infinitive, with suffix, חֲיֹתָם Jos 5⁸. After the prefixes וְ, בְּ, כְּ, לְ, מִ (=מִן) both ה and ח retain the simple Šewâ (§ 28 *b*) and the prefix takes *ĭ*, as elsewhere before strong consonants with *Šewâ*; hence in the *perfect Qal* וִהְיִיתֶם, *imperative* וִהְיוּ, *infinitive* לִהְיוֹת, בִּהְיוֹת &c. (cf. § 16 *f*, ε). The only exception is the 2nd *sing. masc.* of the *imperative* after *wāw*; וֶהְיֵה Gn 12², &c., וֶחֲיֵה Gn 20⁷.

§ 64. *Verbs Middle Guttural*, e.g. שָׁחַט *to slaughter.*

The slight deviations from the ordinary inflexion are confined *a*
chiefly to the following [1] :—

1. When the guttural would stand at the beginning of a syllable
with simple *S͏ͤwâ*, it necessarily takes a *Ḥaṭeph*, and almost always
Ḥaṭeph-Pathaḥ, e.g. *perfect* שַׁחֲטוּ, *imperfect* יִשְׁחֲטוּ, *imperative Niph'al*
הִשָּׁחֲטוּ. In the *imperative Qal*, before the afformatives *î* and *û*, the
original *Pathaḥ* is retained in the first syllable, and is followed by
Ḥaṭeph-Pathaḥ, thus, זַעֲקִי, זַעֲקוּ, &c.; in אֶהֱבוּ the preference of the א
for *S͏ͤghôl* (but cf. also יֶֽאֱחֹֽזֶךָ Jer 13²¹) has caused the change from
ă to *ĕ*; in שְׁחֲרֻ Jb 6²², even *ĭ* remains before a *hard* guttural.

So in the *infinitive Qal fem.*, e. g. אַהֲבָה *to love*, דַּאֲבָה *to pine*; and in the
infinitive with a suffix לְסָעֲדָהּ Is 9⁶; the doubtful form שַׁחֲטָה Ho 5², is better
explained as *infinitive Pi'ēl* (= שַׁחֲתָהּ).

2. Since the preference of the gutturals for the *a*-sound has less *b*
influence on the following than on the preceding vowel, not only is
Ḥolem retained after the middle guttural in the *infinitive Qal* שָׁחֹט
(with the fem. ending and retraction and shortening of the *o* רָחְצָה and
רׇחְקׇה, cf. § 45 *b*), but generally also the *Ṣere* in the *imperfect Niph'al*
and *Pi'ēl*, e.g. יִלָּחֵם *he fights*, יְנַחֵם *he comforts*, and even the more
feeble *S͏ͤghôl* after *wāw consecutive* in such forms as וַיִּלָּחֶם, וַתְּפַעֶם
Gn 41⁸ (cf., however, וַיַּֽעַץ 1 K 12⁶, &c.). But in the *imperative* and
imperfect Qal, the final syllable, through the influence of the guttural,
mostly takes *Pathaḥ*, even in transitive verbs, e.g. שְׁחַט, יִשְׁחַט;
זְעַק, יִזְעַק; בְּחַר, יִבְחַר; with *suffixes* (according to § 60 *c*), *imperative*
שְׁאָלֻנִי, בְּחָנֵנִי, *imperfect* יִנְאָלֹֽהוּ.

With *ō* in the *imperative Qal*, the only instances are נְעֹל 2 S 13¹⁷; *c*
אֱחֹז Ex 4⁴, 2 S 2²¹, *fem.* אֱחׇזִי Ru 3¹⁵ (with the unusual repetition of the
lost *ō* as *Ḥaṭeph-Qameṣ*; 2nd *plur. masc.* in *pause* אֱחֹזוּ Neh 7³; without
the *pause* אֲחֹזוּ Ct 2¹⁵); סְעָד Ju 19⁸. [2] Finally וְעׇמָה for זַֽעֲמָה, Nu 23⁷,
is an example of the same kind, see § 63 *p*. Just as rare are the imperfects in *ō* of verbs *middle guttural*, as יִנְהֹם, יֶאֱחֹז, תִּמְעֹל Lv 5¹⁵, Nu 5²⁷
(but וַיִּמְעַל 2 Ch 26¹⁶); cf. וַתִּשְׁחֲרִ־ Ez 16³³; תִּפְעֹל Jb 35⁶. Also in the
perfect Pi'ēl, *Pathaḥ* occurs somewhat more frequently than in the
strong verb, e.g. נַחַם *to comfort* (cf., however, כִּהָה, כָּחַד, כָּחַשׁ, שָׁחַת);

---

[1] *Hoph'al*, which is not exhibited in the paradigm, follows the analogy of
Qal; *Hiph'il* is regular.

[2] Also Ju 19⁵ (where Qimḥi would read *s͏ͤ'ād*), read *s͏ͤ'ŏd*, and on the use
of the conjunctive accent (here *Darga*) as a substitute for *Metheg*, cf. § 9 *u* (c)
and § 16 *b*.

but אַ and עַ always have *ē* in 3rd *sing*.—On the *infinitive* with suffixes, cf. § 61 *b*.

d 3. In *Piʿēl*, *Puʿal*, and *Hithpaʿēl*, the *Dageš forte* being inadmissible in the middle radical, the preceding vowel, especially before ה, ח, and ע, nevertheless, generally remains short, and the guttural is consequently to be regarded as, at least, *virtually* strengthened, cf. § 22 *c*; e. g. *Piʿēl* שִׁחֵת, נִחֲלוּ Jos 14¹, וּבְעַרְתִּי 1 K 14¹⁰, נִהַג Ex 10¹³ (cf., however, אִחַר Gn 34¹⁹; נָהַלְתָּ Ex 15¹³, but in the *imperfect* and *participle* יְנַהֵל, &c.; in verbs ה״ל, e. g. רְעֵה), *infinitive* שַׂחֵק, *Puʿal* רֻחַץ (but cf. דֹּחוּ ψ 36¹³ from דָּחָה, also the unusual position of the tone in בֹּחַ¹ Ez 21¹⁸, and in the *perfect Hithpaʿēl* הִתְרָחַצְתִּי Jb 9³⁰); *Hithpaʿēl perfect* and *imperative* הִטַּהֲרוּ, &c.; in *pause* (see §§ 22 *c*, 27 *q*, 29 *v*, 54 *k*) הִפָּהֲרוּ Nu 8⁷, 2 Ch 30¹⁸; יִתְנֶחָם Nu 23¹⁹, &c.

e The complete omission of the strengthening, and a consequent lengthening of the preceding vowel, occurs invariably only with ר (כָּתַת) Ez 16⁴ is an exception; כֹּרְתָה also occurs, Ju 6²⁸), e. g. בֵּרַךְ (in *pause* בֵּרֵךְ), *imperfect* יְבָרֵךְ, *Puʿal* בֹּרַךְ. Before אַ it occurs regularly in the stems בֵּאֵר, מֵאֵן, גֵּאַל, פֵּאֵר, and in the *Hithpaʿēl* of ראה, באש, and שׁאה; on the other hand, אַ is *virtually* strengthened in the *perfects*, נִאֵף (once in the imperfect, Jer 29²³) *to commit adultery*, נִאֵץ *to despise* (in the *participle*, Nu 14²³, Is 60¹⁴, Jer 23¹⁷; according to Baer, but not ed. Mant., or Ginsb., even in the *imperfect* יְנַאֵץ ψ 74¹⁰), נִאֵר *to abhor* La 2⁷ (also נֵאַרְתָּה ψ 89⁴⁰) and שֵׁאַל ψ 109¹⁰; moreover, in the *infinitive* יַאֵשׁ Ec 2²⁰, according to the best reading. On the *Mappîq* in the *Puʿal* רֻאָּה Jb 33²¹, cf. § 14 *d*.

f Rem. 1. In the verb שָׁאַל *to ask, to beg*, some forms of the *perfect Qal* appear to be based upon a secondary form *middle e*, which is *Ṣere* when the vowel of the אַ stands in an open syllable, cf. שָׁאֵלְתִּ Gn 32¹⁸, Ju 4²⁰; שְׁאֵלוּנִי ψ 137³; but in a closed syllable, even without a suffix, שְׁאֶלְתֶּם 1 S 12¹³, 25⁵, Jb 21²⁹; שְׁאֶלְתִּיהוּ Ju 13⁶, 1 S 1²⁰. Cf., however, similar cases of attenuation of an original *ă*, § 69 *s*, and especially § 44 *d*. In the first three examples, if explained on that analogy, the *ĭ* attenuated from *ă* would have been lengthened to *ē* (before the tone); in the next three *ĭ* would have been modified to *ĕ*. Also in the *Hiphʿil*-form הִשְׁאֶלְתִּיהוּ 1 S 1²⁸ the אַ is merely attenuated from אַ.

g 2. In *Piʿēl* and *Hithpaʿēl* the lengthening of the vowel before the guttural causes the tone to be thrown back upon the penultima, and consequently the *Ṣere* of the ultima to be shortened to *Sᵉghôl*. Thus (*a*) before monosyllables, according to § 29 *e*, e. g. לְשָׁרֶת שָׁם *to minister there*, Dt 17¹², even in the case of a guttural which is *virtually* strengthened, Gn 39¹⁴, Jb 8¹⁸ (see § 29 *g*). (*b*) after *wāw consecutive*, e. g. וַיְבָרֶךְ *and he blessed*, Gn 1²² and frequently, וַיְגָרֶשׁ *and he drove out*, Ex 10¹¹ וַתְּפָצֵם Dn 2¹.

---

¹ בֹּחַ is explained by Abulwalid as the 3rd pers. *perfect Puʿal*, but by Qimḥi as a noun.

3. The following are a few rarer anomalies; in the *imperfect Qal* יִצְחַק Gn 21⁶ *h* (elsewhere תִּצְחַק, &c., in *pause* יִצְחָק, cf. § 10 *g* (*c*) and § 63 *n*); וַאֵחַר Gn 32⁵ (for וָאֵחַר); in the *perfect Pi'ēl* וַ אֵחֲרוּ Ju 5²⁸ (perhaps primarily for אֵחֲרוּ; according to Gn 34¹⁹ אֵחֲרוּ would be expected), and similarly יְחַמְּתַנִי ψ 51⁷ for יֶחֱמַתְנִי; in the *imperative Pi'ēl* קָרֵב Ez 37¹⁷ (cf. above, § 52 *n*); finally, in the *imperative Hiph'il* הַרְחַק Jb 13²¹ and הַמְעַד ψ 69²⁴, in both cases probably influenced by the closing consonant, and by the preference for *Pathaḥ* in *pause* (according to § 29 *q*); without the pause הַרְחֵק Pr 4²⁴, &c.; but also הַנַּחַת Jo 4¹¹.

4. As *infinitive Hithpa'ēl* with a suffix we find הִתְיַחְשָׂם Ezr 8¹, &c., with *i* a firmly closed syllable, also the *participle* מִתְיַחְשִׂים Neh 7⁶⁴; Baer, however, reads in all these cases, on good authority, הִתְיָחְשָׂם &c.—The quite meaningless *Kethibh* וְנָאשָׁאר Ez 9⁸ (for which the *Qerê* requires the equally unintelligible וְנִשְׁאָר) evidently combines two different readings, viz. וְנִשְׁאָר (*part. Niph.*) and וַאִשָּׁאֵר (*imperf. consec.*); cf. König, *Lehrgebäude,* i. p. 266 f.—In יִתְאָרֲהוּ Is 44¹³ (also יְתָאֲרֵהוּ in the same verse) an *imperfect Pô'ēl* appears to be intended by the Masora with an irregular shortening of the *ô* for ´יְתֹאֲר; cf. § 55 *b* מְלָשְׁנִי ψ 101⁵ *Qerê*; on the other hand Qimḥi, with whom Delitzsch agrees, explains the form as *Pi'ēl*, with an irregular ◌ָ for ◌ֵ, as in the reading אֲלַקֵּטָה Ru 2²·⁷; cf. § 10 *h*.

5. A few examples in which א, as middle radical, entirely loses its consonantal value and quiesces in a vowel, will be found in § 73 *g*.

§ 65. *Verbs Third Guttural,* e.g. שָׁלַח *to send.*[1]

1. According to § 22 *d*, when the last syllable has a vowel incom- *a* patible with the guttural (i.e. *not* an *a*-sound), two possibilities present themselves, viz. either the regular vowel *remains,* and the guttural then takes *furtive Pathaḥ,* or *Pathaḥ* (in pause *Qameṣ*) takes its place. More particularly it is to be remarked that—

(*a*) The unchangeable vowels ◌ִ´—, ◌ֹ, וּ (§ 25 *b*) are always retained, even under such circumstances; hence *inf. abs. Qal* שָׁלוֹחַ, *part. pass.* שָׁלוּחַ, *Hiph.* הִשְׁלִיחַ, *imperf.* יַשְׁלִיחַ, *part.* מַשְׁלִיחַ. So also the less firm *ō* in the *inf. constr.* שְׁלֹחַ is almost always retained: cf., however, שְׁלַח, in close connexion with a substantive, Is 58⁹, and נְגֹעַ Nu 20³. Examples of the *infinitive* with suffixes are בְּבָרְחַךָ Gn 35¹; בִּפְגְעוֹ Nu 35¹⁹; לְרִבְעָהּ Lv 18²³, &c.

(*b*) The *imperfect* and *imperative Qal* almost always have *ă* in the *b* second syllable, sometimes, no doubt, due simply to the influence of the guttural (for a tone-long *ō,* originally *ŭ*), but sometimes as being the original vowel, thus יִשְׁלַח, שְׁלַח, &c.; with suffixes שְׁלָחֵנִי, יִשְׁלָחֵנִי, see § 60 *c*.

---

[1] Verbs ל״ה in which the ה is *consonantal* obviously belong also to this class, e.g. גָּבַה *to be high,* תָּמַהּ *to be astonished,* מָהַהּ (only in *Hithpalpel*) *to delay.*

Exceptions, in the *imperfect* אסלוח Jer 5⁷, K°ᵗʰ. (אֶסְלָח Q°rê) ; in the *imperative* טבֹח Gn 43¹⁶. On such cases as אֶפְשָׁעָה Is 27⁴, cf. § 10 *h*.

c (c) Where *Ṣere* would be the regular vowel of the final syllable, both forms (with *ēᵃ* and *ă*) are sometimes in use ; the choice of one or the other is decided by the special circumstances of the tone, i. e. :—

d Rem. 1. In the *absolute state* of the participle Qal, Pi'ēl and Hithpa'ēl, the forms שֹׁלֵחַ (with suff. שֹׁלְחִי, but שֹׁלְחֵךְ), מְשַׁלֵחַ (with suff. מְשַׁלֵּחֲךָ), and מִשְׁתַּגֵּעַ are used exclusively ; except in verbs ל״ע where we find, in close connexion, also נֹטֵעַ ψ 94⁹, רֹגֵעַ Is 51¹⁵, Jer 31³⁵, רֹקֵעַ Is 42⁵, 44²⁴, רֹוקֵעַ ψ 136⁶, שֹׁגֵעַ Lv 11⁷, all with the tone on the last syllable.—The part. Pu'al is מֻרְבָּע Ez 45² according to the best authorities (Kittel מְרֻבָּע).

e 2. Similarly, in the *imperf.* and *inf.* Niph'al, and in the *perf. inf.* and *imperf.* Pi'ēl the (probably more original) form with *ă* commonly occurs in the body of the sentence, and the fuller form with *ēᵃ* in *pause* (and even with the lesser distinctives, e.g. with D°hi ψ 86⁴ in the imperative Pi'ēl ; with Tiphḥa 1 K 12³² in the infinitive Pi'ēl ; Jer 4³¹ imperfect Hithpa'ēl ; Jer 16⁶ imperfect Niph'al), cf. e.g. יִגְרַע Nu 27⁴, with יִגְרֵעַ 36³ ; וַיִּשְׁבַּע Dt 1³⁴, even with retraction of the tone in the *inf. abs.* Niph'al הִשָּׁבֵעַ Nu 30³ (elsewhere הִשָּׁבַע Jer 7⁹, 12¹⁶ twice, in each case without the pause) ; תְּבַקֵּעַ Hb 3⁹, with תְּבַקַּע Ez 13¹¹ ; בַּלַּע to *devour* Hb 1¹³, Nu 4²⁰ with בַּלַּע La 2⁸ ; for infinitive Hithpa'ēl, cf. Is 28²⁰. The *infinitive absolute* Pi'ēl has the form שַׁלֵּחַ Dt 22⁷, 1 K 11²² ; the *infinitive construct*, on the other hand, when without the pause is always as שַׁלַּח except לְשַׁלֵּחַ Ex 10⁴.— יָזֹבַח Hb 1¹⁶ has *ē*, though not in *pause*, and even וַיִּזְבַּח 2 K 16⁴, 2 Ch 28⁴ ; but *a* in pause in the *imperative* Niph'al הֵאָנַח Ez 21¹¹ ; *jussive* Pi'ēl תְּאַחַר ψ 40¹⁸ ; cf. § 52 *n*. An example of *ă* in the *imperative* Pi'ēl under the influence of a final ר is כַּתֵּר Jb 36², in the *imperfect* Niph'al וַתְּעַצֵּר Nu 17¹³, &c.—In יִפְרַח Jb 14⁹ (cf. ψ 92¹⁴, Pr 14¹¹), Barth (see above, § 63 *n*) finds an *i-imperfect* of Qal, since the intransitive meaning is only found in Qal.

f 3. In the 2nd *sing. masc.* of the *imperative*, and in the forms of the *jussive* and *imperfect consecutive* of Hiph'il which end in gutturals, *a* alone occurs, e.g. הַצְלַח *prosper thou*, יַבְטַח *let him make to trust*, וַיַּצְמַח *and he made to grow* (so in Hithpalpel יִתְמַהְמַהּ, &c., Hb 2³) ; even in *pause* וַיַּצְלַח 1 Ch 29²³ and, with the best authorities, וַיּוֹכַח 1 Ch 12¹⁷ ; וְיֹשַׁעֲךָ Is 35⁴ is perhaps to be emended into וְיֵשַׁע (=וְיֹשִׁיעַ).—In the *infinitive absolute* Ṣere remains, e.g. הַגְבֵּהַּ *to make high*; as *infinitive construct* הוֹכֵחַ also occurs in close connexion (Jb 6²⁶) ; on הֹשֵׁעַ as infinitive construct (1 S 25²⁶·³³), cf. § 53 *k*.

g 2. When the guttural with *quiescent Šewâ* stands at the end of a syllable, the ordinary strong form remains when not connected with suffixes, e. g. שָׁלַחְתָּ, שָׁלַחְתִּי. But in the 2nd *sing. fem. perfect* a *helping-Pathaḥ* takes the place of the *Šewâ*, שָׁבַחַתְּ Jer 13²⁵ (§ 28 *e*) ; also in 1 K 14³ לָקַחַתְּ is to be read, not לָקַחְתְּ.

h Rem. The soft combination with *compound Šewâ* occurs only in the 1st *plur. perfect* with suffixes, since in these forms the tone is thrown one place farther forward, e.g. יְדַעֲנוּךְ *we know thee*, Ho 8² (cf. Gn 26²⁹, ψ 44¹⁸, 132⁶). Before the *suffixes* ךָ and כֶם, the guttural must have —ַ, e.g. אֲשַׁלֵּחֲךָ *I will send thee*, 1 S 16¹ ; וַאֲשַׁלֵּחֲךָ Gn 31²⁷ ; אֲשַׁמִּיעֵךָ Jer 18². On the weak verbs ל״א, see especially § 74.

II. The Weak Verb.[1]

§ 66. *Verbs Primae Radicalis Nûn* (פ״נ), e.g. נָגַשׁ *to approach*

Brockelmann, *Semit. Sprachwiss.*, p. 138 ff.; *Grundriss*, p. 595 ff.

The weakness of initial נ consists chiefly in its suffering *aphaeresis* **a** in the *infinitive construct* and *imperative* in some of these verbs (cf. § 19 *h*). On the other hand, the *assimilation* of the נ (see below) cannot properly be regarded as weakness, since the triliteral character of the stem is still preserved by the strengthening of the second consonant. The special points to be noticed are—

1. The *aphaeresis* of the Nûn (*a*) in the *infinitive construct*. This **b** occurs only (though not necessarily) in those verbs which have *a* in the second syllable of the *imperfect*. Thus from the stem נגשׁ, *imperfect* יִגַּשׁ, *infinitive* properly גַּשׁ, but always lengthened by the feminine termination ת to the segholate form גֶּשֶׁת[2]; with *suffix* גִּשְׁתּוֹ Gn 33³; with the concurrence of a guttural נָגַע *to touch*, imperfect יִגַּע, infinitive גַּעַת (also נְגֹעַ, see below); נָטַע *to plant*, infinitive טַעַת (also נְטֹעַ, see below); on the verb נָתַן *to give*, see especially *h* and *i*. On the other hand, *aphaeresis* does not take place in verbs which have *ō* in the *imperfect*, e.g. נָפַל *to fall*, imperfect יִפֹּל, infinitive נְפֹל, with *suffix* נָפְלוֹ, also נִפְלוֹ; לִנְדֹּר Nu 6², &c.; cf., moreover, לִנְגֹּעַ Gn 20⁶, &c., וּנְגֹעַ Ex 19¹² (even לִנְגּוֹעַ Jb 6⁷; cf. Jer 1¹⁰); with *suffix* בְּנָגְעוֹ Lv 15²³. Also לִנְטֹעַ Is 51¹⁶ (but לָטַעַת Ec 3²); נְשֹׂא Is 1¹⁴, 18³; with *suffix* בְּנָשְׂאִי ψ 28² (elsewhere שְׂאֵת, cf. § 74 *i* and § 76 *b*), לִנְשֹׁק 2 S 20⁹.

(*b*) In the *imperative*. Here the *Nûn* is always dropped in verbs **c** with *a* in the *imperfect*, e.g. נגשׁ, *imperative* גַּשׁ (more frequently with *paragogic* ā, גְּשָׁה; before *Maqqeph* also גֶּשׁ־ Gn 19⁹), *plur.* גְּשׁוּ, &c. Parallel with these there are the curious forms with *ō*, גֹּשִׁי Ru 2¹⁴ (with *retarding* Metheg in the second syllable, and also *nasog 'aḥor*, according to § 29 *e*, before וְחָלֹם) and גֹּשׁוּ Jos 3⁹ (before הֵנָּה), 1 S 14³⁸ (before וְחָלֹם) and 2 Ch 29³¹; in all these cases without the *pause*. With *Nûn* retained, as if in a strong verb, נְהַג *drive*, 2 K 4²⁴ (*imperfect* יִנְהַג), without assimilation of the *Nûn*), וְנִטְעוּ 2 K 19²⁹, Is 37³⁰, Jer 29⁵·²⁸; cf. also the verbs ל״ה, which are at the same time פ״נ; נְחֵה Ez 32¹⁸, נְחֵה Ex 32³⁴, נְמֵה Ex 8¹, &c.; the verb ל״א, נְשָׂא ψ 10¹² (usually שָׂא); cf. § 76 *b*. But, as in the infinitive, the *aphaeresis* never takes place in verbs which have *ō* in the *imperfect*, e.g. נְצֹר, נְתִיק, &c.

---

[1] Cf. the summary, § 41.

[2] The law allowing the addition of the feminine termination to the unlengthened form, instead of a lengthening of the vowel, is suitably called by Barth 'the law of compensation' (*Nominalbildung*, p. xiii).

d 2. When, through the addition of a *preformative*, *Nûn* stands at the end of a syllable, it is readily assimilated to the second radical (§ 19 *c*); thus in the *imperfect Qal*,[1] e.g. יִפֹּל for *yinpōl*, *he will fall*; יִגַּשׁ for *yingaš*; יִתֵּן for *yintēn*, *he will give* (on this single example of an *imperfect* with original *i* in the second syllable, cf. *h*)[2]; also in the *perfect Niph'al* נִגַּשׁ for *ningaš*; throughout *Hiph'il* (הִגִּישׁ, &c.) and *Hoph'al* (which in these verbs always has *Qibbuṣ*, in a sharpened syllable, cf. § 9 *n*) הֻגַּשׁ.

The other forms are all quite regular, e. g. the *perfect, infinitive absolute* and *participle Qal*, all *Pi'ēl*, *Pu'al*, &c.

In Paradigm H, only those conjugations are given which differ from the regular form.

e The *characteristic* of these verbs in all forms with a preformative is *Dageš* following it in the second radical. Such forms, however, are also found in certain verbs פ״י (§ 71), and even in verbs ע״ע (§ 67). The *infinitive* גֶּשֶׁת and the *imperative* גַּשׁ, also גְּשׁ (Gn 19⁹) and תֵּן, resemble the corresponding forms of verbs פ״י (§ 69).—On יִקַּח, קַח, and קַחַת, from לָקַח *to take*, see *g*.—In יָקוּם (*imperfect Niph'al* of קוּם), and in similar forms of verbs ע״ו (§ 72), the *full* writing of the *ô* indicates, as a rule, that they are not to be regarded as *imperfects Qal* of נָקַם, &c.—Also אֶפַּק (ψ 139⁸) is not to be derived from נפק, but stands for אֶסְלַק (with a sharpening of the ס as compensation for the loss of the ל), from סָלַק *to ascend*, see § 19*f*, and Kautzsch, *Gramm. des Bibl.-Aram.*, § 44. Similarly the *Hiph'il*-forms הַשִּׁיקוּ Ez 39⁹, יַשִּׁיק Is 44¹⁵, and the Niph'al נִשְּׁקָה ψ 78²¹ are most probably from a stem שׁלק, not נשׁק.

f Rem. 1. The instances are comparatively few in which the forms retain their *Nûn* before a firm consonant, e. g. נָטַר, imperfect יִנְטוֹר Jer 3⁵ (elsewhere יִפֹּר); also from נָצַר the pausal form is *always* יִנְצֹרוּ (without the *pause* יִצְּרוּ Pr 20²⁸); similarly in Is 29¹, 58³, ψ 61⁸, 68³ (where, however, תִּנְדֹּף is intended), 140²·⁵, Pr 2¹¹, Jb 40²¹, the retention of the *Nûn* is always connected with the *pause*. In *Niph'al* this never occurs (except in the irregular *inf.* כְּהִנָּדֹף ψ 68³, cf. § 51 *k*), in *Hiph'il* and *Hoph'al* very seldom; e. g. לְהַנְתִּיךְ Ez 22²⁰, הִנְתְּכוּ Ju 20³¹; for לַנְפֹּל Nu 5²² read לִנְפֹּל, according to § 53 *q*. On the other hand, the *Nûn* is regularly retained in all verbs, of which the second radical is a guttural, e. g. יִנְחַל *he will possess*, although there are rare cases like יַחַת (also יִנְחַת) *he will descend*, Jer 21¹³ (even תֵּחַת Pr 17¹⁰; without apparent reason accented as *Mil'ēl*), plur. יֵחַתּוּ Jb 21¹³ (cf. § 20 *i*; the Masora, however, probably regards יַחַת and יֵחַתּוּ as *imperfect Niph'al* from חָתַת); *Niph'al* נָחַם for נִנְחַם *he has grieved*.

g 2. The ל of לָקַח *to take* is treated like the *Nûn* of verbs פ״ן (§ 19 *d*). Hence *imperfect Qal* יִקַּח, cohortative (§ 20 *m*) אֶקְחָה, *imperative* קַח, in *pause* and

---

[1] Cf. Mayer Lambert, 'Le futur qal des verbes פ״י, פ״ן, פ״א,' in the *REJ.* xxvii. 136 ff.

[2] An imperfect in *a* (יִגַּשׁ) is given in the Paradigm, simply because it is the actual form in use in this verb.

before *suffixes* קַח (on קָחֶם־נָא Gn 48⁹, see § 61 *g*), *paragogic* form קָחָה; קְחִי,
&c. (but cf. also לְקַח Ex 29¹, Ez 37¹⁶, Pr 20¹⁶, לְקְחִי 1 K 17¹¹, perhaps a
mistake for לָהּ קְחִי, cf. LXX and Lucian); *infinitive construct* קַחַת (once קֹחַת
2 K 12⁹, cf. § 93 *h*); with לָ, לָקַחַת; with *suffix* קַחְתִּי; *Hoph'al* (cf., however,
§ 53 *u*) *imperfect* יֻקַּח; *Niph'al*, however, is always נִלְקַח.—The meaningless
form קָח Ez 17⁵ is a mistake; for the equally meaningless קָחֶם Ho 11³ read
וָאֶקָּחֵם.

3. The verb נָתַן *to give*, mentioned above in *d*, is the only example of a *h*
verb פ״נ with *imperfect* in *ē* (יְתֵן for *yintēn*; נִתֵּן ¹ only in Ju 16⁵, elsewhere
before *Maqqeph* ־יֶתֶּן, &c.), and a corresponding *imperative* תֵּן or (very
frequently) תְּנָה (but in ψ 8² the very strange reading תְּנָה is no doubt
simply meant by the Masora to suggest נְתָנָה); before *Maqqeph* ־תֶּן, *fem.* תְּנִי,
&c. Moreover, this very common verb has the peculiarity that its final *Nûn*,
as a weak nasal, is also assimilated; נָתַתִּי for *nāthántī*, נָתַתָּ or, very
frequently, נָתַתָּה, with a kind of orthographic compensation for the assimilated *Nûn* (cf. § 44 *g*); *Niph'al perfect* נִתַּם Lv 26²⁵, Ezr 9⁷.

In the *infinitive construct* Qal the ground-form *tint* is not lengthened to *tĕneth ĭ*
(as גֶּשֶׁת from נָגַשׁ), but contracted to *titt*, which is then correctly lengthened to תֵּת, with the omission of *Dageš forte* in the final consonant, see § 20 *l*;
but with suffixes תִּתִּי, תִּתּוֹ, &c.; before *Maqqeph* with the prefix לְ = ־לְתֶת,
e. g. Ex 5²¹, and even when closely connected by other means, e. g. Gn 15⁷.
However, the strong formation of the *infinitive construct* also occurs in נְתֹן Nu
20²¹ and ־נְתָן Gn 38⁹; cf. § 69 *m*, note 2. On the other hand, for לְתֵת 1 K 6¹⁹
read either לְתִתּוֹ or simply לָתֵת, just as the *Qᵉrê*, 1 K 17¹⁴, requires תֵּת
for תתן.

In other stems, the נ is retained as the third radical, e. g. זָקַנְתִּי, שָׁבַנְתָּ, cf. *k*
§ 19 *c* and § 44 *o*. On the entirely anomalous aphaeresis of the *Nûn* with a
strong vowel in תֵּתָּה (for נָתַתָּ) 2 S 22⁴¹, cf. § 19 *i*.—On the *passive imperfect*
יֻתַּן, cf. § 53 *u*.

§ 67. *Verbs* ע״ע, e. g. סָבַב *to surround*.

Brockelmann, *Semit. Sprachwiss.*, p. 155 ff.; *Grundriss*, p. 632 ff.

1. A large number of Semitic stems have verbal forms with only *a*
two radicals, as well as forms in which the stem has been made
triliteral by a *repetition of the second radical*, hence called verbs ע״ע.
Forms with two radicals were formerly explained as being due to
contraction from original forms with three radicals. It is more correct

¹ P. Haupt on Ju 16⁵ in his Bible, compares the form of the Assyrian
imperfect *iddan* or *ittan* (besides *inádin*, *inámdin*) from *nadánu* = נתן. But
could this one passage be the only trace left in Hebrew of an imperf. in *a*
from נתן?

to regard them as representing the original stem (with two radicals), and the forms with the second radical repeated as subsequently developed from the monosyllabic stem.[1] The appearance of a general contraction of triliteral stems is due to the fact that in biliteral forms the second radical regularly receives *Dageš forte* before afformatives, except in the cases noted in § 22 *b* and *q*. This points, however, not to an actual doubling, but merely to a strengthening of the consonant, giving more body to the monosyllabic stem, and making it approximate more to the character of triliteral forms.

The development of biliteral to triliteral stems (ע״ע) generally takes place in the 3rd *sing. masc.* and *fem.* and 3rd *plur. perfect Qal* of *transitive* verbs, or at any rate of verbs expressing an activity, e. g. סָבַב, סָבְבָה, סָבְבוּ : חָנַן Gn 33⁵ (but with suffix חַנַּנִי, ver. 11); sometimes with an evident distinction between transitive and intransitive forms, as צָרַר *to make strait,* צַר *to be in a strait*; see further details, including the exceptions, in *aa*. The development of the stem takes place (*a*) necessarily whenever the strengthening of the 2nd radical is required by the character of the form (e. g. חִלֵּל, שֵׁדַּד), and (*b*) as a rule, whenever the 2nd radical is followed or preceded by an essentially long vowel, as, in Qal, סָבוֹב, סָבוּב, in Pôʻēl and Pôʻal, סוֹבֵב, סוֹבַב.

b 2. The biliteral stem always (except in *Hiphʻîl* and the *imperfect Niphʻal*, see below) takes the vowel which would have been required between the *second* and *third* radical of the ordinary strong form, or which stood in the ground-form, since that vowel is characteristic of the form (§ 43 *b*), e. g. תַּם answering to קָטַל, תַּמָּה to the ground-form *qăṭălăt,* תַּמּוּ to the ground-form *qăṭălû*; *infinitive,* סֹב to קְטֹל.

c 3. The insertion of *Dageš forte* (mentioned under *a*), for the purpose of strengthening the second radical, never takes place (see § 20 *l*) in the final consonant of the word, e. g. סֹב, תַּם, not סֹבּ, תַּמּ; but it appears again on the addition of afformatives or suffixes, e. g. תַּמּוּ, סַבּוּנִי, סַבּוּ, &c.

d 4. When the afformative begins with a consonant (נ, ת), and hence the strongly pronounced second radical would properly come at the end of a closed syllable, a *separating vowel* is inserted between the stem-syllable and the afformative. In the *perfect* this vowel is ◌ֹ, in the *imperative* and *imperfect* ◌ֶ, e. g. סַבּוֹת, סַבּוֹנוּ, *imperfect* תְּסֻבֶּינָה (for *sabb-tā, sabb-nû, tasōbb-nā*). The artificial opening of the syllable

---

[1] So (partly following Ewald and Böttcher) A. Müller, *ZDMG.* xxxiii. p. 698 ff. ; Stade, *Lehrbuch,* § 385 *b, c*; Nöldeke, and more recently Wellhausen, 'Ueber einige Arten schwacher Verba im Hebr.' (*Skizzen u. Vorarb.* vi. 250 ff.). Against Böttcher see M. Lambert, *REJ.* xxxv. 330 ff., and Brockelmann, as above.

by this means is merely intended to make the strengthening of the second radical audible.[1]

e The *perfect* תַּמֹּנוּ (for תַּמֹּונוּ) Nu 17²⁸, ψ 64⁷ (Jer 44¹⁸ תַּמְנוּ with *Silluq*), owing to omission of the separating vowel, approximates, if the text is right, to the form of verbs ע"וּ (cf. קָמְנוּ from קוּם).

5. Since the preformatives of the *imperfect Qal*, of the *perfect* *f* *Niph'al*, and of *Hiph'îl* and *Hoph'al* throughout, before a monosyllabic stem form an open syllable, they take a *long* vowel before the tone (according to § 27 *e*), e.g. imperfect *Hiph'îl* יָסֵב for *yă-sēb*, imperative הָסֵב for *hă-sēb*, &c. Where the preformatives in the strong verb have *ĭ*, either the original *ă* (from which the *ĭ* was attenuated) is retained and lengthened, e.g. יָסֹב in *imperfect Qal* for *yă-sōb*, or the *ĭ* itself is lengthened to *ē*, e.g. הֵסֵב *perfect Hiph'îl* for *hĭ-sēb* (see further under *h*). The vowel thus lengthened can be maintained, however, only before the tone (except the *ŭ* of the *Hoph'al*, הוּסַב for *hŭ-săb*); when the tone is thrown forward it becomes *Šewâ*, according to § 27 *k* (under א and ה compound *Šewâ*), e.g. תָּסֹב, but תְּסֻבֶּינָה; *imperfect Hiph'îl* תָּסֵב, but תְּסֻבֶּינָה; *perfect* הֲסִבֹּתִי, &c.

Besides the ordinary form of the imperfects, there is another (common in *g* Aramaic), in which the *imperfect Qal* is pronounced יִסֹּב or יִסַּב, the *first* radical, not the second, being strengthened by *Dageš forte*, cf. יִשֹּׁם 1 K 9⁸, וַיִּקֹּד Gn 24²⁶; with *a* in the second syllable, יִגַּר Lv 11⁷, יִדַּל Is 17⁴, וַיִּשַּׁח Is 2⁹, &c., יִדַּם Am 5¹³ and frequently, וְאֵבַךְ Dt 9²¹, &c., יִסֹּב (*turn intrans.*) 1 S 5⁸, &c., וַיִּקֹּב Lv 24¹¹, יִחֹּם Ez 47¹², &c., יִחַם (with *Dageš forte implicitum*) 1 K 1¹; in the plural, יִתַּמּוּ Nu 14³⁵, &c. (in pause יִתַּמּוּ ψ 102²⁸); perhaps also יִמַּל, יִמַּךְ (unless these forms are rather to be referred to *Niph'al*, like יִדְּמוּ 1 S 2⁹; יִמֹּלוּ Jb 24²⁴); with suffix תִּקְּבֶנּוּ occurs (cf. § 10 *h*) in Nu 23²⁵; *Imperfect Hiph'îl* יַחֵם, *Hoph'al* יֻבַּת, &c. The vowel of the preformative (which before *Dageš* is, of course, short) follows the analogy of the ordinary strong form (cf. also *u* and *y*). The same method is then extended to forms with afformatives or suffixes, so that even before these additions the second radical is not strengthened, e.g. וַיִּקְּדוּ Gn 43²⁸, &c., for וַיִּקְּדוּ *and they bowed the head*; וַיַּכְּתוּ *and they beat down*, Dt 1⁴⁴ (from כָּתַת); וַיִּתַּמּוּ Dt 32⁸; יִדְּמוּ Ex 15¹⁶, Jb 29²¹ (cf., however, וַיִּסֹּבּוּ Ju 18²³, 1 S 5⁸, יֹבַּתוּ Jer 46⁵, Jb 4²⁰). To the same class of apparently strong formations belongs תִּצַּלְנָה (without the separating vowel, for תִּצֹּלְיִנָה, cf. 1 S 3¹¹ and below, *p*) *they shall tingle*, 2 K 21¹², Jer 19³.—On the various forms of the *Niph'al*, see under *t*.

---

[1] Of all the explanations of these separating vowels the most satisfactory is that of Rödiger, who, both for the *perfect* and *imperfect* (Ewald and Stade, for the *imperfect* at least), points to the analogy of verbs ל"ה. We must, however, regard סַבּוֹתָ as formed on the analogy not of גָּלִיתָ, but (with P. Haupt) of a form גָּלוֹתָ (= *gālautā*, cf. Arab. *ǵazauta*), while תְּסֻבֶּינָה follows the analogy of תִּגְלֶינָה. [See also Wright, *Comp. Gr.*, 229 f.]

h   **6.** The original vowel is retained, see *f*, (*a*) in the preformative of the *imperfect Qal* יִסֹב for *yă-sōb* (cf. §§ 47 *b*, 63 *b*, and for verbs ע״יּ § 72); (*b*) in the *perfect Niph'al* נָסַב for *nă-săb* (§ 51 *a*); (*c*) in *Hoph'al* הוּסַב, with irregular lengthening (no doubt on the analogy of verbs פ״וֹ) for *hŏsăb* from *hŭ-sab*, imperfect יוּסַב from *yŭ-sab*, &c.

i   On the other hand, an already attenuated vowel (*i*) underlies the intransitive *imperfects Qal* with *ă* in the second syllable (probably for the sake of dissimilating the two vowels), e. g. יֵמַר for *yĭ-măr* (see *p*); and in the preformative of *Hiph'îl* הֵסֵב from *hĭ-sēb* (ground-form הִקְטֵל, § 53 *a*), as well as of the participle מֵסֵב (ground-form מַקְטֵל), on the analogy of the perfect. In the second syllable of the Perf. the underlying vowel is *ĭ*, attenuated from an original *ă*, which in the strong verb is abnormally lengthened to *î* (§ 53 *a*). The *ē* lengthened from *ĭ* is, of course, only tone-long, and hence when without the tone and before *Dageš forte* we have e. g. הֲסִבּוֹתָ. On the retention of the original *ă* in the second syllable, cf. *v*.

k   **7.** The *tone*, as a general rule, tends to keep to the stem-syllable, and does not (as in the strong verb) pass to the afformatives הָ—ָ, ־ and ־ְ—ִ (2nd *sing. fem. imperfect*); e. g. 3rd *sing. fem. perfect* חַתָּה, in *pause* חָתָה; with ר and gutturals מָרָה (for מַרָה, מָרֲה), שָׂחָה ψ 44²⁶; on the other hand, with *wāw consecutive* וַרַבָּה Is 6¹² (but וְחָיָה Ex 1¹⁶). In the 3rd *plur. perfect* the tone-syllable varies; along with דַּלּוּ, קַלּוּ, we also find דַּלּוּ and קַלּוּ, רַבּוּ Is 59¹², שַׂחוּ Hb 3⁶, &c.; but in *pause* always תַּמּוּ, חָתּוּ, &c. The tone likewise remains on the stem-syllable in the *imperfect Qal* in תָּסֹבּוּ, יָסֹבּוּ; *perfect Hiph'îl* הֵסֵבּוּ, הֵסֵבָּה; *imperfect* יָסֵבּוּ, תָּסֵבִּי, &c. In the forms with separating vowels, the tone is moved forward to these vowels (or to the final syllable, cf. *ee*), e. g. תְּסֻבֶּינָה, סַבּוֹתָ, &c.; except before the endings חֶם and חֶן in the *perfect*, which always bear the tone. This shifting of the tone naturally causes the shortening of the merely tone-long vowels *ē* and *ō* to *ĭ* and *ŭ* (or *ŏ*, see *n*), hence הֲסִבּוֹתֶם from הֵסֵב, תְּסֻבֶּינָה from יָסֹב; on cases in which the vowel of the preformative becomes *S͏ewâ*, see above, *f*.

l   **8.** In several verbs ע״ע, instead of *Pi'ēl*, *Pu'al* and *Hithpa'ēl*, the less frequent conjugation *Pō'ēl*, with its passive and reflexive, occurs (most probably on the analogy of the corresponding forms of verbs ע״וֹ, cf. § 72 *m*), generally with the same meaning,[1] e. g. עוֹלֵל *to ill-treat*, passive עוֹלַל, reflexive הִתְעוֹלֵל (from עָלַל; cf. the *Hithpō'ēl* from רָעַע

---

[1] Sometimes both *Pi'ēl* and *Pō'ēl* are formed from the same stem, though with a difference of meaning, e. g. רִצֵּץ *to break in pieces*, רֹצֵץ *to oppress*; חִנֵּן *to make pleasing*, חוֹנֵן *to have pity*; סִבֵּב *to turn, to change*, סוֹבֵב *to go round, to encompass*.

and פָּרַר Is 24.¹⁹ ᶠ·); in a few verbs also *Pilpēl* (§ 55 *f*) is found, e. g.
גִּלְגֵּל *to roll*, *Hithpalpēl* הִתְגַּלְגֵּל *to roll oneself* (from גָּלַל); imperative
with suffix סַלְסְלֶהָ *exalt her*, Pr 4⁸; שַׁעֲשַׁע *to comfort, to delight in*; passive
שֻׁעֲשַׁע *to be caressed* (from שָׁעַע). These forms cannot appear in a
biliteral form any more than *Pi̇ēl*, *Pu'al*, and *Hithpa'ēl*; cf. עֲוִים
(Is 19¹⁴) and קַוְקוֹ (Is 18²,⁷).—For תִּתְבָּר 2 S 22²⁷ read, according to
ψ 18²⁷, תִּתְבָּרָר.

REMARKS.

I. *On Qal.*

1. In the *perfect*, isolated examples are found with ō in the first syllable, ***m***
which it is customary to refer to triliteral stems with middle ō (like יָכֹל,
§ 43 *a*) ; viz. רֹמּוּ *they are exalted*, Jb 24²⁴ to רָמַם; רֹבּוּ *they shot*, Gn 49²³ to רָבַב;
זֹרוּ Is 1⁶ to זָרַר. But this explanation is very doubtful : זֹרוּ especially is
rather to be classed among the passives of Qal mentioned in § 52 *e*.

2. *Imperfects Qal* with ō in the second syllable keep the original *a* in the ***n***
preformative, but lengthen it to *ā*, as being in an open syllable, hence יָחֹן,
יָמֹד, יָעֹו, יָרֹן, יָרֹעַ (trans. *he breaks in pieces*, but יֵרַע *intrans.=he is evil*);
imperfects with *ă* have, in the preformative, an *ē*, lengthened from *ĭ*. See
the examples below, under *p*, § 63 *c* and *e*, § 72 *h*, and specially Barth in
ZDMG. 1894, p. 5 f.

The *Ḥōlĕm* of the *infinitive, imperative*, and *imperfect* (יָסֹב, סֹב) is only tone-
long, and therefore, as a rule, is written defectively (with a few exceptions,
chiefly in the later orthography, e. g. צוֹר *bind up*, Is 8¹⁶; גּוֹל ψ 37⁵; דּוֹם
ver. 7 ; לְבֹז for לָבוֹז *to plunder*, Est 3¹³, 8¹¹). When this ō loses the tone, it
becomes in the final syllable *ŏ*, in a sharpened syllable *ŭ*, or not infrequently
even *ŏ* (see above, *k*). Examples of *ŏ* are : (*a*) in a toneless final syllable, i. e.
before *Maqqeph* or in the *imperfect consecutive*, רָן־ (*rŏn*) *to rejoice*, Jb 38⁷; וַיָּסָב
Ju 11¹⁸ (once even with *ŭ* in a toneless final syllable, וַיָּרָם Ex 16²⁰) ; on the
other hand, in the *plur.* וַיָּסֹבּוּ, *fem.* וַתְּסֻבֶּינָה ; (*b*) before a tone-bearing
afformative or *suffix*, e. g. *imperative 2nd sing. fem.* רָנִּי, גֻּנִּי (cf. *ff*.), חָנֵּנִי *pity me* ;
סֻלּוּ Jer 50²⁶; יָשֻׁדֵם Pr 11³ *Qerê*; תְּחֻנֵּהוּ Ex 12¹⁴ (for the defective writing,
cf. יֻסַבֻּהוּ Jb 40²²). In יָחֻנְךָ Gn 43²⁹, Is 30¹⁹ (for יְחָנְךָ) this *ŏ* is thrown back
to the preformative.

On the 2nd plur. fem. imperat. עֹרָה *make yourselves naked* Is 32¹¹, cf. the ***o***
analogous forms in § 48 *i*.—Quite abnormal is the *infinitive absolute* רֹעָה Is 24¹⁹
(as ה follows, probably only a case of dittography for רֹעַ, cf. קֹב Nu 23²⁵ and
שֹׁל Ru 2¹⁶); so also are the *imperatives* קָבְה־לִּי Nu 22¹¹.¹⁷, and אָרָה־לִּי 22⁶, 23⁷,.
with ה *paragogic*. We should expect אָ֫רָה, קָ֫בָּה. If these forms are to be
read *qŏballi, 'ŏralli*, they would be analogous to such cases as מִדְבָּ֫רָה (§ 90 *i*),
the addition of the *paragogic* הָ__ causing no change in the form of the word
(קָב־ like רָן־ above). If, however, as Jewish tradition requires, they are to
be read *qābalī, 'āralli*, then in both cases the *Qameṣ* must be explained, with

Stade, as the equivalent of *ō* (לִי-קְבָה), &c.; cf. § 9 *v*). Still more surprising is קָבְנוֹ *curse him*, Nu 23[13], for קָבֵּנּוּ or קָב׳.[1]

p 3. Examples with *Pathaḥ* in the *infinitive*, *imperative*, and *imperfect* are בַּר (in לְבָרָם *to prove them*, Ec 3[18]); רַד Is 45[1]; שֵׁךְ Jer 5[26]; בְּשַׁגָּם *in their error*, Gn 6[3] (so ed. Mant., but there is also good authority for בְּשַׁגָּ, from שֵׁי · = שֵׁי = אֲשֶׁר and בַּ *also*; so Baer and Ginsburg). Also בַּל *take away*, ψ 119[22]; and the *imperfects* יֵחַם *it is hot*, Dt 19[6], &c. (on the *ē* of the preformative cf. *n*); יֵמַר *it is bitter*, Is 24[9]; יֵצַר *it is straitened*; יֵרַךְ *it is soft*, Is 7[4]; תֵּשַׁם *it is desolate*, Ez 12[19] (in pause תֵּשָׁם Gn 47[19]); וַתֵּקַל *she was despised*, Gn 16[4] (but elsewhere in the *impf. consec.* with the tone on the penultima, e. g. וַיֵּצֶר Gn 32[8], &c.; וַיֵּרַע Gn 21[11], &c., cf. Ez 19[7]); in the 1st *sing. imperfect* אִיתַם [2] ψ 19[14], abnormally written fully for אֵתַם, unless אֶתָם is to be read, as in some MSS., on the analogy of the 3rd sing. יֵתַם.—In the *impf. Qal* of שָׁלַל the reading of Hb 2[8] varies between יְשָׁלּוּךְ (Baer, Ginsb.) and יְשָׁלּוּךְ (ed. Mant., Jabl.).— The following forms are to be explained with Barth (*ZDMG*. xliii. p. 178) as imperfects Qal with original *ĭ* in the second syllable, there being no instances of their Hiph'il in the same sense: וַיִּגַּל Gn 29[10]; יָגֵן Is 31[5], &c.; וַיָּסֶךְ Ex 4c[21], ψ 91[4], &c.; perhaps also תִּצְלֶינָה 1 S 3[11] and יָהֵל Jb 31[26], &c.; in accordance with this last form, (בְּ)הָלוֹ Jb 29[3] would also be an *infinitive Qal*, not Hiph'il (for בְּהַהְלוֹ), as formerly explained below, under *w*. Finally the very peculiar form וַתָּרֵץ Ju 9[53] may probably be added to the list.

q Imperfects, with an original *u* in the second syllable, are also found with this *ŭ* lengthened to *û* (instead of *ō*), e. g. יָרוּן, if the text is correct, in Pr 29[6]; יָשׂוּגֵּד ψ 91[6] (unless it be simply an imperfect from שׂוּג *to be powerful, to prevail*); יָרוּץ (if from רצץ) Is 42[4], &c. (also defectively אָרֻץ ψ 18[30]; but in Ec 12[6], according to Baer, יָרֻץ); תֻּתַּם Ez 24[11] (on the sharpening of the תּ cf. *g* above).[3]

r A similar analogy with verbs ע״ו is seen in the infinitives לָבוּר (for בֹּר) Ec 9[1]; בְּחֻקוֹ Pr 8[27] (cf. בְּחוּקוֹ Pr 8[29]) for בְּחֻקּוֹ, and in the *imperfect* אֲמֹשְׁךָ Gn 27[21]. (The forms חַנּוֹת in ψ 77[10], שְׁמוֹת Ez 36[3], חַלּוֹתִי ψ 77[11], formerly treated here as infinitives from ע״ע stems, are rather to be referred to ל״ה stems, with Barth, *Wurzeluntersuchungen*, Lpz. 1902, p. 21.) On other similar cases, see below, under *ee*. For examples of the *aramaïzing imperfect*, see above, *g*.

s 4. In the *participle*, the aramaïzing form שָׁאֲסַיִךְ for שֹׁסַיִךְ occurs in Kᵉthibh, Jer 30[16] (the *Qᵉrĕ* indicates a *participle* from שָׁסָה); רֹעָה Pr 25[19] appears to be a contraction from רְעֹעָה, *part. fem.* = *breaking in pieces*.

---

[1] For נוֹ as suffix of the 3rd person a parallel might be found in יְשֵׁנוֹ, § 100 *o*, and probably also in the *Nûn* of the Phoenician suffix נם: cf. Barth, *ZDMG*. xli. p. 643, and the note on § 100 *o*.

[2] Also in Ez 6[6], instead of תֶּאְשַׁמְנָה, which could only come from יֵשׁם, יֵשׁ is intended, and יֵאְשְׁמוּ in the same verse is probably only an error for יֵשְׁמוּ.

[3] According to Stade, *Grammatik*, § 95, Rem., the pronunciation with *û*, since it also appears in Neo-Punic [and in Western Syriac, see Nöldeke, *Syr. Gramm.*, § 48], was that of everyday life.

II. On Niph'al.

5. Besides the ordinary form of the *perfect* נָסַב with *Pathaḥ* (in *pause* **t** נָסָב) and the *participle* נָסָב with *Qameṣ* in the second syllable, there is also another with *Ṣere*, and a third with *Ḥolem*, e.g. *perfect* נָמֵס *it melts*, Ez 21¹², 22¹⁵; נָסַבָּה (for נָסַבָּה) Ez 26²; *part.* נָמֵס *molten*, 1 S 15⁹, Na 2¹¹; נָקֵל *it is a light thing*, 2 K 20¹⁰, Is 49⁶ (*perf.* נָקֹל); with *ō*, e.g. נָגֹלּוּ *they are rolled together*, Is 34⁴; cf. 63¹⁹, 64², Am 3¹¹, Na 1¹², Ec 12⁶ᵇ. In the *imperfect* with *ō* in the second syllable, on the analogy of verbs ע"וּ (from which König would also explain the *perfects* with *ō*), we find תִּדֹּמִּי *thou shalt be brought to silence*, Jer 48² (unless this form should be referred to Qal with Qimḥi, Olshausen, König); יֵרֹעַ *he suffers hurt*, Pr 11¹⁵, 13²⁰; תָּרֹץ (for *tirrōṣ*) Ez 29⁷; with *ē* in the second syllable תֵּחֵל *she profanes herself*, Lv 21⁹, but וָאֵחַל Ez 22²⁶, and יֵחַל Is 48¹¹, תֵּחַת Is 7⁸, &c. For infinitives, cf. הִמֵּס *to melt*, ψ 68³ (as *inf. constr.*; 2 S 17¹⁰ as *inf. absol.*); again, with compensatory lengthening in the first syllable, הֵחֵל Ez 20⁹, 14²², but with suffix הֵחַלּוֹ Lv 21⁴; also הִבּוֹז *to be plundered*, and הִבּוֹק *to be emptied*, Is 24³; in the *imperative*, only הִבָּרוּ *be ye clean*, Is 52¹¹. On הֵרֹמּוּ *get you up*, Nu 17¹⁰, and the corresponding *imperf.* יֵרֹמּוּ Ez 10¹⁷, &c., cf. 72 *dd*.

Examples of the *perfect* Niph'al with sharpening of the initial syllable are, **u** נִחַל *it is profaned*, Ez 22¹⁶, 25³ (from חָלַל); נִחַר (from חָרַר) ψ 69⁴, 102⁴ (also נָחַר Jer 6²⁹); נִחַת *fractus est* (from חָתַת) Mal 2⁵; cf. with this in the *participle*, נְחָמִים (for *niḥḥāmim*) Is 57⁵, and נֵאָרִים Mal 3⁹: in the *imperative* and *infinitive* Niph'al such a virtual strengthening of the guttural after preformatives never occurs.—The occurrence of *u* instead of *ô* as a separating vowel in the *perfect* נָשַׁדֻּנוּ Mic 2⁴ is abnormal.

III. On Hiph'îl and Hoph'al.

6. The second syllable in *Hiph'îl* sometimes has *Pathaḥ* instead of *Ṣere*, **ⱱ** especially under the influence of ר and the gutturals, e.g. *perfect* הֵמַר *he made bitter*, הֵשַׁח *he bowed*, הֵפַר *he hath broken*, Gn 17¹⁴, in *pause*, cf. § 29 *q*; otherwise הֵפֵר, *plur.* הֵפֵרוּ Is 24⁵. In הֵפִיר ψ 33¹⁰, Ez 17¹⁹, cf. ψ 89³⁴, and in הֵשִׁירוּ Ho 8⁴ (perhaps also in יִחְיַן Hab 2¹⁷, but cf. § 20 *n*) there is an assimilation to the corresponding forms of verbs ע"וּ, see *z*. Also הֵצַר Dt 28⁵², הֵתַן (in pause) Is 18⁵; *inf.* לְהָבַר *to cleanse*, Jer 4¹¹, in *pause*. But also with other consonants, e.g. הֵרַק 2 K 23¹⁵, הֵקַל Is 8²³; הֵרַךְ Jb 23¹⁶; *plur.* הֵסַבּוּ 1 S 5⁹·¹⁰ (and so usually in the 3rd *plur. perf*, except before ר and gutturals, e.g. הֵרֵעוּ); *imper.* הֵשַׁע *besmear*, Is 6¹⁰; *plur.* הָשַׁמּוּ *be astonished*, Jb 21⁵; *imperfect* תָּרַע *Thou dost afflict*; *part.* מֵצַל (on *ē* in the first syllable, see under *i*) *shadowing*, Ez 31³ (but מֵסִיךְ Ju 3²⁴ is assimilated to the form of verbs ע"וּ, unless, with Moore, we simply read מֵסֵךְ, or, with incorrect spelling, מֵסִיךְ. So in the *imperative* הֲמִישֵׁנִי Ju 16²⁶ *Qᵉrê*, and in the *infinitive* הַתְמֵךְ Is 33¹).

The *ē* of the second syllable, when without the tone, may become *ĕ*, e.g. **ⱳ** הֵחֵל בִּי Gn 31⁷ (see also *x*). It is unusual (cf. § 53 *k*) to find the *ē* written fully as in the *infinitive* לְהָפִיר Zc 11¹⁰. Instead of *Ḥaṭeph-Pathaḥ* ᵃ *Ḥaṭeph-*

Sᵉghôl is found under the preformative in הִקְלֹתַנִי 2 S 19⁴⁴, and a *Pathaḥ* occurs before ח (with a virtual sharpening of the ח) in such forms as הַחִתַּת Is 9³; cf. Gn 11⁶, Dt 2³¹, 3²⁴, 1 S 22¹⁵, Est 6¹³—in all these cases before ח.—On בְּהִלוֹ Jb 29³, see above, *p*: on וְהַחִתַּתִי Jer 49³⁷, see below, *dd*.

x 7. In the *imperfect consecutive* of verbs whose second radical is a guttural, *ă* is retained (§ 22 *d*) in the second syllable instead of *ĕ*, e. g. וַיֵּרַע 1 K 16²⁵: so also with ר, as וַיֵּצַר 2 Ch 28²⁰, Dt 2⁹—but cf. also וַיֵּפֶר Neh 4⁹.

y 8. Aramaïzing forms (but cf. Rem. to § 67 *g*) in *Hiph'il* and *Hoph'al* are, וַיֵּסַב Ex 13¹⁸, &c.; cf. Ju. 18²³; אַל־תָּמֵר Ex 23²¹, but read אַל־תֶּמֶר from מָרָה: וַיַּבְתִּי Dt 1⁴⁴ (cf. Nu 14⁴⁵), but וַיֻּכַּבּוּ Ju 18²³, 1 S 5⁸, 2 Ch 29⁶; אָחֵל *profanabo*, Ez 39⁷; תֻּתַּם Jb 22³; without elision of the ה (cf. § 53 *q*), וַיֵּהֶתֵּל 1 K 18²⁷, but Jer 9⁴ יְהָתֵלּוּ, Jb 13⁹ תְּהָתֵלּוּ; with *î* in the second syllable יָשִׁים Jer 49²⁰, 50⁴⁵; cf. וַשִּׁים Nu 21³⁰; in the *perfect* הֵילִילוּ La 1⁸. In *Hoph'al*, הוּמַכּוּ *they are brought low*, Jb 24²¹; יֻכַּת *he is smitten*, Is 24¹² (*plur.* יֻכַּתּוּ Jer 46⁵, Mi 1⁷); in *pause*, יֻחָקּוּ Jb 19²³, but also יֻכַּתּוּ Jb 4²⁰ (so Baer, Ginsb., but ed. Mant., Jabl. יֻכַּתּוּ); with *ŏ* in the initial syllable, הַשַּׁמָּה (*infinitive* with *suffix* = הָשַׁמָּה, cf. § 91 *e*) Lv 26³⁴ f., cf. 2 Ch 36²¹; בְּהָשַׁמָּה, with irregular syncope for בְּהִשַּׁ׳, Lv 26⁴³.

IV. *In General.*

z 9. Verbs ע״ע are most closely related as regards inflexion to verbs ע״וֹ (§ 72). The form of verbs ע״ע is generally the shorter (cf. e. g. יָסֹב and הֵסֵב, and הָקִים, יָקוּם); in a few cases, however, the two classes exactly coincide, e. g. in the *imperfect Qal* and *Hiph'il* with *wāw consecutive*, in *Hoph'al* and in the less common conjugations (see above, *l*).

aa 10. The developed forms (with three radicals), as mentioned in *a*, are especially frequent in the 3rd *sing. masc.* and *fem.*, and the 3rd *plur. perf. Qal* (i. e. in forms without an affirmative or with an affirmative beginning with a vowel) of transitive verbs, or verbs, at any rate, expressing action, e. g. סָבַב, סָבְבוּ (but before a suffix also סַבּוּנִי, as well as סְבָבוּנִי, שַׁדּוּנִי, &c.); אָפַפוּ, זָמֲמָה, זָמָם, &c. Sometimes the contracted, *as well as* the uncontracted form, is found, e. g. בַּז *to plunder*, plur. בָּזְזוּ; in other parts, only בַּזּוֹנוּ Dt 2³⁵, as well as בַּגּוֹנוּ Dt 3⁷; זַמֹּתִי Zc 8¹⁴·¹⁵ and זַמֹּתִי Jer 4²⁸. Other examples of biliteral forms in 2nd *sing. masc.* are Dt 25¹², Pr 30³²; in 1st *sing.*, Jos 5⁹. Apart from Qal the only example of a developed form is וְהַחִתַּתִי Jer 49³⁷.

bb On the other hand, the biliteral forms are the more common in the 3rd *sing.* and *plur.* of perfects which are *intransitive*, and express a state; cf. דַּק Dt 9²¹ (Ex 32²⁰ דָּק; elsewhere always a transitive verb); חַת, *fem.* חַתָּה; מַר, *fem.* מָרָה (for *marrā*); צַר, *fem.* צָרָה (cf. וְחָרָה Ez 24¹¹); שַׁח, *fem.* רַךְ, שַׁחָה, תַּם, &c.; *plur.* חַתּוּ, תַּמּוּ, &c. (but on the tone, cf. *ee* below). Exception, עָשָׁשָׁה ψ 6⁸.

cc The intransitive but developed perfects הָלַל (also דַּלּוּ, דַּלּוּ), חָלַל, נָדְדָה, נָדְדוּ (in *pause* נָדָדוּ), סָרַר, עָשְׁשָׁה (*plur.* in *pause* עָשֵׁשׁוּ ψ 31¹¹), שָׁחֲחוּ, צָלֲלוּ (also שַׁחוּ), almost all have, as Mayer Lambert observes, at least an active, not a stative meaning. Triliteral forms of the *infinitive* after לְ are לִסְבֹּב Nu 21⁴; לִשְׁדוֹד Jer 47⁴; לָנֹז Gn 31¹⁹ (also לָגֹז Gn 38¹³); cf. also לָחֹם Is 47¹⁴, in *subordinate pause*, for לַחֹם; with *suffix* חַנְנְכֶם Is 30¹⁸, and, from the same

form חַן, with retraction and modification of the vowel, לַחֲנֻנָה ψ 102¹⁴; also
שָׁחוֹחַ Is 60¹⁴, בִּגְזָן 1 S 25², כְּמַסֹם Is 10¹⁸, בְּעֻזּוֹ Pr 8²⁸, בִּצְרוֹר Pr 26⁸.—*Imperative*
שָׁדְדוּ Jer 49²⁸ (cf. § 20 b, and ibid. also on חָנְנֵנִי ψ 9¹⁴); in the *imperfect*,
יָדוֹד Na 3⁷ (ψ 68¹³; cf. Gn 31⁴⁰) from נדד; the strong form here, after the
assimilation of the *Nûn*, was unavoidable. On the other hand, יְשָׁדְּדֵם Jer 5⁶ is
anomalous for יָשֹׁדֵם (Pr 11³ Q^erê; the eastern school read the Pô'ēl ישׁודרם
in the K^ethibh); the strengthening of the second radical has been afterwards
resolved by the insertion of a *vocal Š^ewâ*. Cf. also יֶחֱמָן Am 5¹⁵ (elsewhere
יָחֹן). In *Niph'al*, the triliteral form יֻלְבַּב is found, Jb 11¹²; in *Hiph'il*, all
the forms of רנן, thus *imperative* הַרְנִינוּ, *imperfect* תַּרְנִין; *infinitive* הַשְׁמֵם
Mi 6¹³; *participle* מַשְׁמִים Ez 3¹⁵. That the developed (triliteral) forms
possess a certain emphasis is seen from their frequent use in *pause*, as in
ψ 118¹¹ after a biliteral form (סַבּוּנִי נַם־סְבָבוּנִי).

dd　11. The above-mentioned (see g) neglect of the strengthening in aramaïzing
forms, such as יִדְּמוּ and the like, occurs elsewhere tolerably often; in the
perfect Qal תַּמֹּנוּ for תַּמֹּונוּ Nu 17²⁸ (Jer 44¹⁸; cf. above, e); *imperfect* נָבֹלָה
1 S 14³⁶ (ה֫ pa parag. without any influence on the form, cf. o); even with
the firm vowel reduced to *vocal Š^ewâ*; נִבְלָה Gn 11⁷ for נָבְלָה (cohortative
from בְּלַל); יָזְמוּ for יָזֹמּוּ ibid. ver. 6, *they purpose*; following the analogy of
verbs ע״וּ, אָמֻשְׁךָ (see above, r); from *intransitive imperfects Qal*, תֵּצְרִי Is 49¹⁹
(*plur. masc.* Jb 18⁷); יֵרְעוּ Neh 2³; also תְּשִׁימְּנָה Ez 6⁶ (for which read
תָּשֹׁם=תָּשֵׂם) might be explained in the same way.—*Perfect Niph'al* נָסֵבָּה
for נָסַבָּה Ez 41⁷; נָזֹלּוּ Ju 5⁵ for נָזֹלּוּ; נְמַלְתֶּם for נְמֹלְתֶם Gn 17¹¹ (as if from
מָלַל not מוּל to circumcise), cf. Is 19³, Jer 8¹⁴; *imperfect* תִּפָּקַֽדְנָה Zc 14¹²;
participle נְחֻמִים, cf. u. So also נָפֵץ 1 S 13¹¹, נִפֹּצָה Gn 9¹⁹ (cf. Is 33³), are
perfects *Niph'al* from פצץ (= פּוּץ), not *Qal* from נָפֵץ.—In *Hiph'il* הֵֽחֵלֹתָ (for
הֵחִלֹּתָ) Ju 16¹⁰ (2 S 15³⁴); הֶעֱוָה for הֶעֱוָה Pr 7¹³ (cf. Ct 6¹¹, 7¹³).

No less irregular is the suppression of the vowel of the stem-syllable in
לְהַפְרְכֶם Lv 26¹⁵.—On the perfect דַּלְיוּ Pr 26⁷, cf. § 75 u.

12. Cases in which the tone is thrown forward on the afformatives (see *cc*
k) are (a) in the *perfect*, the 1st sing. regularly (but cf. וַהֲצָרֹתִי Jer 10¹⁸ before
לָהֶם) after ו consec., Ex 33¹⁹·²², 2 K 19³⁴, &c., also Is 44¹⁶ (חַמּוֹתִי before ר);
ψ 92¹¹ (but the text is certainly corrupt; see the Lexicon), 116⁶, perhaps also
Jb 19¹⁷, וְחַנֹּתִי (though in this passage, and in ψ 17³, the form might be an
infinitive in *ôth*; see Delitzsch on Jb 19¹⁷); in the 2nd *sing*. וְקַצֹּתָה (before
א) Dt 25¹²; in the 3rd *plural* רַבּוּ *multi sunt*, ψ 3², 104²⁴, Jer 5⁶, 1 S 25¹⁰; רַבּוּ
they are soft, ψ 55²²; קַלּוּ *they are swift*, Jer 4¹³, Hb 1⁸; זַכּוּ *they are pure*, Jb 15¹⁵,
25⁵, La 4⁷; שַׁחּוּ *they did bow*, Hb 3⁶; חָרּוּ *they are burned*, Is 24⁶. A by-form of
שַׁתּוּ (ע״וּ, cf. § 72 dd) is שָׁתּוּ ψ 49¹⁵, 73⁹.

ff　(b) In the *imperative* (a command in an emphatic tone) רָנִּי *sing*, Is 54¹,
Zp 3¹⁴, Zc 2¹⁴; רָנּוּ Is 44²³, 49¹³, Jer 31⁷ (but רֹנִּי *lament*, La 2¹⁹), חָגִּי *keep* (*thy*
feasts), Na 2¹, Jer 7²⁹; עֻזִּה (=עֻזָּה) before א, ψ 68²⁹. On the retention of the
short vowels ŭ (ŏ) and ĭ before *Dageš forte*, in place of the tone-long ō and ē,
see above, k; on the change of the vowel of the preformative into *Š^ewâ*,
when it no longer stands before the tone, see g.

THE WEAKEST VERBS (*Verba Quiescentia*).

§ 68. *Verbs* פ״א e. g. אָכַל *to eat.*

Brockelmann, *Semit. Sprachwiss.*, p. 140 ff. ; *Grundriss*, p. 589 ff.

a So far as א retains its full consonantal value as a guttural, these verbs share all the peculiarities of verbs *primae gutturalis*, mentioned in § 63. They are, however, to be treated as *weak* verbs, when the א loses its value as a consonant, and coalesces with the preceding vowel (originally short) to form one long syllable. This takes place only in the following very common verbs and forms, as if through phonetic decay :—

b 1. In the *imperfect Qal*, five verbs (viz. אָבַד *to perish,* אָבָה *to be willing,* אָכַל *to eat,* אָמַר *to say,* אָפָה *to bake*) regularly make the א quiesce in a long ô, e. g. יֹאכַל.[1] In a few others the ordinary (strong) form is also in use, as יֶאֱחֹז (18 times) and יַאֲחֹז (3 times) *he takes hold;* יֶסֹף (see *h*), also יֶאֱסֹף, *he collects.* This ô has primarily arisen from an obscuring of *â* (§ 9 *q*), and the *â* from אַ—, the weak consonant א coalescing with *ă* to *â* ; cf. § 23 *a*.

c In the second syllable ō (for original *ŭ*) never appears, but either *ē* [2] or *ă* ; and in *pause* almost always *ē*, even before the tone-bearing *heavy* afformative וּן, e. g. יֹאכְלוּן Dt 18¹, without the pause יֹאכְלוּן Dt 4²⁸. In the 3rd *sing. masc.* and 1st *sing.* of אָמַר, however, *ă* is always retained in pause, יֹאמֵר and אֹמַר ; but in the 2nd *masc.* תֹּאמַר 1 K 5²⁰, in the 3rd *fem.* תֹּאמַר Pr 1²¹ ; in the *plural* יֹאמְרוּ Jer 5², ψ 145⁶·¹¹, תֹּאמַרְוּ Jer 23³⁸, with *S°golta* ; cf. also תֹּאכַל 1 S 1⁷, &c. But with conjunctive accents in the body of the sentence, *ă* (as being a lighter vowel) is used, e. g. תֹּאבַד לָעַד ψ 9¹⁹, but in *pause* תֹּאבֵד ψ 1⁶ ; cf. a similar interchange of *ē* and *ă* in § 65 *c*. The 3rd *fem. plur. impf.* always has the form תֹּאבַלְנָה Zc 11⁹.

d When the tone moves back, the final syllable of the *imperfects* of אָבַד and אָכַל, with a conjunctive accent, also always takes *Pathah,* e. g. יֹאבַד יוֹם Jb 3³, וַיֹּאכַל *and he did eat;* in אָמַר the loss of the tone from the final syllable only occurs in the form with *wāw consecutive*

---

[1] So in the modern vulgar Arabic of South Palestine, *ya'kul* (*he eats*) becomes *yôkul.*

[2] On this *ē* (originally *ĭ*) as a dissimilation from ō (originally *ŭ*), cf. § 27 *w*, and F. Philippi, in the *Zeitschrift für Völkerpsychologie und Sprachwissenschaft*, xiv. 178. The latter rightly observes that the existence of an original *u* in the *imperfect* of אָכַל is indicated by the form of the *imperative* אֱכֹל, the Arabic *ya'kul* and the Aramaic יֵאכַל, as well as by the fact that יֶאֱחֹז and יֶאֱסֹף are found along with יַאֲחֹז and יַאֲסֹף.

(but never in the 1st *sing.* וָאֹמַר ; cf. וַיֹּאכַל), and then the final syllable, if without the *pause*, always takes *Seghôl*, וַיֹּאמֶר *and he said* (except וַתֹּאמֶר לוֹ Pr 7¹³).

In *pause*, however, the *imperfect consecutive* (except the 1st pers. of *c* אָכַל, see below) always has the form וַיֹּאכַל (but *plur.* always יֹאכֵלוּ, וַיֹּאמַר(וַיֹּאכֵלוּ); except וַיֹּאמַר in the poetic portion of the book of Job, as 3², 4¹, &c., but not in 32⁶, in the middle of the verse. The weak *imperfect* of אָחַז is always יֹאחֵז and וַיֹּאחֶז, but in the 1st *sing.*, according to § 49 *e*, וָאֹחֵז Ju 20⁶; cf. וָאֹכַל Gn. 3¹²·¹³ in *pause*.—אָבָה and אָפָה are, at the same time, verbs ל"ה, hence *imperfect* יֹאבֶה (§ 75 *c*).

Before *light* suffixes the vowel of the second syllable becomes vocal *Šewâ*, as *f* יֹאכְלֵם, תֹּאכְלֵנוּ, but תֹּאכֲלֵם.—In a few cases, instead of the ô in the first syllable an *ê* is found, which is due to contraction from the group ‾ָ֫‾ (or ‾‾‾) in place of ‾‾‾ ; e.g. תֵּאתֶה *it shall come*, Mi 4⁸, from תֶּאֱתֶה (from אָתָה); אֵהַב (for אֶאֱהַב) *I love*, Pr 8¹⁷, also (four times) אֵהַב Mal 1², &c., with suffixes אֵהָבֵהוּ Ho 11¹, 14⁵, &c. (but only in 1st *sing.*, otherwise יֶאֱהַב , &c., from אֶאֱהַב, אָהַב); וָאֵשֵׁר *and I stayed*, Gn 32⁵. The *infinitive construct* of אָמַר with ל is always לֵאמֹר *dicendo*, for לֶאֱמֹר.—According to Barth (*ZDMG.* 1889, p. 179) וַיֵּאָצֶל Nu 11²⁵ is to be regarded as an *imperfect Qal*, without the obscuring of אֶ‾ to ô, not as *imperfect Hiph'il*, since אצל elsewhere occurs only in the *perfect Qal* and *Niph'al*; on the original *i* in the second syllable, see above, § 67 *p*. For תֵּאָכְלֵהוּ Jb 20²⁶ we should simply emend תֹּאכֵל/; the view that it is *imperfect Pô'el* (which nowhere else occurs) can, as regards the change of ô to ŏ, be supported only by the very doubtful analogies of ψ 62⁴ (see § 52 *q*) and ψ 101⁵ *Qerê* (see § 55 *b*), while the view that it is *Pi'ēl* (תֵּאַבֵּ/=תֵּאַבֵּ=תֵּאַבְּ/) rests on no analogy whatever. It would be more admissible to suppose that תֵּאַבֵּ/ stands for תֵּאַבְּ/, *Pu'al* (cf. אֻכְּלָה for אֻכְּלֶךָ, § 27 *q*); but no reason has been discovered for this departure from the natural punctuation תֵּאַבֵּ/.

2. In the 1st *pers. sing. imperfect*, where two א's would ordinarily *g* come together, the second (which is radical) is regularly dropped (§ 23 *f*), as אֹמַר ¹ (for אֶאֱמֹר), &c., and even *plene* וָאוֹמַר Neh 2⁷, &c., אֹמְרָה ψ 42¹⁰. In the other cases, also, where the א is ordinarily regarded as *quiescing* in ô or ê, it is only retained orthographically, and on etymological grounds. Hence the possibility of its being dropped in the following cases:—

Always in the contracted forms of אָסַף, as תֹּסֵף for תֶּאֱסֹף ψ 104²⁹; וַיֹּסֶף *h* 2 S 6¹ (but for יָאֱסֹף Jb 27¹⁹ read יֹסֵף=יֶאֱסֹף with the LXX); cf. also in

---

¹ The regularity of this orthography indicates that the contraction of אֶא to *â* in this 1st pers. occurred at a time when in the 3rd and 2nd persons the א was still audible as a consonant (which accordingly was almost always retained in writing). Nöldeke (*ZDMG.* xxxii. 593) infers this from the fact that also in Arabic the 3rd and 2nd persons are still written *yā'kŭlŭ, tā'kŭlŭ*, but the 1st pers. *'ákŭlŭ*, not *'ā'kŭlŭ*.

the 1st *pers.* Mi 4⁶ and אֶסְפֵּךְ 1 S 15⁶, which is apparently (from the *Metheg* with the *i*), intended for an imperfect *Hiph'îl*: instead of it, however, read, with the Mantua edition, אֹסְפֵּךְ (with *i*, according to § 60 *f*). But תֵּאָסְפוּן Ex 5⁷ (for 'תֹוֹ), וַיֵּאָסֶף 1 S 18²⁹ (for 'וַיּוֹ), and יֵאָסֵף Jb 27¹⁹ (see above) are due to a mistake, since all three forms must be derived from the stem יָסַף.

Furthermore, יְמָרוּךְ ψ 139²⁰ (where certainly 'יָמָר is to be read) ; תָּבֹא Pr 1¹⁰ (cf. § 75 *hh*) ; וַתֹּפֵהוּ 1 S 28²⁴ ; יֹוכְלוּ Ez 42⁵ ; תֹּמְרוּ 2 S 19¹⁴ ; וַתֹּחֶז 2 S 20⁹ ; תֵּזְלִי *thou gaddest about* (from אָזַל), Jer 2³⁶ ; וַיֵּתֵא Dt 33²¹ (for יֶאֱתָה), according to other readings (on the analogy of the cases mentioned in § 75 *p*) וַיֵּתֵא, וַיֵּתֵא or וַיֵּת.

Paradigm I shows the weak forms of the imperfect *Qal*, and merely indicates the other conjugations, which are regular.

i   Rem. 1. In the derived conjugations only isolated weak forms occur : *Perfect Niphal* נֹאחֲזוּ Nu 32³⁰, Jos 22⁹ ; *Hiph.* וַיָּאצֶל Nu 11²⁵ (but the statement in verse 17 is וְאָצַלְתִּי, therefore Qal) ; equally doubtful is the punctuation of וָיֶּרֶב (for וָיֶּאֱרֹב ?) *and he laid wait*, 1 S 15⁵, and אָזֵין *I listen*, Jb 32¹¹ (on the analogy of verbs ע״ו) ; cf. also אֹוכִיל (ô from â) *I give to eat*, Hos 11⁴ ; אֹבִידָה (ô from â) *I will destroy*, Jer 46⁸ ; וַיֹּחֶר 2 S 20⁵ *Qᵉrê* (for 'וַיֵּאח) ; the *Kᵉthibh* appears to require the *Piʻēl* וַיְיַחֵר, from יחר as a secondary form of אחר ; but וַיְיַחֵר = וַיֵּאָחֵר for וַיְאַחֵר as imperfect Qal is not impossible. On וָאֹצְרָה וַיֵּאחַר Neh 13¹³, cf. § 53 *n.*—*Infinitive* לְהָכִיל Ez 21³³ (= לְהַאֲכִ׳) unless it is rather *infin. Hiph.* from כּוּל) ; *Participle* מֵזִין *giveth ear*, Pr 17⁴ (clearly by false analogy of verbs ע״ו, for מַאֲזִין) ; *Imperative* הֵתָיוּ *bring* (from אָתָה) Jer 12⁹. (On the same form used for the *perfect* in Is 21¹⁴, cf. § 76 *d*.)

k   2. In the *Piʻēl* the א is sometimes elided (like ה in יַהְקְטִיל, יַקְטִיל), thus מַלֵּף (as in Aramaic and Samaritan) *teaching*, for מְאַלֵּף Jb 35¹¹ ; יַהֵל (if not a mere scribal error) for יַאְהֵל Is 13²⁰, וַתְּזְרֵנִי *thou hast girded me*, 2 S 22⁴⁰, for וַתְּאַזְּרֵנִי, as ψ 18⁴⁰ ; וָאַבֶּדְךָ Ez 28¹⁶ ; cf. § 23 *v*.

§ 69. Verbs פ״י. First Class, or Verbs originally פ״ו, e.g. יָשַׁב *to dwell*.

Brockelmann, *Semit. Sprachwiss.*, p. 141 f. ; *Grundriss*, p. 596 ff.

a   Verbs which at present begin with Yôdh when without preformatives are divided into two classes according to their origin and consequent inflexion : (*a*) Verbs which (as still in Arabic and Ethiopic) originally began with *Wāw*, e.g. יָלַד *to give birth to*, Arab. and Eth. *wălădă*. In consequence of a phonetic change which prevails also with few exceptions in the noun, this *Wāw* in Hebrew and Aramaic always becomes a *Yôdh*, at least when it is the initial consonant ; but after preformatives it either reappears, or is again changed into

Yôdh, or, lastly, is altogether elided; (*b*) Verbs which (as in Arabic) originally began with *Yôdh* (called *Verba cum Iod originario*, see § 70). A few verbs again (some with original *Yôdh*, and some with original *Wāw*) form a special class, which in certain forms assimilates the *Wāw* or *Yôdh* to the following consonant on the analogy of the *Nûn* in verbs נ"פ (see § 71).

With regard to verbs ו"פ (i. e. י"פ with original *Wāw*) it is to be *b* noticed that—

1. In the *imperfect, imperative* and *infinitive construct Qal* there is a twofold inflexion, according as the *Wāw* is wholly rejected or only changed into *Yôdh*. The complete rejection (or *elision*) takes place regularly in eight verbs (see *h*) in the following manner:

A. *Imperfect* יֵשֵׁב, יֵרַע with an unchangeable [1] *Ṣere* in the first syllable and original *ĭ* in the second, which in the tone-syllable (according to § 27 c) becomes *ē* (thus יֵלֵד, יֵצֵא, יֵרֵד; יֵלֵךְ, see *x*), or, under the influence of a guttural, with *ă* in the second (יֵרַע, יֵקַע, יֵחַד).

The tone-long *ē* of the second syllable is of course liable to be shortened or to become *S̆ewâ*, e. g. וַיֵּשֶׁב, יֵ֫שְׁבוּ, &c.; in the same way *ă* becomes *S̆ewâ* in such cases as יֵדְעוּ, &c., but is lengthened to *Qameṣ* in *pause* (יֵדָ֫עוּ) and before suffixes (יֵדָעֵם).

B. *Imperative* שֵׁב with *aphaeresis* of the *Wāw* and with tone-long *ē*, from *ĭ*, as in the *imperfect*.

C. *Infinitive* שֶׁבֶת from original *šibh*, by addition of the feminine ending (ת) lengthened to a *segholate* form; as in verbs נ"פ (cf. § 66 b) this lengthening affords a certain compensation for loss of the initial consonant.

Rem. Since the infinitives דֵּעָה, לָדָה (see below, *m*) point to a ground- *c* form *di'at, lidat*, we must, with Philippi (*ZDMG.* xxxii. 42) and Barth (ibid. xli. 606), assign to שֶׁבֶת, &c., the ground-form *šibt* (which, therefore, reappears in שִׁבְתִּי, &c.); the apparent ground-form *šabt* rests upon the law that the *ĭ* of the stem-syllable is changed into *a* whenever the syllable becomes doubly closed by the addition of the vowelless feminine ending.

---

[1] The *e* of the first syllable is really *ê*, not tone-long *ē*, since it is retained not merely before the tone, and in the counter-tone (e. g. וַיֵּדְעָם Ho 14[10]), but also in אֵדָעֲךָ Ex 33[13.17]. It is no objection to this view that the *scriptio plena* of this *ê* occurs (with the exception of יֵיקַר ψ 72[14], elsewhere pointed יֵיקַר) only in Mi 1[8] and Ez 35[9] *K͏eth.*; in ψ 138[6] the Masora prefers to point יֵדָע.—Of the various explanations of the *ê* the most satisfactory is that of Philippi (*ZDMG.* xl. p. 653) that an original *yălĭd*, for example (see above), became *yilid* by assimilation of the vowel of the first syllable to that of the second; this then became *yêlĕd* instead of *yelĕd*, in an attempt to raise the word again in this way (by writing *ê* instead of *ĕ*) to a triliteral form.

d In more than half the number of verbs פ״ו the original *Wāw* in the above-mentioned forms gives place to *Yôdh*, which, unless it suffers aphaeresis (see *f*), appears:—

in the *imperatives* יְצֹק, יְרַשׁ and *infinitives* יְרֹא, יְסֹד, as a strong consonant, but

in the *imperfect* יִירַשׁ, properly *yiyrăš*, merges with the preceding *ĭ* into *î*.

In the second syllable *imperfects* of this form regularly have *ă*.

e (a) That the latter forms are derived from verbs with an original *Wāw* (not *Yôdh*) is shown partly by the inflexion of these verbs in *Niph'al*, *Hiph'il*, and *Hoph'al* (where the original *Wāw* reappears throughout), and partly by the Arabic, in which verbs פ״ו likewise exhibit a twofold formation ; cf. *wălădă*, imperf. *yălĭdu*, with elision of the *Wāw*, and *wăǧĭlă*, *yauǧalu*, with retention of the *Wāw*.

f (b) Sometimes both forms, the weaker and the stronger, occur in the same verb ; cf. צָק 2 K 4⁴¹ and יָצַק *pour*, Ez 24³ (cf. יִצֹּק 1 K 18³⁴ and the *infin.* צֶקֶת Ex 38²⁷) ; רַשׁ *take possession*, Dt 1²¹, 1 K 21¹⁵ (but cf. *s*), רֵשׁ (in *pause* for רַשׁ) Dt 2²⁴·³¹ ; *plur.* רְשׁוּ Dt 1⁸, 9²³, but also, with ה_ *paragogic*, יְרָשָׁה Dt 33²³. In the *imperfect* יִיקַד Dt 32²² and יַקַד Is 10¹⁶ *it shall be kindled* ; וַיִּיקַר *it was precious*, 1 S 18³⁰ and יַקַר ψ 49⁹ (cf. יִיקַר ψ 72¹⁴).—The form וַיֵּחַמוּ Gn 30³⁹, for וַיֵּחַמוּ, beside וַיֵּחַמְנָה verse 38, is remarkable ; cf. § 47 *k*.

g (c) On רַד Ju 19¹¹ for יְרַד and שׁוּב Jer 42¹⁰ for the *infinitive absolute* יָשׁוֹב, cf. § 19 *i*.—But יְרַד Ju 5¹³ (twice) is not intended by the Masora either as *perfect* (for יָרַד, which really should be restored) or as *imperative* of יָרַד, but as an apocopated *imperfect Pi'ēl* from רָדָה (=יְרַדֶּה) *to have dominion*.

h (d) The eight verbs,[1] of which the initial consonant in the above-mentioned forms always suffers elision or aphaeresis, are יָלַד *to bring forth*, יָצָא *to go forth*, יָשַׁב *to sit, to dwell*, יָרַד *to descend*, also הָלַךְ *to go* (cf. below, *x*) ; and with *ă* in the second syllable of the *imperfect*, יָדַע *to know*, יָחַד *to be united*, יָקַע *to be dislocated*. Examples of the other formation (יִירַשׁ, &c.) are יָעֵף *to be wearied*, יָעַץ *to counsel*, יָשֵׁן *to sleep*, יָרֵא (*imperfect* יִירָא, *imperative* יְרָא) *to fear*.

i 2. The original *Wāw* is retained as a firm consonant : (a) in the *infinitive*, *imperative*, and *imperfect Niph'al*, being protected by the strengthening, e. g. הִוָּשֵׁב, יִוָּשֵׁב, which are consequently strong forms like הָקְטֵל, יִקָּטֵל ; (b) in the *Hithpa'el* of some verbs, e. g. הִתְוַדַּע from יָדַע, הִתְוַכַּח from יָכַח, הִתְוַדָּה from יָדָה ; otherwise a radical *Wāw* at the beginning of a word is now found only in a few nouns, e. g. וָלָד *offspring* from יָלַד *to bear*. At the end of a syllable *Wāw* with the homogeneous

---

[1] A ninth יָסַף *to add*, is also to be included. In the Mēša'-inscription, l. 21, the *infinitive* is written לספת (cf. יספתי, l. 29) ; hence read in Is 30¹ (Nu 32¹⁴, Dt 29¹⁸) סֶפֶת for סְפוֹת. The 2nd *plur. masc. imperative* סְפוּ Is 29¹, Jer 7²¹ corresponds to שְׁבוּ ; thus in proof of a supposed סָפָה *addere*, there remains only אָסְפָה Dt 32²³, for which, according to 2 S 12⁸, read אֹסִפָה.

vowel *ŭ* coalesces into *û*; so throughout *Hoph'al*, e.g. הוּשַׁב for *hŭwšabh*; but with a preceding *a* the *Wāw* is contracted into *ô* (וֹ); so in the *perfect* and *participle Niph'al* and throughout *Hiph'îl*, e.g. נוֹשַׁב from an original *nāwšăbh*, הוֹשִׁיב from an original *hăwšîbh*.

The first radical always appears as *Yôdh* in the *perfect* and *participle k* *Qal*, יָשַׁב, &c., יָשֵׁב, יָשׁוּב, even when וְ precedes, e.g. וְיָשַׁב (but וִישַׁבְתֶּם according to § 24 *b*), also throughout *Pi'ēl* and *Pu'al*, e.g. יַחֵל *to wait*, יֻלַּד *to be born*, and in the *imperfect* and *participle* יְיַחֵל, מְיַדֵּעַ *known* (from יָדַע), and, as a rule, also in *Hithpa'el*, e.g. הִתְיַחֵשׂ, הִתְיַצֵּב, הִתְיַלֵּד (as against הִתְוַדַּע, &c., with *Wāw*).

The beginner may recognize verbs פ״י in the *imperfect Qal* partly by the *l* *Ṣere* under the preformatives; in *Niph'al* and *Hiph'îl* by the *Wāw* (וֹ, וִ) before the second radical. (The defective writing, as in הֹלִיד, is rare.) Verbs פ״י have forms like שֵׁב (דַּע), שֶׁבֶת, in common with verbs פ״ן. Similarly *Hoph'al* has the same form as in verbs ע״ע and ע״וּ.

Rem. 1. The *infinitive Qal* of the weaker form (שֶׁבֶת, ground-form *šibt*, *m* רֶשֶׁת; cf. above, *c*) with suffixes is pointed as רִשְׁתוֹ, שִׁבְתִּי (the strong form only in לְיִרְשֵׁנוּ Ju 14[15]). The masculine form is very rare, e.g. דֵּעַ *to know*, Jb 32[6.10], as also the feminine ending ה__, e.g. דֵּעָה[2] Ex 2[4], לֵדָה Is 37[3] (2 K 19[3]); Jer 13[21], Ho 9[11]; רֶרְדָה[2] *to descend*, Gn 46[3], where the change of the *ē* into vocal *Šewâ* is to be explained, with König, from its position between the principal and secondary tone. From יָדַע, under the influence of the guttural, דַּעַת is formed, with *suff.* דַּעְתִּי, &c.; but from יצא צֵאת. From יָרַד there occurs in ψ 30[4] in *Q're* מִיָּרְדִי (the *K'th.* requires מִיּוֹרְדִי) a very remarkable case of the strong form (for מֵרִדְתִּי). For לַת 1 S 4[19] (generally explained as a case of assimilation of ד to ת in the supposed ground-form *ladt*; according to Mayer Lambert pausal of לַת = *lidt*, see above, *c*) read simply לֶדֶת.

Examples of the strong form of the *infinitive* are יְרֹא *to fear*, Jos 22[25], with *n* preposition לִיסֹד Is 51[16] (but 2 Ch 31[7] according to Ben Naphtali לְיִסֹד, where the י is only retained orthographically, but is really assimilated to the ס; the reading of Ben Asher, לִיסוֹד, accepted by Baer, is meaningless); לִישׁוֹן Ec 5[11]; לְרֹא 1 S 18[29] is irregular, but probably לְרֹא (for לִירֹא) is intended. With *suff.* בִּיסְדִי Jb 38[4], cf. Ju 14[15], Ezr 3[12]; with ת *fem.* יְכֹלֶת *to be able*, Nu 14[16]. On וְיָשְׁתָּ, which is likewise usually referred to this class, cf. the note on § 70 *a*.

---

[1] וְשָׁבְתִּי ψ 23[6] can hardly be intended for an *infin.* with suffix from יָשַׁב, but rather for a *perf. consec.* from שׁוּב; but read וְישַׁבְתִּי.

[2] The infinitives דֵּעָה and רְדָה belong to the source marked E (Dillmann's B) in the modern criticism of the Pentateuch. The same document also has נְתֹן *to give*, for תֵּת; הֲלֹךְ *to go*, for לֶכֶת; and עֲשֹׁה *to make*, for עֲשׂוֹת. See Dillmann, *Die BB. Num., Deut., Jos.*, p. 618.

O 2. The imperative Qal frequently has the lengthening by ה‎ָ, e.g. שְׁבָה‎ *sit thou*, רְדָה‎ *descend thou*. From יָהַב‎ *to give*, Arab. *wăhăbă*, only the *imperative* is used in Hebrew; it has the form הַב‎ *give*, lengthened הָבָה‎ generally with the meaning *age, go to*, hence in Gn 11³·⁴ even addressed to several persons (Gn 29²¹ הָבָה‎ before אֵ‎ to avoid the hiatus); *fem.* הָבִי‎ Ru 3¹⁵, *Milra'* on the analogy of the plural הָבוּ‎ (once in Jb 6²² הָבוּ‎ before the tone-syllable ; but cf. Dt 32³), whilst, on the analogy of other *imperatives Qal* of verbs פ״ו‎, הַבִי‎, הַבוּ‎ would be expected.—On דְּעָה‎ Pr 24¹⁴, cf. § 48 *l*.

p 3. The *imperfect* with ו‎ elided takes *ă* in the second syllable, besides the cases mentioned above (under *f*), also in תֵּרַד‎ Jer 13¹⁷ (cf. La 3⁴⁸) and in the pausal form יֵלַךְ‎ Jb 27²¹, &c. (from הָלַךְ‎, see *x*) ; on יֵקַד‎ Is 10¹⁶ see above, *f*. The *ă* in the second syllable, when followed by the afformative נָה‎ (תֵּרַדְנָה‎ &c.), is in accordance with the law mentioned above (under *c*), by which *ă* takes the place of *ĭ* in a doubly closed syllable. Forms with *ē* in the second syllable shorten the *ē* to *Seghôl*, when the tone is drawn back (before a tone-syllable or after *wāw consecutive*), e.g. יֵשֶׁב‎ Gn 44³³ ; וַיֵּרֶד‎, וַיֵּשֶׁב‎; but *ē* is retained in an open syllable, even with Mil'el-tone, in יֵצֵא‎ Ex 16²⁹, Ju 9³⁹, in both cases with *nasog 'aḥor*, § 29 *e*. The *pausal* is either of the form וַיֵּשֵׁב‎ Ru 4¹ or וַיֵּרַד‎ ψ 18¹⁰; the 1st pers. sing., whether in or out of pause, is וָאֵרֵד‎, וָאֵלֵד‎, &c., except וָאֵלֶךְ‎ Jb 19¹⁰, see *x*.—For יֵרַד‎ ψ 138⁶ (cf. the note above, on *b* and the analogous cases in § 70 *d*) יֵרֵד‎ is intended.

q The *imperfect* of the form יִירַשׁ‎ is frequently (especially before afformatives) written defectively, in which case the * î* can always be recognized as a long vowel by the *Metheg* (see § 16 *f*), e.g. יַעֲפוּ‎ Is 40³⁰, יִגְעוּ‎ Is 65²³ ; and so always יִרְאוּ‎ *they fear*, as distinguished from יִרְאוּ‎ *they see* (*imperf. Qal* of רָאָה‎).—On וַיִּישַׁם‎ Gn 50²⁶, 24³³ *Kᵉth*, and יִיסַךְ‎ Ex 30³², see § 73 *f*.

r From יָכֹל‎ *to prevail, to be able*, the *imperfect Qal* is יוּכַל‎, which can only have arisen through a depression of the vowel from יוֹכַל‎ (ground-form *yaukhal = yawkhal*), to distinguish it, according to Qimḥi, from אוֹכַל‎, just as, according to § 47 *b*, אֶקְטֹל‎ is differentiated from יִקְטֹל‎. Cf. the Arabic *yauru'u (yôru'u)* from *waru'a, yauǧalu (yôǧalu)* from *waǧila*, as also the vulgar Arabic (among towns-people) *yûṣal*, &c., from *waṣala*. Others regard יוּכַל‎ as an *imperfect Hophʿal* (*he is enabled = he can*), always used instead of the *imperfect Qal*; cf., however, § 53 *u*.—וַתּוּכַל‎ occurs in Jer 3⁵ as 2nd *sing. fem.* for וְתוּכְלִי‎, according to König because the 2nd *fem.* had been sufficiently indicated previously.— Further יוֹרֶה‎ or יֹרֶה‎ is to be regarded with M. Lambert (*REJ.* xxxvii, no. 73) as *impf. Qal* (not *Hiphʿil*) of יָרָה‎ *to throw, shoot* (the supposed *impf. Qal* וַיִּרָם‎ Nu 21³⁰ is critically very doubtful). This is shown especially by the passages in which the *impf.* יוֹרֶה‎ is immediately preceded by the *imperat. Qal* (2 K 13¹⁷) or *infin. Qal* (ψ 64⁵), or is followed by the *participle Qal* (2 Ch 35²³ ; but in 2 S 11²⁴ by the *participle Hiphʿil*).

s 4. The attenuation of *ă* to *ĭ* in the *perfect* (in a toneless, closed syllable) which is discussed in § 44 *d* (cf. § 64 *f*) occurs in verbs פ״ו‎ in a few forms of יָלַד‎ Nu 11¹², Jer 2²⁷, ψ 2⁷, &c. (always after י‎), as well as of יָרַשׁ‎, e.g. יְרִשְׁתֶּם‎, &c., Dt 4¹, 8¹, 17¹⁴, 19¹, 26¹, 31³ (always after ו‎ for וֹ‎). In both cases the attenuation might be explained from the tendency to assimilate the vowels, especially if the initial י‎ was pronounced, as in Syriac, like *i* (§ 47 *b*). In the case of יָרַשׁ‎, however, a secondary form יָרֵשׁ‎ (cf. § 44 *d*) is probably to be assumed, since in Arabic also the verb is *wăriṭă*. The forms

‏וִירֵשׁוּךְ‎ Ez 36¹² and ‏וִירֵשׁוּהָ‎ ψ 69³⁶, &c., are most simply explained from the return of this *î*.

5. As an exception, the *imperfect Niph'al* sometimes has a ‏ו‎ instead of the *î* ‏ו‎, e. g. ‏וַיִּחָל‎ *and he stayed*, Gn 8¹² (unless the *Pi'ēl* or ‏וַיְחַל‎, as in ver. 10, is to be read), cf. Ex 19¹³ ; 1 S 13⁸ *Kᵉthibh*.—The first person always has the form ‏אִוָּשֵׁב‎, not ‏אֶוָּשֵׁב‎, cf. § 51 *p*.—In the *participle* the plural ‏נוֹגֵי‎ (from ‏יָגָה‎, with depression of *ô* to *û*, cf. § 27 *n*) is found in Zp 3¹⁸ ; cf. La 1⁴. While in these cases some doubt may be felt as to the correctness of the Masoretic pointing, much more is this so in the *perfect* ‏נוּלְּדוּ‎ *nullᵉdhû*, 1 Ch 3⁵, 20⁸, for ‏נוֹלְדוּ‎ which appears to be required by the *wāw* in the initial syllable.

6. In the *imperfect Pi'ēl* elision of the first radical (‏י‎) sometimes takes place after *wāw consec.* (as in the case of ‏א‎, § 68 *k*), e. g. ‏וַיַּגֶּה‎ for ‏וַיְיַגֶּה‎ *and he has grieved*, La 3³³, ‏וַיַּדּוּ‎ for ‏וַיְיַדּוּ‎ *and they have cast*, verse 53, from ‏ירה‎, which may also be a true verb ‏פ״ו‎ (on the other hand, in ‏יַדּוּ גוֹרָל‎ *they have cast lots*, Jo 4³, Ob ¹¹, Na 3¹⁰, a *perfect Qal* of ‏יָדַד‎ is required by the context; but as this, being a *transitive* perfect, ought to have the form ‏יָדְדוּ‎ according to § 67 *a*, perhaps we should read ‏יַדּוּ‎). So from a verb ‏פ״ו‎, of the second class, ‏וַיְּבַשֵּׁהוּ‎ for ‏וַיְיַבְּשֵׁהוּ‎ *and he made it dry*, Na 1⁴; cf. ‏וַיֵּשְׁרַם‎ 2 Ch 32³⁰ *Qᵉrê* (the *Kᵉth*. points either to *Pi'ēl* ‏וַיְיַשְּׁרַם‎ or *Hiph'il* ‏וַיְיַשְּׁרַם‎).

7. The *imperative Hiph'il*, instead of the usual form ‏הוֹשֵׁב‎, sometimes has *i* in the second syllable ; ‏הוֹצִיא‎ Is 43⁸ ; ‏הוֹפִיעַ‎ ψ 94¹ (before ‏ה‎, hence probably a mere mistake for ‏הוֹפִיעָה‎). On the uncertainty of the tone in ‏הוֹשִׁיעָה־נָּא‎ see § 53 *m*. When closed by a guttural the second syllable generally has *ă*, as ‏הוֹדַע‎, ‏הוֹשַׁע‎, cf. also ‏הַכַּר‎ Pr 25¹⁷ (as in the *infin. constr.* ‏הוֹכַח‎ Jb 6²⁶ ; see § 65 *f*). On the other hand, *i* always appears when the syllable is open, thus ‏הוֹשִׁיבִי‎, ‏הוֹשִׁיבָה‎, and so also before suffixes (§ 61 *g*) ; ‏הַיְצֵא‎ Gn 8¹⁷ *Qᵉrê* (*Kᵉth*. ‏הוֹצֵא‎, see § 70 *b*) is irregular.—The *jussive* and the *imperfect consecutive Hiph'il* when the tone is drawn back take *Sᵉghôl* in the second syllable, as in *Qal*, e. g. ‏יֹסֵף‎ *that he may increase*, Pr 1⁵, before ‏לֶקַח‎ ; cf. Ex 10²⁸ and Dt 3²⁶ after ‏אַל־‎ ; ‏וַיֹּסֶף‎ (‏תּוֹסֵף‎) Pr 30⁶ is anomalous) ; in *pause*, however, also ‏תּוֹסַף‎ as jussive, Jb 40³² (usual jussive in *pause* ‏וְיֹשֵׁב‎, &c., which occurs even without the pause after *wāw consecutive*, Gn 47¹¹, Jos 24³, 2 S 8⁴, &c.). With a final guttural ‏יֹדַע‎ and ‏יוֹכַח‎ (*jussive*) ‏וַיֹּכַח‎, &c. ; with a final ‏ר‎ in *pause* ‏וַתֹּתַר‎ Ru 2¹⁴ : on ‏וְיֹשַׁעֲכֶם‎ Is 35⁴, cf. § 65 *f*).—On forms like ‏יְהוֹשִׁיעַ‎, see § 53 *q*.

In *Hoph'al ô* stands instead of ‏ו‎, in ‏הוֹדַע‎ (for ‏הֻדַּע‎) Lv 4²³·²⁸, ‏הוֹנָה‎ 2 S 20¹³, and perhaps in ‏יוֹרָא‎ (for ‏יוּרֶה‎) Pr 11²⁵ ; but cf. Delitzsch on the passage.— *Ptcp.* ‏מוּדַּעַת‎ Is 12⁵ *Qᵉre* ‏מְיֻדַּעַת‎ *Kᵉth*).—An *infinitive Hoph'al* with feminine ending occurs in ‏הֻלֶּדֶת‎ Gn 40²⁰, for ‏הֻלָּדֶת‎ = ‏הֻגָּל־‎ ; cf. above, *t*, on ‏נוּלְּדוּ‎, and § 71 at the end.

8. The verb ‏הָלַךְ‎ *to go*, also belongs in some respects to the ‏פ״ו‎ class, since it forms (as if from ‏וָלַךְ‎) *imperfect* ‏יֵלֵךְ‎, with *wāw consecutive* ‏וַיֵּלֶךְ‎ (in *pause* ‏וַיֵּלַךְ‎ Gn 24⁶¹, &c.), 1st sing. ‏וָאֵלֵךְ‎ (but in Jb 19¹⁰ ‏וָאֵלַךְ‎) ; *infinitive construct* ‏לֶכֶת‎ with suff. ‏לֶכְתִּי‎ (*Sᵉghôl* under the influence of the following palatal, as in ‏נֶכְדִּי‎, cf. also ‏נֶגְדִּי‎) ; *imperative* ‏לֵךְ‎, ‏לֶךְ־‎, in the lengthened form ‏לְכָה‎ (as an interjection referring even to a *feminine*, Gn 19³², or a *plural*, Gn 31⁴⁴) and ‏לֵךְ‎ (Nu 23¹³, Ju 19¹³, 2 Ch 25¹⁷) ; *Hiph.* ‏הוֹלִיךְ‎ (also in Ex 2⁹ ‏הוֹלִיכִי‎ 2nd *fem*. *imperative* is to be read for ‏הֵילִיכִי‎, which probably arose merely through

confusion with the following וַיִּנָּקֵהוּ) ; *imperfect* יוֹלִיךְ, but in the 1st sing. of
the *imperfect consecutive* always וָאֵלֶךְ Lv 26¹³, Am 2¹⁰, &c. Rarely, and almost
exclusively late or in poetry, the regular inflexions of הָלַךְ are also found :
imperf. יֶהֱלַךְ (ψ 58⁹, &c. ; but תְּהֲלַךְ Ex 9²³, ψ 73⁹; cf. § 64 *a* and *h*) ; אֶהֱלֹךְ
Jb 16²², also Mêša‘ inscription, line 14, אהלך; *infin.* הֲלֹךְ (Ex 3¹⁹, Nu 22¹³ f.¹⁶, 1
Ec 6⁸·⁹) ; *imperative plur.* הִלְכוּ Jer 51⁵⁰. On the other hand, the *perfect Qal* is
always הָלַךְ, *participle* הֹלֵךְ, *infinitive absolute* הָלוֹךְ, *Niph‘al* נֶהֱלַךְ, *Pi‘ēl* הִלֵּךְ,
Hithpa‘ēl הִתְהַלֵּךְ, so that a י never appears unmistakably as the first radical.
The usual explanation of the above forms is nevertheless based on a supposed
obsolete יָלַךְ. It is, however, more correct to regard the apparent פ״י
forms of הלך with Praetorius (*ZAW.* ii. 310 ff.) as originating with the
Hiph‘il, of which the ground-form *hahlikh* became *hâlikh*, and this again, on
the analogy of the *imperfect Qal* of verbs פ״א, *hôlikh.* This *hôlikh* being
referred to a supposed *haulikh* (properly *hawlikh*) gave rise to new formations
after the manner of verbs פ״י.

§ 70. Verbs פ״י. Second Class, or Verbs properly פ״י,

e. g. יָטַב *to be good. Paradigm L.*

Brockelmann, *Semit. Sprachwiss.*, p. 143 ff. ; *Grundriss*, p. 603 ff.

Verbs properly פ״י differ from verbs פ״ו in the following points :

a　1. In *Qal* the initial Yôdh never suffers aphaeresis or elision ; hence
the *infinitive* has the form יְבַשׁ,² the *imperfect* יִיטַב, יִיקַץ, יִינַק (in *pause*
יִינָק), also written יִטַב, &c. ; and so always with a tone-bearing *ă* in the
second syllable, even after *wāw consec.*, e. g. וַיִּקַץ, except וַיִּיקֶץ Gn 9²⁴,
and וַיִּיצֶר Gn 2⁷·¹⁹, unless יָצַר is to be included among verbs פ״ו (cf. נוֹצָר
Is 43¹⁰).

b　2. In *Hiph‘îl* the original form הַיְטִיב is regularly contracted to הֵיטִיב
(rarely written הֵטִיב, הֵיטֵב, &c.) ; *imperfect* יֵיטִיב, וַיֵּטֶב. Instances of
the uncontracted form are יְיִשְׁרוּ Pr 4²⁵, according to Barth (see above,
§ 67 *p*), an example of an *i-imperfect* of *Qal*, since the *Hiph‘îl* is otherwise always *causative* ; הַיְשֵׁר (*imperative*) ψ 5⁹ *Q⁰rê* (the *K⁰th.* requires
הוֹשֵׁר according to the form of verbs פ״ו ; cf. Is 45², אוֹשֵׁר *K⁰th.*, אֲיַשֵּׁר
Q⁰rê), cf. Gn 8¹⁷ *Q⁰rê*; מֵימִינִים 1 Ch 12², to be explained as a
denominative from יָמִין; אֲיַסִירֵם Ho 7¹² (§ 24 *f*, note), but perhaps the
punctuation here is only intended to suggest another reading אֲיַסְּרֵם.

---

¹ Cf. above, *m*, note 2.

² This may be inferred from בִּיבֹשׁ (= בְּיְ) Is 27¹¹, which with its fem.
יָבֵשֶׁת Gn 8⁷, is the only example of an infinitive *construct Qal* of these verbs.
No example of the *imperative Qal* is found : consequently the forms יְטַב, &c.
(in Paradigm L of the earlier editions of this Grammar), are only inferred
from the *imperfect.*

Rem. 1. The only verbs of this kind are : יָטַב *to be good* (only in the *C imperfect Qal* and in *Hiph'il*; in the *perfect Qal* טוֹב, a verb ע״ו, is used instead), יָנַק *to suck*, יָקַץ *to awake*, יָצַר *to form* (but see above, *a*), יָלַל only in *Hiph'il* הֵילִיל *to bewail*, יָשַׁר *to be straight, right*, also יָבֵשׁ (Arabic *yābisă*) *to be dry* (but *Hiph'il* הוֹבִישׁ 2 S 19⁶, on the analogy of verbs פ״ו; on Is 30⁵, cf. § 72 *x*), and the *Hiph'il* הֵימִין (denominative from יָמִין), infin. לְהֵמִין 2 S 14¹⁹ *to go to the right*.

2. In some examples of the *imperfect Hiph'il* the preformative has been subsequently added to the contracted form : יֵיטִיב Jb 24²¹; יְיֵלִיל Is 15²·³, 16⁷; אֵילִיל Jer 48³¹; plur. יְיֵלִילוּ Ho 7¹⁴, cf. Is 65¹⁴. Qimḥi and others explain the above forms from a phonetic interchange of *Yôdh* and *He*, arising from the unsyncopated forms יְהֵילִיל, &c. (cf. Is 52⁵). It is, perhaps, more correct to suppose that the regular forms (יֵילִיל, יֵיטִיב) were originally intended, but that in the later pronunciation the syllable was broken up in order to restore artificially the preformative which had become merged in the first radical.

Isolated anomalies are : *perfect Hiph'il* וְהֵיטַבְתִּי Ez 36¹¹ with separating vowel (for הֵיטַבְתִּי) on the analogy of verbs ע״ו; *imperfect* יֵיטִיב for יֵיטִיב 1 K 14⁷; תֵּיטְבִי (*imperfect Qal* for תִּיטְבִי) Na 3⁸; וַתִּינִיקֵהוּ *imperfect Hiph'il* Ex 2⁹, either an error for וַתֵּינִק, or an irregular shortening of the first syllable, caused by the forward movement of the tone. Similarly, the *Hiph'il* הֵקִיץ (from קוּץ) is always used instead of הֵיקִיץ from יָקַץ; hence also הֲקִיצֹתִי, הֲקִיצֹֽות, *imperat.* הָקִיצָה, *infin.* הָקִיץ.—On וַיְבַשֵּׁהוּ Na 1⁴, see § 69 *u*).

§ 71. *Verbs* פ״י. *Third Class, or Verbs with Yôdh assimilated.*

In some verbs פ״י, the *Yôdh* (or the original *Wāw*) does not quiesce in the preceding vowel, but is regarded as a full consonant, and, like *Nûn*,[1] is assimilated to the following consonant. These forms, therefore, belong properly to the class of strong verbs. Assimilation invariably takes place in יָצַע (prop. וצע) *to spread under*; *Hiph'il* הִצִּיעַ, *Hoph'al* הֻצַּע; יָצַת *to burn*, imperfect יִצַּת, *Niph'al* נִצַּת, *Hiph'il* הִצִּית (in Is 27⁴ also אַצִּיתֶנָּה is to be read with König; in 2 S 14³⁰ the Masora has rightly emended the *Kᵉthîbh* והוציתיה, which could only be the 1st sing. perf. of a verb פ״ו, to the imperative וְהַצִּיתֻהָ in agreement with the context and all the early versions); יָצַג, *Hiph'il* הִצִּיג *to place*, *Hoph'al* הֻצַּג; and probably also in the forms ordinarily derived from נָצַב, viz. נִצַּב (*Niph'al*), הֻצַּב, יַצִּיב, הִצִּיב; at any rate a stem יָצַב is implied by the *Hithpa'ēl* הִתְיַצֵּב; instead of the anomalous וַתֵּתַצַּב Ex 2⁴ read with the Samaritan ותתיצב, i.e. וַתִּתְיַצַּב. Besides the common form we find once אֶצָּק in Is 44³ (from יָצַק *to pour*) with a *transitive* meaning, beside וַיִּצֶק *intransitive*, 1 K 22³⁵. Elsewhere the *imperfect*

---

[1] These verbs, like verbs ע״ע (cf. above, note on § 67 *g*), may perhaps have been influenced by the analogy of verbs פ״ן.

consecutive has the form וַיָּצֶק Gn 28¹⁸, 35¹⁴, &c., cf. § 69 *f*, where also other forms of יָצַק are given; וַיִּצֶר and יִצֹר (Is 44¹², 49⁸, Jer 1⁵ *Qᵉrê*), from יָצַר *to form*, are, however, used in the same sense. Cf. also אָפֶרְךָ Ho 10¹⁰; וַיְּשָׁרֶנָה (for וַתִּ׳ according to § 47 *k*) 1 S 6¹²; לִיסֹר 2 Ch 31⁷ (cf. § 69 *n*) and מוּסָר Is 28¹⁶. This assimilation is found always with sibilants (most frequently with צ) except in the case of וַיִּקַּץ 1 K 3¹⁵ (so ed. Mant., Ginsb., Kittel; but Jabl., Baer וַיָּקַץ) and in הֻלֶּדֶת Gn 40²⁰, Ez 16⁵ (cf. הֻלֶּדֶת verse 4), *infinitive Hophʿal* of יָלַד (cf. נוּלְדוּ § 69 *t*).

§ 72. *Verbs* ע״וּ (*vulgo* ע״ו), e. g. קוּם *to rise up*. *Paradigm M*.

Brockelmann, *Semit. Sprachwiss.*, p. 144 ff. ; *Grundriss*, p. 605 ff.

a 1. According to § 67 *a* a large number of monosyllabic stems were brought into agreement with the triliteral form by a strengthening, or repetition, of the second radical, i. e. of the *consonantal* element in the stem. In another large class of stems the same object has been attained by strengthening the *vocalic* element. The ground-form used for these verbs is not, as in other cases (§ 39 *a*), the 3rd *sing. masc. perfect*, but always the *infinitive construct* form (§ 39 *b*), the *û* of which is characteristic also of the *imperative* and of the *imperfect indicative* Qal. These stems are consequently termed verbs ע״וּ or more correctly (see below) ע״י.[1]

---

[1] The term ע״ו was consequent on the view that the *Wāw* (or י in the case of verbs ע״י) in these stems was originally consonantal. This view seemed especially to be supported by the return of the *Wāw* in Piʿēl (עִוֵּר, the ו usually passing into י as in קָיַם, cf. Arabic *qáwwāmă*), and by certain forms of the *absolute state* of the nouns of such stems, e. g. מָוֶת *death*, compared with מוּת *to die*. Hence in explaining the verbal forms a supposed stem *qawam* (in verbs ע״י e. g. *šayat*) was always assumed, and יָקוּם was referred to an original *yaqwŭm*, the *infinitive absolute* קוּם to original *qawôm*, the *participle passive* קוּם to original *qawûm*. It must, however, be admitted: (1) that forms like עוּר, קִים (see *m*) are only to be found in the latest books, and are hence evidently secondary as compared with the pure Hebrew forms קוֹמֵם, &c. ; (2) that to refer the verbal forms invariably to the stem קָוַם, leads in many cases to phonetic combinations which are essentially improbable, whereas the assumption of original *middle-vowel* stems renders a simple and natural explanation almost always possible. These ע״י stems are therefore to be rigidly distinguished from the real ע״ו stems of the strong forms, such as רָוַח, גָּוַע, &c. (see below, *gg*).—As early as the eleventh century the right view with regard to ע״י stems was taken by Samuel Hannagîd (cf. Bacher, *Leben und Werke des Abulwalîd*, p. 16); recently by Böttcher (*Lehrbuch*, § 1112), and (also as to ע״ע stems) especially by Müller, Stade, and Wellhausen (see above, § 67 *a*, note). On the other hand, the old view of ו and י as consonants has been recently revived by Philippi, Barth, M. Lambert, and especially Brockelmann (op. cit.).

2. As in the case of verbs ע״ע, the monosyllabic stem of verbs ע״י *b* generally takes the vowel which would have been required in the *second* syllable of the ordinary strong form, or which belonged to the ground-form, since this is essentially characteristic of the verbal form (§ 43 *b*; § 67 *b*). However, it is to be remarked: (*a*) that the vowel, short in itself, becomes of necessity long in an open syllable as well as in a tone-bearing closed *ultima* (except in *Hoph'al*, see *d*), e. g. 3rd *sing. masc. perf.* קָם, *fem.* קָמָה, *plur.* קָמוּ, but in a closed *penultima* קַמְתְּ, &c.[1]; (*b*) that in the forms as we now have them the lengthening of the original short vowel sometimes takes place irregularly. Cf. *f.*

Intransitive verbs *middle e* in the *perfect Qal* have the form מֵת *he c is dead*; verbs *middle o* have the form אוֹר *he shone*, בּשׁ *he was ashamed*, טוֹב *he was good*.[2] Cf. *n–r.*

3. In the *imperfect Qal, perfect Niph'al*, and throughout *Hiph'îl* and *d Hoph'al* the short vowel of the preformatives in an open syllable before the tone is changed into the corresponding tone-long vowel. In *Qal* and *Niph'al* the original *ă* is the basis of the form and not the *ĭ* attenuated from *ă* (§ 67 *h*; but cf. also *h* below, on יְבשׁ), hence יָקוּם, for *yăqûm*; נָקוֹם for *năqôm*; on the other hand, in the *perfect Hiph'îl* הֵקִים for *hĭqîm*; *participle* מֵקִים (on the Ṣere cf. *z*); *perfect Hoph'al* הֻקַם for *hŭqam*.

A vowel thus lengthened before the tone is naturally changeable and *e e* becomes *vocal Šᵉwâ* when the tone is moved forward, e.g. יְמִיתֶנּוּ *he will kill him*; so also in the 3rd *plur. imperfect Qal* with *Nûn paragogic*; יְמוּתוּן (without *Nûn* יְמוּתוּ). The wholly abnormal *scriptio plena* of *ē* in הַהֵימִיר Jer 2¹¹ (beside הֵמִיר in the same verse) should, with König, be emended to הֲיָמִיר; the incorrect repetition of the interrogative necessarily led to the pointing of the form as *perfect* instead of *imperfect.*—But in *Hoph'al* the *û* is retained throughout as an unchangeable vowel, when it has been introduced by an abnormal lengthening for the tone-long *ō* (as in the *Hoph'al* of verbs ע״ע).

---

[1] In Aramaic, however, always קָמַת; also in Hebrew grammars before Qimḥi קָמְתְּ, יְקָמְתִּי, &c., are found, but in our editions of the Bible this occurs only in *pause*, e. g. קַמְתִּי Mi 7⁸, מַתְנוּ 2 K 7³·⁴.

[2] According to Stade (*Grammatik*, § 385 *e* and *f*) the *e* in מֵת is of the nature of a diphthong (from *ai*, which arose from the union of the vowel *ĭ*, the sign of the intransitive, with the *ă* of the root), and likewise the *o* in אוֹר, &c. (from *au*). But *ô* (from *au*) could not, by § 26 *p*, remain in a closed penultima (בּשְׁתָּ, &c.); consequently the *o* of these forms can only be tone-long, i.e. due to lengthening of an original *ŭ*, and similarly the *ē* of מֵת to lengthening of an original *ĭ*. This is confirmed by the fact that the *ō* in בּשְׁתָּ, בּשְׁתִּי, בּשְׁנוּ is always, and in בּשׁ, 3rd *plur. perfect*, nearly always (the instances are 11 to 2), written defectively. Forms like בּוֹשָׁה, בּוֹשׁוּ, אוֹרוּ, &c., are therefore due to orthographical licence.

f 4. The cases of unusual vowel lengthening mentioned in *b* are : *imperfect Qal* יָקוּם (also in Arabic *yáqûmu*), but *jussive* with normal lengthening (§ 48 *g*), יָקֹם, with retraction of the tone יָקָם (*yāqŏm*), וַיָּקָם (in *pause* וַיָּקֹם); *imperative* קוּם, with normal lengthening of the *ŭ* in the 2nd *plur. fem.* קֹמְנָה, since, according to § 26 *p*, the *û* cannot be retained in a closed penultima; *infinitive construct* קוּם. In *Hiph'îl* the original *ĭ* is naturally lengthened to *î* (הֵקִים, *imperfect* יָקִים, *jussive* יָקֵם, with retraction of the tone וַיָּקֶם, יָקֵם); on the transference of this *î* to the *Hiph'îl* of the strong verb, cf. § 53 *a*.

g The following forms require special consideration : the *participle Qal* קָם is to be traced to the ground-form with *â* unobscured, Arab. *qâtil*, § 9 *q*, and § 50 *b*. On this analogy the form would be *qâim*,[1] which after absorption of the *ĭ* became קָם, owing to the predominating character of the *â*. The unchangeableness of the *â* (*plur.* קָמִים, *constr.* קָמֵי, &c.) favours this explanation.

h In the *imperfect Qal*, besides the forms with original *ŭ* (now *û*) there are also forms with original *ă*. This *ă* was lengthened to *ā*, and then further obscured to *ô*; hence especially יָבֹא (יְבֹא), וַיָּבֹא, &c., from the *perfect* בָּא *he has come.* In the *imperfects* יֵאוֹר (but cf. וַתָּאֹרְנָה 1 S 14²⁷) and יֵבוֹשׁ from the *intransitive perfects* אוֹר, בּשׁ (see above, *c*), most probably also in יֵאָתוּ 2 K 12⁹, נֵאוֹת Gn 34¹⁵ from an unused אוֹת *to consent,* and perhaps in וַתֵּהֹם 1 S 4⁵, &c., as in the cases noticed in § 63 *e* and especially § 67 *n*, the *ē* of the preformative is lengthened from *ĭ* (which is attenuated from original *ă*) and thus *yĭ-băš* became *yĭ-băš*, and finally *yē-bôš*. Finally the *Niph.* נָקוֹם (*nă-qām*), *imperfect* יִקּוֹם from *yiqqām*, originally (§ 51 *m*) *yinqăm*, arises in the same way from the obscuring of *ā* lengthened from *ă*.

i 5. In the *perfect Niph'al* and *Hiph'îl* a ו is inserted before the afformatives beginning with a consonant in the 1st and 2nd persons, and יָ— regularly (but see Rem.) in the *imperfect Qal*, sometimes also in the *imperfect Hiph'îl* (as in תְּבִיאֶינָה Lv 7³⁰, cf. תְּרִימֶנָה Mi 2¹²), before the termination of נָה. As in verbs ע״ע (§ 67 *d* and note) these *separating vowels* serve as an artificial opening of the preceding syllable, in order to preserve the long vowel ; in the *perfect Hiph'îl*, however, before the ו, instead of the *î* an *ē* is somewhat often found[2] (as a normal lengthening of the original *ĭ*), especially after *wāw con-*

---

[1] So in Arabic, prop. *qâ'im*, since the two vowels are kept apart by the insertion of an א, cf. Aram. קָאֵם; but also contracted, as *šâk, hâr,* for *šâ'ik,* &c. (cf. Wright's *Gramm. of the Arabic Language,* 2nd ed. vol. i. p. 164).

[2] וַהֲשִׁיבֹתֶם 1 S 6⁷ (cf. 2 Ch 6²⁵) could only be an orthographic licence for וְהֵשַׁבְתֶּם/ ; perhaps, however, והֵשִׁיב/ was originally intended.

secutive, Dt 4³⁹, 30¹, as well as before the afformatives הֶם and הֶן or before suffixes, Dt 22², 1 S 6⁸, 1 K 8³⁴, Ez 34⁴. For in all these cases the tone is removed from the וֹ to the following syllable, and this forward movement of the tone produces at the same time a weakening of the î to ē; thus הָקִים, הֲקִימֹות (or הֶקֵ׳; on הַעֲרֹתָה Ex 19²³, cf. *x*), but וַהֲקֵמֹת, &c., Ex 26³⁰, &c.; Dt 4³⁹, Nu 18²⁶ (cf., however, וַהֲקֵמֹנוּ Mi 5¹). In the same way in the 1st *pers. sing.* of the *perfect Niph'al*, the ô before the separating vowel is always modified to û (נְקוּמֹותִי); cf. *v*. In the *imperfect Qal* and *Hiph'il* the separating vowel י‒ָ always bears the tone (תְּקוּמֶינָה).

Without the separating vowel and consequently with the tone-long ō and *k* ē instead of û and i we find in *imperfect Qal* תָּבֹאנָה (see § 76 *g*); תְּשֹׁבֶן Ez 16⁵⁵ (also תְּשׁוּבֶינָה in the same verse); וַתִּשְׁבֶּנָה 1 S 7¹⁴ (cf. Ez 35⁹ *Qᵉrê*; on the *Kᵉthibh* תֵּישַׁבְנָה cf. above, note on § 69 *b*); וַתֵּאֹרְנָה 1 S 14²⁷ from אֹור (*Kᵉthibh* וַתִּרְאֶנָה *and they saw*, see § 75 *w*); in *Hiph'il*, e.g. הֵנֵפְתָּ Ex 20²⁵, also הֲנִיפֹותִי Jb 31²¹; וְהִטַּלְתִּי Jer 22²⁶; תְּשֹׁבֶנָה Jb 20¹⁰; with a separating vowel, e.g. תְּבִיאֶינָה Lv 7³⁰ from בֹּוא. *Sᵉghôl* without י occurs in the *imperfect Qal* in תְּמוּתֶנָה Ez 13¹⁹, Zc 1¹⁷; and in *Hiph'il* Mi 2¹²: the Dageš in the *Nûn* is, with Baer, to be rejected in all three cases according to the best authorities. Wholly abnormal is תָּקֹמְנָה Jer 44²⁵, probably an erroneous transposition of ים (for תְּקֹמֶינָה), unless it originates from an incorrect spelling תָּקֵימֶנָה or תְּקֵימֶנָה.

6. The tone, as in verbs ע״ע (cf. § 67 *k*), is also generally retained *l* on the stem-syllable in verbs ע״י before the afformatives ה‒ָ, ו, י‒ְ; thus קָמָה (but also בָּזָה לָךְ 2 K 19²¹, probably for the sake of rhythmical uniformity with the following לָעֲנֶה לָךְ; after *wāw consecutive* וְשָׁבָה Is 23¹⁷); קָמוּ (but also קָמוּ, cf. Is 28⁷, 29⁹, Na 3¹⁸, ψ 76⁶, Pr 5⁶, La 4¹⁸; וְרָצוּ 1 S 8¹¹; so especially before a following א, cf. § 49 *l*, Nu 13³²; וָעֵוּ Is 19¹; before ע, ψ 131¹, Pr 30¹³, La 4¹⁴); יָקוּמוּ תְּקוּמִי, but before a *suffix* or with *Nûn paragogic* וַיְסֻבֹּוּם 2 Ch 28¹⁵; יְקוּמוּן Dt 33¹¹, &c.

7. The formation of the conjugations *Pi'ēl*, *Pu'al*, and *Hithpa'ēl* is, *m* strictly speaking, excluded by the nature of verbs ע״י. It is only in the latest books that we begin to find a few secondary formations, probably borrowed from Aramaic, on the analogy of verbs ע״ו (with consonantal ו, see below, *gg*); e.g. the *Pi'ēl* עֹור to *surround*, only in עֹורְדֵנִי ψ 119⁶¹; and with change of ו to י, קִיֵּם Est 9³¹, קִיְּמוּ Est 9²⁷, *impf.* וַאֲקַיְּמָה ψ 119¹⁰⁶, *infin.* קַיֵּם Ez 13⁶, Ru 4⁷ &c., Est 9²¹ &c., *imperat.* קַיְּמֵנִי ψ 119²⁸; וְחִיַּבְתֶּם Dn 1¹⁰ from חוב to *be guilty*. The *Hithpa'ēl* הִצְטַיָּד Jos 9¹², which belongs to the older language, is probably a denominative from צַיִד. On the other hand the otherwise less common conjugation *Pôlēl* (see § 55 *c*), with its passive and reflexive, is usually

employed in the sense of *Piʿēl* and as a substitute for it, e. g. קוֹמֵם *to set up* from קוּם; מוֹתֵת *to slaughter*, 1 S 14¹³, 17⁵¹, 2 S 1⁹, from מוּת; רוֹמֵם *to exalt*, passive רוֹמַם, from רוּם; reflexive הִתְעוֹרֵר *to stir up oneself* (cf. יִתְעֹרָר Jb 17⁸ in *pause*) from עוּר; reciprocal הִתְבּשֵׁשׁ *to be ashamed before one another*, Gn 2²⁵. The conjugation *Pilpēl* (§ 55 *f*), on the analogy of verbs ע″ע, is less common, e. g, טִלְטֵל *to hurl away* from טוּל; כִּלְכֵּל *to contain* from כּוּל; קִרְקַר *to destroy* from קוּר.

REMARKS.

I. On Qal.

n　1. Of verbs *middle e* and *o*, in which, as in the strong verb, the *perfect* and *participle* have the same form (§ 50. 2), the following are the only examples: מֵת *he is dead, fem.* מֵתָה, 2nd *masc.* מַתָּה (cf. § 44 *g*; § 66 *h*); 1st *sing.* מַתִּי, וָמַתִּי (even in *pause*, Gn 19¹⁹); *plur.* מֵתוּ, 1st *pers.* מַתְנוּ, in *pause* מָתְנוּ; בּשׁ *he was ashamed*, בֹּשְׁתִּי, בֹּשְׁתִּ, בֹּשׁוּ; אוֹר *it has shone*, plur. אוֹרוּ; טוֹב *to be good*, טֹבוּ. Participles מֵת *a dead man* (*plur.* מֵתִים); (מֵתֵי) בּשִׁים *ashamed*, Ez 32³⁰. For נֵד Is 27¹¹ read נָד, or, with LXX, עַד.

o　Isolated anomalies in the *perfect* are : וְשָׁבַת (with the original ending of the *fem.* for שָׁבָה) Ez 46¹⁷ (see § 44 *f*); צָקוּן Is 26¹⁶ (see § 44 *l*).—In בָּנוּ 1 S 25⁸ (for בָּאנוּ from בּוֹא) the א has been dropped contrary to custom. In בָּאוּ Jer 27¹⁸ (instead of בָּאוּ) the Masora seems to point to the *imperfect* יָבֹאוּ which is what would be expected; as *Yôdh* precedes, it is perhaps simply a scribal error.

p　The form קָם occurs (cf. § 9 *b*) with א in the *perfect*, קָאם Ho 10¹⁴, also in the *participles* לָאט *softly*, Ju 4²¹, רָאשׁ *poor*, 2 S 12¹·⁴, Pr 10⁴, *plur.* 13²³; שָׁאטִים *doing despite unto* (unless שָׁאטִים is to be read, from a stem שׁאט whence שָׁאט Ez 25¹⁵, 36⁵), Ez 28²⁴·²⁶; *fem.* 16⁵⁷; also in Zc 14¹⁰ רָאמָה is to be read with Ben-Naphtali for רָאֲמָה. On the analogy of participles of verbs *middle ō* (like בּשִׁים, see above) קוֹמִים occurs for קָמִים 2 K 16⁷ and even with a transitive meaning לוֹט *occultans*, Is 25⁷; בּוֹסִים Zc 10⁵.—*Participle passive,* מוּל *circumcised*; but סוּג *a backslider*, Pr 14¹⁴, and סוּרָה *put aside*, Is 49²¹ (cf. Jer 17¹³ Qᵉrê), are verbal adjectives of the form *qāṭûl* (§ 50 *f*), not passive participles. For חָשִׁים *hastening*, Nu 32¹⁷, read חָמֻשִׁים as in Ex 13¹⁸; for שׁוּבֵי Mi 2⁸ read שָׁבֵי.

q　2. Imperfects in *û* almost always have the corresponding *imperative* and *infinitive construct* in *û*, as יָקוּם, *imperative* and *infinitive* קוּם (also defectively written קָם, יָקֻם); but יָדֹשׁ *he threshes* (*infin.* דּוּשׁ), has *imperative* דּוֹשִׁי (*fem.*), Mi 4¹³; יָמוּט *it slippeth, infinitive* מוֹט (ψ 38¹⁷, 46³); cf. נֹחַ (also נוּחַ) Nu 11²⁵ and נוֹעַ Is 7² (elsewhere נוּעַ) with the *imperfects* יָנוּחַ and יָנוּעַ; לָעוּז Is 30²; שׁוּב Jos 2¹⁶; רוּם Ez 10¹⁷ (verse 16 רֹם).

r　Where the *imperfect* (always intransitive in meaning) has *ó* the *imperative* and *infinitive* also have it; thus *imperfect* יָבֹא (יָבוֹא), *infin.* and *imper.* בֹּא or בֹּא¹; וַיָּאַר 2 S 2³²; אוֹרוּ, אוֹרִי, בּוֹשׁ, &c.—קָקוֹט Jb 8¹⁴ (if it be a verb at all and not rather a substantive) is formed on the analogy of verbs ע″ע,

---

¹ In 1 K 14¹² בְּבֹאָה before a genitive), the text is evidently corrupt : read with Klostermann after the LXX בְּבֹאֵךְ.

since the *imperfect* of קוּט appears as אָקוּט in ψ 95¹⁰. On the other hand
יִקְשׁוּן (as if from קוֹשׁ, on the analogy of יָבוֹא, &c.) occurs as *imperfect* of
יָקֹשׁ (פ״י). The *imperfect* יָדוֹן, with ô, Gn 6³, probably in the sense of *to rule*,
has no corresponding *perfect*, and is perhaps intentionally differentiated
from the common verb יָדִין *to judge* (from דִּין, ע״וּ). Or can יָדוֹן be a *jussive*
after לֹא (cf. § 109 d)? Similarly לֹא תָחוּם עֵינִי (עֵינְךָ) might be taken as
a case of a jussive after לֹא, with irregular *scriptio plena* (as in Ju 16³⁰), in
Dt 7¹⁶, 13⁹, 19¹³·²¹, 25¹², Ez 5¹¹, 7⁴·⁹, 8¹⁸, 9¹⁰. But perhaps in all these cases
לֹא תָחוּם was originally intended, as in Is 13¹⁸, Jer 21⁷, while cases like יָחֹם
ψ 72¹³ are to be explained as in § 109 k.—The *infinitive absolute* always has ô,
e.g. קוֹם יָקוּמוּ Jer 44²⁹.

3. In the *imperative* with afformatives (קוּמוּ, קוּמִי) the tone is on the stem *S*
syllable (cf., however, עוּרִי Ju 5¹² intentionally varied from עֹרִי; also עֹרִי
Zc 13⁷ and Is 51⁹ beside עוּרִי גִּילִי; Zc 9⁹; צוּרִי Is 21², שׁוּבִי ψ 116⁷,
likewise for rhythmical reasons). So also the lengthened form, as שׁוּבָה
Jer 3¹², ψ 7⁸, and עוּרָה verse 7. But if an א follows in close connexion, the
lengthened *imperative* usually has the form קוּמָה, &c.,¹ in order to avoid
a hiatus, e.g. Ju 4¹⁸, ψ 82⁸; hence also before יְהוָה, *Qᵉrê perpetuum* אֲדֹנָי
(§ 17 c), e.g. ψ 3⁸, 7⁷ קוּמָה (cf., however, in the same verse עוּרָה and in Jer 40⁵,
שֻׁבָה before א), and so even before ר ψ 43¹, 74²², &c. (רִיבָה).

4. In the *jussive*, besides the form יָקֹם (see above, *f*), יָקוּם also occurs *t*
(as subjunctive, Ec 12⁴; נָסוּג ψ 80¹⁹ may also, with Delitzsch, be regarded as
a voluntative), incorrectly written *plene*, and יָקֵם (Gn 27³¹; cf. Ju 6¹⁸,
Pr 9⁴·¹⁶), which, however, is only orthographically different from יָקֻם (cf.
Jer 46⁶). In the *imperfect consecutive* (וַיָּקָם, in *pause* וַיָּקֹם, see above, *f*) if there
be a guttural or ר in the last syllable, ă often takes the place of ŏ, e.g.
וַיָּנַח *and he rested*; וַיָּנַע *and it was moved*; וַיָּסַר *and he turned aside*, Ju 4¹⁸, Ru 4¹
(distinguished only by the sense from *Hiph'il* וַיָּסַר *and he removed*, Gn 8¹³); וַיָּצַר
Ex 21⁴, 2 K 5²³, 17⁵ (but also וַיָּגָר from both גּוּר *to sojourn*, and גּוּר *to fear*);
וַיָּעַף (to be distinguished from וַיָּעָף *and he flew*, Is 6⁶) *and he was weary*, Ju 4²¹,
1 S 14²⁸·³¹, 2 S 21¹⁵, but probably in all these cases וַיָּעַף for וַיִּיעַף from יָעֵף
is intended. For ותלש 2 S 13⁸ *Kᵉth.*, the Qᵉrê rightly requires וַתָּלָשׁ. On
the other hand, in an open syllable always וָאָקוּם, וַיָּסֹרוּ, וַיָּקֻמוּ, &c. On וָאָקוּם
(וָאָקֻם), see § 49 e.

Examples of the full plural ending וּן with the tone (see above, *l*) are *u*
תְּמֻתוּן Gn 3³·⁴; יְנֻסוּן ψ 104⁷; יְרוּצוּן Jo 2⁴·⁷·⁹.

II. *On Niph'al.*

5. The form of the 1st *sing. perf.* נְקוּמֹתִי, which frequently occurs (נְסוּגֹתִי, *v*
נְפוּגֹתִי, cf. also the *ptcp. plur.* נְבוּכִים Ex 14³), serves as a model for the
2nd *sing.* נְקוּמֹתָ, נְקוּמוֹת, and the 1st *plur.* נְקוּמֹנוּ given in the paradigm,
although no instances of these forms are found; but of the 2nd *plur.* the

---

¹ Cf. Delitzsch's commentary on ψ 3⁸.

only examples found have *ô* (not *û*), viz. נְפוֹצֹתֶם *ye have been scattered*, Ez 11¹⁷, 20³⁴˙⁴¹, and וּנְקֹטֹתֶם *and ye shall loathe yourselves*, Ez 20⁴³, 36³¹.—To the *ĭ* (instead of *ă*) of the preformative may be traced the *perfect* עֹעוֹר Zc 2¹⁷ (analogous to the *perfect* and *participle* נָמוֹל, see below, *ee*), *imperfect* יֵעוֹר for *yiʿʿōr*.—The *infinitive construct* הַדּוּשׁ occurs in Is 25¹⁰; in לָאוֹר Jb 33³⁰, the Masora assumes the elision of the ה (for לְהָאוֹר); but probably לָאוֹר (*Qal*) is intended (see § 51 *l*).—נָמוֹג Is 14³¹, נָסוֹג Is 59¹³ are to be regarded as *infinitives absolute*.

III. On Hiphʿîl, Hophʿal, and Piʿlēl.

w 6. Examples of the *perfect* without a separating vowel (see above, *k*) are : הֵבֵאת, &c. (see further, § 76 *g*); הֵמַתָּה (from מוּת) for *hēmáth-tā* (cf. § 20 *a*); הֲבֵנוּ 1st *plur. perfect Hiphʿil* from בּוּן 2 Ch 29¹⁹, even הֲמִתֶּם (§ 27 *s*) Nu 17⁶, &c.; cf. 1 S 17³⁵, 2 S 13²⁸, also וַהֲמִתֶן Ex 1¹⁶, and וַהֲמִתִּיהָ Ho 2⁵; but elsewhere, with *wāw consecutive* וַהֲמִתִּי Is 14³⁰; cf. וְהִטַּלְתִּי Jer 16¹³, and וַהֲנִפֹתָ Ex 29²⁴, &c.—In these cases the *ē* of the first syllable is retained in the secondary tone; elsewhere in the second syllable before the tone it becomes —ֵ (1 Ch 15¹², &c.) or more frequently —ֵ, and in the syllable before the antepenultima it is necessarily —ֲ (e. g. וַהֲקִמֹתִי Gn 6¹⁸). Before a suffix in the 3rd *sing. masc.* (except Gn 40¹³) and *fem.*, and in the 3rd *plur.*, the vowel of the initial syllable is *Ḥaṭeph-Seghôl*, in the other persons always *Ḥaṭeph-Pathaḥ* (König); on הֲקִמֹתוֹ 2 K 9², ψ 89⁴⁴, cf. Ex 19²³, Nu 31²⁸, Dt 4³⁹, 22², 27², 30¹, Ez 34⁴, and above, *i*. The 3rd *fem. perf. Hiph.* הָסֵתָּה 1 K 21²⁵ is quite abnormal for הֱסִיתָה from סוּת or סִית.

x As in verbs ע״ע with ח for their first radical (§ 67 *w*), all the forms of עוּר Ex 19²³ (where against the rule given under *i* we find הָעֲרֹתָה with *ē* instead of *i*), Dt 8¹⁹, Neh 9³⁴, Jer 42¹⁹, and עוּר Is 41²⁵, 45¹³, take Pathaḥ in these conjugations instead of —ֵ. The irregular וְהוֹשַׁבֹתִים Zc 10⁶ has evidently arisen from a combination of two different readings, viz. וְהוֹשַׁבֹתִים (from יָשַׁב) and וַהֲשִׁבוֹתִים (from שׁוּב): the latter is to be preferred.—On הֵבִישׁ and הוֹבִישׁ as a (metaplastic) *perfect Hiphʿîl* of בּוֹשׁ, cf. § 78 *b*.

y 7. In the *imperative*, besides the short form הָקֵם (on הָשֵׁב Is 42²² with Silluq, cf. § 29 *q*; but in Ez 21³⁵ for הָשֵׁב read the *infinitive* הָשֵׁב) the lengthened form הָקִימָה is also found. With *suffix* הֲקִימֵנִי, &c. The *imperative* הָבִיא Jer 17¹⁸ is irregular (for הָבֵא Gn 43¹⁶); perhaps הָבִיא (as in 1 S 20⁴⁰; cf. 2 K 8⁶) is intended, or it was originally הָבִיאָה.

z In the *infinitive*, elision of the ה occurs in לָבִיא Jer 39⁷, 2 Ch 31¹⁰ (for לְהָבִיא); ה—ָ *fem.* is added in לְהָנִפָה Is 30²⁸; cf. Est 2¹⁸ and the analogous *infinitive Haphʿel* in biblical Aramaic, Dn 5²⁰.—As *infinitive absolute* הָכִין occurs in Ez 7¹⁴ (perh. also Jos 4³, Jer 10²³).—The *participles* have *ē*, on the analogy of the *perfect*, as the vowel of the preformative, like verbs ע״ע (§ 67 *i*). On מֵבִי 2 S 5², &c. (in *Kethibh*), see § 74 *k*.

aa On the shortened forms of the *imperfect* (יָקֵם, יָקֶם, וַיָּקֶם, but always וַיָּבֵא; in the *jussive* also with retraction of the tone אַל־תִּתֵּב 1 K 2²⁰) see above, *f*. With a guttural or ר the last syllable generally has *Pathaḥ* (as in *Qal*), e. g. וַיָּעַד *and he testified*, 2 K 17¹³; יָרַח *let him smell*, 1 S 26¹⁹; וַיָּרַח Gn 8²¹; וַיָּסַר

and he took away, Gn 8¹³. The 1st *sing.* of the *imperfect consecutive* commonly has the form וָאָשִׁיב Neh 2²⁰, or, more often, defectively וָאָעַד 1 K 2⁴², less frequently the form וָאֵשֶׁב Jos 14⁷.—For אָסֵף Zp 1² (after אָסֹף) and in verse 3, read אֹסֵף from אָסַף, on the analogy of אֹמֵר § 68 *g* : similarly in Jer 8¹³ אֹסְפֵם instead of אֲסִיפֵם.

In the *imperfect Pôlēl* the tone is moved backwards before a following tone-syllable, but without a shortening of the vowel of the final syllable ; e. g. תְּרוֹמֵם גּוֹי Pr 14³⁴ ; תְּחוֹלֵל לוֹ Jb 35¹⁴ ; cf. Pr 25²³, and acc. to Baer וַתִּתְבֹּנֵן בִּי Jb 30²⁰ (ed. Mant., Ginsb. בִּי וַתִּתְבֹּנֵן), always in principal pause ; on the *Metheg* with *Ṣere*, cf. § 16 *f. γ.*—As *Pôlal* cf. יֻרָעַע Is 16¹⁰. *bb*

As *participle Hoph'al* הַמּוּשָׁב occurs in close connexion, Gn 43¹² ; cf. § 65 *d*.

Peculiar contracted forms of *Pôlēl* (unless they are transitives in *Qal*) are וַיְכַנְנוּ Jb 31¹⁵, יְעוֹרְרוּ 41², וַתְּמוֹגְנֵנוּ Is 64⁶ for וַיְכֹנְנוּ, &c. [but read (§ 58 *k*), יְעוֹרְרֵנוּ or יְעִירֵנוּ, and וַתְּמוֹגְנֵנוּ] ; also תְּרֹמֵם Jb 17⁴, for תְּרֹמְמֵם.—In Is 15⁵ יְעֹעָרוּ appears to have arisen from the *Pilpel* יְעַרְעָרוּ, the *ă* after the loss of the ר having been lengthened to *ā*, which has then been obscured to *ô*.—For the strange form בִּתְקוֹמְמֶיךָ ψ 139²¹, which cannot (according to § 52 *s*) be explained as a *participle* with the מ omitted, read בְּמִתְקֹ׳. *cc*

IV. *In General.*

8. The verbs ע״וּ are primarily related to the verbs ע״ע (§ 67), which were also originally biliteral, so that it is especially necessary in analysing them to pay attention to the differences between the inflexion of the two classes. Several forms are exactly the same in both, e. g. *imperfect Qal* and *Hiph'il* with *wāw consecutive*, the whole of *Hoph'al*, the *Pi'lēl* of verbs ע״וּ, and the *Pô'ēl* of verbs ע״ע ; see § 67 *z*. Owing to this close relation, verbs ע״וּ sometimes have forms which follow the analogy of verbs ע״ע, e. g. *perfect Qal* בַּז *he has despised* (from בּוּז, as if from בָּזַז) Zc 4¹⁰ ; *perfect Niph'al* נָמֵר Jer 48¹¹ (for נָמוֹר from מוּר, as if from מָרַר). The same explanation equally applies to נָקֹטָה Jb 10¹ for נָקֹטָה (cf. § 67 *dd*)=נָקוֹטָה from קוּט, and נָקֹטוּ Ez 6⁹ (for נָקוֹטוּ) ; יְרֹמּוּ Ez 10¹⁷ and וַיִּרֹמּוּ verse 15 ; הָרֹמּוּ (imperative) Nu 17¹⁰ ; יָסַג Mi 2⁶ ; *Hiph'il perfect* הֵתַן Is 18⁵ for הֵתֵן (cf. § 29 *q*), which is for הֵתִין from תּוּן. On the other hand the *imperfects* יָמֵר Ez 48¹⁴ (unless it be intended for יָמֵר, cf. ψ 15⁴) and יָפַח Hb 2³, are to be regarded according to § 109 *i*, simply as rhythmically shortened forms of יָמִיר and יָפִיחַ. *dd*

9. In common with verbs ע״ע (§ 67 *g*) verbs ע״וּ sometimes have in *Niph'al* and *Hiph'il* the quasi-Aramaic formation, by which, instead of the long vowel under the preformative, they take a short vowel with *Dageš forte* in the following consonant ; this variety is frequently found even along with the ordinary form, e. g. הֵסִית *to incite*, imperfect יַסִּית (also הֵסִית, יָסִית ; הֵסִיג, imperfect יַסִּיג *to remove* (from סוּג), also *Hoph'al* הֻסַּג Is 59¹⁴ (on הֻסַּם cf. § 29 *g*) ; sometimes with a difference of meaning, as הֵנִיחַ *to cause to rest*,[1] but הִנִּיחַ (*imperfect* יַנִּיחַ, *consecutive* וַתַּנַּח Gn 39¹⁶ ; *imperative* הַנַּח, plur. הַנִּיחוּ) *to set down* ; for וְהִנִּיחָה (Baer, Ginsburg וְהִנַּ׳) Zc 5¹¹ (which at any rate could only be explained as an isolated passive of *Hiph'il* on the analogy of the biblical Aramaic הֳקִימַת Dn 7⁴) we should probably read וְהִנִּיחָה with *ee*

---

[1] As the passive of this *Hiph'il* we should expect the *Hoph'al* הוּנַח, which is, no doubt, to be read for הוּנַּח in La 5⁵.

Klostermann after the LXX. In Dn 8¹¹ the *Kᵉthîbh* הרים is intended for a *perfect Hiph'îl.* There is also a distinction in meaning between יָלִין *to spend the night, to remain,* and יָלִין Ex 16⁷ *Qᵉrê* (*Kᵉthîbh* תְּלוּנוּ; conversely, verse 2 *Kᵉthîbh* יַלִּינוּ, *Qᵉrê* וַיִּלּוֹנוּ), *participle* מַלִּין Ex 16⁸, Nu 14²⁷, 17²⁰, *to be stubborn, obstinate* : in the latter sense from the form יָלִין only וַיָּלֶן is found, Ex 17³. Other examples are *Niph'al* נִמּוֹל *he was circumcised,* Gn 17²⁶ ᶠ·; *participle* 34²² (from מוּל, not נָמַל); נֵעוֹר *he is waked up,* Zc 2¹⁷ (see above, *v*); *Hiph'îl* הַדִּילוּהָ La 1⁸; יַלִּיזוּ Pr 4²¹.

ff   Perhaps the same explanation applies to some forms of verbs *first guttural* with *Dageš forte implicitum,* which others derive differently or would emend, e. g. וַתְּחַשׁ for וַתְּחָשׁ *and she hastened* (from חוּשׁ) Jb 31⁵; וַיָּעַט (another reading is וַיַּעַט), וַהֵּעַט 1 S 15¹⁹, 25¹⁴ (14³² *Qᵉrê*) from עוּט or עִיט *to fly at anything.* Both, as far as the form is concerned, would be correct *apocopated imperfects* from חָשָׂה and עָטָה (ל״ה), but these stems only occur with a wholly different meaning.

gg   10. Verbs with a consonantal *Wāw* for their second radical, are inflected throughout like the strong form, provided the first or third radical is not a weak letter, e. g. חָוַר, *imperfect* יֶחְוָר *to be white* ; גָּוַע, *imperfect* יִגְוַע *to expire* ; רָוַח *to be wide* ; צָוַח *to cry* ; Pi'ēl עִוֵּל, *imperfect* יְעַוֵּל *to act wickedly* ; עָוַת *to bend,* *Hithpa'ēl* הִתְעַוֵּת *to bend oneself* ; and this is especially the case with verbs which are at the same time ל״ה, e. g. צָוָה, Pi'ēl צִוָּה *to command,* קִוָּה *to wait,* רָוָה *to drink,* Pi'ēl רִוָּה (on אֲרַיֵּךְ Is 16⁹, see § 75 *dd*) and *Hiph'îl* הִרְוָה *to give to drink,* &c.

§ 73. *Verbs middle i (vulgo* ע״י*), e. g.* בִּין *to discern.*
Paradigm N.

a   1. These verbs agree, as regards their structure, exactly with verbs ע״וּ, and in contrast to them may be termed ע״י, or more correctly, '*ayin-î* verbs, from the characteristic vowel of the *impf., imper.,* and *infin. constr.* This distinction is justified in so far as it refers to a difference in the pronunciation of the *imperfect* and its kindred forms, the *imperative* and *infin. constr.*—the ע״וּ verbs having *û* lengthened from original *ŭ* and ע״י having *î* lengthened from original *ĭ.* In other respects verbs ע״י simply belong to the class of really monosyllabic stems, which, by a strengthening of their *vocalic* element, have been assimilated to the triliteral form ¹ (§ 67 *a*). In the *perfect Qal* the monosyllabic stem, as in ע״וּ, has *ā* lengthened from *ă,* thus: שָׁת *he has set; infinitive* שִׁית, *infinitive absolute* שׁוֹת, *imperative* שִׁית, *imperfect* יָשִׁית, *jussive* יָשֵׁת (§ 48 *g*), *imperfect consecutive* וַיָּשֶׁת.—The *perfect Qal* of some verbs

---

¹ That verbs ע״וּ and ע״י are developed from biliteral roots at a period before the differentiation of the Semitic languages is admitted even by Nöldeke (*Beiträge zur sem. Sprachwiss.,* Strassburg, 1904, p. 34 ff.), although he contests the view that בִּינֹתִי and רִיבֹתִ are to be referred to *Hiph'îl* with the preformative dropped.

used to be treated as having a double set of forms, a regular series, and others like *Hiph'îl* without the preformative, e. g. בִּין Dn 10¹; בִּינֹ֫תִי Dn 9², also בַּנְתָּ ψ 139²; רִיבֹ֫ותָ *thou strivest*, Jb 33¹³, also רַ֫בְתָּ La 3⁵⁸. The above *perfects* (בִּין, רִיב, &c.) might no doubt be taken as forms *middle ē* (properly *ĭ*), the *ĭ* of which has been lengthened to *î* (like the *ŭ* lengthened to *û* in the *imperfect Qal* of קוּם). It is more probable, however, that they are really shortened forms of *Hiph'îl*. This is supported by the fact that, especially in the case of בִּין, the shortened forms are few and probably all late, while the corresponding unshortened forms with the same meaning are very numerous, e. g. *perfect* הֵבִין (but בִּין only in Dn 10¹), הֲבִינֹתֶם, *infinitive* הָבִין (but *infin. abs.* בִּין only in Pr 23¹), *imperative* הָבֵן (only in Dn 9²³ וּבִין immediately before וְהָבֵן, also בִּ֫ינוּ three times, and בִּ֫ינָה ψ 5²), *participle* מֵבִין.¹ Elsewhere *Hiph'îl*-forms are in use along with actual *Qal*-forms with the same meaning, thus : מֵרִיב (also רָב), מֵשִׂים *placing* (but only in Jb 4²⁰, which, with the critically untenable הָשִׂ֫ימִי Ez 21²¹, is the only instance of שׂוּם in *Hiph'îl*), מֵנִיץ *breaking forth* Ju 20³³, with *infin. Qal* הָחִ֫ישׁוּ; נִ֫יחוֹ *they rushed forth* Ju 20³⁷, with חָשׁ, חַשְׁתִּי; מֵצִיץ *glancing*, also in *perfect* צָץ, הֵקִיא *he spat out*, with *imperat. Qal* קִיא. As *passives* we find a few apparent *imperfects Hoph'al*, which are really (according to § 53 *u*) *imperfects passive* of *Qal*, e. g. יוּחַל Is 66⁸ from חִיל *to turn round*, יוּשַׁר from שִׁיר *to sing*, יוּשַׁת from שִׁית *to set*.

2. The above-mentioned *Hiph'îl*-forms might equally well be derived *b* from verbs ע״י; and the influence of the analogy of verbs ע״י is distinctly seen in the *Niph'al* נָבֹ֫ון (ground-form *nabān*), *Pôlēl* בּוֹנֵן, and *Hithpôlēl* הִתְבּוֹנֵן. The very close relation existing between verbs ע״ו and ע״י is evident also from the fact that from some stems both forms occur side by side in *Qal*, thus from חִיל *to turn round*, *imperative* also חוּלִי Mi 4¹⁰; שִׂים *to place*, *infinitive construct* commonly שׂום (2 S 14⁷ שִׂים *Qᵉre*), *imperfect* יָשִׂים, but Ex 4¹¹ יָשׂום. In other verbs one form is, at any rate, the more common, e. g. גִּיל *to exult* (גּוּל only Pr 23²⁴ *Kᵉthîbh*); from לן (perhaps denominative from לַיְל) *to spend the night*, לְלִין occurs six times as *infinitive construct*, לֻן only in Gn 24²³; but the *imperative* is always לִין, &c.—Of verbs ע״י the most common are שִׁית *to set*, רִיב *to strive*, דִּין *to judge*, שִׂישׂ *to rejoice*; cf. also *perfect* כָּל (*middle*

---

¹ Since בנת ψ 139² might be intended for בָּנֹ֫ת, there remains really no form of בין which must *necessarily* be explained as a Qal, except the *ptcp. plur.* בָּנִים Jer 49⁷. Nevertheless it is highly probable that all the above instances of Hiph'îl-forms, parallel with Qal-forms of the same meaning, are merely due to a secondary formation from the *imperfects Qal* יָשִׂים, יָבִין, &c., which were wrongly regarded as *imperfects Hiph'îl* : so Barth, *ZDMG*. xliii. p. 190 f., and *Nominalbildung*, p. 119 f.

Yôdh in Arabic) *to comprehend, to measure*, Is 40¹²; עִט (as in Arabic and Syriac) *to rush upon*, and the denominative *perfect* קָץ (from קַיִץ) *to pass the summer*, Is 18⁶. On the other hand, וְרִיגוּם *and they shall fish them*, Jer 16¹⁶, generally explained as *perfect Qal*, denominative from דָּג *fish*, probably represents a denominative *Piʿēl*, וְרִיגוּם.

c　Corresponding to verbs properly ע״י, mentioned in § 72 gg, there are certain verbs ע״י with consonantal *Yôdh*, as אָיַב *to hate*, עָיֵף *to faint*, הָיָה *to become, to be*, חָיָה *to live*.

d　Rem. 1. In the *perfect Qal* 3rd *fem. sing.* וְלָנֶה occurs once, Zc 5⁴, for וְלָנָה, with the weakening of the toneless *ā* to *ĕ* (as in the *fem. participle* זֹרֶה Is 59⁵); cf. the analogous examples in § 48 l and § 80 i.—2nd *sing. masc.* שַׁתָּה ψ 90⁸, *Qᵉrê* (before ע; cf. § 72 s); 1st *sing.* once שַׁתִּי ψ 73²⁸, *milraʿ*, without any apparent reason; 1st *plur.* וְלָנוּ Ju 19¹³ for lán-nu. The lengthened *imperative* has the tone on the ultima before gutturals, רִיבָה יהוה ψ 35¹; see further, § 72 s.—Examples of the *infinitive absolute* are: רֹב *litigando*, Ju 11²⁵, Jb 4C²; שׂוֹם Jer 42¹⁵; שֵׂת *ponendo*, Is 22⁷. On the other hand, רִיב יָרִיב (for רֹב) Jer 50³⁴, בִּין תָּבִין Pr 23¹, חוּל תָּחִיל Ez 30¹⁶ *Kᵉth.*, are irregular and perhaps due to incorrect *scriptio plena*; for the last the *Qᵉrê* requires הָגִיל תָּחוּל, but read חוּל; cf. § 113 x.

e　2. The *shortened imperfect* usually has the form יָשֵׂת, יֵשֶׁת, יָבֶן; more rarely, with the tone moved back, e.g. יֶרֶב לוֹ Ju 6³¹, cf. Ex 23¹, אַל־תָּשֶׁת 1 S 9²⁰. So with *wāw consecutive* וַיָּשֶׂם *and he placed*, וַיָּבֶן *and he perceived*; with a middle guttural וַיָּעַט בָּהֶם 1 S 25¹⁴ (see § 72 ee); with ר as 3rd radical, וַתָּשַׁר Ju 5¹. As jussive of לִין תָּלֶן is found in Ju 19²⁰ (in *pause*) and Jb 17², for תָּלֵן.—For אַל־תַּרֹב Pr 3³⁰ *Keth.* (*Qᵉre* תָּרִיב) read תֵּרֶב.

f　3. As *participle active Qal* לָן *spending the night*, occurs once, Neh 13²¹; *participle passive* שִׂים Nu 24²¹, 1 S 9²⁴, Ob⁴; *feminine* שׂוּמָה 2 S 13³², in the *Qᵉrê*, even according to the reading of the Oriental schools (see p. 38, note 2): the *Kᵉthîbh* has שִׂימָה. A *passive of Qal* (cf. above, § 52 e and s, and § 53 u) from שִׂים may perhaps be seen in וַיִּישֶׂם Gn 5C²⁶ (also Gn 24³³ *Kᵉthîbh* וַיִּישֶׂם, *Qᵉrê* וַיִּישֶׂם; the Samaritan in both places has וַיּוּשֶׂם), and also in יֵיסֶךְ Ex 30³², Samaritan יוּסַךְ. Against the explanation of יֵיסֶךְ as a *Hophʿal*-form from סוּךְ, Barth (*Jubelschrift . . . Hildesheimer*, Berlin, 1890, p. 151) rightly urges that the only example of a Hiphʿil of סוּךְ is the doubtful וַיָּסֶךְ, which is probably an *i*-imperfect of *Qal*.—The explanation of יוּשַׂם, &c., as a *passive of Qal* arising from yiysam, &c. = yuysam (so Barth, ibid., note 1), is certainly also unconvincing, so that the correctness of the traditional reading is open to question.

　　　　*　　　*　　　*　　　*　　　*　　　*

g　4. In verbs ע״א the א always retains its consonantal value; these stems are, therefore, to be regarded as verbs *middle Guttural* (§ 64). An exception is יָנָאץ Ec 12⁵ if it be *imperfect Hiphʿil* of נאץ (for יַנְאִיץ); but if the form has really been correctly transmitted, it should rather be referred to נָצַץ, and regarded as incorrectly written for יָנֵץ. On נָאוֹ (from נָאוָה), which was formerly treated here as ע״א, see now § 75 x.

§ 74. *Verbs* אּ״ל, e. g. מָצָא *to find*. *Paradigm O.*

The א in these verbs, as in verbs פּ״א, is treated in some cases as *a* a consonant, i. e. as a guttural, in others as having no consonantal value (as a quiescent or vowel letter), viz.:

1. In those forms which terminate with the א, the final syllable always has the regular vowels, if long, e. g. מֹצֵא, מָצָא, מָצוּא, הִמְצִיא, i. e. the א simply quiesces in the long vowel, without the latter suffering any change whatever. It is just possible that after the altogether heterogeneous vowel *û* the א may originally have preserved a certain consonantal value. On the other hand, if the final א quiesces in a preceding *ă* (as in the *perfect, imperfect,* and *imperative Qal,* in the *perfect Niph'al,* and in *Pu'al* and *Hoph'al*) this *ă* is necessarily lengthened to *ā,* by § 27 *g*, as standing in an open syllable; e. g. מָצָא, יִמְצָ., &c.

The *imperfect* and *imperative Qal* invariably have *ā* in the final syllable, on *b* the analogy of verbs *tertiae gutturalis*; cf., however, § 76 *e*.—In the *imperfect Hithpaʻēl ā* occurs in the final syllable not only (according to § 54 *k*) in the principal pause (Nu 31²³), or immediately before it (Jb 10¹⁶), or with the lesser disjunctives (Lv 21¹·⁴, Nu 19¹³·²⁰), but even out of pause with *Merᵉkha,* Nu 6⁷, and even before *Maqqeph* in Nu 19¹².

2. When א stands at the end of a syllable before an afformative *c* beginning with a consonant (ת, נ), it likewise quiesces with the preceding vowel; thus in the *perfect Qal* (and *Hoph'al,* see below) quiescing with *ă* it regularly becomes *Qameṣ* מָצָאתָ for מָצַאתָ, &c.); but in the *perfect* of all the other active and reflexive conjugations, so far as they occur, it is preceded by *Ṣere* (נִמְצֵאתָ, &c.), and in the *imperative* and *imperfect* by *Sᵉghôl,* תִּמְצֶאנָה, מְצֶאנָה.

(*a*) The *Sᵉghôl* of these forms of the imperfect and imperative might be *d* considered as a modification, and at the same time a lengthening of an original *ă* (see § 8 *a*). In the same way the *ē* of the *perfect* forms in *Pi'ēl,* *Hithpa'ēl,* and *Hiph'îl* might be traced to an original *i* (as in other cases the *ē* and *i* in the final syllable of the 3rd *sing. masc. perfect* of these conjugations), although this *i* may have only been attenuated from an original *ă*. According to another, and probably the correct explanation, however, both the *Ṣere* and the *Sᵉghôl* are due to the analogy of verbs ל״ה (§ 75 *f*) in consequence of the close relation between the two classes, cf. § 75 *nn*.—No form of this kind occurs in *Pu'al*; in the *perfect Hoph'al* only the 2nd *masc. sing.* הֻבָאתָ Ez 40⁴, lengthened according to rule.

(*b*) Before suffixes attached by a connecting vowel (e. g. יִקְרָאֵנִי) the א *e* retains its consonantal value; so before ךָ and כֶם, e. g. אֶמְצָאֲךָ Ct 8¹; הַבְּרַאֲךָ Ez 28¹³ (cf. § 65 *h*), not אֶמְצָאךָ, &c., since these suffixes, by § 58 *f*, are likewise attached to the verb-form by a connecting vowel in the form of *Šᵉwâ mobile*.—As *infinitive Qal* with suffix notice מַחֲאֲךָ Ez 25⁶; *participle* with suffix בֹּרַאֲךָ Is 43¹; *infinitive Pi'ēl* בְּטַמְּאֲכֶם.—The doubly anomalous form יִקְרָאוֹ Jer 23⁶ (for יִקְרָאֵהוּ or יִקְרָאֶנּוּ) is perhaps a *forma mixta* combining the readings יִקְרָאוֹ and יִקְרָאוּ.

f 3. When א begins a syllable (consequently before afformatives which consist of or begin with a vowel, as well as before suffixes) it is necessarily a firm consonant, and the form then follows the analogy of the strong verb, e. g. מָצְאָה *māṣeʾā*, מָצְאוּ, &c. (in *pause* מָצָאוּ, מָצָאָה).

REMARKS.

g 1. Verbs *middle e*, like מָלֵא to be full, retain the Ṣere also in the other persons of the *perfect*, e. g. מָלֵאתִי מָלֵאוּ (מָלֵאת Est 7⁵ has __ owing to its transitive use; for יְרֵאתֶם Jos 4²⁴ read with Ewald יְרָאתֶם). Instead of מָצְאָה the form קָרֵאת she names, on the analogy of the ל״ה-forms noticed in § 75 *m*, occurs in Is 7¹⁴ (from קָרָאת, cf. § 44 *f*), and with a different meaning (*it befalls*) in Dt 31²⁹, Jer 44²³, in both places before א, and hence, probably, to avoid a hiatus (on the other hand, וְחָטָאת Ex 5¹⁶, could only be the 2nd *sing. masc.*; the text which is evidently corrupt should probably be emended to וְחָטָאת לְעַמֶּךָ with the LXX); in *Niphʿal* נִפְלָאת ψ 118²³; in *Hophʿal* הֻבָאת Gn 33¹¹.—The 2nd *fem. sing.* is written קָרָאת by Baer, Gen 16¹¹, &c., according to early MSS.

h 2. The *infin. Qal* occurs sometimes on the analogy of verbs ל״ה (גְּלוֹת, &c., see § 75 *nn*) in the feminine form; so always מְלֹאת to fill (as distinguished from מְלֹא *fullness*), Lv 8³³, 12⁴·⁶, 25³⁰, Jer 29¹⁰, Ez 5², also written מַלְאוֹת Jer 25¹², Jb 20²², &c., and מְלֹאת Est 1⁵. Cf. further, קְרֹאת Ju 8¹; שְׂנֹאת Pr 8¹³; before suffixes, Ez 33¹², and likewise in *Niph.* Zc 13⁴; also in *Piʿēl* לְמַלֹּאת Ex 31⁵, 35³³, or לְמַלֹּאות Dn 9², &c. *Kethibh*; with suffix 2 S 21².—On the (aramaïzing) *infinitives* מַשָּׂאת and מַשָּׂאוֹת, see § 45 *e*; on לִקְרֹאת *obviam*, § 19 *k*.—בִּמְצֹאֲכֶם when ye find, Gn 32²⁰, stands, according to § 93 *q*, for מָצְאֲכֶם. The tone of the lengthened *imperative* רְפָאָה Ps 41⁵ as *Milʿraʿ* (before נַפְשִׁי) is to be explained on rhythmical grounds; cf. the analogous cases in § 72 *s*.—The 2nd *fem. plur. imperative* in Ru 1⁹ has, according to Qimḥi, the form מְצֶאןָ and in verse 20 קְרֶאןָ; on the other hand, the Mantua edition and Ginsburg, on good authority, read מְצֶאןָ, קְרֶאןָ.

i 3. The *participle fem.* is commonly contracted, e. g. מֹצֵאת (for מֹצֵאת) 2 S 18²², cf. Est 2¹⁵; so *Niphʿal* נִפְלֵאת Dt 30¹¹, Zc 5⁷ (but נִשָּׂאָה Is 30²⁵), and *Hophʿal*, Gn 38²⁵; less frequent forms are מוּצֵאת Ct 8¹⁰; נִשֵּׂאת 1 K 10²² (cf. § 76 *b*, שֵׂאת beside לָשֵׂאת as *infinitive construct* from נָשָׂא) and without א (see *k*) יֹצֵת (from יָצָא) Dt 28⁵⁷. In the forms חֹטְאִים sinning, 1 S 14³³, cf. ψ 99⁶; בֹּרְאָם feigning them, Neh 6⁸, the א is elided, and is only retained orthographically (§ 23 *c*) after the retraction of its vowel; see the analogous cases in § 75 *oo*.—On the *plur. masc. ptcp. Niph.* cf. § 93 *oo*.

k 4. Frequently an א which is quiescent is omitted in writing (§ 23 *f*): (a) in the middle of the word, e. g. בָּנוּ 1 S 25⁸; מָצָתִי Nu 11¹¹, cf. Jb 1²¹; צָמֵתִי Ju 4¹⁹, cf. Jb 32¹⁸. In the *imperfect* תִּשֶּׂנָה Jer 9¹⁷, Zc 5⁹, Ru 1¹⁴ (but the same form occurs with *Yôdh* pleonastic after the manner of verbs ל״ה in Ez 23⁴⁹, according to the common reading; cf. § 76 *b* and Jer 50²⁰); in *Piʿēl* אֲחַטֶּנָּה (after elision of the א, cf. § 75 *oo*) Gn 31³⁹; and also in *Niphʿal* נִטְמֵתֶם Lv 11⁴³; cf. Jos 2¹⁶. (b) at the end of the word; וַיְבוֹ 1 K 12¹² *Kethibh*; *Hiphʿil* הֶחֱטִי 2 K 13⁶, cf. Is 53¹⁰ (הֶחֱלִי for הֶחֱלִיא *perfect Hiphʿil* of חָלָה formed after the manner of verbs (ל״א); in the *imperfect Hiph'îl* יִשֵּׁי ψ 55¹⁶ *K^ethîbh*; יָנַי ψ 141⁵; אָבִי 1 K 21¹⁹, Mi 1¹⁵; in the *infinitive*, Jer 32³⁵; in the *participle*, 2 S 5², 1 K 21²¹, Jer 19¹⁵, 39'⁶, all in *K^ethîbh* (מֵבִי, always before א, hence perhaps only a scribal error).

5. In the *jussive, imperfect consecutive*, and *imperative Hiph'îl* a number of cases *l* occur with *i* in the final syllable; cf. יַשְׂא Is 36¹⁴ (in the parallel passages 2 K 18²⁹, 2 Ch 32¹⁵ יַשִּׁיא); וַיְּבִיא Neh 8² (before ע); וַיְּחַטָא 2 K 21¹¹ (cf. 1 K 16², 21²²); וַתַּחְבָּא 2 K 6²⁹; וַיּוֹצֵא Dt 4²⁰, 2 K 11¹², ψ 78¹⁶, 105⁴³; *imperative* הָבִיא Jer 17¹⁸; הוֹצִיא Is 43⁸ (in both cases before ע). If the tradition be correct (which at least in the defectively written forms appears very doubtful) the retention of the *i* is to be attributed to the open syllable; while in the closed syllable of the 3rd *sing. masc.* and *fem.*, and the 2nd *sing. masc.* after ו *consecutive*, the *i* is always reduced to *ē*. In the examples before ע considerations of euphony may also have had some influence (cf. § 75 *hh*).—In Ez 40³, Baer reads with the Western school וַיְּבִיא, while the Orientals read in the *K^ethîbh* ויבוא, and in the *Q^erê* וַיָּבֹא.

On the transition of verbs ל״א to forms of ל״ה see § 75 *nn*.

§ 75. *Verbs* ל״ה, e.g. גָּלָה *to reveal. Paradigm P.*

Brockelmann, *Semit. Sprachwiss.*, p. 149 ff.; *Grundriss*, p. 618 ff.—G. R. Berry, 'Original Waw in ל״ה verbs' in *AJSL*. xx. 256 f.

These verbs, like the verbs פ״י (§§ 69, 70), belong to two different *a* classes, viz. those originally ל״ו and those originally ל״י,[1] which in Arabic, and even more in Ethiopic, are still clearly distinguished. In Hebrew, instead of the original ו or י at the end of the word, a ה always appears (except in the *ptcp. pass. Qal*) as a purely orthographic indication of a final vowel (§ 23 *k*); hence both classes are called ל״ה, e.g. גָּלָה for גָּלֵו *he has revealed*; שָׁלָה for שָׁלֵו *he has rested*. By far the greater number of these verbs are, however, treated as originally ל״י; only isolated forms occur of verbs ל״ו.

שָׁלָה *to be at rest* may be recognized as originally ל״ו, in the forms in which *b* the *Wāw* appears as a strong consonant, cf. 1st *sing. perfect Qal* שָׁלַוְתִּי Jb 3²⁶, the *participle* שָׁלֵו and the derivative שַׁלְוָה *rest*; on the other hand the *imperfect* is יִשְׁלָיוּ (with *Yôdh*). In עָנָה (Arab. עני) *to answer*, and עָנָה (Arab. ענו)[2] *to be afflicted*, are to be seen two verbs originally distinct, which have been assimilated in Hebrew (see the Lexicon, s. v. עָנָה).

---

[1] According to Wellhausen, 'Ueber einige Arten schwacher Verba' in his *Skizzen*, vi. p. 255 ff., the ל״ה verbs, apart from some true ל״ו and some probable ל״י, are to be regarded as originally biliteral. To compensate for their arrested development they lengthened the vowel after the 2nd radical, as the ע״ו verbs did after the 1st radical. But although there is much to be said for this view, it fails to explain pausal forms like חָסָיָה (see *u*). It seems impossible that these should all be *late* formations.

[2] In the Mêša' inscription, line 5, ויענו *and he oppressed* occurs as 3rd *sing. masc. imperfect Pi'êl*, and in line 6, אענו *I will oppress* as 1st *sing.*

Of quite a different class are those verbs of which the third radical is a *consonantal* ה (distinguished by *Mappîq*). These are inflected throughout like verbs *tertiae gutturalis*. Cf. § 65 note on the heading.

c　The grammatical structure of verbs ל״ה (see Paradigm *P*) is based on the following laws :—

1. In all forms in which the original *Yôdh* or *Wāw* would stand at the end of the word, it is dropped (cf. § 24 *g*) and ה takes its place as an orthographic indication of the preceding long vowel. Such an indication would have been indispensable, on practical grounds, in the still unvocalized consonantal text. But even after the addition of the vowel signs, the orthographic rule remained, with insignificant exceptions (see § 8 *k*, and *ā* in קָטַלְתָּ, &c.), that a final vowel must be indicated by a vowel letter. In verbs ל״ה the ה which is here employed as a vowel letter is preceded by the same vowel in the same part of the verb throughout all the conjugations. Thus the endings are—

הָ— in all perfects, גָּלָה, נִגְלָה, גֻּלָּה, &c.

הֶ֫— in all imperfects and participles, גֹּלֶה, יִגְלֶה, &c.

הֵ֫— in all imperatives, גְּלֵה, גַּלֵּה, &c.

הֹ֫— in the infinitive absolute (גָּלֹה, &c.), except in *Hiph'îl, Hoph'al*, and generally also *Pi'ēl*, see *aa* and *ff*.

The *participle passive Qal* alone forms an exception, the original י (or ו, see *v*) reappearing at the end, גָּלוּי; and so also some derived nouns (§ 84*a*, *c*, *ϵ*, &c.).

The *infinitive construct* always has the ending וֹת (with ת *feminine*); *Qal* גְּלוֹת, *Pi'ēl* גַּלּוֹת, &c.; for exceptions, see *n* and *y*.

d　These forms may be explained as follows :—in the *perfect Qal* גָּלָה stands, according to the above, for גָּלַי(וֹ), and, similarly, in *Niph'al, Pu'al*, and *Hoph'al*. The *Pi'ēl* and *Hithpa'ēl* may be based on the forms קַטֵּל, הִתְקַטֵּל (§ 52 *l*; and § 54 *k*), and *Hiph'îl* on the form הַקְטֵל, on the analogy of the *ă* in the second syllable of the Arabic *'áqtălă* (§ 53 *a*). Perhaps, however, the final *ā* of these conjugations simply follows the analogy of the other conjugations.

e　The explanation of the final tone-bearing הֶ֫— of the *imperfect* is still a matter of dispute. As to the various treatments of it, see Barth, *Nominalbildung*, i. p. xxx ff, with § 136, Rem., and *ZDMG*. xliv. 695 f., against Philippi's objections in the *Zeitschrift für Völkerpsychologie*, 1890, p. 356 f. ; also *ZDMG*. lvi. 244, where Barth appeals to the rule that, in the period before the differentiation of the North Semitic dialects, final *iy* becomes —ֶ (*constr.* הֶ֫—), not *î* ; M. Lambert, *Journ. Asiat.* 1893, p. 285 ; Prätorius, *ZDMG*. lv. 365. The most probable explanation now seems to be, first, that the uniform pronunciation of *all* imperfects and participles with *S^eghôl* in the last syllable merely follows the analogy of the *impf. Qal*, and secondly, that the *S^eghôl* of the *impf. Qal* does perhaps ultimately represent a contraction of the original termination י—ֶ (= *ai*), although elsewhere (e.g. in the *imperative* of ל״ה) *ai* is usually contracted to *ê*.

2. When the original *Yôdh* stands at the end of the syllable before *f* an afformative beginning with a consonant (ת, נ) there arises (*a*) in the *perfects*, primarily the diphthong *ai* ('ַ֫י). In the middle of the word this ought always to be contracted to *ê* ('ֵ֫י), but this *ê* is only found consistently in the passive conjugations, whilst regularly in *Qal*, and frequently in the other active and reflexive conjugations (especially in *Piʿēl*), it appears as *î* (cf. *x, z, ee*). This *î*, however, in the *perf.* *Qal* is not to be explained as a weakening of an original *ê*, but as the original vowel of the *intransitive* form. It then became usual also in the *transitive* forms of *Qal* (and in some other conjugations on this analogy), whereas e. g. in Syriac the two kinds of forms are still carefully distinguished.—(*b*) In the *imperfects* and *imperatives*, 'ֶ֫י with the tone always appears before the afformative נָה. On the most probable explanation of this 'ֶ֫י, see above, *e*.

Summary. Accordingly before afformatives beginning with a con- *g* sonant the principal vowel is—

In the perfect *Qal* *î*, e. g. גָּלִ֫יתָ;

In the perfects of the other active and reflexive conjugations, sometimes *ê*, sometimes *î*, גִּלִּ֫יתָ and גִּלֵּ֫יתָ; נִגְלֵ֫יתָ and נִגְלִ֫יתָ;

In the perfects passive always *ê*, e. g. גֻּלֵּ֫יתָ;

In the imperfects and imperatives always 'ֶ֫י, e. g. תִּגְלֶ֫ינָה, גְּלֶ֫ינָה.

The diphthongal forms have been systematically retained in Arabic and Ethiopic; only as an exception and in the popular language is the diphthong contracted. In Aramaic the contracted forms predominate, yet the Syriac, for example, has in *Qal* 2nd *pers. sing.* *gᵉlait* (but 1st *pers. sing.* גְּלִית), and so too the Western Aramaic גְּלִ֫יתָ, but also גְּלֵ֫יתָ.

3. Before the vocalic afformatives (ו, 'ִ֫י, ָה) the *Yôdh* is usually *h* dropped altogether, e. g. גָּלוּ (ground-form *gălăyû*), תִּגְלִי, *participle fem.* גֹּלָה, *plur. masc.* גֹּלִים; yet the old full forms also not infrequently occur, especially in *pause*, see *u*. The elision of the *Yôdh* takes place regularly before *suffixes*, e. g. גְּלָךְ (see *ll*).

4. In the 3rd *sing. fem. perfect*, the original feminine ending ־ת *i* was appended to the stem; hence, after elision of the *Yôdh*, arose properly forms like גָּלָת, with *ā* in the final syllable with the tone. This form, however, has been but rarely preserved (see below, *m*). The analogy of the other forms had so much influence, that the common ending ־ָה was added pleonastically to the ending ־ת. Before the ־ָה the vowel of the ending ־ת, which thus loses the tone, becomes *Šᵉwâ*, and thus there arise such forms as נִגְלְתָה, גָּלְתָה, &c. (but in *pause* גָּלָ֫תָה, &c.).

For similar cases see § 70 *d*; § 91 *m*.

k **5.** Finally, a strongly-marked peculiarity of verbs ל״ה is the rejection of the ending ה‎ָ in forming the *jussive* and the *imperfect consecutive*. This shortening o:curs in all the conjugations, and sometimes also involves further changes in the vocalization (see *o, y, bb, gg*). Similarly, in some conjugations a *shortened imperative* (cf. § 48 *k*) is formed by *apocope* of the final ה‎ָ (see *cc, gg*).

l **6.** The ordinary form of the *imperfect* with the ending ה‎ָ serves in verbs ל״ה to express the cohortative also (§ 48 *c*); cf. Gn 1²⁶, 2¹⁸, 2 Ch 25¹⁷, &c. With a final ה‎ָ there occur only: in *Qal*, אֶשְׁעָה ψ 119¹¹⁷, אֶהֱמָיָה (with the י retained, see below, *u*) ψ 77⁴; and in *Hithpa'ēl* וְנִשָּׁעָה Is 41²³ (with *Ṭiphḥa*, therefore in lesser pause).

REMARKS.

I. *On Qal*.

m 1. The older form of the *fem.* of the 3rd *sing. perf.* גָּלָת, mentioned above, under *i* (cf. § 74 *g*), is preserved in עָשָׂת (before א) Lv 25²¹ (cf. 2 K 9³⁷ *Kethibh*)¹; likewise in *Hiph'il* הִרְצָת (before א) Lv 26³⁴; הֶלְאָת Ez 24¹²; and in *Hoph'al* הָגְלָת (before י) Jer 13¹⁹.—The 2nd *sing. fem.* is also written יִתְ‎__; thus in the textus receptus וְהָיִית 2 S 14², and always in Baer's editions (since 1872), as in most other verbs; חָזִית and גָּלִית Is 57⁸; עָשִׂית Jer 2²³, Ez 16⁴⁸, &c. (so וְהוֹצֵאת 1 K 17¹³ from יָצָא). In the 3rd *pers. plur.* the tone, instead of keeping its usual place (גָּלוּ, &c.), is retracted in ψ 37²⁰, כָּלוּ, both on account of the *pause* and also in rhythmical antithesis to the preceding כָּלוֹ; also in Is 16⁸ תָּעוּ (according to Delitzsch for the sake of the assonance with נָגְעוּ); and in Jb 24¹ חָזוּ.—On the tone of the *perfect consecutive* see § 49 *k*.

n 2. The *infin. absol.* frequently has וֹ (probably a survival of the older orthography) for ה‎ָ__, e.g. הָיוֹ Gn 18¹⁸; עָשֹׂו Jer 4¹⁸, &c., Ez 31¹¹; קָנוֹ 2 S 24²⁴; רָאֹו Gn 26²⁸, Is 6⁹ (cf. 1 S 6¹²), &c., beside רָאֹה. The form שָׁתוֹת Is 22¹³ (beside שָׁתוֹ in the same verse) appears to have been chosen on account of its similarity in sound to שָׁחֹט; so in Is 42²⁰ *Qerē* and Ho 10⁴, אָלוֹת (unless it is a substantive, *oaths*) and כָּרֹת; cf. also עָרוֹת Hb 3¹³.—Conversely, instead of the *infinitive construct* גְּלוֹת such forms are occasionally found as רְאֹה גְּלֹה or גְּלֹה, cf. Gn 48¹¹; קְנֹה Pr 16¹⁶; עֲשֹׂה Gn 50²⁰, ψ 101³, also עֲשֹׂו Gn 31²⁸ (cf. Pr 31⁴), and even with the *suffix* הוֹ the very remarkable form עֲשֹׂהוּ Ex 18¹⁸.²—The feminine form רָאֲוָה (for רְאוֹת) Ez 28¹⁷, analogous to nouns like גַּאֲוָה (cf. § 45 *d*), is strange, but הֱיֵה as *infin.* Ez 21¹⁵ is quite inexplicable.—The forms הֹגוֹ and הֹרוֹ Is 59¹³ are perhaps to be regarded with Barth, *Nominalbildung*, § 51 *a*, as *infinitives absolute* of the *passive* of *Qal* (see above, § 53 *u*), not of *Pōʿēl*.—The 2nd *sing. masc. imperative* וַחֲיֵה occurs in the principal pause in Pr 4⁴ and 7²; but

---

¹ In the Siloam inscription also (see above, § 2 *d*), line 3, היח may be read היָת quite as well as [היָתְה‎.

² All these infinitives construct in *ô*, in the Pentateuch, belong to the document called E; cf. § 69 *m*, second note.

probably these forms are simply to be attributed to ρ Masoretic school, which in general marked the difference between certain forms by the use of ê for ē, and conversely ē for ê; cf. the analogous examples in § 52 n, and especially § 75 hh, also Kautzsch, *Grammatik des Bibl.-Aram.*, § 17, 2, Rem. 1.—On the reading וּרְאֵינָה Ct 3¹¹ (for וּרְאֶינָה, on the analogy of the reading מְצֶאנָה, &c., § 74 h), see Baer's note on the passage.

3. The *shortening* of the *imperfect* (see above, k, and the note on hh) occasions **O** in *Qal* the following changes:

(a) As a rule the first radical takes a helping *S⁰ghôl*, or, if the second radical is a guttural, a helping *Pathaḥ* (according to § 28 e). Thus יֶגֶל for יִגֶל; וַיִּבֶז *and he despised*, Gn 25³⁴; וַיִּבֶן *and he built*; יֵשַׁע *he looks*; וַיִּמַח *and he destroyed*, Gn 7²³.

(b) The ĭ of the preformative is then sometimes lengthened to ē, e.g. יֵרָא **p** *he sees*. This, however, mostly happens only after the preformative ת, whilst after י the homogeneous ĭ remains, e.g. וַתֵּכַל (but וְיִכַל), וַתֵּפֶן (but יִפֶן), וַתֵּרֶב (but וַיִּרֶב); with middle guttural וַתֵּחַה, תֵּחַע Jb 17⁷ (from כָּהָה). The unusual position of the tone in תֵּרָא Zc 9⁵, וְתֵרָא Mi 7¹⁰ (so Baer and Ginsb.; ed. Mant. יֵרָא, וַיֵּרָא) is best explained (except in יֵרָא Gn 41³³, before פ) on the analogy of קוּמָה, &c., § 72 s, as due to the following א. But cf. also hh.

(c) The helping vowel is elsewhere not used under the circumstances mentioned in § 28 d; וַיֵּשְׁבְּ Nu 21¹, Jer 41¹⁰, cf. וַיִּפְתְּ Jb 31²⁷; on the other hand, **q** with ĭ lengthened into ē (see p) וַיֵּשְׁתְּ, וַיֵּרְדְ, וַיִּבְךְ, יֵשַׁתְּ. The form יֵרָא *he sees*, occurs parallel with וַיַּרְא *and he saw* (but 3rd *fem.* always וַתֵּרֶא), the latter with the original *Pathaḥ* on account of the following ר, and identical with the 3rd *sing. masc.* of the *imperf. consec.* Hiph'il, 2 K 11⁴.

(d) Examples of verbs *primae gutturalis* (§ 63), and at the same time לה, **r** are וַיַּעַשׂ, in pause וַיָּעַשׂ *and he made*, from עָשָׂה; וַיַּעַן *and he answered*, from עָנָה (always identical with the corresponding forms in Hiph'il), וַיַּחַץ *and he divided*, from חצה. On some similar forms of אפ see § 76 d.—In the following cases the initial (hard) guttural does not affect the form: וַיֵּחַר *and he was wroth*, וַיֵּחַן *and he encamped* (3rd plur. וַיַּחֲנוּ), יֵחַדְּ (with *Dageš lene* and *Š⁰wâ*) *let it rejoice*, Jb 3⁶; cf. Ex 18⁹.—On וַיֵּט, וַיֵּז (לה) as well as (פן), &c., see § 76 b, c, f.

(e) The verbs הָיָה *to be*, and חָיָה *to live*, of which the shortened imperfects **S** ought to be yihy and yiḥy, change these forms to יְהִי and יְחִי, the second Yôdh being resolved into i at the end of the word; but in pause (§ 29 n) יֶחִי, יֶהִי, with the original ă modified to S⁰ghôl with the tone (cf. also nouns like בְּכִי for bakhy. in pause; בֶּכִי; עֳנִי for 'ŏny, &c., § 84ᵃ c, and § 93 x). For תֵּשַׁי, however, in Dt 32¹⁸, since no verb שָׁיָה exists, we must read either תֵּשׁ, or better תִּשֶּׁה (Samaritan תשׁא), as imperfect Qal of נָשָׁה *to forget*.—Analogous to יְהִי from הָיָה, there occurs once, from הָוָה *to be*, the form יְהוּא for יְהוּ *he will be*, Ec 11³, but no doubt הוּא is the right reading.

The *full* forms (without apocope of the הַ◌ָ, cf. § 49 c) not infrequently **t** occur after *wāw consecutive*, especially in the 1st pers. and in the later books, e.g. וָאֶרְאֶה *and I saw*, twenty times, and Jos 7²¹ in K⁰thibh, but never in the Pentateuch (וָאֵרֶא fifteen times, of which three are in the Pent.); also in the

3rd pers. וַיִּרְאֶה Ez 18²⁸, Jb 42¹⁶ *Q^ere*; וַיַּעְשֶׂה *and he made*, four times (but וַיַּעַשׂ over 200 times); cf. also Ju 19² (וַתִּזְנֶה); 1 K 10²⁹ (וַתַּעֲלֶה); Dt 1¹⁶ (וָאֲצַוֶּה), and Gn 24⁴⁸. So also occasionally for the *jussive*, cf. Gn 1⁹, 41³⁴, Jer 28⁶.—For the well attested, but meaningless תִּירְאוּ Jb 6²¹ (doubtless caused by the following וַתִּרְאוּ), read תִּרְאוּ *ye see*, with Ginsburg.

u 4. The original י sometimes appears even before afformatives beginning with a vowel (cf. above, *h* and *l*), especially in and before the *pause*, and before the full plural ending וּן‎__, or where for any reason an emphasis rests on the word. *Perfect* חָסָיוּ ψ 57², חָסָיוּ Dt 32³⁷, cf. ψ 73² *Q^erê*; *imperative* בְּעָיוּ Is 21¹².

Imperfect יֶאֱתָיוּ Jb 16²², 30¹⁴ (without the *pause*, ψ 68³²); יִשְׁלָיוּ ψ 122⁶, Jb 12⁶, cf. ψ 77⁴; יִרְבָּיֻן Dt 8¹³; ψ 36⁹: more frequently like יִשְׁתָּיוּן ψ 78⁴⁴; Is 17¹², 21¹², 26¹¹, 31³, 33⁷, 41⁵, ψ 36⁸, 39⁷, 83³; before a suffix, Jb 3²⁵. Also in Pr 26⁷ דַּלְיוּ, as *perf. Qal* from דָּלָה, was perhaps originally intended, but hardly דַּלְיוּ, since these full forms, though they may stand out of pause, do not begin sentences; דַּלְיוּ probably points to דָּלֽוּ from דָּלַל as the right reading, since the sense requires an intransitive verb. Cf. further, *v*, *x*, *dd*, *gg*.

v 5. The *participle active* (cf. Vollers, 'Das Qâtil-Partizipium,' *ZA.* 1903, p. 312 ff., and on the participles of ל״ה, *ibid.*, p. 316 ff.), besides feminine forms like עֹלָה Ju 20³¹, &c., רֹאָה Pr 20¹², has also a *feminine* which retains the 3rd radical י, viz. בּוֹכִיָּה (= בֹּכָה) *weeping*, La 1¹⁶; הוֹמִיָּה *tumultuous*, Is 22² (*plur.* Pr 1²¹); צוֹפִיָּה *spying*, Pr 31²⁷, פְּרִיָּה *fruitful*, ψ 128³, *plur.* אֲתִיּוֹת *the things that are to come*, Is 41²³. With the ordinary strong inflexion י appears in עֹטְיָה Ct 1⁷, but perhaps there also עֹטִיָּה was intended, unless it should be טֹעִיָּה *a wanderer*. For רֹאֲנִי Is 47¹⁰, רֹאֵנִי is to be read.—On עֹשֶׂה 1 K 20⁴⁰ for עֹשֶׂה, cf. § 116 *g*, note. —In the *participle passive* the 3rd radical still sometimes appears as ו (§ 24 *b*), cf. עָשׂוּ *made*, Jb 41²⁵, צָפוּ Jb 15²², contracted from עָשׂוּי, צָפוּי; and before a formative ending, it even has its consonantal sound, הֶעָשׂוּם (read הֶעֲשׂוּיִם) 2 K 23⁴; עָשׂוּות (read *ʿasûwôth*) 1 S 25¹⁸ *K^ethibh*, נטוות (read *n^ṭûwôth*) Is 3¹⁶ *K^ethibh*. The shortening of the *û* in רְאִיוֹת Est 2⁹ is irregular.

w 6. The defective writing is rare in such forms as וְהָיִת 2 S 15³³; בָּנֹתִי 1 K 8⁴⁴, cf. 1 K 9⁸; וְתִדְלֶנָה Ex 2¹⁶ (cf. Jer 18²¹, 48⁶, 1 Ch 7¹⁵, Jb 17⁵, &c.), and the pronunciation תִּרְאֶינָה Mi 7¹⁰, cf. תַּעֲנֶנָּה Ju 5²⁹ (unless they are *sing.* with *suff.* of the 3rd *sing. fem.*). Both cases are probably to be explained according to § 20 *i*.

II. *On Niphʿal.*

x 7. Here the forms with ‎י‎__ in the 1st and 2nd pers. *sing.* of the *perfect* predominate (‎י‎__ only in נִקֵּיתָ Gn 24⁸); on the other hand in the 1st *plur.* always ‎י‎__, as נִגְלֵינוּ 1 S 14⁸. No examples of the 2nd *plur.* occur.—With י retained in *pause* נִפְוָּיוּ Nu 24⁶; once with an initial guttural נֶחֶרוּ Ct 1⁶ for נֶחֱרוּ, probably arising from the ordinary strong form *niḥru*, but the harshness of ח immediately followed by ר is avoided by pronouncing the ח with *Ḥaṭeph-Pathaḥ*.—In the 3rd *sing. fem.* נִשְׁתְּוָה Pr 27¹⁵ (in pause for נִשְׁתְּוָה) ו and ת may be transposed for euphonic reasons; but probably we should simply read נִשְׁוָתָה.—Among Niphʿal forms of ל״ה must be classed, with Buxtorf and others (cf. Nöldeke, *ZDMG.* xxx. 185), נָאֲוָה from אָוָה, not Pi'lel of נאה (=נָאוּ ; hence, according to § 23 *d*, נָאווּ *they are beautiful* (for נָאֲווּ) Is 52⁷, Ct 1¹⁰ ; but in ψ 93⁵, where Baer requires נָאֲוָה, read נָאֲוָה with ed. Mant., Ginsb.

8. The *apocope of the imperfect* causes no further changes beyond the rejection *y* of the ה__ , e.g. יִגֶל from יִגְלֶה ; in one verb *middle guttural*, however, a form occurs with the *Qameṣ* shortened to *Pathaḥ*, viz. יִמַח (for יִמְחֶה) ψ 109¹³, as in verbs ע״ע ; but in *pause* תִּמַח verse 14. Cf. *bb*.—The *infinitive absolute* נִגְלוֹת emphasizing an *infinitive construct*, 2 S 6²⁰, is very extraordinary ; probably it is a subsequent correction of an erroneous repetition of הִגָּלוֹת.—The *infin.* *constr.* לִקְרַאת occurs in Ju 13²¹, 1 S 3²¹ for לְהִקָּרֵאת ; cf. above, *n*.—On the *infinitive Niph'al* with the ה elided, see § 51 *l*.—The irregular תֵּעָלוּ Ez 36³ has probably arisen from a combination of the readings תֵּעָלוּ (*Qal*) and תֵּעָלוּ (*Niph'al*). Similarly the solecism נִמְבְּזָה 1 S 15⁹ might be due to a combination of the *participle fem. Niph'al* (נִבְזָה, cf. נַחְלָה, נֶחְפָּה, נֶעֶשְׂתָה) with the *Hoph'al* (מֻבְזָה) ; but it is more correct, with Wellhausen, to explain the מ from a confusion with נמס and to read, in fact, נִבְזֶה וְנִמְאָסְת.

III. On Pi'ēl, Pô'ēl, Pu'al, and Hithpa'ēl.

9. In the 1st and 2nd persons of the *perfect Pi'ēl* the second syllable in ≈ most of the instances has י__ on the analogy of *Qal* (see *f*), as קִוִּיתִי, דִּמִּיתָ ; always so in the first *plur.*, and before *suffixes*, e.g. כִּסִּינוּ Gn 37²⁶, דִּמִּיתָנוּ ψ 44²⁰. The form with י__ is found only in the 1st *sing.* (e.g. Jo 4²¹ ; Is 5⁴, 8¹⁷ along with the form with *î*). On the tone of the *perf. consec. Pi'el* of ל״ה, see § 49 *k*.—*Hithpa'ēl* has (besides י__ Jer 17¹⁶) as a rule י__ (Pr 24¹⁰, 1 K 2²⁶, Jer 50²⁴). On the other hand, *Pu'al* always has י__ , e.g. עֻשֵּׂיתִי ψ 139¹⁵.—A 1st *sing. perfect Pô'ēl* שׁוֹשֵׂתִי (=שׁוֹסַיְתִּי) occurs in Is 10¹³.

10. The *infinitive absolute Pi'ēl* takes the form כַּלֵּה, גַּלֵּה (like קַטֵּל, the more *aa* frequent form even in the strong verb, see § 52 *o*) ; with *ô* only in ψ 40² כַּוֹּה ; with *ôth* Hb 3¹³ עָרוֹת (cf. above, *n*). On הִגֹּו and הֵרֹו, *infinitives absolute* of the passive of *Qal*, not of *Pô'ēl*, see above, *n*.—As *infinitive construct* חַכֵּי occurs in *Pi'ēl*, Ho 6⁹ (only orthographically different from חַכֵּה, if the text is correct) ; לְכַלֵּא Dn 9²⁴ (on the א see *rr*) ; עַד־לְכַלֵּה 2 Ch 24¹⁰, 31¹, for which in 2 K 13¹⁷·¹⁹, Ezr 9¹⁴ עַד־כַּלֵּה with *infin. abs.* ; in *Pu'al* עֻנּוֹת ψ 132¹.

11. The apocopated *imperfect* must (according to § 20 *l*) lose the *Dageš forte* *bb* of the second radical, hence וְיִצַו *and he commanded*, יַֽעַר (for תְּעָרֶה =*tᵉ'arrè*) ψ 141⁸ ; cf. Gn 24²⁰ ; even in the principal pause אַל־תְּגַל Pr 25⁹ ; *Hithpa'ēl* וַיִּתְגַּל *and he uncovered himself*, Gn 9²¹ ; תִּתְרַע Pr 22²⁴ ; cf. ψ 37¹·⁷·⁸. With the lengthening of *Pathaḥ* to *Qameṣ*, וַיְתָו *and he made marks*, 1 S 21¹⁴ (but read with Thenius וַיְתָו, and instead of the meaningless וַיְשַׁנּוּ *ibid.* read וַיְשֶׁן). In *Hithpa'ēl* אַל־תִּתְגָּר, in close connexion, Dt 2⁹·¹⁹ ; תִּשְׁתַּע Is 41¹⁰ ; according to Qimḥi also יִתְאָו, תִּתְאָו ψ 45¹², Pr 23³·⁶, 24¹, 1 Ch 11¹⁷, whilst Baer and Ginsburg read with the best authorities תִּתְאָו, יִתְאָו (but cf. König, *Lehrgebäude*, i. 597).[1]—On אֲחַוְךָ Jb 15¹⁷ (for אֲחַוֶּךָ) cf. § 20 *m* ; on אֹכְלְךָ Ex 33³, see § 27 *q* ;

---

[1] In Nu 34⁷ *f.*, according to verse 10, תִּתְאָו (=תִּתְאַוּוּ) is intended to be read for תִּתָאוּ (*imperfect Pi'ēl* from תָּאָה).

on יָרַד Ju 5¹³, see § 69 *g*. Finally, on דְּלִיּוּ, which is referred to *Pi'ēl* by some, as a supposed *imperative*, see above, *u*.

cc 12. Examples of apocopated *imperatives* in *Pi'ēl* and *Hithpa'ēl* are : צַו, also צַוֵּה *command thou*, גַּל *open thou*, ψ 119¹⁸.²²; כַּן *prepare thou*, ψ 61⁸; נַס for נַסֵּה *prove thou*, Dn 1¹²; הִתְחַל *feign thyself sick*, 2 S 13⁵; cf. Dt 2²⁴.—On רַבָּה Ju 9²⁹, cf. § 48 *l*.—In ψ 137⁷ עָרוּ *rase it*, is found twice instead of עָרוּ (for 'arrû) for rhythmical reasons (cf., however, וְיֵעָרוּ in the *imperfect*, 2 Ch 24¹¹).

dd 13. Examples of forms in which the *Yôdh* is retained are the *imperfects* תְּרַמְּיוּן Is 40¹⁸, cf. verse 25 and 46⁵; יְכַסְּיֻמוּ *they cover them*, Ex 15⁵; *participle Pu'al* מְכֻסְּיָם Is 25⁶; for אֲרַיְוֶךְ Is 16⁹ (from רָוָה) read with Margolis, אֲרַוְּיֵךְ.

IV. *On Hiph'il and Hoph'al.*

ee 14. The 3rd *sing. perfect Hiph'il* sometimes has *S°ghôl* in the first syllable instead of *i* (§ 53 *p*), especially in הִגְלָה (but *perfect consecutive* וְהִגְלָה 2 K 24¹⁴), הֶרְאָה, הֶלְאָה; also with *suffixes*, e. g. הֶגְלָם 1 Ch 8⁷, הֶלְאָנִי Jb 16⁷, וְהִפְדָּהּ Ex 21⁸. The *S°ghôl* also occurs in the 1st *sing.*, e. g. הֶלְאֵתִיךְ Mi 6³. On וְהִרְאֵיתִי Na 3⁵, cf. § 53 *p*. The forms with *ê* in the second syllable (also written defectively, as וְהִכֵּתִי Jer 21⁶) are found throughout in the 1st *sing.* (except Pr 5¹³), rarely in the 2nd *sing. masc.*, and never in the 1st *plur.* In the other persons they are about equally common with *i*, except in the 2nd *plur.*, where *i* predominates. Before *suffixes* the forms with *i* predominate throughout; cf., however, *ê* in Ex 4¹², Mi 6³, Pr 4¹¹. On the tone of the *perf. consec. Hiph.* of ה״ל, see § 49 *k*. In *Hoph'al* only ֵי occurs in the 2nd syllable.

ff 15. In the *infinitive Hiph'il* of רָבָה *to be abundant*, besides the *construct* הַרְבּוֹת we find the *absolute* הַרְבָּה taking the place of the common form הַרְבֵּה, which had come to be used invariably (but König calls attention to its use as *infinitive construct* in Ez 21²⁰) as an adverb, in the sense of *much*; in 2 S 14¹¹ the *Q°rê* requires הַרְבַּת for the *K°thîbh* הַרְבִּית, an evident scribal error for הַרְבּוֹת. Cf. Gn 41⁴⁹, 22¹⁷, Dt 28⁶³; the pointing הַרְבֵּה Jer 42² probably arises from regarding this form as a noun.—On הַמְרוֹת Jb 17² (with *Dageš f. dirimens*) see § 20 *h*.—In 2 K 3²⁴ הַכּוֹת (before א) is probably *infinitive absolute*, used in order to avoid the hiatus, cf. § 113 *x*, and on a similar case in *Qal*, see above, *n*.—On the *infinitives* with elision of the ה, cf. § 53 *q*.

gg 16. The *shortened imperfect Hiph'il* either takes no helping vowel, as יַפְתְּ *let him enlarge*, Gn 9²⁷; יַרְדְּ *he shall subdue*, Is 41²; וַיַּשְׁקְ *and he watered*, Gn 29¹⁰, &c.; וַיַּרְא *and he showed*, 2 K 11⁴ (see § 28 *d*): or else has a helping vowel, as יֶגֶל (for יַגְל, see § 27 *r*), e. g. 2 K 18¹¹; וַיֶּפֶר ψ 105²⁴; וַתֹּאמֶר Ez 5⁶; וַיֵּחַת 2 Ch 33⁹; וארב i. e. probably וָאָרֶב Jos 24³ *K°thîbh* (וָאַרְבֶּה *Q°rê*).—Examples of verbs *first guttural*: וַיַּעַל Nu 23², וָאַעַל, &c., which can be distinguished as *Hiph'il* from the similar forms in *Qal* only by the sense.—The apocopated *imperative Hiph'il* always (except in verbs פ״ן, e. g. הַךְ, הַט, § 76 *c*) has a helping vowel, *S°ghôl* or *Pathaḥ*, e. g. הֶרֶב *increase thou* (for harb, הַרְבֵּה) ψ 51⁴ *Q°rê*, also Ju 20³⁸; where, however, it cannot be explained the text stands; הֶרֶף *let alone* (for הַרְף, הַרְפֵּה Dt 9¹⁴, &c.; הַעַל (for הַעֲלֵה) Ex 8¹, 33¹²; but for הָשַׁע ψ 39¹⁴, which could only be *imperative Hiph'il* of שָׁעַע (= *smear over*, as in Is 6¹⁰), read with Baethgen שְׁעֵה *look away*.—The *imperfect Hiph'il* with *Yôdh* retained occurs only in תּוֹנִיּן Jb 19², from יָנָה. Cf. *u*.

V. *In General.*

17. In Aramaic the *imperfect* and *participle* of all the conjugations terminate *hh* in אֵ__ or יֵ__. The Hebrew *infinitives*, *imperatives*, and *imperfects* in ה__, less frequently אֵ__ or יֵ__, may be due to imitation of these forms. On the *infinitive construct Pi'ēl* חַפֵּי, see above, *aa* ; *imperative Qal* הֱוֵא Jb 37⁶ (in the sense of *fall*) ; *imperfect* יֵרֵא *let him look out*, Gn 41³³ (but see above, *p*) ; יַעֲשֶׂה *he will do*, Is 64³ ; אַל־תִּהְיֶה Jer 17¹⁷ ; אַל־תֹּבֶא *consent thou not*, Pr 1¹⁰ ; אַל־תַּעֲשֶׂה *do thou not*, 2 S 13¹² (the same form in Gn 26²⁹, Jos 7⁹, Jer 40¹⁶ Q°rê) ; אֶהְיֶה (so Baer and Ginsburg, after cod. Hillel, &c.) *I will be*, Jer 31¹ ; וַנַּעֲשֶׂה Jos 9²⁴ ; תֵּרָאֶה Dn 1¹³. Cf. also in *Niph'al* יִמָּצֵה Lv 5⁹ ; תִּבָּנֶה (according to Qimḥi) Nu 21²⁷ ; in *Pi'ēl* תִּנָּלֶה Lv 18⁷·⁸·¹²⁻¹⁷, 20¹⁹, in each case לֹא תִגַּלֶּה, beside תְּנַלֶּה with a minor distinctive; יֵנָּקֵה (Baer יְנַקֶּה) Na 1³ ; אֱזֹרֶה Ez 5¹² (with *Zaqeph* ; Baer אֱזָרֶה). The fact, however, that a great number of these forms occur in *pause* and represent at the same time a *jussive* or *voluntative* (Jos 7⁹), suggests the view that the Ṣere is used merely to increase the emphasis of the pausal form, and at the same time to make a distinction in sound between the *jussive* or *voluntative* and the ordinary *imperfect*.[1] Elsewhere (Gn 26²⁹, Lv 5⁹, Jer 40¹⁶, Dn 1¹³ ; according to Baer also Mi 7¹⁰, Zc 9⁵) the pronunciation with *ê* is probably intended to soften the hiatus caused by a following א or ע ; cf. the analogous cases above, § 74 *l*.

The ending יֵ__ appears to stand for ה__ in the *imperfect Qal* in וַתִּזְנִי־שָׁם *ii* *and there hath she played the harlot*, Jer 3⁶ ; perhaps, however, the 2nd *sing. fem.* is intended, or it may have been introduced into the text of Jeremiah from Ez 16¹⁵, &c. Still more strange is it in the *imperfect Hiph'il* אַל־תֶּרְמִי Jer 18²³ ; but the Mil'ēl-tone probably points to תֶּרֶם as the correct reading (cf. Neh 13¹⁴). The יֵ__ stands for ה__ in the *perfect Hiph'il* הֶחֱלִי *he made sick*, Is 53¹⁰, which is probably for הֶחֱלִיא from חָלָא, a secondary form of חלה ; see *rr*. The *plur.* הֵמַסִּיוּ (Baer הֵמַסִּיו) *they made to melt*, Jos 14⁸, is a purely Aramaic form.

18. In two verbs the rare conjugation Pa'lēl or its reflexive (§ 55 *d*) occurs : *kk* מְשָׁחֲוֵי *archers*, Gn 21¹⁶ (from מָחָה) ; but most frequently in שָׁחָה *to bend*, Pa'ēl שַׁחֲוֶה not in use, whence reflexive הִשְׁתַּחֲוֶה *to bow oneself, to prostrate oneself*, 2nd *pers.* in יֵתָ_. and 1st *pers.* in יֵתִי_., *imperfect* יִשְׁתַּחֲוֶה, consecutive 3rd *sing. masc.* וַיִּשְׁתַּחוּ for *wayyištaḥw* (analogous to the noun-forms, like שָׂחוּ for *saḥw*) ; 3rd *plur.* יִשְׁתַּחֲווּ.—Instead of the aramaizing *infinitive* with *suffix* הִשְׁתַּחֲוָתִי 2 K 5¹⁸ read with König בְּהִשְׁתַּחֲוֹתִי ; in Ez 8¹⁶ מִשְׁתַּחֲוִיתֶם is still more certainly a scribal error for מִשְׁתַּחֲוִים.

19. Before *suffixes* in all forms ending in ה, a connecting vowel is employed *ll* instead of the ה and the connecting vowel which precedes it (§ 58 *f*), e.g. נָחַנִי Gn 24²⁷ ; in *pause* עָנָנִי I K 2³⁰, &c., even with lesser disjunctives, ψ 118⁵, Pr 8²², or with a conjunctive accent, I S 28¹⁵ (but Baer עֲנָנִי), Jb 30¹⁹ ; cf. § 59 *h* ; עֶנְךָ, in *pause* עָנָךְ, Is 30¹⁹ (and even when not in *pause* Jer 23³⁷) or like מָךְ Dt 32⁶ ; וַיִּפְרְךָ, וַיַּרְבֶּךָ Gn 28³ ; cf. also עָנָהוּ, עָנָם, *imperfect* יַעֲנֵהוּ, הַבָּה, הֶעְלָךְ, *Hiph'il* הַבְּנִי, יַעֲנֶךָ.

Only very seldom does the *imperat.* or *impf.* end in יֵ__ before suffixes, e. g. *mm*

---

[1] Possibly these examples (like the cases of S°ghôl in *pause*, see *n*) represent the view of a particular Masoretic school, which was intended to be consistently carried out.

אֶפְאֵיהֶם Dt 32²⁶ ; יְכַבֵּימוֹ ψ 140¹⁰ Q°rê ; הַבֵּינִי *smite me*, 1 K 20³⁵·³⁷ ; cf. Hb 3², Is 38¹⁶. Even in these examples a return to the original ending *ay* might be assumed ; but perhaps they are merely due to a less correct *plene* writing. In the 3rd *sing. perf. fem.* the older form גְּלָת (see *i*) is always used before a suffix, e. g. כְּלָתוּ (for כְּלָתְהוּ) Zc 5⁴ ; *in pause* עֲשָׂתְנִי Jb 33⁴ ; רָאָתֶךָ 42⁵.

VI. *The Relation between Verbs* ל״ה *and* ל״א.

nn 20. The close relation existing between verbs ל״א and ל״ה is shown in Hebrew by the fact that the verbs of one class often borrow forms from the other, especially in the later writers and the poets.

oo 21. Thus there are forms of verbs ל״א—

(a) Which have adopted the vowels of verbs ל״ה, e. g. *perfect Qal* כָּלָאתִי *I have refrained*, ψ 119¹⁰¹ ; *participle* חוֹטֵא (חֹטֵא) *sinning*, Ec 2²⁶, 8¹², 9²·¹⁸ ; cf. Is 65²⁰ ; מוֹצֵא Ec 7²⁶ ; נֹשֵׁא *lending*, 1 S 22² ; *Pi'êl perfect* מִלֵּא *he has filled*, Jer 51³⁴ ; cf. 1 K 9¹¹, Am 4² (where, however, the *perfect Niph.* is perhaps intended), ψ 89¹¹, 143³ ; רִפָּאתִו *I heal*, 2 K 2²¹ ; cf. Jer 51⁹ ; *imperfect* יֶחֱמָא Jb 39²⁴ ; *Niph'al perfect* נִפְלָאתָה (like נִגְלְתָה) *it was wonderful*, 2 S 1²⁶ ; *Hiph'il perfect* הִפְלִא Dt 28⁵⁹ ; הֶחְבִּאָתָה (not אָ_תָה, cf. above, 2 S 1²⁶) *she hid*, Jos 6¹⁷. On the other hand, forms like חֹטִאים 1 S 14³³, קֹרִאים ψ 99⁶, נִרְפָּאוּ Ez 47⁸, תְּרִכָּאוּנֵנִי, according to the correct reading, Jb 19² (cf. Gn 31³⁹ אֲחַטֶּנָה), and יְרָאוּ *imperative plur. masc.* from יָרֵא Jos 24¹⁴, 1 S 12²⁴, ψ 34¹⁰, are due to the elision of the א, see § 74 *i*. On יִשְׁוָא Jer 10⁵ and נָשְׁוָא ψ 139²⁰, see § 23 *i*.

pp (b) Forms in ה, but keeping their ל״א vowels, e. g. *imperfect Qal* אֶרְפֶּה Jer 3²² ; *imperative* רְפֵה *heal thou*, ψ 60⁴ ; *Niph'al* נֵחְבֶּה Jer 49¹⁰ (which must evidently be a *perfect*; read with Ewald the *infinitive absolute* נֵחְבֹּה as in verse 23), and הֵחָבֶה *to hide oneself*, 1 K 22²⁵, cf. Jer 19¹¹ ; *Pi'êl imperfect* יְמַלֶּה *he will fill*, Jb 8²¹.

qq (c) Forms entirely of a ל״ה character, e. g. *perfect Qal* וְצָמֵת *and when thou art athirst*, Ru 2⁹, cf. 2 S 3⁸ ; כָּלוּ *they shut up*, 1 S 6¹⁰ ; cf. 25³³ ; מָלוּ *they are full*, Ez 28¹⁶, cf. 39²⁶ ; *infinitive* חֲטוֹ (see above, *n*) *to sin*, Gn 20⁶ (on מְלֹאת see above, § 74 *h*) ; *imperative sing. fem.* חֲבִי Is 26²⁰ ; *imperfect* יִכְלֶה (for יִכְלָא) *he will keep back*, Gn 23⁶ ; תִּרְפֶּינָה *they heal*, Jb 5¹⁸ ; *participle* בּוֹטֶה Pr 12¹⁸ ; *fem.* יֹצֵא Ec 10⁵ ; *plur.* צֹבֶיהָ Is 29⁷ ; *participle passive* נָשׂוּי ψ 32¹ ; *Niph'al* נִרְפָּתָה Jer 51⁹ ; *thou hast prophesied*, Jer 26⁹ (cf. ψ 139¹⁴, Jb 18³) ; *imperfect* וַיִּרְפּוּ 2 K 2²² (*infinitive* Jer 19¹¹) ; *Pi'êl imperfect* וַיְרַפּוּ Jer 8¹¹, cf. Gn 31³⁹ ; *Hiph'il participle* מַקְנֶה Ez 8³ ; *Hithpa'el* הִתְנַבִּית 1 S 10⁶ ; *infinitive* הִתְנַבּוֹת 1 S 10¹³. For the *K°thibh* לְהִשׁוֹת 2 K 19²⁵, Jablonski and others require as *Q°rê* the form לְהַשְׁאוֹת (so Is 37²⁶) ; the *K°thibh* would have to be read לְהָשׁוֹת, with elision of the א and retraction of the vowel.

rr 22. On the other hand, there are forms of verbs ל״ה, which wholly or in part follow the analogy of verbs ל״א, e. g. in their consonants אָתָא *he comes*, Is 21¹² ; בְּרָא 2 S 12¹⁷ (*textus receptus* בְּרָה) ; וְרָצָאתִי Ez 43²⁷ ; יִשְׁגָּא Jb 8¹¹ ; יִשְׁנָא La 4¹ ; וַיֶּחֱלָא 2 Ch 16¹² ; תִּקְרָאנָה Ex 1¹⁰, Lv 10¹⁹ ; תִּלְאִים Dt 28⁶⁶ (cf. Ho 11⁷) ; נְקֹרָא (*infin. absol. Niph'al beside* נָקְרֵיתִי) 2 S 1⁶ ; שְׁנָא 2 K 25²⁹ ; מְרַפָּא

Jer 38⁴; יִשְׂנָא Ec 8¹: in their vowels, אָתָנוּ Jer 3²²; יִקְרָה Dn 10¹⁴; תִּכְלָה
1 K 17¹⁴: in both, יִקְרָא Gn 49¹; cf. 42⁴, Is 51¹⁹; תִּלְאַם 2 S 21¹² Q°rê;
2 Ch 26¹⁵ (cf. וַיִּרְאוּ הַמּוֹרָאִים 2 S 11²⁴ K°thibh); מֹרָאָה (participle fem. Qal) Zp 3¹;
יַפְרִיא Ho 13¹⁵; מְסֻלָּאִים La 4².—For פֹּרֹאות (so Baer, Ez 17⁶, cf. 31⁸), which can
only be intended for פֹּרָאות participle fem. plur. from פֹּרָה = פֹּרָא, read פֹּארות
branches, according to Ez 31⁵, &c.

§ 76. *Verbs Doubly Weak.*

1. In a tolerably large number of verbs two radicals are weak *a*
letters, and are consequently affected by one or other of the anomalies
already described. In cases where two anomalies might occur, usage
must teach whether one, or both, or neither of them, takes effect.

Thus e.g. from נָדַד *to flee*, the *imperfect* is יִדּוֹד in Na 3⁷ and יִדַּד in Gn 31⁴⁰
(on the analogy of verbs פ״ן); *Hiph'il* הֵנַד (like a verb ע״ע), but the *imperfect*
Hoph'al again יֻדַּד (as פ״ן).

2. The following are examples of difficult forms, which are derived *b*
from doubly weak verbs:

(*a*) Verbs פ״ן and ל״א (cf. § 66 and § 74), e.g. נָשָׂא *to bear*, imperative שָׂא
(נְשָׂא ψ 10¹², of which נְסָה ψ 4⁷ is probably only an orthographic variation);
infinitive construct שְׂאֵת (for שֶׁאֶת; see the analogous noun-formations in § 93 *t*),
also נְשָׂא Is 1¹⁴, 18³; Gn 4¹³; נְשׂוֹא ψ 89¹⁰ שׂוֹא (perhaps only a scribal error);
after the *prefix* לְ always לָשֵׂאת (otherwise the contracted form only occurs in
מָשְׂאֵתו Jb 41¹⁷, with rejection of the א); *imperfect* תִּשֶּׂאנָה for תִּשֶּׂאנָה Ru 1¹⁴;
wholly irregular are תִּשֶּׂאֶינָה Ez 23⁴⁹ (so Baer after Qimḥi; *textus receptus*, and
also the Mantua ed., and Ginsburg, תִּשָּׂאֶינָה) and נְשֵׂאת 2 S 19⁴³ as *infinitive
absolute Niph'al* (on the analogy of the *infinitive construct Qal*?); but most probably
נְשֹׂא is to be read, with Driver.

(*b*) Verbs פ״ן and ל״ה (cf. § 66 and § 75), as נָטָה *to bow, to incline*, נָכָה *to C
smite*. Hence *imperfect* Qal יִטֶּה, apocopated וַיֵּט (Gn 26²⁵ וַיֵּט) *and he bowed*;
וַיֵּן (so, probably, also Is 63³ for וַיֶּז) 2 K 9³³ *and he sprinkled* (from נָזָה); *perfect
Hiph'il* הִכָּה *he smote*, imperfect יַכֶּה, apocopated וַיַּךְ, יַךְ (even with *Athnaḥ* 2 K 15¹⁶;
but also ten times וַיַּכֶּה) וַיַּן Dt 2³³; so also וַיַּן Lv 8¹¹·³⁰; אַל־תַּט ψ 141⁴ (cf.
Jb 23¹¹); *imperative* הַכֵּה, apocopated הַךְ *smite thou* (like הַט *incline*, with הַטֵּה),
infinitive הַכּוֹת, *participle* מַכֶּה; *Hoph'al* הֻכָּה, *participle* מֻכֶּה.

(*c*) Verbs פ״א and ל״ה (cf. § 68 and § 75), as אָבָה *to be willing*, אָפָה *to bake, d
*אָתָה *to come*. E. g. *imperfect* Qal יֹאפֶה, יֹאבֶה, *plur.* יֹאפוּ; וַיֵּתֵא (cf. § 68 *h*) Dt 33²¹
for וַיֶּאֱתָה (= וַיֶּאֱתָה); *imperfect apocopated* וַיֵּאת Is 41²⁵ for וַיֶּאֱתְ; *imperative* אֱתָיוּ
Is 21¹², 56⁹·¹² (cf. אֱפוּ *bake ye*, Ex 16²³) for אֱתָיוּ, אֱתָיוּ (§ 23 *h*; § 75 *u*); *Hiph'il*
perfect הֶאֱתִיו for הֶאֱתִיו (הֶאֱתִיו) Is 21¹⁴; *imperfect apocopated* וַיֹּאֶל *and he adjured*,
1 S 14²⁴, properly יַאֲלֶה (יַאֲלֶה) from אָלָה, whence יָאֶלֶה, and, with the obscuring
to ô, יֹאֶל; instead of the simple *apocope* (וַיַּאַל) the א which had already become

quiescent, is made audible again by the helping Seghôl (unless perhaps there is a confusion with the *imperfect consecutive Hiph'il* of יֵאַל).

e   (*d*) Verbs פ״י and ל״א (cf. § 69, § 70, and § 74), as יָצָא *to go forth, imperative* צֵא *go forth,* with הַ‑ *paragogic* צְאָה Ju 9²⁹ in principal pause for צְאָה; 2nd *fem. plur.* צֶאנָה Ct 3¹¹; *infinitive* צֵאת; *Hiph'il* הוֹצִיא *to bring forth.*—יָרֵא *to fear, imperfect* יִירָא and וַיִּרָא (or וַיֵּרָא), *imperative* יְרָא; *imperfect Niph'al* יִוָּרֵא ψ 130⁴, *participle* נוֹרָא.

f   (*e*) Verbs פ״י and ל״ה (cf. § 69, § 70, and § 75), e.g. יָדָה *to throw,* Hiph'il *to confess, to praise,* and יָרָה *to throw* (both properly verbs פ״ו), and יָפָה *to be beautiful. Infinitive* יְרוֹת, יָרֹה; *imperative* יְרֵה; *imperfect consecutive* וַיִּיף Ez 31⁷ (cf. also וַתִּיפִי 16¹³); with *suffixes* וַיֹּרֻם *we have shot at them* (from יָרָה) Nu 21³⁰; perhaps, however, it should be read with the LXX וְנִינָם *and their race* (also in the very corrupt passage ψ 74⁸ נִינָם is probably a *substantive,* and not the *imperfect Qal* with *suffix* from יָנָה); *Pi'ēl* וַיַּדּוּ for וַיִּדּוּ (§ 69 u). *Hiph'il* הוֹרָה, הוֹרָה; *infinitive* הוֹרֹת (as *infinitive absolute* 2 Ch 7³); *imperfect* יוֹרֶה, cf. אַל־תּוֹרֵנוּ Jer 22³; *apocopated* וַיֹּר 2 K 13¹⁷.

g   (*f*) Verbs ע״ו and ל״א, particularly בּוֹא *to come. Perfect* בָּא, בָּאתָ, בָּאת, or בָּאת (Gn 16⁸, 2 S 14³, Mi 4¹⁰; cf. § 75 m), once בָּאנוּ for בָּאנוּ 1 S 25⁸; for בֹּאוּ Jer 27¹⁸, which is apparently the *perfect,* read יָבֹאוּ. In the *imperfect Qal* the separating vowel occurs תְּבֹאֶינָה instead of the more common תְּבֹאנָה, cf. also תְּבֹאן Gn 30³⁸) only in Jer 9¹⁶, ψ 45¹⁶, and 1 S 10⁷ *Kethibh.*

h   For וַתָּבֵאת 1 S 25³⁴ Qerê (the *Kethibh* ותבאתי evidently combines the two readings וּבָאת and וַתָּבֹאִי; cf. Nestle, *ZAW.* xiv. 319), read וַתָּבֹאִי; on the impossible forms Dt 33¹⁶ and Jb 22²¹ cf. § 48 d.—In the *perfect Hiph'il* הֵבִיא, הֵבֵאת and (only before a suffix) הֲבִיאֹת; the latter form is also certainly intended in Nu 14³¹, where the Masora requires וְהֵבִיאתִי, cf. 2 K 9², 19²⁵, Is 43²³, Jer 25¹³, Ct 3⁴. Before suffixes the ē of the first syllable in the 3rd *sing.* always becomes *Ḥaṭeph-Seghôl,* e.g. הֱבִיאֲךָ, הֱבִיאַנִי; elsewhere invariably *Ḥaṭeph-Paṯaḥ,* e.g. הֲבִיאֹתֶנוּ or הֲבִיאָתָנוּ. On the other hand, ē is retained in the secondary tone in the *perfect consecutive* when without suffixes, e.g. וְהֵבֵאתָ. Cf. moreover, וְהֵקֵאתוֹ (וְהֲקֵאתוֹ) in Opitius and Hahn is altogether incorrect), Pr 25¹⁶, from קִיא; but קִיוּ *spue ye,* Jer 25²⁷ (perhaps only a mistake for קִיאוּ), is not to be referred to קִיא but to a secondary stem קָיָה. In the *imperfect* וַתָּקִא is found once, Lv 18²⁵, besides וַיָּקֵא (analogous to וַיְּבֵא).—On אֲבִי (for אָבִיא), אֲבִיא, יָנִי, מֵבִי, see § 74 k.

i   (*g*) The form חָיַי *to live,* in the *perfect Qal,* besides the ordinary development to חָיָה (*fem.* חָיְתָה), is also treated as a verb ע״ע, and then becomes חַי in the 3rd *pers. perfect,* in *pause* חָי, and with *wāw consecutive* וָחַי Gn 3²², and frequently. In Lv 25³⁶ the contracted form וְחֵי is perhaps *st. constr.* of חַי *life,* but in any case read וָחַי *perfect consecutive* as in verse 35. The form וְחָיָה occurs in Ex 1¹⁶ in *pause* for וְחָיְתָה (3rd *fem.*) with *Dageš* omitted in the י on account of the pausal lengthening of ă to ā.

§ 77. *Relation of the Weak Verbs to one another.*

The close relation which exists between some classes of the weak *a* verbs (e. g. between פ״ו and פ״י, ל״א and ל״ה, ע״ו and ע״י, ע״ע and ל״ה) appears not only in their similarity or identity of inflexion, or their mutual interchange of certain forms, but especially from the fact that frequently the same root (*radix bilittera*, see § 30 *g*) recurs in various weak stems of similar meaning. The meaning accordingly is inherent in the two constant root-consonants, while the third consonant, which is weak (and the particular class of weak verbs with it), does not establish any difference in the meaning. Thus from the root דך there occur with the same meaning דָּבָא, דּוּךְ, דָּכַךְ *to strike, to crush*; and from the root נד there are נוּד, נָדַד, נָדָה *to flee*.

In this manner the following classes are related in form and *b* meaning:

1. Verbs ע״ו and ע״ע in which the first and third consonants are the same in both, as being essential to the meaning; e. g. מוּךְ and מָכַךְ *to become poor*; מוּשׁ and מָשַׁשׁ *to feel*; נוּד and נָדַד *to flee.*

2. Verbs פ״י and פ״ן; e. g. יָצֵב and נָצֵב *to place*, נָקֵשׁ and יָקֹשׁ (*yāqōš*) *to lay C snares.* Moreover, stems belonging to the classes mentioned in 1 (especially ע״ו) are frequently related also to verbs פ״י and פ״ן, e. g. גּוּר and יָגֹר *to fear*; טוֹב and יָטַב *to be good*; נָפַח and פּוּחַ *to blow*; נָפַץ and פּוּץ *to dash to pieces.* Verbs פ״א are less frequently connected with these classes, e. g. אָדַשׁ and דּוּשׁ *to thresh*, &c.

3. Verbs ל״א and ל״ה (in which the first two consonants form the real *d* body of the stem) are sometimes related to each other, and sometimes to the above classes. To each other, in דָּכָא and דָּכָה *to crush*, קָרָא and קָרָה *to meet* (cf. § 75 *nn*); to verbs of the other classes, in מָצָה and מָצַץ *to suck*, דָּחָה and דּוּחַ *to thrust*, &c.

4. Verbs ע״ע and ל״ה, on which cf. Grimm, *Journal of Bibl. Lit.*, 1903, p. 196; *e* e. g. אָנָה and אָנַן *to sigh*, דָּמָה and דָּמַם *to be quiet*, חָנָה and חָנַן *to incline*, בָּלָה and בָּלַל *to end*, קָלָה and קָלַל *to despise*, שָׁנָה and שָׁנַן *to err*, שָׁחָה and שָׁחַח *to bend down*, שָׁסָה and שָׁסַס *to plunder.*

5. Verbs ע״ו and ע״ה; e. g. מוּל and מָהַל (New Hebrew; in O. T. only מָהוּל *f* Is 1²²) *to circumcise*, מוּר and מָהַר *to exchange*, נוּר (in מְנוֹרָה *a light*) and נָהַר *to shine*; cf. also לְהָטִים *secret arts*, Ex 7¹¹ with לָט *secret*, from לוּט.

§ 78. *Verba Defectiva.*

It often happens, when two kindred weak verbs are in use with *a* the same meaning, that both are *defective*, i. e. do not occur in all the forms. Since, however, those tenses and forms which are not in use in the one verb are generally supplied by the other, they mutually complete one another, and thus form together, as it were, an entire

verb, as in Greek ἔρχομαι, aor. ἦλθον, fut. ἐλεύσομαι, and in Latin *fero,
tuli, latum, ferre*, &c., but with this difference, that in Hebrew the
roots of these verbs are almost always closely related.

b　　The most common verbs of this kind are—

בּשׁ *to be ashamed.* *Hiph'il* הֵבִישׁ (inferred from הֵבִישׁוֹת,), but also הֹבִישׁ,
הוֹבִישׁ, as if from יבשׁ, on the analogy of verbs פ״וֹ; also in Is 30⁵ the *Q*ᵉ*rê*
requires הֹבִישׁ, where the *K*ᵉ*thibh* has הִבְאִישׁ from בָּאַשׁ.

טוֹב *to be good.* *Perfect* טוֹב; but *imperfect* יִיטַב and *Hiph'il* הֵיטִיב from יָטַב
(but cf. הֵטִיבֹת 2 K 10³⁰).

יָגֹר *to be afraid.* *Imperfect* יָגוּר (from גּוּר).

יָקַץ *to awake,* only in the *imperf.* יִיקַץ; for the *perfect,* the *Hiph'il* הֵקִיץ is used
(from קוּץ).

נָפַץ *to break in pieces.* *Imperfect* יָפוּץ (from פּוּץ). *Imperative* פּוּץ. *Niph'al*
נָפוֹץ. *Pi'ēl* נִפֵּץ (from נָפַץ). *Pōlēl* פּוֹצֵץ (from פּוּץ). *Reflexive* הִתְפּוֹצֵץ. *Hiph'il*
הֵפִיץ. Also פִּצְפֵּץ Jb 16¹².

נָצַב (*Qal* in post-biblical Hebrew, in Aramaic and Arabic) *to place,* whence
(possibly) *Niph'al* נִצַּב and *Hiph'il* הִצִּיב (see above, § 71); but *Hithpa'ēl* הִתְיַצֵּב.

שָׁתָה *to drink,* used in *Qal;* but in *Hiph.* הִשְׁקָה *to give to drink,* from a *Qal* שָׁקָה
which is not used in Hebrew.

On הָלַךְ (יָלַךְ) *to go,* see above, § 69 *x.*

c　　Rem. I. To the same category belong also, to a certain extent, those cases
where the *tenses* or *moods* not in use in one conjugation, are supplied by forms
having the same meaning in other conjugations of the same verb. Thus:

יָסַף *to add.* The *infinitive* (but cf. § 69 *h*, note) and *imperfect,* unused in *Qal,*
are supplied by the *Hiph'il* הוֹסִיף, יוֹסִיף (on יֹסֵף as *imperfect indicative,* see
§ 109 *d,* cf. also § 109 *i*).

כָּשַׁל *to stumble.* *Perfect* from *Qal, imperfect* from *Niph'al.*

נָגַשׁ *to approach,* unused in *perf.* *Qal,* instead of which *Niph'al* נִגַּשׁ is used;
but *imperfect* יִגַּשׁ, *imperative* גַּשׁ, and *infinitive* גֶּשֶׁת from *Qal* only are in use.

נָחָה *to lead.* *Perfect* usually נָחָה in *Qal,* so *imperative* נְחֵה, but *imperfect* and
infinitive always in *Hiph'il.*

נתך *to be poured out.* *Perfect Niph'al* נִתַּךְ with *imperfect Qal* יִתַּךְ, but the *perfect
Qal* and *imperfect Niph'al* are not in use.

2. The early grammarians often speak of *mixed forms* (*formae mixtae*), i. e.
forms which unite the supposed character and meaning of two different
tenses, genders, or conjugations. Most of the examples adduced are at
once set aside by accurate grammatical analysis; some others appear to have
arisen from misapprehension and inaccuracy, especially from erroneous views
of unusual *plene* forms. Others, again, are either merely wrong readings or
represent an intentional conflation of two different readings.

CHAPTER III

THE NOUN

§ 79. *General View.*

For the literature, see De Lagarde, *Uebersicht über die im Aram., Arab. und Hebr. übliche Bildung der Nomina*, Göttingen, 1889; Index and Additions, 1891; J. Barth, *Die Nominalbildung in den semitischen Sprachen*, first half, *Simple nouns*, Leipzig, 1889; second half, *Nouns with external additions*, 1891; second edition, with indices of words and subjects, 1894; E. König, *Historisch-kritisches Lehrgebäude, &c.*, ii. 1, Leipzig, 1895, see above, § 3 *f.*—Of these three important works the first two especially have given rise to various articles. In support of De Lagarde: Hommel in *ZDMG.* xliv, p. 535 ff. (against De Lagarde and Hommel: Barth, *ibid.*, p. 679 ff.), and dealing with the Index, *ZDMG.* xlv, p. 340 ff.—Against Barth (though with many points of agreement): Philippi in the *Zeitschrift für Völkerpsychologie*, 1890, p. 344 ff. (answered by Barth in *ZDMG.* xliv, p. 692 ff.), and *ZDMG.* xlvi, p. 149 ff. (answered again by Barth, *ibid.*, xlviii, p. 10 ff.), also in the *Beiträge zur Assyriologie*, ii (1892), p. 359 ff. 'Die semitische Verbal- und Nominalbildung,' and lastly, in *ZDMG.* xlix, p. 187 ff.— Cf. also A. Müller, 'Semitische Nomina. Bemerkungen zu de Lagarde und Barth,' *ZDMG.* xlv, p. 221 ff.—The main points at issue in the works of De Lagarde and Barth are indicated below, § 83 *d.*—Brockelmann, *Semit. Sprachwiss.*, p. 104 ff.; *Grundriss*, p. 329 ff.

1. Since, according to § 30 *a*, most word-stems are developed into *a* verbal stems as well as into noun-stems, it has become customary (especially in the Lexicon) to refer the noun to the most simple ground-form of the verbal formation, viz. the 3rd *pers. sing. perfect Qal*, and, as it were, to derive it from that form. This is usual, not only in those noun-stems which can be directly connected with a corresponding verbal stem (*Nomina verbalia* or *derivativa*, § 83 ff.), but also with *Nomina primitiva*, i.e. those of which no verbal stem is now found in Hebrew (see § 82), as well as finally with *Nomina denominativa*, which have evidently been derived from other nouns (§ 86).

The adjective agrees in form entirely with the substantive. On the formation of adjectival ideas by giving to abstracts a concrete sense, see § 83 *c*.

2. A special inflexion of the noun to express the various cases does *b* not exist in Hebrew; only a few ancient and almost extinct traces of case-endings have survived (§ 90). The syntactical relation of a noun can therefore in general only be inferred from its position in the sentence, or from its being joined to prepositions. In either case, the form of the noun undergoes no change (except for the *construct*

state, § 89), and the representation of case-relations belongs therefore almost exclusively to the syntax (§ 117 ff.). The comparative and superlative of adjectives also can be expressed only by a syntactical combination (§ 133). On the other hand, several changes in the forms of nouns are occasioned by the additions of the plural, dual, and feminine terminations, as well as of the pronominal suffixes, and also by the close connexion of two nouns, by means of the *construct state*.[1]

§ 80. *The Indication of Gender in Nouns.*

Brockelmann, *Grundriss*, p. 404 ff.; ' Ueber die Femininendung *at*, *ah*, *ā* ' in *Semit. Sprachwiss.*, p. 106 f.; *Grundriss*, pp. 105, 405 ff.; ' Die Femininendung *T* im Semit.' (*Sitzung d. orient.-sprachwiss. Sektion d. schlesischen Gesellschaft*, Feb. 26, 1903); against him J. Barth, *ZDMG.* 1903, p. 628 ff.; Brockelmann's reply, *ibid.*, p. 795 ff.; and Barth again, *ibid.*, p. 798 ff.

a 1. The Hebrew, like all Semitic languages, recognizes only two genders in the noun, a *masculine* and a *feminine*. Inanimate objects and abstract ideas, which other languages sometimes indicate by the *neuter*, are regarded in Hebrew either as masculine or feminine, more often the latter (see the Syntax, § 122 *q*).

b 2. The *masculine*, as being the more common and important gender, has no special indication.

Feminine nouns are also without an indication of gender when the meaning of the word naturally denotes a feminine, as אֵם *mother*, אָתוֹן *a she-ass*, עֵז *a she-goat*, רָחֵל *an ewe* (cf. § 122 *b*). As a rule, however, the *feminine* had originally the ending ָה—, as in the 3rd *sing. perfect* of verbs (§ 44 *a*). This ָה—, however, is regularly retained in Hebrew only in close connexion with a following genitive or suffix (cf. § 89 *e* and § 91 *o*), except where the form has arisen through the addition of a simple ת [2] (see below, *d*). Otherwise, the feminine ending of the independent form (the *absolute state*, § 89 *a*) is—

c (*a*) Most commonly a tone-bearing ָה—, e.g. סוּס *equus*, סוּסָה *equa*. Of nouns ending in ִי—, like עִבְרִי, the feminine (by § 24 *b*) is עִבְרִיָּה, cf. § 86 *h*. As in the 3rd *sing. fem. perfect* (קָטְלָה, &c.), this ָה— seems to have arisen by the rejection of the final ת, and the lengthening of the ă in the open syllable, whereupon the ה was added as an orthographic indication of the final long vowel: cf. the exactly similar origin of such forms as גָּלָה for גְּלִי, § 75 *c*. It must, however, be

---

[1] To speak of these changes as a declension of the Hebrew noun, as is usually done, is accordingly incorrect.

[2] In Mal 1[14] מָשְׁחַת (so e.g. ed. Mant.) would stand for מָשְׁחָתַת, the ptcp. fem. Hoph'al; but מָשְׁחָת (so Baer and Ginsb.) is also supported by good authority.

noticed that in Arabic (see *m* and note) the pausal form of *at* is *ah*, of which a trace may be preserved in the Hebrew הָ‑ָ.

(*b*) Simple ת with nouns ending in a vowel, e. g. יְהוּדִי *Jew*, יְהוּדִית *d Jewess*. The same ending ת is very frequently added to stems ending in a consonant, but only (except before suffixes) by means of a helping vowel, which, as a rule, is *Sᵉghôl*, but after gutturals *Pathaḥ*, e. g. קֹטֵל, *fem.* קֹטֶלֶת, *killing*; before suffixes, e. g. קְטַלְתִּי, according to the rule given in § 69 *c*, cf. also § 84ᵃ *s*; מוֹדָע *an acquaintance, fem.* מוֹדַעַת. The forms which arise in this way follow in every respect the analogy of the *segholate* forms (§ 94 *f*). The forms which have been developed by means of a helping vowel are retained even in the connective form (*construct state*); except וְיֹלַדְתְּ (for יֹלֶדֶת, which is used elsewhere) Gn 16¹¹, Ju 13⁵·⁷; cf. Jer 22²³ and 51¹³ *Qᵉrê*, also מְשָׁרַת 1 K 1¹⁵, *participle fem. Piʿel*, properly *mᵉšāratt*=מְשָׁרֶתֶת; also מְבַעְתֶּךָ (*participle fem. Piʿel* with suffix) arises from the form מְבַעַתְּ which was developed into מְבַעֶתֶת.

Rem. 1. The fem. form in ת‑ֶ‑ is in general less frequent, and occurs *e* almost exclusively when the form in הָ‑ָ is also in use. It is only in the participles and infinitives that it is the commoner, e.g. קֹטֶלֶת more common than קְטָלָה, לֶדֶת than לֵדָה.

2. *Rarer* feminine endings are—(*a*) ת‑ַ with the tone, e. g. בָּרֶקֶת *emerald*, *f* Ez 28¹³ (also בָּרְקַת Ex 28¹⁷); שִׁפְעַת *a company*, 2 K 9¹⁷, unless the reading is wrong; more frequently in proper names, especially of places among the Canaanites or Phoenicians (in whose language ת‑ַ was the usual fem. ending, § 2 *d*) and other neighbouring tribes,[1] e. g. צָרְפַת *Zarephath*, גִּבְעַת *Gibeath*, קִרְיַת *Kiriath*, אֵילַת *Greek Ailana* in Idumea; אֲחֻזַּת Gn 26²⁶: on the reading גְּלִית cf. *g.* Cf., moreover, נְגִינַת ψ 61¹ (prob. originally נְגִינֹת; חַיַּת (LXX חַיּוֹת) 74¹⁹·ᵃ; פּוּגַת La 2¹⁸; [רַבַּת *much*, in ψ 65¹⁰, 120⁶, 123⁴, 129¹·², is a form borrowed from the Aramaic (Syriac *rabbath*) in which the original *t* of the *fem.* is often retained to form *adverbs*, see Wright, *Comparative Grammar*, p. 135.]

(*b*) ת‑ָ, which likewise occurs in some names of places, e.g. חֶלְקַת, בַּעֲלַת, *g* as well as in the *masc.* proper name גְּלְיָת 1 S 17⁴, &c. (in 17²³, and 21¹⁰, ed. Mant. has גָּלְיַת), and in the *fem.* proper name שִׁמְעָת; otherwise, almost only in poetry, viz. זִמְרָת Ex 15², Is 12², ψ 118¹⁴ (really for זִמְרָתִי *my song*; the absorption of the *î*, however, can scarcely have 'taken place in the Aramaic manner', as suggested by Duhm on Is 12², nor is it due merely to the following *Yôdh*, but is intended 'to facilitate the absorption of יָהּ'; so Geiger, *Urschrift*, p. 277 f.); נַחֲלָת *heritage*, ψ 16⁶ (either again for נַחֲלָתִי *my heritage*, or for נַחֲלָתָהּ, cf. § 90 *g*, as probably also עֶזְרָת *help*, ψ 60¹³, 108¹³ for עֶזְרָתָהּ). These forms are possibly

---

[1] In the list of Palestinian towns taken by Pharaoh Shoshenq, the feminine town-names all end in *t*. Cf. also the Meša' inscription, line 3, הבמת זאת *this high place*; line 26, המסלת *the highway* [see also Driver, *Tenses*, § 181, *note*].

survivals from a period when even final vowels were not supported by a vowel-letter. Cf. also פֹּרָת *fecunda* (*a fruitful tree*) Gn 49²²; יִתְרַת *abundance*, Jer 48³⁶ (before עׇ; but in Is 15⁷ יִתְרָה); שְׁנַת *sleep* (for שֵׁנָה) ψ 132⁴; and (unless the ת is radical) in prose קָאַת *pelican* (which reading is also preferable, in Is 34¹¹, to the form קָאַת), also מׇחֳרָת *the morrow*, but in *construct state* always מׇחֳרַת.¹—תְּהִלָּת Jer 45²⁵ *Qᵉrê* is no doubt intended to indicate the reading תְּהִלָּתִי, parallel to מְשׂוֹשִׂי; cf. above, on זִמְרָת, &c.

h (c) א__, the Aramaic orthography for ה__, chiefly in the later writers; זָרָא *loathing*, Nu 11²⁰; חַגָּא *a terror*, Is 19¹⁷; שֵׁנָא *sleep*, ψ 127²; לְבִיא *a lioness*, Ez 19² (unless לָבִיא is intended); מְטָרָא *a mark*, La 3¹²; cf. also דָּשָׁא *threshing* (*participle Qal* from דּוּשׁ) Jer 50¹¹; מָרָא *bitter*, Ru 1²⁰. On the other hand, according to the western Masora, קׇרְחָה *baldness* is to be read in Ez 27³¹; see Baer on the passage.

i (d) ה__, an obtuse form of ה__ (§ 27 *u*), only in הַוּׄרָה for הַוּׄרָה Is 59⁵ (unless it is again a *forma mixta* combining the active ptcp. masc. הַוּׄרֶה and the passive ptcp. fem. הַוּׄרָה); cf. לָנֶה for לָנָה Zc 5⁴; אָנֶה 1 K 2³⁶·⁴² (§ 90 *i*, and § 48 *d*).

k (e) ה__ without the tone, e. g. רְאֵמָה Dt 14¹⁷ [Lv 11¹⁸; רָחָם]; תַּנּוּר בֹּעֵרָה an oven *heated*, Ho 7⁴; cf. Ez. 40¹⁹, 2 K 15²⁹, 16¹⁸. In all these examples the usual tone-bearing ה__ is perhaps intended, but the Punctuators, who considered the feminine ending inappropriate, produced a kind of *locative* form (see § 90 *c*) by the retraction of the tone. [In 2 K 16¹⁸, Is 24¹⁹, Ez 21³¹ (note in each case the following ה), and in Jb 42¹³, Ho 7⁴, the text is probably in error.]

l (f) י__, as an old feminine termination, preserved also in Syriac (*ai*; see examples in Nöldeke's *Syrische Gram* , § 83), in Arabic and (contracted to *ê*) in Ethiopic, very probably occurs in the proper name שָׂרַי *Sarai*, cf. Nöldeke, *ZDMG*. xl. 183, and xlii. 484; also עֶשְׂרָה *ten* (*fem.*) undoubtedly arises from an original '*esray*; so Wright, *Comparative Grammar*, p. 138; König, *Lehrgebäude*, ii. 427.

m 3. It is wholly incorrect to regard the *vowel*-ending ה__ ² as the original termination of the feminine, and the *consonantal* ending ת__ as derived from it. The Ethiopic still has the ת throughout, so too the Assyrian (*at*, *it*); in Phoenician also the feminines end for the most part in ת, which is pronounced *at* in the words found in Greek and Latin authors; less frequently in א (see Gesenius, *Monumm. Phoen.*, pp. 439, 440; Schröder, *Phön. Sprache*, p. 169 ff.). The ancient Arabic has the obtuse ending (*ah*) almost exclusively in *pause*; in modern Arabic the relation between the two endings is very much as in Hebrew.

---

¹ In 1 S 2c²⁷ also, where the Masora (see Baer on Jos 5¹¹) for some unknown reason requires מׇחֳרַת, read with ed. Mant., Jablonski, Opitius, and Ginsburg, מׇחֳרַת.

² In this ending the ה *h* can only be considered consonantal in the sense that the ת was originally aspirated, and afterwards ' the mute ת was dropped before *h*, just as the old Persian *mithra* became in modern Persian *mihr* '; so Socin, who also points to the Arabic pausal form in *ah*, and observes that among some of the modern Beduin an *h* is still heard as a fem. ending, cf. Socin, *Diwan aus Centralarabien*, iii. 98, ed. by H. Stumme, Lpz. 1901. In Hebrew this consonantal termination was entirely abandoned, at any rate in later times.

§ 81. *Derivation of Nouns.*

Brockelmann, *Grundriss*, p. 329 ff.

Nouns are by their derivation either *primitive*, i. e. cannot be *a*
referred to any verbal stem at present extant (see § 82), such as
אָב *father*, אֵם *mother* (but see both words in the Lexicon; according
to Stade and others אָב, אֵם, &c., are children's words and terms of
endearment, and so really primitive nouns), or *derivative*, i. e. either
Derivativa verbalia (§§ 83–5), e. g. רָם *high*, רָמָה *high place*, מָרוֹם
height, from רוּם *to be high*, or less frequently *Derivativa denominativa*
(§ 86), e. g. מַרְגְּלוֹת *the place at the feet*, from רֶגֶל *foot*.

Rem. 1. The earlier grammarians consider the verb alone as stem, and *b*
therefore *all* nouns as verbals, dividing them into (*a*) *Formae nudae*, i. e. such
as have only the *three* (or *two*) radicals, and (*b*) *Formae auctae*, such as have
formative letters or syllables added at the beginning or end, e. g. מַמְלָכָה,
מַלְכוּת. The formative letters used for this purpose are ה א מ נ ת י ו
(הָאֱמַנְתִּיו),[1] and the treatment of nouns formerly followed this order.

According to the view of *roots* and *stems* presented in § 30 *d*, nouns (other *c*
than *denominatives*) are derived not from the verbal stem, but either from the
(abstract) root or from the still undefined stem. In the following pages,
however, the arrangement according to the verbal stem is retained as being
simpler for the beginner. Cf. § 79 *a*.

2. *Compound* nouns as *appellatives* are very rare in Hebrew, e. g. בְּלִיַּעַל *d*
worthlessness, *baseness*. On the other hand, they very frequently occur as
proper names, e. g. גַּבְרִיאֵל (*man of God*), יְהוֹיָקִים (*Yahwe raises up*), יְהוֹנָתָן (*Yahwe
gave*), &c.[2]

§ 82. *Primitive Nouns.*

The number of *primitive* nouns in the sense used in § 81 is small,
since nouns, which in other languages are represented as independent
noun-stems, can easily be traced back in Hebrew to the verbal idea,
e. g. names of animals and natural objects, as שָׂעִיר *he-goat* (prop.
shaggy, from שָׂעַר), שְׂעֹרָה *barley* (prop. *prickly*, also from שָׂעַר), חֲסִידָה
stork (prop. *pia*, sc. *avis*), זָהָב *gold* (from צָהַב=זָהַב *to shine, to be
yellow*). Thus there remain only a few nouns, e. g. several names of
members of the body in men or beasts, to which a corresponding
verbal stem cannot be assigned at all, or at any rate only indirectly
(from other Semitic dialects), as קֶרֶן *horn*, עַיִן *eye*.

---

[1] From this *vox memorialis* the *nomina aucta* are also called by the older
grammarians *nomina heemantica*.

[2] G. Rammelt (*Über die zusammengesetzten Nomina im Hebr.*, Halle, 1883, and
Leipzig, 1884) recognizes as appellatives only צָפַרְדֵּעַ (cf. below, § 85 *w*) and
צַלְמָוֶת (the latter certainly incorrectly [see, however, Nöldeke, *ZATW.* 1897,
p. 183 ff.]). In p. 8 ff. the author gives a list of 'logical compounds', i. e.
new terms formed by composition with the negatives לֹא, בְּלִי, מִבְלִי.

§ 83. Verbal Nouns in General.

a 1. In Hebrew, as in Greek and Latin, the *verbal nouns* are connected in form and meaning primarily with certain forms of the verb, especially the participles and infinitives, which are themselves, even in their ordinary form, frequently used precisely like nouns, e. g. אֹיֵב *enemy*, דַּעַת *to know, knowledge*. Still oftener, however, certain forms of the infinitive and participle, which are seldom or never found as such in the strong verb, though in use in the weak verb and in the kindred dialects, came to be commonly used for the verbal noun; e. g. the participial form קָטֵל, the infinitives of the (Aramaic) form מִקְטַל (as a *noun* also מִקְטָל), further קְטֹלֶת, קְטָלָה, קַטְלָה, קְטָלָה (§ 45 *d*), &c. Others (as the Arabic shows) are properly intensive forms of the participle.

b 2. As regards their meaning, it follows from the nature of the case that nouns which have the form of the infinitive regularly denote the *action* or *state*, with other closely related ideas, and are therefore mostly *abstract*; while the participial nouns, on the contrary, denote for the most part the *subject* of the action or state, and are therefore *concrete*. Moreover, it is to be noticed, that a particular meaning is attached to many of the special forms of derivative nouns, although it does not appear equally in them all.

c Rem. It need not appear strange, when we consider the analogy of other languages, that a noun which in form is properly *abstract* afterwards acquired a *concrete* sense, and vice versa. So in English, we say *his acquaintance*, for the *persons* with whom he is *acquainted*; the *Godhead* for *God* himself; in Hebrew מוֹדַע *acquaintance* and *an acquaintance*.

d The inner connexion in thought between Semitic noun-forms and the corresponding verbal forms is investigated in the works of De Lagarde and Barth (see the titles at the head of § 79) on very different lines, but with many points of agreement. De Lagarde starts from the fact that language consists of sentences. A sentence which consists of only *one* word is called a verb, and anything which serves as a complement to it is a noun. The oldest form of the sentence is the imperative. Closely related to it are three kinds of sentences of the nature of verbal forms, differing according as the property of the particular object of sense is to be represented as invariable (form *qatula*), or as liable to change (form *qatila*), or, finally, as a circumstance which takes place before our eyes (form *qatala*). Like the imperative, these three forms of sentences have also been transformed into nouns, by means of certain phonetic changes,—especially by the omission of the final vowels and the addition of different terminations to the last consonant of the stem. But just as the forms of the verbal sentence undergo numerous modifications (in the tenses, moods, and conjugations), so also do the nouns, sometimes by assimilation of the unessential to the characteristic vowel (*qutul, qitil*), sometimes by the lengthening of the characteristic vowel (*qatûl, qatîl, qatâl*), or else through the displacement of the accent and the consequent reduction of the noun to a monosyllabic form (*qatl, qutl, qitl*), or, finally, by their being formed from the derived stems (or conjugations), e. g. *qattal, qattâl; qittil, qittâl*, &c. Further modifications arise from the use of the various imperfect and infinitive forms, and also from the employment of the prefix *m*. Lastly, *denominalia* are formed from *deverbalia* by appending certain suffixes.

De Lagarde does not, however, claim to be able to show in the case of each particular noun the sense it conveyed in primitive times ; the origin of a number of nouns can now no longer be detected. In those, however, which are clearly derived from verbs, the original meaning is chiefly determined by the characteristic vowel.

Barth's system is based on the thesis that 'all Semitic nouns, adjectives, and participles are derived from either the perfect or the imperfect stem'. Thus, e. g. קְטֹל is the infinitive of the perfect stem, קְטֹל the infinitive of the imperfect stem, שְׁכַב infinitive of יִשְׁכַּב, &c. In dissyllabic noun-forms the second vowel is always alone characteristic and essential, the first vowel unessential, and therefore variable. Further modifications of the simple form are effected by strengthening (sharpening) the second or third consonant, by lengthening the characteristic vowel (instead of which, however, the feminine termination may also be used), or by 'metaplasm', i. e. by the use of noun-forms derived from one of the two intransitive stems for the other, e. g. *qutl* for *qitl*, and vice versa.

In nouns of the perfect stem, the vowels *i* and *u* indicate intransitive formations, the vowel *a* a transitive sense. In nouns of the imperfect stem on the contrary, *u* and *i*, being characteristic vowels, indicate a transitive and *a* an intransitive sense : for *yaqtŭlŭ* is imperfect of the transitive perfect *qatala*, and *yaqtălŭ* imperfect of the intransitive perfects *qatila* and *qatula*, &c. This explains how nouns, apparently identical in form, may yet in sense belong to different classes : a *qutl*-form from a *u*-imperfect has a transitive meaning, but the same form from a *u*-perfect has an intransitive meaning. This double system of perfect and imperfect forms runs through the whole scheme of noun-formation, not only the forms connected with the conjugations, but also the forms with prefixes and suffixes.

Against the whole theory it has been urged that it postulates for the development of the language a much too abstract mechanism, and further, that the meanings of words as we find them may in many cases be due to a modification of the original sense. But though many of the details (e. g. the alleged unessential character of the vowel of the first syllable) remain doubtful, yet the agreement between the characteristic vowel of certain noun formations and that of the perfect or imperfect stem, is supported by such a number of incontestable instances, that there can be no doubt as to a systematic, intimate connexion between the two. At the same time it must be admitted that De Lagarde has put forward many important and suggestive points, and both scholars agree in laying stress on *one* characteristic vowel as indicative of the meaning.

§ 84ᵃ. *Nouns derived from the Simple Stem.*

Preliminary remark.—From the statement made above, § 83 *d*, it follows that *a* an external similarity between forms is no proof of their similar origin, and, vice versa, external difference does not exclude the possibility of their being closely related both in origin and meaning.

I. *Nouns with One Vowel, originally Short.*

R. Růžička, 'Beiträge zur Erklärung der nomina segolata,' in *Sitz.-ber. d. böhmischen Ges. d. Wiss.*, Prag, 1904.

1. Nouns with one of the three short vowels after the first radical : *present* ground-form *qăṭl, qĭṭl, qŭṭl*.

The supposition of *monosyllabic* ground-forms appeared to be required by the character of forms now existing in Hebrew, as well as in Arabic, &c. But there are strong reasons for believing that at least a large proportion of these forms go back to original dissyllabic bases with a short vowel in each syllable. When formative additions were made, the vowel of the 2nd syllable was dropped, i.e. before case-endings in Assyrian and early Arabic, and before pronominal suffixes in Hebrew. From the forms thus produced, the bases *qaṭl, qiṭl, quṭl* have been assumed, although they never appear in Hebrew except in the singular and then in connexion with suffixes.

In support of this view of a large number of original dissyllabic bases, we must not, however, appeal to the Seghôl or Pathaḥ under the 2nd consonant of the existing developed forms, סֵפֶר, זֶרַע, &c. These are in no sense survivals or modifications of an original full vowel in the 2nd syllable, but are mere helping-vowels (§ 28 *e*) to make the monosyllabic forms pronounceable,[1] and consequently disappear when no longer needed. Under certain circumstances even (e.g. in קֹשְׁטְ) they are not used at all. Actual proofs of such original toneless full vowels in the 2nd syllable of existing Segholates are—

1. Forms like Arab. *málik*, for which rarely *malk*, corresponding to the Hebrew ground-form ; cf. De Lagarde, *Uebersicht*, p. 72 ff.

2. In Hebrew גֶּדֶר, יָרֵךְ, בְּבֶר, כָּתֵף, the connective forms of גֶּדֶר, יָרֵךְ, &c., which latter can only come from ground-forms *gădĭr, yărĭk, kăbĭd, kătĭp.*

3. The forms treated under *e*, which are in many ways related to the Segholates proper, in so far as they are to be referred to original dissyllabic bases.

4. The plurals of Hebrew Segholates, since, with very rare exceptions, they take *Qameṣ* under the 2nd radical before the termination ◌ִים, fem. וֹת◌,

of the *absolute state*, as סְפָרִים, מְלָכוֹת, מְלָכִים, &c. This *Qameṣ* (see note 1 on § 26 *e*) can only be due to a lengthening of an original short vowel in the 2nd syllable, and hence it would seem as though the vowel were always *ă*. This is impossible from what has been said, especially under 1 and 2. Hence the explanation of the consistent occurrence of *Qameṣ* in the plurals of *all* Segholates can only be that the regularly formed plurals (i.e. from singulars with original *ă* in the 2nd syllable) became the models for all the others, and ultimately even for some really monosyllabic forms.[2]

(*a*) From the strong stem the above three ground-forms are further developed to קְטֵל,[3] קֶטֶל, קֵטֶל, קֹטֶל (cf. § 27 *r* and in § 93 the explanations of Paradigm I, *a–c*) ; without a helping vowel (§ 28 *d*) קֹשְׁטְ *truth*. If the second

---

[1] According to Delitzsch (*Assyr. Gram.*, p. 157 f.) the same is true in Assyrian of the corresponding *qaṭl*-forms. Without case-endings they are *kalab, šamas, aban* (= בְּלָב, שָׁמֶשׁ, אָבֶן), with case-endings *kalbu, šamsu, abnu.* On the other hand, acc. to Sievers, *Metrik*, i. 261, Hebrew ground-forms probably have a twofold origin : they are shortened according to Hebrew rules partly from old absolute forms like *kálbu, sifru, qúdšu*, and partly from old construct-forms like the Assyrian types *kalab, sifir, quduš.*

[2] On the other hand, Ungnad, *ZA.* 1903, p. 333 ff., rejecting all previous explanations, maintains that the *a* in *mᵉlākhîm, mᵉlākhôth* is inserted merely to facilitate the pronunciation. From *qaṭlim* arose *qaṭᵃlim*, then *qaṭalim* and finally *qᵉṭālim*. See, however, Nöldeke, 'Zur semit. Pluralendung,' *ZA.* 1904, p. 68 ff., who points out that the Semitic nouns *fa'l, fi'l, fu'l* with their corresponding feminines *fa'la*, &c., on assuming the plural termination commonly take an *a* before the 3rd radical, but that no satisfactory account can be given for it. M. Margolis, 'The plural of Segolates' (*Proc. of the Philol. Assoc. of the Pacific Coast*, San Francisco, 1903, p. 4 ff.), and S. Brooks, *Vestiges of the broken plural in Hebrew*, Dublin, 1883, explain *mᵉlākhim* as a *pluralis fractus.*

[3] It is worthy of notice that St. Jerome also (cf. Siegfried, *ZAW.* iv. 76) frequently represents the vowel of the first syllable by *a*, e.g. *gader, aben, ader, areb*, for גֶּדֶר, אָבֶן, אֶדֶר, חֶרֶב, but *cedem, secel, deber*, &c., for שֶׁקֶל, קֶדֶם, דֶּבֶר, &c.

or third radical be a guttural, a helping *Pathaḥ* takes the place of the helping
Sᵉghôl, according to § 22 *d*, e.g. זֶרַע *seed*, נֶצַח *eternity*, פֹּעַל *work*; but with
middle ה or ח, note לֶחֶם *bread*, רֶחֶם (as well as רַחַם) *womb*, אֹהֶל *tent*, בֹּהֶן *thumb*;
so with final א, פֶּרֶא *a wild ass*, &c.; with a middle guttural also the
modification of the principal vowel *ă* to *è* does not occur, e.g. לֶחַי, נַעַר, רַהַב
(exceptions, again, רֶחֶם, לֶחֶם). On the inflexion, cf. § 93, Paradigm I, *a-f*,
and the explanations. In חֵטְא *sin*, the א has wholly lost its consonantal
value.

Examples of feminines: מַלְכָּה (directly from the ground-form *malk, king*), *b*
סִתְרָה *a covering* (also סֵתֶר), אָכְלָה *food* (also אֹכֶל); with a middle guttural
נַעֲרָה *girl*, טָהֳרָה *purity* (also טֹהַר). Cf. § 94, Paradigm I.

(*b*) From weak stems: (*a*) from stems ע״ן, e.g. אַף *nose* (from '*anp*, hence *c*
with formative additions, e.g. אַפִּי for '*anpî, my nose*); עֵז *a she-goat* (ground-
form '*inz*); fem. חִטָּה *wheat*; (*β*) from stems ע״ע (§ 93, Paradigm I, *l–n*) פַּת
a morsel, עַם *people* (so, when in close connexion with the next word; unconnected עָם; with the article הָעָם, לָעָם, &c.); רַב in the sense of *much*, but רָב *great*,
numerous (in close connexion also רַב); רָע *evil*, with the article in close connexion הָרָע, unconnected הָרַע; with the *ă* always lengthened to *ā*, יָם *sea*;
fem. חַיָּה *life*, and with attenuation of the *ă* to *i*, מִדָּה *measure*; from the
ground-form *qiṭl*, אֵם *mother*; fem. גִּזָּה *a shearing*; from the ground-form *quṭl*,
חֹק *statute*, fem. חֻקָּה. (*γ*) from stems ע״י (Paradigm I, *g* and *i*); מָוֶת *death*
(from *má-ut*, the *u* passing into the corresponding consonant, as in תָּוֶךְ *middle*)
or contracted יוֹם *day*, שׁוֹט *whip*, שׁוֹר *a bull*; fem. עַוְלָה *perverseness* (also contracted עוֹלָה); from the ground-form *quṭl*, צוּר *a rock*; fem. סוּפָה *a storm*.
(*δ*) from stems ע״י (Paradigm I, *h*); זַיִת *an olive-tree* (with a helping *Ḥireq*
instead of a helping Sᵉghôl) from *za-it*, the *i* passing into the corresponding
consonant; or contracted חֵיק *bosom*, חַיִל, 2 K 18¹⁷ (elsewhere חַיִל) *host*; fem.
שֵׂיבָה *grey hair*; from the ground-form *qiṭl*, דִּין *judgement*; fem. בִּינָה *understanding*. (*ε*) from stems ל״ה (Paradigm I, *k*); partly forms such as בְּכֶה
weeping, הֶגֶה *murmuring*, נֶדֶה *a present*, קֶצֶה *the end*, partly such as בְּכִי, אֲרִי
a lion (ground-form *băky, 'ăry*); cf. also the forms from stems originally ל״ו,
שָׂחוּ *swimming* (ground-form *sáḥw*); fem. שַׁלְוָה *rest*, גַּאֲוָה *exaltation*; from stems
ל״י, אַלְיָה *a fat tail*, and with attenuation of *ă* to *i* שִׁבְיָה *captivity*, also שִׁבְית,
formed no doubt directly from the masc. שְׁבִי with the fem. termination ת;
from the ground-form *qiṭl*, חֲצִי (from *ḥiṣy*); fem. חֶדְוָה *joy*, עֶרְיָה and עֶרְוָה
nakedness; from the ground-form *quṭl*, בֹּהוּ (from *bŏhw*) *waste*, תֹּהוּ *emptiness*;
דְּלִי, for דְּלְי, *bucket*; fem. אֳנִיָּה *a ship* (directly from אֳנִי *a fleet*).

The masculines as well as the feminines of these *segholate* forms may have *d*
either an *abstract* or a *concrete* meaning. In the form קְטָל the *passive* or at any
rate the *abstract* meaning is by far the more common (e.g. נֹעַר *youthfulness*,
abstract of נַעַר *boy*; אֹכֶל *food*, &c.).[1]

---

[1] M. Lambert also (*REJ*. 1896, p. 18 ff.), from statistics of the Segholates,
arrives at the conclusion that the *qaṭl*-form is especially used for concretes (in
nouns without gutturals he reckons twenty concretes as against two abstracts), and the *qiṭl*-form, and less strictly the *quṭl*, for abstracts.

e 2. Nouns with one of the three short vowels under the second radical (present ground-form *qᵉṭăl, qᵉṭĭl, qᵉṭŭl*), e. g. דְּבַשׁ *honey*, דְּוַי *sickness*, חֲתַת *terror*; and so always with middle א, בְּאֵר *a well*, זְאֵב *a wolf*, בְּאֹשׁ *stench*. In reality these forms, like the segholates mentioned in No. 1 (see above, *a*), are, probably, for the most part to be referred to original *dissyllabic* forms, but the tone has been shifted from its original place (the penultima) on to the ultima. Thus *dibáš* (originally *dibáš*) as ground-form of דְּבַשׁ is supported both by the Hebrew דִּבְשִׁי (with suffix of the first person), and by the Arabic *dibs*, the principal form ; *bi'ir* (according to Philippi with assimilation of the vowel of the second syllable to that of the first) as ground-form of בְּאֵר is attested by the Arabic *bi'r*; for בְּאֹשׁ (Arabic *bu's*) similarly a ground-form *bu'uš* may be inferred, just as a ground-form *qăṭŭl* underlies the infinitives of the form קְטֹל.[1]

II. *Nouns with an original Short Vowel in both Syllables.*

f 3. The ground-form *qăṭăl*, fem. *qăṭălăt*, developed in Hebrew to קָטָל (§ 93, Paradigm II, *a, b*) and קְטָלָה (§§ 94, 95, Paradigm II, *a, b*), mostly forms intransitive adjectives, as חָכָם *wise*, חָדָשׁ *new*, יָשָׁר *upright* ; but also substantives, as דָּבָר *a word*, and even abstracts, as אָשָׁם *guilt*, רָעָב *hunger*, שָׂבָע *satiety* ; in the fem. frequently abstract, as צְדָקָה [2] *righteousness* ; with an initial guttural אֲדָמָה *earth*.—Of the same formation from verbs ע״ע are בַּדָּד *alone*, עָנָן *cloud* ; passive חָלָל *pierced*.—In verbs ל״ה a final Yôdh is almost always rejected, and the *ă* of the second syllable lengthened to *ê*. Thus שָׂדַי *field*, after rejection of the י and addition of ה as a vowel-letter, becomes שָׂדֶה (cf. § 93, Paradigm II, *f*) ; fem. e. g. שָׁנָה *year* ; cf. § 95, Paradigm II, *c*. From a verb ל״י the strong form עָנָו *afflicted* occurs.

g 4. The ground-form *qăṭĭl*, fem. *qăṭĭlăt*, developed to קָטֵל (§ 93, Paradigm II, *c–e*) and קְטֵלָה, is frequently used as participle of verbs middle *e* (§ 50 *b*), and hence mostly with an intransitive meaning ; cf. זָקֵן *old, an old man* ; כָּבֵד *heavy*, fem. בְּהֵמָה *cattle*, אֲפֵלָה and חֲשֵׁכָה *darkness*.—From verbs פ״י : irregularly, דָּלִיּוֹתָיו *the branches of it*, Jer 11¹⁶, &c., generally referred to a *sing.* דָּלִית (stem דָּלָה), and הָרִיּוֹתָיו Ho 14¹ *their women with child* (from הָרָה, st. constr. הֲרַת, plur. st. absol. and constr. הָרוֹת).—From a verb ל״ו with consonantal Wāw : שְׁלֵו *at ease*, incorrectly written *plene* שְׁלֵיו Jb 21²³.

h 5. The ground-form *qăṭŭl*, developed to קָטֹל (also written קָטוֹל), generally forms adjectives, e. g. אָיֹם *terrible*, בָּרֹד *piebald*, מָתוֹק *sweet*, נָקֹד *speckled*, עָבֹת *interwoven*, עָגֹל *round*, עָמֹק *deep*, עָקֹב *hilly*, צָהֹב *golden* ; קָטֹן *small*, only in sing. masc., with a parallel form קָטָן of the class treated under *f*, fem. קְטַנָּה, plur. קְטַנִּים. These forms are not to be confounded with those in No. III, from

---

[1] On this theory cf. Stade, *Hebräische Grammatik*, § 199 *b* ; De Lagarde, *Übersicht*, p. 57 f. ; A. Müller, *ZDMG.* xlv, p. 226, and especially Philippi, *ZDMG.* xlix, p. 208.

[2] In St. Jerome's time these forms were still pronounced *ṣadaca* (צְדָקָה), *ṣaaca* (צְעָקָה), *nabala* (נְבָלָה), &c., see Siegfried, *ZAW.* iv. 79. Moreover, the numerous abstracts of this form (e. g. even קְצָפָה *a splintering*, צְוָחָה *a crying*, &c.) are undoubtedly to be regarded (with Barth, *Nominalbildung*, p. 87) as feminines of infinitives of the form *qăṭăl*, the lengthening of the second syllable being balanced, as in other cases, by the addition of the feminine termination.

the ground-form *qăṭăl*.—Fem. אֵימָה, כְּבוּדָּה (*glorious*), עֲבָתָה, עֲנֻגָּה (*delicate*), עֲנֻלָּה, עֲמֻקָּה, with sharpening of the third radical, in order to keep the original *ŭ* short, and similarly in the plurals אֲסַפִּים, עֲנָלִים, נְקֻדִּים, בְּרֻדִּים *stores*, &c.

6. The ground-form *qiṭăl* develops to קְטַל (cf. § 93, Paradigm II, Rem. 1), *i* e. g. לֵבָב *heart*, עֵנָב *a bunch of grapes*, שֵׁכָר *strong drink*; from a verb ל״ה, probably of this class is רֵעֶה, generally contracted to רֵעַ *friend*, ground-form *ri'ay*: the full form is preserved in רֵעֵהוּ *his friend*, for רֵעֱיהוּ.

III. *Nouns with an original Short Vowel in the First and a Long Vowel in the Second Syllable.*

7. The ground-form *qăṭăl* in Hebrew always develops to the form קָטוֹל, the *k* *ă* becoming an obscure *ô*. The fact that this form is also written קָטֹל must not lead to the confusion of these forms with those mentioned in No. 5, from the ground-form *qăṭŭl*.[1] Moreover the *qaṭôl*-class includes forms of various origin, and therefore of various meaning, as (*a*) intransitive adjectives like גָּדוֹל *great*, קָדוֹשׁ *holy*, fem. גְּדוֹלָה, the short vowel becoming Šᵉwâ, whereas in גָּדוֹל, &c., *before the tone* it is lengthened to *ă*; (*b*) the *infinitives absolute* of the form קָטוֹל (§ 45 *a*) as representing the abstract idea of the verb, and abstract substantives like כָּבוֹד *honour*, שָׁלוֹם *peace* (Arab. *sălâm*); (*c*) substantives and adjectives in an active sense, as בָּחוֹן *assayer* (of metals), עָשׁוֹק *an oppressor*, חָמוֹץ *oppressing*; in the feminine בְּגוֹדָה *treacherous* Jer 3⁷·¹⁰, the irregular retention of the *ă* in the third syllable from the end is no doubt to be explained, with Brockelmann, from Aramaic influence, the punctuator having in mind the Aramaic nomen agentis *qâṭôl*.

8. The ground-form *qăṭîl* develops to קָטִיל (cf. § 93, Paradigm IV, *a* and *b*). *l* Here also forms of various origin and meaning are to be distinguished: (*a*) adjectives used substantively with a passive meaning to denote duration in a state, as אָסִיר *a prisoner*, מָשִׁיחַ *an anointed one*. These proper *qăṭîl*-forms are parallel to the purely passive *qaṭûl*-forms (see *m*), but others are due to a strengthening of original *qaṭîl*-forms. These are either (*b*) intransitive in meaning, as צָעִיר *small*, and, from ל״י stems, נָקִי *pure*, עָנִי *poor* (see § 93 *vv*), or (*c*) active, as נָבִיא *a speaker* (prophet), פָּקִיד *an overseer*.—Of a different kind again (according to De Lagarde, infinitives) are (*d*) forms like אָסִיף *the ingathering*, בָּצִיר *vintage*, חָרִישׁ *ploughing time*, קָצִיר *harvest*. On *qăṭṭîl*-forms with a kindred meaning, cf. § 84ᵇ *f*.

9. The ground-form *qăṭûl* develops to קָטוֹל. As in the *qaṭăl* and *qaṭîl*-forms *m* (see *k* and *l*), so here forms of various kinds are to be distinguished: (*a*) *qaṭûl*-forms proper, with passive meaning, especially all the passive participles of Qal; fem. e. g. בְּתוּלָה *virgin* (properly *secluded*). On the other hand, by strengthening an original *qaṭûl*-form we get (*b*) certain stative adjectives (§ 50 *f*), as אָנוּשׁ *incurable*, עָצוּם *strong*, עָרוּם *subtil*, or even transitive, as אָחוּז *holding*; (*c*) active substantives, as יָקוּשׁ *a fowler*. Further, some of the forms mentioned in § 84ᵇ *g* belong to this class; see above, the remark on *l*.

10. The ground-form *qiṭăl* or *qăṭăl*[2] in Hebrew changes the *ĭ* to vocal Šᵉwâ, *n*

---

[1] In Na 1³ only the *Qᵉrê* requires גְּדָל־ (in the constr. state) for the *Kᵉthibh* גְּדוֹל.

[2] On the *fu'ăl*-forms (regarded by Wellhausen as original diminutives) see Nöldeke, *Beiträge* (Strassb. 1904), p. 30 ff. He includes among them נָעֹרֶת *tow*, and טְחֹרִים *hemorrhoids*.

and develops to קְטָל (cf. § 93, Paradigm IV, c) or קְטוֹל, with *á* obscured to *ô* (as above, *k*). Cf. שְׁאָר *remnant*, יְקָר *honour*, כְּתָב *book* (Arab. *kitáb*), קְרָב *war* (the last three probably loan-words from the Aramaic); of the other form, חֲלוֹם *a dream*, חֲמוֹר *an ass* (Arab. *ḥimâr*), אֱלוֹהַּ *God* (Arab. *'iláh*); with א prosthetic (§ 19 *m*), אֶזְרוֹעַ *arm* (twice: usually זְרוֹעַ); fem. בְּשׂוֹרָה *good news* (Arab. *bišârăt*); עֲבוֹדָה *service*, כְּתֹבֶת (Arab. *kitâbăt*) *tattooing*.

o 11. The ground-form *qiṭîl* seems to occur e. g. in Hebrew אֱוִיל *foolish*, אֱלִיל *vanity*, בְּדִיל *lead*, כְּסִיל *a fool*, חֲזִיר *a swine* (the prop. name חֲזִיר points to the ground-form *qiṭil*, cf. Arab. *ḥinzîr*).

p 12. The ground-form *qiṭûl* or *quṭûl*, Hebr. קְטוּל, e. g. גְּבוּל *a boundary*, לְבוּשׁ *a garment*; fem. גְּבוּרָה *strength*, אֱמוּנָה *faithfulness*.

q Rem. When the forms *qᵉṭûl* and *qᵉṭôl* begin with א, they almost invariably take in the singular a *Şere* under the א instead of the ordinary *Ḥaṭeph-Sᵉghôl*; cf. אֵבוּס *a crib*, אֵטוּן *thread*, אֵמוּן *faithful*, אֵזוֹב *hyssop*, אֵזוֹר *a waist-band*, אֵסוּר *a bond*, אֵפוֹד *an 'ephod'*; cf. § 23 *h*, and the analogous cases of *Şere* for *Ḥaṭeph-Sᵉghôl* in verbal forms § 52 *n*, § 63 *p*, § 76 *d*.

IV. Nouns with a Long Vocal in the First Syllable and originally a Short Vowel in the Second Syllable.

r 13. The ground-form *qâṭăl*, in Hebrew, always changes the *â* into an obscure *ô*, קוֹטָל (קֹטָל), e. g. עוֹלָם (§ 93, Paradigm III, *a*), Arab. *'âlăm*, *eternity*; חוֹתָם (Arab. *ḥâtăm*) *a seal* (according to Barth a loan-word of Egyptian origin), fem. חֹתֶמֶת (from *ḥôtămt*); תּוֹלֵע *worm* (unless from a stem ולע, like תּוֹשָׁב from ישׁב; see the analogous cases in § 85 *b*). On the participles *Qal* of verbs ל״ה (§ 93, Paradigm III, *c*), cf. § 75 *e*; on the feminines of the participles *Qal*, which are formed with the termination ת, see below, *s*.

Rem. Of a different kind (probably from a ground-form *qauṭal*) are such forms as אוֹפָן (or אוֹפַן Ez 10⁹ in the same verse) *a wheel*; גּוֹזָל *a young bird*, דּוֹנַג *wax*, &c.

s 14. The ground-form *qâṭil* also becomes in Hebrew almost invariably קוֹטֵל (קֹטֵל). Besides *participles active masc. Qal* this class includes also feminines of the form קֹטֶלֶת, if their ground-form *qôṭalt* (§ 69 *c*) goes back to an original *qâṭilt*. The substantives of this form, such as כֹּהֵן *priest* (Arab. *kâhin*), were also originally participles *Qal*. The fem. of the substantives has *ē* (lengthened from *ĭ*) retained before the tone, e. g. יֹלֵדָה *a woman in travail* (cf. also בֹּגֵדָה *the treacherous woman*, Jer 3⁸; הַצֹּלֵעָה *her that halteth*, Mi 4⁶ ᶠ·, Zp 3¹⁹; סֹחֵרָה *a buckler*, ψ 91⁴); the participles as a rule have the form יֹלְדָה, &c., the original *ĭ* having become *Šᵉwâ*; however, the form with *Şere* occurs also in the latter, Is 29⁶·⁸, 34⁹, ψ 68²⁶, 118¹⁶ (all in principal *pause*; in subordinate *pause* 2 S 13²⁰, Is 33¹⁴; with a conjunctive accent, Ct 1⁶).

t 15. The ground-form *qâṭăl*, Hebrew קוּטָל (as יוּבַל *river*, Jer 17⁸) or קֹטָל e. g. עוּגָב *a pipe*, commonly עֻגָב, and to be so read, with Baer, also in ψ 150⁴, not עֻגָב.

V. Nouns with a Long Vowel in each Syllable.

u 16. קִיטוֹל, e. g. קִיטוֹר *smoke*. The few forms of this kind are probably derived from the ground-form *qiṭâl* (*qiṭṭâl*?), i. e. the original *â* has become an obscure *ô*.

§ 84ᵇ. *Formation of Nouns from the Intensive Stem.*

This includes all forms which have arisen, either through the *a*
doubling of the middle radical, or the repetition of one or of two
consonants of the simple stem.

VI. *Nouns with the Middle Consonant sharpened.*

As in the corresponding verbal stems (cf. § 52 *f*), so also in some noun-
formations of this class, the Dageš in the second radical expresses an
intensification of the idea of the stem, either emphasizing the energy of the
action or relation, or else indicating a longer continuance of the relation or
state. Other nouns of this character are evidently only by-forms of the
nouns derived from the simple stem, which were treated in the last section :
cf. the instances adduced under *f* and *g*, and Barth, *Nominalbildung*, Introd., p. x.

17. The ground-form *qăṭṭăl* is mostly lengthened in Hebrew to קַטָּל ; cf. *b*
אַיָל *a stag*, fem. אַיָּלָה, constr. st. אַיֶּלֶת (from '*ăyyălt*) ; cf. also the fem. (originating from *Qal*) לֶהָבָה *a flame* (according to § 27 *q* for *lăhhăbhā*), חָרָבָה *dry land*
(for *ḥarrābhā*), דַּלֶּקֶת and קַדַּחַת *a burning fever*, יַבָּשָׁה and יַבֶּשֶׁת *dry land*, טַבַּעַת
a seal-ring, שַׁחֶפֶת *consumption*. Adjectives of this class ('intensified participles
of the active verb', Barth, *ibid*., § 33) are חַטָּא *sinful*, נַגָּח *wont to gore*, קַנָּא
jealous, כֶּחָשׁ (for *kaḥḥăš*, by § 22 *c*) *lying*. *Nomina opificum* also, curiously
enough, are so treated in Hebrew (at least in the *constr. state* of the sing.),
although the corresponding Arabic form *qăttăl* points to an original (unchange-
able) *ā* in the second syllable ; cf. גַּנָּב *a thief*, דַּיָּן *a judge* (constr. st. דַּיַּן ψ 68⁶),
טַבָּח *a cook*, חָרָשׁ (for *ḥarrăš*) *artificer* (constr. st. חָרַשׁ, but plur. constr. חָרָשֵׁי ; פָּרָשׁ
horseman (for *parrăš*), const. st. פָּרַשׁ Ez 26¹⁰.

18. The ground-form *qĭṭṭăl* appears in צָחֶה *dry*, גֵּאֶה *haughty* (the *ĭ* being *c*
lengthened to *ē* according to § 22 *c*), if these forms go back to original *ṣĭḥḥăy*,
gĭ''ăy. On the analogy, however, of the adjectives denoting defects (see *d*
below), we should rather expect a ground-form *qĭṭṭĭl*; moreover, '*iwwai'*, ground-
form of the fem. אִוֶּלֶת *foolishness*, goes back to an original *iwwilt*, see § 69 *c*.

19. The ground-form *qŭṭṭăl* and *qŭṭṭŭl* ; cf. the fem. כֻּסֶּמֶת *spelt*, כֻּתֹּנֶת *coat*.

20. The ground-form *qăṭṭĭl* ; from the intensive stem, the infinitives Pi'ēl of *d*
the form קַטֵּל.

21. The ground-form *qĭṭṭĭl*, in Hebrew lengthened to קִטֵּל. Of this form
are a considerable number of adjectives which denote a bodily or mental fault
or defect. Cf. אִטֵּר *disabled*, אִלֵּם *dumb*, גִּבֵּן *hump-backed*, עִוֵּר *blind*, חֵרֵשׁ *deaf* (for
ḥirrēš), פִּסֵּחַ *lame*, קֵרֵחַ *bald*, עִקֵּשׁ *perverse* ; פִּקֵּחַ *open-eyed* follows the same
analogy.

22. The ground-form *qăṭṭăl*, cf. the remarks in *b* above, on the *nomina* *e*
opificum ; moreover, to this class belong infinitives Pi'ēl of the Aramaic form
בַּקָּרָה *a searching out* ; בַּקָּשָׁה *a request* ; with middle guttural (see § 22 *c*) נֶאָצָה
contumely ; but cf. also נִאֲצוֹתֶיךָ Ez 35¹², with full lengthening of the original
ă before א ; נֶחָמָה *comfort*. From the attenuation of the *ă* of this form to *ĭ*,
arises undoubtedly :

23. The ground-form *qĭṭṭăl*, e. g. אִכָּר *husbandman* (Arab. '*ăkkăr*).

24. The ground-form *qĭṭṭōl*, most probably only a variety of the form *qăṭṭăl*
with the *ă* attenuated to *ĭ* (as in No. 23), and the *ā* obscured to *ō* (as in *n* and

r); cf. גִּבּוֹר *hero* (Arab. *gäbbár*), יִפּוֹר *caviller*, צִפּוֹר (*piper* or *chirper*) *a bird*, שִׁכּוֹר *drunkard*. On the other hand, יִלּוֹד *born* probably arises from *yullôd*, an old participle passive of *Qal*, the *ŭ* being dissimilated in the sharpened syllable before *ô*: so Barth, *ibid.*, p. 41 f.

f　25. The ground-form *qáṭṭîl*, קַטִּיל, almost exclusively of persons, who possess some quality in an intensive manner, e. g. אַבִּיר *strong*, צַדִּיק *righteous*, בָּרִיחַ *fugitive* (for *barriᵃḥ*), עָרִיץ *violent* (for *'árrîṣ*).

That some of these are only by-forms of the *qăṭîl*-class (see above, remark on *a*), appears from the *constr. st.* פְּרִיץ *ravenous*, Is 35⁹ (but פְּרִיצִים, פְּרִיצֵי always), and according to Barth (*ibid.*, 35 *a*) also from the *constr. st.* אַבִּיר (but also אַבִּיר 1 S 21⁸) of אַבִּיר. However, the form אֲבִיר, as a name of God, may be intentionally differentiated from אַבִּיר, a poetic term for the bull.

In the same way אַסִּיר *prisoner*, סָרִים *eunuch* (*constr. st.* always סָרִים, plur. סָרִיסִים, *constr. st.* סָרִיסֵי Gn 40⁷, but in the book of Esther always סָרִיסֵי, with *suffix* סָרִיסָיו, &c.), and עָתִיק *weaned*, may be regarded as by-forms of the *qăṭîl*-class w·ᵗʰ passive meaning, see § 84ᵃ *l*.

g　26. The ground-form *qăṭṭûl*, קַטּוּל, e. g. חַנּוּן *gracious*, רַחוּם *compassionate* (with virtual strengthening of the ח), חָרוּץ *diligent* (for *ḥarrûṣ*), probably, again, to a large extent by-forms of the *qăṭûl*-class, § 84ᵃ *m*. The same applies to substantives like אַשֻּׁר *a step* (in אַשֻּׁרִי, as well as אֲשֻׁרוֹ, &c.), עַמּוּד *pillar*; fem. חֲבֻרָה *a stripe* (also חֲבֻרָתוֹ), בַּטֻּחוֹת *security* : cf. Barth, *ibid.*, § 84.

h　27. The ground-form *qăṭṭôl*; besides the infinitives absolute *Piʿēl* of the form קַטֹּל, also קַנֹּוא *jealous* (as well as קַנָּא, an obscured form of *qăṭṭâl*, see *e*).

i　28. The ground-form *qĭṭṭûl*, קִטּוּל, e. g. צִפּוּי *a coating of metal*, שִׁלֻּם *requital*, שִׁקּוּי *drink*, שִׁקּוּץ *detestable thing* ; with concrete meaning לִמּוּד *a disciple*, עִזּוּז *strong*; frequently in the plural in an abstract sense, as גִּדּוּפִים *reproach*, מִלֻּאִים *filling* (the induction of a priest), נִחֻמִים *consolations, compassion*, שִׁכֻּלִים *bereavement*, שִׁלֻּחִים *dismissal*, שִׁמֻּרִים *observance*.

VII. *Nouns with the Third Consonant repeated.*

k　29. The ground-form *qăṭlăl*, e. g. שַׁאֲנָן *quiet*, fem. שַׁאֲנַנָּה (with sharpening of the second *Nûn*, in order to keep the preceding vowel short) ; רַעֲנָן *green*, plur. רַעֲנַנִּים.

l　30. The ground-form *qăṭlîl*, in Hebrew קַטְלֵל; of this form are e. g. the infinitives *Piʿlēl* (prop. *Paʿlēl*), cf. § 55 *d*.

m　31. The ground-form *qăṭlŭl*; so the plur. גַּבְנֻנִּים *ridges* (with sharpening of the *Nûn*, as in No. 29).

32. The ground-form *qĭṭlăl*, in פֶּרְחַח *a brood*.

33. The ground-form *qŭṭlăl*, in אֻמְלָל *faint*.

34. The ground-form *qăṭlîl*, e. g. עַבְטִיט *plunder*, סַגְרִיר *rain-storm*, שַׁפְרִיר *glittering tapestry*, Jer 43¹⁰ *Qᵉrê* ; with attenuation of the *ă* to *i* בִּמְרִירִים *all that maketh black*, Jb 3⁵ (but the better reading is כַּמְרִירֵי).

35. The ground-form *qăṭlŭl*, e. g. שַׁפְרוּר Jer 43¹⁰ *Kᵉth.*; נַאֲפוּפִים *adulteries*.

VIII. *Nouns with the Second and Third Consonants repeated.*

n　36-39. *Qᵉṭălṭăl, qᵉʿălṭĭl, qᵉʿălṭŭl; qᵉṭălṭŭl, qᵉṭălṭôl* (in *fem.* and *plur.* often with the last consonant sharpened for the reason given in *a* above); cf. הֲפַכְפַּךְ

crooked, חֲלַקְלַקּוֹת *slippery places,* עֲקַלְקַלּוֹת *crooked (ways)* ; פְּתַלְתֹּל *tortuous* ; also words denoting colours, אֲדַמְדָּם (Lv 13⁴²·⁴⁹ in pause) *reddish,* fem. אֲדַמְדֶּמֶת, plur. אֲדַמְדַּמֹּת ; יְרַקְרַק *greenish,* plur. fem. יְרַקְרַקֹת ; *qᵉṭalṭil,* יְפֵיפִיָּה *very fair* (to be read in Jer 46²⁰ for יׇפְפִיָּה) ; *qᵉṭalṭül,* שְׁחַרְחֹרֶת (fem.) *blackish* ; אֲסַפְסֻף *a rabble* (augmented from אָסוּף *collected*). From a verb פ״י with aphaeresis of the initial syllable צֶאֱצָאִים *offspring.* Moreover, of the same form, probably, is חֲצוֹצְרָה *a trumpet* (for חֲצַרְצְרָה, cf. § 55 e). Also in Is 2²⁰ לַחֲפַרְפֵּרוֹת is to be read instead of לַחְפֹּר פֵּרוֹת (from the *sing.* חֲפַרְפֵּרָה *a digging* or *burrowing* animal, perhaps the *mole*). But פִּקְחָקוֹחַ *opening,* Is 61¹ (ed. Mant., Baer, Ginsb. פְּקַח־קוֹחַ), is an evident mistake due to dittography ; read פְּקֹחַ as in 42⁷.

IX. *Nouns in which the Whole (Biliteral) Stem is repeated.*

Naturally this class includes only isolated forms of the stems ע״וּ and ע״ע *o* (on פִּיפִיּוֹת see § 96 under פֶּה). Thus :—

40. גַּלְגַּל *a wheel,* and, with attenuation of the first *ă* to *ĭ,* גִּלְגָּל (from נלל) ; fem. חַלְחָלָה *anguish* (from חוּל or חיל) ; כָּכָּר (for *kirkar*) *a talent* ; cf. also כּוֹכָב *a star* (from *kăwkăb,* Arabic *kaukăb,* for כַּבְכַּב), טוֹטָפֹת *bands,* for טַפְטָפֹת ; צְלָצַל probably *a whirring locust.*

41. כַּלְכֵּל infin. *Filpēl* (prop. *Palpil*) from כּוּל ; fem. טַלְטֵלָה *a hurling* (from *p* טוּל).

42. כַּרְבֹּד perhaps a *ruby* (for *kădkŭd*), from כרד.

43. קָדְקֹד *the crown of the head* (for *qŭdqŭd*), from קרד ; fem. גֻּלְגֹּלֶת *a skull* (for *gülgült*), from נלל.

44. זַרְזִיר *girded,* from זרר ; בַּקְבּוּק *a bottle,* from בקק ; בַּרְבֻּרִים *fattened birds* (?).

§ 85. *Nouns with Preformatives and Afformatives.*

These include nouns which are directly derived from verbal forms *a* having preformatives (*Hiph'il, Hoph'al, Hithpa'ēl, Niph'al,* &c.), as well as those which are formed with other preformatives (א, י, מ, נ, ת), and finally those which are formed with afformatives. The quadriliterals and quinqueliterals also are taken in connexion with these formations, inasmuch as they arise almost always by the addition or insertion of one or two consonants to the triliteral stem.

X. *Nouns with Preformatives.*

45. Nouns with א prefixed. Cf. the substantives with א *prosthetic* (§ 19 m), *b* such as אֶזְרוֹעַ *arm* (Jer 32²¹, Jb 31²²; elsewhere always זְרוֹעַ) ; אֶצְבַּע *a finger,* אַרְבֶּה *a locust,* אֶגְרוֹף *fist* (others *mattock,* or *clod*), אַשְׁמוּרָה or אַשְׁמֹרֶת *a watch.* In these examples the א is a 'euphonic' prefix (Barth, *ibid.,* § 150 b) ; in other cases it is 'essential' ; cf. especially the adjectives, אַכְזָב *deceitful,* אַכְזָר *cruel,* אֵיתָן *perennial* (for 'aitan) [=the Arab. 'elative', used for expressing the compar. and superl. degrees]. The fem. אַזְכָּרָה *fragrant part*[1] (of the meal-

---

[1] Or perhaps more correctly with Jacob, *ZAW.* 1897, p. 79, 'declaration,' i.e. the part of the meal-offering which 'announces the sacrifice and its object'.

offering) is a *nomen verbale* of *Hiph'il*, answering to the Aramaic infinitive of the causal stem (*'Aph'ēl*), hence with suff. אַזְבַּרְתָּה Lv 2², &c.

c 46. Nouns with ה prefixed. Besides the ordinary infinitives of *Hiph'il* הַקְטֵל and הַקְטִיל, of *Niph'al* הִקָּטֵל, הִקָּטֹל (for *hinq.*), and of the conjugations formed with the prefix הִת, this class also includes some rare *nomina verbalia* derived from *Hiph'il* (cf. § 72 *z*), viz. הַכָּרָה *appearance* (from נָכַר), Is 3⁹; הֲנָפָה *a swinging* (from נוּף), [Is 30²⁸; הֲנָחָה *a rest-giving*, Est 2¹⁸]; הַצָּלָה *deliverance* (from נָצַל), [Est 4¹⁴ an Aram. form : cf. הַזָּרָה Dn 5²⁰]; perhaps also הֵיכָל *palace*, from *haikāl*, unless it is borrowed from the Assyrian ; see the Lexicon.

d 47. Nouns with י prefixed, as יִצְהָר *oil*, יַלְקוּט *wallet*, יַנְשׁוּף *owl*(?) ; from verbs ע״וּ, e. g. יְקוּם *a living thing*, יֶתֶר *a range* ; from a verb ע״ו יָרִיב *an adversary*. Of a different character are the many proper names which have simply adopted the imperfect form, as יִצְחָק, יַעֲקֹב, &c.

e 48. Nouns with מ prefixed. This *preformative Mêm*, which is no doubt connected with מִי *who*, and מָה *what* (see § 37 and § 52 *c*), appears in a very large number of nouns, and serves to express the most varied modifications of the idea of the stem : (1) מ *subjective*, when preformative of the participles *Pi'ēl*, *Hiph'il*, *Hithpa'ēl*, and other active conjugations. (2) מ *objective*, when preformative of the participles *Pu'al*, *Hoph'al*, and other passive conjugations, as well as of numerous nouns. (3) מ *instrumental*, as in מַפְתֵּחַ *a key*, &c. (4) מ *local*, as in מִדְבָּר *a drive for cattle*, &c.

f As regards the formation of these nouns, it is to be remarked that the preformative מ was originally in most cases followed by a short *ă*. This *ă*, however, in a closed syllable is frequently attenuated to *ĭ* ; in an open syllable before the tone it is lengthened to *ā* (so also the *ĭ*, attenuated from *ă*, is lengthened to *ē*), and in מָגֵן *shield* (with suff. מָגִנִּי) it even becomes unchangeable *ā*. But in an open syllable which does *not* stand before the tone, the *a* necessarily becomes *Š^ewā*.

g The following forms are especially to be noticed : (*a*) ground-form *măqtăl*, in Hebrew מַקְטָל,¹ e. g. מַאֲכָל *food* ; fem. מַמְלָכָה *kingdom*, מַאֲכֶלֶת *a knife*, מְלָאכָה (for מַלְאָכָה by § 23 *c*) *business* ; from a verb פ״ן, מַתָּן *a gift* ; from verbs פ״י, מוֹצָא *a going forth*, מוֹשָׁב *a seat* ; from verbs פ״י, מֵיטָב *the best* (from *maităb*) ; with י (or ו) assimilated, מַצָּע *a bed* ; from verbs ע״ע, מָסָךְ *a screen*, and with the shortening of the *ă* under the preformative, מֶמֶר *bitterness* (from מָמַר developed to a segholate), fem. מְשַׁמָּה *desolation* ; from a verb ע״וּ, probably of this class is מָקוֹם *place*, the *ă* lengthened to *ā* and obscured to ô (Arabic *măqâm*) ; from verbs ל״ה, מַרְאֶה *appearance*, מַעַן (for מַעֲנֶה) prop. *intention*, only in לְמַעַן *on account of, in order that*.

h (*b*) Ground-form *miqtăl* (the usual form of the infin. Qal in Aramaic), Hebr. מִקְטָל, e. g. מִדְבָּר (in Jer 2³¹ also, where Baer requires הַמִּדְבָּר, read with ed. Mant., Ginsburg, &c.) הַמְדַבֵּר) *a cattle-drive*, fem. מִלְחָמָה *war*, מֶרְכָּבָה *a chariot* (with *S^eghôl* instead of *ĭ*, but in *constr. st.* מִרְכֶּבֶת Gn 41⁴³ ; cf. מֶרְחָק *distance*), מִשְׁמֶרֶת *a watch* ; from verbs ע״ע, e. g. מֵסַב *surroundings* (from *mĭ-săb* ; *ĭ* in the open syllable being lengthened to *ē* ; but cf. also מַשָּׁק Is 33⁴ as *constr. state* from שׁקק with sharpening of the first radical ; cf. § 67 *g*) ; from verbs ל״ה, מִקְנֶה *a possession*, fem. מִקְנָה.

___

¹ In כְּמֻחַקִּים Ct 5¹⁶, Neh 8¹⁰, the first syllable is artificially opened to avoid the cacophony ; on the *ă* of the second syllable cf. § 93 *ee*.

(c) Ground-form *măqṭŭl*, Hebr. מַקְטֵל, e.g. מַשְׁעֵן *a support* (fem. מִשְׁעֶנֶת), *i*
מַסְגֵּר *a smith*, מַעֲשֵׂר *a tithe*; fem. מַכְשֵׁלָה *a ruin*; from a verb פ"נ, מַגֵּפָה *an
overthrow*, מַצֵּבָה *a pillar*; from verbs ע"ע, מָגֵן *a shield*; fem. מְגִלָּה *a roll* (from
גָּלַל), מְאֵרָה *a curse* (for *me'irrā* from אָרַר); from a verb פ"ו, מוֹקֵשׁ *a snare*
(from *măwqĭš*).

(d) Ground-form *mĭqṭăl*, Hebr. מִקְטָל, e.g. מִסְפֵּד *mourning*, מִזְבֵּחַ *an altar* *k*
(*place of sacrifice*); from a verb ע"ע, e.g. מֵסַב (מֵסָב?) *consessus*; (e) ground-
form *măqṭŭl*, Hebr. מַקְטֹל; fem. מַאֲכֶלֶת *food*, מַשְׂכֹּרֶת *wages*; from a verb ע"ע,
fem. מְסִכָּה *a covering* (from סָכַךְ). Also from ע"ע, according to the Masora,
מָעוֹז *a refuge*, with suffixes מָעֻזִּי and מָעוּזִּי, plur. מָעֻזִּים, but, very probably,
most if not all of these forms are to be referred to the stem עוּז *to flee for safety*,
and therefore should be written מְעוּזִי, &c. The form מָעֹז, if derived from
the stem עָזַז, would mean *stronghold*.—Cf. also מֹרֶךְ *faintness*, developed to a
segholate, probably from מֹרְךְ, for *mărōkh* from רָכַךְ, like מְתֹם *soundness* of
body, from תָּמַם.

With a long vowel in the second syllable : (f) ground-form *maqṭāl*, with *ā* *l*
always obscured to *ō*, e.g. מַחְסוֹר *want*, מַלְקוֹחַ *booty*; from verbs ע"ו, e.g. מָגוֹר
fear, fem. מְגוֹרָה and מְגוּרָה (with the *ō* depressed to *ū* in a toneless syllable;
cf. § 27 *n*), מְהוּמָה, &c., Is 22⁵. (g) Ground-form *mĭqṭāl*, in Hebr. again מִקְטוֹל,
e.g. מִסְתּוֹר *a covert*, מִכְשׁוֹל *a stumbling-block* (cf. above under *i*, *măkhšēlā*); fem.
מִכְמֹרֶת *a fishing-net*; (h) the ground-forms *maqṭĭl*, *miqṭĭl* (cf. מֵקִים) are found
only in participles *Hiph'il*; the fem. מַבְלִיגִית, *cheerfulness*, is a denominative
formed from a participle *Hiph'il*; (i) ground-form *măqṭŭl*, as מַלְבּוּשׁ *a garment*.

Rem. On מ as preformative of the participles of all the conjugations except *m*
Qal and *Niph'al*, cf. § 52 *c*. Many of these participles have become substantives,
as מְזַמֶּרֶת *snuffers*, מַשְׁחִית *destroyer, destruction*.

49. Nouns with נ prefixed. Besides the participles *Niph'al* (ground-form *n*
năqṭāl, still retained e.g. in נוֹלָד for *năwlād*, but commonly attenuated to *nĭqṭāl*,
Hebr. נִקְטָל) and the infinitive *Niph'al* of the form נִקְטֹל, the prefix נ is found
in נַפְתּוּלִים *wrestlings*, Gn 30⁸, which is also to be referred to *Niph'al*, and נָזִיד
boiled pottage (stem זיד).

50. With שׁ prefixed, e.g. שַׁלְהֶבֶת *a flame*. On this *Šaph'ēl* formation, cf. § 55 *i*. *O*

51. Nouns with ת prefixed. Examples of this formation are numerous, *p*
especially from weak stems, for the purpose of strengthening them phoneti-
cally (see Barth, *ibid.*, p. 283), and notably from verbs פ"ו and ע"י. They
may be classified as follows :—(a) the ground-form *tăqṭăl* in תַּחְמָס *ostrich* (?) ;
from verbs פ"ו, תּוֹשָׁב *a settler*; fem. תּוֹחֶלֶת *expectation*, תּוֹכַחַת (from the *Hiph'il*
הוֹכִיחַ) *correction*; from a verb פ"י, תֵּימָן *the south*; from verbs פ"ו and ל"ה,
תּוֹדָה *thanksgiving*, and תּוֹרָה *law*, both from *Hiph'il*; from a verb פ"ו and ל"א,
תּוֹצָאוֹת *issues*; probably belonging to this class, from verbs ע"ע, תֶּבֶל *confusion*,
and תָּמֶס *a melting away* (developed from תְּבַל and תְּמַס, from בָּלַל and מָסַס).

(b) *Tĭqṭăl*, e.g. fem. תִּפְאָרָה and תִּפְאֶרֶת *glory*; from a verb ל"ה, e.g. תִּקְוָה *q*
hope; (c) *tăqṭŭl*, e.g. תַּשְׁבֵּץ *chequer work*; fem. תַּרְדֵּמָה *deep sleep* (probably from
the *Niph'al* נִרְדַּם); from a verb פ"ו, תּוֹכֵחָה *correction* (from the *Hiph'il*-stem,
like the *constr. st. plur.* תּוֹלְדוֹת *generations*); from verbs ע"ע, ל"ה, תְּהִלָּה *praise*, תְּפִלָּה
prayer (from the *Pi'ēl* of the stems הָלַל and פָּלַל).

r　With a long vowel in the second syllable : (*d*) *tiqtâl*, as תְּהוֹם *the ocean, the deep* (for *tihâm* ; in Assyrian the fem. *tiâmtu*, constr. st. *tiâmat*, is the usual word for *sea*), unless it is to be derived with Delitzsch, *Prolegomena*, p. 113, from the stem תהם ; (*e*) *tåqṭil* (in Arabic the usual form of the infinitive of conjugation II. which corresponds to the Hebrew *Pi'ēl*), e.g. from a verb ל״ה, fem. תַּכְלִית *completeness* ; תַּרְבִּית *increase, usury*, with a parallel form מַרְבִּית ; in a passive sense, תַּלְמִיד *a disciple* ; (*f*) תַּקְטוּל, e.g. תַּפּוּחַ *an apple* (for *tånpûªḥ*) ; very frequently used to form abstracts, e.g. תַּגְמוּל *a benefit* (also גְּמוּל) ; from verbs ע״ו, תְּבוּסָה *a treading down*, תְּנוּפָה *a waving* (like תְּרוּמָה *a lifting up*, from the *Hiph'il* stem), תְּשׁוּקָה *a longing*, &c. ; very frequently also as an abstract plural, e.g. תַּהְפֻּכוֹת *perverseness*, תַּחְבֻּלוֹת *guidance*, תַּמְרוּרִים *bitterness*, תַּנְחוּמִים and תַּנְחֻמוֹת *consolation* ; from a verb ע״ו, תְּאֵנִים *toil*.

XI. *Nouns with Afformatives.*

s　52. **Nouns with ל affixed.** Perhaps חַשְׁמַל *amber* (?), and probably בַּרְזֶל *iron*, כַּרְמֶל *garden-land* (*S^eghôl* in both cases is probably a modification of the original *ă* in the tone-syllable), גִּבְעֹל *bloom*, cf. § 30 *q*.—According to Prätorius, *ZDMG*. 1903, p. 530 ff., *al* is an affix of endearment in the proper names מִיכָל, חֲמוּטַל (*little lizard* ?) אֲבִיגַל (also אֲבִיגָיִל).

t　53. **Nouns with ם affixed.** With an original *ăm* as afformative, אוּלָם *vestibule* (although the *â* in the *sing.* remains unchangeable), plur. אֻלַמִּים ; but in כְּנָם *a swarm of gnats*, the ם is radical. With original afformative *ûm*, עֵירֹם (also עָרֹם) *naked* (from עוּר), plur. עֵירֻמִּים Gn 3⁷, parallel form עָרוֹם, plur. עֲרוּמִּים Gn 2²⁵.—To this class also belong the adverbs in *âm* and *ōm*, mentioned in § 100 *g*, and many proper names, as גֵּרְשֹׁם, also גֵּרְשׁוֹם, and גֵּרְשׁוֹן (*patronymic* גֵּרְשֻׁנִּי), מַלְכָּם, עַמְרָם, &c. ; but for פִּדְיוֹם *ransom* (?), Nu 3⁴⁹, probably פְּדוּיִם is to be read.

u　54. **Nouns with ן affixed.** The ן is added by means of a simple helping vowel in כְּנַעַן *Canaan*, and צִפֹּרֶן *a finger nail* ; more frequently the addition is made by means of a tone-bearing *ă*, which in Hebrew is modified to *S^eghôl* (as גַּרְזֶן *axe*) or lengthened to *â* (but cf. also אַחֲרֹנִית and קַדְמֹנִית) ; e.g. קִנְיָן *a possession*, שֻׁלְחָן *a table*, קָרְבָּן *an offering*. From an original *â* being changed into an obscure *ô* we may probably explain such forms as דְּאָבוֹן *a pining away* ; דֵּרָבוֹן (also דָּרְבָן) *a goad* ; רְעָבוֹן *hunger* ; from verbs ל״ה, גָּאוֹן *pride*, הָמוֹן *noise*, חָזוֹן *a vision* ; שִׁרְיוֹן *a coat of mail* ; from a verb פ״ן, מַשָּׁאוֹן *guile* (the only instance with both ם preformative and *ôn* afformative) [1] ; very frequently from the simple stem with an unorganic sharpening of the second radical, e.g. זִכָּרוֹן *memorial*, כִּלָּיוֹן *destruction* (constr. st. זִכְרוֹן and כִּלְיוֹן), &c. ; cf. also הֵרָיוֹן *pregnancy* (for הֶרְיֹ) and § 93 *uu* ; קִיקָלוֹן *shame*, for קַלְקָלוֹן. Proper names occur with the termination *ûn*, as יְשֻׁרוּן, § 86 *g*, and others.

---

[1] The plurals נִצָּנִים *flowers*, Ct 2¹², and קִמְשֹׁנִים *thorns* appear to be formed directly from the singulars נֵץ (cf. נִצָּה) and קִמּוֹשׁ with the insertion of *ăn* (which in קִמֹּ is obscured to *ôn*). See Nöldeke, *Mand. Gr.*, p. 169, Rem. 3 ; similarly, according to Hoffmann, ' Einige phöniz. Inschriften,' p. 15 (*Abh. der Gött. Ges. der Wiss.*, xxxvi), עֶבוֹנִים *wares*, Ez 27¹⁴·¹⁶ from עֹצֶב = עֹצֶב.

Rem. A large number of proper names now ending in הֶ—ֲ or ֹן— used to *v* be classed as nouns originally formed with the affix ֹן—. The subsequent rejection of the final *Nûn* seemed to be confirmed by the form מִגְדּוֹן, once used (Zc 12[11]) for מִגְדּוֹ (and conversely in Pr 27[20] *K*[ethibh] אֲבַדֹּה, *Q*[erê] אֲבַדּוֹ for אֲבַדּוֹן *destruction*), also by the fact that for שְׁלֹמֹה the LXX give the form Σολωμών or Σαλωμών, and especially that in patronymics and tribal names (§ 86 *h*) a *Nûn* appears before the termination *î*, as גִּילֹנִי *Gilonite* from גִּלֹה and שִׁילֹנִי from שִׁילֹה (modern name *Sailûn*). Wetzstein, however (in Delitzsch's *Commentary on Job*, 1st ed., p. 599), explained the *Nûn* in מִגְדּוֹן as a secondary addition to the common old-Palestinian termination *ô* (רִמּוֹנוֹ, עַכּוֹ, יְרִיחוֹ, &c.), and Barth (*Nominalbildung*, § 224 *b*) has since shown the unsoundness of the prevailing view on other grounds: the rejection of the *Nûn* would be much more likely to occur in the numerous appellatives in *ôn* than in proper names, and גִּילֹנִי and שִׁילֹנִי are due to the necessity of avoiding, for euphonic reasons, such forms as *gilô-î, šilô-î*, &c.; cf. also שְׁלָנִי from שֵׁלָה.

On the afformatives ִי—, ַי—, וּת, ִית—, see below, § 86 *h–l*.

XII. *Quadriliterals and Quinqueliterals.*

55. גַּלְמוּד *barren*, חַלָּמִישׁ *a flint*, and the fem זַלְעָפָה *heat*, &c., have probably *w* arisen from the insertion of a ל; חַרְגֹּל *a locust*, קַרְדֹּם *an axe*, סַרְעַפָּה *a branch*, Ez 31[5] (verses 6, 8 סְעַפָּה), שַׂרְעַפִּים (also שְׂעִפִּים) *anxious thoughts*, שַׁרְבִיט *sceptre*, from insertion of a ר, which is common in Aramaic. Cf., moreover, חֶרְמֵשׁ *a sickle*, סְמָדַר *vine-blossom*; with an initial ע, עֲטַלֵּף *a bat*, עַכָּבִישׁ *a spider*, עַכְבָּר *a mouse*, עַקְרָב *a scorpion*,[1] &c.—Quinqueliteral, צְפַרְדֵּעַ *a frog*.

§ 86. *Denominative Nouns.*

1. Such are all nouns formed *immediately* from another noun, *a* whether the latter be primitive or derived from a verb, e. g. קַדְמוֹן *eastern*, immediately from קֶדֶם *the east* (verbal stem קָדַם *to be in front*).

2. Most of the forms which nouns of this class assume have already *b* been given in §§ 84 and 85, since the denominatives, as secondary (although in some cases very old) forms, invariably follow the analogy of the verbal derivatives. As, for instance, the verbals with a prefixed מ (§ 85 *e* to *m*) express the place, &c., of an action, so the denominatives with מ *local* represent the place where a thing is found or its neighbourhood (see *e*).

The most common forms of denominatives are— *c*

1. Those like the *participle Qal* (§ 84[a] *s*), e. g. שֹׁעֵר *a porter*, from שַׁעַר *a gate*; בֹּקֵר *a herdsman*, from בָּקָר *a herd*; כֹּרֵם *a vinedresser*, from כֶּרֶם *a vineyard*.
2. Those like the form *qāṭṭāl* (§ 84[b] *b*), e. g. קַשָּׁת *an archer*, from קֶשֶׁת *a bow*. *d*

---

[1] Derenbourg (*REJ.*, 1883, p. 165) infers from the above examples and a comparison of the Arabic *'uṣfûr, sparrow* (from *ṣafara, to chirp*), that ע was especially employed to form quadriliteral names of animals.

Both these forms (*c* and *d*) indicate customary occupations, inhering in the subject, like Greek nouns in της, τεύς, e. g. πολίτης, γραμματεύς.

e 3. Nouns with מ prefixed, denoting the place where a thing is (cf. § 85 *e*), or its neighbourhood, e. g. מַעְיָן *a place of fountains*, from עַיִן; מַרְגְּלוֹת *the place about the feet*, מַרַאֲשׁוֹת *the place about the head*, from רֶגֶל, רֹאשׁ; מִקְשָׁה (for מִקְשָׁאָה) *a cucumber field*, from קִשֻּׁא *cucumber*. Cf. ἀμπελών from ἄμπελος.

f 4. Nouns with the termination וֹן or וֹ֫ן expressing adjectival ideas: קַדְמוֹן *eastern*, from קֶדֶם; אַחֲרוֹן *posterior*, from אַחַר; חִיצוֹן *exterior*, from חוּץ; probably also לִוְיָתָן *coiled*, hence *coiled animal, serpent*, from לִוְיָה *a winding*; נְחֻשְׁתָּן *brazen*, from נְחֹשֶׁת *brass*. Also abstracts, e. g. עִוָּרוֹן *blindness*, from עִוֵּר. Cf. § 85 *u*.— With a double termination (*ôn* or *ân* with *i*) אַדְמֹנִי *reddish*, יִדְּעֹנִי *a knowing* (spirit); צִפְעֹנִי *basilisk*; רַחֲמָנִיּוֹת *merciful* [fem. plur.].

g וֹ appears to be used as a diminutive ending (cf. the Syriac וֹ) in אִישׁוֹן *little man* (in the eye), *apple of the eye*, from אִישׁ[1]; on the other hand שְׁפִיפֹן *adder*, which was formerly regarded as a diminutive, is properly an adjectival form from שָׁפַף *to rub* (hence, as it were, a *rubbing* creature); in the same way יְשֻׁרוּן is a *denominative* from יָשׁוּר (=יָשָׁר), properly *upright* (*righteous* people), and not a *diminutive* (*pious little people*, and the like); finally, שַׁהֲרוֹן is not *lunula*, but *an artificial moon* (used as an ornament), and צַוְּרֹנִים not *little neck*, but *necklace* (from צַוָּאר *neck*). Cf. Delitzsch on Ct 4[9].

h 5. Peculiar to denominatives is the termination יִ֫, which converts a substantive into an adjective, and is added especially to numerals and names of persons and countries, in order to form *ordinals*, *patronymics*, and *tribal names*; e. g. רַגְלִי *footman*, plur. רַגְלִים, from רֶגֶל *foot*; אַכְזָרִי *cruel*, נָכְרִי *strange*, from נֵכָר *strangeness*, תַּחְתִּי *lower*, from תַּחַת *below*, fem. תַּחְתִּית and תַּחְתִּיָּה, plur. תַּחְתִּיִּים, תַּחְתִּיּוֹת; שִׁשִּׁי *the sixth*, from שֵׁשׁ *six*; מוֹאָבִי *Moabite*, from מוֹאָב, plur. מוֹאָבִים, fem. מוֹאֲבִיָּה and מוֹאָבִית, plur. מוֹאֲבִיּוֹת; עִבְרִי *Hebrew*, plur. עִבְרִים and עִבְרִיִּים, fem. עִבְרִיָּה, plur. עִבְרִיּוֹת; יִשְׂרְאֵלִי *Israelite*, from יִשְׂרָאֵל. When the original substantive is a *compound*, it is resolved again into two words, e. g. בֶּן־יְמִינִי *Benjamite*, from בִּנְיָמִין (cf. on the use of the article in such cases, § 127 *d*).

i Instead of יִ֫ we find in a few cases (*a*) the ending יִ֫ (as in Aram.), e. g. כִּילַי (*crafty*, or, according to others, *churlish*) if it stands for נְכִילַי and is not rather from a stem כלא or כלה; חֹרָי *white cloth*, Is 19[9] in pause; perhaps also גֹּבַי *a swarm of locusts*, Am 7[1] (גּוֹבַי Na 3[17]); hardly נְגִינוֹתַי Is 38[20], Hb 3[19]; but certainly in proper names as בַּרְזִלַּי (*ferreus*) *Barzillai*;[2] and (*b*) ה,

---

[1] Cf. Barth, § 212; König, ii. 1, 413. Diminutives in Semitic languages are, however, most commonly formed by inserting a *y* after the second radical, e. g. Aram. עוּלֵּימָא, Syr. ܟܘܠܝܡܐ, Arab. غُلَيِّم *a very young man, kulaib, a little dog*, &c. Since Olshausen (§ 180), זְעֵיר *a little* (Is 28[10.13], Jb 36[2]) has commonly been regarded as an example of the same form, to which others have added שְׁבִיסִים Is 3[18] (as though a foreign dialectical form for *šumais, little sun*), and אֲמִינוֹן 2 S 13[20], as a contemptuous diminutive form of אַמְנוֹן; cf. Ewald, § 167, W. Wright, *Arab. Gramm.*[2] i. § 269, De Lagarde, *Nominalbildung*, pp. 85–87, König. ii. 1, p. 143 f. The existence of the form in Hebrew is disputed by Barth, § 192 *d*.]

[1] On יִ֫ as an old fem. ending, see above, § 80 *l*.

arising from *ăy,* in אִשֶּׁה *belonging to fire* (אֵשׁ), i. e. *a sacrifice offered by fire* ; לְבֵנָה (prop. *milky*) *the storax-shrub,* Arabic *lubnay.*

6. *Abstract* nouns formed from *concretes* by the addition of וּת, ־ִ[ת] *k* (§ 95 *t*), cf. our terminations *-dom, -hood, -ness,* e.g. יַלְדוּת *youth,* מַלְכוּת *kingdom* (the omission of the *Dageš* in כ shows that the *Š^ewâ* is weakened from a full vowel; on *malik* as underlying the present form מֶלֶךְ cf. § 84[a] *a*) ; אַלְמָנוּת *widowhood,* from אַלְמָן *widower,* אַלְמָנָה *widow.* In Aram. this fem. ending וּת (or וּ with rejection of the ת) is a common termination of the infinitive in the derived conjugations (cf., as substantival infinitives of this kind, הַשְׁמָעוּת *the announcing,* Ez 24[26], and הִתְחַבְּרוּת *the making of a league,* Dn 11[23]) ; in Hebr. וּת as a termination to express abstract ideas (including some which appear to be directly derived from the verbal stem, as סִכְלוּת *folly,* רְפֻאוּת *a healing*[1]) becomes more common only in the later books. It is affixed to adjectives ending in *î* (see above, *h*) in אַכְזְרִיּוּת *cruelty,* and קוֹמְמִיּוּת *upright position* (Lv 26[13], used adverbially).

The ending ־ִית is found earlier, e.g. in שְׁאֵרִית *remainder,* רֵאשִׁית *prin- l cipium,* from רֹאשׁ=רֵאשׁ (*head*) *princeps.* The termination *ôth* seems to occur in חָכְמוֹת *wisdom* (in Pr 1[20], 9[1], joined to a *singular* ; so also חַכְמוֹת Pr 14[1], where, probably, חָכְמוֹת should likewise be read) and in הֹלֵלוֹת Ec 1[17], &c., with the parallel form הוֹלֵלוּת Ec 10[13].

§ 87. *Of the Plural.*

Brockelmann, *Grundriss,* i. 426 ff., and on the feminines, p. 441 ff. ; M. Lambert, 'Remarques sur la formation du pluriel hébreu,' *REJ.* xxiv. 99 ff., and 'Les anomalies du pluriel des noms en Hébreu,' *REJ.* xliii. 206 ff. ; P. Lajčiak, *Die Plural- u. Dualendungen im semit. Nomen,* Lpz. 1903 ; J. Barth, 'Beiträge zur Pluralbildung des Semit.,' *ZDMG.* 1904, p. 431 ff., i. 'the *ai* of the constr. st.'

1. The regular *plural* termination for the *masculine gender* is ־ִים, *a* always with the tone, e. g. סוּס *horse,* plur. סוּסִים *horses*; but also very often written defectively ־ִם, especially when in the same word one of the vowel letters, ו or י, precedes, e. g. Gn 1[21] תַּנִּינִם. Nouns in ־ִי make their plural in ־ִים, e. g. עִבְרִי *a Hebrew,* plur. עִבְרִים (Ex 3[18]) ; but usually contraction takes place, e. g. עִבְרִים ; שָׁנִים *crimson garments,* from שָׁנִי.

Nouns in ־ֶה lose this termination when they take the plural *b* ending, e. g. חֹזֶה *seer,* plur. חֹזִים (cf. § 75 *h*).—In regard to the loss of the tone from the ־ִם in the two old plurals מַיִם *water* and שָׁמַיִם *heaven,* cf. § 88 *d* and § 96.

The termination ־ִים is sometimes assumed also by feminines (cf. *c* נָשִׁים *women,* § 96 under אִשָּׁה ; שָׁנִים *years,* from שָׁנָה ; רְחֵלִים *ewes,* from רָחֵל), so that an indication of gender is not necessarily implied in it (cf. also below, *m–p*).—On the use of this termination ־ִים to express abstract, extensive, and intensive ideas, cf. § 124.

---

[1] [See a complete list of instances in König, *Lehrgebäude,* ii. 1, p. 205 f.]

d The ending *îm* is also common in Phoenician, e. g. צדנם *Sidonii*; Assyrian has *âni* (acc. to P. Haupt originally *âmi*, cf. § 88 *d*); Aramaic has *in*; Arabic *ûna* (nominative) and *ina* (in the oblique cases, but in vulgar Arabic *in* is also used for the nominative); Ethiopic *ân*. Cf. also the verbal ending וֹן in the 3rd plur. perf. (§ 44 *l*) and in the 3rd and 2nd plur. impf. (§ 47 *m*).[1]

e Less frequent, or only apparent terminations of the plur. masc. are—

(*a*) ן‑ָ, as in Aramaic,[2] found almost exclusively in the later books of the O. T. (apart from the poetical use in some of the older and even the oldest portions), viz. מְלָכִין *kings*, Pr 31³, צַדִּיקִין 1 K 11³³, רָצִין *the guard*, 2 K 11¹³, חִטִּין *wheat*, Ez 4⁹; defectively אִיִּן *islands*, Ez 26¹⁸; יָמִין *days*, Dn 12¹³. Cf. also מַדִּין *carpets*, Ju 5¹⁰, in the North-Palestinian song of Deborah, which also has other linguistic peculiarities; עַיִין *heaps*, Mi 3¹² (before ח; cf. § 44 *k*); מִלִּין *words* (from the really Aram. מִלָּה), Jb 4², and twelve other places in Job (beside מִלִּים, ten times in Job); further, חַיִּין Jb 24²², אַחֲרִין 31¹⁰, and שׁוֹמֵמִין La 1⁴, תַּנִּין 4³.—The following forms are doubtful:

f (*b*) י‑ַ (with the ם rejected, as, according to some, in the *dual* יְדֵי for יָדַיִם Ez 13¹⁸, cf. § 88 *c*), e. g. מִנֵּי *stringed instruments*, ψ 45⁹ for מִנִּים (unless it is to be so written)[3]; עַמֵּי *peoples*, ψ 144², and, probably, also La 3¹⁴ (in 2 S 22⁴⁴ it may be taken as עַמִּי *my people*; cf. in the parallel passage ψ 18⁴⁴ עָם; also in Ct 8² the *î* of רִמֹּנִי is better regarded as a *suffix*); see also 2 S 23⁸ as compared with 1 Ch 11¹¹, and on the whole question Gesenius, *Lehrgebäude*, p. 524 ff. More doubtful still is—

g (*c*) י‑ַ (like the constr. state in Syriac), which is supposed to appear in e. g. שָׂרַי *princes*, Ju 5¹⁵ (perhaps *my princes* is intended: read either the constr. st. שָׂרֵי, which also has good authority, or with LXX שָׂרִים); for חֲלוּנֵי וֹס׳ Jer 22¹⁴ (according to others *dual*, see § 88 *c*, or a loan word, cf. *ZA.* iii. 93) read חֲלוּנָיו סָפוֹן. On גּוֹבַי and חוֹרַי, which have also been so explained, see above, § 86 *i*.—חֲשׂוּפֵי Is 20⁴ (where the right reading is certainly חֲשׂוּפֵי) must be intended by the Masora either as a singular with the formative syllable י‑ַ = *bareness* or, more probably, as a constr. st. with the original termination *ay* (cf. § 89 *d*) to avoid the harsh combination *haśûfē śēṯ*⁴; in אֲדֹנָי *the Lord* (prop. *my lord*, from the plur. *majestatis*, אֲדֹנִים *lord*), the *ay* was originally a *suffix*, § 135 *q*.

h (*d*) ם‑ַ a supposed *plural* ending in כְּנָם = כִּנִּם *gnats* (or *lice*), and סֻלָּם *ladder* (supposed by some to be a plur. like our *stairs*); but cf. on the former, § 85 *t*.

i 2. The plural termination of the *feminine gender* is generally indicated by the termination וֹת (often written defectively ת‑, e. g. תְּהִלָּה *song of praise, psalm*, plur. תְּהִלּוֹת (only in post-biblical Hebrew

---

[1] On the connexion between all these endings see Dietrich's *Abhandl. zur hebr. Gramm.*, Leipzig, 1846, p. 51 ff.; Halévy, *REJ.* 1888, p. 138 ff. [cf. also Driver, *Tenses*, § 6, *Obs.* 2].

[2] So also always in the Mêša' inscription, e. g. line 2 שלשׁן *thirty*; line 4 מלכן *kings*; line 5 רבן ימן *many days*, &c.

[3] According to some this *î* is simply due to a neglect of the point (§ 5 *m*), which in MSS. and elsewhere marked the abbreviation of the plur. ending.

[4] Prätorius, *ZDMG.* 1903, p. 525, regards חֲשׂוּפֵי as an instance of the affix of endearment (cf. כְּלוּבַי, אֲחוּמַי) transferred to an appellative, but such an explanation is rendered unlikely by the meaning of this isolated instance.

תְּהִלִּים, as in the headings of the printed editions, as well as סֵפֶר תְּהִלּוֹת *the Book of Psalms*); אִגֶּרֶת *a letter*, plur. אִגְּרוֹת; בְּאֵר *a well*, plur. בְּאֵרוֹת. Feminines in ־ִית form their plural in ־ִיּוֹת, e. g. מִצְרִית *an Egyptian woman*, plur. מִצְרִיּוֹת; and those in וּת either make ־ֻיּוֹת, as מַלְכוּת *kingdom*, plur. מַלְכֻיּוֹת, Dn 8²² (cf. חֲנֻיּוֹת *cells*, Jer 37¹⁶), or are inflected like עֵדְוֺת *testimonies* (pronounced *ʿedhᵉwôth* for *ʿedhŭwôth*).

It is only from a mistake or disregard of these feminine endings וּת and ־ִית that some words ending with them form their plural by the addition of ־ִים or ־וֹת, e. g. חֲנִית *spear*, plur. חֲנִיתִים and חֲנִיתוֹת; זְנוּת *whoredom*, plur. זְנוּתִים (by the side of זְנוּנִים); אַלְמְנֻתִים *widowhood*; שְׁחִיתוֹת *pits*, כְּסָתוֹת *amulets* (if connected with Assyr. *kâsu, to bind*), &c.

The termination *-ôth* stands primarily for *-âth* (which is the form it has in Arab., Eth., in the *constr. st.* of Western Aramaic, in Eastern Syriac, and also in Assyrian; on the change of *â* into an obscure *ô*, see § 9 *q*). On the other hand, it is doubtful whether this *âth* is to be regarded as a lengthened and stronger form of the singular fem. ending *ăth* (cf. § 80 *b*).

How the changeable vowels of a noun are shortened or become *Šᵉwâ* in consequence of the addition of the plural endings is explained in §§ 92–5.

3. Words which in the singular are used both as masculine and feminine (§ 122 *d*), often have in the plural parallel forms with the masculine and feminine terminations, e. g. עָב *cloud*, plur. עָבִים and עָבוֹת; and each form may be treated either as masculine or feminine, according to the usage of the particular word.—But even those words, of which the gender is invariable, sometimes have both plural forms, e. g. דּוֹר masc. *a generation*, plur. דּוֹרִים and דּוֹרוֹת; שָׁנָה fem. *a year*, plur. שָׁנִים and שָׁנוֹת (see the Rem.). In these words the gender of both plural forms remains the same as in the singular, e. g. אֲרִי masc. *a lion*, plur. אֲרָיוֹת masc., Zp 3³, דּוֹרוֹת masc., Jb 42¹⁶.

Sometimes usage makes a distinction between the two plural forms of the same word. Thus, יָמִים *days*, שָׁנִים *years* are the usual, but יָמוֹת (only twice, in the *constr. st.* Dt 32⁷, ψ 90¹⁵) and שָׁנוֹת (also only in the *constr. st.* and before suffixes) are rarer poetic forms.

A difference of meaning appears in several names of members of the body, the dual (see § 88) denoting the living members themselves, while the plur. in וֹת expresses something like them, but without life (§ 122 *u*), e. g. יָדַיִם *hands*, יָדוֹת *artificial hands*, also e. g. the *arms* of a throne; כַּפַּיִם *hands*, כַּפּוֹת *handles* (Lat. *manubria*); פַּעַם *foot*, פְּעָמוֹת *artificial feet* (of the ark), קַרְנַיִם *horns*, קְרָנוֹת *horns* (of the altar); עֵינַיִם *eyes*, עֲיָנוֹת *fountains*; cf. also אֲרָיִים *lions*, אֲרָיוֹת the *figures of lions* on Solomon's throne, תָּמָר *palm*, תִּמֹרָה *a palm-like column*, plur. תִּמֹרִים and תִּמֹרוֹת.

4. A considerable number of masculines form their plural in וֹת, while many feminines have a plural in ־ִים. The gender of the singular, however, is as a rule retained in the plural.

Undoubted instances of masculines with (masculine) plural in וֹת‎ are :

אָב *father,* אוֹצָר *treasure,* בְּאֵר and בּוֹר *cistern,* זָנָב *tail,* חֲלוֹם *dream,* כִּסֵּא *throne,* לֵב and לֵבָב *heart,* לוּחַ *tablet,* לַיִל and לַיְלָה *night,* מִזְבֵּחַ *altar,* מָקוֹם *place,* נֹאד *skin-bottle,* נֵר *lamp,* עוֹר *skin,* קוֹל *voice,* שֻׁלְחָן *table,* שֵׁם *name,* שׁוֹפָר *trumpet.*

q Feminines ending in ה‎ which take in the plural the termination ־ִים‎ are אֵלָה *terebinth,* אֵימָה *terror* (but also אֵימוֹת‎), דְּבֵלָה *a cake of figs,* חִטָּה *wheat,* לְבֵנָה *a brick,* מִלָּה (only in poetry) *a word,* סְאָה *seā, a dry measure,* שְׂעוֹרָה *barley,* and the following names of animals דְּבוֹרָה *a bee* and יוֹנָה *a dove*; also, for בֵּיצִים *fem. eggs,* a singular בֵּיצָה is to be assumed. אֲלֻמָּה *sheaf* and שָׁנָה *year* (see above, *n*) take both ־ִים‎ and וֹת‎ ; cf. finally שִׁבֹּלֶת *an ear of corn,* plur. שִׁבֳּלִים, and without the fem. termination in the singular פִּילֶגֶשׁ *concubine,* plur. פִּילַגְשִׁים.

r **5.** A strict distinction in gender between the two plural endings is found, in fact, only in adjectives and participles, e. g. טוֹבִים *boni,* טוֹבוֹת *bonae,* קְטֻלִים *masc.,* קְטֻלוֹת *fem.* So also in substantives of the same stem, where there is an express distinction of sex, as בָּנִים *filii,* בָּנוֹת *filiae;* מְלָכִים *reges,* מְלָכוֹת *reginae.*

s **Rem. 1.** In some few words there is added to the plural ending וֹת a second (masculine) plural termination (in the form of the *constr. st.* ־ֵי‎ , cf. § 89 *c*), or a dual ending ־ַיִם‎, e. g. בָּמָה *a high p'ace,* plur. בָּמוֹת, *constr. s*. בָּמוֹתֵי (also בָּמֳתֵי *bāmŏthê,* Is 14[14], Jb 9[8], &c., sometimes as *Qerê* to the Kethîbh במותי ; see § 95 *o*) ; מֵרַאֲשֹׁתֵי שָׁאוּל *from Saul's head,* 1 S 26[12] ; חוֹמָה *wall,* plur. חוֹמוֹת *moenia,* whence dual חוֹמֹתַיִם *double walls.* This double indication of the plural appears also in the connexion of suffixes with the plural ending וֹת (§ 91 *m*).

t **2.** Some nouns are only used in the singular (e. g. אָדָם *man,* and collectively *men*) ; a number of other nouns only in the plural, e. g. מְתִים *men* (the old *sing.* מְתוּ is only preserved in proper names, see § 90 *o*; in Eth. the *sing.* is *mět, man*) ; some of these have, moreover, a singular meaning (§ 124 *a*), as פָּנִים *face.* In such cases, however, the same form can also express plurality, e. g. פָּנִים means also *faces,* Gn 40[7], Ez 1[6] ; cf. אֱלֹהִים *God,* and also *gods* (the *sing.* אֱלֹהַּ, a later formation from it, occurs only ten times, except in Job forty-one and in Daniel four times).

§ 88. *Of the Dual.*

Cf. the literature on the Semitic dual in Grünert, *Die Begriffs-Präponderanz und die Duale a potiori im Altarab.* (Wien, 1886), p. 21 ; Brockelmann, *Grundriss,* p. 455 ff.

a **1.** The *dual* is a further indication of number, which originated in early times. In Hebrew, however, it is almost exclusively used to denote those objects which naturally occur in pairs (see *e*). The dual termination is never found in adjectives, verbs, or pronouns. In the noun it is indicated in both genders by the termination ־ַיִם‎

appended to the ground-form,[1] e. g. יָדַיִם *both hands*, יוֹמַיִם *two days*.
In the feminine the dual termination is always added to the old ending
ath (instead of ־ָה), but necessarily with *ā* (since it is in an open syllable
before the tone), thus ־ָתַיִם, e. g. שָׂפָה *lip*, שְׂפָתַיִם *both lips*. From
a feminine with the ending ־ֶ֯ת, e. g. נְחֹשֶׁת (from *neḥušt*) the dual
is formed like נְחֻשְׁתַּיִם *double fetters*.

With nouns which in the singular have not a feminine ending, the *b*
dual termination is likewise really added to the ground-form; but
the latter generally undergoes certain changes in consequence of the
shifting of the tone, e. g. כָּנָף *wing* (ground-form *kănăph*), dual כְּנָפַיִם,
the first *ă* becoming *Šewâ*, since it no longer stands before the tone,
and the second *ă* being lengthened before the new tone-syllable.
In 1 K 16²⁴, 2 K 5²³ᵇ the form כִּבְרַיִם (which should be כִּבְרָיִם) evidently
merely points to the *constr. st.* כִּבְרֵי, which would be expected before
כֶּסֶף; cf. כִּבְרַים in 2 K 5²³ᵃ, and on the syntax see § 131 *d*. In the
segholate forms (§ 84ᵃ *a*) the dual ending is mostly added to the
ground-form, e. g. רֶגֶל *foot* (ground-form *răgl*), dual רַגְלַיִם; cf., however,
קַרְנַיִם (only in the book of Daniel), as well as קַרְנַיִם from קֶרֶן *horn*, and
לְחָיַיִם from לְחִי *cheek* (as if from the plurals לְחָיִם, קְרָנוֹת).—A feminine
dual of an adjective used substantively occurs in עֲצַלְתַּיִם *a sluggish
pair* (of hands) Ec 10¹⁸ from the sing. עָצֵל.

Rem. 1. Certain place-names were formerly reckoned as dual-forms (so in *c*
earlier editions of this Grammar, and still in König's *Lehrgebäude*, ii. 437), viz.—
(*a*) those in ־יִן and ־ַיִם, e. g. דֹּתַיִן Gn 37¹⁷ᵃ (locative דֹּתַיְנָה, but in 17ᵇ דֹּתָן),
and דֹּתָן 2 K 6¹³; קַרְתָּן Jos 21³², identical with קִרְיָתַיִם in 1 Ch 6⁶¹ (cf. also the
Moabite names of towns in the Mêša‘ inscription, line 10 קריתן = Hebrew
קִרְיָתַיִם; line 30 בֵּית דִּבְלָתַיִם=בת דבלתן Jer 48²²; lines 31, 32 חורנן=הֹרֹנַיִם
Is 15⁵, &c.); (*b*) in ־ַם, Jos 15³⁴ הָעֵינָם (= עֵינַיִם Gn 38²¹). The view that
־ַיִן and ־ַם arise from a contraction of the dual terminations ־ַיִן (as in
Western Aramaic, cf. also nom. *áni*, accus. *aini*, of the dual in Arabic) and
־ַיִם seemed to be supported by the Mê‘a‘ inscription, where we find
(line 20) מאתן *two hundred*=מָאתַיִן, Hebrew מָאתַיִם. But in many of these
supposed duals either a dual sense cannot be detected at all, or it does not
agree at any rate with the nature of the Semitic dual, as found elsewhere.
Hence it can hardly be doubted that ־ַיִן and ־ַיִם in these place-names
only arise from a subsequent expansion of the terminations ־ָן and ־ָם: so
Wellhausen, *Jahrbücher für Deutsche Theologie*, xxi. 433; Philippi, *ZDMG*. xxxii.
65 f.; Barth, *Nominalbildung*, p. 319, note 5; Strack, *Kommentar zur Genesis*,
p. 135. The strongest argument in favour of this opinion is that we have
a clear case of such an expansion in the *Qeré perpetuum* (§ 17 *c*) יְרוּשָׁלִַם for
יְרוּשָׁלֵם (so, according to Strack, even in old MSS. of the Mišna; cf. *Urusalim*
in the Tel-el-Amarna tablets, and the Aramaic form יְרוּשְׁלֶם): similarly in

---

[1] On dual endings appended to the plural see § 87 *s* and § 95 *o* at the
beginning.

the Aramaic שִׁמְרָ֫יִן = שָׁמְרָן for the Hebrew שֹׁמְרוֹן *Samaria*.—We may add to this list אֶפְרַ֫יִם, נַהֲרַ֫יִם_ the river country (in the Tel-el-Amarna letters *nârima*, *na'rima*), מִצְרַ֫יִם *Egypt*, Phoenician מצרם ; also the words denoting time, צָהֳרַ֫יִם *midday* (Mêša' inscription, line 15 צהרם), and perhaps עַרְבַּ֫יִם *in the evening*, if the regular expression בֵּין־הָעַרְבַּ֫יִם Ex 12⁶, 16¹², &c., is only due to mistaking עַרְבַּ֫יִם for a dual : LXX πρὸς ἑσπέραν, τὸ δειλινόν, ὀψέ, and only in Lv 23⁵ ἀνὰ μέσον τῶν ἑσπερινῶν. The Arabs also say *el 'iša'ân, the two evenings*, cf. Kuhn's *Literaturblatt*, iii. 48.

Instead of the supposed dual יָדַי Ez 13¹⁸ read יָדָ֫יִם. On חַלּוֹנֵי (generally taken to be *a double window*) Jer 22¹⁴, see above, § 87 *g*.

d　2. Only apparently dual-forms (but really plural) are the words מַ֫יִם *water* and שָׁמַ֫יִם *heaven*. According to P. Haupt in *SBOT.* (critical notes on Isaiah, p. 157, line 18 ff.), they are to be derived from the old plural forms (found in Assyrian) *mâmi, šamâmi*, whence the Hebr. מים, שמים arose by inversion of the *i, mâmi, mâimi, maim*. It is simpler, however, to suppose that the primitive singulars *may* and *šamay*, when they took the plural of extension (§ 124 *b*), kept the tone on the *ay*, thus causing the *im* (which otherwise always has the tone, § 87 *a*) to be shortened to *im*. Cf. the analogous formations, Arab. *tarḍaina*, 2nd *fem. sing. imperf.* of a verb ל״י, for *tarḍay + ina*, corresponding to *taqtulina* in the strong verb ; also bibl.-Aram. בָּנַ֫יִן the *abs. st. plur.* of the *ptcp. Qal* of בָּנָה (ל״י), which otherwise always ends in *in* with the tone, e. g. in the *p'cp. Qal* of the strong verb, דִּבְחִין *sacrificing*.

e　2. The use of the dual in Hebrew is confined, except in the numerals 2, 12, 200, &c. (see § 97), practically to those objects which are by nature or art always found in *pairs*, especially to the double members of the body (but not necessarily so, cf. וְרֵעִים and וְרֵעוֹת *arms*, never in the dual), e. g. יָדַ֫יִם *both hands*, אָזְנַ֫יִם *both ears*, שִׁנַּ֫יִם *teeth* (of both rows), also נַעֲלַ֫יִם_ *a pair of sandals*, מֹאזְנַ֫יִם *a pair of scales*, Lat. *bilanx*, &c.; or things which are at least thought of as forming a pair, e. g. יוֹמַ֫יִם *two* (successive) *days*, Lat. *biduum* ; שְׁבֻעַ֫יִם *two weeks* ; שְׁנָתַ֫יִם *two years* (in succession), Lat. *biennium* ; אַמָּתַ֫יִם *two cubits*.[1]

f　In the former case the dual may be used for a plural, either indefinite or defined by a numeral, where it is thought of in a double arrangement, e. g. אַרְבַּע רַגְלָ֫יִם *four feet*, Lv 11²³ ; שֵׁשׁ כְּנָפַ֫יִם *six wings* (i. e. three pairs), Is 6², Ez 16 ; even שִׁבְעָה עֵינַ֫יִם *seven eyes*, Zc 3⁹, כָּל־בִּרְכַּ֫יִם *all knees*, Ez 7¹⁷ ; כָּל־יָדַ֫יִם *all hands*, Ez 21¹² ; מְצִלְתַּ֫יִם *cymbals*, Ezr 3¹⁰ ; שְׂפָתַ֫יִם *double-hooks*, Ez 40⁴³.—To express a certain emphasis the numeral *two* is used with the dual, as in Ju 16²⁸, Am 3¹².—See some other remarks on the use of the dual in § 87 *o* and *s*.

g　It is not impossible that Hebrew at an earlier period made a more extensive and freer use of the dual, and that the restrictions and limitations of its use, mentioned above, belong to a relatively later phase of development. The

---

[1] But for דְּרָבֹ֑ים Pr 28⁶·¹⁸ (which the Masora takes as two roads leading from the cross-ways) דְּרָכִים is to be read.

Arabic literary language forms the dual in the noun, pronoun, and verb, almost as extensively as the Sanskrit or Greek; but in modern Arabic it has almost entirely disappeared in the verb, pronoun, and adjective. The Syriac has preserved it only in a few stereotyped forms, with which such duals as the Latin *duo, ambo, octo* may be compared. In the same way, the dual of the Sanskrit is lost in the modern Indian languages, and its full use in Old Slavonic has been restricted later, e. g. in Bohemian, just as in Hebrew, to *pairs*, such as hands, feet, eyes, ears. On the Germanic dual, see Grimm's *Gramm.*, 2nd ed., i. p. 814.

§ 89. *The Genitive and the Construct State.*

Philippi, *Wesen und Ursprung des Stat. Constr. im Hebr. . . .*, Weimar, 1871, p. 98 ff : on which cf. Nöldeke in the *Gött. Gel. Anzeigen*, 1871, p. 23.— Brockelmann, *Grundriss*, p. 459 ff.

1. The Hebrew language no longer makes a living use of *case- a endings*,[1] but either has no external indication of case (this is so for the *nominative*, generally also for the *accusative*) or expresses the relation by means of prepositions (§ 119), while the *genitive* is mostly indicated by a close connexion (or interdependence) of the *Nomen regens* and the *Nomen rectum*. That is to say, the noun which as genitive serves to define more particularly an immediately preceding *Nomen regens*, remains entirely unchanged in its form. The close combination, however, of the governing with the governed noun causes the tone first of all to be forced on to the latter,[2] and the consequently weakened tone of the former word then usually involves further changes in it. These changes to some extent affect the consonants, but more especially the vocalization, since vowels which had been lengthened by their position *in* or *before* the tone-syllable necessarily become shortened, or are reduced to *Šᵉwâ* (cf. § 9 *a, c, k*; § 27 *e–m*); e. g. דָּבָר *word*, דְּבַר אֱלֹהִים *word of God* (a sort of compound, as with us in inverted order, *God's-word, housetop, landlord*); יָד *hand*, יַד הַמֶּלֶךְ *the hand of the king*; דְּבָרִים *words*, דִּבְרֵי הָעָם *the words of the people*. Thus in Hebrew only the noun which stands *before a genitive* suffers a change, and in grammatical language is said to be dependent, or in the *construct state*, while a noun which has not a genitive after it is said to be in the *absolute state*. It is sufficiently evident from the above that the *construct state* is not strictly to be regarded as a *syntactical* and *logical* phenomenon, but rather as simply *phonetic* and *rhythmical*, depending on the circumstances of the tone.

---

[1] On some remains of obsolete case-endings see § 90.
[2] The same phenomenon of the tone may also be easily seen in other languages, when two words are closely connected in a similar way. Observe, for example, in German the natural stress on the last word in ' *der Thron des Königs* '; though here the other order of the words (inadmissible in Hebrew) ' *des Königs Thron* ' exhibits the same peculiarity.

b   Very frequently such interdependent words are also united by Maqqeph (§ 16 *a*); this, however, is not necessary, but depends on the accentuation in the particular case. On the wider uses of the *constr. st.* see the Syntax, § 130.

c   **2.** The *vowel* changes which are occasioned in many nouns by the construct state are more fully described in §§ 92–5. But besides these, the *terminations* of the noun in the construct state sometimes assume a special form. Thus:

(*a*) In the *construct state*, plural and dual, the termination is 'ֵ֫, e. g. סוּסִים *horses*, סוּסֵי פַרְעֹה *the horses of Pharaoh*; עֵינַיִם *eyes*, עֵינֵי הַמֶּ֫לֶךְ *the eyes of the king*.

d   Rem. The 'ֵ֫ of the dual has evidently arisen from 'ַ֫ (cf. יָדַ֫יִם), but the origin of the termination 'ֵ֫ in the *constr. st.* plur. is disputed. The Syriac *constr. st.* in *ay* and the form of the plural noun before suffixes (סוּסַי, סוּסֶ֫יךָ, &c., § 91 *h*) would point to a contraction of an original 'ַ֫, as in the dual. But whether this *ay* was only transferred from the dual to the plural (so Olshausen, and Nöldeke, *Beitr. zur sem. Sprachwiss.*, Strassb. 1904, p. 48 ff.), or is to be regarded as the *abstract*, *collective* termination, as in אִשֶּׁה (see *f*) and חוֹרִי (so Philippi, *ThLZ.* 1890, col. 419 ; Barth, *ZDMG.* 1904, p. 431 ff.), must be left undecided.

e   (*b*) The original הַ֫ is regularly retained as the feminine termination in the *construct state* sing. of those nouns which in the *absolute* state end in הָ֫, e. g. מַלְכָּה *queen*, מַלְכַּת שְׁבָא *the queen of Sheba*. But the feminine endings תְּ֫, תִּ֫, and also the plural וֹת, remain unchanged in the *construct state*.

f   (*c*) Nouns in הֶ֫ (cf. § 75 *e*) from verbs ל״ה (§ 93, Paradigm III *c*) form their *constr. st.* in הֵ֫, e. g. רֹאֶה *seer*, constr. רֹאֵה. If this הֶ֫ is due to contraction of the original 'ֶ֫, with ה added as a vowel letter, we may compare דַּי, constr. דֵּי *sufficiency*; חַי, constr. חֵי *life*; גַּיְא (גַּי), constr. גֵּיְא (גֵּי) *valley*.

On the terminations וֹ and 'ִ֫ in the *constr. st.* see § 90.

§ 90. *Real and Supposed Remains of Early Case-endings.*

הָ֫ *local*, וֹ *in compound proper names*, 'ִ֫ *and* וֹ *in the Construct State.*

K. U. Nylander, *Om Kasusändelserna i Hebräiskan*, Upsala, 1882 ; J. Barth, ' Die Casusreste im Hebr.,' *ZDMG.* liii. 593 ff.

a   **1.** As the Assyrian and old Arabic distinguish three cases by special endings, so also in the Hebrew noun there are three endings which, in the main, correspond to those of the Arabic. It is, however, a question whether they are all to be regarded as real remnants of former case-endings, or are in some instances to be explained otherwise. It can hardly be doubted (but cf. *h*, Rem.) that the (locative) termination הָ‎ָ‎ is a survival of the old accusative termination *a*, and that ‍ֹ‍ in certain compound proper names is the old sign of the nominative. The explanation of the *î* as an old genitive sign, which, as being no longer understood in Hebrew, was used for quite different purposes, and the view that ‍ֹ‍ is a form of the nominative termination ‍ֹ‍, are open to grave doubts.

b In Assyrian the rule is that *u* marks the nominative, *i* the genitive, and *a* the accusative,[1] 'in spite of the many and various exceptions to this rule which occur' (Delitzsch, *Assyrische Gramm.*, § 66). Similarly, the Arabic case-endings in the fully declined nouns (*Triptotes*) are: -*u* for the nominative, -*i* for the genitive, and -*a* for the accusative; in the *Diptotes* the ending -*a* represents the genitive also. In modern Arabic these endings have almost entirely disappeared, and if they are now and then used, as among the Beduin, it is done without regularity, and one is interchanged with another (Wallin, in *ZDMG.* v, p. 9, xii, p. 874; Wetzstein, *ibid.*, xxii, p. 113 f., and especially Spitta, *Gramm. des arab. Vulgärdialekts von Ägypten*, Lpz. 1880, p. 147 ff.). Even as early as the Sinaitic inscriptions, their regular use is not maintained (Beer, *Studia Asiatica*, iii. 1840, p. xviii; Tuch, *ZDMG.* iii. 139 f.). Ethiopic has preserved only the -*a* (in proper names -*hâ*), which is, however, still used for the whole range of the accusative, and also (the distinction of case being lost) as a termination of the *constr. st.* to connect it with a following genitive.

c **2.** As remarked above, under *a*, the *accusative* form is preserved in Hebrew most certainly and clearly in the (usually toneless) ending הָ‎ָ‎, originally *â*, as in the old Arabic accusative. This is appended to the substantive:

(*a*) Most commonly to express *direction towards* an object, or motion to a place,[2] e. g. יָמָּה *seaward, westward*, קֵדְמָה *eastward*, צָפוֹנָה *northward*, אַשּׁוּרָה *to Assyria*, בָּבֶלָה *to Babylon*, הָרָה (from הַר) *to the mountain*, Gn 14[10], אַרְצָה *to the earth*, בַּיְתָה *to the house*, תִּרְצָתָה *to Tirzah* (תִּרְצָה) 1 K 14[17], &c., עַזָּתָה *to Gaza* (עַזָּה) Ju 16[1]; with the article הָהָרָה *to the mountain*, הַבַּיְתָה *into the house*, הַחַדְרָה *into the chamber*, 1 K 1[15]; הָאֹהֱלָה[3] *into the tent*, Gn 18[6], &c.; similarly with adverbs, as שָׁמָּה *thither*, אָנָה *whither?*; even with the *constr. st.* before a genitive בֵּיתָה יוֹסֵף *into Joseph's house*, Gn 43[17.24]; אַרְצָה הַנֶּגֶב *toward the land of the south*, Gn 20[1]; אַרְצָה מִצְרַיִם *to the land of Egypt*, Ex 4[20]; מִדְבַּרָה דַמֶּשֶׂק *to the wilderness of Damascus*, 1 K 19[15]; מִזְרְחָה שֶׁמֶשׁ *toward the sun-rising*, Dt 4[41]; and even with the plural כַּשְׂדִּימָה *into Chaldea*, Ez 11[24]; הַשָּׁמַיְמָה *towards the heavens*.

---

[1] This rule is almost always observed in the Tell-el-Amarna letters (see § 2 *f*); cf. the instances cited by Barth, l. c., p. 595, from Winckler's edition.

[2] On this meaning of the accusative see the Syntax, § 118 *d*, and cf. the Latin accusative of motion to a place, as in *Romam profectus est, domum reverti, rus ire*.

[3] הָאֹהֵלָה in Baer's text, Gn 18[6], is an error, according to his preface to Isaiah, p. v.

Rem. The above examples are mostly rendered definite by the article, or by a following genitive of definition, or are proper names. But cases like בֵּיתָה, הֶרָה, יָמָּה show that the locative form *of itself* possessed a defining power.

d (*b*) In a somewhat weakened sense, indicating the place *where* something is or happens (cf. § 118 *d*), e. g. מַחֲנַיְמָה *in Mahanaim*, 1 K 4¹⁴; שָׁמָּה *there* (usually *thither*, see *c*), Jer 18², cf. 2 K 23⁸, and the expression *to offer a sacrifice* הַמִּזְבֵּחָה, properly *towards the altar* for on *the altar*. On the other hand, בָּבֶלָה Jer 29¹⁵, and וְבֵלָה Hb 3¹¹, are to be regarded as ordinary accusatives of direction, *to Babylon, into the habitation*; also expressions like פְּאַת צָפוֹנָה *the quarter towards the north*, Jos 15⁵ (at the beginning of the verse, גְּבוּל קֵדְמָה *the border toward the east*), cf. 18¹⁵·²⁰, Ex 26¹⁸, Jer 23⁸.

e (*c*) The original force of the ending ◌ָה is also disregarded when it is added to a substantive with a preposition prefixed (cf. also עַד־אָנָה *how long ?*), and this not only after לְ, אֶל־ or עַד־ (which are easily explained), e. g. לְמַעְלָה *upwards*, לְמַטָּה *downwards*, לִשְׁאוֹלָה *to Sheol*, ψ 9¹⁸; עַד־אֲפֵקָה *unto Aphek*, Jos 13⁴, אֶל־הַצָּפוֹנָה *toward the north*, Ez 8¹⁴, cf. Ju 20¹⁶; but also after בְּ, and even after מִן, e. g. בַּנֶּגְבָּה *in the south*, Jos 15²¹, cf. Ju 14², 1 S 23¹⁵·¹⁹, 31¹³, 2 S 20¹⁵, Jer 52¹⁰; מִבָּבֶלָה *from Babylon*, Jer 27¹⁶; cf. 1¹³, Jos 10³⁶, 15¹⁰, Ju 21¹⁹, Is 45⁶.

f Rem. Old locative forms (or original accusatives) are, according to the Masora, still to be found in

(*a*) לַיְלָה, in *pause* לָיְלָה, the usual word in prose for *night*, which is always construed as masculine. The nominative of this supposed old accusative[1] appeared to be preserved in the form לַיִל, only used in poetry, Is 16³, constr. st. לֵיל (even used for the *absol. st.* in pause Is 21¹¹). Most probably, however, לַיְלָה is to be referred, with Nöldeke and others, to a reduplicated form לֵילֵי; cf. especially the western Aramaic לֵילְיָא, Syr. *lilya*, &c.—Another instance is מְאוּמָה *something*, probably from מְאֻם, מוּם *spot, point*, generally with a negative = *nothing*. Similarly אַרְצָה Is 8²³ and (in pause) Jb 34¹³, סוּפָתָה Ho 8⁷, and the place-name הָעְצָה 1 Ch 6⁶³, might be explained as accusatives. Elsewhere, however, the toneless ◌ָה can be regarded only as a meaningless appendage, or at the most as expressing poetic emphasis; thus אָרְצָה (in *pause*) Jb 37¹²; הַמָּוְתָה *death*, ψ 116¹⁵; נֶגְדָה־נָּא ψ 116¹⁴·¹⁸; נַחְלָה *stream*, ψ 124⁴; הַחַשְׁמַלָּה *amber*, Ez 8² [in 1⁴ הַחַשְׁמַל, cf. § 80 *k*], &c. In Jos 15¹² הַיָּמָּה is probably only a scribal error (dittography). In Ju 14¹⁸ instead of the quite unsuitable poetic word הַחַרְסָה (towards the sun??) read as in 15¹ הַחַדְרָה *to the bride-chamber*.

---

[1] Brockelmann, *Sem. Sprachwiss.*, p. 113, also takes it as such, *láylā* being properly *at night*, then *night* simply. Barth, however (*Sprachwiss. Abhandlungen*, p. 16, note 1), refers it to an original לֵילָה, like אָנָה from אָנָה.

(*b*) In the termination תָ֫ה often used in poetry with feminines, viz. *g*
אֵימָ֫תָה *terror* (= אֵימָה), Ex 15¹⁶; עֶזְרָ֫תָה *help* (= עֶזְרָה), ψ 44²⁷, 63⁸, 94¹⁷; יְשׁוּעָ֫תָה
salvation (= יְשׁוּעָה), ψ 3³, 80³, Jon 2¹⁰; עַוְלָ֫תָה *unrighteousness* (= עַוְלָה), Ez 28¹⁵,
Ho 10¹³, ψ 125³; עֶלְיָ֫תָה ψ 92¹⁶ K⁽ᵉᵗʰ⁾. Jb 5¹⁶; צָרָ֫תָה ψ 120¹; עֵיפָ֫תָה *darkness*,
Jb 10²²; הַמָּזְפָּ֫תָה Jer 11¹⁵ is corrupt, see the LXX and Commentaries. These
cases are not to be taken as double feminine endings, since the loss of the
tone on the final syllable could then hardly be explained, but they are
further instances of an old accusative of direction or intention. In examples
like עֶזְרָ֫תָה *for help* (ψ 44²⁷) this is still quite apparent, but elsewhere it has
become meaningless and is used merely for the sake of poetical emphasis.[1]

This termination ה־ָ usually has reference to *place* (hence called *h*
ה־ָ *locale*[2]); sometimes, however, its use is extended to time, as in
מִיָּמִים יָמִ֫ימָה *from year to year*. Its use in חָלִ֫ילָה, properly *ad profanum !*=*absit !* is peculiar.

As the termination ה־ָ is almost always toneless (except in מִזְרָ֫חָה *constr. st.* *i*
Dt 4⁴¹; גֻּ֫תָּה and עֻ֫תָּה Jos 19¹³) it generally, as the above examples show,
exercises no influence whatever upon the vowels of the word; in the *constr. st.*
מִדְבָּ֫רָה Jos 18¹², 1 K 19¹⁵, and in the proper names גֵּ֫תָה 1 K 2⁴⁰; דִּבְלָ֫תָה 2 S 24⁶
(so Baer; ed. Mant. and Ginsb., דִּבְלָ֫תָה), צָפְרָ֫תָה 2 Ch 14⁹, צָרְפַ֫תָה 1 K 17⁹, צָרְתָ֫נָה
1 K 4¹², an *ă* is retained even in an open tone-syllable (cf., however, הָ֫רָה
Gn 14¹⁰, פַּדֶּ֫נָה Gn 28² from פַּדָּן, with modification of the *a* to *ĕ*; also כַּרְמֶ֫לָה
1 S 25⁵ from כַּרְמֶל). In segholate forms, as a general rule, the ה־ָ *local* is
joined to the already developed form of the *absol. st.*, except that the helping-
vowel before ה־ָ naturally becomes *šᵉwâ*, e.g. בֵּ֫יתָה, הָאֹ֫הֱלָה Gn 18⁶, &c.;
הַיַּ֫עְרָה Jos 17¹⁵, ³ הַשַּׁ֫עְרָה Ju 20¹⁶, &c., but also נַ֫חְלָה Nu 34⁵ (*constr. st.*; likewise
to be read in the *absolute* in Ez 47¹⁹, 48²⁸) and שֶׁ֫עְרָה Is 28⁶ (with *Silluq*); cf.
נֶ֫גְבָּה Ez 47¹⁹ and גֹּ֫רְנָה (Baer, incorrectly, גֹּרְנָה) Mi 4¹² (both in *pause*).—In
the case of feminines ending in ה־ָ the ה־ָ *local* is added to the original
feminine ending ת־ַ (§ 80 *b*), the *ă* of which (since it then stands in an
open tone-syllable) is lengthened to *â*, e.g. תִּרְצָ֫תָה.—Moreover the termination
ה־ָ is even weakened to ה־ֶ in נֹ֫בֶה *to Nob*, 1 S 21², 22⁹; אָ֫נֶה *whither*, 1 K 2³⁶.⁴²
and דְּדָ֫נֶה *to Dedan*, Ez 25¹³.

3. Of the three other terminations ִי may still be regarded as a *k*
survival of the old nominative ending. It occurs only in the middle

---

[1] The form clings also to a few place-names, as גְּדֵ֫רָה Dt 10⁷; שִׁלֹ֫שָׁה 1 S 9⁴,
2 K 4⁴²; קְהֵלָ֫תָה Nu 33²² ᶠ·; יָטְבָ֫תָה verse 33 f.; תִּמְנָ֫תָה Jos 19⁴³, &c.; אֶפְרָ֫תָה
Mi 5¹, &c.]

[2] Cf. Sarauw, 'Der hebr. Lokativ,' *ZA*. 1907, p. 183 ff. He derives the
ה־ָ from the adverbs שָׁ֫מָּה, אָ֫נָה and holds that it has nothing whatever to
do with the old accusative.

[3] So Qimḥi, and the Mant. ed. (Baer הַשַּׁעֲרָה), i.e. locative from שַׁ֫עַר (Is 7²⁰).
The reading הַשַּׁעֲרָה (Opit., Ginsb.) implies a feminine in ה־ָ.

of a few (often undoubtedly very old) proper names,[1] viz. אֲחוּמַי (if compounded of אָחוּ and מִי), חֲמוּטַל (for which in Jer 52¹ *K^eth.* חֲמִיטַל), מְתוּשָׁאֵל and מְתוּשֶׁלַח (otherwise in Hebrew only in the plur. מְתִים *men*; to מְתוּ corresponds most probably בְּתוּ in בְּתוּאֵל), פְּנוּאֵל Gn 32³¹ (but in ver. 32 פְּנִיאֵל) *face of God* (otherwise only in the plur. פָּנִים *constr. st.* פְּנֵי).[2]—בַּשְׁמוֹ Neh 6⁶ (elsewhere בִּשְׁמָם), is the name of an Arab, cf. 6¹. On the other hand the terminations ִי— and וֹ are most probably to be regarded (with Barth, l. c., p. 597) as having originated on Hebrew soil in order to emphasize the *constr. st.*, on the analogy of the *constr. st.* of terms expressing relationship.

In view of the analogies in other languages (see *b*) there is nothing impossible in the view formerly taken here that the *litterae compaginis* ִי— and וֹ are obsolete (and hence no longer understood) case-endings, *i* being the old genitive and *ô* for the nominative sign *u*. Barth objects that the *i* and *ô* almost invariably have the tone, whereas the accusative ָה— is toneless, and that they are long, where the Arab. *ĭ* and *ŭ* are short. Both these objections, however, lose their force if we consider the special laws of the tone and syllable in Hebrew. The language does not admit a final *ĭ* or *ŭ*, and the necessarily lengthened vowel might easily attract the tone to itself. On the other hand a strong argument for Barth's theory is the fact that these *litterae compaginis* are almost exclusively used to emphasize the close connexion of one noun with another, hence especially in the *constr. st.* Consequently it seems in the highest degree probable that all these uses are based upon forms in which the *constr. st.* is expressly emphasized by a special termination, i. e. the *constr. st.* of terms of relationship, אֲבִי, אֲחִי, חֲמִי from אָב *father*, אָח *brother*, חָם *father-in-law* (cf. § 96). The instances given under *l* and *m* followed this analogy.

Like *i*, וֹ is also used only to emphasize the *constr. st.* (see *o*), and must therefore have a similar origin, but its exact explanation is difficult. According to Barth, this וֹ corresponds to a primitive Semitic *â* (cf. § 9 *q*) and is traceable to *'abâ*, *'aḥâ*, the accusatives of terms of relationship in the *constr. st.*, which have *â* only before a genitive. Against this explanation it may be objected that there is no trace of the supposed Hebrew accusatives אָבוֹ, אָחוֹ, חָמוֹ, and only of the analogous בְּנוֹ. It is also remarkable that so archaic a form should have been preserved (except in בְּנוֹ) only in two words and those in quite late passages. However we have no better explanation to offer in place of Barth's.

Finally we cannot deny the possibility, in some cases, of Barth's explanation of the וֹ in compound proper names like בְּתוּאֵל, &c. (see above), as due to the analogy of terms of relationship with nominative in וֹ. But this in no way militates against the view expressed above, that in some very old names, like פְּנוּאֵל, בְּתוּאֵל, &c., the original common nominative sign has simply been preserved.

---

[1] Cf. the list in L. Kaila, *Zur Syntax des in verbaler Abhängigkeit stehenden Nomens im alttest. Hebr.*, Helsingfors, 1906, p. 54.

[2] The name שְׁמוּאֵל formerly regarded as a compound of שְׁמוֹ = שֵׁם *name* and אֵל, is better explained with Prätorius, *ZDMG.* 1903, p. 777, as a name of affection, for שְׁמוּעַ אֵל = יִשְׁמָעֵאל [but see Driver on 1 S 1²⁰]; similarly, according to Prätorius, פְּתוּאֵל = פְּתוּחַ אֵל and many others.

The instances found are:

(*a*) Of the ending ־ִי: בְּנִי אֲתֹנוֹ *his ass's colt*, Gn 49[11]; עֹזְבִי הַצֹּאן *l* *that leaveth the flock*, Zc 11[17] (cf. the preceding רֹעִי הָאֱלִיל); שֹׁכְנִי סְנֶה *the* *dweller in the bush*, Dt 33[16] (on שְׁכִנִי cf. below Jer 49[16a], Ob[3]); appended to the feminine גְּנֻבְתִי יוֹם וּגְנֻבְתִי לָיְלָה *whether stolen by day or* *stolen by night*, Gn 31[39] (in prose, but in very emphatic speech); מְלֵאֲתִי מִשְׁפָּט *plena iustitiae*, Is 1[21]; רַבָּתִי עָם *full of people*, La 1[1] (on the retraction of the tone before a following tone-syllable, cf. § 29 *e*; in the same verse the second רבתי and שָׂרָתִי, see below, follow the example of רַבָּתִי, although no tone-syllable follows; cf. also Ho 10[11] below); עַל־דִּבְרָתִי מַלְכִּי־צֶדֶק *after the order of Melchizedek*, ψ 110[4]; cf. also ψ 113[9], Jer 49[16b]. To the same category belong the rather numerous cases, in which a preposition is inserted between the *construct state* and its genitive (cf. § 130 *a*), without actually abolishing the dependent relation, e. g. רַבָּתִי בַגּוֹיִם *she that was great among the nations*, שָׂרָתִי בַמְּדִינוֹת *princess among the provinces*, La 1[1]; אֹהַבְתִּי לָדוּשׁ *that loveth to* *tread*, Ho 10[11]; cf. also Jer 49[16a], Ob[3].—In Ex 15[6] נֶאְדָּרִי can only be so explained if it is a vocative referring to יהוה, but perhaps we should read נֶאְדָּרָה as predicate to יְמִינְךָ.

Further, the *Ḥireq compaginis* is found with certain particles which are really also nouns in the *constr. st.*, as זוּלָתִי (=זוּלָת) *except*, מִנִּי (poetical for מִן) *from*, בִּלְתִּי *not*, אַפְסִי *not* (thrice in the formula אֲנִי וְאַפְסִי עוֹד *I am, and there is none else beside me*; but many take the ־ִי as a suffix here), Is 47[8.10], Zp 2[15]. [The above are all the cases in which this ־ִי is attached to independent words in the O.T.; it occurs, however, besides] in compound proper names (again attached to the *constr. st.*), as מַלְכִּי־צֶדֶק (*king of righteousness*), גַּבְרִיאֵל (*man of* *God*), חַנִּיאֵל (*favour of God*), and others (cf. also the Punic name Hannibal, i. e. חַנִּיבַעַל *favour of Baʿal*).

Otherwise than in the *constr. st.* the *Ḥireq compaginis* is only found *m* in participial forms, evidently with the object of giving them more dignity, just as in the case of the construct forms in *î*. We must distinguish, however, between passages in which the participle nevertheless does stand in close connexion, as Gn 49[11], Is 22[16] (הֹצְבִי and חֹקְקִי, also in impassioned speech), Mi 7[14] (probably influenced by Dt 33[16]), ψ 101[5], 113[7]; and passages in which the *î* added to the participle with the article merely serves as an ornamental device of poetic style, e. g. in the late Psalms, 113[5.6.7.9] (on verse 8 see *n*), 114[8], 123[1].

In *K^ethîbh* the termination *î* also occurs four times in יושבתי, i. e. יוֹשַׁבְתִּי, *n* Jer 10[17], 22[23] (before בְּ), Ez 27[3] (before עַל־), La 4[21] (before בְּ). The *Q^ere* always requires for it יוֹשֶׁבֶת (or יֹשְׁ'), except in Jer 22²³ יֹשַׁבְתְּ ; cf. ibid. מִקְנֶנְתִּי *K^{eth.}*,

מְקַנֶּנְתְּ *Q^ere*, and finally Jer 51¹³ שְׁכַנְתְּ *K^{eth.}*, שֹׁכַנְתְּ *Q^ere*. Perhaps יֹשַׁבְתִּי and

שֹׁכַנְתִּי are *formae mixtae*, combining the readings יֹשֶׁבֶת, &c. and יָשַׁבְתְּ (*2nd fem.*

perf.), &c., but מְקַנֶּנְתִּי may be merely assimilated to יֹשַׁבְתִּי which immediately

precedes it.

The following are simply textual errors : 2 K 4²³ הֹלַכְתִּי *K^{eth.}*, due to the

preceding אֹתִי, and to be read הֹלָכֶת as in the *Q^ere* ; ψ 30⁸ (read הַרְרִי), 113⁸

(read לְהוֹשִׁיבוֹ), 116¹ (read קוֹל תַּח', as in five other places). On בְּרִיתִי,

thrice, in Lv 26⁴² , cf. § 128 *d*.

o (*b*) Of the ending וֹ¹ (always with the tone): in prose only in the

Pentateuch, but in elevated style, Gn 1²⁴ חַיְתוֹ־אֶרֶץ *the beast of the earth*

(=אֶרֶץ הָ חַיַּת ver. 25); similarly in ψ 50¹⁰, 79², 104¹¹·²⁰, Is 56⁹ (twice),

Zp 2¹⁴ ; otherwise only in בְּנוֹ צִפֹּר *son of Zippor*, Nu 23¹⁸ ; בְּנוֹ בְעֹר *son*

of Beor, Nu 24³·¹⁵ ; and מַעְיְנוֹ מָיִם *a fountain of waters*, ψ 114⁸.

§ 91. *The Noun with Pronominal Suffixes.*

W. Diehl, *Das Pronomen pers. suffixum 2 u. 3 pers. plur. des Hebr.*, Giessen,
1895 ; A. Ungnad, 'Das Nomen mit Suffixen im Semit.,' *Vienna Oriental Journal*,
xx, p. 167 ff.

a With regard to the connexion of the noun with pronominal suffixes,

which then stand in a genitive relation (§ 33 *c*) and are, therefore,

necessarily appended to the *construct state* of the noun, we shall first

consider, as in the verb (§ 57 ff.), the forms of the suffixes themselves,

and then the various changes in the form of the noun to which they

are attached. The nouns are also tabulated in the Paradigms of the

flexion of the noun in § 92 ff. Cf. also Paradigm A in the Appendix.

We are here primarily concerned with the different forms of the

suffixes when added to the singular, plural, and dual.

b 1. The Suffixes of the singular are—

With nouns ending in a—

	Vowel.		Consonant.	
Sing. 1.	*c.* י		ִי	*my.*
2.	*m.* ךָ		ךָ (*pause* ךָ)	} *thy.*
	f. ךְ		ךְ	
3.	*m.* ו הוּ		וֹ (הוּ), הוּ	*his.*
	f. הָ		הָ, הָ	*her.*

---

¹ Cf. Kaila, l.c., p. 59 ff.

Vowel.		Consonant.	
Plur. 1.	*c.* נוּ	נוּ ֵ ‎	*our.*
2. {*m.* כֶם ‎		כֶם ֵ ‎ }	
{*f.* כֶן ‎		כֶן ֵ ‎ }	*your.*
3. {*m.* הֶם ‎		‍ם ָ ‎	
{מוֹ		(poet. מוֹ ֵ ‎) }	*eorum.*
{*f.* הֶן הֶן (הֵן) ‎		‍ן ָ ‎	*earum.*

Rem. 1. There is less variety of forms in these than in the verbal suffixes; *c* the particular forms are used as follows:—

(*a*) Those without a connecting vowel (on the derivation of these 'connecting vowels' from original stem-vowels, see note on § 58 *f*) are generally joined to nouns of a peculiar form (see § 96), the *constr. st.* of which ends in a vowel, as אָבִיךָ, אָבִיהוּ ‎ and אָבִיו, אָבִיהָ, אָבִיכֶם, אֲבִיכֶן, אֲבִיכֶם, אָבִינוּ, אֲבִיהֶם, אֲבִיהֶן, ‎ sometimes also to segholate forms ending in *î* from ל״ה ‎ stems (see § 93 *x, y*), e. g. פֶּרְיָם ‎ *the fruit of them,* Am 9¹⁴ (also פִּרְיָם ‎ Is 37³⁰, &c.), פִּרְיָהֶן ‎ Jer 29²⁸ (also פִּרְיָן ‎ verse 5); cf., moreover, חֶלְבְּהֶן ‎ Lv 8¹⁶·²⁵ and similar examples with הֵן ‎ (Is 3¹⁷ הֵן ‎) Gn 21²⁸, Ez 13¹⁷, 16⁵³. ¹ Also in Gn 1²¹, 4⁴, Ez 10¹², Nah 2⁸, &c., the *Keth.* perhaps intends the singular, לְמִינֵהֶם, ‎ &c., but the Masora requires the plural with defective *ê.*

(*b*) The forms with connecting vowels (§ 58 *f*) are joined to nouns ending *d* in a consonant. The connecting vowel is regularly *a* in the 3rd sing. *fem.* ‍ה ָ ‎ (for *aha*) and 3rd *plur.* ‍ם ָ ‎ , מוֹ ֵ ‎ , ‍ן ָ ‎ , also in the 3rd sing. *masc.* וֹ (הֹ), ‎ since the *ô* is contracted from *a*[*h*]*û*, and in the pausal form of the 2nd *masc.* ‍ךָ ֵ ‎ (a modification of original ‍ךָ ֵ ‎).

The forms with *ē* in the above-mentioned persons are common only with nouns in ‍ה ָ ‎ (from stems ל״ה ‎), *constr. st.* ‍ה ֵ ‎ (cf. § 89 *f*), e. g. שָׂדֵהוּ ‎ (from *sadaihû*) *his field;* עָלֵהוּ ‎ *its leaf,* Is 1³⁰; מַרְאֵה ‎ *the appearance thereof,* Lv 13⁴ (from *mar'aihā*; on the *Seghôl* see *k*); but שָׂדֶה ‎ *her field.* The orthographic retention of the י, ‎ e. g. מַעֲשֵׂי, מַעֲשָׂיו, ‎ gives to many forms the appearance of plurals; see the instances in § 93 *ss.*

Apart from these ל״ה ‎ forms the connecting vowel *ē* in the 3rd pers. occurs only in isolated cases; אוֹרֵהוּ ‎ *his light,* Jb 25³; לְמִינֵהוּ ‎ *after its kind,* Gn 1¹²·²⁵ [+ 12 times]; Na 1¹³; in Ju 19²⁴ read פִּילַגְשׁוֹ ‎ as in vv. 2, 25. On the other hand ‍ךָ ֵ ‎ in the 2nd sing. *fem.* and נוּ ֵ ‎ in the 1st *plur.* are by far the more common forms, while ‍ךָ ָ ‎ , נוּ ָ ‎ are of rare occurrence; see *e.*—Instead of ‍ךָ ָ ‎ (כָה) ‎ in Gn 10¹⁹, Ex 13¹⁶, Jer 29²⁵, &c., cf. לְכָה, בְּכָה § 103 *g*), כֶם ָ ‎ , כֶן ָ ‎ (with *Šewâ mobile*), if the last consonant of the noun is a guttural, the forms are ‍ךָ ֳ ‎ , כֶם ֳ ‎ , כֶן ֳ ‎ , e. g. רוּחֲךָ ‎ *thy spirit,* בֹּרַאֲךָ ‎ *thy creator,* Is 43¹, רֵעֲכֶם ‎ *your friend,* Jb 6²⁷ (on such cases as בְּחוֹבְכֶם ‎ Hag 2⁵, see § 10 *g*).—With *Nun energicum* (cf. § 58 *i*, and on עֹנֶךָ ‎ Jb 5¹, &c., cf. § 61 *h*) ‍ךָ ֶ ‎ occurs in Pr 25¹⁶, in principal pause.

2. Rare or incorrect forms are—

Sing. 1st pers. נִי ‎ in בְּשׁוּבֵנִי ‎ Ez 47⁷ (certainly only a scribal error, caused *e* by וָשְׁבֵנִי ‎ in verse 6).

_____

¹ Also in Jer 15¹⁰ read (according to § 61 *h*, end) כֻּלְּהֶם קִלְּלוּנִי; ‎ in Ho 7⁶ probably אָפֵהֶם for אֹפֶהֶם. ‎

2nd pers. *m.* in pause כָֿה‎ֶ‎, e.g. כַּפֶּכָה (*thy hand*), ψ 139⁵, cf. Pr 24¹⁰; once חִנְךָ ψ 53⁶ (cf. the analogous cases in the verbal suffix § 7 *f ll*); *fem.* ךְ‎ֵ‎ Ez 5¹² (in 16⁵³ also for שְׁבִיתַיִךְ probably שְׁבִיתֵיךְ is intended), כִֿי‎ֵ‎ Jer 11¹⁵, ψ 103³, 116¹⁹, 135⁹ (corresponding to the Aramaic suffix of the 2nd *fem.* *sing.*; on the wholly abnormal כֶה‎ֵ‎ Na 2¹⁴, cf. *l*), לְכִי *Kᵉth.* 2 K 4², Ct 2¹³. Also ךְ‎ֵ‎ Is 22¹, Ez 23²⁸, 25⁴.

3rd pers. ה‎ָ‎ (cf. § 7 *c*), e.g. אָהֳלֹה Gn 9²¹, 12⁸, 13³, 35²¹ (always with *Qᵉrê* אׇהֳלוֹ); נחֹה Nu 10³⁶; לָחֹה Dt 34⁷; כֻּלֹּה Jer 20⁷, Na 2¹ *Qᵉrê*; קָצֹה 2 K 19²³ *Kᵉth.*, for which קָצוֹ is read in Is 37²⁴; עִירֹה and סוּתֹה Gn 49¹¹, cf. Ex 22²⁶ (*Qᵉrê* עִירוֹ, סוּתוֹ); סֻכֹּה ψ 10⁹, 27⁵ *Kᵉth.*; הַמוֹנֹה Ez 31¹⁸, &c., *Kᵉth.*; תְּבוּאָתֹה Ez 48·⁸ [altogether fourteen times in the Pentateuch, and some forty times in other books: see Driver, *Samuel*, p. xxxv, and on 2 S 2⁹, 21¹].

3rd *fem.* ה‎ָ‎ for הּ‎ָ‎ (with the softening of the *Mappiq*, cf. § 23 *k*, and the analogous cases in § 58 *g*) occurs repeatedly before *Bᵉghadhkᵉphath* and other soft consonants, Ex 9¹⁸ (before וְ, if the text is right), Lv 13⁴ (before לְ), Nu 15²⁸·³¹, 1 S 1⁹ (unless אׇכְלָה, the infin. with fem. termination, is intended; שָׁתָה follows), Ez 16⁴⁴, 24⁶ (before בְּ), 1 S 20²⁰, 2 K 8⁶, Pr 12²⁸ (before אֵ), Na 3⁹ (before וְ), ψ 48¹⁴ (before פְ), Ez 47¹⁰, Jb 31²² twice (before תְ), Is 21², Jer 20¹⁷ (before הֵ), Nu 32⁴², Am 1¹¹ (before גְ), Lv 6² (before עֲ); even in *pause*, Lv 12⁴ ᵃ and ⁵ ᵇ; Is 23¹⁷, Pr 21²², also with Zaqeph, Is 45⁶, Jer 6⁶ (probably), 44¹⁹; on הַשַּׁמָּה Lv 26³⁴, &c., see § 67 *y*. Cf. also אֵ‎ָ‎ Ez 36⁵.—Sometimes the Masora appears (but this is very doubtful) to regard the ה‎ָ‎ with feminines as a shortening of תָה‎ָ‎, e.g. נְצָה Gn 40¹⁰ for נָצָתָה, פֶּנָּה Pr 7⁸ for פִּנָּתָה; also ם‎ָ‎ for תָם‎ָ‎ in כְּתֻבוּם Ho 13², and עָרְמָם Jb 5¹³. The examples, however, are for the most part uncertain, e.g. in Is 28⁴ the reading is simply to be emended to בְּבִכּוּרָה, and in Zc 4² to גֻּלָּה, Jb 11⁹ to מִדָּה, Neh 5¹⁴ to פֶּחָה. [See also, after prepositions, § 103 *g*.]

f Plur. 1st pers. נוּ‎ֵ‎, in *pause* קִימָנוּ Jb 22²⁰ (where, however, קׇמֵנוּ is certainly to be read); cf. Ru 3² [Is 47¹⁰, cf. § 61 *c, h*], and so always כֻּלָּנוּ *all of us*, Gn 42¹¹, &c [cf. עׇמָּנוּ, אִתָּנוּ, לָנוּ, בָּנוּ].

2nd pers. *fem.* בֶּנָה Ez 23⁴⁸·⁴⁹.

3rd pers. *masc.* מוֹ‎ֵ‎ ψ 17¹⁰ (on מוֹ in פִּימוֹ in the same verse, and in ψ 58⁷ see *l*); הֶם‎ַ‎ 2 S 23⁶, according to Sievers probably to call attention to the reading כֻלָּהם. *Fem.* הֶנָה‎ֵ‎ 1 K 7³⁷, Ez 16⁵³ (in *pause*); נָה‎ֶ‎ Gn 41²¹; נָֽה‎ֵ‎ Gn 30⁴¹; נָֽה‎ֶ‎ Ru 1¹⁹; elsewhere generally in *pause* (Gn 21²⁹, 42³⁶, Jer 8⁷, Pr 31²⁹, Jb 39²); finally הֶן as suffix to a noun, only in Is 3¹⁷.

For examples of singulars with plural suffixes see *l*.

g 2. In the *plural masc.* and in the *dual* the suffixes are to be regarded primarily as affixed to the original ending of the *construct state* (ֵי‎, cf. § 89 *d*). This ending, however, has been preserved unchanged only in the 2nd *fem.* In most cases it is contracted to ֵי‎, as in the *constr. st.* without suffixes (so throughout the plur. and in the poetical suffix יהוּ‎ֵ‎ of the 3rd *sing. masc.*); in the 2nd *masc.* and 3rd *fem. sing.* it is ַי‎ (cf. *k*). On the 1st *pers.* and 3rd *masc. sing.* see *i*.—Thus there arise the following

Suffixes of Plural Nouns.   *h*

Singular.		Plural.	
1. *c.* יַ֖ ־, pause יָ֖ ־	*my.*	1. *c.* יֵ֫נוּ	*our.*
2. { *m.* יֶ֫יךָ *f.* יַ֫יִךְ ־, pause יָ֫יִךְ }	*thy.*	2. { *m.* יכֶם *f.* יכֶן }	*your.*
3. { *m.* יָו ־, poet. יֵ֫הוּ *f.* יֶ֫יהָ }	*his.* *her.*	3. { *m.* יהֶם ־, poet. יֵ֫ימוֹ *f.* יהֶן }	*their.*

Thus the original יַ֖ ־ is (*a*) contracted in the 3rd *sing. masc.* *i*
יֵ֫הוּ and throughout the *plural*, as סוּסֵ֫ינוּ, סוּסֵיהוּ, &c.; (*b*) retained
unchanged in the 1st *sing.* סוּסַי, the real suffix-ending י (see *b*) being
united with the final *Yôdh* of the ending יַ֖ ־; and in the 2nd *fem.*
sing. סוּסַ֫יִךְ, with a *helping-Ḥireq* after the *Yôdh*. On the other hand
(*c*) the *Yôdh* of יַ֖ ־ is lost in pronunciation and the ă lengthened to ā
in the 3rd *masc. sing.* סוּסָיו, i.e. *sûsāw* (pronounced *susā-u*).[1] The
2nd *masc. sing.* סוּסֶ֫יךָ and the 3rd *fem. sing.* סוּסֶ֫יהָ were formerly
also explained here as having really lost the י, and modified the *a* of
sûsakā, *sûsahā* to *Sᵉghôl*; but cf. the view now given in *g* and *k*.

Rem. 1. As סוּסֵ֫ינוּ represents *sûsai-nû*, so סוּסֶ֫יךָ and סוּסֶ֫יהָ represent *sûsai-kā*, *k*
sûsai-hā, and the use of *Sᵉghôl* instead of the more regular *Ṣere* is to be explained
from the character of the following syllable,—so P. Haupt who points to
יְקַטְּלָה as compared with יְקַטְלֵ֫הוּ. In support of the view formerly adopted
by us that the י is only orthographically retained, too much stress must not
be laid on the fact that it is sometimes omitted,[2] thereby causing confusion
in an unpointed text with the singular noun. A number of the examples
which follow may be due to an erroneous assumption that the noun is a plural,
where in reality it is a singular, and others may be incorrect readings. Cf.
דְּרָכֶ֑ךָ *thy ways* (probably דַּרְכְּךָ is intended), Ex 33¹³, Jos 1⁸, ψ 119⁸⁷; for other
examples, see Jos 21¹¹ ff. (מִנְרָשֶׁ֑הָ; but in 1 Ch 6⁴⁰ ff. always יהָ ־ּ), Ju 19⁹,
1 K 8²⁹, Is 58¹³, ψ 119⁴¹·⁴³·⁹⁸ (probably, however, in all these cases the *sing.*
is intended); אֶסָרֶ֑הָ Nu 30⁸ (cf. v. 5); מַבֹּאתֶ֑הָ Jer 19⁸, 49¹⁷; מְבִיאֶ֑הָ Dn 11⁶.
For the orthographic omission of י before suffixes cf. רֵעֹה֑וּ for רֵעָ֫יהוּ *his friends*
1 S 30²⁶, Pr 29¹⁸; Jb 42¹⁰ (but it is possible to explain it here as a *collective
singular*); עֲוֹנֵ֫נוּ *our iniquities*, Is 64⁵·⁶, Jer 14⁷; Ex 10⁹, Neh 10¹ (לְוִיִּם from לְוִיִּ֫ם
which is always written defectively); נְסָכֵ֑כֶם Nu 29³³; רָעֹתֶ֫כֶם Jer 44⁹; יְדֵכֶם
ψ 134²; לְמִינֵ֫הֶם *after their kinds*, Gn 1²¹ (but see *c*), cf. 4⁴ and Na 2⁸. The

---

[1] In the papyrus of the decalogue from the Fayyûm, line 16, ויקרשׁין occurs
for ויקרשׁהו Ex 20¹¹. Gall, *ZAW.* 1903, p. 349, takes this as an indication
that the traditional forms of the noun-suffix ׳יו or ׳ו represent *aiŭ* or *eŭ*.
P. Haupt aptly compares the Greek use of the *iota subscript* (ᾳ).

[2] So in the Mêšaʿ inscription, l. 22 מגדלתה *its towers* (along with שׁעריה *its
gates*). Can it have been the rule to omit י after the termination *ôth*? Cf.
below, *n*.

defective writing is especially frequent in the 3rd masc. sing. וֹ‑, which in
Qᵉrê is almost always changed to יו‑, e. g. חִצֹּו *his arrows*, ψ 58⁸, *Qᵉrê* חִצָּיו.
On יַחְדָּו, only three times יַחְדָּיו, cf. § 135 *r*.

l　2. Unusual forms (but for the most part probably only scribal errors) are—
Sing. 2nd pers. *fem* יְ‑ךְ (after אַשְׁרֵי *happy!* Ec 10¹⁷, which has become
stereotyped as an interjection, and is therefore unchangeable; cf. Delitzsch
on the passage) ; יְכִ‑ (cf. Syr. ـכ‑) 2 K 4³, and ⁷ in *Kᵉth.*, ψ 103³⁻⁵, 116⁷
(יְכִ‑ in *pause*).—In Ez 16³¹ יֵ‑ךְ (so כֶם‑ in 6⁸) occurs with an *infin.*
ending in וֹת, the וֹת being therefore treated as a plural ending; similarly,
the plural suffix is sometimes found with the feminine ending וֹת (Nu 14³³,
Is 54⁴, Jer 3⁸, Ez 16¹⁵, 23⁷, as well as in 16²⁰ *Qᵉrê*, and Zp 3²⁰), with the ending
îth (Lv 5²⁴, reading חֲמִשִׁתוֹ), and even with the ordinary feminine ending *ath* ;
Is 47¹³, Ez 35¹¹, ψ 9¹⁵, Ezr 9¹⁵.—Wholly abnormal is מַלְאָכֵכֶה *thy messengers,*
Na 2¹⁴, evidently a case of dittography of the following ה : read מַלְאָכַיִךְ.

3rd masc. יֵהוּ‑ Hb 3¹⁰, Jb 24²³ ; הוּ‑ 1 S 30²⁶, Ez 43¹⁷, Na 2⁴ ; וֹהִי‑ (a
purely Aramaic form) ψ 116¹².—3rd *fem.* יֵהָא‑ Ez 41¹⁵.

Plur. The strange *2nd pers. masc.* תְּפוּצוֹתִיכֶם (with *i*, so Qimḥi ; cf. Norzi)
Jer 25³⁴, is probably a mixed form combining תְּפוּצוּ and הֲפִיצוֹתִיכֶם ; *fem.*
יְכֶנָה‑ Ez 13²⁰.

3rd masc. יְהֶמָה‑ Ez 40¹⁶ ; *fem.* יְהֶנָה‑ Ez 1¹¹.

3. The termination מוֹ‑ (also with the *dual*, e. g. ψ 58⁷, 59¹³), like מוֹ and
מוֹ‑, occurs with the noun (as with the verb, § 58 *g*) almost exclusively in
the later poets [viz. with a substantive in the singular, ψ 21¹¹, 17¹⁰·¹⁰, 58⁷,
59¹³, 89¹⁸ ; with a dual or plural, Dt 32²⁷·³²·³⁷·³⁸, 33²⁹, ψ 2³·³, 11⁷, 35¹⁶, 49¹², 58⁷,
59¹⁴, 73⁵·⁷, 83¹²·¹², 140⁴·¹⁰, Jb 27²³ ; after prepositions, see § 103 *f, o*, notes], and
cannot, therefore, by itself be taken as an indication of archaic language.
On the other hand there can be no doubt that these are revivals of really old
forms. That they are consciously and artificially used is shown by the evidently intentional accumulation of them, e. g. in Ex 15⁵·⁷·⁹, ψ 2³·⁵, and 140⁴·¹⁰,
and also by the fact observed by Diehl (see the heading of this section) that
in Ex 15 they occur *only* as verbal suffixes, in Dt 32 *only* as noun suffixes.

m　**3.** It is clear and beyond doubt that the *Yôdh* in these suffixes
with the plural noun belongs, in reality, to the ending of the *construct
state* of the masculine plural. Yet the consciousness of this fact
became so completely lost as to admit of the striking peculiarity
(or rather inaccuracy) of appending those *suffix*-forms which include
the plural ending ‑ָי‑, even to the feminine plural in סוּסוֹתֵינוּ (זת,
סוּסוֹתֶיךָ, &c.), so that in reality the result is a double indication of
the plural.[1]

n　Such is the rule : the singular suffix, however (see *b*), also occurs with the
ending וֹת (probably through the influence of Aramaic), e. g. עֵדְוֹתִי ψ 132¹²
(unless it be *sing.* for עֵדוּתִי, as, according to Qimḥi in his Lexicon, תְּחִנָּתִי 2 K
6⁸ is for תְּחִנוּתִי) ; מַבְּתְךָ Dt 28⁵⁹ (treated on the analogy of an *infin.* ל״ה) ;

---

[1] See an analogous case in § 87 *s*. Cf. also the double feminine ending in
the 3rd sing. *perf.* of verbs ל״ה, § 75 *i*.

אֲחִיוֹתֵךְ Ez 16⁵² . On the other hand מִצְוֹתֵךְ (so Baer, Ginsb. ; but Opit. ךְ_ ֵ)
ψ 119⁹⁸, Dn 9⁵ is merely written defectively, like גְּרוֹתֵךְ according to Baer
(not Ginsb.) in Pr 1⁹, &c. In the *3rd plur.* the use of the singular suffix is
even the rule in the earlier Books (see the instances in Diehl, l. c., p. 8),
e. g. אֲבוֹתָם (*their fathers*) oftener than אֲבִתֵיהֶם (this only in 1 K 14¹⁵, and in
Jer, Ezr, Neh, and Ch [in 1 K, Jer, Ezr, however, אֲבוֹתָם is more common]) ;
so always שְׁמוֹתָם, שְׁמוֹתָן *their names*, דּוֹרֹתָם *their generations*. From parallel
passages like 2 S 22⁴⁶ compared with ψ 18⁴⁶, Is 2⁴ with Mi 4³, it appears that
in many cases the longer form in הֶם__ ֵי can only subsequently have taken
the place of ם__ ָ .

4. The following Paradigm of a masculine and feminine noun *o*
with suffixes is based upon a monosyllabic noun with one unchangeable
vowel. With regard to the ending ת__ in the *constr. st.* of the fem.
it should be further remarked that the short *ă* of this ending is only
retained before the *grave* suffixes כֶם and כֶן ; before all the others
(the *light* suffixes) it is lengthened to *ā*.

Singular. *p*

	Masculine.		Feminine.	
	סוּס *a horse.*		סוּסָה *a mare.*	
Sing. 1. *com.*	סוּסִי *my horse.*		סוּסָתִי *my mare.*	
2. { *m.*	סוּסְךָ *thy horse.*		סוּסָתְךָ *thy mare.*	
{ *f.*	סוּסֵךְ *thy horse.*		סוּסָתֵךְ *thy mare.*	
3. { *m.*	סוּסוֹ *equus eius (suus).*		סוּסָתוֹ *equa eius (sua).*	
{ *f.*	סוּסָהּ *equus eius (suus).*		סוּסָתָהּ *equa eius (sua).*	
Plur. 1. *com.*	סוּסֵנוּ *our horse.*		סוּסָתֵנוּ *our mare.*	
2. { *m.*	סוּסְכֶם *your horse.*		סוּסַתְכֶם *your mare.*	
{ *f.*	סוּסְכֶן *your horse.*		סוּסַתְכֶן *your mare.*	
3. { *m.*	סוּסָם *equus eorum (suus).*		סוּסָתָם *equa eorum (sua).*	
{ *f.*	סוּסָן *equus earum (suus).*		סוּסָתָן *equa earum (sua).*	

Plural. *q*

	Masculine.		Feminine.	
	סוּסִים *horses.*		סוּסוֹת *mares.*	
Sing. 1. *com.*	סוּסַי *my horses.*		סוּסוֹתַי *my mares.*	
2. { *m.*	סוּסֶיךָ *thy horses.*		סוּסוֹתֶיךָ *thy mares.*	
{ *f.*	סוּסַיִךְ *thy horses.*		סוּסוֹתַיִךְ *thy mares.*	
3. { *m.*	סוּסָיו *equi eius (sui).*		סוּסוֹתָיו *equae eius (suae).*	
{ *f.*	סוּסֶיהָ *equi eius (sui).*		סוּסוֹתֶיהָ *equae eius (suae).*	
Plur. 1. *com.*	סוּסֵינוּ *our horses.*		סוּסוֹתֵינוּ *our mares.*	
2 { *m.*	סוּסֵיכֶם *your horses.*		סוּסוֹתֵיכֶם *your mares.*	
{ *f.*	סוּסֵיכֶן *your horses.*		סוּסוֹתֵיכֶן *your mares.*	
3. { *m.*	סוּסֵיהֶם *equi eorum (sui).*		סוּסוֹתֵיהֶם *equae eorum (suae).*	
{ *f.*	סוּסֵיהֶן *equi earum (sui).*		סוּסוֹתֵיהֶן *equae earum (suae).*	

§ 92. *Vowel Changes in the Noun.*

a 1. Vowel changes in the noun may be caused (*a*) by dependence on a following genitive; (*b*) by connexion with pronominal suffixes, (*c*) by the plural and dual terminations, whether in the form of the absolute state or of the construct (before a following genitive of a noun or suffix).

b 2. In all these cases, the tone of the noun is moved forward either one or two syllables, while the tone of the *construct state* may even be thrown upon the following word. In this way the following changes may arise :—

(*a*) *When the tone is moved forward only one place*, as is the case when the plural and dual endings ִים, וֹת and ַיִם are affixed, as well as with all monosyllabic or paroxytone suffixes, then in dissyllabic nouns the originally short vowel of the first syllable (which was lengthened as being in an open syllable before the tone) becomes *Šewâ*, since it no longer stands before the tone. On the other hand, the originally short, but tone-lengthened vowel, of the second syllable is retained as being now the pretonic vowel ; e. g. דָּבָר *word* (ground-form *dăbăr*), plur. דְּבָרִים ; with a light suffix beginning with a vowel, דְּבָרִי, דְּבָרֵנוּ ; plur. דְּבָרֶיךָ, דְּבָרַי, &c.; כָּנָף *wing*, dual כְּנָפַיִם. With an unchangeable vowel in the second syllable : פָּקִיד *overseer*, plur. פְּקִידִים ; with the suffix of the sing. פְּקִידִי, פְּקִידֵנוּ, &c.; with the suff. of the plur. פְּקִידַי, פְּקִידֶיךָ, &c. With an unchangeable vowel in the first syllable : עוֹלָם *eternity*, plur. עוֹלָמִים, with suff. עוֹלָמִי, &c.[1]

c But in participles of the form קֹטֵל, with tone-lengthened *ē* (originally *ĭ*) in the second syllable, the *ē* regularly becomes *Šewâ mobile* before a tone-bearing affix, e. g. אֹיֵב *enemy*, plur. אֹיְבִים, with suff. אֹיְבִי, &c. Likewise in words of the form קַטֵּל, קִטֵּל, &c. (with *ē* in the second syllable ; § 84^b *d, l, p* ; § 85 *i* and *k*), e. g. אִלֵּם *dumb*, plur. אִלְּמִים.

d (*b*) When the tone of the *construct state*, plural or dual, is carried over to the following word, or, in consequence of the addition of the *grave suffixes* to the constr. st. plur. or dual, *is moved forward two places* within the word itself, in such cases the originally short vowel of the second syllable becomes *Šewâ*, while the vowel of the first syllable reverts to its original shortness, e. g. דִּבְרֵי הָעָם *the words of the people*, דִּבְרֵיכֶם *your words*, דִּבְרֵיהֶם *their words* (in all which instances the *ĭ* of the first syllable is attenuated from an original *ă*).

---

[1] The participles *Niph'al* נִדְחַךְ Dt 30⁴, נִדְחוּ 2 S 14¹³, and some plurals of the participle Niph. of verbs ל״א form an exception ; cf. § 93 *oo*.

In the segholate forms in the singular and mostly in the dual the suffix is *e*
appended to the ground-form (מַלְכִּי *my king*, מַלְכֵּנוּ, &c.) ; on the other hand,
before the endings ־ִים, ־וֹת (sometimes also before ־ַיִם) a *Qameṣ* regularly
occurs,[1] before which the vowel of the first syllable then becomes vocal *Šewâ*
(מְלָכִים, מְלָכוֹת). This *Qameṣ* (on which cf. § 84[a] *a*) remains even before the
light suffixes, when attached to the plur. masc. (מְלָכַי, מְלָכֶיךָ, &c.). On
the other hand, the *constr. st.* plur. and dual, regularly, according to *d*, has
the form מַלְכֵי, with grave suffix מַלְכֵיכֶם,&c., דַּלְתֵי from דְּלָתַיִם *folding-doors.*

(*c*) Before the *Šewâ mobile* which precedes the suffix ךָ when *f*
following a consonant, the *a*-sound, as a rule, is the only tone-
lengthened vowel which remains in the final syllable (being now
in an open syllable *before* the tone), e. g. הֲמָךְ, דְּבָרְךָ, &c. (on the
forms with *ē* in the second syllable, see § 93 *qq*); but before the grave
suffixes ־כֶם and ־כֶן in the same position it reverts to its original
shortness, as דִּבְרְכֶם (*deḇárkhèm*), &c. In the same way the tone-
lengthened *ā* or *ē* of the second syllable in the *constr. st. sing.* also
becomes short again, since the *constr. st.* resigns the principal tone to
the following word, e. g. חֲצַר הַבַּיִת ; דְּבַר אֱלֹהִים (from חָצֵר).

Rem. The Masora (cf. *Diqduqe ha-ṭeamim*, p. 37) reckons thirteen words *g*
which retain *Qameṣ* in the *constr. st.*, some of which had originally *â* and
therefore need not be considered. On the other hand, אֻלָם or אֵלָם 1 K 7[6],
Ez 40[48], &c. (in spite of the *constr. st.* plur. אֵלַמֵּי) ; מִבְטָח ψ 65[6], Pr 25[19] ; מֵצַב
1 S 13[23] (so Baer, but ed. Mant., Ginsburg, &c. מַצַּב) ; מִשְׁקַל Ezr 8[30] and מַתָּן
Pr 18[16] are very peculiar.

3. The vowel changes in the inflexion of *feminine nouns* (§ 95) are *h*
not so considerable, since generally in the formation of the feminine
either the original vowels have been retained, or they have already
become *Šewâ*.

Besides the vowel changes discussed above in *a–g*, which take place according *i*
to the general formative laws (§§ 25–28), certain further phenomena must also
be considered in the inflexion of nouns, an accurate knowledge of which
requires in each case an investigation of the original form of the words in
question (see §§ 84–86). Such are, e. g., the rejection of the ה of ל"ה stems
before all formative additions (cf. § 91 *d*), the sharpening of the final consonant
of ע"ע stems in such cases as חֻקִּי, חֹק, &c.
A striking difference between the vowel changes in the verb and noun is *k*
that in a verb when terminations are added it is mostly the second of two
changeable vowels which becomes *Šewâ* (קָטַל קְטָלָה, קָטְלוּ), but in a noun,
the first (דָּבָר, דְּבָרִי, דְּבָרִים), cf. § 27. 3.

---

[1] For the rare exceptions see § 93 *l* and § 97 *f*, note 2.

§ 93. *Paradigms of Masculine Nouns.*[1]

a　Masculine nouns from the simple stem may, as regards their form and the vowel changes connected with it, be divided into *four* classes. A synopsis of them is given on pp. 264, 265, and they are further explained below. Two general remarks may be premised :

(*a*) That all feminines without a distinctive termination (§ 122 *h*) are treated like these masculine nouns, e. g. חֶרֶב *f. sword,* like מֶלֶךְ *m. king,* except that in the *plural* they usually take the termination וֹת‎—; thus חֲרָבוֹת, *constr.* חַרְבוֹת (and so always before *suffixes,* see § 95). ,

b　(*b*) That in the plural of the first three classes a changeable vowel is always retained even before the light suffixes as a lengthened pretonic vowel, whenever it also stands before the plural ending ־ִים‎. All suffixes, except כֶם, כֶן, הֶם, הֶן (־ֵיכֶם‎, ־ֵיכֶן‎, ־ֵיהֶם‎, ־ֵיהֶן‎), are called *light*. Cf. § 92 *e*.

Explanations of the Paradigms (see pp. 264, 265).

c　1. Paradigm I comprises the large class of *segholate* nouns (§ 84[a] *a–e*). In the first three examples, from a strong stem, the ground-forms, *mǎlk, sǐphr, qǔdš* have been developed by the adoption of a helping *S⁰yhôl* to מֶלֶךְ (with *ǎ* modified to *è*), סֵפֶר (*ǐ* lengthened to *ē*), קֹדֶשׁ (*ǔ* lengthened to *ō*).[2] The next three examples, instead of the helping *S⁰ghôl*, have a helping *Pathaḥ*, on account of the middle (*d, f*) or final guttural (*e*). In all these cases the *constr. st. sing.* coincides exactly with the *absolute*. The singular suffixes are added to the ground-form; but in *c* and *f* an *ŏ* takes the place of the original *ǔ*, and in *d* and *f* the guttural requires a repetition of the *ǎ* and *ŏ* in the form of a *Ḥaṭeph* (פָּעֳלִי, נַעֲרִי); before a following *S⁰wâ* this *Ḥaṭeph* passes into a simple helping vowel (*ǎ, ŏ*), according to § 28 *c*; hence נַעֲרְךָ, &c.

d　In the plural an *a*-sound almost always appears before the tone-bearing affix ־ִים‎ (on the analogy of forms with original *a* in the

---

[1] A sort of detailed commentary on the following scheme of Hebrew declensions is supplied by E. König in his *Hist.-krit. Lehrgeb. der hebr. Spr.*, ii. 1, p. 1 ff.

[2] According to P. Haupt 'The book of Nahum' in the *Journ. of bibl. Lit.*, 1907, p. 29, the *e* in סֵפֶר and the *o* in קֹדֶשׁ are not long but accented, and hence to be pronounced σέφρ, ὄζν (אֹזֶן), a theory unknown at any rate to the Jewish grammarians.

second syllable; cf. § 84ᵃ *a*), in the form of a pretonic *Qameṣ*, whilst the short vowel of the first syllable becomes vocal *Šᵉwâ*. The original *a* of the 2nd syllable is elided in the *construct state*, so that the short vowel under the first radical then stands in a closed syllable. The omission of *Dageš* in a following *Begadkephath* (מַלְכֵי, not מַלְכֵּי, &c.) is due to the loss of a vowel between ל and כ. On the other hand, the pretonic *Qameṣ* of the *absolute state* is retained before the light plural suffixes, whilst the grave suffixes are added to the form of the *construct state*.—The ending of the *absolute state* of the dual is added, as a rule, to the ground-form (so in *a–d* and *h*, but cf. *k*). The *construct state* of the dual is generally the same as that of the plural, except, of course, in cases like *m*.

Paradigms *g* and *h* exhibit forms with middle *u* and *i* (§ 84ᵃ *c*, γ and δ); the ground forms *maut* and *zait* are always contracted to *môth*, *zêth*, except in the *absol. sing.*, where *u* and *i* are changed into the corresponding consonants ו and י.

Paradigm *i* exhibits one of the numerous forms in which the contraction of a middle *u* or *i* has already taken place in the *absol. sing.* (ground-form *šaut*).

Paradigm *k* is a formation from a stem ל״ה (§ 84ᵃ *c*, ε).

Paradigms *l, m, n* are forms from stems ע״ע, and hence (see § 67 *a*) originally biliteral, *yam, 'im, ḥuq*, with the regular lengthening to יָם, אֵם, חֹק. Before formative additions a sharpening, as in the inflexion of verbs ע״ע, takes place in the second radical, e.g. אִמִּי, יַמִּים, &c. (see § 84ᵃ *c*, β).

REMARKS.

1. A. On I. *a* and *d* (ground-form *qaṭl*). In *pause* the full lengthening to *ā* generally takes place, thus כֶּרֶם *vineyard*, זֶרַע *seed* (from זֶרַע), and so always (except ψ 48¹¹), in אֶרֶץ *earth* with the article, הָאָרֶץ, according to § 35 *o* (cf. also in the LXX the forms 'Αβέλ, 'Ιαφέθ for יֶפֶת, הֶבֶל). However, the form with *è* is also sometimes found in pause, along with that in *ā*, e.g. חֶסֶד together with חָסֶד; and very frequently only the form with *Sᵉghôl*, e.g. מֶלֶךְ, דֶּשֶׁא *grass*, נֶצַח *perpetuity*, פֶּלֶא *a wonder*, צֶדֶק *righteousness*, קֶדֶם *the East*, יֶשַׁע *help*, &c.—With two *Sᵉghôls*, although with a middle guttural, we find לֶחֶם *bread* (in pause לָחֶם) and רֶחֶם *womb* (in pause רָחֶם), besides רַחַם Ju 5³⁰ (in pause רֹחַם). A helping *Sᵉghôl* always stands before a final א, as דֶּשֶׁא טֶנֶא (with suff. טַנְאֲךָ), פֶּרֶא, פֶּלֶא (also written פֶּרֶה), except in גֵּיא, see *v*.

B. The *constr. st.* is almost always the same as the *absolute*. Sometimes, however, under the influence of a final guttural or ר, Pathaḥ appears in the second syllable as the principal vowel (see below, *s*), e.g. גֶּבֶר ψ 18²⁶; זֶרַע

Paradigms of

I.

	a.	b.	c.	d.	e.	f.
Sing. absolute	מֶלֶךְ	סֵפֶר	קֹדֶשׁ	נַעַר	נֵצַח	פֹּעַל
	(king)	(book)	(sanctuary)	(a youth)	(perpetuity)	(work)
„ construct	מֶלֶךְ	סֵפֶר	קֹדֶשׁ	נַעַר	נֵצַח	פֹּעַל
„ with light suff.	מַלְכִּי	סִפְרִי	קָדְשִׁי	נַעֲרִי	נִצְחִי	פָּעֳלִי
	מַלְכְּךָ	סִפְרְךָ	קָדְשְׁךָ	נַעַרְךָ	נִצְחֲךָ	פָּעָלְךָ
„ with grave suff.	מַלְכְּכֶם	סִפְרְכֶם	קָדְשְׁכֶם	נַעַרְכֶם	נִצְחֲכֶם	פָּעָלְכֶם
Plur. absolute	מְלָכִים	סְפָרִים	[קָדָשִׁים]	נְעָרִים	נִצָחִים	פְּעָלִים
„ construct	מַלְכֵי	סִפְרֵי	קָדְשֵׁי	נַעֲרֵי	נִצְחֵי	פָּעֳלֵי
„ with light suff.	מְלָכַי	סְפָרַי	[קָדָשַׁי]	נְעָרַי	נִצָחַי	פְּעָלַי
„ with grave suff.	מַלְכֵיכֶם	סִפְרֵיכֶם	קָדְשֵׁיכֶם	נַעֲרֵיכֶם	נִצְחֵיכֶם	פָּעֳלֵיכֶם
Dual absolute	רַגְלַיִם	קֳבָצַיִם	מָתְנַיִם	נַעֲלַיִם		
	(feet)	(two heaps)	(loins)	(sandals)		
		[proper name.]				
„ construct	רַגְלֵי		מָתְנֵי	נַעֲלֵי		

II.

	a.	b.	c.	d.	e.	f.
Sing. absolute	דָּבָר	חָכָם	זָקֵן	כָּתֵף	חָצֵר	שָׂדֶה
	(word)	(wise)	(an old man)	(shoulder)	(court)	(field)
„ construct	דְּבַר	חֲכַם	זְקַן	כֶּתֶף	חֲצַר	שְׂדֵה
„ with light suff.	דְּבָרִי	חֲכָמִי	זְקֵנִי	כְּתֵפִי	חֲצֵרִי	שָׂדִי
	דְּבָרְךָ	חֲכָמְךָ				שָׂדְךָ
„ with grave suff.	דְּבַרְכֶם	חֲכַמְכֶם				
Plur. absolute	דְּבָרִים	חֲכָמִים	זְקֵנִים		חֲצֵרִים	פָּנִים
„ construct	דִּבְרֵי	חַכְמֵי	זִקְנֵי		חַצְרֵי	פְּנֵי
„ with light suff.	דְּבָרַי	חֲכָמַי	זְקֵנַי		חֲצֵרַי	פָּנַי
„ with grave suff.	דִּבְרֵיכֶם	חַכְמֵיכֶם	זִקְנֵיכֶם		חַצְרֵיכֶם	פְּנֵיכֶם
Dual absolute	כְּנָפַיִם	חֲלָצַיִם	יְרֵכַיִם			פָּנִים
	(wings)	(loins)	(thighs)			(face)
„ construct	כְּנָפֵי					

Masculine Nouns.

I.

g.	h.	i.	k.	l.	m.	n.
מָ֫וֶת	זַ֫יִת	שׁוֹט	פְּרִי	יָם	אֵם	חֹק
(death)	(olive)	(whip)	(fruit)	(sea)	(mother)	(statute)
מוֹת	זֵית	שׁוֹט	פְּרִי	יַם, יָם	אֵם	חָק־
מוֹתִי	זֵיתִי	שׁוֹטִי	פִּרְיִי	יַמִּי	אִמִּי	חֻקִּי
מוֹתְךָ	זֵיתְךָ	שׁוֹטְךָ	פֶּרְיְךָ	יַמְּךָ	אִמְּךָ	חָקְךָ
מוֹתְכֶם	זֵיתְכֶם	שׁוֹטְכֶם	פֶּרְיְכֶם	יַמְּכֶם	אִמְּכֶם	חָקְכֶם
[מוֹתִים]	זֵיתִים	שׁוֹטִים	גְּדָיִים	יַמִּים	אִמּוֹת	חֻקִּים
מוֹתִי	זֵיתֵי	שׁוֹטֵי	גְּדָיֵי	יַמֵּי	אִמּוֹת	חֻקֵּי
	זֵיתַי	שׁוֹטַי	(kids)	יַמַּי	אִמּוֹתַי	חֻקַּי
	זֵיתֵיכֶם	שׁוֹטֵיכֶם		יַמֵּיכֶם	אִמּוֹתֵיכֶם	חֻקֵּיכֶם
	עֵינַ֫יִם	יוֹמַ֫יִם	לְחָיַ֫יִם	כַּפַּ֫יִם	שִׁנַּ֫יִם	
	(eyes)	(two days, biduum)	(cheeks)	(hands)	(teeth)	
	עֵינַי	שׁוֹטַי	לְחָיֵי	כַּפֵּי	שִׁנֵּי	

III.

a.	b.	c.
עוֹלָם	אֹיֵב	חֹזֶה
(eternity)	(enemy)	(seer)
עוֹלָם	אֹיֵב	חֹזֶה
עוֹלָמִי	אֹיְבִי	חֹזִי
עוֹלָמְךָ	אֹיִבְךָ	חֹזְךָ
עוֹלָמְכֶם	אֹיִבְכֶם	חֹזְכֶם
עוֹלָמִים	אֹיְבִים	חֹזִים
עוֹלָמֵי	אֹיְבֵי	חֹזֵי
עוֹלָמַי	אֹיְבַי	חֹזַי
עוֹלָמֵיכֶם	אֹיְבֵיכֶם	חֹזֵיכֶם
מֶלְקָחַ֫יִם	מֹאזְנַ֫יִם	
(pair of tongs)	(balance)	
	מֹאזְנֵי	

IV.

a.	b.	c.
פָּקִיד	עָנִי	כְּתָב
(overseer)	(poor)	(writing)
פָּקִיד	עָנִי	כְּתָב
פְּקִידִי		כְּתָבִי
פְּקִידְךָ		כְּתָבְךָ
פְּקִידְכֶם		כְּתָבְכֶם
פְּקִידִים	עֲנִיִּים	[כְּתָבִים]
פְּקִידֵי	עֲנִיֵּי	[כְּתָבֵי]
פְּקִידַי		[כְּתָבַי]
פְּקִידֵיכֶם	עֲנִיֵּיכֶם	[כְּתָבֵיכֶם]
שְׁבֻעַ֫יִם		
(two weeks)		

(only in Nu 11⁷, before Maqqeph), סְחָר‎ ‎חֲדַר‎ Ju 3²⁴ (but Ct 3⁴ חֶדְרִי‎), נֶטַע‎ as
well as זְרַע‎, &c. ; cf., moreover, קָחַת‎ 2 K 12⁹ (for קַחַת‎, *infin. constr.* from לָקַח‎).

i C. The ה‎ָ *locale* is, according to § 90 *i*, regularly added to the already
developed form, e. g. נֶגְדָּה‎ ψ 116¹⁴·¹⁸ : הַפֶּתְחָה‎ Gn 19⁶, *to the door* ; but also with
a firmly closed syllable נֶגְבָּה‎ Ex 40²⁴ ; under the influence of a guttural or ר‎,
אַרְצָה‎, חַדְרָה‎, in *pause* אָרְצָה‎ (cf. זֹרְחָה‎ 1 Ch 14¹⁶, from זֶרַח‎).

k D. The suffixes of the singular are likewise added to the ground-form, but
forms with middle guttural take *Ḥaṭeph-Paṭaḥ* instead of the *Šᵉwâ quiescens* ;
נַעֲרִי‎, &c. (but also לְחָמִי‎, וַעֲמִי‎, &c.). In a rather large number of *qǎṭl*-forms,
however, before suffixes in the sing., as well as in the *constr. st.* plur. and
dual, the *ǎ* of the first syllable is attenuated to *ĭ*,[1] thus בִּטְנִי‎ *my womb*, יִתְרוֹ‎ ;
so in בֶּגֶד‎, בֶּצַע‎, גֵּו‎, זֶבַח‎, טֶבַח‎, פֶּשַׁע‎, פֶּתַח‎, צֶדֶק‎, קֶבֶר‎, קֶרֶב‎, רֶשַׁע‎, שֶׁמֶשׁ‎, and
many others. In some cases of this kind besides the form with *ǎ* there most
probably existed another with original *ĭ* in the first syllable ; thus certainly
with יֵשַׁע‎ beside יִשְׁעֲ‎, נֵצַח‎ beside נִצְחֲ‎, &c. (According to the *Diqduqe ha-ṭᵉamim*,
§ 36, the *absolute st.* in such cases takes *ê*, the *constr. ê* ; cf. נֵדֶר‎ Nu 30⁴ (*absol.*)
and נֶדֶר‎ 30¹⁰ (*constr.*) ; שֵׁבֶר‎ Lv 24²⁰ (*absol.*) and שֶׁבֶר‎ Am 6⁶ (*constr.*). According
to this theory[2] פֶּלֶא‎ (so the best authorities) Is 9⁵ would be the *constr. st.*,
although the accentuation requires an *absol. st.*)—A weakening of the firmly
closed syllable occurs in בִּגְדִי‎, &c. from בֶּגֶד‎ and יָקְבֶךָ‎ Dt 15¹⁴, 16¹³, in both
cases evidently owing to the influence of the palatal in the middle of the
stem. With *Sᵉghôl* for *ĭ* : נֶגְדִּי‎, יֶשְׁעֲךָ‎, הֶבְלִי‎, &c.

l E. In the plural the termination וֹת‎ is found as well as ־ִים‎, e. g. נְפָשׁוֹת‎,
עֲצָמוֹת‎ together with נְפָשִׁים‎ (Ez 13²⁰ [but read חַפְשִׁים‎ ; see comm.]), &c.,
constr. st. נַפְשׁוֹת‎. Other nouns have only the ending וֹת‎, e.g. אֲרָצוֹת‎, *constr.*
אַרְצוֹת‎ from אֶרֶץ‎. Without *Qameṣ* before the ending ־ִים‎ we find רַחֲמִים‎
(*bowels*) *mercy*. On the numerals עֶשְׂרִים‎ *twenty*, &c., cf. § 97 *f*, note 2. Moreover *a* is not inserted before plural suffixes with the tone on the penultima
in אַשְׁרֵיךָ‎, &c., properly *thy happiness!* (a word which is only used in the *constr.
st. pl.* and at an early period became stereotyped as a kind of interjection).

m F. In the *constr. st.* plural a firmly closed syllable is sometimes found,
contrary to the rule, e. g. בְּכַסְפֵּיהֶם‎ Gn 42²⁵·³⁵ ; רִשְׁפֵי‎ Ct 8⁶ (רִשְׁפֵי‎ ψ 76⁴) ; טַרְפֵּי‎
Ez 17⁹ ; צָמְדֵי‎ Is 5¹⁰, and so always in נִסְכֵּיכֶם‎ Nu 29³⁹, נִסְכֵּיהֶם‎, ψ 16⁴, &c. (on
the other hand, according to the best authorities *not* in חַסְדֵי‎ Is 55³, &c.,
though in ψ 107⁴³ Ginsburg reads חַסְדֵי‎) ; cf. § 46 *d*. Even with a middle
guttural בַּעֲלֵיהֶן‎ Est 1¹⁷·²⁰.—The attenuation of *ǎ* to *ĭ* also occurs sometimes
in this form (see above, *k*), e.g. זִבְחֵי‎, &c., even יִלְדֵי‎ Is 57⁴ beside יַלְדֵי‎
Ho 1², &c.

n G. In the *dual absol.* beside forms like רַגְלַיִם‎ *feet*, with suff. רַגְלֶיךָ‎, רַגְלָיו‎, &c.
אַלְפַּיִם‎ *two thousand*, נַעֲלַיִם‎ *sandals*, בִּרְכַּיִם‎ *knees* (*ǎ* attenuated to *ĭ*, *constr. st.* בִּרְכֵּי‎
with a firmly closed syllable), with suffixes בִּרְכַּי‎, בִּרְכֵּי‎, &c. (cf., however, בִּרְכֵּיהֶם‎
Ju 7⁶), forms with pretonic *Qameṣ* are also found (in consequence of the

[1] According to M. Lambert, *REJ*. 1896, p. 21, *a* tends to remain with labials ;
so in 14 cases out of 22 masculines, and in 3 out of 6 feminines.
[2] Probably only a theory of one particular school and not generally accepted,
or at any rate not consistently carried out ; cf. König, *Lehrgeb.*, ii. 22.

tendency to assimilate the dual to the plural in form : so König, *Lehrgeb.*,
ii. 17), as קְרָנַיִם *horns*, with suff. קַרְנָיו (Dn 8³ ᶠᶠ·; elsewhere always קְרָנַיִם,
קַרְנָיו, &c.), and so always דְּלָתַיִם, *constr. st.* דִּלְתֵי *folding-doors*, דְּרָבַיִם (?) *double
way.*

2. On Paradigms *b* and *e*. With a final א rejected (but retained orthographically) we find חֵטְא *sin*. An initial guttural before suffixes generally
receives Sᵉghôl instead of the original *i*, e.g. עֶזְרִי, חֶלְקִי, &c., so in the *constr. st.
plur.* עֶגְלֵי, &c. ; חֵטְא forms חֲטָאִי 2 K 10²⁹, &c., retaining the Qameṣ of חֲטָאִים
before the weak א.—The pausal forms סָתֶר and שָׁבֶט (out of pause always
שֵׁבֶט, סֵתֶר) go back to by-forms סָתֶר, שָׁבֶט.—On עֲשָׂבוֹת (*constr. st.* plur. of עֵשֶׂב)
Pr 27²⁵, cf. § 20 *h* ; שִׁקְמִים *sycamores*, without Qameṣ before the termination
ִים (see above, *l*), is probably from the sing. שִׁקְמָה found in the Mišna.

3. On Paradigms *c* and *f.* קֶשְׁט occurs in Pr 22²¹ without a helping vowel ; *p*
with a middle guttural פֹּעַל, &c., but with ה also אֹהֶל, בֹּהֶן ; with a final
guttural גֹּבַהּ, רֹבַע, &c., but with א, אֹמֶא ; with a firmly closed syllable אֹסְפֵי
Mi 7¹.

Before suffixes the original *u* sometimes reappears in the sing., e.g. גֻּדְלִי *q*
(ψ 150²) beside גָּדְלוֹ, from גֹּדֶל *greatness* ; סֻבְּלוֹ (with Dageš *forte dirimens*, and
the *u* repeated in the form of a Ḥaṭeph-Qameṣ, cf. § 10 *h*) Is 9³, &c. ; וּשְׁמָה
Ez 22²⁴.—Corresponding to the form פָּעֳלְכֶם *pŏ'ŏlkhèm* we find קָטְבֵךְ Ho 13¹⁴,
even without a middle guttural ; similarly קְטָנִי (so Jablonski and Opitius)
1 K 12¹⁰, 2 Ch 10¹⁰, from קֹטֶן *little finger* ; but the better reading is, no doubt,
קָטְנִי (so ed. Mant., 'the ק proleptically assuming the vowel of the following
syllable' ; König, *Lehrgeb.*, ii. 69), and the form is to be derived, with König,
from קֹטֶן, not *qŭtŭn*, as Brockelmann quotes him, in *Grundriss*, p. 103. The
reading קְטָנִי (Baer and Ginsburg) is probably not due to a confusion of the
above two readings, but ְ is merely intended to mark the vowel expressly
as *ŏ*. In the forms פָּעֳלוֹ Is 1³¹ (for פָּעֳלוֹ) and תָּאֳרוֹ Is 52¹⁴ (for תָּאֳרוֹ 1 S 28¹⁴),
the lengthening of the original *u* to *ō* has been retained even before the suffix ;
cf. § 63 *p* and § 74 *h* (בְּמֹצַאֲכֶם Gn 32²⁰).—In the same way *ō* remains before
ה locale, e.g. גֹּרְנָה, הָאֹהֱלָה Gn 18⁶, 24⁶⁷, &c. Dissimilation of the vowel (or
a by-form נֶבַח ?) seems to occur in נְכֹחוֹ Ex 14², Ez 46⁹, for נֹכַח.

In the *absol. st. plur.* the original *u* generally becomes Šᵉwâ before the Qameṣ, *r*
e.g. בְּקָרִים from בֹּקֶר *morning*, פְּעָלִים *works*, רְמָחִים *lances*, שְׁעָלִים *handfuls* (*constr.
st.* שַׁעֲלֵי Ez 13¹⁹) ; on the other hand, with an initial guttural the *u*-sound reappears as Ḥaṭeph Qameṣ, e.g. חֳדָשִׁים *months*, עֳפָרִים *gazelles*, אֳרָחוֹת *ways* ; and
so even without an initial guttural, הַגֳּרָנוֹת *the threshing-floors*, 1 S 23¹, Jo 2²⁴ ;
קֳדָשִׁים *sanctuaries*, and שֳׁרָשִׁים *roots* (*qŏdhāšim*, &c., with *ŏ* for ְ) ; also קֳדָשַׁי
[but קֳדָשָׁיו, קֳדָשָׁיךְ, once קֳ, where, however, the reading frequently fluctuates
between קְ and קֳ ; with the article הַקֳּ, בַּקֳּ, לַקֳּ, according to Baer and
Ginsburg. On these forms cf. especially § 9 *v*. From אֹהֶל *tent*, both
אֹהָלִים and בָּאֳהָלִים (cf. § 23 *h* and פָּעֳלוֹ above) are found ; with light suffixes
אָהֳלִי, &c.; so from אֹרַח *way*, אָרְחֹתַי (also אֳרָחֹתַי)—hence only with initial א,
'on account of its weak articulation' (König, *Lehrgeb.*, ii. 45). It seems that
by these different ways of writing a distinction was intended between the

plural of אׇרְחׇה *caravan*, and of אׇרַח *way*; however, אׇרְחוֹת is also found in the former sense (in *constr. st.* Jb 6¹⁹) and אׇרְחוֹת in the latter (e. g. Jb 13²⁷ according to the reading of Ben Naphtali and Qimḥi); cf. also אׇנִיּוֹת 2 Ch 8¹⁸ *K*ᵉ*th.* (אֳנִי *Q*ᵉ*rê*).—The *constr. st.* plural of בֹּהֶן *thumb* is בְּהֹנוֹת Ju 16 ᶠˑ, as if from a sing. בֹּהֶן: of נֹגַהּ *brightness*, Is 59⁹ נְגֹהוֹת (on these *q*ᵉ*ṭōl*-forms, cf. *t*).—If אׇפְנׇיו Pr 25¹¹ is not dual but plural (see the Lexicon) it is then analogous to the examples, given in *l* and *o*, of plurals without a pretonic *Qameṣ*; cf. בְּטׇנִים *pistachio nuts*, probably from a sing. בׇּטְנׇה. According to Barth, *ZDMG.* xlii, 345 f. אׇפְנׇיו is a sing. (אׇפְנׇי, the ground-form of אׇפְנׇה, with suffix).

In the *constr. st. plur.* the only example with original *ŭ* is רׇכְבֵי ψ 31²¹; otherwise like אׇהֳלֵי, קׇדְשֵׁי, &c.

s　　4. Besides the forms treated hitherto we have to consider also a series of formations, which have their characteristic vowel under the *second* radical, as is ordinarily the case in Aramaic (on the origin of these forms see further, § 84ᵃ *e*). Thus (*a*) of the form קְטַל; דְּבַשׁ *honey*, מְעַט *little*; in pause, דְּבׇשׁ, גְּבַר מְעׇט; גְּבַר *man* (as *constr. st.*, see above, *h*), ψ 18²⁶ (elsewhere always גֶּֽבֶר), and infinitives like שְׁכַב (§ 45 *c*; on קְחַת, see above, *h*); שְׁכֶם *shoulder, ă* being modified to *è* (but in pause שְׁכׇֽם); locative שְׁכֶֽמׇה, also שְׁכֶֽמׇה Ho 6⁹. With suffixes in the usual manner שׇׁכְמִי, שׇׁכְבׇה Gn 19³³·³⁵ (an infin. with suffix, therefore not שְׁכׇבׇהּ). On the other hand, the *ă* is retained in the *plur. absol.* by sharpening the final consonant: אֲגַמִּים (*constr.* אַגְמֵי) *marshes*, הֲדַסִּים *myrtles*, מְעַטִּים *few*.

t　　(*b*) Of the form קְטֵל: בְּאֵר *a well*, זְאֵב *wolf*, &c.¹; *locative* בְּאֵרׇה, with *suff.* בְּאֵרִי, *plur.* זְאֵבִים, זְאֵבֵי; but בְּאֵרוֹת, *constr.* בְּאֵרֹת; on the *infin. constr.* שְׂאֵת, cf. § 76 *b*.

(*c*) of the form קְטֹל: בְּאֹשׁ *stench* (with *suff.* בׇּאְשׁוֹ, just as סׇבְכוֹ occurs in Jer 4⁷ along with the *constr. st.* סְבׇךְ־ ψ 74⁵; cf. for the Dageš, § 20 *h*), perhaps also לְאֹם *nation*, pl. לְאֻמִּים.

u　　5. Paradigms *g-i* comprise the segholate forms with middle ו or י: (*a*) of the form *qaṭl* with *Wāw* as a strong consonant, in which cases the original *ă* is almost always lengthened to *ā* (Paradigm *g*), thus מׇֽוֶת, אׇֽוֶן *vanity*, עׇֽוֶל *iniquity*, תׇּֽוֶךְ *midst*; with final א, שׇׁוְא *falsehood*; cf. however, also רֶֽוַח *space*. In the *constr. st.* contraction always occurs, מוֹת, &c. (from original *maut*), and likewise before suffixes מוֹתִי, &c. Exception, עׇוֶל as *constr. st.* Ez 28¹⁸ (according to Qimḥi) and with suff. עַוְלוֹ. The contraction remains in all cases in the plural (but see below, *w*).

v　　(*b*) Of the form *qaṭl* with consonantal *Yôdh* (Paradigm *h*). With final א, גַּיְא (also גַּיְ), in Is 40⁴ גֵּיְא, in the *constr. st.* (also *absol.* Zc 14⁴) גֵּיְא (also גֵּיְ); plur. 2 K 2¹⁶ and Ez 6³ *K*ᵉ*th.* according to Baer גֵּאׇיוֹת, i. e. doubtless גֵּאׇיוֹת (cf. גֵּיאֹתֶיךׇ Ez 35⁸; according to another reading [and so Ginsburg] גֵּיׇאוֹת,

---

¹ The proposal of Haupt (*SBOT.* 'Proverbs', p. 34, l. 44 ff.) to read זְאֵב בְּאֵר, &c., does not seem to be warranted. The case here is quite different from that in Pr 1²² where the Masora requires תְּאֵהֲבוּ, no doubt on the analogy of בְּאֵר, &c., for תְּאֵהֲבוּ, which was probably intended, see § 63 *m*.

i. e. doubtless גְּאָיוֹת), but in *Qᵉrê*, and all other passages, גֵּאָיוֹת. The uncontracted form (in the *absol. st.* with helping *Ḥireq*) remains also before ה‍ָ‍
locale, e. g. בַּיְתָה (but in the *constr. st.* e. g. בֵּיתָה יוֹסֵף).—עִירֹה (from עִיר) Gn 49¹¹
is peculiar, so also שִׂיחוֹ Is 10¹⁷ (from שִׂיחַ).—In the *plural absol.* uncontracted
forms occur, like חֲיָלִים *hosts*, עֲיָנוֹת *springs*, עֲיָרִים *young asses*, תְּיָשִׁים *he-goats*,
&c.; as *constr. st.* Pr 8²⁸ עֵינוֹת for עֲיָנוֹת.

(*c*) With the contraction of the ו and י even in the *absol. st.* sing. (Paradigm *i*). In this way there arise formations which are unchangeable
throughout; thus from the ground-form *qăṭl*: יוֹם (cf., however, § 96), סוּף,
שׁוֹר, &c.; with middle *Yôdh*, חַיִל 1 Ch 9¹³ (elsewhere חֵיל, הַחַיִל), לֵיל Is 21¹¹ (elsewhere לַיִל, in prose לַיְלָה, see above, § 90 *f*); from the ground-form *qĭṭl*, דִּין,
עִיר, שִׁיר (see, however, § 96); from the ground-form *qŭṭl*, גּוּר, רוּחַ, &c. The
plurals דְּוָדִים *pots*, שְׁוָקִים *streets*, שְׁוָרִים *oxen*, have a strong formation (but for
חֲוָחִים 1 S 13⁶ read חוֹרִים as in 14¹¹). Finally, forms with a quiescent middle
א also belong to this class, such as רֹאשׁ *head* (obscured from רֵאשׁ = *ra'š*, see
§ 96) and צֹאן *sheep*.

6. On Paradigm *k*: segholate forms from לְ״ה stems. Besides the formations
mentioned in § 84ᵃ *c*, ε, like בֶּכֶה, &c., and שָׁחוּ Ez 47⁵, with the original ו
resolved, according to § 24 *d* (cf. the *constr. plur.* חַגְוֵי *clefts*, Ob ³, &c., and קַצְוֵי
ends, ψ 48¹¹, &c., where the ו becomes again a strong consonant,[1] from חֵנְו and
קֵצְו or חָנוּ and קָצוּ), there occur also (*a*) commonly, of the ground-form *qaṭl*,
forms like צְבִי, לְחִי, גְּדִי, בְּכִי, פְּרִי, אֲרִי, &c.; in *pause* פֶּרִי, בֶּכִי, לָחִי, צֶבִי (cf.
§ 29 *m*), but אֲרִי Ju 14¹⁸; with suffixes פִּרְיוֹ (attenuated from *păryó*), בִּכְיִי ψ 6⁹,
but also לֶחְיֶךָ, פֶּרְיֶךָ, &c.; before a grave suffix פֶּרְיְהֶם, but also פְּרִיכֶם. Plur.
גְּדָיִים (constr. גְּדָיֵי, see above, *o*), חֲטָאִים), אֲרָיִים and אֲרָיוֹת; with softening of the
י to א (as elsewhere in בִּלְוֹאֵי Jer 38¹² for which there is בְּלוֹי in verse 11,
according to § 8 *k*; עֶרְבִיאִים 2 Ch 17¹¹, cf. 26⁷ *Kᵉth*.; probably in לְלָאוֹת, דּוּדָאִים
from דּוּדַי and לוּלַי; also חֲלֹבָאִים ψ 10¹⁰ *Kᵉth*., divided into two words by the
Masora, is to be referred to a sing. חֲלְכַּי *hapless*): חֲלָאִים *jewels*, Ct 7² (from
חֲלִי), טְלָאִים *lambs*, Is 40¹¹ (from טְלִי); but instead of פְּתָאִים and צְבָאִים (from
פֶּתִי and צְבִי) the Masora requires פְּתָאִים and צְבָאִים; dual: לְחָיַיִם, *constr. st.*
לְחָיֵי, with *suff.* לְחָיַי, &c. On דַּל *door*, cf. § 95 *f*, and on such formations
generally, see Barth on biliteral nouns in *ZDMG.* 1887, p. 603 ff., and *Nominalbildung* (isolated nouns), p. 1 ff.

(*b*) From the ground-form *qĭṭl*, חֲצִי *half*, in *pause* חֵצִי, with *suff.* חֶצְיוֹ, &c.—
From stems with middle *Wāw* arise such forms as אִי (from *'iwy*), עִי, צִי,
ship, plur. אִיִּים, צִיִּים, &c.; instead of the extraordinary plur. צִים Nu 24²⁴ read
with the Samaritan יֹוְצְאִים, and for בַּצִּים Ez 30⁹ read probably with Cornill
אֳצִים.

(*c*) From the ground-form *qŭṭl* sometimes forms like תֹּהוּ, בֹּהוּ (from *tŭhw*,
bŭhw), sometimes like חֳלִי, עֳנִי, and even without an initial guttural דְּמִי, יְפִי,

---

[1] Nöldeke, *Beiträge*, p. 58: the direct or indirect retention of this ו is hardly
a feature of early Hebrew. The true Hebrew forms from קָצָה would be קָצֶה,
קָצוֹת, the aramaizing forms קָצֶה, קָצָת, קַצְוֹת.

צְרִי (also צֶרִי, יְפִי, דְּמִי (צְרִי), רָאִי, &c ; in *pause* חֹלִי, &c., with suff.חָלְיוֹ, plur. חֳלָיִים.
From עֳפִי *branch*, there occurs in ψ 104¹² the plur. עֳפָאִים (analogous to פְּתָאִים,
&c., see above, *x*) ; the Kᵉth. evidently intends עֳפָאִים (so Opitius and others).
Dual, with *suff.* דָּלְיָו Nu 24⁷, *bucket* (from דְּלִי, for דְּלְיָ), more correctly, with the
Masora, דָּלְיָו with Munaḥ for Metheg. This unusual Metheg is to be treated
as following the analogy of the cases mentioned in § 9 *v*.

aa 7. On Paradigms *l-n* : segholate forms from stems ע״ע (see § 84ᵃ *c*, β).

(*a*) In the *qaṭl*-form the ă of the contracted formation is sometimes lengthened
in the *absol. st.*, sing. as in יָם (so also in the *constr. st.*, except in the combination יַם־סוּף *the Red sea*; and even before *Maqqeph* יָם־הַמֶּלַח *the salt sea*),
sometimes it remains short, e. g. פַּת *morsel*, עַם *people*, but even these formations generally have *Qameṣ* in pause, as well as after the article (e. g. הָעָם).
Adjectives under the influence of a guttural either have forms like לָחִים,
צָחִים or, with *compensatory lengthening*, רָעִים, רֵעֵי. In the *constr. st.* חַי *living*
(in the plural חַיִּים also a substantive, *life*), and דַּי *sufficiency*, are contracted to
חֵי¹ and דֵּי. As a locative form notice הָרָה *to the mountain*, Gn 14¹⁰ (see § 27 *q*)
beside הָהָרָה. The stem is expanded to a triliteral form in הֲרָרִי (unless it is
simply derived from a by-form הָרָר on the analogy of *qāṭāl*-forms) Jer 17³
(but in ψ 30⁸ for הַרְרִי read הֲרֵרִי) and הַרְרָם Gn 14⁶ ; plur. *constr.* הַרְרֵי Nu 23⁷,
&c. (but only in poetical passages), with suffix, הַרְרֶיהָ Dt 8⁹ ; עֲמָמִים Ju 5¹⁴
(where, however, read probably בַּעֲמָקֵיך), Neh 9²² ; עֲמָמֵי Neh 9²⁴ : elsewhere
עֲמָמִים, עַמֵּי.—Before *suffixes* and in the plur. ă is sometimes attenuated to ĭ,
e. g. פִּתִּי, פִּתִּים, from פַּת ; סִפִּים and סִפּוֹת סִפּוֹת (also סִפּוֹת 2 S 17²⁸) from סַף.
Before ה ă is retained in a virtually sharpened syllable, e. g. פַּחִים *traps*.

bb (*b*) *Qiṭl*-forms : אֵם אֵם, אֵשׁ *fire* (with suff. אִשּׁי, but cf. also אֶשְׁבָּה Is 50¹¹),
חֵן *favour*, &c. ; of a triliteral form, the plur. חֲצָצֶיך ψ 77¹⁸.

(*c*) *Quṭl*-forms : כֹּל חֹק *totality*, before *Maqqeph* כָּל־, חָק־, with suff. חֻקִּי, &c.,
with omission of *Dageš forte* (according to § 20 *m*) always חָקְך, חָקְכֶם, but from
עֹז עֻזְּך, עֻזְּכֶם, עֳזְך, for which עֻזִּי and עֻזְּך are also found. חֻקְקִי, expanded to
a triliteral form, Ju 5¹⁵ and Is 10¹, generally explained as a secondary form
of חֻקִּי with abnormal weakening of the ŭ to ĭ, is more probably to be referred
to a *qiṭl*-form = Arabic *ḥiqq*.

cc The forms with assimilated middle *Nûn* likewise follow the analogy of
Paradigms *l-n*, e. g. אַף *nose, anger* (אַפִּי, dual אַפַּיִם, also *face*) for 'anp ; חֵך *palate*
for *ḥink*, זִקִּים *fetters*, עֵז *goat*, plur. עִזִּים, for 'inz, probably also אֵב *green herb*,
for 'inb.

dd 2. Paradigm II comprises all formations with original short vowels,
whether in the first or second syllable ; cf. § 84ᵃ *f-i*, and the general
laws of formation, § 92 *b-g*.

---

¹ חֵי only in Dn 12⁷ as *constr. st.*, since in the asseverative formulae (cf.
§ 149) חֵי נַפְשְׁך, חֵי פַרְעֹה (otherwise only in 2 S 15²¹, after יהוה חַי, and
Amos 8¹⁴), חֵי is a contracted form of the *absol. st.* (prop. *living is Pharaoh !* &c.).
It is evidently only a rabbinical refinement which makes the pronunciation
חַי distinctive of an oath by God (or of God by himself), as in the regular
formulae חַי אָנִי (חַי אָנֹכִי) Dt 32⁴⁰) and חַי יהוה (= חַי אֲדֹנָי).

Rem. 1. On Paradigms *a* and *b*: ground-form *qăṭăl*. The lengthening of the second *ă* to *ā* is maintained in the *constr. st. sing.* only in אָ״ל-forms, e.g. צָבָא *army*, צְבָא. For the construct forms חֲלֵב *milk*, לְבֶן־ *white*, Gn 49[12], instead of the ordinary absolutes חָלָב, לָבָן, a secondary form לְבָן, חֲלָב must be assumed; from עָשָׁן *smoke*, the *constr. st.* עֲשַׁן occurs once, Ex 19[18], beside עֲשַׁן, from הָדָר *ornament* the *constr. st.* הֲדַר Dn 11[20], beside the common form הֲדַר.—The plur. פָּרָשִׁים *horses*, Is 21[7] (instead of פְּרָשִׁים, ground-form *părăš*) is no doubt due to a confusion with the *qaṭṭăl*-form פָּרָשׁ *horseman*.

A. Sometimes a sharpening of the third radical takes place, in order to *ee* keep the preceding vowel short, e.g. גְּמַלִּים *camels*, קְטַנִּים *small ones*, פְּלַגּוֹת *brooks* (see § 20 *a*).—The attenuation of the *ă* of the first syllable to *ĭ* does not take place in the *constr. st. plur.* as a rule after an initial guttural, as חַכְמֵי, עֲנְוֵי, but חִזְקֵי, and never before a middle guttural, e.g. נַהֲרֵי; nor (according to König, owing to the influence of the nasal) in the non-guttural forms זַנְבוֹת *tails*, כַּנְפוֹת, and (in the dual) כַּנְפֵי *wings*, from זָנָב, כָּנָף.—The dual נַהֲרַיִם from נָהָר *river*, shows an abnormal omission of the lengthening of the *ă* before a tone-bearing termination, but cf. § 88 *c*.

B. From ע״ע stems, forms like חָלָל, עָנָן, &c., belong to this class. *ff*

C. The few nouns of the ground-form *qĭṭăl* follow the same analogy, such as *gg* לְבָב *heart*, שֵׁכָר *strong drink*, עֵנָב *grape*, &c. From שֵׂעָר *hair*, in the *constr. st.* besides שְׂעַר the form שַׂעַר is also found (perhaps a survival of a secondary form like those in Paradigm I, *d*); so from צֵלָע *rib*, צְלָע and even צֶלַע 2 S 16[13] (so ed. Mant., Ginsb.; but Baer צֵלַע), both, probably, old secondary forms (also used for the *absol. st.*) of צֵלָע; cf. also צַלְעִי and צַלְעוֹ, as well as the *constr. st. plur.* צַלְעוֹת; also from נֵכָר *strangeness*, the *constr. st.* נֵכַר־ is found, Dt 31[16].

2. On Paradigms *c–e*: ground-form *qăṭĭl*, developed to *qăṭēl*; with a final *hh* guttural, e.g. שָׂבֵעַ *satisfied*. In the *constr. st.* the original *ĭ* of the second syllable, probably on the analogy of the forms discussed in § 69 *c*, becomes *ă*, e.g. זְקַן, חֲדַל, חֲסַר, &c., but not before suffixes כְּתֵפִי, &c., nor in forms from אָ״ל stems, e.g. מָלֵא *full*, מְלָא; cf., moreover, עֲקֵב Gn 25[26] from עָקֵב *heel*, and אֲבֶל־ ψ 35[14], *mourning*. Paradigm *d* represents forms which in the *constr. st.* instead of the ordinary כְּתֵף, &c., have a segholate form, as עֶרֶל, גֹּדֶל, יֶרֶךְ, אֶרֶךְ (Ez 44[9]), *constr. st.* of אָרֵךְ *long*, גֶּדֶר *wall*, יֶרֶךְ *thigh*, גֹּזֶל *robbery*, עֶרֶל *uncircumcised*. In Is 11[14] בְּכָתֵף would be altogether without precedent as a *constr. st.* (for בְּכֶתֶף); most probably the *absol. st.* is intended by the Masora (according to Nöldeke, *Gött. Gel. Anzeigen*, 1871, No. 23 [p. 896] for בכ׳ אֶחָד *with one shoulder*, i.e. *shoulder to shoulder*); [cf. Driver, *Tenses*, § 190, *Obs.*].

In the *plur. constr.* the *ē* lengthened from *ĭ* is frequently retained in verbal *ii* adjectives of this formation, e.g. חֲפֵצֵי, יְשֵׁנֵי, אֲבֵלֵי, שְׂמֵחֵי, שְׁכֵחֵי; cf. also יְתֵדֹתָיו (with *ē* under the protection of the secondary tone) from יָתֵד *tent-peg*. On the other hand from יָרֵא *fearing*, always יִרְאֵי; cf. also רֹעֵי ψ 35[20] from רָעַע.—With *ă* retained in the initial syllable cf. אַחֵר *alius* (with a virtual sharpening of the ה).—From ע״ע stems come forms like מֵת *dead person*, גֵּר *resident stranger*, עֵד *witness*, with unchangeable *Ṣērê*; hence מֵתֵי, מֵתִים, &c.

Kindred in character are the formations from the ground-form *qăṭŭl*. This *kk* ground-form is regularly lengthened to *qāṭōl*, e. g. עָגֹל *round*, עָמֹק *deep*, אָדֹם *red* ; but before formative additions the short *ŭ* returns, protected by the sharpening of the following consonant (see *ee* above), as עֲגֻלִּים, &c. (but in stems with a third guttural or ר, גָּבְהָה (שְׁחֹרִים). The form עָגוֹל, 1 K 10¹⁹, is abnormal ; likewise עֲמוּקָה Pr 23²⁷, Jablonski (ed. Mant. עֲמֻקָה, Baer and Ginsburg עֲמֻקָּה).

ll 3. On Paradigm *f*: ground-form *qăṭăl* from ל״ה stems. As in verbs ל״ה § 75 *h*, the general rule is that before the terminations of the plur. and dual and before suffixes beginning with a vowel, the third radical is usually elided altogether. But besides שָׂדֶה the form שָׂדַי, with the final *Yôdh* retained, is also found in poetry (cf. also the singulars with suffixes, like מִשְׁתֵּיהֶם, in *ss*) ; in the same way final ו is retained in עָנָיו *the poor, constr.* עֲנָיו. The plur. of שָׂדֶה is שָׂדוֹת, *constr.* שְׂדוֹת (also שְׂדֵי, unless this is a *sing.*, contracted from שְׂדָי ; so Barth, *ZDMG*. xlii, p. 351). The *qăṭăl*-form (see § 84ᵃ *i*) רֵעֶה 2 S 15³⁷, 16¹⁶, 1 K 4⁵ is remarkable as a *constr. st.* (the reading רֵעֶה of Opitius and others is opposed to the express statement of the Masora). To the category of these forms also belongs without doubt פָּנִים *face* (only in *plur.*), פְּנֵי, פָּנַי, פְּנֵיכֶם, &c.

mm In a few formations of this kind the vowel of the second syllable appears to have been already lost in the *absol. st. sing.* ; so according to the ordinary view, in יָד *hand, constr.* יַד, with *suff.* יָדוֹ, but יֶדְכֶם ; plur. יָדוֹת, *constr.* יְדוֹת, dual יָדַיִם, with *suff.* יָדַי, יְדֵיכֶם, &c., and in דָּם *blood, constr.* דַּם, with *suff.* דָּמִי, but דִּמְכֶם (*ă* attenuated to *i*), plur. דָּמִים, דְּמֵי. But perhaps both these nouns are to be regarded as primitive (§ 81), and as original monosyllabic formations.

nn 3. Paradigm III comprises forms with an unchangeable vowel in the first syllable, whilst the vowel of the second syllable has been lengthened from an original short vowel and is therefore changeable. The special cases are to be distinguished in which the original short vowel is lengthened both *in* and *before* the tone, but in an open syllable becomes *Šᵉwâ* (Paradigm *a*, but cf. also examples like אוֹפַנִּים *wheels*, for אוֹפָן, and אֻלַמִּים *porches*), secondly, the cases in which the vowel becomes *Šᵉwâ* even *before* the tone (Paradigm *b*), and finally, those in which the termination of ל״ה formations is entirely lost (Paradigm *c*).

oo Rem. 1. On the model of עוֹלָם (which, moreover, is obscured from *ʿâlăm*), the following forms also are inflected : מְקֻטָּל (§ 85 *h*), in some cases with virtual sharpening of the third radical (see § 20 *a*), as מִבְטַחוֹ Jer 17⁷, ψ 40⁵, Jb 8¹⁴, &c. ; ל״א nouns of this form maintain the *Qames* in the *constr. st. plur.*, e. g. מִקְרָאֵי from מִקְרָא¹ ; on the other hand, in the plur. of the *participles Niph.* (§ 85 *n*) of verbs ל״א (which likewise belong to this class), are found not only regular forms like נִקְרָאִים but also נֶחְבָּאִים Jos 10¹⁷, נִטְמָאִים Ez 20³⁰ᶠ·,

---

¹ מְקַדְּשֵׁיהֶם Ez 7²⁴ for מְקַדְּשֹׁ׳ (from מִקְדָּשׁ) is wholly irregular; perhaps, however, the *part. Piʿēl* is intended, without *Dageš* in the ד (according to § 20 *m*).

and so always נְבָאִים (except Ez 13² הַנְּבָּאִים) and נִמְצָאִים 1 S 13¹⁵, 2 K 14¹⁴, &c. (except Ezr 8²⁵ הַנִּמְצָאִים in pause).[1]

Moreover, the other participles in *ā* also follow the analogy of עוֹלָם as *pp* regards the final syllable (מְקֻטָּל, מָקְטָל; cf., however, הַמּוֹשַׁב Gn 43¹² in close connexion; see the analogous cases in § 65 *d*); also שֻׁלְחָן *table* (§ 85 *u*; plur. שֻׁלְחָנוֹת (שֻׁלְחָנוֹת, *constr.* קָרְבָּן, *constr.* קָרְבַּן, hence in plur. *constr.* with *suff.* קָרְבְּנֵיהֶם Lv 7³⁸; עָקְרָב (§ 85 *w*), plur. עַקְרַבִּים (with sharpening of the final consonant for עָקְרָבִים, cf. also עֵירָם *naked*, plur. עֵירֻמִּים Gn 3⁷ [but in 2²⁵ עֲרוּמִּים, according to § 9 *o* an orthographic licence for עֲרֻמִּים from עֵרֹם], *nakedness*, 2 Ch 28¹⁵; קָרְדֹּם, קַרְדֻּמּוֹ; מַעֲמַקֵּי Is 51¹⁰; נִכְבַּדֵּי Is 23⁸ ᶠ; מִשְׁנַבִּי ψ 18³; even with attenuation of the *ā* to *i* מוֹרִגִּים *threshing instruments*, 2 S 24²², 1 Ch 21²³, from מוֹרַג), מַתָּן (§ 85 *g*), מָגֵן (§ 85 *i*), מָעוֹז (§ 85 *k*), inasmuch as they retain the *ā* of the first syllable, contrary to rule, even when not pretonic, e.g. מָעֲזִי, מָעֹז; מוֹשָׁב (§ 85 *g*); תּוֹשָׁב (§ 85 *p*), *constr. st. plur.* תֹּשָׁבֵי 1 K 17¹; also isolated forms according to § 84ᵃ *t*, and § 84ᵇ *b*, *c*, *k*, *m*, *n*, *o*. Cf. finally, צַוָּאר *neck* (from *ṣaw'ăr*), *constr. st.* צַוַּאר Jer 28¹⁰ ᶠᶠ., *constr. st. plur.* צַוְּארֵי Gn 45¹⁴, &c.

2. (Paradigm *b*; cf. § 84ᵃ *s*.) Instead of the original *i* in such forms as *qq* אֹיְבְכֶם (cf. 2 K 22²⁹), the second syllable more frequently has *ĕ*, e.g. יֹצֶרְךָ *thy creator*; with a closing guttural (according to § 91 *d*; but cf. also אֹבֵד Dt 32²⁸) forms are found sometimes like שֻׁלְחָתְךָ, sometimes like בֹּרַאֲךָ; *constr. st.* without *suff.* נֹטֵעַ ψ 94⁹ (according to § 65 *d*); with a middle guttural גֹּאֲלֵךְ Is 48¹⁷; cf. 43¹⁴.—The same analogy also is followed in the flexion of the other participles which have *ē* in the final syllable (מִתְקַטֵּל, מְקַטֵּל, &c.), see further, in § 84ᵇ *d*, גַּבֵּן, &c. (but with exceptions, as שְׁלִשִׁים שְׁלִשִׁים), and ibid. *l*, *p*; § 85 *i*, *k* (מִזְבֵּחַ *altar*, *constr. st.* מִזְבַּח, plur. מִזְבְּחוֹת), and ibid. *q*, but here also there are exceptions like מַקְהֵלִים ψ 26¹².

3. (Paradigm *c*: *part. Qal* of verbs ל״ה, differing from Paradigm II, *f* in the *rr* unchangeableness of the vowel of the first syllable.) In Ez 17¹⁵ *ē* in the *absol. st.* is abnormal, and *Sᵉghôl* in the *constr. st.* in 2 S 24¹¹ (so Opitius, Ginsburg; but Baer חֹזֶה, Ec 2¹⁵ (according to Baer, but not the Mantua ed.; מִקְרֶה Ec 3¹⁹ is in the *absol. st.*). To this class belong, as regards their formation, the ל״ה-forms mentioned in § 84ᵃ *r*, § 85 *g* (with *suff.*, e.g. הַמַּעַלְךָ Dt 20¹, *which brought thee up*), and *h*.

In a few instances, before a suffix beginning with a consonant, the original *ss* *ay* of the termination has been contracted to *ē*, and thus there arise forms which have apparently *plural suffixes*; as מַשְׁתֵּיהֶם Is 5¹², Dn 1¹⁰⋅¹⁶; מַרְאֵיהֶם *their appearance*, Dn 1¹⁵, Gn 41²¹, cf. Na 2⁵; נֹטֵיהֶם *who stretched them forth*, Is 42⁵; *defectively* אֹפֵהֶם Ho 7⁵ (cf. נֹחֵם Ez 34¹⁴); on the other hand, the examples in Is 14¹¹, Gn 47¹⁷, which were formerly classed with the above, are really plurals. But מַחֲנֶיךָ *thy camp*, Dt 23¹⁵ (מַחֲנֶךָ occurs just before),

---

[1] Brockelmann, *Grundriss*, p. 659, observes that except in 2 Ch 5¹¹, 35¹⁷ הַנִּמְצָאִים is always followed by a preposition governing a word, so that the punctuators perhaps intended to indicate a sort of *constr. st.*

מִקְנֶיךָ *thy cattle*, Is 30²³ (probably also שָׂדֶיךָ 1 K 2²⁶), מַרְאֶיךָ Ct 2¹⁴, and מַרְאָיו *the sight of him*, Jb 41¹ (with the ' here retained orthographically), מַעֲלָיו Ez 40³¹, &c., are still to be explained as singulars.—On a few other examples which may perhaps be thus explained, see § 124 *k*. Before the plural ending the original termination *ay* reappears in מֵמְחָים Is 25⁶ (*part. Pu.* from מָחָה).

tt 4. Paradigm IV comprises the forms with a changeable vowel (*a*, *b*), or a vowel which has already become *Šᵉwâ* (*c*), in the first syllable, and an unchangeable vowel in the second. With Paradigm *c* (which, however, for the most part consists merely of forms based on analogy, without biblical parallels) are also connected all the forms which have unchangeable vowels in both syllables, and therefore (like כְּתָב) cannot undergo any vowel changes.

uu Rem. 1. Analogous to פָּקִיד (ground-form *pāqîd*) are § 84ᵃ *k*, גְּדוֹל, &c. (with *ô*, not changeable *ō* for *ŭ*); in substantives like שָׁלוֹם, this *ô* is demonstrably obscured from *â* (Arab. *sălâm*); ibid. *l*, *m*, אָסוּר, אָסִיר, &c. ; § 85 *u*, זִכָּרוֹן, constr. זִכְרוֹן ; חִזָּיוֹן, constr. חֶזְיוֹן ; בִּלָּיוֹן, constr. בִּלְיוֹן (cf., however, the forms in the *constr. st.* עִצָּבוֹן, קִמָּמוֹן, and with the plural suffix עִזְבוֹנַיִךְ Ez 27¹² ff.) ; § 85 *w*, חַלָּמִישׁ, constr. חַלְמִישׁ ; § 85 *l*, מָקוֹם, &c.

vv 2. עָנִי (ground-form '*ăniy*, stem עָנָה) represents forms in which a final *Yôdh* has been resolved into *î* ; before formative additions the original *Yôdh* under the protection of a *Dageš forte* again becomes audible as a firm consonant, whilst the (originally short) vowel of the first syllable becomes *Šᵉwâ* ; cf. § 84ᵃ *l*, נָקִי, plur. נְקִים, and § 87 *a*.

ww 3. כְּתָב with unchangeable *â* in the second syllable, whilst the *Šᵉwâ* is weakened from a short vowel (Arab. *kĭtâb*) ; *constr. st.* כְּתָב־ Est 4⁸ (readings like כְּתַב 2 Ch 35⁴ are incorrect, although יְקַר Est 1¹⁴ and כְּתָב־ 4⁸ are supported by fairly good authority; however, these *qᵉtâl*-forms in Hebrew are probably all loan-words from the Aramaic). The only plural form found in the O. T. is עֲבָדֵיהֶם *their deeds*, Ec 9¹. In a narrower sense the forms enumerated in § 84ᵃ *n–p* belong to this class; in a wider sense all those which have unchangeable vowels throughout, thus § 84ᵃ *u*, § 84ᵇ *e* (קַטָּל, cf., however, the anomalous forms mentioned there), ibid. *f–i*, *m* (No. 34 f.), *n* (No. 39), *p* (No. 44), also partly § 85 *b–w* (especially *l* and *r*).

xx In opposition to the anomalous shortening of the form קַטָל (see above), cases are also found where pretonic vowels are retained even in the ante-penultima (with the secondary tone) ; cf. above, *ii* and *pp*, also of the form קָטִיל (properly *qătîl*) the examples שְׁלִישִׁים, פְּרִיצִים, סָרִיסִים, whilst the *constr. st. sing.* according to the rule, changes the *ā* into *Šᵉwâ* (פְּרִיץ, סָרִיס). (These are not to be confounded with forms like עָרִיץ *tyrant*, which is for עַרִיץ, and consequently has an unchangeable *Qameṣ*.) Of the form קָטוּל (*qâṭûl*) in this class are שָׁבוּעַ *week*, plur. שָׁבֻעִים and שָׁבֻעוֹת, *constr.* שְׁבֻעוֹת, but with *Metheg* of the secondary tone in the fifth syllable from the end, שְׁבֻעֹתֵיכֶם.—On מָעוֹן, מְעוֹנִי, &c., cf. § 85 *k*.

§ 94. *Formation of Feminine Nouns.*

1. The feminine ending ◌ָה, when appended to the masculine *a* forms treated in § 93, effects in almost all cases the same changes as are produced in the masculine forms by the addition of a light suffix, since in both cases the tone is moved one place farther forward (see § 92 *b*). The following scheme is based on the same division into four classes, with their subdivisions, as in § 93; a few special forms will be treated in § 95 in connexion with the paradigms of feminine nouns.

Paradigm I: segholate forms, with the feminine ending always *b* added to the ground-form, (*a*) מַלְכָּה *queen*, כַּבְשָׂה, and with attenuation of *ă* to *ĭ* כִּבְשָׂה *lamb*, רִצְפָּה *hot stone*, Is 6⁶ (from another root רָצְפָּה; see Baer on Ez 40¹⁷), חֶזְקָה *strength* (unless belonging to Paradigm *b*); (*b*) סִתְרָה *covering* (masc. סֵתֶר); עֶדְנָה *pleasure* (עֵדֶן), not to be confounded with the unchangeable forms with a prefixed מ, derived from ל״ה stems, as מִצְוָה *command*, plur. מִצְוֹת; (*c*) חֻלְדָּה, proper name (חֹלֶד *mole*), אָכְלָה *food* (אֹכֶל); (*d*) נַעֲרָה *girl* (נַעַר); (*f*) בָּאְשָׁה *weed*, טָהֳרָה *purity* (טֹהַר); (*g*) עַוְלָה *wrong* (also עוֹלָה, Paradigm *i*); (*i*) צֵידָה *victuals* (masc. צַיִד, cf. Paradigm *h*); from *qiṭl* and *quṭl*-forms, בִּינָה *understanding*, סוּפָה *tempest*; (*k*) אַלְיָה *fat tail* (as if from אֱלִי), שִׁבְיָה (*ă* attenuated to *ĭ*) *captivity* (שְׁבִי), לִוְיָה *wreath* (probably an original *qiṭl*-form); (*l*) חַיָּה *life*, מִדָּה *measure* (attenuated from מַדָּה). Adjectives derived from ע״ע stems also belong in flexion to this class, as רַבָּה *multa*, with middle guttural רָעָה *mala*; (*m*) זִמָּה *plan*; (*n*) חֻקָּה *statute* (חֹק).

Paradigm II: ground-form *qăṭălăt*, &c., (*a*) נְקָמָה *vengeance* (נָקָם); *c* (*b*) אֲדָמָה *earth*; (*c*) נְבֵלָה *corpse*; (*d*) עֲיֵפָה *languida*; (*f*) יָפָה *beautiful*, קָצָה *end* (from קָצֶה, יָפֶה). From stems ע״וּ arise such forms as עֵדָה (masc. עֵד, properly *part. Qal* from עוּד) *female witness*. From the ground-form *qăṭŭl*, עֲמֻקָּה *profunda* (masc. עָמֹק), עֲבֻדָּה *servitude*, &c.

Paradigm III: unchangeable vowel in the first, changeable in the *d* second syllable, (*a*) יֹלֵדָה *a woman with child* (cf. the examples in § 84ᵃ *s*, and the retention of the *ē* in the *part. Piʿēl*, Ex 22¹⁷, 23²⁶; in the *Hithpaʿēl* 1 K 14⁵ᶠ·), but also with the change of the *ē* (originally *ĭ*) into *Šᵉwâ*, יֹשְׁבָה *dwelling*, Na 3⁸. However, in these participial forms the feminine is mostly indicated by ◌ֶת (see below, *h*); (*c*) גּוֹלָה *those of the captivity* (masc. גּוֹלֶה), but also with a return of the final *Yôdh*, הֹמִיָּה *clamorous*, Pr 7¹¹, and the examples in § 75 *v*. On the *ă* of the participles of verbs ע״וּ, which also belong to this class, such as זָרָה *peregrina*, cf. § 72 *g*.

e Paradigm IV: originally changeable vowel in the first syllable, unchangeable in the second, (*a*) גְּדֻלָה *magna*, חֲסִידָה *stork*, properly *pia*; בְּתוּלָה *virgin*, properly *seiuncta*; (*b*) עֲנִיָּה *misera*.

f 2. A simple ת is added as feminine ending in forms like בְּכִית *weeping* (masc. בְּכִי, § 93 *x, a*), בְּרִית *covenant*; but *feminine participles* of verbs ל״א, as יֹצֵאת, מֹצֵאת, may be due to contraction from *yôṣĕʾet*, &c. (hardly to lengthening of the *i* in the ground-form *môṣi*), whilst forms like מוֹצֵאת, נִשֵּׂאת (see § 74 *i*) are to be explained on the analogy of the forms treated in § 93 *t*. Apart from the ל״ה formations, we find the simple ת in the participle מְשָׁרַת 1 K 1¹⁵, contracted from מְשָׁרַתְּ. But וַיֹּלַדְתְּ Gn 16¹¹, Ju 13⁵⁻⁷ is the ground-form of the ptcp. וְיֹלֶדֶת (as in the same connexion in Gn 17¹⁹, Is 7¹⁴), cf. § 80 *d* and the *Qᵉre* שָׁבַתְּ, &c., discussed in § 90 *n*.

g The forms which arise by appending the ת feminine to masculine nouns with a changeable vowel in a closed final syllable are, as a rule, developed exactly in the same way as masculine segholate forms. Thus there arise in Paradigm I (*a*) from גְּבִרְתְּ (for original *gᵉbirt*; § 69 *c*), the form גְּבֶרֶת *mistress* (but only in *construct st.*; in Is 47⁷ also גְּבֶרֶת עַד are to be taken together; the *absolute st.* is גְּבִירָה); from מַלְכְּתְּ, מַלְכַּת *queen* (in Paradigm II, *a*); פֶּחֶתָ (פַּחַת=פַּחַתְּ *pit*) Lv 13⁵⁵; (*c*) גֶּדֶר *wall*, גִּדְרְתְּ (from גִּדְרְתְּ=*gᵉdirt*; cf. זֵקֶן as construct st. of זָקֵן); on the other hand, חֲמֵשֶׁת is construct st. of חֲמִשָׁה *five*, with lengthening of the original *i* of חֲמִשְׁתְּ.

h Formations with a changeable *ō* in the second syllable belonging to this class are נְחֹשֶׁת *bronze* (from נְחֻשְׁתְּ), כֻּתֹּנֶת the constr. st. of כֻּתֹּנֶת *coat*, perhaps also כְּתֹבֶת *writing* (unless it be obscured from כְּתָב, § 93, Paradigm IV, *c*).—Paradigm III, (*a*) חֹתֶמֶת (from חֹתַמְתְּ), masc. חוֹתָם *seal*; (*b*) יוֹנֶקֶת (properly *sucking*) *sprout* (in *pause*, e. g. חֹבָרֶת Ex 26⁴, &c.), and so most feminines of participles קֹטֵל. On this transition of the ground-form *qôṭilt* to קֹטַלְתְּ (regularly before suffixes in יוֹנַקְתּוֹ, יְלַדְתּוֹ, &c.), cf. § 69 *c*; *qôṭalt* serves as the ground-form under the influence of a guttural as well as before suffixes, e. g. יֹדַעַת, feminine of יֹדֵעַ *knowing*; in a wider sense, גֻּלְגֹּלֶת *skull* may also be included here, see § 95, Paradigm IV, *c*.

On the endings וּת and ־ִית, see § 86 *k, l*, § 95 at the end.

§ 95. *Paradigms of Feminine Nouns.*

a In accordance with the general formative laws, stated in § 92 *b–k*, the following cases have chiefly to be considered in the flexion of

feminines also: (1) a tone-lengthened vowel on the removal of the
tone reverts to its original shortness (thus the *ā* of the termination
הָ‎ becomes again *ă* in the *construct st.* תַ‎). On the other hand,
even an originally short vowel is retained as (a long) pretonic vowel
before the endings הָ‎ and וֹת‎ in the *abs. st.*, e. g. צְדָקָה‎‎, צְדָקָה‎; (2) without
the tone or foretone an originally short vowel almost always becomes
Šᵉwâ; on the other hand, *before* a vowel which had thus become *Šᵉwâ*
the *ă* in the first syllable which had hitherto also been reduced to
Šᵉwâ returns, although usually attenuated to *ĭ*, e. g. צִדְקַת‎ from
ṣādhăqăth; (3) in the plural of the feminines of segholate forms before
the termination of וֹת‎ or ־ִים‎, and in formations of the latter kind also
before the light suffixes, a *pretonic Qameṣ* reappears, while the short
vowel of the first syllable becomes *Šᵉwâ*. This short vowel, however,
returns in the *construct st. plur.*, whether ending in וֹת‎ or ־ַי‎; in
formations of the latter kind also before the grave suffixes.

The following Paradigms (with the exception of I, *d*) deal only with
such of the forms treated in § 94 as incur some vowel changes or
other. All forms with unchangeable vowels follow the analogy of
Paradigm I, *d*.

I.

b

	a.	b.		c.	d.	e.
Sing. absolute	מַלְכָּה	[כִּלְיָה]	חֶרְפָּה	חָרְבָּה	חֻקָּה	[גְּבִירָה]
	(queen)	(kidney)	(reproach)	(waste)	(statute)	(mistress)
„ construct	מַלְכַּת		חֶרְפַּת	חָרְבַּת	חֻקַּת	גְּבֶרֶת
„ with light suff.	מַלְכָּתִי		חֶרְפָּתִי	חָרְבָּתִי	חֻקָּתִי	גְּבִרְתִּי
„ with grave suff.	מַלְכַּתְכֶם		חֶרְפַּתְכֶם	חָרְבַּתְכֶם	חֻקַּתְכֶם	גְּבִרְתְּכֶם
Plur. absolute	מְלָכוֹת	כְּלָיוֹת	חֲרָפוֹת	חֳרָבוֹת	חֻקּוֹת	
„ construct	מַלְכוֹת	כִּלְיוֹת	חֶרְפוֹת ¹	חָרְבוֹת	חֻקּוֹת	
„ with suff.	מַלְכוֹתַי	כִּלְיוֹתַי		חָרְבוֹתַי	חֻקּוֹתַי	
Dual absolute			רִקְמָתַיִם			מְצִלְתַּיִם
			(a double piece of embroidery)			(cymbals)

¹ Only in ψ 69¹⁰, contrary to rule, with a firmly closed syllable, cf. § 93 *m*.

c

	II.			III.	
	a.	*b.*	*c.*	*a.*	*b.*
Sing. absolute	צְדָקָה	זְעָקָה	שָׁנָה	יוֹנֶקֶת	גֻּלְגֹּלֶת
	(*righteousness*)	(*outcry*)	(*year*)	(*sprout*)	(*skull*)
,, construct	צִדְקַת	זַעֲקַת	שְׁנַת	יוֹנֶקֶת	גֻּלְגֹּלֶת
,, with light suff.	צִדְקָתִי	זַעֲקָתִי	שְׁנָתִי	יוֹנַקְתִּי	גֻּלְגָּלְתִּי
,, with grave suff.	צִדְקַתְכֶם	זַעֲקַתְכֶם	שְׁנַתְכֶם	יוֹנַקְתְּכֶם	גֻּלְגָּלְתְּכֶם
Plur. absolute	צְדָקוֹת		שָׁנוֹת [1]	[יוֹנְקוֹת]	
,, construct	צִדְקוֹת		שְׁנוֹת	יוֹנְקוֹת	גֻּלְגְּלוֹת
,, with suff.	צִדְקוֹתַי		שְׁנוֹתַי	יוֹנְקוֹתַי	גֻּלְגְּלוֹתַי
Dual absolute	[נְחֻשְׁתַּיִם]		שְׂפָתַיִם		
	(*fetters of brass*)		(*lips*)		
,, construct			שִׂפְתֵי		

REMARKS.

d 1. Paradigm I: feminines of segholate forms. (*a*) The locative of this class has the form גִּבְעָתָה *towards Gibeah* (masc. גֶּבַע). In some cases, especially with an initial guttural, there is no means of deciding whether the form in question is to be referred to a *qăṭl* or a *qiṭl* base, e. g. חָזְקָה *strength* (cf. חָרְפָּה under *b*). A *dual* of this form occurs in שִׁבְעָתַיִם *seven times* (cf. שֶׁבַע *seven*, fem.). Analogous to masculine forms like דְּבַשׁ (§ 93 *s*) is הֲדַס *myrtle*.—From masculines of the form פְּרִי (ל״ה, cf. § 93 I, *k*) arise feminines sometimes like אַלְיָה, שִׁלְיָה, נַאֲוָה (see above, § 94 *b*), sometimes like בְּכִית (§ 94 *f*); occasionally the final ת is retained before the plural ending, as if it belonged to the stem (cf. § 87 *k*), e. g. חֲנִיתוֹת *spears*. Forms like גְּדִיָּה (cf. אֳנִיָּה, a *qăṭl* form) are derived directly from the masculine forms גְּדִי *kid*, אֳנִי *a fleet*.—(*b*) From a stem ע״ו, חִטָּה *wheat* (for חִנְטָה), plur. חִטִּים.—(*c*) From עָרְלָה *foreskin*, the plur. absol. is עֲרָלוֹת (cf. פְּעָלִים, § 93, Paradigm I, *f*), constr. עָרְלוֹת.—(*d*) Example of a feminine segholate form from a stem ע״ע (ground-form *qŭṭl*, like חַיָּה of the form *qăṭl*, זִמָּה of the form *qiṭl*), with ŏ for ŭ, חַגָּא *terror*, Is 19[17] (Aramaic orthography for חָגָּה).

e (*e*) To the list of segholate forms with ת fem. belong also the infinitives of verbs פ״י and פ״ן, which have rejected the weak consonant at the beginning, as שֶׁבֶת (from יָשַׁב), דֵּעַת (from יָדַע), גֶּשֶׁת (from נָגַשׁ), as well as קַחַת (from לָקַח); cf. § 69 *m* and § 66 *b* and *g*. The infinitives of verbs פ״י are, however, also found in the form צֵאָה, לֵדָה, דֵּעָה, and of the same origin also are עֵדָה *congregation* (from יָעַד), עֵצָה *counsel* (from יָעַץ), שֵׁנָה *sleep* (from יָשֵׁן), constr. שְׁנַת, עֲדַת, while in the constr. forms זֵעַת *sweat*, Gn 3[19] (from יָזַע *to flow*), and צֵאַת *excrement*, Ez 4[12], the Ṣere has remained firm.

f From a stem ע״ו (cf. בּוֹשׁ *to be ashamed*) is בֹּשֶׁת *shame*, with suffix בָּשְׁתִּי.

---

[1] On שְׁנוֹת as a less frequent (poetic) form for שָׁנִים see § 87 *n*.

From a stem ל״ה (דְּלָה, cf., however, Barth, *ZDMG*. 1887, p. 607, who assumes a stem ידל) the masculine דַּל appears to have been formed after the rejection of the final *Yôdh*, and afterwards the feminine דֶּלֶת *door*; but in the *plural* דְּלָתוֹת, *constr.* דַּלְתוֹת, the ת of the termination is retained (see above, *d*, חֲנִיתוֹת). In a similar way רְפָתִים *stalls*, Hb 3¹⁷, has arisen, if it is from the stem רפה, and שֹׁקֶת *trough* (from שָׁקָה), of which the masc. must have been שְׁקִי = שֹׁקִי; on the other hand, the *plur. constr.* שִׁקֲתוֹת Gn 30³⁸ (again retaining the feminine ת as an apparent radical) can only be an abnormal formation from the *singular* שֹׁקֶת, not from a kindred form שֶׁקֶת or שְׁקֶת.

2. Paradigm II: ground-form *qăṭălăt*, &c., cf. § 94 *c*, Paradigm II, *a* and *b*. *g* Analogous to the masculine forms like קָטָן, plur. קְטַנִּים, we find קְטַנָּה *parva*, &c.—The *constr.* forms, like צִדְקַת (*ṣidhᵉqăth*), are distinguished by the vocal *Šᵉwâ* (§ 10 *d*) from the segholate forms, like כִּבְשַׂת (*kibh-săth*). Consequently the *constr. st.* בִּרְכַּת Gn 28⁴, &c. (from בְּרָכָה *blessing*), and חֶרְדַּת 1 S 14¹⁵, &c. (from חֲרָדָה *a trembling*), are abnormal.—Under the influence of a guttural (see Paradigm *b*) the original *ă* is retained in the first syllable in the *constr. st.* (cf. also אַדְמַת earth, אֲדָמָה); in other cases it is modified to *Sᵉghôl*, e.g. עֲגָלָה *wagon*, עֶגְלָתוֹ. Frequently from an *absol. st.* in ◌ָה the *constr.* is formed with the termination ת, e.g. עֲטָרָה *crown*, constr. עֲטֶרֶת (from עֲטַרְתְּ); along with עֲצָרָה *assembly*, עֲצֶרֶת is found usually, even in the *absol. st.*; יְבֶמֶת (from יָבָם *levir*) before suffixes is pointed as in יְבִמְתִּי, and thus entirely agrees with גְּבֶרֶת (Paradigm I *e*). From a stem ל״ן (אָמַן) is formed אֱמֶת *truth* (from '*ămant*, and this no doubt for an original '*ămint*, § 69 *c*) before suffixes אֲמִתִּי, &c.

From the masc. form קָטֵל (*qăṭîl*) are formed, according to rule, גְּדֵרָה *wall*, *h* נְבֵלָה *corpse*, constr. נִבְלַת; בְּהֵמָה *cattle*, constr. בֶּהֱמַת (for בְּהֵמַת), with suffix בְּהֶמְתְּךָ Lv 19¹⁹. More frequently, however, the *ē* of the second syllable is retained before the termination *ath* of the *constr. st.*; thus from נְבֵלָה *once* נְבֵלָתִי Is 26¹⁹, and always בְּרֵכַת *pool*, גּוֹלַת *prey*, טְמֵאַת *unclean*, מְלֵאָתִי *full*, Is 1²¹ (with *Ḥireq compaginis*, see § 90 *l*), מְרֵרָתִי Jb 16¹³; שְׁאֵלָתִי 1 S 1²⁷, &c. (with elision of the א, שְׁלָתֵךְ 1 S 1¹⁷), also שְׁאֵלָתִי Jb 6⁸. Cf. the analogous forms of the *constr. st.* מַגֵּפַת *plague*, תַּרְדֵּמַת *deep sleep*, from מַגֵּפָה, תַּרְדֵּמָה.

As dual we find יְרֵכָתַיִם *sides* (cf. יַרְכְתוֹ Gn 49¹³, from the obsolete יְרֵכָה, *i* feminine of יָרֵךְ); the *constr. st.* יַרְכְּתֵי is perhaps to be referred to a segholate form (יַרְכָּה, cf. יֶרֶךְ as *constr. st.* of יָרֵךְ), unless the closed syllable be due to the analogy of בִּרְכַּת and חֶרְדַּת (see *g*).

In the forms with simple ת feminine the ground-form *qăṭilt* is developed *k* (§ 69 *c*) to *qᵉṭalt*, and this again regularly to קְטֶלֶת. Thus the feminine of חָבֵר *companion* is חֲבֶרֶת (with suffix חֲבֶרְתָּהּ Mal 2¹⁴, cf. שְׁבֶנְתָּהּ Ex 3²²), of גֵּר fem. גְּדֵרָה besides גִּדְרַת.—Of ע״וּ stems the segholate forms נַחַת *rest* and שַׁחַת *pit* (from נוּחַ, שׁוּחַ) belong to this class; Böttcher (*Gram.* i. 411) rightly distinguished the latter from שַׁחַת *corruption* (stem שָׁחַת); in the same way also נַחַת *rest* is distinct from נַחַת *a lighting down* (stem נָחַת).

The feminines of the form *qăṭil* from stems ע״וּ, as מֵתָה *mortua*, עֵדָה fem. *l witness* (from מוּת, עוּד), have likewise an unchangeable vowel in the first syllable. Cf., on the other hand, the forms from ע"י stems mentioned above, under *e*, such as שֵׁנָה *sleep*, constr. st. שְׁנַת ; moreover, חֵמָה *anger*, constr. st. חֲמַת (but חֵמַת *a leathern bottle*, in pause חֵמָת [so Baer, Ginsb., but Kittel חֲ] Gn 21¹⁵, constr. st. חֵמַת מַיִם Gn 21¹⁴, perhaps from a stem חמת).

m The feminines of the form *qāṭŭl*, like עֲמֻקָּה (masc. עָמֹק), maintain the original *ŭ* by sharpening the following consonant (cf. § 93 *kk*); on the other hand, by appending the fem. ת, segholate forms arise like נְחֹשֶׁת, before suff. נְחֻשְׁתָּם, &c. Dual נְחֻשְׁתַּיִם (see Paradigm II, *a*); but cf. נְחָשְׁתִּי La 3⁷.

n A few (aramaising) feminines from ל"ה stems (Paradigm II, *c*) are found with the ending *āth*, due to the rejection of the final *Wāw* or *Yôdh* and contraction of the preceding *ă* with the *ă* of the termination *āth*; thus מְנָת *portion* (for *mănăyăth* or *mănăwăth*), קְצָת *end* (also קָצֶה and קָצֶה), plur. מְנָיוֹת (*constr. st.* Neh 12⁴⁷, 13¹⁰) and מְנָאוֹת (Neh 12⁴⁴); קְצוֹת Ex 38⁵; cf. 37⁸ and 39⁴ *Kʰeth*.; on גֵּאָיוֹת *valleys*, see § 93 *v*.—אוֹת *sign* (stem אוה) is obscured from אָת, and this is contracted from *'āyăth* = *'ăwăyăth*; plur. אֹתוֹת, with the double feminine ending; cf. above, *f*, and § 87 *k*.—The retention of the *ā* in the first syllable in אֲלָתִי, &c., Gn 24⁴¹, &c., is abnormal.

O 3. Paradigm III, cf. the various forms in § 94 *d* and *f-h*. The *dual* חוֹמֹתַיִם *two walls*, Is 22¹¹, &c., taken directly from the plur. חוֹמוֹת, for חוֹמָתַיִם, is abnormal (cf. § 87 *s*, and the proper name גְּדֵרֹתַיִם Jos 15³⁶).—Among the forms resembling participles *Qal* of verbs ע"י, such as זָרָה (masc. זָר from *zâir*, hence with unchangeable *â*), must be reckoned also בָּמָה *high place* (from בּוּם), which has for its *constr. st. plur.* the pleonastic form בָּמוֹתֵי, or written defectively בָּמֹתֵי (see § 87 *s*); for this the Masora everywhere requires בָּמֳתֵי, which is to be read *bāmᵒthê* (not *bŏmᵒthê*), with an anomalous shortening of the *ô* to ◌ֳ ; but with suffixes בָּמוֹתֵי, &c.

p In a wider sense the feminines of the form קַטֵּל (§ 84ᵇ *e*) belong to this class, in so far as they shorten the *â* of the second syllable before the termination ת, e.g. דַּלֶּקֶת *inflammation* (from *dalläqt*), with suff. צַדִּקְתֶּךָ Ez 16⁵²; טַבַּעַת *signet*; also fem. of the forms קַטֵּל and קַטֵּל (§ 84ᵇ *c* and *d*), as אִוֶּלֶת *folly* (for *'iwwält*), and of all the forms which have a changeable vowel in the second syllable, and are formed with the prefix מ (§ 85 *g-k*), e.g. מַמְלָכָה *kingdom*, *constr.* always מַמְלֶכֶת; מַזְמֵרָה (not used in the sing.) *pruning-hook*, plur. מַזְמֵרוֹת ; מַשְׂכֹּרֶת *reward*, with suff. מַשְׂכֻּרְתִּי; cf. also the examples given in § 85 *g* and *p*, like מוֹלֶדֶת *birth* (but from ל"א, מוֹצָאָה *outgoing*), תּוֹלֶדֶת *generation*, תּוֹעֵבָה *abomination*, constr. תּוֹעֲבַת, &c.

q Sometimes the plural of these forms is to be traced to a secondary form, e.g. אִגֶּרֶת *a letter*, plur. אִגְּרוֹת (as if from אִגְּרָה); also יוֹנְקוֹת, which is merely formed on the analogy of the other plur. fem. of participles *Qal*, is to be referred to a sing. יוֹנֶקֶת. Cf., moreover, מַחֲרֶשֶׁת *ploughshare*, plur. מַחֲרֵשׁוֹת (as if from מַחֲרֵשָׁה)[1]; on the other hand, כֹּתָרוֹת *capitals* (of columns), and תּוֹכָחוֹת *reproofs*, are the regular plurals of כֹּתֶרֶת and תּוֹכַחַת.

---

[1] עַשְׁתֹּרֶת *Astarte* (plur. עַשְׁתָּרוֹת), which was formerly included among these examples, is most probably due to an intentional alteration of the

In כֻּתֹּנֶת *coat* the original *ŭ* of the first syllable is maintained by the *r̄* sharpening of the following consonant (cf. Arab. *qŭṭŭn*), with suff. כֻּתָּנְתִּי, the constr. st., however, is כְּתֹנֶת (as also in the *absol. st.* in Ex 28³⁹); plur. כֻּתֳּנוֹת, constr. כָּתְנוֹת.—The form גֻּלְגֹּלֶת given in Paradigm III, *b* is a *Pŭlpŭl*-form of the stem גָּלַל, cf. קָדְקֹד, § 84ᵇ *p*.

4. To the fourth class, for which no Paradigm is required, belong all the *s* numerous forms which in classical Hebrew have unchangeable vowels throughout, the originally short vowel of the first syllable having become Šᵉwâ, owing to the tone being thrown forward. Of the forms mentioned in §§ 84 and 85 those from ע״ע stems especially belong to this class, as מְגִלָּה *scroll*, תְּהִלָּה *praise*, תְּפִלָּה *prayer* (§ 85 *i* and *q*), as well as the feminine of the participle *Hiph'il* of verbs ע״וּ, e. g. מְאִירָה *enlightening* (from מֵאִיר), and generally the feminines of ע״וּ stems which are compounded with the *preformative* מ, as מְנוּחָה *rest* (from מָנוֹחַ), see § 85 *l*; from ל״ה stems perhaps also תְּעָלָה *conduit* (constr. st. תְּעָלַת Is 7³, &c.) and תְּלָאָה *travail*. Thus all these forms coincide externally with those which already, in the masculine form, have unchangeable vowels throughout (see the list of them in § 93 *ww*).

5. The feminine ending יִת— (apart from ל״ה-forms like בְּכִית, § 94*f*) arises *t* from the addition of the feminine ת to the ending י—, which is employed to form adjectives, &c., see § 86 *d*, *h*, and *k*. The ending וּת, mentioned there, is attached, in segholate forms, sometimes to the ground-form, as עַשְׁתּוּת Jb 12⁵ (v. l. עֶשְׁתּוֹת), sometimes to forms with a loosely-closed syllable, as מַלְכוּת *kingdom*; from ל״ה stems we find forms sometimes like שְׁבוּת *captivity* (according to others from the stem שׁוּב, like לְזוּת *perverseness* from לוּז), sometimes like בְּכוּת *weeping*, גָּלוּת *exile*, חָזוּת *vision*; the latter retain the *ā* of the first syllable even in the *constr. st.* and before suffixes. From a *qāṭil*-form is formed כְּבֵדוּת *heaviness*; from a *qăṭil*-form פְּקֻדוּת, &c.

In the plural of these forms different methods of treatment may be distin- *u* guished. In some cases the whole ending וּת is retained, as if belonging to the stem (cf. above, *f*), e. g. אַלְמְנוּתָיִךְ from אַלְמָנוּת, in others this ending is resolved, as in מַלְכֻיּוֹת Dn 8²² (no doubt for *mălᵉkhuwwôth*), and עֵדְוֹת *ʿēdᵉwôth*, from עֵדוּת *testimony*, but only with suffixes, עֵדְוֹתֶיךָ ψ 119¹⁴, &c.; עֵדְוֹתָיו 1 K 2³, &c.

§ 96. *Nouns of Peculiar Formation.*

In the following Paradigms,[1] pp. 282 to 284, a number of frequently used nouns are arranged, whose flexion presents more or less striking peculiarities. These peculiarities, however, are almost always subordinate to the usual phonetic laws, and the usual designation of the nouns as *irregular* is, therefore, not justified, when once the ground-forms are properly recognized on which the present forms are based.

---

original עַשְׁתֶּרֶת, like מֹלֶךְ Lv 18²¹, &c. (for מֶלֶךְ), with the vowels of בֹּשֶׁת *shame*, the latter word being substituted in reading for the name of the goddess.

[1] The only omissions from these Paradigms are אָחָד, חָם, and חָמוֹת (on which see the remarks), and all forms which are not found in the O. T.

		(father)	(brother)	(sister)	(man)	(woman)
Sing. *absolute*		אָב	אָח	אָחוֹת	אִישׁ	אִשָּׁה
,,	*construct*	אֲבִי	אֲחִי	אֲחוֹת	אִישׁ	אֵשֶׁת
,,	*with suff. of* 1 *sing.*	אָבִי	אָחִי	אֲחֹתִי	אִישִׁי	אִשְׁתִּי
,,	2 *masc.*	אָבִיךָ	אָחִיךָ	אֲחוֹתְךָ		אִשְׁתְּךָ
,,	2 *fem.*	אָבִיךְ	אָחִיךְ	אֲחוֹתֵךְ	אִישֵׁךְ	
,,	3 *masc.*	אָבִיו (אָבִיהוּ)	אָחִיו (אָחִיהוּ)	אֲחֹתוֹ	אִישׁוֹ	אִשְׁתּוֹ
,,	3 *fem.*	אָבִיהָ	אָחִיהָ	אֲחֹתָהּ	אִישָׁהּ	
,,	1 *Pl.*	אָבִינוּ	אָחִינוּ	אֲחֹתֵנוּ		
,,	2 *masc.*	אֲבִיכֶם	אֲחִיכֶם	[אֲחוֹתְכֶם]		
,,	2 *fem.*	אֲבִיכֶן				
,,	3 *masc.*	אֲבִיהֶם	אֲחִיהֶם	אֲחֹתָם		
,,	3 *fem.*	אֲבִיהֶן				
Plur. *absolute*		אָבוֹת	אַחִים		אֲנָשִׁים	נָשִׁים
,,	*construct*	אֲבוֹת	אֲחֵי		אַנְשֵׁי	נְשֵׁי
,,	*with suff. of* 1 *sing.*	אֲבֹתַי, אֲבַי	אַחַי, *pause* אֶחָי	אַחְיוֹתַי	אֲנָשַׁי	נָשַׁי
,,	2 *masc.*	אֲבֹתֶיךָ	אַחֶיךָ		אֲנָשֶׁיךָ	נָשֶׁיךָ
,,	2 *fem.*		אַחַיִךְ	אַחְיוֹתַיִךְ		
,,	3 *masc.*	אֲבֹתָיו	אֶחָיו	אַחְיוֹתָיו	אֲנָשָׁיו	נָשָׁיו
,,	3 *fem.*		אַחֶיהָ		אֲנָשֶׁיהָ	
,,	1 *Pl.*	אֲבֹתֵינוּ	אַחֵינוּ		אֲנָשֵׁינוּ	נָשֵׁינוּ
,,	2 *masc.*	אֲבֹתֵיכֶם	אֲחֵיכֶם	אַחְיוֹתֵיכֶם		נְשֵׁיכֶם
,,	3 *masc.*	אֲבֹתָם (אֲבֹתֵיהֶם)	אֲחֵיהֶם	אַחְיוֹתֵיהֶם	אַנְשֵׁיהֶם	נְשֵׁיהֶם
,,	3 *fem.*				אַנְשֵׁיהֶן	

REMARKS.

אָב *father* ; the *constr.* אֲבִי, like אֲחִי and בְּנִי (which occurs once), belongs to the connective forms discussed in § 90 k, which serve as the model for the *Ḥireq compaginis.* However, אַב also occurs in compound proper names, e.g. אֲבִשָׁלוֹם, beside אֲבִישָׁלוֹם, &c. ; also Gn 17⁴ ᶠ. אַב־הֲמוֹן for the purpose of explaining the name אַב[ר]הָם. On the plur. אָבוֹת see § 87 p.

אָח *brother.* The plur. *absol.* אַחִים has *Dageš forte implicitum* (§ 22 c); אֶחָיו stands for אַחָיו according to the phonetic law stated in § 27 q, and so also אֶחָי in *pause* for אַחָי. The sharpening of the ח merely serves to keep the preceding *Pathaḥ* short, as in גְּמַלִּים, &c. (§ 93 ee).

אֶחָד *one* (for אַחַד, likewise with *Dageš forte implicitum,* § 22 c, cf. § 27 q), *constr.* and otherwise in close connexion, אַחַד, Gn 48²², 2 S 17²², Is 27¹²,

אָמָה	בַּיִת	בֵּן	בַּת	יוֹם	כְּלִי
(handmaid)	(house)	(son)	(daughter)	(day)	(vessel)
	בֵּית	בֶּן־	בַּת	יוֹם	כְּלִי
אֲמָתִי	בֵּיתִי	בְּנִי	בִּתִּי		
אֲמָתְךָ	בֵּיתְךָ	בִּנְךָ, pause בְּנֶךָ	בִּתְּךָ, pause בִּתֶּךָ		כֶּלְיְךָ
	בֵּיתֶךָ	בְּנֶךָ			
אֲמָתוֹ	בֵּיתוֹ	בְּנוֹ	בִּתּוֹ	יוֹמוֹ	
אֲמָתָהּ	בֵּיתָהּ	בְּנָהּ	בִּתָּהּ		
		בְּנֵנוּ			
	בֵּיתְכֶם		בִּתְּכֶם		
	בֵּיתָם			יוֹמָם	
אֲמָהוֹת	בָּתִּים	בָּנִים	בָּנוֹת	יָמִים	כֵּלִים
אֲמָהוֹת	בָּתֵּי	בְּנֵי	בְּנוֹת	יְמֵי	כְּלֵי
אַמְהֹתַי		בָּנַי	בְּנֹתַי	יָמַי	כֵּלַי
	בָּתֶּיךָ	בָּנֶיךָ	בְּנֹתֶיךָ	יָמֶיךָ	כֵּלֶיךָ
	בָּתַּיִךְ	בָּנַיִךְ	בְּנֹתַיִךְ	יָמַיִךְ	
אַמְהֹתָיו		בָּנָיו	בְּנֹתָיו	יָמָיו	כֵּלָיו
אַמְהֹתֶיהָ		בָּנֶיהָ	בְּנֹתֶיהָ	יָמֶיהָ	כֵּלֶיהָ
	בָּתֵּינוּ	בָּנֵינוּ	בְּנֹתֵינוּ	יָמֵינוּ	כֵּלֵינוּ
אַמְהֹתֵיכֶם	בָּתֵּיכֶם	בְּנֵיכֶם	בְּנֹתֵיכֶם	יְמֵיכֶם	כְּלֵיכֶם
	בָּתֵּיהֶם	בְּנֵיהֶם	בְּנֹתֵיהֶם	יְמֵיהֶם	כְּלֵיהֶם
אַמְהֹתֵיהֶן	בָּתֵּיהֶן	בְּנֵיהֶן			

Ze 11[7]; and especially before מִן (מֵ) Gn 3[22], Ex 30[14], Nu 16[15], Ju 17[5], 1 S 9[3], Ez 18[10]; fem. אַחַת *una* (for אַחְדְּתְּ, according to § 19 *d*), in *pause* אָחָת. Once חַד masc. (by aphaeresis, § 19 *h*), Ez 33[30], as in Aramaic; plur. אֲחָדִים *some,* but also *iidem.*

אָחוֹת *sister,* from *'ăḥăwăt* or *'ăḥăyăt,* with elision of the ו or י, and with the *á,* which has arisen from *ăă,* obscured to *ô.*[1] In Nu 6[7] אֲחֹתוֹ stands for אֲחֹתוֹ (with virtual sharpening of the ח). The plur. *absol.* (אֲחָיוֹת) does not happen

---

[1] This explanation of אָחוֹת (and חָמוֹת q. v.) still seems to us more probable than the assumption that the fem. ending *ăth* is lengthened to compensate for the loss of the 3rd radical (so Wellhausen, *Skizzen,* vi. 258), or that the form is derived from *'aḥâ,* the old-semitic *constr. st.* of the accusative, with ת feminine (so Barth, *ZDMG.* 1899, p. 598).

	[מַי] (water)	עִיר (city)	פֶּה (mouth)	רֹאשׁ (head)	שֵׁם (name)	[שָׁמַי] (heaven)
Sing. absolute	[מַי]	עִיר	פֶּה	רֹאשׁ	שֵׁם	[שָׁמַי]
,, construct		עִיר	פִּי	רֹאשׁ	שֶׁם-, שֵׁם	
,, with suff. of 1 *sing.*		עִירִי	פִּי	רֹאשִׁי	שְׁמִי	
,, 2 *masc.*		עִירְךָ	פִּיךָ	רֹאשְׁךָ רֹאשֶׁךָ	שִׁמְךָ, *pause* שְׁמֶךָ	
,, 2 *fem.*				רֹאשֵׁךְ	שְׁמֵךְ	
,, 3 *masc.*		עִירוֹ	פִּיו, פִּיהוּ	רֹאשׁוֹ	שְׁמוֹ	
,, 3 *fem.*		עִירָהּ	פִּיהָ	רֹאשָׁהּ	שְׁמָהּ	
,, 1 *Pl.*			פִּינוּ	רֹאשֵׁנוּ	שְׁמֵנוּ	
,, 2 *masc.*			פִּיכֶם	רֹאשְׁכֶם	שִׁמְכֶם	
,, 3 *masc.*		עִירָם	פִּיהֶם	רֹאשָׁם	שְׁמָם	
,, 3 *fem.*			פִּיהֶן	רֹאשָׁן		
Plur. absolute	מַיִם	עָרִים	פִּיּוֹת	רָאשִׁים	שֵׁמוֹת	שָׁמַיִם
,, construct	מֵי, מֵימֵי	עָרֵי		רָאשֵׁי	שְׁמוֹת	שְׁמֵי
,, with suff. of 1 *sing.*	מֵימַי	עָרַי				
,, 2 *masc.*	מֵימֶיךָ	עָרֶיךָ				שָׁמֶיךָ
,, 2 *fem.*		עָרַיִךְ				
,, 3 *masc.*	מֵימָיו	עָרָיו		רָאשָׁיו		שָׁמָיו
,, 3 *fem.*	מֵימֶיהָ	עָרֶיהָ		רָאשֶׁיהָ		
,, 1 *Pl.*	מֵימֵינוּ	עָרֵינוּ		רָאשֵׁינוּ		
,, 2 *masc.*		עָרֵיכֶם		רָאשֵׁיכֶם		שְׁמֵיכֶם
,, 3 *masc.*	מֵימֵיהֶם	עָרֵיהֶם		רָאשֵׁיהֶם	שְׁמוֹתָם	
,, 3 *fem.*		עָרֵיהֶן		רָאשֵׁיהֶן	שְׁמֹתָן	

to occur. In Ez 16⁵² אֲחַיוֹתֵךְ occurs (for אֲחִיֹתֵךְ). In the forms אֲחוֹתַי
Jos 2¹³ *Keth.*, אֲחוֹתָיִךְ Ez 16⁵¹·⁵⁵·⁶¹ (to be read also in verse 45 for אֲחוֹתֵךְ, which
has been erroneously assimilated to the singular occurring in vv. 48, 49, 56),
and אֲחוֹתֵיכֶם Ho 2³ (for which, however, read אֲחוֹתְכֶם), the third radical has
been entirely lost.

אִישׁ *man*, according to the common opinion either incorrectly lengthened
for אֵשׁ (from 'iš, with assimilation of the *Nûn* of the ground-form 'inš, which
again has been attenuated from 'anš from the stem אָנַשׁ), or softened directly
from 'inš. It is, however, probable that a separate stem (אִישׁ *to be strong?*) is
to be assumed for the singular[1]; consequently the stem אָנַשׁ *to be sociable*,

---

[1] So already Gesenius in his *Thes. linguae Hebr.*, i. 83 f., and recently again
Friedr. Delitzsch, *Prolegg.*, p. 160 ff., Praetorius in Kuhn's *Orient. L.-B.*, 1884,
p. 196; König, *Lehrgeb.*, ii. 38; while Nöldeke (*ZDMG.* 1886, p. 739 f.), against
Delitzsch, would connect both אִישׁ and נָשִׁים with the stem אָנַשׁ.

would be connected only with the plur. אֲנָשִׁים (אִישִׁים is found only in Is 53³, ψ 141⁴, Pr 8⁴).

אָמָה *slave, handmaid*; with the plur. אֲמָהוֹת, with consonantal ה, cf. in Aram. אֲבָהָן *fathers*, and similarly in Phoen. דלחת from דלת, also Arab. *'abahât* (fathers), *'ummahât* (mothers), with an artificial expansion into a triliteral stem.

אִשָּׁה *woman*, probably for אֲנָשָׁה; from אָנַשׁ i.e. not (as Aram. אִתְּתָא shows) אֲנַשׁ to be sociable (see above, on אִישׁ) but אָנַשׁ to be weak (Arab. *'ănŭṯä*). So De Lagarde, *Uebersicht*, p. 68; König, *Lehrgeb.*, ii. 159 f. The form אֵשֶׁת (for *'išt*, with ח fem., from *'iššt*, after rejection of the doubling and lengthening of the *i* to *ē*) occurs in Dt 21¹¹, 1 S 28⁷, ψ 58⁹, even in *absol. st.* [cf., however, below, § 130. 4, 5].—In ψ 128³ אֶשְׁתְּךָ is found for אִשְׁתְּךָ. Instead of the plur. נָשִׁים, we find in Ez 23⁴⁴ אֶשֶׁת.[1]

בַּיִת *house*, locative בַּיְתָה, הַבַּיְתָה, in *pause* בַּיְתָה, הַבָּיְתָה, *constr.* בֵּית, plur. בָּתִּים (but in Dt 6¹¹, 1 Ch 28¹¹ בָּתִּים without *Metheg*), pronounced *báttim*. The explanation of the Dageš in the ח is still a matter of dispute. The Syriac *bâttin*, however, shows that the *Dageš* is original, and belongs to the character of the form.[2] According to Wright, *Comparative Grammar*, p. 88, בָּתִּים is simply contracted from *bai-tim* (as אַן from אַיִן, אֵן, עֵינַם from עֵינַיִם, &c.), and the Dageš, therefore, is *lene*; König, *Lehrgeb.*, ii. 56, proposes the name *Dageš forte orthoconsonanticum*; on the other hand Rahlfs, *ThLZ.* 1896, col. 587, suggests that the י is assimilated to the ח, while Philippi, *ZDMG.* xlix, p. 206, assumes for the plural a stem distinct from that of the singular. A definite solution is at present impossible. The incorrectness of the formerly common pronunciation *bottim* is sufficiently shown by the Babylonian punctuation (see § 8 *g*, note 3), which leaves no doubt as to the *á*.

בֵּן *son* (Gn 30¹⁹ בֶּן־שִׁשִּׁי) *constr.* usually בֶּן־ (also with a conjunctive accent as an equivalent for *Maqqeph*, Gn 17¹⁷, Is 8², &c., 1 Ch 9²¹; even with smaller disjunctives, especially in the combination מִבֶּן, Ex 30¹⁴, Lv 27³, &c. [מִבֶּן־ only after וְאִם and before חֹדֶשׁ, also in Is 51¹²; see Strack on Ex 30¹⁴]), rarely בֶּן־ (Dt 25², Jon 4¹⁰ twice, Pr 30¹, and so always in the combination בִּן־נוּן, and in the proper names בִּנְיָמִין [but בֶּן־יְמִינִי *Benjamite*] and בֶּן־יִקָה Pr 30¹), once בְּנִי (cf. § 90 *l*) Gn 49¹¹, and בְּנוֹ (§ 90 *o*) Nu 23¹⁸, 24³·¹⁵.—In Gn 49²² בֵּן, for which בֶּן־ ought to be read, is intended by the Masora for the *absol. st.*, not the *constr.*

---

[1] Friedr. Delitzsch (in his Babylonian glosses to Baer's text of Ezekiel, p. xi) on Ez 23⁴⁴ remarks that in Assyro-Babylonian the plur. of *aššatu* (woman) is *aššâti*, corresponding, therefore, to אֶשּׁוֹת, not to the ordinary plur. נָשִׁים. The *a* of נָשִׁים (instead of *i* as in Arab. or *e* as in Syr.) is to be explained with Barth (*Orient. Studien zu Ehren Th. Nöldekes*, Giessen, 1906, p. 792) from the natural connexion of the ideas 'men' and 'women', נָשִׁים and אֲנָשִׁים.

[2] This disposes of the traditional view that the *Dageš* (after a firm Metheg, see § 16 *f* ζ) only serves to distinguish it from בָּתִּים *passing the night*, ptcp. Qal of בּוּת, a stem which never occurs in the O. T. According to P. Haupt the stem is בא *to go in*, ח therefore being the feminine termination, as in *bint daughter*, and the original form *ba'tu*, *bâtu* (entrance) is preserved in the plural *báttim* where the *tt* is to be explained as due to the analogy of trisyllabic stems. In the singular *bât* passed into *bēt* (?), and this was resolved into *bait*, as Yᵉrûšālēm into Yᵉrûšālayim.

בַּת *daughter* (from *bant*, and this again, according to the law stated in § 69 c, for *bint*, fem. of בֵּן), with suff. בִּתִּי for בִּנְתִּי. Plur. בָּנוֹת, from the sing. בָּנָה, comp. בָּנִים *sons*.

חָם *husband's father*, only with suff. חָמִיךָ, חָמִיהָ; and חָמוֹת *husband's mother*, only with suff. חֲמוֹתֵךְ, חֲמוֹתָהּ. Cf. אָח, אָב, and especially אָחוֹת.

יוֹם *day* (Arab. *yaum*),[1] dual יוֹמַיִם; the plur. יָמִים is probably from a different sing. (יָם *yām*), constr. יְמֵי and (poetically) יְמוֹת, Dt 32⁷, ψ 90¹⁵.

כְּלִי *vessel*, in pause כֶּלִי (with suff. כֶּלְיְךָ Dt 23²⁵) from כָּלָה *to contain*, plur. כֵּלִים (as if from כֶּלֶה, כֶּל; according to König, ii. 63, shortened from *kilyim*).

מַיִם *water*; on the plur. cf. § 88 d.

עִיר *city*. The plur. עָרִים is scarcely syncopated from עֲיָרִים, as it is pointed in Ju 10⁴ (no doubt erroneously, in imitation of the preceding עֲיָרִים *ass colts*), but from a kindred sing. עָר, which still occurs in proper names.

פֶּה *mouth*, constr. st. פִּי (for original פֵּי = פֶּה?). Its origin is still disputed. According to Gesenius and König (ii. 103), פֶּה stands for פָּאֶה (ground-form *pi'ay*) from פָּאָה *to breathe, to blow*; according to Olshausen, for פֵּי, from a stem פִּיָה or פָּוָה. But parallel with the Hebrew פֶּה are Assyr. *pû*, Arab. *fû, fam, famm, fumm*, bibl. Aram. פֻּם, פֻּמָּא, Syr. *pûm, pûmā*, so that Barth, *ZDMG*. xli, p. 634, assumes two forms of development from the same stem (פמו), viz. *fm* and *fw*. פִּי *my mouth*, from *pi-y*; for פִּיהֶם we find in ψ 17¹⁰, 58⁷, 59¹³ פִּימוֹ. The supposed plur. פִּים 1 S 13²¹ is generally explained as a contraction from פִּיִּם, but the text is altogether corrupt. The plur. פִּיּוֹת, for the *edges* of a sword, occurs in Pr 5⁴; reduplicated פִּיפִיּוֹת Is 41¹⁵, ψ 149⁶.

רֹאשׁ *head* (obscured from רָאשׁ = *rā'š*); plur. רָאשִׁים (for רְאָשִׁים, § 23 c); רֹאשׁוֹ only in Is 15².

שֶׂה *a head of small cattle* (sheep or goat), constr. st. שֵׂה, with suff. שֵׂיְהוּ 1 S 14³⁴ and שְׂיוֹ Dt 22¹, according to König, ii. 131, from a ground-form *si'ay*, but according to De Lagarde, *Uebersicht*, 81 f., from a stem שׂי (ושׂי) (שֶׂה = *say* = *wisay*).

שֵׁם *name*, constr. generally שֵׁם (only six times שֶׁם־); cf. בֵּן.

שָׁמַיִם *heaven* (§ 88 d).

§ 97. *Numerals.* (a) *Cardinal Numbers.*

Brockelmann, *Sem. Sprachwiss.*, p. 116 ff.; *Grundriss*, i. 484 ff.

a 1. The formation of the cardinal numbers from 3 to 10 (on 1 and 2 see below) has this peculiarity, that numerals connected with a mascu-

---

[1] Cf. Nöldeke, *Beiträge*, p. 58, *yaum*, probably an extension of a biliteral word which has survived in יָמִים, יְמֵי. Barth, however, *Orient. Studien*, p. 791 (see above on אִשָּׁה), sees in יְמֵי, יָמִים, יְמוֹת new formations in Hebrew, caused by the naturally close connexion and association of these plurals with שָׁנִים, שְׁנֵי, שְׁנוֹת *years*, to which they became assimilated in form. The view that יוֹם is merely an incorrect obscuring of יָם, and therefore distinct from the Arab. *yaum*, is contradicted by the invariable spelling יוֹם, &c., notwithstanding the spelling ובים (= וּבְיֹם?) in the Siloam inscription, line 3 (cf. § 7 f), and מִיָּמִים Ho 6². Cf. also the note on § 100 g.

line substantive take the feminine form, and those with a feminine
substantive take the masculine form. The common explanation of this
strange phenomenon used to be that the primary form of the numeral
was an abstract noun in the feminine (cf. § 122 *p*). This was originally
attached in the *constr. st.* to the word qualified, then came to be also
used in apposition to it, and finally was placed after it like an adjective.
The consequence of the appositional, and finally adjectival, construction
was, that for numerals connected with feminine nouns a special shorter
form came to be used, whilst the original forms, with the abstract
feminine ending, were used in connexion with masculine nouns, after
as well as before them.

On this view the historical process would have been that originally the
abstract numerals (like Latin *trias, decas,* Greek πεντάς, δεκάς, &c.) were placed
in the *constr. st.* before masculines and feminines alike, e. g. שְׁלֹשֶׁת בָּנִים *trias
filiorum,* עֲשֶׂרֶת נָשִׁים *decas mulierum.* A trace of this earlier usage was seen in
the examples mentioned under *c*, like שְׁלֹשֶׁת נָשִׁים.—Further, it was possible to
say שְׁלֹשָׁה בָנִים *trias,* sc. *filii,* as well as בָּנִים שְׁלֹשָׁה *filii, trias.* From this
second appositional construction it was only a step to the treatment of
the abstract numeral as an adjective, *filii tres.* Similarly the subsequently
shortened forms of the abstract numeral, which were used in connexion with
feminines, might stand either in the *constr. st.* before, or in apposition before
or after the word numbered, thus שְׁלֹשׁ בָּנוֹת *trias filiarum,* or בָּנוֹת שָׁלֹשׁ *trias,*
sc. *filiae,* or בָּנוֹת שָׁלֹשׁ *filiae, trias,* or adjectivally *filiae tres.*

A different and much more intelligible explanation of the striking
disagreement between the gender of the numeral and that of the word
numbered has recently been given by Reckendorf, *Die syntaktischen
Verhältnisse des Arabischen,* pt. ii, Leiden, 1898, p. 265 ff. He also
considers that the earliest forms were abstract numerals which were
placed in the *constr. st.* before the noun numbered, the latter depending
on them in the genitive. The original form, however, of the abstract
numerals from 3 to 9 is not the feminine, but the masculine, used for
both genders, as it still is in the tens, 20, 30, &c. The feminine
abstract numeral was first distinguished by a special form in the
numbers from 13 to 19 (see further, below) when connected with
masculines, and this distinction was afterwards extended to the numbers
from 3 to 10. This explanation does not affect the view stated above
that the appositional and adjectival use of the abstract numerals was
only adopted later in addition to their use in the genitive construction.

The differentiation of the numerals (originally of common gender) into
masculine and feminine forms in the second decade, was occasioned, according to Reckendorf, by the use of the abstract feminine עֲשָׂרָה in compounds.

So long as it was felt that שְׁלֹשׁ עֶשְׂרֵה simply meant *the three of the decade*, the gender of the noun numbered made no difference. When, however, the consciousness of this meaning became weakened and the combination of units and tens came to be felt as a copulative rather than a genitive relation, it seemed suitable to connect only feminine nouns with the feminine form עֶשְׂרֵה. New forms were therefore invented, both of the units and the tens, for use with masculine nouns. The former, however, no longer had the form of the *constr.* but of the absolute state, clearly showing that the consciousness of the original syntactical relation in שְׁלֹשׁ עֶשְׂרֵה, &c., was lost. On the other hand, after the extension of these new formations to the first decade, the new feminine forms readily came to be used also in the genitive construction (and therefore in the *constr. st.*) on the analogy of the earlier masculine forms.

Of the first two numerals, אֶחָד *one*, with its fem. אַחַת (see § 96), may be recognized, from its form and use, as an adjective, although even so it admits of such combinations as אַחַד הֶהָרִים *unus e montibus*. The numeral two, as would be expected, appears as an abstract in the *dual*, but, like the other numerals, can also stand in apposition to the noun numbered. In form it always agrees with the gender of its noun. Accordingly, the numerals from 1 to 10 are as follows:

b

	With the Masculine.		With the Feminine.	
	Absol.	Constr.	Absol.	Constr.
1.	אֶחָד	אַחַד	אַחַת	אַחַת
2.	שְׁנַיִם	שְׁנֵי	שְׁתַּיִם ¹	שְׁתֵּי
3.	שְׁלֹשָׁה	שְׁלֹשֶׁת	שָׁלֹשׁ	שְׁלֹשׁ
4.	אַרְבָּעָה	אַרְבַּעַת	אַרְבַּע	אַרְבַּע
5.	חֲמִשָּׁה ²	חֲמֵשֶׁת	חָמֵשׁ	חֲמֵשׁ
6	שִׁשָּׁה	שֵׁשֶׁת	שֵׁשׁ	שֵׁשׁ
7.	שִׁבְעָה	שִׁבְעַת	שֶׁבַע	[שְׁבַע] ³
8.	שְׁמֹנָה	שְׁמֹנַת	שְׁמֹנֶה	שְׁמֹנֶה
9.	תִּשְׁעָה	תִּשְׁעַת	תֵּשַׁע	[תְּשַׁע] ³
10.	עֲשָׂרָה	עֲשֶׂרֶת	עֶשֶׂר	עֶשֶׂר

---

¹ Shortened from שְׁנָתַיִם, which would be the regular feminine form of שְׁנַיִם. Nevertheless, the *Dageš* in שְׁתַּיִם, &c. (even after מִן; מִשְׁתַּיִם Jon 4¹¹; cf., however, מִשְׁתֵּי Ju 16²⁸), can by no means be regarded as a *Dageš forte* arising from assimilation of the *Nûn*, for in that case the word could only be שַׁתַּיִם (cf. Arab. *ṯintāni*). This form does occur in the Codex Babylonicus of A.D. 916, but it is only a later correction for שְׁתַּיִם, while in the Berlin MS. or. qu. 680 described by Kahle (Lpz. 1902) there is no trace of the Dageš. It is rather to be read *štáyim*, *štê* (with *Dageš lene*), cf. אֶשְׁתַּיִם, representing the later Palestinian pronunciation (Philippi, *ZDMG.* xlix, p. 206), and Arab. ʾiṯnătāni (with a kind of prosthetic א; cf. § 19 *m*), as a further feminine form of

On the connective forms שְׁבַע, תִּשַׁע, cf. the analogous forms in § 93 *h*.

The other Semitic languages also exhibit the same peculiarity in the C
external differentiation of the numerals from 3 to 10 as regards gender. The
fem. form of the numeral abstracts is only rarely found in connexion with
feminine nouns,[4] e. g. שְׁלֹשֶׁת נָשִׁים Gn 7¹³, 1 S 10³, Jb 1⁴, Ez 7² *K⁽ᵉ⁾th.*; probably
also Jos 17¹¹, where we should read with Dillmann הַנָּפוֹת 'שׁ. In apposition,
Zc 3⁹, 4², cf. Jer 36²³.   From what was said above, under *a*, it follows that
these cases are not a return to original usage, but only an intrusion of the
form used before masculines into the sphere of the feminine.   Conversely in
Gn 38²⁴ שָׁלֹשׁ חֳדָשִׁים (but in the Samaritan שְׁלֹשֶׁת).—For שִׁבְעָה *seven*, there
occurs in Jb 42¹³ the strange form שִׁבְעָנָה, according to Ewald [*Ausführl,
Lehrb.*⁸, § 269 *b*] an old feminine substantive (German *ein Siebend, a set of
seven*), but more probably a scribal error.

2. The numerals from 11 to 19 are formed by placing the units, *d*
without the *copula*, before the number ten (in the form עָשָׂר masc.,
עֶשְׂרֵה fem.), but without the two words being joined into one.   As was
said above, under *a*, and as is proved by the use of אַחַת, אַחַד in the
numeral 11, the feminine numerals from 13 to 19 are to be regarded
as *construct* forms in a genitive connexion.   The connective forms of
the masculine abstracts, like שְׁלֹשֶׁת, &c., are not admitted in combination with עָשָׂר, since they are merely in apposition, and not in a
genitive relation (see the rare exceptions at the end of *e*).   On the
other hand שְׁנֵי and שְׁתֵּי in the numeral 12 are undoubtedly true
constructs, like אַחַד and the fem. numerals 13–19. But instead of שְׁנֵי
(Ex 28²¹, Jos 3¹² and four other places) and שְׁתֵּי (Jos 4⁸ and three times
in Ezek.), we generally find שְׁנֵים and שְׁתֵּים.   Two explanations have
been given of these forms: (1) that the *K⁽ᵉ⁾thîbh* really intends שְׁנַיִם,
שְׁתַּיִם, in the *absol. st.*, which was first introduced in the case of שְׁנַיִם,
on the analogy of עֶשְׂרָה, &c., and then extended to שְׁתַּיִם; the Masora,
however, required שְׁנֵי, שְׁתֵּי (but see below), and therefore pointed
שְׁנַיִם, שְׁתַּיִם as a *Q⁽ᵉ⁾rê perpetuum* (see § 17).—(2) that the *absolute* forms
שְׁנַיִם, שְׁתַּיִם (introduced on the analogy of שְׁלֹשָׁה, &c.) were contracted
to שְׁתַּיִם, שְׁנַיִם to facilitate the pronunciation of the duals when closely

---

'iṭnāni, *duo.*   According to Barth (*Orient. Studien ... Th. Nöldeke,* ii. 792 f.) the
irregularity of שְׁתַּיִם (he takes the Dageš as *Dageš forte*) is due to the complete
assimilation of its vowels to those of the masc. שְׁנַיִם where the Š⁽ᵉ⁾wâ *mobile* is
normal.

² With Dageš probably on the analogy of שִׁשָּׁה, as שֵׁשֶׁת on the analogy of
חֲמֵשֶׁת.   Cf. also J. K. Blake on חֲמִשָּׁה חֲמִשִּׁים in *JAOS.* 1905, p. 117 ff.

³ שְׁבַע and תִּשַׁע appear only as connective forms before עֶשְׂרֵה and מֵאוֹת.

⁴ In the vulgar dialects of Arabic, and in Ethiopic, the feminine form of
the numeral is by far the more common. This form appears also in Hebrew,
when the number is regarded in the abstract, as in the multiplicatives
(see § 97 *h*).

connected with עֶשֶׂר and עֶשְׂרֵה, and that the contraction is founded on an early and correct tradition. The second explanation is supported by the large number of examples of שָׁנִים (66) and שָׁתִים (34). It would be strange if the Masora required the alteration of the far commoner forms on account of isolated instances of שְׁנֵי and שְׁתֵּי. As a matter of fact even in regard to the latter forms the tradition often varies between שְׁנֵי and שְׁנַיִם, &c., cf. e. g. Ginsburg on Jos 3¹². We cannot therefore assume a *Q°rê perpetuum*.

e　Accordingly the numbers from 11 upwards are—

	Masculine.	Feminine.
11.	אַחַד עָשָׂר / עַשְׁתֵּי¹ עָשָׂר	אַחַת עֶשְׂרֵה / עַשְׁתֵּי עֶשְׂרֵה
12.	שְׁנֵים עָשָׂר / שְׁנֵי עָשָׂר	שְׁתֵּים עֶשְׂרֵה / שְׁתֵּי עֶשְׂרֵה
13.	שְׁלֹשָׁה עָשָׂר	שְׁלֹשׁ עֶשְׂרֵה

&c., on the analogy of the last. These numerals regularly have only the above form. In regard to their syntax, cf. § 134 *f*.

Very rarely the units appear in the *masc.* in the *constr. st.*, as חֲמֵשֶׁת עָשָׂר *fifteen*, Ju 8¹⁰, 2 S 19¹⁸ ; שְׁמֹנַת עָשָׂר *eighteen*, Ju 20²⁵.—Connected by וְ we find עֶשְׂרָה וַחֲמִשָּׁה in Ex 45¹².

f　3. The tens from 30 to 90 are expressed by the plural forms of the units (so that the plural here always stands for *ten times* the unit), thus, שְׁלֹשִׁים 30, אַרְבָּעִים 40, חֲמִשִּׁים 50, שִׁשִּׁים 60, שִׁבְעִים 70, שְׁמֹנִים 80, תִּשְׁעִים 90. But *twenty* is expressed by עֶשְׂרִים, plur. of עֶשֶׂר *ten*.² These numerals are all of common gender, and do not admit of the *construct state*.—In compound numerals, like 22, 23, 44, &c., the units

---

¹ עַשְׁתֵּי, which remained for a long time unexplained, was recognized (first by J. Oppert) in the Assyro-Babylonian inscriptions in the form *ištin* or *ištēn* ; cf. Friedr. Delitzsch, *Assyrische Grammatik*, p. 203, and P. Haupt, in the *American Journal of Philology*, viii. 279. Accordingly, עַשְׁתֵּי עָשָׂר is a compound, like the Sansk. *êkádaçan*, ἕνδεκα, *undecim* (analogous to the combination of units and tens in the numerals from 12 to 19), and is used at the same time in the composition of the feminine numeral eleven. On the gradual substitution of עַשְׁתֵּי ע׳ for אַחַד ע׳ and אַחַת ע׳ see Giesebrecht in *ZAW.* 1881, p. 226 ; עַשְׁתֵּי ע׳ occurs only in Jer., Ez., in the prologue to Deuteronomy (1³), in the Priestly Code, and in passages undoubtedly post-exilic, so that it may very well be a loan-word from the Babylonian.

² For עֶשְׂרִים, שִׁבְעִים, תִּשְׁעִים (from the *segholates* עֶשֶׂר שֶׁבַע, תֵּשַׁע), we should expect *ʿᵃsārim*, *šᵉbhāʿim*, *tᵉšāʿim*. Is this very unusual deviation from the common formation (see above, § 93 *l, o, r*) connected with the special meaning of these plurals, or are these survivals of an older form of the plural of segholates?

may precede (*two and twenty*, as in Arabic and English), e. g. Nu 3³⁹, 26¹⁴. Very frequently, however, the reverse order is found (*twenty and two*, as in Syriac, cf. French and English *twenty-two*), e. g. 1 Ch 12²⁸, 18⁵.[1] In all cases the units and tens are connected by the *copula*, ordinarily וְ, but וָ before numerals with the tone on the penultima, וָ before ﬦָ, וִ before *Š*ᵉ*wâ*; see § 104 *d, e, g*.

The remaining numerals are the substantives—

   100 מֵאָה fem., *constr.* מְאַת.   *g*

   200 מָאתַיִם dual (contracted from מְאָתַיִם; cf. § 23 *c*).

   300 שְׁלֹשׁ מֵאוֹת plur. (but in 2 K 11⁴·⁹·¹⁰·¹⁵, *K*ᵉ*th*. הַמֵּאָיוֹת).

   1000 אֶלֶף masc.

   2000 אַלְפַּיִם dual.

   3000 שְׁלֹשֶׁת אֲלָפִים plur., and so on (except עֲשָׂרָה אֲלָפִים in 2 S 18³, 2 K 24¹⁴ *K*ᵉ*th*.; elsewhere always עֲשֶׂרֶת אֲלָפִים).

   10000 רְבָבָה, in the later books the aramaising[2] forms רִבּוֹ, רִבּוֹא, רִבּוֹת (properly *multitude*, cf. μυριάς).

   20000 רִבֹּתַיִם dual (see below, *h*); but שְׁתֵּי רִבּוֹת Neh 7⁷⁰ (also שְׁתֵּי רִבּוֹא Neh 7⁷¹).

   40000 אַרְבַּע רִבּוֹא Neh 7⁶⁶.

   60000 שֵׁשׁ־רִבֹּאוֹת Ezr 2⁶⁹ (Baer and Ginsburg רִבֹּאוֹת, as in Dn 11¹²).

   אַלְפֵי רְבָבָה *thousands of myriads*, Gn 24⁶⁰.

Rem. 1. The dual form which occurs in some of the units has the meaning *h* of our ending -*fold*, e. g. אַרְבַּעְתַּיִם *fourfold*, 2 S 12⁶; שִׁבְעָתַיִם *sevenfold*, Gn 4¹⁵·²⁴, Is 30²⁶, ψ 12⁷, 79¹² (cf. § 134 *r*). The dual רִבֹּתַיִם ψ 68¹⁸ (explained by אַלְפֵי שִׁנְאָן *thousands of duplication*) is not meant to be taken in the sense of *two myriads* or *twice the number of myriads*, but in a multiplicative sense.[3]—Besides the plural which denotes the tens, there are also the plurals אֲחָדִים *some*, also *iidem*, and עֶשָׂרֹות *decades* (not *decem*) Ex 18²¹·²⁵.

2. The *suffixes* to numerals are, as with other nouns, properly genitives, *i* although they are translated in English as nominatives, e. g. שְׁלָשְׁתְּכֶם *your triad*, i. e. *you three*, Nu 12⁴; חֲמִשָּׁיו *his fifty* (i. e. the 50 belonging to him) 2 K 1⁹⁻¹³, and חֲמִשֶּׁיךָ 2 K 1¹⁰·¹².

---

[1] According to the conclusions of König (*De Criticae Sacrae Argumento*, p. 61, and *Lehrgeb.*, ii. p. 215 ff.), the smaller number more commonly precedes in Ezek. and the Priestly Code, but the larger always elsewhere. S. Herner (*Syntax der Zahlwörter im A. T.*, Lund, 1893, p. 71 ff.) arrives at the same conclusion by a full examination of the statistics; cf. also his remarks on König in *ZAW*. 1896, p. 123, and König's reply, *ibid.*, p. 328 f.

[2] Cf. Kautzsch, *Die Aramaismen im A.T.* (Halle, 1902), p. 79 f.

[3] Cf. D. H. Müller, 'Die numeralia multiplicativa in den Amarnatafeln u. im Hebr.,' *Semitica*, i, Wien, 1906, p. 13 ff.

§ 98. *Numerals.* (*b*) *Ordinal Numbers.*

a   The ordinal numbers from 2 to 10 are formed from the corresponding cardinals by adding the termination ִי—ּ (§ 86 *h*), before which another ִי—ּ also is generally inserted between the second and third radicals. They are as follows : שֵׁנִי *second,* שְׁלִישִׁי, רְבִיעִי (like רֶבַע, רֹבַע, רִבְּעִים, without the prosthetic א, which appears in אַרְבַּע, &c.), חֲמִישִׁי or חֲמִשִׁי (which, according to Strack, is always to be read for חֲמִשִׁי), שִׁשִּׁי, שְׁבִיעִי, שְׁמִינִי, תְּשִׁיעִי, עֲשִׂירִי. The ordinal *first* is expressed by רִאשׁוֹן (cf. § 27 *w*), from רֹאשׁ *head, beginning,* with the termination וֹן (§ 86 *f*). On the use of אֶחָד as an ordinal in numbering the days of the month, cf. § 134 *p* ; in such cases as Gn 1⁵, 2¹¹, the meaning of *first* is derived solely from the context.

b   The feminine forms have the termination ִית—ּ, more rarely (and only in the case of 3 and 10) ִיָּה—ּ. They are employed also to express fractions, e. g. חֲמִשִׁית *fifth* or *fifth part,* עֲשִׂירִית and עֲשִׂירִיָּה *tenth part.* Side by side with these, in the same sense, there are also forms like רֹבַע and רֶבַע *a quarter,* חֹמֶשׁ *a fifth part,* and with the afformative וֹן, עִשָּׂרוֹן (plur. עֶשְׂרוֹנִים) *a tenth part* ; these are to be regarded as abstracts, and are denominatives from the cardinal numbers. Cf. finally שָׁבוּעַ ἑβδομάς, *a week* ; עָשׂוֹר *a decade* (of days), and also the *tenth day.*

On the expression of the other relations of number, for which the Hebrew has nò special forms, see the Syntax, § 134 *q* and *r*.

CHAPTER IV

THE PARTICLES

§ 99. *General View.*

Brockelmann, *Grundriss*, i. 492 f.

1. The particles, which in general express the secondary modi- *a*
fications of thought in speech, the closer relation of words to one
another, and the mutual connexion of sentences, are for the most part
either borrowed or derived from noun-forms, sometimes also from
pronouns and verbs (§ 30 *s*). *Primitive* particles (apart from a few
demonstrative forms, see § 100 *i*) can only be so called in the sense
defined in § 81 f.

2. So far as the origin of the particles can be discovered with *b*
certainty, they are either (1) *borrowed* from other parts of speech;
i. e. certain forms of the noun, pronoun, or verb, with more or less
loss of their original meaning, have come to be employed as particles;
cf. in the Indo-Germanic languages, e. g. the Latin *certo, falso, partim,
verum, causa*, the German *statt, anstatt, wegen, weg*, and the English
instead, away; or (2) *derived* from other parts of speech, either (*a*)
by the *addition* of formative syllables, as יוֹמָם *by day*, from יוֹם (cf.,
however, § 100 *g*); or most commonly (*b*) by *abbreviations* effected in
various ways, the extent of their mutilation being in proportion to
the frequency of their use, so that in some cases (see below) the
original stem has become wholly unrecognizable.

Cf. in German *gen*, from *gegen, Gegend*; *seit*, from *Seite*; *weil* (originally
a particle of time, like our *while*), from *Weile*.
Still more violent abbreviations occur in Greek, Latin, and the Romance
languages, e. g. ἀπό, *ab, a*; ἐξ, *ex, e*; *ad*, Fr. *à*; *aut*, Fr. *ou*, Ital. *o*; *super*,
Ital. *su*.[1]

The greatest shortening occurs in those particles which have *c*
entirely lost the character of an independent word, by being reduced
to a single consonant with its vowel (generally short) or *Šewâ*.
According to the laws of syllable formation in Hebrew (§ 26 *m*),

---

[1] Even short phrases are contracted into one word : Lat. *forsitan*, from
fors sit an, δηλονότι, δηλαδή, Fr. *peut-être*, Eng. *prithee* from *I pray thee*. — In
Chinese most of the particles are verbs or nouns ; e. g. *iü* (to give), also the
sign of the dative ; *ï* (to make use of), *to, for* ; *nëi* (the interior), *in*.

such particles cannot stand by themselves, but are united, as prefixes, with the following word (§ 102), very much like the preformatives of the imperfect (§ 47 a–d).

d The view that this shortening of whole words to single letters has actually taken place in the gradual course of linguistic development is rendered highly probable by the fact that similar abbreviations in later Hebrew and in Aramaic, i.e. as the development of the original Semitic speech progresses, become more and more striking and frequent. Thus the Biblical Aramaic דִּי becomes at a later period דְּ; in modern Arabic, e.g. *hallaq* (now) is from *halwaqt*; *lēš* (why?) from *li-ayyi-šaïn*, &c. Cf. also the analogous cases mentioned above from the Western languages. Nevertheless, the use of the simplest particles is found already in the earliest periods of the Hebrew language, or, at any rate, in the earliest documents which have come down to us.

e 3. Less frequently particles are formed by *composition*; as מַדּוּעַ *wherefore?* for מַה־יָדוּעַ *quid edoctus?* (τί μαθών;) or *quid cognitum?*; בִּלְעֲדֵי (from בַּל and עֲדִי) *besides*; מִלְמַעְלָה (from מִן, לְ, מַעְלָה) *from above, above.*

More frequent is the combination of two words into one without contraction, e.g. כִּי־עַל־כֵּן, אַף־כִּי, בִּי־אָם, אַחֲרֵי־כֵן; cf. also the compounds of אֵי with demonstrative pronouns, as אֵי־מִזֶּה *from what?*; אֵי לָזֹאת *wherefore?* [R.V. *how*]. See the lexicon under אֵי.

§ 100. *Adverbs.*

On demonstrative adverbs cf. Brockelmann, *Grundriss*, i. 323; on interrogative adverbs, *ibid.*, i. 328; on adverbs in general, i. 492 ff.

a 1. The negative לֹא *not*, and a few particles of place and time, as שָׁם *there*, are of obscure origin.

b 2. Forms of other parts of speech, which are used adverbially without further change, are—

(*a*) Substantives with prepositions, e.g. בִּמְאֹד (with might) *very*; לְבַד *alone* (prop. *in separation*, Fr. *à part*), with suffix לְבַדִּי *I alone*; מִבַּיִת *from within, within*; cf. also כְּאֶחָד (as one) *together*, לְעֻמַּת and מִלְעֻמַּת (originally *in connexion with*) *near to, corresponding to, like*, &c., cf. § 161 b.

c (*b*) Substantives in the accusative (the adverbial case of the Semites, § 118 m), cf. τὴν ἀρχήν, δωρεάν, e.g. מְאֹד (might) *very*, אֶפֶס (cessation) *no more*, הַיּוֹם (the day) *to-day* (cf. § 126 b), מָחָר [1] *to-morrow*, יַחַד (union) *together*. Several of these continued to be used, though rarely, as substantives, e.g. סָבִיב, plur. סְבִיבִים and סְבִיבוֹת, *circuit*, as adverb

---

[1] Generally derived from the *ptcp.* Pu'al מְאֻחָר *mᵉ'ŏhār* (= *mᵉ'ohhār*) and hence to be read *mŏhār* (cf. מָחֳרָת *morning*); but according to P. Haupt (notes to Esther, p. 159) from יוֹם אַחַר.

circum, around; others have quite ceased to be so used, e.g. כְּבָר (length)
long ago [Aram.: only in Ec.]; עוֹד (repetition, duration) *again* or *further*.

(c) Adjectives, especially in the feminine (corresponding to the *d*
Indo-Germanic neuter), e.g. רִאשׁוֹנָה *primum, formerly* (more frequently
בָּרִאשׁוֹנָה, also לָרִאשׁוֹנָה); רַבָּה and רַבַּת [both rare] *multum, much, enough*;
נִפְלָאוֹת *wonderfully* (properly *mirabilibus*, sc. *modis*), יְהוּדִית *Jewish,*
i.e. in the Jewish language.

(d) Verbs in the infinitive absolute, especially in *Hiph'îl*, which *e*
are likewise to be regarded as accusatives (§ 113 h), e.g. הַרְבֵּה (prop.
a multiplying) *much* [frequent], לְהַרְבֵּה [rare and late] *in multitude*;
הַשְׁכֵּם (*mane faciendo*) *early*; הַעֲרֵב (*vespere faciendo*) *in the evening*.

(e) Pronouns and numerals, e.g. זֶה (prop. *there=at this place*) *here, f*
הֵנָּה *here, hither* (also of time, עַד־הֵנָּה *till now*, cf. the late and rare עֶדֶן
and עֶדֶּנָה = עַד־הֵן); אַחַת, שְׁתַּיִם, שֶׁבַע, מֵאָה *once, twice, seven times, a
hundred times*; שֵׁנִית *for the second time*.

3. Some adverbs are formed by the addition of formative syllables *g*
(most frequently ◌ָם) to substantives or adjectives, e.g. אָמְנָם and
אֻמְנָם *truly* (from אֹמֶן *truth*); חִנָּם (by favour) *gratis* (from חֵן *gratia*) ;
רֵיקָם *in vain, frustra*, but also *empty* (from רֵיק *empty, emptiness,
vanum*), Ru 1²¹, parallel with the *fem.* מְלֵאָה *full*; יוֹמָם *by day* (from יוֹם)¹ ;
with *ô* in the last syllable, פִּתְאֹם, for פִּתְאָם, *in a twinkling, suddenly*
(from פֶּתַע *a twinkling*, the *ô* being probably obscured from an original
â).² —Moreover, cf. אֲחֹרַנִּית *backward*, and קְדֹרַנִּית *darkly attired*, Mal 3¹⁴.
In both these cases, the formative syllable *an* has been first attached
to the stem, and then the feminine ending *îth*, which is elsewhere
used to form adverbs, has been added to it.

The termination ◌ָם occurs also in the formation of substantives, e.g. *h*
אוּלָם *porch*, and hence the above adverbs may equally well be regarded as
nouns used adverbially, so that ◌ָם, ◌ִ-, would correspond to ◌ָן, ◌ֹן (§ 85,
Nos. 53, 54), cf. בְּפִתְאֹם (with prep.) *suddenly*, 2 Ch 29³⁶. According to others,
this *am* is an obsolete accusative ending, to be compared with the indeterminate accusative sing. in *ăn* in Arabic.

---

¹ Is this ◌ָם an instance of the locative or temporal termination (cf.
especially צָהֳרַם) mentioned in § 88 c? Nöldeke, ZDMG. xl. p. 721, considers
יוֹמָם a secondary substantival form (used adverbially like לַיְלָה *noctu*), corresponding to the Phoenician and Aramaic יְמָם, Syr. 'îmâmâ; cf. on the other
hand, König, ii. 255, who follows Olshausen in maintaining that the *âm* is an
adverbial termination.

² דּוּמָם *silent* (an adjective in Is 47⁵, La 3²⁶; a substantive in Hb 2¹⁹), which
was formerly included under this head, is better taken, with Barth (*Nominalbildung*, p. 352, Rem. 2), as a participle formed like שׁוֹבָב, עוֹלָל, so that דּוּמָם
(perhaps assimilated to דּוּמָה) stands for original דֻּמָם.

i   **4.** A number of forms standing in very close relation to the demonstrative pronoun may be regarded as primitive adverbs, since they arise directly from a combination of demonstrative sounds. Some of these have subsequently suffered great mutilation, the extent of which, however, can now very rarely be ascertained with certainty. Such are e. g. אָז *then*, הִנֵּה *here* (according to Barth, *Sprachwiss. Abhandlungen*, p. 16, formed from the two demonstrative elements *hin* and *na*), כֵּן, כָּכָה *thus* (cf. אֵיכָה, אֵיכָכָה, אֵיךְ *how ?*), אַךְ *only*, אָכֵן *truly* (on all these adverbs, see the Lexicon), and especially the interrogative הֲ (*Hē interrogativum*), e. g. הֲלֹא (Dt 3¹¹ הֲלֹה) *nonne ?*, הֲגַם *num etiam ?* This *Hē interrogativum* is perhaps shortened from הֲל, which is still used in Arabic, and, according to the view of a certain school of Masoretes, occurs also in Hebrew in Dt 32⁶.[1]

k   The הֲ interrogative takes—(1) *Ḥaṭeph-Paṭhaḥ* generally before non-gutturals (even before ר), with a firm vowel, e. g. הֲשַׂמְתָּ *hast thou set?* see the interrogative clause, § 150 *c* (הַיִּיטַב Lv 10¹⁹ is an exception).

l   (2) Before a consonant with *S⁽ewâ*, usually *Paṭhaḥ* without a following *Dageš forte*, e. g. הַבְּרָכָה Gn 27³⁸, cf. 18¹⁷, 29⁵, 30¹⁵, 34³¹; less frequently (in about ten passages), *Paṭhaḥ* with a following *Dageš forte*, e. g. הַבְּדֶרֶךְ *num in via*, Ez 20³⁰, הַלְּבֶן Gn 17¹⁷, 18²¹, 37³², Nu 13¹⁹, Jb 23⁶; even in ר, 1 S 10²⁴, 17²⁵, 2 K 6³².

m   (3) Before gutturals, not pointed with either *Qameṣ* or *Ḥaṭeph-Qameṣ*, it takes *Paṭhaḥ*, e. g. הַאֵלֵךְ *shall I go ?*, הַאַתָּה *num tu ?*, הַאִם *num si*; הַאָרְצָה Mal 1¹³; also in Ju 6³¹ read הַאַתֶּם (not 'הָא), likewise הַ in Ju 12⁵, Jer 8¹⁹, Neh 6¹¹.— In הַאִישׁ Nu 16²², the Masora intends the article; read הַאִישׁ, and cf. Dt 20¹⁹; in Ec 3²¹ read הַעֹלָה and הַיֹּרֶדֶת; the article is a correction due to doctrinal considerations.

n   (4) The הֲ takes *S⁽eghôl* before gutturals pointed with *Qameṣ* or (as in Ju 9⁹ᶠ.) *Ḥaṭeph-Qameṣ*, e. g. הֶאָמוֹר Mi 2⁷; הֶאָנֹכִי Jb 21⁴; הֶהָיְתָה Jo 1²; הֶהָשֵׁב Gn 24⁵ (cf. the analogous instances in § 22 *c*, § 35 *k*, § 63 *k*). The place of this interrogative particle is always at the beginning of the clause [but see Jb 34³¹, Neh 13²⁷, Jer 22¹⁵, where one or more words are prefixed for emphasis].

o   **5.** Some adverbs occur also in connexion with suffixes, thus יֶשְׁךָ *thou art there*, 3rd sing. masc. יֶשְׁנוֹ[2] (but see note below), 2nd plur. masc. יֶשְׁכֶם; אֵינֶנִּי *I am not*, 2nd sing. אֵינְךָ, fem. אֵינֵךְ, 3rd sing. אֵינֶנּוּ, fem. אֵינֶנָּה, 2nd plur. אֵינְכֶם, 3rd plur. masc. אֵינָם.—Also עוֹדִי *I am yet* (עוֹדִי only in בְּעוֹדִי and מְעוֹדִי), עוֹדְךָ, עוֹדָךְ, עוֹדֵינוּ (La 4¹⁷ *Q⁽erê*; עוֹדֵינָה

---

[1] The separation of the הֲ at the beginning of Dt 32⁶, expressly noticed by Qimḥi (ed. Rittenb., p. 40 b) as an unique instance, is perhaps a protest against admitting a particle הֲל.

[2] This form, which occurs in Dt 29¹⁴, 1 S 14³⁹, 23²³, Est 3⁸, is textually very doubtful, and cannot be supported by the equally doubtful קְבֻנּוֹ (for קֻבְּנּוּ) Nu 23¹³. Most probably, with Stade, *Gramm.*, § 370 b, and P. Haupt, *SBOT* Numbers, p. 57, line 37, we should read יֶשְׁנּוּ.

K^eth.; the oriental school [see above, p. 38, note 2] recognize only
the reading עוֹרֵינוּ), עוֹרָם.—אַיֶּכָּה *where art thou ?*, אַיּוֹ *where is he ?*, אַיָּם
where are they ? The same applies to הֵן (הֶן־) and הִנֵּה *behold !* (prop.
here, here is; see § 105 *b*), only in Gn 19² הִנֵּה־נָא; with suffixes, הִנְנִי,
once הִנֶּנִּי (Gn 22⁷ with *Munaḥ*), in pause הִנֶּנִּי *behold me* (*here am I*),
הִנְּךָ (*pause* הִנֶּךָּ ψ 139⁸), הִנּוֹ, הִנָּם, and הִנֵּהוּ [both very rare], הִנְנוּ (*behold
us*). and הִנֶּנּוּ (in pause הִנֶּנּוּ), הִנָּם, הִנְּכֶם; [see more fully in the Lexicon,
p. 243].

The usual explanation of these suffixes (especially of the forms with *Nûn* *p*
energicum) as verbal suffixes, which ascribes some power of verbal government
even to forms originally substantival (e.g. יֶשְׁנוֹ *there is, he is*), is at least
inadmissible for forms (like אַיּוֹ, בְּעוֹרִי) which are evidently connected with
noun-suffixes; even for the other forms it is questionable. Brockelmann
suggests that the נ in connexion with these particles is a survival from הנה
corresponding to the Arab. *'ánna* which introduces dependent clauses.

101. *Prepositions.*

Brockelmann, *Grundriss*, i. 494 ff.

1. All words, which by usage serve as prepositions, were originally *a*
substantives, viz.:

(*a*) Substantives in the accusative and in the construct state, so that
the noun governed by them is to be considered as in the genitive,
and in Arabic actually has the genitive ending, cf. in German *statt*
dessen, kraft dessen, in Greek τούτου χάριν, in Latin *huius rei causa*,
or *gratia, montis instar*.¹ Cf. אַחַר (hinder part*) *behind, after* (*Mil'êl*
in אַחַר כֵּן Lv 14³⁶, Dt 21¹³, 1 S 10⁵; אַחַר זֶה 2 Ch 32⁹); אֵצֶל (side)
close by; בֵּין (intermediate space *) *between*; בְּעַד (distance²)
behind, around; זוּלַת, or with *Hireq compaginis* זוּלָתִי (removal, want)
except; יַעַן (purpose) *on account of*; מוֹל (מוֹל) only in Dt 1¹) *before, over*
against; מִן־ (separation; cf. § 119 *v*) *from, out of*; נֶגֶד (coming in
front, that which is over against) *before, over against*; עַד־ (progress,
duration*) *during, until*; עַל (height, upper part*) *upon, over*; עִם־
(connexion ?) *with*; it is doubtful whether this is to be derived from
the same stem as עֲמַת, לְעֻמַּת *near, beside, like*; תַּחַת (under part*)
under, instead of.

(*b*) Substantives in the construct state, but to be regarded as in the *b*
genitive, since they depend on prepositions (especially the inseparable),
e.g. לִפְנֵי (in the face of*) *before*; כְּפִי, לְפִי (according to the mouth,

---

¹ In the examples which follow, the meaning of the noun is added in
parentheses, and, when it is actually in use [though it is mostly in such cases
very rare], is marked with an asterisk.—On a similar use in other languages,
see W. von Humboldt, *Über die Kawisprache*, iii, p. 621.

² So also J. Hoch de Long, *Die hebr. Präpos.* בְּעַד, Lpz. 1905.

i. e. the command of *) *according to*; בְּגְלַל (in the concern of) *on account of*; לְמַעַן (for the purpose of) *on account of*.

c **2.** Substantives used adverbially very frequently become preposi-tions in this way, e. g. בְּלִי, בְּבְלִי, מִבְּלִי, בִּלְתִּי, בְּאֵין, בְּאֶפֶס (with cessation) *without*, בְּעוֹד (in the duration of) *during*; כְּדֵי, כְּדֵי (according to the requirement of) *for*, *according to*.

§ 102. *Prefixed Prepositions.*

a **1.** Of the words mentioned in § 101, מִן *from, out of*, frequently occurs as a prefix (§ 99 c), with its *Nûn* assimilated to the following consonant (by means of *Dageš forte*), e. g. מִיַּעַר *out of a forest*.

b Rem. The separate מִן (always with a following *Maqqeph*) is usual (but not necessary, cf. Ju 20¹⁴ with verse 15, Ez 43⁶, &c.) only before the article, e. g. מִן־הָאָרֶץ, and sometimes occurs before the softer consonants, e. g. מִן־אָז Jer 44¹⁸, מִן־בְּנֵי Jo 1¹², 1 Ch 5¹⁸; cf. Ex 18¹⁴, Lv 1¹⁴, 14³⁰, Ju 7²³, 10¹¹, 19¹⁶, ψ 104⁷ (2 K 23³⁶ before ר; also before ק in ψ 18⁴⁹), and elsewhere in the later books (as in Aramaic) ¹; there is besides a poetic by-form מִנִּי (cf. § 90 m) and מִנֵּי Is 30¹¹. Its form is most commonly מִ with a following Dageš, which may, however, be omitted in letters which have Šᵉwâ (cf. § 20 m). With a follow-ing י the מִ is, as a rule, contracted to מִי, e. g. מִידֵי = מִידֵי or מִידֵי (but cf. מִישְׁנֵי Dn 12²; מִירֻשָּׁתְךָ 2 Ch 20¹¹); before gutturals it becomes מֵ (according to § 22 c), e. g. מֵאָדָם, מֵעָם; before ח the מֵ occurs with the guttural virtually sharpened in מֵחוּץ *on the outside*, and in מֵחוּט Gn 14²³; before ה in מֵהְיוֹת (cf. § 28 b and § 63 q. The closed syllable here is inconsistent with the required virtual sharpening of the ה; probably מֵהְיוֹת is merely due to the analogy of לִהְיוֹת); similarly Is 14³ before ר; but in 1 S 23²⁸, 2 S 18¹⁶ מֵרְדֹף is to be read, according to § 22 s.

c **2.** There are also three other particles, the most commonly used prepositions and the particle of comparison, which have been reduced by abbreviation (§ 99 c) to a single prefixed consonant with Šᵉwâ (but see below, and § 103 e), viz.:

בְּ [poet. בְּמוֹ] *in, at, with.*

לְ [poet. לְמוֹ] *towards*, (belonging) *to, for*, Lat. *ad.*

כְּ [poet. כְּמוֹ] *like, as, according to* (no doubt the remnant of a sub-stantive with the meaning of *matter, kind, instar*).

d With regard to the pointing it is to be observed that—

(*a*) The Šᵉwâ *mobile*, with which the above prefixes are usually pronounced, has resulted from the weakening of a short vowel (an original ă, according to f) ²; the short vowel is regularly retained before Šᵉwâ : before Šᵉwâ *simplex*

---

¹ König, *Einleitung ins A. T.*, p. 393 (cf. also the almost exhaustive statistics in his *Lehrgebäude*, ii. 292 ff.), enumerates eight instances of מִן before a word without the article in 2 Samuel and Kings, and forty-five in Chronicles.

² Jerome (see Siegfried, *ZAW*. iv. 79) almost always represents בְּ by *ba.*

in the form of an *ĭ*, attenuated from *ă*: before a *Ḥateph* the prefix takes the vowel of the *Ḥateph*, e. g. לִפְרִי *for fruit*, כַּאֲרִי *as a lion*, בְּעָנְיִ *bŏʿŏni, in affliction* (sometimes with the syllable subsequently closed, cf. § 28 *b*, and the infinitives with לְ § 63 *i*): before weak consonants it follows the rule given in § 24 *c*, e.g. לְהוּדָה for לְיִ. When the prefixes לְ, כְּ, וּ, בְּ precede אֱלֹהִים *God*, the *Šᵉwâ* and *Ḥateph Sᵉghôl* regularly coalesce in *Ṣērê*, e. g. בֵּאלֹהִים, &c., for בֶּאֱל ; so with suffixes וֵאלֹהָיו, &c. (once also in the sing. לֵאלֹהוּ Hb 1¹¹); also regularly לֵאמֹר *to say*, for לֶאֱמֹר, see § 23 *d*.

(*b*) When the prefixes precede the article, the ה is almost always dropped, and they take its vowel. See further in § 35 *n*.

(*c*) Immediately before the tone-syllable, i. e. before monosyllables and dissyllables with the tone on the penultima (in the fore-tone), they take *Qameṣ* (undoubtedly a lengthening of an original *ă*, cf. § 26 *e*, § 28 *a*), but only in the following cases :

(*aa*) לְ before infinitives of the above-mentioned forms, as לָתֵת *to give*, לָדִין *to judge*, לָבֹז *to plunder*, לָגֹז *to shear*, לָחֹג *to keep a festival*, לָלֶדֶת *to bring forth*, לָלֶכֶת *to go*, לָקַחַת *to take*, except when the infinitive (as a *nomen regens*) is closely connected with another word (especially its subject, § 115 *e*), and consequently, as being in a sort of *constr.* state, loses the principal tone, e. g. לְצֵאת Ex 19¹, לְשֶׁבֶת Gn 16³, and so always לְבֹא חֲמָת Nu 13²¹, &c. (in such cases as לְתֵת־חֶרֶב Ex 5²¹ the *ā* is protected by the secondary tone; before infinitives of verbs ע״וּ, the לְ is retained even in close connexion; cf. Ez 21²⁰·²⁵, 22³);

(*bb*) before many pronominal forms, e.g. בָּזֶה (so also in 1 S 21¹⁰; not בֶּזֶה), לָזֶה, כָּזֶה, לָזֹאת (in close connexion, however, לְזֹאת Gn 2²³; כְּזֹאת Gn 45²³); כָּאֵלֶּה *as these*; and especially כָּכֶם, לָכֶם, בָּכֶם (כְּכֶם) and בָּהֶם, לָהֶם, כָּהֶם (כְּהֶם), see § 103 *e*;

(*cc*) לְ before monosyllables or fore-toned nouns in such combinations as פֶּה לָפֶה *mouth to mouth*, 2 K 10²¹, בֵּין מַיִם לָמָיִם *between waters and waters*, Gn 1⁶ ; לְטֹרַח *for a trouble*, Is 1¹⁴, but always before the principal pause. The instructive example in Dt 17⁸ also shows that the punctuation לְ is only possible with at least the lesser pause after it ; in Is 28¹⁰·¹³ the לְ is twice repeated, even before the small and smallest disjunctives ;

(*dd*) in certain standing expressions, which have become stereotyped almost as adverbs, e. g. לָעַד *to eternity*, לָרֹב *in multitude*, לָבֶטַח *in security*, לָנֶצַח *to eternity*, but לָנֶצַח נְצָחִים *to all eternity*, Is 34¹⁰. Cf. also לָנֶפֶשׁ *for the dead*, Lv 19²⁸, Nu 5², 9¹⁰.

(*d*) With the interrogative מָה they are pointed as in בַּמֶּה ; in *pause* and before א as in בַּמָּה *by what?* (before a following relative clause, as in Ec 3²², בְּמֶה ; cf. Delitzsch, *Jesaia*, 4th ed., on Is 2²²); בַּמָּה *how much?* but also בַּמֶּה 1 K 22¹⁶, in close connexion, and at a greater distance from the *pause*. The *Sᵉghôl* in these forms arises from a modification of the original *ă*, while the מ is sharpened in order to maintain the original *ă* of the prefixes.

When לְ (prop. *la*) is united to מָה, it takes, according to § 49 *f, g*, the form לָמָה (Jb 7²⁰), לָמָה, 1 S 1⁸ לָמֶה, all *Mil'êl*, and hence the *ă* in the tone is lengthened to *ā*) *for what? why?* Before the gutturals א, ה, ע, לָמָה is used for euphonic reasons (exceptions 1 S 28¹⁵, 2 S 14³¹, Jer 15¹⁸, before ה ; 2 S 2²²,

ψ 49[6], before אָ) ; לְמָּה, however, remains before ה. Before letters which are not gutturals, לְמָה is found in ψ 42[10], 43[2] (immediately after a tone-syllable).

m Rem. The divine name יְהֹוָה, which has not its original vowels (יַהְוֶה) but those of אֲדֹנָי (see § 17 *c*), except that the י has simple not compound *Šᵉwá*, takes the prefixes also, after the manner of אֲדֹנָי, thus וַיְהֹוָה, לַיהֹוָה,־בַּיהֹוָה, מֵיְהֹוָה (since they are to be read וַאֲדֹנָי, לַאֲדֹנָי, בַּאֲדֹנָי, מֵאֲדֹנָי); for the א of אֲדֹנָי, as of אֲדֹנָי אֲדֹנִים, &c. (see below), *quiesces* after the prefixes בְּ, בַּ, לְ, וְ, but is *audible* after מֵ (for מִן), שֶׁ (no instance in the O. T.), and הָ (in הָאֲדֹנִים Dt 10[17], ψ 136[3], the article, not הֲ interrog., is intended ; the only example with הֲ interrog.,· Jer 8[19], is to be pointed הַיְהֹוָה, i.e. הַאֲדֹנָי, not הֲיְהֹוָה). Hence the rule, מֹשֶׁה מוֹצִיא *Moses brought out* (i. e. מ, שׁ, ה make the א audible), וְכָלֵב מַכְנִים *and Caleb brought in* (i. e. וְ, כְּ, לְ, בְּ allow it to quiesce).[1]—As regards the other plural forms of אָדֹן, elision of the א always takes place after בְּ, וְ, כְּ, לְ, except in the form אֲדֹנַי, thus לַאֲדֹנָיו, לַאֲדֹנֶיךָ, &c. ; but לַאֲדֹנֵיהֶם, &c., לַאֲדֹנֵינוּ, &c., לַאֲדֹנָי.

§ 103. *Prepositions with Pronominal Suffixes and in the Plural Form.*

a 1. As all prepositions were originally nouns (§ 101) in the accusative, they may be united with the noun-suffixes (§ 91 *b–l*), e. g. אֶצְלִי (prop. at my side) *by me*, אִתִּי (in my proximity) *with me*, תַּחְתָּם (in their place) *instead of them*, like the Latin *mea causa*, *for my sake*.

b Rem. 1. The preposition אֵת (usually אֶת־) *near*, *with*, is distinguished from אֵת (see below, and § 117 *a*, note 4), the sign of the definite accusative (§ 117 *a*), in its connexion with suffixes, by a difference of pointing, the former making אִתִּי, אִתְּךָ, in *pause* אִתָּךְ, 2nd fem. אִתָּךְ (Is 54[10] (אִתֵּךְ), אִתּוֹ, אִתָּהּ, אִתָּנוּ, אִתְּכֶם, אִתָּם (also in the later books, especially in Kings, and always in Jer. and Ezek., incorrectly אוֹתִי *with me* ; מֵאוֹתְךָ *from thee*, 1 K 20[25] ; מֵאוֹתוֹ *from him*, 1 K 22[7] ; אֹתָם *with them*), while the latter retains its ô (obscured from *á*) before the light suffixes, but before grave suffixes is pointed with Sᵉghôl. This Sᵉghôl is to be explained, with Praetorius, *ZDMG.* lv. 369 f., as the modification of an *ä* which again was shortened from original *á* (in 'áthí, 'áthô, &c.) in a closed syllable ('áth-hem, &c.). The same shortening and modification of the original *á* takes place before words in close connexion, hence אֶת־כֹּל, &c. When not in close connexion, the toneless אֶת becomes tone-long אֵת, e.g. אֵת הַשָּׁמַיִם Gn 1[1]. Hence the following forms arise :—

	Sing.		Plur.	
1.	אֹתִי *me.*		אֹתָנוּ *us.*	
2.	*m.* אֹתְךָ, pause אֹתָךְ	thee.	אֶתְכֶם *you.*	
	f. אֹתָךְ		. . . . . .	
3.	*m.* אֹתוֹ *him.*		אֹתָם, rarely אֶתְהֶם	them.
	f. אֹתָהּ *her.*		אֶתְהֶן, rarely אֹתָן	

[1] Another *vox memor.* is כָּל־בּוֹ נֶעְלָם *all is hidden in him.*

Less common are the *plene* forms אוֹתִי, אֹתְךָ, אוֹתְךָ (Nu 22³³) אֹתְכָה before (ה, אוֹתָךְ (Ex 29³⁵), אֹתְכָה, אוֹתוֹ, אוֹתָהּ, אוֹתָנוּ, אֹתָם. Moreover, for אֶתְכֶם we find אוֹתְכֶם Jos 23¹⁵; for אֶתָם, five times אֶתְהֶם (Gn 32¹, Ex 18²⁰, &c.), and in Ez 23⁴⁵ אוֹתְהֶם; for אֶתְהֶן אֶתְהֶן (Gn 19⁸, &c. [13 times]), אֹתָן (only found in Ez 16⁵⁴; Ex 35²⁶ אֹתָנָה) Ez 34²¹ (אוֹתְהֶן), and אוֹתְהֶן Ez 23⁴⁷.—No instance of the 2nd fem. plur. אֶתְכֶן occurs in the O. T.; in Cant 2⁷, &c., אֶתְכֶם is used instead.

2. The preposition עִם *with* (with suffixes on the model of stems ע״ע, עַם, C עִמָּךְ [1 S 1²⁶ [עִמְכָה], in *pause* עִמָּךְ; 2nd fem. עִמָּךְ; עִמּוֹ, עִמָּהּ) is united with the suffixes נוּ, כֶּם, and הֶם by a (pretonic) *Qameṣ*, which causes the sharpening of the *Mêm* to be distinctly audible: עִמָּנוּ, עִמָּכֶם, עִמָּהֶם (so in Nu 22¹², Dt 29¹⁶, both in principal pause, and often in very late passages, otherwise עִמָּם is generally used). In the first person, besides עִמִּי, we also find עִמָּדִי (probably from original עִנְדִי; cf. Arab. *'inda*, beside, with).

3. It is but seldom that prepositions occur with verbal suffixes, as תַּחְתֵּנִי d 2 S 22³⁷·⁴⁰·⁴⁸ (for which ψ 18³⁷·⁴⁰·⁴⁸ ,תַּחְתֵּנָה, תַּחְתָּי Gn 2²¹ and בַּעֲדֵנִי ψ 139¹¹ (here probably for the sake of the rhyme with יְשׁוּפֵנִי).[1]

2. When pronominal suffixes are added to the prefixes (§ 102), there e appears occasionally, especially in the case of the shorter suffixes, an endeavour to lengthen the preposition, so as to give it more strength and body. Hence to כְּ is appended the syllable מוֹ (see below, k), and בְּ and לְ take at least a full vowel, בָּ and לָ (§ 102 d, f).—The following deviations from the analogy of the noun with suffixes are to be noticed (a) in the pausal forms עִמָּךְ, אִתָּךְ, אֹתָךְ, לָךְ, בָּךְ (not *bĕkhā*, &c.); (b) in the similar forms with the suffix of the 2nd sing. fem. (not *bĕkh*, &c.) and in עִמָּנוּ, לָנוּ, בָּנוּ, &c. (not *bēnû*, &c.).

(a) לְ *with Pronominal Suffixes.* f

	Sing.		Plur.
1.	לִי *to me.*		לָנוּ *to us.*
2.	m. לְךָ (לְכָה), in *pause* לָךְ f. לָךְ . . . . } *to thee.*		לָכֶם לְבֶנָה [לָכֶן²] } *to you.*
3.	m. לוֹ *to him.* f. לָהּ *to her.*		לָהֶם, לָהֵמָּה, poet. לָמוֹ [53 times][3] לָהֵנָּה⁴, לָהֶן } *to them.*

[1] *Fini* and *bini* (in me), in vulgar Arabic for *fiyya* and *bi*, are compared by Socin. Brockelmann, *ZA.* xiv. 347, note 1, suggests that תַּחְתֵּנִי, תַּחְתָּנָה, בַּעֲדֵנִי are later formations on the model of מִמֶּנִּי when its origin from the reduplication of the preposition had become obscured, but see below, *m*.

[2] לָכֶן does not occur in the O. T., by a mere accident, no doubt; Ez 13¹⁸ לְבֵנָה.

[For notes 3 and 4 see next page.]

g　בְּ takes suffixes in the same manner : בְּךָ, בִּי (Ex 7²⁹, 2 S 22³⁰, ψ 141⁸ בְּכָה, as in Gn 27³⁷, 2 S 18²², Is 3⁶ לְכָה [for 2nd fem. לָךְ the *K⁽ᵉ⁾thîbh* לכי occurs in 2 K 4², Ct 2¹³, cf. § 91 *e*]), בָּם, &c.; except that for the 3rd plur., besides בָּהֶם (especially in the later books) and בָּהֵמָּה (only in Ex 30⁴, 36¹, Hb 1¹⁶; לָהֵמָּה only in Jer 14¹⁶), the form בָּם is also used; and for the feminine, besides בָּהֵנָּה (three times), בָּהֶן is found fifteen times, and בָּהֵן only in 1 S 31⁷, Is 38¹⁶, Ez 42¹⁴.—According to the Masora, לֹא is found fifteen times for לוֹ (as conversely in 1 S 2¹⁶, 20² לוֹ for לֹא), e. g. Ex 21⁸, 1 S 2³, Is 9², ψ 100³ (and, as has been conjectured, also Jb 41⁴); cf. Delitzsch on ψ 100³.—In Nu 32⁴², Zc 5¹¹, Ru 2¹⁴, the Masora requires לְהּ instead of לָהּ (in all three places before a following tone-syllable; cf. § 23 *k*, and the analogous cases of the loss of *Mappîq* in § 58 *g*, § 91 *e*).

h　　　　　(*b*) כְּ *with Pronominal Suffixes.*

	Sing.	Plur.
1.	כָּמֹנִי⁵ *as I.*	כָּמֹנוּ *as we.*
2.	*m.* כָּמוֹךָ⁵ } *as thou.* *f.* . . .	כָּכֶם, כְּכֶם, rarely כְּמוֹכֶם } *as ye.* . . . . }
3.	*m.* כָּמוֹהוּ *as he.* *f.* כָּמוֹהָ *as she.*	כְּמוֹהֶם, [כָּהֵמָּה, בָּהֶם], בָּהֶם } *as they.* כָּהֵנָּה, [בָּהֶן] }

---

³ The question whether לָמוֹ can also stand for the sing. לוֹ, which Rödiger and recently W. Diehl (*Das Pronomen pers. suff.* . . . *des Hebr.*, p. 20 f.) and P. Haupt (*SBOT.* on Pr 23²⁰, a contraction of *la-humû*) have altogether denied, must be answered in the affirmative unless we conclude with Diehl and Haupt that *all* the instances concerned are due to corruptions of the text. It is true that in such places as Gn 9²⁶·²⁷, Dt 33², Is 30⁵, ψ 73¹⁰ (all *in* or immediately before the principal pause ; in Dt 33² with *Zaqeph qaṭon* at least) לָמוֹ can be better explained as plural (in reference to collective nouns) ; and in Is 53⁸ for נֶגַע לָמוֹ we should read with the LXX נֻגַּע לַמָּוֶת. On the other hand, in Is 44¹⁵ its explanation as plural would be extremely forced. Even then there would remain—presuming the traditional text to be correct— פְּנֵימוֹ ψ 11⁷ and כַּפֵּימוֹ Jb 27²³, as well as עָלֵימוֹ, three times, Jb 20²³, 27²³ (beside עָלָיו), and especially Jb 22². In all these places the most extreme exegetical artifices can only be avoided by simply admitting a singular suffix (= עָלָיו, כַּפָּיו, פָּנָיו).—On the question of the antiquity of the suffixes in מוֹ see § 91 *l*.

⁴ The form לְהֵן in Ru 1¹³ is Aramaic (= *therefore*).

⁵ The use of נִי here for יִ‍֫ (cf. above, *d*) might be due to euphonic reasons.—כָּמֹנִי (defectively) only in the Pentateuch, כָּמֹכָה Ex 15¹¹.

(c) מִן with *Pronominal Suffixes.*

	Sing.	Plur.
1.	מִמֶּנִּי, poet. מִנִּי [4 times], in *pause* also מֶנִּי [6 times] *from me.*	מִמֶּנּוּ *from us.*
2.	*m.* מִמְּךָ, in *pause* וּמִמֶּךָ } *from thee.* *f.* מִמֵּךְ }	מִכֶּם } *from you.* מִכֶּן }
3.	*m.* מִמֶּנּוּ, Jb 4¹² in *pause* מִמֶּנְהוּ, מֶנְהוּ, [מִנֶּהוּ or מִנְהוּ: see below] *from him.* *f.* מִמֶּנָּה *from her.*	מֵהֶם, מֵהֵמָּה [twice], מִנְּהֶם Jb 11²⁰ } *from them.* מֵהֶן, מֵהֶנָּה [7 times] }

The syllable מוֹ (in Arabic *mâ* מָא = Heb. מָה *what*) in כָּמוֹנִי (probably from כְּ בָּמָה אֲנִי, prop. *according to what I*, for *as I*) is, in poetry, appended to the three simple prefixes בְּ, כְּ, לְ, even without suffixes, so that לְמוֹ, כְּמוֹ, בְּמוֹ appear as independent words, equivalent in meaning to בְּ, כְּ, לְ. Poetry is here distinguished from prose by the use of longer forms; in the case of מִן, on the other hand, it prefers the shorter, which resemble the Syriac and Arabic.

The form כָּהֶם, enclosed in brackets above, occurs only in 2 K 17¹⁵ (in *l* pause), כָּהֵמָּה only in Jer 36³² (in *pause*); כָּהֵן (Baer following Qimḥi כָּהֶן) only in Ez 18¹⁴. Cf. Frensdorff, *Massora Magna*, p. 234 ff.—For כָּכֶם *as ye*, Qimḥi requires כָּכֶם (invariably or only in Jb 16⁴?); in Jos 1¹⁵, Ju 8², Ezr 4² Baer gives כָּכֶם.

With regard to מִן with suffixes, מִמֶּנִּי *from me* is usually explained as arising, *m* by a reduplication of מִן, from an original מנמני, just as מִמֶּנּוּ *from him*, from מנמנ-הו, identical in form with מִמֶּנּוּ[1] *from us*, from מנמנ-נו, while מִמֶּנָּה *from her*, goes back to מנמנה. Far simpler, however, is Mayer Lambert's explanation (*REJ.* xxiii. 302 ff.), that מִמֶּנִּי, &c., have arisen from מִנֶּנִּי, &c., and that the forms of the suffixes are to be explained on the analogy of תְּחִתֵּנָּה, אֵינֶנִּי, עוֹדֶנּוּ, יֹרְדֶנּוּ, § 100 *o.*—The bracketed form מִנֶּהוּ, for which Baer, following Qimḥi and others, writes מִנְהוּ, occurs only in ψ 68²⁴, and is there regarded by Delitzsch, Hupfeld, and others (following Simonis) as a substantive (מֶן = *portion*). The expression מִן־הוּא (for מִמֶּנּוּ?) Is 18²·⁷ is very strange.—מֵהֵמָּה occurs only in Jer 10², Ec 12¹² (Jb 11²⁰ מִנְּהֶם); מֵהֶן (so Baer and Ginsburg, following the best authorities, instead of the ordinary reading מֵהֵן) only in Ez 16⁴⁷·⁵².

---

[1] The Babylonian Masora writes מִמֶּנּוּ (to distinguish it from the 3rd sing.), which is justly blamed by Ibn Ezra.

n 3. Several prepositions, especially those which express relations of space and time, are (like the German *wegen*) properly plural nouns (for the reason, see § 124 *a*), and are, therefore, joined with the pronominal suffixes in the form of the plural *construct state*, just like other plural nouns (§ 91 *g*). On the other hand, the apparent connexion of אֶל‍־ ,עַד‍־ ,עַל‍־ with plural suffixes is explained from the ground-forms of those prepositions (from stems ל״ה) עַל (אֱלֵי) ,אֱלַי ,עֲדַי ,עֲלַי (contracted to אֱלֵי ,אֱלַי, &c.).[1]

o Without suffixes these prepositions are—

אַחַר, more frequently אַחֲרֵי (prop. *hinder parts*) *behind, after.*

אֶל‍־,[2] poet. [4 times in Job] also אֱלֵי (*region, direction*), *towards, to, according to.*

בֵּין (*interval*) *between*; the suffixes indicating the singular are added to the singular בֵּין, thus בֵּינְךָ ,בֵּינִי, &c. (Gn 16⁵ בֵּינֶיךָ, the second *Yôdh* is, however, marked with a point as critically doubtful ; בֵּינַי, which occurs three times, is only the Masoretic *Qᵉrê* for בֵּינוֹ, which is found e.g. in Gn 30³⁶). On the other hand, the suffixes indicating a plural are attached to the plural forms בֵּינֵי or בֵּינוֹת.

סָבִיב (*circuit*) *around*, as a preposition, always has the plural form, sometimes masc. סְבִיבָיִךְ, &c. [10 times], but much more frequently in the fem. סְבִיבוֹת (*surroundings*). In Ez 43¹⁷ סָבִיב אוֹתָהּ is a corruption of סְבִיבֹתֶיהָ; [in 1 K 6⁵ סָבִיב אֶת also is so contrary to usage, that it must be due to some textual error].

עַד‍־ (*continuation, duration*, from עָדָה) *as far as, unto*, poet. עֲדֵי [12 times]. In Jb 32¹² עֲרֵיכֶם, with the *ā* retained in the secondary tone, is abnormal. Also in 2 K 9¹⁸ for עַד‍הֶם read עֲדֵיהֶם.

עַל‍־ *upon, over* (cf. the rare subst. עַל *height* [see Lexicon], from עָלָה *to ascend*), poet. עֲלֵי [40 times, and 2 *Qᵉrê*].

תַּחַת *under* (prop. *what is beneath*). On תַּחְתֵּנִי, &c.; cf. above, *d.*

---

[1] The reference of these forms to original plurals has been again expressly supported by De Lagarde, *Symmicta*, ii. 101 ff. ; *Nachrichten der G. g. G.*, 1881, p. 376, cf. *Mittheilungen*, 1884, p. 63 ; also *GGA.* 1884, p. 280 f. According to Barth, *ZDMG.* xlii. p. 348 ff., and *Nominalbildung*, p. 375 ff., תַּחְתֶּיךָ, &c., was only formed on the analogy of עָלֶיךָ, &c., and אַחֲרֶיךָ, &c., only on the analogy of לְפָנַי, &c., since the real plural forms ought to be תִּחְתֶּיךָ ,אֲחַדֶיךָ, &c. ; cf., however, König, *Lehrgebäude*, ii. 305 f.

[2] On the use of this particle see § 119 *g.*

With Suffixes.

	אַחֲרַי (after me)	בֵּינִי (between me)	סְבִיבוֹתַי (around me)	תַּחְתַּי (beneath me)	אֵלַי (to me)	עָדַי (unto me)	עָלַי (on me) p
1 *Sing.*	אַחֲרַי	בֵּינִי	סְבִיבוֹתַי	תַּחְתַּי	אֵלַי	עָדַי	עָלַי
2 *S. m.*	אַחֲרֶיךָ	בֵּינְךָ	סְבִיבוֹתֶיךָ & סְבִיבֶיךָ	תַּחְתֶּיךָ	אֵלֶיךָ	עָדֶיךָ	עָלֶיךָ
2 *S. f.*	אַחֲרַיִךְ		סְבִיבוֹתַיִךְ & סְבִיבַיִךְ		אֵלַיִךְ		עָלַיִךְ
3 *S. m.*	אַחֲרָיו	בֵּינוֹ	סְבִיבוֹתָיו & סְבִיבָיו	תַּחְתָּיו	אֵלָיו	עָדָיו	עָלָיו
3 *S. f.*	אַחֲרֶיהָ		סְבִיבוֹתֶיהָ & סְבִיבֶיהָ	תַּחְתֶּיהָ	אֵלֶיהָ	עָדֶיהָ	עָלֶיהָ
1 *Plur.*	אַחֲרֵינוּ &	בֵּינֵינוּ [1] בֵּינוֹתֵינוּ	סְבִיבוֹתֵינוּ	תַּחְתֵּינוּ	אֵלֵינוּ		עָלֵינוּ
2 *Pl. m.*	אַחֲרֵיכֶם	בֵּינֵיכֶם	סְבִיבוֹתֵיכֶם	תַּחְתֵּיכֶם	אֲלֵיכֶם	עֲדֵיכֶם	עֲלֵיכֶם
3 *Pl. m.*	אַחֲרֵיהֶם	בֵּינֵיהֶם	סְבִיבוֹתֵיהֶם	תַּחְתֵּיהֶם	אֲלֵיהֶם	[עֲדֵיהֶם]	עֲלֵיהֶם [עֲדֵיהֶם]
	& בֵּינוֹתָם		usually סְבִיבוֹתָם & סְבִיבֹתָם	תַּחְתָּם &	אֲלֵהֶם & [אֲלֵימוֹ [2]		[עָלֵימוֹ [2]
3 *Pl. f.*	אַחֲרֵיהֶן			תַּחְתֵּיהֶן	אֲלֵיהֶן & אֲלֵהֶן		עֲלֵיהֶן

§ 104. *Conjunctions.*

1. The conjunctions serve to connect sentences, and to express their *a* relations one to another. They may be either—

(*a*) Original pronouns, e. g. the demonstrative כִּי *that, because, for.*

(*b*) Original substantives, which afterwards were reduced to the rank of pronouns, adverbs, or conjunctions; so perhaps אֲשֶׁר (see § 36), which is sometimes used to express the general idea of relation, sometimes as a relative pronoun (properly a demonstrative), but in many cases stands simply for כִּי; also אַל־ (*nothing*), *that not*; פֶּן *that not* (the Greek μή of *prohibition*), &c. To these may be added the adverbial combination of substantives with prepositions, e. g. בְּטֶרֶם

---

[1] As Mayer Lambert observes, usage (cf. esp. Gn 26[28]) distinguishes between the two forms: בֵּינוֹתֵינוּ means *between us and you*, whereas בֵּינֵינוּ (Jos 22[25.27.28] before וּבֵינֵיכֶם) means *between us on the one side.*

[2] The poetical form אֲלֵימוֹ only in ψ 2[5]; עָלֵימוֹ, on which see note 3 on *f*, 12 times [viz. Dt 32[23], ψ 5[12], 55[16], 64[9], Jb 6[16], 20[23], 21[17.22], 27[23], 29[22], 30[2.5]].

(*in the not yet*) *earlier, before*, for which מִטֶּרֶם is also used. On the combination of two particles to express complex ideas (e. g. אַף־כִּי *added to this, that* = *much more*), see the Syntax, § 163 f.

b　　(*c*) Prepositions, which with the addition of the conjunction אֲשֶׁר or כִּי together form one single conjunction, e. g. יַעַן אֲשֶׁר *because*, prop. *on account of the fact that*; אַחַר אֲשֶׁר, and more frequently אַחֲרֵי אֲשֶׁר, *after that*; כַּאֲשֶׁר *according as* (with כְּ); עֵקֶב כִּי and עֵקֶב אֲשֶׁר *in consequence of the fact that, for the reason that, because*. Sometimes, however, the conjunction in such cases is omitted, and the preposition itself used as a conjunction, e. g. עַל־ (for עַל־אֲשֶׁר) *although*, Jb 16¹⁷.

So, at any rate, according to our linguistic principles. It would, however, be more correct to say, that instead of the intermediary אֲשֶׁר the whole of the succeeding sentence is regarded as *one* substantival idea, under the immediate government of the preposition. In the same way, all prepositions governing the gerund in English may be paraphrased by conjunctions with the finite verb, see §§ 114 and 115, *passim*.

c　　2. Besides those already mentioned, there are certain other small words now used as conjunctions, of which the derivation or original meaning is altogether obscure, thus אוֹ *or*, אִם־ *if* (also *or* before the second member of a double question), אַף *also*, וְ *and*, and others.

d　　Rem. The pointing of the וְ (originally וַ, as still before *Ḥaṭeph Pathaḥ* and—with a following *Dageš forte*—in *wāw consecutive* of the imperfect; cf. § 49 *f*) is in many respects analogous to that of the prefixes בְּ, כְּ, לְ (§ 102 *d–i*), but as being a weak consonant, the *wāw copulative* has some further peculiarities :

(*a*) Usually it takes simple *S°wâ* (וְ).

(*b*) Before words which begin with a guttural having a *compound S°wâ*, it takes the vowel with which the *S°wâ* is compounded (according to § 28 *b*), e. g. וַחֲכַם *and be thou wise*, וַעֲבָדִים *and servants*, וֶעֱזוּז *and strength*, וֶאֱכֹל *and eat thou*, וָחֳלִי *and sickness*. On וֵאלֹהִים, וֵאלֹהַי, &c., see § 102 *d* ; on וַאדֹנָי, &c., see § 102 *m* ; on such cases as וְעָצֹר Jb 4², cf. § 28 *b*.

e　　(*c*) Before words with simple *S°wâ* under the first consonant (except in the cases under *f*), the *Wāw* becomes the vowel *û* (cf. § 26 *a*), e. g. וּלְכֹל *and to all*, so also (except in the case under *g*) before the cognate labials בּ, מ, פ, hence וּמְלָךְ. On the cases in which *simple S°wâ* has become a *Ḥaṭeph* after וְ *copulative* (e. g. וְזָהָב Gn 2¹²), cf. § 10 *g*.

f　　(*d*) With a following יְ the וְ coalesces to form וִי according to § 24 *b*, as וִיהִי *and let him be*. On the peculiar punctuation of the *wāw copulative* before forms with initial *S°wâ* from הָיָה *to be* and חָיָה *to live* (e. g. וִהְיִיתֶם Jos 8⁴, וֶחְיֵה Gn 20⁷), cf. § 63 *q*.

g　　(*e*) Immediately before the tone-syllable it frequently takes *Qameṣ*, like בָּ, כָּ, לָ (see § 102 *f*), but in most cases only at the end of a sentence or clause (but cf. also וָבָא 2 K 22³⁰), e. g. וָמֵת Ex 21¹² (on the other hand, in verse 20

וּמֵת is in closer logical connexion with what follows); 2 K 7⁴ וְשֵׁם, וְמַחְתְּנוּ, וּמֵתָנוּ
and וּמֵתָנוּ; Ru 3³ וְסַבְתְּ; ψ 10¹⁵ זְרֹעַ; 1 S 9⁴ וְאַיִן; 2 S 13²⁶ וָלֹא; Ez 47⁹ וָחָי; cf.
also (with *Tiphḥa*) Gn 33¹³, 2 S 15¹². The very frequent connexion of nouns
expressing kindred ideas, by means of וְ, is due simply to considerations of
rhythm, for even in such cases the *Wāw* must immediately precede the tone-
syllable, which must be marked by a disjunctive accent, e. g. תֹּהוּ וָבֹהוּ Gn 1²,
יוֹם וָלַיְלָה Gn 8²² (see also the previous examples); Gn 13¹⁴ (thrice); Ex 25³
זָהָב וָכֶסֶף; ψ 96⁷ כָּבוֹד וָעֹז; ψ 76⁷ וָרֶכֶב וָסוּס; Gn 7¹³ נֹחַ וְשֵׁם־וְחָם וָיֶפֶת; 1 K 21¹⁰
אֱלֹהִים וָמֶלֶךְ; כֹּה וָכֹה *thus and thus*; Est 1⁸ אִישׁ־וָאִישׁ at the end of the verse,
but in ψ 87⁵ אִישׁ וָאִישׁ in spite of the *Dᵉḥi* with the second אִישׁ, because it is
closely connected with the following predicate. Also with three words
פַּחַד וָפַחַת וָפָח Is 24¹⁷. On the other hand, the rapid pronunciation וְ occurs
before a conjunctive accent (and, when farther removed from the principal
pause, even with the smaller disjunctives, in spite of a following tone-syllable),
e. g. צֹאן וָעֶבֶד Gn 32⁶; cf. Gn 31⁴⁰, Lv 7²³, Dt 2²¹, and among the examples
given above, Gn 7¹³ and ψ 76⁷. (Exceptions : וְקִדְּמָה Gn 13¹⁴, where evidently
the וְ is intended to ensure the slow and solemn recitation of the promise,
but also וָזִיף Jos 15⁵⁵, וָעָתֵר 19⁷, וָבֶטֶן 19²⁵, all immediately before the pause.)
For the same rhythmical reason וְ (not וָ) is used regularly with certain
monosyllables which, by their nature, lean more closely upon the following
word, thus וְלֹא, וְגַם, וְאֵת, וְזֶה (to be distinguished from וָלֹא *if not*, with *Zaqeph*
gadol, 2 K 5¹⁷), and others.

§ 105. *Interjections.*

1. Among the interjections some (as in all languages) are simply *a*
natural sounds, or, as it were, vocal gestures, called forth involuntarily
by certain impressions or sensations, e. g. אֲהָהּ (הָהּ), אָח (Ez 30²), הֶאָח *ah !*
aha ! (cf. this אָח also in אַחֲלַי and אַחֲלֵי *utinam !*), אָנָּא Ex 32³¹, &c.
(Gn 50¹⁷ אָנָּא) *ah !* (from אָח and נָא), otherwise written אָנָּה 2 K 20³,
Jn 1¹⁴, ψ 116⁴; also הַס (in pause הָס, even in the plural הַסּוּ *hold your*
peace ! Neh 8¹¹) *hush !* הוֹי (Am 5¹⁶ הוֹ־הוֹ) *ha ! woe !* אוֹי, אֹויָה (ψ 120⁵),
אִי (in אִילוֹ Ec 4¹⁰; אִי־לָךְ 10¹⁶) *woe !*

2. Others, however, originally expressed independent ideas, and *b*
become interjections only by rapid pronunciation and by usage, e. g.
הָא הֵן (הֵא) or הִנֵּה *behold !* (prop. *here*); רְאֵה *behold !* (prop. imperative);
הָבָה, plur. הָבוּ (prop. *give*, imperative of יָהַב; as to the tone, cf. § 69 *o*),
come, the Latin *age, agite !* לְכָה (also לֶךְ), לְכוּ (prop. *go*, imperative
of הָלַךְ) with the same meaning ¹ ; חָלִילָה *far be it !* (prop. *ad profanum !*)

---

¹ רְאֵה (Dt 1⁸), הָבָה and לְכָה are also used in connexion with the feminine
and the plural, which proves that they have become quite stereotyped as
interjections.

בִּי (see the Lexicon) *I beseech, hear me!* נָא *pray!*[1] used to emphasize a demand, warning, or entreaty, and always placed after the expression to which it belongs.[2]

---

[1] נָא serves to express the most various shades of expression, which are discussed in the various parts of the syntax. It is used especially (*a*) after the *imperative*, either in commands or entreaty, see § 110 *d*; (*b*) with the *imperfect*, either in the cohortative (§ 108 *b*) or jussive (§ 109 *b*); (*c*) once with *perfect*, Gn 40¹⁴; (*d*) after various particles: הִנֵּה־נָא *behold now*; particularly after the conjunctions אַל and אִם: אַל־נָא *ne quaeso* and אִם־נָא *if now,* εἴπερ, εἴποτε, *if*, in a deprecatory sense, expressive of politeness or modesty. In Nu 12¹³ נָא stands after a noun; but we ought certainly to read אַל־נָא.— In polite language this particle is used constantly in all these ways, Gn 18³·⁴, 19⁷·⁸·¹⁹, and 50¹⁷.

[2] Against the usual view which regards נָא as a hortatory particle (= *up! come!* analogous to the original imperatives הָבָה and לְכָה and the Ethiopic *nāʿâ*, properly *hither*, also *come!*), P. Haupt, in the *Johns Hopkins University Circulars*, xiii, no. 114, p. 109, justly observes that we should then expect the particle to be *prefixed* to the imperative, &c. He proposes to describe נָא as an emphatic particle. Haupt's suggested identification of this נָא with the Assyrian, Arabic, and Ethiopic particle *mā* (which is also an enclitic of emphasis), and ultimately with the interrogative *mā*, we shall not discuss here.

THIRD PART

SYNTAX[1]

CHAPTER I

THE PARTS OF SPEECH

I. Syntax of the Verb.

A. USE OF THE TENSES AND MOODS.[2]

§ 106. *Use of the Perfect.*

The perfect serves to express actions, events, or states, which the *a*
speaker wishes to represent from the point of view of completion,
whether they belong to a determinate past time, or extend into the
present, or. while still future, are pictured as in their completed state.

The definition formerly given here (' the perfect serves to express *completed*
actions') applies, strictly speaking, only to some of the varieties of the perfect
discussed under *b–p*: hence the above modification based on the arguments
of Knudtzon (for the title see note 2, and cf. further § 107 *a*).

More particularly the uses of the perfect may be distinguished as
follows :—

1. To represent actions, events, or states, which, after a shorter *b*

---

[1] Recent works on Hebrew syntax are: A. B. Davidson, *Introductory Heb.
Gram.*, vol. ii, *Heb. Syntax*, Edinburgh, 1894; Ed. König. *Hist.-compar. Syntax
der hebr. Sprache*, Lpz. 1897 (see above, § 3 *f*). Important contributions to
Hebrew syntax are also contained in H. Reckendorf's work *Die syntakt.
Verhältnisse des Arab.*, 2 pts., Leiden, 1895, 1898, of which we have already made
use in § 97 *a*. Cf. also the same author's very instructive discussions *Ueber
syntakt. Forschung*, Munich, 1899.

[2] Cf. the sketch of the tenses and moods used in Hebrew in § 40; and on
the general characteristics of the perfect and imperfect see the note on § 47 *a*;
also Driver, *A Treatise on the Use of the Tenses in Hebrew* (Oxford, 1874; 3rd ed.
1892); Bennett, 'Notes on the Use of the Hebrew Tenses' (*Hebraica*, 1886,
vols. ii, iii). A partial modification of the accepted definition of the Semitic
perfect and imperfect was proposed by J. A. Knudtzon, *Om det saakaldte
Perfektum og Imperfektum i Hebraisk*, Kristiania, 1890; of which a summary
entitled 'Vom sogenannten Perf. und Imperf. im Hebr.' appeared in the
Transactions of the Oriental Congress at Stockholm, section sémitique *b*, p. 73 ff.
(Leiden, 1893). Cf. also Knudtzon's articles, 'Zur assyrischen und allgemein
semitischen Grammatik' in the *Zeitschrift für Assyriologie*, especially vi. 422 ff.
and vii. 33 ff.

or longer duration, were terminated in the past, and hence are finally concluded, viz.:

(*a*) Corresponding to the perfect proper in Latin and the English perfect definite, in assertions, negations, confirmations, interrogations, &c., e. g. Gn 18¹⁵ *then Sarah denied, saying, I laughed not* (לֹא צָחַקְתִּי)......; *and he said, Nay, but thou didst laugh* (צָחָקְתְּ); Gn 3¹¹ מִי הִגִּיד לָךְ *who told thee* ....? Cf. 3¹³·¹⁴·¹⁷·²². Also pointing to some undefined time in the past, e. g. Is 66⁸ מִי־שָׁמַע כָּזֹאת *who hath* (*ever yet*) *heard such a thing?*

c Rem. In opposition to this express use of the perfect to emphasize the completion of an event, the imperfect is not infrequently used to emphasize that which is still future, e. g. Jos 1⁵ *as I was* (הָיִיתִי) *with Moses, so will I be* (אֶהְיֶה) *with thee;* Jos 1¹⁷, Ex 10¹⁴, Dt 32²¹, 1 K 2³⁸, Is 46⁴·¹¹, Jo 2², Ec 1⁹.

d (*b*) As a simple *tempus historicum* (corresponding to the Greek *aorist*) in narrating past events, e. g. Gn 4⁴ *and Abel, he also brought* (הֵבִיא), &c.; Gn 7¹⁹ *the waters did prevail* (גָּבְרוּ), &c.; Jb 1¹ *there was a man* (אִישׁ הָיָה) *in the land of Uz*, &c.; even in relating repeated actions, 1 S 18³⁰.

e Rem. As the above examples indicate, the perfect of *narration* occurs especially at the head of an entire narrative (Jb 1¹; cf. Dn 2¹) or an independent sentence (e. g. Gn 7¹¹·¹³), but in co-ordinate sentences, as a rule, only when the verb is separated from the copulative וְ by one or more words (cf. above Gn 4⁴ and 7¹⁹). In other cases, the narrative is continued in the imperfect consecutive, according to § 111 *a*. The direct connexion of the narrative perfect with וְ copulative (not to be confounded with the perfect consecutive proper, § 112) agrees rather with Aramaic syntax (cf. Kautzsch, *Gramm. des Biblisch-Aram.*, § 71, 1 *b*). On the examples (which are in many respects doubtful) in the earlier texts, see § 112 *pp–uu*.

f (*c*) To represent actions, &c., which were already completed in the past, at the time when other actions or conditions took place (pluperfect),[1] e. g. 1 S 28³ *now Samuel was* (*long since*) *dead*[2] ... *and Saul had put away* (הֵסִיר) *those that had familiar spirits ... out of the land.* Both these statements, being as it were in parentheses, merely assign a reason for the narrative beginning at verse 6. Cf. 1 S 9¹⁵, 25²¹, 2 S 18¹⁸.—Gn 20¹⁸ (*for the Lord had fast closed up*, &c.); 27³⁰, 31¹⁹·³⁴, Dt 2¹⁰; and in a negative statement, Gn 2⁵ *for the Lord God had not* (up to that time) *caused it to rain*, &c. This is especially frequent, from the nature of the case, in relative, causal, and temporal clauses, when the main clause contains a tense referring to the past, e. g. Gn 2² *and he rested ... from all his work which he had made* (עָשָׂה); Gn 7⁹,

---

[1] Cf. P. Haupt in the *Notes on Esther*, 9².

[2] Incorrectly, e. g. in the Vulgate, *Samuel autem mortuus est ... et Saul abstulit magos*, &c.

19²⁷, &c.; 29¹⁰ *now when Jacob had seen Rachel* (כַּאֲשֶׁר רָאָה) . . ., *Jacob went near*, &c.; so also in clauses which express the completion or incompleteness of one action, &c., on the occurrence of another, as in Gn 24¹⁵, 27³⁰, &c.; cf. § 164 *b*, with the note, and *c*.

2. To represent actions, events, or states, which, although completed *g* in the past, nevertheless extend their influence into the present (in English generally rendered by the present):

(*a*) Expressing facts which were accomplished long before, or conditions and attributes which were acquired long before, but of which the effects still remain in the present (present perfect), e. g. ψ 10¹¹ הִסְתִּיר פָּנָיו *he hath hidden his face* (*and still keeps it hidden*); ψ 143⁶ פֵּרַשְׂתִּי *I have spread forth my hands* (*and still keep them spread forth*). This applies particularly to a large number of perfects (almost exclusively of intransitive¹ verbs, denoting affections or states of the mind) which in English can be rendered only by the present, or, in the case mentioned above under *f*, by the imperfect.² Thus, יָדַעְתִּי *I know* (prop. *I have perceived, have experienced*) Jb 9², 10¹³, לֹא יָדַעְתִּי *I know not* Gn 4⁹, &c.; on the other hand, e. g. in Gn 28¹⁶, Nu 22³⁴, the context requires *I knew not*; זָכַרְנוּ *we remember* Nu 11⁵; מֵאֲנָה *she refuseth* Jb 6⁷; עָלַז *it exulteth*; שָׂמַחְתִּי *I rejoice* 1 S 2¹; בִּקֵּשׁ *he requireth* Is 1¹²; קִוִּיתִי *I wait* Gn 49¹⁸, ψ 130⁵ (parallel with הוֹחַלְתִּי); חָפַצְתִּי *I delight* ψ 40⁹ (mostly negative, Is 1¹¹, &c.); אָהַבְתִּי *I love* Gn 27⁴; שָׂנֵאתִי *I hate* ψ 31⁷; מָאַסְתִּי *I despise* Am 5²¹; תְּעֵבוּנִי *they abhor me* Jb 30¹⁰; בָּטַחְתִּי *I trust* ψ 25²; חָסִיתִי *I put my trust* ψ 31²; צָדַקְתִּי *I am righteous* Jb 34⁵; פָּקַרְתִּי *I have decided to requite* 1 S 15².—We may further include a number of verbs which express bodily characteristics or states, such as גָּדַלְתָּ *thou art great* ψ 104¹; קָטֹנְתִּי *I am little* Gn 32¹¹; גָּבְהוּ *they are high* Is 55⁹; רָחֲקוּ *they stand aloof* Jb 30¹⁰; טֹבוּ *they are goodly* Nu 24⁵; נָאווּ *they are beautiful* Is 52⁷; זָקַנְתִּי *I am old* Gn 18¹³; יָגַעְתִּי *I am weary* ψ 6⁷; שָׂבַעְתִּי *I am full* Is 1¹¹, &c.

Rem. To the same category probably belong also the perfects after עַד־מָתַי *h* Ex 10³ *how long hast thou* already *been refusing* (and refusest still . . . ? which really amounts to *how long wilt thou refuse?*), ψ 80⁵, Pr 1²² (co-ordinate with the imperf.), and after עַד־אָנָה Ex 16²⁸, Hb 1².

(*b*) In direct narration to express actions which, although really *i* only in process of accomplishment, are nevertheless meant to be repre-

----

¹ With regard to the great but very natural preponderance of intransitive verbs (expressing an existing state), cf. the lists in Knudtzon (see above, p. 309, note 2), pp. 117 and 122 in the Danish text.

² Cf. *novi, odi, memini*; οἶδα, μέμνημαι, ἔοικα, δέδορκα, κέκραγα; in the New Testament, ἤλπικα, ἠγάπηκα.

sented as already accomplished in the conception of the speaker, e. g.
הֲרִמֹ֫תִי *I lift up* (my hand in ratifying an oath) Gn 14²²; נִשְׁבַּ֫עְתִּי *I swear*
Jer 22⁵; הַעִדֹ֫תִי *I testify* Dt 8¹⁹; יָעַ֫צְתִּי *I counsel* 2 S 17¹¹ (but in a
different context in ver. 15, *I have counselled*); אָמַ֫רְתִּי (prop. *I say*)
I decide (*I consider as hereby settled*) 2 S 19³⁰; *I declare* Jb 9²², 32¹⁰.

k   (*c*) To express facts which have formerly taken place, and are still
of constant recurrence, and hence are matters of common experience
(the Greek *gnomic aorist*), e. g. ψ 9¹¹ *for thou, Lord, hast not forsaken*
(לֹֽא־עָזַ֫בְתָּ) *them that seek thee.* Cf. ver. 13, also ψ 10³, 119⁴⁰ and Gn 49¹¹
(כִּבֵּס).

l   Rem. In almost all the cases discussed in No. 2 (included under the English
present) the imperfect can be used instead of the perfect, wherever the action
or state in question is regarded, not as already completed, but as still continuing or just taking place (see § 107 *a*). Thus, לֹא יָכֹ֫לְתִּי *I am not able* ψ 40¹³
and לֹא אוּכַל Gn 31³⁵ have practically the same meaning. Hence also it is very
frequently happens that the imperfect corresponds to such perfects in poetic
or prophetic parallelism, e. g. Is 5¹², ψ 2¹ ᶠ·, Pr 1²², Jb 3¹⁷.

m   3. To express *future* actions, when the speaker intends by an
express assurance to represent them as finished, or as equivalent to
accomplished facts:

(*a*) In contracts or other express stipulations (again corresponding
to the English present, and therefore closely related to the instances
noted under *i*), e. g. Gn 23¹¹ *the field I give* (נָתַ֫תִּי) *thee*; cf. ver. 13 and
48²², 2 S 14²¹, 24²³, Jer 40⁴; in a threat, 1 S 2¹⁶, 2 S 5⁶ (unless, with
Wellhausen, יְסִירְךָ is to be read).—Especially in promises made by God,
Gn 1²⁹, 15¹⁸, 17²⁰, Ju 1².

n   (*b*) To express facts which are undoubtedly imminent, and, therefore,
in the imagination of the speaker, already accomplished (*perfectum
confidentiae*), e. g. Nu 17²⁷ הֵן גָּוַ֫עְנוּ אָבַ֫דְנוּ כֻּלָּ֫נוּ אָבָ֫דְנוּ *behold, we perish, we
are undone, we are all undone.* Gn 30¹³, Is 6⁵ (נִדְמֵ֫יתִי *I am undone* ¹),
Pr 4². Even in interrogative sentences, Gn 18¹², Nu 17²⁸, 23¹⁰, Ju 9⁹·¹¹,
Zc 4¹⁰ (?), Pr 22²⁰. ² This use of the perfect occurs most frequently in
prophetic language (*perfectum propheticum*). The prophet so trans-

---

¹ Cf. the similar use of ὄλωλα (διέφθορας, *Il.* 15. 128) and *perii!* On the
kindred use of the perfect in conditional sentences, cf. below, *p*.

² In Gn 40¹⁴ a *perf. confidentiae* (after כִּי אִם; but cf. § 163 *d*) appears to be
used in the expression of an earnest desire that something may happen (*but
have me in thy remembrance*, &c.). Neither this passage, however, nor the use of
the perfect in Arabic to express a wish or imprecation, justifies us in assuming
the existence of a *precative* perfect in Hebrew. In Jb 21¹⁶, 22¹⁸, also, translate
the counsel of the wicked is far from me. Cf. Driver, *Tenses*³, p. 25 f. In Is 43⁹
either נִקְבְּצוּ is *imperative* (see § 51 *o*) or we must read יִקָּבְצוּ, corresponding to
יֵאָסְפוּ which follows.

ports himself in imagination into the future that he describes the future
event as if it had been already seen or heard by him, e. g. Is 5¹³ *therefore my people are gone into captivity* (גָּלָה); 9¹ᶠᶠ·, 10²⁸, 11⁹ (after כִּי, as
frequently elsewhere); 19⁷, Jb 5²⁰, 2 Ch 20³⁷. Not infrequently the
imperfect interchanges with such perfects either in the parallel member
or further on in the narrative.

(c) To express actions or facts, which are meant to be indicated as *o*
existing in the future in a completed state (*futurum exactum*), e. g.
Is 4⁴ אִם רָחַץ *when he has washed away=when he shall have washed
away* (an *imperfect* follows in the co-ordinate sentence; cf. the conditional sentences in § 107 *x*); Is 6¹¹ (after עַד אֲשֶׁר אִם, as in Gn 28¹⁵,
Nu 32¹⁷; also 2 S 17¹³ after עַד אֲשֶׁר, Gn 24¹⁹ after עַד אִם and elsewhere
frequently after temporal conjunctions); Mi 5² (יָלָדָה); Gn 43¹⁴ וַאֲנִי
כַּאֲשֶׁר שָׁכֹלְתִּי שָׁכָלְתִּי *and I—if I am bereaved* (*orbus fuero*), *I am
bereaved,* an expression of despairing resignation. Cf. Pr 23¹⁵, Est 4¹⁶.

4. To express actions and facts, whose accomplishment in the past *p*
is to be represented, not as actual, but only as possible (generally
corresponding to the Latin imperfect or pluperfect subjunctive), e.g.
Gn 31⁴² *except the God of my father . . . had been with me, surely now
hadst thou sent me away empty* (שִׁלַּחְתָּנִי); Gn 43¹⁰, Ex 9¹⁵ (שָׁלַחְתִּי *I had
almost put forth,* &c.); Nu 22³³, Ju 13²³, 14¹⁸, 1 S 13¹³ (הֵכִין); 2 K 13¹⁹;
so frequently after כִּמְעַט *easily, almost,* Gn 26¹⁰, Is 1⁹ (where כִּמְעַט is
probably to be connected with the word after it), ψ 73², 94¹⁷, 119⁸⁷,
Pr 5¹⁴. Cf. also Jb 3¹³, 23¹⁰ (בְּחָנַנִי), Ru 1¹² (*if I should think,* &c.; cf.
2 K 7⁴); in the apodosis of a conditional sentence, 1 S 25³⁴.—So also
to express an unfulfilled desire, Nu 14² לוּ מַתְנוּ *would that we had
died . . . !* (לוּ with the imperfect would mean *would that we might
die!* 1 S 14³⁰). Finally, also in a question indicating astonishment,
Gn 21⁷ מִי מִלֵּל *who would have said . . . ? quis dixerit? ψ 73¹¹.*

§ 107. *Use of the Imperfect.*[1]

The imperfect, as opposed to the perfect, represents actions, events, *a*
or states which are regarded by the speaker at any moment as still
continuing, or in process of accomplishment, or even as just taking
place. In the last case, its occurrence may be represented as certainly
imminent, or merely as conceived in the mind of the speaker, or
simply as desired, and therefore only contingent (the modal use of the
imperfect).

---

[1] Cf. the literature cited above, p. 309, note 2.

Knudtzon (see above, Rem. on § 106 *a*), comparing the Ass.-Bab. usage, would prefer the term *present* rather than imperfect, on the ground that the tense expresses what is either actually or mentally present. In any case, the essential difference between the perfect and imperfect consists, he argues, in this, that the perfect simply indicates what is actually complete, while the imperfect places the action, &c., in a more direct relation to the judgement or feeling of the speaker.

More precisely the imperfect serves—

1. In the sphere of *past time*:

b (*a*) To express actions, &c., which *continued* throughout a longer or shorter period,[1] e. g. Gn 2⁶ *a mist went up* continually (יַעֲלֶה-), 2²⁵, 37⁷, 48¹⁰, Ex 1¹², 8²⁰, 13²², 15⁶·¹²·¹⁴·¹⁵, Nu 9¹⁵ ⁱ· ²⁰ ⁱ·, 23⁷, Ju 2¹, 5⁸, 1 S 3², 13¹⁷ⁱ·, 2 S 2²⁸, 23¹⁰, 1 K 3⁴, 7⁸, 21⁶, Is 1²¹, 6⁴ (וְיִפָּא:), 17¹⁰ ⁱ·, 51²·², Jer 13⁷, 36¹⁸, ψ 18⁷·¹⁴·¹⁷ ff.³⁸ ff·, 24², 32⁴·⁵ (אוֹרִיעֲךָ), 47⁵, 68¹⁰·¹², 104⁶ ff·, 106¹⁹, 107¹⁸·²⁹, 139¹³, Jb 3¹¹, 4¹²·¹⁵ ⁱ·, 10¹⁰ ⁱ, 15⁷ ⁱ·—very frequently alternating with a perfect (especially with a frequentative perfect; cf. Nu 9¹⁵⁻²³ and § 112 *e*), or when the narration is continued by means of an imperfect consecutive.[2]

c Rem. 1. The imperfect is frequently used in this way after the particles אָז *then*, טֶרֶם *not yet*, בְּטֶרֶם *before*, עַד־ *until*, e. g. Ex 15¹ אָז יָשִׁיר־מֹשֶׁה *then sang Moses*, &c.; Nu 21¹⁷, Dt 4⁴¹, Jos 10¹², 1 K 3¹⁶, 8¹, ψ 126², Jb 38²¹. (The *perfect* is used after אָז when stress is to be laid on the fact that the action has really taken place, and not upon its gradual accomplishment or duration in the past, e. g. Gn 4²⁶ אָז הוּחַל *then began*, &c.; Gn 49⁴, Ex 15¹⁵, Jos 22³¹, Ju 5¹¹, ψ 89²⁰.)[3] After טֶרֶם e. g. Gn 19⁴ טֶרֶם יִשְׁכָּבוּ *before they lay down*; Gn 2⁵, 24⁴⁵, 1 S 3³·⁷, always in the sense of our *pluperfect*. (In Gn 24¹⁵ instead of the perf. כִּלָּה, the imperf. should be read, as in verse 45; so also in 1 S 3⁷ [וְיִגָּלֶה] an imperf. is co-ordinated with ירע). After בְּטֶרֶם (sometimes also simply טֶרֶם Ex 12³⁴, Jos 3¹), e.g. Jer 1⁵ בְּטֶרֶם תֵּצֵא *before thou camest forth*; Gn 27³³, 37¹⁸, 41⁵⁰, Ru 3¹⁴ (perhaps also in ψ 90² an imperf. was intended instead of יֻלָּד; cf. Wellhausen on 2 S 3²; but note also Pr 8²⁵, in a similar context, *before the mountains were settled*, הַטְבָּעוּ, the predicate being separated from בְּטֶרֶם by הָרִים, as in ψ 90²). After עַד־ Jos 10¹³, ψ 73¹⁷ (*until I went*), 2 Ch 29³⁴; on the other

---

[1] Cf. the Mêša‛ inscription, l. 5, כי יאנף כמש בארצה *for Chemosh was angry with his land*. As Driver, *Tenses*, 3rd ed., § 27, 1 *a*, remarks, this vivid realization of the accomplishment of the action is especially frequent in poetic and prophetic style.

[2] According to the Masora such imperfects occur in Is 10¹³ *bis* (where, however, וְאָסִיר might also mean *I am wont to remove*, &c.), Is 48³, 57¹⁷, ψ 18³⁸ ᵃ, also (according to § 49 *c*) in 2 S 1¹⁰ and Ez 16¹⁰. In some other cases ו is no doubt a dogmatic emendation for ו (*imperf. consec.*) in order to represent historical statements as promises; cf. Is 42⁶, 43²⁸ [contrasted with 42²⁵], 51² *bis*, 63³ ff. and the note on § 53 *p*.

[3] After אָז *then* (to announce future events) the imperf. is naturally used in the sense of a future, Gn 24⁴¹, Ex 12⁴⁸, Mi 3⁴, Zp 3⁹, ψ 51²¹.

hand, with the perf., e.g. Jos 2²². As after אָז, so also after בְּטֶרֶם טֶרֶם, and עַד־ the imperf. may be used, according to the context, in the sense of our *future*, e.g. 2 K 2⁹, Is 65²⁴, Jb 10²¹; after עַד־ e.g. Is 22¹⁴. The imperf. is used in the sense of our *present* after טֶרֶם in Ex 9³⁰, 10⁷.

2. Driver (*Tenses*³, p. 35 f.) rightly lays stress upon the inherent distinction *d* between the *participle* as expressing *mere* duration, and the *imperfect* as expressing *progressive* duration (in the present, past, or future). Thus the words וְנָהָר יֹצֵא Gn 2¹⁰ represent the river of Paradise as going out of Eden in a continuous, uninterrupted stream, but יִפָּרֵד, which immediately follows, describes how the parting of its waters is always taking place afresh. In the same way יַעֲלֶה Gn 2⁶ represents new mists as constantly arising, and יִמָּלֵא Is 6⁴ new clouds of smoke. Also those actions, &c., which might be regarded in themselves as single or even momentary, are, as it were, broken up by the imperfect into their component parts, and so pictured as gradually completing themselves. Hence תְּבַלְעֵמוֹ Ex 15¹² (after a *perf.* as in verse 14) represents the Egyptians, in a vivid, poetic description, as being swallowed up one after another, and יַנְחֵנִי Nu 23⁷ the leading on by stages, &c.

(b) To express actions, &c., which were *repeated* in the past, either *e* at fixed intervals or occasionally (the *modus rei repetitae*), e.g. Jb 1⁵ *thus did* (יַעֲשֶׂה) Job *continually* (after each occasion of his sons' festivities); 4³ᶠ·, 22⁶ᶠ·, 23¹¹, 29⁷·⁹·¹²ᶠ·, Gn 6⁴, 29², 30·⁸, 42³¹·³⁹ (*I used to bear* the loss of it), Ex 1¹², 19¹⁹, 33⁷ᶠᶠ· (יַּקַּח *used to take* every time), 40³⁶ᶠᶠ·, Nu 9¹⁷ᶠ· ²⁰ᶠᶠ·, 11⁵·⁹, Ju 6⁴, 14¹⁰, 21²⁵, 1 S 1⁷, 2²², 9⁹, 13¹⁹, 18⁵, 27⁹, 2 S 1²², 12³, 13¹⁸, 1 K 5²⁵ (of tribute repeated year by year), 10⁵, 13³³, 14²⁸, 2 K 4⁸, 8²⁹, 13²⁰, 25¹⁴, Jer 36²³, ψ 42⁵, 44³, 78¹⁵·⁴⁰, 103⁷, Est 2¹⁴; even in a negative dependent clause, 1 K 18¹⁰.

2. In the sphere of *present time*, again   *f*

(a) To express actions, events, or states, which are *continued* for a shorter or longer time,¹ e.g. Gn 37¹⁵ מַה־תְּבַקֵּשׁ *what seekest thou?* 19¹⁹ לֹא־אוּכַל *I cannot*; 24⁵⁰, 31³⁵, Is 1¹³. Other examples are Gn 2¹⁰, 24³¹, 1 S 1⁸, 11⁵, 1 K 3⁷, ψ 2², and in the prophetic formula יֹאמַר יְהֹוָה *saith the Lord*, Is 1¹¹·¹⁸, &c., cf. 40¹. So especially to express facts known by experience, which occur at all times, and consequently hold good at any moment, e.g. Pr 15²⁰ *a wise son maketh a glad father*; hence especially frequent in Job and Proverbs. In an interrogative sentence, e.g. Jb 4¹⁷ *is mortal man just before God?* In a negative sentence, Jb 4¹⁸, &c.

(b) To express actions, &c., which may be *repeated* at any time, *g* including therefore the present, or are *customarily* repeated on a given occasion (cf. above, *e*), e.g. Dt 1⁴⁴ *as bees do* (are accustomed to

---

¹ It is not always possible to carry out with certainty the distinction between *continued* and *repeated* actions. Some of the examples given under *f* might equally be referred to *g*.

do); Gn 6²¹, 32³³, 43³², Ju 11⁴⁰, 1 S 2⁸, 5⁵, 20², 2 S 15³², Is 1²³, 3¹⁶, ψ 1³. So again (see *f*) especially to express facts known by experience which may at any time come into effect again, e. g. Ex 23⁸ *a gift blindeth* (יְעַוֵּר), &c. ; Gn 2²⁴, 22¹⁴, Is 32⁶, Am 3⁷, Mal 1⁶, Jb 2⁴, &c. Of the same kind also is the imperfect in such relative clauses (see § 155), as Gn 49²⁷ *Benjamin is* זְאֵב יִטְרָף *a wolf that ravineth* (properly, is accustomed to ravin). Finally, compare also the formulae יֵאָמֵר *it is* (wont to be) *said* (to introduce proverbial expressions) Gn 10⁹, 22¹⁴, &c. ; לֹא־יֵעָשֶׂה כֵן *it is not* (wont to be) *so done* (and hence *may not, shall not be*, see *u*), Gn 29²⁶, 20⁹, 34⁷, 2 S 13¹².

h　　(*c*) To express actions, &c., which although, strictly speaking, they are already finished, are regarded as still lasting on into the present time, or continuing to operate in it, e. g. Gn 32³⁰ *wherefore is it that thou dost ask* (תִּשְׁאַל) *after my name ?* 24³¹, 44⁷, Ex 5¹⁵, 2 S 16⁹. In such cases, naturally, the perfect is also admissible, and is sometimes found in the same formula as the imperfect, e. g. Jb 1⁷ (2²) מֵאַיִן תָּבֹא *whence comest thou* (just now) ? but Gn 16⁸ (cf. 42⁷) אֵי־מִזֶּה בָּאת *whence camest thou ?* The imperfect represents the coming as still in its last stage, whereas the perfect represents it as an accomplished fact.

i　　3. In the sphere of *future time*. To express actions, &c., which are to be represented as about to take place, and as continuing a shorter or longer time in the future, or as being repeated ; thus :

(*a*) From the standpoint of the speaker's present time, e. g. Ex 4¹ *they will not believe* (יַאֲמִינוּ) me, *nor hearken* (יִשְׁמְעוּ) *unto my voice : for they will say* (יֹאמְרוּ), &c., 6¹, 9⁵, &c.

k　　(*b*) In dependent clauses to represent actions, &c., which from some point of time in the past are to be represented as future, e. g. Gn 43⁷ could we in any wise know *that he would say* (יֹאמַר) ? 2¹⁹, 43²⁵, Ex 2⁴, 2 K 3²⁷ אֲשֶׁר־יִמְלֹךְ *qui regnaturus erat*; 13¹⁴, Jon 4⁵, Jb 3³, Ec 2³, ψ 78⁶ *that the generation to come might know*, בָּנִים יִוָּלֵדוּ *the children which should be born* (*qui nascituri essent*; the imperfect here with the collateral idea of the occurrence being repeated in the future).

l　　(*c*) To represent a *futurum exactum*; cf. Is 4⁴, 6¹¹ (co-ordinated with a perfect used in the same sense, see § 106 *o*); so also sometimes after the temporal particles עַד, ψ 132⁵, and עַד אֲשֶׁר *until*, Gn 29⁸, Nu 20¹⁷, &c.

m　　4. Finally to the sphere of future time belong also those cases in which the (modal) imperfect serves to express actions, events, or states, the occurrence of which is to be represented as willed (or not willed), or as in some way conditional, and consequently only contingent. More particularly such imperfects serve—

(*a*) As an expression of will, whether it be a definite intention and *n* arrangement, or a simple desire, viz.:

(1) Sometimes in positive sentences in place of the cohortative (cf. e. g. ψ 59¹⁷ with verse 18; 2 S 22⁵⁰ with ψ 18⁵⁰; Ju 19¹¹, &c.), of the imperative (Is 18³), or of the jussive (which, however, in most cases, does not differ from the ordinary form of the imperfect), e. g. תֵּרָאֶה *let it appear* Gn 1⁹, 41³⁴, Lv 19²·³, 2 S 10¹² (and so frequently in verbs ל״ה; cf. § 109 *a*, note 2); Zc 9⁵ (תָּחִיל); ψ 61⁷ (תּוֹסִיף); Pr 22¹⁷ (תָּשִׁית); 23¹, Jb 6²³ (co-ordinated with the imperative), 10²⁰ *K^eth.*; so probably also יָדִין *let him judge!* ψ 72².—So also in the 1st pers., to express a wish which is asserted subsequently with reference to a fixed point of time in the past, e. g. Jb 10¹⁸ אֶגְוַע *I ought to* [not *should* as A.V., R.V.] *have,* (then,·immediately after being born) *given up the ghost*; cf. verse 19 אֶהְיֶה and אוּבַל Lv 10¹⁸, Nu 35²⁸. Even to express an obligation or necessity according to the judgement of another person, e. g. Jb 9²⁹ אֶרְשָׁע *I am to be guilty,* 12⁴. Cp. Jb 9¹⁵, 19¹⁶; in a question, ψ 42¹⁰, 43².

(2) To express the definite expectation that something will not *o* happen. The imperfect with לֹא represents a more emphatic form of prohibition than the jussive[1] with אַל־ (cf. § 109 *c*), and corresponds to our *thou shalt not do it!* with the strongest expectation of obedience, while אַל־ with the jussive is rather a simple warning, *do not that!* Thus לֹא with the imperfect is especially used in enforcing the divine commands, e. g. לֹא תִגְנֹב *thou shalt not steal* Ex 20¹⁵; cf. verses 3, 4, 5, 7, 10 ff. So לֹא with the 3rd pers. perhaps in Pr 16¹⁰.

Rem. The *jussive*, which is to be expected after אַל־, does not, as a rule *p* (according to *n*, and § 109 *a*, note 2), differ in form from the simple imperfect. That many supposed jussives are intended as simple imperfects is possible from the occurrence after אַל־ of what are undoubtedly imperfect forms, not only from verbs ל״ה (cf. § 109 *a*, note 2), but also from verbs ע״וּ, to express a prohibition or negative wish, אַל־נָא יָשִׂים, אַל־תָּסוּר Gn 19¹⁷, אַל־תַּבִּיט Jos 1⁷, 1 S 25²⁵. Even with the 1st pers. plur. (after an imperative) וְאַל־נָמוּת *that we die not,* 1 S 12¹⁹. Also to express the conviction that something cannot happen, אַל־יָנוּם *he will not slumber,*[2] ψ 121³; cf. Jer 46⁶, 2 Ch 14¹⁰.

---

[1] As stated in § 46 *a*, a prohibition cannot be expressed by אַל־ and the imperative.

[2] To regard this as an optative (so Hupfeld) is from the context impossible. It is more probably a strong pregnant construction, or fusion of two sentences (such as, *do not think he will slumber!*). Verse 4 contains the objective confirmation, by means of לֹא with the imperf., of that which was previously only a subjective conviction.

q (3) In dependent clauses after final conjunctions (§ 165 b), as אֲשֶׁר, Gn 11⁷ (אֲשֶׁר לֹא יִשְׁמְעוּ *that they may not understand*); בַּעֲבוּר Gn 21³⁰, 27⁴·¹⁹, Ex 9¹⁴, &c.; לְמַעַן אֲשֶׁר Nu 17⁵; לְמַעַן Dt 4¹, ψ 51⁶, 78⁶, and יַעַן אֲשֶׁר[1] Ez 12¹², *in order that*[2]; לְבִלְתִּי *that . . . not*, Ex 20²⁰, 2 S 14¹⁴; also after פֶּן־ *that not, lest*, Gn 3²², 11⁴, 19¹⁵, &c.[3]; cf. also the instances introduced by וְלֹא in § 109 g.—In Lv 9⁶ such an imperfect (or jussive? see the examples in § 109 f) is added to the expression of the command by an asyndeton, and in La 1¹⁹ to the principal clause simply by ו: *while they sought them food* וְיָשִׁיבוּ אֶת־נַפְשָׁם *to refresh their souls* (cf. also La 3²⁶, *it is good and let him hope*, i. e. *that he should hope*); so after an interrogative clause, Ex 2⁷. Finally also in a relative clause, ψ 32⁸ בְּדֶרֶךְ־זוּ תֵלֵךְ *in the way which thou shouldst go*.

r (b) To express actions, &c., which are to be represented as possibly taking place or not taking place (sometimes corresponding to the *potential* of the classical languages, as also to our periphrases with *can, may, should*[4]). More particularly such imperfects are used—

s (1) In a permissive sense, e. g. Gn 2¹⁶ *of every tree of the garden* (אָכֹל תֹּאכֵל) *thou mayest freely eat* (the opposite in verse 17); 3², 42³⁷, Lv 21³·²², Jb 21³. In the 1st pers. ψ 5⁸, 22¹⁸ (*I may*, or *can, tell*); in a negative sentence, e. g. ψ 5⁵.

t (2) In interrogative sentences, e. g. Pr 20⁹ מִי־יֹאמַר *quis dixerit?* Cf. Gn 17¹⁷, 18¹⁴, 31⁴³, 1 S 11¹², 2 K 5¹² הֲלֹא־אֶרְחַץ בָּהֶם *may I not wash in them?* Is 33¹⁴, ψ 15¹, 24³, Ec 5⁵. So especially in a question expressing surprise after אֵיךְ, e. g. Gn 39⁹ *how then can I . . .?* 44³⁴, Is 19¹¹, ψ 137⁴, and even with regard to some point of time in the past, looking forward from which an event might have been expected to take place, e. g. Gn 43⁷ הֲיָדוֹעַ נֵדַע *could we in any wise know . . .?* Cf. 2 S 3³³ (יָמוּת *was Abner to die as a fool*, i. e. *was he destined to die . . .?*), and so probably also Gn 34³¹ (*should he deal . . .?*). Very closely connected with this is the use of the imperfect—

u (3) In a consecutive clause depending on an interrogative clause, e. g. Ex 3¹¹, *who am I* (כִּי אֵלֵךְ) *that I should* (*ought, could*) *go?* 16⁷, Nu 11¹², Ju 9²³, 1 S 18¹⁸, 2 K 8¹³, Is 29¹⁶, Jb 6¹¹, 21¹⁵, similarly after אֲשֶׁר Gn 38¹⁸, Ex 5².

---

[1] But יַעַן אֲשֶׁר in a causal sense (*because, since*), e. g. Ju 2²⁰ (as אֲשֶׁר Gn 34²⁷) is followed by the perfect. On Jos 4²⁴ see above, § 74 g.

[2] R.V. *because he shall not see.*

[3] In 2 K 2¹⁶ פֶּן־ occurs with the perf. in a vivid presentment of the time when the fear is realized and the remedy comes too late. (In 2 S 2c⁶, since a *perfect consec.* follows, read with Driver יִמְצָא.)

[4] By this, of course, is not meant that these finer distinctions were consciously present to the Hebrew mind. They are rather mere expedients for making intelligible to ourselves the full significance of the Semitic imperfect.

Rem. In passages like 1 S 11⁵, ψ 8⁵, 114⁵, the context shows that the
imperfect corresponds rather to our present. In such sentences the perfect
also is naturally used in referring to completed actions, e.g. Gn 20¹⁰, Ju 18²³,
2 S 7¹⁸, Is 22¹.

(4) In *negative sentences* to express actions, &c., which cannot or
should not happen, e.g. Gn 32¹³ אֲשֶׁר לֹא־יִסָּפֵר מֵרֹב *which cannot be
numbered for multitude*; 20⁹ *deeds* (אֲשֶׁר לֹא־יֵעָשׂוּ) *that ought not to
be done* (cf. above, *g*); ψ 5⁵.

(5) In *conditional clauses* (the *modus conditionalis* corresponding
to the Latin present or imperfect conjunctive) both in the protasis
and apodosis, or only in the latter, ψ 23⁴ לֹא־אִירָא רָע ... גַּם כִּי־אֵלֵךְ
yea, though I walk (or *had to walk*) ... *I fear* (or *I would fear*) *no
evil*; Jb 9²⁰ *though I be righteous, mine own mouth shall condemn me*.
After a perfect in the protasis, e.g. Jb 23¹⁰. Very frequently also in
an apodosis, the protasis to which must be supplied from the context,
e.g. Jb 5⁸ *but as for me, I would seek unto God* (were I in thy place);
3¹³·¹⁶, 14¹⁴·ᶠ, ψ 55¹³, Ru 1¹². However, some of the imperfects in these
examples are probably intended as jussive forms. Cf. § 109 *h*.

§ 108. *Use of the Cohortative.*

The cohortative, i.e. according to § 48 *c*, the 1st pers.[1] sing. or
plur. of the imperfect lengthened by the ending הָ‍ֽ,[2] represents in
general an endeavour directed expressly towards a definite object.
While the corresponding forms of the indicative rather express the
mere announcement that an action will be undertaken, the cohortative
lays stress on the determination underlying the action, and the
personal interest in it.

Its uses may be divided into—

1. The cohortative standing alone, or co-ordinated with another
cohortative, and frequently strengthened by the addition of the
particle נָא:

(*a*) To express self-encouragement, e.g. Ex 3³ אָסֻרָה־נָּא וג׳ *I will
turn aside now, and see* ... ! So especially as the result of inward
deliberation (in soliloquies), e.g. Gn 18²¹, 32²¹ (rarely so used after
אַל־, Gn 21¹⁶ *let me not look* ... ! Jer 18¹⁸), and also as a more or less
emphatic statement of a fixed determination, e.g. Is 5¹ *I will sing*[3]
... ! 5⁶, 31⁸. Cf. also Gn 46³⁰ *now let me die* (*I am willing to die*),

---

[1] For the few examples of cohortatives in the 3rd sing., see § 48 *d*.

[2] But verbs לה״, according to § 75 *l*, even in the cohortative, almost always
have the ending הָ‍ֽ; cf. e.g. in Dt 32²⁰ אֶרְאֶה after אַסְתִּירָה.

[[3] R.V. *let me sing*.]

since I have seen thy face; and ψ 31⁸. In the 1st pers. plur. the cohortative includes a summons to others to help in doing something, e. g. ψ 2³ נְנַתְּקָה *come! let us break asunder!* &c., and Gn 11³.

c   (*b*) To express a wish, or a request for permission, that one should be allowed to do something, e. g. Dt 2²⁷ אֶעְבְּרָה *may I be allowed to pass through (let me pass through)!* Nu 20¹⁷ נַעְבְּרָה־נָּא *may we be allowed to pass through!* Jer 40¹⁵ *let me go, I pray thee!* &c.; 2 S 16⁹; so after לֹא 2 S 18¹⁴; after אַל־ 2 S 24¹⁴, Jer 17¹⁸, ψ 25² (אַל־אֵבוֹשָׁה *let me not be ashamed*; cf. ψ 31²·¹⁸, 71¹); 69¹⁵. After אַל־נָא Jon 1¹⁴.

d   2. The cohortative in dependence on other moods, as well as in conditional sentences : (*a*) In dependence (with *wāw copulative*; ψ 9¹⁵ after לְמַעַן) on an imperative or jussive to express an intention or intended consequence, e. g. Gn 27⁴ *bring it to me*, וְאֹכֵלָה *that I may eat*, prop. *then will I eat*; Gn 19⁵, 23⁴, 24⁵⁶, 27²⁵, 29²¹, 30²⁵ᶠ·, 42³⁴, 49¹, Dt 32¹, Ho 6¹, ψ 2⁸, 39¹⁴, Jb 10²⁰ *Qᵉrê*; Is 5¹⁹ *and let the counsel of the Holy One of Israel draw nigh and come*, וְנֵדְעָה *that we may know (it)!* Gn 26²⁸, 1 S 27⁵. Also after negative sentences, Gn 18³⁰·³², Ju 6³⁹, and after interrogative sentences, 1 K 22⁷, Is 40²⁵, 41²⁶, Am 8⁵.

e   (*b*) In conditional sentences (with or without אִם) to express a contingent intention, e. g. Jb 16⁶ אִם־אֲדַבְּרָה *should I determine to speak, my grief is not assuaged,* וְאַחְדְּלָה *and should I forbear, what am I eased?* without אִם Jb 19¹⁸, 30²⁶ (where, however, וְאֵיחִלָה *is probably intended*); ψ 73¹⁶ (unless וָאֲחַ֫שֵּׁב should be read), 139⁸ᶠ·. After the 3rd person, Jb 11¹⁷ *though it be dark,* &c. So perhaps also 2 S 22³⁸ אֶרְדְּפָה *if I determined to pursue, then . . . ,* but cf. ψ 18³⁸.

f   (*c*) Likewise in the apodosis of conditional sentences, e. g. Jb 31⁷ᶠ· *if my step hath turned out of the way . . . ,* אֶזְרָעָה *then let me sow;* cf. 16⁴ᶠ· *I also could speak as ye do, if . . . .!* So even when the condition must be supplied from the context, e. g. ψ 40⁶ *else would I declare and speak of them;* 51¹⁸ *else would I (gladly) give it,* i. e. if thou didst require it (cf. the precisely similar וְאֶשָּׂא ψ 55¹³); Jb 6¹⁰. In the 1st plur. Jer 20¹⁰. To the same category belong the cohortatives after the formula expressing a wish מִי־יִתֵּן, מִי־יִתְּנֵנִי, e. g. Jer 9¹ *oh, that I had . . . ,* וְאֶעֶזְבָה *then (i. e. if I had) should I (or would I) leave my people,* &c.; Ju 9²⁹; without *Wāw* Is 27⁴, ψ 55⁷, Jb 23⁴ (cf. also verse 7).

g   Rem. 1. The question, whether a resolution formed under compulsion (a *necessity*) is also expressed by the cohortative (so, according to the prevailing opinion, in Is 38¹⁰ אֵלְכָה; Jer 3²⁵, 4¹⁹·²¹, 6¹⁰, ψ 55³·¹⁸ (?); 57⁵, where, however, with Hupfeld, שָׁכְבָה should be read; 77⁷, 88¹⁶, and in the 1st plur. Is 59¹⁰), is to be answered in the sense that in these examples the cohortative *form* is used after its meaning has become entirely lost, merely for the sake of its fuller sound, instead of the ordinary imperfect. This view is strongly supported by the rather numerous examples of cohortative forms after *wāw* *consec.* of the imperfect (cf. § 49 *e*, as also ψ 66⁶ שָׁם נִשְׂמְחָה *there did we rejoice* [1] ; ψ 119¹⁶³ וָאֲתַעֵבָה; Pr 7⁷), which can likewise only be explained as forms chosen merely for euphony, and therefore due to considerations of rhythm.

2. The cohortative is strange after עַד־ ψ 73¹⁷ *until I went* . . . אָבִ֫ינָה *I con-* *h* *sidered their latter end* ; possibly a pregnant construction for ' until I made up my mind, saying, I will consider ', &c. (but אָבִינָה Pr 7⁷ is still dependent on the preceding וְ) ; עַד־אֲרוֹגִ֫יעָה Pr 12¹⁹ is at any rate to be explained in the same way (in Jer 49¹⁹, 50⁴⁴ we have כִּי־אִ֫יֹ with a similar meaning), *as long* *as I* (intentionally) *wink with the eyelashes* (shall wink). On the other hand, in Ex 32³⁰ אֲכַפֵּר is to be read, with the Samaritan, instead of אֲכַפְּרָה after אוּלַ֫י.

§ 109. *Use of the Jussive.*

As the *cohortative* is used in the 1st pers., so the *jussive* is especially *a* found in the 2nd and 3rd pers. sing. and plur. to express a more or less definite desire that something should or should not happen (cf. for its form, which frequently coincides with that of the ordinary *imperfect*,[2] § 48 *f, g*). More particularly its uses may be distinguished as follows :

1. The *jussive* standing alone, or co-ordinated with another jussive :

(*a*) In affirmative sentences to express a command, a wish (or a *b* blessing), advice, or a request ; in the last case (the optative or precative) it is frequently strengthened by the addition of נָא. Examples : Gn 1³ יְהִי אוֹר *let there be light!* Gn 1⁶·⁹·¹¹, &c. (the creative commands); Nu 6²⁶ *the Lord lift up his countenance upon thee, and give thee peace!* cf. verse 25. After particles expressing a wish, Gn 30³⁴ לוּ יְהִי *I would* *it might be;* ψ 81⁹ אִם־תִּשְׁמַֽע־לִי *if thou wouldest hearken unto me !* As a humble request, Gn 44³³ . . . וְהַנַּ֫עַר יַ֫עַל . . . יֵ֫שֶׁב־נָא עַבְדְּךָ *let thy servant,* *I pray thee, abide,* &c., *and let the lad go up,* &c., Gn 47⁴.

(*b*) In negative sentences to express prohibition or dissuasion, *c* warning, a negative wish (or imprecation), and a request. The prohibitive particle used before the jussive (according to § 107 *o*) is almost always אַל (in negative desires and requests frequently

---

[1] Analogous to this cohortative (as equivalent to the imperfect) after שָׁם is the use of the historic imperf. after אָז, § 107 *c*.

[2] With regard to verbs ל״ה, it is true that the full form of the imperfect is frequently used with the meaning of the jussive (as also for the cohortative, see § 108 *a*, note 2), e. g. אַל־יִּרְאֶה Jb 3⁹ (but previously יָקוּ *let it look for !*) : especially *in* (Neh 2³) and immediately *before* the principal pause, Gn 1⁹ תֵּרָאֶה; Ju 6³⁹ יְהִיֶה, but previously יְהִי־נָא; Is 47³ תֵּרָאֶה, previously תִּגַּל; ψ 109⁷. On the attempt to distinguish such jussives from the imperfect by means of a special meaning הָ—, see § 75 *hh*.

אַל־נָא); e. g. Ex 34³ אִישׁ אַל־יֵרָא *neither let any man be seen!* Pr 3⁷ *be not* (אַל־תְּהִי) *wise in thine own eyes!* Jb 15³¹ אַל־יַאֲמֵן *ne confidat.* In the form of a request (prayer), Dt 9²⁶ אַל־תַּשְׁחֵת *destroy not!* 1 K 2²⁰, ψ 27⁹, 69¹⁸.

d   Rem. 1. The few examples of לֹא with the jussive could at most have arisen from the attempt to moderate subsequently by means of the jussive (voluntative) form what was at first intended to be a strict command (אַל with imperf. indic.); probably, however, they are either cases in which the defective writing has been misunderstood (as in 1 K 2⁶, Ez 48¹⁴), or (as in Gn 24⁸) instances of the purely rhythmical jussive form treated below, under *k*. Moreover, cf. יֹסֵף לֹא Jo 2² and from the same verb Gn 4¹² (unless it is to be referred to *h*) and Dt 13¹. The same form, however, appears also to stand three times for the cohortative (see below), and in Nu 22¹⁹ for the ordinary imperfect (but see below, *i*). Thus it is doubtful whether an imaginary by-form of the ordinary imperf. is not intended by the Masora in all these cases, and whether consequently יֹסֵף, &c., should not be restored.— On לֹא־תָחוֹס עֵינְךָ, &c., Dt 7¹⁶, 13⁹, &c., Ez 5¹¹, &c., cf. § 72 *r*, according to which תָחוֹס should probably be read in every case.—The jussive appears in the place of the cohortative after לֹא 1 S 14³⁶ וְלֹא־נַשְׁאָר (co-ordinated with two cohortatives), 2 S 17¹²; cf. Is 41²³ *Kᵉth.* (ונרא, i. e. וְנֵרֶא, after another cohortative); also (see above) לֹא אֹסֵף Dt 18¹⁶, Ho 9¹⁵, and even without לֹא Ez 5¹⁶.

e   2. אַל־ with the jussive (or imperf., cf. § 107 *p*) is used sometimes to express the conviction that something cannot or should not happen; cf. Is 2⁹ (where, however, the text is very doubtful) וְאַל־תִּשָּׂא לָהֶם *and thou canst not possibly forgive them* [R.V. *therefore forgive them not*]; ψ 34⁶, 41³, 50³, 121³ (אַל־יִתֵּן); Pr 3²⁵, Jb 5²² אַל־תִּירָא *neither needest thou be afraid*; 20¹⁷, 40³².

f   2. The jussive depending on other moods, or in conditional sentences:
(a) Depending¹ (with *Wāw*) on an imperative or cohortative to express an intention or an assurance of a contingent occurrence, e. g. Gn 24⁵¹ *take her and go, and let her be* (וּתְהִי prop. *and she will be*)...; 30³, 31³⁷, 38²⁴, Ex 8⁴, 9¹³, 10¹⁷, 14², Jos 4¹⁶, Ju 6³⁰, 1 S 5¹¹, 7³, 1 K 21¹⁰, ψ 144⁵, Pr 20²², Jb 14⁶. Also after interrogative sentences, which include a demand, Est 7² (say) *what is thy desire...*, וְתֵעָשׂ *and it shall* (i. e. in order that it may) *be granted!* 1 K 22²⁰, Is 19¹², Jb 38³⁴ᶠ· Depending on a cohortative, e. g. Gn 19²⁰ אִמָּלְטָה נָּא שָׁמָּה *oh, let me escape thither* ... וּתְחִי נַפְשִׁי *that my soul may live;* even after a simple imperf. (cf. below, *g*), 1 K 13³³ *whosoever would, he consecrated him* ... וִיהִי *that he might be a priest* (read כֹּהֵן) *of the high places,* but probably the LXX reading וַיְהִי *is to be preferred.*

---

¹ This does not include the cases in which the jussive is not logically dependent on a preceding imperat., but is merely co-ordinated, e. g. Gn 20⁷, ψ 27¹⁴, &c.

Rem. In 2 Ch 35²¹ a negative final clause with וְאַל־ is dependent on an *g*
imperative, *forbear from* (meddling with) *God . . . that he destroy thee not.*
As a rule, however, negative final clauses are attached to the principal
sentence by means of וְלֹא and a following imperfect; so after an imperative,
Gn 42², 1 K 14², 18⁴⁴; after a jussive, Ex 30²⁰, Neh 6⁹; after a perfect consec.,
Ex 28³⁵·⁴³, 30¹², Nu 18⁵; after לֹא with an imperfect, Lv 10⁶, Nu 18³, Dt 17¹⁷
neither shall he multiply wives unto himself (וְלֹא יָסוּר לְבָבוֹ) *that his heart turn not
away*; 1 S 20¹⁴, 2 S 21¹⁷, Jer 11²¹; after אַל־ with jussive, Lv 10⁹, 11⁴³, 16²,
2 S 13²⁵, Jer 25⁶, 37²⁰, 38²⁴ ᶠ·; after the asseverative אִם with the impft., Gn 14²³;
even after a simple imperfect, Jer 10⁴ *with nails . . . they fasten it* (וְלֹא יָפִיק) *that
it move not*; after a participle, Jb 9⁷.

(*b*) Frequently in conditional sentences (as in Arabic), either in the *h*
protasis or in the apodosis, cf. ψ 45¹² יִתְאָו *should he desire . . . then . . .*;
104²⁰ וִיהִי . . . . תָּשֶׁת *if thou makest darkness, then it is night*; so also in
the protasis, Ex 22⁴, Lv 15²⁴, Is 41²⁸, Ez 14⁷ (וְיָעַל), Jb 34²⁹; in the
apodosis, Ex 7⁹ *then will it* (not, *then shall it*) *become a serpent*; Pr 9⁹
after an imperat. in the protasis; Jb 10¹⁶, 13⁵, 22²⁸. In a negative
apodosis, Gn 4¹² (לֹא־תֹסֵף), but see above, *d*). In 2 K 6²⁷ אַל־יוֹשִׁעֵךְ (*if
the Lord do not help thee*, &c.) is to be explained as a jussive in
a negative protasis.

Rem. Undoubtedly this use of the jussive (in conditional sentences) is based *i*
on its original *voluntative* meaning; let something be so and so, then this or
that must happen as a consequence. Certain other examples of the *jussive*,
however, show that in the consciousness of the language the *voluntative* has
in such cases become weakened almost to a *potential* mood, and hence the
jussive serves to express facts which may happen *contingently*, or may be
expected, e. g. Nu 22¹⁹ (מַה־יֹּסֵף, but cf. above, *d*); Jb 9³³ *there is no daysman
betwixt us, that might lay* (יָשֵׁת), hence plainly a *subjunctive = qui ponat*; also in
Nu 23¹⁹ וִיכַזֵּב *that he should lie* is probably intended as a jussive); Ec 5¹⁴; so
after interrogative sentences, Jer 9¹¹ *who is the wise man*, וְיָבֵן *qui intelligat hoc?*;
Ho 14¹⁰.

Moreover, in not a few cases, the jussive is used, without any collateral *k*
sense, for the ordinary imperfect form. and this occurs not alone in forms,
which may arise from a misunderstanding of the defective writing, as Dt 28²¹·³⁶,
32⁸, 1 K 8¹, Is 12¹, Mi 3⁴, 5⁸, ψ 11⁶, 18¹², 21² Qᵉrê (מַה־יִּגֶּל, Kᵉth. (וְיָגִיל), 25⁹,47⁴,90⁸,
91⁴, 107²⁹, Pr 15²⁵, Jb 13²⁷, 15³³, 18⁹, 20²·⁻ ·ᶦ7²², 33¹¹, 36¹⁴, 38²⁴, Ec 12⁶ (verse 7 יֹשֹׁב,
but immediately afterwards תָּשׁוּב), Dn 8¹²,—but also in shortened forms,
such as יְהִי Gu 49¹⁷ (Sam. וְיִהְיֶה), Dt 28⁸, 1 S 10⁵, 2 S 5²⁴, Ho 6¹, 11⁴, Am 5¹⁴, Mi 1²,
Zp 2¹³, Zc 9⁵, ψ 72¹⁶ᶠ· (after other jussives), 104³¹, Jb 18¹², 20²³·²⁶·²⁸, 2ᴋ⁸, 33²¹, 34³⁷,
Ru 3⁴. This use of the jussive can hardly be due merely to poetic licence, but
is rather to be explained on rhythmical grounds. In all the above-cited
examples, in fact, the jussive stands at the beginning of the sentence (and
hence removed as far as possible from the principal tone), in others it is
immediately before the principal pause (Is 42⁶, 50², ψ 68¹⁵, Pr 23²⁵, Jb 24¹⁴, 29³,
40¹⁹), or actually *in* pause (Dt 32¹⁸, Jb 23⁹·¹¹, La 3⁵⁰), and is then a simply
rhythmical shortening due to the strong influence of the tone. Moreover,
since the jussive in numerous cases is not distinguished in form from the
imperfect (§ 48 *g*), it is frequently doubtful which of the two the writer
intended. This especially applies to those cases, in which a *subjunctive* is to be
expressed by one or other of the forms (cf. § 107 *k* and *m-x*).

§ 110. *The Imperative.*

Mayer Lambert, ‘Sur la syntaxe de l’impératif en hébreu,’ in
REJ. 1897, p. 106 ff.

a 1. The imperative,[1] which, according to § 46, is restricted to the
2nd pers. sing. and plur., and to *positive* commands, &c., may stand
either alone, or in simple co-ordination (as in 1 K 18⁴⁴, Is 56¹, 65¹⁸)
with other imperatives :

(*a*) To express real commands, e. g. Gn 12¹ *get thee out of thy
country;* or (like the jussive) mere admonitions (Ho 10¹²) and requests,
2 K 5²², Is 5³; on the addition of נָא see below, Rem. 1. The imperative
is used in the sense of an ironical challenge (often including a threat)
in 1 K 2²² *ask for him the kingdom also;* 22¹⁵, Ju 10¹⁴, Is 47¹² (with
נָא), Jer 7²¹, Ez 20³⁹, Am 4⁴, Jb 38³ᶠ˙, 40¹⁰ᶠᶠ˙, La 4²¹. The imperative
has a concessive sense in Na 3¹⁵ (though thou *make thyself many*, &c.),
and in the cases discussed under *f,* e. g. Is 8⁹ᶠ˙, 29⁹.

b (*b*) To express permission, e. g. 2 S 18²³ after previous dissuasion,
(then) *run* (as far as I am concerned)! Is 21¹², 45¹¹.

c (*c*) To express a distinct assurance (like our expression, *thou shalt
have it*)[2] or promise, e. g. Is 65¹⁸ *but be ye glad,* &c. (i. e. ye will have
continually occasion to be glad); and Is 37³⁰, ψ 110²; in a threat,
Jer 2¹⁹. So especially in commands, the fulfilment of which is
altogether out of the power of the person addressed, e. g. Is 54¹⁴ *be far
from anxiety* (meaning, thou needst not fear any more); Gn 1²⁸, &c. (for
other examples, such as 1 K 22¹², 2 K 5¹³, see below, *f*). Most clearly
in the case of the *imperative Niph'al* with a passive meaning, e. g.
Gn 42¹⁶ וְאַתֶּם הֵאָסְרוּ *and ye shall be bound;* Dt 32⁵⁰, Is 49⁹ (Is 45²², see
below, *f*).

d Rem. 1. The particle נָא *age!* (§ 105) is frequently added to the imperative,
as to the jussive, sometimes to soften down a command, or to make a request
in a more courteous form (see above, *a*), Gn 12¹³, 24², sometimes to strengthen
an exhortation uttered as a rebuke or threat (Nu 16²⁶, 20¹⁰) or in ridicule
(Is 47¹²).

e 2. The imperative after the desiderative particle לוּ Gn 23¹³ (at the end of
verses 5 and 14 also read לוּ for לוֹ and join it to the following imperative) is
due to an anacoluthon. Instead of the imperfect which would be expected
here after לוּ, the more forcible imperative is used in a new sentence.

f 2. The imperative in logical dependence upon a preceding imperative, jussive (or cohortative), or an interrogative sentence, serves to

---

[1] On the close relation between the imperative and jussive (both in meaning and form), cf. § 46 and § 48 *i*.
[2] Like the threatening formulae in the Latin comic writers, e. g. *vapula,*
Ter. Phorm. v. 6, 10 = *vapulare te iubeo,* Plaut. Curc. vi. 4, 12.

express the distinct assurance or promise that an action or state will ensue as the certain consequence of a previous action. So especially:

(a) The imperative when depending (with *wāw copulative*) upon another imperative. In this case the first imperative contains, as a rule, a condition, while the second declares the consequence which the fulfilment of the condition will involve. The imperative is used for this declaration, since the consequence is, as a matter of fact, intended or desired by the speaker (cf. *divide et impera*), e. g. Gn 42¹⁸ זֹאת עֲשׂוּ וִֽחְיוּ *this do, and live,* i. e. thus shall ye continue to live. Gn 17¹, 1 K 22¹², 2 K 5¹³, Is 36¹⁶, 45²² (וְהִוָּֽשְׁעוּ), Jer 6¹⁶, Am 5⁴·⁶, ψ 37²⁷, Pr 3³ᶠ·, 4⁴, 7², 13²⁰ Kᵉᵗʰ., Jb 2⁹, 2 Ch 20²⁰; in Jer 25⁵, Jb 22²¹ נָא is added to the first imperative. In other cases, the first imperative contains a mocking concession, the second an irrevocable denunciation, e. g. Is 8⁹ רֹעוּ עַמִּים וָחֹתּוּ (continue to) *make an uproar, O ye peoples, and ye shall be broken in pieces*; cf. verse 9 b.

Rem. 1. If a promise or threat dependent on an imperative be expressed in *g* the 3rd pers. then the jussive is naturally used instead of the 2nd imperative Is 8¹⁰, 55².

2. In Pr 20¹³ the second imperative (containing a promise) is attached by *h* asyndeton; elsewhere two imperatives occur side by side without the copula, where the second might be expected to be subordinated to the first, e. g. Dt 2²⁴ הָחֵל רָשׁ (where רָשׁ is virtually, as it were, an object to הָחֵל) *begin, take in possession* for *to take in possession* (cf., however, Ju 19⁶ הֹואֶל־נָא וְלִין *be content, I pray thee, and tarry all night,* and on this kind of co-ordination in general, cf. § 120 d). But such imperatives as קוּמוּ) קוּם (לְכוּ) קוּם, when immediately preceding a second imperative, are for the most part only equivalent to interjections, *come! up!*

(b) The imperative, when depending (with *wāw copulative*) upon *i* a jussive (cohortative), or an interrogative sentence, frequently expresses also a consequence which is to be expected with certainty, and often a consequence which is intended, or in fact an intention; cf. Gn 20⁷ *and he shall pray for thee,* וֶֽחְיֵה *and thou shalt live;* cf. Ex 14¹⁶, 2 K 5¹⁰, Jb 11⁶, ψ 128⁵ *the Lord bless thee ... so that* (or *in order that*) *thou seest,* &c.; Ru 1⁹, 4¹¹; after a cohortative, Gn 12², 45¹⁸, Ex 3¹⁰ וְהֹוצֵא *that thou mayest bring forth;* Ex 18²², 1 S 12¹⁷, 1 K 1¹²; Jer 35¹⁵ (after imperative and jussive); after an interrogative sentence, 2 S 21³ *wherewith shall I make atonement,* וּבָֽרְכוּ *that ye may bless,* &c.—In Nu 5¹⁹ the imperative without וְ (in 32²³ with וְ) is used after a conditional clause in the sense of a definite promise.

Rem. The 2nd sing. masc. occurs in addressing feminine persons in Ju 4²⁰ *k* (עֲמֹד, according to Qimḥi an infinitive, in which case, however, the infinitive absolute עָמֹד should be read; but probably we should simply read עִמְדִי with Moore), Mi 1¹³ and Zc 13⁷ (after עֹֽוּרִי); and in Is 23¹, the 2nd plur. masc. (On the four forms of the 2nd *fem. plur. imperative* in Is 32¹¹, erroneously explained here in former editions, see now § 48 *i*). In Na 3¹⁵ the interchange of masc. and fem. serves to express totality (the nation in all its aspects). Cf., moreover, § 145 *p* on other noticeable attempts to substitute the corresponding masculine forms for the feminine.

§ 111. *The Imperfect with Wāw Consecutive.*

a 1. The *imperfect* with *wāw consecutive* (§ 49 *a–g*) serves to express actions, events, or states, which are to be regarded as the temporal or logical sequel of actions, events, or states mentioned immediately [1] before. The *imperfect consecutive* is used in this way most frequently as the *narrative tense*, corresponding to the Greek *aorist* or the Latin *historic perfect*. As a rule the narrative is introduced by a perfect, and then continued by means of imperfects with *wāw consecutive* (on this interchange of tenses cf. § 49 *a*, and especially § 112 *a*), e. g. Gn 3¹ *now the serpent was* (הָיָה) *more subtil . . . and he said* (וַיֹּאמֶר) *unto the woman*; 4¹, 6⁹ᶠᶠ·, 10⁹ᶠ·, 15¹⁹, 11¹²ᶠᶠ· ²⁷ᶠᶠ·, 14⁵ᶠ·, 15¹ᶠ·, 16¹ᶠ·, 21¹ᶠᶠ·, 24¹ᶠ·, 25¹⁹ᶠᶠ·, 36²ᶠᶠ·, 37².

b Rem. 1. To this class belong some of the numerous *imperfects consec.* after various expressions of time, whenever such expressions are equivalent in meaning to a perfect [2] (viz. הָיָה *it came to pass*), e. g. Is 6¹ *in the year that king Uzziah died, I saw* (וָאֶרְאֶה), &c.; Gn 22⁴, 27³⁴, Ju 11¹⁶, 1 S 4¹⁹′, 17⁵⁷, 21⁶, Ho 11¹: on the use of וַיְהִי to connect expressions of time, see below, *g*.—It is only in late books or passages that we find the simple *perfect* in a clause following an expression of time, as 1 S 17⁵⁵ (cf. Driver on the passage), 2 Ch 12⁷, 15⁸, &c., Dn 10¹¹, 15¹⁹; the *Perfect* after וְ and the subject, 2 Ch 7¹.

c 2. The continuation of the narrative by means of the imperfect consec. may result in a series of any number of such imperfects, e. g. there are forty-nine in Gn. 1. As soon, however, as the connecting *Wāw* becomes separated from the verb to which it belongs, by the insertion of any word, the perfect necessarily takes the place of the imperfect, e. g. Gn 1⁵ *and God called* (וַיִּקְרָא) *the light Day, and the darkness he called* (וְלַחֹשֶׁךְ קָרָא) *Night*; verse 10, 2²⁰, 11³ and frequently.

d 3. Of two co-ordinate *imperfects consecutive* the former (as equivalent to a temporal clause) is most frequently subordinate in sense to the latter, e. g. Gn 28⁸ᶠ· וַיֵּלֶךְ . . . וַיַּרְא עֵשָׂו *when Esau saw that . . ., he went*, &c.; so also, frequently וַיִּשְׁמַע, &c., Gn 37²¹, &c. On the other hand, a second *imperfect consecutive* is seldom used in an explanatory sense, e. g. Ex 2¹⁰ (וַתֹּאמֶר *for she said*); cf. 1 S 7¹². Other examples of the imperfect consecutive, which apparently represent a progress in the narrative, in reality only refer to the same time, or explain what precedes, see Gn 2²⁵ (וַיִּהְיוּ *they were*; but Jos 4⁹, 1 K 8⁸ *they are*); Gn 36¹⁴ (וַתֵּלֶד), 36³² (וַיִּמְלֹךְ), 1 K 1⁴⁴.

---

[1] On an apparent exception (the *imperf. consec.* at the beginning of whole books) see § 49 *b* note.

[2] Cf. Is 45⁴, where the *imperf. consec.* is joined to an abrupt statement of the cause, and Jb 36⁷, where it is joined to an abrupt statement of the place.

4. The imperfect consecutive sometimes has such a merely *external* con- *e* nexion with an immediately preceding perfect, that in reality it represents an antithesis to it, e.g. Gn 32³¹ *and (yet) my life is preserved*; 2 S 3⁸ *and yet thou chargest me*; Jb 10⁸, 32³; similarly in dependence on noun-clauses, Pr 30²⁵ ᶠᶠ.

2. The introduction of independent narratives, or of a new section *f* of the narrative, by means of an *imperfect consecutive*, likewise aims at a connexion, though again loose and external, with that which has been narrated previously. Such a connexion is especially often established by means of וַיְהִי (καὶ ἐγένετο) *and it came to pass*, after which there then follows either (most commonly) an *imperfect con-secutive* (Gn 4³.⁸, 8⁶, 11², Ex 12²⁹, 13¹⁷, &c.), or *Wāw* with the perfect (separated from it), Gn 7¹⁰, 15¹², 22¹, 27³⁰, or even a perfect without *Wāw* (Gn 8¹³, 14¹ᶠ·, 40¹, Ex 12⁴¹, 16²², Nu 10¹¹, Dt 1³, 1 S 18³⁰, 2 K 8²¹, &c.), or finally a noun-clause introduced by *Wāw*, Gn 41¹.

Rem. 1. This loose connexion by means of וַיְהִי¹ is especially common, *g* when the narrative or a new section of it begins with any expression of time, see above, *b*; cf., in addition to the above-mentioned examples (e.g. Gn 22¹ *and it came to pass after these things, that God did prove Abraham*), the similar cases in Gn 19³⁴, 21²², 1 S 11¹¹, Ru 1¹. Elsewhere the statement of time is expressed by בְּ or כְּ with an infinitive (Gn 12¹⁴, 19¹⁷·²⁹ 39¹³, 15¹⁸ᶠ·, Ju 16²⁵) or by an independent sentence with the perfect (equivalent to a pluperfect, cf. § 106*f*), e.g. Gn 15¹⁷, 24¹⁵, 27³⁰, or by a temporal clause introduced by כִּי *when*, Gn 26⁸, 27¹, Ju 16¹⁶, כַּאֲשֶׁר *when*, Gn 12¹¹, 20¹³, מֵאָז *from the time that*, Gn 39⁵; or, finally, by a noun-clause (cf. § 116 *u*), e.g. 2 K 13²¹ וַיְהִי הֵם קֹבְרִים אִישׁ *and it came to pass, as they were* (just) *burying a man* (prop. they burying), *that* . . .; Gn 42³⁵, 2 K 2¹¹ (the apodosis in both these cases being introduced by וְהִנֵּה); 1 S 7¹⁰, 2 S 13³⁰, 2 K 6⁵·²⁶, 19³⁷ (= Is 37³⁸).—In 1 S 10¹¹, 11¹¹, 2 S 2²³, 15² a noun standing absolutely follows וַיְהִי (as the equivalent of a complete sentence; see below, *h*), and then an *imperfect consecutive* follows.

2. Closely related to the cases noticed in *g* are those in which the *imperfect* *h* *consecutive*, even without a preceding וַיְהִי, introduces the apodosis either— (*a*) to whole sentences, or (*b*) to what are equivalent to whole sentences, especially to nouns standing absolutely. As in certain cases of the *perfect consecutive* (see § 112 *x*), so the *imperfect consecutive* has here acquired a sort of independent force. Cf. for (*a*) 1 S 15²³ *because thou hast rejected the word of the Lord*, וַיִּמְאָסְךָ *he hath rejected thee* (cf. Nu 14¹⁶, Is 48⁴, where the causal clause precedes in the form of an infinitive with preposition), Ex 9²¹; for (*b*) Gn 22²⁴ וּפִילַגְשׁוֹ *and* (as to) *his concubine*..., וַתֵּלֶד *she bare*, &c.; Ex 38²⁴, Nu 14³⁶ᶠ·, 1 S 14¹⁹, 17²⁴, 2 S 4¹⁰, 19⁴¹ ᴷᵉᵗʰ·, 21¹⁶, 1 K 9²⁰ᶠ·, 12¹⁷, 2 K 25²², Jer 6¹⁹, 28⁸, 33²⁴, 44²⁵. ²—In 1 K 15¹³, 2 K 16¹⁴ the preceding noun, used absolutely, is even regarded as the object of the following imperfect consecutive, and is therefore introduced by אֵת־.

---

¹ Exhaustive statistics of the use of וַיְהִי in its many and various connexions are given by König in *ZAW*. 1899, p. 260 ff.

² Cf. the Mēša‘ inscription, l. 5 (Omri) *the king of Israel*, וַיְעַנּוּ *he oppressed Moab*, &c.—The peculiar imperfect consecutive in Gn 30²⁷ᵇ (in the earlier editions explained as equivalent to an object-clause) arises rather from a preg-nant brevity of expression: *I have observed and* have come to the conclusion, *the Lord hath blessed me*, &c.—In Gn 27³⁴ read, with LXX, וַיְהִי before כִּשְׁמֹעַ.

i 3. The *imperfect consecutive* serves, in the cases treated under *a–h*, to represent either expressly, or at least to a great extent, a *chronological* succession of actions or events; elsewhere it expresses those actions, &c., which represent the logical consequence of what preceded, or a result arising from it by an inherent necessity. Thus the *imperfect consecutive* is used—

k (*a*) As a final summing up of the preceding narrative, e. g. Gn 2¹, 23²⁰ וג׳ וַיָּקָם הַשָּׂדֶה *so* (in this way) *the field became* (legally) *the property of Abraham*, &c.; 1 S 17⁵⁰, 31⁶.

l (*b*) To express a logical or necessary consequence of that which immediately precedes, e. g. Gn 39², Jb 2³ *and he still holdeth fast his integrity*, וג׳ וַתְּסִיתֵנִי *so that thou thus* (as it now appears) *groundlessly movedst me against him*; ψ 65⁹ *so that they are afraid* . . .; even a consequence which happens conditionally, Jer 20¹⁷ וַתְּהִי *so that my mother should have been* . . . Another instance of the kind perhaps (if the text be correct) is Jer 38⁹ וַיָּמָת *so that he dies* (must die).

m Rem. Such consecutive clauses frequently occur after interrogative sentences, e. g. Is 51¹² *who art thou* (i. e. art thou *so helpless*), וַתִּירְאִי *that thou art* (*must needs be*) *afraid?* ψ 144³ (cf. ψ 8⁵, where in a very similar context כִּי *that* is used with the imperfect); Gn 12¹⁹ (וָאֶקַּח); 31²⁷ וָאֲשַׁלֵּחֲךָ *so that I might have sent thee away.*

4. As regards the range of time it is to be carefully noticed—

n (*a*) That the *imperfect consecutive* may represent all varieties in the relations of tense and mood, which, according to § 107 *a*, follow from the idea of the imperfect;

o (*b*) That the more precise determination of the range of time to which an *imperfect consecutive* relates must be inferred in each case from the character of the preceding tense (or tense-equivalent), to which it is attached, in a more or less close relation, as temporal or logical sequence. Thus the *imperfect consecutive* serves—

p (1) To represent actions, events, or states, which are *past* (or were repeated in past time), when it is united with tenses, or their equivalents, which refer to an actual past.

q Cf. the examples given above, under *a* and *f*, of the imperfect consecutive as an historic tense. The imperfect consecutive also frequently occurs as the continuation of a perfect (*preterite*) in a subordinate clause; e. g. Gn 27¹, Nu 11²⁰, Dt 4³⁷, 1 S 8⁸, 1 K 2⁵, 11³³, 18¹³, &c.; also in Is 49⁷ וַיִּבְחָרֶךָ is the continuation of a preterite, contained, according to the sense, in the preceding אֲשֶׁר נֶאֱמָן.—In Jb 31²⁶·³⁴ the imperfect consecutive is joined to an imperfect denoting the past in a conditional sentence. An imperfect consecutive occurs in dependence on a perfect which has the sense of a pluperfect (§ 106*f*), e. g. in Gn 26¹⁸, 28⁶ ᶠ·, 31¹⁹·³⁴ (*now Rachel had taken the teraphim*, וַתְּשִׂמֵם *and had* *put them*, &c.) ; Nu 14³⁶, 1 S 28³, 2 S 2²³, Is 39¹. Finally there are the cases in which an infinitival or participial construction representing past time, according to § 113 *r*, § 116 *x*, is taken up and continued by an imperfect consecutive.

(2) To represent *present* actions, &c., in connexion with tenses, or *r* their equivalents, which describe actions and states as being either present or lasting on into the present (continuing in their effect) ; so especially,

(*a*) In connexion with the present perfects, described in § 106 *g*, e.g. ψ 16⁹ *therefore my heart is glad* (שָׂמַח) *and my glory rejoiceth* (וַיָּ֫גֶל) ; Is 3¹⁶ (parallel with a simple imperfect). Cf. also such examples as ψ 29¹⁰ וַיֵּ֫שֶׁב (prop. he sat down, *and has been enthroned ever since*), ψ 41¹³.

(*β*) In connexion with those perfects which represent experiences *s* frequently confirmed (see § 106 *k*), e.g. Jb 14² *he cometh up* (יָצָא) *like a flower, and is cut down* (וַיִּמָּל) ; *he fleeth* (וַיִּבְרַח) *also as a shadow*, וְלֹא יַעֲמוֹד *and continueth not* ; Jb 20¹⁵, 24².¹¹, Is 40²⁴, Pr 11².

(*γ*) In connexion with imperfects which, in one of the ways *t* described in § 107. 2, are used in the sense of the present ; e.g. Jb 14¹⁰ *but man dieth* (יָמוּת) *and becometh powerless* (וַיֶּחֱלָשׁ), &c., i. e. remains powerless ; Jb 4⁵, Ho 8¹³, Hb 1⁹ᶠ·, ψ 55¹⁸, 90³, Jb 5¹⁵, 7¹⁸, 11³ (*when thou mockest*), 12²⁵, 34²⁴, 37⁸ (parallel with a simple imperfect) ; 39¹⁵. In the apodosis of a conditional sentence, ψ 59¹⁶, so also after an interrogative imperfect, 1 S 2²⁹, ψ 42⁶ (וַתֶּהֱמִי for which in verse 12 and in 43⁵ we have וּמַה־תֶּהֱמִי *and why art thou disquieted ?*).

(*δ*) In dependence on participles, which represent what at present *u* continues or is being repeated, e.g. Nu 22¹¹, 1 S 2⁶, 2 S 19² *behold the king weepeth* (בֹּכֶה) *and mourneth* (וַיִּתְאַבֵּל) *for Absalom* ; Am 5⁸, 9⁵ᶠ·, Na 1⁴, ψ 34⁸, Pr 20²⁶, Jb 12²²ᶠ·, but cf. e. g. Jb 12⁴ קֹרֵא לֶאֱלוֹהַּ *who called upon God*, וַיַּעֲנֵהוּ *and he answered him*.

(*ε*) In dependence on other equivalents of the present, as in Is 51¹², *v* ψ 144³ (see above, *m*) ; Jb 10²². So especially as the continuation of an infinitive, which is governed by a preposition (cf. § 114 *r*), Is 30¹², Jer 10¹³, ψ 92⁸, &c.

(3) To represent *future* actions, &c., in dependence on—(*a*) an *w* imperfect which refers to the future, ψ 49¹⁵, 94²²ᶠ· ;—(*β*) a perfect consecutive, or those perfects which, according to § 106 *n*, are intended to represent future events as undoubtedly certain, and therefore as though already accomplished (*perf. propheticum*) ; cf. Is 5¹⁵ (parallel with a simple imperfect separated from וֹ) ; 5¹⁶ (cf. 2¹¹·¹⁷, where the same threat is expressed by the perfect consecutive) ; 5²⁵, 9⁵·¹⁰ᶠ·,

13¹⁵·¹⁷ᶠᶠ·, 22⁷ᶠᶠ·, Jo 2²³, Mi 2¹³, Ez 33⁴·⁶, ψ 7¹³, 64⁸ᶠᶠ· ;—(γ) a future participle, Jer 4¹⁶. [1]

x　Rem. An imperfect consecutive in dependence on a perfect or imperfect, which represents an action occurring only conditionally, is likewise used only in a hypothetical sense, e. g. Jb 9¹⁶ אִם־קָרָאתִי וַיַּעֲנֵנִי *if I had called, and he had answered me, yet* . . .; ψ 139¹¹ וָאֹמַר *if I should say* (previously, in verse 8 f., hypothetical imperfects are used).—In Is 48¹⁸ ᶠ· an imperfect consecutive occurs in dependence on a sentence expressing a wish introduced by לוּא *utinam* (וַיְהִי *and it*, or *so that it were*, equivalent to *then should it be*). Cf. also the examples mentioned above, under *l* (Jer 20¹⁷) and *m* (Gn 31²⁷), where the imperfect consecutive expresses facts occurring *contingently*.

§ 112. *The Perfect with Wāw Consecutive.*

G. R. Berry, 'Waw consecutive with the perfect in Hebrew,' in *Bibl. Lit.*, xxii. (1903), pp. 60–69.

a　1. The perfect, like the imperfect (§ 111), is used with *wāw consecutive* (cf. § 49 *a*; on the external differentiation of the perfect consecutive by a change in the position of the tone, see § 49 *h*) to express actions, events, or states, which are to be attached to what precedes, in a more or less close relation, as its *temporal* or *logical* consequence. And as, according to § 111 *a*, the narrative which begins with a perfect, or its equivalent, is continued in the imperfect consecutive, so, vice versa, the perfect consecutive forms the regular continuation to a preceding imperfect, or its equivalent.

b　Rem. 1. This alternation of perfect and imperfect or their equivalents is a striking peculiarity of the *consecutio temporum* in Hebrew. It not only affords a certain compensation for the lack of forms for tenses and moods, but also gives to Hebrew style the charm of an expressive variety, an action conceived as being still in progress (*imperfect*, &c.), reaching afterwards in the *perfect* a calm and settled conclusion, in order to be again exhibited in movement in the imperfect, and vice versa.[2] The strict regularity of this

---

[1] Also in Jer 51²⁹ the imperfects consecutive are attached to the threat virtually contained in the preceding imperatives. On the other hand וַיִּחְלּוּ Ho 8¹⁰ would be very remarkable as expressing a future ; the text is, however, certainly corrupt, and hence the Cod. Babyl. and the Erfurt MS. 3 endeavour to remedy it by וַיְח׳, and Ewald reads וַיָּחֵלּוּ.—In Ez 28¹⁶ (cf. Jer 15⁶ᶠ·) וָאֲחַלֶּלְךָ appears to announce an action irrevocably determined upon, and therefore represented as already accomplished ; cf. the prophetic perfects in verse 17 ff.

[2] It is difficult to give a proper explanation of this phenomenon (according to § 49 *a*, note, to be found only in the Canaanitish group of languages), when we have given up the theory of a special *wāw conversivum* in the unscientific sense mentioned in § 49 *b*, note, at the end, and if we accept the fact that the *perfect* and *imperfect consecutive* cannot possibly be used in a way which contradicts their fundamental character as described in §§ 106 and 107. In other words, even the *perfect consecutive* originally represents a finally completed action, &c., just as the *imperfect consecutive* represents an action which

alternation belongs indeed rather to the higher style, and even then it depends upon the view and intention of the speaker, whether he wishes the action, &c., to be regarded as the logical consequence of what has preceded, or as simply co-ordinate with it, and so in the same tense.

2. A succession of any number of other *perfects consecutive* may be co-or- *C* dinated with a *perfect consecutive* (cf. e. g. Ez 14[18], Am 5[19], Ru 3[3], four perfects in each case, Is 8[7] five, Ex 6[6f.] eight). It is true, however, of the perfect (as conversely of the *imperfect*, § 111 c), that as soon as the *Wāw* is separated by any intervening word from the verb to which it belongs, an *imperfect* necessarily takes the place of the *perfect*, e.g. Gn 12[12] *when the Egyptians shall see thee, they shall say* (וְאָמְרוּ), *This is his wife: and they will kill me* (וְהָרְגוּ אֹתִי) *but thee they will save alive* (וְאֹתָךְ יְחַיּוּ).

2. The perfect consecutive, like the imperfect consecutive, always *d* belongs to the period of time expressed by the preceding tense, or its equivalent, with which it is connected as the temporal or logical consequence. The particular cases may be classed under three heads: (*a*) the perfect consecutive in *immediate* dependence (see *e*), (*b*) in loose connexion (see *x*) with the preceding, and (*c*) the perfect consecutive at the beginning of the apodosis to other sentences, or their equivalents (see *ff*).

3. The perfect consecutive in immediate dependence on the pre- *e* ceding tense, or its equivalent, serves

(*a*) As a frequentative tense to express *past* actions, &c., i.e. actions repeatedly brought to a conclusion in the past, and follows tenses, or their equivalents, representing actions which have *continued* or been *repeated in the past*:

(α) After a simple imperfect, e.g. Gn 2[6] אֵד יַעֲלֶה *there went up a mist* (again and again) *from the earth*, וְהִשְׁקָה *and watered* (as it were, *and ever watered afresh*), &c. This frequentative use of the perfect consecutive is equally evident after frequentative imperfects, Gn 2[10] (וְהָיָה *and it became* again every time; וַיְהִי would mean, and it became so once for all); 29[2f.] (four perfects consecutive referring to actions repeated daily); Ex 33[7-11] יִקַּח *he used to take* at each new encampment *the tent*, וְנָטָה *and to pitch it* again every time *without the camp*; notice, amongst the numerous frequent. perff. consec., the imperf. in vv. 7, 8, 9, 11, always in a frequentative sense; 34[34f.], Nu 9[19.21] (among several simple imperfects), 10[17], Ju 2[19], 1 S 2[19] תַּעֲשֶׂה

---

is only beginning, becoming or still continuing, and hence in any case incomplete. The simplest view is to suppose, that the use of the *perfect consecutive* originated from those cases, in which it had to express the conclusion (or final consequence) of an action which was continued (or repeated) *in past time* (see the examples above), and that this use was afterwards extended to other cases, in which it had to represent the temporal or logical consequence of actions, &c., still in progress, and thus in the end a regular interchange of the two tenses became recognized.

she used to make . . . וְהֶעֱלַתָה *and brought it to him from year to year*; 27⁹ (וְלָקַח), 1 K 14²⁸, 2 K 3²⁵, 12¹⁵ (in verses 16ᶠ· imperfects occur again). So also in dependent sentences, Gn 6⁴ (וְיָלְדוּ) as a continuation of יָבֹאוּ), Jb 31²⁹.[1]

f (β) After an imperfect consecutive, e. g. Ex 39³ (Samaritan וקצצו), 1 S 5⁷ (? see § 112 *rr*), 7¹⁶, 2 S 15²·⁵, 16¹³ *and he threw stones at him*, וְעִפַּר *and cast dust* continually; 12¹⁶·³¹, 2 K 6¹⁰, 12¹¹ ff. 15, Jer 37¹⁵, Jb 1⁵.

g Rem. The frequentative perfect consecutive is sometimes joined even with imperfects consecutive which simply express one *single* action or occurrence in the past; thus Ex 18²⁶, 4ᶜ³¹ᶠ·, 1 S 1⁴, 2 S 15¹ᶠ·, 1 K 14²⁷ (cf. verse 28); 1 K 18⁴, 2 K 12¹⁰. For other examples of a loosely connected frequentative perfect consecutive, see below, *dd*.

h (γ) After a perfect, Gn 37³ (וְעָשָׂה לוֹ, i. e. as often as he needed a new garment)[2]; Gn 31⁷, Nu 11⁸, 1 S 16¹⁴, 2 K 3⁴, ψ 22⁶;[3] in interrogative sentences, 1 S 26⁹ *who has ever*, &c.; ψ 80¹³, Jb 1¹·⁴, Ru 4⁷.

i (δ) After an infinitive, Am 1¹¹ עַל־רָדְפוֹ *because he did pursue his brother*, וְשִׁחֵת *and* (on each occasion) *did cast off all pity* (then an imperfect consecutive); after an infinitive absolute, Jos 6¹³, 2 S 13¹⁹, Jer 23¹⁴.

k (ε) After a participle, Is 6³ (וְקָרָא), &c., frequentative, as a continuation of עֹמְדִים, verse 2); 1 S 2²², 2 S 17¹⁷.[4]

l (ζ) After other equivalents of tenses, e. g. Gn 47²² *the priests had a portion from Pharaoh*, וְאָכְלוּ *and did eat* (year by year), &c.; 1 K 4⁷.

m (*b*) To express *present* actions, &c., as the temporal or logical consequence of actions or events which continue or are repeated in the present, especially such as have, according to experience, been at all times frequently repeated, and may be repeated at any time:

(α) After a simple imperfect, e. g. Gn 2²⁴ *therefore a man leaves* (יַעֲזָב *is accustomed to leave*) . . . וְדָבַק *and cleaves*, &c., here, as frequently elsewhere, clearly with the secondary idea of purpose, i. e. in order to cleave; Is 5¹¹ (if וְהָיָה is to be taken as a continuation

---

[1] Also in Ez 44¹² (where Stade, *ZAW*. v. 293, would read שֵׁרְתוּ and וְיִהְיוּ) the unusual tenses may have been intentionally chosen: *because they continually ministered and so always became afresh* . . .

[2] Driver, on this passage, rightly refers to 1 S 2¹⁹.

[3] Am 4⁷ would also come under this head, if וְהִמְטַרְתִּי is really intended, and the statement refers to the past; מָנַעְתִּי might, however, also be a perfect expressing positive assurance (§ 106 *m*), and the passage would then come under *s*.

[4] That וְהָלְכָה, &c., are frequentatives (*the maidservant used to go repeatedly and tell them*) may be seen from יֵלְכוּ (necessarily an imperfect, since it is separated from וְ by הֵם) and וְיֻכְלוּ; on the other hand in verse 18 וַיִּרְא and וַיֵּלְכוּ of actions which happened only once.

of יַדְלִיֳקֵם); Is 28²⁸, Jer 12³, Ho 4³, 7⁷, ψ 90⁶, Jb 14⁹; also in dependent clauses, Lv 20¹⁸, Is 29⁸·¹¹ᶠ·, Am 5¹⁹.

(β) After a participle, as the equivalent of a sentence representing *n* a contingent action, &c., e. g. Ex 21¹² מַכֵּה אִישׁ וָמֵת (instead of מַכֵּה there is in verse 20, &c. וְכִי יָכֶּה אִישׁ)) *if one smite a man and* (so that) *he die*, &c., Ex 21¹⁶, Is 29¹⁵, Am 6¹, Hb 2¹².

(γ) After an infinitive absolute, Jer 7⁹ᶠ· *will ye steal, murder, and* o *commit adultery* (simple infinitives absolute; cf. § 113 *ee*), וּבָאתֶם *and then come and stand before me . . . and say*, &c.; cf. below, *u*.

(c) To express *future* actions, &c., as the temporal or logical con- *p* sequence of tenses, or their equivalents, which announce or require such future actions or events. Thus—

(a) After imperfects in the sense of a simple future, e. g. Am 9³ᶠ· מִשָּׁם אֲחַפֵּשׂ וּלְקַחְתִּים *I will search and take them out thence*, &c.; Gn 4¹⁴, 40¹³, Ex 7³, 1 S 17³², 2 K 5¹¹, Jb 8⁶ᶠ· (also with a change of subject, Gn 27¹², Ju 6¹⁶, &c.); and in interrogative sentences, Gn 39⁹, Ex 2⁷, 2 S 12¹⁸, 2 K 14¹⁰, Am 8⁸, ψ 41⁶; cf. also Ru 1¹¹; in sentences expressing a wish, 2 S 15⁴; as well as in almost all kinds of dependent clauses. Also in conditional clauses after אִם־ Gn 32⁹, Ex 19⁵, 1 S 1¹¹, or כִּי Gn 37²⁶, or הֵן Jer 3¹; in final clauses after לְמַעַן Gn 12¹³, Nu 15⁴⁰, Is 28¹³; after אֲשֶׁר Dt 2²⁵, or פֶּן־ Gn 3²², 19¹⁹, 32¹², Is 6¹⁰, Am 5⁶; in temporal clauses, Is 32¹⁵, Jer 13¹⁶; and in relative clauses, Gn 24¹⁴, Ju 1¹², 1 S 17²⁶.

(β) After the jussive (or an imperfect in the sense of a jussive or *q* optative) or cohortative, with the same or a different subject, e. g. Gn 1¹⁴ᶠ· יְהִי מְאֹרֹת . . . וְהָיוּ *let there be lights . . . and let them be*, &c.; Gn 24⁴, 28³, 31⁴⁴, 1 K 1², 22¹³, Ru 2⁷, 1 Ch 22¹¹; after a jussive expressing an imprecation, ψ 109¹⁰.

(γ) After an imperative, also with the same or a different subject, *r* e. g. 2 S 7⁵ לֵךְ וְאָמַרְתָּ *go and tell* (that thou mayst tell), &c., and often, *perf. consec.* after לֵךְ (as also the *perf. consec.* of אָמַר and דִּבֶּר very frequently follows other imperatives);. Gn 6¹⁴, 8¹⁷, 27⁴³ᶠ·, 1 S 15³·¹⁸, 1 K 2³⁶, Jer 48²⁶.

(δ) After perfects which express a definite expectation or assurance *s* (cf. § 106 *m* and *n*), e. g. Gn 17²⁰ הִנֵּה בֵּרַכְתִּי אֹתוֹ וְהִפְרֵיתִי אֹתוֹ *behold, I have blessed him, and will make him fruitful*, &c.; Is 2¹¹, 5¹⁴; on Am 4⁷ see above, note 3 on *h*; in an interrogative sentence, Ju 9⁹, 11¹³.

(ε) After a participle, e. g. Gn 7⁴ *for yet seven days*, אָנֹכִי מַמְטִיר *t and I will cause it to rain* . . . וּמָחִיתִי *and I will* (i. e. in order to) *destroy*, &c.; Jer 21⁹; also with a different subject, Gn 24⁴³ᶠ· *the maiden which cometh forth* (הַיּצֵאת) . . . , וְאָמַרְתִּי אֵלֶיהָ *to whom I shall say* . . . , וְאָמְרָה *and she* (then) *shall say*, &c. This use of the perfect consecutive is especially frequent after a participle introduced by הִנֵּה, e.g. Gn 6¹⁷ ᶠ·; with a different subject 1 K 20³⁶, Am 6¹⁴; after a complete noun-clause introduced by הִנֵּה (cf. § 140), Ex 3¹³ *behold, I come* (i.e. if I shall come) . . . , וְאָמַרְתִּי לָהֶם *and shall say unto them* . . . , וְאָמְרוּ *and they* (then) *shall say*, &c.; 1 S 14⁸ᶠᶠ·, Is 7¹⁴, 8⁷ᶠ·, 39⁶.

u (ζ) After an infinitive absolute, whether the infinitive absolute serves to strengthen the finite verb (see § 113 *t*), e.g. Is 31⁵, or is used as an emphatic substitute for a cohortative or imperfect (§ 113 *dd* and *ee*), e.g. Lv 2⁶, Dt 1¹⁶, Is 5⁵, Ez 23⁴⁶ ᶠ·

v (η) After an infinitive construct governed by a preposition (for this change from the infinitive construction to the finite verb, cf. § 114 *r*), e.g. 1 S 10⁸ עַד־בּוֹאִי אֵלֶיךָ וְהוֹדַעְתִּי לְךָ *till I come unto thee* (prop. until my coming) *and show thee*, &c.; Gn 18²³, 27⁴⁵, Ju 6¹⁸, Ez 39²⁷; cf. 1 K 2³⁷,⁴².

w Rem. To the same class belong 1 S 14²⁴, where the idea of time precedes, *until it be evening* and until *I be avenged*, &c., and Is 5⁶, where the idea of place precedes, in both cases governed by עַד־.

x 4. The very frequent use of the perfect consecutive in direct dependence upon other tenses (see above, *d–v*) explains how it finally obtained a kind of independent force—especially for the purpose of announcing future events—and might depend loosely on sentences to which it stood only in a wider sense in the relation of a temporal or logical consequence. Thus the perfect consecutive is used—

(*a*) To announce *future* events, &c., in loose connexion with a further announcement, e.g. Gn 41³⁰ וְקָמוּ and two co-ordinate perfects consecutive, equivalent to *but then shall arise*, &c.; frequently so after הִנֵּה with a following substantive (1 S 9⁸), or a participial clause (cf. the analogous instances above, under *t*), e.g. 1 S 2³¹ *behold, the days come*, וְגָרַעְתִּי *that I will cut off*, &c.; Is 39⁶, Am 4², 8¹¹, 9¹³, and very often in Jeremiah; after an expression of time, Ex 17⁴, Is 10²⁵, 29¹⁷, Jer 51³³, Ho 1⁴. Further, when joined to a statement concerning present or past facts, especially when these contain the reason for the action, &c., expressed in the perfect consecutive; cf. Is 6⁷ *lo, this hath touched thy lips*, וְסָר *therefore thine iniquity shall be taken away*, &c. (not copulative *and it is taken away*, since it is parallel with a simple imperfect), Gn 20¹¹, 26²², Ju 13³ (here in an adversative sense); Ho 8¹⁴. In loose connexion with a noun-clause, a long succession of perfects consecutive occurs in Ex 6⁶ᶠᶠ· Also in Amos 5²⁶ וּנְשָׂאתֶם may be an announcement *yea, ye shall take up*; but cf. below, *rr*.

Rem. 1. Very frequently the announcement of a future event is attached *y* by means of וְהָיָה¹ *and it shall come to pass* (cf. the analogous continuation in the past by means of וַיְהִי, § 111, 2), after which the event announced (sometimes after a long parenthesis) follows in one or more (co-ordinate) perfects consecutive, Gn 9¹⁴, 12¹² (וְהָיָה כִי = *if*, as in 46³³, Ex 1¹⁰, 22²⁶ and frequently), 1 K 18¹², Is 14³ ᶠ·, Am 8⁹ ; or in the imperfect, Gn 4¹⁴, Is 2², 3²⁴, 4³, 7¹⁸.²¹ ff. (cf. 29⁸) ; or in the jussive, Lv 14⁹. It very rarely happens that the verb which is thus loosely added, agrees in gender and number with the following subject, as in Nu 5²⁷, Jer 42¹⁶ וְהָיְתָה (before הַחֶרֶב), and in Jer 42¹⁷ וְיִהְיוּ (before כָּל־הָאֲנָשִׁים).

2. The jussive form וִיהִי occurs (in the sense described in *y*) instead of וְהָיָה *z* in 1 S 10⁵, 2 S 5²⁴ (1 Ch 14¹⁵), 1 K 14⁵, Ru 3⁴, although in the first three places a jussive is wholly inadmissible in the context, and even in Ru 3⁴ (where an admonition follows) וְהָיָה would be expected (see below, *bb*). In 1 K 14⁵ the form is a textual error, and the pointing should simply be וַיְהִי. In the other passages ויהי (always before an infinitive with a preposition) stands at the beginning of the sentence at an unusually long distance from the principal tone, and hence is certainly to be explained according to § 109 *k*, except that in 1 S 10⁵, &c., the simply rhythmical jussive form takes the place, not of the full imperfect form, but (exceptionally) of the perfect consecutive.

(*b*) To introduce a command or wish : Dt 10¹⁹ *love ye therefore the aa stranger* ; 1 S 6⁵, 24¹⁶, 1 K 2⁶ (in Gn 40¹⁴ the precative perfect consecutive, as elsewhere the cohortative, jussive, and imperative, is strengthened by means of נָא). So, also, in loose connexion with participial and other noun-clauses (see above, *x*), Gn 45¹²ᶠ·, 1 K 2²ᶠ·, Ru 3³ ᶠ·, 3⁹.—In Gn 17¹¹ the perfect consecutive (וּנְמַלְתֶּם *and ye shall be circumcised*, &c.) is used to explain a preceding command.

Rem. As in the cases mentioned above under *y*, the connexion may be *bb* made by means of וְהָיָה. Thus with a following perfect consecutive, e. g. Gn 46³³, 47²⁴, Ju 4²⁰. Cf. also Gn 24¹⁴, where the real wish, at least as regards the sense, is contained in the next sentence.

(*c*) To introduce a question, whether in loose connexion with *cc* another interrogative sentence (see above, *p*), e. g. Gn 29¹⁵ *art thou my brother* (equivalent to, *Surely thou art*), וַעֲבַדְתַּנִי *and shouldest thou then serve me for naught ?* or with a positive statement, e. g. Ex 5⁵ וְהִשְׁבַּתֶּם *will ye then make them rest ?*) ; Nu 16¹⁰, 1 S 25¹¹, and (if it is *Milᵉraʻ*) וְהֶחֱרַשְׁתִּי ψ 50²¹).

(*d*) To introduce actions frequently repeated (hence analogous to *dd* the numerous examples of a frequentative perfect consecutive, above, under *e*), e. g. 1 S 1³ (וְעָלָה of annual festival journeys) ; 13²¹ (where, however, the text appears radically corrupt) ; 27⁹ (וְהִכָּה, i. e. every time, therefore continued by means of וְלֹא יְחַיֶּה) ; 1 K 5⁷ (וְכִלְכְּלוּ,

¹ On the various combinations with וְהָיָה see König's statistics in *ZAW*. xix. 272 ff.

parallel with a simple imperfect); 9²⁵, Jer 25⁴, Ho 12¹¹, Dn 8⁴.—In Jb 1⁴ᶠ· a series of frequentative perfects consecutive is interrupted by an imperfect consecutive, while a simple imperfect (as the *modus rei repetitae*) forms the conclusion. In Jer 6¹⁷ a similar perfect is expressly marked, by placing the tone on the final syllable (according to § 49 *h*), as parallel with the real perfects consecutive.

ee   Rem. The loose connexion of *tempora frequentativa* by וְהָיָה (cf. the Rem. on *y* and *bb*) is also very common in this sense; thus with a following perfect consecutive, Gn 30⁴¹ᶠ· (but in verse 42ᵃ, where the verb is separated from the *Wāw* by an insertion, we find לֹא יָשִׂים *he used not to put them in*, according to § 107 *e*); Gn 38⁹, Ex 17¹¹, 33⁷ ᶠᶠ· (see above, *e*), Nu 21⁹, Ju 6³, 19³⁰, 1 S 16²³ (followed by five perfects consecutive); 2 S 15⁵; with a following imperfect (as the *modus rei repetitae*), Ju 2¹⁹, 2 S 14²⁶.—In Ju 12⁵ᶠ· וְהָיוּ, contrary to what would be expected, is continued by means of the imperfect consecutive, and in 1 S 13²² by וְלֹא with the perfect (instead of the imperfect).

ff   **5.** Further, the perfect consecutive is very frequently employed with a certain emphasis to introduce the apodosis after sentences (or their equivalents) which contain a condition, a reason, or a statement of time. Such an apodosis, as in the cases already treated, may represent either future events, or commands and wishes, or even events which have been often repeated in the past. Thus—

(*a*) The perfect consecutive occurs in the apodosis to conditional sentences [1] (§ 159 *g, o, s*):

(α) After אִם with the imperfect, e. g. 2 K 7⁴ᵇ אִם־יְמִיתֻנוּ וָמָתְנוּ *if they kill us,* (well then) *we shall but die;* here the perfect consecutive is used obviously with greater emphasis than the imperfect (נִחְיֶה) which immediately precedes; Gn 18²⁶, 24⁸·⁴¹, 32⁹, Nu 30¹⁵, Ju 4²⁰, 1 S 1¹¹, 20⁶, 1 K 3¹⁴, Na 3¹², Ec 4¹¹.

gg   (β) After אִם with the perfect (in the sense of a *futurum exactum*), Nu 5²⁷, 2 K 5²⁰, 7⁴ᵃ, Is 4⁴ᶠ·; as precative apodosis after אִם־נָא with the *perf. preteritum*, Gn 33¹⁰; as a frequentative perfect consecutive, to represent past events in the apodosis after אִם with a perfect, Gn 38⁹, Nu 21⁹, Ju 6³, Jb 7⁴; after אִם with imperfect, Gn 31⁸.

hh   (γ) After כִּי (*in case, suppose that*) with the imperfect, Gn 12¹², Ex 18¹⁶, Ju 13¹⁷, Is 58⁷, Ez 14¹³. [2] Frequentative with reference to the past, after כִּי with frequentative perfect, Ju 2¹⁸, Jb 7¹³ᶠ·.

---

[1] In a number of the examples of this kind the protasis is already loosely connected by means of והיה, and hence some of them had to be already mentioned above, under *y, bb, ee.*

[2] In 1 S 24¹⁹ a question appears to be expressed by the perfect consecutive, *for if a man find his enemy, will he let him go well away?* Probably, however, with Klostermann, יְמַ should be read for וְכִי.

(δ) After אֲשֶׁר with the imperfect, Gn 44⁹ וָמֵת . . . אֲשֶׁר יִמָּצֵא אִתּוֹ *ii with whomsoever . . . it be found, let him die*; with the perfect, Ex 21¹³ *and if a man lie not in wait*, &c.; Ju 1¹².

(ε) Very frequently after a perfect consecutive (one or more) con- *kk* taining the condition, e. g. Gn 44²⁹ וְהוֹרַדְתֶּם . . . וּלְקַחְתֶּם גַּם־אֶת־זֶה *and if ye take* (or *shall have taken*) *this one also . . . ye shall bring down*, &c.; cf. Gn 33¹³, 42³⁸, 44⁴·²², 47³⁰, Nu 30¹², Ru 2⁹, and probably also Ez 39²⁸.— Also frequentative in reference to the past, e. g. 1 S 17³⁴ᶠ· . . . וּבָא הָאֲרִי וְיָצָאתִי *and when there came* (as sometimes happened) *a lion . . . I went out*, &c.; Ex 33¹⁰, Nu 10¹⁷ᶠᶠ·, 1 K 18¹⁰, Jer 20⁹ (the perfects consecutive being regularly continued in the apodosis by וְלֹא with an imperfect[1]).

Rem. The perfect consecutive may be used also in the protasis to express *ll* a condition when the employment of the perfect consecutive in the apodosis has become impossible, owing to an emphatic word having to stand before it; thus in Ez 14¹⁴ on account of הֵמָּה; 33⁴ on account of דָּמוֹ.—In 1 S 14⁵² the imperfect consecutive, contrary to what might be expected, stands in the apodosis, *and when Saul saw any . . . valiant man, he took him unto him*, where וַיַּאַסְפֵהוּ suggests the special case, rather than a repeated occurrence; cf. 2 S 15². Conversely, in 1 S 2¹⁶ (וַיֹּאמֶר perhaps a mere mistake for וְאָמַר), 17³⁵ ᵇ an imperfect consecutive stands in the protasis.

(ζ) After various equivalents of sentences, which contain a condition; *mm* thus, after a substantive standing absolutely, or a participle (a *casus pendens*), Gn 17¹⁴ וְנִכְרְתָה וג' . . . וְעָרֵל זָכָר *and the uncircumcised male* (in case such an one be found), *he shall be cut off*, &c.; cf. Gn 30³², Ex 12¹⁵, 2 S 14¹⁰, Is 6¹³, and (after an infinitive with a preposition) 2 S 7¹⁴; in a wider sense also Ex 4²¹, 9¹⁹, 12⁴⁴, Is 9⁴, 56⁵.

(b) The perfect consecutive serves as the apodosis to causal clauses; *nn* thus e. g. after יַעַן כִּי with the perfect, Is 3¹⁶ᶠ·; after יַעַן אֲשֶׁר with perfect, 1 K 20²⁸; after עֵקֶב with perfect, Nu 14²⁴; also after what are equivalent to causal clauses, e. g. ψ 25¹¹ (וְסָלַחְתָּ . . . לְמַעַן שִׁמְךָ *for thy name's sake . . . pardon . . .*); Is 37²⁹ after יַעַן with an infinitive.

(c) The perfect consecutive occurs as the apodosis to temporal *oo* clauses or their equivalents, e. g. 1 S 2¹⁵ וּבָא . . . בְּטֶרֶם יַקְטִרוּן אֶת־הַחֵלֶב נַעַר הַכֹּהֵן *before they burnt the fat, the priest's servant came* (used to come), &c., hence a frequentative perfect consecutive relating to the past, as in Ex 1¹⁹; also after participial clauses (§ 116 *w*), e. g. 1 S 2¹³ᶠ· וּבָא . . . כָּל־אִישׁ זֹבֵחַ זֶבַח *when(ever) any man offered sacrifice, then came*,

---

[1] In all these examples (not only in the frequentative perfects consecutive) the original idea of the perfect, which also underlies the perfect consecutive, comes out very distinctly. Gn 44²⁹ (see above) implies in the mind of the speaker, If it ever shall have come to this, that ye *have taken* this one also, then *ye have* thereby brought me down to Sheol.

&c. (so Ju 19³⁰, 2 S 20¹²), with a frequentative perfect consecutive. The perfect consecutive is very frequently used to announce future actions or events after simple expressions of time of any kind; thus Gn 3⁵, Ex 32³⁴ (after בְּיוֹם with the infinitive), cf. also such examples as Gn 44³¹, Ju 16², Jos 6¹⁰, 1 S 1²², 16²³ (numerous frequentative perfects consecutive after the infinitive with a preposition; so 2 S 15⁵, see above, *ee*); 1 S 20¹⁸, 2 S 14²⁶, 15¹⁰, Is 18⁵; moreover, Ex 17⁴, Is 10²⁵, 29¹⁷, 37²⁶; even after single disconnected words, e. g. Ex 16⁶ עֶרֶב וִידַעְתֶּם *at even* (when it becomes evening) *then ye shall know*; cf. verse 7, Lv 7¹⁶, 1 K 13³¹, Pr 24²⁷.

pp 6. Finally there still remains a number of passages which cannot be classed with any of those hitherto mentioned. Of these, some are due to the influence of Aramaic modes of expression, while in others the text is evidently corrupt.[1] In a few instances we can do no more than merely call attention to the incorrectness of the expression. (We are not of course concerned here with the cases—usually occurring in dependent clauses—in which a 2nd pers. *perf.* with Wāw copulative is simply co-ordinate with what precedes, as in Gn 28⁶, and probably Nu 21¹⁵, Dt 33².)

(*a*) The influence of the Aramaic construction of the perfect with וֹ as the narrative tense, instead of the Hebrew imperfect consecutive (cf. Kautzsch, *Gramm. des Bibl.-Aram.*, § 71 *b*), is certainly to be traced in *Qoheleth*, and sporadically in other very late books,[2] perhaps also in a few passages in the books of Kings, which are open to the suspicion of being due to later interpolation; so probably 1 K 12³² וְהֶעֱמִיד; 2 K 11¹ *Keth.* וְרָאתה; 14¹⁴ וְלָקַח (in the parallel passage, 2 Ch 25²⁴, the word is wanting); 2 K 23⁴ וְנָשָׂא, &c.; verse 10 וְטִמֵּא, &c.; verse 12 וְהִשְׁלִיךְ, &c.; verse 15 וְשָׂרַף, &c.[3] Cf. also Ez 37²·⁷·¹⁰.

qq (*b*) The text is certainly corrupt in Is 40⁶ (read with the LXX and Vulgate

---

[1] Mayer Lambert, *REJ.* xxvi. 55, is probably right in pointing some of these forms as *infin. abs.* instead of *perfects.*

[2] In the whole of *Qoheleth* the imperfect consecutive occurs only in 1¹⁷ and 4¹·⁷. Several of the perfects with וֹ can no doubt be explained as frequentatives, e. g. 1¹³, 2⁵·⁹·¹¹·¹³·¹⁵, 5¹⁸, compared with 6²; but this is impossible in such passages as 9¹⁴ ff. In Ezra, Driver reckons only six examples of the historical perfect with וֹ, in Nehemiah only six, and in Esther six or seven.

[3] Stade in *ZAW.* v. 291 ff. and in *Ausgewählte akad. Reden*, Giessen, 1899, p. 194 ff. and appendix p. 199, discusses, in connexion with 2 K 12¹², a number of critically questionable perfects with וֹ. He considers that the whole section, 2 K 23⁴ from וְנָשָׂא to verse 5 inclusive, is to be regarded as a gloss, since the continuation of an imperfect consecutive by means of a perfect with וֹ never occurs in pre-exilic documents, except in places where it is due to corruption of the original text. The theory of frequentative perfects consecutive (even immediately after imperfects consecutive), which has been supported above, under *f* and *g*, by a large number of examples, is quite inconsistent with the character of the action in 2 K 23⁵ וְהִשְׁבִּית, verse 8 וְנָתַץ, and verse 14 וְשִׁבַּר.

וַאֹמַר) ; Jer 38²⁸, where the narrative breaks off in the middle of the sentence ; 40³ (וְהָיָה), &c., wanting in the LXX) ; also in Ju 7¹³ וְנָפַל הָאֹהֶל is altogether redundant ; in 1 S 3¹³ read, with Klostermann, the 2nd *sing. masc.* instead of והגדתי ; in 1 K 21¹² וְהֹשִׁיבוּ is, no doubt, incorrectly repeated from verse 9, where it is an imperative.

Of other questionable instances, (a) the following, at any rate, may also be *rr* explained as frequentatives, Gn 21²⁵, 49²³, Ex 36³⁸, 38²⁸, 39³, 1 S 5⁷, 17²⁰, 24¹¹ (but even so וְאָמְרוּ would be expected) ; 2 K 23¹², Is 28²⁶ (parallel with an imperfect) ; Am 5²⁶ (unless it is rather, *yea, ye shall take up* ; see above, *x*) ; ψ 26³, Ez 8³⁶.

(β) A longer or constant continuance in a past state is perhaps represented *SS* by the perfect with וְ (as a variety of the frequentative perfect with וְ), in Gn 15⁶, 34⁵, Nu 21²⁰, Jos 9¹², 22³ᵇ, Is 22¹⁴, Jer 3⁹. But the unusual *perfects consec.* in Jos 15³⁻¹¹, 16²⁻⁸ (ultimately parallel with an imperf. as in 17⁹, 18²⁰), 18¹²⁻²¹, 19¹¹⁻¹⁴·²²·²⁶⁻²⁹·³⁴, are without doubt rightly explained by Bennett (*SBOT.*, Joshua, p. 23) as originally containing the directions either of God to Joshua or of Joshua to the people ; cf. the evident trace of this in 15⁴ᵇ. A redactor transformed the directions into a description but left the *perfects consec.*, which are to be explained as in *aa*. In the same way וְהָיוּ Ex 36²⁹ is most simply explained as repeated from 26²⁵.

(γ) The following are due to errors in the text, or to incorrect modes of *tt* expression : Ex 36²⁹ ᶠ·, Ju 3²³, ¹ 16¹⁸ (read וַיַּעֲלוּ), 1 S 4¹⁹, 17³⁸, 2 S 16⁵, 19¹⁸ ᶠ· (read צָלְחוּ and וַיַּעַבְרוּ), 1 K 3¹¹ (where וְשָׁאַלְתָּ is, no doubt intentionally, assimilated to the four other perfects) ; 13³, 20²¹ ; 2 K 14⁷ (where, with Stade, וְאֶת־הַפֶּלַע תָּפַשׂ should be read) ; 14¹⁴, 18⁴ (where, at any rate, וְשִׁבַּר might be taken as a frequentative, but not וכרת, &c. ; evidently the perfects are co-ordinated only in form with הוּא הֵסִיר) ; 18³⁶, 21¹⁵, 24¹⁴, Jer 37¹⁵ (where וְהִכּוּ, but not וְנָתְנוּ, might be frequentative) ; Ez 9⁷ (omit וְיָצְאוּ with Stade, and read וְהִכּוּ) ; 20²² והשבתי Mil'ēl before an imperfect consecutive ; Am 7⁴ (וְאָכְלָה after an imperfect consecutive) ; Jb 16¹².

Finally, in 1 S 1¹², 10⁹, 17⁴⁸, 25²⁰, 2 S 6¹⁶, 2 K 3¹⁵, Jer 37¹¹, Am 7² וִיהִי is to be *uu* read throughout instead of וְהָיָה, but in Gn 38⁵ וְהָיָה with the LXX.

B. The Infinitive and Participle.

§ 113. *The Infinitive Absolute.*

Cf. the dissertation of J. Kahan, and, especially, the thorough investigation by E. Sellin, both entitled, *Ueber die verbal-nominale Doppelnatur der hebräischen Participien und Infinitive*, &c., Lpz. 1889 ; F. Prätorius, 'Ueber die sogen. Infin. absol. des Hebr.' in *ZDMG.* 1902, pp. 546 ff.

1. The infinitive absolute is employed according to § 45 to emphasize *a* the idea of the verb *in the abstract*, i.e. it speaks of an action (or state) without any regard to the agent or to the circumstances of time and mood under which it takes place. As the *name* of an action the infinitive absolute, like other nouns in the stricter sense,

---

¹ Or does ונעל, as a frequentative, imply fastening with several bolts ? It is, at all events, to be noticed, that in 2 S 13¹⁸ also ונעל follows an imperfect consecutive.

may form part of certain combinations (as a subject, predicate, or object, or even as a genitive,[1] see below); but such a use of the infinitive absolute (instead of the infinitive construct with or without a preposition) is, on the whole, rare, and, moreover, open to question on critical grounds. On the other hand, the infinitive absolute frequently exhibits its character as an expression of the *verbal idea* by taking an object, either in the accusative or even with a preposition.

b Examples of the use of the infinitive absolute :—

(a) As subject, Pr 25²⁷ אֲכֹל דְּבַשׁ הַרְבּוֹת לֹא טוֹב *it is not good to eat much honey*; Jer 10⁵, Jb 6²⁵, Ec 4¹⁷; epexegetically, after a demonstrative pronoun, Is 58⁵ ᶠ·, Zc 14¹².

c (b) As predicate, Is 32¹⁷ *and the effect of righteousness* (is) הַשְׁקֵט וָבֶטַח *quietness* (prop. *to find rest*) *and confidence*.

d (c) As object, Is 1¹⁷ לִמְדוּ הֵיטֵב *learn to do well*; Is 7¹⁵, Pr 15¹², Jb 9¹⁸; according to the sense also Jer 9²³ ²3¹⁴, as well as Is 5⁵ הָסֵר and פָּרֹץ virtually depend on the idea of the wish contained in עֹשֶׂה); Is 22¹³, where a long series of infinitives absolute is governed by הִנֵּה, and 59¹³ (six infinitives governed by יְדַעֲנוּם in verse 12); Dt 28⁵⁶ is strange since the object precedes the infinitive absolute which governs it,[2] also Is 42²¹, where the statement of place precedes the infinitive absolute.—In Jer 9⁴, Jb 13³ the infinitive absolute as the object of the verb is placed before it for the sake of emphasis (with the verb negatived by לֹא in Is 57²⁰, Jer 49²³), so also in La 3⁴⁵ where it is the remoter object and co-ordinated with a substantive.

e (d) As genitive, Is 14²³ בְּמַטְאֲטֵא הַשְׁמֵד *with the besom of destruction*; so perhaps also 4⁴ בְּרוּחַ בָּעֵר; cf. further, Pr 1³, 21¹⁶. The infinitive absolute is never used in immediate connexion with prepositions[3] (which as being originally substantives govern the genitive), but always the infinitive construct; but if a second infinitive is co-ordinated by ו with such an infinitive construct, it has the form of the infinitive absolute (since it is released from the immediate government of the preposition), e.g. 1 S 22¹³ . . . בְּתִתְּךָ לוֹ לֶחֶם וְשָׁאוֹל לוֹ בֵּאלֹהִים *in that thou hast given him bread . . . and hast enquired of God for him*; Ez 36³; 1 S 25²⁶·³³ (after מֵן); after לְ Ex 32⁶, Jer 7¹⁸, 44¹⁷.

f (e) Governing an accusative of the object, e.g. Is 22¹³ הָרֹג בָּקָר וְשָׁחֹט צֹאן *slaying oxen and killing sheep*; cf. Ex 20⁸, 23³⁰, Dt 5¹², Is 37¹⁹, Ez 23³⁰, and of the examples in *a–d*, Dt 28⁵⁶, Is 5⁵, 58⁶ ᶠ·, Pr 25²⁷, &c.; followed by a preposition, e.g. Is 7¹⁵ מָאוֹס בָּרָע וּבָחוֹר בַּטּוֹב *to refuse the evil and choose the good*; Pr 15¹² (הוֹכֵחַ לוֹ).

g If the object be a personal pronoun, then, since the infinitive absolute can never be united with a suffix (see the note on *a*), it is affixed by means of the accusative-sign אֵת (אֹת), e.g. Jer 9²³ וְיָדֹעַ אֹתִי *and knoweth me*; Ez 36³.

---

[1] The infinitive absolute can never be joined with a genitive or a pronominal suffix.

[2] Perhaps הַצֵּן according to § 53 *k* should be explained as an infinitive construct, or should be written הַצֵּן.

[3] ואחרי שָׁתָה 1 S 1⁹ is impossible Hebrew, and as the LXX shows, a late addition.

2. Analogous to the use of the infinitive absolute as the accusative *h*
of the object, mentioned in *d*, is its employment as a *casus adverbialis*[1]
in connexion with some form of the finite verb, to describe more
particularly the manner or attendant circumstances (especially those
of time and place) under which an action or state has taken place, or
is taking place, or will take place; e. g. Jer 22¹⁹ *he shall be buried
with the burial of an ass,* סָחוֹב וְהַשְׁלֵךְ *a drawing and casting forth,* i. e.
being drawn and cast forth, &c.; Gn 21¹⁶ (הַרְחֵק *a removing,* i. e.
distant; cf. Ex 33⁷, Jos 3¹⁶); Gn 30³², Ex 30³⁶, Nu 6⁵·²³, 15³⁵ (where
a subject is added subsequently; see below, *gg*); Jos 3¹⁷, 1 S 3¹²
(הָחֵל וְכַלֵּה *a beginning and ending,* i. e. from beginning to end); 2 S 8²,
Is 7¹¹ (הַעֲמֵק and הַגְבֵּהַּ, prop. *a making deep . . .,* and *a making high,*
i. e. whether thy request extend to the world below or to the height
above); 57¹⁷ (הַסְתֵּר *in hiding,* sc. my face); Jer 3¹⁵ (דֵעָה וְהַשְׂכִּיל *with
knowledge and understanding*); Hb 3¹³ (עָרוֹת, for the form cf.
§ 75 *aa*); Zc 7³, ψ 35¹⁶ (חָרֹק, to define more precisely קָרְעוּ verse 15);
Jb 15³.[2]

Rem. 1. To an adverbial infinitive absolute of this kind, there may further *i*
be added a *casus adverbialis* (the accusative of state or circumstance), or even
a circumstantial clause, to define more exactly the manner in which the
action is performed, e. g. Is 20² *and he did so* הָלַךְ עָרוֹם וְיָחֵף *walking naked and
barefoot,* prop. in the condition of one naked, &c.; Is 30¹⁴ *a breaking in pieces*
(acc. to the reading כָּתוֹת; the Masora requires כָּתוּת) *without sparing.*

2. A few infinitives of this kind, all of which are in Hiphʿil, have, through *k*
frequent use, come to be treated by the language as simple adverbs; so
especially הַרְבֵּה (cf. § 75 *ff*) *multum faciendo,* i. e. *multum,* very frequently
strengthened by מְאֹד *very* and even used without connexion with a finite
verb (see the Lexicon); also הֵיטֵב *bene faciendo,* i. e. *bene,* used especially to
express the careful and thorough performance of an action (e. g. Dt 13¹⁵); in
Dt 9²¹, 27⁸ it is added epexegetically to another adverbial infinitive absolute,
in Jon 4⁹ it twice precedes the verb for the sake of emphasis. Finally, הַשְׁכֵּם
mane faciendo, i. e. *early in the morning,* then in general *early* with the additional
idea of earnestness; in 1 S 17¹⁶ joined with the infinitive absolute וְהַעֲרֵב
a denominative from עֶרֶב *evening* (*morning and evening,* i. e. *early and late*),
elsewhere (with the exception of Pr 27¹⁴) always joined with the infinitive
absolute of the governing verb, e. g. Jer 11⁷ *for I earnestly protested* (הַעִדֹתִי)
unto your fathers . . . הַשְׁכֵּם וְהָעֵד *rising early and protesting,* i. e. with earnest
protestation; Jer 25³, 26⁵ (where ן should be omitted before ה'); Jer 29¹⁹, 32³³,
2 Ch 16¹⁵.

---

[1] That this *casus adverbialis* also was originally regarded as an accusative,
may be seen from classical Arabic, where an infinitive of this kind expressly
retains the accusative ending. In Latin the ablative of the gerund corresponds in many ways to this use of the infinitive absolute.

[2] Also in 2 K 21¹³ for מָחָה וְהָפַךְ read with Stade and Klostermann מָחֹה וְהָפֹךְ;
similarly, with Stade, וְקָשֹׁה in Ju 4²⁴; וְחָזוֹק in Jer 23¹⁴, and on Is 31⁵ cf. *t.*

l 3. The infinitive absolute occurs most frequently in immediate connexion with the finite verb of the same stem, in order in various ways *to define more accurately* or *to strengthen the idea of the verb*.[1]

m These infinitives absolute joined immediately to the finite verb belong in a sense to the *schema etymologicum* treated in § 117 *p*, i. e. they are objects of the finite verb in question, except that the infinitive absolute (as a *nomen abstractum*) lays stress rather on the actual occurrence or the energy of the action (see the examples below), while the noun proper emphasizes the result or extent of the action ; cf. e. g. Ex 22²² אִם־צָעֹק יִצְעַק אֵלַי *if it actually happens that he cries to me*, with Gn 27³⁴ (as it were, *he cried*, so that *a great cry was heard*).

We must further distinguish —

n (*a*) The infinitive absolute used *before* the verb to *strengthen* the verbal idea, i. e. to emphasize in this way either the certainty (especially in the case of threats) or the forcibleness and completeness of an occurrence. In English, such an infinitive is mostly expressed by a corresponding adverb, but sometimes merely by putting greater stress on the verb ; e. g. Gn 2¹⁷ מוֹת תָּמוּת *thou shalt surely die*, cf. 18¹⁰·¹⁸, 22¹⁷, 28²², 1 S 9⁶ (*cometh surely to pass*); 24²¹, Am 5⁵, 7¹⁷, Hb 2³, Zc 11¹⁷; with the infinitive strengthened by אַךְ Gn 44²⁸ (but 27³⁰ *and Jacob was yet scarce gone out*, &c.); Gn 43³ הָעֵד הֵעִד בָּנוּ *he did solemnly protest unto us*; 1 S 20⁶ נִשְׁאֹל נִשְׁאַל *David earnestly asked leave of me* ; Jos 17¹³, Ju 1²³ וְהוֹרִישׁ לֹא הוֹרִישׁוֹ *and did not utterly drive them out* ; especially typical instances are Am 9⁸ *I will destroy it from off the face of the earth* וג׳ אֶפֶס כִּי לֹא הַשְׁמֵיד אַשְׁמִיד *saving that I will not utterly destroy*, &c.; Jer 30¹¹ *and will in no wise leave thee unpunished* ; cf. further Gn 20¹⁸, 1 K 3²⁶, Jo 1⁷, Jb 13⁵.

o The infinitive absolute is used before the verb with less emphasis :

(1) Frequently at the beginning of the statement; cf. Driver on 1 S 20⁶. However, in these cases a special emphasis on the following verb is sometimes intended ; cf. above, *n*, on Gn 43³, 1 S 20⁶; also Gn 3¹⁶, 26²⁸, 32¹⁷, 1 S 14²⁸, 20³. Elsewhere the infinitive absolute is evidently used only as possessing a certain fullness of sound (hence for rhythmical reasons, like some uses of the separate pronoun, § 135 *a*), as in Gn 15¹³, 43⁷·²⁰, Ju 9⁸, 1 S 10¹⁶, 23¹⁰, 2 S 1⁶, 20¹⁸.

(2) Very frequently in conditional sentences after אִם, &c. The infinitive absolute in this case emphasizes the importance of the con-

---

[1] Cf. A. Rieder, *Die Verbindung des Inf. abs. mit dem Verb. fin . . . im Hebr.*, Lpz., 1872; also his *Quae ad syntaxin Hebraicam . . . planiorem faciendam ex lingua Graeca et Latina afferantur*, Gumbinnen (Programm des Gymnasiums), 1884. G. R. Hauschild, *Die Verbindung finiter und infiniter Verbalformen desselben Stammes in einigen Bibelsprachen*, Frankfurt a. M., 1893, discussing especially the rendering of such constructions in the Greek and Latin versions.

dition on which some consequence depends, e. g. Ex 15²⁶ *if thou wilt diligently hearken*, &c., Ex 19⁵, 21⁵, 22³·¹¹ᶠ·¹⁶·²² (see above, *m*); 23²², Nu 21², Ju 16¹¹, 1 S 1¹¹, 12²⁵; after לֹא 1 S 14³⁰.

The infinitive absolute is used to give emphasis to an antithesis, e. g. *p* 2 S 24²⁴ *nay; but I will verily buy* (קָנוֹ אֶקְנֶה) *it of thee*, &c. (not receive it as a gift); Ju 15¹³ *no; but we will bind thee fast . . . but surely we will not kill thee*; cf. further Gn 31³⁰ (thou art indeed gone=) *though thou wouldst needs be gone* (Vulg. *esto*), *because thou sore longedst*, &c.; ψ 118¹³·¹⁸, 126⁶ (the second infinitive absolute as a supplement to the first—see below, *r*—comes *after* the verb).—Hence also, as permissive, Gn 2¹⁶ᶠ· אָכֹל תֹּאכֵל *thou mayest freely eat*, but, &c. (so that verse 16 is in antithesis to verse 17); or concessive, 1 S 2³⁰ *I said indeed . . .* , 14⁴³.

The infinitive absolute is used to strengthen a question, and *q* especially in impassioned or indignant questions, e. g. Gn 37⁸ הֲמָלֹךְ תִּמְלֹךְ עָלֵינוּ *shalt thou indeed reign over us?* Gn 37¹⁰, 43⁷, Ju 11²⁵, 1 S 2²⁷, 2 S 19⁴³, Jer 3¹, 13¹², Ez 28⁹, Am 3⁵, Zc 7⁵; but cf. also Gn 24⁵ *must I needs bring again?*

(*b*) The infinitive absolute *after the verb*, sometimes (as in *n*) to *r* intensify[1] the idea of the verb (especially after imperatives and participles, since the infinitive absolute can never precede either, e. g. Nu 11¹⁵, Jb 13¹⁷, 21², 37² שִׁמְעוּ שָׁמוֹעַ *hearken ye attentively*; Jer 22¹⁰; after participles, e. g. Is 22¹⁷, also elsewhere, e. g. Nu 23¹¹, 24¹⁰ *thou hast altogether blessed them*; Jos 24¹⁰, 2 K 5¹¹, Dn 11¹⁰, and with the infinitive absolute strengthened by means of גַּם Gn 31¹⁵, 46⁴, Nu 16¹³); sometimes to express the long *continuance* of an action; here again after an imperative, Is 6⁹ שִׁמְעוּ שָׁמוֹעַ *hear ye continually*; after a perfect, Jer 6²⁹; after a participle, Jer 23¹⁷; after an imperfect consecutive, Gn 19⁹, Nu 11³².

To this class belong especially those cases in which a second infini- *s* tive absolute is co-ordinated with the first; the latter then expresses either an accompanying or antithetical action or the aim to which the principal action is directed; e. g. 1 S 6¹² הָלְכוּ הָלֹךְ וְגָעוֹ *lowing as they went* (lowing continually; so after a participle, Jos 6¹³ᵇ *Qᵉrê*); Gn 8⁷ *it went forth to and fro*[2]; Is 19²² *smiting and* (i. e. but also) *healing again*; Jo 2²⁶ (see above, *m*).

Rem. 1. Instead of a second infinitive absolute (see above) there is some- *t* times found a perfect consecutive (Jos. 6¹³ᵃ and 2 S 13¹⁹ [but Stade's וְזָעוֹק is

---

[1] In Arabic also, the intensifying infinitive regularly stands *after* the verb, but in Syriac *before* the verb.

[2] Also in Ez 1¹⁴ for the distorted form רצוא reads simply יָצֹא יֵצֵא.

is preferable], in both places as perfect frequentative; Is 31⁵ referring to the future, unless with Stade, *ZAW.* vi. 189, we read וְהַצִּיל and וְהִמְלִיט), or an imperfect consecutive (1 S 19²³, 2 S 16¹³) or participle (2 S 16⁵); cf. also *u*.

u 2. The idea of long *continuance* is very frequently expressed by the verb הָלַךְ *to go*, along with its infinitive absolute, or even by the latter alone, and this occurs not only when it can be taken in its literal sense (*to go, to walk*, as in the examples given above, Jos 6⁹·¹³, 1 S 6¹², 2 S 3¹⁶, 13¹⁹; cf. also, Is 3¹⁶, where both infinitives stand *before* the verb, and ψ 126⁶, where הָלוֹךְ precedes), but also in cases where הָלַךְ in the sense of *to go on, to continue*, merely performs the function of an adverb. The action itself is added in a second infinitive absolute, or sometimes (see above, *t*) in a participle or verbal adjective.

Examples, Gn 8³ הָלוֹךְ וָשׁוֹב . . . וַיָּשֻׁבוּ הַמַּיִם *and the waters returned . . . continually*; Gn 8⁵, 12⁹, Ju 14⁹, 2 K 2¹¹; with a participle following, Jer 41⁶ (unless we read וּבָכֹה, as in 2 S 3¹⁶); with an adjective following, Gen 26¹³, Ju 4²⁴, 1 S 14¹⁹, 2 S 5¹⁰ (1 Ch 11⁹), 2 S 18²⁵. [1]

On the other hand, in 1 S 17⁴¹ the participle הֹלֵךְ is used instead of the infinitive absolute. Of a different kind are the instances in which the participle הֹלֵךְ is used as predicate along with the co-ordinate adjective (Ex 19¹⁹, 1 S 2²⁶, 2 S 3¹, 15¹², Est 9⁴, 2 Ch 17¹²) or participle (1 S 17¹⁵, Jon 1¹¹, Pr 4¹⁸, Ec 1⁶).

v 3. The regular place of the negative is between the intensifying infinitive absolute and the finite verb,[2] e.g. Ex 5²³ וְהַצֵּל לֹא־הִצַּלְתָּ *neither hast thou delivered at all*, Ju 15¹³, Jer 13¹², 30¹¹; cf. Mi 1¹⁰ (אַל). Exceptions are Gn 3⁴ (where the negation of the threat pronounced in 2¹⁷ is expressed in the same form of words); Am 9⁸, ψ 49⁸.

w 4. With a finite verb of one of the derived conjugations, not only the infinitive absolute of the *same* conjugation may be connected (Gn 28²² Pi‘ēl; 17¹³, Ex 22³ Niph‘al; Gn 40¹⁵ Pu‘al; Ho 4¹⁸ Hiph‘îl; Ez 16⁴ Hoph‘al), but also (especially with Niph‘al, rarely with Pi‘ēl and Hiph‘îl; see Driver on 2 S 20¹⁸) that of Qal as the simplest and most general representative of the verbal idea, 2 S 20¹⁸ (with Pi‘ēl; but in Gn 37³³, 44²⁸ טֹרַף is a passive of Qal, § 52 *e*); 46⁴ (with Hiph‘îl); Ex 19¹³, 21²⁰, 2 S 23⁷, Is 40³⁰, Jer 10⁵, Jb 6² (with Niph‘al); Is 24¹⁹ (with Hithpo‘ēl; רֹעָה in the same verse must also, according to the Masora, certainly be the infinitive absolute Qal; see § 67 *o*), and so always מוֹת יוּמַת *he shall surely be put to death*. Elsewhere the infinitive absolute of a conjugation with kindred meaning is found, Lv 19²⁰, 2 K 3²³ Hoph‘al for Niph‘al (but most probably we should read, with Driver, the *infin. Niph.* in both places, הַפָּרֵה and הֵחָרֵב); 1 S 2¹⁶ (Pi‘ēl for Hiph‘îl, unless יַקְטִרוּן is to be read); Ez 16⁴ (Hoph‘al for Pu‘al).[3] Finally, the infinitive absolute may

---

[1] Cf. in French, *Le mal va toujours croissant, la maladie va toujours en augmentant et en empirant,* ‘ *continually increases and becomes worse and worse.*’

[2] Cf. Rieder, *Quo loco ponantur negationes* לֹא *et* אַל . . . (*Zeitschrift für Gymn.-Wesen,* 1879, p. 395 ff.).

[3] In three passages even the infinitive absolute of another stem of like sound occurs; but in Is 28²⁸ אָדוֹשׁ is no doubt a mere textual error for דּוֹשׁ, and in Jer 8¹³, according to § 72 *aa*, we should read אָסְפֵם, and in Zp 1² אָסֵף. Barth, *Nom.-bildung,* § 49 *b*, sees in אָדוֹשׁ and אָסוֹף infinitives *Hiph‘îl*, exactly corresponding in form to '*aqâm[â]* the Aram. infin. 'Aph‘ēl of קוּם; but there is no more evidence for a *Hiph.* of דּוּשׁ in Hebrew than for a stem אָדַשׁ.

equally well be represented by a *substantive* of kindred stem.[1] In Is 29[14] the substantive intensifying the verb is found *along with* the infinitive absolute.

5. Instead of the infinitive absolute immediately connected with the finite x verb, an infinitive construct form appears (cf. § 73 *d*), in Nu 23[25] (גַּם קֹב); cf. Ru 2[16] (גַּם שֹׁל); Jer 50[34] (רִיב יָרִיב); Pr 23[1] (בִּין תָּבִין). In the last instances the infinitive is probably assimilated to the imperfect, like the infinitive Niph'al in the forms noticed in § 51 *k* and note.—Cf. also 2 K 3[24] וַיָּבֹאוּ בֹא וְהַכּוֹת (read so with the LXX) before א, hence, no doubt due to the dislike of a hiatus; so in ψ 50[21], Neh 1[7] (חָבֹל), all in rapid style; *after* the verb, Jos 7[7], unless הֶעֱבִיר is intended.

4. Finally the infinitive absolute sometimes appears as *a substitute* y *for the finite verb*, either when it is sufficient simply to mention the verbal idea (see *z*), or when the hurried or otherwise excited style intentionally contents itself with this infinitive, in order to bring out the verbal idea in a clearer and more expressive manner (see *aa*).

(*a*) The infinitive absolute as the continuation of a preceding finite z verb. In the later books especially it often happens that in a succession of several acts only the first (or sometimes more) of the verbs is inflected, while the second (or third, &c.) is added simply in the infinitive absolute. Thus after several perfects, Dn 9[5] (cf. verse 11) *we have sinned ... and have transgressed thy law,* וְסוֹר *and have turned aside* (prop. *a turning aside* took place); so after a *perfect* Ex 36[7](?), 1 S 2[28], Is 37[19], Jer 14[5], 19[13], Hag 1[6] (four infinitives), Zc 3[4] (but read with Wellhausen, after the LXX, וְהִלְבַּשְׁתִּ אֹתוֹ), 7[5], Ec 8[9], 9[11], Est 3[13], 9[6.16.18], 12[6ff.], Neh 9[8.13], 1 Ch 5[20], 2 Ch 28[19];[2] after the *perfect consecutive*, Zc 12[10]; after the *perfect frequentative* 1 K 9[25] (unless וְהִקְטִיר be intended); after the simple *imperfect*, Lv 25[14], Nu 30[3], Jer 32[44] (three infinitives), 36[23], 1 Ch 21[24]; after a *cohortative*, Jos 9[20]; after the *imperfect consecutive*, Gn 41[43] (as a continuation of וַיַּרְכֵּב); Ex 8[11], Ju 7[19], Jer 37[21], Neh 8[8], 1 Ch 16[36], 2 Ch 7[3]; with אוֹ *or* after the *jussive*, Dt 14[21], Est 2[3], 6[9]; after the *imperative*, Is 37[30b], Am 4[4f.]; after the *participle*, Hb 2[15] (strengthened by אַף, and regarded, like the participle itself, as an adverbial accusative); Est 8[8].

(*b*) At the beginning of the narrative, or at least of a new section aa of it. The special form of the finite verb which the infinitive absolute represents must be determined from the context. The infinitive

---

[1] On these substantives (and on the use of the infinitive absolute generally as absolute object, see above, *m*), cf. the *schema etymologicum* treated in connexion with the government of the verb in § 117 *p*, *q*.

[2] In Ez 7[14] a perfect appears to be continued by means of an infinitive construct; but the text is quite corrupt; Cornill reads תִּקְעוּ תָקוֹעַ הָבִינוּ הָכֵן.

absolute is most frequently used in this way, corresponding to the infinitive of command in Greek, &c.[1] :—

bb　(*a*) For an emphatic imperative,[2] e. g. שָׁמוֹר (thou shalt, ye shall), *observe* Dt 5¹²; זָכוֹר (thou shalt) *remember*, Ex 13³, 20⁸ (the full form occurs in Dt 6¹⁷ שָׁמוֹר תִּשְׁמְרוּן; 7¹⁸ זָכֹר תִּזְכֹּר); Lv 2⁶, Nu 4², 25¹⁷, Dt 1¹⁶, 2 K 5¹⁰, Is 38⁵, Jer 2², followed by a *perfect consecutive*; Jos 1¹³, 2 K 3¹⁶, Is 7⁴, 14³¹ (parallel with an *imperative*; in Na 2² three imperatives follow). But הַבִּים ψ 142⁵ may be only an incorrect spelling of הַבֵּט imperative.[3]

cc　(β) For the jussive, Lv 6⁷, Nu 6⁵, 2 K 11¹⁵, Ez 23⁴⁶; cf. also Pr 17¹² (*let it* rather *meet*).

dd　(γ) For the cohortative, Is 22¹³ᵇ אָכוֹל וְשָׁתוֹ (the exclamation of the mocker); Ez 21³¹, 23³⁰·⁴⁶; perhaps also Jer 31² (הָלוֹךְ).[4]

ee　(δ) For the imperfect in emphatic promises, e. g. 2 K 4⁴³ *ye shall eat and leave thereof*; 19²⁹ (Is 37³⁰), 2 Ch 31¹⁰; also in indignant questions, Jb 40² *shall he that cavilleth contend with the Almighty ?*[5] (on the addition of the subject cf. the Rem. below); Jer 3¹ *and thinkest thou to return again to me ?* Jer 7⁹ ff. (six infinitives, continued by means of the *perfect consecutive*; cf. § 112 *o*).

ff　(ε) For any historical tense (like the Latin *historic* infinitive) in lively narration (or enumeration) and description, even of what is still taking place in present time, e. g. Hos 4² *swearing and breaking faith, and killing, and stealing, and committing adultery* (in these they are busied); 10⁴ (after a *perfect*); Is 21⁵, 59⁴, Jer 8¹⁵, 14¹⁹, Jb 15³⁵; cf. further Jer 32³³, Ec 4².—In Ez 23³⁰, Pr 12⁷, 15²², and 25⁴, the infinitive absolute is best rendered by the passive.

---

[1] Cf. also such infinitives in French as *voir* (page so and so, &c.), *s'adresser* . . . , *se méfier des voleurs !*

[2] Prätorius, *op. cit.*, p. 547 : the extraordinarily common use of the infinitive form *qāṭōl* in the sense of an imperative, jussive, or cohortative has long since caused it to be compared with the Arab. *fa'āli*. It thus appears that the infin. *qāṭōl* in Hebrew could be used from early times as a kind of fixed, invariable word of command.

[3] In Ez 21³¹, for the infinitives construct הָסִיר, הָרִים, הַשְׁפִּיל (beside הַגְבֵּהַּ) read with Cornill the infinitives absolute הָסֵר, &c. The Kᵉthîbh probably intends הָסִיר, &c.

[4] In 2 S 3¹⁸ the infinitive construct appears to be used instead of the cohortative, but אוֹשִׁיעַ should certainly be read for הוֹשִׁיעַ. Also in 1 K 22³⁰ (2 Ch 18²⁹), which was formerly included under this head (I will *disguise myself and go into the battle*), read אֶתְחַפֵּשׂ וָאבֹא.

[5] In Jb 34¹⁸ in a similar question instead of the infinitive constr. we should rather expect the infinitive absolute (הָאָמֹר), unless with the LXX and Vulg. the participle with the article (הָאֹמֵר) is to be read.

Rem. The subject is sometimes added to the infinitive absolute when it *gg* takes the place of the finite verb, e. g. Lv 6[7], Nu 15[35], Dt 15[2], ψ 17[5], Pr 17[12], Jb 40[2], Ec 4[2], Est 9[1]. So, probably, also in Gn 17[10], Ex 12[48], although here כָּל־זָכָר according to § 121 *a* might also be taken as *an object* with a passive verb; cf. Est 3[13]. In 1 S 25[26.33] the subject follows an infinitive absolute which is co-ordinated with an infinitive construct, see above, *e*.

§ 114. *The Infinitive Construct.*

1. The infinitive construct, like the infinitive absolute, may also *a* represent a *nomen verbale* (§ 45 *a*), but of a much more flexible character than the infinitive absolute (cf. § 113 *a*). Its close relation with nouns properly so called is especially seen in the readiness with which the infinitive construct may be used for any case whatever; thus,

(*a*) As the nominative of the subject, e. g. Gn 2[18] לֹא־טוֹב הֱיוֹת הָאָדָם לְבַדּוֹ, literally, *not good is the being of man in his separation*; Gn 30[15], 1 S 23[20], Is 7[13], Pr 17[26], 25[7.24] (but cf. 21[9] טוֹב לָשֶׁבֶת in the same statement); ψ 32[9] prop. *there is not a coming near unto thee*, but the text is probably corrupt. With a *feminine* predicate, 1 S 18[23], Jer 2[17].

(*b*) As genitive, e. g. Ec 3[4] עֵת סְפוֹד וְעֵת רְקוֹד *a time of mourning b and a time of dancing*; Gn 2[17], 29[7], Neh 12[46], 2 Ch 24[14]. This equally includes, according to § 101 *a*, all those cases in which the infinitive construct depends on a preposition (see below, *d*) [and Driver, *Tenses*, § 206].

(*c*) As accusative of the object, e. g. 1 K 3[7] לֹא אֵדַע צֵאת וָבֹא *I know c not the going out or the coming in* (*I know not* how *to go out and come in*); Gn 21[6], 31[28], Nu 20[21], Is 1[14], 37[28] (even with אֶת), Jer 6[15], Jb 15[22] (cf. for the use of the infinitive absolute as object, § 113 *f*); as accusative with a verb expressing fullness, Is 11[9].

2. The construction of the infinitive with prepositions (as in Greek, *d* ἐν τῷ εἶναι, διὰ τὸ εἶναι, &c.) may usually be resolved in English into the finite verb with a conjunction, e. g. Nu 35[19] בְּפִגְעוֹ־בוֹ *in his meeting him*, i. e. if (as soon as) he meets him; Gn 27[45] (עַד־שׁוּב); Is 30[12] יַעַן מָאָסְכֶם *because ye despise*; Jer 2[35] עַל־אָמְרֵךְ *because thou sayest*; Gn 27[1] *and his eyes were dim* מֵרְאֹת *from seeing*, i. e. so that he could not see.

This use of the infinitive construct is especially frequent in con- *c* nexion with בְּ or לְ to express time-determinations (in English resolved into a temporal clause, as above the combination of the infinitive with יַעַן or עַל־ is resolved into a causal clause), especially after וַיְהִי (see the examples, § 111 *g*), e. g. 1 S 2²⁷ בִּהְיוֹתָם בְּמִצְרָיִם *when they were in Egypt*; Gn 24³⁰ וּכְשָׁמְעוֹ וג׳ . . . וַיְהִי כִרְאֹת אֶת־הַנֶּזֶם *and it came to pass, when he saw* (prop. in the seeing) *the ring* . . . , *and when he heard* (prop. in his hearing), &c.

f But by far the most frequent is the connexion of the infinitive construct with לְ.¹ Starting from the fundamental meaning of לְ, i. e. *direction towards something*, infinitives with לְ serve to express the most varied ideas of purpose or aim, and very commonly also (with a weakening or a complete disregard of the original meaning of the לְ) to introduce the object of an action, or finally even (like the infinitive absolute used adverbially, § 113 *h*, and the Latin gerund in -*ndo*) to state motives or attendant circumstances. See the instances in the Remarks.

g Rem. 1. The original meaning of the לְ is most plainly seen in those infinitives with לְ which expressly state a purpose (hence as the equivalent of a final clause), e. g. Gn 11⁵ *and the Lord came down*, לִרְאֹת אֶת־הָעִיר *to see the city*; also with a change of subject, e. g. 2 S 12¹⁰ *and thou hast taken the wife of Uriah the Hittite* לִהְיוֹת לְךָ לְאִשָּׁה *to be* (i. e. that she may be) *thy wife*; cf. Gn 28⁴, Jer 38²⁶ (לָמוּת).—If there is a special emphasis on the infinitive with לְ, it is placed, with its complement, before the governing verb, e. g. Gn 42⁹, 47⁴, Nu 22²⁰, Jos 2³, 1 S 16² with בּוֹא; Ju 15¹⁰, 1 S 17²⁵ with עָלָה.

h 2. Just as clearly the idea of aiming at a definite purpose or turning towards an object may be seen in the combination of the verb הָיָה *to be*, with לְ and an infinitive. In fact הָיָה לַעֲשׂוֹת may mean, either (*a*) *he was in the act of, he was about to* (as it were, he set himself), *he was ready, to do* something, or (*b*) *he* or *it was appointed* or *compelled*, &c., to do the action in question. In the latter case הָיָה לַעֲשׂוֹת corresponds to the Latin *faciendum erat*, cf. also the English *I am to go*. In both cases הָיָה (as elsewhere when copula) is often omitted.

i Examples of (*a*) Gn 15¹² וַיְהִי הַשֶּׁמֶשׁ לָבוֹא *and when the sun was going down* (just about to set); 2 Ch 26⁵ וַיְהִי לִדְרֹשׁ אֱלֹהִים *and he set himself to seek God* (here with the secondary idea of a continuous action); with the omission of הָיָה Is 38²⁰, יְהֹוָה לְהוֹשִׁיעֵנִי *the Lord is ready to save me*; 1 S 14²¹ (?), Jer 51⁴⁹, ψ 25¹⁴ (*et foedus suum manifestaturus est eis*); Pr 18²⁴ (?), 19⁸ (לִמְצֹא *consecuturus*

---

¹ Cf. § 45 *g*, according to which the close union of the לְ with the first consonant of the infinitive (לִכְתֹּב with a firmly closed syllable, as opposed to בְּכָתֹב, כִּכְתֹב, &c.) seems to point to the formation of a special new verbal form. Quite distinct are the few examples where the infinitive with לְ serves to express time, as Gn 24⁶³ לִפְנוֹת עָרֶב *at the eventide* (prop. at the time of the return of evening); cf. Dt 23¹², Ex 14²⁷, Ju 19²⁶; 2 S 18²⁹ *when Joab sent the king's servant*.

est, unless we simply read יִמָּצֵא with the LXX) [1]; 20²⁵, Ec 3¹⁵ אֲשֶׁר לִהְיוֹת *quod futurum est*; 2 Ch 11²², 12¹² (in a negative statement); in a question, Est 7⁸ (*will he even . . . ?*). Cf. also 1 S 4¹⁹.

Of (*b*) Jos 2⁵ וַיְהִי הַשַּׁעַר לִסְגּוֹר *and the gate was to be shut* (had to be shut) ; *k* Is 37²⁶, ψ 109¹³. [2] Mostly with the omission of הָיָה, e.g. 2 K 4¹³ מֶה לַעֲשׂוֹת לָךְ וג׳ *what is to be done for thee?* (הֲיֵשׁ לְדַבֶּר־לָךְ) *wouldest thou be* (lit. is it to be) *spoken for to the king, &c.*? 2 K 13¹⁹ לְהַכּוֹת *it was to smite* equivalent to *thou shouldest have smitten*; Is 5⁴, ψ 32⁹, 68¹⁹ (?), Jb 30⁶ (*habitandum est iis*), 1 Ch 9²⁵, 10¹⁸, 22⁵, 2 Ch 8¹³ (?), 11²², 19², 36¹⁹ (?), Ho 9¹³, Hb 1¹⁷. In a question 2 Ch 19²; after לֹא 1 Ch 5¹, 15²; after אֵין 1 Ch 23²⁶, 2 Ch 5¹¹ and frequently.

Of the same kind also are the cases, in which the infinitive with לְ depends *l* on the idea of an obligation or permission (or prohibition); especially in such forms of expression as 2 S 18¹¹ עָלַי לָתֶת לְךָ וג׳ it was *upon me*, i.e. it would have been *my duty to give thee, &c.* [3] ; cf. Mi 3¹ (2 Ch 13⁵) *it is not for you to* (i. e. are ye not bound to)? [4] with a negative, 2 Ch 26¹⁸ לֹא לְךָ וג׳ *it pertaineth not unto thee, Uzziah, to burn incense unto the Lord, but* only *to the priests*; also לְ אֵין with an infinitive expresses *it is not permitted* (nefas est), *may not*, e.g. Est 4² כִּי אֵין לָבוֹא *for none might enter*; 8⁸, 1 Ch 15²; [5] אֵין לְ with an infinitive is used in a somewhat different sense, equivalent to *it is not feasible, not possible*, e.g. in ψ 40⁶, Ec 3¹⁴, 2 Ch 5¹¹. [6]—With either meaning לֹא can be used instead of אֵין, e.g. Am 6¹⁰ לֹא לְהַזְכִּיר *nefas est, to make mention* of the name of the Lord : but Ju 1¹⁹ *for it was not possible to drive out, &c.*, perhaps, however, the text originally stood as in Jos 17¹² לֹא יָכְלוּ לְהֹ וג׳ ; 1 Ch 15².

---

[1] P. Haupt (*SBOT.*, Proverbs, p. 52, lines 10 ff. ; *Critical Notes on Esther*, p. 170, on 7⁸) considers it possible that here and in Pr 2⁸, 6²⁴, 7⁵, 16³⁰, 30¹⁴, as well as in 14³⁵, 17²¹ before a noun, the לְ is a survival of the emphatic לְ with an *imperf.*, which is especially common in Arabic. In that case לִמְצֹא must be read לְמָצֵא, i. e. לְ + יִמָּצֵא. But all the above instances can be taken as infinitives with לְ without difficulty.

[2] Somewhat different are the cases where הָיָה לְ with the infinitive (which is then used exactly as a substantive) implies *to become something*, i. e. to meet with a particular fate, as Nu 24²² (cf. Is 5⁵, 6¹³) לְבָעֵר *for wasting*, for which elsewhere frequently לְשַׁמָּה and the like ; probably also לְבַלּוֹת ψ 49¹⁵ is to be explained in this way, the הָיָה being omitted.

[3] 2 S 4¹⁰ (*cui dandum erat mihi*) appears to be similar ; it may, however, be better, with Wellhausen, to omit the אֲשֶׁר.

[4] But in 1 S 23²⁰ after וְלָנוּ *and our part shall be* the infinitive without לְ stands as the subject of the sentence.

[5] Quite different of course are such cases as Is 37³ וְכֹחַ אַיִן לְלֵדָה *and there is not strength to bring forth*; cf. Nu 20⁵, Ru 4⁴.

[6] In 2 S 14¹⁹ אִשׁ (=יֵשׁ *it is, there is*) is used in a similar sense after אִם, the negative particle of asseveration, *of a truth it is not possible to turn to the right hand or to the left*.

m 3. A further class comprises the very numerous cases, in which the infinitive with ל is used as the object[1] of a governing verb, hence, again, for *the direction* which an action takes. The verbs (or conjugations) which occur most frequently in this combination with ל and an infinitive are : הֵחֵל (with an infinitive without ל, e.g. Dt 2²⁵·³¹, Jos 3⁷), הוֹאִיל *to begin*, יָסַף, הוֹסִיף (prop. *to add*) *to continue*, very frequently, even in prose, with an infinitive without ל, as Gn 4¹², 8¹⁰·¹², 37⁵, 1 S 3⁸, Jb 27¹, &c. ; חָדַל *to cease from, to desist*; כִּלָּה *to complete, to make an end of* ; תָּמַם *to be finished* ; הִקְרִיב *to come near to*, Gn 12¹¹ ; מִהַר *to hasten* (with an infinitive without ל Ex 2¹⁸) ; אָבָה *to be willing* (with an infinitive without ל Is 28¹², 30⁹, Jb 39⁹) ; חָפֵץ *to will, to desire* ; מֵאֵן *to refuse (to be unwilling)* ; בִּקֵּשׁ *to seek* ; יָכֹל *to be able* (with an infinitive without ל, e.g. Gn 24⁵⁰, 37⁴, Ex 2³, 18²³, Nu 22³⁸, Jb 4²) ; נָתַן with an accusative of the person in the sense of *to give up to some one, to cause*, or *permit* him to do something, e.g. Gn 20⁶, ψ 16¹¹ (with an infinitive abs. Jb 9¹⁸, see § 113 *d*), יָדַע *to understand* how to do something (in Jb 3⁸ הָעֲתִידִם עֹרֵר is analogous) ; לָמַד *to learn* ; קִוָּה *to wait, expect* (with a change of subject, e.g. Is 5² *and he waited for it to bring forth grapes*).

n We must further mention here a number of verbs in Hiph'îl (partly denominatives), which express an action in some definite direction (cf. § 53 *f*), as הִגְדִּיל *to do greatly*, הִשְׁפִּיל *to make* (it) *low*, הִגְבִּיהַּ *to make* (it) *high*, הֶעֱמִיק *to make* (it) *deep*, הִרְחִיק *to make* (it) *far, distant*, הֵיטִיב *to make* (it) *good* (with an infinitive without ל ψ 33³, but 1 S 16¹⁷, in the same combination, with ל) ; הִשְׁכִּים *to do anything early* (ψ 127², along with its opposite אֵחַר *to do* something *late*, with an infinitive without ל) ; הִרְבָּה *to make* (it) *much*, הִפְלָא *to make* (it) *wonderful* (even with a passive infinitive 2 Ch 26¹⁵),[2] &c.

---

[1] This view is based upon the fact, that in numerous expressions of this kind (see the examples above) the ל may be omitted, and the infinitive consequently stand as an actual accusative of the object (see above, *c*). However, the connexion of the verb with the object is in the latter case closer and more emphatic (hence especially adapted to poetic or prophetic diction), than the looser addition of the infinitive with ל ; thus לֹא אָבוּ שְׁמוֹעַ Is 28¹² is equivalent to *they desired not obeying* (לֹא אָבוּ) also with the infin. abs. in Is 42²⁴; cf. § 113 *d*) ; but לֹא אָבוּ לִשְׁמֹעַ Ez 20⁸ rather expresses *they could not make up their mind as to hearkening.* When connected with ל, the governing verb has a more independent sense than when it directly governs the accusative of the object.

[2] In almost all these examples the principal idea is properly contained in the infinitive, whilst the governing verb strictly speaking contains only a subordinate adverbial statement, and is therefore best rendered in English by an adverb ; e. g. Gn 27²⁰ *how is it that thou hast found it so quickly?* (prop. how thou hast hastened to find !), Gn 31²⁷ *wherefore didst thou flee secretly?* So frequently with הִרְבָּה (= *often, abundantly*), Ex 36⁵, 1 S 1¹², 2 K 21⁶, Is 55⁷, Am 4⁴, ψ 78³⁸, &c. ; with שׁוּב (= *again*), Dt 30⁹, 1 K 13¹⁷, Ho 11⁹, Ezr 9¹⁴ ; cf. also 2 S 19⁴, Jer 1¹², Jn 4², and the analogous instances in § 120 *g* ; also 2 K 2¹ *thou hast asked a hard thing.*

4. Finally, the infinitive with ל is very frequently used in a much looser **O** connexion to state motives, attendant circumstances, or otherwise to define more exactly. In English, such infinitive constructions (like the Latin gerund in *-do*; cf. *f*) must frequently be turned by *that* or a gerund; e.g. 1 S 12[17] לִשְׁאָל לָכֶם מֶלֶךְ *in asking you a king*; 14[33], 19[5], 20[36], Gn 3[22], 18[19], 34[7.15], Ex 23[2], Lv 5[4.22.26], 8[15], Nu 14[36], 2 S 3[10], 1 K 2[3 f.], 14[8], Jer 44[7 f.], ψ 63[3], 78[18], 101[8], 103[20], 104[14 f.], 111[6], Pr 2[8], 8[34], 18[5], Neh 13[18]. Sometimes the infinitive with ל is used in this way simply by itself, e.g. 1 Ch 12[8] *as the roes upon the mountains* לְמַהֵר (as regards hasting) *in swiftness*; Gn 2[3], 2 S 14[25] (לְהַלֵּל); Is 21[1] (לַחֲלוֹף); Jo 2[26], Pr 2[2], 26[2] and so very frequently the infinitive לֵאמֹר *dicendo* which has become stereotyped as an adverb to introduce direct narration (in the sense of *thus, as follows*).[1]

5. In a number of instances—especially in the later books—the infin. **P** constr. with ל appears to be attached by *Wāw* (like the infinitive absolute, § 113 *z*), as the continuation of a previous finite verb. In most examples of this kind it is, however, evident that the infinitive with ל virtually depends on an idea of intention, effort, or being in the act of, which, according to the sense, is contained in what has preceded, whilst the copula, as sometimes also elsewhere, is used in an emphatic sense (*and that too*); thus e.g. Ex 32[29] (if the text be right) *fill your hand to-day* (sc. with an offering) *for the Lord . . . and that to bring a blessing upon you*, i.e. that ye may be blessed; cf. 1 S 25[31] (otherwise in verses 26 and 33 where the infinitive absolute is used, see § 113 *e*); ψ 104[21],[2] Jb 34[8], Ec 9[1], Neh 8[13], 2 Ch 7[17].—In Lv 10[10 f.] וּלֲהַבְדִּיל might be regarded as an explanatory addition to the command contained in verse 9 *b* (=this prohibition of wine before the service shall ye observe, and that in order to put a difference, &c.); but probably the text has been disturbed by a redactor.—In 2 Ch 30[9] וְלָשׁוּב depends on the idea of receiving a favour which lies in לְרַחֲמִים. On the other hand, in 1 S 8[12] it is sufficient to explain *and in order to appoint them unto him for captains of thousands* (sc. he will take them). In Is 44[28] translate *and he (Cyrus) shall perform all my pleasure, and that in saying of Jerusalem*, &c.

3. The period of time to which an action or occurrence represented **q** by the infinitive construct belongs, must sometimes be inferred from the context, or from the character of the principal tenses; cf. e.g. Gn 2[4] *these are the generations of the heaven and of the earth*, בְּהִבָּרְאָם *when they were created* (prop. in their being created); Ju 6[18] עַד־בֹּאִי וג׳ *until*

---

[1] לֵאמֹר is very often so used after וַיְדַבֵּר in the Priestly document (Gn 8[15], 17[3], &c., and numberless times in the legal parts of Exod., Lev., and Num.)—a pleonasm which is not surprising considering the admittedly prolix and formal style of the document.

[2] When Delitzsch on ψ 104[21], referring to Hb 1[17], explains the infinitive with ל as an elliptical mode of expressing the *coniugatio periphrastica* (equivalent to *flagitaturi sunt a deo cibum suum*), this is, in point of fact, certainly applicable to this and a few other places mentioned above; but all these passages, in which the infinitive with וְ follows, are to be distinguished from the cases treated above under *h*, where the infinitive with ל *without Wāw* corresponds to a Latin gerundive, or is actually used to express the *coniugatio periphrastica*.

I come unto thee, and bring forth, &c. Cf. 1 S 18¹⁹ (=*when she should have been given*); 2 K 2¹, Ho 7¹.

r Rem. 1. The constructions of the infinitive with a preposition, described above under *d*, are almost always continued in the further course of the narrative by means of the *finite verb*, i. e. by an independent sentence, not by a co-ordinate infinitive. Such a finite verb *we* regard as governed by a conjunction, which corresponds to the preposition standing before the infinitive. Thus the infinitival construction (frequently even with a change of subject) is continued by a perfect (with אֹל), Jer 9¹² *because they have forsaken* (עַל־עָזְבָם) *my law* . . . וְלֹא שָׁמְעוּ *and have not obeyed my voice*; Gn 39¹⁰, 1 S 24¹², Am 1⁹; without אֹל Jb 28²⁵ (perf. after לְ and infin.); by a perfect with וְ (cf. § 112 *i* and *v*) Am 1¹¹ /וְ רׇדְפוֹ עַל־רׇדְפוֹ *because he did pursue his brother with the sword,* וְשִׁחֵת *and did cast off* continually all pity (a frequentative perfect; for examples of the perfect consecutive proper see Gn 27⁴⁵, Ju 6¹⁸, 1 S 10⁸, 2 K 18³² [Is 36¹⁷], always after עַד־בֹּאִי *until I come*); by a simple imperfect, e. g. Pr 1²⁷ (after בְּ); Is 30²⁶ (after בְּיוֹם *in the day,* a temporal phrase which has here become equivalent to a preposition); Is 5²⁴ (after בְּ), 10², 13⁹, 14²⁵, 45¹, 49⁵, 1 S 2⁸, Pr 2⁸, 5², 8²¹ (always after לְ) ¹; by an imperfect consecutive, e. g. Gn 39¹⁸ *and it came to pass,* וָאֶקְרָא קוֹלִי כַּהֲרִימִי *as I lifted up my voice and cried, that* . . .; 1 K 10⁹, Jb 38¹³ (after לְ); 1 K 18¹⁸, Is 38⁹, Jb 38⁷·⁹ ff· (after בְּ); Is 30¹², Jer 7¹³, Ez 34⁸ (after יַעַן).

s 2. The negation of an infinitive construct, on account of the predominance of the noun-element in its character, is effected not by the verbal negative לֹא (except in the compound בְּלֹא, which has come to be used as a preposition, *without,* Nu 35²³, Pr 19²), but by בִּלְתִּי, originally a substantive (see the Lexicon), with לְ prefixed (but also Nu 14¹⁶ מִבִּלְתִּי), e. g. Gn 3¹¹ לְבִלְתִּי אֲכׇל־מִמֶּנּוּ *not to eat of it*; in a final sense, 4¹⁵ *lest any finding him should smite him*; only in 2 K 23¹⁰ is לְ repeated before the infinitive. In ψ 32⁹ (if the text be right) בַּל negatives, not the infinitive, but the predicate which is understood.

§ 115. *Construction of the Infinitive Construct with Subject and Object.*

a 1. Like the infinitive absolute (see § 113 *a*), the character of the infinitive construct as a *verbal* noun is shown by its power of taking the case proper to its verb, and hence in transitive verbs² *the accusative of the object,* e. g. Nu 9¹⁵ בְּיוֹם הָקִים אֶת־הַמִּשְׁכָּן *on the day the*

---

¹ The great frequency of examples of this kind, especially in the poetical books, is due to a striving after what is called *chiasmus* in the arrangement of the parallel members in the two halves of the verse, i. e. in the instances given, the finite verb *at the end* of the second (co-ordinate) clause is parallel with the infinitive *at the beginning* of the first. In this way the verbal form necessarily became separated from the וְ, and consequently the imperfect had to be used instead of the perfect consecutive. Such a parallelism of the *external* and *internal* members of a verse is frequent also in other cases, and was evidently felt to be an elegance of elevated—poetic or prophetic—style.

² For examples of the accus. of the object with a pass. infin., see § 121 *c*.

tabernacle was reared up; 1 S 19¹ לְהָמִית אֶת־דָּוִד *that they should slay David*; Gn 14¹⁷, 19²⁹, Ex 38²⁷, 1 K 12¹⁵, 15⁴; with a negative, e. g. Lv 26¹⁵ לְבִלְתִּי עֲשׂוֹת אֶת־כָּל־מִצְוֹתַי *so that ye will not do all my commandments*; with the accusative of the personal pronoun, e. g. Dt 29¹² לְמַעַן הָקִים־אֹתְךָ *that he may establish thee*; Gn 25²⁶, Jer 24⁷; with a verbal suffix, e. g. Ex 2¹⁴ לְהָרְגֵנִי *to kill me*; Jer 38²⁶ לְבִלְתִּי הֲשִׁיבֵנִי *that he would not cause me to return* (on the suffix, cf. *c*). In Is 49⁶ the object even precedes the infinitive with לְ; on this order cf. the note on § 114 *r*.— If the verb governs a double accusative, the infinitive may also take the same, e. g. Gn 41³⁹ אַחֲרֵי הוֹדִיעַ אֱלֹהִים אוֹתְךָ אֶת־כָּל־זֹאת *forasmuch as God hath showed thee all this*; Dt 21¹⁶.

Rem. 1. The object after the infinitive construct must also always be *b* regarded as in the accusative, even when it is not expressly introduced (as in all the above examples) by the *nota accusativi* אֶת־, and when therefore the substantive in question might easily be taken as the *genitive of the object* governed by the infinitive (the usual construction in Arabic), e. g. Pr 21¹⁵ עֲשׂוֹת מִשְׁפָּט *to do judgement*. Against regarding it as a genitive, which is in itself possible (*the doing, the executing of judgement*), is the fact (*a*) that elsewhere the *nota accusativi* is so frequently added; (*b*) that in such a case the secondary forms of the infinitive, such as רְאֹה for (פְּנֶיךָ) רְאֹת Gn 48¹¹ (cf. ψ 101³, Pr 16¹⁶), would be unintelligible; (*c*) that certain infinitive forms, if they were to be regarded as in the construct state, could hardly retain the pretonic Qames without exception, whereas, when connected with suffixes (i. e. with real genitives; cf. § 33 *c*), this Qames necessarily becomes *Šewâ*; e. g. Gn 18²⁵ לְהָמִית צַדִּיק *to slay the righteous* (never as לַהֲמִית; cf., on the other hand, above, (הֲשִׁיבֵנִי); 2 K 21⁸, Ez 44³⁰. Similarly in such cases as Is 3¹³ (ψ 50⁴) instead of לָדִין עַמִּים we should rather expect לְדִין, if the infinitive were regarded as in the construct state, and עַמִּים as the genitive. Hence also in cases like Is 58⁹ שְׁלַח (for שְׁלֹחַ) we must assume, with Sellin, op. cit., p. 78, a merely 'external phonetic connexion' and not the genitive construction.

2. The verbal suffixes added to the infinitive are (with the exception of *c* לְהוֹצִיאֵהוּ Jer 39¹⁴) only the suffix of the 1st pers. sing. (besides the above examples cf. also 1 S 5¹⁰, 27¹, 28⁹, Ru 2¹⁰, 1 Ch 12¹⁷, &c.) and plural; e. g. לְהַשְׁמִידֵנוּ *to destroy us*, Dt 1²⁷ (immediately after לָתֵת אֹתָנוּ, so that נוּ־ is doubtless a *verbal* not a *noun*-suffix, although in form it might be either); לַהֲמִיתֵנוּ Nu 16¹³, Ju 13²³ (after חָפֵץ). Elsewhere the pronominal object is appended either by means of the accusative sign (e. g. Gn 25²⁶ בְּלֶדֶת אֹתָם prop. *in the bearing them*; לָדַעַת אֹתִי *to know me*, Jer 24⁷) or in the form of a noun-suffix (as genitive of the object). The latter occurs almost always, whenever the context excludes the possibility of a misunderstanding; e. g. 1 S 20³³ לְהַכֹּתוֹ (prop. for his smiting) *to smite him*, not, as the form might also mean, *in order that he might smite*; cf. 1 K 20³⁵; with the suffix of the 3rd sing. fem. Nu 22²⁵; of the 3rd plur. Jos 10²⁰, 2 S 21², &c. Hence also the suffixes of the 2nd sing. with the infinitive, as לְהַבֹּתְךָ Jer 40¹⁴, cf. Mi 6¹³, and even גַּדֶּלְךָ *to magnify thee*, Jos 3⁷, must certainly be regarded as *nominal* not *verbal* suffixes. The connexion of the noun-suffix, as genitive of the object, with the infinitive, was so fully established, that it could be used not only in such strange cases, as Gn 37⁴ לֹא יָכְלוּ דַּבְּרוֹ לְשָׁלֹם *they could not speak to him peaceably*, cf. Zc 3¹ לְשָׂטְנוֹ *to be an adversary to him*, but ultimately even in the 1st sing., as in Nu 22¹³ לְתִתִּי *to give me leave* [Dt 25⁷ לֹא אָבָה יַבְּמִי *he will not perform the duty of a husband's brother unto me*; 1 Ch 4¹⁰ לְבִלְתִּי עָצְבִּי *that it may not grieve me !*]

d　3. The power of governing like a verb is also retained in those verbal nouns which, although originally secondary forms of the infinitive, have fully acquired the value of nouns, e. g. Is 11⁹ דֵּעָה אֶת־יְהוָֹה (prop. *to know the Lord) the knowledge of the Lord*; לְיִרְאָה אֹתִי *to fear me*, Dt 4¹⁰, 5²⁶, 10¹²; an accusative follows לְאַהֲבָה Dt 10¹².¹⁵, Is 56⁶ (cf. also 1 K 10⁹, Ho 3¹); לְהַנָּפָה Is 30²⁸; בְּשִׂנְאַת יְהוָֹה אֹתָנוּ Dt 1²⁷; after verbal nouns formed with the prefix מ (cf. § 45 *e*), Nu 10², Is 13¹⁹, Am 4¹¹, Ez 7⁹. The accusative of the object likewise remains after infinitives (or their secondary forms) which have the article, e. g. Gn 2⁹, Jer 22¹⁶, or a suffix, e. g. Gn 5⁴, &c., 28⁴.⁶, 29¹⁹ ꜰ., 30¹⁵, 38⁵, 2 S 3¹¹, Is 29¹³.

e　2. The subject of the action represented by the infinitive is mostly placed immediately[1] after it, either in the *genitive* or *nominative*. The subject is in the genitive (§ 33 *c*) whenever it has the form of a noun-suffix, and also when the infinitive has the termination of the constr. st. fem. sing. (see *f*); probably also in many other cases, where the infinitive in form and meaning is used more like a substantive, and accordingly governs like a noun. On the other hand, the subject of the infinitive is certainly to be regarded as a nominative, when it is separated from the infinitive by any insertion, and according to certain indications (see *g*) very probably in many other instances.

f　Rem. 1. Examples of genitives of the subject after infinitives in the connective form are Dt 1²⁷ בְּשִׂנְאַת יְהוָֹה אֹתָנוּ prop. *in the Lord's hating us*; cf. 7⁸, Gn 19¹⁶, 1 K 10⁹, Is 13¹⁹, 47⁹, Ho 3¹, Am 4¹¹. The subject of the infinitive is probably also to be regarded as genitive in such cases as Ex 17¹ *and there was no water* לִשְׁתֹּת הָעָם *for the people to drink* (prop. for the drinking of the people), and in cases like Gn 16¹⁶ (בְּלֶדֶת הָגָר); Gn 16³, Ex 19¹, Nu 20³.⁴, 33³⁸, 1 K 6¹, ψ 133¹, 2 Ch 7³, &c.

g　2. Examples in which the subject is separated from the infinitive by an insertion, and hence must certainly be regarded as a nominative, are Jb 34²² לְהִסָּתֶר שָׁם פֹּעֲלֵי אָוֶן *that the workers of iniquity may hide themselves there* (prop. for the hiding themselves there the workers of iniquity); cf. Gn 34¹⁵, Nu 35⁶, Dt 19³, Ju 9², 2 S 24¹³, ψ 76¹⁰, and below, *i*. The subject is likewise to be regarded as a *nominative*, whenever the Lamedh is prefixed to the infinitive by means of a pretonic Qameṣ (cf. *b* above), e. g. 2 S 19²⁰ לְשׂוּם הַמֶּלֶךְ אֶל־לִבּוֹ,

---

[1] In Gn 24³⁰ the subject of כִּרְאֹת is wanting (but כְּשָׁמְעוֹ follows); the original reading was undoubtedly כְּרֹאתוֹ, and the text is now in a state of confusion; verse 30*a* should come before verse 29*b*. In Gn 19²⁹, 25²⁶, Ex 9¹⁶, 13²¹, 1 S 18¹⁹, Jer 41⁶, ψ 42⁴ the subject, although not indicated, is easily supplied from the context. The infinitive in such cases is best rendered in English by a passive.

since, if the infinitive were used as a *nomen regens*, we should rather expect לָשֹׂוּם according to § 102 *f*. That the subject of the infinitive is regarded elsewhere also as nominative is again (see above, *b*) probable, since in such forms as הָנִיחַ Dt 25[19], Is 14[3], הָמִיר ψ 46[3], &c., the pretonic Qames̥ is retained without exception, whereas on the analogy of הֲנִיחִי Ez 24[13], הֲקִימוֹ Jer 23[20], &c., we should expect הֲנִיחַ, הֲמִיר, &c., if the infinitive were regarded as a *nomen regens*. Or was the retention of the Qames̥ (assuming the thorough correctness of the Masoretic punctuation) rendered possible even before a following genitive, because that vowel was characteristic of the form ? It is at all events certain that owing to the lack of case-endings,[1] a distinction between the genitival and nominatival constructions could not have been consciously made in the case of most infinitives, e. g. in unchangeable forms like קְטֹל, קוּם, &c.

3. When both a *subject* and an *object* are connected with the *h* infinitive, the rule is, that the subject should immediately follow the infinitive, and then the object. The latter, in such a case, is necessarily in the accusative, but the subject (as in *e*) may be either in the genitive or in the nominative. The noun-suffixes again are, of course, to be regarded as genitives, e. g. Gn 39[18] בַּהֲרִימִי קוֹלִי *as I lifted up my voice* (cf. 1 K 13[21], and the examples, Gn 5[4], &c., enumerated above, under *d*), and so also substantives which follow a connective form, Dt 1[27], &c.; see above, *d* and *f*.

On the other hand, the subject appears necessarily to be in the *i* nominative in such cases as Is 10[15] כְּהָנִיף שֵׁבֶט אֶת־מְרִימָיו *as if a rod should shake them that lift it up* (for the plur. מרימיו cf. § 124 *k*), not בַּהֲנִיף, as would be expected (see *g* above), if שֵׁבֶט were in the genitive; cf. 2 S 14[13], Jb 33[17]. And so probably also in other cases, as Gn 5[1], 13[10], Jos 14[7], 1 K 13[4], 2 K 23[10], Is 32[7]. The subject is separated from the infinitive by an insertion (and consequently must necessarily be in the nominative; see *g* above), e. g. in Jer 21[1].

Rem. Less frequently the object is placed immediately after the infinitive, *k* and then the nominative of the subject, as a subsequent complement, e. g. Is 20[1] בִּשְׁלֹחַ אֹתוֹ סַרְגוֹן *when Sargon sent him* ; Gn 4[15], Jos 14[11], 2 S 18[29], Is 5[24], ψ 56[1], Pr 25[8]. In Nu 24[23] the subject follows an infinitive which has a noun-suffix in place of the object.

§ 116. *The Participles.*

Cf. Sellin (see above at the head of § 113), p. 6 ff., and Kahan, p. 11 ff.

1. Like the two infinitives, the participles also occupy a middle *a* place between the noun and the verb. In form they are simple nouns,

---

[1] In Arabic, where the case-endings leave no doubt as to the construction, it is equally possible to say either *qatlu Zaidin* (gen. of subj.) *'Amran* (acc.), literally *Zaid's killing 'Amr*, or *qatlu 'Amrin* (gen. of obj.) *Zaidun* (nom. of subj.), or even *el-qatlu* (with article) *Zaidun* (nom. of subj.) *'Amran* (acc. of obj.).

and most nearly related to the adjective; consequently they cannot in themselves be employed to represent definite relations of tense or mood. On the other hand, their verbal character is shown by their not representing, like the adjectives, a fixed and permanent quality (or state), but one which is in some way connected with an *action* or *activity*. The *participle active* indicates a person or thing conceived as being in the continual uninterrupted *exercise* of an activity. The *participle passive*, on the other hand, indicates the person or thing in a state which has been brought about by external *actions*.

b Rem. That the language was fully conscious of the difference between a state implying action (or effected by external action) and mere passivity, is seen from the fact, that participles proper cannot be formed from the purely stative Qal, but only verbal adjectives of the form *qāṭēl* (מָלֵא, כָּבֵד, &c.) or *qāṭōl* (גָּבֹהַּ, &c.), whereas the *transitive* Qal שָׂנֵא *to hate*, although it coincides in form with the intransitive Qal (as a verb middle *e*), nevertheless forms a participle active שֹׂנֵא, and participle passive שָׂנוּא (cf. the feminine שְׂנוּאָה).— In cases where the participle proper and the verbal adjective both occur, they are by no means synonymous. When the Assyrians are called in Is 28¹¹ לַעֲגֵי שָׂפָה *men of stammering lips*, a character is ascribed to them which is inseparably connected with their personality. On the other hand בַּלֵּה לֹעֵג לִי Jer 20⁷, describes those about the prophet as continually engaged in casting ridicule upon him. Cf. also ψ 9¹⁸ (שְׁבֵחַי) with 50²² (שֹׁכְחֵי).

c On the difference between the participle as expressing *simple* duration and the imperfect as expressing *progressive* duration, cf. what has been stated above in § 107 *d*. Nevertheless the participle is sometimes used—especially in the later books, cf. e. g. Neh 6¹⁷, 2 Ch 17¹¹—where we should expect the action to be divided up into its several parts, and consequently should expect the finite verb. But the substitution of the participle for the *tempus historicum*, which becomes customary in Aramaic (cf. Kautzsch, *Gramm. des Bibl.-Aram.*, § 76. 2, *d* and *e*), is nevertheless quite foreign to Hebrew.

d 2. The period of time indicated by (*a*) a participle active, either as an attribute or predicate, must be inferred from the particular context. Thus מֵת may mean either *moriens* (Zc 11⁹), or *mortuus* (so commonly; with the article הַמֵּת regularly=*the dead man*), or *moriturus* (Dt 4²²); בָּא *coming, come* Gn 18¹¹, &c., *venturus* 1 S 2³¹, &c.; נֹפֵל *falling*, but also *fallen*, Ju 3²⁵, 1 S 5³, and *ready to fall* (threatening ruin, Is 30¹³, Am 9¹¹). For other examples of perfect participles see Gn 27³³, 43¹⁸ הַשָּׁב *that was returned*; cf. Ezr 6²¹, &c., הַשָּׁבִים *which were come again* from the captivity); Gn 35³, Ex 11⁵, Zc 12¹, ψ 137⁷, Pr 8⁹, Jb 12⁴ (קֹרֵא), and see *m* below. For future participles see Gn 41²⁵, 1 K 18⁹, Is 5⁵, Jon 1³, &c., probably also לְקֹחַי Gn 19¹⁴. On the *futurum instans* (esp. after הִנֵּה) see *p* below.

e (*b*) Of the passive participles, that of *Qal* (e. g. כָּתוּב *scriptus*) always corresponds to a Latin or Greek perfect participle passive, those of the other conjugations, especially *Niph'al*, sometimes to

The Participles

a Latin gerundive (or to an adjective in -*bilis*), e. g. נוֹרָא *metuendus*,
to be feared, ψ 76⁸, &c.; נֶחְמָד *desiderandus* (*desiderabilis*) Gn 3⁶,
ψ 19¹¹, &c.; נִבְרָא *creandus* ψ 102¹⁹; נוֹלָד, usually *natus*, but also (like
הַיִּלּוֹד Ju 13⁸) *procreandus, nasciturus* 1 K 13², ψ 22³²; נַעֲרָץ *terribilis*
ψ 89⁸; נִתְעָב *abominable* Jb 15¹⁶; נֶחְשָׁב *aestimandus* Is 2²²; הַנֶּאֱכֶלֶת
that may be eaten (an animal) Lv 11⁴⁷. In *Puʿal* מְהֻלָּל *laudandus,*
worthy to be praised ψ 18⁴. In *Hophʿal,* 2 S 20²¹ מֻשְׁלָךְ; 2 K 11²
הַמּוּמָתִים; Is 12⁵ *Qerê* מוּדַעַת.¹

3. The participles active, in virtue of their partly verbal character, *f*
possess the power of governing like verbs, and consequently, when
used in the absolute state, may take after them an object either in the
accusative, or with the preposition with which the verb in question
is elsewhere usually construed, e. g. 1 S 18²⁹ אֹיֵב אֶת־דָּוִד *hating David*;
Gn 42²⁹; with the suffix of the accusative, e. g. עֹשֵׂנִי *that made me*
Jb 31¹⁵; מִי רֹאֵנוּ *who seeth us ?* Is 29¹⁵ (in Is 47¹⁰ רֹאָנִי is abnormal);
רֹדֵם *ruling them* ψ 68²⁸, sometimes also with the article, e. g. ψ 18³³
הַמְאַזְּרֵנִי *that girdeth me* (LXX ὁ κραταιῶν με); Dt 8¹⁴⁻¹⁶, 13⁶·¹¹, 20¹,
2 S 1²⁴, Is 9¹² (where, however, Cheyne omits the article), 63¹¹, ψ 81¹¹,
103⁴, Dn 11⁶; followed by a preposition, e. g. 1 K 9²³ הָרֹדִים בָּעָם *which*
bare rule over the people; 2 K 20⁵ הִנְנִי רֹפֵא לָךְ *behold, I will heal thee.*²

By an exhaustive examination of the statistics, Sellin (see the title at the
head of § 113), p. 40 ff., shows that the participle when construed as a *verb*
expresses a single and comparatively transitory act, or relates to particular
cases, historical facts, and the like, while the participle construed as a *noun*
(see *g*) indicates repeated, enduring, or commonly occurring acts, occupations,
and thoughts.

So also the verbal adjectives of the form *qāṭēl* may take an
accusative of the person or thing, if the finite verb from which they
are derived governs an accusative, e. g. Dt 34⁹ מָלֵא רוּחַ חָכְמָה *full of*
the spirit of wisdom ; ψ 5⁵ חָפֵץ רֶשַׁע *that hath pleasure in wickedness.*

As a sort of noun the participle may, however, also exercise the *g*
same government as a noun, being in the construct state, and followed
by the object of the action in the genitive (see § 89 *a*; and cf.
§ 128 *x*), e. g. ψ 5¹² אֹהֲבֵי שְׁמֶךָ *that love thy name*; cf. ψ 19⁸ᶠ·; also
when a verbal adjective, e. g. Gn 22¹² and often יְרֵא אֱלֹהִים *one fearing*

---

¹ Such examples as נוֹרָא, נֶחְמָד, מְהֻלָּל show plainly the origin of this
gerundive use of the participle passive. A person or thing *feared, desired,* or
praised at all times is shown thereby to be *terrible, desirable,* or *praiseworthy,* and
therefore also *to be feared,* &c.
² On the other hand, in Is. 11⁹ *as the waters* לַיָּם מְכַסִּים *covering the sea,* the
ל serves only to introduce the object preceding the participle [cf. the Arabic
parallels cited by Driver, *Tenses,* § 135, 7 *Obs.*]. Cf. Hab. 2¹⁴.

God ; Hb 2¹⁵ ; with an infinitive, ψ 127² ; with a noun-suffix (which, according to § 33 *c*, also represents a genitive), e. g. Gn 4¹⁴ כָּל־מֹצְאִי *whosoever findeth me* (prop. my finder; cf. עֹשִׂי *my maker*) ; 12³ מְבָרֲכֶיךָ *that bless thee,* מְקַלֶּלְךָ *that curseth thee* (but read either מְקַלְלָיךְ, or מְבָרֲכֶךָ in the preceding clause) ; 27²⁹, 1 S 2³⁰, Is 63¹³, ψ 18⁴⁹. In Jer 33²² read מְשָׁרְתִים אֹתִי.¹

h Rem. To the class of objective genitives belong also specifications of place after the participles בָּא *iniens* and יֹצֵא *egrediens,* since the verbs בּוֹא and יָצָא, in the sense of *ingredi, egredi,* can be directly connected with an accusative ; e. g. Gn 23¹⁰·¹⁸ בָּאֵי שַׁעַר עִירוֹ *that went in at the gate of his city;* La 1⁴ ; after יֹצְאֵי Gn 9¹⁰, 34²⁴, 46²⁶, &c.—In poetic language the participle in the construct state may be connected not only with a genitive of the object, but also with any other specifications (especially of space) which otherwise can only be made to depend on the verb in question by means of a preposition ; cf. Is 38¹⁸, and frequently, יוֹרְדֵי־בוֹר *they that go down into the pit* (the grave) ; ψ 88⁶ שֹׁכְבֵי קֶבֶר *that lie in the grave;* Dt 32²⁴ (Mi 7¹⁷) ; 1 K 2⁷, 2 K 11⁵·⁷·⁹ *those that came in* (or *went out*) *on the sabbath,* Pr 2⁷, 1 Ch 5¹⁸, &c.; instead of the construction with מִן־, e. g. Is 59²⁰ (*those who turn from transgression*), Mi 2⁸ (cf. § 72 *p*).

i These genitives of nearer definition appear also in the form of a noun-suffix, e. g. ψ 18⁴⁰·⁴⁹ קָמַי (for קָמִים עָלַי) *that rise up against me* ; cf. Ex 15⁷, Dt 33¹¹, ψ 44⁶, Ex 3⁴²⁵, Is 1²⁷ שָׁבֶיהָ *her converts* ; ψ 53⁶ (חֹנָךְ) ; Pr 2¹⁹ כָּל־בָּאֶיהָ *all that go unto her* ; the construction is especially bold in Is 29⁷ כָּל־צֹבֶיהָ וּמְצֹדָתָהּ *all that fight against her and her stronghold* (for כָּל־הַצֹּבְאִים עָלֶיהָ וְעַל־מְ׳) ; ψ 102⁹ even with a participle Poʻal, מְהוֹלָלַי *they that are mad against me* (?), but read perhaps with Olshausen מְחוֹלְלָי *who pierce me.*—In Is 1³⁰ *as a terebinth* נֹבֶלֶת עָלֶהָ *fading as regards its leaf,* it remains doubtful whether נֹבֶלֶת is in the absolute state, and consequently עָלֶהָ in the accusative, or whether it is to be regarded as construct state, and עָלֶהָ as the genitive. In the latter case it would be analogous to Pr 14² (see *k*).

k 4. The passive participles also may either be in the absolute state, and take the determining word in the accusative,² or may be connected

---

¹ When, as in Jb 40¹⁹, the participle with the noun-suffix הָעֹשׂוֹ *he that made him,* also has the article (cf. § 127 *i*), the anomaly is difficult to understand, since a word determined by a genitive does not admit of being determined by the article.—No less remarkable is the use of the constr. st. of the participle before the accusative in Jer 33²² מְשָׁרְתֵי אֹתִי *that minister unto me* (for which there is מְשָׁרְתָי in verse 21). In Am 4¹³ an accusative of the product follows the genitive of the object, עֹשֵׂה שַׁחַר עֵיפָה *maker of the morning into darkness.* In Jer 2¹⁷ בְּעֵת כוֹלְכֵךְ is supposed to mean *at the time when he led thee;* perhaps the perfect (הוֹלֵךְ) should be read as in 6¹⁵. In Ez 27³⁴, the ancient versions read נִשְׁבַּרְתְּ (ה)עַתָּ *now thou art broken,* instead of the difficult עֵת נִשְׁבֶּרֶת. In 1 K 20⁴⁰ read עֹשֶׂה before הִנֵּה וָהֵנָּה.

² On the proper force of this accusative when retained in the passive con-

with it in the construct state, e. g. Ju 18[11], 1 S 2[18], Ez 9[2] לְבֻשׁ בַּדִּים *clothed in linen*, cf. verse 3 הַלָּבֻשׁ הַבַּדִּים; (even with a suffix קָרֻעַ כֻּתָּנְתּוֹ *rent as regards his coat* 2 S 15[32]; with the participle following Ju 1[7]); but Ez 9[11] לְבֻשׁ הַבַּדִּים *the one clothed with linen*; 2 S 13[31] קְרֻעֵי בְגָדִים *rent in respect of clothes*, equivalent to *with their clothes rent* (cf. Jer 41[5]); Nu 24[4], Dt 25[10], Is 3[3], 33[24], Jo 1[8], ψ 32[1] (נְשׂוּי־פֶּשַׁע *forgiven in respect of transgression*, כְּסוּי חֲטָאָה *covered in respect of sin*); with a suffix to the noun, Pr 14[2] נְלוֹז דְּרָכָיו *he that is perverse in his ways*.

Rem. The passive participle occurs in the construct state before a genitive *l* of the *cause*, e. g. in Is 1[7] שְׂרֻפוֹת אֵשׁ *burnt with fire*; cf. Gn 41[6], Ex 28[11], Dt 32[24]; before a genitive denoting the *author*, e. g. Gn 24[31] בְּרוּךְ יְהֹוָה *blessed of the Lord* (but ψ 115[15] בְּרוּכִים לַיהֹוָה, see § 121 *f*); cf. Is 53[4], ψ 22[7], Jb 14[1] (15[14], 25[4]); hence also with noun-suffixes (which are accordingly genitive) Pr 9[18] קְרֻאֶיהָ *her invited ones*, i. e. those invited by her; cf. 7[26], ψ 37[22].

5. The use of the participle as predicate is very frequent in noun- *m* clauses (which, according to § 140 *e*, describe established facts and states), in which the period of time intended by the description must again (see above, *d*) be inferred from the context. Thus:

(*a*) As *present*, in speaking of truths which hold good at all times, e. g. Ec 1[4] *n* דּוֹר הֹלֵךְ וְדוֹר בָּא *one generation goeth, and another generation cometh; and the earth abideth* (עֹמָדֶת) *for ever*; cf. verse 7; also to represent incidental (continuous) occurrences which are just happening, Gn 3[5], 16[8] (*I am fleeing*); 32[12], Ex 9[17], 1 S 16[15], 23[1], 2 K 7[9], Is 1[7]; when the subject is introduced by the emphatic demonstrative הִנֵּה *behold!* (§ 100 *o* and § 105 *b*), e. g. Gn 16[11] הִנָּךְ הָרָה *behold, thou art with child*, &c.; 27[42]; frequently also in circumstantial clauses (connected by *Wāw*), cf. § 141 *e*, e. g. Gn 15[2], &c.

(*b*) To represent *past* actions or states, sometimes in independent noun- *o* clauses, e. g. Ex 20[18] וְכָל־הָעָם רֹאִים אֶת־הַקּוֹלֹת *and all the people saw the thunderings*, &c.; 1 K 1[5]; in negative statements, e. g. Gn 39[23 *a*]; sometimes in relative clauses, e. g. Gn 39[23 *b*], Dt 3[2] (cf. also the frequent combination of the participle with the article as the equivalent of a relative clause, e. g. Gn 32[10] הָאֹמֵר *which saidst*; 12[7], 16[13], 35[1.3], 36[35], 48[16], 2 S 15[31], &c.); sometimes again (see *n*) in *circumstantial* clauses, especially those representing actions or states which occurred simultaneously with other past actions, &c., e. g. Gn 19[1] *and the two angels came to Sodom* וְלוֹט יֹשֵׁב *and* (i. e. *while*) *Lot sat*, &c.; 18[1.8.16.22], 25[26], Ju 13[9], 2 Ch 22[9]; also with the subject introduced by הִנֵּה 37[7], 41[17]. (On הֹלֵךְ with a following adjective or participle to express an action constantly or occasionally recurring, cf. § 113 *u*.)

(*c*) To announce *future* actions or events, e. g. 1 K 2[2], 2 K 4[16] *at this season p when the time cometh round*, אַתְּ חֹבֶקֶת בֵּן *thou shalt embrace a son*; so after a specification of time, Gn 7[4], 15[14], 17[19], 19[13], Hag 2[6] (but in Is 23[15], where, after וְהָיָה we should rather expect a perfect consecutive, it is better to explain

struction cf. below, § 117 *cc*, &c., and § 121 *c, d*. So also Neh 4[12] is to be understood, *and the builders were* אִישׁ חַרְבּוֹ אֲסוּרִים עַל־מָתְנָיו *girded every one with his sword on his side, and building.*

וְנִשְׁבַּחַת, with Qimḥi, as the 3rd sing. fem. of the perfect; on the form, cf. § 44 *f*); or in relative clauses, Gn 41²⁵, Is 5⁵ *what I am doing*, i. e. am in the act of doing ; in a deliberative question, Gn 37³⁰ ; but especially often when the subject is introduced by הִנֵּה (especially also if the subject be attached as a suffix to הִנֵּה as הִנְנִי, הִנְּךָ, &c.), if it is intended to announce the event as imminent, or at least near at hand (and sure to happen), when it is called *futurum instans*, e. g. Gn 6¹⁷, 15³, 20³, 24¹³ ᶠ·, 48²¹, 50⁵, Ex 3¹³, 8²⁵, 9³, 34¹⁰, Jos 2¹⁸, Ju 7¹⁷, 9³³, 1 S 3¹¹, 2 K 7², Is 3¹, 7¹⁴, 17¹, Jer 30¹⁰, Zc 2¹³, 3⁸ ; with a participle passive, 2 S 20²¹ : cf. also § 112 *t*.

q Rem. 1. As the above examples show, a noun-clause with a participle as predicate may have for its subject either a substantive or a personal pronoun ; in both cases the participle, especially if there be a certain emphasis upon it, may precede the subject. Also in noun-clauses introduced by הִנֵּה the subject may be either a substantive, or (e. g. Gn 37⁷) a separate personal pronoun, or a suffix attached to הִנֵּה. In the same way, the subject may also be introduced by יֵשׁ (*est*, see the Lexicon) with a suffix, and in negative sentences by אֵין (*non est*) with a suffix, e. g. Ju 6³⁶ אִם־יֶשְׁךָ מוֹשִׁיעַ *if thou wilt save* ; Gn 43⁵ אִם־אֵינְךָ מְשַׁלֵּחַ *if thou wilt not send* ; 1 S 19¹¹.—In such cases as Is 14²⁷ יָדוֹ הַנְּטוּיָה *the stretched out hand is his*, הַנְּטוּיָה is not, like נְטוּיָה in 9¹¹·¹⁶, &c., the predicate (in which case the participle could not take the article), but the subject ; cf. Gn 2¹¹, 45¹², Is 66⁹, Ez 20²⁹, Zc 7⁶ (cf. § 126 *k*), where the participle with the article likewise refers to the present, also Nu 7², Dt 3²¹, 4³, &c., 1 S 4¹⁶, where it refers to the past. In 1 K 12⁸ and 21¹¹ even in relative clauses after אֲשֶׁר.

r 2. To give express emphasis to an action continuing in the *past*, the perfect הָיָה in the corresponding person is sometimes added to the participle, and similarly the imperfect יִהְיֶה (or the jussive יְהִי, or the imperfect consecutive) is used to emphasize an action continuing in the *future*, e. g. Jb 1¹⁴ הַבָּקָר הָיוּ חֹרְשׁוֹת *the oxen* (cows) *were plowing* ; Gn 37², 39²², Ex 3¹, Dt 9²⁴, Ju 1⁷, 1 S 2¹¹, 2 S 3⁶ ; the same occurs with a passive participle, e. g. Jos 5⁵, Zc 3³ ; יְהִי with a participle is found e. g. in Is 2² ; the jussive in Gn 1⁶, ψ 109¹² ;1 and וִיהִי with a participle in Ju 16²¹, Neh 1⁴.

s 3. The *personal pronoun* which would be expected as the subject of a participial clause is frequently omitted, or at least (as elsewhere in noun-clauses, cf. Is 26³, ψ 16⁸, Jb 9³²) the pronoun of the 3rd pers. הוּא, e. g. Gn 24³⁰, 37¹⁵, 38²⁴, 41¹, 1 S 10¹¹, 15¹², Is 29⁸ (the participle always after הִנֵּה); cf., moreover, Gn 32⁷, Dt 33³, 1 S 17²⁵, 20¹, Is 33⁵, 40¹⁹, ψ 22²⁹, 33⁵, 55²⁰, Jb 12¹⁷·¹⁹ ᶠᶠ·, 25², 26⁷.— הִיא is omitted in Lv 18²⁸ ; הֵמָּה in Is 32¹², Ez 8¹², Neh 9³ ; in a relative clause, Gn 39²², Is 24².—The personal pronoun of the 2nd pers. masc. (אַתָּה) is omitted in Hb 2¹⁰ ; the 2nd fem. (אַתְּ) in Gn 20¹⁶ (where, however, for the participle וְנֹכַחַת the 2nd fem. perf. וְנֹכַחַתְּ is to be read) ; the pronoun of the 1st sing. in Hb 1⁵ (?), Zc 9¹², Mal 2¹⁶ ; the 2nd plur. (אַתֶּם) 1 S 2²⁴ (if the text be right), 6³, Ez 13⁷ (?). But these passages are all more or less doubtful.

t Of a different kind are the cases in which some undefined subject is to be supplied with the participle ; e. g. Is 21¹¹ אֵלַי קֹרֵא *there is one calling unto me* (= one calleth ; § 144 *d*) ; cf. Is 30²⁴, 33⁴.—So with participles in the plur., e. g. Ex 5¹⁶ אֹמְרִים sc. the taskmasters) ; Jer 38²³ (in 33⁵ the text is corrupt), Ez 13⁷ (?), 36¹³, 37¹¹ (equivalent to *sunt qui dicant*).

---

¹ A jussive is practically to be supplied also in the formulae of blessing and cursing, בָּרוּךְ *blessed be* . . . Gn 9²⁶, &c. ; אָרוּר *cursed art thou* . . . 3¹⁴, &c.

4. We must mention as a special class those noun-clauses which occur at *u* the beginning of a period, and are intended to lay stress upon the fact that the first action still continues on the occurrence of the second (always introduced by וְ) ; e. g. Jb 1¹⁶ ᶠ· עוֹד זֶה מְדַבֵּר וְזֶה בָא *he was yet speaking, and* (= *when*) *another came*, &c.[1] ; cf. Gn 29⁹, 1 S 9¹¹·²⁷, 20³⁶, 1 K 14¹⁷ *she was entering the threshold of the house, when the child died* ; 2 K 2¹³, 4⁵, Dn 9²⁰ ᶠ· ; also in Ju 19²², 1 S 9¹⁴, 17²³, 1 K 1⁴², Jb 1¹⁸ ᶠ·, in all which passages the apodosis is introduced by וְהִנֵּה.—On the other hand, in 1 K 1¹⁴ the noun-clause itself is introduced by הִנֵּה (as in verse 22 by וְהִנֵּה), and denotes an action only just impending.[2] Finally, when the whole sentence is introduced by means of וַיְהִי (cf. § 111 *g*), and the apodosis by וְהִנֵּה, Gn 42³⁵, 2 K 2¹¹, 13²¹ ; without הִנֵּה in the apodosis, 1 S 7¹⁰, 2 K 19³⁷ (Is 37³⁸).

Participles active, which are used in the sense of the perfect participle, and *v* also *participles passive*, in accordance with their meaning, express in such noun-clauses a state still continuing on the occurrence of the principal action, e. g. Gn 38²⁵ הוּא מוּצֵאת וְהִיא שָׁלְחָה *she was being brought forth, when she sent,* &c. ; cf. Gn 50²⁴. [See further in Driver, *Tenses*, §§ 166–169.]

5. Different from the examples treated in *u* and *v* are the instances in *w* which a participle (either alone or as the attribute of a noun) stands at the beginning of the sentence as a *casus pendens* (or as the subject of a *compound noun-clause*, see § 143 *c*) to indicate a condition, the contingent occurrence of which involves a further consequence ; e. g. Gn 9⁶ שֹׁפֵךְ דַּם הָאָדָם בָּאָדָם דָּמוֹ יִשָּׁפֵךְ *shedding man's blood*, i. e. if any one sheddeth man's blood, *by man shall his blood be shed* ; Ex 21¹², ψ 75⁴, Pr 17¹⁴, Jb 41¹⁸ ; so especially if כָּל־ *every* precedes the participle, Gn 4¹⁵, 1 S 3¹¹ (2 K 21¹²), 2 S 5⁸ (*whosoever smiteth*), 1 Ch 11⁶. The apodosis is very often introduced by וְ (*wāw apodosis*), e. g. Ex 12¹⁵ (with a following perfect consecutive), Nu 35³⁰ ; 1 S 2¹³ כָּל־אִישׁ זֹבֵחַ זֶבַח וּבָא נַעַר הַכֹּהֵן *when any man offered sacrifice, the priest's servant came*, &c. ; 2 S 14¹⁰ (participle with article) ; 22⁴¹ (where, however, the text is to be emended in accordance with ψ 18⁴¹) ; 2 S 23³ ᶠ·, Pr 23²⁴ *Keth.* ; 29⁹.—As in the instances discussed under *u*, such sentences are sometimes preceded by וַיְהִי, cf. 1 S 10¹¹, 11¹¹, 2 S 2²³ וַיְהִי כָל־הַבָּא *and it came to pass, that as many as came,* &c. [or by וְהָיָה, frequentative, Ju 19³⁰].—On the other hand, וְהַנִּשְׁבֶּרֶת Dn 8²² is a mere catchword (equivalent to *and as for that which was broken*) to call to mind the contents of verse 8.

6. On the use of the participle after the infinitive absolute הָלוֹךְ cf. § 113 *u*.

7. Almost as a rule the participial construction beginning a sentence (like *x* the infinitival constructions according to § 114 *r*) is continued by means of a finite verb with or without וְ, before which the English construction requires us to supply the relative pronoun implied in the participle; thus,

---

[1] The independent noun-clause here lays stress upon the simultaneous occurrence (and consequently the overlapping) of the events far more forcibly than could be done by a subordinate expression of time (as e. g. וַיְהִי בְדַבְּרוֹ). In English it may be represented by *scarcely had he finished speaking when*. . . . As the above examples show, the apodosis also frequently consists of a noun-clause.

[2] At the same time the preceding עוֹד *still* shows that what is announced is not merely a future event, but a future event *contemporaneous* with something else; the case thus entirely differs from the examples given in § 112 *t*, where הִנֵּה refers to the following participle, while here it belongs properly to the apodosis, before which it is therefore generally placed; see the examples.

continued by means of a perfect, Is 14¹⁷ שָׂם תֵּבֵל כַּמִּדְבָּר וְעָרָיו הָרָס *that made the world as a wilderness, and overthrew the cities thereof* ¹; 43⁷, Ez 22³, ψ 136¹³ ᶠᶠ·, Pr 2¹⁷; by a perfect without *Wāw*, Gn 49¹¹; by a simple imperfect (as the *modus rei repetitae* in the present), Is 5²³, 46⁶, Pr 7⁸, Jb 12¹⁷·¹⁹ ᶠᶠ·, 24²¹; by an imperfect without *Wāw*, e. g. 1 S 2⁸, Is 5⁸, Pr 2¹⁴, 19²⁶; by an imperfect consecutive, Gn 27³³, 35³, 1 S 2⁶, Jer 13¹⁰ (after several participles), ψ 18³³, 136¹⁰ᶠ·

C. THE GOVERNMENT OF THE VERB.

§ 117. *The Direct Subordination of the Noun to the Verb as Accusative of the Object. The Double Accusative.*

L. Kaila, *Zur Syntax des in verbaler Abhängigkeit stehenden Nomens im alttest. Hebr.*, Helsingfors, 1906.

a 1. The simplest way in which a noun is subordinated to a verbal form is by the addition of an accusative of the object to a transitive verb.² In the absence of case-endings,³ this accusative can now be recognized only from the context, or by the particle אֶת־ (אֵת, before suffixes also אֹת, אֹות)⁴ prefixed to it. The use of this *nota accusativi*

---

¹ On the parallelism between the *external* and *internal* members, which appears here and in many other examples of this kind, see the note on § 114 r.

² The verb in question may either have been originally transitive, or only have become transitive by a modification of its original meaning. Thus the vocalization shows that חָפֵץ (*to have pleasure*, usually with בְּ) *to desire*, מָלֵא (*to be full* of something, also transitive) *to fill*, were originally intransitive. Cf. also such cases as בָּכָה *to weep* (generally with עַל־, אֶל־ or לְ), but also *to bewail* with an accusative; יָשַׁב *to dwell* (usually with בְּ), but also *to inhabit* with an accusative (cf. further, under *u*).—The examples are different in which verbs of motion such as בּוֹא *intrare*, also *aggredi*, יָצָא *egredi* (cf. § 116 *h* above), שׁוּב *redire*, Is 52⁸, take an accusative of the aim of the motion, while בּוֹא according to the Old Semitic usage, even takes an accusative of the person (at least in poetry, equivalent to בּוֹא אֶל־ in prose).

³ On traces of these endings, especially the remains of a former accusative ending in *a*, cf. § 90 c.

⁴ אֶת־ (toneless owing to the following Maqqeph), and אֵת (with a tone-long *ē*, אֵת only in Jb 41²⁶), אֹת or אֹות before the light suffixes (on all these forms cf. § 103 b: the underlying form *āth* was obscured in Hebrew to *ôth*, shortened to *ăth* before suffixes beginning with a consonant and then modified to אֶת־, whence finally the secondary form אֵת with the tone), Phoenician אִית i. e. probably *iyyāth* (for the Phoenician form, cf. G. Hoffmann, *Einige phönik. Inschriften*, Göttingen, 1889, p. 39 f.), Punic *yth* or (according to Euting) pronounced even as a mere prefixed *t*, Arabic, before suffixes, *'iyyā*, Aram. יָת, יָת. It was no doubt originally a substantive, meaning *essence, substance, self* (like the Syriac *yāth*; on the other hand, any connexion with the Hebrew אוֹת, Syriac *'ātā*, Arabic *'āyat, a sign*, must, with Nöldeke, *ZDMG.* xl. 738, be rejected), but now united in the construct state with a following noun or suffix stands for the pronoun *ipse*, αὐτός. In common use, however (cf. Wilson, 'The particle אֵת in Hebrew,' *Hebraica*, vi. 2, 3, and the precise statistics of the use

is, however, somewhat rare in poetry, and even in prose it is not invariably necessary but is restricted to those cases in which the accusative of the object is more closely determined by being a proper name, or by having the article, or by a following determinate genitive (hence also by the suffixes), or in some other way (see below, *c*), e. g. Gn 4¹ *and she bare* אֶת־קַיִן *Cain* ; 6¹⁰, 1¹ *God created* אֵת הַשָּׁמַיִם וְאֵת הָאָרֶץ *the heaven and the earth* (but 2⁴ אֶרֶץ וְשָׁמַיִם); 1²⁵ *and God made* אֶת־חַיַּת הָאָרֶץ *the beast of the earth* ; 2²⁴.

Rem. 1. The rare occurrence of the *nota accusativi* in poetic style (e. g. it *b* never occurs in Ex 15²⁻¹⁸, Dt 32, Ju 5, 1 S 2, &c., though it is frequent in the late Psalms) may be explained from the fact that in this as in other respects (cf. § 2 *q*) poetry represents a somewhat more archaic stage of the language than prose. The need of some external means of indicating the accusative could only have been felt after the case-endings had become wholly extinct. Even then the אֵת would probably have been used at first to indicate only an object placed *before* the verb (when it followed, it was already sufficiently characterized by its position as depending on the verb), or proper names.[1] Finally, however, the *nota accusativi* became so customary everywhere in prose, that even the pronominal object was expressed rather by אֵת with suffixes than by verbal suffixes, even when none of the reasons mentioned under *e* can be assigned for it; cf. Giesebrecht in *ZAW*. 1881, p. 258 ff., and the statistics of H. Petri, cited above at the head of § 58. Such examples as כְּכֹל אֲשֶׁר־צִוָּהוּ אֹתוֹ צִוָּה אֹתוֹ אֱלֹהִים Gn 6²² in the *Priestly Code*, beside כְּכֹל אֲשֶׁר־צִוָּהוּ יְהֹוָה 7⁵ in the *Jahvist*, are especially instructive.

2. As accusatives determined in other ways, we have in the first place to *c* consider the collectives introduced by כֹּל *entirety*, without a following article or determinate genitive, inasmuch as the meaning of כֹּל includes a deter-minative sense, cf. e. g. Gn 1²¹·³⁰, 8²¹, Dt 2³⁴, 2 K 25⁹. אֶת־כֹּל is used absolutely in Gn 9³, cf. 39²³; similarly, מִי is determinate of itself, since it always denotes a person, hence אֶת־מִי *quem?* e. g. Is 6⁸, 37²³, &c., but never אֶת־מָה *quid?* So also the relative אֲשֶׁר in the sense of *eum qui* or *quem*, &c., e. g. 1 S 16³, or *id quod*, Gn 9²⁴, &c. Cf. also such examples as Jos 2¹⁰, 1 S 24¹⁹, where אֵת אֲשֶׁר is equivalent to *the circumstance, that*, &c.—Elsewhere אֵת stands before nouns which are determinate in sense, although the article is omitted, which according to § 126 *h* is very frequently the case in poetic or otherwise elevated style; thus Lv 26⁵, Jos 24¹⁴·¹⁵, Is 41⁷ (to distinguish the object from the subject); 50⁴ (with the first of two accusatives, also for the sake of clearness); Ez 13²⁰, 43¹⁰, Pr 13²¹ (where the צַדִּיקִים are to be regarded as a distinct class); Jb 13²⁵

---

of אֵת on p. 140 ff.), it has so little force (like the oblique cases αὐτοῦ, αὐτῷ, αὐτόν, sometimes also *ipsius, ipsum*, and the Germ. *desselben*, &c.) that it merely serves to introduce a determinate object; אֵת הַשָּׁמַיִם prop. αὐτὸν τὸν οὐρανόν (cf. αὐτὴν Χρυσηΐδα, Iliad i. 143) is no stronger than the simple הַשָּׁמַיִם τὸν οὐρανόν. Cf., further, P. Haupt on Pr 18²⁴ in his Rainbow Bible, and also in the *Notes on Esther*, p. 191.

[1] Thus, in Dt 33, אֵת occurs only in verse 9 (twice, with an object preceding the verb), in Gn 49 in the blessing of Jacob only in verse 15 with a co-ordinate second object (consequently farther removed from the verb). Of the thirteen instances of אֵת in the Mêša‘ inscription, seven stand directly and four indirectly before proper names.

(unless, with Beer and others, we read וְאִם for (וְאֶת־); also Ec 7⁷ may be a quotation of an ancient maxim.

d On the other hand אֵת occurs very seldom in prose before a noun actually or apparently undetermined. In 1 S 24⁶ כְּנָף is more closely defined by means of the following relative clause; in 2 S 4¹¹ אִישׁ צַדִּיק refers to Ishbosheth (as if it were *him, who was an innocent man*); in 1 K 6¹⁶ עֶשְׂרִים אַמָּה refers to the particular twenty cubits. In Ex 21²⁸ (otherwise in verse 29) perhaps the אֶת־ is used in order to avoid the combination אִישׁ שׁוֹר (as in Nu 21⁹ to avoid the cacophony אִישׁ הַנָּחָשׁ נָשַׁךְ ?); in Lv 7⁸ and 20¹⁰ the accusatives are at any rate defined by the context.—In Nu 16¹⁵ אֶת־אַחַד מֵהֶם probably means *even a single one* (and then *ipso facto* a definite one) *of them*, as also in 1 S 9³ אֶת־אַחַד מֵהַנְּעָרִים may refer to some definite one of the men-servants. In Gn 21³⁰ we should read אֶת־שֶׁבַע הַכְּבָשֹׂת with the Samaritan, since the seven lambs have been already mentioned; in Ex 2¹ translate with Meyer, *Die Israeliten*, p. 79, אֶת־בַּת־לֵוִי *the daughter of Levi*; in Ex 28⁹ read הַשֵּׁהַם with the Samaritan; in Lv 20¹⁴ אֶת־אִשָּׁה is probably a scribal error due to וְאֶת־אִמָּה; in 1 S 26²⁰ read נַפְשִׁי with the LXX for פַּרְעֹשׁ אֶחָד; in 2 S 5²⁴ read הַצְּעָדָה as in 1 Ch 14¹⁵; in 2 S 15¹⁶ the אֶת־ is incorrectly inserted from 20³, where it refers to the women already mentioned; in 2 S 18¹⁸ read הַמַּצֶּבֶת, or omit both אֶת־ and אֲשֶׁר with the LXX and Lucian; in 1 K 12³¹ omit אֶת־; in 2 K 23²⁰ probably אֶת־עַצְמוֹתָם is to be read; in 2 K 25⁹ the text is corrupt. In Ez 16³² אֶת־זָרִים might refer to *the strangers in question*; but see Smend on the passage.

e 3. The pronominal object *must* be represented by את with a suffix (instead of a verbal suffix), when (*a*) it precedes the verb, e.g. Nu 22³³ אֹתְכָה הָרַגְתִּי וְאוֹתָהּ הֶחֱיֵיתִי *I had slain thee and saved her alive*; Gn 7¹, Lv 22²⁸, 1 S 8⁷, Is 43²², 57¹¹, Jer 4¹⁷·²², 7¹⁹; (*b*) when a suffix is already attached to the verb, and as a rule when a second accusative with וְ follows, e.g. 2 S 15²⁵ וְהִרְאַנִי אֹתוֹ *and he will show me it*; Ex 17³ לְהָמִית אֹתִי וְאֶת־בָּנַי *to kill us and our children*; Nu 16³², 1 S 5¹¹, 2 S 14¹⁶ (but cf. also Dt 11⁶, 15¹⁶, &c., and Driver on 1 S 5¹⁰); (*c*) after an infinitive absolute, see above § 113 *a* note; (*d*) after an infinitive construct, when it is immediately followed by the subject, e.g. Gn 41³⁹, or when the combination of a suffix with the infinitive might lead to a misunderstanding, e.g. Gn 4¹⁵ לְבִלְתִּי הַכּוֹת־אֹתוֹ *lest one should smite him*, &c., where לְבִלְתִּי הַכּוֹתוֹ might also mean *lest he should smite*.

f 4. The pronominal object is very frequently omitted, when it can be easily supplied from the context; so especially the neuter accusative referring to something previously mentioned (the English *it*) after *verba sentiendi* (שָׁמַע) and *dicendi*, e.g. Gn 9²², &c., וַיַּגֵּד *and he told* (it); also after נָתַן *to give*, Gn 18⁷, 24⁴¹, &c., לָקַח *to take*, הֵבִיא *to bring*, שִׂים *to lay*, Gn 9²³, &c., מָצָא *to find*, Gn 31³³, &c. A personal object is omitted, e.g. in Gn 12¹⁹, 24⁵¹ (after לָקַח).—The omission of the plural object is remarkable, because it leaves an opportunity for a misunderstanding, in Gn 37¹⁷ שָׁמַעְתִּי אֹמְרִים¹ *I heard* them *saying*; perhaps, however, we should read שָׁמַעְתִּים with the Samaritan.

g 5. In common formulae the substantival object is also sometimes omitted

---

¹ According to the ordinary rules of syntax (cf. § 116 *t*) we should translate, *I heard men who said*, &c.

(an elliptical expression); thus e.g. כָּרַת 1 S 20[16], &c. (see the Lexicon) stands for כָּרַת בְּרִית like the English *to close* (sc. a bargain) with any one; נָטַר *to keep* (sc. אַף *anger*) equivalent to *to be resentful*, ψ 103[9], &c.; so also שָׁמַר Jer 3[5] (beside נָטַר); נָשָׂא for נָשָׂא קוֹל *to lift up the voice*, Is 3[7]; נָשָׂא לְ for נָשָׂא עָוֺן לְ *to take away any one's sin* (to forgive), Gn 18[24.26], Is 2[9]; שָׁלַח *to put forth* (sc. יָד *the hand*) equivalent to *to reach after something*, 2 S 6[6], ψ 18[17].

6. *Verba sentiendi* may take a second object, generally in the form of a parti- *h* ciple or adjective and necessarily indeterminate, to define more exactly the action or state in which the object is perceived, e.g. Nu 11[10] וַיִּשְׁמַע מֹשֶׁה אֶת־הָעָם בֹּכֶה *and Moses heard the people weeping*; Gn 7[1] אֹתְךָ רָאִיתִי צַדִּיק *thee have I seen righteous*. Frequently, however, the second object is expressed by a separate clause. This is especially frequent with רָאָה *to see*, e.g. Gn 1[4] *and God saw the light, that it was good*; Gn 6[2], 12[14], 13[10], 49[15], Ex 2[2], ψ 25[19], Pr 23[31], Jb 22[12], Ec 2[24], 8[17]; so with יָדַע *to know*, Ex 32[22], 2 S 3[25], 17[8] (with two objects); 1 K 5[17].

7. In certain instances אֵת serves apparently to introduce or to emphasize *i* a nominative. This cannot be regarded as a reappearance of the original substantival meaning of the אֵת, since all unquestionable examples of the kind belong to the later Books of the Old Testament. They are rather (apart from textual errors or other explanations) cases of virtual dependence on an implied *verbum regens* understood. The constant use of אֵת to indicate a clause governed by the verb, necessarily led at length to the use of אֵת generally as a defining particle irrespective of a governing verb. So in the Hebrew of the Mishna[1] (see above, § 3 a) אֹתוֹ and אֹתָהּ are prefixed even to a nominative without any special emphasis.

Naturally the above does not apply to any of the places in which אֵת is not *k* the *nota accusativi*, but a preposition (on אֵת *with*, cf. § 103 b), e.g. Is 57[15], 1 S 17[34] (וְאֶת־הַדּוֹב) *and that, with a bear*; אֶת־ here, however, has probably been interpolated from verse 36, where it is wanting); nor the places in which the accusative is subordinate to a passive (according to § 121 c) or to a verb of wanting as in Jos 22[17] and Neh 9[32], see below, *z*. In Ez 43[17] סָבִיב *about* governs like a verb, being followed by אֹתָהּ.

Other cases are clearly due to attraction to a following relative pronoun in *l* the accusative (Ez 14[22], Zc 8[17]; but Hag 2[5a], to מִמִּצְרַיִם, must be omitted, with the LXX, as a later addition), or the accusative depends on a verbal idea, virtually contained in what has gone before, and consequently present to the speaker's mind as governing the accusative. Thus Nu 3[26] (the verbal idea contained in וּמִשְׁמֶרֶת verse 25 is *they had to take charge of*); in Jos 17[11] וַיְהִי לְ implies *it was given up* or *they gave him*; 1 S 26[16] *see where* is equivalent to *search now for*; in 2 S 11[25] אַל־יֵרַע בְּעֵינֶיךָ is used in the sense of *noli aegre ferre*[2]; Jer 36[33] *and he had the brazier before him*; in Ec 4[3] a verb like *I esteem* is mentally supplied before אֵת אֲשֶׁר. On Jos 22[17], Neh 9[32], see below, *aa*.— Aposiopesis occurs in Dt 11[2] *for not your children* (do I mean); still more boldly in Zc 7[7], where either שְׁמַעְתֶּם or תִּשְׁמְעוּ (תַּעֲשׂוּ) is to be supplied.

Setting aside a few undoubtedly corrupt passages[3] there still remain the *m*

---

[1] Cf. Weiss, משפט לשון המשנה (Vienna, 1867), p. 112.

[2] So also in 1 S 20[13] the Qal (יֵיטַב) is, with Wellhausen, to be read instead of the Hiph'il.

[3] Thus 1 S 26[16], where וְאֵי is to be read for וְאֵת; 1 K 11[25], where at present the predicate of the relative clause is wanting; in 2 K 6[5] the אֵת is probably

following examples, in which אֶת־ in the later Hebrew manner (almost in the sense of the Latin *quod attinet ad*) introduces a noun with more or less emphasis, Nu 3⁴⁶, 5¹⁰, 35⁶, Ju 20⁴⁴·⁴⁶, Ez 17²¹, 20¹⁶, 35¹⁰, 44³, Neh 9¹⁹·³⁴, Dn 9¹³, 2 Ch 31¹⁷.—In Ez 47¹⁷⁻¹⁹ (cf. also 43⁷) it is simplest to emend וְזֹאת for אֶת־, according to verse 20. However, even the LXX, who have ταῦτα only in verse 18, càn hardly have known any other reading than אֵת ; consequently in all these passages אֵת must be regarded as virtually dependent on some governing word, such as *ecce* (LXX 43⁷ ἑώρακας), and 47¹⁷ᶠ· as equivalent to *thou shalt have* as a border, &c.

n 8. Another solecism of the later period is finally the introduction of the object by the preposition לְ (prop. *in relation to, in the direction of*), as sometimes in Ethiopic[1] and very commonly in Aramaic.[2] Less remarkable is this looser connexion of the object with a participle, as with אֹכַל La 4⁵, אֹסֵף Nu 10²⁵, זָקֵף ψ 145¹⁴ (but cf. 146⁸), צָרַר Nu 25¹⁸, הַשְׁגִּיא and שֹׁמֵט Jb 12²³ ; *before* the participle Is 11⁹.—To introduce an object *preceding* the finite verb לְ is employed in Jb 5² (cf. also Dn 11³¹); also *after* אָהֵב Lv 19¹⁸·³⁴; הַאֲרִיךְ ψ 129³ ; הַבְדִּיל Ezr 8²⁴, 2 Ch 25¹⁰ ; הֵבִין Jb 9¹¹ ; בֵּרַךְ 1 Ch 29²⁰ (immediately before with an accusative), 136¹⁹ᶠ·; הִגְלָה 1 Ch 5²⁶ ; דָּרַשׁ Ezr 6²¹, 1 Ch 22¹⁹, 2 Ch 17¹³ ; הֶחֱיָה Gn 45⁷, where, however, read פְּלֵיטָה with the LXX for לִפְלֵיטָה and take לָכֶם as a *dativus commodi* ; הִלֵּל 1 Ch 16³⁶, 2 Ch 5¹³ ; הָרַג 2 S 3³⁰, ψ 135¹¹ (verse 10 with accusative), 136¹⁹ᶠ·; חָבַשׁ (*to bind up*) Is 61¹ (Ez 34⁴ *before* the verb) ; יָדַע ψ 69⁶ ; כָּבֵד ψ 86⁹; לָקַח Jer 40², 2 Ch 23¹ ; הִמְלִיךְ and מָשַׁח 1 Ch 29²² ; נָהַל 2 Ch 28¹⁵ ; סָמַךְ ψ 145¹⁴; עָזַב 1 Ch 16³⁷; הֶעֱלָה Ez 26³ ; פָּתַח ψ 116¹⁶; רָדַף Jb 19²⁸ ; הַצְּדִיק Is 53¹¹ ; שָׁבַר 2 Ch 24¹² (previously accusatives) ; שִׂים 1 S 22⁷ (but probably וְכִלְּכֶם is to be read) ; הֵשִׁיב (in the connexion,לְ דָבָר הֵשִׁיב) 2 Ch 10⁶ (but verse 9 and 1 K 12⁹ with an accusative) ; שָׁחַת Nu 32¹⁵, 1 S 23¹⁰ ; שִׁית ψ 73¹⁸ ; שָׁלַח Ezr 8¹⁶, 2 Ch 2¹², 17⁷; שָׁמַר 1 Ch 29¹⁸, 2 Ch 5¹¹.

o 9. Sometimes the verb, on which an accusative of the object really depends, is contained only in sense in the verb which apparently governs, e.g. Is 14¹⁷ אֲסִירָיו לֹא־פָתַח בֵּיתָה *his prisoners he let not loose* nor sent them back *to their home*. On this *constructio praegnans* in general, see § 119.*ff.*

p **2.** With the proper accusatives of the object may also be classed what is called the *internal* or *absolute object* (also named *schema etymologicum* or *figura etymologica*), i.e. the addition of an object in the form

---

derived from a text which read the Hiph'îl instead of נָפַל. In Jer 23³³ instead of the artificial explanation *what a burden* (is, do ye ask ?) we should read with the LXX and Vulg. אַתֶּם הַמַּשָּׂא *ye are the burden*. In Ez 10²² מַרְאֵיהֶם וְאוֹתָם is unintelligible; in 37¹⁹ read with Hitzig אֶל־ for את ; in Hag 2¹⁷ for אתכם read with the LXX שְׁבֶכֶם [or אֶינְכֶם ; for the לְ cf. 2 K 6¹¹, Jer 15¹, Ez 36⁹].

[1] Dillmann, *Grammatik der äthiopischen Sprache*, p. 349.

[2] With regard to Biblical Aramaic, see Kautzsch's *Grammatik des Bibl.-Aram.*, p. 151 f. In other ways, also, a tendency may be observed in later Hebrew to make use of the looser connexion by means of prepositions instead of the closer subordination of the noun in the accusative.

of a noun derived from the same stem,[1] e.g. ψ 14⁵ פָּחַד פָּֽחֲדוּ *they feared a fear* (i.e. they were in great fear), Pr 15²⁷; also with the object preceding, e.g. La 1⁸ חֵטְא חָטְאָה יְרוּשָׁלַ͏ִם *Jerusalem hath sinned a sin*; with a double accusative (see below, *cc*), e.g. 1 K 1¹² אִיעָצֵךְ נָא עֵצָה *let me, I pray thee, give thee counsel*; 1 K 1¹².[2]

Rem. (*a*) Strictly speaking the only cases of this kind are those in which *q* the verbal idea is supplemented by means of an *indeterminate* substantive (see the examples above). Such a substantive, except in the case of the addition of the internal object to denominative verbs (see below), is, like the infinitive absolute, never altogether without force, but rather serves like it to strengthen the verbal idea. This strengthening is implied in the indeterminateness of the internal object, analogous to such exclamations as, *this was a man!* [3] Hence it is intelligible that some intensifying attribute is very frequently (as in Greek usually) added to the internal object, e.g. Gn 27³⁴ וַיִּצְעַק צְעָקָה גְדֹלָה וּמָרָה עַד־מְאֹד *he cried* (with) *an exceeding great and bitter cry*; cf. the Greek νοσεῖν νόσον κακήν, ἐχάρησαν χαρὰν μεγάλην (Matt. 2¹⁰); *magnam pugnare pugnam, tutiorem vitam vivere,* &c.

Examples of an internal object *after* the verb, and without further addition, are Ex 22⁵, 2 S 12¹⁶, Is 24²², 35², 42¹⁷, Ez 25¹⁵, 26¹⁵, 27³⁵, Mic 4⁹, Zc 1², Pr 21²⁶; with an intensifying attribute, Gn 27³³, Ex 32³¹, Ju 15⁸, 2 S 13³⁶, 1 K 1⁴⁰ (cf. Jon 4⁶, 1 Ch 29⁹); Is 21⁷, 45¹⁷, Jon 1¹⁰, Zc 1¹⁴, 8²ᵃ, Dn 11³; along with an object proper the internal object occurs with an attribute in Gn 12¹⁷, 2 S 13¹⁵; cf. also Is 14⁶, Jon 4¹.—An internal object without an attribute *before* the verb: Is 24¹⁶, Jer 46⁵, Hb 3⁹, Jb 27¹²; with an attribute *before* the verb: Jer 14¹⁷, Zc 1¹⁵ (cf. also Gn 30⁸, Jer 22¹⁹, 30¹⁴, ψ 139²²). Instead of the substantive which would naturally be expected, another of kindred meaning is used in Zc 8².

(*b*) Only in a wider sense can the *schema etymologicum* be made to include *r* cases in which the denominative verb is used in connexion with the noun from which it is derived, e.g. Gn 1¹¹, 9¹⁴, 11³, 37⁷, Ez 18², ψ 144⁶, probably also Mi 2⁴, or where this substantive, made determinate in some way, follows its verb, e.g. Gn 30³⁷, Nu 25¹¹, 2 K 4¹³, 13¹⁴, Is 45¹⁷, La 3⁵⁸, [4] and, determinate at least in sense, Jer 22¹⁶; or precedes it, as in 2 K 2¹⁶, Is 8¹², 62⁵, Zc 3⁷; cf. also Ex 3⁹. In both cases the substantive is used, without any special emphasis, merely for clearness or as a more convenient way of connecting the verb with other members of the sentence.

3. Verbs which denote *speaking* (*crying out, weeping*), or any *s* external act, frequently take a direct accusative of the organ or means by which the action is performed. In this case, however, the accusative must be more closely determined by an attributive adjective or a noun in the genitive. This fact shows the close relation between these accusatives and the *internal objects* treated under *p*, which also,

---

[1] On a kindred use of the infinitive absolute as an *internal object*, see above, § 113 *w*.

[2] Cf. βουλὰς βουλεύειν, Iliad x. 147.

[3] The Arab grammarians assign to the indeterminate cases generally an intensive sense in many instances; hence the commentators on the Qorān usually explain such cases by adding *and what . . . !* see § 125 *b*.

[4] Also in ψ 13⁴ *lest I sleep the* sleep *of death*, הַמָּוֶת is only used pregnantly for שְׁנַת הַמָּוֶת (cf. Jer 51³⁹), as צְדָקוֹת Is 33¹⁵ for דֶּרֶךְ צְדָקוֹת. On the similar use of הָלַךְ תָּמִים in ψ 15², see § 118 *n*.

according to *q*, mostly take an intensifying attribute. On the other hand, they must not be regarded as adverbial (instrumental) accusatives, nor are they to be classed with the second (neuter) subjects treated below in § 144 *l*.

t Examples of the accusative following the verb are וַיִּזְעַק קוֹל־גָּדוֹל *and I cried a loud voice*, i. e. with a loud voice, Ez 11¹³, 2 S 15²³ (after the proper object, Dt 5¹⁹, 1 K 8⁵⁵) ; ψ 109² *they have spoken unto me* לְשׁוֹן שֶׁקֶר *a tongue of deceit*, i. e. with a lying tongue ; Pr 10⁴ *he becometh poor* עֹשֶׂה כַף־רְמִיָּה *dealing a slack hand*, i. e. who dealeth with a slack hand ; cf. the German *eine schöne Stimme singen*, to sing a fine voice, *eine tüchtige Klinge schlagen*, to smite a trusty sword, *Schlittschuhe laufen*, to run skates (i. e. to skate), and our *to write a good hand, to play ball*, &c.—Examples of the accusative preceding are שְׂפָתֵי רְנָנוֹת יְהַלֶּל־פִּי *my mouth shall praise* with *joyful lips*, ψ 63⁶ ; cf. ψ 12³, where a *casus instrumenti* with בְּ follows the accusative.

u 4. Many verbs originally intransitive (sometimes even in form ; see *a*, note 2) may be used also as transitives, in consequence of a certain modification of their original meaning, which has gradually become established by usage ; cf. e. g. רִיב *to strive*, but also with an accusative *causam alicuius agere* (so even in Is 1¹⁷, &c.; elsewhere with לְ of the person for whom one strives) ; יָכֹל absolutely *to be able*, with an accusative *to prevail over* any one ; חָפֵץ *to be inclined* and רָצָה *to have pleasure* (usually with בְּ), with an accusative *to wish for some one* or *something* ; שָׁכַב *cubare*, then in the sense of *concumbere*, originally joined with עִם *cum*, but quite early also with the accusative, equivalent to *comprimere* (*feminam*), &c. So in 2 S 13¹⁴, &c., unless in all or some of the passages the preposition אֵת is intended, e. g. אֹתָהּ for אִתָּהּ ; in the earlier passages עִם־ is the more usual.

v Rem. 1. It is certainly difficult to decide whether some verbs, which were afterwards used absolutely or joined with prepositions, were not nevertheless originally *transitive*, and consequently it is only the supposed original meaning, usually assigned to them in English, which causes them to appear *intransitive*.[1] In that case there is of course no syntactical peculiarity to be considered, and a list of such verbs would at the most be requisite only for practical purposes. Moreover, it is also possible that certain verbs were originally in use at the same time both as transitive and intransitive, e. g. perhaps לָבֵשׁ *to be clothed* along with לָבַשׁ *to put on* (a garment). Finally, the analogy of certain transitives in constant use may have led to intransitives of kindred meaning being also united directly with the accusative, so that, in other words, whole classes of verbs came to be regarded in a particular aspect as transitives. See below, *y*.

---

[1] Thus e. g. עָנָה *to reply to* (ἀμείβεσθαί τινα), *to answer any one* ; צָוָה *to command* (iubere aliquem) ; זָכַר *to remember* ; קָוָה (also with לְ) *to wait for any one* (to expect any one) ; בִּשַּׂר *to bring glad tidings to any one* (see the Lexicon) ; נָאַף and נָאַף *to commit adultery* (adulterare matronam) ; עָבַד *to serve* (colere) ; עָרַב *to become surety for* . . ., and many others.

2. The modification of the original meaning becomes especially evident *w* when even reflexive conjugations (*Niph'al, Hithpa'ēl,* &c.) take an accusative (cf. § 57, note 2); e.g. נִבָּא *to prophesy,* Jer 25¹³; נָסַב (prop. *to put oneself round*) *to surround,* Ju 19²²; נִלְחַם *to fight,* ψ 109³ (where, however, the Qal וַיִּלָּחֲמוּנִי should be read; cf. ψ 35¹); also הִתְגַּלַּח *to shave* (something) *for oneself,* Num 6¹⁹; הִתְנַחֵל *to take* some one *for oneself as a possession,* Is 14²; הִתְנַכֵּל *to make* some one *an object of craft,* Gn 37¹⁸; הִתְנַצֵּל *to strip* a thing *off oneself,* Ex 33⁶; הִתְעַבֵּר *to bring on oneself the anger* of any one, *to anger* him; הִתְבּוֹנֵן *to consider* something, Jb 37¹⁴; הִתְפָּרֵק *to break* something *off from oneself,* Ex 32³. In Gn 34⁹ after הִתְחַתְּנוּ *make ye marriages,* read אִתָּנוּ instead of אֹתָנוּ. Cf. § 54 *f.*

3. So also it is only owing to a modification of the original meaning of *x* a verb (except where the expression is incorrect, and perhaps derived from the popular language), when sometimes the remoter object (otherwise introduced by לְ) is directly subordinated in the form of an accusative suffix, e.g. Zc 7⁵ הֲצוֹם צַמְתֻּנִי אָנִי *did ye fast at all unto me, even to me?* as though to say, have ye *be-fasted* me? have ye reached me with your fasting? Still more strange is Jb 31¹⁸ גְּדֵלַנִי כְאָב *he* (the orphan) *grew up to me as to a father;* cf. Is 27⁴, 65⁵, Jer 31³, and in Aramaic Dn 5⁶; but אֶרֶץ הַנֶּגֶב נְתַתָּנִי Jos 15¹⁹ is to be regarded as a double accusative after a verb of *giving,* see *ff.* In 1 S 2²⁵ read וּפִלְלוּ for וּפִלְלוֹ; in Is 44²¹, instead of the Niph'al, read תִּנָּשֵׁנִי; in Ez 29³ either עֲשִׂיתִיו is to be read with Olshausen or עֲשִׂיתִים (and previously יְאֹרִי) with Smend; in ψ 42⁵ אֶדַּדֵּם or אַדַּדֵם; in ψ 55²³ (where König takes יְהָבְךָ as *he has given it to thee*) we must certainly assume a substantive יְהָב (= *fate?*).

4. Whole classes of verbs, which, according to *v* above, are regarded as *y* transitive, either on account of their original meaning or (for the sake of analogy) by a modification of that meaning, are—

(*a*) Verba *induendi* and *exuendi,* as לָבֵשׁ *to put on,* פָּשַׁט *to put off* a garment, עָדָה *to put on* ornaments, *to adorn oneself with* (cf. also זָהָב מִשְׁבְּצִים *enclosed in gold,* Ex 28²⁰). Also in poetic expressions such as ψ 65¹⁴ לָבְשׁוּ כָרִים הַצֹּאן *the pastures are clothed with flocks,* cf. ψ 109²⁹; 104² (עָטָה); 65¹⁴ᵇ (עָטַף), &c.[1]

(*b*) Verba *copiae* and *inopiae* (also called verba *abundandi* and *deficiendi*), as *z* מָלֵא, *to be full of* something, Ex 8¹⁷; here, and also frequently elsewhere, construed with אֶת־, and hence evidently with an accusative; Gn 6¹³; with a personal object, Ex 15⁹ *my lust shall be satisfied upon them;* with an accusative *preceding* the verb for the sake of emphasis, e.g. Is 1¹⁵ *your hands* דְּמִים מָלֵאוּ *are full of blood,* cf. Is 22²; so also the *Niph.* נִמְלָא *to fill oneself with* something, e.g. Gn 6¹¹, Ex 1⁷ (where the object is connected by אֵת); Is 2⁷ᶠ, 6⁴, Pr 3¹⁰; נִזְרַע *to be fructified with,* Nu 5²⁸; שָׁרַץ *to swarm with,* Gn 1²⁰·²¹ Ex 7²⁸; שָׂבַע (שָׂבֵעַ) *to be full of,* Is 1¹¹, Jo 2¹⁹, Pr 12¹¹; גָּבַר *to become strong, to wax mighty in* something, Jb 21⁷; פָּרַץ *to overflow with* something, Pr 3¹⁰ (with the object preceding); יָרַד prop. *to descend,* poetically also *to pour down, to overflow with* something (cf. in Greek προρέειν ὕδωρ, δάκρυα στάζειν), e.g. La 3⁴⁸ פַּלְגֵי מַיִם תֵּרַד עֵינִי *mine eye runneth*

---

[1] From the idea of *covering oneself with* something, we might also, if necessary, explain Ex 30²⁰ יִרְחֲצוּ מַיִם *they shall wash themselves with water;* but the reading is simply to be emended to the ordinary בַּמַּיִם.

down (*with*) *rivers of water*; 1¹⁶, Jer 9¹⁷, 13¹⁷, ψ 119¹³⁶; so also הָלַךְ *to run over with, to flow with*, Jo 4¹⁸; נָזַל *to gush out with*, Jer 9¹⁷; נָטַף *to drop, to overflow with*, Ju 5⁴, Jo 4¹⁸ᵃ; פָּרַח *to break forth*, Ex 9⁹; שָׁטַף *to overflow*, but also (transitively) *to overflow with*, probably in Is 10²²; נוּב *to bud with*, Pr 10³¹; so perhaps also עָבַר *to pass over, to overflow with*, Jer 5²⁸; יָצָא *to go forth with*, Am 5³.—Especially bold, but still on the analogy of the above examples, is Is 5⁶, where it is said of a vineyard וְעָלָה שָׁמִיר וָשַׁיִת *but it shall come up* (it shall be overgrown) *with briers and thorns*; cf. Pr 24³¹, and still more boldly, Is 34¹³.

aa   With the opposite idea, חָסֵר *to be in want of, to lack*, Gn 18²⁸; שָׁכַל *to be bereaved of* (as though it were *to lose*), Gn 27⁴⁵.—In Jos 22¹⁷ even הַמְעַט־לָנוּ (prop. *was there too little for us of* . . . ?) as being equivalent to a verbum inopiae (= *had we too little of* . . . ?) is construed with an accusative; cf. Neh 9³².

bb   (*c*) Several verbs of *dwelling*; the accusative in this case expresses either the place or the thing *at* which or *with* which any one tarries; thus Gn 4²⁰, ψ 22⁴ after יָשַׁב, cf. § 118 *g*; Ju 5¹⁷, Is 33¹⁴ after גּוּר; ψ 57⁵ after שָׁכַב; ψ 68⁷, Pr 8¹², Is 33¹⁶ with שָׁכַן; or even the person (the people) with whom any one dwells or is a guest, as ψ 5⁵, 120⁵ after גּוּר, Gn 30²⁰ after זָבַל, ψ 68¹⁹ with שָׁכַן.

cc   **5.** *Two accusatives* (usually one of the person and one of the thing) are governed by—

     (*a*) The causative conjugations (*Piʿēl, Hiphʿîl*, sometimes also *Pilpel*, e.g. כִּלְכֵּל Gn 47¹², &c.) of verbs which are simply transitive in *Qal*, and hence also of *verba induendi* and *exuendi*, &c. (cf. above *a* and *u*, and also *y, z*), e.g. Ex 33¹⁸ הַרְאֵנִי נָא אֶת־כְּבֹדֶךָ *show me, I pray thee, thy glory*. Thus very frequently הוֹדִיעַ *to cause* some one *to know* something; לִמַּד *docere aliquem aliquid*, &c.; cf. further, Gn 41⁴² וַיַּלְבֵּשׁ אֹתוֹ בִגְדֵי־שֵׁשׁ *and he caused him to put on vestures of fine linen* (*he arrayed him in vestures*, &c.); cf. in the opposite sense, Gn 37²³ (both accusatives after הִפְשִׁיט introduced by אֵת); so with מִלֵּא *to fill, to fill up with something*, Gn 21¹⁹, 26¹⁵, Ex 28³; אָזַר *to gird* some one *with something*, ψ 18³³; עִטֵּר *to crown*, ψ 8⁶, &c.; חִסֵּר *to cause* some one *to lack something*, ψ 8⁶; הֶאֱכִיל *to feed* some one *with something*, Ex 16³²; הִשְׁקָה *to make* some one *drink something*, Gn 19³² ᶠᶠ.

dd   (*b*) Many verbs (even in *Qal*) which express an influence upon the object through some external means. The latter, in this case, is attached as a second object. They are especially—

ee   (*a*) Verbs which express *covering, clothing, overlaying*, חָגַר Ex 29⁹, צִפָּה Ex 26²⁹, &c., טוּחַ Ez 13¹⁰ ᶠᶠ., עָטַר ψ 5¹³; cf. also אֶבֶן רָגַם Jos 7²⁵, &c.; hence also verbs which express *sowing* (זָרַע Jud 9⁴⁵, Is 17¹⁰, 30²³), *planting* (Is 5²), *anointing* (ψ 45⁸) *with anything*.

ff   (*β*) Expressions of *giving*, thus נָתַן Jos 15¹⁹ where the accusative of the thing precedes; *endowing*, זָבַד Gn 30²⁰; and its opposite *taking away*, as קָבַע Pr 22²³; בֵּרַךְ *to bless some one with something*, Gn 49²⁵, Dt 15¹⁴; *to give graciously*, חָנַן Gn 33⁵; *to sustain* (i.e. to support, to maintain, to furnish) *with anything*, e.g. Gn 27³⁷, ψ 51¹⁴ (סָמַךְ); Ju 19⁵ (סָעַד); *to do something to one,* גָּמַל Gn 50¹⁵·¹⁷, 1 S 24¹⁸; cf. also קִדֵּם *to come to meet any one with* something, ψ 21⁴, שָׁלֵּם *to repay some one with* something (with two accusatives, ψ 35¹², Pr 13²¹), and for the accusative of the person cf. εὖ, κακῶς πράττειν τινά. In a wider sense we may also include such phrases as *they hunt every man his brother with a net,* Mi 7²; *to shoot at one with arrows,* ψ 64⁸ (though this is against the accents); Pr 13²⁴ *seeks him early* (with) *discipline,* i.e. *chastises him betimes,* &c.

(γ) Expressions of *asking* some one *for* something, *desiring* something *from* some one (שָׁאַל Dt 14²⁶, ψ 137³); *answering* any one anything (עָנָה Mi 6⁵, &c.; cf. in the other conjugations הֵשִׁיב דָּבָר prop. *verbum reddere,* with an accusative of the person, 1 K 12⁶, &c., also in the sense of *announcing*; sometimes also הִגִּיד *to declare* something *to* some one, Jb 26⁴, &c., for הִגִּיד לְ); צִוָּה *to enjoin* a person something, Ex 34³², Dt 1¹⁸, 3²⁴⁶, Jer 7²³.

(δ) Expressions which mean *to make, to form, to build* something *out of* something; in such cases, besides the accusative of the object proper, another accusative is used for the material of which the thing is made, e.g. Gn 2⁷ וַיִּיצֶר יְהוָה אֱלֹהִים אֶת־הָאָדָם עָפָר מִן־הָאֲדָמָה *and the Lord formed man of the dust of the ground*; so with יָצַר also in 1 K 7¹⁵; further Ex 38³ כָּל־כֵּלָיו עָשָׂה נְחֹשֶׁת *all the vessels thereof made he of brass* (for another explanation of the accusative נְחֹשֶׁת [*into brass*], linguistically possible but excluded by the context, see below, *ii* with *kk*); cf. Ex 25¹⁸·²⁸, 26¹·¹⁴ ᶠ·²⁹, 27¹, 36⁸, 1 K 7²⁷; with a preceding accusative of the material, Ex 25²⁹, 29², Dt 27⁶ אֲבָנִים שְׁלֵמוֹת תִּבְנֶה אֶת־מִזְבַּח יְהוָה *of unhewn stones shalt thou build the altar of the Lord.*

(c) Verbs which express *making, preparing, forming into* anything, along with the object proper, take a second accusative of the product, e.g. Gn 27⁹ אֶעֱשֶׂה אֹתָם מַטְעַמִּים *I will make them* (the kids) *into savoury meat*; cf. Gn 6¹⁴·¹⁶, Ex 26¹ᵇ, 30²⁵, 32⁴, Is 44¹⁵, Ho 8⁴, 1 K 18³² וַיִּבְנֶה אֶת־הָאֲבָנִים מִזְבֵּחַ *and he built the stones* (into) *an altar*; cf. 10¹². So also אָפָה, with two accusatives, *to bake* something *into* something, Ex 12³⁹, Lv 24⁵; שִׂים (prop. *to set up for* something, cf. Gn 27³⁷, 28¹⁸, ψ 39⁹, and similarly הֵרִים Gn 31⁴⁵) *to change into* something, Jos 8²⁸, Is 50², 51¹⁰, Mi 1⁷, 4¹³; with two accusatives of the person (*to appoint, promote* any one to the position of a . . .), Is 3⁷; נָתַן is also used in the same sense with two accusatives, Gn 17⁵, and שִׂית 1 K 11³⁴; as a rule, however, the description of the office, and also frequently of the product, is introduced by לְ *to,* § 119 *t*; also שִׂית *to make a thing so and so* (Is 5⁶, 26¹; with a personal object, ψ 21⁷, ¹ 91⁹); הֶחֱשִׁיךְ *to make dark,* Am 5⁸. Of the same class also are instances like Jb 28² אֶבֶן יָצוּק נְחוּשָׁה *a stone they smelt into brass*; 1 K 11³⁰ וַיִּקְרָעֶהָ שְׁנֵים עָשָׂר קְרָעִים *and rent it* (the garment) *into twelve pieces*; cf. Is 37²⁶, accusative of the product before the object proper, after לְהַשְׁאוֹת *to lay waste.*

---

¹ Cf. a very pregnant expression of this kind in ψ 21¹³ כִּי תְשִׁיתֵמוֹ שֶׁכֶם *for thou shalt make them* (as) *a neck,* i.e. *thou shalt cause them to turn their necks* (backs) *to me*; similarly ψ 18⁴¹ (2 S 22⁴¹, Ex 23²⁷); אֹיְבַי נָתַתָּה לִּי עֹרֶף *thou hast given mine enemies unto me as a back*; cf. Jer 18¹⁷.

On a second object with *verba sentiendi* (as יָדַע *to know* something *to be* something, Ec 7²⁵; רָאָה *to see, find to be,* Gn 7¹; חָשַׁב *to esteem* one *to be* something, Is 53⁴, elsewhere always construed with לְ or כְּ), cf. *h.*

kk Rem. At first sight some of the examples given above appear to be identical in character with those treated under *hh*; thus it is possible, e. g. in 1 K 18³², by a translation which equally suits the sense, *he built from the stones an altar,* to explain מִזְבֵּחַ as the nearer object and אֶת־הָאֲבָנִים as an accusative of the material, and the construction would then be exactly the same as in Dt 27⁶. In reality, however, the fundamental idea is by no means the same. Not that in the living language an accusative of the material in the one case, and in the other an accusative of the product were consciously distinguished. As Driver (*Tenses,* § 195) rightly observes, the remoter accusative in both cases is, strictly speaking, in apposition to the nearer. This is especially evident in such examples as Ex 20²⁵ *thou shalt not build them* (the stones of the altar) גָּזִית as *hewn stones,* cf. also Gn 1²⁷. The main point is, which of the two accusatives, as being primarily affected (or aimed at) by the action, is to be made the more prominent; and on this point neither the position of the words (the nearer object, mostly determinate, as a rule follows immediately after the verb), nor even the context admits of much doubt. Thus in 1 K 18³² the treatment of the stones is the primary object in view, the erection of the altar for which they were intended is the secondary; in Dt 27⁶ the case is reversed.

ll (*d*) Finally, the second accusative sometimes more closely determines the nearer object by indicating the part or member specially affected by the action,[1] e. g. ψ 3⁸ *for thou hast smitten all mine enemies* לְחִי (as to) *the cheek bone,* equivalent to *upon the cheek bone*; cf. Gn 37²¹ *let us not smite him* נֶפֶשׁ in *the life,* i. e. let us not kill him; Dt 22²⁶, 2 S 3²⁷; also with שׁוּף Gn 3¹⁵; with רָעָה Jer 2¹⁶; in poetry the object specially concerned is, by a bold construction, even placed first, Dt 33¹¹ (with מָחַץ).

§ 118. *The Looser Subordination of the Accusative to the Verb.*

a 1. The various forms of the looser subordination of a noun to the verb are distinguished from the different kinds of the accusative of the object (§ 117) by their specifying not the persons or things directly affected by the action, but some *more immediate circumstance* under which an action or an event takes place. Of such circumstances the most common are those of *place, time, measure, cause,* and finally the *manner* of performing the action. These nearer definitions are, as a rule, placed *after* the verb; they may, however, also precede it.

b Rem. That the cases thus loosely subordinated to the verb are to be regarded as *accusatives* is seen first from the fact that in certain instances the *nota accusativi* (את) is prefixed; secondly from the fact that in one form of

---

[1] Analogous to this is the σχῆμα καθ' ὅλον καὶ κατὰ μέρος in Greek epic poetry, e. g. ποῖόν σε ἔπος φύγε ἕρκος ὀδόντων.

the *casus loci* a termination (הָ‎‗) is employed, in which (according to § 90 c) the old accusatival ending is preserved ; and finally from the consistency with which classical Arabic puts these nearer definitions in the accusative (which may be recognized by its form) even under circumstances in which one would be rather inclined to expect a nominative in apposition.

The relation subsisting ˏbetween the circumstantial accusative and the *C* accusative of the object is especially apparent when the former (as e.g. in a statement of the goal after a verb of motion) is immediately connected with its verb. But even the more loosely connected circumstantial definitions are certainly to be regarded as originally objects of a governing word habitually omitted, only that the consciousness of this closer government was at length lost, and the accusative more and more acquired an independent value as a *casus adverbialis*.

2. The accusative serves to define more precisely the *place* (*accus.* *d* *loci*), either (*a*) in answer to the question *whither ?* after verbs of motion,[1] or (*b*) in answer to the question *where ?* after verbs of *being, dwelling, resting,* &c. (but also after transitive verbs, see the examples), or finally (*c*) to define more precisely the *extent* in space, in answer to the question *how far ? how high ? how much ?*, &c.

Instead of the simple accusative, the locative (see above, § 90 c)[2] is fre- *e* quently found in the cases mentioned under *f* (sometimes also in those under *g*) or the preposition אֶל‎-,[3] especially before persons as the aim of the movement, or בְּ‎, usually, to express being *at* a place.

Examples of (*a*) : נֵצֵא הַשָּׂדֶה‎ *let us go out into the field,* 1 S 20¹¹ ; cf. Gn 27³, 31⁴, *f* Jb 29⁷ ; לָלֶכֶת תַּרְשִׁישׁ‎ *to go to Tarshish,* 2 Ch 20³⁶ ; cf. Gn 10¹¹, 13⁹, 24²⁷, 26²³, 31²¹, Ex 4⁹, 17¹⁰, Ju 1²⁶, 2 K 11¹⁹, Na 1⁸ (?), ψ 134² ; with לָקַח‎ Nu 23¹⁴ ; with נָתַן‎ Jos 6²⁴ ; with the *accus. loci* emphatically preceding (cf. Driver on 1 S 5⁸), 1 K 2²⁶, Is 23¹², Jer 2¹⁰, 20⁶, 32⁵ ; with בּוֹא‎ (in the sense of *aggredi,* equivalent to בּוֹא‎ עַל‎-, cf. § 117 a, note 2) the *personal* aim also is poetically added in the accusative, Ez 32¹¹, 38¹¹, Pr 10²⁴, 28²², Jb 15²¹, 20²² ; but in the last passage it is better taken as an accusative of the object (cf. the German *einen ankommen, überkommen*). See also Nu 10³⁶ (where שׁוּב‎ can hardly be transitive) ; Ju 11²⁹, 1 S 13²⁰ (where, however, אֶל‎- has probably fallen out after יִשְׂרָאֵל‎ ; so Strack).—Finally, cf. also the use of אֲשֶׁר‎ for שָׁמָּה . . . אֲשֶׁר‎ *whither,* Nu 13²⁷.—The *accus. loci* occurs after a passive, e.g. Gn 12¹⁵.

Examples of (*b*) : Gn 38¹¹ *remain a widow* בֵית אָבִיךְ‎ *in thy father's house* ; cf. *g* Gn 24²³, 1 S 17¹⁵, 2 S 2³², Is 3⁶, Hos 12⁵, Mi 6¹⁰, 2 Ch 33²⁰ ; פֶּתַח הָאֹהֶל‎ *in the tent door,* Gn 18¹·¹⁰, 19¹¹, and frequently. As observed by Driver on 1 S 2²⁹, accusatives of this kind are almost without exception (but cf. 1 K 8³², Is 16², 28⁷, 2 Ch 33²⁰) connected with a noun in the genitive. In all the above examples, however, the accusative may have been preferred to the natural construction with בְּ‎ (which is not rare even with בֵּית‎ and פֶּתַח‎) for euphonic reasons, in order to avoid the combination of such sounds as בְּבֵ'‎ and בְּפֶ'‎ ; cf., moreover, Gn 2¹⁴, 4¹⁶, Ex 18⁵, Lv 6⁸ (הַמִּזְבֵּחַ‎ instead of the usual הַמִּזְבֵּחָה‎

---

[1] So commonly in Sanskrit ; in Greek only poetically, e. g. Iliad i. 317 κνίσῃ δ' οὐρανὸν ἷκεν : in Latin, e. g. *rus ire, Romam proficisci.*

[2] Hence e. g. in 1 S 9²⁶ the Masora requires הַגָּגָה‎ instead of the *Kͤth.* הַגָּג‎.

[3] So in Ju 19¹⁸ for י'‎ אֶת‎-בֵּית‎ the better reading is אֶל‎-בֵּ'‎.

Ex 29¹³, &c.); Dt 1². ¹⁹, ¹ 2 S 17²⁶, 1 K 7⁸, Pr 8³, 9¹⁴. On Is 1³⁰ see § 116 *i*; on יָשַׁב, with the accus. *loci*, see § 117 *bb*. On the other hand, in Dt 6³, according to the LXX, a verb of *giving* has dropped out before אֶרֶץ.

h Examples of (*c*): Gn 7²⁰ *fifteen cubits upward did the waters prevail*; Gn 31²³, 41⁴⁰ רַק הַכִּסֵּא אֶגְדַּל מִמֶּךָּ *only in the throne will I be greater than thou*; Dt 1¹⁹ *we went* (through) *all that great and terrible wilderness*; cf. Jb 29³. Of the same kind also are such cases as Ex 16¹⁶ (*according to the number of your persons*, for which elsewhere לְמִסְפַּר־ is used); 1 S 6⁴ (with the accus. preceding); 6¹⁸, 2 S 21²⁰, Jb 1⁵.—A statement of weight is put in the accusative in 2 S 14²⁶.

i 3. The accusative is employed to determine more precisely the *time* (*accus. temporis*), (*a*) in answer to the question *when ?* e.g. הַיּוֹם *the day*, i.e. *on the day* (in question), *at that time*, but also *on this day*, i.e. *to-day*, or finally *by day*, equivalent to יוֹמָם, like עֶרֶב *at evening*, לַיְלָה *noctu*, בֹּקֶר *in the morning, early*, ψ 5⁴, &c., צָהֳרַיִם *at noonday*, ψ 91⁶; יוֹם אֶחָד *on one and the same day*, Gn 27⁴⁵; שֵׁנָא *in sleep*, ψ 127²; תְּחִלַּת קְצִיר שְׂעֹרִים (Qᵉrê בְּתְ) *at the beginning of barley harvest*, 2 S 21⁹; in stating a date, Gn 11¹⁰, 14⁴ *in the thirteenth year*.

k (*b*) In answer to the question *how long ?* e.g. Gn 3¹⁴, &c., כָּל־יְמֵי חַיֶּיךָ *all the days of thy life*; 7⁴ *forty days and forty nights*; 7²⁴, 14⁴, 15¹³, 21³⁴, 29¹⁸, Ex 20⁹ (*for six days*); 23¹⁵, 31¹⁷; עוֹלָמִים *for ever*, 1 K 8¹³; also with the accusative made determinate, Ex 13⁷ אֵת שִׁבְעַת הַיָּמִים *throughout the seven days* in question, mentioned immediately before; cf. Ju 14¹⁷, Dt 9²⁵.

l 4. The accusative is sometimes used of abstract ideas to state the reason (*accus. causae*), e.g. Is 7²⁵ *thou shalt not come thither* יִרְאַת שָׁמִיר *for fear of briers*.

m 5. Finally the accusative is used very variously (as an *accus. adverbialis* in the narrower sense), in order to describe more precisely the *manner* in which an action or state takes place. In English such accusatives are mostly rendered by *in, with, as, in the form* or *manner of . . ., according to, in relation to, with regard to.* For more convenient classification we may distinguish them as—

n (*a*) Adjectives expressing *state*, placed *after* the verb to describe more accurately some bodily or other external condition, e.g. Is 20² *walking* עָרוֹם וְיָחֵף *naked and barefoot*; cf. verse 3, 8²¹, Gn 15², 33¹⁸ (שָׁלֵם), Ju 8⁴, Mi 1⁸, ψ 107⁵ (but in 15² תָּמִים is rather a substantive directly dependent on הוֹלֵךְ = *he that walketh in uprightness*; cf. § 117 *r*, note); Jb 30²⁸. After an accusative, e.g. Dt 15¹⁸; to specify some mental state, e.g. Gn 37³⁵ (אָבֵל).—*Before* the verb (and then with a certain emphasis), Am 2¹⁶, Jb 1²¹, Ec 5¹⁴; Lv 20²⁰, Jb 19²⁵, 27¹⁹, 31²⁶

---

¹ In ψ 2¹² דֶּרֶךְ is not to be taken as an *accus. loci* (*on the way*), but as an *accus. of respect* (*with regard to the way*); see below, *m*.

(unless יָקָר be a substantive); Ru 1²¹ (מְלֵאָה parallel with the adverb רֵיקָם).
In Mi 2⁷ the text is clearly corrupt.

Those examples are especially instructive in which the adjective expressing O
a state, although referring to several, is nevertheless used in the singular,
e.g. Jb 24¹⁰ עָרוֹם הִלְּכוּ *naked*, i.e. in the condition of one naked, *they go about*;
cf. verse 7 and 12¹⁷. In Is 20⁴ the singular occurs *after* a plural object, and
in Is 47⁵ the *masc.* after the 2nd sing. *fem.* imperative, which clearly proves
that the term expressing the state is not conceived as being in apposition,
but as an indeclinable adverb.

(*b*) Participles, again either *after* the verb, Nu 16²⁷, Jer 2²⁷, 43², ψ 7³, Jb 24⁵, p
Ct 2⁸, or *before* it, Gn 49¹¹, Is 57¹⁹, Ez 36³⁵, ψ 56², 92¹⁴, Pr 20¹⁴ ; cf. also the
substantival use of the participles Niph'al נוֹרָאוֹת *in a fearful manner* (ψ 139¹⁴)
and נִפְלָאוֹת *in a wonderful manner*, Jb 37⁵, Dn 8²⁴.—Also participles in connexion with genitives, as מִתְהַלֵּךְ Gn 3⁸ (cf. also בָּאָה 1 K 14⁶), are to be
regarded as expressing a state and not as being in apposition, since in the
latter case they would have to take the article.—In 2 S 13²⁰, 1 K 7⁷ and Hb 2¹⁰
the *explicative Wāw* (equivalent to *and that too*) is also prefixed to the
participle. In ψ 69⁴ for מְיַחֵל read מְיַחֵל.—On 1 K 11⁸, 2 K 10⁶, 19², Hag 1⁴,
cf. the note on § 131 *h*.

(*c*) Substantives[1] in the most varied relations : thus, as describing an q
external state, e.g. Mi 2³ וְלֹא תֵלְכוּ רוֹמָה *neither shall ye walk haughtily* (as
opposed to שָׁחוֹחַ Is 60¹⁴) ; Lv 6⁹ (accus. before the verb = as *unleavened cakes*),
Dt 2⁹, 4¹¹, Ju 5²¹, Is 57², Pr 7¹⁰, Jb 31²⁶, La 1⁹ ; as stating the position of a
disease, 1 K 15²³ *he was diseased* אֶת־רַגְלָיו in *his feet* (2 Ch 16¹² בְּרַגְלָיו), analogous
to the cases discussed in § 117 *ll* and § 121 *d* (*d*) ; as describing a spiritual,
mental, or moral state, e.g. Nu 32¹⁴, Jos 9² פֶּה אֶחָד *with one accord*, 1 K 22¹³ ;
cf. Ex 24³, Zp 3⁹), 1 S 15³², 2 S 23³, Is 41³ (unless שָׁלוֹם is adjectival, and the
passage is to be explained as in *n*); Jer 31⁷, Ho 12¹⁵, 14⁵, ψ 56⁸, 58², 75³, Pr 31⁹,
Jb 16⁹, La 1⁹ ; Lv 19¹⁶, &c., in the expression הָלַךְ רָכִיל *to go up and down* as
a tale-bearer ; also בְּטַח *unawares*, Gn 34²⁵, Ez 30⁹ ; מֵישָׁרִים *uprightly*, ψ 58², 75³
(in both places *before* the verb); as stating the age, e.g. 1 S 2³³ (if the text be
right) יָמוּתוּ אֲנָשִׁים *they shall die as men*, i.e. *in the prime of life* ; cf. 1 S 2¹⁸
(נַעַר), Is 65²⁰, and Gn 15¹⁶ ; as specifying a number more accurately, Dt 4²⁷,
1 S 13¹⁷, 2 K 5², Jer 31⁸ [in Jer 13¹⁹ שְׁלוֹמִים *wholly* (?) is corrupt; read גָּלוּת שְׁלֵמָה
with LXX for שׁ׳ הָגְלַת] ; as stating the consequence of the action, Lv 15¹³, &c.

The description of the external or internal state may follow, in poetry, in r
the form of a comparison with some well-known class, e.g. Is 21⁸ וַיִּקְרָא אַרְיֵה
and he cried as a lion; cf. ψ 22¹⁴, Is 22¹⁸ (כַּדּוּר *like a ball*) ; Is 24²², Zc 2⁸, ψ 11¹
(unless צִפּוֹר be vocative) ; 58⁹ᵇ (unless the force of the preceding כְּ is carried
on, as in ψ 90⁴) ; ψ 144¹², Jb 24⁵ פְּרָאִים, before the verb) ; 41⁷ *shut up together*
as with *a close seal*.[2]

6. To the expressions describing a state belong finally those nouns s
which are introduced by the comparative particle כְּ,[3] since the כְּ is to

---

[1] Cf. above, § 100 *c*, on certain substantives which have completely become
adverbs ; and § 113 *h* and *k* on the adverbial use of the infinitive absolute.

[2] It is, as a matter of fact, permissible to speak of the above examples as
comparatio decurtata, but it must not be assumed that the comparative particle
כְּ, which is otherwise regularly prefixed (see *s*), has actually dropped out.

[3] On the use of כְּ as a prefix, cf. § 102 *c*.

be regarded as originally a substantive [1] in the sense of *amount, kind* (*instar*), standing in the accusative (so that כְּ is equivalent to *as a kind of, after the manner of, according to*), while the following noun represents a genitive governed by the כְּ. From this, which is the proper meaning of the כְּ, may be explained its power of representing a great many pregnant relations, which in English can only be rendered by the help of prepositions.[2] Thus the comparison may refer to—

t (*a*) The *place*, e.g. Is. 5[17] כִּדְבָרָם *after the manner of*, i. e. *as in their pasture*; 23[15] *as* (it is said) *in the song of the harlot*; 28[21], 29[7] כַּחֲלוֹם *as in a dream*.

u (*b*) The *time*, especially in the combination כַּיּוֹם *after the manner of the day*, equivalent to *as in the day*, Is 9[3], Ho 2[5]; כִּימֵי *as in the days of*. . ., Is 51[9], Ho 2[17], 9[9], 12[10], Am 9[11]; cf. moreover, Lv 22[13], Ju 20[39], Is 17[6], Jb 5[14], 29[2], and the expressions כְּיוֹם בְּיוֹם *as day by day* = *as in the former days*, 1 S 18[10]; כְּפַעַם בְּפַעַם *as at other times*, 1 S 3[10], &c. ; כְּשָׁנָה בְשָׁנָה *as in former years*, 2 K 17[4]; cf. § 123 *c.* Of a different character is the use of כְּ as a simple particle of time, e.g. Gn 18[10] כָּעֵת חַיָּה *at this time* (not *about the time*), when it lives again, i. e. at the end of a year ; כָּעֵת מָחָר *to-morrow at this time* ; cf. Is 23[5], and the frequent connexion of כְּ with the infinitive construct to express a definite time (in the sense of a pluperfect), Gn 12[14], 27[34], Ex 9[29], &c.

v (*c*) The *person*, e.g. Gn 34[31] *should he deal with our sister as with a harlot?*

w (*d*) The *thing*, e. g. Is 10[14], ψ 33[7], Jb 28[5] כְּמוֹ־אֵשׁ *as a fire*, i. e. *as it were by fire* (cf. Is 1[25] כַּבֹּר *as with lye*) ; Jb 29[23] כַּמָּטָר *as for the rain* (they waited for me) ; Jb 38[14] (*as in a garment*) ; 38[30] כָּאֶבֶן *as to stone* (the waters are solidified in freezing).

x Rem. According to the earlier grammarians, כְּ is sometimes used pleonastically, i. e. not to indicate a similarity (as in Lv 14[35] *as it were*, i. e. *something like*), but simply to introduce the predicate (*Kaph veritatis*), e.g. Neh 7[2] *for he was* כְּאִישׁ אֱמֶת *a faithful man*; cf. 1 S 20[3] כְּפֶשַׂע, La 1[20] כַּמָּוֶת. Such a pleonasm is of course out of the question. At the most a *Kaph veritatis* can only be admitted in the sense that the comparison is sometimes introduced by כְּ with a certain emphasis (equivalent to *in every respect like*) ; thus כְּאִישׁ אֱמֶת in Neh 7[2] means simply *of the nature of a faithful man*, i. e. *as* only a faithful man can be; cf. Nu 11[1], Is 1[7], 13[6], Ho 4[4], 5[10], Ob 11, Jb 24[14], 27[7], La 1[20], 2[4]; also כִּמְעַט in such passages as ψ 105[12] *yea, very few*; but e. g. in Is 1[9] *only just, a very small* . . .

---

[1] Schwabe (כְּ *nach seinem Wesen und Gebrauch im alttestam. Kanon gewürdigt*, Halle, 1883) contests this explanation (which is defended especially by Fleischer and is certainly indisputable). He, with Gesenius and Ewald, places כְּ as a preposition on the same footing as בְּ and לְ, and believes it to be probably connected with the stem כֵּן as well as with כִּי and כֵּן. The above view of כְּ as a substantive of course does not imply that the language as we have it is still in every case conscious of the substantival meaning.—On כְּ in numerical statements, in the sense of *about, nearly*, see the Lexicon.

[2] It would be altogether unsuitable here also (see above, note 2 on *r*) to assume a loss of the preposition. Such examples as Is 1[26] כְּבָרִאשֹׁנָה and כְּבַתְּחִלָּה), Lv 26[37] (כְּמִפְּנֵי) are to be explained from the fact that here the

§ 119. *The Subordination of Nouns to the Verb by means of Prepositions.*

1. In general. As is the case with regard to the looser subordina- *a* tion of nouns to the verbal idea (§ 118), so also their subordination by means of prepositions is used to represent the more immediate circumstances (of place, time, cause, purpose, measure, association, or separation) under which an action or event is accomplished. In the case of most prepositions some idea of a relation of *space* underlies the construction, which then, in a wider sense, is extended to the ideas of time, motive, or other relations conceived by the mind.

On the origin of the prepositions and the original case-relation in which they stand to the nouns governed by them, cf. § 101, where a list of the prepositions is given with their original meanings. Cf. also § 102 on the prefixes, and § 103 on the union of prepositions with suffixes.

2. A not unimportant part is played in Hebrew by the *compounding* *b* of prepositions to represent more accurately the relations of place, which either precede or follow the action. In the former case מִן‎־, and in the latter (which is not so frequent) אֶל‎־ occurs before other prepositions of place; cf. e. g. Am 7¹⁵ *the Lord took me* מֵאַחֲרֵי הַצֹּאן‎ *from behind the flock*; 2 K 9¹⁸ *turn thee* אֶל‎־אַחֲרָי‎ *to behind me*, i.e. *turn thee behind me*; מֵעִם‎, מֵאֵת‎ *from being with* . . ., as in French *de chez, d'après quelqu'un.*[1] For further examples, see *c*.

Rem. 1. We must *not* regard as combined prepositions in the above sense *c* either those *substantives* which have become prepositions only by their union with prefixes, as לִפְנֵי‎ *before*, מִפְּנֵי‎, לְמַעַן‎ *on account of* (but e.g. מִלִּפְנֵי‎ *from before*, Gn 4¹⁶, &c., is such a compound); nor *adverbs*, which are also formed by combining words which were originally substantives (also used as prepositions) with prepositions, as מִחוּץ‎ *without*, מִתַּחַת‎ in the sense of *below*,[2] מֵעַל‎

preposition and substantive had already become simply *one* word before the בְּ‎ was prefixed. We find also בְּעַל‎ Is 59¹⁸, 63⁷, ψ 119¹⁴, and 2 Ch 32¹⁹; cf. Driver on 1 S 14¹⁴ (כְּבַבְצֵי‎), where the text is wholly corrupt.

[1] In other cases French, as well as English and German, can only emphasize *one* of the two combined ideas; thus, such expressions as *il prend le chapeau sur la table*, German and English *er nimmt den Hut vom Tisch, he takes his hat from the table*, all regard the action from one point of view only; the Hebrew here brings out both aspects of it by means of מֵעַל‎־ *from upon*, cf. e.g. Is 6⁶.

[2] Hence not to be confounded with מִתַּחַת‎ *from under*, in such examples as Pr 22²⁷, which is a real compound preposition. In the above-mentioned adverbs also the מִן‎־ was *originally* by no means pleonastic; מִתַּחַת‎ denotes properly the locality, regarded primarily as a place *from beneath* which something proceeds, and so on. This original sense of the מִן‎־, however, has become so much obscured by its regular combination with words of place to form independent adverbs, that it is even prefixed (evidently only on the analogy of such common adverbs as מֵעַל‎־, מִתַּחַת‎) in cases where it is really inadmissible, owing to the meaning of the adverb, e. g. in מִבַּלְעֲדֵי‎, מִלְּבַד‎

above (so also in Gn 27³⁹, 49²⁵, not *from above*). These adverbs of place, however, may become prepositions by the addition of לְ, e.g. מִחוּץ לְ *outside as regards* . . . , i.e. *outside of something*, in 1 K 21¹³ even after a transitive verb of motion ; מִתַּחַת לְ *below as regards* . . ., i.e. *under something* (cf. עַד־מִתַּחַת לְ *until they came under* . . ., 1 S 7¹¹), מֵעַל לְ *over something*, &c. ; לְבַד prop. *in separation* ; לְבַד מִן־ *in separation from*, i.e. *apart from, besides.* Only rarely in such a case is the לְ omitted for the sake of brevity, e.g. Jb 26⁵ מִתַּחַת מַיִם *beneath the waters* ; Neh 3²⁸ (מֵעַל־).

d 2. Real combinations of prepositions (each retaining its full force) occur—

(*a*) With מִן־, in מֵאַחַר, מֵאַחֲרֵי (see above) *from behind something* ; מֵאֵת and מֵעִם *from with* (see above) ; מִבֵּין or מִבֵּינוֹת *from between something* (with motion in either direction, see e.g. Gn 49¹⁰) ; מִלִּפְנֵי *from before* (see above) ; sometimes also מִמּוּל Lv 5⁸, &c. ; מֵעַל־ *from upon*, i.e. *off from* ; מִתַּחַת *away from under* (see footnote 2 on p. 377).

e (*b*) With אֶל־, in אֶל־אַחֲרֵי *to behind*, אֶל־בֵּינוֹת *to between* ; אֶל־מִבֵּית לְ *forth between* 2 K 11¹⁵, אֶל־מִחוּץ לְ *forth without*, i.e. *out in front of*, Nu 5³ ; אֶל־תַּחַת *down under.*[1]—In Jb 5⁵ the two prepositions of motion are combined in a peculiarly pregnant construction, אֶל־מִצִּנִּים (he goes thither and takes it) *out of the thorns*, i.e. he taketh it *even out of the thorns*, but the text is hardly correct.

f 3. A general view of the union of certain verbs, or whole classes of verbs, with particular prepositions, especially in explanation of certain idioms and pregnant expressions.[2]

g (*a*) אֶל־ (אֱלֵי)[3] *towards*, properly an expression of *motion* or at least *direction towards something* (either in the sense of *up to* = עַד, or *into* = אֶל־תּוֹךְ), is used after verbs not only in answer to the question *whither?* but by a specially pregnant construction, in answer to the question *where?* e.g. Jer 41¹² they

---

without, cf. also such examples as מְבַלִּי, מִמּוּל, מִנֶּגֶד, מִשָּׁם (*there*), &c. Since a מִן־ is not usually repeated after מִלְּבַד, it appears as if מִלְּבַד by a transposition of the מִן־ stood for the usual לְבַד מִן־. In reality, however, the preposition which forms the adverb into a preposition is omitted here, as in מִתַּחַת, מֵעַל, without a following לְ (see above). Properly מִלְּבַד has a purely adverbial meaning = *taken by itself*, like מִלְמַעְלָה מִמַּעַל (Syriac *men le'ēl*) *above* (adv.), as distinguished from מִמַּעַל לְ or מֵעַל־לְ (Syriac *le'ēl men*), *over, upon something.*—Also לְמִן־ *from . . . onward* is not for מִן־לְ, but the לְ serves merely (just like the Latin *usque* in *usque a, usque ad, usque ex*) to indicate expressly the starting-point, as an exact *terminus a quo* (of place or time).

[1] Also in 1 S 21⁵ אֶל־תַּחַת by a pregnant construction is virtually dependent on the idea of *coming into*, contained in the preceding אֵין־.

[2] A summary of *all* the relations and senses in which a preposition may be used, belongs not to the Grammar but to the Lexicon.

[3] Cf. Mitchell, 'The preposition *el*,' in the *Journal of the Society of Biblical Literature and Exegesis*, 1888, p. 143 ff., and especially A. Noordtzij, *Het hebreeuwsche voorzetsel* אֶל, Leiden, 1896, a thorough examination of its uses, and especially of the relation between אֶל־ and עַל־.

found him אֶל־מַיִם רַבִּים *by the great waters*; cf. Dt 16⁶, 1 K 13²⁰, and a still
more remarkable instance in 8³⁰ אֶל־מְקוֹם שִׁבְתְּךָ אֶל־הַשָּׁמַיִם. This combination of *two* different ideas, of motion *to* a place and being or acting *in* the place
(very plainly seen in Dt 16⁶ *but to the place which the Lord thy God shall choose...*
shalt thou bring thine offering and *there shalt thou sacrifice*, &c.), is the same
as the Greek use of εἰς, ἐς for ἐν, the Latin *in potestatem, in amicitiam ditionemque
esse, manere* (Cic. Verr. 5, 38 ; Div. 2, 14, &c.) ; cf. also the common German
expressions *zu* Hause, *zu* Leipzig sein, *zu* Bette liegen, &c.

(*b*) בְּ.[1] Underlying the very various uses of this preposition is either the *h*
idea of being or moving within some definite region, or some sphere of space
or time (with the infinitive, a simultaneous action, &c.), or else the idea of
fastening on something, *close connexion with* something (also in a metaphorical
sense, following some kind of pattern, e.g. the advice or command of some
one בִּדְבַר פ׳, בַּעֲצַת פ׳, or in a comparison, as in Gn 1²⁶ בְּצַלְמֵנוּ כִּדְמוּתֵנוּ *in
our image, after our likeness*; cf. 1²⁷, 5¹·³), or finally the idea of *relying* or *depending* upon . . ., or even of merely *striking* or *touching* something.

Thus the use of בְּ is explained— *i*

(1) In the sense of *among* (in the domain of), e.g. Mi 7² יָשָׁר בָּאָדָם אָיִן
there is none upright among men; in the sense of *consisting of*, in specifying the
constituents of a collective idea, e.g. Gn 7²¹ *and all flesh died . . . in* (=con-
sisting of) *fowl*, &c. 8¹⁷, 9¹⁰, Ho 4³. Also after ideas of *appearing, manifesting
oneself, representing, being*, in the sense of *as, in the capacity of* (prop. in the
sphere, after the manner of, see above), *consisting of . . ., tanquam*, the בְּ *essentiae*
of the earlier grammarians, corresponding to the Greek ἐν, the Latin *in*,[2] and
the French *en*, e.g. Ex 6³ *I appeared unto Abraham . . .* בְּאֵל שַׁדָּי *as El Shaddai*;
Jb 23¹³ וְהוּא בְאֶחָד *but he is* (manifests himself as) *one*, i.e. he remains always
the same; Dt 26⁵, 28⁶² בִּמְתֵי מְעָט *in the condition of being few*, cf. 10²² *to the
number of seventy*; Is 40¹⁰, ψ 39⁷.—Cf. also such examples as Ex 18⁴ (ψ 35², 146⁵)
בְּעֶזְרִי *as my help*; Dt 26¹⁴ *being unclean*; Is 28¹⁶ *in Sion* (i.e. *I make Sion a foundation*); Ez 20⁴¹ *as a sweet savour*; Pr 3²⁶, perhaps also Ex 3² *in* (i.e. *as*) *a flame
of fire*; Is 66¹⁵ *with* (i.e. *like*) *fire*; ψ 31²², 37²⁰ (102⁴). For the origin of all
these forms of expression ψ 54⁶ is especially instructive, since אֲדֹנָי בְּסֹמְכֵי נַפְשִׁי
is not meant to refer to the Lord as *belonging to* the סֹמְכִים, but only to ascribe
to him a similar character, i.e. *the Lord is one who upholds my soul*; so also
ψ 99⁶, 118⁷, Ju 11³⁵ [the plur. as in § 124 *g-i*].[3]—Cf. Gesenius, *Thes. Linguae
Hebr.*, i. 174 f., and Delitzsch on ψ 35².

(2) To introduce the object after transitive verbs, which denote *touching*, *k*
striking, reaching to (thus to some extent a fastening on, see above) something,
in English sometimes rendered by *at, on*, &c., and in German generally by
compounds with *an*, e.g. *anfassen* = אָחַז בְּ, *anrühren* = נָגַע בְּ, &c. To the same
category belongs also the construction of verbs denoting *authority* (מָשַׁל, מָלַךְ,
רָדָה, נָגַשׂ, the last prop. *to tread on* . . .) with בְּ, inasmuch as the exercise of
the authority is regarded as a laying hold of the person ruled ; so also, the
introduction of the object by בְּ after certain *verba dicendi*, or when the mental
action is to be represented as extending *to* some one or something : e.g.

---

[1] Cf. Wandel, *De particulae Hebr.* בְּ *indole, vi, usu*, Jena, 1875.

[2] e.g. *res in praeda captae*, i.e. things taken as spoil ; see Nägelsbach, *Lat.
Stilistik*, § 123⁴. On the Hebrew בְּ *essentiae*, see Hauschild in the *Festschrift zur
Einweihung des Goethegymn.* Frankf. a. M. 1897, p. 163.

[3] Other instances formerly cited here (Is 26⁴, ψ 55¹⁹, where בְּ is used before
the subject) as well as ψ 68⁵ בְּיָהּ שְׁמוֹ *Jah is his name*, are textually very
uncertain. Cf. Cheyne, *SBOT.* Isaiah, p. 173, on Is 26⁴.

קָרָא בְ to call on some one, נִשְׁבַּע בְּ *iurare per aliquem*, שָׁאַל בְּ to enquire of some one. Again; רָאָה בְ to look upon, שָׁמַע בְּ to hearken to (but cf. also *m*), generally with the secondary idea of participation, or of the pleasure with which one sees or hears anything, especially pleasure at the misfortunes of others, hence רָאָה בְ to see his desire on any one or anything ; cf. however, Gn 21¹⁶ *let me not look upon the death of the child* ; 1 S 6¹⁹ *because they had looked* [irreverently] *at the ark of the Lord.*

Closely related to this is the use of בְּ :

l (3) To introduce the person or thing, which is the object of a *mental* act, e. g. הֶאֱמִין בְּ to trust in (to cleave trustingly *to*) somebody or something ; בָּטַח בְּ to have confidence in . . . ; שָׂמַח בְּ to rejoice in or at something, &c. ; דִּבֶּר בְּ *to speak of (about)* some one or something, Dt 6⁷, 1 S 19³ ᶠ·, &c.

m (4) The idea of an action as extending *to* something, with at the same time the secondary idea of participation *in* something, underlies finally the *partitive* use of בְּ, e. g. אָכַל בְּ to share in eating something, Ex 12⁴³ ᶠᶠ·, Lv 22¹¹ ; also simply *to eat, to taste of* something, Ju 13¹⁶, Jb 21²⁵ ; so also בְּ לֶחֶם *to eat of*, and שָׁתָה בְ¹ *to drink of* something, Pr 9⁵ ; שָׁמַע בְּ *to hear* a whisper *of something*, Jb 26¹⁴ ; מָצָא בְּ *they found remaining of her only* . . ., 2 K 9³⁵ ; נָשָׂא בְ *to bear a share of* something, Nu 11¹⁷, Ez 18²⁰, Jb 7¹³. Cf. also חָלַק בְּ *to give a share of* something, Jb 39¹⁷ ; בָּנָה בְ *to do building to*, Neh 4⁴.

n (5) With the idea of *touching, striking against anything* is naturally connected that of proximity and vicinity *near*, and further that of association *with* something ; cf. Gn 9⁴ בְּנַפְשׁוֹ *with the life thereof* ; 15¹⁴, 32¹¹ בְּמַקְלִי *with my staff*. Sometimes בְּ combined with a verb of motion (*to come with* something), expresses the idea of *bringing*, e. g. Ju 15¹ Samson *visited his wife with a kid*, i. e. he brought her a kid ; Dt 23⁵, ψ 66¹³, 1 Ch 15¹⁹ ᶠᶠ·, 16⁶.

o (6) From the idea of connexion with something, being accompanied by something (see *n*), is developed, finally, the *instrumental* use of בְּ, which represents the means or instrument (or even the personal agent), as something *with which* one has associated himself in order to perform an action ; cf. Mi 4¹⁴ בַּשֵּׁבֶט *they smite with the rod* ; Is 10²⁴ ; ψ 18³⁰ בְּךָ *by thee* (so also 44⁶, parallel with בְּשִׁמְךָ) ; Is 10³⁴, Ho 1⁷, 12¹⁴ ; cf. also עָבַד בְּ *to labour by means of* some one, i. e. to cause him to labour at it, Ex 1¹⁴, &c. On בְּ with the passive to introduce the means or the author, see § 121 *f*.

p A variety of the בְּ *instrumenti* is בְּ *pretii* (the price being considered as the *means* of acquiring a thing), cf. Gn 23⁹, 29¹⁸ (בְּרָחֵל) ; 30¹⁶, 33¹⁹, 34¹⁵ (בְּזֹאת) on this condition) ; 37²⁸ ; also, in a wider sense, Gn 18²⁸ בְּ *for the sake of* ; 1 S 3¹³.

q Rem. The use of בְּ *instrumenti* to introduce the object is peculiar in such expressions as ψ 44²⁰ *and thou coveredst over us* בְּצַלְמָוֶת *with the shadow of death* ; Jb 16¹⁰ פָּעֲרוּ עָלַי בְּפִיהֶם *they have opened wide their mouth against me* (prop. *have made an opening with their mouth*) ; cp. ψ 22⁸, Ex 7²⁰ *he lifted up* בַּמַּטֶּה *the rod* ; Lv 16⁴ חָגַר and צָנַף followed by בְּ ; Jos 8¹⁸, La 1¹⁷. Analogous to some English expressions we find both *to gnash the teeth*, ψ 35¹⁶, and *to gnash with the teeth*, Jb 16⁹ ; *to wink the eye*, Pr 10¹⁰, and *to wink with the eye*, Pr 6¹³ ; *shake the head*, ψ 22⁸, and *to shake with the head*, Jer 18¹⁶, Jb 16⁴.—In all these instances

---

¹ To be distinguished from שָׁתָה בְ = *to drink from* (a cup, &c., Gn 44⁵, Am 6⁶), as in Arabic and Aramaic (Dn 5²). Cf. also ἐν ποτηρίοις (Xen. Anab. vi. 1, 4), ἐν χρυσώμασι πίνειν (3 Ezr 3⁶), *venenum in auro bibitur*, Seneca, Thyestes 453, and the French *boire dans une tasse.*

the verb (intransitive) construed with בְּ has a greater independence, and consequently more emphasis than the verb construed with a direct accusative ; the latter conveys a sort of necessary specification of the action, while the noun introduced by בְּ is used rather as a merely adverbial complement.

An instructive example of this is נָתַן קוֹל *vocem emittere, to utter a voice,* also *to thunder,* while in נָתַן בְּקוֹלוֹ ψ 46⁷ (68³⁴, Jer 12⁸), נָתַן has an independent sense = *he thundered with his voice* (i. e. mightily).

(c) לְ[1] *to,* a very general expression of *direction towards* anything, is used to *r* represent the most varied *relations* of an action or state with regard to a person or thing. On the use of לְ as a periphrasis for the *genetivus possessoris* or *auctoris* (the idea of belonging to), see § 129 ; on לְ with the passive, to introduce the author or the cause, see § 121 *f*; on לְ in a purely local sense (e. g. לִימִינֶךָ *at thy right hand,* prop. *towards thy right hand*), or temporal (e. g. לָעֶרֶב *at evening,* &c.) or distributive, see the Lexicon.

The following uses of לְ properly belong to the government of the verb :

(1) As a *nota dativi*[2] to introduce the remoter object ; also *s*

(2) To introduce the *dativus commodi.* This *dativus commodi* (or *incommodi,* e. g. Ez 37¹¹) is used—especially in colloquial language and in later style— in the form of a pronoun with לְ, as an apparently pleonastic *dativus ethicus,* with many verbs, in order to give emphasis to the significance of the occurrence in question *for* a particular subject. In this construction the person of the pronoun must always agree with that of the verbal form.[3] By far the most frequent use of this לְ is with the pronoun of the 2nd person after imperatives, e. g. לֶךְ־לְךָ *go, get thee away,* Gn 12¹, 22², Dt 2¹³ (also in the feminine, Ct 2¹⁰·¹³) ; וּמֵה לָךְ *turn thee aside,* 2 S 2²¹ ; סְעוּ לָכֶם *take your journey,* Dt 1⁷ ; עִבְרוּ לָכֶם *pass ye over* ; בְּרַח־לְךָ *flee* (to save thyself), Gn 27⁴³ ; עֲלִי־לָךְ *get thee up,* Is 40⁹ ; פְּנוּ לָכֶם *turn you,* Dt 1⁴⁰ ; שֻׁבוּ לָכֶם *return ye,* Dt 5²⁷ ; קוּמִי לָךְ *rise up,* Ct 2¹⁰ ; שְׁבוּ לָכֶם *abide ye,* Gn 22⁵ ; חֲדַל לָךְ *forbear thee,* 2 Ch 35²¹ (in the plural, Is 2²²) ; הָבוּ לָכֶם *take you,* Dt 1¹³, Jos 18⁴, Ju 20⁷, 2 S 16²⁰, and so almost regularly הִשָּׁמֶר לְךָ (see above, § 51 *n*) *cave tibi!* and הִשָּׁמְרוּ לָכֶם *take heed to yourselves* ; דְּמֵה לְךָ *be thou like,* Ct 2¹⁷ (cf. verse 9), 8¹⁴, is remarkable ; after a perfect consecutive, 1 K 17,³ 1 S 22⁵ ; after an imperfect consecutive, e. g. Is 36⁹ וְתִבְטַח לְךָ *and puttest thy trust.*—In the 3rd person, e. g. וַתֵּשֶׁב לָהּ *and sat her down,* Gn 21¹⁶, cf. 22⁵, Ex 18²⁷, ψ 120⁶, 123⁴, Jb 6¹⁹ ; even after a participle, Ho 8⁹.—In the 1st person plural, Ez 37¹¹.

(3) To introduce the result after verbs of making, forming, changing, *t* appointing *to* something, esteeming *as* something ; in short, in all those cases in which, according to § 117 *ii*, a second *accusative* may also be used.

(4) In loose connexion with some verbal idea in the sense of *in reference to, u with regard to* ... (§ 143 *e*) ; so after a *verbum dicendi,* Gn 20¹³ ; 1 K 10²³, cf.

---

[1] Cf. Giesebrecht, *Die hebr. Präpos. Lamed,* Halle, 1876.

[2] Just as in the Romance languages the Latin preposition *ad* (Italian *a,* before vowels *ad,* French *à,* Spanish *á*) and in English *to* are used as a periphrasis for the dative.—On the introduction of the nearer object by לְ, cf. § 117 *n*.

[3] Such expressions as the analogous English *he plucked me ope his doublet, but me no buts,* and the like, are accordingly inadmissible in Hebrew.

Is 36⁹ ; even before the verb, Jer 9². — To the same class belongs also the *Lamedh inscriptionis* (untranslatable in English, and hardly more than a mere quotation-mark) which introduces the exact wording of an inscription or title ; thus Is 8¹ *write upon it . . .* (the words) וגו׳ שָׁלָל מַהֵר (cf. verse 3, where the לְ naturally is not used) ; Ez 37¹⁶.

v   (*d*) מִן, originally (according to § 101 *a*) *separation*,[1] represents both the idea of *distance, separation* or *remoteness from* something, and that of *motion away from* something, hence also *descent, origin from* a place, Am 1¹.

w   (1) From the idea of *separation* is naturally derived on the one hand the sense of *(taken) from among . . ., e numero*, e. g. Gn 3¹ *subtil as none other of the beasts,* &c. ; cf. 3¹⁴, Dt 33²⁴, 1 S 15³³, Ju 5²⁴ (so especially after the idea of choosing *out of*[2] a larger class, 1 S 2²⁸ ; cf. Ex 19⁵, &c.), and on the other hand, the sense of *without* (separated, free from . . .), e. g. Is 22³ מִקֶּשֶׁת אֻסָּרוּ *without the bow* (i. e. without one needing to bend a bow against them) *they were made prisoners* ; cf. Jer 48⁴⁵ מִכֹּחַ *without strength* ; Ho 6⁶, as the first half-verse shows, not *more than burnt offerings* (as R. V.), but *and not burnt offerings* ; Mi 3⁶, ψ 52⁵, Jb 11¹⁵, 19²⁶, 21⁹, also such examples as Nu 15²⁴ *far from the eyes,* i. e. unobserved by the congregation ; Pr 20³.

x   Here also belongs the use of מִן after the ideas of *restraining, withholding from, refusing to* any one, frequently in pregnant expressions, which we can render only by complete final or consecutive clauses, e. g. 1 S 15²³ *he hath rejected thee* מִמֶּלֶךְ *away from* (being) *king,* instead of מִהְיוֹת מ׳ (as in verse 26), *that thou be no longer king* ; cf. 1 K 15¹³, Is 17¹ מֵעִיר *so that it is no longer a city* ; Jer 17¹⁶, Jb 28¹¹ *he bindeth the streams* מִבְּכִי *that they trickle not* ; Gn 16², 23⁶ מִקְּבֹר *that thou shouldst not bury thy dead* ; Is 24¹⁰.

y   The מִן has a still more pregnant force in those examples in which the idea of precluding from anything is only indirectly contained in the preceding verb, e. g. Gn 27¹ *his eyes were dim* מֵרְאֹת *away from seeing,* i. e. *so that he could not see* ; Is 7⁸ *Ephraim shall be broken in pieces* מֵעָם *that it be not a people* (just as in Is 23¹, Jer 48².⁴², ψ 83⁵) ; Lv 26¹³, Is 5⁶, 49¹⁵, 54⁹, Ezr 2⁶² (for other pregnant constructions with מִן see below, *ff*)[3] ; on מִבְּלִי and מֵאֵין *without,* cf. § 152 *y*.

---

[1] Cf. O. Molin, *Om prepositionen min i Bibelhebreisken,* Upsala, 1893, and especially N. Zerweck, *Die hebr. Praep.* min, Leipzig, 1893, who, instead of the partitive meaning (formerly accepted by us also), more correctly takes ' separation ' as the starting-point of its various uses.

[2] All the *partitive* uses of מִן also come most naturally under this idea of separation *out of* a larger class. Thus מִן is used in the sense of *some, something,* and even *one,* in such expressions as *and he slew . . . also* מִשָּׂרֵי יִשְׂרָאֵל (*divers*) *of the princes of Israel,* 2 Ch 21⁴ ; מִבְּל־ Lv 4² ; 1 K 18⁵ ; מִדַּם הַפָּר *some of the blood of the bullock,* Ex 29¹², &c. ; Jb 27⁶ *my heart doth not reproach me* מִיָּמָי *for any,* i. e. *for one, of my days* ; 38¹² מִיָּמֶיךָ *one of thy days,* i. e. *ever in thy life* (this explanation is confirmed by 1 K 1⁶ ; cf. also 1 S 14⁴⁵, 25²⁸). In this way also, the frequently misunderstood Hebrew (and Arabic) idiom is to be explained, by which מִן before אַחַת, אֶחָד is equivalent to *ullus* ; e. g. Lv 4² *and shall do* מֵאַחַת מֵהֵנָּה *any one of these things* ; 5¹³, Dt 15⁷, Ez 18¹⁰ ; so before a *nomen unitatis* (see § 122 *t*), 1 S 14⁴⁵ (2 S 14¹¹, 1 K 1⁵²) מִשַּׂעֲרַת רֹאשׁוֹ *not one hair of his head.* — מִן is used in the sense of the Arabic *min el-beyân* or explicative *min* (often to be simply translated by *namely*), e. g. in Gn 7²² *of all that was,* i. e. *so far as it was,* probably also Gn 6² (= *whomsoever they chose*).

[3] On the use of מִן to express the comparative, which likewise depends on the idea of *distance from . . .,* cf. below, § 133 *a* ; on מִן as expressing the

(**2**) On the sense of *motion away from* anything depends the use of מִן after ‏≋‏ such ideas as *to take away from, to beware, to be afraid of, to flee, to escape, to hide oneself from* (cf. καλύπτω ἀπό, *custodire ab*), sometimes again in pregnant expressions, e. g. Is 33[15]. On the idea of *starting from* anything depends finally the very frequent *causative* use of מִן *on account of, in consequence of* (cf. our *that comes from . . .*), *prae*, e. g. מֵרֹב *for multitude,* 1 K 8[5].

(*e*) עַל־.[1] The two original local meanings of this preposition are *upon* aa (ἐπί)[2] and *over* (ὑπέρ, *super*).

(1) From the original meaning *upon* is explained the use of עַל־ after ideas of *commanding, commissioning* (פָּקַד עַל־), &c., inasmuch as the command, obligation, &c., is *laid upon* the object. The construction is self-evident in the case of *to lie, rest, lean, rely, press upon* something; cf. also, for the last, such examples as Is 1[14], Jb 7[20], 23[2], and especially 2 S 18[11] וְעָלַי prop. *upon me* would it have been, it would have been incumbent *upon me,* &c.

(2) From the original meaning *over* is explained the use of עַל־ after ideas bb of *covering, protecting, guarding* בָּסָה עַל־, גָּנַן עַל־; also the combinations רָחַם עַל־ *to have compassion upon . . .,* חוּס עַל־, חָמַל עַל־ *to spare* some one, arise from the idea of a compassionate or protective *bending over* something. Cf. also נִלְחַם עַל־ Ju 9[17] = *to fight for* some one, i. e. in his defence.

(3) Moreover עַל־ is used after verbs of *standing* and *going,* to express cc a towering *over* some one or something, sometimes in phrases, in which the original local idea has altogether fallen into the background, and which are therefore to be rendered in English by means of other prepositions (*by, with, before, near*), e. g. Gn 41[1], &c., *Pharaoh . . . stood* עַל־הַיְאֹר *by the Nile* (above the water level; cf. ψ 1[3]), and so especially עָמַד עַל־ in the pregnant sense *to stand serving before* some one (prop. *over* one who sits or reclines at table) Zc 4[14] (cf. Is 6[2], where מִמַּעַל לְ is used for עַל־); הִתְיַצֵּב עַל־ *to present oneself* by command *before* some one, Jb 1[6], &c. Cf. also עַל־יַד, עַל־יְדֵי (Jb 1[14]) *near, at (on) the side* of some one or something.

(4) From the original meaning *above* (not, as formerly explained, *on to* dd something, *at* something) there arise finally all the various constructions with עַל־ in the sense of *towards, against.* The original idea (which in many of these constructions has become wholly unrecognizable) starts from the view that the assailant endeavours to take up his position *over* the person attacked, so as to reach him from above, or to *overpower* him; cf. especially קוּם עַל־ to rise up *over,* i. e. *against* some one, then with a transference of

---

distance of time from a fixed limit, in the sense of *after,* e. g. ψ 73[20] מְהָקִיץ *after awaking* (cf. ἐξ ἀρίστου, *ab itinere*), or *after the lapse of . . .,* e. g. Gn 38[24], Ho 6[2], and very frequently מִקֵּץ *from the end of,* i. e. *after the lapse of . . .,* see the Lexicon; also for the use of מִן to represent *resting beside* anything, like the Latin *prope abesse ab . . .*

[1] Cf. Budie, *Die hebr. Präpos. 'Al* (עַל), Halle, 1882.

[2] Since the placing *upon* anything is an addition to it, עַל־ also implies *in addition to* something, cf. Gn 28[9] (31[50]); 30[40], 32[12] (probably a proverbial saying = *mother and children*); Dt 22[6]. Also עַל *notwithstanding* is no doubt properly *in addition to,* e. g. Jb 10[7] *although thou knowest,* prop. *in addition to thy knowing.* — From the original meaning *upon* is also derived that of *on account of* (prop. *upon the ground of*) and *in agreement with, according to,* since the pattern is regarded as the foundation *upon* which a thing stands or rests.

thought applied to any kind of hostile approach, נִלְחַם עַל־ *to fight against* ... , חָנָה עַל־ *to encamp against* ... , נֶאֱסַף עַל־ *to be gathered together, to assemble against* (Mi 4¹¹ ; cf. ψ 2²), &c. ; even after verbs which express a mental action, e. g. חָשַׁב רָעָה עַל־ *to imagine evil against* any one, &c.

ee **4.** Sometimes a preposition appears to be under the immediate government of a verb, which, by its meaning, excludes such a union. In reality the preposition is dependent on a verb (generally a verb of motion), which, for the sake of brevity, is not expressed, but in sense is contained in what is apparently the governing verb.

ff Various examples of this *constructio praegnans* have been already noticed above in x and y under מִן־ ; for מִן־ cf. also ψ 22²² וּמִקַּרְנֵי רֵמִים עֲנִיתָנִי *and thou hast answered* and saved *me from the horns of the wild oxen* (in Is 38¹⁷, which Delitzsch translates by thou hast loved and delivered *my soul from the pit*, read חָשַׁכְתָּ with the LXX) ; Gn 25²³, 2 S 18¹⁹, Jb 28¹² ; cf. also זָנָה מִן־ ψ 73²⁷ *to go a whoring from* any one i. e. *to be unfaithful to him* ; רָשַׁע מִן־ ψ 18²² = *to depart wickedly from God* ; חָרַשׁ מִן ψ 28¹ *to be silent from* one (to turn away in silence) ; cf. Jb 13¹³ [; so with מֵעַל Jb 30¹⁷·³⁰].

gg Pregnant constructions with אַחֲרֵי : Nu 14²⁴ equivalent to וַיְמַלֵּא לָלֶכֶת אַחֲרֵי *and he made full to walk* i. e. walked fully *after me* ; in 1 S 13⁷ read with the LXX חָרְדוּ מֵאַחֲרָיו *they trembled*, i. e. *went trembling away from him* ; with דָּרַשׁ אֶל־ Gn 43³³ תָּמַהּ אֶל־ *to turn in astonishment to* some one (cf. Is 13⁸) ; Is 11¹⁰, &c., *to turn inquiringly to* some one ; הֶחֱרִישׁ אֶל־ Is 41¹ *to turn in silence to* some one ; חָרַד אֶל־ Gn 42²⁸ *to turn trembling to* some one (cf. חָרַד לִקְרַאת *to come trembling to meet*, 1 S 21² [also with שַׂאג, הֵרִיץ, שָׂמַח and other verbs, Ju 14⁵, 15¹⁴, 19³ ; see Lexicon]) ; cf. further Jer 41⁷, ψ 7⁷, 2 Ch 32¹ ; with בְּ ψ 55¹⁹ *he hath redeemed* and hath put *my soul in peace*, exactly like ψ 118⁵ ; with לְ ψ 74⁷ *they have profaned* and cast... *even to the ground* ; cf. 89⁴⁰.

hh **5.** In poetic parallelism the governing power of a preposition is sometimes extended to the corresponding substantive of the second member ;[1] e. g. בְּ Is 40¹⁹, 48¹⁴ *he shall perform his pleasure* בְּבָבֶל *on Babylon, and his arm shall be* כַּשְׂדִּים (for בַּכַּשְׂדִּים) *on the Chaldaeans* ; Jb 15³ ; לְ Is 28⁶, 42²² (but probably לְ has fallen out after another לְ), Ez 39⁴, Jb 34¹⁰ (perhaps also Gn 45⁸ ; מֹשֵׁל may, however, be taken here as a second accusative according to § 117 *ii*) ; לְמַעַן Is 48⁹ ; מִן־ Is 58¹³, ψ 141⁹ (unless וּמִמְּקֻשׁוֹת is to be read) ; עַד־ Is 15⁸ ; תַּחַת Is 61⁷.

ii **6.** Adverbs which have acquired a substantival value are sometimes governed by prepositions, e. g. אֶל־חִנָּם *in vain*, Ez 6¹⁰ ; אַחֲרֵי־כֵן *after this* ; בְּכֵן (Ec 8¹⁰, Est 4¹⁶) *then, on this condition* ; לְכֵן and עַל־כֵּן *therefore* ; עַד־כֵּן *hitherto.*

---

[1] Similarly the force of a negative is sometimes extended to the parallel member ; see § 152 *z*.

§ **120.** *Verbal Ideas under the Government of a Verb.*
Co-ordination of Complementary Verbal Ideas.

1. When a *relative* verb (incomplete in itself) receives its necessary *a* complement in the form of a verbal idea, the latter is, as a rule, subordinated in the infinitive construct (with or without לְ), less frequently in the infinitive absolute, in a few instances in the form of a participle (or verbal adjective), or finally in the imperfect without the copula. In these combinations the principal idea is very frequently represented by the subordinate member of the sentence, whilst the governing verb rather contains a mere definition of the manner of the action; cf. *d* and *g* below, and § 114 *n*, note 2.

(*a*) On the subordination of an infinitive construct as an accusative of the *b* object, and as the complement of relative verbal ideas, see above, § 114 *c*, and the numerous examples given in § 114 *m*; on the infinitive absolute as object, see § 113 *d*.—The complement in the form of a participle (as in Greek, and also frequently in Syriac) occurs in Is 33¹ שֹׁדֵד כַּהֲתִמְךָ (cf. for the form, § 67 *v*) *when thou hast ceased as a spoiler*, i. e. to spoil; Jer 22³⁰ יֹשֵׁב ... לֹא יִצְלַח *he shall never prosper, sitting*, i. e. so as to sit, &c.; Jon 1⁶ *what meanest thou, sleeping?* i. e. that thou sleepest; [1] by a verbal adjective, 1 S 3² *now his eyes* הֵחֵלּוּ כֵהוֹת *had begun being dim*, i. e. to wax dim (unless we read לִכְהוֹת=כְּהוֹת, cf. § 114 *m*); by a substantive, Gn 9²⁰ *and Noah began to be an husbandman* (omitting the article before אֲדָמָה).

(*b*) Examples of the subordination of the complementary verbal idea in the *c* imperfect[2] (in English usually rendered by *to, in order to* or *that*) are—(1) with both verbs in the same person: after the perfect, Is 42²¹ יַגְדִּיל ... יְהֹוָה חָפֵץ *it pleased the Lord ... to magnify*, &c.; Jb 30²⁸, 32²² לֹא יָדַעְתִּי אֲכַנֶּה *I know not to give flattering titles*; after a perfect consecutive, 1 S 20¹⁹ (where for תֵּרֵד we should read with the LXX תִּפָּקֵד); after an imperfect, ψ 88¹¹, 102¹⁴, Jb 19³, 24¹⁴; after an imperf. consec., Jb 16⁸; after a participle, Is 5¹¹ᵃ.—(2) with a difference in the persons: after a perfect, Lv 9⁶ *this is the thing* אֲשֶׁר־צִוָּה יְהֹוָה תַּעֲשׂוּ *which the Lord commanded (that) ye should do*; a negative imperfect follows צִוָּה in La 1¹⁰; after the imperfect, Is 47¹ (⁵) כִּי לֹא תוֹסִיפִי עוֹד יִקְרְאוּ־לָךְ *for thou shalt no more continue (that) they call thee*, i. e. thou shalt no longer be called, &c.; Ho 1⁶ לֹא אוֹסִיף עוֹד אֲרַחֵם *I will no longer continue (and) have mercy*, i. e. *I will no more have mercy*; Is 52¹, Pr 23³⁵.—Nu 22⁶ *peradventure I shall prevail (that) we may smite them, and (that) I may drive them out of the land* (אוּכַל may, however, be a scribal error for נוּכַל, due to the preceding אוּלַי, and in that case the example would belong to No. 1); after a participle,

---

[1] In יֵדַע מְנַגֵּן 1 S 16¹⁶, which appears to be a case of this kind, two different readings are combined, יֵדַע לְנַגֵּן and the simple מְנַגֵּן.

[2] This kind of subordination is frequent in Arabic and in Syriac (cf. e. g. the Peshiṭtâ, Luke 18¹³); as a rule, however, a conjunction (corresponding to our *that*) is inserted. Cf. moreover, the Latin *quid vis faciam?* Terence; *volo hoc oratori contingat*, Cicero, Brut. 84; and our *I would it were*; *I thought he would go*.

2 S 21⁴.—A perfect is possibly subordinated in La 1¹⁰; but the explanation of בָּאוּ as a relative clause is preferable.

d 2. Instead of subordination (as in the cases mentioned in *a–c*), the *co-ordination* of the complementary verbal idea in the finite verb (cf. above, *c*) frequently occurs, either—

(*a*) With the second verb co-ordinated in a form exactly corresponding to the first (but see below, *e*) by means of וְ (וַ, וְ).¹ As a rule, here also (see above, *a*) the principal idea is introduced only by the second verb, while the first (especially שׁוּב, יָסַף,² הוֹסִיף) contains the definition of the manner of the action, e. g. Gn 26¹⁸ וַיָּשָׁב וַיַּחְפֹּר *and he returned and digged*, i. e. he digged again; 2 K 1¹¹·¹³; in the perfect consecutive, Is 6¹³; with הוֹסִיף, e. g. Gn 25¹ *and Abraham added and took a wife*, i. e. again took a wife; Gn 38⁵ and frequently; with הוֹאִיל in the jussive, Jb 6⁹; in the imperative (cf. § 110 *h*), Ju 1 ⁶ הוֹאֶל־נָא וְלִין *be content, I pray thee, and tarry all night* (cf. the English *he was persuaded and remained*, for *to remain*); 2 S 7²⁹; with מָהַר Gn 24¹⁸·²⁰, &c.; with חָפֵר Ct 2³.

e Rem. 1. Instead of an exact agreement between co-ordinate verbal forms, other combinations sometimes occur, viz. imperfect and perfect consecutive (cf. § 112 *d*), e. g. Dt 31¹² *that they* יִלְמְדוּ וְיָרְאוּ אֶת־יְהוָֹה *may learn, and fear the Lord*, i. e. *to fear the Lord*; Is 1¹⁹, Ho 2¹¹, Est 8⁶, Dn 9²⁵ᵇ; perfect and imperfect, Jb 23³ (*O that I knew how I might find him*); perfect and imperfect consecutive, Jos 7⁷, Ec 4¹·⁷; jussive and imperative, Jb 17¹⁰; cf., finally, Gn 47⁶ וְאִם־יָדַעְתָּ וְיֶשׁ־בָּם *and if thou knowest and there are among them*, &c., i. e. that there are among them.

f 2. Special mention must be made of the instances in which the natural complement of the first verb is suppressed, or is added immediately after in the form of an historical statement, e. g. Gn 42²⁵ *then Joseph commanded and they filled* ³ (prop. that they should fill, and they filled . . . ; cf. the full form of expression in Gn 50²); a further command is then added by means of לְ and the infinitive; Ex 36⁶; another instance of the same kind is Gn 30²⁷ *I have divined and the Lord hath blessed me*, &c., i. e. that the Lord hath blessed me for thy sake.

g (*b*) With the second verb (which, according to the above, represents the principal idea) attached *without the copula* ⁴ in the same mood, &c, In this construction (cf. § 110 *h*) the imperatives קוּמִי, קוּמָה, קוּם,

---

¹ Cf. the English colloquial expression *I will try and do it.*

² Of a different kind are the cases in which יָסַף with a negative is co-ordinated with a verb to emphasize the non-recurrence of the action; cf. Nu 11²⁵ *they prophesied and added not*, sc. *to prophesy*, i. e. *but they did so no more*; Dt 5¹⁹, Jb 27¹⁹ (reading וְלֹא יֹאסִיף).

³ Cf. the analogous examples in Kautzsch's *Gramm. des Bibl. Aram.*, § 102.

⁴ To be distinguished, of course, from the cases in which two equally important and independent verbs are used together without the copula in vigorous poetic imagery, e. g. Ex 15⁹, Jb 29⁸, &c,

&c.) and לֵךְ (לְכָה, לְכִי, &c.) are exceedingly common with the sense of interjections, before verbs which express a movement or other action, e.g. קוּם הִתְהַלֵּךְ *arise, walk*, Gn 13^{17}, 19^{15}, 27^{43}; in the plural, Gn 19^{14}; Ex 19^{24} לֶךְ־רֵד *go, get thee down*; 1 S 3^{9}; with a following cohortative, 1 S 9^{10} לְכָה נֵלְכָה *come, let us go*; Gn 31^{44} and frequently.—Also with שׁוּב (a periphrasis for *again*) in the perfect, Zc 8^{15}; in the imperfect, Mi 7^{19}, ψ 7^{13}, 59^{7}, 71^{20}; in the jussive, Jb 10^{16}; in the cohortative, Gn 30^{31}; in the imperative, Jos 5^{2}, 1 S 3^{5} *lie down again*; הוֹאִיל (sometimes to express the idea of *willingly* or *gladly*) in the perfect, Dt 1^{5}, Ho 5^{11}; in the imperative, Jb 6^{28}; הִרְבָּה = *much*, 1 S 2^{3} אַל־תַּרְבּוּ תְדַבְּרוּ גְבֹהָה *do not multiply* and *talk,* i.e. talk not so much *arrogancy*; in the imperative, ψ 51^{4}; הֵחֵל, Dt 2^{24} הָחֵל רָשׁ *begin, possess*; יָכֹל, La 4^{14} בְּלֹא יוּכְלוּ יִגְּעוּ *without men's being able to touch*, &c.; מִהַר = *quickly*, in the perfect, ψ 106^{13}; in the imperative, Gn 19^{22}, Ju 9^{48}, Est 6^{10}.—Other examples are: Ho 9^{9} הֶעְמִיק = *deeply, radically*; Zp 3^{7} הִשְׁכִּים = *early* (even in the participle, Ho 6^{4}, 13^{3}); Is 29^{4} שָׁפֵל = *low*, cf. Jer 13^{18}; Jos 3^{16} תָּמַם = *wholly*; ψ 112^{9} פִּזַּר = *plentifully*.

Rem. This co-ordination without the copula belongs (as being more *h* vigorous and bolder) rather to poetic or otherwise elevated style (cf. e.g. Is 52^{1}, Ho 1^{6}, 9^{9} with Gn 25^{1}, &c.). Asyndeton, however, is not wanting even in prose; besides the above examples (especially the imperatives of קוּם and הָלַךְ Gn 30^{31}, Dt 1^{5}, 2^{24}, Jos 3^{16}, 1 S 3^{5}) cf. also Neh 3^{20}, 1 Ch 13^{2}. For special reasons the verb representing the principal idea may even come first; thus Is 53^{11} יִרְאֶה יִשְׂבָּע *he shall see, he shall be satisfied* (sc. with the sight), for the satisfaction does not come until after the enjoyment of the sight; Jer 4^{5} קִרְאוּ מַלְאוּ *cry, fill*, i.e. cry with a full (loud) voice.

§ 121. *Construction of Passive Verbs.*

Blake, 'The internal passive in Semitic,' *JAOS.* xxii.

1. Verbs which in the active take *one* accusative (either of the *a* proper object, or of the *internal* object, or of some other nearer definition; cf. § 117 *a, p, u*) may in the passive, according to our mode of expression, be construed *personally*, the object of the active sentence now becoming the subject, e.g. Gn 35^{19} וַתָּמָת רָחֵל וַתִּקָּבֵר *and Rachel died, and was buried*, &c. The passive, however, is also used *impersonally* (in the 3rd sing. masc.), either absolutely, as Dt 21$^{3f.}$, Is 16^{10}, Ez 16^{34} (with a dative added, 2 S 17^{16}, Is 53^{5}, La 5^{5}), or, more frequently, with the object of the active construction still subordinated in the accusative,[1] e.g. Gn 27^{42} וַיֻּגַּד לְרִבְקָה אֶת־דִּבְרֵי עֵשָׂו *and there were told.*(i.e. one told) *to Rebekah the words of Esau*; 2 S 21^{11}, 1 K 18^{13}.

---

[1] When this is not recognizable either by the *nota accusativi*, or by its disagreement with the passive form in gender, number, and person, it

b Other examples are : after Niph., Gn 4¹⁸ וַיִּוָּלֵד לַחֲנוֹךְ אֶת־עִירָד *and unto Enoch was born Irad* (cf. Nu 26⁶⁰, and after an infinitive, Gn 21⁵) ; Gn 17⁵, 21⁸ (after an infinitive) ; 29²⁷ (unless וְנִתְּנָה is 1st plur. cohortative) ; Ex 21²⁸, 25²⁸, Lv 6¹³, Nu 7¹⁰ (after an infinitive) ; 26⁵⁵ (cf. verse 53) ; Dt 20⁸ (where, however, for יִמַּס the Hiph. יַמֵּס should be read, according to § 128) ; Jos 7¹⁵, Is 16¹⁰ ; with the object preceding, Ex 13⁷, Lv 2⁸, 19²⁰, Nu 16²⁹, Dan 9²⁴.¹—Also after Puʻal, Jer 50²⁰ ; *before* Puʻal, Is 14³ (אֲשֶׁר equivalent to the internal object עֲבֹדָה = *which they have caused to be served by thee*) ; Jb 22⁹ ; according to the Masoretic text also Gn 46²², where, however, the Samaritan and LXX read יֻלְּדָה for יֻלַּד ; the Samaritan in Gn 35²⁶ and 46²⁷ also reads יֻלְּדוּ, and this (or יֻלְּדוּ) should certainly be read instead of ילדו in 2 S 21²².—After Hoph., Ex 10⁸, 27⁷, Lv 10¹⁸, 16²⁷, Nu 32⁵, 1 K 2²¹, Pr 16³³, Jb 30¹⁵ ; after the infinitive Hoph., Gn 40²⁰, Ez 16⁴ᶠ·, 27⁷ ; *before* Hoph., Is 17¹, 21², Ho 10⁶, Zc 13⁶ ; after the infinitive Hothpaʻel, Lv 13⁵⁵ᶠ·.

c 2. Verbs which in the active take two accusatives (§ 117 *cc*) retain in the passive construction at least *one* accusative, namely that of the second or remoter object, whilst the nearer object now becomes the subject. Thus, corresponding to אֲשֶׁר אַרְאֶךָ *which I will show thee* (Gn 12¹) the passive is אֲשֶׁר אַתָּה מָרְאֶה (Ex 25⁴⁰) *which thou hast been shown*, i. e. which has been shown to thee ; cf. Ex 26³⁰ (but in Lv 13⁴⁹ with an accusative of the person) ; Jb 7³. In ψ 22¹⁶ מָדְבָּק מַלְקוֹחָי depends on an assumed transitive הִדְבִּיק governing two accusatives (= *my tongue is made to cleave to my jaws*) ; also in Is 1²⁰ חֶרֶב תְּאֻכְּלוּ *ye shall be devoured with the sword*, חֶרֶב is not an *accus. instrumenti*, but most probably an accusative of the object retained from the active construction.²

d Rem. 1. Examples of the retention of the second accusative are—(a) with *verba induendi* and *exuendi* (§ 117 *cc*), ψ 80¹¹ כֻּסּוּ הָרִים צִלָּהּ *the mountains were covered with the shadow of it* (the vine) ; Pr 19²³. So also some of the examples in § 116 *k* of passive participles of these verbs, Ju 18¹¹, 1 S 2¹⁸, 17⁵, 1 K 22¹⁰,

---

naturally cannot be determined whether the construction is really impersonal. The construction itself can only be explained by supposing that while using the passive form the speaker at the same time thinks of some author or authors of the action in question, just as on the theory of the Arab grammarians a *concealed agent* is included in every passive. This accounts for the possibility (cf. § 144 *g*) of using the active without a specified subject as a periphrasis for the passive.

¹ In 2 K 18³⁰ יִנָּתֵן is to be read or אֵת is to be omitted, as in the parallel passage Is 36¹⁵.

² In the active, the sentence would be *I will cause the sword to devour you* ; by the rule stated above, under *c*, this would become in the passive, *the sword* (nom.) *shall be made to devour you* (acc.). Instead of this, the remoter object is here made the subject, and the nearer object is retained in the accusative. Otherwise, the only possible explanation would be, according to the Arabic idiom, *to cause one to devour the sword* (remoter object), i. e. to give him over to it. It would then be simplest to read תְּאַכְלוּ.

Ez 9[2.3] ;[1] with the accusative preceding, Neh 4[12].—(b) with *verba copiae* and *inopiae*, Ex 1[7], Is 38[10] (equivalent to *I must forego the residue of my years*); Is 40[20].—(c) an accusative of the result (§ 117 *ii*) with the passive, Is 6[11], Zc 14[4], Jb 28[2] ; with the accusative preceding, Is 24[12], Mi 3[12] (Jer 26[18]), Jb 15[7], 22[16].[2] Also in Ez 40[17] and 46[23], the accusative preceding עָשׂוּי (in 41[18] follow- ing it) can only be taken as the accusative of the result ; some general idea, such as that of *place*, is to be understood as the subject of עָשׂוּי.—(d) an accusative of the member or part specially affected by the action (§ 117 *ll*), Gn 17[11], 14[24], Ju 1[7] (accusative *before* part. pass.) ; 2 S 15[32] (accusative with suffix after the part. pass.).

2. Both accusatives are retained in an unusual manner after the passive of *e* a *verbum implendi* in Nu 14[21] ; instead, however, of the *Niph.* וַיִּמָּלֵא the *Qal* (which is sometimes used transitively elsewhere) should simply be read with the LXX ; similarly in ψ 72[19], although there the LXX also translate the passive.

3. The efficient cause (or personal agent) is, as a rule, attached to *f* the passive by לְ (thus corresponding to the Greek and Latin dative), e. g. Gn 25[21] וַיֵּעָתֶר לוֹ יְהוָה *the Lord let himself be intreated by him* ; cf. Lv 26[23], ψ 73[10] and the blessing בָּרוּךְ הוּא לַיהוָה *blessed be he of the Lord* Ru 2[20] ; cf. Gn 14[19], Ju 17[2b], 1 S 15[13] ; also in the plural, 1 S 23[21] (2 S 2[5], ψ 115[15]).—*Before* the verb, Pr 14[20] and frequently ; less com- monly by מִן־ (called מִן־ of origin=*coming from*), e. g. Gn 9[11] ; *before* the verb, ψ 37[23], Jb 24[1] ; by בְּ (*instrumenti*) [rarely, König § 106], Gn 9[6] בָּאָדָם *by man*) ; Nu 36[2], Is 14[3 b] [but ?=*wherewith it was worked* (§ 52 e) *with thee* ; cf. Dt 21[3], König § 106 ; and see בְּ עָבַד in the Lexicon], Ho 14[4], always to introduce a personal agent.—On the con- nexion of the passive participle with a genitive of the agent, cf. § 116 *l*.

II. Syntax of the Noun.

§ 122. *Indication of the Gender of the Noun.*

Cf. F. Schwabe, *Die Genusbestimmung des Nomens im bibl. Hebr.*, Jena, 1894, and especially the thorough investigation by K. Albrecht, 'Das Geschlecht der hebr. Hauptwörter,' in *ZAW.* 1895, p. 313 ff., and 1896, p. 61 ff. H. Rosenberg, 'Zum Geschlecht der hebr. Hauptwörter,' in *ZAW.* 1905, p. 325 ff. (supple- menting Albrecht's work by a treatment of the gender of many nouns in the Mishna) ; and his 'Notizen aus der tannaitischen Literatur...' *ZAW.* 1908, p. 144 ff.

1. According to § 80 *a*, Hebrew, like the other Semitic languages, *a* distinguishes only a *masculine* and *feminine* gender. To indicate the

---

[1] Analogous to הַלָּבֻשׁ הַבַּדִּים *who was clothed in linen*, Ez 9[3], would be וְהַנּוֹתָר אֶת־הֶהָמוֹן הַזֶּה 2 Ch 31[10] ; but we must certainly read there וְנוֹתָר with the LXX.—Still less can ψ 87[3] be so explained, נִכְבָּדוֹת being not an accusative, but the subject of a noun-clause. On the other hand, שָׁלוּחַ 1 K 14[6] may be explained with Ewald in the sense of *being charged with* something, so that, like צֻוָּה, it may be construed with an accusative.

[2] In reality וַיָּרֻם Ex 16[20.26] (*it became putrid*) is equivalent to a passive (*it was changed*), to which תּוֹלָעִים is added as an accusative of the result.

latter a special feminine ending is generally used (§ 80 *b* and § 87 *i*)
both in the singular and plural (see, however, § 87 *p*), its use being
most consistent in adjectives and participles; cf. § 87 *r*. The employment of these special endings is most natural when by means of them
the feminine names of persons or animals are distinguished from the
masculine of the same stem and the same formation, e. g. אָח *brother*,
אָחוֹת *sister*; עֶלֶם *a young man*, עַלְמָה *a young woman, maid*; פַּר
iuvencus, פָּרָה *iuvenca*; עֵגֶל *vitulus*, עֶגְלָה *vitula*. On the other hand,
the feminine plays an important part in denoting the gender of whole
classes of ideas (see below, *p*, &c.), which the Hebrew regards as
feminine. The language, however, is not obliged to use the feminine
ending either for the purpose of distinguishing the *sex* of animate
objects (see *b*), or as an indication of the (*figurative*) gender of inanimate things which are regarded as feminine (see *h*).

b 2. The distinction of *sex* may be effected even without the feminine
ending, (*a*) by the employment of words of different stems for the
masculine and feminine; (*b*) by the different construction (either as
masculine or feminine) of the same word (*communia*). But the distinction may also, (*c*) in the case of names of animals, be entirely
neglected, all examples of a species being included under one particular
gender, either masculine or feminine (*epicoena*).

c Examples of (*a*) are: אָב *father*, אֵם *mother*; אַיִל *ram*, רָחֵל *ewe*; תַּיִשׁ *he-goat*,
עֵז *she-goat*; חֲמוֹר *he-ass*, אָתוֹן *she-ass*; אַרְיֵה *lion*, לָבִיא *lioness*. Sometimes
with the feminine ending as well, e. g. עֶבֶד *male slave, man-servant*, אָמָה or
שִׁפְחָה *female slave, maid*; חָתָן *bridegroom*, כַּלָּה *bride*.

d Of (*b*): גָּמָל *camel*. Plur. גְּמַלִּים construed as masculine, Gn 24⁶³; as
feminine, Gn 32¹⁶; בָּקָר collect. *oxen*, Ex 21³⁷, construed as masculine, but in
Gn 33¹³, Jb 1¹⁴ as feminine. In Jer 2²⁴ the construction of פֶּרֶה *wild ass*,
changes directly from the masculine (intended as epicene) to the feminine.
Cf. the Greek ὁ, ἡ παῖς· ὁ, ἡ βοῦς.

e Of (*c*): analogous to the epicene nouns of other languages, many species of
animals which are strong and courageous, are regarded in Hebrew as always
masculine, while the weak and timid are feminine; cf. ὁ λύκος, ἡ χελιδών,
and the German *der Löwe, der Adler*, &c., but *die Katze, die Taube*, &c. Similarly in Hebrew, e. g. אַלּוּף *ox* (ψ 144¹⁴ even referring to cows when pregnant),
דֹּב *bear*, Ho 13⁸ דֹּב שַׁכּוּל (*a bear that is bereaved of her whelps*; cf., however,
2 K 2²⁴, Is 11⁷), זְאֵב *wolf*, כֶּלֶב *dog*, all masculine; but אַרְנֶבֶת *hare*, יוֹנָה *dove*,
חֲסִידָה *stork*, דְּבוֹרָה *bee*, נְמָלָה *ant*, &c., feminine.

f Rem. 1. Masculine nouns which either have a separate feminine form or
might easily form one, are but seldom used as epicene; such are, חֲמוֹר *ass*,
2 S 19²⁷ for אָתוֹן; אַיִל *hart*, ψ 42² for אַיָּלָה. In Gn 23³ ᶠᶠ. מֵת *a dead body*, refers
more especially to the body of a woman; אָמוֹן *a master workman*, in Pr 8³⁰
refers to wisdom (חָכְמָה feminine, cf. Plin. 2, 1 *natura omnium artifex*; and our

use of *friend, teacher, servant, neighbour,* either as masculine or feminine; in German, *Gemahl*[1] spouse, also for fem. *Gemahlin,* &c.).

2. Of words denoting persons נַעַר *παῖς,* according to the formerly common *g* opinion, was in early times used as epicene (see, however, above, § 2 *n*). The use of the plural נְעָרִים in Jb 1[19] and Ru 2[21] in the sense of *young people* (of both genders) does not, however, prove this. In this and in similar cases (cf. e.g. אֹתָם Gn 1[27] and אֶתְהֶם 32[1]) the masculine as *prior gender* includes the feminine.[2]

3. The following classes of ideas are usually regarded as feminine,[3] *h* although the substantives which express them are mostly without the feminine ending:[4]

(*a*) Names of *countries* and *towns,* since they are regarded as the mothers[5] and nurses of the inhabitants; e.g. אַשּׁוּר *Assyria,* אֱדֹם *Idumaea,* צֹר *Tyre;* cf. also such expressions as בַּת בָּבֶל, בַּת צִיּוֹן *daughter of Babylon, daughter of Zion,* &c. On the other hand appellatives which are originally masculine, remain so when used as place-names, e.g. Am 5[5] הַגִּלְגָּל, בֵּית־אֵל, &c.

Rem. The same proper nouns, which as names of countries are regarded *i* as feminine, are frequently used also as names of the people, and may then, like national names in other languages, be construed as masculine (the national name almost always being used also as the personal name of the supposed ancestor of the people); thus יְהוּדָה masc. Is 3[8], &c., *Judaei;* but

---

[1] So in early Arabic, *ba'l* (lord) and *zauġ* (conjux) are used both for *maritus* and *uxor;* *'arūs* for *bridegroom* and *bride;* the later language, however, distinguishes the feminine from the masculine in all these cases generally by the ending *a* (*at*). In early Arabic also the feminine ending is commonly omitted in such participles as *ḥāmil, bāṭin* (gravida), and the like, which from the nature of the case can only be used of females. Thus also אָמֵן, at least in Nu 11[12] (Is 49[23]?), probably means *nurse* (for אֹמֶנֶת 2 S 4[4], &c.), not *nursing-father.*

[2] The Arab grammarians call this use of the masculine plural and dual (e.g. *el-abawāni,* the two fathers, i.e. *parentes*) *taghlib* or *the making* (the masculine) *prevail* (over the feminine).—Cf. M. Grünert, *Die Begriffs-Präponderanz und die Duale a potiori im Altarab.,* Vienna, 1886.

[3] The masculine gender is attributed 'by the Hebrews and the Semites generally to whatever is dangerous, savage, courageous, respected, great, strong, powerful . . .; the feminine to whatever is motherly, productive, sustaining, nourishing, gentle, weak, . . . subject, &c.' (Albrecht, *ZAW.* 1896, p. 120 f.).

[4] When, on the other hand, words *with* a feminine-ending, such as קֶשֶׁת a *bow* (stem קוש), עֵת *time* (see the Lexicon), are sometimes construed as masculine, this is owing probably in some cases to a misunderstanding of the formation of the word, the ת of the feminine being regarded as a radical.

[5] Cf. *a city and a mother* (אֵם) *in Israel,* 2 S 20[19]. In the same way אֵם (like μήτηρ, *mater*) on Phoenician coins stands for *mother-city,* μητρόπολις. The same figure is used in such expressions as *sons of Zion,* ψ 149[2]; *sons of Babylon,* Ez 23[15], &c., as also in speaking of the suburbs of a city as its *daughters,* e.g. Jos 15[45 ff.], &c.—The comparison of Jerusalem to a woman is especially frequent in allegorical descriptions, e.g. Ez 16[23], La 1[1], &c.

Is 7⁶, fem., *Judaea*; אֱדוֹם masc., *Idumaei*, Nu 20²⁰; fem., *Idumaea*, Jer 49¹⁷.
Nevertheless, it sometimes happens that by a very common transference of
thought (just as we say *Turkey concludes peace*) these names are construed as
feminine, even when they denote not the country but the inhabitants; so
יְהוּדָה La 1³; cf. Gn 41⁸, Ex 10⁷, 12³³, 1 S 17²¹, 2 S 8², 24⁹, Is 7², 21², 42¹¹,
Jer 50¹⁰, Jb 1¹⁵. Hence the frequent personification of nations (as well as of
countries and towns, see *h*, note 5) as female beings, e. g. Is 50¹, 54¹ ᶠᶠ·,
and the use of the expressions בַּת בָּבֶל Is 47¹ ᶠ·, בַּת צִיּוֹן &c. (see above) as
collective poetical personifications of the people.

k　(*b*) Appellative nouns, which denote a *circumscribed space*, such as
אֶרֶץ *earth, land*, תֵּבֵל *world*, שְׁאֹל *the abode of the dead*, כִּכָּר *circle* (of
the Jordan valley), עִיר *a town*, בְּאֵר *a well*, צָפוֹן *the north*, תֵּימָן *the south*.

l　In the majority of nouns denoting place the gender is variable, e. g. אֹרַח
and דֶּרֶךְ *a way* (usually feminine; the masculine gender only begins to predominate with Ezekiel; cf. Albrecht, l. c., 1896, p. 55), גֵּי (גַּיְא) *valley*, גַּן *garden*
(fem. Gn 2¹⁵, unless לְעָבְדָהּ, &c., is to be read), הֵיכָל *palace, temple*, חָצֵר *court*,
כֶּרֶם *vineyard*, שַׁעַר *door*,¹ &c.; also מָקוֹם *place*, at least in Gn 18²⁴ (referring to
Sodom), Jb 20⁹, and 2 S 17¹² *Kᵉthibh*, is construed as feminine. The mountains
and hills commanding the surrounding country are almost without exception
masculine (see Albrecht, l. c., p. 60 f.).

m　(*c*) The names of *instruments, utensils*, and (on the same analogy)
members and *parts of the body* in man or beast, since these are all
regarded as subservient and subordinate (consequently as feminine).

n　Thus חֶרֶב *sword*, יָתֵד *tent-peg*, בַּד *bucket*, כּוֹס *cup*, נַעַל *shoe*, עֶרֶשׂ *bed*, &c.; in
other cases, as אֲרוֹן *chest, ark* (with the article הָאָרוֹן), תַּנּוּר *oven*, the gender is
variable. ('Instruments for binding or holding, girdles and the like, as
constraining and mastering, are masculine,' Albrecht, l. c., p. 89.)—Also
אֹזֶן *ear* (and in general, members occurring in pairs, Albrecht, l. c., p. 73 f.),
אֶצְבַּע *finger* (and so probably בֹּהֶן *thumb, great toe*), יָד and כַּף *hand*, יָמִין *right
hand*, רֶגֶל *foot*, בֶּרֶךְ *knee*, יָרֵךְ *thigh*, כָּתֵף *shoulder*, לְחִי *cheek*, בֶּטֶן *belly*, כָּנָף *wing*,
קֶרֶן *horn*, שֵׁן *tooth*; as a rule also זְרוֹעַ *arm* (masc. Is 17⁵, &c.), לָשׁוֹן *tongue* (masc.
ψ 22¹⁶, Pr 26²⁸, &c.), עַיִן *eye* (masc. Zc 3⁹, &c.), שׁוֹק *thigh* (masc. Ex 29²⁷).²

o　(*d*) Certain names of natural forces or substances are feminine,
being probably regarded as instruments, while the names of the
heavens, the heavenly bodies and natural phenomena, the masculine
generally predominates (cf. Albrecht, l. c., p. 323 ff.); thus feminine
are שֶׁמֶשׁ *sun* (but often also *masc.*, ψ 19⁶, 104¹⁹); אֵשׁ (Ethiopic *'ĕsât*)

---

¹ מַחֲנֶה *camp* is feminine only when it is a collective, denoting the persons
in a camp.

² אַף *nose*, גִּיד *sinew*, זָנָב *tail*, חֵךְ *palate*, כָּבֵד *liver*, לֵב, לֵבָב *heart*, מֵעִים, רַחֲמִים
bowels, מֵצַח *forehead*, עוֹר *skin*, עֹרֶף *back of the neck*, פֶּה *mouth*, צַוָּאר *neck*, רֹאשׁ *head*,
שְׁכֶם *shoulder*, also רֶחֶם *womb*, except in Jer 20¹⁷, are invariably construed as
masculine.—עֶצֶם *bone* is common.

fire (rarely *masc.*); נֹגַהּ *brightness,* אֶבֶן *a stone,* as a rule also רוּחַ *wind, spirit;* נֶפֶשׁ *breath, soul;* also אוֹר *light* in Jer 13¹⁶, Jb 36³², and others.

4. The following classes of ideas, which are also regarded as *p* feminine in Hebrew (see above, *h*), are usually indicated by the feminine *form*, notwithstanding their occasional transference to masculine persons (see *r* and *s*):

(*a*) Abstracts[1] (sometimes along with masculine forms from the same *q* stem, as נְקָמָה *vengeance,* as well as נָקָם, עֶזְרָה *help,* as well as עֵזֶר), e. g. אֱמוּנָה *firmness, faithfulness,* גְּבוּרָה *strength,* גְּדוּלָה *greatness,* מְלֵאָה *fullness,* מֶמְשָׁלָה *dominion,* &c. Similarly, the feminine (sing. and plur.) of adjectives and participles is used substantively in the sense of the Latin and Greek *neuter,* e. g. נְכוֹנָה *stedfastness,* ψ 5¹⁰, טוֹבָה *goodness,* רָעָה *evil,* Gn 50²⁰, נְקַלָּה *a light thing* (i. e. a trifling thing), Jer 6¹⁴; so especially in the plural, e. g. גְּדֹלוֹת *great things,* ψ 12⁴; הַנֶּהֱרָסוֹת *the ruined places,* Ez 36³⁶, along with הַנְּשַׁמָּה *that which was desolate,* טֹבוֹת *kindnesses,* 2 K 25²⁸, נְכֹחוֹת *uprightness, honesty,* Is 26¹⁰, נְעִימוֹת *amoena,* ψ 16¹¹ (but in verse 6 in the same sense נְעִימִים), נִפְלָאוֹת *wonderful things,* Ex 34¹⁰ and frequently, קָשׁוֹת *hard things, roughly,* Gn 42⁷·³⁰ (but cf. also רֵיקִים *vain things,* Pr 12¹¹, 28¹⁹). Cf. moreover, the very frequent use of זֹאת, הִיא (as well as זֶה and הוּא), Ju 14⁴, ψ 118²³, &c., in the sense of *hoc, illud* (also הֵנָּה equivalent to *illa,* Is 51¹⁹): also the use of the feminine form of the verb in Is 7⁷ לֹא תָקוּם וְלֹא תִהְיֶה *it shall not stand, neither shall it come to pass;* cf. Jer 10⁷; so too the suffixes Gn 15⁶, Ex 10¹¹, Jb 38¹⁸, referring back to a whole statement.[2]

(*b*) Titles and designations of office, properly a subdivision of the abstract *r* ideas treated above, under *q,* and specially noticed here only on account of their peculiar transference to concrete male persons. Thus we have קֹהֶלֶת Ec 1¹, &c. (as a title of Solomon), properly no doubt *that which takes part in or speaks in a religious assembly,* hence LXX ἐκκλησιαστής, i. e. *concionator, preacher;* the proper names סֹפֶרֶת Ezr 2⁵⁵, Neh 7⁵⁷, and פֹּכֶרֶת Ezr 2⁵⁷, Neh 7⁵⁹, and the foreign word פֶּחָה *viceroy;* in the plural כְּנָוֹת prop. *cognomina,* then *like-named, colleagues;* פַּרְעוֹת *princes* (if this be the true meaning).[3] All these words, in accordance with their meaning, are construed as masculine (in Ec 7²⁷ instead of אָמְרָה ק׳ the words should rather be divided as אָמַר הַקּ׳; cf. 12⁸).

---

[1] Cf. the list of masculine and feminine abstracts in Albrecht, l. c., 1896, p. 111 ff.

[2] While in all these instances it is simplest to speak of the *feminine* in Hebrew as being used *for the neuter* (which in Latin, Greek, and German is commonly employed for similar purposes), it must yet not be forgotten that since the language is wholly wanting in *neuters,* the Semitic mind regarded the above-mentioned forms primarily as actual feminines. Hence the Arab commentators are accustomed to explain the feminines of adjectives and participles (which would be neuter in Latin, &c.) by supplying a feminine substantive.

[3] This use of the feminine form is far more frequent in Arabic, Ethiopic, and Aramaic; cf. e. g. in Arabic *ḥalīfa* (fem. from *ḥalīf,* following after, taking the place of) in the sense of *the* successor or representative (of Muḥammad), and ʿ*allāma* (*great wisdom*) as a title of learned men. Analogous to this is the Latin *magistratus, magistracy,* for *magistrate,* and our *his Majesty, Excellency, Highness,* &c.

s Abstract ideas include also—

(c) *Collectives* in the fem. form,[1] generally fem. participles used substantivally, especially as the comprehensive designation of a number of *persons*, e. g. אֹרְחָה (fem. of *travelling*), prop. *the travelling* (company), i. e. travelling persons (a caravan) ; גּוֹלָה (fem. of גֹּלֶה *one going into exile*) *the company of exiles* (also frequently used of those who had returned home again) ; יוֹשֶׁבֶת (that which inhabits) i. e. *the population*, Is 12⁶, Mi 1¹¹ ᶠ· ; אֹיֶבֶת (prop. that which is hostile) *the enemy*, Mi 7⁸·¹⁰ (cf. Mi 4⁶ ᶠ· *the halting, cast off, driven away*, i. e. *those who halt*, &c.) ; דַּלָּה (the abject) *the poorest sort* ; of living beings which are not persons, cf. חַיָּה (that which lives) in the sense of *cattle, beasts* ; דְּגָה *a shoal of fish*, Gn 1²⁶ (but in Jon 2² as a *nomen unitatis*, cf. *t*, for דָּג *a fish*, which in verses 1 and 11 is used as the *nomen unitatis*). Cf., moreover, נְבֵלָה *dead body*, Is 26¹⁹, &c. (construed as masculine), for *a heap of dead bodies*.—On the collective poetic personification of a nation, by means of בַּת *daughter*, in בַּת עַמִּי, בַּת בָּבֶל (equivalent to בְּנֵי עַמִּי) *my countrymen*, see above, *i*.

t (d) Conversely the feminine form of substantives is sometimes used (as in Arabic) as a *nomen unitatis*, i. e. to indicate a *single* example of a class which is denoted by the masculine form ; cf. אֳנִי *a fleet* (1 K 9²⁶), אֳנִיָּה *a single ship* (Jon 1³ ᶠᶠ·) ; צַיִד *hunting, game,* צֵידָה Gn 27³ Kᵉth. (צַיִד Qᵉrè) *a piece of venison* ; שֵׂעָר *hair* (coll.), שַׂעֲרָה *a single hair* (Ju 20¹⁶ ; in the plural, ψ 40¹³, 69⁵) ; שִׁיר *a poem*, frequently collective, שִׁירָה *a single song* ; so probably also תְּאֵנָה *a fig* (the corresponding masculine *tin* is collective in Arabic) ; שׁוֹשַׁנָּה *a lily* (also שׁוֹשָׁן) ; לְבֵנָה *a brick* (Arab. *libina*, but *libin* collective), &c.

u (e) The feminine is also used for things *without life* (as being weaker or less important), which are named from their resemblance to *organic* things expressed by the corresponding masculine form ; cf. יָרֵךְ *side* (of the body), *thigh*, יַרְכָּה or יְרֵכָה *back part, border* (of a country, house, &c.) ; מֵצַח *forehead*, מִצְחָה *greaves*. On a similar distinction between the masculine for natural, and the feminine for artificial objects, see § 87 *o*.

v Rem. The juxtaposition of the masculine and feminine from the same stem serves sometimes to express entirety ; e. g. Is 3¹ מַשְׁעֵן וּמַשְׁעֵנָה *stay and staff*, i. e. every kind of support (unless we omit verse 1ᵇ as a gloss and take *staff* as = *staff-bearer, official* ; the list of officials begins in verse 2) ; cf. Is 16⁶, Pr 8¹³. For similar groupings in the case of persons, see Is 43⁶, 49²², 60⁴ (*sons and daughters*) ; 49²³, Ec 2⁸.

§ 123. *The Representation of Plural Ideas by Means of Collectives, and by the Repetition of Words.*

a Besides the plural endings treated in § 87 *a–i*, the language employs other means to express a plurality of living beings or things :

(a) Certain words employed exclusively in a collective sense, while the individual members of the class are denoted by special words (*nomina unitatis*, but not in the same sense as in § 122 *t*).

---

[1] Cf. in Greek ἡ ἵππος, *the cavalry* (as well as τὸ ἱππικόν), ἡ κάμηλος, Hdt. 1, 80, &c., *the camel corps*.

Thus בָּקָר *cattle, oxen* [1] (even joined with numerals, e. g. Ex 21³⁷ חֲמִשָּׁה בָקָר *five head of cattle*), but שׁוֹר *an ox* ; צֹאן *small cattle*, i. e. sheep and goats (μῆλα), cf. Jb 1³ שִׁבְעַת אַלְפֵי־צֹאן *seven thousand sheep*; but שֶׂה *a single head of small cattle* (a sheep or a goat). Other more or less common collectives are : זִין (prop. *that which prowls or roams*) *wild beasts*, טַף (perhaps prop. *tripping*) *a number of little children* ; דֶּשֶׁא *fresh green herb*, i. e. young plants, יֶרֶק *green*, i. e. vegetation in general ; עוֹף *birds, fowl* ; רֶכֶב *chariots* or *cavalcade*, רִמָּה *worms*, רֶמֶשׂ *creeping things* (of small creatures), שֶׁרֶץ *swarming things.*

(*b*) The collective use of substantives which at the same time serve as *nomina unitatis* ; thus, אָדָם (never in plur.) means both *man* (homo) and *men* (homines) ; אִישׁ *a man* (vir) and *men* (viri) ; אִשָּׁה *woman* and *women* (Ju 21¹⁶, 1 S 21⁶) ; אַרְבֶּה *a locust*, but usually *a swarm of locusts* ; נֶפֶשׁ *soul* and *souls* (persons) ; מַקֵּל *staff* and *staves* (Gn 30³⁷) ; עַיִט *a bird of prey* and *birds of prey* ; עָלֶה *a leaf* and *foliage* ; עֵשֶׂב *a plant* and *plants, herbs* ; עֵץ *a tree* and *trees* (as it were *foliage*) ; פְּרִי *fruit* and *fruits* ; שִׂיחַ *a shrub* and *shrubs* ; in isolated instances also nouns like עֶבֶד *man-servant*, שִׁפְחָה *maid-servant*, חֲמוֹר *ass*, שׁוֹר *ox* (cf. Gn 32⁶).—On the singular (especially of gentilic names) with the article (which may, however, be omitted in poetry, cf. e. g. ψ 12² חָסִיד, Pr 11¹⁴ יוֹעֵץ) to include all individuals of the same species, cf. § 126 *l*. On the special meaning of the plurals formed from certain collectives, see § 124 *l*.

(*c*) The feminine ending ; see § 122 *s*.

(*d*) The repetition of single words, and even of whole groups of words, especially to express entirety, or in a distributive sense. The following cases are more particularly to be noticed :

1. The repetition of one or more words to express the idea of *every, all*, as יוֹם יוֹם Gn 39¹⁰, &c., *day by day, every day* ; שָׁנָה שָׁנָה *year by year*, Dt 14²² ; אִישׁ אִישׁ *every man*, Ex 36⁴ ; with בְּ before each, as בַּבֹּקֶר בַּבֹּקֶר Ex 16²¹ *every morning* (and similarly before a group of words, Lv 24⁸), for which the *distributive* לְ is also used, לַבֹּקֶר לַבֹּקֶר 1 Ch 9²⁷, and with *one* plural לִבְקָרִים ψ 73¹⁴, לִבְקָרִים Jb 7¹⁸ parallel with לִרְגָעִים *every moment*. Somewhat different are the instances with בְּ before the second word only, e. g. יוֹם בְּיוֹם *day by day*, 1 Ch 12²² ; שָׁנָה בְשָׁנָה *year by year*, Dt 15²⁰, 1 S 1⁷ (but in verse 3 מִיָּמִים יָמִימָה), Nu 24¹, Ju 16²⁰, 20³⁰ᶠ·, 1 S 3¹⁰ *as at other times*. Also with the two words united by means of *wāw copulative*, אִישׁ וָאִישׁ ψ 87⁵, or אִישׁ וָאִישׁ Est 1⁸ ; דּוֹר וָדוֹר *all generations*, Dt 32⁷ ; יוֹם וָיוֹם Est 3⁴ ; cf. Est 8⁹,

---

[1] The plural form בְּקָרִים from בָּקָר is found only in very late Hebrew, Neh 10³⁷ (where according to the Mantua edition, Ginsburg, &c., even צֹאנֵינוּ *our sheep*, is also to be read ; Baer, however, has צֹאנֵנוּ), and 2 Ch 4³. In Am 6¹² read, with Hitzig, בַּבָּקָר יָם.

Ezr 10¹⁴, 1 Ch 26¹³ and often (cf. Cheyne, *Bampton Lectures*, 1889, p. 479, according to whom the use of the וֹ copulative with the second word is especially common in Ch and Est, and therefore belongs to the later language; Driver, *Introd.*⁶, p. 538, No. 35); sometimes (but with the exception of ψ 45¹⁸ only in very late passages) with a pleonastic כָּל־ preceding, ψ 145¹³, Est 2¹¹, 9²⁸, 2 Ch 11¹², &c.

d 2. Repetition of words in an expressly *distributive* sense¹ (which may to some extent be noticed in the examples under *c*) equivalent to *one each*, &c., e. g. Nu 14³⁴ *forty days* יוֹם לַשָּׁנָה יוֹם לַשָּׁנָה *counting for every day a year*; cf. Ez 24⁶, Ex 28³⁴ (three words repeated); also with the addition of לְבַד *apart*, עֵדֶר עֵדֶר לְבַדּוֹ *every drove by itself*, Gn 32¹⁷; cf. Zc 12¹². Most frequently with the addition of a numeral (for the simple repetition of numerals for the same purpose, cf. § 134 *q*), and with the words not only in groups of two (Lv 24⁸, Nu 13², 31⁴) or three (Nu 7¹¹, 17²¹), but even of six (Ex 26³) or seven (Ex 25³³, 26¹⁹·²¹·²⁵); in Ex 25³⁵ five words even three times repeated.²

e 3. Repetition to express an exceptional or at least superfine quality; e. g. 2 K 25¹⁵ *which were of gold, gold, of silver, silver*, i. e. made of pure gold and pure silver; Dt 2²⁷ בַּדֶּרֶךְ בַּדֶּרֶךְ *only along by the* high *way*; cf. Nu 3⁸, 8¹⁶ *they are given, given to him*, i. e. given exclusively for his service, for his very own. Also with a certain hyperbole in such examples as 2 K 3¹⁶ גֵּבִים גֵּבִים *nothing but trenches*; Gn 14¹⁰ בֶּאֱרֹת בֶּאֱרֹת חֵמָר *all asphalt-pits.*—Repetition serves to intensify the expression to the highest degree in Ju 5²² *by reason of the violent pransings of his strong ones*, Ex 8¹⁰ (*countless heaps*), and Jo 4¹⁴ (*countless multitudes*); cf. also מְעַט מְעַט Ex 23³⁰ *by little and little, very gradually*; cf. § 133 *k*.

f 4. Repetition with the copula to express *of more than one kind*; thus Dt 25¹³ (Pr 20¹⁰) אֶבֶן וָאָבֶן *a weight and a weight*, i. e. two kinds of weight (hence the addition *great and small*); ψ 12³ בְּלֵב וָלֵב *with two kinds of heart*, i. e. *with a double-dealing heart*; cf. the opposite בְּלֹא לֵב וָלֵב 1 Ch 12³³.

§ 124. *The Various Uses of the Plural-form.*³

a 1. The plural is by no means used in Hebrew solely to express a number of individuals or separate objects, but may also denote them collectively. This use of the plural expresses either (*a*) a combination of various external constituent parts (plurals of *local extension*), or (*b*) a more or less intensive focusing of the characteristics inherent in the idea of the stem (*abstract plurals*, usually rendered in English by forms in *-hood, -ness, -ship*). A variety of the plurals described under (*b*), in which the secondary idea of *intensity* or of an *internal*

---

¹ Cf. in the New Testament St. Mark 6³⁹ f. συμπόσια συμπόσια, πρασιαὶ πρασιαί (Weizsäcker, *tischweise, beetweise*).

² These repetitions of larger groups of words belong entirely to the *Priestly Code* in the Pentateuch, and are unquestionably indications of a late period of the language. Of quite a different kind are such examples as Ez 16⁶, where the repetition of four words serves to give greater solemnity to the promise, unless here, as certainly in 1²⁰, it is a mere *dittography*; the LXX omit the repetition in both passages.

³ Cf. Dietrich, 'Über Begriff und Form des hebr. Plurals,' in the *Abhandl. zur hebr. Grammatik*, Leipzig, 1846, p. 2 ff.

multiplication of the idea of the stem may be clearly seen, is (*c*) the *pluralis excellentiae* or *pluralis maiestatis*.

Examples of (*a*): Plurals of *local extension* to denote localities in general, but *b* especially level surfaces (the *surface*-plural), since in them the idea of a whole composed of innumerable separate parts or points is most evident, as שָׁמַיִם (§ 88 *d*) *heaven* (cf. also מָרוֹמִים *heights* of heaven, Is 33¹⁶, Jb 16¹⁹; elsewhere מָרוֹם); מַיִם *water*; יַמִּים (the broad surface of the sea) poetically for יָם *sea*; פָּנִים (prop. the side *turned towards* any one, then) *surface* in general, usually *face*; אֲחוֹרִים the *back*, Ex 26¹², 33²³, &c., צַוְּארִים *neck, nape of the neck* [1]; also מְרַאֲשׁוֹת *the place at the head*, מַרְגְּלוֹת *place at the feet*; עֲבָרִים *place on the other side* (of a river); מַעֲמַקִּים *depth*, מֶרְחַקִּים (also מֶרְחָק) *distance*, מִשְׁכָּבִים *bed*, Gn 49⁴ (unless, with Dillmann, it is to be explained in the sense of *double bed*, i.e. *torus*), מִשְׁכָּנִים ψ 46⁵, and מִשְׁכָּנוֹת 43³, 84², 132⁶, *dwelling* (perhaps also אֹהָלִים *encampment*, in passages like 1 S 4¹⁰). The last four belong, however, to poetic style, and are better reckoned amongst the *plurals of amplification* treated under *d-f*. So perhaps יְצֻעִים *bed* (ψ 63⁷, Jb 17¹³; but Gn 49⁴, ψ 132³, &c., in the singular); probably, however, יְצֻעִים (prop. *strata*) refers to a number of coverings or pillows.

The plural of extension is used to denote a lengthened period of *time* in עוֹלָמִים *eternity* (everlasting ages).

Rem. The plural of extension includes also a few examples which were *c* formerly explained as simply poetic plurals, e.g. Jb 17¹ קְבָרִים לִי *graves are* (ready) *for me*, i.e. the place where there are many of them (as it were *the graveyard*) is my portion, Jb 21³², 2 Ch 16¹⁴; cf. 2 K 22²⁰.

Of (*b*): the tolerably numerous abstract plurals, mostly of a particular *d* form (*qᵉṭûlîm, qiṭṭûlîm*, &c.), may be divided into two classes. They sum up either the *conditions* or *qualities* inherent in the idea of the stem, or else the various single *acts* of which an action is composed. Cf. for the first class, בְּחוּרִים and בְּחוּרוֹת *youth*, זְקֻנִים *old age*, נְעוּרִים *youth*; בְּתוּלִים *maidenhood*, כְּלוּלוֹת *bridal state*; מְגוּרִים *condition of a sojourner*, בְּשָׂרִים *fleshliness* (only in Pr 14³⁰), חַיִּים *life* (the abstract idea of the qualities of a living being); שְׁכּוּלִים *childlessness*, סַנְוֵרִים *blindness*, עִוְּעִים *perverseness*.

There are also a number of plurals, found almost exclusively in poetry *e* (sometimes along with the singular), which are evidently intended to intensify [2] the idea of the stem (plural of amplification), as אוֹנִים *might*, Is 40²⁶; אֱמוּנִים (as well as אֱמוּנָה) and אֱמוּנוֹת *faithfulness*; אַשְׁרֵי (according to § 93 *l*, only in the construct state plural or with suffixes = *the happiness of*), *happy*; כֹּשָׁרוֹת (complete) *prosperity*, ψ 68⁷; בִּינוֹת Is 27¹¹ and תְּבוּנוֹת Is 40¹⁴, &c. (keen) *understanding*; עֵצוֹת (true) *counsel*, Dt 32²⁸; דֵּעִים Jb 37¹⁶ and דֵּעוֹת

---

[1] Cf. the same use of the plural in τὰ στέρνα, τὰ νῶτα, τὰ τράχηλα, *praecordia, cervices, fauces*; on plurals of extension in general, cf. the prepositions of place and time in the plur. form, § 103 *n*. סְפָרִים is not a case in point, in the sense of *letter* (properly a sheet folded into several pages; elsewhere also סֵפֶר 1 K 21⁸ ff., 2 K 10¹, 19¹⁴ (Is 37¹⁴; referred to afterwards by the *singular* suffix); Is 39¹, Jer 29²⁵, 32¹⁴ (*after* being folded, previously סֵפֶר).

[2] Cf. A. Ember, 'The pluralis intensivus in Hebrew,' *AJSL.* 1905, p. 195 ff.

1 S 2³ (thorough) *knowledge*; בַּטֻּחוֹת Jb 12⁶ and מִבְטַחִים Is 32¹⁸ (full) *confidence*; בְּרָכוֹת (abundant) *blessing*, ψ 21⁷; גְּבוּרוֹת (exceptional) *strength*, Jb 41⁴; הַוּוֹת ψ 5¹⁰ (very) *wickedness*; חֲמוּדוֹת Dn 9²³ (greatly) *beloved*; חֲמוֹת ψ 76¹¹, &c. (fierce) *wrath*; חֲרָפוֹת Dn 12² (utter) *contempt*; יְשֻׁעוֹת (real) *help*, Is 26¹⁸, &c.; מַרְאֹת Gn 46² (an important) *vision*; מֵישָׁרִים *uprightness*; תַּהְפֻּכוֹת *perversity*; נְקָמוֹת (complete) *vengeance*, Ju 11³⁶, &c.; חֲשֵׁכִים and מַחֲשַׁכִּים (thick) *darkness*; מִסְתָּרִים a (close) *hiding-place*; נְגִידִים *nobility*; שְׁמָנִים Is 28¹ *fatness*; צִחְצָחוֹת (complete) *aridity*; מַמְתַקִּים *sweetness*; מַחֲמַדִּים *preciousness*; שַׁעֲשֻׁעִים *delight*; עֲדָנִים and תַּעֲנֻגִים *pleasure*; רַחֲמִים *compassion*; מְנֻחֹת ψ 23² *refreshment*; מְהוּמֹת Am 3⁹ *tumult*. Probably also יְדִידֹת (heartfelt) *love*, ψ 45¹; מְרֹרוֹת (extreme) *bitterness*, Jb 13²⁶; מִרְמוֹת (base) *deceit*, ψ 38¹³; צְדָקוֹת (true) *righteousness*, Is 33¹⁵, &c.; שְׂמָחוֹת (the highest) *joy*, ψ 16¹¹. On the other hand, חָכְמוֹת *wisdom* (Pr 1²⁰, &c.) can hardly be a *plural* (=the essence of wisdom, or wisdom personified), but is a singular (see § 86 *l*).

A further extension of this plural of amplification occurs according to P. Haupt's very probable suggestion (*SBOT*. Proverbs, p. 40, line 50, &c.) in יְאֹרִים *the great river* (of the Nile, generally יְאֹר) Is 7¹⁸, 19⁶ (though with the predicate in the plural), Ez 30¹², ψ 78⁴⁴, but in Is 37²⁵, Ez 29³ the usual explanation, *arms* or *channels of the Nile*, can hardly be avoided; also in נְהָרוֹת ψ 24² of the ocean, which encircles the earth, 137¹ of the *great river*, i. e. the Euphrates, but in Is 18¹ נַהֲרֵי כוּשׁ is evidently a numerical plural.—In Pr 16¹³ מְלָכִים (acc. to P. Haupt=the *great king*) is very doubtful. In נְשִׂיאֵי Ez 19¹ the second *yôdh* is evidently due to dittography, since יִשְׂרָאֵל follows.

f　The summing up of the several parts of an action is expressed in חֲנֻטִים *embalming*, כִּפֻּרִים *atonement*, מִלֻּאִים (prop. *filling*, sc. of the hand) *ordination to the priesthood*, שִׁלֻּחִים *dismissal*, שִׁלֻּמִים *retribution*, פִּתֻּחִים *engraving* (of a seal, &c.); אַהֲבִים *fornication*, זְנוּנִים *whoredom*, נִאֻפִים *adultery*; נִחֻמִים (prop. no doubt, warm compassion) *consolation*, תַּחֲנוּנִים *supplication*, נְדֻדִים Jb 7⁴ (restless) *tossing to and fro*, פְּלָאִים *wonder* La 1⁹, עֹלֵלוֹת *gleaning*; perhaps also נְגִינוֹת ψ 4¹, 6¹, &c., if it means *the playing on stringed instruments*, and שִׁלְמֹנִים Is 1²³ *bribery*, unless it be a plural of number.[1]

g　Of (*c*): the *pluralis excellentiae* or *maiestatis*, as has been remarked above, is properly a variety of the abstract plural, since it sums up the several characteristics[2] belonging to the idea, besides possessing the secondary sense of an *intensification* of the original idea. It is thus closely related to the plurals of amplification, treated under *e*, which are mostly found in poetry.

---

[1] Mayer Lambert in *REJ*. xxiv. 106 ff., enumerates no less than ninety-five words ending in *îm*, which in his opinion are to be regarded as *pluralia tantum*.

[2] The Jewish grammarians call such plurals רִבּוּי הַכֹּחוֹת *plur. virium* or *virtutum*; later grammarians call them *plur. excellentiae*, *magnitudinis*, or *plur. maiestaticus*. This last name may have been suggested by the *we* used by kings when speaking of themselves (cf. already 1 Macc. 10¹⁹, 11³¹); and the plural used by God in Gn 1²⁶, 11⁷, Is 6⁸ has been incorrectly explained in this way. It is, however, either *communicative* (including the attendant angels; so at all events in Is 6⁸, cf. also Gn 3²²), or according to others, an indication of *the fullness of power and might* implied in אֱלֹהִים (see Dillmann on Gn 1²⁶); but it is best explained as a plural of *self-deliberation*. The use of the plural as a form of respectful address is quite foreign to Hebrew.

So especially אֱלֹהִים *Godhead, God* (to be distinguished from the numerical plural *gods*, Ex 12¹², &c.). The supposition that אֱלֹהִים is to be regarded as merely a remnant of earlier polytheistic views (i. e. as originally only a numerical plural) is at least highly improbable, and, moreover, would not explain the analogous plurals (see below). That the language has entirely rejected the idea of numerical plurality in אֱלֹהִים (whenever it denotes *one* God), is proved especially by its being almost invariably joined with a singular attribute (cf. § 132 *h*), e.g. אֱלֹהִים צַדִּיק *ψ* 7¹⁰, &c. Hence אֱלֹהִים may have been used originally not only as a numerical but also as an abstract plural (corresponding to the Latin *numen*, and our *Godhead*), and, like other abstracts of the same kind, have been transferred to a concrete single god (even of the heathen).

To the same class (and probably formed on the analogy of אֱלֹהִים) belong *h* the plurals קְדֹשִׁים *the Most Holy* (only of Yahweh), Ho 12¹, Pr 9¹⁰, 30³ (cf. אֱלֹהִים קְדֹשִׁים Jos 24¹⁹, and the Aram. עֶלְיוֹנִין *the Most High*, Dn 7¹⁸·²²·²⁵); and probably תְּרָפִים (usually taken in the sense of *penates*) the image of a god, used especially for obtaining oracles. Certainly in 1 S 19¹³·¹⁶ only *one* image is intended; in most other places a single image *may* be intended [1]; in Zc 10² alone is it most naturally taken as a numerical plural. In Ec 5⁷ גְּבֹהִים *supremus* (of God) is doubtful; according to others it is a numerical plural, *superiores*.

Further, אֲדֹנִים, as well as the singular אָדוֹן, (lordship) *lord*, e.g. אֲדֹנִים קָשֶׁה *i a cruel lord*, Is 19⁴; אֲדֹנֵי הָאָרֶץ *the lord of the land*, Gn 42³⁰, cf. Gn 32¹⁹; so especially with the suffixes of the 2nd and 3rd persons אֲדֹנֶיךָ, אֲדֹנָיו *ψ* 45¹², אֲדֹנֵינוּ, &c., also אֲדֹנֵינוּ (except 1 S 16¹⁶); but in 1st sing. always אֲדֹנִי.[2] So also בְּעָלִים (with suffixes) *lord, master* (of slaves, cattle, or inanimate things; but in the sense of *maritus*, always in the singular), e.g. בְּעָלָיו Ex 21²⁹, Is 1³, &c.[3]

On the other hand, we must regard as doubtful a number of participles in *k* the plural, which, being used as attributes of God, resemble *plurales excellentiae*; thus, עֹשַׂי *my Maker*, Jb 35¹⁰; עֹשֶׂךָ Is 54⁵; עֹשָׂיו *ψ* 149²; עֹשֶׂיהָ Is 22¹¹; נוֹטֵיהֶם *stretching them out*, Is 42⁵; for all these forms may also be explained as singular, according to § 93 *ss.*[4] נֹגְשָׂיו Is 3¹² might also be regarded as another instance, unless it be a numerical plural, *their oppressors*; moreover, מְרִימָיו *him who lifteth it up*, Is 10¹⁵ (but read probably מְרִימוֹ); שֹׁלְחָיו *him who sendeth him*, Pr 10²⁶, 22²¹ (so Baer, but Ginsburg שֹׁלְחֶךָ), 25¹³ (in parallelism with אֲדֹנָיו). These latter plurals, however (including מְרִימָיו), may probably be more simply explained as indicating an indefinite individual, cf. *o* below.—For שֹׁמְרֶיךָ *ψ* 121⁵ (textus receptus) and בּוֹרְאֶיךָ Ec 12¹ (textus receptus) the singular should be read, with Baer.

---

[1] Even in Gn 31³⁴, notwithstanding the plural suffix in וַתְּשִׂמֵם and עֲלֵיהֶם, since the construction of these abstracts as numerical plurals is one of the peculiarities of the E-document of the Hexateuch; cf. Gn 20¹³, 35⁷, and § 145 *i*.

[2] On אֲדֹנִי (for אֲדֹנָי) as a name of God, cf. § 135 *q*.

[3] Euting, *Reise in Arabien*, p. 61, mentions the interesting fact that the subjects of the Emir of Ḥâyel commonly speak of their ruler as *šiyûkh*, a plur. majestatis = *the great sheikh*.

[4] בְּעָלֶיךָ, which in Is 54⁵ is in parallelism with עֹשֶׂךָ, must then be explained as merely formed on analogy.

l Rem. 1. (*a*) Coherent substances, &c., are mostly regarded as *single*, and are, accordingly, almost always represented by nouns in the singular, cf. אָבָק *fine dust,* אֵפֶר *ashes,* בַּד *linen,* בְּדִיל *lead,* זָהָב *gold,* כֶּסֶף *silver,* נְחֹשֶׁת *brass,* חָלָב *milk,* יַיִן *wine,* עָפָר *dust, the ground,* עֵץ *wood.* Plurals are, however, formed from some of these words expressing materials in order to denote separate portions taken from the whole in manufacture (*plurals of the result*) or parts otherwise detached from it; thus, בַּדִּים *linen garments;* כְּסָפִים *silver pieces,* Gn 42²⁵·³⁵; נְחֻשְׁתַּיִם (dual) *fetters of brass;* עֵצִים *ligna (timber* for building or *sticks* for burning); also in a wider sense, בְּדִילִים *particles of alloy* to be separated by smelting, Is 1²⁵; עֲפָרוֹת *fragments of earth,* Pr 8²⁶, cf. Jb 28⁶ עַפְרֹת זָהָב *dust of gold.*

m (*b*) To the class of *plurals of the result* belong also a few names of natural products, when represented in an artificial condition; thus, חִטִּים *wheat in grain* (threshed wheat), as distinguished from חִטָּה *wheat* (used collectively) *in the ear;* cf. the same distinction between כֻּסְּמִים and כֻּסֶּמֶת *spelt;* עֲדָשִׁים and עֲדָשָׁה (the singular preserved only in the Mishna) *lentils;* שְׂעֹרִים and שְׂעֹרָה *barley;* also פִּשְׁתִּים *linen,* פֵּשֶׁת (to be inferred from פִּשְׁתִּי) *flax.*

n (*c*) Finally, the distinction between דָּם *blood* and דָּמִים requires to be specially noticed. The singular is always used when the blood is regarded as an organic unity, hence also of menstrual blood, and the blood of sacrifices (collected in the basin and then sprinkled), and in Nu 23²⁴ of the blood gushing from wounds. On the other hand, דָּמִים as a sort of plural of the result and at the same time of local extension, denotes *blood which is shed,* when it appears as blood-stains (Is 1¹⁵) or as blood-marks (so evidently in Is 9⁴). But since blood-stains or blood-marks, as a rule, suggest blood shed in murder (although דָּמִים also denotes the blood which flows at childbirth or in circumcision), דָּמִים acquired (even in very early passages) simply the sense of a *bloody deed,* and especially of *bloodguiltiness,* Ex 22¹ᶠ·, &c.

o In some few cases the plural is used to denote an indefinite singular; certainly so in Dt 17⁵ אֶל־שְׁעָרֶיךָ *unto one of thy gates;* Zc 9⁹ בֶּן־אֲתֹנוֹת (cf. Ct 2⁹); Ex 21²² יְלָדֶיהָ (where evidently only *one* child is thought of, though certainly in connexion with a contingency which may be repeated); cf. also Ec 4¹⁰ (*if one of them fall*).—So probably also Gn 8⁴, 1 S 17⁴³, Dn 2¹, Neh 3⁸, 6²; but *not* Gn 19²⁹, since the same document (Gn 13¹²) makes Lot dwell *in the cities* of the Jordan valley; in Gn 21⁷ בָּנִים denotes the class with which the action is concerned. In Ju 12⁷ instead of the unusual בְּעָרֵי גִלְעָד *in the cities of Gilead* (formerly explained here as in *one of the cities of Gilead*) we should most probably read, with Moore (*SBOT.* Judges, p. 52), בְּעִירוֹ בְּמִצְפֶּה גִלְעָד *in his city, in Mizpeh* (in) *Gilead.*

p 2. When a substantive is followed by a genitive, and the compound idea thus formed is to be expressed in the plural, this is done—

(*a*) Most naturally by using the plural of the *nomen regens,* e. g. גִּבּוֹרֵי חַיִל *mighty men of valour* (prop. heroes of strength), 1 Ch 7²·⁹; so also in compounds, e. g. בְּנֵי יְמִינִי 1 S 22⁷, as the plur. of בֶּן־יְמִינִי *Benjamite;* but also

q (*b*) By using the plural of *both* nouns,[1] e. g. גִּבּוֹרֵי חֲיָלִים 1 Ch 7⁵;

---

[1] Cf. König, *Lehrgebäude,* ii. 438 f., according to whom the plural of the principal word exercises an influence on the determining genitive.

וּבְבָתֵּי כְלָאִים *and in prison houses*, Is 42²²; cf. Ex 34¹, &c., שְׁנֵי־לֻחֹת אֲבָנִים *two tables of stone* (but Ex 31¹⁸ לֻחֹת אֶבֶן); Nu 13³², Dt 1²⁸, Jos 5², 6⁴, 2 K 14¹⁴, 25²³, Is 51⁹, Jer 41¹⁶, Ezr 3³, &c. עַמֵּי הָאֲרָצוֹת *the people of the country*; 2 Ch 26¹⁴; so perhaps בְּנֵי אֵלִים *sons of God*, ψ 29¹, 89⁷ (according to others *sons of gods*); or finally even

(c) By using the plural of the *nomen rectum*;[1] e. g. בֵּית אָבוֹת Ex 6¹⁴, *r* Nu 1²·⁴ᶠᶠ·, &c., as plur. of בֵּית אָב *father's house, family*; בֵּית הַבָּמוֹת *the houses of the high places*, 2 K 17²⁹ (also בָּתֵּי הַבָּמוֹת 23¹⁹); בֵּית עֲצַבֵּיהֶם *the houses of their idols*, 1 S 31⁹, Ez 46²⁴; cf. also Ju 7²⁵ *the head of Oreb and Zeeb*, i. e. the heads, &c.

Rem. When a substantive (in a distributive sense) with a suffix refers *S* back to a plural, the singular form of the substantive suffices, since the idea of plurality is already adequately expressed by the suffix, e. g. פִּימוֹ *os* (for *ora*) *eorum*, ψ 17¹⁰; יְמִינָם *their right hand*, ψ 144⁸ [so in the English RV.], for *hands*.

§ 125. *Determination of Nouns in general. Determination of Proper Names.*

Brockelmann, *Grundriss*, i. 466 ff.

1. A noun may either be determinate in itself, as a proper name *a* or pronoun (see below, *d* and *i*), or be made so by its context. In the latter case, the determination may be effected either by prefixing the article (see § 126), or by the connexion of the noun (in the construct state) with a following determinate genitive, and consequently also (according to § 33 c) by its union with a pronominal suffix (§ 127 a). It is to be taken as a fundamental rule, that the determination can only be effected in *one* of the ways here mentioned; the article cannot be prefixed to a proper name, nor to a noun followed by the genitive, nor can a proper name be used in the construct state. Deviations from this rule are either only apparent or have arisen from a corruption of the text.

Rem. Only in a few passages is a noun made expressly *indeterminate* by the *b* addition of אֶחָד in the sense of our indefinite article; cf. Ex 16³³, Ju 9⁵³, 13², 1 S 1¹, 7⁹·¹², 1 K 13¹¹, 19⁴, 20¹³, 22⁹, 2 K 4¹, 8⁶, 12¹⁰, Ez 8⁸, Dn 8³, 10⁶ (in 8¹³ אֶחָד קָדוֹשׁ i. e. *one*, viz. *a holy one*, is opposed to another).

It is further to be noticed, that in Hebrew the phenomenon sometimes *C* occurs, which the Arab grammarians call *indeterminateness for the sake of amplification*; e. g. Is 31⁸ *and he shall flee* מִפְּנֵי־חֶרֶב *from a sword*, i. e. *from an irresistible sword* (God's sword); cf. Is 28² בְּיָד; 2 S 6² שָׁם; Ho 3¹ אִשָּׁה *such a woman*, without doubt to be referred to the Gomer mentioned in cap. 1;

---

[1] Cf. Brockelmann, *Grundriss*, i. 482.

Am 6¹⁴ גּוֹי ; ψ 77¹⁶ בְּזֹרֵעַ ; Pr 21¹² צַדִּיק, if with Delitzsch it is to be referred to God ; Jb 8¹⁰ מִלִּים meaning *important words*, but in 15¹³ מִלִּין *reproachful words*. Cf. on this point, § 117 *q*, note 3, and Delitzsch, *Psalmen*, ed. 4, p. 79.

d **2.** Real *proper nouns*, as being the names of things (or persons) only *once* met with, are sufficiently determinate in themselves. Such names, therefore, as יהוה, דָּוִד, יַעֲקֹב, כְּנַעַן, סְדֹם do not admit of the article,¹ nor can they be in the construct state. On the other hand, not only *gentilic* names (as denoting the *various* individuals belonging to the same class), but also all those proper names, of which the appellative sense is still sufficiently evident to the mind, or at least has been handed down from an earlier period of the language, frequently (often even as a rule) take the article (according to § 126 *e*), and may even be followed by a genitive.

e Examples. Like the above-mentioned proper names of individuals, countries, and cities, so also national names, which are identical in form with the name of the founder of the race (e.g. מוֹאָב, אֱדוֹם, יִשְׂרָאֵל), are always determinate in themselves. Of gentilic names (e.g. הָעִבְרִי *the Hebrew*, הָעִבְרִים *the Hebrews*, Gn 40¹⁵ ; הַכְּנַעֲנִי *the Canaanite*) the plural פְּלִשְׁתִּים, even when meaning *the* Philistines, is generally used without the article (but in 1 S 4⁷, &c., הַפְּ׳) ; so always כַּפְתֹּרִים.—Evident appellatives (like such modern names as *the Hague*, *le Havre*) are הַגִּבְעָה *the hill*, in the construct state גִּבְעַת שָׁאוּל, i. e. *the Gibeah named after Saul* to distinguish it from others; הָרָמָה *the height* ; הָעַי *the heap* ; הַלְּבָנוֹן (prop. *the white mountain*) *the Lebanon* ; הַיְאֹר (prop. *the river*) *the Nile*, cf. Am 8⁸ כִּיאוֹר מִצְרַיִם *like the river of Egypt*; הַיַּרְדֵּן *the Jordan* (according to Seybold, *Mittheil. und Nachr. des DPV.*, 1896, p. 11, probably *the drinking-place* [ירד, Arab. *warada*, meaning orig. *to go down to drink*]).

f Rem. 1. In a few instances original appellatives have completely assumed the character of real proper names, and are therefore used without the article ; thus אֱלֹהִים *God*, to denote the one true God (as elsewhere יהוה) Gn 1¹ and so generally in this document of the Pentateuch up to Ex 6, elsewhere sometimes הָאֱלֹהִים ὁ θεός (cf. § 126 *e*) ; also the sing. אֱלוֹהַּ *God*, עֶלְיוֹן *the Most High*, and שַׁדַּי *the Almighty* never take the article.—Moreover, אָדָם *Adam* from Gn 5¹ onwards (previously in 2⁷, &c., הָאָדָם *the first man*) ; שָׂטָן *Satan*, 1 Ch 21¹ (but Zc 3¹, Jb 1⁶, &c., הַשָּׂטָן *the adversary*) ; cf. אֹהֶל מוֹעֵד *the tent of revelation* (i. e. the tabernacle), always without the article.

g To the class of nouns originally appellative, which the language regards

---

¹ Consequently, הַמְנַשֶּׁה Dt 3¹³, Jos 1¹², &c. (In the Deuteronomist) in the combination שֵׁבֶט הַמְנַשֶּׁה (for which elsewhere שֵׁבֶט מְנַשֶּׁה) is to be regarded *not* as a proper name but as a gentilic name (= *the tribe of the Manassites*), for which in Dt 29⁷ הַמְנַשִּׁי שׁ׳ is used, as in 10⁸ הַלֵּוִי שׁ׳ *the tribe of the Levites*, and in Ju 18¹ הַדָּנִי שׁ׳ *the tribe of the Danites*.—In Jos 13⁷ הַמְנַשֶּׁה (like gentilic names in ־ִי) is even used adjectivally.

as proper names, and which consequently never take the article, belong also
certain archaic words mostly used only by poets, such as שְׁאוֹל *Hades*, תֵּבֵל
world, תְּהוֹם *ocean*, of the body of water which encircles the earth, Gn 1², &c. ;
but Is 63¹³, ψ 106⁹ בַּתְּהֹמוֹת *through the depths*, viz. of the Red Sea.¹

2. When nouns which the usage of the language always treats as proper *h*
names occasionally appear to be connected with a following genitive, this is
really owing to an ellipse whereby the noun which really governs the
genitive, i. e. the appellative idea contained in the proper name, is suppressed.
So evidently in the case of יְהֹוָה צְבָאוֹת *Yahweh* (the God) *of hosts* ; the fuller
form יהוה אֱלֹהֵי צְבָאוֹת 2 S 5¹⁰, &c., or יהוה אֱלֹהֵי הַצְּבָאוֹת Am 3¹³, &c., is
a secondary expansion of the original יְהֹוָה צְבָאוֹת; אֱלֹהִים in ψ 59⁶,
80¹⁵·²⁰, 84⁹ is due to the mechanical substitution of אֱלֹהִים for יהוה affected in
the 2nd and part of the 3rd book of the Psalms. So also in geographical
names such as אוּר כַּשְׂדִּים *Ur* (the city) *of the Chaldees*, Gn 11²⁸; אֲרַם נַהֲרַיִם
Aram (the region) *of the two rivers*; בֵּית לֶחֶם יְהוּדָה *Bethlehem* (the city) *of
Judah*; אָבֵל בֵּית מַעֲכָה 2 S 20¹⁴, &c., to distinguish it from אָבֵל מַיִם *Abel by
the water*, 2 Ch 16⁴; יָבֵישׁ גִּלְעָד 1 S 11¹, &c.; יַרְדֵּן יְרֵחוֹ Nu 22¹, 26³·⁶³, &c.; on
Ju 8³² cf. § 128 c; צִיּוֹן קְדוֹשׁ יִשְׂרָאֵל *the Zion of the Holy One of Israel*, Is 60¹⁴; but
in 1 S 1¹ for צוֹפִים read צוּפִי *a Zuphite*. Some of these examples (cf. also
Am 6²) come very near to the actual construct state (cf. above, גִּבְעַת שָׁאוּל),
since e. g. the addition of the genitive serves to distinguish the place from
four others called Aram (see the Lexicon), or from another Bethlehem.
Aram, Bethlehem, &c., are accordingly no longer names found only in one
special sense, and therefore also are no longer proper names in the strictest
sense.

3. Of the pronouns, the personal pronouns proper (the separate *i*
pronouns, § 32) are always determinate in themselves, since they can
denote only definite individuals (the 3rd person, also definite things).
For the same reason the demonstrative pronouns (§ 34) are also
determinate in themselves, when they stand *alone* (as equivalent to
substantives), either as subject (Gn 5²⁹) or as predicate (e. g. זֶה הַיּוֹם
this is the day, Ju 4¹⁴; אֵלֶּה הַדְּבָרִים *these are the words*, Dt 1¹), or as
object (e. g. אֶת־זֹאת 2 S 13¹⁷), or as genitive (מְחִיר זֶה 1 K 21²), or
finally when joined to a preposition (לָזֹאת Gn 2²³; בָּזֶה 1 S 16⁸, see
§ 102 *g*).

So also the personal pronouns הוּא, הִיא, הֵם, הֵמָּה, הֵנָּה when they *k*
are used as demonstratives (= *is, ea, id, ille*, &c.) are always determinate in themselves, e. g. הוּא הַדָּבָר *that is the thing*, Gn 41²⁸. They

---

¹ That various other words, such as אֱנוֹשׁ *man*, צַלְמָוֶת *deep darkness*, רוֹזֵן
prince, שָׂדַי *field*, תּוּשִׁיָּה *effectual working*, are always found without the article
is not to be attributed to any special archaism, but is to be explained from
the fact that they belong solely to poetic language, which avoids the article ;
in other cases, such as תַּרְדֵּמָה *deep sleep*, there is no occasion for the article in
the passages we possess.

are made determinate by the article, when they are joined like adjectives (see § 126 *u*) with a determinate substantive, e. g. הָאִישׁ הַזֶּה *this man*; הָאֲנָשִׁים הָאֵלֶּה *these men*; בַּיָּמִים הָהֵמָּה וּבָעֵת הַהִיא *in those days, and in that time*, Jo 4¹. The demonstrative, however, even in this case, is frequently used *without* the article, as being sufficiently determinate in itself (cf. § 126 *y*).

§ 126. *Determination by Means of the Article.*

a 1. The article (הֲ, הָ, הַ, § 35) was originally, as in other languages (clearly in the Romance; cf. also ὁ, ἡ, τό in Homer), a demonstrative pronoun. The demonstrative force of the article, apart from its occasional use as a relative pronoun (see § 138 *i*), appears now, however, only (*a*) in a few standing phrases, and (*b*) in a certain class of statements or exclamations.

b (*a*) Cf. הַיּוֹם *this day, hodie* (§ 100 *c*); הַלַּיְלָה *this night*, Gn 19³⁴; הַפַּעַם *this time*, Gn 2²³; הַשָּׁנָה *this year* (= in this year) Is 37³⁰, Jer 28¹⁶.

(*b*) includes those instances in which the article, mostly when prefixed to a participle, joins on a new statement concerning a preceding noun. Although such participles, &c., are no doubt primarily regarded always as in apposition to a preceding substantive, the article nevertheless has in some of these examples almost the force of הוּא (הִיא, הֵמָּה) as the subject of a noun-clause; e.g. ψ 19¹⁰ *the judgements of the Lord are true* . . ., verse 11 הַנֶּחֱמָדִים וגֹ׳ prop. *the more to be desired than gold*, i.e. *they are more to be desired*, or *even they, that are more to be desired*,[1] &c.; cf. Gn 49²¹, Is 40²² ᶠ·, 44²⁷ ᶠ·, 46⁶, Am 2⁷, 5⁷, ψ 33¹⁵, 49⁷ הַבֹּטְחִים in the parallel half of the verse continued by a finite verb); ψ 104³, Jb 6¹⁶, 28⁴, 30³, 41²⁵ and frequently. When such a participle has another co-ordinate with it, the latter is used *without* the article, since according to the above it strictly speaking represents a second predicate, and as such, according to *i*, remains indeterminate; e.g. Jb 5¹⁰ *who giveth* (הַנֹּתֵן) *rain*, &c., *and sendeth* (וְשֹׁלֵחַ), &c.

c The article is sometimes used with similar emphasis before a substantive, which serves as the subject of a compound sentence (§ 140 *d*); e.g. Dt 32⁴ הַצּוּר תָּמִים פָּעֳלוֹ i.e. as a fresh statement (not in apposition to the preceding dative), really equivalent to *he is a rock, perfect in his work* (i. e. *whose work is perfect*); cf. ψ 18³¹.

d 2. The article is, generally speaking, employed to determine a substantive wherever it is required by Greek and English; thus:

(*a*) When a person or thing already spoken of is mentioned again, and is consequently more definite to the mind of the hearer or reader; e. g. Gn 1³ *and God said, Let there be light*: verse 4 *and God saw the light* (אֶת־הָאוֹר); 1 K 3²⁴ *fetch me a sword: and they brought the sword*; Ec 9¹⁵. (In 2 S 12² therefore לְעָשִׁיר must be read.)

---

[1] On the analogous use of the article before participles which have a verbal suffix, as in ψ 18³³, &c., cf. above, § 116 *f*.

(*b*) With a title understood and recognized by every one, e. g.
הַמֶּלֶךְ שְׁלֹמֹה ὁ βασιλεὺς Σαλωμών : Gn 35⁸ *under the oak* (the well-known oak which was there).

(*c*) With appellatives to denote persons or natural objects which are unique, e. g. הַכֹּהֵן הַגָּדוֹל *the high priest*, הַשֶּׁמֶשׁ *the sun*, הָאָרֶץ *the earth*.

(*d*) When terms applying to whole classes are restricted (simply by *e* usage) to particular individuals (like ὁ ποιητής, meaning Homer) or things, e. g. שָׂטָן *adversary*, הַשָּׂטָן *the adversary*, Satan ; בַּעַל *lord*, הַבַּעַל *Baal* as proper name of the god ; הָאָדָם *the* (first) *man*, *Adam* ; הָאֱלֹהִים [1] or הָאֵל ὁ θεός, *the one true God* (cf. also ὁ Χριστός in the New Testament); also הַנָּהָר *the river*, i. e. *Euphrates* ; הַכִּכָּר *the circle*, sc. of the Jordan, *the Jordan plain* [Gn 19¹⁷, &c.].

(*e*) Very often with the vocative, e. g. 2 S 14⁴ הוֹשִׁעָה הַמֶּלֶךְ *help, O king*; Zc 3⁸ יְהוֹשֻׁעַ הַכֹּהֵן הַגָּדוֹל *O Joshua the high priest* ; 1 S 17⁵⁸, 24⁹, 2 K 9⁵; in the plural, Is 42¹⁸, Jo 1²·¹³; but cf. also Jos 10¹², Is 1², 49¹³ (שָׁמַיִם and אֶרֶץ); 23¹⁶, Ho 13¹⁴, Jo 1⁵, ψ 34¹², Ec 10¹⁷, 11⁹, &c. [2] The vocative occurs *without* the article in Is 22², since it has been already defined by a preceding accusative.

Rem. Strictly speaking in all these cases the substantive with the article *f* is really in apposition to the personal pronoun of the 2nd person, which is either expressly mentioned or virtually present (in the imperative), e. g. 1 S 17⁵⁸ *thou, the young man*. But such passages as Is 42¹⁸, where the vocative precedes the imperative, prove that in such cases the substantive originally in apposition eventually acquired the value of a complete clause.

(*f*) With words denoting classes (see particulars under *l*). *g*

(*g*) In a peculiar way, to specify persons or things, which are so far definite as to be naturally thought of in connexion with a given case, and must be assumed accordingly to be there (see *q–s*).

(*h*) With adjectives (also ordinal numbers and demonstrative pronouns used adjectivally) which are joined to substantives determined in some way (see *u*).

Rem. The article may be omitted in *poetry* in all the above-mentioned *h* cases; in general it is used in poetry far less frequently than in prose. Its use or omission probably often rests on rhythmical grounds ; [3] it is sometimes omitted also for rhetorical reasons. Cf. e. g. אֶרֶץ for הָאָרֶץ ψ 2²; מְלָכִים as vocative, verse 10; מֶלֶךְ for הַמֶּלֶךְ 21²; שְׁמָךְ גָּדוֹל וְנוֹרָא (contrary to *u*, *v*) 99³. In the instances in which the ה of the article is omitted after a prefix (§ 35 *n*), the vowel of the article is often retained after the prefix even in poetry, e. g. בַּשָּׁמַיִם ψ 2⁴, &c.

---

[1] On the subsequent change of שָׂטָן, אָדָם, אֱלֹהִים into real proper names by the omission of the article, cf. above, § 125 *f*.

[2] For further exceptions see Nestle, *ZAW.* 1904, p. 323 ff.

[3] Cf. the useful statistics of J. Ley in the *Neue Jahrbücher für Philologie und Pädagogik*, 2te Abteilung, 1891, Heft 7–9, and M. Lambert, 'L'article dans la poésie hébr.,' *REJ.* 37, 263 ff.

i (*i*) On the other hand, the article is always omitted when a person or thing is to be represented as indefinite (or indefinable) or as yet unknown ; consequently also before the predicate, since this is from its nature always a general term, under which the subject is included, e.g. Gn 29⁷ עוֹד הַיּוֹם גָּדוֹל *as yet the day is great*, i.e. it is yet high day; 33¹³, 40¹⁸, 41²⁶, Is 66³.

k Rem. 1. As exceptions to the above rule it is usual to regard those examples in which a determinate adjective or participle (equivalent to a relative clause) is used apparently as a predicate, e.g. Gn 2¹¹ הוּא הַסֹּבֵב *it is the compassing*, i. e. *that is it which compasseth* ; 42⁶, 45¹², Ex 9²⁷, Dt 3²¹, 8¹⁸, 11⁷, 1 S 4¹⁶, Is 14²⁷, Mal 3² (cf. in Greek, e.g. St. Mat. 10²⁰, where Winer, *Gram. des neutest. Sprachidioms*, § 58, 2, Rem., explains οἱ λαλοῦντες as a predicate with the article). In reality, however, these supposed predicates are rather subjects (acc. to § 116 *q*), and the only peculiarity of these cases is that the subject is not included under a general idea, but is equated with the predicate.

2. Sometimes the article is used with only one of two parallel words, as Na 1⁵ הֶהָרִים and הַגְּבָעוֹת, 2 Ch 3¹⁷ מִיָּמִין and מֵהַשְּׂמֹאול.

l 3. The use of the article to determine the *class* is more extensive in Hebrew than in most other languages. In this case the article indicates universally known, closely circumscribed, and therefore well defined classes of persons or things. The special cases to be considered are—

m (*a*) The employment of general names as collectives in the singular, to denote the *sum total* of individuals belonging to the class (which may, however, be done just as well by the plural) ; e.g. *the righteous, the wicked man*, Ec 3¹⁷ ; *the woman*, i.e. *the female sex*, 7²⁶ ; הָאֹיֵב *th. enemy*, i. e. *the enemies* (?) ψ 9⁷ ; הָאֹרֵב *the lier in wait*, i.e. *the liers in wait* ; הֶחָלוּץ *the armed man*, i.e. *soldiers* ; הַמְאַסֵּף *the rearguard* ; הַמַּשְׁחִית *the spoiler*, 1 S 13¹⁷ ;[1] so also (as in English) with names of animals, when something is asserted of them, which applies to the whole species, e.g. 2 S 17¹⁰ *as the courage of* הָאַרְיֵה *the lion*. Especially also with gentilic names, e.g. *the Canaanite*, Gn 13⁷ (cf. 15¹⁹ᶠ·) ; so in English *the Russian, the Turk*, &c., in Attic writers ὁ Ἀθηναῖος, ὁ Συρακόσιος, &c.

n (*b*) Names of materials known everywhere, the elements and other words denoting classes, even though only a part and not the whole of them is considered, in which case in other languages, as e.g. in English, the article is usually omitted (cf., however, our *to fall into the water, into the fire*, &c.), e. g. Gn 13² *and Abram was very rich* בַּמִּקְנֶה בַּכֶּסֶף וּבַזָּהָב *in cattle, in silver and in gold* ; Jbs 11⁹ *and he burnt their chariots* בָּאֵשׁ *with fire* ; cf. Gn 6¹⁴, 41⁴² (unless this means, *the chain* necessarily belonging to the official dress) ; Ex 2³, 31⁴ (35³²), Is 1²², &c, and בַּשֶּׁמֶן *with oil*[2] very commonly in the sacrificial laws, Ex 29²,

---

[1] But in Ex 12²³ המ׳ is either to be explained as *the destroyer* (now mentioned for the first time) according to *q*, or a particular angel is meant whose regular function it was to inflict punishments. Others again take המ׳ even in Ex 12²³ impersonally = *destruction*.

[2] In nearly all the above examples the presence of the article is only indicated by the vowel of the prefix (בְּ, בַּ, לְ) and might therefore be merely

&c., and also Dt 33²⁴, 2 S 1²¹, Is 1⁶, ψ 23⁵, &c. Similarly the article is used with terms of measurement, as הָאֵפָה Ex 16³⁶, &c.: הַחֹמֶר and הַבַּת Ez 45¹¹; הָעֹמֶר Ex 16²²; בַּחֶבֶל 2 S 8².

(*c*) The expression of abstract ideas of every kind, since they are likewise used to represent whole classes of attributes or states, physical or moral defects, &c.; e.g. Pr 25⁵ (בַּצֶּדֶק); Gn 19¹¹ *and they smote the men* . . . בַּסַּנְוֵרִים *with blindness*; Am 4⁹, &c.; but in הַחֹשֶׁךְ Is 60² the article is no doubt due to dittography of the ה, and the parallel וַעֲרָפֶל has no article.

(*d*) *Comparisons*, since the object compared is treated not (as usually in English) individually but as a general term, e. g. Is 1¹⁸ *white* כַּשֶּׁלֶג *as snow*, כַּצֶּמֶר *as wool*; *red* כַּתּוֹלָע *like crimson*; Is 34⁴ *and the heavens shall be rolled together* כַּסֵּפֶר *as a scroll*; cf. Nu 11¹², Ju 8¹⁸, 16⁹ *as* פְּתִיל־הַנְּעֹרֶת *a string of tow is broken*; 1 S 26²⁰, 1 K 14¹⁵, Is 10¹⁴, 24²⁰, 27¹⁰, 29⁸, 53⁶, Na 3¹⁵, ψ 33⁷, 49¹⁵; cf. also such examples as Gn 19²⁸, Ju 14⁶, where the object compared is determined by a determinate genitive which follows (according to § 127 *a*).

Examples of indeterminate comparisons are rare, and perhaps due only to the Masora,—so at least in the case of singulars, while in such plurals as those in Gn 42³⁰, 1 K 10²⁷, Jo 2⁴·⁷, the omission of the article may be explained by the ordinary rules. On the other hand, the article is regularly omitted when the object compared is already defined by means of an attribute (or relative clause, Jer 23⁹, ψ 17¹²), e. g. Is 16² כְּעוֹף נוֹדֵד קֵן מְשֻׁלָּח *as wandering birds*, (as) *a scattered nest* (but cf. 10¹⁴ (בְּקֵן); 14¹⁹, 29⁵ כְּמֵץ עֹבֵר (but ψ 1⁴ (כַּמֹּץ); Jer 2³⁰, Pr 7⁸, Jb 29²⁵, 30¹⁴.—In comparisons with persons also the Masora seems to avoid the use of the article, as in כְּגִבּוֹר Jb 16¹⁴ and seven other places (כַּגִּבּוֹר only in Is 42¹³), כְּאָב Jb 31¹⁸, כְּגֶבֶר Jb 38³, 40⁷.

4. Peculiar to Hebrew¹ is the employment of the article to denote a single person or thing (primarily one which is as yet unknown, and therefore not capable of being defined) as being present to the mind under given circumstances. In such cases in English the indefinite article is mostly used.

Thus Am 5¹⁹ *as if a man did flee from a lion* (הָאֲרִי, i.e. the particular lion pursuing him at the time), *and a bear* (הַדֹּב) *met him*, &c., cf. 3¹², 1 K 20³⁶ (John 10¹²); also Gn 8⁷ᶠ·, 14¹³ הַפָּלִיט, i. e. *one that had escaped*, the particular one who came just then; so also Ez 24²⁶, 33²¹; cf. 2 S 15¹³); Gn 15¹·¹¹, 18⁷ *the servant*, who is regarded as being constantly at hand and awaiting his commands; cf. 2 S 17¹⁷ (but הַנַּעַר Nu 11²⁷ is used like הַפָּלִיט above); Gn 19³⁰, unless בִּמְעָרָה means in *the* well-known *cave*; בַּמָּקוֹם Gn 28¹¹, according to Dillmann, upon *the* place suitable for passing the night, or the right place, but it may possibly also refer to *the* sanctuary of Bethel afterwards so sacred and celebrated; Gn 42²³, 46², 50²⁶, Ex 2¹⁵, 3², 4²⁰, 21²⁰ (2 S 23²¹), Lv 23⁴², 24¹⁰ (Samaritan יִשְׂרָאֵלִי without the article); Nu 17¹¹, 21⁶·⁹, 25⁶, Dt 19⁵, Jos 2¹⁵, Ju 4¹⁸, 8²⁵, 13¹⁹, 16¹⁹, 19²⁹, 20¹⁶, 1 S 17³⁴, 19¹³, 21¹⁰, 2 S 17¹⁷, 1 K 6⁸, 13¹⁴ (? most

---

due to the masoretic punctuation. There is, however, no reason to doubt the correctness of the tradition. The same is true of the examples under *n* and *o*.

¹ Cf., however, analogous examples in biblical Aramaic in Kautzsch's *Gramm. des Bibl. Aram.*, § 79 *f*, e. g. Dn 2¹⁴, 3², &c.

probably a particular tree is meant) ; 19⁹, Is 7¹⁴ (הָעַלְמָה, i. e. *the* particular *maiden*, through whom the prophet's announcement shall be fulfilled ; we should say *a maiden* [cf. Driver on 1 S 1⁴, 6⁸, 19¹³] ; Jb 9³¹.

s So always *to write in the book* (or *on the scroll*, Nu 5²³, Jer 32¹⁰), i.e. not in *the* book already in use, but in the book which is to be devoted to that purpose, equivalent to *in a book, on a scroll*, Ex 17¹⁴, 1 S 10²⁵, Jb 19²³. Especially instructive for this use of the article is the phrase וַיְהִי הַיּוֹם, which does not simply refer back to the previous narrative in the sense of *the same day*, but is used exactly like our *one day* (properly meaning on the particular day when it happened, i. e. *on a certain day*), 1 S 1⁴, 14¹, 2 K 4⁸, 11¹⁸, Jb 1⁶·¹³. In Gn 39¹¹ even כְּהַיּוֹם הַזֶּה.

t The article is sometimes used in this way before collectives in the singular, which are not meant to denote (like the examples given under *l*) a whole class, but only that part of it which applies to the given case ; thus הָעֹרֵב, הַצְּרָעָה Gn 8⁷, הַיּוֹנָה Ex 23²⁸.

u **5.** When a substantive is defined by the article, or by a suffix, or by a following genitive determinate in any way (see the examples below), the attribute belonging to it (whether adjective, participle, ordinal, or demonstrative pronoun) necessarily takes the article (see, however, the Rem.), e.g. Gn 10¹² הָעִיר הַגְּדֹלָה *the great city* ; Dt 3²⁴ יָדְךָ הַחֲזָקָה *thy strong hand*. A genitive following the substantive may, according to § 127 *a*, be determined either by the article, e.g. 1 S 25²⁵ אִישׁ הַבְּלִיַּעַל הַזֶּה *this worthless man* (prop. *man of worthlessness*; cf. also such examples as 2 Ch 36¹⁸, where the article is prefixed only to a second genitive following the noun) ; or as a proper name, e. g. Dt 11⁷ מַעֲשֵׂה יְהֹוָה הַגָּדֹל *the great work of the Lord* ; or by a suffix, e.g. Is 36⁹ עַבְדֵי אֲדֹנִי הַקְּטַנִּים *the least of my master's servants*.

v When several attributes (whether connected by *Wāw* or not) follow a determinate substantive, each of them takes the article, e. g. Dt 10¹⁷ הָאֵל הַגָּדֹל הַגִּבֹּר וְהַנּוֹרָא *the great God, the mighty, and the terrible*. Cf. also Ex 3³, Dt 1¹⁹, in both of which places a demonstrative with the article also follows the adjective,[1]

Rem. 1. The article is, however, not infrequently used also—

w (*a*) With the attribute alone, when it is added to an originally indefinite substantive as a subsequent limitation ; so always with ordinal numbers after יוֹם,[2] e. g. Gn 1³¹ (cf. 2³, Ex 20¹⁰, &c.) יוֹם הַשִּׁשִּׁי *the sixth day* (prop. *a day* namely

---

[1] The demonstrative used adjectivally is generally placed *after* the adjective proper ; in such cases as עַמְּךָ הַזֶּה הַגָּדוֹל 2 Ch 1¹⁰ the adjective forms a further (fresh) addition to עַמְּךָ הַזֶּה.

[2] Cf. Driver, *Tenses*, 3rd ed., § 209 ; M. Lambert, *REJ.* 31, 279 f.—The omission of the article from the substantive is not to be regarded in *this* instance as an indication of late style, and consequently cannot be put forward as a proof of the late origin of the ' Priestly Code ' (cf. Dillmann on Gn 1³¹, Holzinger, *Einl. in d. Hexateuch*, p. 465, and especially Driver in the *Journal of Philology*, xi. 229 f., against Giesebrecht in *ZAW.* 1881, p. 265 f.). On the other hand, the common omission of the article from the substantive before a determinate adjective (e. g. כְּנֶסֶת הַגְּדוֹלָה *the great synagogue*, in the Mishna ; cf. Segal, *Mišnaic Hebrew*, p. 19 ff.) is certainly a later idiom.

the sixth ; but יוֹם שֵׁנִי‎ *a second day,* Gn 1⁸) ; Ex 12¹⁵ מִיּוֹם הָרִאשֹׁן‎ *from the first day onward* (not before Dn 10¹² and Neh 8¹⁸ is מִן־הַיּוֹם הָרִאשׁוֹן‎ used instead of it). On the other hand, the article is *always* found after בְּ‎, hence בַּיּוֹם הַשִּׁשִּׁי‎, &c., although it is possible that the original reading in these cases was בְּיוֹם‎, and that the article is only due to the Masora. In Ju 6²⁵ the text is evidently corrupt (see verse 26).—Especially also in certain frequently recurring combinations as in particularizing the gates in Jer 38¹⁴, Ez 9², &c., Zc 14¹⁰, and courts in 1 K 7⁸·¹², &c., Ez 40²⁸ ; and very often when the attribute consists of a participle, e.g. Dt 2²³, Ju 21¹⁹, 1 S 25¹⁰, Jer 27³, 46¹⁶ חֶרֶב הַיּוֹנָה‎ *the sword which oppresses* (?) ; Ez 14²², Zc 11² *Ḳeth.* (*the impenetrable forest?*) Pr 26¹⁸, ψ 119²¹.

Of the other examples, Gn 21²⁹ (where, however, the Samaritan reads הכבשות‎), 41²⁶ (but cf. verse 4), Nu 11²⁵, Ju 16²⁷, 1 S 17¹⁷ may at any rate be explained on the ground that the preceding cardinal number is equivalent to a determinant ; in Gn 1²¹, 28⁹·¹⁰, &c., the substantive is already determined by כָּל־‎, and in 1 S 14²⁹ (וְדִבַשׁ‎) by מְעַט‎.—In 1 S 12²³, 2 S 12⁴, Is 7²⁰ (where, however, הַשְּׂכִירָה‎ might also be understood as a subsequent explanation of בְּתַעַר‎) and Neh 9³⁵, the omission of the article after the preposition is certainly due merely to the Masora. In 1 S 16²³ (unless רוּחַ אֱלֹהִים‎ is to be read twice), Zc 4⁷ (where however אֶת הָהָר‎ is probably meant), ψ 104¹⁸ (where a ה‎ precedes הָרִים‎, hence probably a case of haplography), the omission of the article before א‎, ר‎ (?) and ה‎ may be due to a regard for euphony (see *z* below). On the other hand, in 1 S 6¹⁸ (read הָאֶבֶן הַגּ׳‎), 17¹² הַזֶּה‎ is a later addition), 19²² (cf. the LXX), Jer 17², 32¹⁴, 40⁸ *Ḳeth.*, Ez 2³ (read גּוֹי‎ or omit גּוֹיִם‎ with Cornill), Mi 7¹¹, ψ 62⁴, either the text is corrupt, or the expression incorrect. But in 2 K 20¹³, Jer 6²⁰, Ct 7¹⁰ acc. to D. H. Müller (*Anzeiger der Wiener Akad.,* phil.-hist. Kl. 1902, no. x) הַטּוֹב‎ is the genitive of a substantive, *aromatic oil, sweet cane* (in Jer 6²⁰ read וְקָנֶה‎), *like spiced wine.* In Is 39² read שֶׁמֶן הַטּוֹב‎ and in ψ 133² הַטּ׳ כְּשֶׁמֶן‎.

(*b*) *No* article with the attribute, while the substantive is determined either by the article, or a suffix, or a following genitive. Thus the article is sometimes omitted with demonstratives, since they are already to a certain extent determined by their meaning (cf. also the Mêša‘ inscription, l. 3, הבמת זאת‎ *this high place*); as with הוּא‎ Gn 19³³ (evidently for euphony, and so probably often); 30¹⁶, 32²³, 1 S 19¹⁰; with הִיא‎ Gn 38²¹; with זוּ‎ ψ 12⁸ (according to the Masora זוּ‎ is a relative pronoun here, as always elsewhere); with אֵלֶּה‎ 1 S 2²³, according to the present corrupt text (the original reading כָּל־עַם יהוה‎ became כָּל־עַם אֱלֹהִים‎, and אֱלֹהִים‎ was then corrupted to אֵלֶּה‎); so, almost without exception, when the substantive is determined only by a suffix, e.g. Jos 2²⁰, Ju 6¹⁴, 1 K 10⁸, 2 K 1² and 8⁸ᶠ·, where חֳלִי‎, as in Jer 10¹⁹, has arisen by contraction from חָלְיִי‎, or we should simply read חָלְיִי‎ (in all these passages with זֶה‎) ; Gn 24⁸ (with זֹאת‎) ; Ex 10¹, 1 K 22²³, Jer 31²¹ (with אֵלֶּה‎).

The article is sometimes omitted also with the attributes referring to proper names,[1] as צִידוֹן רַבָּה‎ Jos 11⁸, 19²⁸, חֲמָת רַבָּה‎ Am 6². Other examples are Jos 16³·⁵, 18¹³, 1 K 9¹⁷ (but in 1 Ch 7²⁴, 2 Ch 8⁵ with the article). In Gn 7¹¹, &c., תְּהוֹם רַבָּה‎ is also a case of this kind, תְּהוֹם‎ being used (almost always without the article) as a sort of proper name; cf. also אֵל עֶלְיוֹן‎ *the most high*

---

[1] Cf. Nöldeke, *Beiträge zur semit. Sprachwiss.,* p. 48, n. 1.

God and אֱלֹהִים חַי *the living God.* In Ju 1¹⁵ גֻּלֹּת עִלִּית and גֻּלֹּת תַּחְתִּית are strange; Jos 15¹⁹ has גֻּלֹּת עִלִּיּוֹת and גֻּלֹּת תַּחְתִּיּוֹת.

z   Of the remaining examples Is 11⁹ explains itself; the direct connexion of the attribute with its substantive is broken by the insertion of לַיָּם. In Ez 34¹², Hag. 1⁴ (as Wellhausen says, a good instance of a Hebrew adjective in the stative form = סְפוּגִים וְהֵם), ψ 143¹⁰, Ct 6¹²(?) the substantive is also (see above) determined by a suffix, and consequently the attribute is less closely attached ; the same applies to Gn 37², 42¹⁹, 43¹⁴, ψ 18¹⁸, except that in these passages the omission of the article before ר, א, ע may at the same time be due to considerations of euphony (as also in Jos 16¹ before ע, Nu 14³⁷ before ר, 28⁴, Ez 10⁹ before א, 21¹⁹ before ח).¹ In 1 S 13¹⁷ᶠ· (אֶחָד) and 2 K 25¹⁶ (שְׁנַיִם after a determinate substantive), the attribute again, being a numeral, is determinate in itself (see above, x); in Is 65² the לֹא prevents the use of the article; finally, in 2 Ch 26¹⁵ בְּחָצִים and בַּאֲבָנִים are to be read, as in Jer 2²¹ גֶּפֶן for הַגֶּפֶן, in 22²⁶ אֶרֶץ for הָא׳ ; in 2 S 6³ omit חֲדָשָׁה, and in Ez 39²⁷ omit רַבִּים. Without any apparent reason the article is omitted in Dn 8¹³ and 11³¹.

aa   2. When, as in Mi 7¹² (יוֹם הַהוּא *in that day?*), the article is omitted from both substantive and demonstrative, and in Ezr 3¹², the demonstrative even precedes (הַבַּיִת הַזֶּה=זֶה הַבַּיִת), this is obviously due in both cases to a radical corruption of the text (not only in the words quoted). In Jos 9¹² לַחְמֵנוּ is either in apposition to the independent demonstrative זֶה (= *this our bread*, &c.), as in verse 13 נֹאדוֹת is to אֵלֶּה, or they are complete sentences, *this is our bread*, &c. So also in Ex 32¹ מֹשֶׁה (= *that* [*iste*] *Moses*, &c.), and in ψ 48¹⁵ אֱלֹהִים are to be taken in apposition to זֶה. On ψ 68⁸ and Is 23¹³ cf. § 136 d.

§ 127. *The Noun determined by a following Determinate Genitive.*

Brockelmann, *Grundriss*, i. 475.

a   When a genitive, determined in any way, follows a *nomen regens*, it also determines the *nomen regens*, which, according to § 89 a, is always in the construct state. Moreover, every pronominal suffix attached to a substantive is, according to § 33 c, to be considered as a genitive determinate by nature. An independent genitive may be determinate—

(*a*) By its character as a *proper name* (according to § 125 a), e. g. דְּבַר יְהֹוָה *the word of the Lord.*

(*b*) By having the article, e. g. אִישׁ הַמִּלְחָמָה (prop. the man of the war) *the soldier* (but אִישׁ מִלְחָמָה Jos 17¹, *a soldier*) ; אַנְשֵׁי הַמִּלְחָמָה

---

¹ The same reason no doubt also favoured the omission of the article before הוּא and אֵלֶּה, see above, under y. Also in Is 23⁷ (*is this your joyous* . . . ?) the article is omitted before עַלִּיזָה probably only for euphony.

Nu 31⁴⁹, *the soldiers*; דְּבַר הַנָּבִיא *the word of the prophet*, Jer 28⁹ (but
e. g., on the other hand, מִצְוֺת אֲנָשִׁים מְלֻמָּדָה *a commandment of men
which hath been taught*, Is 29¹³; דְּבַר־שֶׁקֶר *word of falsehood*, Pr 29¹²).

(*c*) By the addition of a pronominal suffix (see above), e. g. בֵּית־אָבִי
my father's house.

(*d*) By construction with another genitive determined in some way,
e. g. Gn 3² מִפְּרִי עֵץ־הַגָּן *of the fruit of the trees of the garden*. Thus in
Is 10¹² four, and in 21¹⁷ even five, members of a series are determined
by a concluding determinate genitive.

Rem. 1. The above explains also the various meanings of כֹּל (prop. a *b*
substantive in the sense of *aggregate, whole*), according as it is followed by
a determinate or indeterminate genitive. In the former case כֹּל has the
meaning of *the entirety*, i. e. *all, the whole* (like the French *tous les hommes, toute
la ville*), e. g. כָּל־הָאָרֶץ *the whole* (prop. the entirety of the) *earth*, כָּל־הָאָדָם
all men;[1] Ex 18²², Nu 15¹³, Jer 4²⁹, and cases like Nu 4²³·⁴⁷, 21⁸ where כָּל
is followed by a singular participle with the article. On the other hand,
before an indeterminate genitive כֹּל is used in the more indefinite (in-
dividualizing) sense of *of all kinds, any* (cf. *tout homme, à tout prix*), or
distributively *each, every*, e. g. כָּל־עֵץ *every* (kind of) *tree*, Gn 2⁹; cf. 4²², 24¹⁰,
1 Ch 29²; כָּל־דָּבָר *any thing*, Ju 19¹⁹; בְּכָל־יוֹם *every day, every time*, ψ 7¹².

It is, however, to be observed— *c*
(*a*) That the article may in this case also (see § 126 *h*) be omitted in poetic
style, although the substantive is to be regarded as determinate, e. g.
כָּל־שֻׁלְחָנוֹת *all* (the) *tables*, Is 28⁸.

(*b*) That the meaning *every* is frequent even before singulars used collectively;
afterwards the idea of *quisque* passes naturally into that of *totality*, e. g. כָּל־חַי
each living thing, i. e. *every* (not *every kind of*) *living thing*; כָּל־בָּשָׂר *all flesh*, i. e.
all men or *all living creatures* (with the article only in Gn 7¹⁵ before a relative
clause, and in Is 40⁶); sometimes also כָּל־עֵץ *all trees*, כָּל־עוֹף *all birds*;
finally—

(*c*) That before the names of members of the human body, כָּל־ frequently
(as being determinate in itself) denotes the entirety, e. g. Is 1⁵ *the whole head,
the whole heart* (the sense required by the context, not *every head*, &c., which
the expression *in itself* might also mean); 9¹¹, 2 K 23³, Ez 29⁷ *all* (i. e. *the
whole of) their shoulders . . . all* (*the whole of) their loins*; 36⁵.—On כֹּל with
a suffix when it follows a noun in apposition (e. g. Is 9⁸ הָעָם כֻּלּוֹ *the people,
all of it*, i. e. *the whole nation*, more emphatic than כָּל־הָעָם, cf. Driver on 2 S 2⁹),
as well as when it follows absolutely in the genitive (= *all men, every one*, e. g.
Gn 16¹²),[2] see the Lexicon, pp. 481ᵇ, 482ᵇ.

2. Gentilic names (or patronymics), derived from compound proper names *d*
(consisting of a nomen regens and genitive), are determined by inserting the
article before the second part of the compound (since it contains the original

---

[1] הָאָדָם being a collective, cf. כָּל־הָאִישׁ 2 S 15², *all men*, כָּל־הַבֵּן Ex 1²² *all
sons*, כָּל־הַבַּת *all daughters*; in itself כָּל־הָאָדָם could also mean *the whole man*.

[2] In Ezr 10¹⁷ instead of בְּכֹל אֲנָשִׁים read simply בְּכָל־הָאֲנָשִׁים.

genitive), e.g. בֶּן־יְמִינִי (see § 86 *h*) *a Benjamite*; בֶּן־הַיְמִינִי Ju 3¹⁵, &c., *the Benjamite*; בֵּית־הַלַּחְמִי *the Bethlehemite*, 1 S 16¹, &c. (cf., however, 1 Ch 27¹²
Qᵉʳê בֵּית־הַשִּׁמְשִׁי (לְבֵן יְמִינִי) *the Beth-shemite*, 1 S 6¹⁴; אֲבִי הָעֶזְרִי *the Abiezrite*, Ju 6¹¹, &c., cf. 1 K 16³⁴.

e 3. In a few instances the nomen regens appears to be used indefinitely notwithstanding a following determinate genitive; it is not so, however, in Gn 16⁷, where the reference is to a well-known fountain; 21²⁸, where in the original context there must have been some reason for *the seven ewe lambs of the flock*; 2 S 12³⁰ *the spoil found in the city*; but it often is so before a proper name, as in Ex 10⁹ חַג יְהֹוָה *a feast of the Lord* (unless it is *the* spring festival), Dt 7²⁵, and frequently תּוֹעֲבַת יְהֹוָה *an abomination unto the Lord*; cf. also Gn 46³⁴, Dt 22¹⁹ *a virgin of Israel*; 1 S 4¹² *a man of Benjamin*; Pr 25¹, Ct 2¹, 3⁹; similarly before appellatives with the article (or before a genitive determined by a suffix, as in Lv 14³⁴), 1 S 20²⁰ *three arrows*; 2 S 23¹¹ חֶלְקַת הַשָּׂדֶה *a plot of the ground* (but see Gn 33¹⁹, Jos 24³²); Ju 13⁶, Jer 13⁴, 41¹⁶, Ct 1¹¹·¹³ ᶠ·, 5¹³, 7³, 8². On the other hand, שִׁיר הַמַּעֲלוֹת in the titles of Psalms 120 to 134 (except 121¹, שִׁיר לַמַּעֲלוֹת) was most probably originally the title of a collection, in the sense of '*the pilgrimage-songs*' (according to § 124 *r*), and was subsequently added to these Psalms severally.—In Ex 20²⁴ בְּכָל־הַמָּקוֹם *in all the place*, sc. of the sanctuary, is a dogmatic correction of בְּכָל־מָקוֹם, *in every place*, to avoid the difficulty that several holy-places are here authorized, instead of the one central sanctuary. In Gn 20¹³ also כָּל־הַמָּקוֹם (unless it means *in the whole place*) is remarkable, since elsewhere *every place* is always (8 times) כָּל־מָקוֹם.

f 4. The deviations mentioned under *e*, from a fundamental rule of syntax, are in some cases open to suspicion on textual grounds, but much more doubtful are the instances in which the article is found before a noun already determined in some other way, as—

(*a*) Before a noun which appears to be determined by a following independent determinate genitive. The least questionable are the instances in which the genitive is a *proper name*, since these may be elliptical forms of expression like the apparent construction of proper names with a genitive, noticed in § 125 *h*, e.g. Nu 21¹⁴ הַנְּחָלִים אַרְנוֹן *the valleys*, namely the valleys *of Arnon*; 2 K 23¹⁷ הַמִּזְבַּח בֵּית־אֵל *the altar*, namely the altar of *Bethel* (i.e. with the suppression of the real nomen regens, מִזְבַּח without the article; by the pointing הַמִּזְבַּח the Masora evidently intends to allow the choice either of reading הַמִּזְבֵּחַ or correcting it to מִזְבַּח); הָאֵל בֵּית־אֵל *the God of Beth-el*[1] (equivalent to אֵל בּ'), Gn 31¹³ (the LXX read הָאֵל הַנִּרְאֶה אֵלֶיךָ בַּמָּקוֹם *the God who appeared to thee in the* holy *place*); הַמֶּלֶךְ אַשּׁוּר *the king of Assyria*, Is 36¹⁶ (probably a scribal error due to verse 13; it does not occur in the parallel passage, 2 K 18³¹), cf. Jos 13⁵, 2 K 25¹¹, Jer 38⁶, Ez 47¹⁵; in the vocative, Jer 48³², La 2¹³. On the other hand, שָׂרָה אִמּוֹ Gn 24⁶⁷ is no doubt

---

[1] According to Philippi (*St. Constr.*, p. 38) בֵּית־אֵל is rather a case of ' subposition ' in the accusative, as also הַדֶּרֶךְ חֶתְלוֹן Ez 47¹⁵ (for which, however, in 48¹ there is the correct reading דֶּרֶךְ חֶתְלוֹן) *by the way to Hethlon*; and in fact, Ez 47¹⁵ may without difficulty be explained in this way; so שֵׁשׁ Ex 39²⁷ as an accusative of the material.

only a subsequent insertion; so also יִשְׂרָאֵל Jos 8³³ᵇ (cf. LXX), 2 S 20²³, 2 K 7¹³, הַמֶּלֶךְ 1 S 26²² after הַחֲנִית (simplified by the Masora to חֲנִית Qᵉrê); עֲלִיַּת אָחָז 2 K 23¹², אַשּׁוּר Is 36⁸ (cf. 2 K 18²³), הַקֹּדֶשׁ Ez 46¹⁹ (unless the article with לִשְׁכוֹת is to be omitted), also הַתָּמִיד Dn 8¹³, and עֹדֵר הַנְּבִיא 2 Ch 15⁸. In Ex 9¹⁸ read with the Samaritan לְמִיּוֹם; in 2 S 19²⁵ לֶכֶת might possibly be taken in apposition to לְמִן הַיּוֹם; in 2 K 10¹ restore אֶת־בְּנֵי, with the LXX and Lucian, before אַחְאָב; in 2 K 25¹⁹ omit the article, as in Jer 52²⁵, before סֹפֵר.

A similar ellipse must also be assumed in 2 K 23¹⁷ *the sepulchre is the* *g* sepulchre *of the man of God* (but most probably קֶבֶר has dropped out after הַקֶּבֶר) and ψ 123⁴ (cf., however, the LXX, and observe that in the parallel member the genitive is paraphrased by לְ).—In Jos. 3¹⁴ הַבְּרִית (verse 17 בְּרִית יהוה) has been added to the original הָאָרוֹן by a redactor; cf. similar syntactically impossible additions in verse 11 (also in 1 S 4³, &c., where the LXX still had simply אֲרוֹן יהוה); in הַיָּתֵד Ju 16¹⁴ the Masora evidently combines two different readings הַיָּתֵד and הָאָרֶג; יְתַד הָאָרֶג; and similarly in Jer 25²⁶ (where הָאָרֶץ was only subsequently introduced into the text), the two readings הַמַּמְלָכוֹת and מַמְלְכוֹת הָא׳ are combined.—In Jos 8¹¹, 1 K 14²⁴, Jer 31⁴⁰, Ez 45¹⁶ the article, being usual after כָּל־, has been mechanically added, and so also in 2 Ch 8¹⁶ after עַד־; in 2 K 9⁴ the second הַנַּעַר (instead of נַעַר) is occasioned by the first; in Ez 7⁷ מְהוּמָה belongs as a nominative to what follows; in Ez 8²⁹ the meaning perhaps is *in the chambers, in the house of the Lord*, or the article is to be omitted; in 1 Ch 15²⁷ the text is manifestly corrupt.

Of another kind are the instances in which a determinate noun is followed *h* by a definition of the material *in apposition* (hence, not in the genitive; cf. § 131), e.g. Zc 4¹⁰ הָאֶבֶן הַבְּדִיל *the weight, the lead,* i.e. *the leaden weight;* Ex 39¹⁷, 2 K 16¹⁴ (הַנְּחֹשֶׁת, both here and in verse 17, is probably only a later addition, while הַמְּסֹגְרוֹת הַמְּכֹנוֹת in verse 17 has arisen from a confusion of two readings, מִסְגְּרוֹת הַמְּכֹנוֹת and מְסֹגְרוֹת מְכֹנוֹת). In Jer 32¹² also הַמִּקְנָה (unless the article is simply to be omitted) is in apposition to הַסֵּפֶר.

(*b*) Before a noun with a suffix (which likewise represents a determinate *i* genitive; see above, at the beginning of this section). This does not apply to cases in which a *verbal* (i.e. *accusative*) suffix is affixed to a participle which has the article, e.g. הַמַּכֵּהוּ Is 9¹², *the one smiting him*; in Dt 8¹⁵, 13⁶ also ךְ is a verbal suffix, but hardly the וֹ in הָעֹשׂוֹ for הָעֹשֵׂהוּ Job 40¹⁹, nor the ה in הַיַּלְדָּה Dn 11⁶; § 116 *g*. For הַעֲרִכְךָ Lev 27²³, read עֶרְכְּךָ as in verses 2, 3, 5, 7, 13, &c., twelve times (but cf. also the note on § 128 *d*).—Of the remaining examples כַּגֻּבְרְתָּהּ Is 24² (probably an intentional alliteration with the eleven other words beginning with כ), לַמַּעֲנֵהוּ Pr 16⁴, and בָּעֲרֵינוּ (so Baer, following the best authorities) Ezr 10¹⁴, rest only on the authority of the Masoretes, not of the authors. So also in הָאָהֳלִי Jos 7²¹, הַחֲצִיֹו Jos 8³³ (previously חֲצִיֹו), הָהֳרוֹתֶיהָ 2 K 15¹⁶ (dittography of the ה), the article is simply to be omitted as syntactically impossible; the וֹ of הַדַּבְּרוּ Mi 2¹² is the copula belonging to the next word.

§ 128. *The Indication of the Genitive Relation by means of the Construct State.*

Cf. especially Philippi's work cited at the head of § 89.

a 1. The genitive relation is regularly expressed (see § 89) by the close connexion of the *nomen regens* (in the construct state) with the *nomen rectum* (in the genitive). Since only *one* nomen regens can be immediately connected with a nomen rectum, it follows that the same genitive cannot depend on two or more *co-ordinate* nouns, but a second (sometimes even a third, &c.) regens must be added with a suffix referring to the nomen rectum, e. g. בְּנֵי דָוִד וּבְנֹתָיו *the sons of David and his daughters* (not בְּנֵי וּבְנוֹת דָּוִד); cf. 1 K 8²⁸. [1] The language also prefers to avoid a series of several co-ordinate [2] genitives depending upon one and the same nomen regens (such as occur in Gn 14¹⁹, Nu 20⁵, 31⁵⁴ [1 Ch 13¹], 1 S 23⁷, 2 S 19⁶, Is 22⁵, ψ 5⁷, 8³), [3] and rather tends to repeat the nomen regens, e. g. Gn 24³ אֱלֹהֵי הַשָּׁמַיִם וֵאלֹהֵי הָאָרֶץ *the God of heaven and the God of the earth* (so in Jer 8¹ the regens is five times repeated). A lengthened series of genitives may, however, be formed by a nomen rectum serving at the same time as *regens* to a genitive depending on it (cf. § 127 *a* [*d*]); e. g. Gn 47⁹ יְמֵי שְׁנֵי חַיֵּי אֲבֹתַי *the days of the years of the life of my fathers*; cf. Jb 12²⁴, where there are three genitives, Is 10¹² four, and 21¹⁷ five (unless the last three are in apposition). As a rule, indeed, such an inconvenient accumulation of genitives is avoided by means of a circumlocution in the case of one of them (see § 129 *d*).

b Rem. As the fundamental rules stated above are the necessary consequence not merely of *logical* but more especially of *rhythmical* relations (see § 89 *a*), we must feel the more hesitation in admitting examples in which genitives are supposed to be loosely attached to forms other than the construct state. Some of these examples (the supposed genitives following a regens which is determined by the article) have been already discussed in § 127 *f–h*. Compare, moreover :

c (*a*) Genitives after the absolute state, e. g. Is 28¹ גֵּיא־שְׁמָנִים הֲלוּמֵי יָיִן *the fat valley of them that are overcome with wine.* The usual explanation that גֵּיא־שְׁמָנִים forms *one* single idea (in German *Fettigkeitstal*), on which the

---

[1] Very rare, and only possible in very rapid utterance, are such exceptions as Ez 31¹⁶ (מִבְחַר וְטוֹב־לְבָנוֹן) ; Pr 16¹¹.—In Is 11² *the spirit of knowledge and of the fear of the Lord,* דַּעַת may at any rate also be taken as an absolute genitive, so also כֹּפֶר Dn 1⁴.

[2] In ψ 114¹ a second genitive is added even without the copula, but the parallelism of the members renders any misunderstanding impossible.

[3] In almost all these instances the two (or three) genitives form one closely connected whole, as *heaven and earth, sons and daughters.*

genitive הַלּוּמֵי יָ֫ן then depends, in reality explains nothing; the text is almost certainly corrupt. In Dt 15[18] מִשְׁנֶה would be expected; in Jos 3[11] הַבְּרִית is a later addition; in Is 32[13] (מָשׂוֹשׂ), and ψ 68[22] (שֵׂעָר), the absolute for the construct state probably rests only on the authority of the Masoretes. In Ju 6[25 ff.] the text is obviously in confusion. In Ju 8[32] (cf. 6[24]) בְּעָפְרָה should come either after וַיִּקָּבֵר or at the end of the verse, unless, with Moore, we omit אֲבִי הָע׳ as a gloss (from 6[24]); in Is 63[11] מֹשֶׁה is probably a gloss on יְמֵי־עוֹלָם which has crept into the text; in 2 S 4[2] לְאִישׁ־בֹּ֫שֶׁת, according to the LXX, has dropped out before בֵּן; in Ez 6[11] רָעוֹת is to be omitted with the LXX; if originally in the text, it could only be genitive (= *all abominations of evils*), not an adjective; Pr 21[6] the text is altogether uncertain (the LXX read מְבַקְשֵׁי for (מְבַקֵּשׁ); in 1 Ch 9[13] the preposition לְ (after a לְ) has dropped out before מְלֶ֫אכֶת (cf. 12[25]).—Elsewhere (Dt 3[5], 1 K 4[13], 2 Ch 8[5]) the supposed genitives are to be taken rather as words of nearer definition standing in apposition, i.e. *with high walls, gates, and bars.* In Jer 8[5] ירושלים is either in apposition to הָעָם הַזֶּה or is better (since not in the LXX) omitted as a gloss.

(*b*) Genitives after a noun with a suffix (where the suffix prevents the direct *d* government by the *nomen regens*). Thus in Lv 27[3.5.6], where הַזָּכָר after עֶרְכְּךָ[1] might be taken, contrary to the accents, as subject of the following clause; in Lv 5[15.25] the suffix may refer to Moses. In Lv 6[3] מִדּוֹ בַד *his garment*, namely the garment *of linen*, unless simply in apposition, cf. § 131 *d* (or read מִדֵּי?); Lv 26[42], where בְּרִיתִי יַעֲקוֹב וגו׳ could at most be explained as an ellipse for בְּרִיתִי בְּרִית יַעֲקֹב, cf. § 125 *h* (probably, however, it is a case of dittography of the י, which was repeated also before אברהם; so Valeton, *ZAW.* xii. 3); equally strange is בְּרִיתִי הַיּוֹם Jer 33[20], &c. On the other hand, אִם יִהְיֶה נְבִיאֲכֶם יְהֹוָה Nu 12[6] could not possibly mean *if your prophet be a prophet of the Lord*; the text is manifestly corrupt (probably נְבִיאֲךָ מִיהֹוָה is to be read, with Marti). In ψ 45[7] כִּסְאֲךָ אֱלֹהִים (usually explained as *thy divine throne*), אלהים is most probably a later addition [another suggestion is to read כֵּאלֹהִים *like God('s throne)*: cf. § 141 *d*, note]. In Jer 52[20] two readings are probably combined, לִנְחֹשֶׁת כָּל־הַכֵּלִים without any addition, and לְנֻשְׁתָּם. In Nu 25[12] שָׁלוֹם is in apposition to בְּרִיתִי. On דַּרְכֵּךְ וְזִמָּה Ez 16[27], cf. § 131 *r*.

(*c*) The interposition of a word is assumed between כָּל־ (*the whole*; cf. *e* § 127 *b*) and the genitive governed by it in 2 S 1[9], Jb 27[3] (עוֹד), and, if the text is correct, in Hos 14[3] (תִּשָּׂא). In reality, however, in all three places the genitive relation is destroyed by the transposition of the words (instead of עוֹד כָּל־, &c.), and כָּל־ is rather to be taken adverbially (equivalent to *wholly*), e. g. 2 S 1[9] *because my life is yet wholly in me*, i.e. my whole life; cf. Philippi, *Stat. Constr.*, p. 10.—On the instances in which the original construct state אַ֫יִן *non-existence* is used without a following genitive, see the negative sentences, § 152 *o*.

2. The dependence of the nomen rectum on the nomen regens by *f* no means represents merely what is, properly speaking, the genitive relation (see the examples under *g–i*). Very frequently the nomen

---

[1] Halévy, *J. A.* xiv. 548, removes the difficulty by pointing עֲרָבְּךָ.

rectum only adds a nearer definition of the nomen regens, whether by giving the name, the genus or species, the measure, the material, or finally an attribute of it (*genit. epexegeticus* or *appositionis*,[1] see the examples under *k–q*).

Examples. The *nomen rectum* represents—

g   (*a*) A *subjective genitive*, specifying the possessor, author, &c., e. g. בֵּית־הַמֶּלֶךְ *the king's house*; דְּבַר יְהֹוָה *the word of the Lord*.

h   (*b*) An *objective genitive*, e. g. Ob[10] מֵחֲמַס אָחִיךָ *for the violence done to thy brother*[2] (but in Ez 12[19] מֵחֲמַס is followed by a subjective genitive); Pr 20[2] אֵימַת מֶלֶךְ *the terror of a king*; Gn 18[20] זַעֲקַת סְדֹם *the cry concerning Sodom*; Is 23[5] שֵׁמַע צֹר *the report of (about) Tyre*, cf. 2 S 4[4]; Am 8[10] אֵבֶל יָחִיד *the mourning for an only son*; Dt 20[14] שְׁלַל אֹיְבֶיךָ *praeda hostibus tuis erepta*: cf. Is 3[14]. In a wider sense this includes such examples as דֶּרֶךְ עֵץ הַחַיִּים *the way of* (i. e. *to*) *the tree of life*, Gn 3[24]; cf. Pr 7[27], Jb 38[20]; דֶּרֶךְ הַיָּם *the way of* (*by*) *the sea*, Is 8[23]; זִבְחֵי אֱלֹהִים *the sacrifices of* (i. e. *pleasing to*) *God*, ψ 51[19]; שְׁבֻעַת יְהֹוָה *the oath of* (i. e. *sworn before*) *the Lord*, 1 K 2[43]; דִּבְרֵי לְמוּאֵל *the words of* (i. e. *addressed to*) *L.*, Pr 31[1].

i   (*c*) A *partitive genitive*; this includes especially the cases in which an adjective in the construct state is followed by a general term, e. g. חַכְמוֹת שָׂרוֹתֶיהָ *the wisest of her ladies*, Ju 5[29]; cf. for this way of expressing the superlative, § 133 *h*, and also *r* below.

k   Merely formal genitives (*genit. explicativus* or *epexegeticus*, *genit. appositionis*) are those added to the construct state as nearer definitions—

(*d*) Of the *name*, e. g. נְהַר פְּרָת *the river Euphrates*; אֶרֶץ כְּנַעַן *the land of Canaan*; בְּתוּלַת יִשְׂרָאֵל *the virgin Israel* (not *of Israel*), Am 5[2].

l   (*e*) Of the *genus*, e. g Pr 15[20] (21[20]) כְּסִיל אָדָם *a fool of a man* (= *a foolish man*); cf. Gn 16[12], Is 1[4], 29[19], Ho 13[2], Mi 5[4], &c.

m   (*f*) Of the *species*, e. g. אֲחֻזַּת קֶבֶר *a possession of a burying-place*, i. e. hereditary sepulchre, Gn 23[4], &c.; תְּאֵנֵי הַבַּכֻּרוֹת *the early figs*, Jer 24[2]; אֹהֶל בֵּיתִי *the tabernacle of my house*, i. e. my dwelling-place, ψ 132[3].

n   (*g*) Of the *measure, weight, extent, number*, e. g. מְתֵי מִסְפָּר *people of number*, i. e. *few in number*, Gn 34[30], Dt 26[5]; cf. also Ez 47[3-5] *waters of the ankles, waters of the loins, waters of swimming*, i. e. which reached up to the ankles, or loins, or necessitated swimming; but in verse 4 in apposition (?) מַיִם בִּרְכָּיִם.

o   (*h*) Of the *material*[3] of which something consists, e. g. כְּלִי חָרֶשׂ *a vessel of earthenware*, Nu 5[17]; כְּלֵי כֶסֶף *vessels of silver* (cf. the French *des vases d'or*); אֲרוֹן עֵץ *an ark of wood*; שֵׁבֶט בַּרְזֶל *a rod of iron*, ψ 2[9]; cf. Gn 3[21], 6[14], Ju 7[13], &c.

---

[1] The latter term is preferred especially by König, *Theol. Stud. und Krit.*, 1898, p. 528 ff.

[2] Cf. in Latin a similar use of the genitive after *iniuria* (Caes. *B. G.* 1, 30), *metus* (*hostium, Pompeii*, &c.), *spes*, and other words. In Greek, cf. εὔνοια τῶν φίλων, πίστις τοῦ θεοῦ, ὁ λόγος ὁ τοῦ σταυροῦ, 1 Cor. 1[18].

[3] In the almost entire absence of corresponding adjectives (אֲרוֹן *made of cedar*, a denominative from אֶרֶז, and נָחוּשׁ *brazen* are the only examples), the language regularly has recourse to the above periphrasis. On the form *qāṭûl*, as expressing an inherent property, cf. § 50 *f*; cf. also the proper name, בַּרְזִלַּי *ferreus*.

(*i*) Of the *attribute* of a person or thing, e. g. Gn 17⁸ אֲחֻזַּת עוֹלָם *an everlasting p possession* ; Pr 17⁸ *a precious stone* ; cf. Nu 28⁶, Is 13⁸, 28⁴, ψ 23², 31⁸, Pr 5¹⁹, 14⁵, Jb 41¹⁹, and the examples of the genitive with a suffix given in § 135 *n*. Such a periphrasis for the expression of attributes frequently occurs, even when the corresponding adjectives are in use. Thus especially קֹדֶשׁ *holiness* very frequently serves as a periphrasis for the adjective קָדוֹשׁ (e. g. בִּגְדֵי הַקֹּדֶשׁ *the holy garments*, Ex 29²⁹), since קָדוֹשׁ is used almost exclusively in reference to persons (hence also with עַם and גּוֹי *people*, and with שֵׁם the *name* of a person) ; the only exceptions are מָקוֹם קָדוֹשׁ *holy place*, Ex 29³¹, &c. ; מַיִם קְדֹשִׁים *holy water*, Nu 5¹⁷ ; קָדוֹשׁ as the predicate of יוֹם *day*, Neh 8¹⁰ ᶠ·, and of מַחֲנֶה *camp*, Dt 23¹⁵. So also the use of צַדִּיק *righteous* is always confined to persons, except in Dt 4⁸ ; elsewhere the periphrasis with צֶדֶק or צְדָקָה is always used, e. g. מֹאזְנֵי צֶדֶק *just balances*, Lv 19³⁶.

In a wider sense this use of the genitive also includes statements of the *q* purpose for which something is intended, e. g. צֹאן טִבְחָה *sheep for the slaughter*, ψ 44²³ ; מוּסַר שְׁלוֹמֵנוּ *the chastisement designed for our peace*, Is 53⁵ ; cf. 51¹⁷ (*the cup which causes staggering*), ψ 116¹³ ; finally, also, the description of the material, with which something is laden or filled, e. g. 1 S 16²⁰ חֲמוֹר לֶחֶם וְנֹאד יַיִן *an ass laden with bread and a bottle of wine* (but probably עֲשָׂרָה is to be read for חֲמוֹר); cf. Gn 21¹⁴, Pr 7²⁰, &c.

Rem. 1. Certain substantives are used to convey an attributive idea in the *r* construct state before a partitive genitive; thus מִבְחָר *choice, selection*, as in Gn 23⁶ מִבְחַר קְבָרֵינוּ *the choice of our sepulchres*, i. e. our choicest sepulchres ; Ex 15⁴, Is 22⁷, 37²⁴; other examples are, Is 1¹⁶ *the evil of your doings*, emphatically, *for your evil doings* ; Is 17⁴, 37²⁴ (= *the tall cedars thereof*), ψ 139²², Jb 15²⁶.— This is the more common construction with the substantive כֹּל *entirety*, for *all, the whole, every*, see § 127 *b* ; it is also frequent with מְעַט *a little*, for *few*, 1 S 17²⁸, &c.

2. To the periphrases expressing attributive ideas (see *p* above) by means *s* of a genitive construction may be added the very numerous combinations of the construct states אִישׁ *a man*, בַּעַל *master, possessor*, בֶּן־ *son*, and their feminines and plurals (including מְתֵי *men*, used only in the plural), with some appellative noun, in order to represent a person (poetically even a thing) as possessing some object or quality, or being in some condition. In English, such combinations are sometimes rendered by single substantives, sometimes by circumlocution.

Examples :—

(*a*) Of אִישׁ, &c. : אִישׁ דְּבָרִים *an eloquent man*, Ex 4¹⁰ (but אִישׁ שְׂפָתַיִם Jb 11² *t a man of lips*, i. e. *a boaster*) ; אִישׁ לָשׁוֹן = *a slanderer*, ψ 140¹² ; אִישׁ דַּעַת *a man of knowledge*, Pr 24⁵ ; אִישׁ חֵמָה *a wrathful man*, Pr 15¹⁸ ; אִישׁ דָּמִים *a man of blood*, 2 S 16⁷, ψ 5⁷ ; cf. further, 1 S 16¹⁸, 1 K 2²⁶, Is 53³, Pr 19⁶, 26²¹, 29¹, Ezr 8¹⁸ ; also אֵשֶׁת מִדְיָנִים *a contentious woman*, Pr 27¹⁵ ; in the plural, e. g. Gn 6⁴ אַנְשֵׁי הַשֵּׁם *the men of renown, famous*; cf. Gn 47⁶, Is 41¹¹, Jb 34⁸·¹⁰ (אַנְשֵׁי לֵבָב *men of understanding*) ; with מְתֵי, e. g. Is 5¹³ (מְתֵי רָעָב *famished men*; but read probably מְזֵי רָעָב *weak with hunger*) ; ψ 26⁴, Jb 11¹¹, 22¹⁵.

(*b*) Of בַּעַל, &c. : בַּעַל שֵׂעָר *hairy*, 2 K 1⁸ ; בַּעַל הַחֲלֹמוֹת *the dreamer*, Gn 37¹⁹ ; *u* cf. Na 1², Pr 1¹⁷, 18⁹ (*a destroyer*), 22²⁴, 23² (*disposed to eat, greedy*), 24⁸ ; feminine

בַּעֲלַת־אוֹב *a woman that hath a soothsaying spirit*, 1 S 28⁷; cf. Na 3⁴; in the plural, e.g. בַּעֲלֵי חִצִּים *archers*, Gn 49²³, בַּעֲלֵי בְרִית *confederates*, Gn 14¹³; בַּעֲלֵי שְׁבוּעָה *sworn supporters*, Neh 6¹⁸.

v (c) Of בֶּן־, &c. : בֶּן־חַיִל *a hero, warrior*, 1 K 1⁵²; בֶּן־מֶשֶׁק *heir*, Gn 15²; בֶּן־שָׁנָה *yearling*, Ex 12⁵, &c. ; בֶּן־מֵאַת שָׁנָה *centum annos natus*, Gn 21⁵; בֶּן־מָוֶת *worthy to die*, 1 S 2c³¹ (Luther, 2 S 12⁵ *ein Kind des Todes*) ; cf. Dt 25² בִּן־הַכּוֹת *worthy to be beaten*. Feminine, e. g. בַּת־בְּלִיַּעַל *a wicked woman*, 1 S 1¹⁶ ; frequently also בְּנֵי ב׳, /אַנְשֵׁי ב׳, אִישׁ בְּלִיַּעַל, and even simply בְּלִיַּעַל, like the Latin *scelus* for *scelestissimus*, 2 S 23⁶, Jb 34¹⁸. Plural masculine, e. g. בְּנֵי מְרִי *children of rebellion*, Nu 17²⁵. בֶּן־ is used poetically of things without life, e. g. Is 5¹ בֶּן־שֶׁמֶן *a fat*, i. e. a fruitful (hill); Jon 4¹⁰ בִּן־לָיְלָה i. e. *grown in a night*; Jb 41²⁰ *son of the bow* (i. e. an arrow); so also בְּנֵי רֶשֶׁף = *sparks*, Jb 5⁷; La 3¹³; בְּנוֹת Ec 12⁴ *the daughters of song*, probably meaning the individual notes.

There is another use of בֶּן־ or בְּנֵי to denote membership of a guild or society (or of a tribe, or any definite class). Thus בְּנֵי הָאֱלֹהִים or בְּנֵי אֱלֹהִים Gn 6²·⁴, Jb 1⁶, 2¹, 38⁷ (cf. also בְּנֵי אֵלִים ψ 29¹, 89⁷) properly means not *sons of god(s)*, but beings of the class of אֱלֹהִים or אֵלִים; בְּנֵי־הַנְּבִיאִים 1 K 20³⁵ (singular in Am 7¹⁴) persons *belonging to the guild of prophets*; בֶּן־הָרַקָּחִים Neh 3⁸ *one of the guild of apothecaries*, cf. 3³¹ where בֶּן־הַצֹּרְפִים is to be read. Similarly בְּנֵי שְׁלֹשִׁים Gn 50²³ are most probably not *great-grandsons* but *grandsons*, i. e. those belonging to the third generation. Cf. also בְּנֵי הַגֵּרְשֻׁנִּי Nu 4²⁷ ᶠ· *Gershonites*, בְּנֵי הַקְּהָתִים 2 Ch 20¹⁹, &c., *Kohathites*; בְּנֵי קֶדֶם *dwellers in the East*.

w 3. Special mention must be made of the not infrequent idiom by which adjectives (sometimes also ordinals, see § 134 *o*) are added in the genitive, like substantives, rather than as attributes in the same state, gender, and number as the noun which they qualify; thus, Is 28⁴ צִיצַת נֹבֵל *the flower of that which fades*, for which verse 1 has צִיץ נֹבֵל *the fading flower*; cf. further, Is 22²⁴, Jer 22¹⁷ (?), 52¹³, ψ 73¹⁰, 74¹⁵ (but אֵיתָן may be a substantive), 78⁴⁹; also the use of רַע as a substantive, e.g. in Pr 2¹⁴ ᵇ, 6²⁴ (רַע אֵשֶׁת),&c.. analogous to the New Testament phrase ὁ οἰκονόμος τῆς ἀδικίας, Luke 16⁸, and the French *un homme de bien*.[1]—Finally, an adverb (treated as a substantive) may likewise be used as an epexegetical genitive; cf. דְּמֵי חִנָּם *blood shed without cause*, 1 K 2³¹; Pr 24²⁸, 26²; Ez 30¹⁶ (יוֹמָם).

x 3. The epexegetical genitives include finally the numerous nearer definitions which follow the construct state of adjectives (and of active and passive participles, or verbal adjectives, cf. § 116 *f–l*). For, while the word of nearer definition is added to the verb in the accusative (e. g. חָלָה אֶת־רַגְלָיו *he was diseased in his feet*, 1 K 15²³), it may, with participles and verbal adjectives, be either in the accusative

---

[1] On the other hand, in such passages as Is 36² (2 K 18¹⁷), Zc 14⁴, Ec 8¹⁰, &c., there is no apparent reason why the Masora requires the construct state instead of the absolute; hence חֵיל Is 36² and גֵּיא Zc 14⁴ must be intended as forms of the absolute state, shortened in consequence of their close connexion.

(§ 116 f and k) or in the genitive, the case of a word depending on a noun. Such a genitive relation is usually termed an *improper annexion.* The nearer definition contains a statement either of the *material,* e. g. Ex 3⁸, &c., אֶרֶץ זָבַת חָלָב וּדְבַשׁ *a land flowing with milk and honey;* or of the *means,* e. g. חַלְלֵי־חֶרֶב *slain with the sword,* Is 22²; or the *cause,* Ct 2⁵ *sick of love;* or of the *scope* of the attribute,[1] e. g. Gn 39⁶ יְפֵה־תֹאַר *fair of form;* cf. Gn 41²·⁴, Ex 34⁶, Is 1⁴, Jer 32¹⁹, Na 1³, ψ 119¹, Jb 37¹⁶; or of the *manner,* e. g. ψ 59⁶ אָוֶן בֹּגְדֵי *faithless ones of wickedness* (wickedly faithless).

Especially frequent is the use of this genitive to name the part of y the body described as being affected by some physical or mental condition, e. g. ψ 24⁴ נְקִי כַפַּיִם *clean as regards hands,* &c.; 2 S 9³, Is 6⁵, Jb 17⁹; Is 19¹⁰ אַגְמֵי־נָפֶשׁ *grieved in soul;* 1 S 1¹⁰, Jb 3²⁰. Also such examples as Am 2¹⁶, Pr 19¹, where a suffix is attached to the substantive, must be regarded as instances of the genitive construction, on the analogy of Pr 14², see § 116 k.

§ 129. *Expression of the Genitive by Circumlocution.*

Besides the construction of a nomen rectum dependent upon a nomen a regens in the construct state (§§ 89 and 128), the connexion of two nouns may also be effected otherwise, either by simply attaching the dependent noun by means of the preposition לְ, which, according to § 119 r, expresses, besides other ideas, like that of *belonging to,*[2] or by the addition of a relative clause (לְ אֲשֶׁר, see h below).

1. The introduction of a genitive by לְ sometimes occurs even when the b construction with the construct state would be equally possible, e. g. 1 S 14¹⁶ הַצֹּפִים לְשָׁאוּל *the watchmen of Saul;* ψ 37¹⁶, 2 Ch 28¹⁸ (where indeed the circumlocution makes the sense much plainer); as a rule, however, this use is restricted to the following cases:—

(a) To prevent a nomen regens being determined by a following determinate c genitive, e. g. 1 S 16¹⁸ בֵּן לְיִשַׁי *a son of Jesse* (בֶּן־יִשַׁי would be, according to § 127 a, *the son of Jesse);* cf Gn 14¹⁸, 36¹², 41¹², Nu 16²² (27¹⁶), 1 S 17⁸, 2 S 19²¹, ψ 122⁵. Hence, regularly מִזְמוֹר לְדָוִד (ψ 3¹, &c.) *a psalm of David* (properly belonging to David as the author), for which לְדָוִד *of David* is used alone elliptically in ψ 11¹, 14¹, &c. Such a case as לְדָוִד מִזְמוֹר (ψ 24¹, &c.) is not to

---

[1] Cf. the Latin *integer vitae scelerisque purus ; tristes animi,* &c.

[2] Cf. the σχῆμα Κολοφώνιον in Greek, e. g. ἡ κεφαλή τῷ ἀνθρώπῳ for τοῦ ἀνθρώπου (Bernhardy's *Syntax,* p. 88). The Arab grammarians distinguish a twofold genitive, one of which may be resolved by לְ, and the other by מִן [see Wright's *Arabic Grammar,* vol. ii, § 75 ff.]. The *de* of the Romance languages is a development of the latter idea ; the Gascon, however, says e. g. *la fille à Mr. N..* laying stress upon the idea of *belonging to* and not that of *origin,* as in *la fille de . . .* of the literary language.

be regarded as a transposition, but מִזְמוֹר is used epexegetically for the
general term omitted before לְדָוִד (as it were, a poem *of David, a psalm*).
Moreover, the introduction of the author, poet, &c., by this *Lamed auctoris* is
the customary idiom also in the other Semitic dialects, especially in Arabic.

d   (*b*) When a genitive is to be made dependent on a nomen regens, which is
itself composed of a nomen regens and rectum, and represents, as a compound, one united idea, e. g. Ru 2³ חֶלְקַת הַשָּׂדֶה לְבֹעַז *the portion of field belonging
to Boaz* (שְׂדֵה בֹעַז חֶ׳) would be *the portion of the field of Boaz*) ; 2 K 5⁹ *at the house-
door of Elisha*. This especially applies to the cases in which the compound
regens represents a term in very common use, the fixed form of which
cannot be altered, e. g. 1 K 14¹⁹ עַל־סֵפֶר דִּבְרֵי הַיָּמִים לְמַלְכֵי יִשְׂרָאֵל *in the book
of the chronicles of the kings of Israel*; 15²³, &c.; cf. also Jos 19⁵¹.

e   (*c*) When for any other reason the construction with the nomen regens in
the construct state is inadmissible ; cf. e. g. Lv 18²⁰, where שְׁכָבְתְּךָ, on account
of the suffix, cannot be used in the construct state ; but Lv 15¹⁶ ᶠᶠ., &c.,
שִׁכְבַת־זֶרַע ; Ju 3²⁸ *the Jordan fords of Moab* (יַרְדֵּן as a *proper name* cannot be used
in the construct state) ; Ex 20⁵ *upon the third and upon the fourth generation of
them that hate me*; וְעַל־רִבֵּעִים must be kept in the absolute state for the sake
of conformity with עַל־שִׁלֵּשִׁים, and for the same reason also לַאֲלָפִים לְאֹהֲבַי.

f   (*d*) After statements of number in such cases as Gn 8¹⁴ בְּשִׁבְעָה וְעֶשְׂרִים יוֹם
לַחֹדֶשׁ *on the seven and twentieth day of the month*; cf. 7¹¹, 16³ and frequently, or
as in Hag 1¹ בִּשְׁנַת שְׁתַּיִם לְדָרְיָוֶשׁ *in the second year of Darius*; the numeral here
is always one compound idea with the substantive numbered, and con-
sequently (as in the examples under *b*) does not admit of being in the constr.
st. with a genitive. The same naturally applies also to such examples as
1 K 3¹⁸ בַּיּוֹם הַשְּׁלִישִׁי לְלִדְתִּי *on the third day of my giving birth* (i. e. after my
giving birth). Cf also the standing phrase בְּאֶחָד לַחֹדֶשׁ *on the first* (day) *of the
month*, Gn 8⁵ and frequently.

g   Rem. In cases like 2 S 3² *and his firstborn was Amnon* לַאֲחִינֹעַם *of Ahinoam*,
the genitive expressed by circumlocution with לְ is in reality dependent
on a regens which is omitted (בֶּן לַאֲחִינֹעַם *a son of Ahinoam*) ; cf. 2 S 3³·⁵,
1 K 14¹³, Am 5³ (unless לְבֵית יִשְׂרָאֵל originally depended on *thus spake the
Lord*), and the remarks on לְדָוִד מִזְמוֹר under *c* above.

h   2. The periphrastic expression of the genitive by means of אֲשֶׁר לְ is used
principally to state the *possessor*, e.g. Gn 29⁹ הַצֹּאן אֲשֶׁר לְאָבִיהָ *her father's sheep*
(prop. *the sheep which belonged to her father*) ; Gn 47⁴ and frequently. So also
(according to § 128 *a*) when a genitive depends on more than one substantive,
e.g. Gn 40⁵ *the butler and the baker who* (belonged) *to the king of Egypt* (וְאֹפֶה מֶלֶךְ
מִצְרַיִם would indicate only the baker as belonging to the king) ; or when
a genitive (as in the examples under *d* above) is added to a compound, which
expresses one united idea (Ru 4³) ; or when, as a fixed term (e. g. a title),
it appears always in the same form, e.g. Ct 1¹ שִׁיר הַשִּׁירִים אֲשֶׁר לִשְׁלֹמֹה *the
Song of songs, of Solomon* ; 1 S 21⁸, 2 S 2⁸, 1 Ch 11¹⁰; cf. also Gn 41⁴³.[1]

---

[1] In New Hebrew שֶׁל (derived from שֶׁלְ = אֲשֶׁר לְ, see § 36, and cf. Ct 1⁶,
3⁷ שֶׁלִּשְׁלֹמֹה, שֶׁלִּי) is used like the simple relative דִּי, דְּ in Aramaic, as an
independent sign of the genitive.

§ 130. *Wider Use of the Construct State.*

The construct state, which, according to § 89 a, primarily represents *a*
only the immediate government by one substantive of the following
word (or combination of words), is frequently employed in rapid
narrative as a connecting form, even apart from the genitive relation;
so especially—

(1) Before prepositions,[1] particularly in elevated (prophetic or
poetic) style, especially when the nomen regens is a participle. Thus
before בְּ, שִׂמְחַת בַּקָּצִיר *the joy in the harvest*, Is 9², 2 S 1²¹, ψ 136⁸ᶠ·;
in participles, Is 5¹¹, 9¹, 19⁸, ψ 84⁷, and especially often when בְּ with
a suffix follows the participle, e. g. ψ 2¹² כָּל־חוֹסֵי בוֹ ; cf. Na 1⁷, Jer 8¹⁶
(ψ 24¹) ; ψ 64⁹ (unless רָאָה should be read) ; 98⁷.²—Before לְ, Ho 9⁶
(but read probably מִחֲמַדֵּי כַסְפָּם) ; ψ 58⁵ (before לְמוֹ) ; Pr 24⁹, Jb 18²,
La 2¹⁸ (before לָךְ) ; 1 Ch 6⁵⁵, 23²⁸ ; in participles, Ez 38¹¹, Jb 24⁵ ;
before לְ with an infinitive, Is 56¹⁰, and again before לְ with a suffix,
Gn 24²¹, Is 30¹⁸, 64³ ;³—before אֶל־, Is 14¹⁹, Ez 21¹⁷ ;—before אֵת (*with*),
Is 8⁶ ;—before מִן, Gn 3²², Is 28⁹ (a participle) ; Jer 23²³, Ez 13², Ho 7⁵ ;—
before עַל־, Ju 5¹⁰ ;—before בִּלְתִּי, Is 14⁶ ;—before the *nota accus.* את,
Jer 33²² ;—before a locative (which in such cases also serves as a
genitive), Ex 27¹³, Jer 1¹⁵.

(2) Before *wāw copulative*, e. g. Ez 26¹⁰ ; but חָכְמַת Is 33⁶, גִּילַת 35², *b*
and שְׁכֻרַת 51²¹ may be cases of an intentional reversion to the old
feminine ending *ath*, in order to avoid the hiatus (וִ) וְ הַ‑.

(3) When it governs the (originally demonstrative) pronoun אֲשֶׁר ; *c*
so especially in the combination מְקוֹם אֲשֶׁר, Gn 39²⁰, 40³, *the place where*
(prop. *of that in which*) *Joseph was bound* ; cf. § 138 *g* ; or בִּמְקוֹם אֲשֶׁר
Lv 4²⁴·³³, 2 S 15²¹, 1 K 21¹⁹, Jer 22¹², Ez 21³⁵, Ho 2¹. We should expect
הַמָּקוֹם אֲשֶׁר, בַּמָּקוֹם אֲשֶׁר, as in Gn 35¹³, &c., *at the place which . . .*, cf.
§ 138 ; but אֲשֶׁר is treated as a nomen rectum instead of as an attribute.

---

[1] Cf. König, ' Die Ueberwucherung des St.-constr.-Gebrauchs im Semit.,'
ZDMG. 53, 521 ff.

[2] In Ju 8¹¹ the article is even used before a construct state followed by בְּ,
in order to determine the whole combination שְׁכוּנֵי בָאֳהָלִים *tent-dwellers*, taken
as one word ; cf., however, the remarks in § 127 *f-i* on similar grammatical
solecisms.

[3] These are to be distinguished from the cases where לְ follows a construct
state, which in conjunction with מִן (and the following לְ) has become a sort
of preposition or adverb of place ; thus, we have מִבֵּית־לְ Ex 26³³ (for which in
Ez 1²⁷ merely בֵּית לְ) meaning simply *within* ; מִימִין לְ (2 K 23¹³, Ez 10³) *on the
right hand* (i.e. *south*) *of* ; מִצָּפוֹן לְ (Jos 8¹¹·¹³, &c., Ju 2⁹) *on the north of* ; cf. also
Jos 15²¹ and לִפְנֵי מִן Neh 13⁴.

Cf. also אֵ מִיּוֹם followed by a *perfect* in 1 S 29⁸, and אֵ יְמֵי Lv 13⁴⁶, Nu 9¹⁸.[1]

d (4) When it governs independent sentences (cf. § 155), which virtually stand to the construct state (as nomen regens) in a sort of genitive relation, e. g. Ex 4¹³ בְּיַד־תִּשְׁלָח prop. *by the hand of* him whom *thou wilt send*; Nu 23³ דְּבַר מַה־יַּרְאֵנִי *the matter of* that *which he shall show me*, i. e. whatever he shall; Is 29¹ קִרְיַת חָנָה דָוִד *the city where David encamped*; Jer 48³⁶, ψ 16³ (if the text be right), 65⁵ (Pr 8³²), ψ 81⁶, Jb 18²¹ *the place of him that knoweth not God*; Jb 29¹⁶, La 1¹⁴ (if the text be right) *into the hands* of those against whom *I cannot stand*.[2] In Gn 39⁴ (כָּל־יֶשׁ־לוֹ) the כָּל ־ takes after it a noun-clause, and in Ex 9⁴, still more boldly, a subst. with לְ.—Very often a *time-determination* governs the following sentence in this way; thus אַחֲרֵי followed by a perfect, Lv 25⁴⁸, 1 S 5⁹; בְּיוֹם ψ 102³ (before a noun-clause), Ex 6²⁸, Nu 3¹, Dt 4¹⁵, 2 S 22¹, ψ 18¹, 59¹⁷, 138³ (in every case before a following *perfect*), ψ 56¹⁰ (before an imperfect); מִיּוֹם followed by the perfect, Jer 36²; כָּל־יְמֵי Lv 14⁴⁶, 1 S 25¹⁵, Jb 29² כִּימֵי *as in the days when ...*[3]; cf. כִּימוֹת and שְׁנוֹת before a perfect, ψ 90¹⁵); בְּעֵת before a perfect, Jer 6¹⁵ (cf. 49⁸, 50³¹); before an imperfect, Jb 6¹⁷; תְּחִלַּת before a perfect, Ho 1².

e (5) Connected with a following word in apposition; certainly so in such cases as בְּתוּלַת בַּת־צִיּוֹן *the virgin, the daughter of Zion*, Is 37²²; cf. 23¹², Jer 14¹⁷; also 1 S 28⁷ אֵשֶׁת בַּעֲלַת־אוֹב *a woman, possessor of a soothsaying spirit*; cf. Dt 21¹¹.—Gn 14¹⁰, Ju 19²² (but read probably אֲנָשִׁים with Moore, as in Dt 13¹⁴, Ju 20¹³, 1 K 21¹⁰); 2 K 10⁶, 17¹³ Qʻrê; Jer 46⁹, ψ 35¹⁶ (?), 78⁹, Jb 20¹⁷ᵇ (unless נָהֲרוּ or נַהֲלֵי be a gloss).

f Rem. Some of the above passages may also be explained by supposing that there exists a real genitive relation towards the preceding construct state, which has been, as it were, provisionally left *in suspenso*, in consequence of the insertion of some interrupting word, e. g. Is 37²², &c.; Jb 20¹⁷ᵃ. Elsewhere (Dt 33¹⁹, ψ 68³⁴) the *nomen regens* probably governs the following construct state directly.[4]

---

[1] In Dt 23⁵ the construct state governs a sentence introduced by the *conjunction* (עַל־דְּבַר אֲשֶׁר) אֲשֶׁר *by reason of the fact that*, i. e. *because*); so also in 1 S 3¹³.

[2] Probably Gn 22¹⁴ is also to be so explained (contrary to the accents), and certainly (contrary to the very unnatural division of the verses) 2 Ch 30¹⁸, which should read on thus : יְהֹוָה הַטּוֹב יְכַפֵּר בְּעַד כָּל־לְבָבוֹ הֵכִין *the good Lord pardon every one that setteth his heart to seek God.* [See Wickes' *Accentuation of the Twenty-one Prose Books of the Old Testament*, p. 140.]

[3] Cf. Na 2⁹ מִימֵי הִיא, usually explained to mean *from the days that she hath been*, but the text is evidently very corrupt.

[4] So also Is 28¹⁶ *a corner stone of the preciousness* (יִקְרַת) is a *substantive* not an *adjective*) *of a fixed foundation*, i. e. a precious corner stone of surest foundation.—In 2 S 20¹⁹ the text is wholly corrupt; in ψ 119¹²⁸ read כָּל־פִּקּוּדֶיךָ.

(6) The numeral אַחַד *one* for אֶחָד in close connexion, and even with *g* small disjunctives, e. g. Gn 3²², 48²², 1 S 9³, 2 S 17²², Is 27¹², Zc 11⁷.

The character of these passages shows that the numeral here cannot be in the construct state, but is merely a rhythmical shortening of the usual (tone-lengthened) form.

§ 131. *Apposition.*

1. Apposition in the stricter sense is the collocation of two sub- *a* stantives in the same case in order to define more exactly (or to complete) the one by the other, and, as a rule (see, however, below, under *g*), the former by the latter. Apposition in Hebrew (as in the other Semitic languages[1]) is by no means confined to those cases in which it is used in English or in the classical languages. It is not infrequently found when either the *subordination* of one substantive to the other or some more circumstantial kind of epexegetical addition would be expected.

2. The principal kinds of apposition in Hebrew are:—

(*a*) The collocation of *genus* and *species*, e. g. אִשָּׁה אַלְמָנָה *a woman b* (who was) *a widow*, 1 K 7¹⁴; נַעֲרָה בְתוּלָה *a damsel* (that is) *a virgin*, Dt 22²³·²⁸, Ju 4⁴, 19¹, 21¹², 1 S 30¹⁷, 1 K 1²; cf. Gn 13⁸, 21²⁰ (where, however, קֶשֶׁת is probably an explanatory gloss); Ex 24⁵ (1 S 11¹⁵), 2 S 15¹⁶, 1 K 3¹⁶, 5²⁹ (but probably סֵבֶל should be read instead of סַבָּל); Is 3²⁴ (unless מַעֲשֶׂה is to be read), Jer 20¹. Perhaps also כֹּהֵן הָרֹאשׁ *the priest* (who is) *the chief man*, 2 K 25¹⁸, &c.; others take כֹּהֵן as constr. st.—In 2 S 10⁷ read כָּל־צְבָא הַגִּבֹּ' with the LXX, as in the parallel passage 1 Ch 19⁹ for כָּל־צָבָא הַגִּ', which is evidently meant to refer to the reading in 2 S.

(*b*) Collocation of the *person* or *thing* and the *attribute*, e. g. Jb 20²⁹ *c* (27¹³) זֶה חֵלֶק־אָדָם רָשָׁע *this is the portion of a man*, (who is) *a wicked man* (but רָשָׁע might also be an adject.); cf. Pr 6¹².—Lv 6¹³, 16⁴ (where, however, לֹבֶשׁ is probably a gloss); Pr 22²¹ אֲמָרִים אֱמֶת *words* (which are) *truth*; (immediately after אִמְרֵי אֱמֶת) cf. 1 S 2¹³, Mi 1¹¹ (where, however, בֹּשֶׁת is most probably a gloss on עֶרְיָה); Zc 1¹³ (= *comfortable words*); ψ 45⁵ (?), 68¹⁷ (cf. verse 16). In a wider sense this includes also such cases as ψ 60⁵ יַיִן תַּרְעֵלָה *wine* which is *staggering* (intoxicating drink), which causes staggering[2]; 1 K 22²⁷, 2 Ch 18²⁶ מַיִם לַחַץ (in

---

[1] On certain uses of apposition peculiar to the Semitic languages, cf. the exhaustive discussion by Fleischer, 'Ueber einige Arten der Nominalapposition im Arab.' (*Kleine Schriften*, ii. 16); [and see also Driver, *Tenses*, Appendix IV.]

[2] Unless it is to be translated *thou gavest us intoxication to drink as wine* (and so in 1 K 22²⁷ *give him affliction to eat as bread*, &c.); cf. ψ 80⁶ and the analogous examples of apposition in the form of a second accusative in § 117 *kk*. More-

Is 30²⁰ parallel with צָר לֶחֶם) *water* which is *affliction*, drunk in trouble (imprisonment). Still more boldly, 1 K 5³ בָּקָר רְעִי *oxen* which were taken out of the *pastures*, and 1 K 6⁷ *undressed stones* which come from the *quarry*, probably a corruption of מִמַּסָּע. A person and a condition are in apposition in Ez 18⁶ (unless בְּנִדָּתָה is to be read).— In 1 S 4¹ read הָעֵזֶר אֶבֶן, as in 5¹, 7¹².

d (c) Collocation of the *person* (Dt 28³⁶) or *thing* (form) and *material*,[1] or of the *place* or *measure* and its *contents*, e. g. 1 Ch 15¹⁹ בִּמְצִלְתַּיִם נְחֹשֶׁת *with cymbals* which were *brass*, i. e. of brass; cf. Ex 26²⁵, Dn 11⁸, 1 Ch 28¹⁵·¹⁸ (?); Ex 28¹⁷ *four rows*, namely *stones* (for which 39¹⁰ has אָבֶן טוּרֵי); cf. 2 Ch 4¹³, Lv 6³ (see, however, § 128 *d*); 2 K 7¹ סֹלֶת סְאָה *a seah* of *fine flour*; cf. 2 K 7¹⁶·¹⁸, Gn 18⁶, Ex 16³³, Lv 5¹¹, Ru 2¹⁷, 1 K 16²⁴, 2 K 5²³ כֶּסֶף כִּכְּרַיִם *two talents* of *silver*;[2] cf. 5¹⁷, Ex 39¹⁷, Ez 22¹⁸ (if the text be right). With the *material* placed before the *measure*, Ex 30²³ᶠ.—A *period of time* and its contents are placed in apposition יָמִים חֹדֶשׁ *a month* of *days*, i. e. a month's time=for a whole month, Gn 29¹⁴, Nu 11²⁰·²¹, cf. Dt 21¹³, 2 K 15¹³, and יָמִים שְׁנָתַיִם *two years' time*, i. e. two full years, Gn 41¹, 2 S 13²³, 14²⁸, Jer 28³·¹¹, Dn 10²ᶠ.

Finally, under this head may be included all the cases in which a numeral (regarded as a substantive) is followed by the object numbered in apposition, e. g. בָנִים שְׁלֹשָׁה *trias* sc. *filii*, § 97 *a* and § 134 *b*.

e (d) Collocation of the *thing* and the *measure* or *extent*, *number*, &c., e. g. Nu 9²⁰ מִסְפָּר יָמִים *days*, (a small) *number*, i. e. only a few days; מִשְׁנֶה כֶּסֶף *money*, *repetition*, i. e. twice as much money, Gn 43¹² (unless כֶּסֶף be constr. st.); בִּרְכַּיִם מַיִם *water* which was of the measure of the *knees*, which reached to the knees, Ez 47⁴ (also מָתְנַיִם מֵי *water that was to the loins*, in the same verse). This likewise includes the cases in which a noun is followed in apposition by a numeral (see § 134 *c*) or an adverb, originally conceived as a substantive, e. g. Neh 2¹² אֲנָשִׁים מְעַט *men*, a *few*, i. e. some few men; 1 K 5⁹ הַרְבֵּה תְּבוּנָה *understanding*, *much-making*, i. e. much understanding, unless הַרְבֵּה is to be taken as an adverb with וַיִּתֵּן, as in 2 S 8⁸ with לָקַח.

---

over, having regard to הָרֶקַח יַיִן *spiced wine*, Ct 8², and פֶּרֶא עַיִר *a wild ass's colt*, Jb 11¹² (in which passages יַיִן and עַיִר must certainly be in the construct state) we cannot but ask whether the Masora does not intend the יַיִן in ψ 60⁵ to be taken as construct state (for which elsewhere יֵין).

[1] Cf. also the examples treated above in § 127 *h*.

[2] On the anomalous form כִּכְּרַיִם (instead of כִּכָּרַיִם; cf. כִּכָּרִים immediately before), see § 88 *b*.

(e) Collocation of the *thing* and its *name*, e. g. בְּהַרְרָם שֵׂעִיר *in their* **f** *mountainous district, Seir* (perhaps only a later gloss), Gn 14⁶; הָאָרֶץ כְּנַעַן *the land Canaan* (כנען probably only a later gloss), Nu 34²; cf. Ezr 9¹, 1 Ch 5⁹ (see under *g* below).—For examples of nouns in the construct state before a noun in apposition, see § 130 *e*.

Rem. 1. Only in certain combinations does the noun of nearer definition **g** come first, e. g. הַמֶּלֶךְ שְׁלֹמֹה, הַמֶּלֶךְ דָּוִד *king David, king Solomon* (less frequently דָּוִד הַמֶּלֶךְ as in 2 S 13³⁹, 1 K 2¹⁷, 12², 2 K 8²⁹, 9¹⁵, and in late Hebrew, Hag 1¹·¹⁵ [cf. the Aramaic order דריוש מלכא], and often in Chron.).—A chiasmus occurs in Is 45⁴, the name standing after the defining noun in the first part of the verse, and before it in the parallel clause.

2. When the *nota accusativi* (אֵת, אֶת־) or a preposition precedes the first **h** substantive, it *may* be repeated before the noun in apposition, e. g. Gn 4², 22², 24⁴, 47²⁹, Is 66²¹; this usually occurs when the nearer definition precedes a *proper name*. As a rule, however, the repetition does not take place (Dt 18¹, Jer 33¹⁸, 1 S 2¹⁴). A noun in apposition is made determinate, even after a noun with a prefix, in the ordinary way, e. g. 2 Ch 12¹³ בִּירוּשָׁלַיִם הָעִיר *in Jerusalem, the city which,* &c.[1]

3. Sometimes a second adjective is used in apposition to a preceding **i** adjective, in order to modify in some way the meaning of the first, e. g. Lv 13¹⁹ בַּהֶרֶת לְבָנָה אֲדַמְדָּמֶת *a white-reddish* (light red) *bright spot.*

4. *Permutation* is to be regarded as a variety of apposition. It is not com- **k** plementary like apposition proper (see *a* above), but rather *defines* the preceding substantive (or pronoun, see below), in order to prevent any possible misunderstanding. This includes cases like Gn 9⁴ *with the life thereof* (which is) *the blood thereof*; Ex 22³⁰, Dt 2²⁶, 1 S 7⁹, 2 K 3⁴ *an hundred thousand rams, the wool,* i. e. the wool of the rams; Jer 25¹⁵ *this cup of the wine,* that is *of fury* (but הַחֵמָה is probably a gloss); Is 42²⁵ *he poured upon him fury,* namely *his anger* ;[2] but especially the examples in which such a permutative is added to a preceding pronoun, viz.—

(a) To a separate pronoun, e. g. Ex 7¹¹; with regard to the vocative, cf. **l** § 126 *f*.

(b) To an accusative suffix, e. g. Ex 2⁶ *she saw him, the child* (unless אֶת־הַיֶּ׳ **m** be a later gloss); Ex 35⁵, Lv 13⁵⁷ᵇ, 1 K 19²¹ (where, indeed, הַבָּשָׂר appears to be a late gloss); 21¹³, 2 K 16¹⁵ *Keth.*, Jer 9¹⁴, 31², Ez 3²¹, Ec 2²¹ (according to Delitzsch rather a double accusative).[3]

(c) To a noun-suffix, e. g. Ez 10³ בְּבֹאוֹ הָאִישׁ *when he went in, the man*; 42¹⁴; **n** cf. Pr 13⁴ (?), Ez 3¹²; so also after a preposition with suffix, e. g. Ec 4¹⁰ אִי לוֹ הָאֶחָד *woe to him, the one alone*; with a repetition of the preposition, Nu 32³³, Jos 1² לָהֶם לִבְנֵי יִשְׂרָאֵל *to them, to the children of Israel*; Ju 21⁷, Jer 51⁵⁶,

---

[1] In 1 K 11⁸ participles after לְכָל־נָשָׁיו, as in 2 K 10⁶ after אֶת־גְּדֹלֵי הָעִיר, in 19² after a determinate accusative, and in Hag 1⁴ after בְּבָתֵּיכֶם, are used *without* the article; these, however, are probably to be explained not as in apposition, but according to § 118 *p*.

[2] But מַיִם Gn 6¹⁷ (cf. 7⁶) is to be regarded as a later gloss upon the archaic מַבּוּל.

[3] For וַיִּשַּׁנּוּ 1 S 21¹⁴ either וַיְשַׁנֶּה is to be read or the *Kethibh* is to be explained according to § 75 *b*, note. Also יַלְבִּדֻנוּ Pr 5²² has hardly preserved the correct form.

Ez 42⁵ (?), Dn 11¹¹, 1 Ch 4⁴², 2 Ch 26¹⁴.¹—Cf. finally, Ct 3⁷, where the suffix precedes the genitive periphrastically expressed by שֶׁלְּ, as in Ez 9¹, where the genitive is expressed by לְ.²

o Of a different kind are the cases in which the permutative with its proper suffix follows as a kind of correction of the preceding suffix, e. g. Is 29²³ *when he* (or rather) *his children see*, &c. (but יְלָדָיו is clearly a gloss); cf. ψ 83¹²; in Jb 29³ read בְּהִלּוֹ (infin. Hiph.) or at least its syncopated form בַּהִלּוֹ.

p 5. Cases of apposition in a *wider sense* are those in which the nearer definition added to the noun was originally regarded as an *adverbial accusative*; on its use with the verb and on the relative correctness of speaking of such an accusative in Hebrew, cf. § 118 *a* and *m*. Owing to the lack of case-endings, indeed, it is in many instances only by analogies elsewhere (especially in Arabic) that we can decide whether the case is one of apposition in the narrower or in the wider sense; in other instances this must remain quite uncertain. However, the following are probably cases of apposition in the wider sense :—

q (*a*) Such phrases as מִשְׁנֶה כֶּסֶף *a double amount in money*, Gn 43¹⁵; cf. Jer 17¹⁸; 1 S 17⁵ *five thousand shekels in brass*, but this might also be taken (as in *d*) *shekels* which were *brass*; certainly such cases as Jb 15¹⁰ *older than thy father in days*, and the expression of the superlative by means of מְאֹד (originally a substantive), e. g. טוֹב מְאֹד *very good*, Gn 1³¹ (cf. also Ec 7¹⁶ צַדִּיק הַרְבֵּה *righteous over much*), and the very frequent הַרְבֵּה מְאֹד prop. *a much-making exceedingly*, i. e. *exceedingly great*, Gn 15¹, 41⁴⁹, also Pr 23²⁹ פְּצָעִים חִנָּם *wounds without cause*,³ perhaps also Gn 34²⁵ (בֶּטַח).

r (*b*) A few examples, in which an expexegetical substantive is added to a substantive with a suffix; thus, Ez 16²⁷ מַדְרְכֵּךְ זִמָּה *of thy conduct in lewdness* (but it is also possible to explain it (as in *c*) *of thy conduct*, which is *lewdness*); cf. Ez 24¹³, 2 S 22³³ מָעוּזִּי חָיִל *my fortress in strength*, i. e. *my strong fortress* (cf., however, ψ 18³³); Hb 3⁸, ψ 71⁷. While even in these examples the deviation from the ordinary usage of the language (cf. § 135 *n*) is strange, it is much more so in חֲבֹלָתוֹ חוֹב Ez 18⁷, i. e. according to the context *his pledge for a debt*; Ezr 2⁶² כְּתָבָם הַמִּתְיַחֲשִׂים, i. e. *their register*, namely of *those that were reckoned by genealogy* (but perhaps הַמִּתְיַ׳ is in apposition to the suffix in כְּתָבָם), also the curious combinations (mentioned in § 128 *d*) of בְּרִיתִי with a proper name (Lv 26⁴²), and in Jer 33²⁰ with הַיּוֹם.⁴

---

¹ But in Is 17⁶ we should certainly divide the words differently and read בִּסְעִפֶי הַפֹּרִיָּה, in Jer 48⁴⁴ read אֵלָה for אֵלֶיהָ, and in Pr 14¹³ אַחֲרִית הַשִּׂמְחָה; in Gn 2¹⁹ נֶפֶשׁ חַיָּה is a late gloss upon לוֹ, and in Ez 41²⁵ אֶל־דַּלְתוֹת הַהֵיכָל a gloss on אֲלֵיהֶן.

² Some of the examples given above are textually (or exegetically) doubtful, whilst in the case of others, especially those from the later Books, we cannot help asking whether such a prolepsis of the genitive by means of a suffix (as e. g. Ez 10³) is not due to the influence of Aramaic, in which it is the customary idiom; cf. Kautzsch's *Gramm. des Biblisch-Aram.*, § 81 *e* and § 88.

³ In ψ 69⁵ חִנָּם (like שֶׁקֶר *in a false way, falsely*, ψ 35¹⁹ and 38²⁰) is used as an *adverbial accusative* with a participle; cf. § 118 *q*.

⁴ But in Nu 25¹² שָׁלוֹם may also be explained, according to *c*, as really in apposition. Cf. on the whole question Delitzsch, *Psalmen*, 4th ed., p. 203, note 1.

6. In Dt 33⁴ (מוֹרָשָׁה, perhaps מוֹר׳ לְקְהִלַּת is to be read), 33²⁷ (מְעֹנָה), Ju 7⁸ S (צֵדָה), the absolute state appears to be used instead of the construct to govern a following logical genitive; this, however, cannot be explained either as a special kind of apposition, or (with Hitzig) as a peculiarity of the dialect of Northern Palestine, but is merely a textual corruption. On the other hand, in Jb 31¹¹ עָוֹן is evidently intended to combine the readings עָוֹן פְּלִילִים and עָוֹן פְּלִילִי (as in verse 28).—The remarkable combination אֱלֹהִים צְבָאוֹת in ψ 80⁸·¹⁵ is due to the fact that in ψψ 42–83 אֱלֹהִים has almost throughout been subsequently substituted by some redactor for the divine name יהוה; on יהוה צְבָאוֹת cf. § 125 *h*. In ψ 59⁶, 80⁵·²⁰, and 84⁹ יהוה has been reinstated in the text before אֱלֹהִים צְבָאוֹת.¹

7. Lastly, the nearer definition (qualification) of a noun may be effected by *t* means of a preposition (either with a suffix or with an independent noun), but must then be distinguished from the cases in which the preposition is dependent on a verb or verbal idea, e. g. Gn 3⁶ *and she gave also* לְאִישָׁהּ עִמָּהּ *unto her husband with her* (= *her husband who was with her*); in Gn 9¹⁶ (*that I may remember the everlasting covenant between God and every living creature of all flesh*) and other places, the qualification of the noun is itself also qualified.

§ 132. *Connexion of the Substantive with the Adjective.*²

1. The adjective (like the participle used adjectivally), which serves *a* as an *attribute* of a substantive, stands *after* the substantive, and agrees with it in *gender* and *number*, e. g. אִישׁ גָּדוֹל *a great man*, אִשָּׁה יָפָה *a beautiful woman*. If the substantive is immediately connected with a genitive, the attribute follows the latter, since, according to § 89 and § 128 *a*, the construct state and the genitive belonging to it are inseparably united, e. g. Est 8¹⁵ עֲטֶרֶת זָהָב גְּדוֹלָה *a great crown of gold.*— On the attribute when attached to a *determinate* substantive, see above, § 126 *u*.

---

¹ Without this assumption it would be inconceivable that יהוה אֱלֹהֵי צְבָאוֹת should not have been written; that the author of these Psalms regarded צְבָאוֹת already as an independent name of God (so Gesenius and Olshausen) is out of the question.

² On the expression of attributive ideas by substantives, cf. above, § 127 *h*, and § 128 *o*, with the note; § 135 *n* and § 141 *c* (substantives for adjectives as predicates of noun-clauses) and § 152 *u* (periphrases for negative qualities). On the use of the feminine of adjectives (and participles) to express abstract ideas, see § 122 *q*. It remains to mention further the employment (mostly only in poetry) of certain epithets in place of the substantives to which the quality in question belongs; e. g. אָבִיר *the strong one*, i. e. *God*; אַבִּיר *the strong one*, i. e. *the bull* (in Jer 8¹⁶, &c., *the horse*); קַל *swift* = *the runner* (of the horse, Is 30¹⁶); לְבָנָה *alba*, i. e. *luna*; פֹּרִיָּה (*fructifera*) *a fruitful tree*, Is 17⁶ (so בָּרֻת Gn 49²²); רֹבֵץ *a croucher*, i. e. *a crouching beast of prey*, Gn 4⁷. Cf. also רֹזֵן (*gravis, augustus*) and נָשִׂיא (*elatus*?), i. e. *a prince*. The use of adjectives and participles for substantives is much more extensive in Arabic. In Greek and Latin poetical language cf. such examples as ὑγρή = *the sea*; *merum* for *vinum*, &c.

b Rem. 1. Where an adjectival attribute appears to stand *before* its substantive (according to the usual explanation, for the sake of special emphasis) the relation is really appositional in character; thus, Is 10³⁰ עֲנִיָּה עֲנָתוֹת *O thou poor one, Anathoth!* (but probably עֲנִיָּה *answer her*, is to be read); cf. 23¹², 53¹¹ (*a righteous man, my servant*; but in 28²¹ זָר and נָכְרִי are *predicates* preceding the substantives); Jer 3⁶·¹⁰ ᶠ·, ψ 18⁴ *him who is worthy to be praised will I call upon, the Lord*; 92¹² (apposition after participles).—But רַבִּים and רַבּוֹת *many*, are sometimes placed, like numerals, before the substantive, Jer 16¹⁶, Neh 9²⁸ (in ψ 145⁷ רַב is a *subst. regens*, in 89⁵¹ the text is corrupt); an appositional relation can scarcely be intended in these instances.

c 2. In a few expressions (mostly poetic) the adjective appears not as an attribute *after* the substantive, but in the construct state governing it; so in the singular, Ex 15¹⁶ (unless גֻּדְל should be read); 1 S 16⁷ (*the height of his stature*); in the plural, 1 S 17⁴⁰ חַלְּקֵי אֲבָנִים *smooth ones of* (among) *stones*, i. e. *smooth stones*; Is 35⁹, Ez 7²⁴, ψ 46⁵, and with a following collective instead of a plural, e. g. Is 29¹⁹ אֶבְיוֹנֵי אָדָם *the poor among men*, i. e. *poor men*; Jer 49²⁰, Zc 11⁷; cf. in Latin *canum degeneres*. However, in almost all these cases the adjective which is made into a *regens* is strongly emphatic, and is frequently equivalent to a superlative (see below, § 133 *g*).

d 3. When *two* adjectives follow a feminine, sometimes only that standing next to the noun takes the feminine termination, e. g. 1 K 19¹¹ רוּחַ גְּדֹלָה וְחָזָק וגו' (but read גְּדוֹל); 1 S 15⁹ (but cf. § 75 *y*); Jer 20⁹, ψ 63². A similar dislike of the feminine form may also be observed in the case of verbal predicates referring to feminine subjects, cf. § 145 *p* and *t*.

When an attribute qualifies several substantives of different genders, it agrees with the masculine, as being the *prior gender* (cf. § 146 *d*), e. g. Neh 9¹³ חֻקִּים וּמִצְוֹת טוֹבִים; Jer 34⁹, Zc 8⁵.

When *three* attributes follow a substantive, the first two may stand without a conjunction, and the last be attached by *wāw copulative*, cf. Zc 1⁸.

e 4. After ·feminines plural ending in ־ִים (§ 87 *p*) the adjectival attribute (in accordance with the fundamental rule stated above, under *a*) takes the ending ־וֹת, e. g. Is 10¹⁴ בֵּיצִים עֲזֻבוֹת *forsaken eggs*; Gn 32¹⁶. For a strange exception see Jer 29¹⁷ (differently in 24²).

f 5. With regard to *number* it is to be remarked that—

(*a*) Substantives in the *dual* are followed by adjectives (or participles) in the *plural*, e. g. ψ 18²⁸ (Pr 6¹⁷) עֵינַיִם רָמוֹת *haughty eyes*; Is 35³, Jb 4³ ᶠ·, cf. § 88 *a*.

g (*b*) *Collective* ideas are not infrequently joined with the *plural* of the adjective or participle (*constructio ad sensum*); thus, e. g. צֹאן *sheep* [with *fem. plur.*], Gn 30⁴³, 1 S 25¹⁸; עַם = *men*, 1 S 13¹⁵, Is 9¹; כָּל־יִשְׂרָאֵל = *all the Israelites*, 1 S 2¹⁴; גָּלוּת = *the exiles*, Jer 28⁴; cf. also נֶפֶשׁ שְׁנַיִם *two souls*, Gn 46²⁷.¹ Cf. similar phenomena in the connexion of collectives with plural predicates in § 145 *c*.

h (*c*) The *pluralis excellentiae* or *pluralis maiestatis* is joined, as a rule, to the singular of the attribute, e. g. ψ 7¹⁰ אֱלֹהִים צַדִּיק; 2 K 19⁴·¹⁶ (= Is 37⁴·¹⁷); Is 19⁴; but cf. אֱלֹהִים חַיִּים ² Dt 5²³, 1 S 17²⁶·³⁶, Jer 10¹⁰, 23³⁶, perhaps also

---

¹ But it is impossible to take תְּמִימִם in Ez 46⁶ as an attribute of בָּקָר; probably it is a correction intended to harmonize the passage with Nu 28¹¹, where *two* young bullocks are required.

² Cf. 1 S 28¹³, where אֱלֹהִים (in the sense of *a spirit*) is followed by עֹלִים as a second accusative; conversely in 1 S 19¹³·¹⁶, a singular suffix refers back

Ex 20³ אֱלֹהִים אֲחֵרִים = *another god*, and Jos 24¹⁹ אֱלֹהִים קְדֹשִׁים (but cf. above, § 124 *g–k*). On the other hand, 1 S 4⁸ is to be explained as having been said by the Philistines, who supposed that the Israelites had several gods. On the connexion of אֱלֹהִים with a plural predicate, see § 145 *i*.

2. On the adjective (in the construct state) governing a following genitive, see § 128 *x*; for the participle in the same construction, see § 116 *f–l*.

§ 133. *The Comparison of Adjectives. (Periphrastic Expression of the Comparative and Superlative.)*

A. Wünsche, ' Der Komparativ im Hebr. im Lichte der arab. Gramm.,' in *Vierteljahrsschrift für Bibelkunde*, 1904, p. 398 ff.

1. Hebrew possesses no special forms either for the comparative or a superlative of the adjective.[1] In order to express a comparative, the person or thing which is to be represented as excelled in some particular quality is attached to the attributive word by the preposition מִן (מִי־), e. g. 1 S 9² גָּבֹהַּ מִכָּל־הָעָם *higher than any of the people*. The fundamental idea evidently is, *tall away from all the people* (beyond all the people); cf. Ju 14¹⁸ מַה־מָּתוֹק מִדְּבַשׁ וּמֶה עַז מֵאֲרִי *what is sweeter than honey? and what is stronger than a lion?* Ez 28³, Am 6². Frequently an infinitive appears as the object of the comparison, e. g. Gn 29¹⁹ *it is better that I give her to thee, than that I should give her*, &c.; Ex 14¹², ψ 118⁸ᶠ·².

Rem. 1. This use of מִן is also very common when the attributive idea is b represented by an intransitive verb, e. g. 1 S 10²³ וַיִּגְבַּהּ מִכָּל־הָעָם *and he was higher than any of the people*; Na 3⁸, Jb 7⁶. Elsewhere, especially after transitive verbs, מִן rather represents (on its different senses see § 119 *v–z*) the idea

---

to תְּרָפִים *household god* (but not so in Gn 31³⁴), as in ψ 46⁴ to the plural of amplification יַמִּים *sea*. On the other hand, it is very doubtful whether רַבָּה ψ 78¹⁵ is to be regarded as an attribute of תְּהֹמוֹת and not rather as the adverb, *abundantly*.

[1] There is in Arabic a special form of the adjective (the *elative*) for the comparative and superlative, which in Hebrew would have the form אַקְטַל. Instances of it, perhaps, are אַכְזָר *daring, cruel*, אַכְזָב *deceptive* (of a brook drying up), and its opposite אֵיתָן (contracted from 'aitan) *constantly flowing, perennis*. These forms are, however, used without any perceptible emphasis, and cannot be regarded as more than isolated relics of an elative formation which has become obsolete, much as the Latin comparative disappears in Italian, and still more so in French, and is supplanted by the circumlocution with *più, plus*.

[2] In Ju 11²⁵ the adjective is specially intensified by repetition, *art thou so much better than Balak?* It would also be possible, however, to translate *art thou really better . . . ?*

of a *separation, distinction* or *superiority* of one person or thing *from* or *over* others.[1]　This is evident in such cases as בָּחַר מִן־ *to choose* something (to prefer it) *before* something else, e. g. Jb 7[15], cf. Dt 14[2] (also מִן־ . . . יִתְרוֹן *the excellence of . . . over . . .*, Ec 2[13]); it is also seen in examples like Gn 37[3] וְיִשְׂרָאֵל אָהַב אֶת־יוֹסֵף מִכָּל־בָּנָיו *now Israel loved Joseph more than all his* (other) *children*; 29[30], 1 S 2[29], Ho 6[6].[2]

c　2. A somewhat different idea underlies the use of מִן־ after adjectives, or intransitive verbs possessing an attributive sense, when the thought to be expressed is that the quality is *too little* or *too much* in force for the attainment of a particular aim or object, e. g. Is 7[13] הַמְעַט מִכֶּם *is it a small thing* (i. e. too little) *for you to . . . ?* Jb 15[11]; after an intransitive verb, e. g. Gn 32[11] *I am too insignificant* (קָטֹנְתִּי) *for all the mercies* (I am not worthy of . . .), &c.; cf. also the expressions כָּבֵד מִן־ *to be too heavy for one*, Ex 18[18], Nu 11[14], ψ 38[5]; קָשָׁה מִן־ *to be too hard for one*, Dt 1[17]; מָעַט מִן־ *to be too few for something*, Ex 12[4]; גָּבַר מִן־ *to be too strong for one*, ψ 65[4]; עָצַם מִן־ *to be too mighty for one*, Gn 26[16]; רוּם מִן־ *to be too high for one*, ψ 61[3]; צַר מִן־ *to be too narrow for one*, Is 49[19]; קָצַר מִן־ *to be too short for something*, Is 50[2], and very frequently נִפְלָא מִן־ *to be too wonderful for one* (and, consequently, inconceivable or unattainable), Gn 18[14], Dt 17[8], 30[11], Jer 37[17], Pr 30[18]; in ψ 139[6] פְּלִיאָה in the same sense is followed by מִן.—This use is especially seen in the numerous instances in which the attribute is followed by מִן־ with an infinitive, e. g. 1 K 8[64] *the brazen altar . . . was* קָטֹן מֵהָכִיל *too little to receive* (to be able to receive) *the burnt offering*, cf. Gn 4[13], 36[7] *too great for them to dwell together*; after verbs, e. g. Ex 12[4], Is 28[20], ψ 40[6]. Finally, cf. רַב לָכֶם מִן־, followed by the infinitive, *it is enough* (prop. *too much*) *for you to . . .*, meaning *ye have . . . long enough*, 1 K 12[28]; cf. Ex 9[28] and Ez 44[6] (מִן followed by a substantive).[3]

d　In all these instances מִן־ expresses either the *removal* of a thing *from* a person, or the *severance* of the person from some aim or object; cf. also the expression לֹא־יִבָּצֵר מֵהֶם כֹּל וגו׳ *nothing will be unattainable for them* (prop. there shall not be cut off from them anything which, &c.), Gn 11[6], Jb 42[2].

e　3. The attributive idea, on which מִן־ logically depends, must sometimes, in consequence of a pregnant use of the מִן־ (see the analogous examples in § 119 *f*), be supplied from the context, e. g. Is 10[10] וּפְסִילֵיהֶם מִירוּשָׁלִָם *whose graven images were more numerous than* those at *Jerusalem*, &c.;[4] Mi 7[4] *worse than a thorn hedge*; ψ 62[10] *lighter than a breath*; Jb 11[17] *clearer than the noonday*; Ec 4[17] *better than*, &c.

---

[1] Cf. the Latin ablative with the comparative; also the etymology of such words as *eximius, egregius*, and the Homeric ἐκ πάντων μάλιστα, Il. 4, 96; ἐκ πασέων, 18, 431.

[2] On the other hand, the phrase צָדֵק מִן־ expresses not a comparison, but only a relation existing between one person and another; thus, in Gn 38[26] צָדְקָה מִמֶּנִּי means, *she is in the right as against me*; cf. ψ 139[12], Jb 4[17], 32[2].—In Pr 17[12] *rather* (to meet with so and so) *than . . .* is expressed by וְאַל־ before the second member.

[3] Cf. also 2 K 4[3], where the idea of *doing something too little* is paraphrased by the Hiph. הַמְעִיט = *do not too little*, sc. לִשְׁאֹל *in borrowing empty vessels*.

[4] With this *comparatio decurtata*, cf. the still bolder pregnant construction in ψ 4[8], מֵעֵת *greater gladness than at the time*, &c.

2. The correlative comparatives *greater—less* (*older—younger*) are *f*
expressed by the simple adjective with the article (*the great,* equivalent
to *the greater,* &c.); Gn 1[16], 19[31.34], 27[15], 29[16.18.26].

3. To express the *superlative* it is also sufficient (see above, *f*) to *g*
make the adjective determinate, either by means of the ar.icle or
a following partitive genitive (or suffix); in this case the article
or genitive indicates that the attribute in question belongs especially
to one or more definite individuals; [1] e. g. 1 S 9[21] הַצְּעִרָה *the least*; 16[11]
הַקָּטֹן *the little one,* i. e. the *youngest* of eight sons; 17[14] *David was*
הַקָּטֹן *the youngest, and the three great,* i. e. elder, &c.; Gn 42[13], 44[2],
Ct 1[8].—So also with a qualifying adjective, e. g. Gn 9[24] בְּנוֹ הַקָּטָן *his*
youngest son; cf. Jos 14[15]; also with a following genitive, 2 Ch 21[17]
קְטֹן בָּנָיו *the youngest of his sons:* Pr 30[24] *the least upon the earth;* with
suffix, Mi 7[4] טוֹבָם *their good one,* i. e. the best of them; Jon 3[5] מִגְּדוֹלָם
וְעַד־קְטַנָּם *from the greatest of them even to the least of them;* cf. the
inverse order in Jer 6[13], 31[34].

Rem. 1. The above examples apply only to the most common *relative h*
attributes (*great, small, good*), and to expressions which by usage easily came to
be recognized as periphrases for the superlative. Other adjectives, however,
when followed by a partitive genitive, also acquire the sense of a superlative ;
this appears from the context, e. g. Dt 33[19] *the most hidden treasures of the sand* ;
Ju 5[29] *the wisest amongst her ladies* ; Is 14[30], 19[11], 23[8f.], 29[19], Jer 49[20], Ez 28[7],
Zc 11[7], ψ 45[13], Jb 30[6] (*in the most horrible of valleys*), 41[22] ; probably also ψ 35[16].
On this government by the adjective generally, cf. § 132 *c.*—Moreover, the
combination of a substantive in the construct state with an adjective used
substantivally (§ 128 *w*) sometimes serves as a periphrasis for the superlative,
e. g. Is 22[24] כֹּל כְּלֵי הַקָּטָן *all the smallest vessels.* On Ct 7[10] see § 126 *x.*

2. Other periphrases for the superlative are the use of a substantive in the *i*
construct state before the plural of the same word (which is naturally to be
regarded as a partitive genitive ; cf. our *book of books*), e. g. Ex 26[33] קֹדֶשׁ הַקֳּדָשִׁים
the most holy place ; שִׁיר הַשִּׁירִים (Ct 1[1]) *the most excellent song* ; cf. Gn 9[25] (= *servus*
servorum, the lowest servant) ; Nu 3[32], Dt 10[17] (ψ 136[2.3]) [2] ; 1 K 8[27], Is 34[10] (cf.
Gal 1[5], Rev 22[5]) ; Jer 3[19], Ez 16[7], 26[7] (*king of kings,* of Nebuchadrezzar ;
cf. 1 Tim 6[15], Rev 17[14], 19[16], and another kind of periphrasis in ψ 95[3]) ; Ec 1[2].
Similarly in Jer 6[28] two participles are combined, and in Ho 10[15] two
substantives in the singular. Finally, the same object is attained by connecting one substantive in the construct state with another of the same stem
(שַׁבַּת שַׁבָּתוֹן *a sabbath of solemn rest,* i. e. an obligatory day of rest, Ex 31[15], &c.)
or of the same meaning (e. g. חֹשֶׁךְ אֲפֵלָה *a thick darkness,* Ex 10[22]).

3. The intensification of attributes by means of repetition belongs rather *k*
to rhetoric than to syntax, e. g. Ec 7[24] עָמֹק עָמֹק *exceeding deep* ; 1 S 2[3], Pr 20[14] ;
the adjective is even used three times in Is 6[3].—Cf. the repetition of adverbs
for the same purpose in Gn 7[19], Nu 14[7] (מְאֹד מְאֹד *exceedingly,* also בִּמְאֹד מְאֹד
Ex 1[7], &c.) ; Ez 42[15].—On the other hand, in Dt 28[43] the repetition expresses

---

[1] Cf. also עֶלְיוֹן *the one above,* i. e. *the Most High.*

[2] *God of gods, and Lord of lords,* just as the supreme god of the Babylonians
is called *bēl bēlī* (Tiele, *Compend. der Rel.-Gesch.,* p. 87).

a continuous progress, *higher and higher* ... *lower and lower*; in Dt 2²⁷ (see § 123 *e*) and 16²⁰ (*nothing but justice*) the constancy of the action. Cf. Ex 23³⁰ מְעַט מְעַט *little by little, very gradually*.[1]

l The repetition of substantives serves also as a periphrasis for the superlative in such cases as לְדֹר דֹּר (Ex 3¹⁵) = *to the remotest generations*; cf. 17¹⁶, Jer 6¹⁴, 8¹¹ (*perfect peace*); Ez 21³² (עַוָּה three times);[2] 35⁷, Na 1²; cf. also Ho 2²¹ ⁴· and the emphatic combination of synonymous verbs in Is 33¹⁰. Sometimes the completeness of an action or state is expressed by placing together two or even three substantives of the same stem and of similar sound, cf. Is 22⁵, Ez 6¹⁴ (33²⁸ ⁴·, 35⁵); 32¹⁵, Na 2¹¹, Zp 1¹⁵ (Jb 30³, 38²⁷).

§ 134. *Syntax of the Numerals.*

Cf. the exhaustive statistics collected by Sven Herner, *Syntax der Zahlwörter im A. T.*, Lund, 1893. E. König, ' Zur Syntax der Zahlwörter im A. T.,' *AJSL.* xviii. 129 ff.

a 1. The numerals from 2 to 10, as being originally abstract substantives,[3] may be connected with their substantives in three different ways. They may stand either—

(*a*) In the construct state *before* the substantive (the object numbered being consequently in the genitive), e. g. שְׁלֹשֶׁת יָמִים *a triad of days*, i. e. three days; שְׁנֵי הָאֲנָשִׁים *the two men*; or

b (*b*) In the absolute state *before* it (the object numbered being in apposition, § 131 *d*), e. g. שְׁלֹשָׁה בָנִים *a triad*, viz. *sons*, i. e. three sons; שְׁנַיִם אֲנָשִׁים *two men*; or

c (*c*) In the absolute state (likewise in apposition) *after* the object numbered, e. g. בָּנוֹת שָׁלוֹשׁ. So especially in long lists, since in these the substantives naturally come first, e. g. Gn 32¹⁵. Nu 7¹⁷, 28¹⁹. Apart from such cases, the frequency of this order in the later Books is due to the fact that the character of the numeral tended more and more to become adjectival rather than substantival.[4]

---

[1] Adverbs of the same stem are connected in this way in Nu 6⁹, Is 29⁵, 30¹³; of different stems in Is 5²⁶ and Jo 4⁴. In Nu 12² the particles רַק אַךְ appear to be placed together for a similar purpose, equivalent to *simply and solely*.

[2] Different in kind from the triple utterance of the same words in 2 S 18³³, Jer 7⁴ and 22²⁹, and the double exclamation in Jer 4¹⁹ and La 1¹⁶ (?).

[3] Cf. § 97 *a*, where it is shown that the masculine is the original form of the numerals (used for both genders), and that the feminine was afterwards differentiated and used with masc. nouns, primarily in the second decade and then in the first as well.

[4] From Herner's tables (op. cit., pp. 55–66) it appears, according to p. 68, that in the documents J, E, D of the Pentateuch, and in Jos 1–12, Judges, Samuel, Isaiah, Jeremiah, the Minor Prophets, Psalms, Megilloth, and Job, the numeral never, or very rarely, stands *after* its noun; in Kings and Ezekiel it stands several times *after*; in the Priestly Code nearly always *after*; in Chronicles, Ezra, Nehemiah, and Daniel, nearly as often *after* as *before* the noun. In Ex· 28¹⁰ the Masora makes the numeral in the genitive follow the construct state of the substantive numbered; we should, however, read וְאֶת־שְׁמוֹת הַשִּׁשָּׁה; for the omission of the article before שֵׁ׳, cf. § 126 *w*.

Rem. In Lv 24²² אֶחָד follows the construct state מִשְׁפָּט, but here as in *d* Nu 15¹⁶ מִשְׁפָּט should be read. In Gn 42¹⁹ אֶחָד is in apposition to a substantive with a suffix (= *one of you brethren* ; but verse 33 *the one of you brethren*). In Nu 31²⁸ אֶחָד precedes the substantive in the Aramaic manner (= *one each*). —For מֵאָה־שָׁנָה (Gn 17¹⁷, &c.) we find regularly in the Priestly Code (except in Gn 17¹⁷, 23¹) מְאַת שָׁנָה (Gn 5³, &c.) *an hundred years*. On the connexion of abstract numerals with suffixes, as שְׁנֵיהֶם *their duality*, i. e. *they two*, Gn 2²⁵, &c. (also with a strengthening separate pronoun, as שְׁנֵינוּ אֲנַחְנוּ 1 S 20⁴²), cf. § 97 *i*.

2. The numerals from 2 to 10 take the object numbered in the *e* plural,[1] with very few exceptions, such as Ex 16²² (where שְׁנֵי הָעֹמֶר = *the double of an omer*), 2 K 22¹, Ez 45¹, cf. 2 K 8¹⁷ and 25¹⁷ *Keth*. The numerals from 11 to 19 generally take the plural, but with certain substantives frequently used with numerals the singular is more common (see further, under *f*). The tens (from 20 to 90), when they precede, take the singular (in the accusative, cf. § 131 *p*) of certain nouns frequently used with numerals (אֶלֶף *a thousand*, אִישׁ, שֶׁקֶל, נֶפֶשׁ, בֹּר, יוֹם—but only in Ezekiel and the Priestly Code), otherwise the plural, as עָרִים, בָּנוֹת, בָּנִים (but cf. also Ju 11⁵³), &c.; on the other hand, the plural is necessary when they follow the object numbered in apposition (e. g. אַמּוֹת עֶשְׂרִים *twenty cubits*, 2 Ch 3³ ⁱ·; with the exception of 2 S 24²⁴, only in late Books). After מֵאָה and אֶלֶף the substantive numbered may be used either in the singular or plural, see further under *g*.

Rem. 1. After the numerals from 11 to 19 the singular is used, as a rule, *f* with יוֹם *day*, שָׁנָה *year*, אִישׁ *man*, נֶפֶשׁ *soul* (person), שֵׁבֶט *tribe*, מַצֵּבָה *pillar* (Ex 24⁴), sometimes with אַמָּה *cubit*, חֹדֶשׁ *month*, עִיר *city*, שֶׁקֶל *shekel* (compare our *four-year-old, ten pound*), e. g. Dt 1² אַחַד עָשָׂר יוֹם (cf., however, such exceptions as Dt 1²³, Jos 4², &c.).—Substantives other than these are used in the plural with the numerals from 11 to 19, and the numeral may even follow the substantive, especially in later passages, as Nu 7⁸⁷ ⁱ·, 1 Ch 4²⁷, 25⁵.

2. After מֵאָה (מְאַת [so almost exclusively in the Priestly Code, e. g. always *g* מְאַת אֶלֶף,] מֵאוֹת, מָאתַיִם) and אֶלֶף (אֲלָפִים, אַלְפֵי, אַלְפַּיִם) the substantives אִישׁ, אֶלֶף, אַמָּה (except in Ez 40²⁷), יוֹם, רַגְלִי, צֶמֶד are regularly used in the singular, generally also שֶׁקֶל (בֹּר, כִּכַּר, שָׁנָה (with the exception of Jos 7²¹, 2 S 14²⁶, &c.); cf., moreover, Gn 33¹⁹, 24⁶⁰ (אַלְפֵי רְבָבָה), Est 1¹, Ju 21¹², Dt 7⁹, 1 K 5¹², 2 Ch 9¹⁵.—Examples of the *plural* after מֵאָה are Gn 26¹², 1 S 18²⁵, 2 S 16¹, 1 K 18⁴; after מְאַת Ex 38²⁷; after מֵאוֹת Ju 15⁴, 2 S 8⁴, 1 K 10¹⁷,

---

[1] On examples such as Gn 46²⁷ (נֶפֶשׁ שְׁנַיִם *two souls*), cf. § 132 *g* (collectives joined with the plural of the adjective).

Ez 42^{17}; after מֵאתַ֫יִם 1 S 25^{18}, 1 K 7^{20}; after אֶ֫לֶף 1 S 25^{2}, 1 K 3^{4}, 5^{6}, 2 K 3^{4}, ψ 90^{4}; after אֲלָפִים 1 S 17^{5}, Jb 42^{12}; after אַלְפֵי Mi 6^{7}; after אֲלָפִים Is 36^{8}.—
In Dn 12^{11} the plural יָמִים precedes the numeral *twelve hundred*.

h 3. Numerals compounded of tens and units (like 21, 62) take the object numbered either *after* them in the singular (in the accusative), e. g. Gn 5^{20} שְׁתַּ֫יִם וְשִׁשִּׁים שָׁנָה *two and sixty years* (שָׁנָה in the singular, according to *e*, since it conforms to the ten immediately preceding; but also שְׁלֹשִׁים וּשְׁמֹנֶה שָׁנָה Dt 2^{14}), or *before* them in the plural, especially in the later Books, Dn 9^{26}, &c.; or the object is repeated (but only in 1 K 6^{1}, and the Priestly Code; sometimes even several times, e. g. Gn 23^{1}, 25$^{7.17}$ thrice) in the plural with the units, and in the singular with the tens and hundreds, e. g. Gn 12^{4} חָמֵשׁ שָׁנִים וְשִׁבְעִים שָׁנָה *seventy and five years*; Gn 23^{1} מֵאָה שָׁנָה וְעֶשְׂרִים שָׁנָה וְשֶׁ֫בַע שָׁנִים *an hundred and twenty and seven years*. Cf. Gn 5^{6} ff.

i Rem. 1. It may further be remarked with regard to the order, that the thousand or thousands always precede the hundreds, &c., and the hundreds almost always come before the smaller numbers (in Kings and Ezekiel sometimes, and in the Priestly Code usually, after the smaller numbers), the tens in the earlier Books (documents J and D of the Pentateuch, in Joshua 1-12, Judges, Samuel, Isaiah, and also in Ezra and Nehemiah) *before* the units, but in Jeremiah, Ezekiel, the Priestly Code, Joshua 13-24 *after* the units (see Herner, op. cit., p. 73). After the hundreds the smaller number is very frequently added without ן, especially in Ezra, Nehemiah, and Daniel.

On the syntax of the cardinals in general:—

k 2. The cardinals are determined by the article, when they refer back (without being connected with the object numbered; cf., however, Lv 25^{10} f., Nu 16^{35}, Jos 4^{4}, 2 S 23^{13}) to a number or list already mentioned, e. g. Gn 2^{11} שֵׁם הָֽאֶחָד פִּישׁוֹן *the name of the one* (the first) *is Pishon*; Gn 14^{9} *four kings against the five* (enumerated in verse 2); cf. 1 Ch 11^{20} f., and the determinate tens in Gn 18$^{29.31}$ f. A demonstrative with the article may also be added to a numeral determined in this way, e. g. Dt 19^{9} (but cf. also Gn 9^{19}, 22^{23}, where the numeral and demonstrative are practically determinate in themselves). In the case of the numerals from 11 to 19 the article may stand either before the unit (1 Ch 25^{19}, 27^{15}) or before עֶשָׂר (Jos 4^{4}); it is used before all three members of a compound number (273) in Nu 3^{46}.

l In apposition with any determinate substantive the cardinal number is used *without* the article, not only when it precedes the substantive, as in Jos 15^{14} אֶת־שְׁלֹשָׁה בְּנֵי הָֽעֲנָק, where שְׁלֹשָׁה is equivalent to a substantive determinate in itself; cf. Gn 18^{28}, Jos 6$^{8.22}$, 1 S 17^{14}, 1 K 11^{31}, and the passages discussed above in § 126 *x*, Gn 21^{29}, &c.), but also when it follows the substantive, e. g. 1 K 7$^{27.43}$ f. עָשָׂר and עֲשָׂרָה; the omission of the article may here, as in the cases noticed in § 126 *z*, be also due to the dislike of a hiatus, but cf. also שְׁנָ֫יִם 2 K 25^{16} after a determinate substantive. The fact that it is by nature determinate would also be a very simple explanation of אֶחָד Nu 28^{4}, 1 S 13^{17} f., Jer 24^{2}, Ez 10^{9}, instead of the more usual הָֽאֶחָד, and of אַחַת 1 S 1^{2} for הָֽאַחַת.

Such cases as שִׁבְעַת הַיָּמִים Ju 14¹⁷ (which is determined by a following *m* determinate genitive) are explained from § 127 *b* ; 1 Ch 9²⁵ perhaps from § 126 *q* ; in Is 30²⁶ probably the light of all the seven days of the week is meant ; on the other hand, in 1 S 9²⁰ and 25³⁸ the article is, with Wellhausen, to be omitted.

3. Certain specifications of *measure, weight,* or *time,* are commonly omitted *n* after numerals, e. g. Gn 20¹⁶ אֶלֶף כֶּסֶף *a thousand* (shekels) *of silver* ; so also before זָהָב Gn 24²², 1 K 10¹⁶, Is 7²³, cf. ψ 119⁷². Moreover, Ru 3¹⁵ שֵׁשׁ שְׂעֹרִים *six* (ephahs) *of barley* ; 1 S 10⁴ שְׁתֵּי־לֶחֶם *two* (sc. *loaves,* see verse 3) *of bread,* cf. 17¹⁷ עֲשָׂרָה לֶחֶם ; 2 S 16¹, where before קַיִץ a measure, or perhaps some term like *cakes,* is to be supplied.—The number of cubits is stated in the Priestly Code (Ex 26², &c.) and in 1 K 6 and 7 (otherwise only in Ez 40⁵·²¹, 47³. Zc 5², 1 Ch 11²³, 2 Ch 4² *f.*) by the addition of בָּאַמָּה prop. *by the cubit.* Also in Ex 27¹¹ the Samaritan and LXX read בָּאַמָּה after אֹרֶךְ, and in 27¹⁵ אַמָּה after עֶשְׂרֵה.

4. The *ordinals* above 10 have no special forms, but are expressed *o* by the corresponding cardinals, which may then stand either before or after the object numbered, e. g. Gn 7¹¹ בְּשִׁבְעָה עָשָׂר יוֹם *on the seventeenth day* ; Dt 1³ בְּאַרְבָּעִים שָׁנָה *in the fortieth year* ; cf. Gn 14⁵, 2 K 25²⁷, and, with repetition of שָׁנָה in a compound number, 1 K 6¹ ; such a cardinal occurs without בְּ (and therefore in the *accus. temporis,* according to § 118 *k*) in Gn 14⁴ (the Samaritan, however, has ובשלש) ; with the article (but without a numbered object, see under *k*), 1 K 19¹⁹. ¹—On the position of the numeral as a genitive following its noun, cf. e. g. 1 K 16¹⁰ בִּשְׁנַת עֶשְׂרִים וָשֶׁבַע *in the twenty and seventh year,* and with a determinate numeral, Ex 12¹⁸, Nu 33³⁸, Dt 15⁹. In this case, however, שָׁנָה is very frequently repeated, e. g. Gn 7¹¹, 2 K 13¹⁰ ; after a determinate numeral, Lv 25¹⁰. ²

Rem. In numbering days of the month and years, the cardinals are very *p* frequently used instead of the ordinals even for the numbers from 1 to 10, e. g. בִּשְׁנַת שְׁתַּיִם 1 K 15²⁵ ; בִּשְׁנַת שָׁלֹשׁ 2 K 18¹, &c., cf. Dt 15⁹. The months themselves are always numbered by the ordinals (בָּרִאשׁוֹן, הַשֵּׁנִי, &c., up to בָּעֲשִׂירִי), but not the days of the month, e. g. בְּאַרְבָּעָה אֶחָד לַחֹדֶשׁ Gn 8⁵, &c., בַּחֲמִשָּׁה לַחֹדֶשׁ Ez 1¹, &c., בְּשִׁבְעָה לַחֹדֶשׁ 2 K 25⁸, בִּתְשִׁעָה לַחֹדֶשׁ Zc 7¹ ; Lv 23³² (always, however, בֶּעָשׂוֹר לַחֹדֶשׁ *on the tenth day of the month*). On the

---

¹ Somewhat different from this is Ex 19¹⁵ *be ready* לִשְׁלֹשֶׁת יָמִים prop. *after three days,* i. e. *on the third day* (in verses 11 and 16 and in Ezr 10⁸ the ordinal is used), also 1 S 30¹³ כִּי חָלִיתִי הַיּוֹם שְׁלֹשָׁה *because three days agone I fell sick,* prop. *to-day three* (days).

² All these expressions may indeed be explained by supposing that, e. g. in Lv 25¹⁰, the proper meaning is *the year of the fifty years* which it completed, i. e. the fiftieth year ; but it is more correct to regard שְׁנַת or בִּשְׁנַת in such cases not as a real *nomen regens,* but simply as a connective form to be explained on the analogy of the cases mentioned in § 128 *k*.

omission of יוֹם in all these cases see under *n*; only in late passages is יוֹם added, e. g. 2 Ch 29¹⁷ בְּיוֹם שְׁמוֹנָה לַחֹדֶשׁ; Ezr 3⁶ מֵיּוֹם אֶחָד לַחֹדֶשׁ.—Finally, when the year is stated by בִּשְׁנַת governing a determinate ordinal, viz. 2 K 17⁶ בִּשְׁנַת הַתְּשִׁיעִית *in the ninth year*; 2 K 25¹ (in Jer 52⁴ בְּשָׁנָה), Jer 28¹ *K^eth.*, 32¹ *K^eth.*, 46², 51⁵⁹, Ezr 7⁸; בִּשְׁנַת in such cases is again (see note 2 on *o*) to be explained according to § 128 *k*. This is supported by the fact that the Masora on Jer 28¹, 32¹ requires in the *Q^erê* בַּשָּׁנָה for בשנת.

q **5.** *Distributives* are expressed either by repetition of the cardinal number, e. g. Gn 7⁹ˑ¹⁵ שְׁנַיִם שְׁנַיִם *two and two*; 2 S 21²⁰ שֵׁשׁ וָשֵׁשׁ *six each*; with the numbered object also repeated, e. g. Jos 3¹² אִישׁ אֶחָד אִישׁ אֶחָד לַשֵּׁבֶט *for every tribe a man*; Nu 13², 34¹⁸ (אֶחָד מָן, as in Neh 11¹, *one out of every ten*); cf. § 123 *d*; or a periphrasis with אֶחָד לְ is used, Nu 17¹⁸, Dt 1²³, cf. Is 6² לְאֶחָד after *six wings* twice repeated; the simple distributive לְ is, however, sufficient (as in לַבְּקָרִים, § 123 *c*), e. g. לְמֵאוֹת וְלַאֲלָפִים *by hundreds and by thousands*.

r **6.** The *multiplicatives* are expressed either (like the ordinals above 10, see under *o*) by the cardinals (in the feminine, probably owing to the omission of פַּעַם, פְּעָמִים; so König, *Lehrgeb.*, ii. 228), as שְׁתַּיִם *twice*, Jb 40⁵; שֶׁבַע *seven times*, Lv 26²¹ˑ²⁴, Pr 24¹⁶; cf. also אַחַת *once*, 2 K 6¹⁰, Jb 40⁵, for which in Jb 33¹⁴ בְּאַחַת¹ along with בִּשְׁתַּיִם (the latter also in 1 S 18²¹); or by the *dual* of the numeral, thus שִׁבְעָתַיִם Gn 4¹⁵ (in verse 24 along with the cardinal 77 for 77 times); Is 30²⁶, ψ 12⁷, 79¹²; אַרְבַּעְתַּיִם 2 S 12²;² or periphrastically by פַּעַם *a time* (prop. *a step*, with the article, הַפַּעַם *this time*; cf. also בַּפַּעַם הַזֹּאת, with בְּ, like בְּאַחַת above), as פַּעַם אַחַת *once* (Neh 13²⁰ פַּעַם וּשְׁתַּיִם *once and twice*), בַּעֲמַיִם *twice*, שָׁלֹשׁ פְּעָמִים (for which in Ex 23¹⁴, Nu 22²⁸ˑ³² שָׁלֹשׁ רְגָלִים) *three times*; cf. Ez 41⁶ *thirty-three times*; 2 S 24³ *an hundred times*; Dt 1¹¹ *a thousand times*; 1 K 22¹⁶ עַד־כַּמֶּה פְעָמִים *until how many times*, i. e. how often. Cf. also עֲשֶׂרֶת מֹנִים *ten times*, Gn 31⁷ˑ¹⁴, and רַבּוֹת עִתִּים *many times*, Neh 9²⁸.—In Gn 43³⁴, *five times* is expressed by חָמֵשׁ יָדוֹת (prop. *five hands*),³ and in Ex 16⁵ the *double* is expressed by מִשְׁנֶה עַל־ (prop. *a repetition over and above that which*, &c.).—Of the ordinals שֵׁנִית is used as a numeral adverb, Gn 22¹⁵, &c., *a second time*, cf. the Latin *tertium consul*; בַּשְּׁלִישִׁת *the third time*, 1 S 3⁸; פַּעַם חֲמִישִׁת *a fifth time*, Neh 6⁵; בַּשְּׁבִעִית *at the seventh* (time), 1 K 18⁴⁴, and בַּפַּעַם הַשְּׁבִיעִי Jos 6¹⁶.

---

¹ But בְּאַחַת Nu 10⁴ is to be translated *on one* (trumpet).

² Probably also כְּפְלַיִם Jb 11⁶ (from כָּפַל *doubling*) does not mean *doubled* but *manifold*.

³ But אַרְבַּע הַיָּדוֹת Gn 47²⁴ means *the* (other) *four parts*; cf. 2 K 11⁷, Neh 11¹.

Rem. The collocation of a numeral with the next above it (either in the *S* same or in different sentences) is a rhetorical device employed in *numerical sayings* to express a number, which need not, or cannot, be more exactly specified. It must be gathered from the context whether such formulae are intended to denote only an insignificant number (e. g. Is 17⁶, *two or* at the most *three*), or a considerable number, e. g. Mi 5⁴. Sometimes, however, this juxtaposition serves to express merely an indefinite total, without the collateral idea of intensifying the lower by means of the higher number. Thus *one* and *two* are connected by וְ, Dt 32³⁰, Jer 3¹⁴, Jb 33¹⁴, 40⁵ (without וְ, ψ 62¹²); *two* and *three*, Is 17⁶ (Sirac 23¹⁶, 26²⁸, 50²⁵), and without וְ, 2 K 9³², Ho 6², Am 4⁸; *three* and *four*, Jer 36²³, Am 1³⁻¹¹, Pr 30¹⁸, 21²⁹ (Sirac 26⁵), and without וְ, Pr 30¹⁵; *four* and *five*, without וְ, Is 17⁶; *six* and *seven*, Jb 5¹⁹, Pr 6¹⁶; *seven* and *eight*, Mi 5⁴, Ec 11²; (*nine* and *ten*, Sirac 25⁷).

III. Syntax of the Pronoun.

§ 135. *The Personal Pronoun.*

1. The *separate* pronouns,—apart from their employment as the *a* subject in noun-clauses (cf. § 141 *a*) and the idiom mentioned under *d–h*,—are used, according to § 32 *b*, as a rule, only to give express emphasis to the subject; e. g. Gn 16⁵, 2 S 24¹⁷ אָנֹכִי i. e. *I myself*, so also אֲנִי 2 S 12²⁸, 17¹⁵ (after the verb), Ez 34¹⁵, ψ 2⁶;[1] but 1 S 10¹⁸, 2 S 12⁷, Is 45¹² אָנֹכִי *I* and none else; cf. also אֲנִי אֲנִי *I, I !* Ho 5¹⁴, &c.; אַתָּה Gn 15¹⁵, Ju 15¹⁸, 1 S 17⁵⁶ (as in 20⁸, 22¹⁸, Ex 18¹⁹, Dt 5²⁴, Ju 8²¹, after the imperative); 1 K 21⁷; אַתֶּם Gn 9⁷, Ex 20¹⁹ (after the verb, Ju 15¹²); fem. Gn 31⁶; הוּא 1 S 22¹⁸; הִיא Gn 3²⁰, Ju 14³; הֵמָּה Jer 5⁵.— Sometimes, however, the separate pronoun appears to be placed before the verb more on rhythmical grounds, i. e. in order to give the statement a fuller sound than that of the bare verbal form (cf. the similar use of the infinitive absolute, § 113 *o*). Thus Gn 14²³, ψ 139², and most clearly in such passages as Gn 21²⁴, 47³⁰, Ex 8²⁴, Ju 6¹⁸, 11⁹, 1 S 12²⁰, 2 S 3¹³, 21⁶, 1 K 2¹⁸ (in solemn promises). The same explanation applies to אֲנִי at the beginning of sentences, e. g. Gn 24⁴⁵, Ho 5³, 10¹¹, 12¹¹, ψ 39¹¹, 82⁶, Jb 5³.[2]

Rem. 1. Different from this is the pleonastic addition of the separate *b* pronoun immediately *after* the verb (according to Delitzsch on Ct 5⁵ perhaps

---

[1] Also הוּא, הִיא *he himself, she herself* (of persons and things), e.g. Is 7¹⁴ אֲדֹנָי הוּא *the Lord himself*; Est 9¹ הַיְּהוּדִים הֵמָּה *the Jews themselves*. In the sense of *the same* (ὁ αὐτός) or (*one and) the same*, הוּא is used in Is 41⁴, 43¹⁰·¹³, 46⁴, 48¹² (always הוּא אֲנִי), ψ 102²⁸ (אַתָּה הוּא), and probably also Jb 3¹⁹.—The position of הֵמָּה, as an accusative of the object, before a perfect in 1 Ch 9²², can at most be explained on the analogy of Aramaic (Ezr 5¹²).

[2] As early as the Mêša‘ inscription (line 21 ff.) אָנֹךְ frequently stands at the beginning of a new sentence after the dividing stroke.

a trace of popular language), e.g. 1 S 23²² (?), Ct 5⁵, and (like other indications of the very late origin of the book) very frequently in Ecclesiastes, e.g. 1¹⁶, 2^{1.11.15}, 3^{17f.} and thirteen other places; in Aramaic, Dn 5¹⁶.

c 2. Substantival subjects also are somewhat frequently resumed, and thus expressly emphasized, by the insertion of the corresponding separate pronoun of the 3rd person before the predicate is stated, e.g. Gn 3¹² *the woman whom thou gavest to be with me, she* (הִיא) *gave me*, &c.; 14²⁴ (הֵם); 15⁴, 24⁷, &c.; but הוּא in Is 7¹⁴ after the predicate and subject is equivalent to *he himself*.[1]

d 2. Not infrequently the separate pronoun serves to give strong emphasis to a suffix of the same person which precedes (or sometimes even to one which follows), whether the suffix be attached to a verb (as accusative) or to a noun or preposition (as genitive). In English such an emphasis on the pronoun can generally be rendered only by laying greater stress upon it, or sometimes by repeating it; cf., on the contrary, the French *mon livre à moi*. The separate pronoun in such instances is not to be regarded as a *casus obliquus* (accusative or genitive), but as the subject of an independent sentence, the predicate of which must in each case be supplied according to the context.

e Examples of emphasis :—

(*a*) On a *verbal* suffix by means of אֲנִי (אָ֫נִי), Gn 27³⁴ בָּרֲכֵ֫נִי גַם־אָ֫נִי *bless me, even me also* (prop. *bless me, I also* would be blessed); Zc 7⁵; cf. also Ez 6³, 34^{11.20} הִנְנִי אָ֫נִי; by אַתָּה (אָ֫תָּה) Pr 22¹⁹ (but the text is most probably corrupt). —The separate pronoun *precedes* in Gn 24²⁷ (אָנֹכִי); 49⁸ (אַתָּה, not *Judah, thou art he* whom, but *Judah thee, thee thy brethren shall praise !*), and Ec 2¹⁵ גַּם אָ֫נִי.

f (*b*) On a noun-suffix with a substantive, by means of אֲנִי 2 S 19¹, Pr 23¹⁵; by אַתָּה 1 K 21¹⁹ אֶת־דָּמְךָ גַּם־אָ֫תָּה *thy blood, even thine*; by הוּא 2 S 17⁵, Jer 27⁷, Mi 7³; by אֲנַ֫חְנוּ 1 S 20⁴², after שְׁנֵ֫ינוּ, but without special stress; Neh 5²(?); by אַתֶּם Nu 14³²; by הֵם ψ 38¹¹ (without special stress), הֵ֫מָּה ψ 9⁷.—The separate pronoun *precedes* in Jb 21⁴ (אָנֹכִי); Gn 40¹⁶, Is 45¹², 1 Ch 28² (אֲנִי); Zc 9¹¹ (אַתְּ); Jos 23⁹ (אַתֶּם); Ez 33¹⁷ (הֵ֫מָּה).—In ψ 89⁴⁸, where אֲנִי might be taken as strengthening חֶלֶד (equivalent in sense to חֶלְדִּי), we should read אֲדֹנָי for אֲנִי, as in verse 51.

g (*c*) On a suffix united with a preposition, 1 S 25²⁴ בִּי אֲנִי *upon me, upon me*; 1 K 1²⁶ אֲנִי . . . לִי; 2 Ch 35²¹ לֹא־עָלֶ֫יךָ אַתָּה *not against thee*; 1 S 19²³ עָלָיו גַּם הוּא *upon him also*; Dt 5³ כִּי אִתָּ֫נוּ אֲנַ֫חְנוּ *but with us, even us*; Hag 1⁴ לָכֶם אַתֶּם *for you yourselves*; Jer 25¹⁴ בָּם גַּם־הֵ֫מָּה.—The separate pronoun *precedes* in 1 S 12²³ לִי . . . אָנֹכִי; 1 K 1²⁰ עָלֶ֫יךָ . . . אַתָּה; Mi 5¹ מִמְּךָ . . . אַתָּה, and 2 Ch 28¹⁰ אַתֶּם עִמָּכֶם.

h The same principle also explains Gn 4²⁶ לְשֵׁת גַּם־הוּא *to Seth, to him also* (not גַּם־לוֹ); cf. 10²¹, and Ex 35³⁴, Nu 4²².

---

[1] Analogous to this is the resumption of a noun dependent on a preposition, by means of a pronominal suffix united with the same preposition, e.g. Gn 2¹⁷, 2 S 6²², 2 K 22¹⁸, or of an object by means of the *nota accusativi* אֵת with suffix, e.g. 1 S 15⁹ (where וְנִמְאֶ֫סֶת is certainly to be read), Is 8¹³.

3. The *oblique* cases of the personal pronouns expressed by means of i a preposition (or the *nota accus.* את) with a suffix may be used either in a demonstrative or reflexive sense,[1] as לֹ *to him*, but also *to himself*, e. g. Ju 3[16] *and Ehud made* לֹ *for himself a sword*, cf. Gn 33[17]; so also לָהֶם *sibi*, Is 3[9]; אֵלָיו *unto him*, and Gn 8[9] *unto himself*; אִתּוֹ *with him*, and Gn 22[3] *with himself*; עִמָּהּ *with her*, and 1 S 1[24] *with herself*; also apparently as a pleonastic *dativus ethicus* (see § 119 *s*), Jb 12[11], 13[1].

Rarely, and only when marked emphasis is intended, is the *accusative* k of the reflexive pronoun represented by the *nota accusativi* את with a suffix (this being ordinarily expressed by the reflexive conjugations *Niph'al* and *Hithpa'ēl*[2]); thus, אֹתָם *se ipsos*, Ex 5[19], Jer 7[19] in sharp antithesis to הָאֹתִי; Ez 34[2.8.10]. Cf. § 57 at the end, together with note 2.

Rem. There is a similar emphasis in Is 49[26] on בְּשָׂרָם and דָּמָם in the l sense of *their own flesh, their own blood*. On the sometimes demonstrative, sometimes reflexive meaning of noun-suffixes of the 3rd person singular and plural, cf. § 91, *p* and *q*. For other circumlocutions to express the idea of *self*, see § 139 *f*.

4. The *possessive pronouns* are, according to § 33 *c*, expressed by m the *suffixes of the noun* (in the genitive),[3] which may represent either a *subjective genitive*, or (like the genitives proper, § 128 *h*) an *objective genitive*, e. g. חֲמָסִי *the wrong done against me*, Gn 16[5], Jer 51[35]; cf. Gn 9[2], 18[21], 27[13] (2 S 16[12] *K^eth.*); Gn 30[23], 39[21] (cf. Ex 3[21], &c.); 50[4], Ex 20[20], 21[35], Ju 4[9], 13[12] (מַעֲשֵׂהוּ *the treatment of him*); Is 56[7], Jer 9[7], Na 3[19], Pr 1[27], 24[22], Jb 20[29], 23[14], 34[6]. Cf. also such pregnant expressions as ψ 20[3] יִשְׁלַח עֶזְרְךָ *he will send thy help* (*help for thee*), i. e. he will send thee help; Gn 30[18], 39[21], Ex 2[9], Is 1[26] (*and I will restore judges for thee*); Ez 37[15].

When several substantives are co-ordinated, the pronominal suffix must be attached to each singly, e. g. Gn 36[6] *and Esau took* אֶת־נָשָׁיו וְאֶת־בָּנָיו וְאֶת־ בְּנֹתָיו *his wives and his sons and his daughters*, &c.; 38[18], &c. In 2 S 23[5] the text is hardly correct.

---

[1] As in Luther's Bible *jm* (*ihm*), *jr* (*ihr*) for *sich*, and in our version *him, her* for *himself, herself*.

[2] *Niph'al* according to § 51 *e* (like *Hithpa'ēl* according to § 54 *f*) may also include the *dative* of the reflexive pronoun.

[3] Like the substantival genitive, according to § 129 *h*, the possessive pronoun may also be paraphrased by a relative clause, e. g. Ru 2[21] הַנְּעָרִים אֲשֶׁר לִי *the young men, which are to me*, i. e. *my young men*; so especially, when the substantive, which should take a genitive suffix, is already followed by a genitive, e. g. 1 S 17[40]. In this case, however, the suffix also is sometimes attached pleonastically, e. g. Ct 1[6] כַּרְמִי שֶׁלִּי *my vineyard, which* belongs *to me*. Cf. Ct 3[7], and the analogous pleonasms in 2 S 22[2] (but see ψ 18[2]) and ψ 27[2].

n **5.** When the genitive, following a construct state, is used periphrastically to express the idea of a material or attribute (§ 128 *o* and *p*), the pronominal suffix, which properly belongs to the compound idea (represented by the *nomen regens* and genitive), is, like the article (§ 127), attached to the second substantive (the genitive), e. g. הַר־קָדְשִׁי prop. *the hill of my holiness*, i. e. *my holy hill*, ψ 2⁶, &c.; עִיר קָדְשֶׁךָ *thy holy city*, Dn 9²⁴; אֱלִילֵי כַסְפּוֹ *his idols of silver*, Is 2²⁰, 30²², 31⁷; ¹ cf. Dt 1⁴¹, Is 9³, 28⁴, 41¹¹, Ez 9¹ᶠ·, ψ 41¹⁰, 150¹, Jb 18⁷ צַעֲדֵי אוֹנוֹ *his steps of strength*; 38⁶; after an adjective as *nomen regens*, Is 13³ (Zp 3¹¹) עַלִּיזַי גַּאֲוָתִי *my proudly exulting ones.*—On the same analogy is the use of

e e. g. כְּלֵי מִלְחַמְתּוֹ Dt 1⁴¹ *his weapons of war* [cf. Is 41¹²]; Is 56⁷ בֵּית תְּפִלָּתִי *my house of prayer*, although the genitive here does not convey the idea of an attribute.

o **Rem. I.** Through a weakening in the distinction of gender, which is noticeable elsewhere (cf. § 110 *k*, 144 *a*, 145 *p, t, u*) and which probably passed from the colloquial language ² into that of literature, *masculine* suffixes (especially in the plural) are not infrequently used to refer to *feminine* substantives; thus a noun-suffix in the singular, Ex 11⁶, 25¹⁹, Ju 11³⁴; ³ in the plural, Gn 31⁹, 32¹⁶, 41²³, Ex 1²¹, 2¹⁷, Nu 2₇⁷ (but the feminine suffix twice immediately after, and so the Samaritan also in verse 7); 36⁶ (Samaritan אֲבִיהֶן, but also בְּעֵינֵיהֶם); Ju 19²⁴, 21²², 1 S 6⁷·¹⁰ᵇ (בְּנֵיהֶם); 9²⁰, Is 3¹⁶, Ez 23⁴⁵ ᶠᶠ· (alternating with הֵן); Am 4¹ᶠ· (but afterwards a feminine suffix); Jb 1¹⁴, 39³ חֶבְלֵיהֶם in parallelism with יַלְדֵיהֶן; 42¹⁵, Ct 4², 6⁶, Ru 1⁸ ᶠᶠ· (along with feminine suffixes); Dn 1⁵, 8⁹. Verbal suffixes in the singular, Ex 22²⁵; in the plural, Ju 16³, Pr 6²¹, Jb 1¹⁵. But Gn 26¹⁵·¹⁸, 33¹³, Ex 2¹⁷, 1 S 6¹⁰ᵃ are to be explained according to § 60 *h*. On הֵמָּה as feminine, see § 32 *n*. On the use of the masculine in general as the *prior gender*, see § 122 *g*.

p **2.** The suffix of the 3rd person singular feminine (as also the separate pronoun הִיא Nu 14⁴¹, Jos 10¹³, Ju 14⁴) sometimes refers in a general sense to the verbal idea contained in a preceding sentence (corresponding to our *it*); thus the verbal suffix, Gn 15⁶, Nu 23¹⁹, 1 S 11², 1 K 11¹², Is 30⁸, Am 8¹⁰; cf. Gn 24¹⁴ (בָּהּ *thereby*), 42³⁶, 47²⁶, Ex 10¹¹ (אֹתָהּ *that*), Is 47⁷. Elsewhere the suffix of the 3rd singular feminine refers to the plurals of things, e. g. 2 K 3³

---

¹ On the other hand, more explicitly in prose, Gn 44² אֶת־גְּבִיעִי גְּבִיעַ הַכֶּסֶף *my cup, the silver cup.*

² According to Diehl (see the title at the head of § 91 *a*), who adduces numerous instances on pp. 44 ff., 54 ff., 67 f., many of these cases may be set down to corruption of the traditional text, while the sudden (and sometimes repeated) change of gender in suffixes is mainly due to the influence exercised on the copyists by the Mishnic and popular Aramaic dialects, neither of which recognizes such distinctions. Such influence, however, is insufficient to explain the large number of instances of this weakening, occurring even in the earlier documents.

³ The Masora reckons six instances of מִמֶּנּוּ, where מִמֶּנָּה would be expected (Ju 11³⁴, where, however, the text is most probably corrupt), Ex 25¹⁵ (?), Lv 6⁸, 7¹⁸, 27⁹, Jos 1⁷; almost all these passages can, however, be easily explained in other ways.

[but see Kittel; so 13[2.6.11]; 10[26], but LXX מַצֶּבַת], Jer 36[23], Jb 6[20] (if the text is correct), 39[15] (read תְּחָמֵם in v. 14), and to the plurals of names of animals, Is 35[7], Ezr 11[5]. Conversely, plural suffixes refer to collective singulars, e.g. in Gn 15[13], Nu 16[3], 1 S 2[8], Zp 2[7] [but read עַל הַיָּם]; and to a verbal idea contained in the preceding clause, in Ez 33[18], Jb 22[21] (בָּהֶם *thereby*), Ez 18[26], 33[19] (עֲלֵיהֶם *on that account, thereby*).[1] But the suffix in נְתָנוֹ Dt 21[10] refers to the collective idea contained in אֹיְבֶיךָ; in Jon 1[3] עִמָּהֶם refers to the sailors included in sense under the term אֲנִיָּה. In Jos 2[4] read וַתִּצְפְּנֵם; in Is 30[6] (מֵהֶם), 38[16], ψ 19[5] (בָּהֶם) the text is most probably corrupt.

3. In a few examples the force of the noun-suffix or possessive pronoun *q* has become so weak that the language appears to be almost entirely unconscious of it. Thus in אֲדֹנָי *my Lord*, usually explained as being from the *pluralis maiestatis* אֲדֹנִים (§ 124 *i*) with the suffix of the 1st singular (always with Qameṣ to distinguish it from אֲדֹנַי *my lords*, Gn 19[2]; but see note below), used exclusively of God, not only in addressing him (Gn 15[2], 18[3], ψ 35[23]), but ultimately (see, however, the note below), without any regard to the pronoun, as equivalent to *the Lord*.[2] On אֲדֹנָי as a *Qᵉrê perpetuum* of the Masoretes for יהוה see § 17 *c* and § 102 *m*.

A similar loss of vitality in the suffix is generally assumed in יַחְדָּו prop. *in his unitedness*, i.e. *he &c. together*, e.g. כָּל־הָעָם יַחְדָּו Ex 19[8]; then, without regard to the suffix, even after the 1st person אֲנַחְנוּ יַחְדָּו 1 K 3[18] in reference to two women; Is 41[1], Jb 9[32], Neh 6[2.7]; after the 2nd person, Is 45[20], &c. But the supposed pronominal suffix is perhaps rather to be explained, with Brockelmann, *ZA.* xiv. 344 f., as an old adverbial ending, which survives in the Arabic adverbs in *u* and in Assyrian.—Cf. further כֻּלָּם prop. *their entirety*, but also after the 2nd person equivalent to *all together*, 1 K 22[28], Mi 1[2] (*hear, ye peoples, all of you*; cf. § 144 *p*), and even before the 2nd person, Jb 17[10] (in 1 S 6[4] read לָכֶם with the LXX).—On the redundant suffix in הַעֲרִכְךָ Lv 27[23], cf. § 127 *i*.

---

[1] In 2 K 7[10] for שֹׁעֵר (the LXX had שַׁעַר) read שֹׁעֲרֵי.

[2] Cf. the same weakening of the force of the possessive pronoun in רַבִּי prop. *my master*, from the second century A.D. onwards *the master*; so also in Syriac מָרִי *my lord*, and ultimately as a title *the lord*; in Italian *Madonna*, French *Madame*, *Notre Dame*, *Monsieur*, *Monseigneur*, &c. It can, however, hardly be doubted that the regular distinction between אֲדֹנָי as a holy name, and אֲדֹנַי as an ordinary appellative is merely due to the practice of the later Rabbis. G. H. Dalman, *Der Gottesname Adonaj und seine Geschichte* (Berlin, 1889), in an exhaustive discussion, shows that apart from the book of Daniel and the eight critically doubtful passages, in which אֲדֹנָי is used by God himself, there is nowhere any necessity to regard the suffix as *entirely meaningless*, since אדני is always used either in an address *to* or (like אֲדֹנִי, which also is never a mere phrase or title) in reverent language *about* God— as the Lord of the speaker—like the Assyrian *bēli-ia, my lord*. Against any original distinction between אֲדֹנָי and אֲדֹנַי it may be urged especially that when unconnected with suffixes the singular אָדוֹן is always used of God, and not the *pluralis maiestatis* presupposed by אֲדֹנָי.

§ 136. *The Demonstrative Pronoun.*

a　　The *demonstrative pronouns* are זֶה, fem. זֹאת, plur. אֵלֶּה (§ 34), *hic, haec (hoc), hi*, &c., and the personal pronoun הוּא, likewise used as a demonstrative, fem. הִיא, plur. masc. הֵמָּה, fem. הֵנָּה (§ 32 *b*), *is, ea (id)*, or *ille*, &c., *ii, eae* or *illi*, &c. The distinction between them in usage is that זֶה (like *hic*, ὅδε) almost always points out a (new) person or thing present, while הוּא (like *is, ille*, αὐτός, ἐκεῖνος) refers to a person or thing already mentioned or known (see the examples below).[1]

b　　Rem. 1. Compare the instructive examples in Gn 32³, Ju 7⁴ *of whom I say unto thee, this* (זֶה) *shall go with thee, he* (הוּא) *shall go with thee* (so afterwards with negatives). Moreover, הַיּוֹם הַזֶּה *this day*, i.e. the actual day on which one is speaking or writing (Gn 26³³, &c.), but הַיּוֹם הַהוּא the day or period of which the historian has just been speaking (Gn 15¹⁸, 26³²) or of which the prophet has just been foretelling (Is 5³⁰, 7¹⁸·²⁰ ff.) and of which he continues to speak or foretell. Nevertheless זֶה and אֵלֶּה are also found in certain common combinations where הוּא and הֵמָּה would be expected, and vice versa; thus almost always הַדָּבָר הַזֶּה, plur. הַדְּבָרִים הָאֵלֶּה, but בַּיָּמִים הָהֵמָּה or בַּיָּמִים הָהֵם.—With a secondary sense of contempt (like Latin *iste*) זֶה occurs, e.g. in 1 S 10²⁷, 21¹⁶, 1 K 22²⁷, Is 6¹⁰, &c. In the sense of the neuter, *this*, זֹאת is more common than זֶה, as Is 5²⁵, 43⁹, &c., but הוּא more common than הִיא.

c　　2. Both זֶה and הוּא are sometimes used almost as enclitics to emphasize interrogative words (like the Latin *nam* in *quisnam*; cf. also *quis tandem*); e.g. Jb 38² מִי זֶה *who now* (darkeneth, &c.) . . . ? 1 S 17⁵⁵ f., Is 63¹, Jer 49¹⁹, ψ 24⁸, 25¹², &c ; מַה־זֶּה *what now?* 1 S 10¹¹; *how now?* Gn 27²⁰; *why now?* Ju 18²⁴; but before the verb עָשָׂה it is usually מַה־זֹּאת Gn 3¹³, 12¹⁸, Ex 14⁵, Ju 15¹¹; לָמָּה־זֶּה *wherefore now?* Gn 18¹³, 25²², 1 S 17²⁸, 2 S 12²³, &c.—So also מִי־הוּא Is 50⁹, Jb 4⁷ ff.; and still more emphatically מִי הוּא־זֶה ψ 24¹⁰, Jer 30²¹.

d　　3. זֶה is likewise used as an enclitic (see *c* above): (*a*) *of place*, in such passages as Gn 27²¹ הַאַתָּה זֶה וגו׳ *whether thou* (that art here) *be my son Esau?* 2 S 2²⁰ *is it thou?* הִנֵּה־זֶה *behold, here*, 1 K 19⁵, Is 21⁹;[2] cf. also the strengthen-

---

[1] On זֶה and הוּא standing separately as determinate in themselves, see § 125 *i*. On the use of determinate demonstratives as adjectives, see § 126 *u*.

[2] On the other hand, it is very questionable whether זֶה in ψ 104²⁵ (זֶה הַיָּם), Is 23¹³ (זֶה הָעָם), Ju 5⁵, ψ 68⁹ (זֶה סִינַי) can be taken, according to the common explanation, simply as a prefixed demonstrative particle (*the sea yonder*, &c.). In ψ 104²⁵ הַיָּם may be in apposition to זֶה; cf. § 126 *aa*, on Ex 32¹, and Zc 5⁷, where אַחַת אִשָּׁה is in apposition to זֹאת depending on הִנֵּה, and also Ez 40⁴⁵, where הַלִּשְׁכָּה is in apposition to זֹה; otherwise it is most naturally taken as the subject, *this is the sea*. Is 23¹³, Ju 5⁵, 1 K 14¹⁴, and ψ 68⁹ might also be explained in the same way; but in these passages the text is almost certainly

ing of the separate pronoun by הוּא Is 43²⁵ (אָנֹכִי), 1 S 7²⁸, Is 37¹⁶, ψ 44⁵ (אַתָּה), and אֵלֶּה הֵם *these are*, Gn 25¹⁶, 1 S 4⁸; (b) *of time*: עַתָּה זֶה *now*, 1 K 17²⁴; *just now*, 2 K 5²²; and rather frequently before words denoting number, e. g. Gn 27³⁶ זֶה פַעֲמַיִם *twice, now*; cf. 31³⁸, 2 S 14², Jb 1¹², 7³, 19³; separated from the numeral in Gn 31⁴¹ זֶה־לִּי elliptically for *this*, i. e. this present period, *is to me*, i. e. makes altogether, *twenty years*, &c. The other examples are similarly elliptical.

§ 137. *The Interrogative Pronoun.*

The interrogative pronoun מִי *who* may refer either to a masculine *a* or feminine person (Ct 3⁶), or even to a plural, e. g. מִי אַתֶּם *who are ye?* Jos 9⁸; מִי־אֵלֶּה Gn 33⁵, Nu 22⁹ (more minutely, מִי וָמִי Ex 10⁸, i. e. *who exactly, who in particular?*). It is used of the neuter only when the idea of a person is implied, e. g. מִי־שְׁכֶם *who are the Shechemites?* Ju 9²⁸, 13¹⁷, Gn 33⁸, Mi 1⁵; even more boldly, with the repetition of a מִי used personally, in 1 S 18¹⁸, 2 S 7¹⁸.—Another interrogative is אֵי־זֶה *which, what?*; of persons only in Est 7⁵.

Moreover, מִי may also be used in the sense of a genitive, e. g. *b* בַּת־מִי אַתְּ *whose daughter art thou?* Gn 24²³, 1 S 17⁵⁵,⁵⁶,⁵⁸; דְּבַר מִי *whose word?* Jer 44²⁸, 1 S 12³; in the accusative, אֶת־מִי *quemnam?* 1 S 28¹¹, Is 6⁸; with prepositions, e. g. בְּמִי 1 K 20¹⁴ (in an abrupt question *by whom?*); לְמִי Gn 32¹⁸; אַחֲרֵי מִי 1 S 24¹⁵.—Similarly מָה, מַה־, מֶה, *what?* is used for the nominative, or accusative, or genitive (Jer 8⁹), or with prepositions, e. g. עַל־מָה *whereupon?* Is 1⁵, Jb 38⁶; *why?* Nu 22³², &c.; עַד־מָה *quousque?* ψ 74⁹.¹

Rem. Both מִי and מָה are used also in indirect questions (on the merely *c* relative distinction between direct and indirect questions in Hebrew, see the *Interrogative Sentences*), e. g. Gn 39⁸ (but read מְאוּמָה with Samar. and LXX), 43²², Ex 32¹.—On the meaning of מִי and מָה as interrogatives is based also their use as *indefinite pronouns* (equivalent to *quisquis, quodcunque* or *quicquam*), e. g. Ex 32²⁶, Ju 7³, 1 S 20⁴, Is 50¹⁰ (read יִשְׁמַע in the apodosis), 54¹⁵, Pr 9⁴·¹⁶, 2 Ch 36²³; even שָׂמְרוּ־מִי *have a care, whosoever ye be*, 2 S 18¹² (unless לִי is to be read, with the LXX, for מִי); so also מָה (*whatever it be*) Jb 13¹³, 1 S 19³, 2 S 18²²·²³; cf. Nu 23³ וּדְבַר מַה־יַּרְאֵנִי *and whatsoever he showeth me*. Cf. also מִי אֲשֶׁר *whosoever* Ex 32³³, 2 S 20¹¹, and מִי־הָאִישׁ אֲשֶׁר *any man who* Dt 2c⁵ᶠᶠ·,

---

corrupt. In Ju 5⁵ in fact זֶה סִינַי is most probably to be regarded with Moore as a very early gloss, which subsequently found its way from this passage into ψ 68.

¹ A quite different use of מָה was pointed out (privately) by P. Haupt in Ct 5⁸ *will ye not tell him?* i. e. *I charge you that ye tell him*, and 7¹ = *look now at the Shulamite*, corresponding to the late Arabic *mā tarā, just see! mā taqûlu*, say *now!* It has long been recognized that מָה is used as a negative in Ct 8⁴.

Ju 10¹⁸. A still further weakening of the *indefinite* use of מַה is the combination מַה־שֶּׁ· *that which*, Ec 1⁹, 3¹⁵ (just like the Syriac דְּ מָא) ; cf. Est 8¹, and
מָה . . . בְּל Pr 9¹³, מָה . . . לֹא Neh 2¹², *nothing whatever*.—On מְאוּמָה *quicquam*,
anything at all (usually with a negative), and as an adverb *in any way*, 1 S 21³,
see the Lexicon.

§ 138. *The Relative Pronoun.*

Cf. Philippi, *Stat. constr.* (see heading of § 89), p. 71 f., and especially
V. Baumann, *Hebräische Relativsätze*, Leipzig, 1894.

a　Relative clauses are most frequently (but not necessarily; cf. § 155 *b*)
introduced by the indeclinable אֲשֶׁר (see § 36).[1] This is not, however,
a relative pronoun in the Greek, Latin, or English sense, nor is it
a mere *nota relationis*,[2] but an original *demonstrative* pronoun [as
though *iste, istius*, &c.].[3]　Hence it is used—

(1) In immediate dependence on the substantival idea to be defined,
and virtually in the same case as it (hence belonging syntactically to
the main clause); e. g. Gn 24⁷ . . . הוּא יִשְׁלַח . . . יְהוָֹה אֲשֶׁר לְקָחַנִי *the
Lord, iste, he took me . . . he shall send*, &c. (=*who took me*); Gn 2²
and God finished מְלַאכְתּוֹ אֲשֶׁר עָשָׂה *his work, istud, he had made* (it).
Such qualifying clauses may be called *dependent relative clauses*.

b　Rem. 1. In the above examples אֲשֶׁר in Gn 24⁷ is virtually in the nominative, in Gn 2² in the accusative. A further distinction between the examples
is that in Gn 24⁷ the main idea (יהוה), to which אֲשֶׁר is added in apposition,
is only resumed in the qualifying clause by the subject (*he*) inherent in

---

[1] The etymology of the word is still a matter of dispute. Against the
identification of אֲשֶׁר, as an original substantive, with the Arabic *'aṯar, trace*,
Aram. אֲתַר *place, trace*, Nöldeke urges (*ZDMG*. xl. 738) that the expression *trace
of*. . . could hardly have developed into the relative conjunction, while the
meaning of *place* has been evolved only in Aramaic, where the word is never used
as a relative. According to others, אֲשֶׁר is really a compound of several pronominal roots ; cf. Sperling, *Die Nota relationis im Hebräischen*, Leipzig, 1876,
and König, *Lehrgeb.*, ii. 323 ff., who follows Ewald and Böttcher in referring
it to an original אֲשֶׁל. According to Hommel (*ZDMG*. xxxii. 708 ff.) אֲשֶׁר
is an original substantive, to be distinguished from שֶׁ· and שַׁ· (an original
pronominal stem), but used in Hebrew as a *nota relationis*, or (as זֶה and זוּ
are also sometimes used, see below, *g* and *h*) simply for the *relative pronoun*.
Baumann (op. cit., p. 44) sees in the Assyrian *ša*, Phoenician, Punic, and
Hebrew שֶׁ, the ground-forms, of which the Phoenician and Punic אֵשׁ (see
above, § 36 note) and the Hebrew אֲשֶׁר are developments.

[2] E. g. like Luther's use of *so*, in *die fremden Götter, so unter euch sind*,
Gn 35².

[3] This is the necessary conclusion both from the analogy of the Arabic
'allaḏi, which is clearly a demonstrative (like the Hebr. הַלָּז, הַלָּזֶה), and
from the use of זֶה and זוּ as relatives.

לְקָחֻנִי, while in Gn 2² it is not resumed at all. This suppression of the retrospective pronoun[1] takes place especially when it (as in Gn 2²) would represent an accusative of the object, or when it would be a separate pronoun representing a nominative of the subject in a noun-clause, e. g. Gn 1⁷ הַמַּיִם אֲשֶׁר מִתַּחַת לָרָקִיעַ *the waters, those, under the firmament*, &c. In negative sentences, however, the retrospective pronoun is not infrequently added, e.g. Gn 17¹² הוּא; 7² הִיא; 1 K 9²⁰ הֵמָּה; Dt 20¹⁵ הֵנָּה; but cf. also אֲשֶׁר הוּא חָי Gn 9³. The addition of הִיא in a verbal clause, 2 K 22¹³, is unusual.

The very frequent omission of the retrospective pronoun is noticeable in cases where the predicate of the qualifying clause is a *verbum dicendi*, e.g. Nu 10²⁹ *we are journeying unto the place,* אֲשֶׁר אָמַר יְהוָֹה אֹתוֹ אֶתֵּן לָכֶם *that place, the Lord said* (of it), *It will I give to you*; cf. Nu 14⁴⁰, Ju 8¹⁵, 1 S 9¹⁷·²³, 24⁵, 1 K 8²⁹, Jer 32⁴³.

2. When the substantive, followed by אֲשֶׁר and the qualifying clause, *c* expresses an idea of *place*, it may also be resumed by the adverbs of place שָׁם *there*, שָׁמָּה *thither*, מִשָּׁם *thence*, e.g. Gn 13³ עַד־הַמָּקוֹם אֲשֶׁר־הָיָה שָׁם אָהֳלֹה *unto the place, that one, his tent had been there*, i.e. *where his tent had been*; cf. Gn 3²³ מִשָּׁם, Ex 21¹³ שָׁמָּה. But even in this case the retrospective word may be omitted, cf. Gn 35¹⁴, Nu 20¹³, Is 64¹⁰, where שָׁם would be expected, and Gn 30³⁸, Nu 13²⁷, 1 K 12², where שָׁמָּה would be expected.—When the appositional clause is added to a word of time, the retrospective pronoun is always omitted, e. g. 1 S 20³¹ *for all the days,* אֲשֶׁר בֶּן־יִשַׁי חַי *those—the son of Jesse is living* (*in them*); cf. Gn 45⁶, Dt 1⁴⁶, 9⁷, 1 K 11⁴²; see Baumann, op. cit., p. 33.

3. If the governing substantive forms part of a statement made in the *d* first or second person, the retrospective pronoun (or the subject of the appositional clause) is in the same person, e.g. Gn 45⁴ *I am Joseph,* אֲשֶׁר־מְכַרְתֶּם אֹתִי *he—ye sold me*, i.e. *whom ye sold*; Nu 22³⁰, Is 49²³; 41⁸ *thou, Jacob,* אֲשֶׁר בְּחַרְתִּיךָ *he—I have chosen thee*; Jer 32¹⁹, Ec 10¹⁶ᶠ·; Gn 15⁷ *I am the Lord,* אֲשֶׁר הוֹצֵאתִיךָ *he—I brought thee out*, &c., Ex 20² (Dt 5⁶).

(2) Not depending (adjectivally) on a governing substantive, but *e* itself expressing a substantival idea. Clauses introduced in this way may be called *independent relative clauses.* This use of אֲשֶׁר is generally rendered in English by *he who, he whom,* &c. (according to the context), or *that which,* &c., or sometimes *of such a kind as* (*qualis*), cf. Ex 14¹³ᵇ, and in a dependent relative clause Is 7¹⁷. In reality, however, the אֲשֶׁר is still a demonstrative belonging to the construction of the main clause as subject or object, or as a genitive dependent on a noun or preposition, e.g. Nu 22⁶ אֲשֶׁר תָּאֹר יוּאָר *iste—thou cursest* (him)—*is cursed*, i. e. *he whom thou cursest,* &c.; Ex 22⁸; ² אֲשֶׁר as object, Gn 44¹,

---

[1] The instances in which, instead of a retrospective pronoun, the main idea itself is repeated (Gn 49³⁰, 50¹³, Jer 31³²) are most probably all due to subsequent amplification of the original text by another hand.

² The absolute use of אֲשֶׁר is very peculiar in the formula אֲשֶׁר הָיָה דְבַר יְ׳ אֶל־ *this* (is it)—*it came as the word of the Lord to* . . ., Jer 14¹, 46¹, 47¹, 49³⁴.

49¹, 1 S 16³ᶠᶠ·, Mi 6¹ (אֵת אֲשֶׁר); and even preceding the verb, e. g.
Is 52¹⁵, ψ 69⁵; אֲשֶׁר as genitive, Ez 23²⁸ *I will deliver thee* בְּיַד אֲשֶׁר
שָׂנֵאת *into the hand of those—thou hatest* (them); depending on a preposition, e. g. לַאֲשֶׁר Gn 44⁴, 2 K 10²²; בַּאֲשֶׁר Gn 21¹⁷, בַּאֲשֶׁר הוּא שָׁם *in
that* (place)—*he is there*, i. e. *where he is*; cf. Ju 17⁸ and Ru 1¹⁶ אֶל־אֲשֶׁר
whither; ¹ 1 K 18¹² עַל־אֲשֶׁר *whither*; מֵאֲשֶׁר Ex 5¹¹.

f   From these examples it follows that in independent relative clauses the
retrospective suffix, or adverb of place, may be, and in fact generally is,
omitted. As a rule, however (as in the dependent relative clause), this does
not apply to cases in which the retrospective pronoun, by the construction
of the sentence, depends on a preposition,² e. g. Gn 44⁹ᶠ· . . . אֲשֶׁר יִמָּצֵא אִתּוֹ וָמֵת
he—it (the cup) *is found with him,—shall die* (for the *Wāw* of the apodosis in
וָמֵת cf. § 143 *d*). In such cases אֲשֶׁר preceded by the preposition is quite
anomalous, as in Gn 31³² עִם אֲשֶׁר תִּמְצָא *with whomsoever thou findest*, where
אֲשֶׁר is a relative pronoun in the English sense; on the other hand, in
Is 47¹² (and probably also 56⁴) בַּאֲשֶׁר is to be explained (with Baumann,
op. cit., p. 37) by reference to 47¹⁵, as a demonstrative pronoun, *stand now
with thine enchantments . . . , with those—thou hast laboured* (with them).

[With regard to the preceding explanation of אֲשֶׁר, the student will of
course understand that, in Hebrew as we know it, אֲשֶׁר never occurs as
a mere demonstrative. A particle which, whatever its origin, is uniformly
used with reference to something in another, contiguous clause, will naturally
have acquired in practice that force which we denote by the term 'relative'.]

g   Like the original demonstrative pronoun אֲשֶׁר, the demonstratives
proper זֶה, זוֹ, זוּ (the last commonly),³ and sometimes the article, are
used somewhat frequently in poetic language to introduce both
dependent and independent relative clauses. With regard to the
construction of זֶה, &c., the remarks on אֲשֶׁר, under *a* and *e*, also
hold good.

Examples:—
(*a*) זֶה in apposition to a governing substantive in the nominative, ψ 104²⁶
לִוְיָתָן זֶה־יָצַרְתָּ (there is) *leviathan, he—thou hast formed* (him), i. e. *whom thou hast
formed*; Is 42²⁴ (זוּ); in the accusative, Is 25⁹, ψ 74² (in both cases with a
retrospective pronoun; זוּ is used without it in ψ 132¹²); in apposition to
a genitive dependent on a preposition, Pr 23²² שְׁמַע לְאָבִיךָ זֶה יְלָדֶךָ *hearken
unto thy father, him—he begat thee*, i. e. *who begat thee*; ψ 17⁹ (זוּ).—In ψ 104⁸
אֶל־מְקוֹם זֶה יָסַדְתָּ לָהֶם *unto the place which thou hadst founded for them* (cf. § 130 *c*),
זֶה is in the genitive after the construct state מְקוֹם *to the place of that, thou hadst*

---

¹ In Zc 12¹⁰ also, instead of the unintelligible אלי את אשר, we should
probably read אֶל־אֲשֶׁר, and refer the passage to this class.

² Such a strong ellipse as in Is 31⁶, where מִמֶּנּוּ would be expected after
העמיקו, is only possible in elevated poetic or prophetic language.

³ The etymological equivalent דִּי, דְּ in Aramaic is always a relative.

founded (it) *for them*; on the same analogy we may also take, with Baumann (op. cit., p. 48), ψ 78⁵⁴ (חַר זֶה) and Ex 15¹³ (עַם־זוּ נָאלְתָּ), 15¹⁶, Is 43²¹, ψ 9¹⁶, 10², 31⁵, 32⁸, 62¹², 142⁴, 143⁸ (all examples of זוּ).

To introduce independent relative clauses זֶה is used as a nominative in *h* Jb 19¹⁹; as accusative, Jb 15¹⁷ and זוֹ Hb 1¹¹, ψ 68²⁹ (after a preposition, זֶה Ex 13⁸; but the text is evidently corrupt).

(*b*) More certain examples of the use of the article as a relative pronoun *i* (more correctly, perhaps, of the demonstrative which is otherwise used as article) are 1 Ch 26²⁸ כֹּל הַהִקְדִּישׁ שְׁמוּאֵל *all that Samuel had dedicated*, &c.; 1 Ch 29⁸ (where נִמְצָא can only be *perfect Niph'al*); 2 Ch 29³⁶, Ezr 10¹⁴. In connexion with a plural, Jos 10²⁴ *the chiefs of the men of war* הַהֹלְכוּ אִתּוֹ *who went with him*; Ezr 8²⁵, 10¹⁷, 1 Ch 29¹⁷. Finally, in the sense of *id quod*, Jer 5¹³ (where, however, we should read with the LXX הַדָּבָר). Cf. moreover, 1 S 9²⁴ *the thigh* וְהֶעָלֶיהָ *and that which was upon it* (but see *k* below); 2 Ch 1⁴ בַּהֵכִין equivalent to בַּאֲשֶׁר הֵכִין *to the place, that he had prepared.*

In all the examples adduced except 1 S 9²⁴ (where וְהָאַלְיָה should probably *k* be read for וְהֶעָלֶיהָ) the הַ is followed by undoubted perfects; almost all the examples, moreover, belong to the latest Books (Ezra and Chronicles). On the other hand, another series of instances (even in the older texts) is extremely doubtful, in which the Masora likewise requires perfects, either by placing the tone on the penultima, as in Gn 18²¹, 46²⁷, Jb 2¹¹ הַבָּאָה; Is 51¹⁰ הַשָּׂמָה; Ez 26¹⁷ הַהֲלָלָה Ru 1²², 2⁶ and 4³ הַשָּׁבָה, or by the punctuation, Gn 21³ הַנּוֹלַד; 1 K 11⁹, Dn 8¹ הַנִּרְאָה; Is 56³ הַנִּלְוָה, while no doubt the authors in all these cases intended participles (and in fact perfect participles, cf. § 116 *d*) with the article, thus הַבָּאָה, &c., Ez 26¹⁷ הַהֲלָלָה for הַמְהֻלָּלָה according to § 52 *s*, and in the other examples הַנִּלְוָה, הַנִּרְאָה, הַנּוֹלַד.

§ 139. *Expression of Pronominal Ideas by means of Substantives.*

Analogous to the periphrases for expressing materials and attributes *a* by means of substantives (§ 128 *o* and *p*), is the use of substantives to represent certain kinds of pronominal ideas, for which no special expressions exist. Thus—

1. אִישׁ, אִשָּׁה *man, woman*, are used to express— *b*

(*a*) The idea of *each, every* (in the sense of each severally) with reference to persons,[1] and even animals (Gn 15¹⁰), e.g. Gn 10⁵, feminine Ex 3²²; אִישׁ is the object, e.g. in Jer 12¹⁵. On אִישׁ־אִישׁ cf. § 123 *c*.

In a few passages אִישׁ in the above sense is placed for the sake of emphasis *c* before the governing noun (always a substantive with a suffix), thus מִיַּד אִישׁ אָחִיו Gn 9⁵, according to the usual explanation, stands for מִיַּד אֲחִי אִישׁ *at the hand of the brother of every man*. But although the explanation seems to be

---

[1] As a rule אִישׁ is used in the particularizing sense of *each man*, with the plural of the verb, e.g. Gn 44¹¹; sometimes, however, as subject to a verb in the singular, e.g. Gn 44¹³.

supported by Gn 42²⁵ and Nu 17¹⁷, it is inconceivable that such an inversion of *nomen regens* and *rectum* should occur. It is more likely, either that the second substantive is in apposition to אִישׁ (thus Gn 9⁵ *at the hand of every man, his brother,* [unless it is a combination of the two readings אִישׁ מִיַּד and מִיַּד הָאָדָם]; similarly 15¹⁰ *and he laid each* or, more exactly, *one piece of it,* &c., and so probably also Nu 17¹⁷ *every one,* sc. *his name*), or אִישׁ precedes as a kind of *casus pendens,* and only receives its nearer definition from the following substantive with suffix; thus Gn 41¹², 42²⁵ (according to the context = *to every one in his sack*); 42³⁵, where צְרוֹר־כַּסְפּוֹ בְּשַׂקּוֹ is virtually the predicate of אִישׁ; Ex 12⁴, 28²¹, Nu 5¹⁰, 26⁵⁴, 2 K 23³⁵, and especially Zc 7¹⁰.[1]

d (b) *Any one, some one,* e.g. Gn 13¹⁶, Ct 8⁷, with a negative *no one*;[2] so after אַל־ Ex 16¹⁹·²⁹; before לֹא Gn 23⁶ and frequently.—Instead of אִישׁ we sometimes find in a similar sense אָדָם *man, homo,* e. g. Lv 1² (cf. הָאָדָם כְּאַחַד *as any one else,* Ju 16⁷·¹¹), נֶפֶשׁ (*soul*) *person,* Lv 2¹, 5¹, &c., and in a neuter sense דָּבָר (prop. *word, thing*) for *anything,* Gn 18¹⁴, or כָּל־דָּבָר Lv 5², Nu 31²³. With a negative דָּבָר means *nothing*; thus after אַל־ Gn 19⁸; after לֹא Ec 8⁵.— Cf. finally, מֵאַחַד *any one,* Dt 15⁷; *anything,* Ez 18¹⁰ (but in Lv 4², 5¹³ מֵאַחַת) and the expressions noticed in § 144 *e.* The latter include also instances like Ez 18³² *I have no pleasure* בְּמוֹת הַמֵּת *in the death of him that dieth,* i. e. *of any man.*

e (c) In connexion with אָחִיו *his brother* or רֵעֵהוּ *his neighbour,* אִישׁ *one,* masc. (as אִשָּׁה *one,* fem., in connexion with אֲחוֹתָהּ *her sister* or רְעוּתָהּ *her neighbour*) is used to represent the ideas of *alter—alter, the one—the other*[3] (in reference to persons, animals, or things without life; see the Lexicon) or the idea of *one another,* e.g. Gn 13¹¹ *and they separated themselves* אִישׁ מֵעַל אָחִיו *the one from the other* ; Ex 26³ *five curtains* (יְרִיעֹת fem.) *shall be coupled together* אִשָּׁה אֶל־אֲחֹתָהּ *one to another.*

f 2. נֶפֶשׁ *soul, person* expresses the idea of *self,*[4] both in the singular, Pr 19⁸·¹⁶, 29²⁴, Jb 18⁴ (in all cases נַפְשׁוֹ equivalent to *himself*) and in the plural, Jer 37⁹, &c. Similar to this is the use of בְּקִרְבָּהּ Gn 18¹² (prop. *in her inward part*) in the sense of *within herself.*[5]

---

[1] Cf. on the whole question the thorough discussion by Budde, *Die bibl. Urgeschichte,* p. 283 ff. : according to him, the words in Gn 9⁵ are to be rendered *at the hand of one another* (from men mutually) *will I require it.* [In support of this view, Budde points to Zc 7¹⁰ וְרָעַת אִישׁ אָחִיו אַל־תַּחְשְׁבוּ בִּלְבַבְכֶם, which in the light of 8¹⁷, וְאִישׁ אֶת־רָעַת רֵעֵהוּ אַל־תַּחְשְׁבוּ בִּלְבַבְכֶם, can only, he observes, be rendered 'and devise not *the hurt of one another* in your heart'. So also König, *Syntax,* § 33.]

[2] Cf. also אֵין־אִישׁ Gn 39¹¹. On the expression of the idea of *no one* by means of אַיִן with a following participle, see the *Negative Sentences,* § 152 *l.*

[3] Elsewhere זֶה . . . זֶה are used in a similar sense, Ex 14²⁰, Is 6³; also הָאֶחָד . . . הָאֶחָד 2 S 14⁶, or the substantive is repeated, e.g. Gn 47²¹ (*from one end . . . to the other end*).

[4] On the representation of this idea by pronouns, separate and suffixed, see § 135 *a, i* and *k.*

[5] In a similar way the idea of *self* in Arabic, as in Sanskrit (*átman*), is paraphrased by *soul, spirit*; in Arabic also by *eye*; in Rabbinic by גּוּף *body,*

3. עֶצֶם *bone* (then metaphorically for *substance*) expresses the idea of *self,* *g* *selfsame, very same,* in reference to *things* (as נֶפֶשׁ to persons, e. g. בְּעֶצֶם הַיּוֹם הַזֶּה *in the selfsame day,* Gn 7¹³, cf. Jos 10²⁷, Ez 24²; בְּעֶצֶם הַשָּׁמַיִם לָטֹהַר *as it were the very heaven for clearness,* Ex 24¹⁰; בְּעֶצֶם תֻּמּוֹ *in the very fullness of his strength* (= *in the midst of his full strength*), Jb 21²³.

4. The simple plural of words denoting time sometimes includes also the *h* idea of *a few, some;*[1] thus יָמִים *a few days,* Gn 24⁵⁵, 40⁴ (here even of a longer period, = *for some time*); Is 65²⁰, Dn 8²⁷ (on the other hand, Gn 27⁴⁴, 29²⁰ יָמִים אֲחָדִים; see § 96 under אֶחָד); שָׁנִים *some years,* Dn 11⁶·⁸.

גֶּרֶם or עֶצֶם *bone,* in Ethiopic and Amharic by *head,* in Egyptian by *mouth, hand,* &c.; cf. also the Middle High German *min lip, din lip,* for *ich, du.* However, נֶפֶשׁ in such cases is never (not even in Is 46² נַפְשָׁם *they themselves*) a merely otiose periphrasis for the personal pronoun, but always involves a reference to the *mental* personality, as affected by the senses, desires, &c.

[1] *Some* in reference to persons in Ex 16²⁰ is expressed by אֲנָשִׁים, and in Neh 5²⁻⁴ by יֵשׁ אֲשֶׁר *sunt qui,* with a participle following.

CHAPTER II

THE SENTENCE

I. The Sentence in General.

§ 140. *Noun-clauses, Verbal-clauses, and the Compound Sentence.*

a 1. Every sentence, the subject and predicate of which are nouns or their equivalents (esp. participles), is called a *noun-clause*, e. g. יְהֹוָה מַלְכֵּנוּ *the Lord is our king*, Is 33²²; וְאַנְשֵׁי סְדֹם רָעִים וְחַטָּאִים *now the men of Sodom were wicked and sinners*, Gn 13¹³; פֶּה לָהֶם *a mouth is theirs*, ψ 115⁵; see further, § 141.

b 2. Every sentence, the subject of which is a noun (or pronoun included in a verbal-form) and its predicate a finite verb, is called a *verbal-clause*, e. g. וַיֹּאמֶר אֱלֹהִים *and God said*, Gn 1³; וַיַּבְדֵּל *and he divided,* 1⁷; see further, § 142.

c Rem. In the last example the pronominal subject is at least indicated by the preformative (י), and in almost all forms of the perfect by afformatives. The 3rd pers. sing. perf. however, which contains no indication of the subject, must also be regarded as a full verbal-clause.

d 3. Every sentence, the subject or predicate of which is itself a full clause, is called a *compound sentence*, e. g. ψ 18³¹ הָאֵל תָּמִים דַּרְכּוֹ *God—his way is perfect*, equivalent to *God's way is perfect*; Gn 34⁸ שְׁכֶם בְּנִי חָשְׁקָה נַפְשׁוֹ בְּבִתְּכֶם *my son Shechem—his soul longeth for your daughter*; see further, § 143.

e 4. The above distinction between different kinds of sentences—especially between noun- and verbal-clauses—is indispensable to the more delicate appreciation of Hebrew syntax (and that of the Semitic languages generally), since it is by no means merely external or formal, but involves fundamental differences of meaning. Noun-clauses with a substantive as predicate, represent something *fixed*, *a state* or in short, *a being* so and so; verbal-clauses on the other hand, something *moveable* and *in progress*, an *event* or *action*. The latter description is indeed true in a certain sense also of noun-clauses with a participial predicate, except that in their case the event or action (as distinguished from that expressed by the verbal-clause) is of a fixed and abiding character.

Rem. By the Arab grammarians every clause beginning with an inde- *f* pendent subject is regarded as a noun-clause, and every clause beginning with a finite verb as verbal. If a finite verb follows the noun-subject the two together (since the verb comprises its own subject and is thus a complete verbal-clause) form a compound noun-sentence, just as when the predicate consists of an independent noun-clause. Though this definition of the different kinds of sentence, which we formerly accepted (in § 144 *a* of the 22nd to the 24th German editions of this Grammar), is rejected above, *a–d*, we must, nevertheless, mention here the point in which this more complicated view of the Arab grammarians may be regarded as at least relatively correct, namely, in classifying verbal-clauses according as the subject precedes or follows the verb, a distinction which is often of great importance in Hebrew also; see further, in § 142 *a*.

§ 141. *The Noun-clause.*

1. The *subject* of a noun-clause (see § 140 *a*) may be— *a*

(*a*) A substantive, e. g. וְנָהָר יֹצֵא מֵעֵדֶן *and a river went out* (was going out) *of Eden*, Gn 2¹⁰.

(*b*) A pronoun, e. g. Gn 7⁴ אָנֹכִי מַמְטִיר *I will cause it to rain*; 14¹⁸ וְהוּא כֹהֵן *and he was priest*; 2²³ (זֹאת) before a feminine predicate, as אֵלֶּה before a plural in Ex 32⁴); מִי חָכָם *who is wise?* Ho 14¹⁰.—In 1 Ch 5² וּלְנָגִיד מִמֶּנּוּ *and of him* one became *a prince*, the subject is contained in מִמֶּנּוּ.[1]

2. The *predicate* of a noun-clause may be— *b*

(*a*) A substantive, e. g. Dt 14¹ בָּנִים אַתֶּם וגו' *ye are children of the Lord your God*; Gn 42¹³. Specially characteristic of the Semitic mode of expression are the cases in which both subject and predicate are substantives, thus emphasizing their identity ('the thing is its measure, material, or equivalent'), e. g. Ez 41²² הַמִּזְבֵּחַ עֵץ . . . וְקִירֹתָיו עֵץ *the altar* (was) *wood . . ., and the walls thereof* (were) *wood*, i. e. of wood. Cf. below, *c*.

(*b*) An adjective or participle, e. g. Gn 2¹² וּזְהַב הָאָרֶץ הַהִיא טוֹב *and the gold of that land is good*; וְעֶפְרוֹן יֹשֵׁב *now Ephron was sitting*, &c., Gn 23¹⁰.[2] Very frequently such noun-clauses, attached by *Wāw* to a verbal-clause, are used to represent a state *contemporaneous* with the principal action; cf. *e* below.

(*c*) A numeral, e. g. Gn 42¹³ שְׁנֵים עָשָׂר עֲבָדֶיךָ *the twelve* (of us) *are thy servants.*

---

[1] For other remarkable instances of ellipse in the Chronicler, see Driver, *Introduction*, ed. 8, p. 537, no. 27.

[2] Cf. the numerous examples in § 116 *n–p.*

(*d*) A pronoun, e. g. Gn 10¹² (הִיא), Ex 9²⁷ (אֲנִי), Gn 24⁶⁵ (מִי), 1 K 9¹³ (מָה).[1]

(*e*) An adverb or (esp. if formed with a preposition) any specification of time, place, quality, possessor, &c., which may be regarded as the equivalent of a noun-idea, e. g. שָׁם הַבְּדֹלַח *there is the bdellium*, Gn 2¹²; אֵי הֶבֶל *where is Abel ?* 4⁹; לְעוֹלָם חַסְדּוֹ *his mercy endureth for ever*, ψ 136¹ᶠ·; עֹשֶׁר בְּבֵיתוֹ *riches are in his house*, ψ 112³; לוֹ אֲנַחְנוּ *we are his*, ψ 100³ Qᵉrê.

C **Rem. 1.** The employment of a substantive as predicate of a noun-clause is especially frequent, either when no corresponding adjective exists (so mostly with words expressing the material; cf. § 128 o) or when the attribute is intended to receive a certain emphasis. For in all cases there is a much greater stress upon a substantival predicate,[2] since it represents something as *identical* with the subject (see above, *b* [*a*]), than upon an adjectival or verbal predicate; cf. Ct 1¹⁰; ψ 25¹⁰ *all the paths of the Lord are* חֶסֶד וֶאֱמֶת *lovingkindness and truth* (i. e. *wholly lovingkindness*, &c.; cf. Jer 10¹⁰); Ez 38⁵, ψ 10⁵, 19¹⁰, 23⁵, 88¹⁹, Pr 3¹⁷,[3] Jb 22¹², 23², 26¹³, Ru 3². Sometimes the emphasis on the predicate is obtained by the use of the plural form (according to § 124 e), e.g. ψ 110³ *thy people are* נְדָבֹת *altogether willingness*; Ct 5¹⁶, Dn 9²³.

d Sometimes the boldness of such combinations is modified by the repetition of the subject, as *regens* of the predicate, e. g. Jb 6¹² אִם־כֹּחַ אֲבָנִים כֹּחִי *is my strength the strength of stones?* Pr 3¹⁷. That the language, however—especially in poetry—is not averse even to the boldest combinations in order to emphasize very strongly the unconditional relation between the subject and predicate, is shown by such examples as ψ 45⁹ *myrrh and aloes and cassia* are *all thy garments* (i. e. so perfumed with them that they seem to be composed of them); Ct 1¹⁵ *thine eyes* are *doves*, i. e. dove's eyes (but 5¹² כְּיוֹנִים);[4] ψ 23⁵, 109⁴, Jb 8⁹, 12¹², Ct 2¹³. In prose, e. g. Ex 9³¹, Ezr 10¹³ הָעֵת גְּשָׁמִים *the season is rain showers*, i. e. *the rainy season*; with a bold enallage of the number, Gn 34³⁰ וַאֲנִי מְתֵי מִסְפָּר *and I* (with my family) *am persons few in number*. For similarly bold expressions with הָיָה cf. Gn 11¹, 12², Ex 17¹², Is 5¹², Jer 2²⁸, and again with a bold enallage of the number, Jb 29¹⁵ *I was eyes to the blind, and feet was I to the lame*, but in prose, Nu 10³¹ *and thou shalt be to us* לְעֵינָיִם.

---

[1] Why in these examples the pronouns, notwithstanding appearances to the contrary, are to be considered as predicates and not as subjects, may be seen from what has been remarked above, § 126 k.

[2] The same naturally applies to most of those cases which are not pure noun-clauses, but have the substantival predicate connected with the subject by הָיָה (e. g. Gn 1² *and the earth was a waste and emptiness*; cf. ψ 35⁶, Pr 8³⁰, Jb 3⁴) or where a preposition precedes the substantival predicate, as ψ 29⁴ *the voice of the Lord is with power*, i. e. *powerful*.

[3] שָׁלוֹם here, as in Jb 21⁹, is evidently a substantive after a plural subject; on the other hand, it is doubtful whether שָׁלֹם in such passages as Gn 43²⁷, 2 S 20⁹, ψ 120⁷, &c., is not rather to be regarded as an adjective.

[4] As a rule, in such comparisons כְּ (which is then to be regarded as *nominative*) stands before the predicate, e. g. Is 63² *wherefore* are *thy garments* כְּדֹרֵךְ בְּגַת *like those of one that treadeth in the wine-press ?* (prop. *the like of one that treadeth, instar calcantis*); Jer 50⁹. The comparison is then much less emphatic than in the noun-clauses cited above.

2. The noun-clause connected by *wāw copulative* to a verbal-clause, or its *e* equivalent, always describes a state *contemporaneous* with the principal action, or (when the predicate is a transitive participle) an action represented in constant duration (cf. § 107 *d*, as well as § 116 *n* and *o*), e.g. Gn 19¹ *and the two angels came to Sodom at even,* וְלוֹט יֹשֵׁב *while Lot sat,* &c.; 18¹·⁸·¹⁶·²², 25²⁶, Ju 13⁹, 1 S 1⁶, 2 S 4⁷, 11⁴ (always with a participle); with an adjectival predicate, Gn 18¹²; with a substantival predicate, 18²⁷; with an adverbial predicate, 9²³. Not infrequently such a *circumstantial* clause indicates at the same time some contradictory fact, so that וְ is equivalent to *whereas, whilst, although,* e.g. Gn 15², 18²⁷, 2 c³, 48¹⁴ (*although he was the younger*); Ju 16¹⁵ *how canst thou say, I love thee,* וְלִבְּךָ אֵין אִתִּי *whereas thine heart is not with me?* 2 S 3³⁹, ψ 28³ *whilst mischief is in their hearts.* These clauses describing a state are, however, only a subdivision of the large class of circumstantial clauses, on which see § 156.

3. As the examples given under *a* and *b* show, the syntactical *f* relation existing between the subject and predicate of a noun-clause is as a rule expressed by simple juxtaposition, without a *copula* of any kind. To what period of time the statement applies must be inferred from the context; e.g. 1 K 18²¹ יְהֹוָה הָאֱלֹהִים *the Lord* is *the* true *God*; 1 S 9¹⁹; Is 31² גַּם־הוּא חָכָם *yet he also* is *wise*; Gn 42¹¹; on the other hand, Gn 19¹ וְלוֹט יֹשֵׁב *and* (=while) *Lot was sitting*; Ez 28¹⁵; Gn 7⁴ אָנֹכִי מַמְטִיר *I am raining,* i.e. *I will rain.* Sometimes even a jussive or optative is to be supplied as predicate, Gn 27¹³ *upon me be thy curse*; Gn 11³, 20¹³, Ex 12². Cf. § 116 *r*, note.

Not infrequently, however, a connexion is established between subject *g* and predicate (*a*) by adding the separate pronoun of the 3rd person singular or plural, expressly resuming and therefore strengthening the subject, or (*b*) (especially for the sake of a more exact specification of time) by the help of the verb הָיָה. The first of these will be a *compound* sentence, since the predicate to the main subject consists of an independent clause.

Examples of (*a*): Gn 41²⁶ *the seven good kine* שֶׁבַע שָׁנִים הֵנָּה *they* are *seven h years*; Dt 1¹⁷, 4²⁴; Ec 5¹⁸ זֶה מַתַּת אֱלֹהִים הִיא *this—it* is *a gift of* God; Nu 3²⁷ אֵלֶּה הֵם; in a question, Gn 27³⁸. Sometimes הוּא is used in this way to strengthen a pronominal subject of the first or second person, and at the same time to connect it with the predicate which follows,[1] e.g. אָנֹכִי אָנֹכִי הוּא Is 43²⁵ *I, even I,* am *he that blotteth out,* &c.; 51¹²; אַתָּה הוּא 2 S 7²⁸, Is 37¹⁶, ψ 44⁵, Neh 9⁶·⁷; in an interrogative sentence, Jer 14²²;[2] in Jer 49¹² הוּא in a *verbal*-clause strengthens אַתָּה.

---

[1] On a similar use of the separate pronoun of the third person in Aramaic (Dn 2³⁸, Ezr 5¹¹, &c.) see Kautzsch, *Gramm. des Bibl. Aram.*, § 87. 3.

[2] This is of course to be distinguished from the use of הוּא (to be inferred from the context) as predicate in the sense of ὁ αὐτός; see above, § 135 *a*, note 1; or such cases as Dt 32³⁹ *see now* אֲנִי אֲנִי הוּא *that I, even I,* am *he*; 1 Ch 21¹⁷.

i Of (*b*): naturally this does not apply to the examples, in which הָיָה, in the sense of *to become, to fare, to exist*, still retains its full force as a verb, and where accordingly the sentence is verbal, and not a noun-clause; especially when the predicate precedes the subject. On the other hand, such examples as Gn 1² *and the earth was* (הָיְתָה) *waste and emptiness*, can scarcely be regarded as properly verbal clauses; הָיְתָה is used here really only for the purpose of referring to past time a statement which, as the description of a state, might also appear in the form of a pure noun-clause; cf. Gn 3¹. This is especially true of the somewhat numerous instances in which הָיָה occurs as a connecting word between the subject and the participial predicate; e. g. Ju 1⁷, Jb 1¹⁴ (immediately afterwards a pure noun-clause). The imperfect of הָיָה announces what is future in Nu 14³³, &c.; cf. § 116 *r*. However, especially in the latter case, הָיָה is not wholly without verbal force, but comes very near to being a mere copula, and this use is more frequent in the later books[1] than in the earlier.

k Rem. On the employment of יֵשׁ *existence*, and אַיִן *non-existence*, which were originally substantives (on their tendency to be used as verbs, equivalent to *est*, and *non est*, cf. § 100 *o*, and the *Negative Sentences*, § 152) as a connecting link between a pronominal subject and a participial predicate (especially in conditional and interrogative sentences, Gn 24⁴²·⁴⁹, 43⁴, &c.), see above, § 116 *q*, and the various kinds of subordinate clauses mentioned in §§ 150, 159.

l 4. The natural *arrangement* of words in the noun-clause, as describing a state, is *subject—predicate*; the principal stress falls on the former since it is the object of the description. Very frequently, however (and not merely in poetry, where greater freedom is naturally allowed in the arrangement of words), the reverse order is found, i. e. *predicate—subject*. The latter order *must* be used when special emphasis is laid on the predicate,[2] or when it consists of an interrogative word; thus with a substantival predicate, e. g. Gn 3¹⁹ עָפָר אַתָּה *dust thou art*; 4⁹, 12¹³ (*my sister*, not my wife); 20²·¹², 29¹⁴, Is 6³ᵇ, Jb 5²⁴, 6¹²; with an adjectival predicate, e. g. Is 6³ᵃ, 28²¹, Jer 10⁶; with a participle, Gn 30¹, 32¹²; with an interrogative pronoun, e. g. Gn 24⁶⁵;[3] with an adverbial interrogative, e. g. Gn 4⁹.

m Rem. On the above cf. the exhaustive investigations of C. Albrecht, ' Die Wortstellung im hebr. Nominalsatze,' *ZAW*. vii. 218 ff. and viii. 249 ff.; with a complete list of the exceptions to the order *subject—predicate*, p. 254 ff. The predicate *must* precede for the reasons stated (an *adjectival predicate* is particularly emphatic when it has the force of a comparative, e. g. Gn 4¹³; the predicate expressed by means of a preposition precedes most frequently when it serves to convey the ideas of *having, possessing*, e. g. Gn 18¹⁴, 29¹⁶, &c.; cf. also 26²⁰, 31¹⁶·⁴³).

n The predicate *may* precede: (*a*) when the subject is a pronoun, for 'the person assumed to be generally known, does not excite the same interest as

---

[1] According to Albrecht, *ZAW*. viii. 252, especially in Deuteronomy and in the Priestly Code.

[2] For the same reason specifications of place (e. g. Gn 4⁷) or other adverbial qualifications may stand at the beginning of the sentence.

[3] The only exceptions, according to Albrecht (see the Rem. above), are Ex 16⁷·⁸.

that which is stated about him ;' (*b*) 'in order not to be a mere appendage to a subject which consists of several words,' e. g. 2 K 20¹⁹ ; (*c*) in interrogative sentences (with a substantival or adjectival predicate or one compounded with a preposition), e. g. 1 S 16⁴ ; finally (*d*) in a relative clause, when the predicate is adverbial or compounded with a preposition, as a rule closely united (by Maqqeph) with אֲשֶׁר, e.g. Gn 2¹¹ אֲשֶׁר־שָׁם ; 1²⁹ᶠ· אֲשֶׁר־בּוֹ.

§ 142. *The Verbal-clause.*

1. By § 140 *f* there is an essential distinction between verbal- *a* clauses, according as the subject stands before or after the verb.　In the verbal-clause proper the principal emphasis rests upon the action which proceeds from (or is experienced by) the subject, and accordingly the verb naturally precedes (*necessarily* so when it is in the perf. consec. or imperf. consec.).　Nevertheless, the subject does sometimes precede even in the verbal-clause proper, in the continuation of the narrative, e.g. Gn 7¹⁹, 1 S 18¹, 2 S 19¹² ; especially so if there is special emphasis upon it, e. g. Gn 3¹³ (it is not I who am to blame, but) *the serpent beguiled me*, cf. Gn 2⁵, &c.[1] In the great majority of instances, however, the position of the subject at the beginning of a verbal-clause is to be explained from the fact that the clause is not intended to introduce a new fact carrying on the narrative, but rather to describe a *state*.　Verbal-clauses of this kind approximate closely in character to noun-clauses, and not infrequently (viz. when the verbal form might just as well be read as a participle) it is doubtful whether the writer did not in fact intend a noun-clause.

The particular *state* represented in the verb may consist—　　　*b*

(*a*) Of an act completed long before, to which reference is made only because it is necessary for understanding the sequel of the principal action. If the predicate be a perfect (as it almost always is in these cases), it is generally to be rendered in English by a pluperfect ; cf. the examples discussed above in § 106 *f* (1 S 28³, &c.); also Gn 6⁸ (not *Noah found grace*) ; 16¹, 18¹⁷, 20⁴, 24¹, 39¹ (*and Joseph* in the meanwhile *had been brought down to Egypt*) ; 41¹⁰, Ju 1¹⁶, 1 S 9¹⁵, 14²⁷, 25²¹, 1 K 1¹, &c.—In a wider sense this applies also to such verbal-clauses as Gn 2⁶ (see further, § 112 *e*), since when they serve to represent an action continuing for a long period in the past, and thus to some extent a state.

(*b*) Of a fact, contemporaneous with the principal events or continuing as *C* the result of them.　To the former class belong all those instances in which the predicate is combined with הָיָה (provided that הָיָה has not, as in Gn 1², 3¹, &c., been weakened to a mere copula, in which case the precedence of the subject is fully explained from the character of the clause as a noun-clause ; cf. § 141 *i*, and the examples of הָיָה, &c., with a participle, § 116 *r*) ; as an example of the second class, cf. e. g. Gn 13¹² אַבְרָם יָשַׁב בְּאֶרֶץ־כְּנַעַן וגו׳ *Abraham* accordingly *continued to dwell in the land of Canaan*, but *Lot dwelt, &c.*

---

[1] This of course applies also to the cases, in which the subject consists of a strongly emphasized personal pronoun, e.g. Gn 32¹³ אַתָּה *thou thyself*; 33³ הוּא *he himself.*

d Rem. 1. The close relation between verbal-clauses beginning with the subject and actual noun-clauses, is seen finally from the fact that the former also are somewhat frequently added with וְ (or subordinated) to a preceding sentence in order to lay stress upon some accompanying circumstance; on such noun-clauses describing a *state* or *circumstance*, cf. § 141 *e*. This is especially the case, again, when the circumstantial appendage involves an antithesis ; cf. Gn 18¹⁸ *seeing that* nevertheless *Abraham shall surely become*, &c. ; 24⁵⁶, 26²⁷, Is 29¹³, Jer 14¹⁵, ψ 50¹⁷, Jb 21²², and such examples as Gn 4²·⁴, 29¹⁷, where by means of וְ a new subject is introduced in express antithesis to one just mentioned. Moreover, in the examples treated above, under *b* and *c* (1 S 28³, &c.), the subject is frequently introduced by וְ, which then corresponds to the Greek δέ, used to interpose an explanation, &c., see Winer. *Gramm. des neutest. Sprachidioms*, § 53. 7 *b*.

e 2. By a peculiar construction verbal-clauses may be joined by means of וְ and a following subject to participial clauses, e. g. Gn 38²⁵ הִיא מוּצֵאת וְהִיא שָׁלְחָה *she was already brought forth, when she sent*, &c. ; 44³·⁴, Ju 18³, 19¹¹, 2 S 20⁸; for other examples, see § 116 *u* (where it is pointed out, note 1, that the apodosis also frequently appears in the form of a *noun*-clause, a further proof of the close relation between verbal-clauses beginning with the subject and noun-clauses proper). Without doubt there is in all these cases a kind of inversion of the principal clause and the temporal subordinate clause ; the latter for the sake of greater emphasis being raised to an independent noun-clause, while the real principal action is added as though it were an accompanying circumstance, and hence in the form of an ordinary circumstantial clause. [Cf. Driver, *Tenses*, § 166 ff.]

f 2. According to what has been remarked above, under *a*, the natural *order of words* within the verbal sentence is : *Verb—Subject*, or *Verb—Subject—Object*. But as in the noun-clause (§ 141 *l*) so also in the verbal-clause, a variation of the usual order of words frequently occurs when any member of the sentence is to be specially emphasized by priority of position.[1] Thus the order may be :—

(*a*) *Object—Verb—Subject* : Gn 30⁴⁰, 37⁴, 1 S 15¹, 2 K 23¹⁹ and frequently. Naturally the examples are far more numerous, in which the object precedes a verbal form which includes the subject in itself, e. g. Gn 3¹⁰·¹⁴·¹⁸, 6¹⁶, 8¹⁷, 9¹³, Ex 18²³, Ju 14³, 1 S 18¹⁷, 20⁹, 21¹⁰, 2 K 22⁸, Pr 13⁵, &c.

(*b*) *Verb—Object—Subject* : Gn 21⁷, Nu 5²³, 1 S 15³³, 2 S 24¹⁶ (but הַמַּלְאָךְ is probably only a subsequent addition) ; Is 19¹³, ψ 34²², Jb 11¹⁹, &c.

(*c*) *Subject—Object—Verb* : Is 3¹⁷, 11⁸, 13¹⁸, Ho 12¹¹, ψ 6¹⁰, 11⁵, Jb 29²⁵.[2]

---

[1] Not infrequently also the striving after *chiasmus* mentioned in § 114 *r*, note, occasions a departure from the usual arrangement of words.

[2] This sequence occurs even in prose (Gn 17⁹, 23⁶, &c.) ; it is, however, more doubtful here than in the above prophetical and poetical passages, whether the preceding subject should not be regarded rather as the subject of a compound sentence (§ 143), the predicate of which is an independent verbal-clause ; this would explain why the verbal-clause is usually separated from the subject by one of the greater disjunctives.—On the other hand, the sequence *Subject—Object—Verb* is quite common in Aramaic (e.g. Dn 2⁷·¹⁰) ; cf.

(d) *Object—Subject—Verb* (very rarely): 2 K 5¹³, Is 5¹⁷, 28¹⁷, ψ 51⁵, Pr 13¹⁶ (read כֹּל).¹

(e) A substantival complement of the verb היה is placed first in Is 18⁵ וּבֹסֶר גֹּמֵל יִהְיֶה נִצָּה *and a ripening grape the flower becometh.*

Rem. Of specifications compounded with a preposition those of *place* stand *g* regularly after the verb, unless they are specially emphatic as e. g. Gn 19², 30¹⁶, 32⁵, Mi 5¹, Est 9¹² ; in Gn 29²⁵ בְּרָחֵל with בְּ *pretii* precedes for the sake of emphasis. Cf., however, in Gn 35¹³ the order *verb*—specification of *place*—*subject.*—The remoter object precedes for the sake of emphasis, e. g. in Gn 13¹⁵ (26³), 15³ ; even before the interrogative, Gn 27³⁷ (cf. Jer 22¹⁵ where the subject precedes an interrogative, and 1 S 20⁸, Jb 34³¹ where a prepositional specification precedes). — Prepositional specifications of *time*, such as בְּרֵאשִׁית (Gn 1¹), בְּיוֹם, בַּיּוֹם הַהוּא, &c. (but not בְּרֵאשֹׁנָה, nor the simple רִאשֹׁנָה, בַּתְּחִלָּה, לְעוֹלָם), stand, as a rule, before the verb, provided it be not in the perf. consec. or imperf. consec. ; so also certain adverbs of time, such as אָז, עַתָּה, אָן, whilst others like עוֹד, תָּמִיד regularly follow the verb.

§ 143. *The Compound Sentence.*

A compound sentence (§ 140 d) is formed by the juxtaposition of *a* a subject ² (which always precedes, see *c*) and

(a) An independent noun-clause, which (α) refers to the principal subject by means of a pronoun, e. g. Na 1³ יְהֹוָה בְּסוּפָה דַרְכּוֹ *the Lord—in the storm is his way*; 2 S 23⁶, ψ 18³¹, 104¹⁷, 125², Ec 2¹⁴; cf. also Gn 34²³, where the predicate is an interrogative clause.—A personal pronoun is somewhat frequently used as the principal subject, e. g. Is 59²¹ וַאֲנִי זֹאת בְּרִיתִי אֹתָם *and as for me, this is my covenant with them,* &c.; Gn 9⁹, 17⁴, Is 1⁷, 1 Ch 28²;³ with an interrogative noun-clause, Gn 37³⁰, Jb 21⁴, 38¹⁹:—or (β) is without a retrospective suffix (in which case naturally the connexion between the subject and predicate is much looser), e. g. 1 S 20²³ *and as touching the matter which,* &c. . . . *behold the Lord is between thee and me for ever*; Pr 27².

Gesenius, *Comm.* on Is 42²⁴, and Kautzsch's *Gramm. des Bibl. Aram.*, § 84. 1 *b.* The pure Aramaic usage of placing the *object* before the *infinitive* occurs in Hebrew in Lv 19⁹, 21²¹, Dt 28⁵⁶, 2 S 11¹⁹, Is 49⁶, 2 Ch 28¹⁰, 31⁷, 36¹⁹ (?).

¹ This sequence occurs more frequently in noun-clauses with a participial predicate, e. g. Gn 37¹⁶, 41⁹, 2 S 13⁴, &c., in interrogative sentences, e. g. 2 K 6²², Jer 7¹⁹ ; in all which cases the emphasized object is placed before the natural sequence of *subject—predicate.* [Cf. Driver, *Tenses,* § 208.]

² In Gn 31⁴⁰ a verbal-clause (הָיִיתִי *I was*) occurs instead of the subject, and is then explained by another verbal-clause.

³ In 1 Chr 28² (cf. also 22⁷ אֲנִי הָיָה עִם־לְבָבִי) אֲנִי might also be taken as strengthening the pronominal suffix which follows (equivalent to *I myself had it in my mind*), as e. g. Ez 33¹⁷ *whereas their own way is not equal*; cf. § 135 *f.*

b   (*b*) An independent verbal-clause: (*a*) with a retrospective suffix,[1] e. g. Gn 9⁶ (cf. § 116 *w*); 17¹⁵ *as for Sarai thy wife, thou shalt not call her name Sarai*; 26¹⁵, 28¹³, 34⁸, Ex 30³⁷, 32¹, 1 S 2¹⁰, 2 K 10²⁹, Is 9¹, 11¹⁰, Ez 33², Ho 9¹¹, ψ 11⁴, 46⁵, 65⁴, 74¹⁷, Dn 1¹⁷; with a pronoun as the principal subject, Gn 24²⁷; (*β*) without a retrospective suffix, Is 19¹⁷ *every one* that *mentions it* (Judah) *to it* (Egypt), *it* (Egypt) *is afraid.*

c   Rem. 1. In all the above examples prominence is given to the principal subject (by its mere separation from the context by means of a greater disjunctive, as a *casus pendens*[2]) in a manner which would be quite impossible in a simple noun or verbal-clause (e. g. Na 1³ if it were בְּסוּפָה יְהֹוָה דַּרְכּוֹ); cf. the French *c'est moi qu'on a accusé*. But the statement or question contained in the clause which forms the predicate also receives greater weight. For the same purpose other members of the sentence also are sometimes placed at the beginning and resumed again by a following suffix; thus the object, Gn 13¹⁵, 21¹³, 35¹², 47²¹ (with the Samaritan and LXX read perhaps הֶעָבִיר); 1 S 25²⁹; a specification of place, Gn 2¹⁷, 2 K 22¹⁸, &c.; a substantive with לְ, 1 S 9²⁰, 2 S 6²³; cf. the examples in § 135 *a*.—In Nu 15²⁹ a dative is co-ordinated with the *casus pendens*, i. e. there is a transition to a different construction.

d   2. To compound sentences belong also the numerous examples already treated in the account of the tenses, where the predicate of a *casus pendens* is introduced by the *wāw apodosis*. The isolation and prominence of the principal subject is in this case still more marked than in the instances treated above; on the *casus pendens* with a following imperfect consecutive (e. g. Jer 6¹⁹, 33²⁴), cf. § 111 *h*; with a following perfect consecutive (e. g. Ex 4²¹, 12⁴⁴, Nu 23³, 1 S 25²⁷, 2 S 14¹⁰, Is 9⁴, 56⁶ ᶠ·), § 112 *t* and *mm*; on the participle as *casus pendens*, § 112 oo and § 116 *w*.—In Jb 15¹⁷ *wāw apodosis* follows with the cohortative; in Jb 23¹², ψ 115⁷, the imperfect is separated by לֹא from the *wāw apodosis*; in Jb 4⁶ as for *thy* hope, it is *the integrity of thy ways*, 36²⁶, Ec 5⁶, an incomplete noun-clause is appended by *wāw apodosis*. On *wāw apodosis* after disconnected specifications of time, cf. § 112 oo at the end, and Gn 40⁹, 2 S 15³⁴ וְעַתָּה וַאֲנִי עַבְדֶּךָ *and now* (so far as the present is concerned) *I will be thy servant*, Nu 12¹², Jer 4¹ (*me thou needest not fear*).

e   3. Sometimes a substantive introduced by לְ (*in respect to*; cf. § 119 *u*) serves the same purpose as the *casus pendens* beginning the sentence, as Nu 18⁸ (unless the לְ here serves to introduce the object, according to § 117 *n*); Is 32¹ (where, however, וְשָׂרִים should most probably be read); Ec 9⁴, 1 Ch 7¹, 24²⁰ ᶠᶠ·, 2 Ch 7²¹. On the other hand, ψ 16³, 17⁴, 32⁶, 89¹⁹, 119⁹¹, are very doubtful. The suggestion of P. Haupt (*Johns Hopkins University Circulars*, xiii. no. 114; Baltimore, 1894) also deserves attention, that in passages like Ec 9⁴, and in לְכֹל Gn 9¹⁰, 23¹⁰, Ex 27³·¹⁹, Ez 44⁹, &c., לְ is not the preposition, but an emphasizing particle, answering to the Arab. *lä, surely*; Assyrian *lû*; with כֹּל it is equivalent to *in short*. Cf. also לְ--לְ *sive—sive, et—et*, Jos 17¹⁶, Ezr 1¹¹, Assyrian *lû—lû*.

---

[1] Cf. the Mêša‘ inscription, l. 31, *and Horonain, therein dwelt*, &c.

[2] But this term must not (any more than that formerly used 'the subject preceding *absolutely*') be misunderstood to mean that the principal subject is, as it were, floating in the air, and that the whole sentence results in an anacoluthon. On the contrary, to the Semitic mind, such sentences appear quite as correctly formed as ordinary noun- and verbal-clauses.

§ 144. *Peculiarities in the Representation of the Subject (especially in the Verbal-clause).*

1. According to § 40 ff. most forms of the finite verb include a *a* specification of the subject in the form of *personal afformatives* (in the imperfect also in the form of preformatives). Not infrequently, however, masculine forms are used in referring to feminines, e. g. וִידַעְתֶּם Ez 23⁴⁹; עֲשִׂיתֶם Ru 1⁸; in the imperfect, Jo 2²², Ct 2⁷; in the imperative, Am 4¹, Zc 13⁷ (for other examples, see § 110 *k*). On emphasizing the pronominal subject by the addition of the separate pronoun, see § 135 *a* and *b*.

On the masculine as *prior gender*, cf. § 122 *g*; on similar anomalies in the use of the personal pronoun, § 135 *o*, in the connexion between substantive and adjective, § 132 *d*, between subject and predicate, § 145 *p*, *t*, *u*.

2. The third person singular is often used impersonally, especially *b* in the masculine, e. g. וַיְהִי *and it came to pass*, וְהָיָה *and it shall come to pass*; חָרָה followed by לְ, &c., *it became hot to him*, i. e. *he became angry*, Gn 4⁶, &c.; וַיֵּצֶר לוֹ lit. *and it became strait to him, he was distressed*, Gn 32⁸;¹ also in the feminine, e. g. 1 S 30⁶ (Ju 10⁹) וַתֵּצֶר לְדָוִד; Ju 11³⁹, Jer 7³¹, Ez 12²⁵, Jb 15³² (unless תְּמוּרָתוֹ in verse 31 be the subject); cf. also the impersonal passives, Is 1⁶ (רֻכָּכָה), 29⁶ (תִּפָּקֵד). Scmewhat different are the instances in which the 3rd singular feminine occurs as the predicate of a feminine subject which is not mentioned, but is before the mind of the speaker, e. g. Is 7⁷, 14²⁴, Jer 10⁷, Jb 4⁵, 18¹⁵ (in 2 K 24⁷ כָּל־אֲשֶׁר is used in this way with a feminine predicate, and in Jer 19⁵ אֲשֶׁר alone); different, too, are the instances in which the 3rd singular masculine refers to an act just mentioned, e. g. Gn 17¹¹ וְהָיָה *and this* (the circumcision) *shall be a token of a covenant*, &c.

Rem. The expressions for natural phenomena may be either in the 3rd *c* sing. masculine or feminine, e. g. אוֹר *it becomes light*, 1 S 29¹⁰ (but with an explicit subject, Gn 44³); וַיֵּאֹר *and it became light*; so also יַחְשַׁךְ *it grows dark*, Jer 13¹⁶; but וְחָשְׁכָה Mi 3⁶; תְּעֻפָּה *though there be darkness*, Jb 11¹⁷; תַּמְטִיר *it rains*, Am 4⁷ (where, however, the context requires the reading אַמְטִיר); ψ 50³ נִשְׂעֲרָה *it is tempestuous.*

---

¹ In Arabic and Ethiopic the masculine is commonly used in this case, in Syriac the feminine.—The forms חַם *hot*, טוֹב *good, well*, מַר *bitter*, צַר *narrow*, רַע *evil* (frequently joined by לִי, לוֹ, &c.), which many regard as impersonal, are no doubt to be regarded in most cases not as forms of the 3rd pers. sing. perf., but, with Hupfeld on ψ 18⁷, as adjectives.

d 3. The indefinite personal subject (our *they, one*, the French *on*, and the German *man*[1]) is expressed—

(*a*) By the 3rd person singular masculine, e. g. קָרָא *one* (sc. any *one who named* it, see the Rem.) *called* (or *calls*) it, Gn 11⁹, 16¹⁴, 19²², Ex 15²³; וַיִּקְרָא Gn 35⁸·¹⁰, 2 S 2¹⁶, Is 9⁵; וַיֹּאמֶר *one said*, Gn 48¹, 1 S 16⁴;[2] other examples are Gn 38²⁸ *one put out a hand*; Nu 23²¹, 1 K 22³⁸, Is 6¹⁰ וְרָפָא לֹו *and one heals them*; 8⁴ (יִשָּׂא); 46⁷ (יִצְעַק); Am 6¹², Mi 2⁴, Jb 27²³; by the 3rd singular feminine (יְלָדָה) Nu 26⁵⁹.

e Rem. The Jewish commentators, following the Arab grammarians, usually explain these singulars by the addition of the participle (generally determinate) of the same stem, e. g. קָרָא הַקֹּרֵא. This view is supported by the fact that such a complement sometimes occurs, e. g. Is 16¹⁰ יְדֹרֹךְ הַדֹּרֵךְ *the treader treads out*, for *one treads out*; 28⁴·²⁴ (*doth one plow continually?*); Dt 17⁶ (Ez 18³²), Dt 22⁸, 2 S 17⁹ (Ez 33⁴), Jer 9²³; with an indeterminate participle (as in Arabic, e. g. *qāla qā'ilun, a sayer says*, i. e. *some one says*), e. g. Nu 6⁹, Am 9¹; cf. above, § 116 *t*, and, on the whole question, Driver on 1 S 16⁴.

f (*b*) Very frequently by the 3rd plural masculine, e. g. Gn 29² *for out of that well* יַשְׁקוּ *they* (i. e. people generally) *watered the flocks*; 26¹⁸, 35⁵, 41¹⁴, 49³¹, 1 K 1², Is 38¹⁶, Ho 12⁹, Jb 18¹⁸, 34²⁰, Est 2², Neh 2⁷.

g Rem. The 3rd plur. also is sometimes used to express an indefinite subject, where the context does not admit of a human agent or at least not of several, e. g. Gn 34²⁷. In such a case the 3rd plur. comes to be equivalent to a passive, as very commonly in Aramaic (see Kautzsch's *Gramm. des Bibl. Aram.*, § 96. 1 *c*); e. g. Jb 7³ *wearisome nights* מִנּוּ־לִי *have they allotted to me* (equivalent to *were allotted to me*; to make 'invisible powers' the subject is a merely artificial device); Jb 4¹⁹, 6², 18¹⁸, 19²⁶, 34²⁰, Ez 32²⁵, ψ 63¹¹, Pr 2²² (in parallelism with a passive); 9¹¹.

h (*c*) By the 2nd singular masculine, e. g. Is 7²⁵ לֹא־תָבוֹא שָׁמָּה *one will* (or *can*) *not come thither* (prop. *thou wilt* . . .); Jer 23³⁷, Pr 19²⁵, 30²⁸ (unless the reading should be תִּתְפֹּשׂ). Cf. also עַד־בֹּאֲךָ or simply בֹּאֲךָ (Gn 10¹⁹·³⁰, 13¹⁰ בֹּאֲכָה) prop. *until thy coming*, i. e. *until one comes*.

i (*d*) By the plural of the participle, e. g. Jer 38²³ *and all thy wives and thy children* מוֹצִאִים (prop. *are they bringing out=*) *they will bring out*, &c.; cf. Is 32¹², Ez 13⁷, Neh 6¹⁰ (*for some are coming to slay thee*)

---

[1] In 1 S 9⁹ הָאִישׁ (prop. *the man*) is used in exactly the same sense as our *one*.

[2] Elsewhere in such cases וַיֹּאמְרוּ usually occurs (but not in the perfect, e. g. 1 S 23²²), so that it is doubtful whether the present reading of Gn 48¹, &c., would not be better explained according to § 7 *d*, note. In Gn 48² for the extraordinary וַיַּגֵּד the common form וַיֻּגַּד is to be read; so in 50²⁶ for וַיִּישֶׂם (after a plural) either וַיּוּשַׂם or the 3rd plur.; in 2 K 21²³ וַיִּקְבְּרוּ.

and the passages discussed above, § 116 *t*.[1] In 1 K 5[1] the text is corrupt.

(*e*) By the passive, e. g. Gn 4[26] אָז הוּחַל לִקְרֹא *then (was it begun=) k began men to call upon*, &c. (but read זֶה הֵחֵל *he began*).

4. A peculiar idiom, and one always confined to poetic language, *l* is the not infrequent occurrence of two subjects in a verbal sentence,[2] one of the person and the other of the thing. The latter then serves —whether it precedes or follows—to state the instrument, organ, or member by which the action in question is performed, and may be most often rendered in English by an adverb, as a nearer definition of the manner of the action. All the examples of this kind have this in common, that the subject denoting the thing takes a suffix in the same person as the personal subject.[3] They are thus distinguished from the *accusatives* treated in § 117 *s*, with which they are often confused.

(*a*) Examples where the subject denoting the *thing* precedes, קוֹלִי אֶל־יְהוָה *m* אֶקְרָא *my voice—I cry unto the Lord*, i. e. *I cry aloud unto the Lord*, ψ 3[5], 27[7], 142[2]; פִּי־קָרָאתִי *my mouth—I cried*, i.e. *I cried aloud*, ψ 66[17] (cf. 17[10]); Is 26[9] נַפְשִׁי *with my soul*, i. e. *fervently*, and parallel with it אַף־רוּחִי; but נַפְשִׁי ψ 57[5] is rather a periphrasis for the 1st pers. *I*.

(*b*) Where the subject denoting the *thing* follows, צַהֲלִי קוֹלֵךְ *cry—thy voice* (i. e. aloud), Is 10[30]; so also after an imperative, ψ 17[13] (חַרְבֶּךָ) and verse 14 (יָדְךָ); 60[7], 108[7] (יְמִינֶךָ); after a perfect, Hb 3[15] (סוּסֶיךָ); after a cohortative, ψ 108[2] (אַף־כְּבוֹדִי). The subject denoting the *thing* stands between the personal subject and the predicate in ψ 44[3] אַתָּה יָדְךָ.[4]

Rem. 1. Sometimes (as in other languages) an action is ascribed to a *n* subject which can only have been performed at his direction by another

---

[1] That this form of expression also (see *g*) comes to be equivalent to a passive is seen from the analogy of such Aramaic passages as Dn 4[22], which exclude any idea of human agency. Cf. Kautzsch, *Gramm. des Bibl. Aram.*, § 76. 2 *e* at the end, and in post.-bibl. Hebrew, e. g. *Pirqe Aboth* 2, 16; 3, 5, &c.

[2] Two subjects occur in a noun-clause in ψ 83[19].

[3] In Ex 6[3] שְׁמִי is subordinated to the following passive נוֹדַעְתִּי (§ 121 *b*); in 1 S 25[26.33] יָדְךָ, יָדִי are subjects to the infinitive absolute הוֹשֵׁעַ, according to § 113 *gg*. In ψ 69[11] read וָאֶעֱנֶה for וָאֶבְכֶּה.

[4] In several of the above examples it might naturally be supposed that the subject denoting the thing (especially when it follows the verb) is to be explained rather as a *casus instrumentalis*, i.e. as an accusative, analogous to the adverbial accusatives in § 118 *q*. But although it is true that the subject denoting the thing often defines more closely the manner in which the action is performed, and although in similar (but still different) examples, ψ 89[2], 109[30], Jb 19[16], פִּי occurs with בְּ *instrumentale*, the explanation given above must nevertheless be accepted.

person ; cf. e. g. Gn 40²² (41¹³), 41¹⁴, 43³⁴ (*and he commanded to set before them,* &c.) ; 46²⁹, 2 S 12⁹.

o 2. Supposed ellipses of a definite subject are due either to a misunderstanding of the passage, or to a corruption of the text. Thus in I S 24¹¹ after וְתְחָם either עֵינִי has dropped out (through confusion with עָלֶיךָ) or we should read with the LXX וָאֹחֵם. In 2 S 13³⁹ (וַתְּכַל דָּוִד) the text is obviously corrupt.

p 3. In poetic (or prophetic) language[1] there sometimes occurs (supposing the text to be correct) a more or less abrupt transition from one person to another. Thus from the 2nd to the 3rd (i. e. from an address to a statement), Gn 49⁴ (?), Is 31⁶ (?), 42²⁰, 52¹⁴, 61⁷, Mal 2¹⁵ (where, however, for יָבוֹד we should undoubtedly read תְּבֹּד) ; ψ 22⁹ [and regularly after a vocative, Is 22¹⁶, 47⁸, 48¹, 54¹·¹¹, Jer 22¹⁶, 49⁴·¹⁶, Am 5⁶ᶠ·, Mic 1² (= I K 22²⁸), Mal 3⁹, 2 K 9³¹ ; and after הוּ Is 5⁸, 29¹⁵, Jer 22¹³]. From the 3rd to the 2nd pers., Dt 32¹⁵, Is 1²⁹ (but read probably חֶמְדַּתְכֶם for חֲמַדְתֶּם, which has caused the insertion of אֲשֶׁר), 5⁸, Jer 29¹⁹, Jb 16⁷, cf. also Dt 32¹⁷. From the 1st to the 3rd pers., La 3¹ (in a relative clause). In Jb 13²⁸ the 3rd pers. וְהוּא is probably employed δεικτικῶς for the 1st.

§ 145. *Agreement between the Members of a Sentence, especially between Subject and Predicate, in respect of Gender and Number.*

a 1. As in other languages, so also in Hebrew, the predicate in general conforms to the subject in gender and number (even when it is a pronoun, e. g. זֹאת בְּרִיתִי *this is my covenant,* Gn 17¹⁰). There are, however, numerous exceptions to this fundamental rule. These are due partly to the *constructio ad sensum* (where attention is paid to the meaning rather than to the grammatical form ; see *b–l* below), partly to the position of the predicate (regarded as being without gender) *before* the subject.

b 2. Singular nouns which include in themselves a collective idea (§ 123 *a*), or which occasionally have a collective sense (§ 123 *b*), may readily, in accordance with their meaning, be construed with the plural of the predicate, whether it precedes or follows. This is also the case, when the collective is itself feminine but represents, exclusively or at least generally, masculine persons.

Examples :—

c (*a*) Of collectives proper (cf. § 132 *g*) : (α) with the predicate preceding, Gn 30³⁸ תֵּבֹאןָ הַצֹּאן (cf. 30³⁹, 31⁸ and 33¹³) ; Ju 1²²ᶠ· בֵּית representing persons belonging to the tribe ; Mi 4³ גּוֹי ; 2 K 25⁵ חַיִל *army* ; Pr 11²⁶ לְאֹם

---

[1] In prose, Lv 2⁸ ; but וְהִקְרִיבָה here is hardly the original reading. Different from this is Gn 26⁷, where there is a transition to direct narration.

the people; Nu 10³ כָּל־הָעֵדָה *all the congregation* (cf. 1 K 8⁵); 1 K 1⁴⁰, Is 9⁸, 25³, Am 1⁵ עַם; 1 S 17⁴⁷, Ezr 10¹² קָהָל *assembly*. Cf. also the construction of national names, as אֲרָם (§ 122 i), e.g. 1 K 20²⁰ וַיָּנֻסוּ אֲרָם *and the Syrians fled*; 1 S 4⁵.—(β) with the predicate following, 1 K 8⁵ צֹאן וּבָקָר *sheep and oxen*, construed with the plural in the following relative clause; Jb 1¹⁴ הַבָּקָר הָיוּ חֹרְשׁוֹת *the cattle* (cows) *were ploughing*; 2 S 3¹ and 1 Ch 10⁶ בַּיִת =*family* (in 1 S 6¹³ בֵּית שֶׁמֶשׁ on the analogy of names of countries, is used for *the inhabitants of Bethshemesh*); Ho 11⁷, Ezr 4⁴ עַם; ψ 68¹¹ חַיָּה *herd* [if correct, figuratively for *people*]; Is 26¹⁹ נְבֵלָה *dead bodies*; Is 27¹¹ קָצִיר *boughs*; 1 S 4¹ יִשְׂרָאֵל, preceded by a predicate in the singular.

(b) Of substantives occasionally used as collectives: (a) with the predicate *d* preceding, Gn 34²⁴ זָכָר; Ju 9⁵⁵, 15¹⁰ אִישׁ; Is 16⁴ רֹמֵס *the treader down.*—(β) with the predicate following, Jb 8¹⁹ אַחֵר =*others*; Ez 28³ סָתוּם *a secret*; [ψ 9⁷, and even after זֶה Jb 19¹⁹.]

(c) Of feminines as collective terms denoting masculine persons: (a) with *e* the predicate preceding, 1 S 17⁴⁶ וְיֵדְעוּ כָּל־הָאָרֶץ *that all the earth may know*, i.e. all the inhabitants of the earth; cf. Dt 9²⁸, ψ 66¹, 96¹.⁹, &c.; Am 1⁸ שְׁאֵרִית *remnant*; (ψ 33⁸ כָּל־הָאָרֶץ).—(β) with the predicate following, Gn 41⁵⁷, 2 S.15²³, 1 K 10²⁴, Gn 48⁶ מוֹלֶדֶת *issue*; 1 S 2³³ כָּל־מַרְבִּית *all the increase*; Jb 30¹² פִּרְחַח *rabble*. In Hag 2⁷ read חֶמְדַת with the LXX.

Examples of predicates in the singular, notwithstanding the collective *f* meaning of the subject, occur in Gn 35¹¹, Ex 10²⁴, 14¹⁰, Dt 1³⁹, &c.—For examples of bold enallage of the number in noun-clauses with a substantival predicate, see above, § 141 c.

Rem. Not infrequently the construction begins in the singular (especially *g* when the predicate precedes; see o below), but is carried on, after the collective subject has been mentioned, in the plural; e.g. Ex 1²⁰ וַיִּרֶב הָעָם וַיַּעַצְמוּ מְאֹד *and the people multiplied, and waxed very mighty*; 33⁴.

3. On the other hand, plurals which have a singular meaning *h* (§ 124 a) are frequently construed with the singular, especially the *pluralis excellentiae* or *maiestatis* (§ 124 g–i; on the union of these plurals with attributes, cf. § 132 h), as אֱלֹהִים Gn 1¹.³, &c. (but see the Rem.), אֲדֹנִים *master*, Ex 21⁴ בְּעָלִים *master, owner*, Ex 21²⁹; cf., moreover, פָּנִים with the singular, Jb 16¹⁶ *K*ᵉth., רַחֲמִים Pr 12¹⁰.—So feminine forms with a masculine meaning are construed with a masculine predicate, e.g. Ec 12⁹ הָיָה קֹהֶלֶת חָכָם *the preacher was wise*.

Rem. The construction of אֱלֹהִים *God* with the plural of the predicate may *i* be explained (apart of course from such passages as 1 K 19², 20¹⁰, where the speakers are heathen, and אֱלֹהִים may, therefore, be a numerical plural) partly as an acquiescence in a polytheistic form of expression, partly from the peculiar usage of one of the early documents of the Hexateuch, called *E* by Wellhausen, &c., *B* by Dillmann; cf. his commentary on Numbers—Joshua, p. 618, and above, § 124 g, note 2. So Gn 20¹³ (but in conversation with a heathen); 31⁵³, 35⁷, cf. also Jos 24¹⁹. That this construction was afterwards studiously avoided from fear of misconception, is shown by such passages as Neh 9¹⁸ compared with Ex 32⁴.⁸, and 1 Ch 17²¹ compared with 2 S 7²³. Cf. Strack's excursus on Gen 20¹³ in *Die Genesis*, Munich, 1905, p. 77.

k 4. Plurals of names of animals or things, and of abstracts, whether they be masculine or feminine, are frequently construed with the feminine singular of the verbal predicate [1] (on the collective sense of the feminine form, cf. § 122 *s*); thus Jo 1²⁰ בַּהֲמוֹת שָׂדֶה תַּעֲרֹג *the beasts of the field long*; Jer 12⁴ (where the predicate precedes), cf. also Jb 12⁷; names of things with the predicate preceding occur in 2 S 24¹³, Is 34¹³, Jer 4¹⁴, 51²⁹, ψ 18³⁵, 37³¹, 73² *Keth.*, 103⁵ (unless הִמְחַדֵּשׁ is to be read for תִּתְחַדֵּשׁ), Jb 14¹⁹, 27²⁰; with the predicate following, Gn 49²² (בָּנוֹת=*branches*); Dt 21⁷, 1 S 4¹⁵ (וְעֵינָיו קָמָה),[2] 2 S 10⁹, Is 59¹², Jer 2¹⁵ *Keth.*, 48⁴¹, 49²⁴, Pr 15²², 20¹⁸, Jb 41¹⁰.[3]

l 5. Moreover, the plural of persons (especially in the participle) is sometimes construed with the singular of the predicate, when instead of the whole class of individuals, each severally is to be represented as affected by the statement. Undoubted examples of this *distributive* singular are Gn 27²⁹ (Nu 24⁹) אֹרְרֶיךָ אָרוּר וּמְבָרְכֶיךָ בָּרוּךְ *those that curse thee, cursed be* every one of them, *and those that bless thee, blessed be* every one of them; Ex 31¹⁴, Lv 17¹¹ and 19⁸ (in both places the Samaritan has אֹכְלוֹ); Is 3¹² unless נְשָׁיו is to be regarded as a *pluralis maiestatis* according to § 124 *k*; Pr 3¹⁸·³⁵ (?), 18²¹ (?), 21²⁷ᵇ, 27¹⁶, 28¹ᵇ, 28¹⁶ *Keth.*

m Rem. Analogous to the examples above mentioned is the somewhat frequent[4] use of suffixes in the singular (distributively) referring to plurals; cf. the *verbal*-suffixes in Dt 21¹⁰, 28⁴⁸, Am 6¹⁰; and the *noun*-suffixes in Is 2⁸, 30²², Jer 31¹⁴, Ho 4⁸ (but since וֹ follows, נַפְשׁוֹ is undoubtedly a dittography for נֶפֶשׁ), Zc 14¹², ψ 5¹⁰ (where, however, פִּימוֹ is clearly to be read with all the early versions); 62⁵, 141¹⁰ (?), Jb 38³², Ec 10¹⁵ [but LXX הַכְּסִיל]; finally, the suffixes with prepositions in Is 2²⁰ אֲשֶׁר־עָשׂוּ־לוֹ *which they made* each one *for himself* (according to others, *which they (the makers) made for him*); 5²⁶, 8²⁰, Jb 24⁵, in each case לוֹ; in Gn 2¹⁹ לוֹ refers to the collectives חַיָּה and עוֹף; cf. further, Jos 24⁷, Is 5²³ מִמֶּנּוּ after צַדִּיקִים (but read probably צַדִּיק with the LXX, &c.). Conversely in Mi 1¹¹ עָבְרִי לָכֶם [cf. Jer 13²⁰ *Keth.*], but the text is undoubtedly corrupt.

---

[1] Cf. in Greek the construction τὰ πρόβατα βαίνει; in Attic Greek the plural of the predicate is allowed only when the neuter denotes actual persons, as τὰ ἀνδράποδα ἔλαβον. In Arabic also the *pluralis inhumanus* (i. e. not denoting persons) is regularly construed with the feminine singular of the attribute or predicate, as are all the *plurales fracti* (properly collective forms).

[2] On the possibility of explaining forms like קָמָה as 3rd plural feminine, cf. above, § 44 *m*; but this explanation would not apply to all the cases under this head, cf. Jo 1²⁰, ψ 37³¹, 103⁵.

[3] In Pr 14¹ an abstract plural חָכְמוֹת (to be read thus with 9¹, &c., instead of חַכְמוֹת) is construed with the singular; but cf. § 86 *l*, § 124 *e*, end.

[4] In several of the above examples the text is doubtful, and hence Mayer Lambert (*REJ*. xxiv. 110) rejects the theory of distributive singulars generally. [Cf. Driver, *Jeremiah*, p. 362, on 16⁷.]

6. Subjects in the dual are construed with the plural of the predicate, *n* since verbs, adjectives, and pronouns, according to § 88 *a*, have no dual forms; thus עֵינַיִם, Gn 29¹⁷ וְעֵינֵי לֵאָה רַכּוֹת *and Leah's eyes were dull*; 2 S 24³, Is 30²⁰, Jer 14⁶, Mi 7¹⁰, ψ 18²⁸, 38¹¹ (on the other hand, in 1 S 4¹⁵ the predicate is in the feminine singular *after* the subject, and in Mi 4¹¹ *before* it; on both constructions cf. *k* above); so also אָזְנַיִם *ears*, 2 Ch 6⁴⁰; יָדַיִם *hands*, Is 1¹⁵, Jb 10⁸, 20¹⁰ (in Ex 17¹² even with the plural masculine כְּבֵדִים; cf. *p*); שְׂפָתַיִם *lips*, 1 S 1¹³, Jb 27⁴; שָׁדַיִם *breasts*, Ho 9¹⁴.

7. Variations from the fundamental rule (see above, *a*) very fre- *o* quently occur *when the predicate precedes the subject* (denoting animals or things ¹). The speaker or writer begins with the most simple form of the predicate, the uninflected 3rd singular masculine, and leaves us without indication as to which of the following subjects (and so which gender or number) is to define the predicate thus left temporarily indefinite.² Thus inflexions are omitted in—

(*a*) The verb, with a following singular feminine, Is 2¹⁷ וְשַׁח גַּבְהוּת הָאָדָם *and bowed down shall be the loftiness of man*; 9¹⁸, 14¹¹, 28¹⁸, 47¹¹; 1 S 25²⁷ (see note 1 below); 1 K 8³¹ᵇ, 22³⁶, 2 K 3²⁶, Jer 51⁴⁶, Ec 7⁷; with a following plural masc., Is 13²² וְעָנָה אִיִּים *and there shall cry wolves*, &c.; Ju 13¹⁷ *Keth.*, 20⁴⁶, 1 S 1², 4¹⁰, 2 S 24¹⁵, 1 K 13³³, Jer 51⁴⁸, ψ 124⁵, Est 9²³ (see note 1 below); Gn 1¹⁴ יְהִי מְאֹרֹת *let there be lights*; with a following plural feminine, Dt 32³⁵, 1 K 11³ᵃ, Is 8⁸, Jer 13¹⁸, Mi 2⁶, ψ 57²; before collectives and mixed subjects, e. g. Gn 12¹⁶, 13⁵, 30⁴³, 32⁶, &c.; before a following dual, Is 44¹⁸, ψ 73⁷ (where, however, with the LXX עֵינֵימוֹ should be read).

Rem. 1. The instances in which a preceding predicate appears in the *p* plural masculine before a plural (or collective singular) feminine of persons (Ju 21²¹, 1 K 11³ ᵇ), of animals (Gn 30³⁹ where however צָא may refer specially to male animals) or of things (Lv 26³³, Jer 13¹⁶, Ho 14⁷, ψ 16⁴, Jb 3²⁴, Ct 6⁹), or before a dual (2 S 4¹, Zp 3¹⁶, 2 Ch 15⁷) are to be explained not on the analogy of the examples under *o*, but from a dislike of using the 3rd plur. fem. imperf., for this is the only form concerned in the above examples (cf., however, Na 3¹¹ תְּהִי instead of תְּהִיֶ); cf. the examples of a following predicate in the 3rd plur. masc., instead of the fem., under *t* and *u*, and on an analogous phenomenon in the imperative, see § 110 *k*.

2. As in the case of verbs proper so also the verb הָיָה, when used as a *q* copula, frequently remains uninflected before the subject; cf. Gn 5²³ ᶠᶠ·, 39⁵,

---

¹ Only rarely does an uninflected predicate precede a personal subject, as 1 S 25²⁷ (but הֲבִיאָה should probably be read, as in verse 35); Est 9²³ (before a plur. masc.). Such examples as Jb 42¹⁵ are to be explained according to § 121 *a*.

² In a certain sense this is analogous to the German *es kommt ein Mann, eine Frau*, &c.

Dt 21³ (according to the accents) ; 22²³, Is 18⁵ וּבֹסֵר גֹּמֵל יִהְיֶה נִצָּה *and a ripening grape the flower becometh.*

r (*b*) The adjective in a noun-clause, e. g. ψ 119¹³⁷ יָשָׁר מִשְׁפָּטֶיךָ *upright are thy judgements* ; cf. verse 155.¹—On the other hand, רֹעֶה in רֹעֵה צֹאן עֲבָדֶיךָ *thy servants are shepherds*, Gn 47³, is either an unusual orthography or simply a misspelling for רֹעֵי.

s Rem. 1. As soon as a sentence which begins with an uninflected predicate is carried on after the mention of the subject, the gender and number of the subsequent (co-ordinate) predicates must coincide with those of the subject, e. g. Gn 1¹⁴ וְהָיוּ . . . יְהִי מְאֹרֹת (see *o* above) ; Nu 9⁶, Ez 14¹ ; cf. also Gn 30³⁹ (see *p* above).

t 2. The dislike mentioned in *p* above, of using the feminine form (cf., further, § 144 *a*, with the sections of the Grammar referred to there, and below, under *u*), is exemplified sometimes by the fact that of several predicates only that which stands next to the feminine substantive is inflected as feminine (cf. the treatment of several attributes following a feminine substantive, § 132 *d*) ; thus in Is 14⁹ רָגְזָה, and afterwards עוֹרֵר (but עוֹרֵר is better taken as an infin. abs. = *excitando*, reading הֵקִים for הֵקִים) ; 33⁹ אָבַל אֻמְלְלָה אָרֶץ *mourneth, languisheth the land.* Cf. Jer 4³⁰, Jb 1¹⁹, and the examples (§ 47 *k*) where only the first of several consecutive forms of the 2nd sing. fem. imperf. has the afformative *î*, Is 57⁸, Jer 3⁵, Ez 22⁴, 23³² (תִּהְיֶה after תִּשָׁתִּי) ; on the converse sequence of genders in imperatives, Na 3¹⁵, cf. § 110 *k*.—Of a different kind are instances like Lv 2¹, 5¹, 20⁶, where נֶפֶשׁ *person* (fem.) as the narrative continues, assumes (in agreement with the context) the sense of a masculine person.

u 3. The instances in which the gender or number of the *following* predicate appears to differ from that of the subject are due partly to manifest errors in the text, e. g. Gn 32⁹ read with the Samaritan הָאֶחָד instead of הָאַחַת ; וְהָיָה then follows correctly ; 1 S 2²⁰ read with Wellhausen שָׁאַל, according to 1²⁸, instead of שָׁאַל ; 1 S 16⁴ read וַיֹּאמְרוּ ; Ez 18²⁹ instead of יִתָּכֵן read the plural as in verse 25 ; so also Ez 20³⁸ for יָבוֹא,² and in Jb 6²⁰ for בָּטַח ; in La 5¹⁰ read נִכְמָר, and cf. in general, § 7 *d*, note ; 1 Ch 2⁴⁸ read יָלְדָה ; in Jer 48¹⁵ also the text is certainly corrupt. Other instances are due to special reasons. The anomalies in Is 49¹¹, Ho 14¹, Pr 1¹⁶ (after רַגְלָיו), ψ 11⁴ (after עֵינָיו), 63⁴, Pr 5², 10²¹·³², 18⁶, 26²³, Jb 15⁶ (all after שְׂפָתַיִם), Pr 3² (after מִצְוֹתַי), ψ 102²⁸, Jb 16²² (after שָׁנוֹת), Dn 11⁴¹ (read וְרִבּוֹת), and perhaps Gn 20¹⁷ are also to be explained (see *p*) from the dislike of the 3rd plur. fem. imperf. ; moreover, in Jer 44¹⁹, Pr 26²³ the plur. masc. even of a participle occurs instead of the plur. fem.—In Gn 31⁸ ᶠ· יִהְיֶה, after a plural subject, is explained as a case of attraction to the following singular predicate.³—In Gn 4⁷ רֹבֵץ

---

¹ This does not include such cases as Jb 24⁷·¹⁰, where עָרוֹם is rather to be explained as an accusative denoting a state, § 118 *n*.

² יָבוֹא probably an error for יָבֹאוּ. The Masora on Lv 11³⁴ reckons fourteen instances of יָבֹא, where we should expect the plural.

³ So also the pronoun הוּא emphatically resuming the subject (see § 141 *h*) is attracted to the predicate in number in Jos 13¹⁴ . . . הוּא נַחֲלָתוֹ אִשֵּׁי יְהוָה *the offerings of the Lord . . . that is his inheritance* ; in number and gender, Lv 25³³ Qᵉrê ; Jer 10³.

is a substantival participle (*a lurker, a coucher*). In Gn 47²⁴ יִהְיֶה remains undefined in gender (masc.), although the noun precedes for the sake of emphasis; so also in Gn 28²², Ex 12⁴⁹, 28⁷·³², Nu 9¹⁴, 15²⁹, Jer 50⁴⁶, Ec 2⁷ (הָיָה לִי as if the sentence began afresh, *and servants born in my house . . . there fell to my lot* this possession also). In Jb 20²⁶ לֹא־נֻפַּח may (unless אֵשׁ is regarded as masculine, § 122 *o*) be taken impersonally, *fire, without its being blown upon.*—In Is 16⁸ and Hb 3¹⁷ the predicate in the singular is explained from the collective character of שְׁדֵמוֹת (see *h* above); on the other hand, the masculine form of the predicate is abnormal in ψ 87³, Pr 2¹⁰, 12²⁵, 29²⁵, Jb 8⁷, 36¹⁸.

§ 146. *Construction of Compound Subjects.*

1. When the subject is composed of a nomen regens (in the construct *a* state) with a following genitive, the predicate sometimes agrees in gender and number not with the nomen regens, but with the genitive, when this represents the principal idea of the compound subject.[1] Thus 1 S 2⁴ קֶשֶׁת גִּבֹּרִים חַתִּים *the bow of the mighty men is broken*, as if it were *the mighty men with their bow are broken*; Ex 26¹², Lv 13⁹, 1 K 1⁴¹ (but the text is clearly very corrupt), 17¹⁶, Is 2¹¹, 21¹⁷, Zc 8¹⁰, Jb 15²⁰, 21²¹, 29¹⁰, 32⁷ (רֹב שָׁנִים equivalent to *many years*); 38²¹; with the predicate preceding, 2 S 10⁹, unless it is to be explained according to § 145 *k*.

Rem. 1. The cases in which קוֹל (*voice, sound*) with a following genitive *b* stands at the beginning of a sentence, apparently in this construction, are really of a different kind. The קוֹל is there to be taken as an exclamation, and the supposed predicate as in apposition to the genitive, e.g. Gn 4¹⁰ *the voice of thy brother's blood, which crieth* (prop. *as one crying*) . . . ! = *hark! thy brother's blood is crying*, &c.; Is 13⁴, 66⁶. In Is 52⁸ an independent verbal-clause follows the exclamation *the voice of thy watchmen!*; in Jer 10²² and Ct 2⁸ an independent noun-clause; in Is 40³ קוֹל קֹרֵא *the voice of one that crieth!* i.e. *hark! there is one crying* is followed immediately by direct speech; in Mi 6⁹ קוֹל *hark!* may be used disconnectedly (cf. the almost adverbial use of קוֹל in § 144 *m*) and יְהֹוָה be taken as the subject to יִקְרָא.

2. When the substantive כֹּל (כָּל־) *entirety* is used in connexion with a *c* genitive as subject of the sentence, the predicate usually agrees in gender and number with the genitive, since כֹּל is equivalent in sense to an attribute (*whole, all*) of the genitive; hence, e.g. with the predicate preceding, Gn 5⁵ וַיִּהְיוּ כָּל־יְמֵי אָדָם *and all the days of Adam were*, &c. (in 5²³, 9²⁹ וַיְהִי; but the Samaritan reads ויהיו here also); Ex 15²⁰; with the predicate following, ψ 150⁶, &c. Exceptions are, e.g. Lv 17¹⁴ (but cf. § 145 *l*), Jos 8²⁵, Is 64¹⁰, Pr 16², Na 3⁷. On the other hand, in such cases as Ex 12¹⁶ the agreement of the

---

[1] Sometimes, however, the attraction of the predicate to the genitive may be merely due to juxtaposition.

predicate with ‫־כָּל‬ is explained from the stress laid upon the latter, ‫כָּל־מְלָאכָה‬ ‫לֹא‬ being equivalent to *the whole of work* (is forbidden).

d **2.** When the subject of the sentence consists of several nouns connected by *wāw copulative*, usually

(*a*) The predicate *following* is put in the plural, e. g. Gn 8²² *seed time and harvest, and cold and heat* . . . *shall not cease* (‫לֹא יִשְׁבֹּתוּ‬); after subjects of different genders it is in the masculine (as the *prior gender*, cf. § 132 *d*), e. g. Gn 18¹¹ ‫אַבְרָהָם וְשָׂרָה זְקֵנִים‬ *Abraham and Sarah were old*; Dt 28³², 1 K 1²¹.

e Rem. Rare exceptions are Pr 27⁹ ‫שֶׁמֶן וּקְטֹרֶת יְשַׂמַּח־לֵב‬ *ointment and perfume rejoice the heart*, where the predicate agrees in gender with the masculine ‫שֶׁמֶן‬ (as in Is 51³ with ‫שָׂשׂוֹן‬); on the other hand, in Ex 21⁴ (where ‫הָאִשָּׁה‬ ‫וִילָדֶיהָ‬ are the subjects) it agrees with ‫הָאִשָּׁה‬ as being the principal person; in the compound sentence, Is 9⁴, it agrees with the feminine subject immediately preceding.[1]

f (*b*) The predicate *preceding* two or more subjects may likewise be used in the plural (Gn 40¹, Jb 3⁵, &c.); not infrequently, however, it agrees in gender and number with the first, as being the subject nearest to it. Thus the predicate is put in the singular masculine before several masculines singular in Gn 9²³, 11²⁹, 21³², 24⁵⁰, 34²⁰, Ju 14⁵; before a masculine and a feminine singular, e. g. Gn 3⁸, 24ʰ⁵ *then said* (‫וַיֹּאמֶר‬) *her brother and her mother*; 33⁷; before a masculine singular and a plural, e. g. Gn 7⁷ ‫וַיָּבֹא נֹחַ וּבָנָיו‬ *and Noah went in, and his sons*, &c.; Gn 8¹⁸ (where feminines plural also follow); 44¹⁴, Ex 15¹, 2 S 5²¹; before collectives feminine and masculine, 2 S 12².

g Similarly, the feminine singular occurs before several feminines singular, e. g. Gn 31¹⁴ ‫וַתַּעַן רָחֵל וְלֵאָה‬ *then answered Rachel and Leah*; before a feminine singular and a feminine plural, e. g. Gn 24⁶¹; before a feminine singular and a masculine singular, Nu 12¹ ‫וַתְּדַבֵּר מִרְיָם‬ ‫וְאַהֲרֹן‬ *then spake Miriam and Aaron*; Ju 5¹; before a feminine singular and a masculine plural, e. g. Gn 33⁷ (cf., on the other hand, ψ 75⁴ ‫נְמֹגִים אֶרֶץ וְכָל־יֹשְׁבֶיהָ‬ *dissolved are the earth and all the inhabitants thereof*). The plural feminine occurs before a plural feminine and a plural masculine in Am 8¹³.—In Jer 44²⁵ for ‫אַתֶּם וּנְשֵׁיכֶם‬ read ‫אַתֶּם‬ ‫הַנָּשִׁים‬ with the LXX, and cf. verse 19.

h (*c*) When other predicates follow after the subjects have been mentioned, they are necessarily put in the plural; cf. Gn 21³², 24⁶¹, 31¹⁴, 33⁷, &c., and § 145 *s*.

---

[1] Similarly with a mixed object, Gn 33² *he put* . . . *Leah and her children after*; ‫אַחֲרֹנִים‬ agrees with the masculine immediately preceding. ‫אַחֲרֹנִים‬

§ 147. *Incomplete Sentences.*

1. Sentences are called *incomplete*, in which either the subject or *a*
the predicate or both must in some way be supplied from the context.[1]
Besides the instances enumerated in § 116 *s* (omission of the personal
pronoun when subject of a participial clause) and the periphrases for
negative attributes § 152 *u*, this description includes certain (noun-)
clauses introduced by הִנֵּה (see *b* below), and also a number of exclamations of the most varied kinds (see *c* below).

Rem. Incomplete sentences are very common in Chronicles, but are
mostly due to the bad condition of the text; cf. Driver, *Introd.*[6], p. 537,
no. 27. Thus in 2 Ch 11[22 b] restore חָשַׁב, with the LXX, before לְהַמְלִיכוֹ; in
35[21] add בָּאתִי, with the LXX, after הַיּוֹם and read פְּרָת for בֵּית; in 2 Ch 19[6]
and 28[21] the pronoun הוּא is wanted as subject, and in 30[9] the predicate
יִהְיֶה; cf. also the unusual expressions in 1 Ch 9[33] (Ezr 3[3]), 1 Ch 15[13] (*ye were
not present?*), 2 Ch 15[3], 16[10.12 (bis)], 18[3].

2. The demonstrative particle הֵן, הִנֵּה *en, ecce* may be used either *b*
absolutely (as a kind of interjection, cf. § 105 *b*) before complete noun-
or verbal-clauses, e. g. Gn 28[15] וְהִנֵּה אָנֹכִי עִמָּךְ *and, behold! I am with
thee*; 37[7], 48[21], Ex 3[13], 34[10], or may take the pronoun, which would
be the natural subject of a noun-clause, in the form of a suffix, see
§ 100 *o*. Whether these suffixes are to be regarded as in the accusative
has been shown to be doubtful in § 100 *p*. However, in the case of
הִנֵּה the analogy of the corresponding Arabic demonstrative particle
'inna (followed by an accusative of the noun) is significant.[2] If הִנֵּה
with a suffix and a following adjective or participle (see the examples
in § 116 *p* and *q*) forms a noun-clause, the subject proper, to which
הִנֵּה with the suffix refers, must, strictly speaking, be supplied again
before the predicate.[3] Sometimes, however, the pronoun referring to
the subject is wanting, and the simple הִנֵּה takes the place of the

---

[1] This does not apply to such cases as Gn 33[8], where an infinitive with
לְ appears alone in answer to a question, the substance of the question being
presupposed as a main clause; cf. also Gn 26[7], where הִיא must again be
supplied after אִשְׁתִּי.

[2] On the same analogy any substantive following הִנֵּה would have to be
regarded as originally a virtual accusative. Since, however, Hebrew does
not possess case-terminations (as the Arabic does, and uses the accusative
necessarily after *'inna*), it is very doubtful whether, and how far, substantives
following הִנֵּה were felt to be accusatives.

[3] That these are real noun-clauses and that the participle (e.g. מֵת in
הִנְּךָ מֵת Gn 20[8]) cannot be taken as a second accusative (as it were *ecce
te moriturum*), is also shown by the analogy of Arabic, where after *'inna* with
an accusative the predicate is expressly in the *nominative*.

subject and copula (as Gn 18⁹ הִנֵּה בָאֹהֶל *behold* she is *in the tent*; 42²⁸), or there is no indication whatever of the predicate, so that the sentence is limited to הִנֵּה with the suffix, as in the frequent use of הִנְנִי, הִנֵּנִי *here am I*, in answer to an address. Elsewhere a substantive follows הִנֵּה (or הֶן Gn 11⁶, Jb 31³⁵), and הִנֵּה then includes the meaning of a demonstrative pronoun and the copula, e. g. Gn 22⁷ הִנֵּה הָאֵשׁ וְהָעֵצִים *here is the fire and the wood*, &c.; 12¹⁹ *behold* thou hast *thy wife!* Ex 24⁸; with reference to the past, e. g. Am 7¹ וְהִנֵּה לֶקֶשׁ וג׳ *and lo, it was the latter growth*, &c. By a very pregnant construction the simple הִנֵּה is used as the equivalent of a sentence in Jb 9¹⁹, *lo, here am I!*

C   3. Examples of exclamations (threatening, complaining, triumphing, especially warlike or seditious) in which, owing to the excitement of the speaker, some indispensable member of the sentence is suppressed, are—(*a*) with suppression of the predicate (which has frequently to be supplied in the form of a jussive), e.g. Ju 7²⁰ *a sword for the Lord and for Gideon!* (verse 18 without חֶרֶב); 2 S 20¹ and 2 Ch 10¹⁶ (cf. also 1 K 22³⁶) *every man to his tents, O Israel!* (i. e. let every man go to or remain in his tent); without אִישׁ 1 K 12¹⁶; moreover, Is 1²³, 13⁴ (on the exclamatory קוֹל equivalent to *hark!* cf. § 146 *b*); 28¹⁰, 29¹⁶ (הַפְכְּכֶם *O your perversity!* i. e. how great it is!); Jer 49¹⁶ (if תִּפְלַצְתְּךָ be equivalent to *terror be upon thee!*); Jo 4¹⁴, Mal 1¹³ (הִנֵּה מַתְּלָאָה *behold what a weariness!*); Jb 22²⁹; perhaps also Gn 49⁴ פַּחַז כַּמַּיִם *a bubbling over as water* (sc. happened), unless it is better to supply a subject אַתָּה (*thou wast*).—(*b*) With suppression of the subject, Ju 4²⁰, cf. § 152 *k*; Jb 15²³ אַיֵּה *where* sc. is bread?—(*c*) With suppression of both subject and predicate, Ju 7¹⁸ (see above); 1 K 12¹⁶ (see above); 2 K 9²⁷ גַּם אֹתוֹ *him also!* explained immediately afterwards by הַכֻּהוּ *smite him!* Ho 5⁸ *after thee, Benjamin!* sc. is the enemy (differently in Ju 5¹⁴); ψ 6⁴, 90¹³, Hb 2⁶ עַד־מָתַי; ψ 74⁹ עַד־מָה.—On וְלֹא *and if not* (unless וְלוּ is to be read), 2 S 13²⁶, 2 K 5¹⁷, see § 159 *dd*.

D   Rem. 1. To the class of incomplete sentences naturally belong exclamations introduced by interjections אֲהָהּ, אוֹי, הוֹי, הַס;¹ cf. § 105. After the first two the object of the *threat* or *imprecation* follows regularly with לְ (cf. *vae tibi*) or אֶל־ or עַל־, e. g. אוֹי לָנוּ *woe unto us!* 1 S 4⁸, Is 6⁵; cf. also אֲהָהּ לַיּוֹם *alas for the day!* Jo 1¹⁵; on the other hand, the object of *commiseration* (after הוֹי) follows mostly in the vocative, or rather in the accusative of exclamation (cf. *vae te* in Plautus); so in lamentation for the dead, הוֹי אָחִי *alas, my brother!* 1 K 13³⁰,

---

¹ We do not consider here the cases in which these interjections (e. g. הַס Ju 3¹⁹, Am 6 ⁹) stand quite disconnectedly (so always אָח and הֶאָח).

Jer 22[18] ; הוֹי גּוֹי חֹטֵא *ah, sinful nation!* Is 1[4], 5[8.11.18.20.22] (*ah! they that . . .*).—
For הַס cf. Hb 2[20], Zp 1[7], Zc 2[17].

2. Finally, instances of noun-clauses shortened in an unusual manner *e*
may perhaps occur in יְדֵיהֶם and רַגְלֵיהֶם ψ 115[7], for יָדַיִם לָהֶם *they have hands,*
&c.; cf. verses 5 and 6 פֶּה־לָהֶם, &c. Perhaps also וּפִילַגְשׁוֹ Gn 22[24], and
וְחָלְיוֹ Ec 5[16] are to be regarded in the same way, but hardly נְבִיאֵכֶם Nu 12[6] ;
cf. § 128 *d* above.

II. Special Kinds of Sentences.

§ 148. *Exclamations.*

The originally interrogative מָה is used to introduce exclamations *a*
of wonder or indignation=*O how!* or ridicule, *why! how!* sometimes
strengthened by זֶה or זֹאת according to § 136 *c*.—Astonishment or
indignation at something which has happened is introduced by אֵיךְ
how (likewise originally interrogative) with the perfect; the indignant
refusal of a demand by אֵיךְ (but also by מָה Jb 31[1]) with the imperfect;
an exclamation of lamentation by אֵיכָה, less frequently אֵיךְ *how!*; in
Jo 1[18] by מָה.

Examples :—
מָה (or מַה־ with a following *Dageš*, see § 37) expressing admiration (or *b*
astonishment) before verbal-clauses, e.g. Gn 27[20] (מַה־זֶּה) ; 38[29], Nu 24[5] (*how
goodly are . . .!*); ψ 21[2], Ct 7[2]; before the predicate of noun-clauses, e.g.
Gn 28[17], ψ 8[2]; mockingly before the verb, 2 S 6[20] (*how glorious was . . .!*);
Jer 22[23], Jb 26[2 f.] ; indignantly, Gn 3[13] (מַה־זֹּאת) ; 4[10], 20[9], 31[26] *what hast thou
done!*
אֵיךְ with the perfect, e.g. Gn 26[9], ψ 73[19] ; in scornful exclamation, Is 14[4.12] ;
in a lament (usually אֵיכָה), 2 S 1[25.27]; with the imperfect, in a reproachful
question, Gn 39[9], 44[8], ψ 11[1], 137[4] ; in a mocking imitation of lament, Mi 2[4].
אֵיכָה with the perfect, Is 1[21], La 1[1] ; with the imperfect, La 2[1], 4[1].

Rem. 1. The close relation between a question and an exclamation appears *c*
also in the interrogative personal pronoun מִי in such cases as Mi 7[18] מִי־אֵל כָּמוֹךָ
who is a God like unto thee? and so in general in *rhetorical* questions as the
expression of a forcible denial; similarly in the use of an interrogative
sentence to express a wish, see §§ 150 *d*, 151 *a*.
2. A weaker form of exclamation is sometimes produced by the insertion *d*
of a corroborative כִּי *verily, surely,* before the predicate, Gn 18[20]; cf. 33[11],
Is 7[9], and the analogous cases in the apodoses of conditional sentences,
§ 159 *ee*.

§ 149. *Sentences which express an Oath or Asseveration.*

The particle אִם, in the sense of *certainly not,* and אִם־לֹא (rarely כִּי *a*
Gn 22[16]) in the sense of *certainly,* are used to introduce promises or
threats confirmed by an oath (especially after such formulae as חַי־יְהוָה,

בִּי נִשְׁבַּעְתִּי ,חַי אָנִי, חֵי־נַפְשֶׁך¹, &c., as well as after imprecations, see below), and also simple asseverations, e.g. 1 S 2³⁰, 2 S 20²⁰, Jb 27⁵ after לִ חָלִילָה *far be it from me*, but mostly without any introductory formula.

b Rem. No certain explanation of these particles has yet been given. According to the usual view, phrases expressing an oath depend on the suppression of an imprecation upon oneself, e.g. *the Lord do so unto me, if I do it* equivalent to *I certainly will not do it*; then naturally אִם־לֹא properly *if I do it not* equivalent to *I certainly will do it*. It is indeed difficult to understand such self-imprecations, put into the mouth of God, as in Dt 1³⁴ f·, Is 14²⁴, 22¹⁴, Jer 22⁶, Ez 3⁶, 35⁶, ψ 95¹¹. Possibly, however, the consciousness of the real meaning of the formula was lost at an early period, and אִם־לֹא simply came to express *verily*, אִם *verily not*.—In 1 S 25²², where, instead of a self-imprecation, a curse is pronounced upon others, read לְדָוִד with the LXX for לְאֹיְבֵי דָוִד.

Examples :—

c (*a*) The particles אִם and אִם־לֹא used after the utterance of an oath and after formulae of swearing, e.g. 2 S 11¹¹ (see note on *a*) חַי־יְהֹוָה וְחֵי נַפְשֶׁךָ אִם־אֶעֱשֶׂה אֶת־הַדָּבָר הַזֶּה *as the Lord liveth, and as thy soul liveth, I will not do this thing*; 1 S 14⁴⁵, 2 K 5¹⁶ (after חַי יְהֹוָה; in 1 S 14³⁹ and 29⁶ חי־ is followed by a simple כִּי); Ct 2⁷, 3⁵ (after הִשְׁבַּעְתִּי *I adjure you*); cf. also Gn 14²³, 21²³, 26²⁹; spoken by God, Dt 1³⁴ f·, 1 S 3¹⁴, ψ 95¹¹; similarly אִם־לֹא Gn 24³⁷ f· ; spoken by God, Is 14²⁴, where אִם־לֹא occurs first with the perfect in the sense of a prophetic perfect, § 106 *n*, but in the parallel clause with the imperfect ; Jer 22⁶; in Gn 31⁵² the negative oath introduced by אִם־אָנִי, אִם־אַתָּה is immediately afterwards continued by לֹא with the imperfect.— In Ez 34¹⁰ the threat introduced in verse 8 by אִם־לֹא is, after a long parenthesis, resumed with הִנְנִי.

d (*b*) אִם and אִם־לֹא after formulae of cursing, e.g. 1 S 3¹⁷ כֹּה יַעֲשֶׂה־לְּךָ אֱלֹהִים וְכֹה יוֹסִיף אִם־תְּכַחֵד מִמֶּנִּי דָּבָר וג' *God do so to thee, and more also !* *thou shalt not hide anything from me*, &c. ; cf. 1 S 25²². On the other hand, כִּי follows the curse, in 1 S 14⁴⁴, 1 K 2²³ (here with a perfect), and in 2 S 3³⁵ כִּי אִם; in 1 S 25³⁴ the preceding כִּי is repeated before אִם; in 1 S 20¹³ the purport of the asseveration is repeated (after the insertion of a conditional sentence) in the perfect consecutive.

e (*c*) אִם and אִם־לֹא as simple particles of asseveration, e.g. Ju 5⁸ מָגֵן אִם־יֵרָאֶה וָרֹמַח וג' *truly, there was not a shield and spear seen*, &c. ; Is 22¹⁴, Jb 6²⁸ (in the middle of the sentence) ; after חָלִילָה חָלִילָה *absit*, 2 S 20²⁰ ; אִם־לֹא with the imperf. Is 5⁹, with the perfect, Jb 22²⁰.

---

¹ Also combined חַי־יְהֹוָה וְחֵי נַפְשֶׁךָ 1 S 20⁸, 25²⁶ *as the Lord liveth, and as thy soul* (i.e. *thou*) *liveth !* (Also in 2 S 11¹¹ read חַי־יהוה instead of the impossible חֵיך). On חַי and חֵי in these noun-clauses (prop. *living is the Lord*, &c.), cf. § 93 *aa*, note.

§ 150. *Interrogative Sentences.*

H. G. Mitchell, 'The omission of the interrogative particle,' in *Old Test. and Sem. Studies in memory of W. R. Harper*, Chicago, 1907, i, 113 ff.

1. A question need not necessarily be introduced by a special *a* interrogative pronoun or adverb. Frequently [1] the natural emphasis upon the words is of itself sufficient to indicate an interrogative sentence as such; cf. Gn 27²⁴ אַתָּה זֶה בְּנִי עֵשָׂו *thou art my son Esau ?* (but cf. note 1 below) Gn 18¹², Ex 33¹⁴ (פָּנַי י׳); 1 S 11¹² שָׁאוּל יִמְלֹךְ עָלֵינוּ *Saul shall reign over us ?* 1 S 22⁷, 2 S 16¹⁷, 18²⁹ שָׁלוֹם לַנַּעַר *is it well with the young man ?* (but cf. note 1); 1 S 16⁴, 1 K 1²⁴, Is 28²⁸, Ho 4¹⁶, Zc 8⁶ (*should it also be marvellous in mine eyes ?*); Pr 5¹⁶. So especially, when the interrogative clause is connected with a preceding sentence by וְ, e.g. Jn 4¹¹ וַאֲנִי לֹא אָחוּס *and I should not have pity ?* Ex 8²² *will they not stone us ?* Ju 11²³, 14¹⁶, 1 S 20⁹, 24²⁰, 25¹¹, 2 S 11¹¹, 15²⁰, Is 37¹¹, 44¹⁹ᵇ, Jer 25²⁹, 45⁵, 49¹², Ez 20³¹, Jb 2¹⁰, 10⁹; or when (as in some of the examples just given) it is negative (with לֹא for הֲלֹא *nonne ?*), 2 K 5²⁶ (but cf. note 1), La 3³³. [2]

Rem. The statement formerly made here that the interrogative particle is *b* omitted especially before gutturals, cannot be maintained in view of Mitchell's statistics (op. cit. p. 123 f.). The supposed considerations of euphony are quite disproved by the 118 cases in which הַ or הֲ occurs before a guttural.

2. As a rule, however, the simple question is introduced by *He c* interrogative הֲ (הַ; as to its form, cf. § 100 *k–n*), *ne ? num ?* the disjunctive question by הֲ (*num ? utrum ?*) in the first clause, and אִם [3] (also וְאִם, less frequently אוֹ) *an ?* in the second, e.g. 1 K 22¹⁵ הֲנֵלֵךְ . . .

---

[1] Mitchell (op. cit.) restricts the number of instances to 39, of which he attributes 12 (or 17) to corruption of the text. Thus in Gn 27²⁴ he would read, with the Samaritan, הַאַתָּה as in verse 21, in 1 S 16⁴ הֲשָׁלֹם, in 2 S 18²⁹ הֲשָׁלוֹם as in verse 32; similarly he would read the interrogative particle in 2 K 5²⁶, Ez 11³, Jb 40²⁵, 41¹; 1 S 30⁸, 2 K 9¹⁹, Ez 11¹³, 17⁹.

[2] But in 1 S 27¹⁰ instead of אַל־ (which according to the usual explanation would expect a negative answer) read either עַל־מִי (אֶל־מִי) with the LXX, or better, אָן (אָנָה) *whither?* with the Targum. In 2 S 23⁵ read חֶפְצִי הֲלֹא with Wellhausen.

[3] Quite exceptional is the use of the particle אַיִן *num?* (common in Aramaic) in 1 S 21⁹ וְאִין יֶשׁ־פֹּה *num est hic?* The text is, however, undoubtedly corrupt; according to Wellhausen, *Text der Bücher Sam.*, the LXX express the reading רְאֵה הֲיֵשׁ; but cf. the full discussion of the passage by König, *ZAW.* xviii. 239 ff.—The above does not apply to interrogative sentences introduced by interrogative pronouns (§ 37) or by the interrogatives compounded with מָה *what?* such as בַּמֶּה *how many?* לָמָּה *why?* (see § 102 *k*), מַדּוּעַ *why?* (§ 99 *e*), or by אַיֵּה *where?* אֵיךְ, אֵיכָה *how?* (§ 148), &c. On the transformation of

נֶחְדָּֽל ¹ אִם *shall we go . . . or shall we forbear ?* Cf. also אָן *where ?*
whither ? אָ֫נָה *whither,* and J. Barth, *Sprachwiss. Untersuchungen,*
i. 13 ff.

d　The particular uses are as follows :—

(*a*) The particle הֲ stands primarily before the simple question, when the
questioner is wholly uncertain as to the answer to be expected, and may be
used either before noun-clauses, e. g. Gn 43⁷ הַעוֹד אֲבִיכֶם חַי הֲיֵשׁ לָכֶם אָח
is your father yet alive? have ye another *brother?* for שׁ הֲיֵשׁ cf. Gn 24¹³, 1 S 9¹¹ ;
for הֲכִי *is it that?* Jb 6²² ; for יֵשׁ־ הֲכִי יֵשׁ *is there yet?* 2 S 9¹ (but in 2 S 23¹⁹ for
הֲכִי read הֻנּוּ with 1 Ch 11²⁵) ; for הַאֵין *is there not?* 1 K 22⁷, &c. ; or before
verbal-clauses, e. g. Jb 2³ *hast thou considered* (הֲשַׂ֫מְתָּ לִבְּךָ) *my servant Job?*
In other cases הֲ (= *num ?*) is used before questions, to which, from their tone
and contents, a negative answer is expected, e. g. Jb 14¹⁴ *if a man die,* הֲיִחְיֶה
shall he indeed *live* again ? Sometimes a question is so used only as a rhetorical
form instead of a negative assertion, or of a surprised or indignant refusal,²
e. g. 2 S 7⁵ הַאַתָּה תִּבְנֶה־לִּי בַ֫יִת *shalt thou build me an house?* (in the parallel
passage 1 Ch 17⁴ וְגֹ לֹא אַתָּה *thou shalt not,* &c.) ; Gn 4⁹ הֲשֹׁמֵר אָחִי אָנֹכִי *am I my
brother's keeper?* cf. 2 K 5⁷, and the two passages where הֲ is used before the
infinitive (*constr.* Jb 34¹⁸, *absol.* Jb 40² ; on both, see § 113 *ee,* with the note).
—On the other hand, in 1 K 16³¹ for הֲנָקֵל (after וַיְהִי) read הֲנָקֵל.

e　Rem. 1. A few passages deserve special mention, in which the use of the
interrogative is altogether different from our idiom, since it serves merely to
express the conviction that the contents of the statement are well known
to the hearer, and are unconditionally admitted by him. Thus, Gn 3¹¹ *surely
thou hast eaten* ; Gn 27³⁶ הֲכִי קָרָא prop. *is it so that one names ?* &c., i. e. *of a truth
he is rightly named Jacob* ; Gn 29¹⁵ *verily thou art my brother* ; Dt 11³⁰, Ju 4⁶,
1 S 2²⁷ *I did indeed,* &c. ; 20³⁷, 1 K 22³ *ye know surely . . .* ; Mi 3¹, Jb 20⁴.—
In 1 S 23¹⁹ (cf. ψ 54²) a surprising communication is introduced in this way
(by הֲלֹא) in order to show it to be absolutely true, and in Am 9⁷ a concession
is expressed by הֲלוֹא *I have, it is true,* &c. Finally, we may include the
formula of quotation הֲלֹא הִיא כְתוּבָה Jos 10¹³ or הֲלֹא־הֵם כְּתֻבִים equivalent
to *surely it is, they are* written (the latter in 1 K 11⁴¹, 14²⁹, and very often
elsewhere in the books of Kings and Chronicles), synonymous with the
simple formula of assertion הִנֵּה כְתוּבָה 2 S 1¹⁸, and הִנָּם כְּתוּבִים 1 K 14¹⁹,
2 K 15¹¹, 2 Ch 27⁷, 32³².

Of very frequent occurrence also are questions introduced by לָ֫מָּה, which
really contain an affirmation and are used to state the reason for a request or
warning, e. g. 2 S 2²² *turn thee aside . . . wherefore should I smite thee to the ground ?*
i. e. *otherwise I will* (or *must*) *smite,* &c. ; cf. 1 S 19¹⁷, and Driver on the passage ;
2 Ch 25¹⁶ ; also Gn 27⁴⁵, Ex 32¹² (Jo 2¹⁷, ψ 79¹⁰, 115²)) ; Ct 1⁷, Ec 5⁵, 7¹⁷, Dn 1¹⁰.

---

pronouns and adverbs into interrogative words by means of a prefixed אֵי, see
the Lexicon.

¹ On the use of the *imperfect* in deliberative questions, see § 107 *t* ; on the
perfectum confidentiae in interrogative sentences, see § 106 *n.*

² Analogous to this is the use of the interrogative מָה in the sense of a
reproachful remonstrance instead of a prohibition, as Ct 8⁴ מַה־תָּעִ֫ירוּ *why
should ye stir up?* i. e. *pray, stir not up* ; cf. also Jb 31¹ ; see above, § 148.

2. The rare cases in which a *simple* question is introduced by אִם (as some- *f* times in Latin by *an? is it?*) are really due to the suppression of the first member of a double question; thus 1 K 1²⁷, Is 29¹⁶, Jb 6¹², 39¹³.

(*b*) Disjunctive questions are, as a rule, introduced by הַ—אִם (*utrum—an?*) *g* or sometimes by הַ—וְאִם¹, e. g. Jo 1², Jb 21⁴ (even with הַ repeated after וְאִם in a question which implies disbelief, Gn 17¹⁷). In Jb 34¹⁷, 40⁸ ᶠ· special emphasis is given to the first member by הַאַף prop. *is it even?* The second member is introduced by אוֹ *or* in 2 K 6²⁷, Jb 16³, 38²⁸, 31³⁶ (Mal 1⁸ הַ אוֹ), in each case before טוֹב, and hence no doubt for euphonic reasons, to avoid the combination אִם טוֹב; cf. also Ju 18¹⁹, Ec 2¹⁹.

Double questions with הַ—אִם (וְאִם) need not always be mutually exclusive; *h* frequently the disjunctive form serves (especially in poetic parallelism; but cf. also e. g. Gn 37⁸) merely to repeat the same question in different words, and thus to express it more emphatically. So Jb 4¹⁷ *shall mortal man be just before God? or* (אִם) *shall a man be pure before his Maker?* Jb 6⁵ ᶠ·, 8³, 10⁴ ᶠ·, 11²·⁷, 22³, Is 10¹⁵, Jer 5²⁹. The second member may, therefore, just as well be connected by a simple וְ, e. g. Jb 13⁷, 15⁷ ᶠ·, 38¹⁶ ᶠ· ²²·³²·³⁹; cf. also ψ 85⁵ after מָה; Jb 21¹⁷ ᶠ· after בַּמֶּה; or even without a conjunction, Jb 8¹¹, 22⁴; after מָה ψ 144³.

(*c*) With regard to *indirect* questions² after verbs of inquiring, doubting, *i* examining,³ &c., simple questions of this kind take either הַ *whether*, Gn 8⁸,⁴ or אִם Gn 15⁵, 2 K 1², Ct 7¹³; even before a noun-clause, Jer 5¹; in 1 S 20¹⁰ the indirect question is introduced by אִן, i. e. probably *if perchance*. In disjunctives (*whether—or*) הַ—אִם Nu 13¹⁸ at the end (or אִם־לֹא—הַ Gn 24²¹, 27²¹, 37³², Ex 16⁴), and הַ—הַ Nu 13¹⁸, which is followed by הַ—אִם; also הַ—אוֹ Ec 2¹⁹. The formula מִי יוֹדֵעַ אִם has an affirmative force, *who knows whether . . . not*, like the Latin *nescio an*, Est 4¹⁴.

In Jon 1⁷·⁸ the relative pronouns שֶׁ and אֲשֶׁר owing to the following *k* לְמִי have become also interrogative, *for whose cause?*

(*d*) זֶה and הוּא (cf. § 136 *c*) immediately after the interrogative serve to *l* give vividness to the question; so also אֵפוֹא (for which אֵפוֹ five times in Job) *then, now*, Gn 27³³ מִי־אֵפוֹא הוּא *who then is he?* Ju 9³⁸, Is 19¹², Jb 17¹⁵; אַיֵּה אֵפוֹ

---

¹ וְאִם occurs in Pr 27²⁴ after a negative statement; we should, however, with Dyserinck read וְאַיִן. Not less irregular is הֲלֹא instead of אִם לֹא in the second clause of Ju 14¹⁵, but the text can hardly be correct (cf. Moore, *Judges*, New York, 1895, p. 337); in 1 S 23¹¹ the second הַ introduces a fresh question which is only loosely connected with the first.—In Nu 17²⁸ and in the third clause of Jb 6¹³, הַאִם is best taken with Ewald in the sense of הֲלֹא, since אִם from its use in oaths (see above, § 149 *b*) may simply mean *verily not*.

² It should here be remarked that the distinction between direct and indirect questions cannot have been recognized by the Hebrew mind to the same extent as it is in Latin or English. In Hebrew there is no difference between the two kinds of sentence, either as regards mood (as in Latin) or in tense and position of the words (as in English). Cf. also § 137 *c*.

³ In Gn 43⁶ the הַ after לְהַגִּיד is explained from the fact that the latter, according to the context, implies *to give information upon a question.*

⁴ Also in Ec 3²¹ we should read הָעֹלָה and הַיֹּרֶדֶת (*whether—whether*) instead of the article which is assumed by the Masora.

where then is . . .? However, אֵפוֹא may also be placed at the end of the entire question (Ex 33¹⁶, Is 22¹; also Ho 13¹⁰, since either אֱהִי is a dialectical form of אַיֵּה, or אַיֵּה should be read instead of it) or at the beginning of the question proper, after a strongly emphasized word, as in Gn 27³⁷.¹

m　(e) Sometimes one interrogative governs two co-ordinate clauses, the first of which should rather be subordinated to the second, so that the interrogative word strictly speaking affects only the second; thus Is 5⁴ after מַדּוּעַ *wherefore looked I . . . and it brought forth?* i.e. wherefore brought it forth, while I looked, &c.; Is 50²; after הֲ Nu 32⁶, Jer 8⁴, also Nu 16²² (read הַאִישׁ); after הֲלֹא Jos 22²⁰; after לָמָּה Is 58³, 2 Ch 32⁴; after אֶל־מִי Is 40²⁵.² But הֲ Jb 4² and הֲלֹא 4²¹ are separated from the verb to which they belong by the insertion of a conditional clause.

n　3. The affirmative answer is generally expressed, as in Latin, by repeating the emphatic word in the question (or with the second person changed to the first, Gn 24⁵⁸, 27²⁴, 29⁵, Ju 13¹¹), Gn 29⁶, 37³²ᶠ·, 1 S 23¹¹, 26¹⁷, 1 K 21¹⁰, Jer 37¹⁷. (On וָיֵשׁ *if it be so* in the corrected text of 2 K 10¹⁵, see § 159 *dd*.) As a negative answer the simple לֹא is sometimes sufficient, as in Gn 19², 1 K 3³², &c.; cf. § 152 *c*; and in Ju 4²⁰ the simple אַיִן equivalent to *no* or *no one.*

§ 151. *Desiderative Sentences.*

a　A wish may be expressed not only by the simple imperfect (§ 107 *n*), cohortative (§ 108, especially with נָא § 108 *c*), jussive (§ 109; with נָא § 109 *b*), imperative (§ 110 *a*), perfect consecutive (§ 112 *aa*) or by a simple noun-clause (§ 116 *r*, note, and § 141 *g*) but also in the following ways :—

1. By exclamations in the form of *interrogative* clauses:³ especially sentences with מִי followed by the imperfect as being the mood of that which is still unfulfilled but possible, and hence also of that which is desired, e.g. 2 S 15⁴ מִי־יְשִׂמֵנִי שֹׁפֵט *who maketh me judge?* i.e. *O that I were made judge!* 1 S 20¹⁰, 2 S 23¹⁵. On the other hand, מִי with the perfect (Gn 21⁷, Nu 23¹⁰, 1 S 26⁹, Is 53¹, &c.) or participle (ψ 59⁸, Pr 24²², &c.), rather expresses a rhetorical question, i.e. a denial, cf. § 150 *d*. Especially frequent is the use of מִי־יִתֵּן (prop. *who gives?*) to introduce all kinds of desiderative clauses (see under *b*).—In Mal 1¹⁰ the desiderative clause proper is co-ordinated with an interrogative clause,

---

¹ On the other hand, in Jb 9²⁴ and 24²⁵ אֵפוֹא is not prefixed to the מִי, but appended to the conditional sentence.

² Cf. the analogous sentences after יַעַן *because*, Is 65¹², Jer 35¹⁷; after causal אֲשֶׁר 1 S 26²³; after כִּי Is 12¹; likewise after גַּם § 153 at the end; after פֶּן־ Dt 8¹²⁻¹⁴, 25³, Jos 6¹⁸, 2 S 12²⁸.

³ The transition from a question to a wish may be seen, e.g. in Nu 11⁴ *who shall give us flesh to eat?* i.e. *O that we had flesh to eat!*

מִי נִם־בָּכֶם וְיִסְגֹּר דְּלָתַיִם *would that one were among you and would shut the doors*, i. e. O that one would shut the doors!

Rem. Sometimes the original sense of מִי־יִתֵּן is still plainly discernible, *b* e. g. Ju 9²⁹ מִי־יִתֵּן אֶת־הָעָם הַזֶּה בְּיָדִי *who gives this people into my hand?* equivalent to, O that this people were given into my hand! cf. ψ 55⁷. In these examples, however, מִי־יִתֵּן is still equivalent to *O had I!* and in numerous other instances the idea of *giving* has entirely disappeared, מִי־יִתֵּן having become stereotyped as a mere desiderative particle (*utinam*). Its construction is either—

(*a*) With the *accusative* (in accordance with its original meaning) of a substantive, Dt 28⁶⁷ *would that it were even! . . . morning!* Ju 9²⁹, ψ 14⁷ (53⁷), 55⁷ ; with an accusative and a following infinitive, Jb 11⁵ ; with two accusatives, Nu 11²⁹, Jer 8²³ ; with the accusative of an infinitive, Ex 16³, 2 S 19¹ מִי־יִתֵּן מוּתִי אֲנִי תַחְתֶּיךָ *would that I had died for thee* (for אֲנִי cf. § 135 *f*) ; of a participle, Jb 31³⁵ ; of a personal pronoun (as a suffix), Jb 29² (with a following כְּ ; but מִי־יִתְּנֵנִי Is 27⁴ and Jer 9¹ with a following accusative is not simply equivalent to מִי־יִתֵּן לִי, but is properly *who endows me with*, &c. ; cf. § 117 *ff*).—With a still greater weakening of the original meaning מִי־יִתֵּן is used with an adjective in Jb 14⁴ *could a clean thing but come out of an unclean!* i.e. *how can a clean thing come*, &c. ; similarly in Jb 31³¹ *who can find one that hath not been satisfied!*

(*b*) With a following perfect, Jb 23³ (cf. § 120 *e*) ; with a perfect consecutive, *c* Dt 5²⁶ *O that they had such an heart!*

(*c*) With a following imperfect, Jb 6⁸, 13⁵, 14¹³ ; in Jb 19²³ the imperfect is *d* twice added with *Wāw* (cf. *a* above, on Mal. 1¹⁰).

On the cohortative in the apodosis to such desiderative clauses, cf. § 108 *f*.

2. The wish may also be expressed by the particles אִם (ψ 81⁹, 95⁷, *e* 139¹⁹, Pr 24¹¹, 1 Ch 4¹⁰ ; always with a following imperfect) and לוּ (for which in ψ 119⁵ we have אַחֲלַי, 2 K 5³ אַחֲלֵי, from אָח *ah!* and לֻ=לוּ ; both with a following imperfect) *si, o si! utinam.*[1] לוּ is followed by the imperfect, Gn 17¹⁸, Jb 6² ; by the jussive, Gn 30³⁴ (rather concessive, equivalent to *let it be so*) ; by the perfect, as the expression of a wish that something might have happened in past time (cf. § 106 *p*), Nu 14² לוּ מַתְנוּ *would that we had died*; 20³ and Jos 7⁷ (both times וְלוּ) ; on the other hand, Is 48¹⁸ and 63¹⁹ (both times לוּא) to express a wish that something expected in the future may already have happened.—On לוּ with the imperative (by an anacoluthon) Gn 23¹³ cf. § 110 *e*. On the perfect after כִּי אִם Gn 40¹⁴, 2 K 5²⁰, cf. § 106 *n*, note 2.

---

[1] Cf. a similar transition from a conditional to a desiderative particle, in consequence of the suppression of the apodosis, in the English, *O if I had!* and the like ; e.g. Nu 22²⁹ *if there were* (לוּ יֶשׁ־) *a sword in my hand now had I surely killed thee!*

§ 152. *Negative Sentences.*

a 1. Besides the use of rhetorical questions (§§ 150 *d*, 151 *a*), independent sentences are made negative by the adverbs לֹא (Jb 6²¹, where instead of the *Kᵉth.* לוֹ we must evidently read לֹא; perhaps preserved as a substantive)=the Greek οὐ, *not*, אַל־=μή (Jb 24²⁵ as a substantive), אֵין (*it is*) *not*; טֶרֶם *not yet*, אֶפֶס *not*, אַפְסִי (cf. § 90 *m*) *not*. The forms בַּל, בְּלִי, בִּלְתִּי *not* belong almost entirely to poetry.—With regard to לֹא and אֵין the main distinction is that verbal-clauses (rarely noun-clauses, see *e*) are regularly negatived by לֹא (besides its use as negativing *single* words[1]), while אֵין is used exclusively with noun-clauses (see the examples below).

b The conjunctions פֶּן־ and לְבִלְתִּי *that not*, serve to negative dependent clauses. The particular uses of these particles are as follows:—

(*a*) לֹא (less frequently לוֹא), like οὐ, οὐκ, is used regularly for the *objective, unconditional* negation, and hence is usually connected with the perfect or imperfect (as indicative); on לֹא with the imperfect to express an unconditional prohibition, see § 107 *o*; on its use with the jussive, see § 109 *d*.—On הֲלֹא for הֲלֹא *nonne*, in interrogative sentences, cf. § 150 *a*. In connexion with בָּל־ (=*any*), לֹא is used to express an *absolute* negation, *nullus, none whatever* (cf. the French *ne . . . personne, ne . . . rien*), usually in the order לֹא . . . כֹּל, e.g. Gn 3¹ לֹא תֹאכְלוּ מִכֹּל עֵץ הַגָּן *ye shall not eat of any tree of the garden*; 9¹¹, Ex 10¹⁵, 20¹⁰, Lv 7²³, Dt 8⁹, Jer 13⁷, 32¹⁷, לֹא . . . כָּל־דָּבָר *nothing at all*; cf. the same statement in the form of a rhetorical question, Jer 32²⁷); Pr 12²¹, 30³⁰

---

[1] Especially in compounds, e.g. לֹא־אֵל lit. *a no-God* (Germ. *Ungott*) who is indeed called a god, but is not really a god, Dt 32²¹; לֹא אֱלֹהַּ verse 17, cf. Jer 5⁷, 2 Ch 13⁹; לֹא־עָם lit. *a not-people* (Germ. *Unvolk*), Dt 32²¹; לֹא דָבָר *a nothing*, Am 6¹³; לֹא עֵץ lit. *not-wood*, Is 10¹⁵; לֹא־אִישׁ, לֹא־אָדָם lit. *not-man, superhuman* (of God), Is 31⁸; לֹא־צֶדֶק *unrighteousness*, Jer 22¹³, cf. Ez 22²⁹; לֹא־סְדָרִים *disorder*, Jb 10²²; לֹא־חָמָם *not-violence*, 16¹⁷; after לֹ Jb 26²ᶠ. (לֹא־כֹחַ, לֹא־עֹז *helplessness*, לֹא חָכְמָה *insipientia*); cf. also Is 55² בְּלוֹא לְשָׂבְעָה *for what is unsatisfying*; ψ 44¹³, Jb 8¹¹, 15³², 1 Ch 12³³.—In Nu 20⁵ a construct state with several genitives is negatived by לֹא.—Also לֹא is used with an infinitive, Nu 35²³; with an adjective, לֹא חָכָם *unwise*, Dt 32⁶, Ho 13¹³; לֹא־חָסִיד *impius*, ψ 43¹; לֹא־עָז and לֹא־עָצוּם *not strong*, Pr 30²⁵ᶠ.; לֹא־כֵן *unsuitably*, 2 K 7⁹; לֹא־טוֹב *not-good*, Is 65², Ez 20²⁵, &c.; לֹא טָהוֹר *not-clean*, 2 Ch 30¹⁷; with a participle, e.g. Jer 2² (*unsown*); 6⁸, Ez 4¹⁴, 22²⁴, Zp 2¹, 3⁵; the Masora, however, requires נֻחָמָה in Is 54¹¹, נֶעֱזָבָה in 62¹², נוֹשָׁבָה in Jer 6⁸, רֻחָמָה in Ho 1⁶, i.e. always 3rd sing. fem. perf. in pause = *she was not comforted*, &c., and consequently not compounds, but either relative clauses instead of (Is 54¹¹, Ho 1⁶, and especially 2²⁵) main clauses instead of proper names.—On the above compounds generally, cf. the dissertation mentioned in § 81 *d*, note 2; on their use in sentences expressing a state, to convey attributive ideas, see *u* below.

מִפְּנֵי־כֹל . . . לֹא and turneth *not* away *for any*; 2 Ch 32[15]; but cf. also the inverted order, Ex 12[16] כָּל־מְלָאכָה לֹא־יֵעָשֶׂה *no manner of work shall be done*; 12[43], 15[26], 22[21], Lv 16[17], Jb 33[13], Dn 11[37]. The meaning is different when כֹּל by being determinate is used in the sense of *whole*, e. g. Nu 23[13] כֻּלּוֹ לֹא תִרְאֶה *thou shalt not see them all*, but only a part.

Analogous to כֹּל . . . , לֹא is the use of לֹא . . . אִישׁ Gn 23[6], &c., in verbal-clauses in the sense of *no one at all, not a single one*. On אֵין־כֹּל *nothing at all*, see under *p*.

Rem. 1. The examples in which לֹא is used absolutely as a negative answer, *c* equivalent to *certainly not! no!* must be regarded as extremely short verbal-clauses, e. g. Gn 19[2] (לֹא) according to the context for לֹא נָסוּר &c.); 23[11], 42[10], Hag 2[12], Jb 23[6], sometimes with a following כִּי *but*, Gn 19[2] (see above); Jos 5[14], 1 K 3[22].

2. The negation of *noun-clauses* by לֹא (as opposed to the regular negation *d* by אֵין) always includes a certain emphasis, since the force of the negation falls rather upon a particular word (cf. e.g. Ez 36[32]), than upon the whole clause. In 2 S 3[34] יָדֶיךָ לֹא־אֲסֻרוֹת *thy hands* were *not bound*, a participle is thus specially negatived by לֹא; cf. ψ 74[9], where, however, לֹא is separated from the participle by אָתָּנוּ, and Jb 12[3]. As a rule, noun-clauses with a pronominal subject are thus negatived by לֹא, Gn 20[12], Nu 35[23] (Dt 4[42], 19[4]); 1 S 15[29], 2 S 21[2], Jer 4[22], ψ 22[7], Jb 28[14], parallel with אֵין; generally with לֹא before a substantival predicate, e.g. Ex 4[10] לֹא אִישׁ דְּבָרִים אָנֹכִי *I* am *not a man of words*; Am 5[18].—Noun-clauses with a substantival subject, Gn 29[7], Nu 23[19], Is 22[2], 44[19], Hag 1[2], ψ 22[3], Jb 9[32], 18[17], 21[9], 22[16], 36[26] (with וְ of the apodosis); 41[2]; in Jb 9[33] even לֹא יֵשׁ *non est* is used instead of אֵין.—In Pr 18[5] לֹא is used before an adjectival predicate; in 1 S 20[26] (where a preceding noun-clause is negatived by בִּלְתִּי) read לֹא טֹהַר with the LXX, for לֹא טָהוֹר. On לֹא for אֵין in circumstantial clauses to express attributive ideas, see *u* below.

3. As a rule לֹא stands immediately before the verb, but sometimes is *e* separated from it (frequently to bring into special prominence another word which follows it); thus Jb 22[7], Ec 10[10] before the object and verb; Nu 16[29] before the subject and verb; Dt 8[9], 2 S 3[34], ψ 49[18], 103[10], Jb 13[16], 34[23] before a complementary adjunct. In Dt 32[5] לֹא according to the accentuation even stands at the end of the clause (*they offend him not*); but undoubtedly לֹא בָנָיו are to be taken together.—On the position of לֹא with the infinitive absolute, see § 113 *v*.

(*b*) אַל־ is used like μή and *ne* to express a *subjective* and *conditional* negation, *f* and hence especially in connexion with the jussive (§ 109 *c* and *e*) to introduce prohibitions, warnings, negative desires, and requests. On אַל־ with the imperfect, see § 107 *p*; with the cohortative, see § 108 *c*; on 2 K 6[27], see § 109 *h*.

Rem. 1. אַל־ (like לֹא, see note on *a* above) may be used to form a compound *g* word, as in Pr 12[28] אַל־מָוֶת *not-death* (immortality); though all the early versions read אֶל־מָוֶת. The instances in which אַל appears to stand absolutely, equivalent to *no, certainly not* (like μή for μὴ γένηται), e. g. Ru 1[13] אַל בְּנֹתַי *nay, my daughters*, and Gn 19[18], 33[10] (אַל־נָא), are also due (see under *c*) to extreme shortening of a full clause (in 2 S 13[25] such a clause is repeated immediately afterwards); thus in 2 S 1²¹, Is 62², ψ 83² יְהִי is evidently to be supplied, and in Jo 2¹³, Am 5¹⁴, Pr 8¹⁰ the corresponding jussive from the preceding imperatives, in Pr 17¹² from the preceding infinitive absolute.

h 2. אַל־, like לֹא, regularly stands immediately before the verb, but in Is 64⁸, Jer 10²⁴, 15¹⁵, ψ 6², 38² before another strongly emphasized member of the sentence.[1]

i (c) אֵין construct state (unless it be sometimes merely a contracted connective form, cf. שְׁנֵי for שְׁנַיִם § 97 *d*) of אַיִן *non-existence* (as also the absolute state, see below) is the negative of יֵשׁ *existence*; cf. e.g. Gn 31²⁹ with Neh 5⁵. As יֵשׁ (*he, she, it is, was,* &c.) includes the idea of *being* in all tenses, so אַיִן, אֵין includes the idea of *not being* in all tenses. Hence—

k (1) The absolute state אַיִן, with an evident transition to the meaning of a verbal predicate, *there does not exist,* always *follows* the word negatived, e.g. Is 37³ (2 K 19³) וְכֹחַ אַיִן לְלֵדָה *and strength does not exist to bring forth*; Gn 2⁵ אַיִן *was not* present; Ex 17⁷ אִם־אָיִן or *is he not?* after הֲיֵשׁ *is he . . . ?* (cf. Nu 13²⁰); Lv 26³⁷, Nu 20⁵, Ju 4²⁰ (אָיִן *no*). In 1 S 9⁴ and 10¹⁴ אַיִן is used in reference to a plural; 1 K 18¹⁰, Is 41¹⁷, 45²¹, 59¹¹, Mi 7², Pr 13⁴, 25¹⁴, Jb 3⁹ וְאַיִן *and let there be none, let none come!* Ec 3¹⁹.—Cf. finally אִם־אַיִן *if it be not so,* Gn 30¹, Ex 32³², Ju 9¹⁵, 2 K 2¹⁰.—Quite anomalous is אָיִן Jb 35¹⁵ before a perfect as an emphatic negation; the text, however, can hardly be correct.

l (2) The construct state אֵין stands in its natural position immediately before the substantive whose non-existence it predicates, or before the subject of the sentence which is to be negatived. To the former class belong also the very numerous instances in which אֵין is joined to a participle, e.g. 1 S 26¹² וְאֵין רֹאֶה וְאֵין יוֹדֵעַ וְאֵין מֵקִיץ *and there was not one seeing,* &c., i.e. *and no man saw it, nor knew it, neither did any awake*; so especially וְאֵין with a participle in subordinate *circumstantial* or *descriptive* clauses, such as Is 5²⁹ וְיַפְלִיט וְאֵין מַצִּיל *and he shall carry it away, while there is none delivering,* i.e. *without any one's delivering it*; ψ 7³, &c.; Lv 26⁶ &c., וְאֵין מַחֲרִיד *without any one's making you afraid*; cf. § 141 *e.* אֵין is used as the negation of an entire noun-clause, e.g. in Gn 39²³, Nu 14⁴² אֵין יְהֹוָה בְּקִרְבְּכֶם *the Lord is not among you*; Gn 37²⁹ אֵין־יוֹסֵף בַּבּוֹר *Joseph was not in the pit.*

m (3) When the subject which is to be negatived is a personal pronoun, it is joined as a suffix to אֵין, according to § 100 *o*, e.g. אֵינֶנִּי *I am not, was not, shall not be*; אֵינְךָ, fem. אֵינֵךְ, *thou art not,* &c.; אֵינֶנּוּ, fem. אֵינֶנָּה *he, she is, is not,* &c.; also absolutely, Gn 42¹³ *he is* (5²⁴ *he was*) no longer *alive*; אֵינָם *they are not,* &c. When the accompanying predicate is a verb, it follows again (see *l*) in the form of a participle, since אֵין always introduces a noun-clause, e.g. Ex 5¹⁰ אֵינֶנִּי נֹתֵן *I will not give*; 8¹⁷, Dt 1³².

n Rem. In Neh 4¹⁷ אֵין אֲנִי for אֵינֶנִּי is due to its being co-ordinate with three other (substantival) subjects; these are again expressly summed up in אֵין־אֲנַחְנוּ.—In Hag 2¹⁷ אֵין אֶתְכֶם the pronominal complement of אֵין appears

---

[1] In Jer 51³ the pointing אֶל־ occurs twice instead of אַל־, and is thus, in the opinion of the Masoretes, equivalent to *against* him that *bendeth*; but undoubtedly we should read אַל־.

to follow with the sign of the accusative;[1] but most probably we should read with the LXX שֶׁבְכֶם for אֶתְכֶם.

(4) The fact that אֵין (like אַל) always includes the idea of a verb (*is not, O was not,* &c.) led finally to such a predominance of the verbal element, that the original character of אֵין as a construct state (but cf. *i* above) was forgotten, and accordingly it is very frequently separated from its noun (substantive or participle); especially so by the insertion of shorter words (of the nature of enclitics), e.g. בּוֹ Is 1⁶, לוֹ Lv 11¹⁰·¹², לָהּ Gn 11³⁰, גַּם ψ 14³, שָׁם Ju 18¹⁰, Ex 12³⁰; but cf. also ψ 5¹⁰, 6⁶, 32², and אֵין used absolutely in Ex 22², 1 K 8⁹, Ru 4⁴.—Hence, finally, even the transposition of אֵין and its noun became possible, e.g. Gn 40⁸ and 41¹⁵ וּפֹתֵר אֵין אֹתוֹ *and an interpreter there is not of it*; Gn 47¹³, Ju 14⁶, 1 S 21², Is 1³⁰, Jer 30¹³, Hb 2¹⁹, Pr 5¹⁷ (וְאֵין =*neve sint*; cf. *k* above, on Jb 3⁹); 30²⁷.—In Gn 19³¹, Ex 5¹⁶ אֵין is placed between the subject and predicate.

Rem. 1. Like בַּל . . . לֹא or לֹא . . . בַּל (see *b* above) so also אֵין בָּל *p* expresses an *absolute* negation, e.g. Ec 1⁹ אֵין כָּל־חָדָשׁ *there is no new thing,* &c.; 2 S 12³, Dn 1⁴ (cf. also מְאוּמָה אֵין *there is nothing,* 1 K 18⁴³, Ec 5¹³); as also אֵין . . . כָּל־ Hb 2¹⁹; cf. מְאוּמָה אֵין Ju 14⁶.

2. Undoubtedly akin to אֵין in origin is the negative syllable אִי occurring *q* in the two compounds אִי כָבוֹד (as a proper name, 1 S 4²¹; Baer אִי־כָבוֹד) and אִי־נָקִי *not innocent,* Jb 22³⁰; but the proper name אִיתָמָר is doubtful, and the fem. אִיזֶבֶל very doubtful. In Ethiopic this אִי is the most common form of negation, prefixed even to verbs.

(*d*) טֶרֶם *not yet,* when referring to past time is used, as a rule (§ 107 *c*), *r* with the imperfect, Gn 2⁵ טֶרֶם . . . בַּל *none . . . yet;* see *b* and *p* above; Gn 19⁴, 24⁴⁵, Jos 2⁸, 1 S 3³; with the imperfect in the sense of a present, Ex 10⁷ הֲטֶרֶם תֵּדַע *knowest thou not yet?* Ex 9³⁰; but cf. Gn 24¹⁵, and בְּטֶרֶם with the perfect in ψ 90² (but see § 107 *c*), Pr 8²⁵.

(*e*) אֶפֶס (prop. a substantive, *cessation*) *no longer,* including the verbal idea *S* of *existing,* cf. Dt 32³⁶, Is 45⁶·¹⁴, 46⁹; used absolutely, Am 6¹⁰ in the question הַאֶפֶס עוֹד אִישׁ *is there none left?* &c., 2 S 9³; frequently also in the sense of *non nisi;* with ִ‍‑ paragogic (§ 90 *m*) אַפְסִי Is 47⁸·¹⁰, Zp 2¹⁵ אֲנִי וְאַפְסִי עוֹד *I am, and there is none else.*

(*f*) בַּל,[2] in poetic and prophetic style, and with a certain emphasis, = לֹא, *t* is used with the imperfect, e.g. Is 26¹⁴, 33²⁰·²³ (immediately afterwards with a perfect); Ho 7², ψ 49¹³, Pr 10³⁰ (but Is 14²¹ before the jussive, = אַל־); before an adjective, Pr 24²³; before a preposition, ψ 16², Pr 23⁷.

(*g*) בְּלִי with a perfect, Gn 31²⁰, Is 14⁶; with an imperfect, Jb 41¹⁸; to negative a participle, Ho 7⁸, ψ 19⁴; to negative an adjective, 2 S 1²¹.

(*h*) בִּלְתִּי to negative an adjective, 1 S 20²⁶; on בִּלְתִּי Ez 13³, see *x*; on

---

[1] According to De Lagarde, *Novae psalterii graeci editionis specimen,* p. 26, יְשׁוּעָתָה ψ 3³ is also an accusative after אֵין.

[2] Evidently from בָּלָה *to waste away,* from which stem also בְּלִי and בֶּלֶת (whence בִּלְתִּי § 90 *m*), originally substantives, are formed.

לְבִלְתִּי as the regular negative with the infinitive construct, see § 114 *s*; on לְבִלְתִּי as a conjunction, see *x* below.

On אִם as a negative particle in oaths (*verily not*), see § 149 *c* above.

u Rem. on בְּלִי, אַיִן, לֹא. To the category of negative sentences belongs also the expression of negative attributes by means of בְּלִי, לֹא *not* (both so used almost exclusively in poetic language) or אַיִן with a following substantive, mostly in the simplest form of circumstantial clause; e.g. 2 S 23⁴ בֹּקֶר לֹא עָבוֹת *a morning* when there are *not clouds*, i.e. *a cloudless morning*; cf. Jb 12²⁴, 26²ᵇ, 38²⁶ (לֹא־אִישׁ *where no man is*, i.e. *uninhabited*); 1 Ch 2³⁰.³² לֹא בָנִים *childless*; so also בְּלִי e.g. Jb 24¹⁰ and אַיִן e.g. ψ 88⁵ *I am as a man* אֵין־אֱיָל *there is not help*, i.e. *like a helpless man*; Is 9⁶ אֵין־קֵץ *endless*; 47¹, Ho 7¹¹; אֵין־מִסְפָּר *countless*, Ct 6⁸, &c., but usually (ψ 104²⁵, &c.) like a proper circumstantial clause (cf. § 141 *e*) connected by *Wāw*, וְאֵין־מִסְפָּר.—Less frequently such periphrases take the form of relative clauses (cf. § 155 *e*), e.g. Jb 30¹³ לֹא עֹזֵר לָמוֹ they *for whom there is no helper*, i.e. *the helpless* (but probably עֹזֵר is only an intrusion from 29¹², and we should read עֹצֵר *without any one's restraining them*; in 29¹² translate *the fatherless and him that had none to help him*; in ψ 72¹² וְאֵין־עֹזֵר is used in the same sense); Hb 1¹⁴; with אַיִן Is 45⁹ *thy work* is that of a man *who hath no hands*; Zc 9¹¹ *out of the waterless pit*.[1]

v How far such compounds finally came to be regarded by the language simply as negative adjectives, may be seen partly from the fact that they (as also relative clauses analogous to the above) are frequently co-ordinated with real adjectives, Jo 1⁶, ψ 72¹², Jb 29¹²; cf. also Is 59¹⁰, where כְּאֵין־עֵינַיִם is parallel with בַעְוֵרִים; partly from their being introduced by the sign of the dative לְ, e.g. Is 40²⁹ (= *and to the powerless*); Jb 26² ᵃ.³, Neh 8¹⁰.

w (*i*) פֶּן *lest, that not*, at the beginning of a clause expressing a fear or precaution, hence especially after such ideas as *fearing*, Gn 32¹², &c. (cf. δείδω μή, *vereor ne*), *taking heed*, frequently after הִשָּׁמֶר, הִשָּׁמְרוּ Gn 24⁶, 31²⁴, &c., *taking care*, 2 K 10²³, &c. Not infrequently the idea on which פֶּן depends, is only virtually contained in the main clause, e.g. Gn 19¹⁹ *I cannot escape to the mountain* (because I am afraid), פֶּן־תִּדְבָּקַנִי הָרָעָה *lest some evil overtake me*; Gn 26⁹, 38¹¹; also in Gn 44³⁴ from the rhetorical question *how shall I . . .?* we must understand *I cannot*, governing פֶּן. This is especially the case after an appeal to do or not to do an action by which something may be prevented (in which case פֶּן is simply equivalent to the final *ne*); cf. e.g. Gn 11⁴, 19¹⁵, Nu 20¹⁸ (where פֶּן *lest* is separated from the verb by a strongly emphasized substantive); Ju 15¹² after *swear unto me*; Pr 24¹⁸.—In Gn 3²² *and now, lest he put forth his hand*, &c., פֶּן is to be regarded as virtually dependent on a cohortative, which immediately afterwards (verse 23) is changed into an historic tense; cf. also Gn 26⁷, 31³¹, 42⁴ Ex 13¹⁷, 1 S 13¹⁹, 27¹¹, ψ 38¹⁷, in every case after כִּי אָמַרְתִּי, כִּי אָמַר, &c. = *I thought*, &c., *I must beware lest*, &c.

Rem. According to § 107 *q*, פֶּן is naturally followed by the imperfect; for the exceptions, 2 S 20⁶, 2 K 2¹⁶, see § 107 *q*, note 3; cf. moreover, 2 K 10²³ רְאוּ פֶּן־יֶשׁ־פֹּה *look lest there be here*, &c.

---

[1] In Pr 9¹³ (perhaps also 14⁷; but see Delitzsch on the passage) a verbal-clause is used co-ordinately in this way as a periphrasis for an adjective.

(k) לְבִלְתִּי *that . . . not*, with the imperfect, Ex 20²⁰, 2 S 14¹⁴ (in Jer 23¹⁴ 𝑥
read the infinitive שׁוּב for שָׁבוּ, in 27⁸ יָבֹאוּ for בֹּאוּ). In Ez 13³ בִּלְתִּי רָאוּ
is a relative clause governed by לְ = *according to* things which *they have not seen.*

2. Two negatives in the same sentence do not neutralize each other 𝑦
(as in *nonnulli, non nemo*), but make the negation the more emphatic
(like οὐκ οὐδείς, οὐκ οὐδαμῶς, *nulli—non, nemo non*); e. g. Zp 2² (if the
text is correct) בְּטֶרֶם לֹא־יָבוֹא *before there shall* (not) *come.*[1] This
especially applies to the compounds formed by the union of אֵין or בְּלִי
with מִן־ *without* (§ 119 *y*), e. g. Is 5⁹ (6¹¹) מֵאֵין יוֹשֵׁב (for which in
Jer 2¹⁵ מִבְּלִי יֹשֵׁב), prop. *without no inhabitant*, i. e. *so that no inhabitant
is left there.* On the other hand, in Is 50² מֵאֵין מַיִם the מִן־ is causative,
because there is no water; as also in Ex 14¹¹ הֲמִבְּלִי אֵין־ *is it because
there were no . . . ?* 2 K 1³·⁶·¹⁶. In Ec 3¹¹ מִבְּלִי אֲשֶׁר לֹא *except that (yet
so that man cannot*, &c.).

3. The negative sometimes extends its influence from the first to 𝑧
a second negative sentence parallel with it (which may or may not
have *Wāw*); e. g. 1 S 2³ *talk not so much arrogancy; let* (not) *boasting
come out of your mouth;* Ex 28⁴³, Lv 19¹², 22⁹·¹⁵ᶠ·, Nu 16¹⁴, 23¹⁹, Dt 7²⁵,
Is 23⁴, 28²⁷, 38¹⁸, 47¹⁴, Ez 16⁴⁷, ψ 9¹⁹, 13⁵, 35¹⁹, 38², 44¹⁹, 75⁶, Jb 28¹⁷ (so
לָמָּה לֹא *why . . . not ?* in Jb 3¹¹ also affects the parallel clause).

§ 153. *Restrictive and Intensive Clauses.*

The particles אַךְ, רַק *only*, serve to introduce restrictive clauses, and
גַּם, אַף *also, besides, even*, intensive clauses. It is to be observed that
the force of these particles does not necessarily affect the word which
immediately follows (as is the case with אַךְ Gn 7²³, 34¹⁵; רַק Gn 6⁵,
Am 3²; even אַף הֲרַק *hath he indeed only ?* Nu 12²; גַּם Gn 27³⁴, Jb 7¹¹;
אַף Dt 15¹⁷), but very frequently extends to the whole of the following
sentence. Thus with אַךְ, e. g. Nu 14⁹, 1 K 17¹³, Pr 17¹¹, Jb 13¹⁵, 14²²,
16⁷, 23⁶; רַק Gn 20¹¹, 24⁸, ψ 32⁶, Pr 13¹⁰; גַּם Gn 27³³, 32²¹ (גַּם הִנֵּה), 44¹⁰;
1 S 22⁷, 28²⁰, Zc 9¹¹, Pr 17²⁶, 20¹¹; אַף Jb 14³, 15⁴.—In Mal 1¹⁰ and
Jb 2¹⁰ גַּם is placed before two co-ordinate sentences, although, strictly
speaking, it applies only to the second. Cf. the analogous examples
in § 150 *m*.

---

[1] In 1 K 10²¹ אֵין־כֶּסֶף goes with what precedes and must be emended,
with the LXX and Lucian, to כִּי הַכֶּסֶף.

§ 154. *Sentences connected by Wāw.*

a *Wāw copulativum* [1] (ן) serves to connect two or more sentences, or single words (on its various vocalization, cf. § 104 *d–g*). Its use, however, is by no means restricted merely to joining sentences which

---

[1] For further particulars of the use of *wāw copulativum*, see Gesenius' *Thesaurus*, i. 393 ff. On its use in the co-ordination of similar tenses and moods (e. g. five imperfects consecutive in Gn 25³⁴, five perfects with וְנָם) as well as of dissimilar tenses and moods, the remarks made in the treatment of the tenses will suffice. With regard to the connexion of single *nouns* by ן (which strictly speaking is always really a contraction of so many clauses into a single sentence) the following observations may be made :—

(*a*) Contrary to English usage, which in lengthy enumerations uses the *and* to connect only the last member of the series, in Hebrew *polysyndeton* is customary, as in Gn 12¹⁶ wāw copulativum six times, 24³⁵ seven times, 15¹⁹ ff. nine times, and in Jos 7²⁴ ten times. Sometimes, however, only the last two words are joined (so in a series of three members, Gn 5³², 10¹, 11²⁶, 13², 14¹, 30³⁹, &c.; the last three out of a series of four, Jer 2²⁶) ; less frequently only the first two, ψ 45⁹; cf. § 132 *d*. The formula תְּמוֹל שִׁלְשׁוֹם *yesterday* (and) *the day before yesterday*, Ex 5⁸, &c., is always without the copula. On the other hand, the *constructio asyndetos* in a series of verbs is used as a rhetorical expedient to produce a hurried and so an impassioned description ; e.g. Ju 5²⁷ *at her feet he bowed, he fell, he lay* ; Ex 15⁹, Dt 32¹⁵, 1 S 15⁶, Jer 4⁷, Am 5²¹, ψ 10¹⁰, 14¹, 45⁵, Jb 20¹⁹, 28⁴, 29⁸, Ct 2¹¹, 5⁶, &c.

(*b*) Frequently *wāw copulativum* is also *explanatory* (like *isque, et—quidem*, and the German *und zwar*, English *to wit*), and is then called *wāw explicativum*, e.g. Gn 4⁴ *and* (i.e. *namely*) *of the fat thereof* (unless it is simply copulative) ; Ex 24¹², 25¹² (*to wit two*) ; 27¹⁴, 28²³, Ju 17³ (in וּמַסֵּכָה ; here as often elsewhere, to introduce an explanatory gloss, cf. Is 17⁸, Ez 3¹⁵, and especially P. Haupt, *SBOT.* Isaiah, p. 90, l. 21 ff.), 1 S 17³⁴ *and that too with the bear* ; 2 S 13²⁰, Is 57¹¹, Jer 17¹⁰, Am 3¹¹, 4¹⁰, Ze 9⁹, Pr 3¹², Neh 8¹³, 2 Ch 23¹⁰ (but in 1 S 28³ the ן before בְּעִירוֹ is to be omitted with the LXX); cf. also such combinations as מִן—וְעַד *from . . . and even to . . .* , Gn 13³, 14²³, 19⁴·¹¹, &c.—In 1 S 6¹¹ (see Driver on the passage), 2 S 1²³, &c., ן is equivalent to *yea, and*; in Is 32⁷ *even*.

ן is used to express emphasis (= *and especially*), e.g. in Gn 3¹⁶ וְהֵרֹנֵךְ ; Is 2¹, ψ 18¹, perhaps also in Jb 10¹⁷ *yea*, a whole *host* ; 2 Ch 16¹⁴.—An undoubted example of what is called *wāw concomitantiae* occurs in Jb 41¹² *a seething pot* וְאַגְמֹן *with burning rushes*; cf. Ex 10¹⁰ (*with your little ones*), 12⁸, Lv 1¹², Is 42⁵. In Arabic this *wāw concom.* is followed by the accusative.

ן—ן is used in the sense of *both—and* in ψ 76⁷, Dn 1³, 8¹³. On ן—ן as meaning *sive—sive*, cf. § 162 *b*.

(*c*) See the Lexicon on adverbs used in a copulative sense, such as גַּם *also, moreover*, summing up a number, c. g. גַּם־שְׁנֵיהֶם *both together*, Gn 27⁴⁵, Pr 17¹⁵ ; גַּם־כֹּל *all together* ; as an intensive *and*, e.g. Gn 30⁸, 37⁷, 1 S 30⁸ ; cf. also such examples as 1 S 24¹² *see, yea see!* גַּם—גַּם or וְגַם—גַּם Gn 24⁴⁴ = *both—and* ; גַּם occurs three times in Gn 24²⁵ and 32²⁰ ; also אַף, which is generally still more intensive, in the sense of *also, in addition to this, even*, and belongs rather to poetry, and to the later language; frequently also equivalent to a mere *and*, but sometimes adversative *but now*, ψ 44¹⁰, &c.; and אַף—אַף (also three times), equivalent to *both—and*; cf. וְאַף גַּם *and even*, Lv 26⁴⁴ ; אַף־כִּי prop. *add to this also that*, equivalent to *not to mention*, according to the context either *quanto magis* or *quanto minus*.

are actually co-ordinate. Frequently the language employs merely the simple connexion by *Wāw*, even to introduce an antithesis (Gn 17²¹, 19¹⁹, Lv 2¹², Jb 6²⁵, and very frequently in circumstantial noun-clauses), or when one of the two clauses is not co-ordinated, but subordinated to the other. On the use of וְ to introduce circumstantial clauses, cf. especially § 141 e and § 142 d; introducing causal clauses, § 158 a; comparative clauses, § 161 a; final clauses, § 165 a; consecutive clauses, § 166 a. On *wāw apodosis*, cf. § 143 d, and the sections there cited; on the use of *Wāw* in numerical sayings, cf. § 134 s.

Rem. Sometimes wāw copulativum joins a sentence apparently to what *b* immediately precedes, but in reality to a sentence which is suppressed and which must, therefore, be supplied from the context. So especially וְ with imperatives to express inferences, e.g. 1 K 2²² וְשַׁאֲלִי *ask now rather*; Ez 18³² *for I have no pleasure in the death of him that dieth . . .*, וְהָשִׁיבוּ *wherefore turn yourselves*. Also at the beginning of a speech in loose connexion with an act or speech of another person, e. g. Ex 2²⁰, 2 S 18¹¹, 24³, 2 K 4¹⁴·⁴¹, 7¹³, 2 Ch 25⁹; cf. also Jos 7⁷ (וְלוּ), ψ 2¹⁰, 4⁴, Is 8⁷. Sometimes the suppression of the protasis is due to passionate excitement or haste, which does not allow time for full expression; this is especially illustrated by Nu 12¹⁴, 20³ (וְלוּ), 1 S 10¹², 15¹⁴, 22¹⁴, 28¹⁶, 2 S 18¹², 24³, 1 K 2²² (וְלָמָּה), 2 K 1¹⁰, 7¹⁹ (cf. verse 2); Is 3¹⁴, Zc 2¹⁰, ψ 2⁶ (at the same time a circumstantial clause *whereas I = and yet I have*, &c.); cf. also a new clause beginning with the formula of wishing יְמִי Nu 11²⁹, Ju 9²⁹; on the disconnected use of וְלֹא and וְיֵשׁ cf. § 159 dd.

§ 155. *Relative Clauses.*

See V. Baumann, *Hebräische Relativsätze*, Leipzig, 1894 (cf. the heading of § 138 above); G. Bergsträsser, 'Das hebr. Präfix שׁ,' *ZATW*. 1909, p. 40 ff.[1]

1. By § 138 a, e, relative clauses are divided into two classes: those *a* which are used for the nearer definition of a noun (substantive or pronoun), and those which are not dependent on a noun. The former may be called *incomplete*, the latter *complete* relative clauses.

Complete relative clauses, as a rule (see the exceptions under *n*), *b* are introduced by the originally demonstrative pronoun אֲשֶׁר; see further in § 138 e. Similarly, incomplete relative clauses may also be introduced by אֲשֶׁר, or by some other demonstrative pronoun; see further in § 138 a and g-k. Very frequently, however, especially

---

[1] In this exhaustive article the author shows that between שׁ (on the pronunciation see § 36) and אֲשֶׁר there is syntactically no primary difference, but only a secondary distinction which arose in the course of the development of the language, namely that אֲשֶׁר is preferred in combinations which are customary in the old literary language, and שׁ in those which are derived from the popular language or from Aramaic.

in poetic style, the attributive relation is expressed by simple co-ordination.[1]

c The governing substantive or pronoun is frequently (in certain cases *always*) resumed by a pronominal suffix or an adverb. The resumption may, however, be omitted, just as in relative clauses introduced by אֲשֶׁר, &c.; see § 138 *f*.

d In Arabic a distinction is made between relative clauses used for the nearer definition of a *determinate* substantive (*ṣila*), and those which are attached to an *indeterminate* substantive (*ṣifa*). The former must be introduced by the demonstrative pronoun *alladi*, the latter are always simply co-ordinated. The same distinction was no doubt originally observed in Hebrew, since simply co-ordinated relative clauses are most commonly found after *indeterminate* substantives (see the examples below), and in cases like Dt 28⁴⁹ (גּוֹי אֲשֶׁר לֹא־תִשְׁמַע לְשֹׁנוֹ) *a nation whose tongue thou shalt not understand* ; cf. Is 66¹³, and especially 1 S 3¹¹), the addition of אֲשֶׁר is explained from the special stress laid on the indeterminate substantive,[2] *a nation of such a kind, thou understandest not their tongue.* On the other hand, in poetic style at least, אֲשֶׁר is somewhat frequently omitted even after a determinate noun, but only rarely in prose (except by the Chronicler; cf. 1 Ch 9²², 12²³, 29¹ (read prob. אֲשֶׁר for אֶחָד), 2 Ch 15¹¹ ; after בָּר־ 1 Ch 29³, 2 Ch 18²³, 30¹⁷, 31¹⁹, Ezr 1⁵, but also Gn 39⁴ ; for further instances, see Driver, *Introd.*⁸, p. 537, no. 30); so Ex 18²⁰, Ju 8¹, 20¹⁵, 1 K 13¹² (=which way), so 2 K 3⁸, 2 Ch 18²³ ; Neh 13²³ ; after a pronominal subject, 1 S 6⁹. In Jer 52¹² for עָמַד read עֹמֵד with the LXX.

e 2. If the nearer definition of a substantive or pronoun is effected by simple co-ordination of the relative clause, it may take the form—

(*a*) Of a noun-clause, e. g. 2 S 20²¹ *a man of the hill country of Ephraim* שֶׁבַע שְׁמוֹ *whose name was Sheba* ; Zc 6¹², Jb 1¹, 3¹⁵ *with princes* זָהָב לָהֶם *that had gold* ; ψ 11⁴, Pr 22¹¹ ; when referring to a noun-suffix, e. g. ψ 49¹⁴ זֶה דַרְכָּם כֵּסֶל לָמוֹ *this is the way of them who have* (self-)*confidence.*—On periphrases of this kind to express negative attributes, as in Jb 38²⁶ עַל־אֶרֶץ לֹא־אִישׁ *on a land where no man is*, see § 152 *u*, and cf. for this very short form of the relative clause, Gn 15¹³ בְּאֶרֶץ לֹא לָהֶם *in a land* that belongs *not to them* ; Dt 32¹⁷ (לְשֵׁדִים לֹא אֱלֹהַּ); Hb 1⁶, Pr 26¹⁷ (לֹא־לוֹ).

f (*b*) Of a verbal clause.

Here we must distinguish the cases in which the retrospective pronoun—

(1) Is the subject of the relative clause, and is contained in the

---

[1] The old view that all these cases arise from the *omission* of אֲשֶׁר is incorrect. These co-ordinated attributive clauses are rather a mere subdivision of the various kinds of circumstantial clauses (see § 156) which may be attached to a *nomen regens.* Cf. in English *this is the letter* (which) *he wrote to me.*

[2] So Baumann, op. cit., p. 14 f., following Böttcher, *Lehrbuch*, ii. 80.

verb; so after a determinate substantive, ψ 34⁹ *happy is the man* יְחֱסָה־בּוֹ *that trusteth in him*; Jb 3³ᵇ הַלַּיְלָה אָמַר *the night which said*; after כָּל־ ψ 71¹⁸; referring to a vocative, which is determinate in itself even without the article, Is 54¹, or to a noun-suffix (see under *e*), ψ 16⁴; after an indeterminate substantive, e. g. Jb 31¹² *it is a fire* (that) *devoureth unto Abaddon*; Dt 32¹⁷ᵇ, 1 S 6⁹, Is 55¹³, 56², ψ 68³¹, 78⁶, Pr 30¹⁷, La 1¹⁰, 2 Ch 28⁹; referring to the suffix in הִנְנִי Is 28¹⁶, prop. *behold me, who have laid*, &c., but perhaps the participle יֹסֵד is to be read; 29¹⁴, 38⁵ (but probably again the participle יֹסֵף should be read instead of the imperfect); Ez 25⁷. The relative clause is used in this way especially to supply the place of an adjective, e. g. Gn 49²⁷ זְאֵב יִטְרָף *a wolf that ravineth*, i. e. *a ravining wolf*; Is 51¹²; to express a negative quality, e. g. Is 40²⁰, Ho 4¹⁴ עָם לֹא־יָבִין *an undiscerning people.*

Rem. Very frequently such relative sentences are attached to substantives *g* which have the particle of comparison כְּ, e. g. Jb 7² כְּעֶבֶד יִשְׁאַף־צֵל *as a servant that earnestly desireth the shadow*, &c.; Dt 32¹¹, Is 62¹, Jer 23²⁹, Ho 6³, ψ 42², 83¹⁵, Jb 9²⁶, 11¹⁶; so also after כְּמוֹ ψ 58⁵; after a determinate substantive, e. g. Is 53⁷ (but the better reading is כַּעֲשֶׂה without the article), 61¹⁰ᶠ·, Hb 2¹⁴, ψ 49¹³·²¹, 125¹; see also the examples under *h*. Sometimes it seems simpler in such cases, to take the verb directly as predicate to the preceding substantive, and to explain כְּ (for כַּאֲשֶׁר; see *Comparative Clauses*, § 161 *b*) as a conjunction—a view which even Hupfeld was ready to accept, at least as regards ψ 90⁵, 125¹, Is 53⁷, 61¹¹, but it can hardly be right.

(2) The cases in which the retrospective pronoun represents an *h* accusative of the object, or would do so if not suppressed, as it usually is in such cases in relative clauses with אֲשֶׁר, cf. § 138 *b*. Examples with the retrospective pronoun are, Dt 32¹⁷ אֱלֹהִים לֹא יְדָעוּם *gods whom they knew not* (see also the end of the verse); after a substantive with כְּ (see above, *g*), Jer 23⁹, Jb 13²⁸. Without a retrospective pronoun, after a determinate substantive, Ju 8¹, ψ 33¹² (preceded by a relative clause with אֲשֶׁר); Jb 28¹. Other examples of this kind, though the article is omitted according to poetic usage, are Is 15⁷ יִתְרָה עָשָׂה, for which Jer 48³⁶ יִתְרַת עָשָׂה with the substantive in the construct state governing the relative clause, see § 130 *d*), ψ 7¹⁶, 51¹⁰, La 1²¹.—Without the retrospective pronoun, after an indeterminate substantive, e. g. Is 6⁶ רִצְפָּה בְּמֶלְקָחַיִם לָקַח מֵעַל הַמִּזְבֵּחַ *a live coal which he had taken with the tongs from off the altar*; Ex 15¹⁷, Is 42¹⁶ (48¹⁷, ψ 25¹², all after בְּדֶרֶךְ; but ψ 32⁸ בְּדֶרֶךְ־זוּ תֵלֵךְ); Is 64²; Ec 10⁵ (in 6¹ the same clause with אֲשֶׁר); moreover, in Jer 14¹⁸ read with the LXX אֶל־אֶרֶץ לֹא יָדָעוּ *into a land* (that) *they know not.*

(3) The cases in which the retrospective pronoun is dependent on *i* a preposition, or its place is taken by the adverb שָׁם, as in Jer 2⁶ end.

Thus after a determinate substantive, ψ 18³ צוּרִי אֶחֱסֶה־בּוֹ *my rock in which I take refuge*; Ex 18²⁰, Is 42¹; in Jb 3³ᵃ also, the omission of the article with יוֹם is only a poetic licence. After an indeterminate substantive, Jer 2⁶, last clause but one; ψ 32².

k In this case also the retrospective word is not infrequently suppressed, giving rise to extremely short, bold expressions, such as Is 51¹ *look unto the rock* חֻצַּבְתֶּם (whence) *ye were hewn, and to the hole of the pit* נֻקַּרְתֶּם (whence) *ye were digged*; Jb 21²⁷ *the devices* (wherewith) *ye act violently against me.*—A retrospective adverb is suppressed in Jb 38¹⁹ *where is the way* (to the place where) *the light dwelleth?* cf. 38²⁴.

l Rem. 1. The omission of the retrospective word occurs most frequently in relative clauses which are governed by the construct state of a preceding substantive (especially an expression of time) and hence are virtually in the genitive. In addition to the instances already given in § 130 *d*, cf. the following : after בְּיוֹם Lv 7³⁵, ψ 56¹⁰; after מִיּוֹם Jer 36²; after simple יוֹם ψ 56⁴ (אִירָא יוֹם *on the day* when *I am afraid*); after בְּעֵת 2 Ch 29²⁷ בְּעֵת הָחֵל הָעוֹלָה *at the time* when *the burnt offering began*); 20²², 24¹¹, Jb 6¹⁷; after לְעֵת Dt 32³⁵; after עַד־עֵת Mi 5²; after מֵעֵת ψ 4⁸ *thou hast put gladness in my heart more than* (their gladness) *at the time* (when) *their corn and their wine are increased*.

m 2. The agreement (§ 138 *d*) of the retrospective pronoun with a pronominal regens in the 1st or 2nd person also takes place in a simple co-ordinated relative clause in 1 S 26¹⁴ *who art thou* (that) *criest?* Cf., however, Is 63¹⁹ *we are become as they over whom* (בָּם not בָּנוּ) *thou no longer bearest rule.*

n 3. Occasionally—chiefly in poetic or otherwise elevated style—even *independent* relative clauses are simply co-ordinated with a regens, whereas we should expect them always to be preceded by a demonstrative pronoun, on the analogy of the examples in § 138 *e*. The suppressed pronoun would stand—

(*a*) As subject, Is 41²⁴ *an abomination* (is he) *that chooseth you* (but read perhaps לִבְחֹר); Jb 30¹³, cf. § 152 *u*.

(*b*) As object, Is 41², with a retrospective pronoun; Mal 2¹⁶ וְכִסָּה *and him that covereth* (or read וְכֹסֶה?); Jb 29¹² *I delivered . . . the fatherless also, and him that had none to help him.*

(*c*) In the genitive governed by a substantive (cf. § 130 *d*), Ex 4¹³ שְׁלַח־נָא בְּיַד־תִּשְׁלָח *send, I pray thee, by the hand of* him *whom thou wilt send*, i. e. by the hand of some one else; ψ 65⁵ and Pr 8³², verbal-clauses after אַשְׁרֵי *O the happiness of* the man, &c.; ψ 81⁶, 141⁹, Jb 29¹⁶, La 1¹⁴; after כָּל־ Gn 39⁴, but we must certainly read here, with the Samaritan and LXX, כָּל־אֲשֶׁר יֶשׁ־לוֹ as in verses 5 and 8; Ex 9⁴; verbal-clauses after בְּכָל־ 1 Ch 29³, 2 Ch 30¹⁹, 31¹⁹, Ezr 1⁵.

(*d*) Governed by a preposition; so verbal-clauses after אַחֲרֵי Jer 2⁸; after אֶל־ (= *to the place where*), 1 Ch 15¹², but Ex 23²⁰ before the same verb אֲשֶׁר הַמָּקוֹם-אֶל ; after בְּ Jer 2[11], 2 Ch 1[4] (בַּהֲכִין=בְּהֵה'=*to the place where*); after לְ Is 65[1] שָׁאֲלוּ לְלֹא by them *that asked not for me . . .* בִקְשֻׁנִי לְלֹא them *that sought me not*; Ez 13[3] that which *they have not seen*, but the text is hardly correct; after עַל ψ 119[136], cf. § 158 *b*; after עַם 2 Ch 16[9].—A noun-clause follows לְ in Neh 8[10]. An analogous instance in Aramaic is Ezr 5[14] *to one whose name was Sheshbazzar* [so in the papyri, see the Lexicon, p. 1116 [a]].

§ 156. *Circumstantial Clauses.*

1. The statement of the particular circumstances under which *a* a subject appears as performing some action, or under which an action (or an occurrence) is accomplished, is made especially (apart from relative clauses, see § 155) by means of noun-clauses connected by *Wāw* with a following subject (see further on this kind of *circumstantial clause* in § 141 *e*), and by verbal-clauses (see § 142 *d*). Very frequently, however, such statements of the particular circumstances are subordinated to the main clause by being simply attached, without *Wāw*, either as noun-clauses, sometimes extremely short (see *c*), or as verbal-clauses (see *d–g*).

Rem. Among relative clauses of this kind the commonest are the various *b* noun-clauses, which are most closely subordinated to a preceding substantive without אֲשֶׁר, e. g. Gn 16[12]; also statements of weight, Gn 24[22]; of name, Jb 1[1] (also introduced by וּשְׁמוֹ Gn 24[29], 1 S 1[1], &c., or וּשְׁמָהּ Gn 16[1], 22[24], &c.); of a condition of body, Ju 1[7], and others.—Noun-clauses which begin with *wāw* and the *predicate* have a somewhat more independent character than those introduced by *wāw* and the *subject*[1] (Gn 19[1], &c.). The former, however, are also to be regarded as circumstantial clauses, in so far as they describe a *state* which is simultaneous with the principal action; thus Is 3[7] *I will not be an healer*, לֶחֶם אֵין וּבְבֵיתִי *while in my house is neither bread nor clothing*; Is 6[6] (Am 7[7]); 2 S 13[18], 16[1]. Cf. also the instances in § 152 *l* of וְאֵין followed by a participle, as מַצִּיל וְאֵין, &c.

2. Characteristic examples of circumstantial *noun*-clauses are Gn 12[8] *c* *and pitched his tent* מִקֶּדֶם וְהָעַי מִיָּם בֵּית-אֵל with *Bethel on the west and Ai on the east*; Nu 22[24], 2 S 18[14] *through the heart of Absalom*, עוֹדֶנּוּ חַי while *he was yet alive*; Jer 30[6], Ez 9[2] (cf. Ct 3[8]), Na 3[8], Zc 14[5], 2 Ch 23[10]; with the predicate preceding, e. g. 1 S 26[13], ψ 32[8].—In Gn 41[29] a noun-clause serves to announce a state in the future.—We may also include here certain set phrases, as פָּנִים אֶל-פָּנִים *face to face* (prop. while *face* was turned *towards face*), Gn 32[31], Ex 33[11], Dt 34[10],

---

[1] In Dt 32[31] this form of sequence appears to be selected for another purpose, *and indeed our enemies are judges* thereof, with *wāw emphatic*; to take it as a circumstantial clause is too artificial.

&c.;[1] so also· *to cast oneself down,* אַפַּיִם אַרְצָה *the face* being turned to *the earth,* Gn 19[1], &c. (for אַרְצָה we find אֶרֶץ in 1 K 1[31], Is 49[23]).[2]—Cf. finally the formula אֵם עַל־בָּנִים *mother with children,* Gn 32[12]; cf. Ho 10[14] and § 119 *aa* note 2.

Rem. On circumlocutions of this kind to express negative attributes by means of short noun-clauses (complete or incomplete), cf. § 152 *u.*

d 3. As circumstantial *verbal*-clauses,[3] we find (1) sometimes affirmative clauses (see below), but far more frequently (2) negative clauses (see *f*), and among these (3) a certain number of expressions which may be regarded simply as equivalent to negative adverbial ideas (see *g*).

Examples of (1) Is 5[11 b] woe unto them, that tarry late in the evening, יַיִן יַדְלִיקֵם *while wine inflames them*; Is 1[5], 10[24], 30[31], Jer 7[26], 20[15], ψ 4[3], 5[12], 21[13], 62[5]. The circumstantial verbal-clause is used to particularize an action which has before been expressed generally, in Gn 44[12], 48[14] = *crossing his hands*; Dt 2[27], Ju 6[19]; antithetically, 1 K 13[18] כִּחֵשׁ לוֹ *wherewith however he lied unto him.* The verbal-clause seems to assign a reason in ψ 7[7] מִשְׁפָּט צִוִּיתָ *since thou hast commanded judgement*; a consequence in ψ 103[5].[4]

e Rem. On the cases in which an imperfect in the sense of a final clause is subordinated to a verb of motion (generally קוּם), see § 120 *c.*

f Of (2), subordinate verbal-clauses with לֹא (in English usually rendered by *without* and the gerund, if the subject be the same as in the principal clause), e.g. Lv 1[17] לֹא יַבְדִּיל *without dividing it asunder*; Jb 31[34]; לֹא with the perfect is so used in Gn 44[4], Ex 34[28], 1 S 30[2], Jb 20[26] (*without its being blown upon it*). With a different subject, equivalent to a consecutive clause in English, Is 27[9] לֹא־יָקֻמוּ *so that they shall rise up no more.*—Moreover, verbal-clauses in the same sense (*without* doing, &c.) are frequently connected by וְלֹא; cf. 1 S 20[2], Jb 24[22], 42[3]; in a concessive sense, Is 33[1], ψ 44[18].

g Of (3), cf. לֹא יָדַע (prop. *he knows it not*) *unawares,* ψ 35[8], Pr 5[6] לֹא יַחְמֹל *unsparingly,* Is 30[14] (after an infinitive absolute); Hb 1[17], Jb 6[10] (but וְלֹא יַחְמֹל Jb 16[13], 27[22]; see *f* at the end); לֹא כִחֵדוּ (prop. *they hide not*) *openly,* Is 3[9] (but

---

[1] The expression הִתְרָאָה פָנִים *to look one another in the face* (i. e. to contend in combat) 2 K 14[8.11], 2 Ch 25[17.21], is probably only a shortened form for הִתְרָאָה פָנִים אֶל־פָּנִים.

[2] That אַרְצָה (אֶרֶץ) is really to be regarded as a virtual predicate to אַפַּיִם, and not אַפַּיִם as a *casus instrumenti,* is seen from Is 49[23], where אַפַּיִם אֶרֶץ precedes the verb.

[3] Some examples of these have been already discussed in another connexion above, § 120 *a-c.*

[4] In Gn 21[14] the circumstantial verbal-clause שָׂם עַל־שִׁכְמָה is only due to a harmonizing transposition; read וְאֶת־הַיֶּלֶד שׂ' ע' שׁ'. According to the source used in cap. 21 Ishmael was still a young child; according to 17[25] he was about 16 or 17 years old.

Jb 15¹⁸ (וְלֹא כִחֲדוּ) ; בְּלִי חָשָׂךְ (prop. *he restrains not*) *unceasingly*, Is 14⁶ ; בַּל־יִמּוֹט
Jb 41¹⁵ (ψ 93¹ בַּל־תִּמּוֹט) and לֹא יִמּוֹט Is 40²⁰ (*without tottering*) *immovably* ; cf.
also לֹא אֶמְעָד *without wavering*, ψ 26¹.

§ 157. Object-Clauses (*Oratio Obliqua*).

Clauses which depend on a transitive verb, especially on what are *a*
called *verba cordis*, i. e. verbs denoting any mental act, such as *to see,
to hear, to know, to perceive, to believe, to remember, to forget, to say, to
think*, &c., may be subordinated to the governing verb without the
help of a conjunction by simple juxtaposition (§ 120 *a*), or they may
be co-ordinated with it either with or without *wāw copulative*
(§ 120 *d–h*). As a rule, however, the objective clause is introduced
by the conjunction כִּי *that*, less frequently by אֲשֶׁר *that*.[1]

Examples:—
(*a*) Object-clauses without a conjunction. Besides the passages mentioned
in § 120 (especially under *e*) there are a number of examples, in which
a clause depending on a *verbum dicendi* or *sentiendi* (the oratio obliqua of the
Latin and English Grammar) is added in the form of an independent noun-
clause or verbal-clause ; e. g. Gn 12¹³ אִמְרִי־נָא אֲחֹתִי אָתְּ *say, I pray thee, thou
art my sister* ; ψ 10¹³, Jb 25⁸ᵃ.¹⁴, Neh 6⁶ ; Zc 8²³ (after שָׁמַע) ; ψ 9²¹ (after יָדַע) ;
verbal-clauses, e. g. ψ 50²¹ *thou thoughtest* הֱיוֹת־אֶהְיֶה כָמוֹךָ *I was surely like thyself*
[but read הָיוֹ for הֱיוֹת] ; Gn 41¹⁵, Ju 9⁴⁸ *what ye have seen me do* ; Is 48⁸, Ho 7².

(*b*) Object-clauses introduced by כִּי, e. g. Gn 6⁵ וַיַּרְא יְהוָֹה כִּי רַבָּה רָעַת הָאָדָם *b*
and the Lord saw that the wickedness of man was great, &c.—Direct narration also
is very frequently introduced by כִּי (analogous to the ὅτι *recitativum*; frequently,
indeed, with the secondary idea of a particle of asseveration, as in Gn 26⁹,
27²⁰), e. g. Gn 21³⁰, 22¹⁶ᶠ·, 26²², 29³², 37³⁵, Jos 2²⁴, &c., even when the direct
narration is not expressly indicated, Gn 4²⁵, 32³¹, 41⁵¹ᶠ·, Ex 18⁴.—On the
expression of a second object by means of a clause introduced by כִּי, see
§ 117 *h*.[2]

(*c*) Object-clauses introduced by אֲשֶׁר, e. g. Est 3⁴ כִּי־הִגִּיד לָהֶם אֲשֶׁר־הוּא *c*
יְהוּדִי *for he had told them that he was a Jew* ; 1 S 18¹⁵, Ez 20²⁶, Ec 8¹²,[3] even before
direct narration, 1 S 15²⁰, 2 S 1⁴. Somewhat frequently אֲשֶׁר is preceded by

---

[1] On these clauses with כִּי and אֲשֶׁר and generally on clauses which we
should render as subordinate, cf. P. Dörwald ' Zur hebr. Syntax ' in *Neue
Jahrbb. für Philol. und Pädag.* 1890, p. 115 ff.

[2] Instead of a complete objective clause we sometimes find a kind of
accusative and infinitive construction, especially after נָתַן (prop. *to give up*)
in the sense of *to allow*, e. g. Nu 21²³ וְלֹא־נָתַן סִיחֹן אֶת־יִשְׂרָאֵל עֲבֹר בִּגְבֻלוֹ *and
Sihon did not suffer Israel to pass through his border*; 20²¹; followed by an
infinitive with לְ, e. g. Gn 20⁶, 31⁷, Ex 3¹⁹.—Cf. also the analogous examples
in Dt 28⁵⁶ (after נִסָּה *to venture*; see § 113 *d*); Ju 11²⁰ (after הֶאֱמִין *to trust*);
1 K 19⁴ (after שָׁאַל *to request*).

[3] In Jer 28⁹ a *subject*-clause is thus introduced by אֲשֶׁר instead of the
usual כִּי.

the *nota accusativi* אֶת־ (equivalent to *the circumstance, the fact, that*), e. g. Jos 2¹⁰, 1 S 24¹¹·¹⁹, 2 S 11²⁰, Is 38³, but in Gn 30²⁹, Dt 29¹⁵ equivalent to *the way in which*.

§ 158. *Causal Clauses.*

a　A complete clause, assigning the reason for statements, demands, threats, &c., sometimes follows with the simple *wāw copulative*, e. g. ψ 60¹³ *give us help against the adversary, and* (for) *vain is the help of man*; Gn 6¹⁷ (וַאֲנִי), 22¹², Ex 23⁹, Jb 22¹², perhaps also ψ 7¹⁰; or even without *Wāw*, e. g. Gn 17¹⁴. As a rule, however, special conjunctions in various combinations are used to introduce causal clauses.

b　The most common causal conjunctions are יַעַן כִּי Is 3¹⁶, &c., and יַעַן אֲשֶׁר *because*, prop. *on account of the fact that*; both, however, may also be shortened to the simple יַעַן Nu 20¹², &c., or to כִּי *because*, Gn 3¹⁴·¹⁷, &c., or to אֲשֶׁר Gn 30¹⁸, 31⁴⁹, 34¹³·²⁷, 1 S 15¹⁵, 20⁴², 26¹⁶·²³, 1 K 3¹⁹, 8³³, Ho 14⁴, Zc 1¹⁵; also בַּאֲשֶׁר Gn 39⁹·²³. On the other hand, the simple יַעַן is sometimes repeated for emphasis, יַעַן וּבְיַעַן (something like the German *sintemal und alldieweil*) Lv 26⁴³, Ez 13¹⁰ (without וּ 36³); also עַל־אֲשֶׁר 2 S 3³⁰, and עַל־כִּי¹ Dt 31¹⁷, Ju 3¹², Mal 2¹⁴ *on the ground that*; עַל־דְּבַר אֲשֶׁר *because of the circumstance that*, Dt 23⁵; עַל־כָּל־אֹדוֹת אֲשֶׁר *for this very cause that*, Jer 3⁸. But just as the simple יַעַן is used for יַעַן אֲשֶׁר, so also the simple עַל־ with the perfect stands for עַל־אֲשֶׁר ψ 119¹³⁶, Ezr 3¹¹; cf. עַל־בְּלִי Gn 31²⁰ and מִבְּלִי Dt 28⁵⁵ both with the perfect, equivalent to *because . . . not*.—Cf. further עֵקֶב אֲשֶׁר Gn 22¹⁸, 26⁵, 2 S 12⁶, all with the perfect, and עֵקֶב כִּי (2 S 12¹⁰ with the perfect; Am 4¹² with the imperfect) prop. *in return for the fact that*; similarly again the simple עֵקֶב Nu 14²⁴ with the perfect, and Dt 7¹², 8²⁰ with the imperfect; finally, מֵאֲשֶׁר Is 43⁴ *arising from the fact that*, = *because*; תַּחַת אֲשֶׁר 1 S 26²¹, &c., and תַּחַת כִּי Dt 4³⁷, Pr 1²⁹ *for the reason that*.

c　Rem. 1. The preposition עַל־ (*because of, on account of*) with the infinitive (§ 114 *e*) is frequently used as the equivalent of a full causal clause; cf. e. g. Am 1³·⁶·¹³, 2¹·⁶. Such a construction with the infinitive may, however, according to § 114 *r*, be continued by means of a finite verb, in which case עַל־ governs the verb as a conjunction; e. g. Am 1⁹ . . . וְלֹא זָכְרוּ עַל־הַסְגִּירָם *because they delivered up . . . and remembered not*, &c.; 1¹¹, 2⁴; without *Wāw*, Is 30¹⁴.

d　2. The choice of tense is regulated by the general principles stated in § 106 ff., viz. the perfect (cf. especially § 106 *f*) refers to causes already brought fully into effect, the imperfect to those which may contingently arise; cf. e. g. Dt 7¹², 8²⁰, 1 K 8³³, where the imperfect leaves the possibility still open that the persons addressed will perhaps escape the threatened punishments by avoiding disobedience.—Cf. further, § 111 *h* on the imperfect consecutive, and § 112 *nn* on the perfect consecutive in the apodosis to causal clauses.

---

¹ Also כִּי־עַל־כֵּן prop. *for therefore*, Gn 18⁵, 19⁸, 33¹⁰, 38²⁶, Nu 10³¹, 14⁴³, 2 S 18²⁰ Q°rê, and אֲשֶׁר עַל־כֵּן Jb 34²⁷, always mean *forasmuch as.*

§ 159. *Conditional Sentences.*

Cf. H. Ferguson, ' The Use of the Tenses in Conditional Sentences in Hebrew ' (*Journal of the Society of Bibl. Lit. and Exeg.*, Middletown, Conn., June and September, 1882).—P. Friedrich, *Die hebr. Conditionalsätze*, Königsberg, 1884 (Inaug.-Diss.).—Driver, *Use of the Tenses*, 3rd ed., p. 174 ff.

1. The great variety of construction in conditional sentences is *a* owing to the fact that it frequently depends on the subjective judgement of the speaker, whether he wishes a condition to be regarded as *capable of fulfilment* (absolutely, or at least possibly), thus including those already fulfilled, or as *incapable of fulfilment.* On this distinction depends the choice both of the conditional particle to be used (see below), and especially (as also in Greek and Latin) of the tense. The use of the latter is naturally determined according to the general principles laid down in § 106 ff.[1] In the following sketch, for the sake of clearness, conditional sentences *without* conditional particles will be first discussed (under *b*), and afterwards sentences *with* these particles (under *l*).

2. The relation between condition and consequence may be expressed, *b* as in English, by the simple juxtaposition of two clauses. At the same time, it is to be observed in general as a fundamental rule (in accordance with the original character of the two tenses), that the *imperfect,* with its equivalents (the jussive, cohortative, imperative, perfect consecutive, and participle), is used to express a condition and consequence which are regarded as being *capable of fulfilment* in present or future time, while the *perfect* represents a condition already fulfilled in the past, and its consequence as an accomplished fact. The other use of the perfect—to represent conditions regarded as *impossible*—occurs only in connexion with particles.

Examples :—

(*a*) *Imperfect* (cf. § 107 *x*) in protasis and apodosis, Jos 22[18], ψ 104[28 ff.] *C* יִלְקֹטוּן [2] תִּתֵּן לָהֶם (if) *thou givest unto them, they gather*, &c. ; ψ 139[18], Pr 12[17], Jb 20[24], Ec 1[18], Neh 1[8] ; with an interrogative imperfect in the apodosis, Ju 13[12] ; with the jussive, Jb 10[16] ; with the cohortative, Pr. 1[23] ; with the perfect, Is 26[10] (*yet will he not learn righteousness* ; the apodosis forcibly denies

---

[1] It may, moreover, happen that a different idea is introduced in the apodosis, from that with which the protasis started—a source of many further variations.

[2] On the termination וּן- cf. § 47 *m*. In verse 28 *b* also יְשֵׁבֵעוּן is probably to be explained from its immediately preceding the greater *pause*. These terminations in verses 28–30 and ψ 139[18] can scarcely have any connexion with the conditional sentence, although it is strange that וּן- in Nu 32[23] appears after אִם־לֹא in the protasis. In Nu 16[29], 32[20] וּן. as before א (as in Jb 31[10] in the apodosis) is to be explained from the dislike of hiatus.

what the imperfect in the protasis had represented as still conceivable ; cf. Ho 8¹²) ; with the perfect consecutive, Gn 47²⁵, Ex 33⁵ ; with the protasis suppressed, Jb 5⁸ (see § 107 *x*).

d   (*b*) *Jussive* in protasis (cf. § 109 *h, i*) and apodosis, ψ 104¹⁰ תְּשֶׁת־חֹשֶׁךְ וִיהִי לָיְלָה (if) *thou makest darkness, it is night*; imperfect in the apodosis, ψ 104²⁹ *b* ; cohortative Pr 1²³.   Also in Ex 7⁹ יְהִי לְתַנִּין *it shall become a serpent*, is the apodosis to a suppressed protasis *if thou cast it down*; so in 2 K 5¹⁰ וְיָשֹׁב is the apodosis to a protasis *if thou wash*, contained in what precedes.

e   (*c*) *Cohortative* (see § 108 *e*) in the protasis ; perfect in the apodosis, ψ 40⁶ ; imperfect consecutive, Jb 19¹⁸ אָקוּמָה וַיְדַבְּרוּ־בִי (if) *I arise, they speak against me* ; on the cohortative in the apodosis, cf. § 108 *f*.

f   (*d*) *Imperfect consecutive* in the protasis (§ 111 *x*), ψ 139¹¹ וָאֹמַר *if I say*, &c. (with a noun-clause as the apodosis) ; with a frequentative perfect consecutive in the apodosis, 1 S 2¹⁶.

g   (*e*) *Perfect consecutive* in the protasis and apodosis (see the examples, § 112 *kk* and *ll*), Gn 44²² וְעָזַב אָבִיו וָמֵת *and should he leave his father, his father would die* ; 9¹⁵, 44²⁹, Ex 4¹⁴, 12¹³, 1 S 16², 19³, 2 S 13²⁸, 1 K 8³⁰ ; with frequentative perfects, Ex 16²¹ (referring to the past, Jer 20⁹) ; with imperfect in the apodosis (being separated from the *Wāw* by לֹא), Nu 23²⁰, Jb 5²⁴ ; introduced by an infinitive absolute, 1 K 2³⁷ ; an interrogative clause in the apodosis, Lv 10¹⁹ ; a noun-clause, ψ 37¹⁰, Jb 7²¹.

h   (*f*) *A simple perfect* (to represent actions which are to be regarded as completed) in the protasis and apodosis, Pr 18²² מָצָא אִשָּׁה מָצָא טוֹב *has one found a wife, he has found a good thing* ; an imperfect in the apodosis, Jb 19⁴, 23¹⁰ ; an imperfect consecutive, Ex 20²⁵, Pr 11², Jb 3²⁵, 23¹³ *b*, 29¹¹ ; an interrogative clause, Nu 12¹⁴, Jb 7²⁰ *if I have sinned* (prop., well, now I have sinned !) *what can I do unto thee?* 21³¹, 35⁶, Am 3⁸ ; a noun-clause, Jb 27¹⁹.

i   (*g*) *A participle* as *casus pendens* (cf. § 143 *d*, and the sections of the Grammar there cited, esp. § 116 *w*) or a complete noun-clause in the protasis ; the apodosis mostly introduced by *wāw apodosis*, e.g. Pr 23²⁴ *K*ᵉᵗʰ. יֹלֵד חָכָם וְיִשְׂמַח בּוֹ *if one begetteth a wise child, he shall have joy of him* ; with perfect frequentative in the apodosis, 1 S 2¹³, &c. ; but also with a simple imperfect, e.g. Ex 21¹² (cf. § 112 *n*) ; with an interrogative imperfect, 2 K 7².¹⁹ ; with an interrogative perfect, Ju 6¹³.

k   (*h*) *Infinitive with preposition* (also as the equivalent of a conditional clause) in the protasis, and a perfect consecutive in the apodosis (cf. § 112 *mm*), e.g. 2 S 7¹⁴ ff. בְּהַעֲוֺתוֹ וְהֹכַחְתִּיו וגו' *if he commit iniquity, I will correct him*; Ex 34³⁴ f. (with imperfect, followed by perfects frequentative in the apodosis).

Rem. On the expression of condition and consequence by means of two co-ordinate *imperatives*, see § 110 *f*.

l   **3.** Particles used to introduce conditional sentences are אִם (for which in the later and latest Books sometimes הֵן, see below, under *w*) and לוּ¹ (1 S 14³⁰, Is 63¹⁹ לוּא ; Ec 6⁶, Est 7⁴ אִלּוּ, from אִם לוּ) *if*, negative אִם לֹא and לוּלֵא (לוּלֵי) *unless* ; כִּי *supposing that* (Lat. *ut*), *in case that*, sometimes used almost in the same sense as אִם.   With regard to the difference between אִם (אִם לֹא) and לוּ (לוּלֵא), the fundamental rule is that אִם is used if the condition be regarded either as already fulfilled, or if it, together with its consequence, be thought of as possibly (or

_____

¹ On לוּ cf. Kohler in Geiger's *Zeitschr. für Wiss. und Leben*, vi (1868), p. 21 ff.

probably) occurring in the present or future. In the former case, אִם
is followed by the perfect, in the latter (corresponding to the Greek
ἐάν with the present subjunctive) by the imperfect or its equivalent
(frequently in the apodosis also). On the other hand, לוּ (לוּלֵא) is used
when the condition is to be represented as *not fulfilled* in the past,
or as *not capable of fulfilment* in the present or future, and the consequence accordingly as not having occurred or never occurring. In the
former case, לוּ and לוּלֵא are necessarily followed by the perfect (mostly
also in the apodosis) corresponding to the Greek εἰ with the indicative
of an historic tense, and the Latin imperfect or pluperfect subjunctive.
In the latter case (which is extremely rare) the perfect, or the participle, or even the imperfect, may be used.

Rem. Since it again frequently depends on the subjective judgement of the *m*
speaker (see under *a*), whether a condition is to be regarded as possible or
impossible, we cannot wonder that the distinction between אִם and לוּ is not
always consistently observed. Although naturally לוּ and לוּלֵא cannot take
the place of אִם and אִם לֹא (on the strange use of לוּ in Gn 50¹⁵ see below),
yet conversely אִם is sometimes used where לוּ would certainly be expected ;
cf. e.g. ψ 50¹², 137⁵, 139⁸, Ho 9¹² (cf. verse 11). These examples, indeed (אִם
with the imperfect), may without difficulty be explained from the fact that
the connexion of לוּ with the imperfect was evidently avoided, because the
imperfect by its nature indicates a still unfinished action, and consequently
(as opposed to לוּ) a still open possibility. But אִם is also used for לוּ in connexion with the perfect, especially when an imprecation is attached by the
apodosis to the condition introduced by אִם, e.g. ψ 7⁴ ᶠᶠ. . . . אִם־עָשִׂיתִי זֹאת
יְרַדֹּף וגו׳ *if I have done this . . . , let the enemy pursue my soul*, &c., cf. Jb 31⁹ ᶠᶠ.
The speaker assumes for a moment as possible and even actual, that which
he really rejects as inconceivable, in order to invoke the most severe punish-
ment on himself, if it should prove to be the case.
On the frequent addition of an infinitive absolute to the verb in clauses
with אִם see § 113 *o* above.

Examples :—
A. אִם 1. with *perfect* in the protasis to express conditions, &c., which have *n*
been completely fulfilled in the past or which will be completely fulfilled in
the future (the perfect is here equivalent to the *futurum exactum*, § 106 *o*).
The apodosis [1] takes—

(*a*) A *perfect* also, e.g. Pr 9¹² אִם־חָכַמְתָּ חָכַמְתָּ לָּךְ *if thou art wise, thou art wise
for thyself*; ψ 73¹⁵ (see below on לוּ).

(*b*) *Imperfect*, e.g. Dt 32⁴¹ אִם־שַׁנּוֹתִי *if I whet my glittering sword . . .* אָשִׁיב
I will render vengeance, &c.; Jb 9¹⁵ ᶠ. ³⁰ (in both cases we should expect
לוּ rather than אִם; so also in ψ 44²¹ ᶠ., with an interrogative imperfect in
the apodosis); Jb 11¹³ (the apodosis is in verse 15).

(*c*) *Jussive* (or *optative*), e.g. Jb 31⁹ ᶠᶠ. (see *m* above) ; Gn 18³.

---

[1] We are not here concerned with the fact that the logical apodosis (the
consequence of the condition) is sometimes mentioned before the condition ;
as in Gn 18²⁸·³⁰, Ju 11¹⁰, ψ 63⁶ ᶠ., 137⁶, and according to Dillmann Is 4⁴.

o　　(*d*) *Perfect consecutive* (see the examples in § 112 *gg*), e. g. Gn 43⁹ אִם־לֹא הֲבִיאֹתִיו וג׳ *if I bring him not . . . then I shall have sinned*, &c. ; Ju 16¹⁷, 2 S 15³³, 2 K 7⁴. On the other hand, e. g. Gn 47⁶, Mi 5⁷, Jb 7⁴ refer to actions already completed ; in Gn 38⁹ and Nu 21⁹ the perfect with וְ is a perfect frequentative and refers to past time.

　　(*e*) *Imperfect consecutive* (see § 111 *q*), e. g. Jb 8⁴ *if thy children have sinned* (חָטָאוּ) . . . , וַיְשַׁלְּחֵם *he has delivered them*, &c.

　　(*f*) *Imperative*, e. g. Gn 50⁴ אִם־נָא מָצָאתִי חֵן בְּעֵינֵיכֶם דַּבְּרוּ־נָא וג׳ *if now I have found grace in your eyes, speak, I pray you*, &c. ; the imperative precedes in Gn 47¹⁶ and Jb 38⁴·¹⁸.

p　　(*g*) A (complete or incomplete) noun-clause, e. g. Jer 14¹⁸ (a vivid realization of the future) *if I have gone forth into the field* (= *if I go*, &c.), *then, behold, the slain with the sword !* &c. ; Pr 24¹⁴ (apodosis with *wāw apodosis*).

q　　2. אִם with *imperfect* in the protasis, to express what is possible in the present or future, as well as (according to § 107 *b*) what has continued or been repeated in the past. The apodosis takes—

　　(*a*) The *perfect*, e. g. Nu 32²³ וְאִם־לֹא תַעֲשׂוּן כֵּן הִנֵּה חֲטָאתֶם *but if ye will not do so, behold, ye have sinned* ; here the apodosis represents the time when the consequence has already taken place ; so also Jb 20¹²⁻¹⁴. On the other hand, Nu 16²⁹ (as also 1 S 6⁹ and 1 K 22²⁸) is a case of a pregnant construction, *if these men die as all men die, then* (it will follow from this) *the Lord hath not sent me.*

r　　(*b*) The *imperfect*, e. g. 2 K 7⁴ אִם־יְחַיֻּנוּ נִחְיֶה *if they save us alive, we shall live*, &c. ; Gn 13¹⁶, 18²⁸·³⁰, 28²⁰ ff., Ex 20²⁵ (the second imperfect is equivalent to a jussive) ; Is 1¹⁸, 10²², Am 9²⁻⁴, ψ 50¹² (where אִם ironically represents an impossibility as possible) ; Jb 8⁵ ᶠ· (with the insertion of a second condition in the form of a noun-clause) ; 9³·²⁰, 14⁷ ; a frequentative imperfect referring to the past, Gn 31⁸ אִם־כֹּה יֹאמַר *if* (ever) *he said thus . . .*, וְיָלְדוּ *then they bare . . .* ; Ex 40³⁷. In Gn 42³⁷ the consequence (on תָּמִית cf. § 107 *s*) precedes the condition.

　　(*c*) The *jussive* (or *optative*), e. g. ψ 137⁵ ; cf. § 109 *h*.

　　(*d*) The *cohortative*, e. g. Gn 13⁹, Jb 31⁷ ; cf. § 108 *f*.

s　　(*e*) The *perfect consecutive* (see the examples in § 112 *ff* and *gg*), e. g. 1 S 20⁶ אִם־פָּקֹד יִפְקְדֵנִי אָבִיךָ וְאָמַרְתָּ *if thy father miss me at all, then shalt thou say*, &c. ; Gn 24⁴¹, Ju 4²⁰ ; with a frequentative perfect consecutive, Gn 31⁸ *if he said* (as often happened) *. . . , then*, &c.

　　(*f*) The *imperfect consecutive* ; so perhaps ψ 59¹⁶, if וִילִינוּ is to be explained according to § 111 *t*.

　　(*g*) The *imperative*, e. g. Gn 31⁵⁰, 1 S 20²¹ (with *wāw apodosis*, but in verse 22 simply לֵךְ), 21¹⁰, Jb 33⁵.

t　　(*h*) A noun-clause, e. g. Gn 4⁷, ψ 139⁸, Jb 8⁶, 31²⁶ ᶠ·

　　3. אִם with *cohortative*, e. g. Gn 30³¹ ; cf. the passages in § 108 *e*.

u　　4. אִם with *infinitive*, Jb 9²⁷ אִם־אָמְרִי prop. *if my saying is* (but probably we should read אָמַרְתִּי).

v　　5. אִם with a noun-clause, e. g. Dt 5²² (in the apodosis a perfect with *wāw apodosis*), Gn 27⁴⁶, Ju 9¹⁵ (imperative in the apodosis) ; 11⁹ (imperfect in the apodosis) ; 2 S 12⁸ (cohortative in the apodosis) ; Ho 12¹² ; especially if the subject of the conditional clause be a personal pronoun. In an affirmative sentence this pronoun is often joined to יֵשׁ, in a negative sentence to אֵין (cf. on both, § 100 *o*), while the predicate (cf. § 116 *q*) is represented by a participle, usually expressing the future, e. g. Ju 6³⁶ ᶠ אִם־יֶשְׁךָ מוֹשִׁיעַ

if thou wilt save, &c. ; Gn 24⁴⁹ אִם־יֶשְׁכֶם עֹשִׂים *if ye will deal*, &c. ; 1 S 23²³. In Gn 24⁴²ᶠ· the condition is expressed in a more humble form by the addition of נָא. With אֵין Gn 43⁵ וְאִם־אֵינְךָ מְשַׁלֵּחַ *but if thou wilt not send*, &c. ; 20⁷ (with imperative in the apodosis) ; Ex 8¹⁷, 9²ᶠ·, 1 S 19¹¹ (all with a participle also in the apodosis). But יֵשׁ and אַיִן may also be used after אִם without a suffix ; thus יֵשׁ Gn 23⁸, 1 S 20⁸, 2 K 9¹⁵, &c., אִם־אַיִן (*if it be not the case*) Gn 30¹, Ex 32³², Ju 9¹⁵, 2 K 2¹⁰ ; cf. also אִם־כֵּן *if it be so*, Gn 25²².

B. הֵן *if*, generally supposed to be originally identical with הֵן *behold!*[1] *w* Probably, however, הֵן *if*, is a pure Aramaism, and since the Aramaic word never has the meaning *behold*, it is at least improbable that it had originally any connexion with הֵן or הִנֵּה. Cf. Ex 8²², Lv 25²⁰, Is 54¹⁵, Jer 3¹, Hag 2¹², 2 Ch 7¹³, and frequently in Job, as 9¹¹·¹², 12¹⁴·¹⁵, 19⁷, 23⁸, 40²³, always with wāw apodosis following, except in 13¹⁵, where consequently the meaning *see* is no doubt preferable.

C. לוּ *if*, לוּלֵא (לוּלֵי) *if not.* *x*

1. With *perfect* in the protasis and apodosis (cf. § 106 p), e.g. Ju 8¹⁹ ; לוּ is used in the same sense as לְוּ in Est 7⁴, cf. Ec 6⁶ (with a question in the apodosis).—With the perfect in protasis and apodosis after לוּלֵא Gn 31⁴², 43¹⁰, Ju 14¹⁸, 1 S 25³⁴, 2 S 2²⁷, Is 1⁹. On the other hand, in Dt 32²⁹ לוּ with a perfect is followed by an imperfect in the apodosis, *if they were wise, they would understand this* ; in Mi 2¹¹ by a perfect consecutive.

2. With *imperfect* after לוּלֵא Dt 32²⁷ אָגוּר probably as the *modus rei repetitae,* *y* *were it not that I ever and again feared*, &c. ; so also the imperfect after לוּ with the apodosis suppressed, Gn 50¹⁵ *supposing that Joseph should hate us* ; since, according to the context, the danger was real, the use of לוּ here is strange ; conversely in other cases, e. g. ψ 73¹⁵, Jb 9¹⁵ᶠ·³⁰, לוּ would be more natural than אִם.

3. A noun-clause occurs after לוּ 2 S 18¹², 2 K 3¹⁴, ψ 81¹⁴, all with imperfect *z* in the apodosis ; Jb 16⁴ לוּ יֵשׁ, with cohortative in the apodosis.

D. כִּי *supposing that, if* :—

1. כִּי with *perfect* in the protasis, e.g. Nu 5²⁰ וְאַתְּ כִּי שָׂטִית *but thou, if thou* *aa* *hast gone astray*, &c. ; with a frequentative perfect consecutive in the apodosis, Jb 7¹³ᶠ· ; with an imperfect consecutive, Jb 22²⁹.

2. כִּי with *imperfect* in the protasis, e.g. ψ 23⁴ גַּם כִּי־אֵלֵךְ *yea, though I walk* *bb* (have to walk) . . ., *I will fear no* (לֹא־אִירָא) *evil* ; 37²⁴ ; Ex 21² כִּי־תִקְנֶה עֶבֶד עִבְרִי וְגוֹ׳ *if thou buy an Hebrew servant, six years shall he serve* (but in verses 3–5 a series of definite conditions with definite consequences is introduced by אִם ; so also the כִּי in verse 7 is followed in verses 8–11 by the special cases with אִם ; cf. also verse 17 ff.) ; cf. Gn 4²⁴, 24⁴¹, Jb 38⁵ ; with a perfect consecutive in the apodosis, Gn 32¹⁸ᶠ·, Ex 18¹⁶ ; with a noun-clause, Is 1¹⁵.

3. כִּי with a *noun-clause* (and imperfect in the apodosis), 2 S 19⁸.

REMARKS.

1. In 2 K 5¹³ the particle אֲבִי (Masora אָבִי, probably in the sense of *my* *cc* *father*) appears exceptionally for לוּ ; its meaning here is unquestionable, but

---

[1] There could be no doubt of their identity if וְהִנֵּה in 1 S 9⁷, 2 S 18¹¹, simply meant *if*. We must, however, keep to the meaning *but behold*.

its origin is obscure. Cf. the exhaustive discussion of Delitzsch and Wetzstein on Jb 34³⁶, where this אִבַי appears to be used as a desiderative particle.—Sometimes when one case has been already discussed, another of the same character is added by means of אוֹ *or*, e.g. Ex 21²⁶ אוֹ נוֹדַע וג׳ *or* (another possible case) *it is known that*, &c., i.e. *but if it be known*, &c., LXX ἐὰν δέ, Vulg. *sin autem*; cf. Lv 4²³·²⁸, 5¹, 25⁴⁹, 2 S 18¹³; with a following imperfect, Ez 14¹⁷ᶠ.—On the hypothetical use of אֲשֶׁר (which is interchangeable with כִּי in other senses also) Lv 4²² (in verses 3 and 27 אִם), Dt 11²⁷ (verse 28 אִם), Jos 4²¹, see the Lexicon.

dd 2. The conditional sentence is frequently found in an abridged form, where the suppressed clauses can be easily supplied from the context; cf. Gn 13⁹, 24⁴⁹, 1 S 2¹⁶ וְאִם־לֹא *and if not*, i.e. *and if thou wilt not give it to me, then I take it* (perfect according to § 106 *n*) *by force*; cf. 1 S 6⁹. The use of וַיֵּשׁ alone in Ju 6¹³ is peculiar, as also וַיֵּשׁ in 2 K 10¹⁵ (where read with the LXX וַיֹּאמֶר יֵהוּא וַיֵּשׁ) in the sense of *if it be so*.—In 2 S 13²⁶, 2 K 5¹⁷ וְלֹא alone appears to be used in the sense of *if really . . . not*, in each case with a following jussive equivalent to *may there at least*, &c. (cf. § 143 *d*); but perhaps with Matthes, *ZAW*. 1903, p. 122 ff., following Kuipers, we should read וְלוּ *would that!*—In 1 S 13¹³, Jb 3¹³ the condition must be supplied from the preceding clause to complete the sentence introduced by כִּי עַתָּה, in Jb 31²⁸ by כִּי, in 2 K 13¹⁹ by אָז.—The apodosis also appears sometimes in an abridged form (e.g. Gn 4²⁴, Is 43²) or is entirely suppressed, e.g. Gn 30²⁷, 38¹⁷, 50¹⁵ (see *y* above), Ex 32³², ψ 27¹³, Jb 38⁵, where properly הִגֵּד must be supplied with כִּי תֵדַע as in verses 4 and 18; cf. § 167 *a*.—In ψ 8⁴, instead of the apodosis *I exclaim* which we should expect, the exclamation itself follows.

ee 3. The absolute certainty with which a result is to be expected is frequently emphasized by the insertion of כִּי Is 7⁹; כִּי אָז 2 S 2²⁷, 19⁷, Jb 11¹⁵; or כִּי עַתָּה *now verily*, Nu 22²⁹, 1 S 14³⁰ after לוּ, Gn 31⁴², 43¹⁰ after לוּלֵי, Jb 8⁶ after אִם. On this *corroborative* כִּי cf. such passages as Gn 18²⁰, &c., and § 148 *d*. On כִּי אִם after an oath cf. 163 *d*.

ff 4. Sometimes the force of a hypothetical particle extends beyond the apodosis to a second conditional clause, as in the case of אִם Pr 9¹², Jb 10¹⁵, 16⁶, 22²³, and כִּי Is 43².

gg 5. In Ex 33²⁰ a negative statement takes the place of a condition with a negative consequence, *for a man doth not see me and live*, instead of *for if a man sees me, he does not live*; cf. the similar passages, Dt 22¹·⁴ *thou shalt not see . . . and hide thyself*, instead of *if thou seest . . . thou shalt not hide thyself*.

§ 160. *Concessive Clauses.*

a Besides the use of the imperative in the sense of a concession, meant either seriously (§ 110 *a*) or mockingly (§ 110 *f*), and of concessive circumstantial clauses (§ 141 *e*, § 142 *d*, and § 156 *f*), concessive clauses may be introduced—

(a) By a simple אִם *if*: thus Jb 9¹⁵ with perfect, *if* (=*though*) *I had been in the right*; Is 1¹⁸ and 10²² with imperfect in reference to a contingent event.

b (b) By כִּי גַם *yea though*, Is 1¹⁵ with imperfect; for which we find simply גַם in Is 49¹⁵ with imperfect, *yea, though these may forget, yet . . .*; on the other hand, with perfect, Jer 36²⁵, ψ 95⁹, Neh 6¹; finally כִּי גַם *even if, though*, Ec 4¹⁴.

(c) By the preposition עַל governing a complete noun-clause, as Jb 16¹⁷ C עַל לֹא־חָמָס בְּכַפַּי *notwithstanding* that *no violence is in mine hands*, or a verbal-clause, Is 53⁹. On עַל with the infinitive in a similar sense (equivalent to *in addition to the fact* that= *notwithstanding* that), cf. § 119 aa, note 2.

§ 161. *Comparative Clauses.*

1. A comparison between two facts is sometimes established by *a* simply uniting them with *wāw copulative*, especially in gnomic poetry, when facts of a moral nature are compared with those of the physical world, e. g. Jb 5⁷ *man is born unto trouble, and the sons of flame fly upward*, i. e. as the sparks by nature fly upward, so man, &c.; Jb 12¹¹ (in an interrogative form; in 34³ the same comparison as a statement); 14¹¹ ᶠ·, Pr 17³, 25³, 26³·⁹·¹⁴, 27²¹, &c.¹ Even without the connecting וְ Jb 24¹⁹ *drought and heat consume the snow waters*, שְׁאוֹל חָטָאוּ so doth *Sheol* those who *have sinned* (cf. § 155 n); cf. Jer 17¹¹.

2. The conjunction כַּאֲשֶׁר (cf. § 155 g; the simple אֲשֶׁר occurs in the *b* same sense in Ex 10⁶, 14¹³, 34¹⁸) *as, quemadmodum*, is used as a comparative conjunction (Ob ¹⁵), frequently with כֵּן *so*, corresponding to it in the apodosis, Is 31⁴, 52¹⁴ᶠ·. Sometimes, however, כֵּן (*so also*) occurs even after independent statements, Is 55⁹, Jer 3²⁰.—Exact coincidence of two facts is expressed in Ec 5¹⁵ by כָּל־עֻמַּת שֶׁ ² *in all points as.*

Rem. On the use of כְּ *as*, with single nouns or pronouns to introduce C comparisons, cf. 118 s; on the alleged use of כְּ as a conjunction (equivalent to כַּאֲשֶׁר), cf. § 155 g.—It is to be further remarked that כְּ—כְּ when used in correspondence with one another, *as—so* (e. g. Lv 7⁷, Ju 8¹⁸, Is 24², Ho 4⁹; also *so—as*, Gn 18²⁵, 44¹⁸, Dt 1¹⁷, 1 K 22⁴; in Jos 14¹¹, 1 S 30²⁴ כְּ—וּכְ; ψ 127⁴ and often, כְּ—כְּ, cf. Jo 2⁴), are not to be regarded as conjunctions, but as virtual substantives with a following genitive; כָּכֶם כַּגֵּר יִהְיֶה Nu 15¹⁵ properly means *the like of you shall be the like of the stranger*, i. e. *your duty shall be* (also) *the stranger's duty*; cf. Lv 24²².

---

¹ On this *wāw adaequationis*, and in general on these proverbial comparisons, see Delitzsch, *Das Salomonische Spruchbuch*, p. 9 f. Moreover, instead of entire clauses, the nouns alone (without predicates) are frequently grouped together, e. g. Pr 25²⁵, 26²¹, 27²¹ (called by Delitzsch, the 'emblematic Mashal'). The expressions נֶחְשַׁב עִם prop. *to be counted with some one*, ψ 88⁵, and נִמְשַׁל עִם *to be likened with some one*, ψ 28¹, 143⁷, also arise from the idea of comparison implied in grouping things together. On this use of עִם cf. Jb 9²⁶, where *with* is equivalent to *like*.

² In spite of its form this particle has originally nothing to do with כֹּל, כָּל־ *all*. The expression is compounded of כְּ and לְעֻמַּת, like the Aramaic כָּל־קֳבֵל for כְּלָקֳבֵל; cf. M. Lambert, *REJ.* xxx. 47.

§ 162. *Disjunctive Sentences.*

a　The introduction of another possible case, excluding that which preceded, is effected by אוֹ *or*, e. g. Ex 21³⁶, equivalent to the Latin *vel*; but also equivalent to *aut* with an exclusive antithesis, 2 K 2¹⁶; so Is 27⁵ אוֹ=*it would then happen that*, for which elsewhere כִּי אוֹ.

b　In the sense of *sive—sive* we find אוֹ—אוֹ, or אִם—אָם, or אִם—אִם־וְאָם (see the examples in the Lexicon), also וְ—וְ Lv 5³, Nu 9¹⁴, Dt 24⁷, Is 2¹³ᶠ·, Jer 32²⁰, ψ 76⁷, Jb 34²⁹, perhaps also Ex 21¹⁶ (but not Pr 29⁹; cf. Delitzsch on the passage), and לְ—לְ (see § 143 *e*); cf. also גַּם—גַּם (in Gn 24⁴⁴ גַּם־וְגַם) *both—and*; but גַּם לֹא—גַּם לֹא (in Gn 21²⁶ וְגַם־לֹא גַם לֹא; Zp 1¹⁸ גַּם—גַּם...לֹא) *neither—nor*. On disjunctive questions, see § 150 *g*.

§ 163. *Adversative and Exceptive Clauses.*

a　1. After negative sentences (especially after prohibitions) the antithesis (*but*) is introduced by כִּי אִם, e. g. 1 S 8¹⁹ *and they said, Nay, but we will have a king over us*; ψ 1², &c.; frequently also by כִּי alone, e. g. Gn 18¹⁵, 19², or even simply connected with וְ, Gn 17⁵, וְהָיָה as perfect consecutive; 42¹⁰; cf. Ex 5¹⁸.

b　Rem. Sometimes the negation is only virtually contained in the preceding sentence, e. g. in the form of a rhetorical question (Mi 6³ᶠ·) or of conditions which are to be regarded as not having been fulfilled (Jb 31¹⁸); כִּי or כִּי אִם in such cases becomes equivalent to *nay, rather.*

c　2. *Exceptive* clauses, depending on another sentence, are introduced by אֶפֶס כִּי *except that*, and (again after negative sentences, see *a* above) כִּי אִם[1] *unless*; especially כִּי אִם with the perfect (equivalent to *unless previously*) after imperfects which contain a declaration, e. g. Gn 32²⁷ *I will not let thee go, except thou hast* previously *blessed me*; Lv 22⁶, Is 55¹⁰, 65⁶, Am 3⁷, Ru 3¹⁸. Finally, בִּלְתִּי אִם *unless*, Am 3⁴ (with perfect after a rhetorical question), or simply בִּלְתִּי Gn 43³ with a noun-clause, *except your brother be with you*; Is 10⁴ after a rhetorical question, with a verbal-clause.

---

[1] Very probably this use of כִּי אִם arises from the original meaning *for if, surely if* (כִּי in an affirmative sense); so evidently in Ex 22²² as a forcible resumption of the preceding אִם. Thus, e. g. Ju 15⁷ is simply *surely when I have been avenged of you, after that I will cease*, equivalent to, I will not cease, until I have, &c. When the exception follows, an ellipse must be assumed, e. g. Ru 3¹⁸ *surely* (or *for*) *when he has finished it* (then the man will rest). It is far less natural to assume such an ellipse with כִּי אִם *but* (before entire clauses as before single nouns); see *a* above.

Rem. The principal statement, to which כִּי אִם appends an exception, *d*
must sometimes be supplied from the context ; thus, Gn 40¹⁴ (I desire
nothing else) *except that thou remember me*, equivalent to *only do thou remember*, &c.
(cf. § 106 *n*, note 2 ; but it is probably better to read אַךְ for כִּי). Cf. Mi 6⁸,
where כִּי אִם, equivalent to *nothing but*, is used before an infinitive, and
Jb 42⁸, equivalent to *only*, before a noun. Similarly when כִּי אִם after an
oath introduces an emphatic assurance, e. g. in 2 K 5²⁰ *as the Lord liveth* (I can
do nothing else) *except I run after him*, &c. ; cf. 2 S 15²¹ K*eth*., Jer 51¹⁴, Ru 3¹²
K*eth*., and even without the oath, Ju 15⁷ ; cf. the Rem. on *c*.

§ 164. *Temporal Clauses*.

1. The relations of time existing between two different actions or *a*
events are frequently expressed without the aid of a conjunction simply
by juxtaposition :—

(*a*) Actions or events are represented as wholly or in part *simultaneous* by
connecting a noun-clause with another noun-clause or verbal-clause introduced by וְ (or וְהִנֵּה), e. g. Gn 7⁶ *and Noah was six hundred years old* (prop.
a son of six hundred years), וְהַמַּבּוּל הָיָה and (i. e. *when*) *the flood was*. This is
especially the case when the predicate of the noun-clause (frequently introduced by עוֹד *still*) is expressed by an active participle, e. g. Jb 1¹⁶ ᶠ· עוֹד זֶה
מְדַבֵּר וְזֶה בָא וּג' *he was yet speaking, and there came another*, &c. ; see the
numerous examples in § 111 *g* and § 116 *u*. Instead of a complete noun-
clause there often occurs a simple *casus pendens* after כָּל־ with a participial
attribute in the sense of *whenever any one . . .*, e. g. 1 S 2¹³ כָּל־אִישׁ זֹבֵחַ זֶבַח
וּבָא וּג' *whenever any man offered sacrifice, then came*, &c. ; 2 S 2²³, &c. ; see the
examples (in which the second member is generally introduced by *wāw
apodosis*) in § 116 *w*.

(*b*) Sequence is expressed by the juxtaposition   *b*
(1) of two imperfects consecutive, e. g. Gn 24¹⁹ וַתְּכַל לְהַשְׁקֹתוֹ וַתֹּאמֶר *and
when she had done giving him drink, she said*, &c. ; 28⁸ ᶠ·, 29³¹, 30⁹, 32²⁶, &c. ;
cf. § 111 *d* ;
(2) of a noun-clause with a passive participle as predicate, and a verbal-
clause attached by וְ, e. g. Gn 38²⁵ ; cf. § 116 *v* ; in Gn 49²⁹ an imperative
follows without וְ ;
(3) of two perfects (frequently with the secondary idea of rapid succession[1]
of the two actions or events in past time), e. g. Gn 19²³ הַשֶּׁמֶשׁ יָצָא . . . וְלוֹט בָּא וּג'
the sun was just risen . . ., *and* (=when) *Lot came*, &c., cf. 1 S 9⁵, 2 S 2²⁴ ;
Gn 44³ ᶠ·, Ju 3²⁴, 15¹⁴, 20³⁹ ᶠ·.—In all these examples the subject follows
immediately after the connective *Wāw*, and then the (simple) perfect. On
the other hand,
(4) a perfect consecutive follows another perfect consecutive to express
the contingent succession of future actions, e. g. Gn 44⁴ וְהִשַּׂגְתָּם וְאָמַרְתָּ אֲלֵהֶם

---

[1] This secondary idea is implied here by the mere co-ordination of two
independent *verbal*-clauses, just as the idea of simultaneous occurrence
(according to § 116 *u*, note 1) is implied in the co-ordination of a *noun*-clause
with another clause. In Gn 27³⁰ the immediate succession is especially
emphasized by אַךְ and the infinitive absolute, *Jacob was yet scarce gone out . . .
then Esau his brother came* ; in 1 K 9²⁴ by אַךְ only · in ψ 48⁶ by כֵּן and the
addition of two more perfects without וְ.

and when thou dost overtake them (as soon as thou shalt have overtaken), *thou shalt say unto them.* Naturally, examples of this kind are very closely related to conditional sentences; see, therefore, the examples in § 112 *kk* and § 159 *g*. On the connexion of an imperfect consecutive or a perfect with detached expressions of time (as equivalent to complete clauses), cf. § 111 *b*; on the imperfect consecutive after וַיְהִי and a statement of time, cf. § 111 *g*; on the perfect consecutive following a detached statement of time, as in Ex 16⁶, cf. § 112 *oo*.—In 1 S 29¹⁰ an imperative with וְ follows the perfect consecutive.

c (5) The fact that one action or event has not yet taken place on the occurrence of another, is expressed by טֶרֶם (an adverb, not a conjunction) with the imperfect (according to § 107 *c*). The apodosis, which may consist of a subject and perfect or even of a noun-clause (Gn 24¹⁵),[1] is then connected by וְ (or וְהִנֵּה) as in the examples above, under no. 3, e.g. Gn 19⁴ (cf. Jos 2⁸) טֶרֶם יִשְׁכָּבוּ וְאַנְשֵׁי הָעִיר . . . נָסַבּוּ וג׳ *they had not yet lain down, and* (= when) *the men of the city . . . compassed,* &c.; Gn 24²⁵.

d 2. Conjunctions used to introduce temporal clauses are כִּי (with perfect, e.g. Gn 6¹, Ju 1²⁸, 16¹⁶, 1 S 1¹²; with imperfect, Gn 4¹², 12¹², 24⁴¹, Ex 3²¹, Lv 21⁹, Dt 31²¹, Is 1¹², 8¹⁹) and אֲשֶׁר[2] *when* (כִּי with the imperfect also = *as often as*, ψ 8⁴; with perfect Jb 1⁵); less frequently אִם[3] (joined with a perfect), e.g. Gn 38⁹, Nu 21⁹, Ju 6³, ψ 41⁷, 94¹⁸, cf. also Is 24¹³ = *quotiescunque*; also in the same sense with an imperfect, Nu 36⁴; with a perfect, equivalent to the *futurum exactum*, Is 4¹. Other conjunctions of time are the compounds כְּמוֹ *when,* Gn 19¹⁵; כַּאֲשֶׁר *when, after that*; עַד־כִּי, עַד־אֲשֶׁר *until* (also the simple עַד, e.g. Gn 38¹¹, Jos 2²², 1 S 1²² [with the imperfect = *only when,* as in 2 S 10⁵]); 2⁵, &c.; especially in the formula עַד־בִּלְתִּי הִשְׁאִיר לוֹ *until there was none left remaining to him* (where indeed it would be very natural to read הַשְׁאִיר the infin. constr., as elsewhere after בִּלְתִּי, § 114 *s*) Nu 21³⁵, Dt 3³, Jos 8²², 11⁸ (but 1 S 14¹⁹ *while, as long as*); עַד אֲשֶׁר לֹא *before that,* Ec 12¹·²·⁶ with an imperfect, as in Pr 8²⁶ עַד with a perfect; עַד־אִם, עַד־אֲשֶׁר אִם *until the time when;* אַחֲרֵי־אֲשֶׁר (for which in Ez 40¹ אַחַר־אֲשֶׁר; Lv 25⁴⁸, 1 S 5⁹ simply אַחֲרֵי; Lv 14⁴³, Jer 41¹⁶, Jb 42⁷ simply אַחַר) *after that;* מֵאָז (prop. *since that time*; the dependent clause is attached to it in the same way as the attributive clause to the demonstrative אֲשֶׁר § 138 *e*) *since,* Gn 39⁵; בְּטֶרֶם (and simply טֶרֶם § 107 *c*) *before;* קַדְמַת (for קַדְמַת אֲשֶׁר) *before,* ψ 129⁶.

e Rem. 1. With regard to the tenses used with the above conjunctions, the rules used are practically the same as those given in § 158 *d* for causal clauses. The perfect indicates actions completed in the past or future (in the former case corresponding to the Latin pluperfect, § 106 *f*, and in the latter to the

---

[1] On the perfect in the protasis, which is critically doubtful, cf. § 107 *c*.

[2] On אֲשֶׁר as an original demonstrative, cf. § 138 *a*; hence עַד־אֲשֶׁר נָשׁוּב is properly *up to that* (moment)—*we shall return.*

[3] Cf. the frequent use of *wenn* [prop. *if*] for *wann* [= *when*] in German.

Latin *futurum exactum,* § 106 *o*), the imperfect denotes actions occurring contingently in the future. On בְּטֶרֶם, טֶרֶם, and עַד with the imperfect as a *tempus historicum,* cf. 107 *c.*

2. Clauses introduced by עַד, עַד־פִּי, or עַד־אֲשֶׁר, sometimes express a limit *f* which is not absolute (terminating the preceding action), but only relative, beyond which the action or state described in the principal clause still continues; thus, עַד with the imperfect, ψ 110¹; עַד־פִּי with the perfect, Gn 26¹³, with impf. 49¹⁰; עַד־אֲשֶׁר with the perfect, Gn 28¹⁵; with the imperfect, ψ 112⁸.—Like the Arab. عَدّ, عَدّ may even introduce a main clause; e.g. Ex 15¹⁶ עַד־יַעֲבֹר prop. no doubt = thus it came to this—*they passed through,* i.e. *so they passed through.*

3. The infinitive construct governed by a preposition (§ 114 *d, e*) is very *g* frequently used as the equivalent of a temporal clause; the infinitive with בְּ may usually be rendered by *when, as,* or *whilst;* the infinitive with כְּ by *when, as soon as* (in Pr 10²⁵ followed by a noun-clause introduced by *wāw apodosis*), or, when referring to the future, by *if;* the infinitive after מִן by *since.* According to § 111 *g* such statements of time are generally preceded by וִיהִי and the apodosis follows in the imperfect consecutive; hence in 1 S 17⁵⁵ (cf. Driver on the passage) וְכִרְאוֹת with a simple perfect following, is unusual. On the continuation of these infinitival constructions by means of the perfect consecutive, cf. § 112 *v,* and in general, § 114 *r.*—With the participle, בְּ appears to be used as the equivalent of a conjunction in כִּמְשִׁיב *as he drew back,* Gn 38²⁹ (unless we should read כְּהָשִׁיב [or כְּמוֹ הֵשִׁיב, cf. Gn 19¹⁵]), and in כְּפֹרַחַת *when it budded,* 40¹⁰.

§ 165. *Final Clauses.*[1]

1. Like most of the dependent clauses hitherto treated, the final *a* clause may also be joined by a simple *wāw copulative* to the main clause, unless the final clause is directly subordinated to the governing verb.

Examples of the connexion: (*a*) of a final imperfect (or jussive?) with a perfect by means of וְ, La 1¹⁹, see § 107 *q;* with an interrogative sentence, 2 S 9¹·³, Jb 38²⁴; with an optative, ψ 51⁹; with an imperative, 1 K 11²¹; (*β*) of a cohortative with an imperative by וְ, Gn 29²¹, 1 S 15¹⁶, or a jussive, Neh 2⁵ (§ 108 *d*); (*γ*) of a jussive with an imperative by וְ, Ex 9¹, 2 S 16¹¹, 1 K 5⁵⁰, ψ 59¹⁴, 86¹⁷; with a jussive, Jb 21¹⁹, or cohortative, § 109 *f, g* (cf. also 2 S 24²¹ the infinitive with לְ, Jon 1¹¹ מַה with the 1st plur. imperf., and 2 Ch 29¹⁰ עִם־לְבָבִי, which are equivalent to cohortatives); (*δ*) of an imperative with a jussive, cohortative, or interrogative sentence by וְ, § 110 *i;* (*ε*) of a perfect consecutive after another perfect consecutive, Lv 14³⁶; after an imperfect, § 112 *m* and *p;* similarly after a jussive, § 112 *q;* after an imperative, § 112 *r.*—On negative final clauses joined by וְלֹא to the imperfect (so Ex 28⁴³, 30²⁰; and 2 S 13²⁵ after אַל־נָא with a jussive in the main clause) see the Rem. on § 109 *g.* In Ex 28³², 39²³ the negative final clause is simply connected by לֹא.—On the use of an historical statement after verbs of command-

---

[1] Cf. H. G. T. Mitchell, *Final Constructions of Biblical Hebrew,* Leipzig, 1879.

ing, where we should expect a final clause (e.g. Neh 13⁹ *then I commanded, and they cleansed*, equivalent to *that they should cleanse, and they cleansed* ; in Jb 9⁷ a negative final clause is connected in this way by וְלֹא), cf. § 120 *f.*

For examples of the direct subordination of the final imperfect (without וְ) see § 120 *c.*

b 2. Final conjunctions are לְמַ֫עַן אֲשֶׁר *to the end that*; also simply לְמַ֫עַן Gn 12¹³, 27²⁵, Ex 4⁵, ψ 51⁶, &c.; בַּעֲבוּר אֲשֶׁר prop. *for the purpose that*, Gn 27¹⁰, and simply בַּעֲבוּר Gn 27⁴, Ex 9¹⁴, 20²⁰; also the simple אֲשֶׁר [1] Dt 4¹⁰·⁴⁰, 6³, 32⁴⁶, Jos 3⁷, Neh 8¹⁴·ᶠ·; negatively, אֲשֶׁר לֹא Gn 11⁷, 24³, 1 K 22¹⁶; or שֶׁ· Ec 3¹⁴; also negatively, עַל־דִּבְרַת שֶׁלֹּא *for the matter (purpose) that . . . not*, Ec 7¹⁴; לְבִלְתִּי with imperfect, Ex 20²⁰, 2 S 14¹⁴ *that . . . not.*—Quite exceptional is the use of מִן (if the text be right) in Dt 33¹¹ מִן־יְקוּמוּן, with the imperfect, equivalent to *that . . . not* [in prose, מִקּוּם].

c Rem. All the conjunctions here mentioned are naturally always used with the imperfect, see § 107 *q* (on the apparent exception in Jos 4²⁴, see § 74 *g*).— On the negative conjunctions אַל and פֶּן *that not, lest*, see § 152 *f* and *w*. On the infinitive with לְ [2] (also לְמַ֫עַן Gn 18¹⁹, 37²², &c.) as the equivalent of a final clause (Gn 11⁵, 28⁴, &c.), see § 114 *f, h, p.* On the continuation of such infinitival constructions by means of the finite verb, see § 114 *r.* On the negation of the final infinitive by לְבִלְתִּי, § 114 *s.* On the preposition מִן with a substantive or infinitive as the equivalent of a negative final clause (Gn 31²⁹, 1 S 15²³, &c.), see § 119 *x* and *y.*

§ 166. *Consecutive Clauses.*

a 1. Consecutive clauses are added by means of simple *wāw copulative* with the jussive,[3] especially after negative and interrogative sentences, e.g. Nu 23¹⁹ לֹא אִישׁ אֵל וִיכַזֵּב וּבֶן־אָדָם וְיִתְנֶחָם *God is not a man, that he should lie, and* (i. e. neither) *the son of man, that he should repent* ; Is 53² וְנֶחְמְדֵהוּ; Ho 14¹⁰ מִי חָכָם וְיָבֵן אֵלֶּה נָבוֹן וְיֵדָעֵם *who is wise, that he may understand these things ? prudent, that he may know them ?* Jb 5¹² וְלֹא=*so that . . . not*; in Pr 30³ וְ is separated from the predicate by the object. In Gn 16¹⁰ a negative consecutive clause comes after a cohortative, and in Ex 10⁵ after a perfect consecutive.—On the other hand, in Jb 9³²·³³ the jussive in the sense of a consecutive clause is attached without *Wāw* to the preceding negative sentence (in

---

[1] In Ez 36²⁷ a final clause is introduced by אֵת אֲשֶׁר, thus at the same time taking the form of an object-clause.

[2] On לְ as a supposed conjunction (equivalent to the Arabic *li*) 1 K 6¹⁹, see § 66 *i.*

[3] That such examples as וִיכַזֵּב are to be regarded as jussive is probable from the analogy of Ho 14¹⁰ and Jb 9³³.

verse 32 a second jussive follows, likewise without *Wāw, for he is not
a man, as I am, that I should answer him, that we should come together
in judgement*). On the imperfect consecutive as expressing a logical
consequence, see § 111 *l*; on the perfect consecutive as a consecutive
clause after a participle, see § 112 *n*.

2. Conjunctions introducing consecutive clauses are again (see *b*
§ 157 *c*, note 3) יִּ and אֲשֶׁר=*so that*; especially again after interrogative sentences, according to § 107 *u;* cf. Nu 16¹¹, יִּ with the
imperfect, *that ye murmur*; but in Gn 20¹⁰ with the perfect, in reference
to an action already completed. On אֲשֶׁר with the imperfect (or jussive)
equivalent to *so that*, cf. further Gn 13¹⁶, 22¹⁴; with perfect and
imperfect, 1 K 3¹²ᶠ·, with the demonstrative force clearly discernible,
depending on כ֫ב; on אֲשֶׁר לֹא=*ut non*, cf. Dt 28³⁵, 1 K 3⁸, 2 K 9³⁷.

On מִן with a substantive or infinitive as the equivalent of a consecutive
clause, see § 119 *y*.

§ 167. *Aposiopesis, Anacoluthon, Involved Series of Sentences.*

1. *Aposiopesis* is the concealment or suppression of entire sentences *a*
or clauses, which are of themselves necessary to complete the sense,[1]
and therefore must be supplied from the context. This is especially
frequent after conditional clauses; besides the examples already given
in § 159 *dd*, cf. also Ex 32³² (the LXX and Samaritan supply שָׂא);
Nu 5²⁰, Ju 9¹⁶ (in verse 19, after a long parenthesis, an imperative
follows as the apodosis to this conditional clause); 1 S 12¹⁴ᶠ·, 2 S 5⁸
(where indeed the text is probably very corrupt; cf. the addition in
1 Ch 11⁶); 2 S 23¹⁷, ψ 27¹³, 1 Ch 4¹⁰. For other examples of various
kinds, see § 117 *l*, and especially § 147; in Aramaic, Dn 3¹⁵.—On
Gn 3²², cf. § 152 *w* at the end.

2. *Anacoluthon* is the change from a construction which has been *b*
already begun to one of a different kind. It is found especially after
long parentheses, because the speaker has either lost sight of the
beginning of his sentence, or for the sake of clearness purposely makes
a new beginning; thus Gn 20¹³, 31⁵² and Ez 34¹⁰ (cf. § 149 at the
end); Nu 14²¹ᶠᶠ·, 32²⁰ᶠᶠ·, Dt 17²ᶠᶠ·, 24¹ᶠᶠ·, 29²¹ᶠᶠ·, Ju 10¹¹ (where, after
a series of intermediate sentences, the predicate *I saved you* is sup-

---

[1] But those cases are not to be regarded as examples of aposiopesis, in
which the answer, being closely connected with the question, is given simply
in the infinitive with לֹ; cf. § 147 *a*, note 1.

pressed; but the text can hardly be correct); perhaps also Is 66[18] (cf., however, Delitzsch on the passage, which is certainly corrupt).[1]　On Gn 23[13] (לֹו with the imperative), see § 110 e.

c　**3.** We may mention as instructive examples of *involved series* of sentences Gn 24[14] and [42 ff.], and Gn 28[6 ff.]

---

[1] On the other hand, from the Semitic point of view the various kinds of compound sentences are *not* to be regarded as instances of anacoluthon, e.g. Gn 17[14.17], nor even Gn 31[40] (cf. § 143).

THE PARADIGMS.

In the paradigms of the verbs, those forms which are to be especially noticed by the beginner are marked throughout by an asterisk as model forms. Thus e.g. in the strong verb the 3rd *sing. fem.* קָטְלָה is the model for קָטְלוּ, which likewise has only a vocalic afformative, and קָטַלְתָּ is the model for קָטַלְתִּי, קָטַלְתְּ and קָטַלְנוּ, which in the same way have a toneless afformative beginning with a consonant. On the other hand, the forms קְטַלְתֶּם and קְטַלְתֶּן, where the affix beginning with a consonant has the tone, stand by themselves.— In the table of the pronouns the asterisk has a different meaning; see the footnote there.—The bracketed forms (from Paradigm G onwards) are merely analogous formations not occurring in the Old Testament.

The newly added paradigm (Q) consists of forms actually found, belonging to various verbs.

A. The Personal

Nominative of the Pronoun, or *Pronomen separatum.*	Accusative of the Pronoun,
	A. Simple form.
Sing. 1. *comm.* אָנֹכִי, in pause אָנֹכִי ; אֲנִי, in pause אָנִי *I.*	נִי ; נִי⸍ ; נִי⸍ *me.*

2. ⎰ *m.* אַתָּה (אַתְּ), in pause
  { אָתָּה
  ⎱ *f.* אַתְּ (אַתִּי) � *thou.*
	ךְ ; ךְ⸍, in pause ךְ⸍,
	ךָ⸍
	ךְ ; ךְ⸍ ; ךְ⸍, ךְ⸍ } *thee.*

3. ⎰ *m.* הוּא *he.* ⎱ *f.* הִיא *she.*	הוּ, וֹ ; הוּ⸍ (ה), וֹ ; הוּ⸍ *him.* הָ ; הָ⸍ ; הָ⸍ *her (eam).*
Plur. 1. *comm.* אֲנַחְנוּ (נַחְנוּ), in pause אֲנָחְנוּ (נָחְנוּ) *we.*	נוּ ; נוּ⸍ ; נוּ⸍ *us.*
2. ⎰ *m.* אַתֶּם ⎱ *f.* אַתֵּנָה, אַתֵּן } *you.*	כֶם ; כֶם⸍ [כֶן ; כֶן⸍] } *you.*
3. ⎰ *m.* הֵמָּה, הֵם ⎱ *f.* הֵנָּה } *they.*	(הֶם), ם ; ם⸍, ם⸍, מוֹ⸍* ; ם⸍, (ם⸍), מוֹ⸍* *them (eos).* [הֶן], ן ; ן⸍,(ן⸍); [ן⸍] *them (eas).*

Pronoun.[1]

or *Suffixum Verbi.*	Genitive of the Pronoun, or *Suffixum Nominis* (*Pron. possessivum*).	
B. With *Nûn energicum.*	**A.** Attached to a sing. noun.	**B.** Attached to a noun plur. or dual.
־ֵ֫נִּי ; ־ֵ֫נִּי	יִ־ *my* (prop. gen. *mei*).	יִ־ *my.*
־ֶ֫ךָּ, (־ֶ֫נְךָ) not found.	ךָ, ־ְךָ, in pause ־ָ֫ךְ ⎱ *thy* ךְ, ־ֵ־, ((־ָ֫ךְ)) ⎰ (prop. *tui*).	־ֶ֫יךָ ⎱ *thy.* ־ַ֫יִךְ ⎰
(־ֶ֫נּוּ ־ְ), ־ֶ֫נּוּ ; (נוּ)	הוּ, ־ֵ֫הוּ ־ְ, וֹ (־ֹה) *his* (*eius* and *suus*).	־ָיו, ־ֶ֫יהוּ ־ְ *) *his.*
־ֶ֫נָּה	הָ; ־ָ֫הּ; ־ֶ֫הָ *her.*	־ֶ֫יהָ *her.*
־ֶ֫נּוּ ? (see § 58 *k*)	נוּ; ־ֵ֫נוּ; (־ָ֫נוּ) *our.*	־ֵ֫ינוּ *our.*
these forms are not found.	כֶם; ־ְכֶם ⎱ *your.* כֶן; ־ְכֶן ⎰	־ֵיכֶם ⎱ *your.* ־ֵיכֶן ⎰
	הֶם; ־ָם, מוֹ ־ָ * ⎱ *their.* הֶן, ־ָן, ־ָ ⎰	־ֵיהֶם, ־ֵ֫ימוֹ * ⎱ *their.* ־ֵיהֶן ⎰

[1] Forms with an asterisk are exclusively poetic, those in parentheses ( ) are rare, those in brackets [ ] do not occur (cf. § 58 *a*, note).

B. Strong

		Qal.			Niph'al.	Pi'ēl.
Perf. Sing.	3. *m.*	*קָטַל	*כָּבֵד	*קָטֹן	*נִקְטַל	*קִטֵּל, קִטֵּל
	3. *f.*	*קָטְלָה	*כָּבְדָה	*קָטְנָה	*נִקְטְלָה	*קִטְּלָה
	2. *m.*	*קָטַלְתָּ	*כָּבַדְתָּ	*קָטֹנְתָּ	*נִקְטַלְתָּ	*קִטַּלְתָּ
	2. *f.*	קָטַלְתְּ	כָּבַדְתְּ	קָטֹנְתְּ	נִקְטַלְתְּ	קִטַּלְתְּ
	1. *c.*	קָטַלְתִּי	כָּבַדְתִּי	קָטֹנְתִּי	נִקְטַלְתִּי	*קִטַּלְתִּי
Plur.	3. *c.*	קָטְלוּ	כָּבְדוּ	קָטְנוּ	נִקְטְלוּ	קִטְּלוּ
	2. *m.*	*קְטַלְתֶּם	*כְּבַדְתֶּם	*קְטָנְתֶּם	נִקְטַלְתֶּם	קִטַּלְתֶּם
	2. *f.*	קְטַלְתֶּן	כְּבַדְתֶּן	קְטָנְתֶּן	נִקְטַלְתֶּן	קִטַּלְתֶּן
	1. *c.*	קָטַלְנוּ	כָּבַדְנוּ	קָטֹנּוּ	נִקְטַלְנוּ	קִטַּלְנוּ

Inf.		*שְׁכַב, קְטֹל			*הִקָּטֵל	קַטֵּל
Inf. absol.		*קָטוֹל			*הִקָּטֹל, נִקְטֹל	*קַטּוֹל, קַטֵּל

Imp. Sing.	2. *m.*	*קְטֹל	*כְּבַד		*הִקָּטֵל	*קַטֵּל
	2. *f.*	*קִטְלִי	*כִּבְדִי		*הִקָּטְלִי	*קַטְּלִי
Plur.	2. *m.*	קִטְלוּ	כִּבְדוּ		הִקָּטְלוּ	קַטְּלוּ
	2. *f.*	*קְטֹלְנָה	*כְּבַדְנָה		*הִקָּטַלְנָה	*קַטֵּלְנָה

Impf. Sing.	3. *m.*	*יִקְטֹל	*יִכְבַּד	*יִקְטַן	*יִקָּטֵל	*יְקַטֵּל
	3. *f.*	תִּקְטֹל	תִּכְבַּד		תִּקָּטֵל	תְּקַטֵּל
	2. *m.*	תִּקְטֹל	תִּכְבַּד		תִּקָּטֵל	תְּקַטֵּל
	2. *f.*	*תִּקְטְלִי	*תִּכְבְּדִי		*תִּקָּטְלִי	*תְּקַטְּלִי
	1. *c.*	אֶקְטֹל	אֶכְבַּד		אֶקָּטֵל	אֲקַטֵּל
Plur.	3. *m.*	יִקְטְלוּ	יִכְבְּדוּ		יִקָּטְלוּ	יְקַטְּלוּ
	3. *f.*	*תִּקְטֹלְנָה	*תִּכְבַּדְנָה		*תִּקָּטַלְנָה	*תְּקַטֵּלְנָה
	2. *m.*	תִּקְטְלוּ	תִּכְבְּדוּ		תִּקָּטְלוּ	תְּקַטְּלוּ
	2. *f.*	תִּקְטֹלְנָה	תִּכְבַּדְנָה		תִּקָּטַלְנָה	תְּקַטֵּלְנָה
	1. *c.*	נִקְטֹל	נִכְבַּד		נִקָּטֵל	נְקַטֵּל

Shortened Impf. (*Jussive*).

Part. act.		*קֹטֵל	כָּבֵד	קָטֹן	*נִקְטָל	*מְקַטֵּל
pass.		*קָטוּל				

Verb.

Pu'al.	Hiph'îl.	Hoph'al.	Hithpa'ēl.
*קֻטַּל	*הִקְטִיל	*הָקְטַל	*הִתְקַטֵּל
*קֻטְּלָה	*הִקְטִילָה	*הָקְטְלָה	*הִתְקַטְּלָה
*קֻטַּלְתְּ	*הִקְטַלְתְּ	*הָקְטַלְתְּ	*הִתְקַטַּלְתְּ
קֻטַּלְתְּ	הִקְטַלְתְּ	הָקְטַלְתְּ	הִתְקַטַּלְתְּ
קֻטַּלְתִּי	הִקְטַלְתִּי	הָקְטַלְתִּי	הִתְקַטַּלְתִּי
קֻטְּלוּ	הִקְטִילוּ	הָקְטְלוּ	הִתְקַטְּלוּ
קֻטַּלְתֶּם	הִקְטַלְתֶּם	הָקְטַלְתֶּם	הִתְקַטַּלְתֶּם
קֻטַּלְתֶּן	הִקְטַלְתֶּן	הָקְטַלְתֶּן	הִתְקַטַּלְתֶּן
קֻטַּלְנוּ	הִקְטַלְנוּ	הָקְטַלְנוּ	הִתְקַטַּלְנוּ
wanting.	*הַקְטִיל	wanting.	*הִתְקַטֵּל
*קֻטַּל	*הָקְטֵל	*הָקְטֵל	*הִתְקַטֵּל
	*הַקְטֵל		*הִתְקַטֵּל
wanting.	*הַקְטִילִי	wanting.	*הִתְקַטְּלִי
	הַקְטִילוּ		הִתְקַטְּלוּ
	*הַקְטֵלְנָה		*הִתְקַטֵּלְנָה
*יְקֻטַּל	*יַקְטִיל	*יָקְטַל	*יִתְקַטֵּל
תְּקֻטַּל	תַּקְטִיל	תָּקְטַל	תִּתְקַטֵּל
תְּקֻטַּל	תַּקְטִיל	תָּקְטַל	תִּתְקַטֵּל
*תְּקֻטְּלִי	*תַּקְטִילִי	*תָּקְטְלִי	*תִּתְקַטְּלִי
אֲקֻטַּל	אַקְטִיל	אָקְטַל	אֶתְקַטֵּל
יְקֻטְּלוּ	יַקְטִילוּ	יָקְטְלוּ	יִתְקַטְּלוּ
*תְּקֻטַּלְנָה	*תַּקְטֵלְנָה	*תָּקְטַלְנָה	*תִּתְקַטֵּלְנָה
תְּקֻטְּלוּ	תַּקְטִילוּ	תָּקְטְלוּ	תִּתְקַטְּלוּ
תְּקֻטַּלְנָה	תַּקְטֵלְנָה	תָּקְטַלְנָה	תִּתְקַטֵּלְנָה
נְקֻטַּל	נַקְטִיל	נָקְטַל	נִתְקַטֵּל
	*יַקְטֵל		
	*מַקְטִיל		*מִתְקַטֵּל
*מְקֻטָּל		*מָקְטָל	

C. Strong Verb

Suffixes		1 Sing.	2 Sing. m.	2 Sing. f.	3 Sing. m.
Perf. Qal	3. m.	קְטָלַ֫נִי שְׁכָחַ֫נִי	קְטָֽלְךָ	קְטָלֵ֫ךְ	קְטָלָ֫הוּ קְטָלוֹ
	3. f.	קְטָלַ֫תְנִי	קְטָלָ֫תְךָ	קְטָלָ֫תֶךְ	קְטָלָ֫תְהוּ קְטָלָ֫תּוּ
	2. m.	קְטַלְתַּ֫נִי	—	—	קְטַלְתָּ֫הוּ קְטַלְתּוֹ
	2. f.	קְטַלְתִּ֫ינִי	—	—	קְטַלְתִּ֫יהוּ
	1. c.	—	קְטַלְתִּ֫יךָ	קְטַלְתִּ֫יךְ	קְטַלְתִּ֫יו קְטַלְתִּ֫יהוּ
Plur.	3. c.	קְטָל֫וּנִי	קְטָל֫וּךָ אֲהֵב֫וּךָ	קְטָל֫וּךְ	קְטָל֫וּהוּ
	2. m.	קְטַלְתּ֫וּנִי	—	—	קְטַלְתּ֫וּהוּ
	1. c.	—	קְטַלְנ֫וּךָ	קְטַלְנ֫וּךְ	קְטַלְנ֫וּהוּ

Inf. Qal	קָטְלִ֫י קָטְלֵ֫נִי	כָּתְבְּךָ קָטְלְךָ	קָטְלֵ֫ךְ	קָטְלוֹ

Imp. Qal 2.		קָטְלֵ֫נִי	—	—	קָטְלֵ֫הוּ

(from an *Imperf.* in *a* שְׁמָעֵ֫נִי, שְׁלָחֵ֫נִי)

Impf. Qal	3. m.	יִקְטְלֵ֫נִי יִלְבָּשֵׁ֫נִי	יִקְטָלְךָ יִלְבָּשְׁךָ	יִקְטְלֵ֫ךְ יִלְבָּשֵׁךְ	יִקְטְלֵ֫הוּ יִלְבָּשֵׁ֫הוּ
	3. m. with *Nûn energ.*	יִקְטְלַ֫נִּי	יִקְטָלֶ֫ךָּ	—	יִקְטְלֶ֫נּוּ
	Plur. 3. m.	יִקְטְל֫וּנִי	יִקְטְל֫וּךָ	יִקְטְל֫וּךְ	יִקְטְל֫וּהוּ יִנְאָל֫וּהוּ

Perf. Piˊēl	3. m.	קִטְּלַ֫נִי	קִטֶּלְךָ	קִטְּלֵ֫ךְ	קִטְּלוֹ

with Suffixes.

3 *Sing. f.*	1 *Plur.*	2 *Plur. m.*	2 *Plur. f.*	3 *Plur. m.*	3 *Plur. f.*
קְטָלָהּ	קְטָלָנוּ	wanting.	wanting.	{ קְטָלָם / לְבֵשָׁם }	קְטָלָן
קְטָלַתָּה	קְטָלַתְנוּ	—	—	קְטָלַתַם	wanting.
קְטַלְתָּהּ	קְטַלְתֶּנוּ	—	—	קְטַלְתָּם	wanting.
קְטַלְתִּיהָ	קְטַלְתִּינוּ	—	—	קְטַלְתִּים	wanting.
קְטַלְתִּיהָ	—	קְטַלְתִּיכֶם	wanting.	קְטַלְתִּים	קְטַלְתִּין
קְטָלוּהָ	קְטָלוּנוּ	wanting.	wanting.	קְטָלוּם	קְטָלוּן
wanting.	קְטַלְתּוּנוּ	—	—	wanting.	wanting.
קְטַלְנוּהָ	—	קְטַלְנוּכֶם	wanting.	קְטַלְנוּם	wanting.
קָטְלָהּ	קָטְלֵנוּ	{ בְּתָבְכֶם / קָטְלְכֶם }	wanting.	קָטְלָם	קָטְלָן
{ קָטְלָהָ / קָטְלָהּ }	קָטְלֵנוּ	—	—	קָטְלֵם	—
{ יִקְטְלָהּ / יִלְבָּשֶׁהָ / יִקְטְלָהּ }	{ יִקְטְלֵנוּ / יִלְבָּשֶׁנּוּ }	יִקְטְלְכֶם	wanting.	יִקְטְלֵם	wanting.
יִקְטְלָנָּה	יִקְטְלֶנּוּ	—	—	—	—
יִקְטְלוּהָ	יִקְטְלוּנוּ	יִקְטְלוּכֶם	wanting.	יִקְטְלוּם	wanting.
קָטְלָהּ	קָטְלֵנוּ	wanting.	wanting.	קָטְלָם	קָטְלָן

D. Verbs primae gutturalis

	Qal		Niph'al	Hiph'il	Hoph'al
Perf. Sing. 3. *m.*	עָמַד		*נֶעֱמַד	*הֶעֱמִיד	*הָעֳמַד
3. *f.*	עָמְדָה		*נֶעֶמְדָה	הֶעֱמִ֫ידָה	*הָעֳמְדָה
2. *m.*	עָמַ֫דְתָּ		נֶעֱמַ֫דְתָּ	הֶעֱמַ֫דְתָּ	הָעֳמַ֫דְתָּ
2. *f.*	עָמַדְתְּ		נֶעֱמַדְתְּ	הֶעֱמַדְתְּ	הָעֳמַדְתְּ
1. *c.*	עָמַ֫דְתִּי		נֶעֱמַ֫דְתִּי	הֶעֱמַ֫דְתִּי	הָעֳמַ֫דְתִּי
Plur. 3. *c.*	עָמְדוּ		נֶעֶמְדוּ	הֶעֱמִ֫ידוּ	הָעֳמְדוּ
2. *m.*	*עֲמַדְתֶּם		נֶעֱמַדְתֶּם	הֶעֱמַדְתֶּם	הָעֳמַדְתֶּם
2. *f.*	*עֲמַדְתֶּן		נֶעֱמַדְתֶּן	הֶעֱמַדְתֶּן	הָעֳמַדְתֶּן
1. *c.*	עָמַ֫דְנוּ		נֶעֱמַ֫דְנוּ	הֶעֱמַ֫דְנוּ	הָעֳמַ֫דְנוּ
Inf.	*עֲמֹד		*הֵעָמֵד	*הַעֲמִיד	
Inf. absol.	עָמוֹד	*נַעֲמוֹד, הַאָסֹף		*הַעֲמֵד	*הָעֲמֵד
Imp. Sing. *m.*	*עֲמֹד	*חֲזַק	*הֵעָמֵד	הַעֲמֵד	
f.	עִמְדִי	חִזְקִי	הֵעָמְדִי	הַעֲמִ֫ידִי	
Plur. *m.*	עִמְדוּ	חִזְקוּ	הֵעָמְדוּ	הַעֲמִ֫ידוּ	wanting.
f.	*עֲמֹ֫דְנָה	*חֲזַ֫קְנָה	הֵעָמַ֫דְנָה	הַעֲמֵ֫דְנָה	
Impf. Sing. 3. *m.*	*יַעֲמֹד	*יֶחֱזַק	*יֵעָמֵד	*יַעֲמִיד	*יָעֳמַד
3. *f.*	תַּעֲמֹד	תֶּחֱזַק	תֵּעָמֵד	תַּעֲמִיד	תָּעֳמַד
2. *m.*	תַּעֲמֹד	תֶּחֱזַק	תֵּעָמֵד	תַּעֲמִיד	תָּעֳמַד
2. *f.*	*תַּעַמְדִי	*תֶּחֶזְקִי	*תֵּעָמְדִי	תַּעֲמִ֫ידִי	*תָּעָמְדִי
1. *c.*	*אֶעֱמֹד	אֶחֱזַק	אֵעָמֵד	אַעֲמִיד	אָעֳמַד
Plur. 3. *m.*	*יַעַמְדוּ	*יֶחֶזְקוּ	*יֵעָמְדוּ	יַעֲמִ֫ידוּ	יָעָמְדוּ
3. *f.*	תַּעֲמֹ֫דְנָה	תֶּחֱזַ֫קְנָה	תֵּעָמַ֫דְנָה	תַּעֲמֵ֫דְנָה	תָּעֳמַ֫דְנָה
2. *m.*	תַּעַמְדוּ	תֶּחֶזְקוּ	תֵּעָמְדוּ	תַּעֲמִ֫ידוּ	תָּעָמְדוּ
2. *f.*	תַּעֲמֹ֫דְנָה	תֶּחֱזַ֫קְנָה	תֵּעָמַ֫דְנָה	תַּעֲמֵ֫דְנָה	תָּעֳמַ֫דְנָה
1. *c.*	נַעֲמֹד	נֶחֱזַק	נֵעָמֵד	נַעֲמִיד	נָעֳמַד
Shortened Impf. (Jussive).				יַעֲמֵד	
Part. act.	עֹמֵד		*נֶעֱמָד	*מַעֲמִיד	
pass.	עָמוּד				מָעֳמָד

E. Verbs mediae gutturalis.

	Qal.	Niph'al.	Pi'ēl.	Pu'al.	Hithpa'ēl.
Perf. Sing. 3. m.	שָׁחַט	נִשְׁחַט	*בֵּרַךְ	*בֹּרַךְ	*הִתְבָּרֵךְ
3. f.	*שָׁחֲטָה	*נִשְׁחֲטָה	בֵּרְכָה	[בֹּרְכָה]	הִתְבָּרְכָה
2. m.	שָׁחַטְתָּ	נִשְׁחַטְתָּ	בֵּרַכְתָּ	בֹּרַכְתָּ	הִתְבָּרַכְתָּ
2. f.	שָׁחַטְתְּ	נִשְׁחַטְתְּ	בֵּרַכְתְּ	בֹּרַכְתְּ	הִתְבָּרַכְתְּ
1. c.	שָׁחַטְתִּי	נִשְׁחַטְתִּי	בֵּרַכְתִּי	בֹּרַכְתִּי	הִתְבָּרַכְתִּי
Plur. 3. c.	*שָׁחֲטוּ	*נִשְׁחֲטוּ	בֵּרְכוּ	בֹּרְכוּ	הִתְבָּרְכוּ
2. m.	שְׁחַטְתֶּם	נִשְׁחַטְתֶּם	בֵּרַכְתֶּם	בֹּרַכְתֶּם	הִתְבָּרַכְתֶּם
2. f.	שְׁחַטְתֶּן	נִשְׁחַטְתֶּן	[בֵּרַכְתֶּן]	בֹּרַכְתֶּן	הִתְבָּרַכְתֶּן
1. c.	שָׁחַטְנוּ	נִשְׁחַטְנוּ	בֵּרַכְנוּ	בֹּרַכְנוּ	הִתְבָּרַכְנוּ
Inf.	שְׁחֹט	הִשָּׁחֵט	*בֵּרֵךְ	wanting.	*הִתְבָּרֵךְ
Inf. absol.	שָׁחוֹט	נִשְׁחוֹט	*בָּרֵךְ		
Imp. Sing. m.	*שְׁחַט	הִשָּׁחֵט	*בָּרֵךְ		*הִתְבָּרֵךְ
f.	*שַׁחֲטִי	*הִשָּׁחֲטִי	*בָּרְכִי	wanting.	[הִתְבָּרְכִי]
Plur. m.	שַׁחֲטוּ	הִשָּׁחֲטוּ	בָּרְכוּ		[הִתְבָּרְכוּ]
f.	שְׁחַטְנָה	הִשָּׁחַטְנָה	*בָּרֵכְנָה		הִתְבָּרֵכְנָה
Impf. Sing. 3. m.	*יִשְׁחַט	יִשָּׁחֵט	*יְבָרֵךְ	*יְבֹרַךְ	*יִתְבָּרֵךְ
3. f.	תִּשְׁחַט	תִּשָּׁחֵט	תְּבָרֵךְ	תְּבֹרַךְ	תִּתְבָּרֵךְ
2. m.	תִּשְׁחַט	תִּשָּׁחֵט	תְּבָרֵךְ	תְּבֹרַךְ	תִּתְבָּרֵךְ
2. f.	*תִּשְׁחֲטִי	*תִּשָּׁחֲטִי	תְּבָרְכִי	[תְּבֹרְכִי]	[תִּתְבָּרְכִי]
1. c.	אֶשְׁחַט	אֶשָּׁחֵט	אֲבָרֵךְ	אֲבֹרַךְ	אֶתְבָּרֵךְ
Plur. 3. m.	יִשְׁחֲטוּ	יִשָּׁחֲטוּ	יְבָרְכוּ	יְבֹרְכוּ	יִתְבָּרְכוּ
3. f.	תִּשְׁחַטְנָה	תִּשָּׁחַטְנָה	תְּבָרֵכְנָה	תְּבֹרַכְנָה	תִּתְבָּרֵכְנָה
2. m.	תִּשְׁחֲטוּ	תִּשָּׁחֲטוּ	תְּבָרְכוּ	תְּבֹרְכוּ	תִּתְבָּרְכוּ
2. f.	תִּשְׁחַטְנָה	תִּשָּׁחַטְנָה	תְּבָרֵכְנָה	תְּבֹרַכְנָה	תִּתְבָּרֵכְנָה
1. c.	נִשְׁחַט	נִשָּׁחֵט	נְבָרֵךְ	נְבֹרַךְ	נִתְבָּרֵךְ
Impf. with Suff.	יִשְׁחָטֵהוּ				
Part. act.	שֹׁחֵט	נִשְׁחָט	*מְבָרֵךְ		*מִתְבָּרֵךְ
pass.	שָׁחוּט			*מְבֹרָךְ	

F. Verbs

	Qal.	Niph'al.	Pi'ēl.
Perf. Sing. 3. m.	שָׁלַח	נִשְׁלַח	‏*שִׁלַּח
3. f.	שָׁלְחָה	נִשְׁלְחָה	שִׁלְּחָה
2. m.	שָׁלַחְתָּ	נִשְׁלַחְתָּ	שִׁלַּחְתָּ
2. f.	*שָׁלַחַתְּ	*נִשְׁלַחַתְּ	*שִׁלַּחַתְּ
1. c.	שָׁלַחְתִּי	נִשְׁלַחְתִּי	שִׁלַּחְתִּי
Plur. 3. c.	שָׁלְחוּ	נִשְׁלְחוּ	שִׁלְּחוּ
2. m.	שְׁלַחְתֶּם	נִשְׁלַחְתֶּם	שִׁלַּחְתֶּם
2. f.	שְׁלַחְתֶּן	נִשְׁלַחְתֶּן	שִׁלַּחְתֶּן
1. c.	שָׁלַחְנוּ	נִשְׁלַחְנוּ	שִׁלַּחְנוּ
Inf.	*שְׁלֹחַ	*הִשָּׁלַח	*שַׁלַּח
Inf. absol.	שָׁלוֹחַ	נִשְׁלוֹחַ	שַׁלֵּחַ
Imp. Sing. m.	*שְׁלַח	*הִשָּׁלַח	*שַׁלַּח
f.	שִׁלְחִי	הִשָּׁלְחִי	*שַׁלְּחִי
Plur. m.	שִׁלְחוּ	הִשָּׁלְחוּ	שַׁלְּחוּ
f.	*שְׁלַחְנָה	הִשָּׁלַחְנָה	*שַׁלַּחְנָה
Impf. Sing. 3. m.	*יִשְׁלַח	*יִשָּׁלַח	*יְשַׁלַּח
3. f.	תִּשְׁלַח	תִּשָּׁלַח	*תְּשַׁלַּח
2. m.	תִּשְׁלַח	תִּשָּׁלַח	תְּשַׁלַּח
2. f.	תִּשְׁלְחִי	תִּשָּׁלְחִי	תְּשַׁלְּחִי
1. c.	אֶשְׁלַח	אֶשָּׁלַח	אֲשַׁלַּח
Plur. 3. m.	יִשְׁלְחוּ	יִשָּׁלְחוּ	יְשַׁלְּחוּ
3. f.	*תִּשְׁלַחְנָה	*תִּשָּׁלַחְנָה	*תְּשַׁלַּחְנָה
2. m.	תִּשְׁלְחוּ	תִּשָּׁלְחוּ	תְּשַׁלְּחוּ
2. f.	תִּשְׁלַחְנָה	תִּשָּׁלַחְנָה	תְּשַׁלַּחְנָה
1. c.	נִשְׁלַח	נִשָּׁלַח	נְשַׁלַּח

Shortened Impf. (Jussive).

Impf. with Suff.   יִשְׁלָחֵנִי

| **Part. act.** | *שֹׁלֵחַ | נִשְׁלָח | *מְשַׁלֵּחַ |
| pass. | *שָׁלוּחַ | | |

tertiae gutturalis.

Pu'al.	Hiph'îl.	Hoph'al.	Hithpa'ēl.
שֻׁלַּח	*הִשְׁלִיחַ	הָשְׁלַח	*הִשְׁתַּלַּח
שֻׁלְּחָה	הִשְׁלִיחָה	הָשְׁלְחָה	הִשְׁתַּלְּחָה
שֻׁלַּחְתָּ	הִשְׁלַחְתָּ	הָשְׁלַחְתָּ	הִשְׁתַּלַּחְתָּ
*שֻׁלַּחַתְּ	*הִשְׁלַחַתְּ	*הָשְׁלַחַתְּ	*הִשְׁתַּלַּחַתְּ
שֻׁלַּחְתִּי	הִשְׁלַחְתִּי	הָשְׁלַחְתִּי	הִשְׁתַּלַּחְתִּי
שֻׁלְּחוּ	הִשְׁלִיחוּ	הָשְׁלְחוּ	הִשְׁתַּלְּחוּ
שֻׁלַּחְתֶּם	הִשְׁלַחְתֶּם	הָשְׁלַחְתֶּם	הִשְׁתַּלַּחְתֶּם
שֻׁלַּחְתֶּן	הִשְׁלַחְתֶּן	הָשְׁלַחְתֶּן	הִשְׁתַּלַּחְתֶּן
שֻׁלַּחְנוּ	הִשְׁלַחְנוּ	הָשְׁלַחְנוּ	הִשְׁתַּלַּחְנוּ
	*הַשְׁלִיחַ		*הִשְׁתַּלֵּחַ
	*הַשְׁלֵחַ	*הָשְׁלֵחַ	
	הַשְׁלַח		*הִשְׁתַּלַּח
wanting.	הַשְׁלִיחִי	wanting.	הִשְׁתַּלְּחִי
	הַשְׁלִיחוּ		הִשְׁתַּלְּחוּ
	הַשְׁלַחְנָה		*הִשְׁתַּלַּחְנָה
יְשֻׁלַּח	*יַשְׁלִיחַ	יָשְׁלַח	יִשְׁתַּלַּח
תְּשֻׁלַּח	תַּשְׁלִיחַ	תָּשְׁלַח	תִּשְׁתַּלַּח
תְּשֻׁלַּח	תַּשְׁלִיחַ	תָּשְׁלַח	תִּשְׁתַּלַּח
תְּשֻׁלְּחִי	תַּשְׁלִיחִי	תָּשְׁלְחִי	תִּשְׁתַּלְּחִי
אֲשֻׁלַּח	אַשְׁלִיחַ	אָשְׁלַח	אֶשְׁתַּלַּח
יְשֻׁלְּחוּ	יַשְׁלִיחוּ	יָשְׁלְחוּ	יִשְׁתַּלְּחוּ
תְּשֻׁלַּחְנָה	תַּשְׁלַחְנָה	תָּשְׁלַחְנָה	*תִּשְׁתַּלַּחְנָה
תְּשֻׁלְּחוּ	תַּשְׁלִיחוּ	תָּשְׁלְחוּ	תִּשְׁתַּלְּחוּ
תְּשֻׁלַּחְנָה	תַּשְׁלַחְנָה	תָּשְׁלַחְנָה	תִּשְׁתַּלַּחְנָה
נְשֻׁלַּח	נַשְׁלִיחַ	נָשְׁלַח	נִשְׁתַּלַּח
	יַשְׁלַח		
	*מַשְׁלִיחַ		*מִשְׁתַּלֵּחַ
מְשֻׁלָּח		מָשְׁלָח	

G. *Verbs mediae geminatae*

			Qal.	Niph'al.
Perf. Sing.	3.	*m.*	*סָבַב, תַּם	*נָסַב, נָמֵס
	3.	*f.*	סָבְבָה, תַּמָּה	*נָסַבָּה
	2.	*m.*	*סַבּוֹתָ	*נְסַבּוֹתָ
	2.	*f.*	סַבּוֹת	נְסַבּוֹת
	1.	*c.*	סַבּוֹתִי	נְסַבּוֹתִי
Plur.	3.	*c.*	סָבְבוּ, תַּמּוּ	נָסַבּוּ
	2.	*m.*	סַבּוֹתֶם	נְסַבּוֹתֶם
	2.	*f.*	סַבּוֹתֶן	נְסַבּוֹתֶן
	1.	*c.*	סַבּוֹנוּ	נְסַבּוֹנוּ
Inf.			*סֹב	*הִסֵּב
Inf. absol.			סָבוֹב	הָמֵס, הִסּוֹב
Imp. Sing.	*m.*		*סֹב	הִסֵּב
	f.		*סֹבִּי	*הִסַּבִּי
Plur.	*m.*		סֹבּוּ	הִסַּבּוּ
	f.		[סֻבֶּינָה]	[הִסַּבֶּינָה]
Impf. Sing.	3.	*m.*	*יָסֹב (§ 67 *p*) *יִסֹּב	*יִסַּב
	3.	*f.*	תָּסֹב	תִּסֹּב	תִּסַּב
	2.	*m.*	תָּסֹב	תִּסֹּב	תִּסַּב
	2.	*f.*	*תָּסֹבִּי	תִּסְבִּי	*תִּסַּבִּי
	1.	*c.*	אָסֹב	אֶסֹּב	אֶסַּב
Plur.	3.	*m.*	יָסֹבּוּ	יִסֹּבוּ	יִסַּבּוּ
	3.	*f.*	*תְּסֻבֶּינָה	[תִּסֹּבְנָה]	[תִּסַּבֶּינָה]
	2.	*m.*	תָּסֹבּוּ	תִּסֹּבוּ	תִּסַּבּוּ
	2.	*f.*	[תְּסֻבֶּינָה]	[תִּסֹּבְנָה]	[תִּסַּבֶּינָה]
	1.	*c.*	נָסֹב	נִסֹּב	נִסַּב
Impf. with Wāw consec.			*וַיָּסָב (pause וַיִּסֹּב)		
Impf. with Suff.			*יְסֻבֵּנִי		
Part. act.			סֹבֵב	נָסָב	
	pass.		*סָבוּב	(*fem.* נְסַבָּה)	

or double ע.

Hiph'îl.	Hoph'al.	Po'ēl.	Po'al.
*הֵסֵב, הֵסַב	*הוּסַב	*סוֹבֵב	*סוֹבַב
*הֲסִבָּה	הוּסַבָּה	סוֹבְבָה	[סוֹבֲבָה]
*הֲסִבּוֹתָ	[הוּסַבּוֹתָ]	סוֹבַבְתָּ	סוֹבַבְתָּ
הֲסִבּוֹת	הוּסַבּוֹת	סוֹבַבְתְּ	סוֹבַבְתְּ
הֲסִבּוֹתִי	[הוּסַבּוֹתִי]	סוֹבַבְתִּי	סוֹבַבְתִּי
הֵסַבּוּ, הֵחֵלּוּ	הוּסַבּוּ	סוֹבְבוּ	סוֹבְבוּ
הֲסִבּוֹתֶם	[הוּסַבּוֹתֶם]	סוֹבַבְתֶּם	סוֹבַבְתֶּם
הֲסִבּוֹתֶן	הוּסַבּוֹתֶן	סוֹבַבְתֶּן	סוֹבַבְתֶּן
הֲסִבּוֹנוּ	[הוּסַבּוֹנוּ]	סוֹבַבְנוּ	[סוֹבַבְנוּ]

| *הָסֵב | | סוֹבֵב | |
| הָסֵב | הַשָּׁמָּה | סוֹבֵב | [סוֹבַב] |

*הָסֵב		סוֹבֵב	
הָסֵבִּי	wanting.	[סוֹבְבִי]	wanting.
הָסֵבּוּ		סוֹבְבוּ	
[הֲסִבֶּינָה]		סוֹבֵבְנָה]	

*יָסֵב, יָסֵב	*יוּסַב, יֻסַב	יְסוֹבֵב	[יְסוֹבַב]
תָּסֵב	[תּוּסַב]	תְּסוֹבֵב	תְּסוֹבַב
תָּסֵב	תּוּסַב	תְּסוֹבֵב	תְּסוֹבַב
[תָּסֵבִּי]	*תּוּסַבִּי	[תְּסוֹבְבִי]	תְּסוֹבְבִי
אָסֵב	[אוּסַב]	אֲסוֹבֵב]	אֲסוֹבַב
יָסֵבּוּ, יָסֵבּוּ	יוּסַבּוּ	יְסוֹבְבוּ	יְסוֹבְבוּ
*תְּסִבֶּינָה	*[תּוּסַבֶּינָה]	[תְּסוֹבֵבְנָה]	תְּסוֹבֵבְנָה
תָּסֵבּוּ	תּוּסַבּוּ	תְּסוֹבְבוּ	תְּסוֹבְבוּ
תְּסִבֶּינָה	תּוּסַבֶּינָה	[תְּסוֹבֵבְנָה]	תְּסוֹבֵבְנָה
נָסֵב	[נוּסַב]	[נְסוֹבֵב]	נְסוֹבַב]

| וַיָּסֵב | | | |

| *יִסְּבֵּנִי (יְסֻבְּכֶם) | | יְסוֹבְבֵנִי | |

| *מֵסֵב | | מְסוֹבֵב | |
| | מוּסָב | | מְסוֹבָב |

H. Verbs פ״ן.

	Qal.		Niph'al.	Hiph'il.	Hoph'al.
Perf. Sing. 3. *m.*	[נָגַשׁ]	נָפַל	נִגַּשׁ*	הִגִּישׁ*	הֻגַּשׁ*
3. *f.*			נִגְּשָׁה	הִגִּישָׁה	הֻגְּשָׁה
2. *m.*			נִגַּשְׁתָּ	הִגַּשְׁתָּ	הֻגַּשְׁתָּ
2. *f.*			נִגַּשְׁתְּ	הִגַּשְׁתְּ	הֻגַּשְׁתְּ
1. *c.*	regular.		נִגַּשְׁתִּי	הִגַּשְׁתִּי	הֻגַּשְׁתִּי
Plur. 3. *c.*			נִגְּשׁוּ	הִגִּישׁוּ	הֻגְּשׁוּ
2. *m.*			נִגַּשְׁתֶּם	הִגַּשְׁתֶּם	הֻגַּשְׁתֶּם
2. *f.*			נִגַּשְׁתֶּן	הִגַּשְׁתֶּן	הֻגַּשְׁתֶּן
1. *c.*			נִגַּשְׁנוּ	הִגַּשְׁנוּ	הֻגַּשְׁנוּ
Inf.	גֶּשֶׁת*	נְפֹל*	הִנָּגֵשׁ	הַגִּישׁ*	הֻגַּשׁ*
Inf. absol.	נָגוֹשׁ		נִגּוֹף, הִנָּגֵשׁ	הַגֵּשׁ*	הֻגֵּשׁ*
Imp. Sing. m.	גַּשׁ*	נְפֹל*	הִנָּגֵשׁ	הַגֵּשׁ*	
f.	גְּשִׁי	נִפְלִי	הִנָּגְשִׁי	הַגִּישִׁי	*wanting.*
Plur. m.	גְּשׁוּ	נִפְלוּ	הִנָּגְשׁוּ	הַגִּישׁוּ	
f.	גַּשְׁנָה	נְפֹלְנָה	הִנָּגַשְׁנָה	הַגֵּשְׁנָה	
Impf. Sing. 3. *m.*	יִגַּשׁ*	יִפֹּל*	[יִנָּגֵשׁ]	יַגִּישׁ*	יֻגַּשׁ*
3. *f.*	תִּגַּשׁ	תִּפֹּל		תַּגִּישׁ	תֻּגַּשׁ
2. *m.*	תִּגַּשׁ	תִּפֹּל		תַּגִּישׁ	תֻּגַּשׁ
2. *f.*	תִּגְּשִׁי	תִּפְּלִי		תַּגִּישִׁי	תֻּגְּשִׁי
1. *c.*	אֶגַּשׁ	אֶפֹּל		אַגִּישׁ	אֻגַּשׁ
Plur. 3. *m.*	יִגְּשׁוּ	יִפְּלוּ	regular.	יַגִּישׁוּ	יֻגְּשׁוּ
3. *f.*	תִּגַּשְׁנָה	תִּפֹּלְנָה		תַּגֵּשְׁנָה	תֻּגַּשְׁנָה
2. *m.*	תִּגְּשׁוּ	תִּפְּלוּ		תַּגִּישׁוּ	תֻּגְּשׁוּ
2. *f.*	[תִּגַּשְׁנָה]	[תִּפֹּלְנָה]		[תַּגֵּשְׁנָה]	[תֻּגַּשְׁנָה]
1. *c.*	נִגַּשׁ	נִפֹּל		נַגִּישׁ	נֻגַּשׁ
Shortened Impf. (*Jussive*).				יַגֵּשׁ*	
Part. act.	נֹגֵשׁ		נִגָּשׁ*	מַגִּישׁ*	
pass.	נָגוּשׁ				מֻגָּשׁ

I. Weak Verbs, פ״א.

	Qal.	Niph'al.	Hiph'il.	Hoph'al.
Perf.	אָכַל	*נֶאֱכַל	*הֶאֱכִיל	*הָאֳכַל

Like Verbs *primae gutturalis.*

	Qal.	Niph'al.	Hiph'il.	Hoph'al.
Inf.	*אֱכֹל, אֲכָל	הֵאָכֵל	הַאֲכִיל	הָאֳכַל
Inf. absol.	אָכוֹל	הֵאָכֹל	wanting.	wanting.
Imp. Sing. m.	*אֱכֹל	הֵאָכֵל	הַאֲכֵל	
f.	אִכְלִי	&c.	&c.	wanting.
Plur. m.	אִכְלוּ			
f.	[אֱכֹלְנָה]			
Impf. Sing. 3. *m.*	*יֹאכַל (in pause	*יֵאָכֵל	*יַאֲכִיל	*יָאֳכַל
3. *f.*	תֹּאכַל יֹאכֵל)	&c.	&c.	&c.
2. *m.*	תֹּאכַל			
2. *f.*	תֹּאכְלִי			
1. *c.*	*אֹכַל			
Plur. 3. *m.*	יֹאכְלוּ			
3. *f.*	תֹּאכַלְנָה			
2. *m.*	תֹּאכְלוּ			
2. *f.*	[תֹּאכַלְנָה]			
1. *c.*	נֹאכַל			
Impf. with Wāw consec.	*וַיֹּאמֶר / *וַיֹּאכַל			
Part. act.	אֹכֵל	נֶאֱכָל	מַאֲכִיל	
pass.	אָכוּל			מָאֳכָל

K. Weak Verbs,

		Qal.		Niph'al.
Perf. Sing	3. m.	יָשַׁב		*נוֹשַׁב
	3. f.			*נוֹשְׁבָה
	2. m.			נוֹשַׁבְתָּ
	2. f.			נוֹשַׁבְתְּ
	1. c.	regular.		נוֹשַׁבְתִּי
Plur. 3. c.				נוֹשְׁבוּ
	2. m.			נוֹשַׁבְתֶּם
	2. f.			נוֹשַׁבְתֶּן
	1. c.			נוֹשַׁבְנוּ
Inf.		יְסֹר, רֶשֶׁת, *שֶׁבֶת		*הִוָּשֵׁב
Inf. absol.		יָשׁוֹב		wanting.
Imp. Sing. m.		*שֵׁב, דַּע		*הִוָּשֵׁב
	f.	שְׁבִי		הִוָּשְׁבִי
Plur. m.		שְׁבוּ		הִוָּשְׁבוּ
	f.	שֵׁבְנָה		[הִוָּשַׁבְנָה]
Impf. Sing. 3. m.	*יֵשֵׁב	*יִירַשׁ	*יִוָּשֵׁב
	3. f.	תֵּשֵׁב	תִּירַשׁ	תִּוָּשֵׁב
	2. m.	תֵּשֵׁב	תִּירַשׁ	תִּוָּשֵׁב
	2. f.	תֵּשְׁבִי	תִּירְשִׁי	תִּוָּשְׁבִי
	1. c.	אֵשֵׁב	אִירַשׁ	*אִוָּשֵׁב
Plur. 3. m.	יֵשְׁבוּ	יִירְשׁוּ	יִוָּשְׁבוּ
	3. f.	תֵּשַׁבְנָה	[תִּירַשְׁנָה]	[תִּוָּשַׁבְנָה]
	2. m.	תֵּשְׁבוּ	תִּירְשׁוּ	תִּוָּשְׁבוּ
	2. f.	[תֵּשַׁבְנָה]	[תִּירַשְׁנָה]	[תִּוָּשַׁבְנָה]
	1. c.	נֵשֵׁב	נִירַשׁ	נִוָּשֵׁב

Shortened Impf. (Jussive).
Impf. with Wāw consec. *וַיֵּשֶׁב

| **Part. act.** | יֹשֵׁב | | *נוֹשָׁב |
| **pass.** | יָשׁוּב | | |

פ״י (*for* פ״ו).   **L.** *Verbs properly* פ״י.

Hiph'il.	Hoph'al.	Qal.	Hiph'il.
*הוֹשִׁיב	*הוּשַׁב	יָטַב	*הֵיטִיב
הוֹשִׁיבָה	הוּשְׁבָה		הֵיטִיבָה
הוֹשַׁבְתָּ	הוּשַׁבְתָּ		הֵיטַבְתָּ
הוֹשַׁבְתְּ	הוּשַׁבְתְּ		הֵיטַבְתְּ
הוֹשַׁבְתִּי	הוּשַׁבְתִּי	regular.	הֵיטַבְתִּי
הוֹשִׁיבוּ	הוּשְׁבוּ		הֵיטִיבוּ
הוֹשַׁבְתֶּם	הוּשַׁבְתֶּם		הֵיטַבְתֶּם
הוֹשַׁבְתֶּן	הוּשַׁבְתֶּן		הֵיטַבְתֶּן
הוֹשַׁבְנוּ	הוּשַׁבְנוּ		הֵיטַבְנוּ
*הוֹשֵׁיב	*הוּשַׁב	יְטֹב	*הֵיטִיב
*הוֹשֵׁב		יָטוֹב	*הֵיטֵב
*הוֹשֵׁב			*הֵיטֵב
הוֹשִׁיבִי	wanting.		הֵיטִיבִי
הוֹשִׁיבוּ			הֵיטִיבוּ
[הוֹשֵׁבְנָה]			[הֵיטֵבְנָה]
יוֹשִׁיב	*יוּשַׁב	*יִיטַב	*יֵיטִיב
תּוֹשִׁיב	תּוּשַׁב	תִּיטַב	תֵּיטִיב
תּוֹשִׁיב	תּוּשַׁב	תִּיטַב	תֵּיטִיב
תּוֹשִׁיבִי	תּוּשְׁבִי	תִּיטְבִי	תֵּיטִיבִי
אוֹשִׁיב	אוּשַׁב	אִיטַב	אֵיטִיב
יוֹשִׁיבוּ	יוּשְׁבוּ	יִיטְבוּ	יֵיטִיבוּ
[תּוֹשֵׁבְנָה]	תּוּשַׁבְנָה	תִּיטַבְנָה	[תֵּיטֵבְנָה]
תּוֹשִׁיבוּ	תּוּשְׁבוּ	תִּיטְבוּ	תֵּיטִיבוּ
[תּוֹשֵׁבְנָה]	[תּוּשַׁבְנָה]	[תִּיטַבְנָה]	תֵּיטֵבְנָה
נוֹשִׁיב	נוּשַׁב	נִיטַב	[נֵיטִיב]
*יוֹשֵׁב			יֵיטֵב
וַיֹּשֶׁב		וַיִּיטַב	וַיֵּיטֵב
*מוֹשִׁיב		יֵטֵב	מֵיטִיב
	*מוּשָׁב	יָטוֹב	

M. Weak

		Qal.		Niph'al.	Hiph'il.
Perf. Sing.	3. *m.*	‏קָם*‏	‏מֵת*‏	‏נָקוֹם*‏	‏הֵקִים*‏
	3. *f.*	‏קָ֫מָה*‏	‏מֵ֫תָה*‏	‏נָק֫וֹמָה*‏	‏הֵקִ֫ימָה*‏
	2. *m.*	‏קַ֫מְתָּ*‏	‏מַ֫תָּה*‏	‏נְקוּמֹ֫ותָ]‏	‏הֲקִימֹ֫ותָ*‏
	2. *f.*	‏קַמְתְּ‏	‏[מַתְּ]‏	‏[נְקוּמוֹת]‏	‏הֲקִימוֹת‏
	1. *c.*	‏קַ֫מְתִּי‏	‏מַ֫תִּי‏	‏נְקוּמֹ֫ותִי‏	‏הֲקִימֹ֫ותִי‏
Plur.	3. *c.*	‏קָ֫מוּ‏	‏מֵ֫תוּ‏	‏נָק֫וֹמוּ‏	‏הֵקִ֫ימוּ‏
	2. *m.*	‏קַמְתֶּם‏	‏[מַתֶּם]‏	‏נְקוּמֹתֶם‏	‏הֲקִימֹתֶם‏
	2. *f.*	‏[קַמְתֶּן]‏	‏[מַתֶּן]‏	‏[נְקוּמֹתֶן]‏	‏[הֲקִימֹתֶן]‏
	1. *c.*	‏קַ֫מְנוּ‏	‏כַּ֫תְנוּ]‏	‏[נְקוּמֹ֫ונוּ]‏	‏הֲקִימֹ֫ונוּ‏
Inf.		‏קוּם*‏		‏*הִקּוֹם‏	‏*הָקִים‏
Inf. absol.		‏קוֹם*‏		‏*הִקּוֹם, נָסוֹג‏	‏הָקֵם*‏
Imp. Sing. m.		‏קוּם*‏		‏*הִקּוֹם‏	‏הָקֵם*‏
f.		‏ק֫וּמִי*‏		‏[הִקּ֫וֹמִי]‏	‏הָקִ֫ימִי*‏
Plur. m.		‏ק֫וּמוּ‏		‏הִקּ֫וֹמוּ‏	‏הָקִ֫ימוּ‏
f.		‏קֹ֫מְנָה*‏			‏[הָקֵ֫מְנָה]‏
Impf. Sing. 3. *m.*		‏*יָקוּם, יָבוֹא‏		‏יִקּוֹם*‏	‏*יָקִים‏
3. *f.*		‏תָּקוּם‏		‏תִּקּוֹם‏	‏תָּקִים‏
2. *m.*		‏תָּקוּם‏		‏תִּקּוֹם‏	‏תָּקִים‏
2. *f.*		‏*תָּק֫וּמִי‏		‏[תִּקּ֫וֹמִי]‏	‏*תָּקִ֫ימִי‏
1. *c.*		‏אָקוּם‏		‏אִקּוֹם‏	‏אָקִים‏
Plur. 3. *m.*		‏יָק֫וּמוּ‏		‏יִקּ֫וֹמוּ‏	‏יָקִ֫ימוּ‏
3. *f.*		‏*תְּקוּמֶ֫ינָה, תָּשֹׁבְנָה‏			‏*תְּקֹמְנָה, תְּקִימֶ֫ינָה‏
2. *m.*		‏תָּק֫וּמוּ‏		‏תִּקּ֫וֹמוּ‏	‏תָּקִ֫ימוּ‏
2. *f.*		‏תְּקוּמֶ֫ינָה‏			‏[תְּקֵ֫מְנָה]‏
1. *c.*		‏נָקוּם‏		‏נִקּוֹם‏	‏נָקִים‏
Shortened Impf.		‏*יָקֹם‏			‏*יָקֵם‏
Impf. with Wāw consec.		‏וַיָּ֫קָם‏ (pause ‏*וַיָּקֹם‏)			‏*וַיָּ֫קֶם‏
Impf. with Suff.		‏*יְשׁוּפֶ֫נִי‏			‏*יְקִימֶ֫נִי‏
Part. act.		‏קָם*‏		‏*נָקוֹם‏	‏*מֵקִים‏
pass.		‏קוּם*‏			

	Verbs, ע״ו.			N. Weak Verbs, ע״י.	
Hoph'al.	Pôlēl.	Pôlal.	Qal.	Niph'al.
*הוּקַם	*קוֹמֵם	*קוֹמַם	*בָּן	*נָבוֹן
[הוּקְמָה]	קוֹמְמָה	[קוֹמְמָה]	*בָּנָה	[נָבוֹנָה]
הוּקַמְתָּ	קוֹמַמְתָּ	קוֹמַמְתָּ	*בַּנְתָּ	נְבוּנֹת
הוּקַמְתְּ	[קוֹמַמְתְּ]	[קוֹמַמְתְּ]	בַּנְתְּ	[נְבוּנוֹת]
[הוּקַמְתִּי]	קוֹמַמְתִּי	קוֹמַמְתִּי	[בַּנְתִּי]	נְבוּנוֹתִי
הוּקְמוּ	קוֹמְמוּ	קוֹמְמוּ	בָּנּוּ	
[הוּקַמְתֶּם]	[קוֹמַמְתֶּם]	[קוֹמַמְתֶּם]	בַּנְתֶּם	See
הוּקַמְתֶּן	קוֹמַמְתֶּן	קוֹמַמְתֶּן	[בַּנְתֶּן]	Verbs ע״ו.
[הוּקַמְנוּ]	[קוֹמַמְנוּ]	[קוֹמַמְנוּ]	בַּנּוּ	
*הוּקַם	קוֹמֵם		*בִּין	
			*בֹּן	
	קוֹמֵם		*בִּין	
	[קוֹמֲמִי]		בִּינִי	
	קוֹמֲמוּ	wanting.	בִּינוּ	
	[קוֹמֵמְנָה]		—	
*יוּקַם	יְקוֹמֵם	יְקוֹמַם	יָגִיל	
תּוּקַם	תְּקוֹמֵם	[תְּקוֹמַם]	תָּגִיל	
[תּוּקַם]	תְּקוֹמֵם	תְּקוֹמַם	תָּגִיל	
תּוּקְמִי	[תְּקוֹמֲמִי]	תְּקוֹמֲמִי	תָּגִילִי	
[אוּקַם]	אֲקוֹמֵם	[אֲקוֹמַם]	אָגִיל	
יוּקְמוּ	יְקוֹמֲמוּ	יְקוֹמֲמוּ	יָגִילוּ	
[תּוּקַמְנָה]	תְּקוֹמֵמְנָה	תְּקוֹמַמְנָה	תְּגֵלֶנָה	
תּוּקְמוּ	תְּקוֹמֲמוּ	[תְּקוֹמֲמוּ]	תָּגִילוּ	
[תּוּקַמְנָה]	תְּקוֹמֵמְנָה	תְּקוֹמַמְנָה	תְּגֵלֶנָה	
נוּקַם	[נְקוֹמֵם]	נְקוֹמַם	נָגִיל	
			יָגֵל	
			וַיָּגֶל	
			יְרִיבֵנִי	
	מְקוֹמֵם		לָנִים, שָׁב	נָבוֹן
*מוּקָם		מְקוֹמָם	שִׂים, שׂוּם	

O. Weak

	Qal.		Niph'al.	Pi'ēl.
Perf. Sing. 3. m.	מָצָא*	מָלֵא	נִמְצָא*	דָּכָא, מִצָּא
3. f.	מָצְאָה	מָלְאָה	נִמְצְאָה	[מִצְּאָה]
2. m.	מָצָאתָ*	מָלֵאתָ	נִמְצֵאתָ*	מִצֵּאתָ*
2. f.	מָצָאת	מָלֵאת	נִמְצֵאת	[מִצֵּאת]
1. c.	מָצָאתִי	מָלֵאתִי	נִמְצֵאתִי	מִצֵּאתִי
Plur. 3. c.	מָצְאוּ	מָלְאוּ	נִמְצְאוּ	מִצְּאוּ
2. m.	מְצָאתֶם	מְלֵאתֶם	נִמְצֵאתֶם	מִצֵּאתֶם
2. f.	[מְצָאתֶן]	[מְלֵאתֶן]	[נִמְצֵאתֶן]	[מִצֵּאתֶן]
1. c.	מָצָאנוּ	מָלֵאנוּ	[נִמְצֵאנוּ]	מִצֵּאנוּ
Inf.	מְצֹא		הִמָּצֵא	מַצֵּא
Inf. absol.	מָצוֹא		נִמְצֹא	מַצֹּא
Imp. Sing. m.	מְצָא*		הִמָּצֵא	מַצֵּא
f.	מִצְאִי		[הִמָּצְאִי]	[מַצְּאִי]
Plur. m.	מִצְאוּ		הִמָּצְאוּ	מַצְּאוּ
f.	מְצֶאנָה*		[הִמָּצֶאנָה]	[מַצֶּאנָה]
Impf. Sing. 3. m.	יִמְצָא*		יִמָּצֵא*	יְמַצֵּא
3. f.	תִּמְצָא		תִּמָּצֵא	תְּמַצֵּא
2. m.	תִּמְצָא		תִּמָּצֵא	תְּמַצֵּא
2. f.	תִּמְצְאִי		תִּמָּצְאִי	[תְּמַצְּאִי]
1. c.	אֶמְצָא		אֶמָּצֵא	אֲמַצֵּא
Plur. 3. m.	יִמְצְאוּ		יִמָּצְאוּ	יְמַצְּאוּ
3. f.	תִּמְצֶאנָה*		תִּמָּצֶאנָה*	תְּמַצֶּאנָה*
2. m.	תִּמְצְאוּ		תִּמָּצְאוּ	[תְּמַצְּאוּ]
2. f.	תִּמְצֶאנָה		תִּמָּצֶאנָה	תְּמַצֶּאנָה
1. c.	נִמְצָא		[נִמָּצֵא]	נְמַצֵּא
Shortened Impf. (Jussive).				
Impf. with Suff.	יִמְצָאֲךָ, יִמְצָאֵנִי			יְמַצְּאֵנִי
Part. act.	מֹצֵא		נִמְצָא	מְמַצֵּא
pass.	מָצוּא			

Verbs, ל"א.

Pu'al.	Hiph'îl.	Hoph'al.	Hithpa'ēl.
קְרָא [מֻצָּא	הִמְצִיא	[הֻמְצָא]	[הִתְמַצָּא
מֻצְּאָה	הִמְצִיאָה	הֻמְצְאָה	הִתְמַצְּאָה
מֻצֵּאתָ	*הִמְצֵאתָ	*[הֻמְצֵאתָ	*הִתְמַצֵּאתָ
מֻצֵּאת	הִמְצֵאת	הֻמְצֵאת	[הִתְמַצֵּאת]
מֻצֵּאתִי	הִמְצֵאתִי	הֻמְצֵאתִי	הִתְמַצֵּאתִי
מֻצְּאוּ	הִמְצִיאוּ	הֻמְצְאוּ	הִתְמַצְּאוּ
מֻצֵּאתֶם	הִמְצֵאתֶם	הֻמְצֵאתֶם	[הִתְמַצֵּאתֶם
מֻצֵּאתֶן	[הִמְצֵאתֶן	הֻמְצֵאתֶן	הִתְמַצֵּאתֶן
[מֻצֵּאנוּ]	הִמְצֵאנוּ]	[הֻמְצֵאנוּ]	[הִתְמַצֵּאנוּ]
wanting.	הַמְצִיא	wanting.	הִתְמַצֵּא
	הַמְצֵא		wanting.
	הַמְצֵא		[הִתְמַצֵּא
wanting.	הַמְצִיאִי	wanting.	הִתְמַצְּאִי
	הַמְצִיאוּ		הִתְמַצְּאוּ
	[הַמְצֶאנָה]		[הִתְמַצֶּאנָה
יְמֻצָּא	יַמְצִיא	[יֻמְצָא]	יִתְמַצֵּא
[תְּמֻצָּא	תַּמְצִיא	תֻּמְצָא	תִּתְמַצֵּא
תְּמֻצָּא	תַּמְצִיא	תֻּמְצָא	תִּתְמַצֵּא
תְּמֻצְּאִי	תַּמְצִיאִי	תֻּמְצְאִי	[תִּתְמַצְּאִי
אֲמֻצָּא	אַמְצִיא	אֻמְצָא	[אֶתְמַצֵּא]
יְמֻצְּאוּ	יַמְצִיאוּ	יֻמְצְאוּ	יִתְמַצְּאוּ
*תְּמֻצֶּאנָה	*תַּמְצֶאנָה	*תֻּמְצֶאנָה	[תִּתְמַצֶּאנָה]
תְּמֻצְּאוּ	תַּמְצִיאוּ	תֻּמְצְאוּ	תִּתְמַצְּאוּ
תְּמֻצֶּאנָה	תַּמְצֶאנָה	תֻּמְצֶאנָה	[תִּתְמַצֶּאנָה]
[נְמֻצָּא]	נַמְצִיא	נֻמְצָא	[נִתְמַצֵּא]
	יַמְצֵא		
	יַמְצִיאֵנִי		
	מַמְצִיא		מִתְמַצֵּא
מְמֻצָּא		מֻמְצָא	

P.   Weak

			Qal.	Niph'al.	Pi'ēl.
Perf. Sing.	3.	m.	*גָּלָה	*נִגְלָה	*גִּלָּה
	3.	f.	*גָּלְתָה	נִגְלְתָה	*גִּלְּתָה
	2.	m.	*גָּלִיתָ	*נִגְלֵיתָ, ־ֵיתָ,	*גִּלִּיתָ
	2.	f.	גָּלִית	נִגְלֵית	גִּלִּית
	1.	c.	*גָּלִיתִי	נִגְלֵיתִי	גִּלִּיתִי, גִּלֵּיתִי
Plur.	3.	c.	*גָּלוּ	נִגְלוּ	גִּלּוּ
	2.	m.	גְּלִיתֶם	[נִגְלֵיתֶם]	גִּלִּיתֶם
	2.	f.	גְּלִיתֶן	[נִגְלֵיתֶן]	[גִּלִּיתֶן]
	1.	c.	גָּלִינוּ	נִגְלֵינוּ	גִּלִּינוּ
Inf.			*גְּלוֹת	*הִגָּלוֹת	*גַּלּוֹת
Inf. absol.			גָּלֹה	נִגְלֹה, הִגָּלֵה	גַּלֵּה, גַּלֹּה
Imp. Sing.		m.	*גְּלֵה	*הִגָּלֵה	*גַּלֵּה, גַּל
		f.	*גְּלִי	*הִגָּלִי	*גַּלִּי
Plur.		m.	גְּלוּ	הִגָּלוּ	גַּלּוּ
		f.	*גְּלֶינָה	[הִגָּלֶינָה]	[גַּלֶּינָה]
Impf. Sing.	3.	m.	*יִגְלֶה	*יִגָּלֶה	*יְגַלֶּה
	3.	f.	תִּגְלֶה	תִּגָּלֶה	תְּגַלֶּה
	2.	m.	תִּגְלֶה	תִּגָּלֶה	תְּגַלֶּה
	2.	f.	*תִּגְלִי	[תִּגָּלִי]	*תְּגַלִּי
	1.	c.	אֶגְלֶה	אֶגָּלֶה, אֶגָּ'	אֲגַלֶּה
Plur.	3.	m.	יִגְלוּ	יִגָּלוּ	יְגַלּוּ
	3.	f.	*תִּגְלֶינָה	*תִּגָּלֶינָה	*תְּגַלֶּינָה
	2.	m.	תִּגְלוּ	תִּגָּלוּ	תְּגַלּוּ
	2.	f.	תִּגְלֶינָה	תִּגָּלֶינָה	תְּגַלֶּינָה
	1.	c.	נִגְלֶה	[נִגָּלֶה]	נְגַלֶּה
Shortened Impf.			*יִגֶל	*יִגָּל	*יְגַל
Impf. with Suff.			יִגְלְךָ, *יִגְלֵנִי		יְגַלְךָ, *יְגַלֵּנִי
Part. act.			*גֹּלֶה	*נִגְלֶה	*מְגַלֶּה
pass.			*גָּלוּי		

Verbs, ל״ה.

Pu'al.	Hiph'il.	Hoph'al.	Hithpa'el.
*גֻּלָּה	*הִגְלָה	*הֻגְלָה	*הִתְגַּלָּה
*גֻּלְּתָה	*הִגְלְתָה	*הֻגְלְתָה	[הִתְגַּלְּתָה]
*גֻּלֵּיתָ	*הִגְלֵיתָ, ־ֵ־יתָ	*הָגְלֵיתָ	*הִתְגַּלֵּיתָ
[גֻּלֵּית]	הִגְלֵית, ־ֵ־ית	[הָגְלֵית]	[הִתְגַּלֵּית]
גֻּלֵּיתִי	הִגְלֵיתִי, ־ֵ־יתִי	הָגְלֵיתִי	הִתְגַּלֵּיתִי
גֻּלּוּ	הִגְלוּ	הָגְלוּ	הִתְגַּלּוּ
[גֻּלֵּיתֶם]	הִגְלֵיתֶם, ־ֵ־יתֶם	[הָגְלֵיתֶם]	הִתְגַּלֵּיתֶם
גֻּלֵּיתֶן	[הִגְלֵיתֶן]	הָגְלֵיתֶן	[הִתְגַּלֵּיתֶן]
[גֻּלֵּינוּ]	הִגְלֵינוּ	[הָגְלֵינוּ]	[הִתְגַּלֵּינוּ]
*גֻּלּוֹת	*הַגְלוֹת		*הִתְגַּלּוֹת
	הֻגְלֵה	*הָגְלֵה	
	*הַגְלֵה		[הִתְגַּלֵּה] הִתְגַּל
wanting.	*הַגְלִי	wanting.	הִתְגַּלִּי
	הַגְלוּ		הִתְגַּלּוּ
	[הַגְלֶינָה]		[הִתְגַּלֶּינָה]
*יְגֻלֶּה	*יַגְלֶה	*[יָגְלֶה]	*יִתְגַּלֶּה
תְּגֻלֶּה	תַּגְלֶה	תָּגְלֶה	[תִּתְגַּלֶּה]
תְּגֻלֶּה	תַּגְלֶה	תָּגְלֶה	תִּתְגַּלֶּה
[תְּגֻלִּי]	*תַּגְלִי	*תָּגְלִי	*תִּתְגַּלִּי
[אֲגֻלֶּה]	אַגְלֶה	*אָגְלֶה	אֶתְגַּלֶּה
יְגֻלּוּ	יַגְלוּ	יָגְלוּ	יִתְגַּלּוּ
[*תְּגֻלֶּינָה]	*תַּגְלֶינָה	*תָּגְלֶינָה	[תִּתְגַּלֶּינָה]
תְּגֻלּוּ	תַּגְלוּ	תָּגְלוּ	תִּתְגַּלּוּ
תְּגֻלֶּינָה	תַּגְלֶינָה	תָּגְלֶינָה	[תִּתְגַּלֶּינָה]
[נְגֻלֶּה]	נַגְלֶה	[נָגְלֶה]	נִתְגַּלֶּה
	*יֶגֶל		*יִתְגַּל
	יַגְלֶךָ, *יַגְלֵנִי		
	*מַגְלֶה		*מִתְגַּלֶּה
*מְגֻלֶּה		*מֻגְלֶה	

M m

Q. *Verbs* ל״ה

	1. Sing.	2. Sing. m.	2. Sing. f.
Perf. Qal. 3. m.	נָחַנִי	רָאַךָ, עָשְׂךָ	
	P. עָשָׂנִי	*P.* סָנֵּךָ, עָנְךָ	
3. f.	עָשַׂתְנִי		
2. m.	רְאִיתַנִי		
	P. עֲנִיתָנִי		
2. f.	*Pi.* רְמִיתָנִי		
1. c.		רְאִיתִיךָ	עִנִּתֵךְ
Plur. 3. c.	עָשׂוּנִי	רָאוּךָ	*Pi.* כְּסוּךְ
1. c.		*Pi.* קִינּוּךָ	
Imper. 2. m.	נְחֵנִי } עֲנֵנִי		
2. f.	*Hiph.* הַרְאִינִי		
Plur. 2. m.	*Pi.* כַּסּוּנִי		
Impf. 3. m.	יִרְאֵנִי	יִפְדְּךָ } יַחְתְּךָ	
3. f.		תִּשְׁבֶּךָ	
2. m.	תִּרְאֵנִי		
2. f.			
1. c.		אֶרְאֶךָ	אֶעֱרֵךְ
		אֶעֶנְךָ	
Plur. 3. m.	יַעֲשׂוּנִי	*Pi.* יְפַתּוּךָ	
2. m.	תִּצַוֻּנִי		
1. c.			

with Suffixes.

3. Sing. m.	3. Sing. f.	1. Plur.	3. Plur. m.
עָשָׂהוּ	רָאָה	עָשָׂנוּ	עָשָׂם
Pi. כִּלַּתּוּ	*Pi.* צִוְּתָה		*Hiph.* הֶעֱלָתַם
Pi. כִּסִּיתוֹ	עָשִׂיתָה	*Pi.* דִּפִּיתָנוּ	עֲנִיתָם
(עֲשִׂיתִיהוּ (רְאִיתִיו	רְאִיתִיהָ		רְעִיתִים
עֲשִׂוּהוּ *Pi.* קִוִּיֻנָהוּ	רָאוּהָ		שְׁבוּם
		Hiph. הַרְאֵנוּ	רְעֵם
תְּלוּהוּ			*Hiph.* הַכֻּם
(יִרְאֶהוּ (יְלֵוּוּ *Hiph.* תַּשְׁקֵהוּ	(יִרְאֶהָ (יִרְאֶנָה	*Pi.* יְצַוֵּנוּ	(יְחָצֵם (יַעֲשֵׂם
תַּעֲשֵׂנּוּ	תַּעֲשֵׂהָ	*Hiph.* תַּתִיעָנוּ	תְּזֹרֵם *Pi.* תְּכַסִּים
אֶרְאֶנּוּ אֶעֱנֵהוּ	אֶעֱשֶׂנָּה		אֶפְדֵם
Pi. יְפַתּוּהוּ	יַעֲשׂוּהָ	*Pi.* יַעֲנוּנוּ	
נַשְׁקֵנּוּ	נַעֲשֶׂנָּה		תְּצַוֵּם

M m 2

I

INDEX OF SUBJECTS

---

[1] Cf. Driver, *Introd.*[8], p. 466: Segal, *Mišn. Hebr.*, p. 63.

INDEX OF HEBREW WORDS AND FORMS

The numbers refer to the sections : the 'superior' figures after the letters refer to the notes. Doubtful forms are marked ? Corrupt forms with †.

בְּמֹצַאֲכֶם 61 d, 74 h, 93 q	+בְּתִקְוֺמֲמֵיךְ 72 cc	דֹּאשִׁי 72 q
בְּמֵתֵי 87 s, 95 o	גֵּאֶה 84ᵇ c	דֹּחוּ 64 d
בֵּן 96	גִּבְהָא 44 f	דְּחִיק 20 c
בָּנוּ 72 o, 76 g	גְּבֹהִים 124 h	דַּגֵּךְ 91 d
בְּנוּ 90 o	גֻּבִּי 86 i, 87 g	דִּיָּן 84ᵇ b
בְּנֵיהֶם 23 k	בִּגְעֹל 85 s	דַּל 93 x, 95 f
בְּנֵיהֶם 60 h	גְּרִיִּים 93 x	דַּלְיוּ 67 dd, 75 u, bb
בנת (Moab.) for בְּנֹתִי 7 d¹	גׇּרְחָיִם 95 o	דׇּלְיוּ 93 z
בִּנְתְּ 73 a	גֵּוֶה 23 f	דְּלִיּוֹתָיו 84ᵃ g
בְּעַדְנִי 103 d	גּוֹזָל 84ᵃ r	דֲּלָלוּ 67 cc
בְּעֹטֶף 51 l	גּוֹי 8 k	דְּלָתוֹת 95 f
בְּעָיוּ 29 t, 75 u	גּוֹיׅ 8 k	דְּלָתָם 93 n
בָּעִיר (ψ 73²⁰) 53 q	גּוֹל 67 n	דָּם 93 mm
בַּעֲלֵיהֶן 93 m	גֻּוַּע 65 a	דָּמִים 124 n
בְּעָלִים 145 h	גֵּיא 93 g, v	דׇּנַּגִּי 58 i, 59 f
בֹּעֵרָה 80 k	גִּילֹנִי 85 v	דֵּעַ 69 m
בַּעֲשֵׂר 53 k	גֻּלְגֹּלֶת 95 r	דֵּעָה 69 c, m²
בַּעֲשֶׂק 35 g	? גֻּלָּה 91 e	דְּעָה 48 l
? בְּעֵת מׇלְכֶך 116 g¹	גָּלִיַת 80 f, g	דַּק 67 bb
? בָּצִים 93 y	גׇּלְתָה 44 f	דֶּרָבוֹן 85 u
בְּצָעָם 61 g	גַּם intensive 153,	דְּרָכִים 93 n
בְּקָרׇב־ 10 g³	154 a¹(c); (וְ)גַּם...ibid.;	? דְּרָכֶּךְ 91 k
בְּקָרִים 123 a¹	גַּם (כִּי) concessive 160 b	דֶּשֶׁא 80 h
(בָּרָה) בָּרָא 75 rr	גַּנֵּב 84ᵇ b	דֶּשֶׁא 22 e
בַּרְזֶל 85 s	גַּרְגְּרֹתֶךָ 91 n	
בִּרְכֵיהֶם 93 n	גׇּרְנָה 90 i	
בִּרְכַּת 95 g	גֶּשׁ־ 66 c	
בְּרֹקֶת 80 f	גְּשׁוּ 66 c	
בֹּשׁ 72 c², n, 78 b	גְּשִׁי 66 c	
בִּשְׁנֵם 67 p	נִשְּׁמוּ 90 k	
? וּבְשׇׁבְּנִי 91 e		
בַּת 96; to per-	דְּאָבוֹן 85 u	
sonify a people 122 i	+דְּאַג 9 b	
בַּת for בֵּית 7 f	דׇּבְקָה 44 c	
בְּתוּאֵל 90 k	דִּבֶּר 52 o	
בְּתוֹכְכֶם 10 g, 91 d	דּוּדָאִים 93 x	
בָּתִּים 9 u; p. 285	דּוֹם 67 n	
s.v. בַּיִת	דּוּמָם 100 g²	
	דּוֹנַג 84ᵃ r	

ה with Mappiq 14, as a weak consonant 23 k, l, in verbs ל״ה 75, as a mere vowel-letter 6 d, 7 b, c, 24 g

ה locale, origin 90 b, use 90 c–i, with constr. st. before a genitive 90 c, sometimes otiose 90 e, mere poetic ornament 90 f, g, in place-names 90 g¹, added in segholate nouns to the developed form 90 i, 93 i

הַ (Article) punc-

tuation 35, syntax 126:
see Article in Index I

הֲ interrog. 100,
origin and pointing 100
i-n, uses of 150; אִם (!) ... הֲ
150 h

הַ־ (with the tone),
ending of fem. nouns 80 c

הָ־ (toneless), end-
ing of the Cohortative and
Imperative 48 c, d, i; an old
case-ending 90 a-i

הָ־ 3rd masc. sing.
pronominal suffix 91 e

הָ־ (without Map-
pîq) anomalous 3rd fem.
sing. pronom. suff. 91 e

הָא 105 b
הָאָזְכֶּה (Mi 6¹¹) 47 b¹
הָאֲנִיחוּ 53 g
הָאוֹקִים 35 d
הָאָח 105 a
הָאִישׁ one, 144 d¹
הָאֵל בֵּית־אֵל 127 f¹
הָאָנָח 65 e
הָאָרוֹן 35 o
הֵבֵאת 74 g
הֵבֵאתָה 74 d
הֵבֵאתָ 72 w
הֵבָה 105 b
הֵבִיא 72 y, 74 l
הֱבִישׁוֹתָה 78 b
הֵבִישׁ 72 x, 78 b
הבמת זאת (Moab.) 80 f¹
הִפְרוּ 67 t
הַבְרָכָה 10 g (end)
הִבְרָכָה 16 g
הַבָּנָה Qᵉrê for הַגֵּן 118 e²
הֹנַח 69 w

הֹנוּ 75 n, aa
הַגְּרָנוֹת 93 r
הֹדוּשׁ 72 v
הַדְּרֵךְ חֶתְלֹו 127 f¹
הַדִּשְׁנָה 54 h
הַהֵימִיר ? 72 e
+ההלכתי 90 n
הַהִלָּה 52 s
הִיא, הוּא 32 k; הוּא with
Qᵉrê הִיא 17 c, הוּא as fem.,
not an archaism 32 l
(הֵמָּה, הִיא) הוּא =
ipse or idem 135 a¹, demonstrative 136, for the copula
141 h, resuming the sub-
ject 145 u³, in questions
136 e (end), 150 l
הֵוא 75 hh
הוֹבִישׁ 72 x
הוֹדַע 69 w
הוּי 105 a
הוֹכַח 65 f
הוּלֶּדֶת 71
הוֹלְלוֹת 86 l
הוֹלָם פַּעַם 29 f
הֻנַּח ? 72 ee¹
הוֹפִיעַ ? 69 v
הוֹצִיא 74 l
הוֹרַדְתֶּנּוּ 59 h
הוֹשַׁע 65 f
הַוּוֹרָה ? 80 i
הַוִּלּוֹהַּ 67 y, 72 ee
הֻזְּכּוּ 54 d
הַזְכַּרְכֶם 53 l
הֶחְבָּאתָה 75 oo
הֶחְבָּה 75 pp
הֶחְדַּלְתִּי 63 k
הֶחֱי, הָחַי 35 f, 27 q
הֶחֱל 67 t
הֶחֱלִי 74 k, 75 ii

הַחֲמָנִים 35 f
הַחֲרִיטִים 35 f
הַחֲרָסָה 90 f
הַחָתֹאת 67 w
הִטָּהֲרוּ 27 q
הִיא 32 k
הָיָה 16 f, 63 q, 75 s,
with participle 116 r, with
לְ before infin. 114 h-k, as
copula 141 g-i. Cf. חָיָה.
הֱיֵה 75 n
הַיּוֹם = one day
126 s
הַיּוֹם שְׁלִשָׁה 134 o¹
הֵיטֵב 113 k
הֵיכָל 9 i, 85 c
הֵילִיכִי ? 69 x, 78 b
הַיָּמָּה ? 90 f
הַיָּצֵא 69 v
הֵיקִיץ 70 e
הֵישַׁר 24 f², 70 b
הית 75 m¹
הַבּוֹת (inf. abs.) 75 ff
הֲכִי 150 d, e
הָכִין 72 z
הַבִּינִי 75 mm
הֶכְלַמְנוּ 53 p
הֵבֵנוּ 72 w
הֲלֹא expressing
assurance 150 e
הֻלֶּדֶת 69 w, 71
הַלֹּוּ 34 f
הַלֵּזֶה 34 f
הַלֵּזוּ 34 f
הָלַךְ inflexion o[f]
69 x, use of, to express continuance 113 u
הֲלַךְ 69 m²
הֲלְכוּא ? 23 i

הִתַּמַהְמְהוּ ? 55 g
הִתְעַמָּךְ 67 v
הִתְנַבּוֹת 75 qq
הִתְנַבִּית 75 qq
הִתְפָּקְדוּ 54 l
הָתְפָּקְדוּ 54 l
הִתְרָאָה פָנִים 156 c¹
הִתְרֹחַצְתִּי 64 d

ו as a vowel-letter 5 b¹, 7 b-g, 8 h-m, 9 n-s, its changes 24, initial 26 a; a firm consonant in verbs ע"ו 72 gg, in verbs orig. ל"י 75 a, b, kk, cf. in nouns 93 x

ו pointing of 104 d-g, connecting sentences 154, = *and that*, or *and especially* 114 p, 154 a¹ (b), introducing predicate 143 d; וֹ introducing predicate 111 h, or apodosis (rare) 111 q, 159 o (e), s (f). 143 d; ו with perf. introducing predicate or apodosis 112 ff-oo, 143 d, 159 o, s. See also Wāw in Index I.

וָאֲבָרֶךְ 23 d, 68 k
וַאֲבָרְכֶם: 60 d
+וָאֲגָרֵשׁ 49 c
וַאדֹנָי 23 d, 26 g, 102 m, 104 d
וָאֶצְרָה. 53 n, g, 68 i
וָאֹחֵז 68 e
וָאֲחַלְּךָ 111 w¹
וָאֹמַר 64 h, 68 e
+וְאַחֲרֵי שָׁתֹה 113 e³
וָאֲחַשְׁבָה ? 49 e
וָאֵירְחֲלָה ? 49 e

וַיֹּאכַל 68 e
וָאֲכַלֶּה 49 e
וָאֲכַסֶּךְ 49 c
וְאַל- = *rather than* 133 b²
וָאֵלֶךְ 69 p
וָאלֹהִים 102 d, 104 d
וָאֶסְחָבָה (Moab.) 7 c
וְאָעִידָה ? 49 e
וָאָקוּם 49 e, 72 t
וָאֶקְרָאֶה ? 48 d
ואֹרֵב 75 gg
וָאָרֶץ 29 i¹
וָבְטֶן 104 g
וְדִיגוּם 73 b
וְהֶאֱזִנִיחוּ 53 g
וַהֲבִיאֹתִי 76 h
וְהִגְלָה 75 ee
וְחֹשְׁבוֹתִים ? 72 x
וְהַחְתִּתִּי 67 dd
וְהִטַּלְתִּי 72 k, w
וְהָיָה in prophetic style 112 y, z
וְהָיָה 28 b
וְהָיִי 28 b
וְהִטְבַּלְתִּי 70 e
וְהָיִיתֶם 63 q, 104 f
וְהִמְטַרְתִּי (Am 4⁷) 112 h³
וְהֵמַתִּי 72 w
וַהֲמִתִּיהָ 72 w
וַהֲמִתֶּן 72 w
וְהִנִּיחָה ? 72 ee
וְהֵנַפְתּ 72 w
וְהַצִּיתוּה 71
וַהֲצַלְתִּי 67 ee
וַהֲקֵאתוֹ 76 h
וְהִקְדַּשְׁנוּ 29 l
וְהֵקַמֹנוּ 72 i
וְהִרְאִיתִי 53 p, 75 ee

וַהֲשִׁיבֹתָם 72 i²
וְהִתְשׁוֹטַטְנָה 54 b
וְזָהָב 16 e, 104 e
חָיִף 104 g
וְחָטָאת (Ex 5¹⁶) 74 g
וְחַי ? 76 i
חַי 76 i
וְחִיבַכְתֶּם 72 m
וְהָיָה 67 k
וְחָיָה with ě for ĭ 28 b, 63 q, 104 f, in pause sometimes וָחָיָה 75 n
וְחָצֹתִי 67 ee
וָאֵל 76 d
וַיֹּאמַר : (in Jb) 68 e
+וַיֹּאסֶף 68 h
וַיֹּאסֹר 23 b
וַיֹּאצֶל 23 d, 68 e
וַיַּאת 23 d
וַיָּבִיא 74 l
וַיֵּבְךְ 75 q
וַיְבָרֶךְ 64 g
וַיַּבְשִׁחֻהוּ 69 u, 70 e
וַיַּגֵּהּ 69 u
וַיָּגֶל 67 p
וַיְגָרְשֵׁם 7 c
וַיְדַבְּקִף 53 n
וַיֵּדוּ 69 u
וַיִּדְרְכוּ 53 n
וַיִהֹוָה 102 m
וַיְהִי 104 f
וַיְהִי 16 g; as a narrative formula 111 f-h
וַיִּהְיוּ שָׁם 29 g
וַיָּהֶל 67 y
וַיֹּוחָר ? 68 i
וַיִּנַּע 64 b
וַיֹּצִיא 74 l
וַיִּז 75 r

מ as preformative of participles 52 c, sometimes dropped 52 s; of infin. (rare) 45 e; of nouns 85 e–m

Deuteronomy

1	24	120 h
	27 . .	115 c, 115 f
	28	124 q
	33	53 q
	34 . . .	65 e, 149 b
	40	119 s
	41	135 n
	44 . 67 g, 67 y, 107 g	
	46	138 c
2	9 . .	75 bb, 118 q
	13	119 s
	14	134 h
	23	126 w
	24	20 g, 69 f, 75 cc, 110 h, 120 g, h
	27	108 c, 123 e, 133 k, 156 d
	28	49 m
	31 . . .	67 w, 69 f
3	3	164 d
	5	128 c
	11	100 i
	13 . . .	125 d N.
	21	126 k
	26	69 v
4	1 . . .	44 d, 69 s
	8	128 p
	10 . .	115 d, 165 b
	15 . .	52 o, 130 d
	20	74 l
	21	54 k
	26	51 k
	36	61 d
	39 . . .	2 i, 72 w
	41	90 c
5	3	135 g
	6 . .	15 p, 138 d
	9	60 b
	12	113 bb
	19 . . .	120 d N.
	23	132 h
	24	32 h
	26 . . .	115 d, 151 c
6	3 . .	118 g, 165 b
	7	119 l
	11 . .	49 m, 96
	17	58 g
7	5	52 n
	15	60 d
	16 . .	72 r, 109 d
	24	53 l
	25	127 e
8	3 . . .	44 l, 72 o
	5	61 h
	9	93 aa
	13	75 u
	14	116 f
	15	127 i
	16 . .	44 l, 72 o
	19	106 i

Deuteronomy

9	7	138 c
	8	54 k
	18	54 k
10	5	29 g
	17	102 m, 126 v, 133 i
	19	112 aa
	22	119 i
11	2	117 l
	15	49 m
	30	150 e
12	3	52 n
	14	61 h
13	1	109 d
	3	60 b
	6	116 f
	9	109 d
14	17	80 k
15	2	113 gg
	7 .	119 w N., 139 d
	14	93 k
	18 . .	128 c, 133 k
16	6	119 g
	13	93 k
	20	133 k
17	2	167 b
	5	124 o
	6	144 e
	8	102 h
	14 . .	44 d, 49 m
	17	109 g
18	1 . .	68 c, 131 h
	16	109 d
19	5	126 r
20	2	61 d
	5	137 c
	8	121 b
	14	128 h
21	3 . .	121 a, 145 q
	4	121 a
	7 . .	44 m, 145 k
	8	55 k
	10 . .	135 p, 145 m
	11	49 m, 96, 130 e
	13	101 a
22	1	159 gg
	19 . .	17 c, 127 e
	23	131 b
23	5 .	61 d, 130 c N1
	11	20 h
	15 . .	93 ss, 128 p
	25	96
24	1	167 b
	4	54 h
	8	51 n
	10	23 d
	13	58 i
25	2 . .	96, 128 v
	12	67 ee
	13	123 f
26	5	119 i
	12	53 k

Deuteronomy

27	2	72 w
	6	117 hh
	9	16 b
28	24	58 g
	36	131 d
	43	133 k
	48 . .	53 l, 145 m
	49	155 d
	52	67 v
	56 .	113 d, 142 f N.
	57	74 i
	59	91 n
	62	119 i
	66	75 rr
	67	151 b
29	14 . . .	100 o N.
	15	157 c
	18	69 h N.
	21	167 b
	28	5 n
30	4	92 b N.
31	12	120 e
	16	93 gg
	21	164 d
	29	74 g
32	1 .	2 r, 91 l, 117 b
	3	69 o
	4	126 c
	5 . .	13 c, 152 e
	6	20 g, 75 ll, 100 i, 152 a N.
	7 .	60 f, 87 n, 123 c
	8 . .	53 k, 109 k
	10 . .	58 i, 58 k
	11 . .	52 n, 155 g
	15	20 g, 144 p, 154 N (a)
	17	144 p, 152 a N., 155 e, 155 f, 155 h
	18 . . .	75 s, 109 k
	20	108 a
	21	152 a N.
	22	69 f
	24 . .	116 h, 116 l
	26 .	58 a N., 75 mm
	27	139 y
	28	50 e, 93 qq, 124 e
	29	159 x
	30	134 s
	31 . . .	156 b N.
	32	20 h
	35	52 o, 145 o, 155 l
	36 .	29 v, 44 f, 152 s
	37 . . .	29 t, 75 u
	39 . . .	141 h N2
	40 . . .	93 aa N.
	41	159 n
	46 . .	117 gg, 165 b
	50	110 c
33	2	112 pp

Judges		Judges		1 Samuel	
7 8	131 *s*	**14** 15	9 *v*, 69 *n*, 150 *g* N.	**1** 1	49 *b* N., 125 *b*, 125 *h*, 156 *b*
12	36	17	134 *m*	2	134 *l*, 145 *o*
13	112 *qq*	18	37 *d*, 90 *f*, 93 *x*, 133 *a*	3	112 *dd*, 123 *c*
19	113 *z*	**15** 1	119 *n*	4	112 *g*, 126 *s*
20	147 *c*	7	163 *c*, 163 *d* N.	6	20 *h*, 22 *s*, 59 *g*, 117 *p*
23	102 *b*	12	152 *w*	7	107 *e*, 123 *c*
25	124 *r*	13	113 *p*	8	37 *e*, 102 *l*
8 1	74 *h*, 155 *d*, 155 *h*	14	164 *b*	9	91 *e*, 113 *e* N., 141 *e*
2	20 *m*	**16** 5	66 *h*	10	128 *y*
4	118 *n*	9	126 *o*	11	113 *o*
10	97 *e*	10	67 *dd*	12	112 *uu*, 114 *n* N., 164 *d*
11	130 *a* N.	11	113 *o*	13	20 *g*
18	126 *o*, 161 *c*	13	28 *c* N.	14	47 *o*
19	63 *q*, 159 *x*	14	127 *g*	16	128 *v*
32	125 *h*, 128 *c*	15	141 *e*	17	23 *f*, 95 *h*
9 8	113 *o*	16	10 *g*, 52 *d*, 60 *d*, 164 *d*	20	44 *d*, 64 *f*
9	63 *k*, 100 *n*, 106 *n*	18	112 *tt*	22	112 *oo*
10	46 *d*, 46 *e*	20	123 *c*	24	135 *i*
15	159 *v*	25	52 *n*	27	95 *h*
16	167 *a*	26	67 *v*	28	64 *f*
17	119 *bb*	27	126 *x*	**2** 1	2 *r*, 106 *g*
28	137 *a*	28	34 *a* N., 88 *f*, 97 *b* N.	3	103 *g*, 120 *g*, 124 *e*, 133 *k*, 152 *z*
29	48 *l*, 76 *e*, 151 *b*, 154 *b*	30	72 *r*	4	146 *a*
39	69 *p*	**17** 2	32 *h*, 121 *f*	6	111 *u*, 116 *x*
41	35 *d*	3	154 N.	8	107 *g*, 116 *x*, 135 *p*
45	117 *ee*	**18** 3	142 *e*	9	67 *g*
48	157 *a*	19	20 *g*, 150 *g*	13	112 *oo*, 116 *w*, 131 *c*, 159 *i*, 164 *a*
53	27 *o*, 67 *p*, 125 *b*	23	67 *g*, 67 *y*	14	131 *h*, 132 *g*
55	145 *d*	29	52 *q*	15	112 *oo*
10 4	96	30	5 *n*	16	103 *g*, 106 *m*, 112 *ll*, 113 *w*, 159 *f*, 159 *dd*
11	167 *b*	**19** 1	131 *b*	18	116 *k*, 118 *q*, 121 *d*
18	137 *c*	2	75 *t*	19	112 *e*
11 5	21 *b*	5	9 *u*, 64 *c* N., 117 *ff*	20	145 *u*
10	159 *n* N.	6	110 *h*, 120 *d*	22	112 *k*
18	47 *m*	8	64 *c*	23	126 *y*
20	157 *b* N.	9	91 *k*	24	116 *s*
25	51 *i*, 133 *a* N.	11	19 *i*	25	117 *x*
29	118 *f*	13	69 *x*, 73 *d*	26	113 *u*
33	134 *e*	18	118 *e* N.	27	113 *q*, 114 *e*, 150 *e*
34	135 *o*, 135 *o* N.	20	29 *q*, 73 *e*	28	49 *e*, 113 *z*, 119 *w*
35	119 *i*	22	54 *c*, 130 *e*	29	133 *b*
36	124 *e*	30	112 *ee*, *oo*, 116 *w*	30	113 *p*, 116 *g*, 149 *a*
39	144 *b*	**20** 2	29 *f*	31	112 *x*, 116 *d*
12 5	100 *m*, 112 *ee*	15	54 *l*, 155 *d*	33	53 *q*, 118 *q*, 145 *e*
6	2 *w*	16	90 *i* N.	**3** 2	107 *b*, 120 *b*
7	124 *o*	31	66 *f*	3	107 *c*, 152 *r*
13 2	125 *b*	32	20 *h*	5	46 *c*, 120 *g*, 120 *h*
5	80 *d*	38	75 *gg*	7	107 *c*
6	44 *d*, 64 *f*, 127 *e*	39	118 *u*	10	54 *k*, 118 *u*, 123 *c*
8	52 *s*	43	22 *s*	11	67 *g*, 67 *p*, 116 *w*, 155 *d*
12	135 *m*	44	117 *m*	12	113 *h*
16	119 *m*	**21** 7	131 *n*		
21	75 *y*	9	54 *l*		
23	90 *h* N.	16	123 *b*		
25	61 *c*	21	145 *p*		
14 2	90 *e*				
3	135 *a*				
4	122 *q*, 135 *p*				
6	152 *p*				

PRINTED IN GREAT BRITAIN
AT THE UNIVERSITY PRESS, OXFORD
BY VIVIAN RIDLER
PRINTER TO THE UNIVERSITY